Frommer's

Florida

2005

by Lesley Abravanel

with Laura Lea Miller

Here's what the critics say about Frommer's:

"Amazingly easy to use. Very portable, very complete."

—*Booklist*

"Detailed, accurate, and easy-to-read information for all price ranges."

—*Glamour Magazine*

"Hotel information is close to encyclopedic."

—*Des Moines Sunday Register*

"Frommer's Guides have a way of giving you a real feel for a place."

—*Knight Ridder Newspapers*

WILEY

Wiley Publishing, Inc.

Published by:

Wiley Publishing, Inc.

111 River St.
Hoboken, NJ 07030-5774

ISBN 0-7645-6897-3

Editor: Kendra L. Falkenstein
Production Editor: Ian Skinnari
Cartographers: John Decamillis, Elizabeth Puhl, Roberta Stockwell
Photo Editor: Richard Fox
Production by Wiley Indianapolis Composition Services

Front cover photo: Hammock and palm trees on Little Palm Island
Back cover photo: Islands of Adventure, Universal Orlando, Incredible Hulk Coaster

For information on our other products and services or to obtain technical support, please contact our Customer Care Department within the U.S. at 800/762-2974, outside the U.S. at 317/572-3993 or fax 317/572-4002.

Wiley also publishes its books in a variety of electronic formats. Some content that appears in print may not be available in electronic formats.

Manufactured in the United States of America

5 4 3 2 1

Contents

List of Maps

About the Authors

Lesley Abravanel is a freelance journalist and a graduate of the University of Miami School of Communication. When she isn't combing South Florida for the latest hotels, restaurants, and attractions, she is on the lookout for vacationing celebrities, about whom she writes in her weekly nightlife and gossip column, "Velvet Underground," for the *Miami Herald.* She is a contributor to *Condé Nast Traveller, Time Out,* all three illustrious supermarket tabloids, reviews restaurants for AOL/Digital City South Florida, is the Miami correspondent for *Black Book Magazine,* and is the author of *Frommer's South Florida* and *Frommer's Portable Miami.*

To Mommy, Daddy, Mags, Winston, and my so-called posse,
you know who you are. —Lesley

Laura Lea Miller is a freelance writer based in Buffalo, New York, though she's spent countless hours scouring Central Florida's theme parks over the years—both with and without her husband and five kids. A family-travel expert who religiously makes an annual pilgrimage to the Land the Mouse built, she is currently researching and writing a guide to Florida for families.

Acknowledgments

To my mother and father, without whose influence, encouragement, and support I would never have ended up in Miami doing what I'm doing.

To all the publicists and proprietors for putting up with the endless e-mails, inquiries, and spur-of-the-moment visits, I thank you for your cooperation and eagerness to answer pressing questions about hair dryers, irons, hours, and credit cards.

Thanks to Kendra Falkenstein, my fabulous editor, for being on the same page as me, "getting it," and, most especially, for being so, ahem, Internet savvy.

Thanks to Gabe Berman and Ronna Gradus. Your help is most appreciated, even though I know you still want to kill me.

Thanks to all my friends and colleagues who know that I'm much more than a party girl and accept my quirkiness, compulsive behavior, and genuine penchant for all things bizarre.

Thank you, Mrs. Ritchie, for inspiring me to express myself and aspire to greatness.

And, last but not at all least, thanks to my Swede for putting up with me and my inanity and my insanity. Mwah!

—Lesley Abravanel

An Invitation to the Reader

In researching this book, we discovered many wonderful places—hotels, restaurants, shops, and more. We're sure you'll find others. Please tell us about them, so we can share the information with your fellow travelers in upcoming editions. If you were disappointed with a recommendation, we'd love to know that, too. Please write to:

Frommer's Florida 2005
Wiley Publishing, Inc. • 111 River St. • Hoboken, NJ 07030-5774

An Additional Note

Please be advised that travel information is subject to change at any time—and this is especially true of prices. We therefore suggest that you write or call ahead for confirmation when making your travel plans. The authors, editors, and publisher cannot be held responsible for the experiences of readers while traveling. Your safety is important to us, however, so we encourage you to stay alert and be aware of your surroundings. Keep a close eye on cameras, purses, and wallets, all favorite targets of thieves and pickpockets.

Frommer's Star Ratings, Icons & Abbreviations

Every hotel, restaurant, and attraction listing in this guide has been ranked for quality, value, service, amenities, and special features using a **star-rating system.** In country, state, and regional guides, we also rate towns and regions to help you narrow down your choices and budget your time accordingly. Hotels and restaurants are rated on a scale of zero (recommended) to three stars (exceptional). Attractions, shopping, nightlife, towns, and regions are rated according to the following scale: zero stars (recommended), one star (highly recommended), two stars (very highly recommended), and three stars (must-see).

In addition to the star-rating system, we also use **seven feature icons** that point you to the great deals, in-the-know advice, and unique experiences that separate travelers from tourists. Throughout the book, look for:

Finds	Special finds—those places only insiders know about
Fun Fact	Fun facts—details that make travelers more informed and their trips more fun
Kids	Best bets for kids and advice for the whole family
Moments	Special moments—those experiences that memories are made of
Overrated	Places or experiences not worth your time or money
Tips	Insider tips—great ways to save time and money
Value	Great values—where to get the best deals

The following **abbreviations** are used for credit cards:

AE	American Express	DISC	Discover	V	Visa
DC	Diners Club	MC	MasterCard		

Frommers.com

Now that you have the guidebook to a great trip, visit our website at **www.frommers.com** for travel information on more than 3,000 destinations. With features updated regularly, we give you instant access to the most current trip-planning information available. At Frommers.com, you'll also find the best prices on airfares, accommodations, and car rentals—and you can even book travel online through our travel booking partners. At Frommers.com, you'll also find the following:

- Online updates to our most popular guidebooks
- Vacation sweepstakes and contest giveaways
- Newsletter highlighting the hottest travel trends
- Online travel message boards with featured travel discussions

What's New in Florida

MIAMI After the Miami hotel boom started to settle down in 2003, the city got hungry for new restaurants. On any given day, a new eatery seems to open, assuring everyone that while they may have blown their food budget on a swank boutique hotel, they don't necessarily have to starve in the city. And, to compete with the restaurant as nightlife trend, several bars and lounges have opened, offering more than just beer nuts and chips as snacks.

Accommodations The **Ritz-Carlton South Beach** (1 Lincoln Rd.; ✆ **800/241-3333**) is the last of three Ritz-Carltons to open in Miami (fall of '03). Two more locations, on Key Biscayne and in Coconut Grove, have already established themselves as magnets for celebrities looking to avoid the South Beach limelight. Ian Schrager, the Midas of hip hotels, bought into the hyper-hip **Shore Club** (1901 Collins Ave.; ✆ **877/640-9500**), which, thanks to the addition of some personality that brought more life into the place, plus Robert DeNiro's Ago restaurant and the L.A.-imported Skybar, is the new Delano—a trend that is likely to stick as long as orange as the new black did. Miami's first **Four Seasons Hotel and Tower** (1435 Brickell Ave.; ✆ **305/358-7758**) opened in the summer of 2003, and, in the summer of 2004, was joined by neighbor **Conrad Miami** (1395 Brickell Ave.; ✆ **305/503-6500**), a 36-story, 308-room tower that's part of the Hilton's chichi

luxe brand. Andre Balazs, owner of L.A.'s Chateau Marmont and Standard hotels (among others), has purchased South Beach's legendary **Raleigh Hotel** (1775 Collins Ave.; ✆ **800/848-1775**), which he is in the process of renovating and restoring to its original Art Deco glory, fusing it with his distinct brand of boutique hotel hip. In Sunny Isles Beach, Donald Trump established his gaudy presence with his **Trump International Sonesta Beach Resort** (18001 Collins Ave.; ✆ **800/SONESTA**), whose bland interior should have Trump screaming, "You're fired" to whomever the interior designer was. Not too far away will be the Le Meridien Hotels and Resorts' first Miami property, **Le Meridien Beach Resort and Spa** (18683 Collins Ave.; ✆ **800/543-4300**), a 25-story, 210 unit resort set to open in December 2004, featuring a second Miami location of the swank Italian restaurant **Bice,** which should bring fine dining to the chain restaurant-spotted area.

Also, Miami Beach's first ever hotel, **The Browns Hotel** (112 Ocean Dr.; ✆ **305/674-7977**), which opened in 1915, has been restored to its old Florida fabulousness featuring original beams of Dade County Pine floorboards and exterior clapboard. The hotel, of course, is a boutique hotel with a requisite see and be seen steakhouse, **Prime 112** (✆ **305/532-8112**).

Dining Still on the verge of becoming a major food city, Miami recently introduced a handful of dining options, most on the more upscale side. The tony Nuevo Latino **Ola** (5061 Biscayne Blvd.; ✆ **305/758-9195**) brings the return of star chef Douglas Rodriguez to his former stomping grounds, not to mention the city's best *mojitos* and *típicos* (traditional Latin-American dishes). Food Network star Emeril Lagasse started in Miami with his usual "bam!" with the opening of **Emeril's Miami Beach** (Loews Hotel, 1601 Collins Ave.; ✆ **305/695-4540**). Yet another star chef, **David Bouley,** will soon take over the restaurant at the **Ritz-Carlton South Beach** (1 Lincoln Rd.; ✆ **786/276-4000**), opening his first signature restaurant out of Manhattan.

After Dark   At press time, the hottest nightspots are located on the still sizzling South Beach. However, over the causeway, a burgeoning nocturnal buzz is emanating from the once desolate area of **downtown Miami,** off of Biscayne Boulevard, thanks to cheaper rents and 24-hour liquor licenses. Among them, **I/O** (30 NE 14th St.; ✆ **305/358-8007**), a dance club where indie music fanatics hang out; and **Grass Restaurant and Lounge** (12 NE 40th St.; ✆ **305/573-5003**) brings a taste of Tiki-chic to the Design District with thatched-roof banquettes and a decidedly artsy crowd. Back on South Beach, Motley Crue-man Tommy Lee opened **Rok Bar** (1905 Collins Ave.; ✆ **305/538-7171**) in May of 2004, a rock 'n' roll themed bar where Lee will make surprise appearances as guest DJ and musician.

FLORIDA KEYS   Islamorada's swank **Cheeca Lodge and Spa** (✆ **800/327-2888;** www.cheeca.com) is in the process of receiving a $15 million renovation to the main lodge, grounds, spa, and pool areas. The resort has also gone condo, converting nearly half of its 202 rooms into luxury apartments.

THE GOLD COAST   While the Gold Coast's beaches remain less congested

than those in Miami, the area isn't impervious to development—especially when it comes to resorts, restaurants, and nightlife. Whereas the Gold Coast used to be a sleepy beachfront, today it's slowly en route to rivaling the liveliness of a big city like Miami.

Accommodations   Fort Lauderdale opened the posh 132-suite **Atlantic** hotel/condo, 601 N. Ft. Lauderdale Beach Blvd. (✆ 954/567-8020), managed by Starwood's Luxury Collection, in the summer of 2004. Opened in the summer of 2004, the $200 million **Seminole Hard Rock Hotel & Casino,** 1 Seminole Rd., Hollywood (✆ **954/327-7625**), offers 500 luxury rooms as well as a lakeside beach club, 130,000 sq. ft. casino, and European Health Spa. It's sort of just like the Hard Rock in Vegas, only without Blackjack, slots, and all other forms of "bet against the house" gambling. Well, there's always bingo. . .

Dining   Delray Beach is proving itself to be a hip dining destination with places such as **Gotham City Restaurant and Bar** (16950 Jog Rd.; ✆ **561/381-0200**), a supper club slash steakhouse with live entertainment and DJ. In West Palm Beach's CityPlace, **Tsunami** (651 Okeechobee Blvd.; ✆ **561/835-9696**) is a see and be seen sushi place that looks as if it came right off the set of *Sex and the City,* with main plate and sushi prices that are nearly the equivalent of a pair of Manolo Blahniks.

Shopping   Shabby chic types are saying hallelujah over the fact that Swedish home furnishing giant **Ikea** has chosen Davie as the site for Florida's first ever outpost (even though ground hasn't even broken yet). No phone or address just yet. For true shopaholics, **Activity Planners** (✆ **954/525-9194**) will arrange a water taxi, limousine, or Town Car for your own private shopping tour through the Greater Fort Lauderdale area. **The Mall at Wellington**

Green (10300 W. Forest Hill Blvd., Wellington; © 561/227-6900) is Palm Beach's newest shopping center, featuring 140 specialty stores and department stores. City Place is adding more home furnishing and accessories stores such as an 8,600 square foot Roche Bobois (700 S. Rosemary Ave.; © 561/514-9650) showroom.

SOUTHWEST FLORIDA All telephone numbers in Fort Myers, Fort Myers Beach, Sanibel and Captiva islands, Naples, and Marco Island all are now in area code 239. Boca Grande and Charlotte County remain in area code 941.

Sanibel & Captiva Islands Dolphin Watch and Wildlife Adventure Cruise (© 239/472-5300), offered by Captiva Cruises, is a 90-minute tour by boat that leaves daily at 4pm from South Seas Resort on Captiva Island. Explore the wildlife in and around picturesque Pine Island Sound, which is home to birds, dolphins, manatees, and more. The cost is $20 for adults and $10 for children ages 3 through 10. Reservations required; group outings and private charters also are available. Captain Mike Fuery (© 239/466-3649) now leads walking and snorkeling tours, which have been featured in National Geographic. The 3-hour charters leave from 'Tween Waters Inn on Captiva Island and include a 30-minute boat trip through waters ideal for spotting dolphin, manatee, otters, osprey, and other local wildlife. Split charters can be arranged at a cost of $50 per person with a maximum of four people; private charters for up to four are $180.

Naples The luxurious Bellasera (221 9th St. S., Naples; © 888/612-1115), an Italian-style boutique hotel, has opened and features luxe chenille robes, Aveda products, and a washer and dryer in every room. The hotel's restaurant, Zizi Restaurant and Lounge, offers Tuscan-inspired fusion dishes.

Fort Meyers Royal Palm Tours, in Fort Myers, now offers the Cracker Culinary Tour (© 800/296-0249; www.royalpalmtours.com), which will first and foremost explain what a Florida Cracker is (a pioneer or cattle hunter). Then it will take you from Palmdale, Florida to Gatorama, a famous roadside attraction off of Highway 27 (www.gatorama.com); La Belle, a honey and bee shop; Flora and Ella's Restaurant, known for its homemade chocolate, coconut, and peanut butter cream pies; on to a citrus refinery, an old school grocery, a food and agricultural science research station, and a farmers' market. The cost for the tour is $200 per person, including lunch and an overnight stay at Admiral Leigh High Golf Resort (225 Joel Blvd; © 239/369-2121).

THE TAMPA BAY AREA Busch Gardens (© 888/800-5447 or 813/987-5283; www.buschgardens.com) unveiled its latest, scream worthy five-story family roller coaster, Cheetah Chase, featuring 1,200 feet of track, speeds up to 22 mph, drops, turns, and corkscrews. Downtown, the Florida Aquarium (© 813/273-4000; www.flaquarium.net) added Explore a Shore, a 2.2-acre outdoor aquatic discovery zone for kids featuring sealife models, a pirate ship, waterslide, water cannons, and live animals. The two-story, 24-foot-long pirate ship will allow kids to fire water cannons from the deck, climb across cargo nets, view a shipwreck through a telescope, and take the helm to follow a map to buried treasure. Kids can also climb on a 10-foot eel reef rock structure, slide through tunnels, and crawl through an 8-by-4-foot wave in the Surf's Up Wave Tunnel.

The Philadelphia Phillies (© 727/442-8496 or 215/436-1000; www.phillies.mlb.com) moved to new spring training digs in Clearwater—Bright House Networks Field (601 Old Coachman Rd.; © 727/442-8496).

The **Hyatt Sarasota** (1000 Blvd. of the Arts; ✆ **800/233-1234** or 941/953-1234) has received a $9.5 million renovation, giving the hotel a more updated look as well as a lagoon pool featuring a 30-foot waterfall and 12-person whirlpool spa.

WALT DISNEY WORLD & ORLANDO Disney's Saratoga Springs Resort and Spa (✆ 407/827-1100 or 407/407/939-6244; www.disneyworld.com), the latest Disney Vacation Club venture, opened in spring 2004 and features a state-of-the-art spa, and a decor scheme inspired by 19th-century upstate New York. Meanwhile, Disney's **Pop Century Resort** (✆ **407/938-4000** or 407/939-6000; disneyworld.com), opened in December 2003, is Mickey's newest budget property and features themed buildings decorated with larger-than-life memorabilia from the past 50 years.

On the restaurant front, **Tchoup Chop** (✆ **407/503-2467**; www.emerils.com) is the most noteworthy new arrival in town. It's Emeril Lagasse's second Orlando eatery and located in Universal's Royal Pacific Resort.

In the theme parks, Disney raised ticket prices $2 to $54.75 for adults. Epcot's new out-of-this-world (literally) attraction, **Mission: Space,** opened in August 2003 to great acclaim—even NASA astronauts have voiced approval of this simulator.

Universal Studios Florida (✆ **800/837-2273;** www.universalorlando.com) welcomed two new attractions. **Shrek 4-D** is a 20-minute show that can be seen, heard, felt, and smelled thanks to film and motion simulators, Ogre-Vision glasses, and other special effects, including water spritzers. **Jimmy Neutron's Nicktoon Blast** lets riders board a spinning, careening adventure

that includes a battle against Yokians—evil, egg-shaped aliens.

SeaWorld (✆ **800/327-2424** or 407/351-3600; www.seaworld.com) is diving deeper into the restaurant game with **Dine with Shamu,** a reservations-only seafood buffet served poolside with Shamu as a special guest and **Sharks Underwater Grill,** where diners can dig into Florida and Caribbean treats while watching denizens of the deep swim by in the Terrors of the Deep exhibit. SeaWorld also has added a new shark encounter that lets snorkelers and divers have limited contact with some of the 58 sharks in its Terrors of the Deep area ($125).

Universal and SeaWorld also raised their ticket prices ($53.75 adults at SeaWorld and $54.75 at Universal Orlando).

NORTHEAST FLORIDA Believe it or not, there is something scarier in Daytona than half naked, mullet-sporting/bikini-wearing teenagers. **Haunts of Daytona** (✆ **386/253-6034;** www.hauntsofdaytona.com) is the only ghost tour in Florida that is owned and operated by a certified ghost hunter and active certified paranormal researcher. Tours begin at 7:30pm. Tickets are $8 per person; children under 6 are free.

NORTHWEST FLORIDA: THE PANHANDLE In July 2003, Pensacola Beach received a $16 million, 6-month beach nourishment project, restoring 200 feet of beach along an 8-mile stretch of coastline. With special attention paid to matching the new sand's color and grain size to the area's existing trademark sugar-white sand, the project brought sand from an off-shore borrow site, along with enough shells to keep beachcombers busy for quite some time.

The Best of Florida

Although it's the state nickname, describing Florida as just The Sunshine State is like calling Katie Couric "perky." Sure, it's true, but not all the time—and it doesn't nearly begin to describe the state's other marketable assets. There's a lot more to the state than just sunshine—which, by the way, isn't even a 24/7 given; it does rain here. Weather aside, choosing the best of Florida is by no means simple. While millions of visitors flock to Florida to escape the bleakness of winter and being landlocked, they don't all come down just for sun, fun, and Mickey Mouse. Sure, the promise of (mostly) clear skies and 800 miles of sparkling, sandy beaches is alluring, as are the animatronics and roller coasters in Orlando and Tampa, but there's much more to the state than that. In fact, in many ways, Florida is like a beautiful, blonde beauty queen who everyone thinks is all fluff until they find out she also happens to be a Rhodes scholar. Okay, so we're not saying that Florida is brilliant, per se, but what we are saying is that there's more than meets the eye that makes this one of the country's most popular year-round vacation destinations.

Here you can choose from a colorful, often kitschy assortment of accommodations, from deluxe resorts to mom-and-pop motels. You can visit remote little towns like Apalachicola or a multicultural megalopolis like Miami. Devour fresh seafood, from amberjack to oysters—and then work off those calories in such outdoor pursuits as bicycling, golfing, or kayaking. Despite overdevelopment in many parts of the state, Floridians have maintained thousands of acres of wilderness areas, from the little respite of Clam Pass County Park in downtown Naples to the magnificent Everglades National Park, which stretches across the state's southern tip.

Choosing the "best" of all this is a daunting task, and the selections in this chapter are only a rundown of some of the highlights. You'll find numerous other outstanding resorts, hotels, destinations, activities, and attractions described in the pages of this book. With an open mind and sense of adventure, you should be able to come up with some bests of your own.

1 The Best Beaches

- **Virginia Key** (Key Biscayne): The producers of *Survivor* could feasibly shoot their show on this ultra-secluded, picturesque, and deserted key, where people go purposely not to be found. See p. 118.
- **Bill Baggs Cape Florida State Park** (Key Biscayne): The pot of gold at the end of the rainbow, Bill Baggs Cape Florida State Park

radiates serenity with 1¼ miles of sandy beach, nature trails, and even a historic lighthouse that recalls an era before pristine places like this one gave way to avaricious developers and pollutants. See p. 125.
- **Lummus Park Beach** (South Beach): This beach is world renowned, not necessarily for its pristine sands, but for its more

Florida

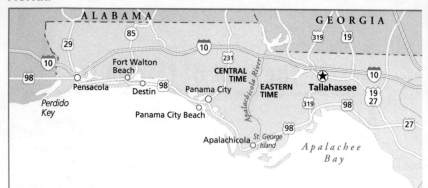

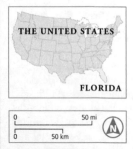

Gulf of Mexico

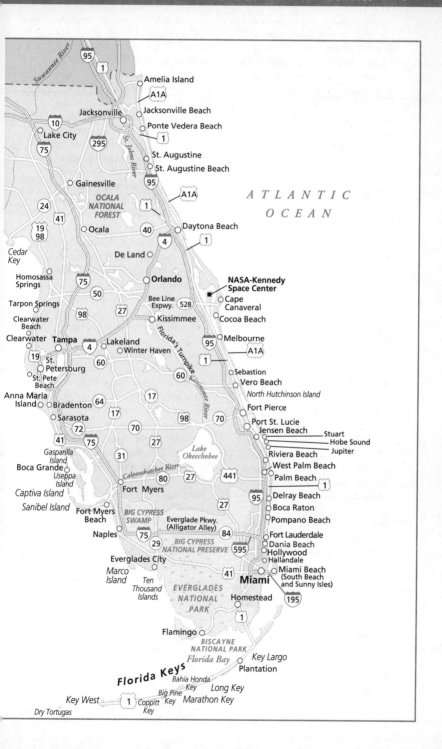

common name of **South Beach,** on which seeing, being seen, and, at times, the obscene, go hand in hand with the sunscreen and beach towels. The 12th Street section of this beach is the beach of choice for gay residents and travelers who come to show off just how much time they've spent in the gym and, of course, catch up on the latest gossip and upcoming must-attend parties and events. Oftentimes, this beach is the venue for some of the liveliest parties South Beach has ever seen. See p. 118.

- **Haulover Beach** (Miami Beach): Nestled between the Intracoastal Waterway and the ocean, especially at the north end, is the place to be for that all-over tan: Haulover is the city's only clothing-optional— aka nude—beach. See p. 132.

- **Bahia Honda State Park** (Bahia Honda Key): One of the nicest and most peaceful beaches in Florida, located amidst 635 acres of nature trails and even a portion of Henry Flagler's railroad. See p. 185.

- **John U. Lloyd Beach State Park** (Dania Beach): Unfettered by high-rise condominiums, T-shirt shops, and hotels, this wonderful beach boasts an untouched shoreline surrounded by a canopy of Australian pine to ensure complete seclusion. See p. 243.

- **Lover's Key State Park** (Fort Myers Beach): You'll have to walk or take a tram through a bird-filled forest of mangroves to this gorgeous, unspoiled beach just a few miles south of busy Fort Myers Beach. Although Sanibel Island gets all the accolades, the shelling here is just as good, if not better. See p. 332.

- **Cayo Costa State Park** (off Captiva Island): These days, deserted tropical islands with great beaches are scarce in Florida, but this 2,132-acre barrier strip of sand,

pine forests, mangrove swamps, oak hammocks, and grasslands provides a genuine get-away-from-it-all experience. Access is only by boat from nearby Gasparilla, Pine, and Captiva islands. See p. 358.

- **Naples Beach** (Naples): Many Florida cities and towns have beaches, but few are as lovely as the gorgeous strip that runs in front of Naples' famous Millionaires' Row. You don't have to be rich to wander its length, peer at the mansions, and stroll on historic Naples Pier to catch a sunset over the Gulf. See p. 365.

- **Caladesi Island State Park** (Clearwater Beach): Even though 3½-mile-long Caladesi Island is in the heavily developed Tampa Bay area, it has a lovely, relatively secluded beach with soft sand edged in sea grass and palmettos. Dolphins cavort in offshore waters. In the park itself, there's a nature trail, and you might see one of the rattlesnakes, black racers, raccoons, armadillos, or rabbits that live here. The park is accessible only by ferry from Honeymoon Island State Recreation Area off Dunedin. See p. 422.

- **Fort DeSoto Park** (St. Petersburg): Where else can you get a good tan *and* a history lesson? At Fort DeSoto Park, you not only have 1,136 acres of five interconnected islands and 3 miles of unfettered beaches, but a fort, for which the park was named, that's listed on the National Register of Historic Places, nature trails, fishing piers, a 2¼-mile canoe trail, and spectacular views of Tampa Bay and the Gulf. See p. 424.

- **Canaveral National Seashore** (Cape Canaveral): Midway between the crowded attractions at Daytona Beach and the Kennedy Space Center is a protected stretch of coastline 24 miles long, backed by cabbage palms, sea grapes, and palmettos. See p. 518.

- **Gulf Islands National Seashore** (Pensacola): You could argue that all of Northwest Florida's Gulf shore is one of America's great beaches—an almost-uninterrupted stretch of pure white sand that runs the entire length of the Panhandle, from Perdido Key to St. George Island. The Gulf Islands National Seashore preserves much of this natural wonder in its undeveloped state. Countless terns, snowy plovers, black skimmers, and other birds nest along the dunes topped with sea oats. East of the national seashore and equally beautiful are **Grayton Beach State Park** near Destin and **St. George Island State Park** off Apalachicola. See p. 584.

- **St. Andrews State Park** (Panama City Beach): With more than 1,000 acres of dazzling white sand and dunes, this preserved wilderness demonstrates what Panama City Beach looked like before motels and condominiums lined its shore, with lacy, golden sea oats swaying in Gulf breezes and fragrant rosemary growing wild. The area is also home to foxes, coyotes, and a herd of deer. See p. 615.

2 The Best Fishing

- **The Keys:** The Keys boast some world-class deep-sea fishing; the prize is such big-game fish as marlin, sailfish, and tuna. There's reef fishing as well, for "eating fish" like snapper and grouper, and backcountry fishing for bonefish, tarpon, and other "stalking" fish. Dozens of charter-fishing boats operate from Key West marinas and from other less-popular keys. Islamorada, in the Upper Keys, is the sport-fishing capital of the world. Anglers compete for trophy sailfish, marlin, wahoo, and kingfish at many annual big-money tournaments. Seven-Mile Bridge, linking the Middle and Lower Keys, is known as "the longest fishing bridge in the world"; it's also a favorite spot for local fishers who wait for barracuda, yellowtail, and dolphin to bite. See p. 175.

- **Lake Okeechobee:** Many visitors to the Treasure Coast come to fish, and they certainly get their fill off the miles of Atlantic shore and on the inland rivers. If you want to fish freshwater and nothing else, head for Lake Okeechobee, the state's largest lake, which is chock-full of good eating fish. It covers more than 467,000 acres; that's more than 730 square miles. At one time, the lake supported an enormous commercial fishing industry. Due to a commercial fishing-net ban, however, much of that industry has died off, leaving the sport fishers all the rich bounty of the lake. See p. 317.

- **Stuart:** Known as the "Sailfish Capital of the World," Stuart is an angler's haven. The fish bite year-round, but peak months are December through March and June through July. Sailfishing is an art of its own—beginners need to learn to feel that exact moment to let the reel drag so that the fish run with the lure. See p. 300.

- **Boca Grande:** The deep, shadowy holes of Boca Grande Pass, between Gasparilla and Cayo Costa islands off Fort Myers, harbor the mighty tarpon, the "silver king of the seas." Teddy Roosevelt and his rich buddies used to bag tarpon in these waters, and anglers from around the globe still compete every July in the World's Richest Tarpon Tournament. See p. 358.

- **Destin:** Florida's largest charter-boat fleet, with more than 140 vessels, is based in this Panhandle town, which calls itself the "World's Luckiest Fishing Village."

Anglers here have landed championship catches of grouper, amberjack, snapper, mackerel, cobia, sailfish, wahoo, tuna, and blue marlin. See p. 600.

3 The Best Golf Courses

- **Biltmore Hotel** (Miami): The beautiful, rolling 18-hole golf course designed by Donald Ross and located at the majestic Biltmore Hotel in Coral Gables is open to the public and is a favorite of Bill Clinton's. See p. 84.
- **Doral Golf Resort and Spa** (Miami): Four championship courses make the Doral one of Miami's best golf destinations. One course, the legendary Blue Monster, is the site of the annual Doral-Ryder Open. See p. 81.
- **Turnberry Isle Resort and Club** (Aventura, North Miami Beach): These two courses by Robert Trent Jones Sr. are open only to guests but are among the city's best. See p. 83.
- **The Inn at Boca Teeca** (Boca Raton): For over 3 decades, this inn has been attracting golf fanatics who could care less about the small, but comfortable, rooms because they're too busy out on the superb 27-hole golf course at the Inn's Boca Teeca Country Club, open only to members and guests of the inn. See p. 268.
- **PGA National Resort & Spa** (Palm Beach): This rambling resort, the national headquarters of the PGA, is a premier golf destination, with five 18-hole courses on more than 2,300 acres. See p. 295.
- **Emerald Dunes Golf Course** (West Palm Beach): This gorgeous Tom Fazio–designed course (featuring 60 acres of water and stunning views of the ocean) is pricey but one of only a few in the area open to the public. See p. 276.
- **Champions Club at Summerfield** (Stuart): The best in the area, this rural, somewhat-challenging championship course was designed by Tom Fazio and built in 1994. It also offers great glimpses of wildlife amid the wetlands. See p. 300.
- **Tiburón Golf Club** (Naples): Greg Norman designed the 36 championship holes at this course to play like a British Open—but without the thick thatch rough. The course is now home to the luxurious Ritz-Carlton Golf Resort, Naples. See p. 365.
- **Naples Beach Hotel & Golf Club** (Naples): One of the state's oldest, this resort course is relatively flat, but small greens and masterful bunkers will test your skills. In addition, one of Florida's most charming resort hotels is across the street. See p. 369.
- **Mangrove Bay Golf Course** (St. Petersburg): One of the nation's top 50 municipal courses, the Mangrove Bay course hugs the inlets of Old Tampa Bay and offers 18-hole, par-72 play. Facilities include a driving range; lessons and golf-club rental are also available. See p. 413.
- **The Westin Innisbrook Resort** (Tarpon Springs): *Golfweek* has called Innisbrook's Copperhead Course, former home of the annual JCPenney Classic, number one in Florida. One thousand students a year go through Innisbrook's Golf Institute, and golfers from around the world come to play the 600 acres of courses. See p. 431.

- **Walt Disney World** (Orlando): The resorts surrounding the theme parks have 99 regulation holes that let you walk in the footsteps (and share the frustrations) of the game's greatest players. Those with a shorter stroke can play the master miniature courses: Fantasia Gardens and Winter Summerland. See p. 509.
- **Ladies Professional Golf Association/LPGA International** (Daytona Beach): This "women-friendly" course (unless you're Anika Sorenson) has multiple tee settings, unrestricted tee times, a great pro shop, and state-of-the-art facilities. Designed by Rees-Jones, the older of the two courses here was chosen as one of the "Top Ten You Can Play" by *Golf* magazine. See p. 529.
- **TPC at Sawgrass** (Ponte Vedra Beach, near Jacksonville): With 99 holes, Pete Dye's Tournament Players Club (TPC) at Sawgrass makes top-10 lists everywhere. The 17th hole, on a tricky island, is one of the most photographed holes in the world. See p. 561.
- **Ocean Hammock Golf Club** (Palm Coast, between Daytona Beach and St. Augustine): Opened in late 2000 with six of its holes actually skirting the Atlantic Ocean, this Jack Nicklaus–designed course is the first authentic seaside links built in Florida since the 1920s. See p. 548.
- **Amelia Island Plantation** (Amelia Island): This exclusive resort has three of the state's best courses. Long Point Club, designed by Tom Fazio, is the most beautiful and challenging. Pete Dye's Amelia Links is another oceanfront course. Both are open only to resort guests. See p. 574.
- **Marriott's Bay Point Resort Village** (Panama City Beach): Thirty-six holes of championship golf at this Marriott include the Lagoon Legends course, one of the country's most difficult. Nearby is The Hombre, an 18-holer where O. J. Simpson played a round right after his acquittal. See p. 620.

4 The Best Small Towns

- **Sebastian** (Treasure Coast): Known as one of the last remaining fishing villages in Florida, Sebastian is located at the northern tip of the Treasure Coast region in Indian River County. The area's small-town feel and laid-back, relaxed atmosphere is one of its biggest draws. See p. 310.
- **Boca Grande** (Southwest Florida): Founded in the 1880s, this little village on Gasparilla Island retains the flavor of those Victorian times. Luxurious mansions coexist with simple homes of fishermen who guide rich folks in search of tarpon, just as their ancestors did a century ago. The du Ponts, Mellons, and Astors once arrived, for the wintertime "social season," at the town's railway depot, which has been restored and now houses shops and the Loose Caboose Restaurant and Ice Cream Parlor. See p. 358.
- **Olde Naples** (Naples): Started in 1886 as a real-estate development, the original part of Naples retains much of Old Florida's charm, with tree-lined streets dividing many of the original clapboard homes. With the houses on Millionaires' Row virtually hidden by dense foliage and with no high-rises in sight, Naples Beach seems far removed from today's modern city. See p. 365.

- **Tarpon Springs** (Southwest Florida): Tarpon Springs calls itself the "Sponge Capital of the World," because immigrants from Greece settled here in the late 1800s to harvest the sponges that grew in abundance offshore. Their descendants make Tarpon Springs a fascinating center of transplanted Greek culture. Sponges still arrive at the historic Sponge Docks, where a lively, carnival-like atmosphere and Greek cuisine prevail. Restored Victorian homes facing Spring Bayou also make this one of the most picturesque towns in the state. See p. 434.

- **Fernandina Beach** (Northeast Florida): You can stay at two of Florida's ritziest resorts on Amelia Island, but the real charm here is in the quaint town of Fernandina Beach, where a 50-block area of Victorian and Queen Anne homes is listed on the National Register of Historic Places. See p. 570.

- **Apalachicola** (Northwest Florida): Located at the mouth of the Apalachicola River, this Gulf-shore town was a major cotton port before the Civil War, and a later timber boom resulted in the fine Victorian homes that still grace Apalachicola's uncurbed streets. It was here that Dr. John Gorrie invented the forerunner of the air conditioner, which revolutionized Florida's tourism industry. Today, the major industry is seafood, with famous Apalachicola oysters eaten fresh off the boats. See p. 624.

- **Pensacola** (Northwest Florida): One of America's oldest communities, Pensacola has preserved its Spanish, French, and English heritage in the Seville Historic District and Historic Pensacola Village. Spanish-named streets are bordered by both French-style wrought-iron balconies reminiscent of New Orleans and English colonial churches like those in Williamsburg, Virginia. See p. 580.

5 The Best Luxury Resorts

- **Ritz-Carlton Key Biscayne** (Key Biscayne; © 800/241-3333 or 305/365-4500): In addition to the Ritz's consistently superior services and amenities, this British-colonial–style version of the Ritz rises above its casual Key Biscayne surroundings with a stellar view of the Atlantic Ocean, not to mention an equally impressive 20,000-square-foot spa. See p. 76.

- **Mandarin Oriental, Miami** (Brickell Key, Miami; © 305/913-8288): The swank and stunning Mandarin Oriental features a waterfront location, residential-style rooms (most with balconies), superb service, a spa frequented by J-Lo, and several upscale dining and bar facilities previously unknown to its nearby downtown Miami locale. See p. 80.

- **Ritz-Carlton** (South Beach; © 800/241-3333 or 786/276-4000): Taking the concept of swanky South Beach to a very literal level, the Ritz-Carlton South Beach may be a landmark building restored to its original 1950s Art Moderne style, but in terms of the hotel's standout service, amenities, and oceanfront, everything else is very much in the immediate present. See p. 66.

- **The Breakers** (Palm Beach; © 800/833-3141 or 561/655-6611): This stately, historic hotel epitomizes la dolce vita, Palm Beach style, featuring expansive manicured lawns, an elegant lobby, the state's oldest and very scenic golf course, and impeccable service. See p. 282.

- **Four Seasons Resort Palm Beach** (Palm Beach; ℂ **800/432-2335** or 561/582-2800): "Exquisite" is the adjective most often used to describe this posher than Posh Spice and David Beckham combined luxe hotel. Luxurious but hardly stuffy, this hotel was the stay of choice for quintessential aging rockers Aerosmith, who took great advantage of post-concert pampering. See p. 283.
- **LaPlaya Beach & Golf Resort** (Naples; ℂ **800/237-6883** or 239/597-3123): More intimate than the Ritz, the equally luxe LaPlaya Beach & Golf Resort offers spacious rooms, each with a completely private balcony with seating and lighting overlooking the pristine waters of the Gulf or Vanderbilt Bay. New to the completely renovated property are four uniquely designed swimming pools, two lagoons and an outdoor whirlpool, Tiki Bar, retail shop, the 4,500-square-foot Spa-Terre, 2,700-square-foot fitness center, 234-seat Gulf-view Baleen Restaurant and bar, and a 6,907-yard championship layout 18-hole golf course designed by Bob Cupp and David Leadbetter Golf School. See p. 370.
- **The Ritz-Carlton Golf Resort, Naples** (Naples; ℂ **888/856-4372** or 239/593-2000): This luxurious new Mediterranean-style resort takes full advantage of the Greg Norman–designed Tiburón Golf Club. Guests here can use the beach and spa at The Ritz-Carlton, Naples, nearby. See p. 371.
- **The Ritz-Carlton, Naples** (Naples; ℂ **888/856-4372** or 239/598-3300): This opulent 14-story Mediterranean-style hotel at Vanderbilt Beach is a favorite of affluent guests who like standard Ritz-Carlton amenities such as imported marble floors, antique art, Oriental rugs, Waterford crystal chandeliers, and afternoon British-style high tea. Guests relax in high-backed rockers on the verandas or unwind by the heated swimming pool set in a landscaped terrace, but they must walk through a narrow mangrove forest to reach the beach. See p. 372.
- **Don CeSar Beach Resort & Spa** (St. Pete Beach; ℂ **866/728-2206** or 727/360-1881): Dating back to 1928 and listed on the National Register of Historic Places, this "Pink Palace" tropical getaway is so romantic you may bump into six or seven honeymooning couples in one weekend. The lobby has classic high windows and archways, crystal chandeliers, marble floors, and original artworks. Most rooms have high ceilings and offer views of the Gulf or Boca Ciega Bay. See p. 427.
- **Disney's Grand Floridian Resort & Spa** (Orlando; ℂ **407/934-7639**): This magnificent Victorian inn has an opulent five-story lobby complete with a Chinese Chippendale aviary. An orchestra plays big-band music every evening near Victoria & Albert's, the resort's five-star restaurant. See p. 464.
- **Hyatt Regency Grand Cypress Resort** (Orlando; ℂ **800/233-1234** or 407/239-1234): This standout has some impressive treats, including a half-acre pool with a dozen waterfalls and three spas, 12 tennis courts, four Jack Nicklaus–designed golf courses, and a 45-acre nature walk. All that adds up to luxury. See p. 470.
- **Amelia Island Plantation** (Amelia Island; ℂ **888/261-6161** or 904/261-6161): Set amid magnolias, oak trees, and the Atlantic Ocean, this gracious resort is straight out of the Deep South. It's more rustic than the nearby Ritz, but it has excellent hiking and biking paths,

tennis, swimming, horseback riding, and boating. Golfers can enjoy exclusive use of two of the top courses in Florida. See p. 574 and "The Best Golf Courses," in section 3, earlier in this chapter.

6 The Best Romantic Hideaways

- **Hotel Place St. Michel** (Coral Gables; ℂ **800/848-HOTEL** or 305/444-1666): This European-style hotel in the heart of Coral Gables is one of the city's most romantic options. The accommodations and hospitality are very old-world European, complete with dark wood-paneled walls, cozy beds, beautiful antiques, and a quiet elegance that seems startlingly out of place in trendy Miami. See p. 85.

- **Hotel Impala** (Miami Beach; ℂ **800/646-7252** or 305/673-2021): During the heyday of 1990s excess, Miami Beach was known for the fabulous parties thrown by the eclectic designer Gianni Versace. The late Versace desired an intimate European-styled guesthouse that would please well-seasoned travelers, and the Impala is the result. His personal touch on this renovated Mediterranean inn is still evident, from the Greco-Roman frescoes and friezes to an intimate garden that is perfumed with the scents from carefully hanging lilies and gardenias. See p. 69.

- **Abbey Hotel** (South Beach; ℂ **888/61-ABBEY** or 305/531-0031): This '40s-revival boutique hotel, tucked away in a mostly residential neighborhood, is a haven from the neighboring South Beach hoopla. See p. 69.

- **Jules' Undersea Lodge** (Key Largo; ℂ **305/451-2353**): Submerge yourself in this single-room Atlantis-like hotel that offers a surprisingly comfortable suite 30 feet underwater. Don't worry; there's plenty of breathing room. See p. 177.

- **Little Palm Island** (Little Torch Key; ℂ **800/343-8567** or 305/872-2524): Accessible only by boat, this private 5-acre island is not only remote, it's romantic, featuring no TVs, telephones, or faxes in the luxurious thatched cottages. See p. 187.

- **Marquesa Hotel** (Key West; ℂ **800/869-4631** or 305/292-1919): Don't be fooled by the Marquesa's location on heavily populated Key West: This charming B&B is in a wonderful world of its own, far enough from the tumult, yet close enough if you want it. See p. 206.

- **The Gardens Hotel** (Key West; ℂ **800/526-2664** or 305/294-2661): A well kept, hidden secret—until now, The Gardens Hotel is an exotic, lush, serene, and sultry escape from the frat boy madness that ensues on nearby Duval Street. See p. 204.

- **Sundy House** (Delray Beach; ℂ **877/439-9601** or 561/272-5678): With just 11 suites surrounded by over 5,000 species of exotic plants and flowers, gazebos and rolling streams, Sundy House is a gorgeous getaway close enough to the beach, but safely hidden from the mood-ruining madness and conventionality of your typical tourist-class beach hotel. See p. 267.

- **Island's End Resort** (St. Pete Beach; ℂ **727/360-5023**). Sitting right on Pass-a-Grille, where the Gulf of Mexico meets Tampa Bay, this little all-cottage retreat is a great hideaway from the maddening crowds of St. Pete Beach. You won't have an on-site restaurant, bar, and other such amenities, but you can step from your cottage right onto the beach. And if you get the unit with two living rooms, you'll have a whirlpool tub and your own private Gulf-side swimming pool. See p. 429.

- **Turtle Beach Resort** (Siesta Key, off Sarasota; ℂ **941/349-4554**): Sitting beside the bay, this intimate little charmer began life years ago as a traditional Old Florida fishing camp, but today it's one of the state's most romantic retreats. It's a tightly packed little place, but high wooden fences surround each unit's private outdoor hot tub, and one-way mirror walls let you lounge in bed while passersby see only reflections of themselves. See p. 449.

- **Disney's Wilderness Lodge** (Lake Buena Vista; ℂ **407/934-7639**): This property is reminiscent of the lodge at Yellowstone. The geyser out back, the mammoth stone hearth in the lobby, the dining room's 360–degree view of Bay Lake, and the nightly electric water pageants are just a few of the reasons to stay here. Some guest rooms have patios or balconies overlooking the lake, woodlands, or a meadow. See p. 466.

- **The Villas of Grand Cypress** (Orlando; ℂ **800/835-7377** or 407/239-4700): This luxury condominium resort offers lush grounds dotted with bougainvillea and hibiscus, lakes fat with largemouth bass and bream, and grounds speckled with trumpeter swans, wood ducks, and the occasional fox or bobcat. It shares a golf academy, racquet club, and equestrian center with the Hyatt Regency Grand Cypress. Best of all, the

woodsy grounds make you feel as if you're far, far from Disney, which is right next door. See p. 471.

- **The Lodge & Club at Ponte Vedra Beach** (Jacksonville; ℂ **800/ 243-4304** or 904/273-9500): Every unit at this intimate hotel in upscale Ponte Vedra Beach has a romantic seat built in front of its oceanview window, plus there's a big bathroom with a two-person tub and a separate shower. Gas fireplaces in most units add even more charm. One of the three swimming pools and whirlpools here is reserved exclusively for couples. You can also get married in the semicircular meeting room overlooking the Atlantic. See p. 565.

- **Henderson Park Inn** (Destin; ℂ **800/336-4853** or 850/837-4853): Nestled against the eastern edge of lovely Henderson Beach State Recreation Area, this Cape Hatteras–style bed-and-breakfast offers romantic escapes without screaming kids. The individually decorated rooms ooze Victorian charm, with high ceilings, fireplaces, Queen Anne furniture, and Gulf views from private balconies. Some even have canopy beds. See p. 603.

- **Seaside** (near Destin; ℂ **800/277-8696** or 850/231-1320): If residents of Northwest Florida don't stay at the Henderson Park Inn for their getaways, they head for the romantic Gulf-front cottages at Seaside. Built in the 1980s but evoking the 1880s, the Victorian-style village of Seaside (a short drive east of Destin) has several of its cozy cottages designed especially for honeymooners. See p. 606.

7 The Best Moderately Priced Accommodations

- **Abbey Hotel** (South Beach; ℂ **888/61-ABBEY** or 305/531-0031): Off the beaten path, this '40s-revival boutique hotel gives

good reason to get off the main drag and revel in its quiet elegance. See p. 69.

- **Hotel Leon** (South Beach; ☎ **305/ 673-3767**): A true value, this charismatic and hip sliver of a property has won the loyalty of fashion industrialists and romantics alike. Built in 1929 and restored in 1996, the hotel still retains many original details such as facades, woodwork, and even fireplaces. See p. 70.
- **The Creek** (South Beach; ☎ **866/ 445-4800** or 305/538-1951): Part Playboy's Penthouse and part Jetsons, The Creek Hotel is a kitschy, 81-room haven for hipsters who don't feel the need to spend $400 a night for a hip hotel. Of the three types of rooms—shared, Cabana, and Waterway Standard—the latter is the way to go, with 18 signature rooms designed by local artists and designers. An 8,000-square-foot pool deck with a 40-foot fully stocked bar, outdoor barbecues, Ms. Pacman, pool tables, and theater, The Creek is somewhere you wouldn't mind being stuck without a paddle. See p. 72.
- **Pelican Hotel** (South Beach; ☎ **800/7-PELICAN** or 305/673-3373): Owned by the creative owners of the Diesel Jeans company, the Pelican is South Beach's only self-professed "toy-hotel," in which each of its 30 rooms and suites is decorated as outrageously as some of the area's more colorful drag queens. See p. 71.
- **Indian Creek Hotel** (Miami Beach; ☎ **800/491-2772** or 305/531-2727): A charming Key West–style hotel that's full of character, the Indian Creek Hotel takes you back in time, with period furnishings, attitude-free service, and a quaint pool and garden, completely lacking water slides, Tiki huts, or calypso bands. See p. 74.
- **Whitelaw Hotel** (South Beach; ☎ **305/398-7000**): With a slogan that reads "clean sheets, hot water, and stiff drinks," the Whitelaw Hotel stands apart from the other boutique hotels with its fierce sense of humor, but it never compromises on the fabulous amenities found at some of the area's more serious properties. See p. 72.
- **Conch Key Cottages** (Marathon; ☎ **800/330-1577** or 305/289-1377): This oceanfront hideaway offers rustic but immaculate and well-outfitted cottages that are especially popular with families. Each has a hammock, barbecue grill, and kitchen. See p. 178.
- **Banyan Marina Resort** (Fort Lauderdale; ☎ **954/524-4430**): These fabulous waterfront apartments located on a beautifully landscaped residential island may have you vowing never to stay in a hotel again. See p. 252.
- **Hotel Biba** (West Palm Beach; ☎ **561/832-0094**): The mod squad has adopted—and adapted—this '40s-style motel into a Jetsonian, jet-set hangout that provides swank and sleek shelter from the upper-crusty hotels that surround it. See p. 286.
- **Island's End Resort** (St. Pete Beach; ☎ **727/360-5023**): A wonderful respite from the maddening crowd, and a great bargain to boot, this little all-cottage hideaway sits right on the southern tip of St. Pete Beach, smack-dab on Pass-a-Grille, where the Gulf of Mexico meets Tampa Bay. You can step from the six contemporary cottages right onto the beach. One unit even has its own private swimming pool. See p. 429.
- **Best Western Lake Buena Vista Hotel** (Lake Buena Vista; ☎ **800/ 348-3765** or 407/828-2424): This 12-acre, 18-story lakefront hotel is

well kept and immaculate, with more upscale rooms and public areas than you might expect at a Best Western. And it has a great location next to Walt Disney World. See p. 469.

- **Disney's Caribbean Beach Resort** (Lake Buena Vista; ☎ **407/934-7639** or 407/934-3400): Here's good value by Disney standards. Units on the 200-acre resort are grouped in five villages around a duck-filled lake. The welcoming rooms feature oak furniture and chintz bedspreads. There are also seven swimming pools, a 1½-mile promenade, and a festive food court. See p. 466.

- **Staybridge Suites** (Lake Buena Vista; ☎ **800/866-4549** or 407/238-0777): Close to the action of Downtown Disney and the theme parks, this resort's one- and two-bedroom suites have full kitchens and are larger and more comfortable than most of the competition's. And to help you relax, the resort will do your grocery shopping for you, so you don't have to deal with the hassle. See p. 472.

- **Casa Monica Hotel** (St. Augustine; ☎ **800/648-1888** or 904/827-1888): Built in 1888 as a luxury hotel, this Spanish-style building was gutted and restored to its previous elegance in 1998. Most interesting of the guest quarters are suites installed in two tile-topped towers and a fortresslike central turret. One suite in the turret has a half-round living room with gun-port windows overlooking St. Augustine's historic district. See p. 549.

- **Gibson Inn** (Apalachicola; ☎ **850/653-2191**): Built in 1907 as a seaman's hotel and gorgeously restored in 1985, this cupola-topped inn is such a brilliant example of Victorian architecture that it's listed on the National Register of Historic Inns. No two guest rooms are alike (some still have the original sinks in the sleeping area), but all are richly furnished with period reproductions. Grab a drink from the bar and relax in one of the high-backed rockers on the old-fashioned veranda. See p. 627.

2

Planning Your Trip to Florida

Whether you plan to spend a day, a week, 2 weeks, or longer in Florida, you'll need to make many "where," "when," and "how" choices before you leave home. This chapter explains how best to plan your trip.

1 The Regions in Brief

The first decision you'll have to make is where to go in Florida. Contrary to popular belief, it's not all sun, sand, and hanging chads—there are countless cultural, culinary, and nocturnal diversions as well. Of course, you will find ample sun, sea, and sand all along the 800 miles of shoreline here, but not every place in the Sunshine State is warm all the time. Many Florida beaches are lined with flashy hotels and condominiums, whereas others are pristinely preserved in their natural states. You can spend your days in busy cosmopolitan cities or while them away in picturesque small towns steeped in history. You can take the kids to see Mickey Mouse, or you can find a romantic retreat far from the madding crowds. The choice is yours.

Here is a brief rundown of the state's regions to help get you started.

MIAMI & MIAMI BEACH Sprawling across the southeastern corner of the state, metropolitan Miami is a city that prides itself on benefiting from its multiple, vibrant personalities, and its no passport necessary international flair. Here you will hear a cacophony of Spanish and many other languages, not to mention accents, spoken all around you, for this cosmopolitan area is a melting pot of immigrants from Latin America, the Caribbean, and, undeniably, the northeastern United States in particular.

Cross the causeways and you'll come to the sands of Miami Beach, long a resort mecca and home to the hyper-trendy South Beach, famous for its Art Deco architecture, electric nightlife, and celebrity sightings. See chapters 4 and 5 for more on the Miami area and p. 53 for descriptions of the different districts within Miami.

THE KEYS From the southern tip of the Florida mainland, U.S. 1 travels through a 100-mile-long string of islands stretching from Key Largo to the famous and funky yet laid-back "Conch Republic" of Key West, only 90 miles from Cuba and the southernmost point in the United States (it's always warm down here). While some of the islands are crammed with strip malls and tourist traps, most are dense with unusual species of tropical flora and fauna. The Keys don't have the best beaches in Florida, but the waters here—all in a vast marine preserve—offer the state's best scuba diving and snorkeling and some of its best deep-sea fishing. See chapter 6, "The Keys & the Dry Tortugas," for more information on this region.

THE EVERGLADES & BISCAYNE NATIONAL PARK This is not your B-movie swamp. In fact, no excessive Hollywood studio budget could afford to replicate the stunning beauty found in this national landmark.

Encompassing more than 2,000 square miles and 1.5 million acres, Everglades National Park covers the entire southern tip of Florida. The park, along with nearby Big Cypress National Preserve, protects a unique and fragile "River of Grass" ecosystem teeming with wildlife that is best seen by canoe, by boat, or on long or short hikes. To the east of the Everglades is Biscayne National Park, preserving the northernmost living-coral reefs in the continental United States. See chapter 7 for more information on these parks.

THE GOLD COAST North of Miami, the Gold Coast is aptly named, for here are booming Hollywood and Fort Lauderdale and ritzy Boca Raton and Palm Beach—sun-kissed, glitzy, glammy, and sandy playgrounds of the rich and famous. Beyond its dozens of gorgeous beaches, the area offers fantastic shopping, entertainment, dining, boating, golfing, tennis, and many places to relax in beautiful settings. With some of the country's most famous golf courses and even more tennis courts, this area also attracts big-name tournaments. See chapter 8 to learn more about the Gold Coast.

THE TREASURE COAST Despite gaining unprecedented numbers of new residents in recent years, the beach communities running from Hobe Sound north to Sebastian Inlet have successfully and blissfully managed to retain their small-town feel. In addition to a vast array of wildlife (not to be mistaken with nightlife, which is intentionally absent from these parts), the area has a rich and colorful history. Its name stems from a violent 1715 hurricane that sunk an entire fleet of treasure-laden Spanish ships. The sea around Sebastian Inlet draws surfers to the largest swells in the state, and the area has some great fishing as well. See chapter 9 for more information on the Treasure Coast.

SOUTHWEST FLORIDA Ever since inventor Thomas Alva Edison built a home here in 1885, some of America's wealthiest families have spent their winters along Florida's southwest coast. They are attracted by the area's subtropical climate, shell-strewn beaches, and intricate waterways winding among 10,000-plus islands. Many charming remnants of Old Florida coexist with modern resorts in the sophisticated riverfront towns of Fort Myers and Naples and on islands like Gasparilla, Useppa, Sanibel, Captiva, and Marco. And thanks to some timely preservation, the area has many wildlife refuges, including the "backdoor" entrance to Everglades National Park. See chapter 10, "Southwest Florida."

THE TAMPA BAY AREA Halfway down the west coast of Florida lies Tampa Bay, one of the state's most densely populated areas. A busy seaport and commercial center, the city of Tampa is home to Busch Gardens Tampa Bay, which is both a major theme park and one of the country's largest zoos. Boasting a unique pier and fine museums, St. Petersburg's waterfront downtown is one of Florida's most pleasant. Most visitors elect to stay near the beaches skirting the narrow barrier islands running some 25 miles between St. Pete Beach and Clearwater Beach. Across the bay to the south lies Sarasota, one of Florida's prime performing-arts venues, the riverfront town of Bradenton, and another string of barrier islands with great beaches and resorts spanning every price range. See chapter 11 for more information.

WALT DISNEY WORLD & ORLANDO Walt Disney announced plans to build the Magic Kingdom in 1965, a year before his death and 6 years before the theme park opened, changing forever what was then a sleepy Southern town. Walt Disney

World claims four distinct parks, two entertainment districts, enough hotels and restaurants to fill a small city, and several smaller attractions including water parks and miniature-golf courses. And then there are the rapidly expanding Universal Studios Orlando and SeaWorld, as well as many more non-Disney attractions. Orlando is Florida's most popular tourist destination thanks not only to an animated rodent but also to those enterprising entertainment venues that have risen to the mouse's challenge. See chapter 12.

NORTHEAST FLORIDA The northeast section of the state contains the oldest permanent settlement in America—St. Augustine, where Spanish colonists arrived and settled more than 4 centuries ago. Today, its history comes to life in a quaint historic district. St. Augustine is bordered to the north by Jacksonville, an up-and-coming Sunbelt metropolis with miles of oceanfront beach and beautiful marine views along the St. Johns River. Up on the Georgia border, Amelia Island has two of Florida's finest resorts and its own historic town of Fernandina Beach. To the south of St. Augustine, Daytona Beach is the home of the Daytona International Speedway and is a maddening, spring-break mecca for the MTV generation.

Another brand of excitement is offered down at Cape Canaveral, where the Kennedy Space Center launches all manned U.S. space missions. See chapter 13.

NORTHWEST FLORIDA: THE PANHANDLE Historic roots run deep in Florida's narrow northwest extremity; and Pensacola's historic district, which blends Spanish, French, and British cultures, is a highlight of any visit to today's Panhandle. Despite that, however, the accents here are decidedly Deep South. So, too, are the powdery, dazzlingly white beaches that stretch for more than 80 miles past the resorts of Pensacola Beach, Fort Walton Beach, Destin, and Panama City Beach. The Gulf Islands National Seashore has preserved much of this beach and its wildlife, and inland are state parks that offer some of the state's best canoeing adventures. All this makes the area a favorite summertime vacation destination for residents of neighboring Georgia and Alabama, with whom Northwest Floridians share many Deep South traditions. Sitting in a pine and oak forest just 30 miles from the Georgia line, the state capital of Tallahassee has a moss-draped, football-loving charm all its own. See chapter 14 for more information.

2 Visitor Information

Your best sources for detailed information about a specific destination in Florida are the **local visitor information offices.** They're listed under "Orientation" or "Essentials" in the following chapters.

Contact **Visit Florida,** P.O. Box 1100, Tallahassee, FL 32302-1100 (© **888/7-FLA-USA;** www.flausa.com), the state's official tourism marketing agent, for a free comprehensive guide to the state. Florida State Parks have a new website at www.florida stateparks.org. Visit Florida also operates **welcome centers** 16 miles west of Pensacola on I-10, 4 miles north of Jennings on I-75, 7 miles north of Yulee on I-95, and 3 miles north of Campbellton on U.S. 231. There's also a walk-in information office in the west foyer of the New Capitol Building in Tallahassee (see chapter 14).

3 Money

How much money you spend on your Florida vacation will depend on your own desires and choices, when you go, and most definitely *where* you go.

The state has a wide range of accommodations, from some of the country's most luxurious and expensive beachfront resorts to no-frills but friendly mom-and-pop motels sitting right by the beach. If you can do without the luxuries, you needn't spend a fortune.

Tourism is Florida's biggest industry, and the economic law of supply and demand dictates that the prices of hotel rooms are highest during the seasons when tourists invade Florida: the winter months in the southern half of the state and during summertime up north.

See "When to Go," below, for details about Florida's high, low, and in-between seasons.

CREDIT CARDS & ATMS

The easiest way to pay for almost everything in Florida is with a credit card. MasterCard and Visa credit and debit cards are accepted almost everywhere. American Express, Diner's

Club, and Discover cards also are accepted, although not as widely as MasterCard and Visa.

The best way to get cash while you're traveling in Florida is to use your debit or credit cards at **ATMs.** Of the big national banks, **First Union Bank** and **Bank of America** have offices with ATMs throughout Florida.

Most ATMs are linked to a national network that most likely includes your bank at home. **Cirrus** (© 800/424-7787;www.mastercard.com/atmlocator) and **Plus** (© 800/843-7587; www.visa.com/atms) are the two most popular networks; check the back of your ATM card to see which network your bank belongs to. Use the toll-free numbers or check online to locate ATMs in your destination. Be sure to check your bank's daily withdrawal limit and your credit limits before leaving home.

Also be sure to have your personal identification number (PIN), which you will need to activate the cash withdrawal functions at all ATMs.

4 When to Go

To a large extent, the timing of your visit will determine how much you'll spend—and how much company you'll have—once you get to Florida. That's because room rates can more than double during the high seasons, when countless visitors migrate to Florida.

The weather determines the high seasons (see "Climate," below). In subtropical Southern Florida, it's during the winter, from mid-December to mid-April. On the other hand, you'll be rewarded with incredible bargains if you can stand the heat and humidity of a South Florida summer between June and early September. In North Florida,

the reverse is true: Tourists flock here during the summer, from Memorial Day to Labor Day.

Presidents' Day weekend in February, Easter week, Memorial Day weekend at the end of May, the Fourth of July, Labor Day weekend at the start of September, Thanksgiving, Christmas, and New Year's are busy throughout the state, and especially at Walt Disney World and the other Orlando area attractions, which can be packed anytime school's out (see chapter 12 for more information on these areas).

Northern and southern Florida share the same "shoulder seasons": April and

The Boys of Spring

Major-league baseball fans can watch the Florida Marlins in Miami and the Tampa Bay Devil Rays in St. Petersburg throughout their seasons April through September, but the entire state is a baseball hotbed from late February to the end of March, when many other teams tune up for the regular season with "Grapefruit League" exhibition games.

Most of Florida's spring-training stadiums are relatively small, so fans can see their favorite players up close, maybe even get a handshake or an autograph. Also, tickets are priced from $5 to $12, a bargain when compared with admission for regular-season games. Many games sell out by early March, so don't wait until you're in Florida to buy tickets.

The teams can move from year to year, so contact the **Florida Sports Foundation**, 2390 Kerry Forest Pkwy., Suite 101, Tallahassee, FL 32309 (© 850/488-8347; fax 850/922-0482; www.flasports.com), which usually posts the Grapefruit League schedules on its website late in January. The main office of **Major League Baseball**, 350 Park Ave., New York, NY 10022 (www.mlb.com), is another place to find out where your favorite teams will be playing.

Here's where the teams played in 2004. See the outdoor activities sections in subsequent chapters for specifics.

Atlanta Braves, Lake Buena Vista, near Orlando (© 407/939-GAME; www.braves.mlb.com); **Baltimore Orioles,** Fort Lauderdale (© 954/776-1921;

May and from September to November, when the weather is pleasant throughout Florida and hotel rates are considerably less than during the high seasons. If price is a consideration, these months of pleasant temperatures and fewer tourists are the best times to visit.

See the accommodations sections in the chapters that follow for specifics about the local high, shoulder, and off seasons.

CLIMATE Northern Florida has a temperate climate, and even in the warmer southern third of the state, it's subtropical, not tropical. Accordingly, Florida sees more extremes of temperatures than, say, the Caribbean islands.

Spring (late Mar–May) sees warm temperatures throughout Florida, but it also brings tropical showers.

Summer runs from May to September in Florida, when it's hot and very

humid throughout the state. If you're in an inland city during these months, you may not want to do anything too taxing when the sun is at its peak. Coastal areas, however, reap the benefits of sea breezes. Severe afternoon thunderstorms are prevalent during the summer heat (there aren't professional sports teams here named *Lightning* and *Thunder* for nothing), so schedule your activities for earlier in the day, and take precautions to avoid being hit by lightning during the storms.

Autumn (from about Sept–Nov) is a great time to visit—the hottest days are gone, and the crowds have thinned out. Unless a hurricane blows through, November usually is Florida's driest month. August through November is hurricane season here, but even if one threatens, the National Weather Service closely tracks the storms and gives ample warning if there's need to evacuate coastal areas.

www.orioles.mlb.com); **Boston Red Sox,** Fort Myers (✆ 877/733-7699; www.redsox.mlb.com); **Cincinnati Reds,** Sarasota (✆ 941/954-4464; www.reds.mlb.com); **Cleveland Indians,** Winter Haven (✆ 863/ 293-3900; www.indians.mlb.com); **Detroit Tigers,** Lakeland (✆ 813/ 287-8844 or 407/839-3900; www.tigers.mlb.com); **Florida Marlins,** Jupiter (✆ 561/966-3309; www.marlins.mlb.com); **Houston Astros,** Kissimmee, near Orlando (✆ 407/839-3900; www.astros.mlb.com); **Kansas City Royals,** Davenport (✆ 800/326-4000; www.royals.mlb.com); **Los Angeles Dodgers,** Vero Beach (✆ 772/569-6858; www.dodgers.mlb. com); **Minnesota Twins,** Fort Myers (✆ 800/338-9467; www.twins. mlb.com); **Montreal Expos,** Melbourne (✆ 321/633-4487; www.expos. mlb.com); **New York Mets,** Port St. Lucie (✆ 772/871-2115; www. mets.mlb.com); **New York Yankees,** Tampa (✆ 813/879-2244; www. yankees.mlb.com); **Philadelphia Phillies,** Clearwater (✆ 727/442-8496; www.phillies.mlb.com); **Pittsburgh Pirates,** Bradenton (✆ 941/748-4610; www.pirates.mlb.com); **St. Louis Cardinals,** Jupiter (✆ 561/775-1818, ext. 7; www.cardinals.mlb.com); **Tampa Bay Devil Rays,** St. Petersburg (✆ 888/FAN-RAYS or 727/825-3250; www.devilrays.mlb.com); **Texas Rangers,** Port Charlotte (✆ 800/326-4000; www.rangers.mlb.com); **Toronto Blue Jays,** Dunedin (✆ 800/707-8269; www.bluejays.mlb.com).

Winter can get a bit nippy throughout the state, and sometimes downright cold in Northern Florida. Although snow is rare, a flake or two has been known to fall as far south as Miami. The "cold snaps" usually last only a few days in the southern half of the state, however, and daytime temperatures quickly return to the 70s.

For up-to-the-minute weather info, tune in to cable TV's Weather Channel, or click onto its website: www.weather.com.

Average Temperatures in Selected Florida Cities (°F/°C)

	Jan	Feb	Mar	Apr	May	June	July	Aug	Sept	Oct	Nov	Dec
Key West	69/21	72/22	74/23	77/25	80/27	82/28	85/29	85/29	84/29	80/27	74/23	72/22
Miami	69/21	70/21	71/22	74/23	78/26	81/27	82/28	84/29	81/27	78/26	73/23	70/21
Tampa	60/16	61/16	66/19	72/22	77/25	81/27	82/28	82/28	81/27	75/24	67/19	62/17
Orlando	60/16	63/17	66/19	71/22	78/26	82/28	82/28	82/28	81/27	75/24	67/19	61/16
Tallahassee	53/12	56/13	63/20	68/20	72/22	78/26	81/27	81/27	77/25	74/23	66/19	59/15

FLORIDA CALENDAR OF EVENTS

January

FedEx Orange Bowl Classic, Miami. Football fanatics flock down to the big Orange Bowl game (oddly taking place not at the Orange Bowl in seedy downtown, but at the much more savory Pro Player Stadium) on New Year's Day, featuring two of the year's best college football teams. Call ✆ **305/ 341-4700** for tickets, but call early as they sell out quickly.

Key West Literary Seminar, Key West. Literary types get a good reason to put down the books and head to Key West. This annual 3-day event features a different theme every year, and a roster of incredible authors, writers, and other literary types. The event is so popular it sells out well in advance, so call early for tickets (available for individual lectures or events, or the entire 3-day conference). For information call ℭ **888/293-9291** or visit www.keywestliteraryseminar.org.

February

Gasparilla Pirate Fest, Tampa. Hundreds of boats and rowdy "pirates" invade the city and then parade along Bayshore Boulevard, showering crowds with beads and coins. ℭ **813/353-8108;** www. gasparillapiratefest.com. Early February.

Everglades Seafood Festival, Florida City. What seems like schools of fish-loving people flock down to Florida City for a 2-day feeding frenzy, in which Florida delicacies from stone crab to gator tails are served from shacks and booths on the outskirts of this quaint Old Florida town. Free admission, but you pay for the food you eat, booth by booth (ℭ **239/695-2561;** www.evergladesseafood festival.com). First full weekend in February.

Miami Film Festival. Though not exactly Cannes, the Miami Film Festival, sponsored by the Film Society of America, is an impressive 10-day celluloid celebration, featuring world premieres of Latin American, domestic, and other foreign and independent films. Actors, producers, and directors show up to plug their films and participate in Q&A sessions with the audiences. Call ℭ **877/888-MIFF** or visit www.miamifilmfestival.com. Early to mid-February.

Speedweeks, Daytona. Nineteen days of events with a series of races that draw the top names in NASCAR stock car racing, all culminating in the Daytona 500. All events take place at the Daytona International Speedway. Especially for the **Daytona 500,** tickets must be purchased even a year in advance. ℭ **386/254-2700;** www. daytonaintlspeedway.com. They go on sale January 1 of the prior year. First 3 weeks of February.

Miami International Boat Show, Miami Beach. If you don't like crowds, beware, as this show draws a quarter of a million boat enthusiasts to the Miami Beach Convention Center. Some of the world's priciest megayachts, speedboats, sailboats, and schooners are displayed for purchase or for gawking. Call ℭ **954/441-3231;** www. discoverboating.com. Mid-February.

March

Bike Week, Daytona Beach. An international gathering of motorcycle enthusiasts draws a crowd of more than 200,000. In addition to major races held at Daytona International Speedway (featuring the world's best road racers, motorcrossers, and dirt trackers), there are motorcycle shows, beach parties, and the Annual Motorcycle Parade, with thousands of riders. ℭ **800/854-1234;** www.officialbikeweek. com. First week in March.

Spring Break, Daytona Beach, Miami Beach, Panama City Beach, Key West, and other beaches. College students from all over the United States and Canada flock to Florida for endless partying, wet T-shirt and bikini contests, free concerts, volleyball tournaments, and more. Three weeks in March.

Calle Ocho Festival, Little Havana. What Carnivale is to Rio, the Calle Ocho Festival is to Miami.

This 10-day extravaganza, also called Carnival Miami, features a lengthy block party spanning 23 blocks, live salsa music, parades, and, of course, tons of savory Cuban delicacies. Those afraid of mob scenes should avoid this party at all costs (✆ **305/644-8888**). Mid-March.

Winter Party, Miami Beach. Gays and lesbians from around the world book trips to Miami as far as a year in advance to attend this weekend-long series of parties and events benefiting the Dade Human Rights Foundation. Travel arrangements can be made through Different Roads Travel, the event's official travel company, by calling ✆ **888/ROADS-55,** ext. 510. For information on the specific events and prices, call ✆ **305/538-5908** or visit www.winterparty.com. Early March.

April

Black College Reunion, Daytona Beach. Some 75,000 students from 115 predominantly African-American universities bring a sometimes-rowdy end to the spring-break season. ✆ **800/854-1234;** www.daytonabeach.com. Mid-April.

PGA Seniors Golf Championship, Palm Beach Gardens. This is the oldest and most prestigious of the senior golf tournaments in which aging swingers prove they've still got spunk in their swing. ✆ **561/624-8400.** Mid-April.

July

World's Richest Tarpon Tournament, Boca Grande. Some $175,000 is at stake in the great tarpon waters off Southwest Florida. ✆ **941/964-0568;** www.bocagrandechamber.com. Second Wednesday and Thursday in July.

Lower Keys Underwater Music Fest, Looe Key. When you hear the phrase "the music and the madness," you may want to think of this amusing aural aquatic event in which boaters head out to the underwater reef at the Looe Key Marine Sanctuary, drop speakers into the water, and pipe in all sorts of music, creating a disco-diving spectacular. Considering the heat at this time of year, underwater is probably the coolest place for a concert. Call ✆ **800/872-3722.** Early July.

Blue Angels Air Show, Pensacola. World-famous navy pilots do their aerial acrobatics just 100 yards off Pensacola Beach. ✆ **800/874-1234** or 850/434-1234; www.visit pensacola.com or www.blueangels. navy.mil. Early July.

September

Labor Day Pro-Am Surfing Festival, Cocoa Beach. One of the largest surfing events on the East Coast draws pros and amateurs from around the country. There are also rock 'n' roll bands and swimsuit contests. ✆ **321/459-2200;** www.space-coast.com. Labor Day weekend.

October

Biketoberfest, Daytona. Road-racing stars compete at the CCS Motorcycle Championship at Daytona International Speedway. There are also parties, parades, concerts, and more. ✆ **386/253-RACE;** www.biketober fest.org. Mid-October.

Clearwater Jazz Holiday, Clearwater. Top jazz musicians play for 4 days and nights at bayfront Coachman Park in this free musical extravaganza. ✆ **727/461-5200;** www.clearwaterjazz.com. Mid-October.

Columbus Day Regatta, Miami. On the day that Columbus discovered America, the party-hearty discover their fellow Americans' birthday suits, as this bacchanalia in the middle of Biscayne Bay encourages participants in this so-called regatta (there is a boat race at some point during the day, but most people are too preoccupied to notice) to strip down to their bare necessities and party at the sandbar in the middle of the bay. You may not need a bathing suit, but you will need a boat to get out to where all the action is. Consider renting one on Key Biscayne, which is the closest to the sandbar.

Halloween Horror Nights, Orlando. Universal Studios transforms its grounds for 19 nights into haunted attractions with live bands, a psychopath's maze, special shows, and hundreds of ghouls and goblins roaming the streets. The studio closes at dusk, reopening in a new macabre form at 7pm. Full admission is charged for the event, which is geared toward adults. ✆ 800/837-2273 or 407/363-8000; www.universalorlando.com. Mid-October through Halloween.

Mickey's Not-So-Scary Halloween Party, Orlando. At Walt Disney World, guests are invited to trick or treat in the Magic Kingdom, starting at 7pm. The party includes parades, storytelling, live music, and a bewitching fireworks display. Call ✆ 407/934-7639 for information; www.disneyworld.com. End of October.

Fantasy Fest, Key West. Mardi Gras takes a Floridian holiday as the streets of Key West are overtaken by wildly costumed revelers who have no shame and no parental guidance. This weeklong, hedonistic, X-rated Halloween party is not for children under 18. Make reservations in Key West early, as hotels tend to book up quickly during this event. Call ✆ 305/296-1817. Last week of October.

November

Miami Bookfair International, downtown Miami. Bibliophiles, literati, and some of the world's most prestigious and prolific authors

descend upon downtown Miami for a weeklong homage to the written word, which also happens to be the largest book fair in the United States. The weekend street fair is the best attended of the entire event, in which regular folk mix with wordsmiths such as Tom Wolfe and Jane Smiley while indulging in snacks, antiquarian books, and literary gossip. All lectures are free, but they fill up quickly, so get there early. Call ✆ 305/237-3258 for lecture schedules. Mid-November.

Blue Angels Homecoming Air Show, Pensacola. World-famous navy pilots do their aerial acrobatics just 100 yards off the beach. ✆ 800/874-1234 or 850/434-1234; www.visitpensacola.com or www.blueangels.navy.mil. Second weekend in November.

American Sandsculpting Festival, Fort Myers Beach. Some 50,000 gather to sculpt or see the world's finest sand castles. ✆ 239/454-7500; www.fmbchamber.com. First weekend in November.

White Party Week, Miami and Fort Lauderdale. This weeklong series of parties to benefit AIDS research is built around the main event, the White Party, which takes place at Villa Vizcaya and sells out as early as a year in advance. Philanthropists and celebrities such as Calvin Klein and David Geffen join thousands of white-clad mostly gay men (and some women) in what has become one of the world's hottest and hardest-to-score party tickets. Visit www.whitepartyweek.com for a schedule of parties and events. Thanksgiving week.

December

Edison/Ford Winter Homes Holiday House, Fort Myers. Christmas music and thousands of lights hail the holiday season here. At the same time, candles create a spectacular Luminary Trail along the full length of Sanibel Island's Periwinkle Way. © **239/334-7419;** www.edison-ford-estate.com. First week of December.

Christmas at Walt Disney World, Orlando. As you would imagine, all of the Disney properties get into the holiday spirit. In the Magic Kingdom, Main Street is lavishly decked out with lights and holly and an 80-foot glistening tree. Call © **407/824-4321** for holiday events, or 407/934-7639 for special travel packages; www.disneyworld.com. Throughout December.

British Night Watch & Grand Illumination Ceremony, St. Augustine. Torchlight procession through the Spanish Quarter kicks off a month of Christmas festivities and the "Nights of Lights," in which 1.25 million twinkling bulbs bathe the Old City. © **800/OLD-CITY;** www.visitoldcity.com. First Saturday in December; Nights of Lights to January 31.

Winterfest Boat Parade, Fort Lauderdale. People who complain that the holiday season just isn't as festive in South Florida as it is in colder parts of the world haven't been to this spectacular boat parade along the Intracoastal Waterway. Forget decking the halls. At this parade, the decks are decked out in magnificent holiday regalia as they gracefully—and boastfully—glide up and down the water. If you're not on a boat, the best views are from waterfront restaurants or anywhere you can squeeze in along the water. Call © **954/767-0686.** Mid-December.

5 Health & Safety

THE HEALTHY TRAVELER

Florida doesn't present any unusual health hazards for most people. Folks with certain medical conditions such as liver disease, diabetes, and stomach ailments, however, should avoid eating raw **oysters,** which can carry a natural bacterium linked to severe diarrhea, vomiting, and even fatal blood poisoning. Cooking kills the bacteria, so, if in doubt, order your oysters steamed, broiled, or fried.

Florida has millions of **mosquitoes** and invisible biting **sand flies** (known as "no-see-ums"), especially in the coastal and marshy areas. Fortunately, neither insect carries malaria or other diseases (though there were a few cases of mosquitoes carrying West Nile virus in the Panhandle, it's really not a problem in Florida). Keep these pests at bay with a good insect repellent.

It's especially important to protect yourself against **sunburn.** Don't underestimate the strength of the sun's rays down here, even in the middle of winter. Use a sunscreen with a high protection factor and apply it liberally.

WHAT TO DO IF YOU GET SICK AWAY FROM HOME

In most cases, your existing health plan will provide the coverage you need. But double-check; you may want to buy **travel medical insurance** instead. Always bring your insurance ID card with you when you travel.

Pack **prescription medications** in your carry-on luggage, and carry prescription medications in their original containers, with pharmacy labels—otherwise they won't make it through airport security. Also bring along copies of your prescriptions in case you lose your pills or run out. And don't forget sunglasses and an extra pair of contact lenses or prescription glasses.

If you get sick, consider asking your hotel concierge to recommend a local doctor—even his or her own. You can also try the emergency room at a local hospital; many have walk-in clinics for emergency cases that are not life threatening. You may not get immediate attention, but you won't pay the high price of an emergency room visit.

THE SAFE TRAVELER

While tourist areas in Florida are generally safe, you should always stay alert. This is particularly true in the large cities such as Miami, Orlando, Tampa, and St. Petersburg. It is wise to ask your hotel's front-desk staff or the city's or area's tourist office if you're in doubt about which neighborhoods are safe.

Remember also that hotels are open to the public, and in a large hotel, security may not be able to screen everyone entering. Always lock your room door. Don't assume that once inside your hotel you are automatically safe and no longer need to be aware of your surroundings.

6 Specialized Travel Resources

FOR GAY & LESBIAN TRAVELERS

Florida is not without its intolerant contingent, but there are active gay and lesbian groups in most cities here. In fact, the editors of *Out and About,* a gay and lesbian newsletter, have described Miami's **South Beach** as the "hippest, hottest, most happening gay travel destination in the world." For many years that could also be said of **Key West,** which still is one of the country's most popular destinations for gays. **Fort Lauderdale**—where gays own more than 20 motels, 40 bars, and numerous other businesses—is definitely also on the gay-friendly map.

You can contact the **Gay, Lesbian & Bisexual Community Services of Central Florida,** 946 N. Mills Ave., Orlando, FL 32803 (© **407/228-8272;** www.glbcc.org), whose welcome packets usually include the latest issue of the *Triangle,* a quarterly newsletter dedicated to gay and lesbian issues, and a calendar of events pertaining to the gay and lesbian community. Although not a tourist-specific packet, it includes information and ads for the area's gay and lesbian clubs.

Watermark, P.O. Box 533655, Orlando, FL 32853 (© **407/481-2243;** fax 407/481-2246; www.watermark online.com), is a biweekly tabloid newspaper covering the gay and lesbian scene, including dining and entertainment options, in Orlando, the Tampa Bay area, and Daytona Beach.

SENIOR TRAVEL

With one of the largest retired populations of any state, Florida offers a wide array of activities and benefits for seniors. Don't be shy about asking for discounts, but always carry some kind of identification, such as a driver's license, that shows your age/date of birth. Mention the fact that you're a senior when you make your travel reservations. In most cities, people over the age of 60 qualify for reduced admission to theaters, museums, and other attractions, as well as discounted fares on public transportation.

Members of **AARP** (formerly known as the American Association of Retired Persons), 601 E St. NW, Washington, DC 20049 (© **888/ 687-2277** or 202/434-2277; www. aarp.org), get discounts on hotels, airfares, and car rentals. AARP offers members a wide range of benefits, including *AARP: The Magazine* and a monthly newsletter. Anyone over 50 can join.

The **U.S. National Park Service (NPS)** offers a **Golden Age Passport** that gives seniors 62 years or older lifetime entrance to all properties administered by the National Park Service—national parks, monuments, historic sites, recreation areas, and national wildlife refuges—for a one-time processing fee of $10, which must be purchased in person at any NPS facility that charges an entrance fee. For more information, go to www.nps.gov/fees_passes.htm or call ☎ **888/467-2757.**

FAMILY TRAVEL

Florida is a great family destination, with Walt Disney World leading the list of theme parks geared to young and old alike. Consequently, most Florida hotels and restaurants are willing if not eager to cater to families traveling with children. Many hotels and motels let children 17 and under stay free in their parent's room (be sure to ask when you reserve).

At the beaches, it's the exception rather than the rule for a resort not to have a children's activities program (some will even mind the youngsters while the parents enjoy a night off!). Even if they don't have a children's program of their own, most will arrange babysitting services.

You may also want to consult *The Unofficial Guide to Florida with Kids* as well as *The Unofficial Guide to Walt Disney World with Kids.* Additionally, *How to Take Great Trips with Your Kids* (The Harvard Common Press) is full of good general advice that can apply to travel anywhere.

7 Getting There

BY PLANE

Most major domestic airlines fly to and from many Florida cities. Choose from **American** (☎ 800/433-7300; www.aa.com), **Continental** (☎ 800/525-0280; www.continental.com), **Delta** (☎ 800/221-1212; www.delta-air.com), **Northwest/KLM** (☎ 800/225-2525; www.nwa.com), **United** (☎ 800/241-6522; www.united.com), and **US Airways** (☎ 800/428-4322; www.usairways.com).

Of these, Delta and US Airways have the most extensive network of commuter connections within Florida (see "Getting Around," later in this chapter).

Several so-called no-frills airlines—low fares but few if any amenities—also fly to Florida. The biggest and best is **Southwest Airlines** (☎ **800/435-9792;** www.southwest.com), which has flights from many U.S. cities to Fort Lauderdale, Jacksonville, Orlando, and Tampa.

Others flying to Florida include **AirTran** (☎ 800/AIR-TRAN; www.airtran.com); **American Trans Air** (☎ 800/435-9282; www.ata.com); **Carnival Air** (☎ 800/824-7386), an arm of the popular cruise line; **JetBlue** (☎ 800/538-2583; www.jetblue.com); **Midwest Express** (☎ 800/452-2022; www.midwestexpress.com); **PanAm** (☎ 800/FLY-PANAM; www.flypanam.com); and **Spirit** (☎ 800/722-7117; www.spiritair.com).

Internet resources such as **Travelocity** (www.travelocity.com) and **Microsoft Expedia** (www.expedia.com) make it relatively easy to compare prices and even purchase tickets.

BY CAR

Florida is reached by **I-95** along the east coast, **I-75** from the central states, and **I-10** from the west. **The Florida Turnpike,** a toll road, links Orlando, West Palm Beach, Fort Lauderdale, and Miami (it's a shortcut from Wildwood on I-75 north of Orlando to Miami). **I-4** cuts across the state from Cape Canaveral through Orlando to Tampa.

See "Getting Around," later in this chapter, for more information about driving in Florida and the car-rental firms operating here.

If you're a member, your local branch of the **American Automobile Association (AAA)** will provide a free trip-routing plan. AAA also has nationwide emergency road service for

---

Tips Saving with Golf & Tennis Packages

Many Florida hotels and resorts and even some motels offer **golf and tennis packages,** which bundle the cost of room, greens and court fees, and sometimes equipment, into one price. These deals usually don't include airfare, but they do represent savings over paying for the room and golf or tennis separately. See the accommodations sections in the following chapters for hostelries offering special packages to their guests.

Summer, early fall, and the first 3 weeks of December are good times to search for discounted deals in Southern Florida. For example, the Naples Beach Hotel & Golf Club in Naples (p. 369) has offered bed-and-breakfast specials for about $125 a night per room, including a full breakfast buffet, during September and December. Regular autumn room rates are more than twice that amount, without breakfast.

---

its members (© **800/AAA-HELP;** www.aaa.com).

BY TRAIN

Amtrak (© **800/USA-RAIL;** www. amtrak.com) offers train service to Florida from both the East and West Coasts. It takes some 26 hours from New York to Miami, 68 hours from Los Angeles to Miami, and Amtrak's fares aren't much less—if not more—than many of the airlines' lowest fares.

Amtrak's *Silver Meteor* and *Silver Star* both run twice daily between New York and either Miami or Tampa, with intermediate stops along the East Coast and in Florida. Amtrak's Thruway Bus Connections are available from the Fort Lauderdale Amtrak station and Miami International Airport to Key West; from Tampa to St. Petersburg, Treasure Island, Clearwater, Sarasota, Bradenton, and Fort

Myers; and from Deland to Daytona Beach. From the West Coast, the *Sunset Limited* runs three times weekly between Los Angeles and Orlando. It stops in Pensacola, Crestview (north of Fort Walton Beach and Destin), Chipley (north of Panama City Beach), and Tallahassee. Sleeping accommodations are available for an extra charge.

If you intend to stop off along the way, you can save money with Amtrak's **Explore America** (or All Aboard America) fares, which are based on three regions of the country.

Amtrak's **Auto Train** runs daily from Lorton, Virginia (12 miles south of Washington, D.C.), to Sanford, Florida (just northeast of Orlando). You ride in a coach while your car is secured in an enclosed vehicle carrier. You should make your train reservations as far in advance as possible.

8 Special-Interest Trips

Bird-watching, boating and sailing, camping, canoeing and kayaking, fishing, golfing, tennis—you name it, the Sunshine State has it. In fact, you'll find these activities almost everywhere you go in Florida. Of course, beach lovers and watersports enthusiasts can indulge their passions almost anywhere along the state's lengthy coastlines.

Merely head east or west, and you'll easily find plenty to do—or viewed another way, Florida's multitudinous watersports operators will find you.

These and other activities are described in the outdoor activities sections of the following chapters, but here's a brief overview of some of the best places to move your muscles, with tips on how to get more detailed information.

The **Florida Sports Foundation,** 2390 Kerry Forest Pkwy., Suite 101, Tallahassee, FL 32309 (© **850/488-8347;** fax 850/922-0482; www.fla sports.com), publishes free brochures, calendars, schedules, and guides to outdoor pursuits and spectator sports throughout Florida. I've noted some of its specific publications in the sections below.

For excellent color maps of state parks, campgrounds, canoe trails, aquatic preserves, caverns, and more, contact the **Florida Department of Environmental Protection,** Office of Communications, 3900 Common-wealth Blvd., Tallahassee, FL 32399 (© **850/245-2118;** www.dep.state. fl.us). Some of the department's publications are mentioned below.

ACTIVITIES A TO Z
BIKING & IN-LINE SKATING Florida's relatively flat terrain makes it ideal for riding bikes and in-line skating. You can bike right into the **Ever-glades National Park** along the 38-mile-long Main Park Road, for example, and bike or skate from St. Petersburg to Tarpon Springs on the 47-mile-long converted railroad bed known as the **Pinellas Trail.** Many towns and cities have designated routes for cyclists, skaters, joggers, and walkers, such as the paved pathways running the length of Sanibel Island, the lovely Bayshore Boulevard in **Tampa,** and the bike lanes from downtown **Sarasota** out to St. Armands, Lido, and Longboat Keys. We've detailed all the many options in the following chapters.

BIRD-WATCHING With hun-dreds of both land- and sea-based species, Florida is one of America's best places for bird-watching—if you're not careful, pelicans will even steal your picnic lunch on the historic **Naples Pier.** The **J. N. ("Ding")** **Darling National Wildlife Refuge** is great for watching, and it shares Sani-bel Island with luxury resorts and fine restaurants.

With its Northeast Florida section now open, the **Great Florida Birding Trail** will eventually cover some 2,000 miles throughout the state. Fort Clinch State Park on Amelia Island and Merritt Island National Wildlife Refuge in Cape Canaveral are gate-ways to the northeast trail. Informa-tion is available from the Birding Trail Coordinator, Florida Fish & Wildlife Conservation Commission, 620 S. Meridian St., Tallahassee, FL 32399-1600 (© **850/922-0664;** fax 850/488-1961; www.floridabirding trail.com). You can download trail maps from their website.

Many of the state's wildlife pre-serves have gift shops that carry books about Florida's birds, including the *Florida Wildlife Viewing Guide,* in which authors Susan Cerulean and Ann Morrow profile 96 great parks, refuges, and preserves throughout the state. The guide is also available directly from the publisher, Falcon Press, at © **888/922-0789;** www. falcbooks.com.

BOATING & SAILING With some 1,350 miles of shoreline, it's not surprising that Florida is a boating and sailing mecca. In fact, you won't be anyplace near the water very long before you see flyers and other adver-tisements for rental boats and for cruises on sailboats. Many of them are mentioned in the following chapters.

The Moorings, the worldwide sail-boat charter company, has its head-quarters in Clearwater and its Florida yacht base nearby in St. Petersburg (© **888/952-8420** or 727/530-5651; www.moorings.com). From St. Pete, experienced sailors can take its bare-boats as far as the Keys and the Dry Tortugas, out in the Gulf of Mexico.

Key West keeps gaining prominence as a world sailing capital. *Yachting* magazine sponsors the largest winter regatta in America here each January, and smaller events take place regularly.

Even if you've never hauled on a halyard, you can learn the art of sailing at **Steve and Doris Colgate's Offshore Sailing School,** headquartered at the South Seas Plantation Resort & Yacht Harbour on Captiva Island, with an outpost in St. Petersburg (www.offshore-sailing.com). The prestigious **Annapolis Sailing** has bases in St. Petersburg and on Marathon in the Keys (http://annapolissailing.com).

The free *Florida Boating & Fishing,* which has tips about safe boating in the state and is available from the **Florida Sports Foundation** (see the introduction to this section, above), is a treasure trove of regulations; locations of marinas, hotels, and resorts; marine products and services; and more, in magazine format.

CAMPING   Florida is literally dotted with RV parks (if you own such a vehicle, it's the least-expensive way to spend your winters here). But for the best tent camping, look to Florida's national preserves and 110 state parks and recreation areas. Options range from luxury sites with hot-water showers and cable TV hookups to primitive island and beach camping with no facilities whatsoever.

Regular and primitive camping in **St. George Island State Park** near Apalachicola, in fact, is a birdwatcher's dream, and you'll be on one of the nation's most magnificent beaches. Equally great are the sands at **St. Andrews State Park** in Panama City Beach (with sites right beside the bay). Other top spots are **Fort DeSoto Park** in St. Pete Beach (more gorgeous bayside sites), the remarkably preserved **Cayo Costa Island State Park** between Boca Grande and Captiva Island in Southwest Florida, **Canaveral**

National Seashore near the Kennedy Space Center, **Anastasia State Park** in St. Augustine, **Fort Clinch State Park** on Amelia Island, and **Bill Baggs Cape Florida State Park** on Key Biscayne in Miami. Down in the Keys, the oceanside sites in **Long Key State Park** are about as nice as it gets.

In all these popular campgrounds, reservations are essential, especially in the high seasons. All of Florida's state parks take bookings up to 11 months in advance.

The **Florida Department of Environmental Protection,** Division of Recreation and Parks, Mail Station 535, 3900 Commonwealth Blvd., Tallahassee, FL 32399-3000 (© 850/245-2118; www.dep.state.fl.us), publishes an annual guide of tent and RV sites in Florida's state parks and recreation areas.

Pet owners note: Pets are permitted at some—but not all—state park beaches, campgrounds, and food service areas. Before bringing your animal, check with the department or with the individual parks to see if your pet will be allowed. And bring your pet's rabies certificate, which is required.

For private campgrounds, the **Florida Association of RV Parks & Campgrounds,** 1340 Vickers Dr., Tallahassee, FL 32303 (© 850/562-7151; fax 850/562-7179; www.floridacamping.com), issues an annual *Camp Florida* directory with locator maps and details about its member establishments throughout the state.

CANOEING & KAYAKING Canoers and kayakers have almost limitless options here: picturesque rivers, sandy coastlines, marshes, mangroves, and gigantic Lake Okeechobee. Exceptional trails run through several parks and wildlife preserves, including **Everglades National Park,** the **J. N. ("Ding") Darling National Wildlife Refuge** on Sanibel Island, and the **Briggs Nature Center,** on the edge of the Everglades near Marco Island.

According to the Florida state legislature, however, the state's official "Canoe Capital" is the Panhandle town of **Milton,** on U.S. 90 near Pensacola. Up there, Blackwater River, Coldwater River, Sweetwater Creek, and Juniper Creek are perfect for tubing, rafting, and paddleboating, as well as canoeing and kayaking.

Another good venue is the waterways winding through the marshes between **Amelia Island** and the mainland.

Many conservation groups throughout the state offer half-day, full-day, and overnight canoe trips. For example, **The Conservancy of Naples** (✆ **239/262-0304;** www.conservancy. org) has a popular series of moonlight canoe trips through the mangroves, among other programs.

Based during the winter at Everglades City, on the park's western border, **North American Canoe Tours, Inc.** (✆ **239/695-3299;** www.everglades adventures.com), offers weeklong, guided canoe expeditions through the Everglades.

Thirty-six creek and river trails, covering 950 miles altogether, are itemized in the excellent free *Canoe Trails* booklet published by the **Florida Department of Environmental Protection,** Office of Communications, 3900 Commonwealth Blvd., Tallahassee, FL 32399 (✆ **850/ 245-2118;** www.dep.state.fl.us).

Specialized guidebooks include *A Canoeing and Kayaking Guide to the Streams of Florida:* Volume 1, *North Central Florida and Panhandle,* by Elizabeth F. Carter and John L. Eearch, and Volume 2, *Central and Southern Peninsula,* by Lou Glaros and Dough Sphar. Both are published by Menasha Ridge Press (www.menasha ridge.com).

ECOADVENTURES If you don't want to do it yourself, you can observe Florida's flora and fauna on guided field expeditions—and contribute to conservation efforts while you're at it.

The **Sierra Club,** America's oldest and largest grassroots environmental organization, offers ecoadventures through its Florida chapters. Recent outings have included canoeing or kayaking through the Everglades, hiking the Florida Trail in America's southernmost national forest, camping on a barrier island, and exploring the sinkhole phenomenon in North Central Florida. You do have to be a Sierra Club member, but you can join at the time of the trip. Contact the club's national outings office at 85 Second St., Second Floor, San Francisco, CA 94105-3441 (✆ **415/977- 5500;** www.sierraclub.org).

The Florida chapter of **The Nature Conservancy** has protected 578,000 acres of natural lands in Florida and presently owns and manages 36 preserves. For a small fee, you can join one of its field trips or work parties that take place periodically throughout the year; fees vary from year to year, event to event, so call for more information. Participants get a chance to learn about and even participate in the preservation of the ecosystem. For details of all the preserves and adventures, contact The Nature Conservancy, Florida Chapter, 222 S. Westmonte Dr., Suite 300, Altamonte Springs, FL 32714 (✆ **407/682-3664;** fax 407/682-3077; http://nature.org).

A nonprofit organization dedicated to environmental research, the **Earthwatch Institute,** 3 Clocktower Place, Suite 100 (P.O. Box 75), Maynard, MA 01754 (✆ **800/776-0188** or 978/ 461-0081; www.earthwatch.org), has excursions to survey dolphins and manatees around Sarasota and to monitor the well being of the captive-raised whooping cranes that have been released in the wilds of Central Florida. Another research group, the **Oceanic Society,** Fort Mason Center, Building E, San Francisco, CA 94123 (✆ **800/ 326-7491** or 415/441-1106; fax 415/ 474-3395; www.oceanic-society.org), also has Florida trips among its expeditions, including manatee monitoring in the Crystal River area north of Tampa.

FISHING In addition to the amberjack, bonito, grouper, mackerel, mahimahi, marlin, pompano, redfish, sailfish, snapper, snook, tarpon, tuna, and wahoo running offshore and in its inlets, Florida has countless miles of rivers and streams, plus about 30,000 lakes and springs stocked with more than 100 species of freshwater fish. Indeed, Floridians seem to fish everywhere: off canal banks and old bridges, from fishing piers and fishing fleets. You'll even see them standing alongside the Tamiami Trail (U.S. 41) that cuts across the Everglades—one eye on their line, the other watching for alligators.

Anglers age 16 and older need fishing licenses for any kind of saltwater or freshwater fishing, including lobstering and spearfishing. Licenses are sold at bait-and-tackle shops around the state or online at www.wildlife license.com/fl.

The **Florida Department of Environmental Protection,** 3900 Commonwealth Blvd., Tallahassee, FL 32399-3000 (© **850/245-2118;** www. dep.state.fl.us), publishes the annual *Fishing Lines,* a free magazine with a wealth of information about fishing in Florida, including regulations and licensing requirements. It also distributes free brochures with annual freshwater and saltwater limits. And the **Florida Sports Foundation** (see the introduction to this section, above) publishes *Florida Fishing & Boating,* another treasure trove of information.

HIKING Although you won't be climbing any mountains in this relatively flat state, there are thousands of beautiful hiking trails in Florida. The ideal hiking months are October through April, when the weather is cool and dry and mosquitoes are less prominent. Like anywhere else, you'll find trails that are gentle and short and others that are challenging—some trails in the Everglades require you to wade waist-deep in water!

If you're venturing into the backcountry, watch out for gators, and don't ever try to feed them (or any wild animal). You risk getting bitten (they can't tell the difference between the food and your hand). You're also upsetting the balance of nature, since animals fed by humans lose their ability to find their own food. Most Florida snakes are harmless, but a few have deadly bites, so it's a good idea to avoid them all.

The **Florida Trail Association,** 5415 SW 13th St., Gainesville, FL 32608 (© **877/HIKE-FLA** or 352/ 378-8823; www.florida-trail.org), maintains a large percentage of the public trails in the state and puts out an excellent book packed with maps, details, and color photos.

For a copy of *Florida Trails,* which outlines the many options, contact Visit Florida (see "Visitor Information," earlier in this chapter). Another resource is *A Guide to Your National Scenic Trails,* Office of Greenways and Trails, Department of Environmental Protection, 3900 Commonwealth Blvd., Tallahassee, FL 32399 (© **50/245-2118;** www.dep.state.fl. us/gwt). You can also contact the office of **National Forests in Florida,** Woodcrest Office Park, 325 John Knox Rd., Suite F-100, Tallahassee, FL 32303 (© **850/523-8500;** www. southernregion.fs.fed.us/florida). And *Hiking Florida,* by M. Timothy O'Keefe (Falcon Press; www.falcbooks. com), details 132 hikes throughout the state, with maps and photos.

GOLF Florida is the unofficial golf capital of the United States—some would say the world—since the **World Golf Hall of Fame** is located near St. Augustine. This state-of-the-art museum and shrine is worth a brief visit even if you're not in love with the game.

One thing's for certain: Florida has more golf courses than any other state—more than 1,150 at last count and growing. We picked the best in chapter 1, but suffice it to say that you can tee off almost anytime there's daylight. The highest concentrations of excellent courses are in Southwest Florida around Naples and Fort Myers (more than 1,000 holes!), in the Orlando area (Disney alone has 99 holes open to the public), and in the Panhandle around Destin and Panama City Beach. It's a rare town in Florida that doesn't have a municipal golf course—even Key West has 18 great holes.

Greens fees are usually much lower at the municipal courses than at privately owned clubs. Whether public or private, greens fees tend to vary greatly depending on the time of year. You could pay $150 or more at a private course during the high season, but less than half that when the tourists are gone. The fee structures vary so much that it's best to call ahead and ask, and always reserve a tee time as far in advance as possible.

You can learn the game or hone your strokes at one of several excellent golf schools in the state. **David Ledbetter** has teaching facilities in Orlando and Naples, **Fred Griffin** is in charge of the Grand Cypress Academy of Golf at Grand Cypress Resort in Orlando, and you'll find **Jimmy Ballard**'s school at the Ocean Reef Club on Key Largo. The Westin Innisbrook Resort at Tarpon Springs has its **Innisbrook Golf Institute.** Amelia Island (near Jacksonville) is home to **Amelia Island Plantation Golf School.**

You can get information about most Florida courses, including current greens fees, and reserve tee times through **Tee Times USA,** P.O. Box 641, Flagler Beach, FL 32136 (© **888/GOLF-FLO** or 904/386-439-0001; www.teetimesusa.com). This company also publishes a vacation guide that includes many stay-and-play golf packages.

Florida Golf, published by the **Florida Sports Foundation** (see the introduction to this section), lists every course in Florida. It's the state's official golf guide and is available from Visit Florida (see the "Visitor Information" section, earlier in this chapter).

Golfer's Guide magazine publishes monthly editions covering most regions of Florida; it is available free at all the local visitor centers and hotel lobbies, or you can contact the magazine at 2 Park Lane, Suite E, Hilton Head Island, SC 29928 (© **800/864-6101** or 843/842-7878; fax 843/842-5743; www.golfersguide.com). Northwest Florida is covered by *South Coast Golf Guide,* published by Tee and J's Ent. LLC, P.O. Box 11278, Pensacola, FL 32524-1278 (© **850/505-7553;** fax 850/505-0057; www.southcoastgolfguide.com).

You can also get more information from the **Professional Golfers' Association (PGA),** 400 Ave. of the Champions, Palm Beach Gardens, FL 33418 (© **800/633-9150;** www.pga.com), or the **Ladies Professional Golf Association (LPGA),** 100 International Golf Dr., Daytona Beach, FL 32124 (© **904/254-6200;** www.lpga.com).

More than 700 courses are profiled in *Florida Golf Guide* by Jimmy Shacky (Open Roads Publishing; $20), available at bookstores.

SCUBA DIVING & SNORKELING

Divers love the Keys, where you can see magnificent formations of tree-sized elkhorn coral and giant brain coral, as well as colorful sea fans and dozens of other varieties, sharing space with 300 or more species of rainbow-hued fish. Reef diving is good all the way from Key Largo to Key West, with plenty of tour operators, outfitters, and dive shops along the way.

Particularly worthy are **John Pennekamp Coral Reef State Park** in Key Largo and **Looe Key National Marine Sanctuary** off Big Pine Key. *Skin Diver* magazine picked Looe Key as the number-one dive spot in North America. Also, the clearest waters in which to view some of the 4,000 sunken ships along Florida's coast are in the Middle Keys and the waters between Key West and the Dry Tortugas. Snorkeling in the Keys is particularly fine between Islamorada and Marathon.

In Northwest Florida, the 100-fathom curve draws closer to the white, sandy Panhandle beaches than to any other spot on the Gulf of Mexico. It's too far north here for coral, but you can see brilliantly colored sponges and fish and, in Timber Hole, discover an undersea "petrified forest" of sunken planes, ships, and even a railroad car. And the battleship USS *Massachusetts* lies in 30 feet of water just 3 miles off Pensacola. Every beach town in Northwest Florida has dive shops to outfit, tour, or certify visitors.

In the Crystal River area, north of the St. Petersburg and Clearwater beaches, you can snorkel with the manatees as they bask in the warm spring waters of Kings Bay.

If you want to keep up with what's going on statewide, you can subscribe to *Florida Scuba News,* a monthly magazine published in Jacksonville (✆ **904/783-1610;** www.scubanews.com). You might also want to pick up a specialized guidebook. Some good ones include *Coral Reefs of Florida,* by Gilbert L. Voss (Pineapple Press; www.pineapplepress.com), and *The Diver's Guide to Florida and the Florida Keys,* by Jim Stachowicz (Windward Publishing).

TENNIS   Year-round sunshine makes Florida great for tennis. There are some 7,700 places to play throughout the state, from municipal courts to exclusive resorts. Even some of the municipal facilities—Cambier Park Tennis Center in Naples leaps to mind—are equal to those at expensive resorts, and they're either free or close to it.

If you can afford it, you can learn from the best in Florida. **Nick Bollettieri** has sports academies in Bradenton. Safety Harbor Resort and Spa near St. Petersburg hosts the **Phil Green Tennis Program.** Amateurs can hobnob with the superstars at **ATP Tour International Headquarters** in Ponte Vedra Beach, near Jacksonville. **Mary Jo Fernandez** is affiliated with the **Arthur Ashe Tennis Center** at the Doral Golf Resort & Spa in Miami. And **Chris Evert, Robert Seguso,** and **Carling Basset** have their own center in Boca Raton.

The three hard courts and seven clay courts at the Key Biscayne Tennis Association, 6702 Crandon Blvd. (✆ **305/361-5263**), get crowded on weekends, since they're some of Miami's most beautiful. You'll play on the same courts as Lendl, Graf, Evert, McEnroe, and other greats; this is the venue for one of the world's biggest annual tennis events, the Nasdaq 100 Open (p. 135). There's a pleasant, if limited, pro shop, plus many good pros. Only four courts are lit at night, but if you reserve at least 48 hours in advance, you can usually take your pick. They cost $6 per person per hour. The courts are open daily from 8am to 9pm.

Famous as the spot where Chris Evert got in her early serves, the **Jimmy Evert Tennis Center,** 701 NE 12th Ave. (off Sunrise Blvd.), Fort Lauderdale (✆ **954/828-5378**), has 18 clay and 3 hard courts (15 lighted). Her coach and father, James Evert, still teaches young players here, though he is very picky about whom he'll accept. Nonresidents of Fort Lauderdale pay $3.50 (singles) to $4.50 (doubles) per hour. Reservations are accepted after 2pm for the following day but cost an extra $3.

Lights are also an extra $3 per hour and are available only for the clay courts.

Other top places to learn and play are **Amelia Island Plantation** on Amelia Island; **Colony Beach and Tennis Resort** on Longboat Key off Sarasota (which *Tennis* magazine picked as the number-two tennis resort in the nation); **Sanibel Harbour Resort & Spa** in Fort Myers, whose 5,500-seat stadium has hosted Davis Cup matches; **South Seas Plantation Resort & Yacht Harbour** on Captiva Island; and **The Registry Resort** in Naples.

9 Getting Around

Having a car is the best and easiest way to see Florida's sights, or just to get to and from the beach. Public transportation is available only in the cities and larger towns, and even there it may provide infrequent or even inadequate service. When it comes to getting from one city to another, cars and planes are the ways to go.

BY PLANE

The commuter arms of **Continental** (📞 **800/525-0280;** www.flycontinental. com), **Delta** (📞 **800/221-1212;** www. delta.com), and **US Airways** (📞 **800/ 428-4322;** www.usairways.com) provide extensive service betweenFlorida's major cities and towns. Fares for these short hops tend to be reasonable.

Cape Air (📞 **800/352-0714;** www. flycapeair.com) flies between Key West, Fort Myers, and Naples, which means you can avoid backtracking to Miami from Key West if you're touring the state. (You can also take a boat between Key West and Fort Myers Beach, Naples, or Marco Island during the winter months; see p. 322.) **Paradise Aviation** (📞 **305/743-4222;** www.flyparadiseair.com) connects Fort Lauderdale with Marathon.

BY CAR

Jacksonville is about 350 miles north of Miami and 500 miles north of Key West, so don't underestimate how long it will take you to drive all the way down the state. The speed limit is either 65 mph or 70 mph on the rural interstate highways, so you can make good time between cities. Not so on U.S. 1, U.S. 17, U.S. 19, U.S. 41, and U.S. 301; although most have four lanes, these older highways tend to be heavily congested, especially in built-up areas.

CAR RENTALS

Every major car-rental company is represented here, including **Alamo** (📞 **800/327-9633;** www.goalamo. com), **Avis** (📞 **800/331-1212;** www. avis.com), **Budget** (📞 **800/527-0700;** www.budgetrentacar.com), **Dollar** (📞 **800/800-4000;** www.dollarcar. com), **Enterprise** (📞 **800/325-8007;** pickenterprise.com), **Hertz** (📞 **800/654-3131;** www.hertz.com), **National** (📞 **800/227-7368;** www. nationalcar.com), and **Thrifty** (📞 **800/ 367-2277;** www.thrifty.com).

If you decide to rent a car, shop around and ask a lot of questions. Reservations clerks are used to being asked for the lowest rate available, and most will find it in order to get your business. You may have to try different dates, different pickup and drop-off points, and different discount offers to find the best deal. It changes constantly. Also, if you're a member of any organization (AARP, Costco, or AAA, for example), be sure to ask if you're entitled to discounts.

Check the rental firms' websites. Most will automatically bring up the lowest available rate, and there are boxes to click if you are an association member or have a discount coupon or ID number. You can comparison shop on Internet sites such as **Travelocity** (www.travelocity.com) and **Expedia** (www.expedia.com), which will make reservations for you once you've found the best deal.

State and local **taxes** will add as much as 20% to your final bill. You'll pay an additional $2.05 per day in statewide use tax, and local sales taxes will tack on at least 6% to the total, including the statewide use tax (the state is being sued over this tax-on-a-tax practice). Some airports add another 35¢ per day and as much as 10% in "recovery" fees. You can avoid the recovery fee by picking up your car in town rather than at the airport. Budget and Enterprise both have numerous rental locations away from the airports. But be sure to weigh the cost of transportation to and from your hotel against the amount of the fee.

Competition is so fierce among Florida rental firms that most have now stopped charging **drop-off fees** if you pick up a car at one place and leave it at another. For example, I recently picked up a car at Tampa and dropped it off at Fort Myers for the same price I would have paid had I returned it to Tampa. Be sure to ask if there's a drop-off fee.

You must have a **valid credit card** (not a debit or check card) in your name, and most companies require you to be at least 25 years old to rent a car. Some also set maximum ages and may deny cars to anyone with a bad driving record. Ask about rental requirements and restrictions when you book in order to avoid problems when you get there.

BY TRAIN & BY BUS

You'll find that train travel isn't terribly feasible within Florida, and it's not much less expensive than flying, if at all. See "Getting There," earlier in this chapter, for Florida towns served by **Amtrak** (© 800/USA-RAIL; www.amtrak.com). For bus travel, see the "Essentials" and "Getting There" sections in the following chapters.

FAST FACTS: Florida

American Express There are a number of American Express offices in Florida. Call Cardmember Services (© 800/528-4800; www.americanexpress.com) for the location nearest you.

ATM Networks ATMs are as ubiquitous in Florida as the palm trees. Machines are found on nearly every street corner, main shopping area and, in most cases, supermarkets, and even in convenience stores.

Banks Banks are usually open Monday through Friday from 9am to 3 or 4pm, and most have automated teller machines (ATMs) for 24-hour banking. You won't have a problem finding a Cirrus or PLUS machine. See "Money," earlier in this chapter, for more information.

Car Rentals See "Getting Around," above.

Emergencies To reach the police, ambulance, or fire department, dial © 911 from any phone. No coins are needed. Emergency hot lines include **Crisis Intervention** (© 305/358-HELP or 305/358-4357) and the **Poison Information Center** (© 800/222-1222).

Liquor Laws You must be 21 to purchase or consume alcohol in Florida. This law is strictly enforced, so if you look young, carry some photo identification that gives your date of birth. Minors can usually enter bars where food is served but are not allowed to drink alcohol.

Newspapers/Magazines Most cities of any size have a local daily paper. The well-respected *Miami Herald* is generally available all over the state, with regional editions available in many areas. In the major cities, you can also find coin-operated boxes for *USA Today*, *The Wall Street Journal*, and *The New York Times*.

Safety Whenever you're traveling in an unfamiliar city, stay alert. Be aware of your immediate surroundings. Always lock your car doors and the trunk when your vehicle is unattended, and don't leave any valuables in sight. See "Health & Safety," earlier in this chapter, for more information.

Taxes The Florida state sales tax is 6%. Many municipalities add 1% or more to that, and most levy a special tax on hotel and restaurant bills. In general, expect at least 9% to be added to your final hotel bill. There are also hefty taxes on rental cars here (see "Getting Around," above).

Time Zones The Florida peninsula observes Eastern Standard Time, but most of the Panhandle, west of the Apalachicola River, is on Central Standard Time, 1 hour behind the rest of the state.

Weather Hurricane season runs August through November. For an up-to-date recording of current weather conditions and forecast reports, call ℂ **305/229-4522**. Online, you can check www.intellicast.com or www. weather.com.

3

For International Visitors

Whether it's your 1st visit or your 10th, a trip to the United States may require an additional degree of planning. This chapter will provide you with essential information, helpful tips, and advice for the more common problems that some visitors encounter.

1 Preparing for Your Trip

ENTRY REQUIREMENTS

Check at any U.S. embassy or consulate for current information and requirements. You can also obtain a visa application and other information online at the **U.S. State Department**'s website, at **www.travel.state.gov**.

VISAS The U.S. State Department has a **Visa Waiver Program** allowing citizens of certain countries (information is available from any U.S. embassy or consulate) to enter the United States without a visa for stays of up to 90 days. Citizens of these countries need only a valid passport and a round-trip air or cruise ticket in their possession upon arrival. Canadian citizens may enter the United States without visas; they need only proof of residence.

Citizens of all other countries must have (1) a valid passport that expires at least 6 months later than the scheduled end of their visit to the United States, and (2) a tourist visa, which may be obtained without charge from any U.S. consulate.

To obtain a visa, the traveler must submit a completed application form (either in person or by mail) with a 1½-inch-square photo, and must demonstrate binding ties to a residence abroad. Usually you can obtain a visa at once or within 24 hours, but it may take longer during the summer rush June through August. If you cannot go in person, contact the nearest U.S. embassy or consulate for directions on applying by mail. Your travel agent or airline office may also be able to provide you with visa applications and instructions. The U.S. consulate or embassy that issues your visa will determine whether you will be issued a multiple- or single-entry visa and any restrictions regarding the length of your stay.

British subjects can obtain up-to-date visa information by calling the **U.S. Embassy Visa Information Line** (© 0891/200-290) or by contacting the U.K. Passport Service (© 0870/521-0410; www.passport. gov.uk).

Irish citizens can obtain up-to-date passport and visa information through the **Embassy of USA Dublin,** 42 Elgin Rd., Dublin 4, Ireland (© 353/1-668-8777), or by checking the visa page on the website at www.usembassy.ie.

Australian citizens can obtain up-to-date visa information by contacting the **U.S. Embassy Canberra,** Moonah Place, Yarralumla, ACT 2600 (© 02/6214-5600) or by checking the embassy's website at http://usembassy-australia.state.gov.

Citizens of **New Zealand** can obtain up-to-date visa information by contacting the **U.S. Embassy New Zealand,** 29 Fitzherbert Terr., Thorndon, Wellington (© **644/462-6000**), or get the information directly from the "Services to New Zealanders" section of the website at http://usembassy.org.nz.

MEDICAL REQUIREMENTS

Unless you're arriving from an area known to be suffering from an epidemic (particularly cholera or yellow fever), inoculations or vaccinations are not required for entry into the United States. If you have a medical condition that requires **syringe-administered medications,** carry a valid signed prescription from your physician—the Federal Aviation Administration (FAA) no longer allows airline passengers to pack syringes in their carry-on baggage without documented proof of medical need. If you have a disease that requires treatment with **narcotics,** you should also carry documented proof with you—smuggling narcotics aboard a plane is a serious offense that carries severe penalties in the U.S.

DRIVER'S LICENSES Foreign driver's licenses are mostly recognized in the U.S., although you may want to get an international driver's license if your home license is not written in English.

PASSPORT INFORMATION

Safeguard your passport in an inconspicuous, inaccessible place like a money belt. Make a copy of the critical pages, including the passport number, and store it in a safe place, separate from the passport itself. If you lose your passport, visit the nearest consulate of your native country as soon as possible for a replacement. Passport applications are downloadable from the Internet sites listed below.

Note that the International Civil Aviation Organization (ICAO) has recommended a policy requiring that *every* individual who travels by air have his or her own passport. In response, many countries are now requiring that children must be issued their own passport to travel internationally, where before those under 16 or so may have been allowed to travel on a parent or guardian's passport.

CUSTOMS
WHAT YOU CAN BRING IN

Every visitor more than 21 years of age may bring in, free of duty, the following: (1) 1 liter of wine or hard liquor; (2) 200 cigarettes, 100 cigars (but not from Cuba), or 3 pounds of smoking tobacco; and (3) $100 worth of gifts. These exemptions are offered to travelers who spend at least 72 hours in the United States and who have not claimed them within the preceding 6 months. It is altogether forbidden to bring into the country foodstuffs (particularly fruit, cooked meats, and canned goods) and plants (vegetables, seeds, tropical plants, and the like). Foreign tourists may bring in or take out up to $10,000 in U.S. or foreign currency with no formalities; larger sums must be declared to U.S. Customs on entering or leaving, which includes filing form CM 4790. For more specific information regarding U.S. Customs and Border Protection, contact your nearest U.S. embassy or consulate, or the **U.S. Customs** office (© **202/927-1770** or www.customs.ustreas.gov).

WHAT YOU CAN TAKE HOME

U.K. citizens should contact HM Customs & Excise at © **0845/010-9000** (from outside the U.K., 020/8929-0152), or consult their website at www.hmce.gov.uk for more information. **Canadian citizens** can contact the **Canada Customs and Revenue Agency** (© **800/461-9999** in Canada, or 204/983-3500; www.ccra-adrc.gc.ca). **Australians** should call the **Australian Customs Service**

at © **1300/363-263,** or log on to
www.customs.gov.au. Those from
New Zealand can get more information from **New Zealand Customs,**
The Customhouse, 17–21 Whitmore
St., Box 2218, Wellington (© **0800/
428-786** or 04/473-6099; www.
customs.govt.nz).

HEALTH INSURANCE

Although it's not required of travelers,
health insurance is highly recommended. Unlike many European
countries, the United States does not
usually offer free or low-cost medical
care to its citizens or visitors. Doctors
and hospitals are expensive, and in
most cases will require advance payment or proof of coverage before they
render their services. Policies can cover
everything from the loss or theft of
your baggage and trip cancellation to
the guarantee of bail in case you're
arrested. Good policies will also cover
the costs of an accident, repatriation,
or death. See "Health & Safety" in
chapter 2 for more information. Packages such as **Europ Assistance's
"Worldwide Healthcare Plan"** are
sold by European automobile clubs
and travel agencies at attractive rates.
Worldwide Assistance Services, Inc.
(© **800/777-8710;** www.worldwide
assistance.com) is the agent for Europ
Assistance in the United States.

Though lack of health insurance
may prevent you from being admitted
to a hospital in nonemergencies, don't
worry about being left on a street corner to die: The American way is to fix
you now and bill the living daylights
out of you later.

MONEY

CURRENCY The U.S. monetary
system is very simple: The most common **bills** are the $1 (colloquially, a
"buck"), $5, $10, and $20 denomina-
tions. There are also $2 bills (seldom
encountered), $50 bills, and $100
bills (the last two are usually not welcome as payment for small purchases).

All the paper money was recently
redesigned, making the famous faces
adorning them disproportionately large.
The old-style bills are still legal tender.

There are seven denominations of
coins: 1¢ (1 cent, or a penny); 5¢ (5
cents, or a nickel); 10¢ (10 cents, or a
dime); 25¢ (25 cents, or a quarter);
50¢ (50 cents, or a half dollar); the
new gold "Sacagawea" coin worth $1;
and, prized by collectors, the rare,
older silver dollar.

Note: The "foreign-exchange bureaus"
so common in Europe are rare even at
airports in the United States, and nonexistent outside major cities. It's best
not to change foreign money (or traveler's checks denominated in a currency other than U.S. dollars) at a
small-town bank, or even a branch in
a big city; in fact, leave any currency
other than U.S. dollars at home—it
may prove a greater nuisance to you
than it's worth.

TRAVELER'S CHECKS Though
traveler's checks are widely accepted,
make sure that they're denominated in
U.S. dollars, as foreign-currency
checks are often difficult to exchange.
The three traveler's checks that are
most widely recognized—and least
likely to be denied—are **Visa, American Express,** and **Thomas Cook.** Be
sure to record the numbers of the
checks, and keep that information in a
separate place in case they get lost or
stolen. Most businesses are pretty
good about taking traveler's checks,
but you're better off cashing them in
at a bank (in small amounts, of
course) and paying in cash. *Remember:* You'll need identification, such as
a driver's license or passport, to change
a traveler's check.

CREDIT CARDS & ATMS Credit
cards are the most widely used form of
payment in the United States: **Visa**
(Barclaycard in Britain), **MasterCard**
(EuroCard in Europe, Access in
Britain, Chargex in Canada), **American Express, Diners Club,** and

Discover. There are, however, a handful of stores and restaurants that do not take credit cards, so be sure to ask in advance. Most businesses display a sticker near their entrance to let you know which cards they accept. (*Note:* Businesses may require a minimum purchase, usually around $10, to use a credit card.)

It is strongly recommended that you bring at least one major credit card. You must have a credit or charge card to rent a car. Hotels and airlines usually require a credit card imprint as a deposit against expenses, and in an emergency a credit card can be priceless.

You'll find **automated teller machines (ATMs)** on just about every block—at least in almost every town—across the country. Some ATMs will allow you to draw U.S. currency against your bank and credit cards. Check with your bank before leaving home, and remember that you will need your personal identification number (PIN) to do so. Most accept Visa, MasterCard, and American Express, as well as ATM cards from other U.S. banks. Expect to be charged up to $3 per transaction, however, if you're not using your own bank's ATM.

One way around these fees is to ask for cash back at grocery stores that accept ATM cards and don't charge usage fees. Of course, you'll have to purchase something first.

ATM cards with major credit card backing, known as "debit cards," are now a commonly acceptable form of payment in most stores and restaurants. Debit cards draw money directly from your checking account. Some stores enable you to receive "cash back" on your debit card purchases as well.

SAFETY
GENERAL   SUGGESTIONS
Although tourist areas are generally safe, U.S. urban areas tend to be less safe than those in Europe or Japan.

You should always stay alert. This is particularly true of large American cities. If you're in doubt about which neighborhoods are safe, don't hesitate to make inquiries with the hotel front desk staff or the local tourist office.

Avoid deserted areas, especially at night, and don't go into public parks after dark unless there's a concert or similar occasion that will attract a crowd.

Avoid carrying valuables with you on the street, and keep expensive cameras or electronic equipment bagged up or covered when not in use. If you're using a map, try to consult it inconspicuously—or better yet, study it before you leave your room. Hold onto your pocketbook, and place your billfold in an inside pocket. In theaters, restaurants, and other public places, keep your possessions in sight.

Always lock your room door—don't assume that once you're inside the hotel you are automatically safe and no longer need to be aware of your surroundings. Hotels are open to the public, and in a large hotel, security may not be able to screen everyone who enters.

DRIVING SAFETY Driving safety is important, too, especially given the highly publicized carjackings of foreign tourists in Florida. Question your rental agency about personal safety and ask for a traveler-safety brochure when you pick up your car. Obtain written directions—or a map with the route clearly marked—from the agency showing how to get to your destination. (Many agencies now offer the option of renting a cellular phone for the duration of your car rental; check with the rental agent when you pick up the car.) And, if possible, arrive and depart during daylight hours.

If you drive off a highway and end up in a dodgy-looking neighborhood, leave the area as quickly as possible. If you have an accident, even on the highway, stay in your car with the doors locked until you assess the situation or until the police arrive. If you're bumped from behind on the street or are involved in a minor accident with no injuries, and the situation appears to be suspicious, motion to the other driver to follow you. Never get out of your car in such situations. Go directly to the nearest police precinct, well-lit service station, or 24-hour store. You may want to look into renting a cellphone on a short-term basis. One recommended wireless rental company is **InTouch USA** (© 800/872-7626; www.intouchusa.com).

Park in well-lit and well-traveled areas whenever possible. Always keep your car doors locked, whether the vehicle is attended or unattended. Never leave any packages or valuables in sight. If someone attempts to rob you or steal your car, don't try to resist the thief/carjacker. Report the incident to the police department immediately by calling © **911.**

2 Getting to the U.S.

A number of U.S. airlines offer service from Europe and Latin America to Florida, including American, Delta, Northwest, and United (see "Getting There," in chapter 2). Many of the major international airlines, such as **British Airways** (www.british-airways.com), **KLM Royal Dutch Airlines** (www.klm.com), and **Lufthansa** (www.lufthansa.com), also have direct flights from Europe to various Florida cities, either in their own planes or in conjunction with an American "partner" airline (Northwest/KLM, to name one such partnership). You can get here from Australia and New Zealand via **Air New Zealand** (www.airnz.com), **Qantas** (www.qantas.com), **American** (www.aa.com), and **United** (www.ual.com), with a change of planes in Los Angeles. Call the airlines' local offices or contact your travel agent, and be sure to ask about promotional fares and discounts.

From Great Britain, **Virgin Atlantic Airways** (© 800/862-8621 in the U.S., or 08/703-80-20-07 in the U.K.; www.virgin-atlantic.com) has attractive deals on its flights from London and Manchester to Miami and Orlando. From Germany, **LTU International Airways** (© 866/266-5588 in the U.S., or 941-8888 in Germany; www.ltu.com) frequently has reduced fares to Miami, Orlando, and Fort Myers from Frankfurt, Munich, and Düsseldorf. From Johannesburg and Cape Town, **South African Airways** and **Delta Airlines** (www.delta.com) fly to Fort Lauderdale.

Canadians should check with **Air Canada** (© 888-247-2262; www.aircanada.ca), which offers service from Toronto and Montreal to Miami, Tampa, West Palm Beach, Fort Lauderdale, and Fort Myers. Also ask your travel agent about **Air Transat** (© 866/847-1112; www.airtransat.com), which has wintertime charter flights to several Florida destinations.

AIRLINE DISCOUNTS   The smart traveler can find numerable ways to reduce the price of a plane ticket simply by taking time to shop around. For example, overseas visitors can take advantage of the APEX (Advance Purchase Excursion) reductions offered by all major U.S. and European carriers. For more money-saving airline advice, see "Getting There," in chapter 2, beginning on p. 29. For the best rates, compare fares and be flexible with the dates and times of travel.

IMMIGRATION AND CUSTOMS CLEARANCE   Visitors arriving by air, no matter what the port of entry, should cultivate patience and resignation before setting foot on U.S. soil. Getting through immigration control can take as long as 2 hours on some days, especially on summer weekends, so be sure to carry this guidebook or something else to read. This is especially true in the aftermath of the World Trade Center attacks, when security clearances have been considerably beefed up at U.S. airports.

3 Getting Around the U.S.

The United States is one of the world's largest countries, with vast distances separating many of its key sights. If you fly from Europe to New York, for example, you still have a trip of more than 1,350 miles to Miami. Accordingly, flying is the quickest and most comfortable way to get around the country.

BY PLANE   Some large airlines (for example, Northwest and Delta) offer travelers on their transatlantic or transpacific flights special discount tickets under the name **Visit USA,** allowing mostly one-way travel from one U.S. destination to another at very low prices. These discount tickets are not on sale in the United States and must be purchased abroad in conjunction with your international ticket. This system is the best, easiest, and fastest way to see the United States at low cost. You should obtain information well in advance from your travel agent or the office of the airline concerned, since the conditions attached to these discount tickets can be changed without advance notice.

BY TRAIN   International visitors (excluding Canada) can also buy a **USA Rail Pass,** good for 15 or 30 days of unlimited travel on Amtrak (© **800/USA-RAIL;** www.amtrak. com). The pass is available through many foreign travel agents. Prices in 2004 for a 15-day pass were $295 off-peak, $440 peak; a 30-day pass costs $385 off-peak, $550 peak. With a foreign passport, you can also buy passes at some Amtrak offices in the United States, including locations in San Francisco, Los Angeles, Chicago, New York, Miami, Boston, and Washington, D.C. Reservations are generally required and should be made for each

part of your trip as early as possible. Regional rail passes are also available.

BY BUS   Although bus travel is often the most economical form of public transit for short hops between U.S. cities, it can also be slow and uncomfortable—certainly not an option for everyone (particularly when Amtrak, which is far more luxurious, offers similar rates). **Greyhound/Trailways (© 800/231-2222;** www.greyhound.com), the sole nationwide bus line, offers an **International Ameripass** that must be purchased before coming to the United States, or by phone through the Greyhound International Office at the Port Authority Bus Terminal in New York City (© **212/971-0492**). The pass can be obtained from foreign travel agents or through Greyhound's website (order at least 21 days before your departure to the U.S.) and costs less than the domestic version. Passes for 2004 cost as follows: 7 days $209, 10 days $259, 15 days $309, 21 days $359, 30 days $399, 45 days $459, or 60 days $569. You can get more info on the pass at the website, or by calling © **00/231-2222** or 402/330-8552 (for international callers who don't have toll-free access). In addition, special rates are available for seniors and students.

BY CAR   Unless you plan to spend the bulk of your vacation time in a city where walking is the best and easiest way to get around (read: New York City or New Orleans), the most cost-effective, convenient, and comfortable way to travel around the United States is by car. The interstate highway system connects cities and towns all over the country; in addition to these high-speed, limited-access roadways, there's an extensive network of federal, state, and local highways and roads. Some of the national car-rental companies include **Alamo** (© 800/462-5266; www.alamo.com), **Avis** (© 800/230-4898; www.avis.com), **Budget** (© 800/527-0700; www.budget.com), **Dollar** (© 800/800-3665; www.dollar.com), **Hertz** (© 800/654-3131; www.hertz.com), **National** (© 800/227-7368; www.nationalcar.com), and **Thrifty** (© 800/847-4389; www.thrifty.com).

If you plan to rent a car in the United States, you probably won't need the services of an additional automobile organization. If you're planning to buy or borrow a car, automobile-association membership is recommended. **AAA, the American Automobile Association** (© 800/222-1134), is the country's largest auto club and supplies its members with maps, insurance, and, most important, emergency road service. The cost of joining runs from $60 for singles, add another for $30, but if you're a member of a foreign auto club with reciprocal arrangements, you can enjoy free AAA service in America. See "Getting There," in chapter 2, beginning on p. 29 for more information.

FAST FACTS: **For the International Traveler**

Business Hours Offices are usually open weekdays from 9am to 5pm. Banks are open weekdays from 9am to 3pm or later and sometimes Saturday mornings. Stores typically open between 9 and 10am and close between 5 and 6pm from Monday through Saturday. Stores in shopping complexes or malls tend to stay open late: until about 9pm on weekdays and weekends, and many malls and larger department stores are open on Sundays.

Drinking Laws The legal age for purchase and consumption of alcoholic beverages is 21; proof of age is required and often requested at bars, nightclubs, and restaurants, so it's always a good idea to bring ID when you go out. On South Beach, in particular, the clubs and bars have become stricter since they raised the minimum age of entry from 18 to 21. Beer and wine can often be purchased in supermarkets, but liquor laws vary throughout the state.

Do not carry open containers of alcohol in your car or any public area that isn't zoned for alcohol consumption. The police can fine you on the spot. And nothing will ruin your trip faster than getting a citation for DUI ("driving under the influence"), so don't even think about driving while intoxicated.

Electricity Like Canada, the United States uses 110 to 120 volts AC (60 cycles), compared to 220 to 240 volts AC (50 cycles) in most of Europe, Australia, and New Zealand. If your small appliances use 220 to 240 volts, you'll need a 110-volt transformer and a plug adapter with two flat parallel pins to operate them here. Downward converters that change 220 to 240 volts to 110 to 120 volts are difficult to find in the United States, so bring one with you.

Embassies & Consulates All embassies are located in the nation's capital, Washington, D.C. Some consulates are located in major U.S. cities, and most nations have a mission to the United Nations in New York City. If your country isn't listed below, call for directory information in Washington, D.C. (© 202/555-1212) or log on to **www.embassy.org/embassies**.

In South Florida, the **Canadian Consulate** is located at 200 S. Bayshore Dr., Miami, FL 33131 (© 305/579-1600). The **British Consulate** is located at the Brickell Bay Tower, Suite 2110, 1001 S. Bayshore Dr., Coconut Grove, FL 33131 (© 305/374-1522). The **French Consulate** is located at 1 Biscayne Tower, Suite 1710, Miami, FL 33131 (© 305/372-9799); the **Italian Consulate** is located at 1200 Brickell Ave., Miami, FL 33131 (© 305/374-6322); the **Israeli Consulate** is located at 100 N. Biscayne Blvd., Miami, FL 33132 (© 305/925-9400); the **German Consulate** is located at 100 N. Biscayne Blvd., Suite 2200, Miami, FL 33132 (© 305/358-0290); the **Australian Consulate** is located at 2525 SW Third Ave., Suite 208, Miami, FL 33129 (© 305/858-7633); and **Brazil's Consulate General** is located at 2601 S. Bayshore Dr., Suite 800, Coconut Grove, FL 33133 (© 305/285-6200).

Emergencies Call © 911 to report a fire, call the police, or get an ambulance anywhere in the United States. This is a toll-free call. (No coins are required at public telephones.)

If you encounter serious problems, contact the **Traveler's Aid Society International** (© 202/546-1127; www.travelersaid.org) to help direct you to a local branch. This nationwide, nonprofit, social-service organization geared to helping travelers in difficult straits offers services that might include reuniting families separated while traveling, providing food and/or shelter to people stranded without cash, or even emotional counseling. If you're in trouble, seek them out.

Gasoline (Petrol) Petrol is known as gasoline (or simply "gas") in the United States, and petrol stations are known as both gas stations and service stations. Gasoline costs about half as much here as it does in Europe (though, at around $2 per gallon at presstime, prices are steeply rising), and taxes are already included in the printed price. One U.S. gallon equals 3.8 liters or .85 Imperial gallons. A majority of gas stations in Florida are now actually convenience grocery stores with gas pumps outside. They do not service your automobile for you; all but a very few stations have self-service gas pumps.

Holidays Banks, government offices, post offices, and many stores, restaurants, and museums are closed on the following legal national holidays: January 1 (New Year's Day), the third Monday in January (Martin Luther King Jr. Day), the third Monday in February (Presidents' Day, Washington's Birthday), the last Monday in May (Memorial Day), July 4 (Independence Day), the first Monday in September (Labor Day), the second Monday in October (Columbus Day), November 11 (Veterans' Day/ Armistice Day), the fourth Thursday in November (Thanksgiving Day), and December 25 (Christmas). Also, the Tuesday following the first Monday in November is Election Day and is a federal government holiday in presidential-election years (held every 4 years, and next in 2004).

Legal Aid If you are "pulled over" for a minor infraction (such as speeding), never attempt to pay the fine directly to a police officer; this could be construed as attempted bribery, a much more serious crime. Pay fines by mail, or directly into the hands of the clerk of the court. If accused of a more serious offense, say and do nothing before consulting a lawyer. Everyone has the right to remain silent, whether he or she is suspected of a crime or actually arrested. Once arrested, a person can make one telephone call to a party of his or her choice. Call your embassy or consulate.

Mail If you aren't sure what your address will be in the United States, mail can be sent to you, in your name, c/o General Delivery at the main post office of the city or region where you expect to be. (Call ℂ **800/ 275-8777** for information on the nearest post office.) The addressee must pick up mail in person and must produce proof of identity (driver's license, passport, and so on.). Most post offices will hold your mail for up to 1 month, and are open Monday through Friday from 8am to 6pm, and Saturday from 9am to 3pm.

At press time, domestic postage rates were 23¢ for a postcard and 37¢ for a letter. For international mail, a first-class letter of up to ½ ounce costs 80¢ (60¢ to Canada and Mexico); a first-class postcard costs 70¢ (50¢ to Canada and Mexico); and a preprinted postal aerogramme costs 70¢.

Taxes The United States has no value-added tax (VAT) or other indirect tax at the national level. Every state, county, and city has the right to levy its own local tax on all purchases, including hotel and restaurant checks, airline tickets, and so on. For Florida's sales taxes, see "Fast Facts: Florida," in chapter 2.

Telephone, Telegraph, Telex & Fax The telephone system in the United States is run by private corporations, so rates, especially for long-distance service and operator-assisted calls, can vary widely. Generally, hotel surcharges on long-distance and local calls are astronomical, so you're usually better off using a **public pay telephone,** which you'll find clearly marked in most public buildings and private establishments as well as on the street. Convenience grocery stores and gas stations always have them. Many convenience groceries and packaging services sell **prepaid calling cards;** these can be the least expensive way to call home. **Local calls** made from public pay phones in Florida cost 35¢. Pay phones do not accept pennies, and few will take anything larger than a quarter.

Most long-distance and international calls can be dialed directly from any phone. **For calls within the United States and to Canada,** dial 1 followed by the area code and the seven-digit number. **For other international calls,** dial 011 followed by the country code, city code, and the telephone number of the person you are calling.

Calls to area codes **800, 888, 866,** and **877** are toll-free. However, calls to numbers in area codes **700** and **900** (chat lines, bulletin boards, "dating" services, and so on) can be very expensive—usually a charge of 95¢ to $3 or more per minute, and they sometimes have minimum charges that can run as high as $15 or more.

For **reversed-charge or collect calls,** and for person-to-person calls, dial 0 (zero, not the letter O) followed by the area code and number you want; an operator will then come on the line, and you should specify that you are calling collect, or person-to-person, or both. If your operator-assisted call is international, ask for the overseas operator.

For **local directory assistance** ("information"), dial 🕐 411; for long-distance information, dial 1, then the appropriate area code and 555-1212.

Most hotels have **fax machines** available for guest use (be sure to ask about the charge to use it). Many hotel rooms are even wired for guests' fax machines. A less expensive way to send and receive faxes may be at stores such as The UPS Store/Mail Boxes Etc., a national chain of packing service shops. (Look in the Yellow Pages directory under "Packing Services.")

Time The continental United States is divided into **four time zones:** Eastern Standard Time (EST), Central Standard Time (CST), Mountain Standard Time (MST), and Pacific Standard Time (PST). Alaska and Hawaii have their own zones. For example, noon in Miami (EST) is 11am in Pensacola (CST), 10am in Denver (MST), 9am in Los Angeles (PST), 8am in Anchorage (AST), and 7am in Honolulu (HST). Most of Florida observes Eastern Standard Time, though the Panhandle west of the Apalachicola River is on Central Standard Time (1 hr. earlier than Tallahassee, Orlando, and Miami).

Daylight savings time is in effect from 1am on the first Sunday in April through 1am on the last Sunday in October, except in Arizona, Hawaii, part of Indiana, and Puerto Rico. Daylight savings time moves the clock 1 hour ahead of standard time.

Tipping Tips are a very important part of certain workers' salaries, so it's necessary to leave appropriate gratuities.

Here are some rules of thumb:

In hotels, tip **bellhops** at least $1 per bag ($2–$3 if you have a lot of luggage) and tip the **chamber staff** $3 per day (more if you've left a disaster area for him or her to clean up, or if you're traveling with kids and/or pets). Tip the **doorman** or **concierge** only if he or she has provided you with some specific service (for example, calling a cab for you or obtaining difficult-to-get theater tickets). Tip the **valet parking attendant** $1 every time you get your car.

In restaurants, bars, and nightclubs, tip **service staff** 15% to 20% of the check, tip **bartenders** 10% to 15%, tip **checkroom attendants** $1 per garment, and tip **valet-parking attendants** $1 per vehicle. Tip the **doorman** only if he has provided you with some specific service (such as calling a cab for you).

As for other service personnel, tip **cab drivers** 15% of the fare; tip **skycaps** at airports at least $1 per bag ($2–$3 if you have a lot of luggage); and tip **hairdressers** and **barbers** 15% to 20%.

4

Getting to Know Miami

A week in Miami is not unlike watching an episode of, say, *Access Hollywood* with a little *CNN* thrown in for good measure. Miami: the city to which J-Lo fled when she and Ben Affleck were on the outs; the place where the paparazzi camps out for days hoping to catch a glimpse of something or someone fabulous; the place where former President Bill Clinton kibitzes with the head of a top modeling agency at a St. Tropez-ish beach club; where Janet Reno throws a politically driven dance party at a South Beach nightclub. And that's just a small sampling of the surreal, Felliniesque world that exists way down here at the bottom of the map. Nothing in Miami is ever what it seems.

What used to be a relatively sleepy beach vacation destination has awakened from its humid slumber, upped its tempo, and finally earned its place in the Palm Pilots of cutting-edge jet-setters worldwide. But don't be fooled by the hipper-than-thou, celebrity-drenched playground known as South Beach. While the chic elite do, indeed, flock to Miami's coolest enclave, it is surprisingly accessible to the average Joe, Jane, or José. For every Phillippe Starck–designed, bank-account-busting boutique hotel on South Beach, there's a kitschy, candy-coated Art Deco one that's much less taxing on the pockets. For each Pan-Mediterranean-Asian haute cuisinerie, there's

always the down-home, no-nonsense Cuban bodega offering hearty food at ridiculously cheap prices.

Beyond the whole glitzy, *Entertainment Tonight*-meets-beach-blanket-bacchanalia-as-seen-on-TV, Miami has an endless number of sporting, cultural, and recreational activities to keep you entertained. Our sparkling beaches are beyond compare. Plus, there's excellent shopping and nightlife activities that include ballet, theater, and opera (as well as all the celebrity-saturated hotels, restaurants, bars, and clubs that have helped to make Miami so famous).

Leave Miami, be it for the Keys, the Gold Coast, or the Treasure Coast, and you'll expose yourself not only to more UV rays, but to a world of cultural, historical, and sybaritic surprises where you can take in a spring baseball game, walk in the footsteps of Hemingway, get up close and personal with the area's sea life, soak up the serenity of unspoiled landscapes, catch the filming of *CSI: Miami* or a big-budget Hollywood flick, and much more.

Forget what you've heard about South Florida being Heaven's Waiting Room. That slogan is as passé as the concept of early bird dinners (which you can still get—they just no longer define the region). In fact, according to some people, South Florida *is* heaven. So what are *you* waiting for?

1 Orientation

ARRIVING

Originally carved out of scrubland in 1928 by Pan American Airlines, **Miami International Airport (MIA)** has become 2nd in the United States for

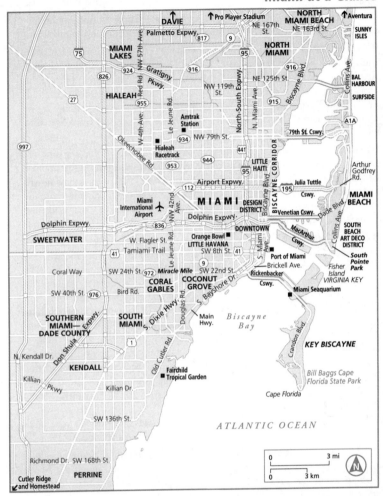

international passenger traffic and 10th in the world for total passengers. Despite the heavy traffic, the airport is quite user-friendly and not as much of a hassle as you'd think. You can change money or use your ATM card at Nation's Bank of South Florida, located near the exit. Visitor information is available 24 hours a day at the **Miami International Airport Main Visitor Counter,** Concourse E, second level (✆ **305/876-7000**). Information is also available at **www.miami-airport.com.** Because MIA is the busiest airport in South Florida, travelers may want to consider flying into the less crowded **Fort Lauderdale–Hollywood International Airport (FLL)** (✆ **954/359-1200**), which is closer to north Miami than MIA, or the **Palm Beach International Airport (PBI)** (✆ **561/471-7420**), which is about 1½ hours from Miami.

GETTING INTO TOWN

Miami International Airport is located about 6 miles west of downtown and about 10 miles from the beaches, so it's likely you can get from the plane to your hotel room in less than half an hour. Of course, if you're arriving from an international destination, it will take more time to go through Customs and Immigration.

BY CAR   All the major car-rental firms operate off-site branches reached via shuttles from the airline terminals. See the "Rentals" section, under "Getting Around," on p. 58 for a list of major rental companies in Miami. Signs at the airport's exit clearly point the way to various parts of the city, but the car-rental firm should also give you directions to your destination. If you're arriving late at night, you might want to take a taxi to your hotel and have the car delivered to you the next day.

BY TAXI   Taxis line up in front of a dispatcher's desk outside the airport's arrivals terminals. Most cabs are metered, though some have flat rates to popular destinations. The fare should be about $20 to Coral Gables, $18 to downtown, and $24 to South Beach, plus tip, which should be about 15% (add more for each bag the driver handles). Depending on traffic, the ride to Coral Gables or downtown takes about 15 to 20 minutes and to South Beach, 20 to 25 minutes.

BY VAN OR LIMO   Group limousines (multipassenger vans) circle the arrivals area looking for fares. Destinations are posted on the front of each van, and a flat rate is charged for door-to-door service to the area marked.

   SuperShuttle (© **305/871-2000;** www.supershuttle.com) is one of the largest airport operators, charging between $9 and $40 per person for a ride within the county. Its vans operate 24 hours a day and accept American Express, MasterCard, and Visa. This is a cheaper alternative to a cab (if you are traveling alone or with one other person), but be prepared to be in the van for quite a while, as you may have to make several stops to drop passengers off before you reach your own destination. SuperShuttle also has begun service from Palm Beach International Airport to the surrounding communities. The door-to-door, shared-ride service operates from the airport to Stuart, Fort Pierce, Palm Beach, and Broward counties.

   Private limousine arrangements can be made in advance through your local travel agent. A one-way meet-and-greet service should cost about $50.

BY PUBLIC TRANSPORTATION   Public transportation in South Florida is a major hassle bordering on a nightmare. Painfully slow and unreliable, buses heading downtown leave the airport only once per hour (from the arrivals level), and connections are spotty at best. It could take about an hour and a half to get to South Beach via public transportation. Journeys to downtown and Coral Gables, however, are more direct. The fare is $1.25, plus an additional 25¢ for a transfer.

VISITOR INFORMATION

The most up-to-date information is provided by the **Greater Miami Convention and Visitor's Bureau,** 701 Brickell Ave., Suite 700, Miami, FL 33131 (© **800/ 933-8448** or 305/539-3000; fax 305/530-3113; www.tropicoolmiami.com).

   If you arrive at the Miami International Airport, you can pick up visitor information at the airport's main visitor counter on the second floor of Concourse E: It's open 24 hours a day.

   Always check local newspapers for special events during your visit. The city's only daily, the *Miami Herald,* is a good source for current-events listings, particularly the "Weekend" section in Friday's edition and the paper's entertainment weekly offshoot, *The Street,* available free every Friday in freestanding boxes anchored to city streets. Even better is the free weekly alternative paper, the *Miami New Times,* available in bright red boxes throughout the city.

Information on everything from dining to entertainment in Miami is available on the Internet at www.miami.citysearch.com, www.digitalcity.com/south florida, www.miaminewtimes.com, or at www.herald.com.

CITY LAYOUT

Miami may seem confusing at first, but it quickly becomes easy to navigate. The small cluster of buildings that makes up the downtown area is at the geographical heart of the city. In relation to downtown, the airport is northwest, the beaches are east, Coconut Grove is south, Coral Gables is west, and the rest of the city is north.

FINDING AN ADDRESS   Miami is divided into dozens of areas with official and unofficial boundaries. Street numbering in the city of Miami is fairly straightforward, but you must first be familiar with the numbering system. The mainland is divided into four sections (NE, NW, SE, and SW) by the intersection of Flagler Street and Miami Avenue. Flagler divides Miami from north to south and Miami Avenue divides the city from east to west. It's helpful to remember that avenues generally run north-south, while streets go east-west. Street numbers (1st St., 2nd St., and so forth) start from here and increase as you go farther out from this intersection, as do numbers of avenues, places, courts, terraces, and lanes. Streets in Hialeah are the exceptions to this pattern; they are listed separately in map indexes.

Getting around the barrier islands that make up Miami Beach is somewhat easier than moving around the mainland. Street numbering starts with 1st Street, near Miami Beach's southern tip, and increases to 192nd Street, in the northern part of Sunny Isles. Collins Avenue makes the entire journey, from head to toe of the island. As in the city of Miami, some streets in Miami Beach have numbers as well as names. When they are part of listings in this book, both name and number are given.

The numbered streets in Miami Beach are not the geographical equivalents of those on the mainland, but they are close. For example, the 79th Street Causeway runs into 71st Street on Miami Beach.

It's easy to get lost in sprawling Miami, so a reliable map is essential. The **Trakker Map of Miami** is a four-color accordion map that encompasses all of Dade County. Some maps of Miami list streets according to area, so you'll have to know which part of the city you are looking for before the street can be found. All the listings in this book include area information for this reason.

THE NEIGHBORHOODS IN BRIEF

South Beach—The Art Deco District South Beach's 10 miles of beach are alive with a frenetic, circuslike atmosphere and are center stage for a motley crew of characters, from eccentric locals, seniors, snowbirds, and college students to gender benders, celebrities, club kids, and curiosity-seekers: Individuality is as widely accepted on South Beach as Visa and MasterCard.

Bolstered by a Caribbean-chic cafe society and a sexually charged,

tragically hip nightlife, people-watching on South Beach (1st St.–23rd St.) is almost as good as a front-row seat at a Milan fashion show. And although the beautiful people do flock to South Beach, the models aren't the only sights worth drooling over: The thriving Art Deco District within South Beach contains the largest concentration of Art Deco architecture in the world (in 1979, much of South Beach was listed in the National

Register of Historic Places). The pastel-hued structures are super-models in their own right—only *these* models improve with age.

Miami Beach In the fabulous '50s, Miami Beach was America's true Riviera. The stamping ground of choice for the Rat Pack and notorious mobsters such as Al Capone, its huge self-contained resort hotels were vacations unto themselves, providing a full day's worth of meals, activities, and entertainment. Then, in the 1960s and 1970s, people who fell in love with Miami began to buy apartments rather than rent hotel rooms. Tourism declined, the Rat Pack fled to Vegas, Capone disappeared, and many area hotels fell into disrepair.

However, since the late 1980s and South Beach's renaissance, Miami Beach (24th St. and up) has experienced a tide of revitalization. Huge beach hotels are finding their niche with new international tourist markets and are attracting large convention crowds. New generations of Americans are quickly rediscovering the qualities that originally made Miami Beach so popular, and they are finding out that the sand and surf now come with a thriving international city.

Surfside, Bal Harbour, and **Sunny Isles** make up the north part of the beach (island). Hotels, motels, restaurants, and beaches line Collins Avenue and, with some outstanding exceptions, the farther north one goes, the cheaper lodging becomes. All told, excellent prices, location, and facilities make Surfside and Sunny Isles attractive places to stay, although, despite a slow-going renaissance, they are still a little rough around the edges. However, a revitalization is in the works for these areas, and, while it's highly unlikely they will ever become as chic as South Beach,

there is potential for this, especially as South Beach falls prey to the inevitable spoiler: commercialism. Keep in mind that beachfront properties are at a premium, so many of the area's moderately priced hotels have been converted to condominiums, leaving fewer and fewer affordable places to stay.

In exclusive and ritzy Bal Harbour, where well-paid police officers are instructed to ticket drivers who go above the 30 mph speed limit, few hotels remain amid the many beachfront condominium towers. Instead, fancy homes, tucked away on the bay, hide behind gated communities, and the Rodeo Drive of Miami (known as the Bal Harbour Shops) attracts shoppers who don't flinch at four-, five-, and six-figure price tags.

Note that **North Miami Beach,** a residential area near the Dade-Broward County line (north of 163rd St.; part of N. Dade County), is a misnomer. It is actually northwest of Miami Beach, on the mainland, and has no beaches, though it does have some of Miami's better restaurants and shops. Located within North Miami Beach is the posh residential community of **Aventura,** best known for its high-priced condos, the Turnberry Isle Resort, and the Aventura Mall.

Note: South Beach, the historic Art Deco District, is treated as a separate neighborhood from Miami Beach.

Key Biscayne Miami's forested and secluded Key Biscayne is technically one of the first islands in the Florida Keys. However, this island is nothing like its southern neighbors. Located south of Miami Beach, off the shores of Coconut Grove, Key Biscayne is protected from the troubles of the mainland by the long Rickenbacker Causeway and its $1 toll.

Largely an exclusive residential community, with million-dollar homes and sweeping water views, Key Biscayne also offers visitors great public beaches, some top (read: pricey) resort hotels, and several good restaurants. Hobie Beach, adjacent to the causeway, is the city's premier spot for windsurfing, sailboarding, and jet-skiing (see the "Miami's Beaches" and "Watersports" sections in chapter 5). On the island's southern tip, Bill Baggs State Park has great beaches, bike paths, and dense forests for picnicking and partying.

Downtown Miami's downtown boasts one of the world's most beautiful cityscapes. Unfortunately, that's about all it offers—for now. During the day, a vibrant community of students, businesspeople, and merchants makes its way through the bustling streets where vendors sell fresh-cut pineapples and mangos while young consumers on shopping sprees lug bags and boxes. However, at night, downtown is mostly desolate (except for NE 11th St., where there is a burgeoning nightlife scene) and not a place in which you'd want to get lost. The downtown area does have a mall (Bayside Marketplace, where many cruise passengers come to browse), some culture (Metro-Dade Cultural Center), and a few decent restaurants, as well as the sprawling American Airlines Arena (home to the Miami Heat). Additionally, a downtown revitalization project is in the works, in which a cultural arts center, urban chic dwellings and lofts, and an assortment of hip boutiques, eateries, and bars are starting to bring downtown back to a life it never really had.

Design District With restaurants springing up between galleries and furniture stores galore, the Design District is, as locals say, the new South Beach, adding a touch of New York's SoHo to an area formerly known as downtown Miami's "Don't Go." The district, which is a hotbed for furniture-import companies, interior designers, architects, and more, has also become a player in Miami's ever-changing nightlife, with bars, lounges, clubs, and restaurants ranging from uber chic and retro to progressive and indie that have helped the area become hipster central for South Beach expatriates and artsy bohemian types. In anticipation of its growing popularity, the district has also banded together to create an up-to-date website, www.designmiami.com, which includes a calendar of events, such as the internationally lauded Art Basel, which attracts the who's who of the art world, and is chock-full of information. The district is loosely defined as the area bounded by NE 2nd Avenue, NE 5th Avenue East and West, and NW 36th Street to the south.

Biscayne Corridor From downtown, near Bayside, to the 70s (affectionately known as the Upper East Side), where trendy curio shops and upscale restaurants are slowly opening, Biscayne Boulevard is aspiring to reclaim itself as a safe thoroughfare where tourists can wine, dine, and shop. Previously known for sketchy, dilapidated 1950s- and 1960s-era hotels that had fallen on hard times, residents fleeing the high prices of the beaches in search of affordable housing are renovating Biscayne block by block, trying to make this once-again famous boulevard worthy of a Sunday drive. With the trendy Design District immediately west of 36th and Biscayne by 2 blocks, there is hope for the area.

Little Havana If you've never been to Cuba, just visit this small section of Miami and you'll come pretty close. The sounds, tastes, and rhythms are very reminiscent of Cuba's capital city, and some even jokingly say you don't have to speak a word of English to live an independent life here—even street signs are in Spanish and English.

Cuban coffee shops, tailor and furniture stores, and inexpensive restaurants line "Calle Ocho" (pronounced *Ka*-yey *O*-choh), SW 8th Street, the region's main thoroughfare. In Little Havana, salsa and merengue beats ring loudly from old record stores while old men in *guayaberas* (loose-fitting cotton or gauzy shirts, short sleeved, used to keep cool in Cuba and now a fashion statement in Miami) smoke cigars over their daily game of dominoes. The spotlight focused on the neighborhood during the Elián González situation in 2000, but the area was previously noted for the groups of artists and nocturnal types who have moved their galleries and performance spaces here, sparking a culturally charged neobohemian nightlife.

Coral Gables "The City Beautiful," created by George Merrick in the early 1920s, is one of Miami's first planned developments. This is not Levittown: The houses here were built in a Mediterranean style along lush, tree-lined streets that open onto beautifully carved plazas, many with centerpiece fountains. The best architectural examples of the era have Spanish-style tiled roofs and are built from Miami oolite, native limestone commonly called "coral rock." The Gables's European-flaired shopping and commerce center is home to many thriving corporations. Coral Gables also has landmark hotels, great golfing, upscale shopping to rival Bal Harbour, and some of the city's best restaurants, headed by world-renowned chefs.

Coconut Grove An arty, hippie hangout in the psychedelic '60s, Coconut Grove has given way from swirls of tie-dyes to the uniform color schemes of the Gap. Chain stores, theme restaurants, a megaplex, and bars galore make Coconut Grove a commercial success, but this gentrification has pushed most alternative types out. Ritzier types have now resurfaced here, thanks, in part, to the anti-boho Ritz-Carlton Coconut Grove (p. 86). The intersection of Grand Avenue, Main Highway, and McFarlane Road pierces the area's heart. Right in the center of it all is CocoWalk and the Shops at Mayfair, filled with boutiques, eateries, and bars. Sidewalks here are often crowded, especially at night, when University of Miami students (who frequent this adopted college town) come out to play.

Southern Miami–Dade County To locals, South Miami is both a specific area, southwest of Coral Gables, and a general region that encompasses all of southern Dade County, including Kendall, Perrine, Cutler Ridge, and Homestead. For the purposes of clarity, this book has grouped all these southern suburbs under the rubric "Southern Miami–Dade County." Similar attributes unite the communities: They are heavily residential and packed with strip malls amid a few remaining plots of farmland. Tourists don't usually stay in these parts, unless they are on their way to the Everglades or the Keys. However, Southern Miami–Dade County contains many of the city's top attractions (see chapter 5), meaning that you're likely to spend at least some of your time in Miami here.

2 Getting Around

Officially, Dade County has opted for a "unified, multimodal transportation network," which basically means you can get around the city by train, bus, and taxi. However, in practice, the network doesn't work very well. Things may improve when the city hopefully completes its transportation center in 2005, but until then, unless you are going from downtown Miami to a not-too-distant spot, you are better off in a rental car or taxi.

With the exception of downtown Coconut Grove and South Beach, Miami is not a walker's city. Because it is so spread out, most attractions are too far apart to make walking between them feasible. In fact, most Miamians are so used to driving that they do so even when going just a few blocks.

BY PUBLIC TRANSPORTATION

BY RAIL   Two rail lines, operated by the **Metro-Dade Transit Agency** (© 305/ 770-3131 for information; www.co.miami-dade.fl.us/mdta), run in concert with each other.

Metrorail, the city's modern high-speed commuter train, is a 21-mile elevated line that travels north-south, between downtown Miami and the southern suburbs. Locals like to refer to this semiuseless rail system as Metro*fail.* If you are staying in Coral Gables or Coconut Grove, you can park your car at a nearby station and ride the rails downtown. However, that's about it. There are plans to extend the system to service Miami International Airport, but until those tracks are built, these trains don't go most places tourists go, with the exception of Vizcaya (p. 125) in Coconut Grove. Metrorail operates daily from about 6am to midnight. The fare is $1.25.

Metromover, a 4½-mile elevated line, circles the downtown area and connects with Metrorail at the Government Center stop. This is a good way to get to Bayside (a waterfront marketplace) if you don't have a car. Riding on rubber tires, the single-car train winds past many of the area's most important attractions and its shopping and business districts. You may not go very far on the Metromover, but you will get a beautiful perspective from the towering height of the suspended rails. System hours are daily from about 6am to midnight, and the ride is free.

BY BUS   Miami's suburban layout is not conducive to getting around by bus. Lines operate and maps are available, but instead of getting to know the city, you'll find that relying on bus transportation will acquaint you only with how it feels to wait at bus stops. In short, a bus ride in Miami is grueling. You can get a bus map by mail, either from the Greater Miami Convention and Visitor's Bureau (see "Visitor Information," earlier in this chapter) or by writing the Metro-Dade Transit System, 3300 NW 32nd Ave., Miami, FL 33142. In Miami, call © 305/770-3131 for public-transit information. The fare is $1.25.

BY CAR

Tales circulate about vacationers who have visited Miami without a car, but they are very few indeed. If you are counting on exploring the city, even to a modest degree, a car is essential. Miami's restaurants, hotels, and attractions are far from one another, so any other form of transportation is relatively impractical. You won't need a car, however, if you are spending your entire vacation at a resort, are traveling directly to the Port of Miami for a cruise, or are here for a short stay centered in one area of the city, such as South Beach, where everything is within walking distance and parking is a costly nightmare.

When driving across a causeway or through downtown, allow extra time to reach your destination because of frequent drawbridge openings. Some bridges open about every half-hour for large sailing vessels to make their way through the wide bays and canals that crisscross the city, stalling traffic for several minutes.

RENTALS   It seems as though every car-rental company, big and small, has at least one office in Miami. Consequently, the city is one of the cheapest places in the world to rent a car. Many firms regularly advertise prices in the neighborhood of $140 per week for their economy cars. You should also check with the airline you have chosen to get to Miami: There are often special discounts when you book a flight and reserve your rental car simultaneously. A minimum age, generally 25, is usually required of renters, while some rental agencies have also set maximum ages!

National car-rental companies, with toll-free numbers, include **Alamo** (✆ 800/327-9633; www.goalamo.com), **Avis** (✆ 800/331-1212; www.avis.com), **Budget** (✆ 800/527-0700; www.budget.com), **Dollar** (✆ 800/800-4000 or 800/327-7607; www.dollar.com), **Hertz** (✆ 800/654-3131; www.hertz.com), **National** (✆ 800/328-4567; www.nationalcar.com), and **Thrifty** (✆ 800/367-2277; www.thrifty.com). One excellent company that has offices in every conceivable part of town and offers extremely competitive rates is **Enterprise** (✆ 800/325-8007; www.enterprise.com). Call around and comparison-shop before you make any decisions—car-rental prices can fluctuate more than airfares. For information on car-rental insurance, see "Getting There," in chapter 2, beginning on p. 29.

Many car-rental companies also offer cellular phones or electronic map rentals. It might be wise to opt for these additional safety features (the phone will definitely come in handy if you get lost), although the cost can be exorbitant.

Finally, think about splurging on a convertible (at most companies, the price for convertibles is approximately 20% more). Not only are convertibles one of the best ways to see the beautiful surroundings, but they're also an ideal way to perfect a tan!

PARKING   Always keep plenty of quarters on hand to feed hungry meters. Or, on Miami Beach, stop by the chamber of commerce at 1920 Meridian Ave. or any Publix grocery store to buy a magnetic **parking card** in denominations of $10, $20, or $25. Parking is usually plentiful (except on South Beach and Coconut Grove), but when it's not, be careful: Fines for illegal parking can be stiff, starting at $18 for an expired meter and going way up from there.

In addition to parking garages, valet services are commonplace and often used. Because parking is such a premium in bustling South Beach as well as in Coconut Grove, prices tend to be jacked up—especially at night and when there are special events (day or night). You can expect to pay an average of $5 to $15 for parking in these areas.

BY TAXI

If you're not planning on traveling much within the city (and especially if you plan on spending your vacation within the confines of South Beach's Art Deco District), an occasional taxi is a good alternative to renting a car and the parking hassles that come with renting your own car. Taxi meters start at $1.70 for the first quarter-mile and cost $2.20 for each additional mile. There are standard flat-rate charges for frequently traveled routes—for example, Miami Beach's Convention Center to Coconut Grove will cost about $16.

Major cab companies include **Yellow Cab** (☎ **305/444-4444**) and, on Miami Beach, **Central** (☎ **305/532-5555**).

BY BIKE

Miami is a biker's paradise, especially on Miami Beach, where the hard-packed sand and boardwalks make it an easy and scenic route. However, unless you are a former New York City bike messenger, you won't want to use a bicycle as your main means of transportation.

For more information on bicycles, including where to rent the best ones, see chapter 5, "What to See & Do in Miami."

FAST FACTS: Miami

American Express You'll find American Express offices in downtown Miami at 100 N. Biscayne Blvd. (☎ **305/358-7350**; open Mon–Fri 9am–5pm); 9700 Collins Ave., Bal Harbour (☎ **305/865-5959**; open Mon–Sat 10am–6pm); and 32 Miracle Mile, Coral Gables (☎ **305/446-3381**; open Mon–Fri 9am–5pm and Sat 10am–4pm). To report lost or stolen traveler's checks, call ☎ **800/221-7282**.

Area Code The original area code for Miami and all of Dade County was 305. That is still the code for older phone numbers, but all phone numbers assigned since July 1998 have the area code 786 (SUN). For all local calls, even if you're just calling across the street, you must dial the area code (305 or 786) first. Even though the Keys still share the Dade County area code of 305, calls to there from Miami are considered long distance and must be preceded by 1-305. (Within the Keys, simply dial the seven-digit number.) The area code for Fort Lauderdale is 954; for Palm Beach, Boca Raton, Vero Beach, and Port St. Lucie, it's 561.

Business Hours Banking hours vary, but most banks are open weekdays from 9am to 3pm. Several stay open until 5pm or so at least 1 day during the week, and most banks feature automated teller machines (ATMs) for 24-hour banking. Most stores are open daily from 10am to 6pm; however, there are many exceptions (noted in "Shopping," in chapter 5, beginning on p. 142). As far as business offices are concerned, Miami is generally a 9-to-5 town.

Dentists **A&E Dental Associates**, 11400 N. Kendall Dr., Mega Bank Building (☎ **305/271-7777**), offers round-the-clock care and accepts MasterCard and Visa.

Doctors In an emergency, call an ambulance by dialing ☎ 911 (a free call) from any phone. The Dade County Medical Association sponsors a **Physician Referral Service** (☎ **305/324-8717**), weekdays from 9am to 5pm. **Health South Doctors' Hospital**, 5000 University Dr., Coral Gables (☎ **305/666-2111**), is a 285-bed acute-care hospital with a 24-hour physician-staffed emergency department.

Drugstores See "Pharmacies," below.

Emergencies To reach the police, ambulance, or fire department, dial ☎ 911 from any phone. No coins are needed. Emergency hot lines include **Crisis Intervention** (☎ **305/358-HELP** or 305/358-4357) and the **Poison Information Center** (☎ **800/222-1222**).

Eyeglasses **Pearle Vision Center,** 7901 Biscayne Blvd. (© **305/754-5144**), can usually fill prescriptions in about an hour.

Hospitals See "Doctors," above.

Internet Access Internet access is available at **Kafka's Cyber Cafe,** 1464 Washington Ave., South Beach (© **305/673-9669**), the **South Beach Internet Cafe,** 1106 Collins Ave. (© **305/532-4331**), and, no joke, the swanky all-in-one **Mobil Station,** at 2500 NW 87th Ave., Doral (© **305/477-2501**).

Laundry/Dry Cleaning For dry cleaning, self-service machines, and a wash-and-fold service by the pound, call **All Laundry Service,** 5701 NW 7th St. (© **305/261-8175**); it's open daily from 7am to 10pm. **Clean Machine Laundry,** 226 12th St., South Beach (© **305/534-9429**), is convenient to South Beach's Art Deco hotels and is open 24 hours a day. **Coral Gables Laundry & Dry Cleaning,** 250 Minorca Ave., Coral Gables (© **305/446-6458**), has been dry cleaning, altering, and laundering since 1930. It offers a lifesaving same-day service and is open weekdays from 7am to 7pm and Saturday from 8am to 3pm.

Liquor Laws Only adults 21 or older may legally purchase or consume alcohol in the state of Florida. Minors are usually permitted in bars, as long as the bars also serve food. Liquor laws are strictly enforced; if you look young, carry identification. Beer and wine are sold in most supermarkets and convenience stores. The city of Miami's liquor stores are closed on Sundays. Liquor stores in the city of Miami Beach are open daily.

Newspapers/Magazines The **Miami Herald** is the city's only English-language daily. It is especially known for its extensive Latin American coverage and has a decent Friday "Weekend" entertainment guide. The most respected alternative weekly is the giveaway tabloid called **New Times,** which contains up-to-date listings and reviews of food, films, theater, music, and whatever else is happening in town. Also free, if you can find it, is **Ocean Drive,** an oversize glossy magazine that's limited on text (no literary value) and heavy on ads and society photos. It's what you should read if you want to know who's who and where to go for fun; it's available at a number of chic South Beach boutiques and restaurants. It is also available on newsstands. For a meatier look at South Beach society, look for **Lincoln Road Magazine,** a freebie with some substance.

For a large selection of foreign-language newspapers and magazines, check with any of the large bookstores or try **News Cafe** at 800 Ocean Dr., South Beach (© **305/538-6397**). Adjacent to the **Van Dyke Cafe,** 846 Lincoln Rd., South Beach (© **305/534-3600**), is a fantastic newsstand with magazines and newspapers from all over the world. Also check out **Eddie's News,** 1096 Normandy Dr., Miami Beach (© **305/866-2661**), and **Worldwide News,** 1629 NE 163rd St., North Miami Beach (© **305/940-4090**).

Pharmacies **Walgreens Pharmacy** has dozens of locations all over town, including 8550 Coral Way (© **305/221-9271**), in Coral Gables; 1845 Alton Rd. (© **305/531-8868**), in South Beach; and 6700 Collins Ave. (© **305/861-6742**), in Miami Beach. The branch at 5731 Bird Rd. at SW 40th Street (© **305/666-0757**) is open 24 hours, as is **Eckerd Drugs,** 6460 S. Dixie Hwy., in South Miami (© **305/661-0778**).

Police For emergencies, dial ☏ **911** from any phone. No coins are needed for this call. For other police matters, call ☏ **305/595-6263.**

Post Office The **Main Post Office,** 2200 Milam Dairy Rd., Miami, FL 33152 (☏ **800/275-8777**), is located west of the Miami International Airport. Conveniently located post offices include 1300 Washington Ave. in South Beach and 3191 Grand Ave. in Coconut Grove. There is one central number for all post offices: ☏ **800/275-8777.**

Radio On the AM dial, 610 (WIOD), 790 (WNWS), 1230 (WJNO), and 1340 (WPBR) are all talk. There is no all-news station in town, although 940 (WINZ) gives traffic updates and headline news in between its talk shows. WDBF (1420) is a good big-band station and WPBG (1290) features golden oldies. Switching to the FM dial, the two most popular R&B stations are WEDR/99 Jams (99.1) and Hot 105 (105.1). The best rock stations on the FM dial are WZTA (94.9), WBGG/Big 106 (105.9), and the progressive college station WVUM (90.5). WKIS (99.9) is the top country station. Top-40 music can be heard on WHYI (100.3) and hip-hop on Mega 103 (103.5). For club music, Party 93.1 (WPYM) is the station, and for more hip-hop and dance music, and Power 96 (96.5) WPOW will help to get your groove on. WGTR (97.3) plays easy listening, WDNA (88.9) has the best Latin jazz and multiethnic sounds, and public radio can be heard either on WXEL (90.7) or WLRN (91.3).

Religious Services Miami houses of worship are as varied as the city's population and include St. Patrick Catholic Church, 3716 Garden Ave., Miami Beach (☏ **305/531-1124**); Coral Gables Baptist Church, 5501 Granada Blvd. (☏ **305/665-4072**); Temple Judea, 5500 Granada Blvd., Coral Gables (☏ **305/ 667-5657**); Coconut Grove United Methodist, 2850 SW 27th Ave. (☏ **305/ 443-0880**); Christ Episcopal Church, 3481 Hibiscus St., Coconut Grove (☏ **305/442-8542**); Plymouth Congregational Church, 3400 Devon Rd., at Main Highway, Coconut Grove (☏ **305/444-6521**); Masjid Al-Ansar (Muslim), 5245 NW 7th Ave., Miami (☏ **305/757-8741**); and Buddhist Temple of Miami, 15200 SW 240th St., Homestead (☏ **305/245-2702**).

Safety As always, use your common sense and be aware of your surroundings at all times. Don't walk alone at night, and be extra wary when walking or driving though downtown Miami and surrounding areas.

Reacting to several highly publicized crimes against tourists several years ago, both local and state governments have taken steps to help protect visitors. These measures include special highly visible police units patrolling the airport and surrounding neighborhoods and better signs on the state's most tourist-traveled routes.

Taxes A 6% state sales tax (plus 0.5% local tax, for a total of 6.5% in Miami–Dade County [from Homestead to North Miami Beach]) is added on at the register for all goods and services purchased in Florida. In addition, most municipalities levy special taxes on restaurants and hotels. In Surfside, hotel taxes total 10.5%; in Bal Harbour, 9.5%; in Miami Beach (including South Beach), 11.5%; and in the rest of Dade County, a whopping 12.5%. In Miami Beach, Surfside, and Bal Harbour, the resort (hotel) tax also applies to hotel restaurants and restaurants with liquor licenses.

Television The local stations are channel 4, WFOR (CBS); channel 6, WTVJ (NBC); channel 7, WSVN (FOX); channel 10, WPLG (ABC); channel 17, WLRN (PBS); channel 23,.WLTV (independent); and channel 33, WBFS (independent). Channel 39 is the WB (WBZL) and channel 33 is UPN (WBFS).

Time Zone Miami, like New York, is in the Eastern Standard Time zone. Between April and October, daylight savings time is adopted, and clocks are set 1 hour ahead. America's eastern seaboard is 5 hours behind Greenwich Mean Time. To find out what time it is, call ⓒ **305/324-8811**.

Weather Hurricane season in Miami runs August through November. For an up-to-date recording of current weather conditions and forecast reports, call ⓒ **305/229-4522**. Also see the "When to Go" section in chapter 2 for more information on the weather.

3 Where to Stay in Miami

As much a part of the landscape as the palm trees, many of Miami's hotels are on display as if they were contestants in a beauty pageant. The city's long-lasting status on the destination A-list has given rise to an ever-increasing number of upscale hotels, and no place in Miami has seen a greater increase in construction than Miami Beach. Since the area's renaissance, which began in the late 1980s, the beach has turned what used to be a beachfront retirement home into a sand-swept hot spot for the Gucci and Prada set. Contrary to popular belief, however, the beach does not discriminate, and it's the juxtaposition of the chic elite and the hoi polloi that contributes to its allure.

While the increasing demand for rooms on South Beach means increasing costs, you can still find a decent room at a fair price. In fact, most hotels in the Art Deco District are less Ritz-Carlton than they are Holiday Inn, unless, of course, they've been renovated (many hotels in this area were built in the 1930s for the middle class). Unless you plan to center your vacation entirely in and around your hotel, most of the cheaper Deco hotels are adequate and a wise choice for those who plan to use the room only to sleep. Smart vacationers can almost name their price if they're willing to live without a few luxuries, such as an oceanfront view.

Many of the old hotels from the 1930s, 1940s, and 1950s have been totally renovated, giving way to dozens of "boutique" (small, swanky, and independently owned) hotels. Keep in mind that when a hotel claims that it was just renovated, it can mean that they've completely gutted the building—or just applied a coat of fresh paint. Always ask what specific changes were made during a renovation, and be sure to ask if a hotel will be undergoing construction while you're there. You should also find out how near your room will be to the center of the nightlife crowd; trying to sleep directly on Ocean Drive or Collins and Washington avenues, especially during the weekend, is next to impossible, unless your lullaby of choice happens to include throbbing salsa and bass beats.

The best hotel options in each price category and those that have been fully upgraded recently are listed below. You should also know that along South Beach's Collins Avenue, there are dozens of hotels and motels—in all price categories—so there's bound to be a vacancy somewhere. If you do try the walk-in routine, don't forget to ask to see a room first. A few dollars extra could mean all the difference between flea and fabu.

While South Beach may be the nucleus of all things hyped and hip, it's not the only place with cool and swanky hotels. The advantage to staying on South Beach as opposed to, say, Coral Gables or Coconut Grove, is that the beaches are within walking distance, the nightlife and restaurant options are aplenty, and, basically, everything you would need is right there. However, staying there is definitely not for everyone. If you're wary, don't worry: South Beach is centrally located and only about a 15- to 30-minute drive from most other parts of Miami.

For a less expensive stay that's only a 10-minute cab ride from South Beach, Miami Beach proper (the area north of 23rd St. and Collins Ave. all the way up to 163rd St. and Collins Ave.) offers a slew of reasonable stays, right on the beach, that won't cost you your kids' college education fund.

For a less frenetic, more relaxed, and more tropical experience, the resorts on Key Biscayne exude an island feel, even though, if you look across the water, a cosmopolitan vibe beckons, thanks to the shimmering, spectacular Miami skyline.

Those who'd rather bag the beach in favor of shopping bags will enjoy North Miami Beach's proximity to the Aventura Mall as much as tan-o-holics are drawn to the sand on South Beach. And for Miami with an old-world European flair, Coral Gables and its charming hotels and exquisite restaurants provide a more prim and proper, well-heeled perspective of Miami than the trendy boutique hotels on South Beach.

SEASONS & RATES   South Florida's tourist season is well defined, beginning in mid-November and lasting until Easter. Hotel prices escalate until about March, after which they begin to decline. During the off season, hotel rates are typically 30% to 50% lower than their winter highs.

But timing isn't everything. In many cases, rates also depend on your hotel's proximity to the beach and how much ocean you can see from your window. Small motels a block or two from the water can be up to 40% cheaper than similar properties right on the sand.

Rates below have been broken down into two broad categories: winter (generally, Thanksgiving–Easter) and off-season (about mid-May to Aug). The months in between, the shoulder season, should fall somewhere in between the highs and lows, while rates always go up on holidays. Remember, too, that state and city taxes can add as much as 12.5% to your bill in some parts of Miami, and don't forget that parking is a pricey endeavor. Some hotels, especially those in South Beach, also tack on additional service charges.

PRICE CATEGORIES   The hotels below are divided first by area, then by price, using the following guidelines: **very expensive,** over $250; **expensive,** $180 to $250; **moderate,** $90 to $180; and **inexpensive,** below $90. Prices are based on published rates (or rack rates) for a standard double room during the high season. You should also check with the reservations agent, since many rooms are available above and below the category ranges listed below. Also ask about packages, since it's often possible to get a better deal than these "official" rates. Most important, always call the hotel to confirm rates, which may be subject to change without notice because of special events, holidays, or blackout dates.

LONG-TERM STAYS   If you plan to visit Miami for a month, a season, or more, think about renting a condominium apartment or a room in a long-term hotel. Long-term accommodations exist in every price category, from budget to deluxe, and in general are extremely reasonable, especially during the off season. Check with the reservation services below, or write a short note to the chamber of commerce in the area where you plan to stay. In addition, many local real estate agents also handle short-term rentals (meaning less than a year).

RESERVATION SERVICES   **Central Reservation Service** (© **800/950-0232** or 305/274-6832; www.reservation-services.com) works with many of Miami's hotels and can often secure discounts of up to 40%. It also gives advice on specific locales, especially in Miami Beach and downtown. During holiday time, there may be a minimum of a 3- to 5-day stay to use their services. Call for more information.

For bed-and-breakfast information throughout the state, contact **Florida Bed and Breakfast Inns** (© **800/524-1880**; www.florida-inns.com).

SOUTH BEACH

Choosing a hotel on South Beach is similar to deciding whether you'd rather pay $1.50 for french fries at Denny's or $8.50 for the same fries—but let's call them *pomme frites*—in a pricey haute cuisinerie. Fortunately, for every chichi hotel in South Beach—and there are many—there are just as many moderately priced, more casual options.

Prices mentioned here are rack rates—that is, the price you would be quoted if you walked up to the front desk and inquired about rates. The actual price you will end up paying is usually less than this. Many hotels on South Beach have stopped quoting seasonal and off-season rates and have, instead, chosen to go with a low-to-high rate representing the hotel's complete pricing range.

If status is important to you, as it is to many South Beach visitors, then you will be quite pleased with the number of haute hotels in the area, which are as popular as nightclubs and restaurants are on South Beach. But the times may be achangin': Not so long ago, Courtyard by Marriott (© **800/321-2211** or 305/604-8887) debuted a 90-room, moderately priced hotel on a seedy stretch of Washington Avenue, smack in the middle of clubland, a horror to many a South Beach trendoid.

Note: Art Deco hotels, while pleasing to the eye, may be a bit run-down inside. Par for the course on South Beach, where appearances are, at times, deceiving.

For a map of the hotels in this section, see the "South Beach" map on p. 64.

VERY EXPENSIVE

The Delano ⚡ *(Overrated)*   Before Ian Schrager revamped (emphasis on the vamp) the neighboring The Shore Club hotel, the Delano was the reigning force in the hierarchy of hip hotel royalty. But that was then. Today, the Delano, a place where smiles from staffers were as rare as snow in Miami, is kinder and gentler, which, for some, takes away the whole cache of staying here. But it certainly still is amusing to look at—with 40-foot sheer white billowing curtains hanging outside, mirrors everywhere, Adirondack chairs, and faux-fur–covered beds. The rooms are done up sanitarium style: sterile, yet terribly trendy, in pure white save for a perfectly crisp green Granny Smith apple in each room—the only freebie you're going to get here. A bathroom renovation recently took place in all of the rooms—but they remain small and spartan.

An attractive, white-clad staff looks as if they were hand picked from last month's *Vogue*. While they may sigh if you ask for something, eventually they'll get it for you. The gym here is great, but it costs $15 a day, even if you are a guest. The fantastic wading pool, thankfully, is free, but get out early to snag a chair. The Blue Door restaurant, formerly part-owned by Madonna, serves lots of attitude with its pricey haute cuisine, and for a quick bite of pricey sashimi,

South Beach

To Central Miami Beach ↑

The Bass Museum of Art

COLLINS PARK

22nd St.

20th St.

Park Ave.

19th St.

Miami Beach Convention Center

18th St.

Dade Boulevard

Jackie Gleason Theater of Performing Arts

17th St.

James Ave.

Lincoln Road Mall

Lincoln Rd.

Collins Ave.

16th St.

15th St.

Española Way

14th St.

Miami Beach Post Office ✉

13th St.

12th St.

Drexel Ave.

Pennsylvania Ave.

Beach Patrol Station

Alton Rd.

Lenox Ave.

Michigan Ave.

Jefferson Ave.

Meridian Ave.

FLAMINGO PARK

11th St.

10th St.

9th St.

8th St.

7th St.

Euclid Ave.

Washington Ave.

Ocean Dr.

Art Deco Welcome Center

6th St.

5th St.

4th St.

3rd St.

2nd St.

1st St.

Commerce St.

Collins Ave.

LUMMUS PARK

ATLANTIC OCEAN

Biscayne St.

FLORIDA

Miami Beach

Miami

SOUTH POINTE PARK

0   1/4 mi

0   1/4 km

N

WHERE TO STAY 🏨
Abbey Hotel **4**
The Clinton Hotel **44**
The Creek **2**
Crest Hotel Suites **21**
The Delano **22**
The Hotel **47**
Hotel Astor **39**
Hotel Impala **35**
Hotel Leon **47**
Pelican Hotel **47**
Raleigh Hotel **14**
The Ritz-Carlton South Beach **25**
The Sagamore **22**
The Shore Club **9**
The Tides **36**
Townhouse **11**
Whitelaw Hotel **47**

WHERE TO DINE ◆
Balan's **16**
Barton G. The Restaurant **26**
BED **43**
Big Pink **55**
Bond St. Lounge **10**
Café Cardozo **33**
China Grill **53**
11th Street Diner **38**
El Rancho Grande **24**
Escopazzo **32**
Front Porch Café **31**
Grillfish **28**
Joe Allen **12**
Joe's Stone Crab Restaurant **57**
La Sandwicherie **29**
L'Entrecote de Paris **52**
Lincoln Road Café **17**
Macaluso's **15**
Mama Vieja **1**
Mark's South Beach **37**
Nemo **56**
News Café **48**
Nobu **9**
Pacific Time **18**
Pao **44**
Pizza Rustica **27, 45**
Puerto Sagua **50**
Shoji Sushi **56**
Spiga **35**
Sport Café **49**
Talula **1**
Tuscan Steak **51**
Twelve Twenty **36**
Van Dyke Cafe **19**
Wish **29**

ATTRACTIONS ⬤
Art Deco Welcome Center **42**
Bass Museum of Art **3**
Collins Park **6**
Colony Theater **16**
Fritz's Skate Shop **20**
Holocaust Memorial **7**
Miami Beach Bicycle Center **51**
Miami Beach Botanical Garden **8**
Miami Beach public courts at Flamingo Park **34**
Miami Beach Regional Library **5**
Sanford L. Ziff Jewish Museum of Florida **54**
Wolfsonian-Florida International University **40**

grab a seat at the communal eat-in-kitchen table at **Blue Sea**, the hotel's superb sushi bar. The lobby's **Rose Bar** is command central for the chic elite who don't flinch at paying in excess of $10 for a martini. Salvation from the hotel's mod version of *Age of Innocence*-esque social mores (or lack thereof) is Agua, the rooftop spa, where, if you can afford it, an hour massage while overlooking the ocean is blissful.

1685 Collins Ave., South Beach, FL 33139. (© 800/555-5001 or 305/672-2000. Fax 305/532-0099. www. ianschragerhotels.com. 195 units, 1 penthouse. Winter $425–$675 standard; $1,050–$2,100 suite; $2,000–$3,000 bungalow or 2-bedroom; $2,900–$3,800 penthouse. Off-season $345–$525 standard; $950–$2,000 suite; $1,500–$3,000 bungalow or 2-bedroom; $2,400–$3,000 penthouse. Additional person $25. AE, DC, DISC, MC, V. Valet parking $25. **Amenities:** 3 restaurants (featuring the acclaimed Blue Door); bar; large outdoor pool; state-of-the-art David Barton gym; extensive watersports equipment; children's programs; concierge; business center; room service; in-room massage; same-day dry cleaning and laundry service. *In room:* A/C, TV/VCR, minibar, hair dryer, safe, CD player.

The Ritz-Carlton South Beach ★★★ *Kids* The luxe life comes to a congested and somewhat seedy corner of South Beach in the form of this beachfront, lushly landscaped Ritz-Carlton. Debuting in the fall of 2003, this Ritz has restored the landmark Morris Lapidus–designed 1950s DiLido Hotel to its original Art Moderne style and filled it with the hotel's signature five-star service. An impressive $2 million art collection consisting of original works by Joan Miro, among others, will be on permanent loan to the hotel from Diana Lowenstein Fine Art, which also happens to have a gallery in the hotel. Though South Beach is better known for its trendy boutique hotels, the Ritz-Carlton offers comfort to those who might prefer 100% cotton Frette sheets and goose-down pillows to high-style minimalism. The best rooms, by far, are the 72 poolside and ocean view lanai rooms. Why choose club level rooms and hibernate inside, indulging in five food and drink courses all day, when you could be outside enjoying the stunning views? Oh yeah, and there's also a tanning butler who will spritz you with SPF and water whenever you want.

With impeccable service, an elevated pool that provides unobstructed views of the Atlantic, an impressive stretch of sand with a fabulous beach club run by Michael Capponi (Miami Beach's most popular promoter), an oceanfront Ritz Kids pavilion, and a world-class 13,000-square-foot spa and wellness center, the Ritz-Carlton kicks sand in the faces of some of the smaller hotels that think they're doing *you* a favor by allowing you to sleep there.

1 Lincoln Rd., South Beach, FL 33139. (© 800/241-3333 or 786/276-4000. Fax 786/276-4001. www. ritzcarlton.com. 375 units. Winter $450–$720 double–suite; off-season $245–$545 double–suite. AE, DISC, MC, V. Valet parking $30. **Amenities:** 3 restaurants; 3 bars; outdoor heated pool; health club; spa; extensive watersports rentals; children's program; 24-hr. business center; salon; 24-hr. room service; babysitting; overnight laundry service; beach service. *In room:* A/C, TV, dataport, minibar, hair dryer, iron, safe.

The Sagamore ★★★ Located just two doors down from the hauter-than-thou Delano Hotel is The Sagamore, quietly fabulous in its own right, with an ultramodern lobby cum art gallery that's infinitely warmer than your typical pop art exhibit at the Museum of Modern Art. And although the lobby and its requisite bar and lounge areas have become command central for the international chic elite and celebrities such as Will Smith, The Sagamore's all-suite, apartment-like rooms are havens from the hype with all the cushy comforts of home and then some. It's hard not to think you're in a museum when walking through the lobby, but once you hit those rooms or the sprawling outdoor lawn leading up to the pool and beachfront, you'll realize that this is yet another of South Beach's ways of making you realize that you're not in Kansas anymore. At press time, there wasn't a restaurant in the hotel, but plans for one helmed by a star chef are underway.

1671 Collins Ave., South Beach, FL 33139. ⓒ 87/SAGAMORE or 305/535-8088. Fax 305/535-8185. www.sagamorehotel.com. 93 units. Winter $435–$1,072 suite; off-season $215–$1,050 suite. AE, DC, DISC, MC, V. Valet parking $20. **Amenities:** Bar; pool bar; pool; spa and fitness center; concierge; room service. *In room:* A/C, TV, VCR, DVD/CD player, dataport, full kitchen, minibar, coffeemaker, hair dryer, iron, safe.

The Shore Club ⓐ   What used to be a concrete canyon, a mod-version of the eerily deserted house in *The Shining,* is now *the* hottest and hautest stay in South Beach thanks to one thing in particular: hip hotelier Ian Schrager rescued it from its first, floundering owner. That, not to mention Florida's first ever Nobu sushi restaurant and cocktail lounge (a major hit in New York, Las Vegas, Paris, and London), and a celebrity clientele that would fill up an entire issue of *Us Weekly* have made The Shore Club a sure thing. Because this hotel is infinitely more cavernous than its (not as) hipster neighbor, The Delano (see above), publicity-shy celebs such as Janet Jackson and Denzel Washington have been known to call this place their home away from home. Then again, publicity hog Leonardo DiCaprio also had no qualms slumber partying with his posse here. Neither did Britney Spears, Beyonce Knowles, Jay-Z, and, well, you get the picture. Stellar crowd aside, the hotel's interior still leaves a lot to be desired, especially amongst those who marvel in Shrager Hotels' signature-Starck-designed lobbies—the lobby here is sorely lacking in personality. But that's all forgotten once you reach the centerpiece and focal point of the place—the resplendent oasis of chic out back. A Miami outpost of L.A.'s celeb-laden SkyBar reigns supreme with a Marrakech-meets-Miami motif that stretches throughout the hotel's sprawling pool, patio, and garden areas. Beware of surly doormen if you're not a hotel guest. In March 2003, L.A.'s hottest Italian eatery, Ago (and its *extremely* pricey pasta), opened here with much fanfare and an appearance by co-owner Robert DeNiro, who hasn't been back since.

The Shore Club also boasts that 80% of its 325 rooms have an ocean view. Contrary to the cold, cavernous lobby, exquisite gardens draw guests toward the beach through courtyards and reflecting pools. Rooms are loaded with state-of-the-art amenities, not to mention 400-thread-count linen bedding, Mexican sandstone flooring in the bathroom with custom-designed glass, and an enclosed "wet area" with bathtub, shower, and teak bench. (Molton Brown bathroom amenities are worth bringing an extra bag for.) If you can't afford the penthouse or a poolside cabana, consider an Ocean View room, which is stellar in its own right, with its massive, two-nozzled shower-tub combo that's almost better than a day at the beach. If you are wondering whether to choose the still somewhat hip mainstay, the Delano, over this hotel, consider that The Shore Club is much larger, newer, hungrier for the hipsters, and its rooms boast a bit more personality than the Delano's.

1901 Collins Ave., Miami Beach, FL 33139. ⓒ 877/640-9500 or 305/695-3100. Fax 305/695-3299. www. shoreclub.com. 325 units, 8 cabanas. Winter $525–$775 double, $1,125 suite, $2,500 cabana; off-season $425–$675 double, $1,025 suite, $1,500 cabana. AE, DC, MC, V. Valet parking $20. **Amenities:** 3 restaurants; 4 bars; outdoor reflecting pools with poolside dataports; health club with steam room and outdoor equipment; spa; concierge; 24-hr. room service. *In room:* A/C, TV, fax, minibar, Intrigue System w/digitally downloaded movies and high-speed Internet access, CD player, stereo.

The Tides ⓐⓐⓐ   This 12-story Art Deco masterpiece (recently accepted into the exclusive Leading Small Hotels of the World club) is reminiscent of a gleaming ocean liner, with porthole windows and lots of stainless steel and frosted glass. Rooms are starkly white but much more luxurious and comfortable than those at the Delano (see above). Also, all rooms are at least twice the size of a typical South Beach hotel room and have a view of the ocean. They feature king beds, spacious closets, large bathrooms, and even a telescope from which to view the vast ocean. The penthouses on the 9th and 10th floors are situated at the highest point on Ocean Drive, allowing for a priceless panoramic view of the ocean, the skyline, and the beach. Even if you can't afford it, you must ask for a tour of the Goldeneye Suite, a room suited for James Bond and his Bond girls, with hot tub in the middle, private deck, and high-tech toys. Although small, the freshwater pool is a welcome plus for those who aren't in the mood to feel the sand between their toes; but it really doesn't fit with the rest of the hotel, lacking in ambience and view (it overlooks an alley). The hotel's restaurant, Twelve Twenty, is an elegant, excellent, and pricey eatery with seating in the lobby. The Terrace is a less expensive outdoor cafe. The Tides is a place where celebrities like Ben Affleck, Jennifer Lopez, and Bono come to stay for some R&R, but you won't find gawkers or paparazzi lurking in the lobby, just an elegant clientele and staff who are respectful of people's privacy and desire for peace and quiet.

1220 Ocean Dr., South Beach, FL 33139. © **866/43-TIDES** or 305/604-5070. Fax 305/604-5180. www. thetideshotel.com. 45 units. Winter $550 suite, $3,000 penthouse; off-season $420 suite, $3,000 penthouse. Additional person $25. Pets $100 one time fee. AE, DC, DISC, MC, V. Valet parking $18. **Amenities:** 2 restaurants; lounge; bar; outdoor heated pool; daily passes to large nearby gym or yoga studio; concierge; 24-hr. room service; in-room massage; laundry and dry cleaning service; beach lounge service. *In room:* A/C, TV/VCR, dataport, minibar, hair dryer, iron, safe, stereo/CD player with selection of music, video rentals.

EXPENSIVE

The Hotel 🏵🏵🏵   Kitschy fashion designer Todd Oldham whimsically restored this 1939 gem (formerly the Tiffany Hotel) as he would have a vintage piece of couture. He laced it with lush, cool colors, hand-cut mirrors, and glass mosaics from his ready-to-wear factory, then added artisan detailing, terrazzo floors, and porthole windows. The small, soundproof rooms are very comfortable and incredibly stylish, though the bathrooms are a bit cramped. There's no need to pay more for an oceanfront view—go up to the rooftop, where the pool is located, and you'll see an amazing view of the Atlantic. The hotel's restaurant, Wish (p. 92), is one of South Beach's best.

801 Collins Ave., South Beach, FL 33139. © **877/843-4683** or 305/531-2222. Fax 305/531-3222. www. thehotelofsouthbeach.com. 53 units. Winter $275–$405 double; off-season $215–$355 double. AE, DC, DISC, MC, V. Valet parking $18. **Amenities:** Restaurant; bar; pool bar; small pool; health club; concierge; business center; room service. *In room:* A/C, TV/VCR, dataport, minibar, coffeemaker, hair dryer, stereo system with CD and cassette players, Kiehl's products, video library.

Hotel Astor 🏵🏵🏵   Cozy-mod best describes this diminutive Deco hotel built in 1936. A 1995 renovation greatly improved on the original design of this simple three-story property, which has hosted the likes of Cameron Diaz and Madonna, and a 2002 renovation, that added a more urban, industrial feel to the place with dark woods, backlit glass, and very sleek contemporary furniture, continues to attract a lively local crowd to the small but sleek lobby bar and basement level hot spot, Metro Kitchen + Bar. Though the hotel hasn't been as sceney (a la the Delano; see above) as it once was, it has already begun to experience a hipster revival thanks to the fact that Metro, as it's more commonly known, is co-owned by Nicola Siervo, the owner of South Beach's celeb central Mynt. Another plus is that what used to be a minute pool has been converted into an outdoor dining garden.

The hotel's rooms are still small but very soothing, featuring plush and luxurious details—brand new Frette linens and towels, new carpeting, funky custom mood lighting with dimmer switches, and incredibly plush mattresses that are difficult to leave. I especially recommend the rooms overlooking the courtyard, for their views and for a bit more serenity than that which is afforded in rooms overlooking the street. Views are probably the worst thing about this hotel, as most rooms face the street or a neighboring seedy hotel. The hotel staff is known for its extreme attentiveness.

956 Washington Ave., South Beach, FL 33139. © **800/270-4981** or 305/531-8081. Fax 305/531-3193. www.hotelastor.com. 40 units. Winter $165–$500 double; off-season $145–$390 double. AE, DC, MC, V. Valet parking $20. **Amenities:** Restaurant; 2 bars; access to nearby health club; 24-hr. concierge service; secretarial services; room service; in-room massage; babysitting; laundry and dry cleaning service. *In room:* A/C, TV, dataport, minibar, fridge, hair dryer, safe.

Hotel Impala *Finds*   This renovated Mediterranean inn is one of the area's best, and it's just beautiful, from the Greco-Roman frescoes and friezes to an intimate garden that is perfumed with the scents from carefully hung lilies and gardenias. Rooms are really, really small despite their super-cushy sleigh beds, sisal floors, wrought-iron fixtures, imported Belgian cotton linens, wood furniture, and fabulous looking, but also incredibly small, bathrooms done up in stainless steel and coral rock. Adjacent to the hotel is Spiga (p. 96), an intimate, excellent Italian restaurant. Enclaves like this one are rare on South Beach.

1228 Collins Ave., South Beach, FL 33139. © **800/646-7252** or 305/673-2021. Fax 305/673-5984. www.hotelimpalamiamibeach.com. 17 units. Winter $185–$225 double, $300–$400 suite; off-season $145–$195 double, $250–$325 suite. AE, DC, MC, V. Valet parking $18. Small pets permitted. **Amenities:** Restaurant; concierge; room service. *In room:* A/C, TV/VCR, dataport, hair dryer, stereo, CD player, complimentary videos.

Raleigh Hotel 🌟🌟   Upon entering the lobby of this oceanfront Art Deco hotel, you will feel like you've stepped back into the 1940s. Polished wood, original terrazzo floors, and an intimate martini bar add to the fabulous atmosphere that's favored by fashion photographers and production crews, for whom the hotel's fleur-de-lis pool is the favorite subject. Rooms are tidy and efficient (those overlooking the resplendent pool and ocean are the most peaceful), nothing too elaborate, but that's not why people stay here. It's the Raleigh's romantic Deco lure that has people skipping over from the chilly, antiseptic Delano a few blocks up for much needed warmth. And now, the Raleigh is even hotter, since hip hotelier Andre Balazs (of Los Angeles's Chateau Marmont and Standard hotels fame), the high profile, new owner of the Raleigh, started implementing extensive renovations that will undoubtedly push the hotel back in the limelight as one of *the* places to be on South Beach yet again.

1775 Collins Ave., Miami Beach, FL 33139. © **800/848-1775** or 305/534-6300. Fax 305/538-8140. www. raleighhotel.com. 111 units. Winter $339–$769 double; off-season $209–$609 double. Rates are cheaper if booked on the hotel's website. AE, DC, DISC, MV, V. Valet parking $20. **Amenities:** Restaurant; bar; coffee bar; fantastic large outdoor pool; concierge; business services; room service (24-hr. in winter, limited off-season); massage; overnight laundry service. *In room:* A/C, TV/VCR, dataport, minibar, fridge, hair dryer, iron, safe, CD player.

MODERATE

Abbey Hotel 🌟🌟 *Finds*   This charming, off-the-beaten-path '40s-revival boutique hotel is possibly the best deal on the entire beach. A haven for artists looking for quiet inspiration, the Abbey has recently undergone a $2.5 million renovation that restored its original Deco glory. Rooms are furnished with over-sized earth-toned chairs and chrome beds that are surprisingly comfortable. Soft white-covered chairs and candles grace the lobby, which doubles as a chic Mediterranean-style restaurant (earning an "exceptional" from the *Miami Herald*), the Abbey Dining Room. It's extremely quiet at this hotel, as it is located in the midst of a sleepy residential neighborhood, but it's only 1 block from the beach and within walking distance of the Jackie Gleason Theater, the Convention Center, the Bass Museum of Art, and the Miami City Ballet.

300 21st St., Miami Beach, FL 33139. ℂ 888/61-ABBEY or 305/531-0031. Fax 305/672-1663. www.abbeyhotel. com. 50 units. Winter $155–$225 double, $225 studio; off-season $99–$130 double, $130 studio. AE, DC, DISC, MC, V. Off-site parking $17. Pets accepted for $25 for the 1st 3 days and $5 for each additional day. **Amenities:** Restaurant; bar; exercise room; concierge; business services; room service; laundry and dry cleaning service. *In room:* A/C, TV/VCR, dataport, hair dryer, iron; safe and stereo w/CD player in studios only.

The Clinton Hotel ⭐ The former president has nothing to do with this chic boutique hotel, but once he gets a gander of the model types who hang here, he may want to endorse it as his own. The Clinton Hotel is South Beach's newest renovated standout, a formerly decrepit building that has benefited from a $12 million renovation that brings a space-age meets South Beach vibe to the area thanks to funky furniture, a requisite hipster lobby bar, the pricey designer boutique Ona Saez, and a stylish yet vintage Cantonese restaurant, Pao. Although boutique hotels are becoming a dime a dozen as, say, Holiday Inns, this one manages to stand out from the rest thanks to its inner sanctum of serenity that includes a sleek pool, private sunning deck, and rooftop spa.

825 Washington Ave., South Beach, FL 33139. ℂ 305/538-1471. Fax 305/538-1472. www.clintonsouth beach.com. 88 units. Winter $149–$679 suite; off-season $135–$399 suite. AE, DC, DISC, MC, V. Valet parking $16. **Amenities:** Restaurant; coffee and sandwich bar; bar; pool bar; pool; spa and fitness center; concierge; room service. *In room:* A/C, TV, dataport, minibar, hair dryer, iron, safe.

Crest Hotel Suites ⭐ *Finds* One of South Beach's best-kept secrets, the Crest Hotel is located next to the pricier, trendier Albion Hotel (and around the corner from Lincoln Road, in the heart of the Art Deco District) and features a quietly fashionable, contemporary, relaxed atmosphere with fantastic service. Built in 1939, the Crest was restored to preserve its Art Deco architecture, but the interior of the hotel is thoroughly modern, with rooms resembling cosmopolitan apartments. All suites have a living room/dining room area, kitchenette, and executive work space. An indoor/outdoor cafe with terrace and poolside dining isn't besieged with trendy locals, but does attract a younger crowd.

1670 James Ave., Miami Beach, FL 33139. ℂ 800/531-3880 or 305/531-0321. Fax 305/531-8180. www.crestgrouphotels.com/CrestHotelSuites.htm. 64 units. Winter $155 double, $235 suite; off-season $115 double, $175 suite. Packages available and 10% discount offered if booked on website. AE, MC, V. **Amenities:** Restaurant; cafe; pool; laundry and dry cleaning service. *In room:* A/C, TV, dataport, kitchenette, fridge, coffeemaker (select units).

The Lily Leon Hotel ⭐ *Finds* A great hotel with little attitude, which recently merged with the neighboring Lily Guesthouse, the Lily Leon Hotel (formerly known as the Hotel Leon) is like a reasonably priced high-fashion garment found hidden on a rack full of overpriced threads. This charismatic sliver of a property has won the loyalty of fashion industrialists and romantics alike. Built in 1929 and restored in 1996, the hotel still retains many original details such as facades, woodwork, and even fireplaces (every room has one, not that you'll need to use it). The very central location (1 block from the ocean) is a plus, especially since the Leon lacks a pool. Most of the spacious and stylish rooms are immaculate and reminiscent of a loft apartment; spacious bathrooms with large, deep tubs are especially enticing.

Wood floors and simple, pale furnishings are appreciated in a neighborhood where many others overdo the Art Deco motif. However, some rooms are dark and have not seen such upgrades (we have gotten complaints) and are to be avoided; do not hesitate to ask to change rooms. Service is warm, friendly, and accommodating. We've also gotten complaints about the music coming from the hotel next door, but you have to realize that if you're staying on Collins or Washington avenues, you're going to hear noise: South Beach isn't known for its quiet, peaceful demeanor! The lobby has an informal bar and restaurant, not to mention a large communal table at which guests—production crews, fashion photographers, Europeans, and young hipsters—tend to mix and mingle. Because its entrance is not directly on pedestrian-heavy Collins Avenue, the Hotel Leon remains one of South Beach's most understated, yet coolest, stays.

841 Collins Ave., South Beach, FL 33139. © 305/673-3767. Fax 305/673-5866. www.lilyguesthouse.com. 18 units. Winter $145–$245 suite, $395 penthouse; off-season $100–$195 suite, $335 penthouse. Additional person $10. AE, DC, MC, V. Valet parking $18. "Well-behaved" pets accepted for $10 per night. **Amenities:** Restaurant and lobby bar; reduced rates at local gym; concierge; business services; room service (breakfast). *In room:* A/C, TV, minibar, hair dryer, safe, CD player.

Pelican Hotel ★★   Owned by the same creative folks behind the Diesel Jeans company, the Pelican (whose brazen, albeit appropriate, motto is "A myth in its own limelight") is South Beach's only self-professed "toy-hotel," in which each of its 30 rooms and suites is decorated as outrageously as some of the area's more colorful drag queens. Each room has been designed daringly and rather wittily by Swedish interior decorator Magnus Ehrland, whose countless trips to antiques markets, combined with his wild imagination, have turned room no. 309, for instance, into the "Psychedelic(ate) Girl," room no. 201 into the "Executive Fifties" suite, and room no. 313 into the "Jesus Christ Megastar" room. But the most popular room is the tough-to-score room no. 215, or the "Best Whorehouse," which is said to have made even former Hollywood madam Heidi Fleiss red with envy.

826 Ocean Dr., Miami Beach, FL 33139. © 800/7-PELICAN or 305/673-3373. Fax 305/673-3255. www. Pelicanhotel.com. 30 units. Winter $180–$250 double, $300–$350 oceanfront suite; off-season $135–$155 double, $225 oceanfront suite. AE, DC, MC, V. Valet parking $16. **Amenities:** Restaurant; bar; access to area gyms; concierge; business services; room service; same-day laundry and dry cleaning service. *In room:* A/C, TV/VCR, dataport, fridge, hair dryer, iron, safe, stereo/CD player.

Townhouse ★★   New York hipster Jonathan Morr felt that Miami Beach had lost touch with the bons vivants who gave the city its original cachet, so he decided to take matters into his own hands. His solution: this 72-room, five-story hotel in which standard rooms started at just $99 during its opening in the fall of 2000. The $99 rate proved too good to be true, but even the revised starting rates of $175 during season and $130 off season are still a great deal. The charm of this hotel is found in its clean and simple yet chic design with quirky details: exercise equipment that stands alone in the hallways, free laundry machines in the lobby, and a water bed–lined rooftop. Comfortable, shabby chic rooms boast L-shaped couches for extra guests (for whom you aren't charged). Though the rooms are all pretty much the same, consider the ones with the partial ocean view. The hotel's basement features the hot New York import, Bond St. Lounge (p. 94).

150 20th St., South Beach, FL 33139. © 877/534-3800 or 305/534-3800. Fax 305/534-3811. www.town househotel.com. 72 units. Winter $175–$225 double, $450 penthouse; off-season $130–$155 double, $395

penthouse. Rates include Parisian-style (coffee and pastry) breakfast. AE, MC, V. Valet parking $18. **Ameni-ties:** Restaurant; bar; workout stations; bike rental; free laundry; rooftop terrace with water beds. *In room:* A/C, TV/VCR, dataport, fridge, hair dryer, safe, CD player.

Whitelaw Hotel ⭐   With a slogan that reads "clean sheets, hot water, and stiff drinks," the Whitelaw Hotel stands apart from the other boutique hotels with a fierce sense of humor, but never compromises on its fabulous amenities. Only half a block from Ocean Drive, this hotel, like its clientele, is full of distinct personalities, pairing such disparate elements as luxurious Belgian sheets with shag carpeting to create a completely innovative setting. All-white rooms manage to be homey and plush and not at all antiseptic. Bathrooms are large and well stocked with just about everything you may have forgotten at home. Complimentary cocktails in the lobby every night from 7 to 8pm contribute to a very social atmosphere.

808 Collins Ave., Miami Beach, FL 33139. ℭ **305/398-7000.** Fax 305/398-7010. www.whitelawhotel.com. 49 units. Winter $165–$190 double, $210 mini-suite; off-season $125–$145 double, $145–$160 mini-suite. Rates include complimentary continental breakfast and free cocktails in the lobby (7–8pm daily). AE, DC, MC, V. Parking $18. **Amenities:** Lounge; concierge; business services; laundry service; free airport pickup (to and from MIA); complimentary passes to area nightclubs. *In room:* A/C, TV, dataport, minibar, hair dryer, safe, CD player.

INEXPENSIVE

The Creek   This funky and arty hostel-like hotel, formerly known as the Banana Bungalow, is cheap, campy, and quintessentially Miami Beach. Popular with the MTV set, The Creek is a redone (to the tune of $1 million that provoked the hotel to challenge other renovations, saying "Bob Villa is a wuss.") 1950s two-story motel where it's always Spring Break. The hotel's clever website humanizes the hotel, saying it "Thinks it's in an episode of Playboy's Penthouse," but also calls it a Jetsonian space age hotel. The Creek is one of those that you have to see to fully appreciate, but in the wise words of the hotel itself, "Why does style and cool and fun have to cost you $400 a night? The Creek is a laid back, kick your feet up on the table, hunker down for a cold beverage, relax in the sun, chow down on a burger type place."

The lobby is a retro fabulous homage to the '50s. Contradictions at the Creek abound, which makes the place all the more amusing and ironic. The hotel surrounds an 8,000-square-foot pool deck complete with underwater music, top of the line DJ equipment, and a fully stocked, 40-foot open air bar where everyone hangs out. Oh, and you'll also find a Ms. Pac Man video game, a theater with movies available for viewing at the front desk, a guest kitchen, and a dining room.

There are three types of rooms here: The Waterway Standard, no frills rooms that face a narrow canal where motorboats and kayaks are available for a small charge; the noisier Cabana Room, which opens to the pool deck (which boasts a serious sound system that the hotel turns off around midnight); and the Signature Rooms, 18 "altered living spaces" designed by artists and on the second floor facing the pool deck. I highly recommend the Signature Rooms in terms of decor and privacy, something you won't have if you face out onto the buzzing pool deck. There also happen to be 25 shared rooms with 4 to 6 bunk beds for backpackers on a serious budget.

2360 Collins Ave., Miami Beach, FL 33139. ℭ **866/445-4800** or 305/538-1951. Fax 305/531-3217. www.thecreeksouthbeach.com. 85 units. Winter $20 per person in shared units, $79–$139 double; off-season $18 per person in shared units, $50–$60 double. MC, V. Parking $5. **Amenities:** Cafe; bar; large pool; access to nearby health club; game room; coin-op laundry; Internet access; theater. *In room:* A/C, TV, fridge.

MIAMI BEACH: SURFSIDE, BAL HARBOUR, SUNNY ISLES & NORTH BEACH

The area just north of South Beach, known as Miami Beach, encompasses Surfside, Bal Harbour, and Sunny Isles. Unrestricted by zoning codes throughout the 1950s, 1960s, and especially the 1970s, area developers went crazy, building ever-bigger and more brazen structures, especially north of 41st Street, which is now known as "Condo Canyon." Consequently, there's now a glut of medium-quality condos, with a few scattered holdouts of older hotels and motels casting shadows over the beach by afternoon. In April of 2003, Donald Trump unveiled his Trump International Sonesta Beach Resort (© **800/SONESTA**), a 390-room Sunny Isles monstrosity done up in the typically bombastic Trump style, setting a glitzier standard for its much less glamorous neighbors (though it's totally devoid of personality or style).

For a map of the hotels in this section, see the "Where to Stay & Dine in Miami Beach, Surfside, Bal Harbour, Sunny Isles & North Beach" map on p. 75.

VERY EXPENSIVE

Beach House Bal Harbour ★★ *Finds*   The Beach House Bal Harbour is the closest thing the city has to a summer beach home—comfortable, unpretentious, and luxurious, yet decidedly low-key. In place of an elaborate hotel lobby, the public spaces of the Rubell-owned Beach House are divided into a series of intimate homey environments, from the wicker-furnished screened-in porch to the Asian-inspired Bamboo Room, with overstuffed Ralph Lauren leather couches and Japanese bric-a-brac. The 24-hour Pantry, inspired by Long Island's Sagaponack General Store, is packed with all the needs of the hotel's "unplugged" urban clientele. The ultraspacious rooms (those ending in 04 are the most spacious) are literally brimming with the comforts of home. The 200-foot private beach, hammock grove, and topiary garden are so lush, they're said to have caused several New York hipsters to renege on their summer shares in the Hamptons in favor of this Beach House.

9449 Collins Ave., Surfside, FL 33154. © **877/RUBELLS** or 305/535-8606. Fax 305/535-8602. www.rubell hotels.com. 170 units. Winter $215–$315 double, $245–$305 junior suite; off-season $180–$210 double, $230–$270 junior suite; year-round $350 1-bedroom suite. AE, DC, DISC, MC, V. Valet parking $15. **Amenities:** Restaurant; pantry; bar (until 11pm); heated pool; health club and spa; watersports equipment; children's playground; business center. *In room:* A/C, TV, dataport, fridge, hair dryer, iron, stereo/CD player, wireless TV Web access.

Eden Roc Renaissance Resort and Spa ★★   Just next door to the mammoth Fontainebleau Hilton, this large Morris Lapidus–designed flamboyant hotel, opened in 1956, seems almost intimate by comparison. The nautical Deco decor is a bit gaudy, but nonetheless reminiscent of Miami Beach's Rat-Packed glory days of the '50s. The 55,000-square-foot modern Spa of Eden has excellent facilities and exercise classes, including yoga. The big, open, and airy lobby is often full of name-tagged conventioneers and tourists looking for a taste of Miami Beach kitsch. The rooms, uniformly outfitted with purple and aquatic-colored interiors and retouched 1930s furnishings, are unusually spacious, and the bathrooms boast Italian marble bathtubs. Because of the hotel's size, you should be able to negotiate a good rate unless there's a big event going on. Harry's Grille specializes in seafood and steaks. From Aquatica, the poolside bar and restaurant, bikini-clad patrons can enjoy casual meals and priceless ocean views.

4525 Collins Ave., Miami Beach, FL 33140. ℂ **800/327-8337** or 305/531-0000. Fax 305/674-5555. www.edenrocresort.com. 349 units. Winter $299–$359 double, $485 suite, $2,500 penthouse; off-season $159–$224 double, $379 suite, $1,500 penthouse. Additional person $15. Packages available. AE, DC, DISC, MC, V. Valet parking $20. Pets under 25 lb. accepted for no fee. **Amenities:** 2 restaurants; lounge; bar; 2 outdoor pools; squash courts; racquetball courts; basketball courts; health club and spa; watersports equipment; concierge; tour desk; car-rental desk; business center; salon; limited room service; in-room massage; babysitting; laundry and dry cleaning service; rock-climbing arena. *In room:* A/C, TV, VCRs for rent, dataport, kitchenettes (in suites and penthouse), minibar, coffeemaker, hair dryer, safe.

Fontainebleau Hilton *(Overrated) (Kids)*   In many ways, this is the quintessential Miami Beach hotel. Also designed by the late and legendary Morris Lapidus, who oversaw an expansion in 2000, this grand monolith symbolizes Miami decadence. Since its opening in 1954, the Fontainebleau has hosted presidents, pageants, and movie productions, including the James Bond thriller *Goldfinger.* This is where all the greats, including Sinatra and his pals, performed in their prime, and to pay homage to the Rat Pack, the hotel has redone its lobby bar to reflect the era of swagger, attitude, raffish cool, and panache, featuring large, bordering on tacky but still swell silhouettes of Frank, Sammy, Dino, Joey, and Peter, and the live music of The Pack, a really good Rat Pack cover band. Club Tropigala is reminiscent of Ricky Ricardo's Tropicana and features a Las Vegas–style floor show with dozens of performers and two orchestras. Rooms are luxurious and decorated in various styles from 1950s to ultramodern; bathrooms are done up in Italian marble a la Caesar's Palace. In 2001, the hotel underwent a $10 million food and beverage renovation, introducing the massive, cruise-ship-esque 150-seat Bleu View Mediterranean restaurant and cocktail lounge. Adding to the Fontainebleau's opulence is the 7,000-square-foot Cookie's World water park; the water slide and river-raft ride bring a bit of Disney to Deco-land, which, along with supervised children's activities, is catered toward (though not reserved for) the little ones.

4441 Collins Ave., Miami Beach, FL 33140. ℂ **800/HILTONS** or 305/538-2000. Fax 305/674-4607. www.fontainebleau.hilton.com. 876 units. Winter $289–$459 double; off-season $209–$329 double. Year-round $525–$1,300 suite. Additional person $30. Packages available. AE, DC, DISC, MC, V. Overnight valet parking $17. Pets accepted at no extra cost. **Amenities:** 4 restaurants; 3 cocktail lounges; 2 large outdoor pools; 7 lighted tennis courts (after next year's renovations); state-of-the-art health club; 3 whirlpool baths; watersports rentals; children's programs; game rooms; concierge; tour desk; car-rental desk; business center; shopping arcade; salon; room service; in-room massage; babysitting; laundry and dry cleaning service. *In room:* A/C, TV, fax, dataport, minibar, coffeemaker, hair dryer, iron, safe.

MODERATE

Indian Creek Hotel *(Finds)*   Located off the beaten path, the Indian Creek Hotel is a meticulously restored 1936 building featuring one of the beach's first operating elevators. It's also the most charming hotel in the area. Besides that, the service is impeccable. Because of its location facing the Indian Creek waterway and its lush landscaping, this place feels more like an old-fashioned Key West bed-and-breakfast than your typical Miami Beach Art Deco hotel. The rooms are outfitted in Art Deco furnishings, such as an antique writing desk, pretty tropical prints, and small but spotless bathrooms. All the rooms have been completely renovated. Just 1 short block from a good stretch of sand, the hotel is also within walking distance of shops and restaurants and has a landscaped pool area that is a great place to lounge in the sun. If you're looking for charm, friendly service, and peace and quiet, stay away from the South Beach hype and come here instead.

Where to Stay & Dine in Miami Beach, Surfside, Bal Harbour, Sunny Isles & North Beach

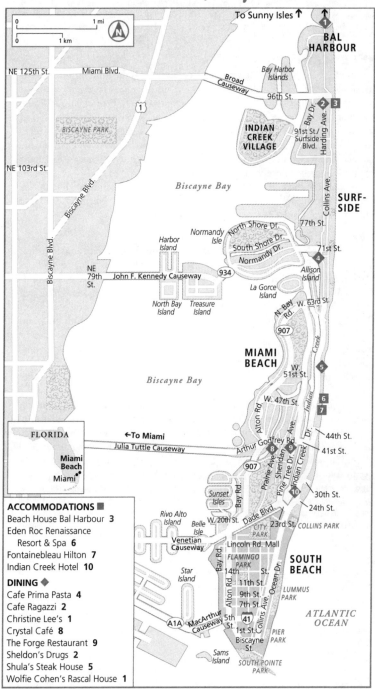

ACCOMMODATIONS ■
Beach House Bal Harbour **3**
Eden Roc Renaissance
    Resort & Spa **6**
Fontainebleau Hilton **7**
Indian Creek Hotel **10**

DINING ◆
Cafe Prima Pasta **4**
Cafe Ragazzi **2**
Christine Lee's **1**
Crystal Café **8**
The Forge Restaurant **9**
Sheldon's Drugs **2**
Shula's Steak House **5**
Wolfie Cohen's Rascal House **1**

2727 Indian Creek Dr. (1 block west of Collins Ave. and the ocean), Miami Beach, FL 33140. ℂ 800/
491-2772 or 305/531-2727. Fax 305/531-5651. www.indiancreekhotel.com. 61 units. Winter $150–$240
double; off-season $90–$150 double. Additional person $25. Group packages and summer specials available.
AE, DC, DISC, MC, V. **Amenities:** Restaurant; bar; pool; concierge; car-rental desk; limited room service; laundry
and dry cleaning service. *In room:* A/C, TV/VCR, dataport, fridge (in suites), hair dryer, CD player.

KEY BISCAYNE

Locals call it the Key, and, technically, Key Biscayne is the northernmost island
in the Florida Keys even though it is located in Miami. A relatively unknown
area until an impeached Richard Nixon bought a home here in the '70s, Key
Biscayne, at 1¼ square miles, is an affluent but hardly lively residential and
recreational island known for its pricey homes, excellent beaches, and actor
Andy Garcia, who makes his home here. The island is far enough from the
mainland to make it feel semiprivate, yet close enough to downtown for guests
to take advantage of everything Miami has to offer.

For a map of the hotels in this section, see the "Where to Stay & Dine in Key
Biscayne, Downtown Miami, West Miami, Airport Area, North Dade, Little
Havana, Coral Gables & Coconut Grove" map on p. 77.

VERY EXPENSIVE

Ritz-Carlton Key Biscayne ★★★ *(Kids)*   Described by some as an oceanfront
mansion, the Ritz-Carlton takes Key Biscayne to the height of luxury with 44
acres of tropical gardens, a 20,000-square-foot European-style spa, and a world-
class tennis center under the direction of tennis pro Cliff Drysdale. Decorated
in British colonial style, the Ritz-Carlton looks as if it came straight out of
Bermuda, with its impressive flower-laden landscaping. The Ritz Kids programs
provide children ages 5 to 12 with fantastic activities, and the 1,200-foot beachfront offers everything from pure relaxation to fishing, boating, or windsurfing.
Spacious and luxuriously appointed rooms are elegantly Floridian, featuring
large balconies overlooking the ocean or the lush gardens. Unlike many behemoth hotels, the Ritz-Carlton is as much a part of the aesthetic value of the
island as is its natural beauty, and its oceanfront Mediterranean-style restaurant,
Aria, is exquisite. The best spa in Miami is also here, with 20,000 square feet of
space that overlooks the Atlantic Ocean. It features unheard-of treatments such
as the Fountain of Youth Ocean Balance treatment (in which you attain total
relaxation while floating in the water) and the Key Lime Coconut Body Scrub.

455 Grand Bay Dr., Key Biscayne, FL 33149. ℂ 800/241-3333 or 305/365-4500. Fax 305/365-4501. www.
ritzcarlton.com. 402 units. Winter $450–$590 double–suite; off-season $260–$490 double–suite. AE, DC,
DISC, MC, V. Valet parking (call for fees). **Amenities:** Restaurant; pool grill; spa cafe; 3 bars; 2 outdoor heated
pools; tennis center w/lessons available; spa and fitness center; watersports equipment; children's programs;
business center; concierge; 24-hr. room service; overnight laundry service. *In room:* A/C, TV, dataport, minibar,
hair dryer, safe.

Sonesta Beach Resort Key Biscayne ★★ *(Kids)*   The Sonesta is an idyllic,
secluded resort on Key Biscayne—like a souped-up summer camp. Families and
couples alike love this place for its oceanfront location and its many high-caliber
amenities, which make it almost impossible to want to venture off the property.

Each of the plush 292 rooms, also recently upgraded, has a private balcony or
terrace. There are also 12 one- and two-bedroom suites. Room no. 828 is particularly appealing, with its sweeping views of the ocean, comfortable (to say the
least) king bed, and top-floor location.

Known for having the best piña coladas in the entire city, the pool and beach
bars are popular with locals and vacationers alike. The hotel's Two Dragons

Where to Stay & Dine in Key Biscayne, Downtown Miami, West Miami, Airport Area, North Dade, Little Havana, Coral Gables & Coconut Grove

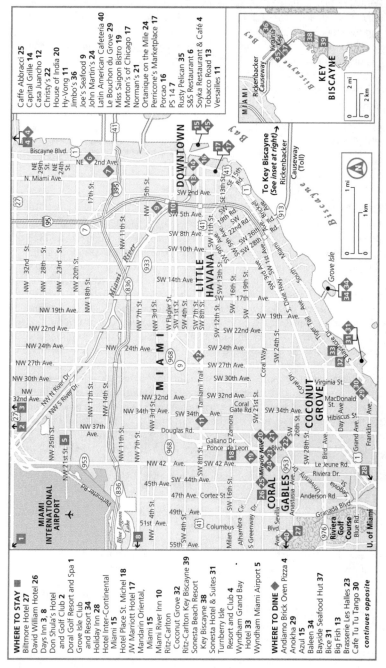

restaurant is good, featuring Chinese, Thai, and Japanese food. A fantastic, free, and fully supervised kids' program (ages 3–12) will actually allow parents to have a vacation of their own, perhaps at the resort's 10,000-square-foot spa or at the Water Tai Chi Program in the outdoor, heated Olympic pool. Although you may not want to leave the lush grounds, Bill Baggs State Recreation Area (p. 125) and the area's best beaches are nearby and worth the trip. Travelers here are only about 15 minutes from Miami Beach and even closer to the mainland and Coconut Grove. A fun new addition to the hotel is the Relay Segway Excursion Center, where you can rent high-tech Segway Human Transporters on which you can tool around the hotel on your own or take guided tours for $25 to $100.

350 Ocean Dr., Key Biscayne, FL 33149. © **800/SONESTA** or 305/361-2021. Fax 305/361-3096. www.sonesta.com. 292 units. Winter $295–$445 double, $635–$1,070 suite; off-season $179–$330 double, $435–$950 suite. 15% gratuity added to food and beverage bills. Special packages available. AE, DC, DISC, MC, V. Valet parking $15. **Amenities:** 4 restaurants; 2 bars; lounge; outdoor heated Olympic-size pool; access to nearby golf; 9 tennis courts; fitness center; full-service spa; 2 waterfront Jacuzzis; extensive watersports equipment rental; bike and moped rental; children's programs; shuttle service to shopping and entertainment; business center; salon; limited room service; laundry and dry cleaning service; sports court; sailing lessons. *In room:* A/C, TV, dataport, minibar, coffeemaker, hair dryer, iron, safe.

DOWNTOWN

If you've ever read Tom Wolfe's *Bonfire of the Vanities,* you may understand what downtown Miami is all about. If not, it's this simple: Take a wrong turn and you could find yourself in some serious trouble. Desolate and dangerous at night, downtown is trying to change its image, but it's a long, tedious process. Recently, however, part of the area has experienced a renaissance in terms of nightlife, with several popular dance clubs and bars opening up in the environs of NE 11th Street off Biscayne Boulevard. Most downtown hotels cater primarily to business travelers and pre- and postcruise passengers. Although business hotels are expensive, quality and service are of a high standard. Look for discounts and packages for the weekend, when offices are closed and rooms often go empty. If you're the kind of person who digs an urban setting, you may enjoy downtown, but if you're looking for shiny, happy Miami, you're in the wrong place (for now). As posh, pricey lofts keep going up in the area faster than the nation's deficit, this area is about to experience the renaissance it has been waiting for. Keep your eyes peeled on this area. You read it here first: Like orange being the new black, Downtown Miami is the new South Beach.

For a map of the hotels in this section, see the "Where to Stay & Dine in Key Biscayne, Downtown Miami, West Miami, Airport Area, North Dade, Little Havana, Coral Gables & Coconut Grove" map on p. 77.

VERY EXPENSIVE

Conrad Miami ✦✦✦   Although you won't find ubiquitous Hilton heiresses Paris and Nicky at this business oriented hotel (they hang out on South Beach), you will find luxury-lovers who have no interest in minimalism and J-Lo spottings and, instead, prefer to bask in the Hilton brand of luxury. This 203-room, 36-floor skyscraper, located in the heart of Miami's financial district, opened in January 2004. While at first you may feel as if you're in an office building, once you walk over the bridge across a sparkling pool, visions of cramped cubicles and bad lighting will immediately disappear. The lobby is located on the 26th floor, which is illuminated by a magnificent atrium that shares the attention with a restaurant, lounge, and bar and splits the difference between the 203-guest rooms and the 116-fully serviced luxury apartments. All rooms feature hyper-high-tech amenities such as flat screen TVs, and, best of all, INNCOM, a bedside remote that controls all lights, thermostat, and do not disturb signs in the room. Because this is a condo-hotel, expect nothing but the best in amenities, including a superbly-equipped fitness center, two tennis courts, and a remarkable swimming pool.

1395 Brickell Ave., Miami, FL 33131. © **305/503-6500.** Fax 305/533-7177. www.conradmiami.com. 203 units. Winter $269–$319 double; off-season $159–$239 double. AE, DC, DISC, MC, V. Valet parking $20. **Amenities:** 2 restaurants; 2 bars; rooftop pool; fitness center; full-service spa; outdoor Jacuzzi; concierge; babysitting; 24-hr. business center; laundry service. *In room:* A/C, TV/VCR/DVD, dataport, coffeemaker, minibar, hair dryer, iron, safe.

The Four Seasons ★★★ *Kids*   Deciding between the hyper luxe Mandarin Oriental or the equally luxe, albeit somewhat museum-like (the artwork in the lobby, including originals by Fernando Botero render most guests as silent as if they were examining the Mona Lisa) Four Seasons is almost like trying to tell the difference between Ava and Zsa Zsa Gabor. Both are spectacular in their own rights. While the architecturally striking Mandarin is located on the semi-private Brickell Key, the equally striking, albeit in an office-building kind of way, 70-story Four Seasons is located on the more bustling Brickell Avenue, the thoroughfare of business transactions. Both have water views that are spectacular. The 221 rooms and 39 suites are luxuriously appointed, and, like the Mandarin, service here is paramount. It's much quieter here at the Four Seasons, the favored stay of camera-shy, agoraphobic celebrities and business moguls. Most rooms overlook Biscayne Bay and while all rooms are cushy, thanks to the hotel's signature "untucked" beds, the bland decor leaves little to be desired, really. The best rooms are the corner suites with views facing both south and east over the water. The hotel's restaurant, Acqua, serves fantastic, surprisingly affordable, Italian fare, with floor to ceiling windows overlooking the pool area, but has yet to surpass the excellence coming out of the kitchen at the Mandarin's deservedly lauded Azul (p. 104). The 40,000 square foot Splash Spa and Sports Club LA here is inimitable, but if you prefer a spa that's not as sprawling and a bit less harried, the Mandarin's got it beat. What the Four Seasons has over the Mandarin, however, are two more pools—a total of three gorgeous pools spread out on over 2 acres (this explains why the Mandarin Oriental recently debuted its sprawling beach club, an amenity the Four Seasons does not have). Bahia, the Latin-American influenced pool bar complete with pre-Castro Cuban musical trio, is the scene for young, upscale movers and shakers. A phenomenal kids program makes the Four Seasons more desirable than the Mandarin, where kids are typically bored. It's hard to choose between the two uber luxurious properties, but one thing that remains consistent at both is that you won't be deprived of the lavish, luxe treatment that you're paying so dearly for.

1435 Brickell Avenue, Miami, FL 33131. © **305/458-3535.** Fax 305/358-7758. www.fourseasons.com/miami. 221 units. Year-round $325 double; $725–$4,000 suite. AE, DC, DISC, MC, V. Valet parking $24. **Amenities:** 2 restaurants; martini bar; outdoor bar; 3 outdoor pools; Sports Club/LA fitness center; full-service spa; outdoor Jacuzzi; concierge; 24-hr. business center. *In room:* A/C, TV, dataport, minibar, hair dryer, iron, safe.

Hotel Inter-Continental Miami ★   This hotel presents a serious catch-22: It's got a front-row view of all of Miami Beach, Biscayne Bay, the Miami River, and the Atlantic Ocean, but it is also located in downtown Miami. If it's a view that you want, then you should stay here; but if you're more interested in location, you may want to reconsider.

With the decidedly threatening presence of the hyperluxurious Mandarin Oriental just over the Brickell Bridge, the Inter-Continental had no choice but to keep up with the competition. A $34 million renovation has brought it up to speed, rendering it downtown proper's swankiest hotel. It boasts more marble than the Liberace Museum (both inside and out), but it is warmed by bold colors and a fancified Florida flavor. Perfectly designed for business travelers, each room is outfitted with a desk and Internet-ready telephone lines, but is not fabulous. They're really just swankier versions of the rooms in a typical chain hotel, albeit a little more froufrou and elaborate, with marble bathrooms, upholstered seating areas, and sit-in windowsills. *Note:* Construction on several new condominiums adjacent to the Inter-Continental may disturb the deafening silence common to downtown Miami.

100 Chopin Plaza, Miami, FL 33131. © 800/327-3005 or 305/577-1000. Fax 305/577-0384. www.miami.interconti.com. 641 units. Winter $199–$359 double; off-season $119–$249 double. Year-round $550–$3,000 suite. Additional person $30. Weekend and other packages available. AE, DC, DISC, MC, V. Valet parking $20. **Amenities:** 3 restaurants; 2 lounges; Olympic-size outdoor heated pool; access to nearby golf course; spa; concierge; tour desk; car-rental desk; large business center; shopping arcade; salon and barbershop; 24-hr. room service; coin-op washers and dryers; 24-hr. laundry and dry cleaning service. *In room:* A/C, TV/VCR, minibar, coffeemaker, hair dryer, CD player.

Mandarin Oriental, Miami ★★★   Corporate big shots and celebrities not in the mood for the South Beach spotlight finally have a high-end luxury hotel to stay in while wheeling and dealing their way through Miami. Catering to business travelers, conventioneers, big time celebrities (J-Lo, Jacko, and so on), and the occasional leisure traveler who doesn't mind spending in excess of $500 a night for a room, the swank Mandarin Oriental features a waterfront location, residential-style rooms with Asian touches (most with balconies), and several upscale dining and bar facilities. The waterfront view of the city is the hotel's best asset, both priceless and absolutely stunning. Much of the hotel's staff was flown in from Bangkok and Hong Kong to demonstrate the hotel's unique brand of superattentive Asian-inspired service. The hotel's two restaurants, the high-end Azul and the more casual Café Sambal, are up to Mandarin standards and are both wonderful, as is the 15,000-square-foot The Spa at Mandarin Oriental in which traditional Thai massages and Ayurvedic treatments are your tickets to nirvana. At press time, the Mandarin Oriental Miami had just opened its 20,000-foot white sand beach club, complete with beds with white cushions and canopies, beach butlers, and beachside cabana treatments, which is nice considering the hotel is 15 minutes from the beach. *Celeb tidbit:* Michael Jackson felt it necessary to autograph one of the paintings inside his suite even though he didn't paint it.

500 Brickell Key Dr., Miami, FL 33131. © 305/913-8288. Fax 305/913-8300. www.mandarinoriental.com. 329 units. Year-round $575 single; $600 double; $1,200–$5,000 suite. AE, DC, DISC, MC, V. Valet parking $24. **Amenities:** 2 restaurants; bar; outdoor pool; beach; beach club; state-of-the-art fitness center; full-service holistic spa; outdoor Jacuzzi; concierge; 24-hr. business center. *In room:* A/C, TV, dataport, minibar, hair dryer, iron, safe.

MODERATE

JW Marriott Hotel ★★   Located smack in the middle of the business-oriented Brickell Avenue near downtown Miami, the JW Marriott is a *really* nice Marriott catering mostly to business travelers, but located conveniently enough between Coconut Grove and South Beach that it isn't a bad choice for vacationers, either. A small but elegant lobby features the classy, appropriately named Drake's Power Bar. The buzz of business deals being sealed amid clouds of cigar smoke contributes to the smoky, but not staid, atmosphere here. Rooms are equipped with every amenity you might need. A lovely outdoor pool, fitness center, sauna, and hot tub should become everybody's business at this hotel. Next door is the area's bustling brewery, Gordon Biersch, which attracts well-heeled, young professional types who gather for postwork revelry.

1109 Brickell Ave., Miami, FL 33131. © **800/228-9290** or 305/374-1224. Fax 305/374-4211. www.marriott. com. Winter $259 deluxe room, $299 concierge room, $399 junior suite; off-season $209 deluxe room, $249 concierge room, $349 junior suite. AE, DC, DISC, MC, V. Valet parking $18; self-parking $16. **Amenities:** 2 restaurants; bar; outdoor pool; health club; spa; sauna; concierge; tour desk; business center; laundry service. *In room:* A/C, TV, dataport w/free Internet access, minibar, coffeemaker, hair dryer, iron, safe.

Miami River Inn ★★★ *Finds*   The Miami River Inn, listed on the National Register of Historic Places, is a quaint country-style hideaway (Miami's *only* bed-and-breakfast!) consisting of four cottages smack in the middle of downtown Miami. In fact, it's so hidden that most locals don't even know it exists, which only adds to its panache. Every room has hardwood floors and is uniquely furnished with antiques dating from 1908. In one room, you might find a hand painted bathtub, a Singer sewing machine, and an armoire from the turn of the 20th century, restored to perfection. Thirty-eight rooms have private bathrooms—4 have a shower only, 6 have a tub only, and 28 have a splendid shower and tub combo. One- and two-bedroom apartments are available as well. In the foyer, you can peruse a library filled with books about old Miami, with histories of this land's former owners: Julia Tuttle, William Brickell, and Henry Flagler. It's close to public transportation, restaurants, and museums, and only 5 minutes from the business district.

118 SW South River Dr., Miami, FL 33130. © **800/468-3589** or 305/325-0045. Fax 305/325-9227. www.miamiriverinn.com. 40 units. Winter $99–$229 double; off-season $69–$109 double. Rates include continental breakfast. Additional person $15. AE, DC, DISC, MC, V. Free parking. Pets accepted for $25 per night. **Amenities:** Small, lushly landscaped swimming pool; access to nearby YMCA facilities; Jacuzzi; babysitting; coin-op washers and dryers; laundry and dry cleaning service. *In room:* A/C, TV, hair dryer (upon request), iron (upon request).

WEST MIAMI/AIRPORT AREA

As Miami continues to grow at a rapid pace, expansion has begun westward, where land is plentiful. Several resorts have taken advantage of the space to build world-class tennis and golf courses. While there's no sea to swim in, a plethora of facilities can definitely make up for the lack of an ocean view.

For a map of the hotels in this section, see the "Where to Stay & Dine in Key Biscayne, Downtown Miami, West Miami, Airport Area, North Dade, Little Havana, Coral Gables & Coconut Grove" map on p. 77.

EXPENSIVE

Doral Golf Resort and Spa ★   This recently renovated (to the tune of $40 million) 650-acre golf and tennis resort is in the middle of nowhere, and even though it still looks stuck in the '70s, it deserves a star just for its legendary golf course. If it weren't for the golf course, I'd never recommend anyone stay here. It's dull and the area in which it's located is not one anyone needs to see while in Miami. While the pamperings in the spa are nothing to sneer at, the next-door golf resort hosts world-class tournaments and boasts the Blue Monster course as well as the Great White Course—the Southeast's first desert-scape course, designed by The Shark himself, Greg Norman. *Note:* Repeat guests usually book the season well in advance. The Blue Lagoon water park features two

80,000-gallon pools with cascading waterfalls, a rock facade, and a 125-foot water slide. Rooms here, like the hotel itself, are spacious, all with private balconies, many overlooking a golf course or garden. Much-needed renovations to the rooms reveal a plantation-style decor with lots of wicker and wood. Spacious bathrooms are done up in marble. Enhancements to the golf courses, spa suites, and driving range have also brought the resort up to speed with its competition. The spa's restaurant serves tasty, healthy fare—so good you won't realize it's health food, actually. For a spa or golf vacation, the Doral is an ideal choice. Otherwise, consider investing your money in a hotel that's better located.

4400 NW 87th Ave., Miami, FL 33178. ✆ **800/71-DORAL** or 305/592-2000. Fax 305/594-4682. www.doral resort.com. 693 units. Winter $350 double, $450 suite, $550 1-bedroom suite, $900 2-bedroom suite; off-season $150 double, $230 suite, $330 1-bedroom suite, $480 2-bedroom suite. Additional person $35. Golf and spa packages available. AE, DC, DISC, MC, V. Valet parking $17. **Amenities:** 5 restaurants; 6 pools and a 125-ft. water slide; 5 golf courses and driving range; 10 tennis courts; health club and world-class spa; bike rental; concierge; business center; room service; babysitting; laundry and dry cleaning service. *In room:* A/C, TV, dataport, minibar, coffeemaker, hair dryer, iron, safe, CD player.

Miccosukee Resort and Convention Center ✪   Located on the edge of the Everglades, about 30 to 40 minutes west of the airport, the Miccosukee Resort is the closest thing South Florida's got to Las Vegas, but accommodations really are just a step above a Holiday Inn. The Miccosukee tribe was originally part of the lower Creek Nation, which lived in areas now known as Alabama and Georgia. After the final Seminole War in 1858, the last of the Miccosukees settled in the Everglades. Following the lead set recently by many other Native American tribes, they built the resort to accumulate gambling revenue. Although many tourists go out to the resort solely to gamble, it also has expansive meeting and banquet facilities, spa services, great children's programs, entertainment, and excursions to the Florida Everglades. Guest rooms are standard, furnished with custom pieces made exclusively for the resort, but if you're here, you're not likely to spend that much time in your room.

500 SW 177th Ave. (at intersection with SW 8th St.), Miami, FL 33194. ✆ **877/242-6464** or 305/221-8623. Fax 305/925-2556. www.miccosukee.com. 309 units. Year-round $109 double; $135 suite; $325 presidential suite. All rooms sleep up to 3 people, suites sleep 4–6 people. AE, DC, DISC, MC, V. Free parking. **Amenities:** 5 restaurants; 24-hr. deli; indoor heated pool; state-of-the-art health club and spa; game room; 24-hr. room service; dry cleaning and self laundry service. *In room:* A/C, TV, dataport, minibar, coffeemaker, hair dryer, in-room movies; some suites have whirlpool and wet bar.

MODERATE

Don Shula's Hotel and Golf Club   Guests come to Shula's mostly for the golf, but there's plenty here to keep nongolfers busy, too. Opened in 1992 to much fanfare from the sports and business community, Shula's resort is an all-encompassing oasis in the middle of the planned, quaint residential neighborhood of Miami Lakes, complete with a Main Street and nearby shopping facilities—a good thing, since the site is more than a 20-minute drive from anything. The guest rooms, located in the main building or surrounding the golf course, are plain but pretty in typical, uninspiring Florida decor—pastels, wicker, and light wood. As expected, the hotel's Athletic Club features state-of-the-art equipment and classes, but costs hotel guests $10 per day or $35 per week. The award-winning Shula's Steak House (p. 100) and the more casual Steak House Two get high rankings nationwide. They serve huge Angus beef steaks and seafood, which can be worked off with a round of golf the next day.

6842 Main St., Miami Lakes, FL 33014. ✆ **800/24-SHULA** or 305/821-1150. Fax 305/820-8094. www. donshulahotel.com. 330 units. Winter $129–$289 suite; off-season $99–$209 suite. Additional person $10.

Business packages available. AE, DC, MC, V. **Amenities:** 2 restaurants; 1 bar; 2 pools; golf course and driving range; 9 tennis courts; sporting courts; health club; Jacuzzi; saunas; room service. *In room:* A/C, TV/VCR, dataport, coffeemaker, hair dryer, iron.

BARGAIN CHAINS

If you must stay near the airport, consider any of the dozens of moderately priced chain hotels. You'll find one of the cheapest and most recommendable options at either of the **Days Inn** locations at 7250 NW 11th St. or 4767 NW 36th St. (© **800/329-7466** for both or 305/888-3661 or 305/261-4230, respectively), each about 2 miles from the airport. The larger property on 36th Street offers slightly cheaper rates with singles starting as low as $49. The 11th Street locale may charge more for weekends, but prices usually start at $70. Prices include free transportation from the airport.

A more luxurious option is the **Wyndham Miami Airport,** at 3900 NW 21st St. (© **305/871-3800**), with rates from $100 to $225.

NORTH DADE

For a map of the hotels in this section, see the "Where to Stay & Dine in Key Biscayne, Downtown Miami, West Miami, Airport Area, North Dade, Little Havana, Coral Gables & Coconut Grove" map on p. 77.

Fairmont Turnberry Isle Resort & Club ★★★   One of Miami's classiest resorts (along the lines of the Mandarin Oriental), this gorgeous 300-acre compound, owned by the Mandarin Oriental Hotel group, has every possible facility for active guests, particularly golfers. You'll pay a lot to stay here—but it's worth it. The main attractions are two Trent Jones courses, available only to members and guests of the hotel. A new seven-story Jasmine wing looks like a Mediterranean village and is surrounded by tropical gardens that are joined by covered marble walkways to the other wings. Treat yourself to a "Turnberry Retreat" at the Turnberry Spa, which recently underwent a $10 million renovation. The spa comprises three levels of deluxe pampering and includes aerobics and fitness classes, stress reduction, massage therapy, and a juice bar designed for complete rejuvenation. Impeccable service from check-in to checkout consistently brings loyal fans back to this resort for more. Its location in the well-manicured residential and shopping area of North Miami Beach known as Aventura means you'll find excellent shopping and some of the best dining in Miami right in the neighborhood. Unless you're into boating, the higher-priced resort rooms (instead of the yacht club) are where you'll want to stay; you'll be steps from the spa facilities and the renowned Veranda restaurant. The well-proportioned rooms are gorgeously tiled to match the Mediterranean-style architecture. The huge bathrooms even have a color TV mounted within reach of the whirlpool bathtubs and glass-walled showers. The only drawback to this hotel is that you'll need to take a shuttle to the beach. *Celeb alert:* You never know who may stay here. Paul McCartney and his new wife Heather Mills were here just before they tied the knot and allegedly had a huge enough fight that Mills threw her rock of an engagement ring out the window. A week later, Sir Paul paid for a staffer to personally fly the ring back to his estate in the U.K.

19999 W. Country Club Dr., Aventura, FL 33180. © **800/327-7028** or 305/936-2929. Fax 305/933-6560. www.turnberryisle.com. 395 units. Winter $395–$495 double, $605–$1,200 suite; off-season $175–$275 double, $375–$730 suite; year round $4,000 grand presidential suite. AE, DC, DISC, MC, V. Valet parking $12; free self-parking. **Amenities:** 6 restaurants; numerous bars and lounges; 2 outdoor pools; 2 golf courses; 2 tennis complexes; state-of-the-art spa; extensive watersports equipment rental; concierge; secretarial services; 24-hr. room service; babysitting. *In room:* A/C, TV/VCR, fax, dataport, minibar, hair dryer, iron, safe, CD player; fridge and coffeemaker on request.

CORAL GABLES

Translated appropriately as "City Beautiful," the Gables, as it's affectionately known, was one of Miami's original planned communities and is still among the city's prettiest, pedestrian-friendly, albeit preservation-obsessed, neighborhoods. Pristine with a European flair, Coral Gables is best known for its wide array of excellent upscale restaurants of various ethnicities, as well as a hotly contested (the quiet city didn't want to welcome new traffic) mega-shopping complex featuring upscale stores such as Nordstrom.

If you're looking for luxury, Coral Gables has a number of wonderful hotels, but if you're on a tight budget, you may be better off elsewhere. Two popular and well-priced chain hotels in the area are a **Holiday Inn** (© **800/HOLIDAY** or 305/667-5611) at 1350 S. Dixie Hwy., with rates between $89 and $189, and a **Terrace Inn** (© **305/665-7501**) at 1430 S. Dixie Hwy., with rates ranging from $59 to $89. Both are located directly across the street from the University of Miami and are popular with families and friends of students.

For a map of the hotels in this section, see the "Where to Stay & Dine in Key Biscayne, Downtown Miami, West Miami, Airport Area, North Dade, Little Havana, Coral Gables & Coconut Grove" map on p. 77.

VERY EXPENSIVE

Biltmore Hotel ✸✸✸   A romantic sense of old-world glamour combined with a rich history permeate the Biltmore as much as the pricey perfume of the guests who stay here. Built in 1926, it's the oldest Coral Gables hotel and a National Historic Landmark—one of only two operating hotels in Florida to receive that designation. Rising above the Spanish-style estate is a majestic 300-foot copper-clad tower, modeled after the Giralda bell tower in Seville and visible throughout the city. Over the years, the Biltmore has passed through many incarnations (including a post–World War II stint as a VA hospital), but it is now back to its original 1926 splendor. More intriguing than scary is the rumor that ghosts of wounded soldiers and even Al Capone, for whom the Everglades Suite is nicknamed, roam the halls here. But don't worry. The hotel is far from a haunted house. It is warm, welcoming, and extremely charming. Now under the management of the Westin Hotel group, the hotel boasts large Moorish-style rooms decorated with tasteful period reproductions and some high-tech amenities. The enormous lobby, with its 45-foot vaulted ceilings, makes a bold statement of elegance. Always a popular destination for golfers, including former President Clinton (who stays in the Al Capone suite), the Biltmore is situated on a lush, rolling 18-hole course that is as challenging as it is beautiful. The spa is fantastic and the enormous 21,000-square-foot winding pool (surrounded by arched walkways and classical sculptures) is legendary—it's where a pre-*Tarzan* Johnny Weismuller broke the world's swimming record. Even if you don't stay at the Biltmore Hotel, definitely take a tour of it (call © **305/445-1926** for more information; p. 129) to learn about its fascinating history and mystery.

1200 Anastasia Ave., Coral Gables, FL 33134. © **800/727-1926** or 305/445-1926. Fax 305/442-9496. www.biltmorehotel.com. 280 units. Winter $339–$509 double; off-season $259–$379 double; year-round specialty suites $569–$2,850. Additional person $20. Special packages available. AE, DC, DISC, MC, V. Valet parking $14; free self-parking. **Amenities:** 4 restaurants; 4 bars; outdoor pool; 18-hole golf course; 10 lighted tennis courts; state-of-the-art health club; full-service spa; sauna; concierge; car rental through concierge; elaborate business center and secretarial services; salon; 24-hr. room service; babysitting; laundry and dry cleaning service; wine cellar. *In room:* A/C, TV, VCR on request, fax, dataport, kitchenette (in tower suite), minibar, hair dryer, iron, safe.

EXPENSIVE

David William Hotel ⭑⭑ This sister hotel to the Biltmore shares many of the same amenities without the Biltmore's price. You can even take a shuttle from here to the Biltmore to play a round of golf, enjoy the health club and spa, play tennis, or take a dip in the pool. The luxurious one- and two-bedroom suites are extremely spacious and have eat-in kitchens for extended stays. For a spectacular view of Miami, go up to the roof and have a drink by the pool. The hotel, which has undergone a recent external renovation, is directly across the street from the Granada Golf Course, less than 5 miles from the airport, and only 20 minutes from Miami Beach. Carmen the Restaurant is the hotel's sublime eatery owned by chef Carmen Gonzalez, whose Nuevo Latino cooking is outstanding. If you want luxury without the price, this is your best alternative in the Gables.

700 Biltmore Way, Coral Gables, FL 33134. ℂ **800/757-8073** or 305/445-7821. Fax 305/913-1933. www. davidwilliamhotel.com. 65 units. Winter $179–$499 double; off-season $99–$399 double. AE, DISC, MC, V. Valet parking $12, limited free self-parking. **Amenities:** Restaurant; rooftop pool; room service (dinner only). *In room:* A/C, TV, kitchenette (in deluxe rooms), minibar, coffeemaker, hair dryer, iron, safe.

Hotel Place St. Michel ⭑⭑⭑ This European-style hotel, in the heart of Coral Gables, is one of the city's most romantic options. The accommodations and hospitality are straight out of old-world Europe, complete with dark wood–paneled walls, cozy beds, beautiful antiques, and a quiet elegance that seems startlingly out of place in trendy Miami. Everything here is charming—from the brass elevator and parquet floors to the paddle fans. One-of-a-kind furnishings make each room special. Bathrooms are on the smaller side but are hardly cramped. All have shower/tub combos except for two, which have either or. If you're picky, request your preference. Guests are treated to fresh fruit upon arrival and enjoy perfect service throughout their stay. The exceptional Restaurant St. Michel is a very romantic dining choice.

162 Alcazar Ave., Coral Gables, FL 33134. ℂ **800/848-HOTEL** or 305/444-1666. Fax 305/529-0074. www. hotelplacestmichel.com. 27 units. Winter $165 double, $200 suite; off-season $125 double, $160 suite. Additional person $10. Rates include continental breakfast and fruit basket upon arrival. AE, DC, MC, V. Self-parking $7. **Amenities:** Restaurant; lounge; access to nearby health club; concierge; room service; laundry and dry cleaning service. *In room:* A/C, TV, dataport, hair dryer, iron (available upon request).

COCONUT GROVE

This waterfront village hugs the shores of Biscayne Bay, just south of U.S. 1 and about 10 minutes from the beaches. Once a haven for hippies, head shops, and arty bohemian characters, the Grove succumbed to the inevitable temptations of commercialism and has become a Gap nation, featuring a host of fun, themey restaurants, bars, a megaplex, and lots of stores. Outside of the main shopping area, however, you will find the beautiful remnants of old Miami in the form of flora, fauna, and, of course, water.

Also see the last paragraph of the Sonesta Beach Resort Key Biscayne listing, on p. 76, for a review of the new Sonesta Hotel & Suites Coconut Grove.

For a map of the hotels in this section, see the "Where to Stay & Dine in Key Biscayne, Downtown Miami, West Miami, Airport Area, North Dade, Little Havana, Coral Gables & Coconut Grove" map on p. 77.

VERY EXPENSIVE

Grove Isle Club and Resort ⭑ Hidden away in the bougainvillea and lushness of the Grove, the Grove Isle Resort is off the beaten path on its own lushly landscaped 20-acre island, just outside the heart of Coconut Grove. The isolated exclusivity of this resort contributes to a country club vibe, though, for the most part, the people here aren't snooty; they just value their privacy and precious relaxation time. Everyone dresses in white and pastels, and if they're not on their way to a set of tennis, they're not in a rush to get anywhere. You'll step into rooms that are elegantly furnished with mosquito-netted canopy beds and a patio overlooking the bay. You'll need to reserve early here—rooms go very fast. Baleen (p. 110), a fantastic yet pricey haute cuisinerie, serves fresh seafood and other regional specialties in a spectacular, elegant dining room, or, better yet, outside on the water.

4 Grove Isle Dr., Coconut Grove, FL 33133. ✆ **800/88-GROVE** or 305/858-8300. Fax 305/854-6702. www. groveisle.com. 49 units. Winter $409 suite; off-season $199–$219 suite. Rates include breakfast with certain packages only. AE, DC, MC, V. Valet parking $17. **Amenities:** Large outdoor heated pool; 12 outdoor tennis courts; deluxe health club; concierge; secretarial services; salon; room service; in-room massage; babysitting; laundry and dry cleaning service. *In room:* A/C, TV/VCR, dataport, minibar, hair dryer, iron, safe.

Ritz-Carlton Coconut Grove   The third and smallest of Miami's Ritz-Carlton hotels opened with a quiet splash in fall 2002, and it is hands down the most intimate of its properties, surrounded by 2 acres of tropical gardens and overlooking Biscayne Bay and the Miami skyline. Decorated in an Italian Renaissance design, the hotel's understated luxury is a welcome addition to an area known for its gaudiness. In addition to the usual Ritz-Carlton standard of service and comfort, the hotel has an excellent, extremely elegant restaurant (with footstools for women to put their purses on, how classy!), Biscaya Grill, whose executive chef, Willis Loughhead, hails from South Beach's much friskier (and since he left, less stellar) Tantra restaurant.

3300 SW 27th Ave., Coconut Grove, FL 33133. ✆ **800/241-3333** or 305/644-4680. Fax 305/644-4681. www.ritzcarlton.com. 115 units. Winter $385–$650 double–suite; off-season $215–$400 double–suite. AE, DC, DISC, MC, V. Valet parking. **Amenities:** Restaurant; pool grill; 3 bars; outdoor heated pool; fitness center; spa; concierge; business center; boutique; 24-hr. room service; babysitting; overnight laundry service. *In room:* A/C, TV, dataport, minibar, hair dryer, safe.

Wyndham Grand Bay Hotel 🐸🐸🐸   Grand in size and stature, the Grand Bay Hotel looks like it belongs in Acapulco with its ziggurat structure and tropical landscaping, but once you see the massive bright red sculpture/structure done by late *Condé Nast* editorial director Alexander Lieberman in the driveway, you know you're not in Mexico. Ultraluxurious, the Grand Bay is quietly elegant, and, as a result, has hosted the likes of privacy fanatics such as Michael Jackson. British singer George Michael filmed his "Careless Whisper" video here because of its sweeping views of Biscayne Bay. Rooms are superb, with views of the bay and the Coconut Grove Marina, and they're decorated in soft peach tones with a country French theme. Bathrooms are equally luxurious. Service is outstanding, and the clientele ranges from families to international jet-setters. Bice (p. 110), a sublime northern Italian restaurant, is the hotel's most popular dining option.

2669 S. Bayshore Dr., Coconut Grove, FL 33133. ✆ **305/858-9600.** Fax 305/859-2026. www.wyndham.com. 177 units. Winter $279–$400 suite; off-season $149–$349 suite. Additional person $20. AE, DC, MC, V. Valet parking $18. **Amenities:** Restaurant; outdoor pool; 24-hr. health club; Jacuzzi; sauna; concierge; business center; babysitting. *In room:* A/C, TV, fax, dataport, minibar, coffeemaker, hair dryer, iron, safe, CD player.

4 Where to Dine in Miami

Don't be fooled by the plethora of superlean model types you're likely to see posing throughout Miami: Contrary to popular belief, dining in this city is as much a sport as the in-line skating on Ocean Drive. With over 6,000 restaurants to choose from, dining out in Miami has become a passionate pastime for locals and visitors alike. Our star chefs have fused Californian-Asian with Caribbean and Latin elements to create a world-class flavor all its own: *Floribbean.* Think mango chutney splashed over fresh swordfish or a spicy sushi sauce served alongside Peruvian ceviche.

Formerly synonymous with early-bird specials, Miami's new-wave cuisine, 10 years in the making, now rivals that of San Francisco—or even New York. Nouveau Cuban chef Douglas Rodriguez may have fled his Miami kitchen in favor of one in Manhattan, but he's coming back to a yet-to-open restaurant at 5061 Biscayne Blvd. In addition, other Food Network–caliber stellar chefs such as the Food Network's own Michelle Bernstein, Mark Militello, Allen Susser, Norman van Aken, and Jonathan Eismann remain firmly planted in the city's culinary scene, fusing local ingredients into edible masterpieces. Indulging in this New World cuisine is not only high in calories, it's high in price. But if you can manage to splurge at least once, it'll be worth it.

Thanks to a thriving cafe society in both South Beach and Coconut Grove, you can also enjoy a moderately priced meal and linger for hours without having a waiter hover over you. In Little Havana, you can chow down on a meal that serves about six for less than $10. And since seafood is plentiful, it doesn't have to cost you an arm and a leg to enjoy the appendages of a crab or lobster. Don't be put off by the looks of our recommended seafood shacks in places such as Key Biscayne—oftentimes these spots get the best and freshest catches.

Whatever you're craving, Miami's got it—with the exception of decent Chinese food and a New York–style slice of pizza. If you're craving a scene with your steak, then South Beach is the place to be. Like many cities in Europe and Latin America, it is fashionable to dine late in South Beach, preferably after 9pm, sometimes as late as midnight. Service on South Beach is notoriously slow and arrogant, but it comes with the turf. (Of course, it is possible to find restaurants that defy the notoriety and actually pride themselves on friendly service.) On the mainland—especially in Coral Gables, and, more recently, downtown and on Brickell Avenue—you can also experience fine, creative dining without the pretense.

The biggest complaint when it comes to Miami dining isn't the haughtiness, but rather the dearth of truly moderately priced restaurants, especially in South Beach and Coral Gables. It's either really cheap or really expensive; the in-between somehow gets lost in the culinary shuffle. Quick-service diners don't really exist here as they do in other cosmopolitan areas. I've tried to cover a range of cuisines in a range of prices. But with new restaurants opening on a weekly basis, you're bound to find a savory array of dining choices on every budget.

Many restaurants keep extended hours in season (roughly Dec–Apr) and may close for lunch and/or dinner on Mondays when the traffic is slower. Always call ahead, since schedules do change. Also, always look carefully at your bill—many Miami restaurants add a 15% gratuity to your total. *Feel free to adjust it* if you feel your server deserves more or less.

SOUTH BEACH

The renaissance of South Beach started in the early '90s and is still continuing as classic cuisine gives in to mod-temptation by inevitably fusing with more chic, nouveau developments created by faithful followers and devotees of the Food Network school of cooking. The ultimate result has spawned dozens of first-rate restaurants. In fact, big-name restaurants from across the country have capitalized on South Beach's international appeal and opened, and continue to open, branches here with great success. A few old standbys remain from the *Miami Vice* days, but the flock of newcomers dominates the scene, with places going in and out of style as quickly as the tides.

The Lincoln Road area is packed with places offering good food and a great atmosphere. Since it's impossible to list them all, I recommend strolling and browsing: Most restaurants post a copy of their menu outside.

With very few exceptions, the places on Ocean Drive are crowded with tourists and priced accordingly. You'll do better to venture a little farther into the pedestrian-friendly streets just west of Ocean Drive.

For a map of the restaurants in this section, see the "South Beach" map on p. 65.

VERY EXPENSIVE

BED ★★ ECLECTIC   BED—that's Beverage, Entertainment, Dining—is one of the most gimmicky dining lounges to land in South Beach in a very long time. So gimmicky, in fact, that an episode of *Sex and the City* featured a fictional New York branch (which is set to become non-fiction at some point) of the sexy South Beach establishment. When you walk inside, you'll feel as if you've entered a Buddhist temple. An array of inviting mosquito-netted beds awaits diners. You'll rest your head against soft cushiony pillows. A DJ spins Euro mood music and some techno. You'll have no problem appreciating the taste and aroma of the exquisite (and exquisitely priced) cuisine, featuring dishes such as pan seared foie gras with caramelized mango and cranberry with French toast, and Florida Red Snapper with garlic mash, matchstick asparagus (a fancy way of saying thin asparagus), and a choice of caper beurre noisette or Vermouth cream sauce. For dessert, try the Ménage à Trois—three sorbets including champagne, sour cherry, and mango—or indulge in some Fire and Ice—molten chocolate cake with rum vanilla ice cream and caramel sauce. Beware of crumbs in the sheets, as they aren't always changed between customers, and for the crowd-phobic, do not go to BED on a weekend or on its most popular Wednesday night—it's a nightmare. Go for the food, but if you really want to enjoy the food, make sure you go to the 8pm seating or else you may be sharing that food with several hundred of your closest (by proxy) friends.

929 Washington Ave., South Beach. ✆ **305/532-9070.** Reservations required, accepted only on the day you plan to dine here. Main courses $32–$40. AE, DC, MC, V. Mon–Sat: first lay (no actual seats) 8pm; second lay 10:30pm. Lounge 11pm–3am.

Casa Tua ★★★ *Finds* ITALIAN   The stunning Casa Tua is a sleek and chic country Italian-style establishment set in a refurbished 1925 Mediterranean-style house cum hotel. It has several dining areas, including a resplendent outdoor garden, comfy Ralph Lauren-esque living room, and a communal eat-in kitchen. The lamb chops are stratospheric in price ($42) but sublime in taste. Service is, as always with South Beach eateries, inconsistent, ranging from ultra professional to absurdly lackadasical. For these prices, they should be wiping our mouths for us. After or before dinner, head upstairs to the lounge area, where the beautiful people convene over $15 cocktails.

1700 James Ave., South Beach. ✆ **305/673-1010.** Reservations required. Main courses $24–$42. AE, DC, MC, V. Mon–Sat 7pm–midnight.

China Grill ★★ PAN-ASIAN   If ever a restaurant could be as cavernous as, say, the Asian continent, this would be it. Formerly a hub of hype and pompous circumstance, China Grill has calmed on the coolness meter despite the infrequent appearance of the likes of J-Lo and Enrique Iglesias (separately, of course), but its cuisine is still sizzling, if not better than ever. With an incomparable, and dizzying, array of amply portioned dishes (such as the outrageous crispy spinach, wasabi mashed potatoes, seared rare tuna in spicy Japanese pepper, broccoli rabe dumplings, lobster pancakes, and a sinfully delicious dessert sampler complete with sparklers), an epicurean journey into the world of near perfect Pan-Asian cuisine is well worth a stop on any foodie's itinerary. Keep in mind that China Grill is a family-style restaurant and that dishes are meant to be shared. For those who can't stay away from sushi, China Grill recently introduced Dragon, a 40-seat "sushi den" in a private back room with one-of-a-kind rolls such as the Havana Roll, which consists of yellowtail snapper, rum, coconut, avocado, and red tobiko, and cocktails such as the Lemongrass Saketini.

404 Washington Ave., South Beach. © 305/534-2211. Reservations strongly recommended. Main courses $25–$59. AE, DC, M, V. Mon–Thurs 11:45am–midnight; Fri 11:45am–1am; Sat 6pm–1am; Sun 6pm–midnight.

Emeril's Miami Beach ★ CREOLE   It was only a matter of time before, bam!, Emeril Lagasse set up shop in South Beach. If only it were a few years sooner. Not that we're knocking Emeril's culinary skills, but it just seems that amidst a bunch of trendy, innovative restaurants that Emeril's is just an upscale cross between Red Lobster and TGI Friday's. At any rate, if you've never dined at Emeril's original restaurant(s) in New Orleans and you're craving Creole cuisine, dine here. Elaborately (bordering on gaudily) designed, the 8,000 square foot restaurant replaces the much lauded Gaucho Room at the Loews Hotel. Signature dishes include New Orleans Barbecue Shrimp with a Petite Rosemary Biscuit; Niman Ranch Double-Cut Pork Chop with Tamarind Glaze, Carmelized Sweet Potatoes and Green Chili Mole Sauce; and Banana Cream Pie with Banana Crust, Caramel Sauce, and Chocolate Shavings. Order a few of those and, bam!, suddenly, your waistline is bigger and your wallet thinner.

In the Loews Hotel, 1601 Collins Ave., South Beach. © 305/695-4550. Reservations required. Main courses $18–$30. AE, MC, V. Daily 11:30am–2pm; Sun–Thurs 5:30–10pm; Fri–Sat 5:30–11pm.

Escopazzo ★★★ ITALIAN   Escopazzo means "I'm going crazy" in Italian, but the only sign of insanity in this primo Northern Italian eatery is the fact that it only seats 90. The wine bottles have it better—the restaurant's cellar holds 1,000 bottles of various vintages. Should you be so lucky to score a table at this romantic local favorite (choose one in the back dining room that's reminiscent of an Italian courtyard complete with water fountain and faux windows; it's not cheesy at all), you'll have trouble deciding between dishes that will have you swearing off the Olive Garden with your first bite. Among these, squid ink pasta with ragout of mussels, clams and calamari in a crispy pasta basket, or Smithfield pork tenderloin filled with smoked mozzarella in a Madeira, sage, and amarene cherry sauce. The hand-rolled pastas and risotto are near perfection. Eating here is like dining with a big Italian family—it's never boring (the menu changes five or six times a year), the service is excellent, and nobody's happy until you are blissfully full.

1311 Washington Ave., South Beach. © 305/674-9450. Reservations required. Main courses $18–$32. AE, MC, V. Mon–Fri 6pm–midnight; Sat 6pm–1am; Sun 6–11pm.

Joe's Stone Crab Restaurant ★★ SEAFOOD   Unless you grease the palms of one of the stone-faced maitre d's with some stone-cold cash, you'll be waiting for those famous claws for up to 2 hours—if not more. As much a

Miami landmark as the beaches themselves, Joe's is a microcosm of the city, attracting everyone from T-shirted locals to a bejeweled Ivana Trump. Whatever you wear, however, will be eclipsed by a kitschy, unglamorous plastic bib that your waiter will tie on you unless you say otherwise. Open only during stone-crab season (Oct–May), Joe's reels in the crowds with the freshest, meatiest stone crabs and their essential accouterments: creamed spinach and excellent sweet-potato fries. The claws come in medium, large, or jumbo. Some say size doesn't matter; others swear by the jumbo (and more expensive) ones. Whatever you choose, pair them with a savory mustard sauce (a perfect mix of mayo and mustard) or hot butter. Not feeling crabby? The fried chicken and liver and onions on the regular menu are actually considered by many as far superior—they're definitely far cheaper—to the crabs. Oh yeah, and save room for dessert. The Key lime pie here is the best in town. If you don't feel like waiting, try Joe's Take Away, which is located next door to the restaurant—it's a lot quicker and just as tasty.

11 Washington Ave. (at Biscayne St., just south of 1st St.), South Beach. (℃ **305/673-0365** or 305/673-4611 for takeout. www.joesstonecrab.com. Reservations not accepted. Market price varies but averages $63 for a serving of jumbo crab claws, $43 for large claws. AE, DC, DISC, MC, V. Daily 11:30am–2pm; Sun 4–10pm, Mon–Thurs 5–10pm; Fri–Sat 5–11pm. Open mid-Oct to mid-May.

Mark's South Beach ✶✶ NEW WORLD/MEDITERRANEAN   Named after owner and chef Mark Militello, this is one of the best restaurants in all of Miami. But because celebrities don't go here, it's not on the A-list as far as scene is concerned, and for true foodies, this is a blissful thing. A cozy, contemporary restaurant nestled in the basement of the quietly chic Hotel Nash, Mark's New World and Mediterranean-influenced menu changes nightly. What doesn't change is the consistency and freshness of the restaurant's exquisite cuisine. The roasted rack of Colorado lamb with semolina gnocchi is exceptional and worth every bit of cholesterol it may have. Crispy-skin yellowtail snapper with shrimp, tomato, black olives, oregano, and crumbled feta cheese is in a school of its own. Desserts, including an impressive cheese cart, are outrageous, especially the pistachio cake with chocolate sorbet. Unlike many South Beach eating establishments, the knowledgeable servers are here because of their experience in the restaurant—not modeling—business. If you're expecting to spot celebs and be part of the "scene," then Mark's is not the place for you. For a few bucks extra and a trip over the causeway, go to Azul at the Mandarin Oriental Miami instead.

In the Hotel Nash, 1120 Collins Ave., South Beach. (℃ **305/604-9050**. Reservations recommended. Main courses $26–$41. AE, DC, DISC, MC, V. Wed–Sun 7–11am and noon–3pm; Wed–Sat 7pm–midnight, Sun 7–11pm.

Nobu ✶✶✶ SUSHI   When Madonna ate here, no one really noticed. Same thing happened when Justin Timberlake and Cameron Diaz canoodled here. Not because they were purposely trying not to notice, but because the real star at Nobu is the sushi. The raw facts: Nobu has been hailed as one of the best sushi restaurants in the world, with always-packed eateries in New York, London, and Los Angeles. The Omakase, or Chef's Choice—a multicourse menu entirely up to the chef for $70 per person and up—gets consistent raves. And although you won't wait long for your food to be cooked, you will wait forever to score a table here.

At the Shore Club Hotel, 1901 Collins Ave., South Beach. (℃ **305/695-3232**. Reservations for parties of 6 or more. Main courses $10–$30. AE, MC, V. Sun 7–11pm; Mon–Thurs 7pm–midnight; Fri–Sat 7pm–1am.

Pacific Time ✶✶ PAN-ASIAN   When Pacific Time opened on a desolate Lincoln Road in 1993, people thought former model turned chef Jonathan Eismann was insane. Eleven years later, Lincoln Road is a bustling place to be and Pacific Time's dishes remain stunning hybrids of Chinese, Japanese, Korean, Vietnamese, Korean, Mongolian, and Indonesian flavors. Everything is fresh and the restaurant prides itself on not owning a single can opener or microwave. One of the best appetizers is the Indochine beef salad, seared Angus beef with a spicy satay vinaigrette. For a main course, the ever-changing menu offers many locally caught fish specialties such as Szechuan grilled mahimahi served on a bed of shredded shallots and ginger with a sweet sake-infused sauce and tempura-dunked sweet-potato slivers on the side. The famous chocolate bomb is every bit as decadent as they say, with hot bittersweet chocolate bursting from the cup-cakelike center—order it as soon as you sit down. The wine list is quite extensive and includes red and white wines from Italy, France, the Napa Valley, Australia, Argentina, New Zealand, and South Africa. The restaurant's best deal is its pretheater menu, a three-course dinner for only $30, available nightly from 6 to 7:30pm—one good reason to go early bird.

915 Lincoln Rd. (between Jefferson and Michigan aves.), South Beach. ✆ **305/534-5979.** Reservations recommended. Main courses $24–$32. AE, DC, MC, V. Sun–Thurs 6–11pm; Fri–Sat 6pm–midnight.

Pao ★ CHINESE   As the Asian contagion continues to sweep South Beach's culinary scene, it's hard to imagine how all the restaurants manage to coexist peacefully. It helps to be housed in a chic boutique hotel, like Pao is at the Clinton, and it also helps to have a mono-monikered native Chinese chef, like Pao does with Chef Kiki. Despite the modern setting, the food here is traditional, but this is not your average Sunday takeout. The prices here are astronomical for eat-out-of-the-carton Chinese, but not too high for the likes of Cher, who, while in town, ordered several hundred dollars worth of takeout for her and her crew. Barbecued pork spareribs, hot and sour snapper, and roast duck are among the best dishes here. Pao is an MSG-free restaurant, but that's about all that's free here. Be prepared to shell out major bucks for this chic Chinese.

Clinton Hotel, 825 Washington Ave., South Beach. ✆ **305/695-1957.** Reservations recommended. Main courses $16–$28, noodle and rice dishes $5–$14. AE, DC, MC, V. Daily 6–11pm.

Prime 112 ★★★ STEAKHOUSE   Part of the ever expanding culinary empire of Nemo, Big Pink, and Shoji Sushi, Prime 112 is the latest darling to join the exclusive group of restaurants in the hot South of Fifth Street area of South Beach. A sleek steakhouse ambiance and bustling bar (complete with dried strips of bacon in lieu of nuts) plays second fiddle to the beef, which is arguably the best in the entire city. The 12-ounce filet mignon is seared to perfection and can be enhanced with optional dipping sauces (for a price)—truffle, garlic herb, foie gras, and chipotle. The 22-ounce bone-in rib eye is fabulous, as is the gigantic 48-ounce porterhouse. Prime 112 also features a Kobe beef burger, a $30 version of sheer ecstasy, although fries are extra at $8, as are all the side dishes (the broccoli rabe sauteed in garlic is outstanding as are the scalloped potatoes)—typical in a steakhouse, but the prices here are hefty. A powerhouse crowd gathers here for lunch and dinner and reservations are more rare than the yellowfin tuna tartare appetizer, but should you be lucky enough to score such a, um, prime reservation, take it without hesitation.

112 Ocean Dr. (in The Browns Hotel), South Beach. ✆ **305/532-8112.** www.prime112.com. Reservations recommended. Main courses $28–$42. AE, DISC, MC, V. Daily 6:30pm–midnight; Mon–Fri 11:30am–3pm.

Tuscan Steak ★★ ITALIAN/STEAK   This excellent northern Italian restaurant, a member of the China Grill scion, is all about meat served Italian style, in large family-style portions. With a rich wood interior, the atmosphere is reminiscent of the dining room of a well-connected family—ornate and very loud.

The house salad is a massive undertaking of the classic antipasto, filled with shredded slices of salami and pepperoni, chunks of mozzarella, and a delicate vinaigrette. Be sure to order the sautéed spinach with garlic and the onion mashed potatoes with whichever steak you choose. All steaks are big enough for at least three people to share. The house specialty is a delicious T-bone steak served with pungent garlic purée. On any given weekend night, reservations are secondary to being friends with the ultratanned host, so expect a long wait for a table. The bar is the only place to wait if you can find a spot there, and drinks are rather pricey. The background music is straight out of Studio 54 and so is the flashy crowd. Despite the long waits, after one meal here, you'll likely want to kiss the ring of the true boss of this culinary mob scene—the chef.

433 Washington Ave., South Beach. ☎ 305/534-2233. Reservations strongly recommended on weekends. Main courses $20–$65. Family-style meals $50 per person, including appetizer and main course. AE, DISC, MC, V. Sun–Thurs 6–11pm; Fri–Sat 6pm–midnight.

Twelve Twenty 🌟🌟 AMERICAN PROGRESSIVE   The name is simple, but the cuisine at The Tides' swank Twelve Twenty restaurant is hardly that. Unlike the other flashy, splashy restaurants in the area, Twelve Twenty is quietly fabulous. No need for neon signs, a star chef who can juggle while he cooks, or other ridiculous gimmicks—it's all about the food here. The dining room exudes an elegance not found anywhere else on Ocean Drive, where the sounds of hushed conversation flow steadily amidst a backdrop of live piano music. Start with the astounding trio of tartars appetizer, tuna, salmon, and smoked marlin with a red chili lemon oil, seaweed salad, wasabi, and sesame; and then make room on the table for the Colossal Pacific Shrimp, a plate of crustaceans the size of small lobsters with pigeon pea ragout. For dessert, save room, because you will want to try the restaurant's signature Key lime cannoli or tropical Popsicle martinis such as the apricot-and-ginger version that comes complete with a mini Popsicle cum stirrer made of lychee; a pineapple-basil martini comes with a Guanabana Popsicle. An all-you-can-eat Sunday brunch may be pricey at $40, but you're paying for delicious food and soothing ambience that's the epitome of the phrase "easy like Sunday morning." Unlike the oft-harried atmospheres of other South Beach eateries—where scene serves as an aperitif—at Twelve Twenty, the only scene happening is the one that's on your plate.

In the Tides Hotel, 1220 Ocean Dr., South Beach. ☎ 305/604-5130. Reservations recommended. Main courses $21–$37. AE, MC, V. Sun–Thurs 7–11pm; Fri–Sat 7pm–midnight.

Wish 🌟🌟🌟 ECLECTIC/BRAZILIAN/FRENCH   Wish got its start as a haute vegetarian restaurant, located in the stylish Todd Oldham–designed The Hotel. It was, and still is, a terrific setting (request an outside table in the serene, umbrella-covered courtyard), but the foodies couldn't bear a meal without meat. First culinary whiz Andrea Curto came on board and redirected the meaty menu and then passed her whisk on to E. Michael Reidt, one of *Food & Wine* magazine's Ten Best New Chefs of 2001, whose own culinary wishes have come true in the form of fantastic French Brazilian cuisine. Three of Wish's finest are cachaca-marinated tuna over jicama-quinoa salad on spicy charred watermelon; tomato watermelon gazpacho with red pepper, cucumber, and Laura Chenel goat cheese; and pan-seared beef tenderloin on a truffled taro-root purée with stewed carrots and grilled asparagus.

In The Hotel, 801 Collins Ave., South Beach. ☎ 305/674-9474. Reservations recommended. Main courses $25–$33. AE, DC, DISC, MC, V. Daily noon–3pm; Tues–Sun 6pm–midnight.

EXPENSIVE

Barton G. The Restaurant ★★★ AMERICAN   For those who are jaded by Pan-fusion, Pan-everything cuisine these days, Barton G. The Restaurant is the culinary ticket to creative and delectable salvation. Located on a residential block on the west side of South Beach, Barton G., named after its owner who happens to be one of Miami's best known, most over the top event planners, is a place that looks like a trendy restaurant but eats like a show. Here, presentation is paramount. Take, for instance, the popcorn shrimp appetizer. This is not your average Red Lobster popcorn shrimp. Served on a plate full of, yes, popcorn, with field greens and the plump shrimp stuffed into an actual popcorn box, this dish is one of many awe-inspiring—and tasting—items you'll find in this, the most unique restaurant in Miami. A grilled sea bass that is light and flavorful is served in a brown paper bag with laundry clips keeping the steam in until your server unclips them and releases the flavor within. Desserts are equally outrageous, including three actual pints of homemade ice cream on a plate with all the toppings on the side, a giant plume of cotton candy reminiscent of drag diva Dame Edna's hair surrounded by three white-, dark-, and milk chocolate–covered popcorn balls, which, when cracked, reveal a sinful chocolate truffle inside. There's nothing ordinary about this seemingly ordinary restaurant. An elegant, well-lit indoor dining room is popular with the members of the socialite set, for whom Barton G. has done many an affair, while the bar area and outdoor courtyard is the place to be for the younger trendoids who appreciate what's on their plates as much as they do who's sitting next to them.

1427 West Ave., South Beach. ⓒ **305/672-8881.** Reservations suggested. Main courses $8–$30. AE, DC, DISC, MC, V. Daily 6pm–midnight.

Nemo ★★ PAN-ASIAN   Located on the quickly developing South Beach area known as SoFi (for "south of Fifth Street"), Nemo is a funky, high-style eatery with an open kitchen and an outdoor courtyard canopied by trees and lined with an eclectic mix of model types and foodies who haven't had that hard a time getting over the exit of former executive chef Michael Schwartz. Among the reasons to eat in this restaurant, whose name is actually "omen" spelled backward: grilled Indian-spiced pork chop; grilled local mahimahi with citrus and grilled sweet-onion salad, kimchi glaze, basil and crispy potatoes; and an inspired dessert menu by Hedy Goldsmith that's not for the faint of calories. Seating inside is comfy-cozy but borders on cramped. On Sunday mornings, the open kitchen is converted into a buffet counter for the restaurant's unparalleled brunch. Be prepared for a wait, however, which tends to spill out onto the street.

100 Collins Ave., South Beach. ⓒ **305/532-4550.** Reservations recommended. Main courses $22–$36; Sun brunch $29. AE, MC, V. Mon–Fri noon–3pm and 7pm–midnight; Sun 11am–3pm and 6–11pm. Valet parking $10 or $20 for curbside.

Shoji Sushi ★ SUSHI   Despite the sushi saturation on South Beach, Shoji stands apart from the typical sashimi and California roll routine with expertly prepared, exquisitely fresh, and innovative top-notch rolls. The sleek sister to its next-door neighbor Nemo, Shoji is known for its authentic Japanese box sushi technique, in which the sushi, rice, and ingredients are packed into a tidy, tasty cake that won't crumble into your lap. Among the rolls I can't seem to get enough of here are the hamachi jalapeño—cilantro, daikon sprout, asparagus, avocado, and jalapeños—and the spicy lobster roll, which consists of mango, avocado, scallion, shiso, salmon egg, and huge chunks of lobster. Wash it all down with the saketinis and my personal fave, the gingertini, which is made with ginger, vodka, triple sec, ginger ale, and pickled ginger juice.

100 Collins Ave., South Beach. ⓒ 305/532-4245. Reservations recommended. Main courses $20–$25. AE, MC, V. Mon–Fri noon–3pm; Mon–Thurs 6pm–midnight; Fri–Sun 6pm–1am. Valet parking $10.

Talula ⭐⭐⭐ CREATIVE AMERICAN   Take two star chefs and combine their epicurean efforts and you've got Talula, one of the most creative, refreshing restaurants to come onto the South Beach scene since Barton G. The Restaurant (see above). Owned by husband and wife team Andrea Curto-Randazzo, formerly of Wish, and Frank Randazzo, formerly of the now defunct Gaucho Room, Talula is a blissful marriage of many flavors, as seen in such signature dishes as grilled Sonoma foie gras, with caramelized figs, blue corn cakes, chile syrup, and candied walnuts, and grilled Atlantic salmon with potato-smoked bacon hash, asparagus, and a Dijon garlic vinaigrette. Daily specials always include a chopped salad, soup, risotto, and meat or fish dish. The wine list is well balanced, featuring 85 vintages from California, Italy, France, Australia, and South America. Wines by the glass are a reasonable, un-South Beach like $6 to $9. As to be expected with any restaurant in South Beach, Talula is cool looking, with an unpretentious, warm decor and outdoor garden patio. An exhibition kitchen is a tempting seating option, with five seats allowing a priceless view of the culinary action.

210 23rd St., South Beach. ⓒ 305/672-0778. Reservations recommended. Main courses $18–$32. AE, MC, V. Tues–Thurs 6:30–11pm; Fri–Sat 6:30–11:30pm; Sun 6–10pm; open for lunch Tues–Fri noon–2:30pm. Happy hour Tues–Sun 5–7pm.

MODERATE

Balan's ⭐ MEDITERRANEAN   Balan's provides undeniable evidence that the Brits actually do know a thing or two about cuisine. A direct import from London's hip Soho area, Balan's draws inspiration from various Mediterranean and Asian influences, labeling its cuisine "Mediterrasian." With a brightly colored interior straight out of a mod '60s flick, Balan's is a local favorite among the gay and arty crowds. The moderately priced food is rather good here—especially the sweet-potato soufflé with leeks and roasted garlic; fried goat cheese and portobello mushrooms; and the Chilean sea bass with roasted tomato. When in doubt, the restaurant's signature lobster club sandwich is always a good choice. Adding to the ambience is the restaurant's people-watching vantage point on Lincoln Road.

1022 Lincoln Rd. (between Lenox and Michigan), South Beach. ⓒ 305/534-9191. Reservations accepted, except for weekend brunch. Main courses $7–$25 (breakfast and dinner specials weekdays). AE, DISC, MC, V. Sun–Thurs 8am–midnight; Fri–Sat 8am–1am; Sat–Sun brunch noon–3:30pm.

Bond St. Lounge ⭐ SUSHI   A New York City import, the sceney Bond St. Lounge is located in the basement of the shabby chic Townhouse Hotel and is packing in hipsters as tightly as the crab meat in a California roll. Despite its tiny size, Bond St. Lounge's superfresh nigiri and sashimi and funky sushi rolls such as the sun-dried tomato and avocado or the arugula crispy potato are worth cramming in for. As the evening progresses, however, Bond St. becomes more of a bar scene than a restaurant, but sushi is always available at the bar to accompany your sake Bloody Mary.

Townhouse Hotel, 150 20th St., South Beach. ⓒ 305/398-1806. Reservations recommended. Sushi $6–$15. AE, MC, V. Daily 6pm–2am.

Grillfish ⭐⭐ SEAFOOD   From the beautiful Byzantine-style mural and the gleaming oak bar, you'd think you were eating in a much more expensive restaurant, but Grillfish manages to pay the exorbitant South Beach rent with the help of a loyal local following who come for fresh, simple seafood in a relaxed but upscale atmosphere.

The servers are friendly and know the menu well. The barroom seafood chowder is full of chunks of shellfish, as well as some fresh whitefish filets in a tomato broth. The small ear of corn, included with each entree, is about as close as you'll get to any type of vegetable offering besides the pedestrian salad. Still, at these prices, it's worth a visit to try some local fare including mako shark, swordfish, tuna, marlin, and wahoo.

1444 Collins Ave. (corner of Española Way), South Beach. (℃) **305/538-9908.** www.grillfish.com. Reservations for 6 or more only. Main courses $9–$26. AE, DC, DISC, MC, V. Daily 11:30am–4pm and 5:30pm–midnight.

Joe Allen ⭐ *Finds* AMERICAN   It's hard to compete in a city with haute spots everywhere you look, but Joe Allen, a restaurant that has proven itself in both New York and London, has stood up to the challenge by establishing itself off the beaten path in possibly the only area of South Beach that has managed to remain impervious to trendiness and overdevelopment. Located on the bay side of the beach, Joe Allen is nestled in an unassuming building conspicuously devoid of neon lights, valet parkers, and fashionable pedestrians. Inside, however, one discovers a hidden jewel: a stark yet elegant interior and no-nonsense, fairly priced, ample-portioned dishes such as meatloaf, pizza, fresh fish, and salads. The scene has a homey feel favored by locals looking to escape the hype without compromising quality.

1787 Purdy Ave./Sunset Harbor Dr. (3 blocks west of Alton Rd.), South Beach. (℃) **305/531-7007.** Reservations recommended, especially on weekends. Main courses $15–$25. MC, V. Open daily 11:30am–11:30pm.

L'Entrecote de Paris ⭐ FRENCH   New York's got the Statue of Liberty and Miami's got L'Entrecote de Paris. We don't complain. Everything in this little piece of Paris, a classy, albeit recently expanded, little bistro, is simple. For dinner, it's either steak, chicken, or seafood—I'd stick to the steaks, particularly the house special, L'Entrecote's French steak, with all-you-can-eat french fries (or *pommes frites,* rather). The salmon looks like spa cuisine, served with a pile of bald steamed potatoes and a salad with simple greens and an unmatchable vinaigrette. The steak, on the other hand, is the stuff cravings are made of, even if you're not a die-hard carnivore. Its salty sharp sauce is rich but not thick, and full of the beef's natural flavor. I loved the *profiteroles au chocolat,* a perfect puff pastry filled with vanilla ice cream and topped with a dark bittersweet chocolate sauce. Most diners are very Euro and pack a petit attitude. If you want a quiet dinner, come early, because as the night grows long, L'Entrecote transforms itself into a lounge, with DJs who do *not* spin Edith Piaf's Greatest Hits.

419 Washington Ave., South Beach. (℃) **305/673-1002.** Reservations recommended on weekends. Main courses $16–$24. DC, MC, V. Tues–Sun 7pm–midnight; bar stays open later when there's a crowd.

Macaluso's ⭐⭐ ITALIAN   This restaurant epitomizes the Italians' love for—and mastery of—savory, plentiful, down-home Staten Island–style food. While the storefront restaurant is intimate and demure in nature, there's nothing delicate about the bold mix of flavors in every meat and pasta dish here. Catch the fantastic clam pie when in season—the portions are huge. Pricier items vary throughout the season, but will likely feature fresh fish hand picked by Chef (and owner) Michael, the Don of the kitchen, who is so accommodating he'll take special requests or even bring to your table a complimentary signature meatball. If he doesn't, don't hesitate to ask your waiter for one, he'll be glad to bring it to you. Everyone will recommend perennial favorites such as the rigatoni and broccoli rabe. There are also delicious desserts that range from homemade anisette cookies to Patricia Scott's pastries. The wine list is also good. The Georges Dubœuf Beaujolais, at $22 a bottle, is a steal, when you consider that it comes nicely chilled with slices of luscious Georgia peaches, which make a great and affordable dessert by themselves. *Celeb alert:* Macaluso's is where Demi Moore and tadpole Ashton Kutcher made their official debut as a couple while in Miami.

1747 Alton Rd., Miami Beach. ⓒ 305/604-1811. No reservations accepted. Main courses $14–$28; pizza $8–$13. MC, V. Tues–Sat 6pm–midnight; Sun 6–11pm. After 10:30pm, only pies are served. Closed Mon.

Spiga ★★ ITALIAN   If you want a side of scene with your spaghetti, don't even think of dining at Spiga, a place that's so on the down low that many of South Beach's most ostentatious hipsters have never even heard of it, which is why people like Julia Roberts choose to eat here rather than Ago while in town. The complimentary bruschetta with grilled eggplant, served to you at one of the few tables inside or out, is the first of many culinary treats. The simple gnocchi with tomato and basil is a garlicky sensation, not to mention a most filling entree. The fresh asparagus baked in Parmesan cheese is so fresh that gourmands insist that Alice Waters, the queen of organic cooking, had something to do with it, and the red snapper with calamata olives, fresh tomatoes, capers, and onions is a refreshingly simple departure from the fusion variety that can be found in almost any area restaurant. The place is extremely romantic and vaguely reminiscent of a Florentine trattoria.

Hotel Impala, 1228 Collins Ave., South Beach. ⓒ 305/534-0079. Reservations accepted. Main courses $7–$20. AE, DC, MC, V. Daily 6pm–midnight.

Van Dyke Cafe ★ AMERICAN   News Cafe's younger, less harried sibling, Van Dyke is a locals' favorite, at which people-watching is also premium, but attitude is practically nonexistent. Like News, the menu here is pretty cut and dry—sandwiches, salads, eggs, and so on, but the Van Dyke's warm, wood-floored interior, upstairs jazz bar, accessible parking, and intense chocolate soufflé make it a less taxing alternative. Also, unlike News, Van Dyke turns into a sizzling nightspot, featuring live jazz nearly every night of the week (a $5 cover charge is added to your bill if you sit at a table; the bar's free). Outside there's a vast tree-lined seating area that provides a front row seat to the people-watching. Those allergic to or afraid of dogs may want to reconsider eating here, as Van Dyke is also a canine hot spot.

846 Lincoln Rd., South Beach. ⓒ 305/534-3600. Reservations recommended for dinner. Main courses $9–$17. AE, DC, MC, V. Daily 8am–2am.

MODERATE
Big Pink ★ *Kids* AMERICAN   Real Food for Real People is the motto to which this restaurant strictly adheres. Located on what used to be a gritty corner of Collins Avenue, Big Pink—owned by the folks at the higher-end Nemo—is quickly identified by a whimsical Pippi Longstocking–type mascot on a sign outside. Scooters and motorcycles line the streets surrounding the place, which is a favorite among beach bums, club kids, and those craving Big Pink's comforting and hugely portioned pizzas, sandwiches, salads, and hamburgers. The

fare is above average at best, and the menu is massive, but it comes with a good dose of kitsch, such as their "gourmet" spin on the classic TV dinner, which is done perfectly, right down to the compartmentalized dessert. Televisions line the bar area, and family-style table arrangement (there are several booths, too) promotes camaraderie among diners. Outdoor tables are available. Even picky kids will like the food here, and parents can enjoy the family-friendly atmosphere (not the norm for South Beach) without worrying if their kids are making too much noise.

157 Collins Ave., Miami Beach. © **305/532-4700**. Main courses $13–$20. AE, DC, MC, V. Sun–Thurs 9am–1am; Fri–Sat 9am–2am.

El Rancho Grande ★★ MEXICAN   Hidden on a side street off of Lincoln Road, El Rancho Grande is a favorite local cantina that has attracted the likes of Cher and Matt Damon thanks to its ultra fresh fare and unassuming ambience. With a Pottery Barn meets Acapulco decor, El Rancho Grande doesn't hold anything back when it comes to the cuisine. The Aztec Soup, a hot and spicy blend of chicken and tortilla strips, is some of the best I've had. The salsa here is not at all watery and is freshly made—a tongue tickling blend of spices, cilantro, tomatoes, onions, and peppers, and the Mexican favorites of burritos, enchiladas, and fajitas are all very well represented at this restaurant. All portions are huge and can be shared or taken home for extra meal mileage. There is a scene here, but it's very relaxed. Margaritas are a little weak when frozen and better ordered on the rocks. Expect a wait at the small bar for your table, especially on weekends. Limited outdoor seating is also available.

1626 Pennsylvania Ave., Miami Beach. © **305/673-0480**. Main courses $10–$19. AE, DC, MC, V. Daily 11am–11pm.

INEXPENSIVE

11th Street Diner AMERICAN   The only real diner on the beach, the 11th Street Diner is the antidote to a late night run to Denny's. Be forewarned that some of Miami's most colorful characters, especially the drunk ones, convene here at odd hours and your greasy spoon experience can quickly turn into a three ring circus. Uprooted from its 1948 Wilkes-Barre, Pennsylvania, foundation, the actual structure was dismantled and rebuilt on a busy—and colorful (a gay bar is right next door so be on the lookout for very flamboyant drag queens) corner of Washington Avenue. Although it can use a good window cleaning, it remains a popular round-the-clock spot that attracts all walks of life. If you're craving french fries, order them smothered in mozzarella with a side of gravy—a tasty concoction that I call disco fries because of its popularity amongst starving clubbers.

1065 Washington Ave., South Beach. © **305/534-6373**. Items $8–$15. AE, MC. Daily 24 hr.

Front Porch Café ★ AMERICAN   Located in an unassuming, rather dreary-looking Art Deco hotel, the Front Porch Café is a relaxed local hangout known for cheap breakfasts. Some of the servers tend to be a bit attitudinal and lackadaisical (many are bartenders or club kids by night), so this isn't the place to be if you're in a hurry, especially on the weekends, when the place is packed all day long and lines are the norm. Enjoy home-style French toast with bananas and walnuts, omelets, fresh fruit salads, pizzas, and classic breakfast pancakes that put IHOP to shame. If you're looking to avoid the tourists and prefer to dine with the locals, Front Porch is where it's at for breakfast, lunch, and even dinner.

In the Penguin Hotel, 1418 Ocean Dr., South Beach. © **305/531-8300**. Main courses $5–$16. AE, DC, DISC, MC, V. Daily 8am–10:30pm.

La Sandwicherie SANDWICHES   You can get mustard, mayo, or oil and vinegar on sandwiches elsewhere in town, but you'd be missing out on all the local flavor. This gourmet sandwich bar, open until the crack of dawn, caters to ravenous club kids, biker types, and the body artists who work in the tattoo parlor next door. For many people, in fact, no night of clubbing is complete without capping it off with a turkey sub from La Sandwicherie.

229 14th St. (behind the Amoco station), South Beach. ℂ 305/532-8934. Sandwiches and salads $6–$12. AE, MC, V. Daily 9am–5am. Delivery 9:30am–11pm.

Lincoln Road Café ✦ *Value* CUBAN   The Van Dyke Cafe (p. 96) is good for people-watching and reliable food, but if you're starving, not in the mood to wait for a table, and don't want to spend more than $10 for breakfast, head over to the Lincoln Road Café. Although it harkens back to the days of old South Beach, before the trendoids came and took over Lincoln Road with minimalistic, ultra modern decor and uncomfortable chairs, Lincoln Road Café remains a local hotspot for cheap breakfasts, lunches, and dinners. Breakfast is the real bargain, however, where for a mere $6, you can gorge yourself on eggs, bacon, ham, sausage, Cuban toast, and a mind blowing, brain buzzing café con leche. For lunch and dinner, there are hefty portions of Cuban faves from black beans and rice to arroz con pollo, all at low, low prices. Lincoln Road Café doesn't need Philippe Starck's designs to help bring in crowds: Thanks to cheap, good food, this unassuming eatery is a hotspot in its own right.

941 Lincoln Rd., South Beach. ℂ 305/538-8066. Items $7–$11. AE, DC, MC, V. Daily 8am–midnight.

Mama Vieja ✦ COLOMBIAN   This funky Colombian hangout looks like a total dive from the outside, but once inside you will want to dive right in to the supremely fresh national specialties such as *pargo rojo estofado a la mama vieja* (red snapper stuffed with a supercreamy and delicate seafood sauce in a rice base). Brightly painted walls and elevated porches look out onto a large-screen TV showing music videos from the old country. The walls and ceilings are decorated with hundreds of hats that have been donated by customers and signed in exchange for a free meal. Bring in an interesting hat and mention it to the server before placing your order so that he or she can bring you to the attention of the owner. All the dishes here are worth trying and are so reasonably priced that it's easy to order a lot. Try to save room for the milky sweet desserts and a good strong coffee—you'll need it if you want to dance it off after at Lola, the very popular, unpretentious hot spot next door. If not, there's live music here, too.

235 23rd St. (just west of Collins Ave.), South Beach. ℂ 305/538-2400. Main courses $4.95–$15. AE, DC, DISC, MC, V. Mon and Wed noon–11pm; Thurs–Sun noon–midnight. Closed Tues. Nightclub midnight–5am Thurs–Sun.

News Cafe ✦ AMERICAN   This South Beach cafe cum landmark hasn't fallen off the radar as far as buzz and hype are concerned. The quintessential South Beach experience, News is still au courant, albeit swarming with mostly tourists. Unless it's appallingly hot or rainy out, you should wait for an outside table, which is where you need to be to fully appreciate the experience. Service is abysmal and often arrogant (perhaps because the tip is included), but the menu is reliable, running the gamut from sandwiches and salads to pasta dishes and omelets. My favorite here is the Middle Eastern platter, a dip lover's paradise, with hummus, tahini, tabouleh, babaganoush, and fresh pita bread. If it's not too busy, feel free to order just a cappuccino—your server may snarl, but that's what News is all about; creative types like to bring their laptops and sit here all day (or all night—this place is open 24 hr. a day). If you're by yourself and need something to read, there's an extensive collection of national and international newspapers and magazines at the in-house newsstand. News Cafe also opened another clone, Café Cardozo, at the Cardozo Hotel at 1300 Ocean Dr. on South Beach, in case 5 blocks is too much to walk to the original.

800 Ocean Dr., South Beach. (C) 305/538-6397. Items $5–$20. AE, DC, MC, V. Open 24 hr.

Pizza Rustica ⭐ PIZZA It's four in the morning and there's a line out the door at Pizza Rustica, not because they're short staffed, but because Pizza Rustica has become a nutritional mainstay for Miami's nocturnal set. Why wait on line at the crack of dawn when there are countless other late night slice spots? The pizza here is *that* good. So good they had to open another Pizza Rustica just blocks away. Day or night—and morning, this place is always slammed with people who must fulfill their craving for meal-sized slices of moan-inducing Tuscan-style pizza. Spinach and Gorgonzola cheese blend blissfully with a touch of olive oil and garlic that will last for a few hours to remind you of just how good their pizza is. Other designer varieties include four cheese, arugula, chicken, and rosemary-potato. Pizza Rustica's slices are made so that you can either scarf down an entire slab, which is the size of a floor tile, or ask them to cut the slice into fours, creating dainty, bite-sized installments. If the original spot is too busy, try your luck at their second location at 1447 Washington Ave. (between 8th and 9th sts.), South Beach (© **305/538-6009**) and 667 Lincoln Rd. (© **305/ 672-2334**). Whatever location, it's worth the wait.

863 Washington Ave., South Beach. (C) 305/674-8244. Slice $3.75. No credit cards. Daily 11am–6am.

Puerto Sagua ⭐ CUBAN/SPANISH This brown-walled diner is one of the only old holdouts on South Beach. Its steady stream of regulars ranges from *abuelitos* (little old grandfathers) to hipsters who stop in after clubbing. It has endured because the food is good, if a little greasy. Some of the less heavy dishes are a super-chunky fish soup with pieces of whole flaky grouper, chicken, and seafood paella, or marinated kingfish. Also good are most of the shrimp dishes, especially the shrimp in garlic sauce, which is served with white rice and salad.

This is one of the most reasonably priced places left on the beach for simple, hearty fare. Don't be intimidated by the hunched, older waiters in their white button-down shirts and black pants. Even if you don't speak Spanish, they're usually willing to do charades. Anyway, the extensive menu, which ranges from BLTs to grilled lobsters to yummy fried plantains, is translated into English. Hurry, before another boutique goes up in its place.

700 Collins Ave., South Beach. (C) 305/673-1115. Main courses $6–$24; sandwiches and salads $5–$10. AE, DC, MC, V. Daily 7:30am–2am.

Sport Café ⭐ ITALIAN If you're in the mood for great Italian food—nothing fancy—but don't feel like dressing up and dealing with surly hosts and "reservations only" rudeness, look no further than Sport Café, known for its delicious, down home, reasonably priced, and homemade Italian food. Seating is either inside the casual dining room or outside in the more romantic, less sporty private outdoor garden. The menu is pretty simple—penne al arrabiata, spaghetti, and so on—but always check the daily specials. The vibe here ranges from quiet and intimate to frenetic, especially when the soccer matches being broadcast on the restaurant's televisions kick the crowd into a European-style frenzy. Make sure to ask if the owners' mama is in the kitchen, where she cooks her not-always-offered secret lasagna and fabulous gnocchi.

560 Washington Ave., South Beach. (C) 305/674-9700. Reservations accepted for 4 or more. Main courses $7–$20; sandwiches and pizzas $6–$9. AE, MC, V. Daily noon–12:30am.

MIAMI BEACH, SURFSIDE, BAL HARBOUR & SUNNY ISLES

The area north of the Art Deco District—from about 21st Street to 163rd Street—had its heyday in the 1950s when huge hotels and gambling halls blocked the view of the ocean. Now, many of the old hotels have been converted into condos or budget lodgings, and the bayfront mansions have been renovated by and for wealthy entrepreneurs, families, and speculators. The area has many more residents, albeit seasonal, than visitors. On the culinary front, the result is a handful of superexpensive, traditional restaurants as well as a number of value-oriented spots.

For a map of the restaurants in this section, see the "Where to Stay & Dine in Miami Beach, Surfside, Bal Harbour, Sunny Isles & North Beach" map on p. 75.

VERY EXPENSIVE

The Forge Restaurant ★★★ STEAK/AMERICAN   English oak paneling and Tiffany glass suggest high prices and haute cuisine, and that's exactly what you get at The Forge. Each elegant dining room possesses its own character and features high ceilings, ornate chandeliers, and European artwork. The atmosphere is elegant but not too stuffy. On Wednesday night (the party night here), however, it's pandemonium as the who's who of Miami society gather for dinner, dancing, and schmoozing. Like the rest of the menu, appetizers are mostly classics, from Beluga caviar to baked onion soup to shrimp cocktail and escargot. When they're in season, order the stone crabs. For the main course, any of the seafood, chicken, or veal dishes are recommendable, but The Forge is especially known for its award-winning steaks. Its wine selection is equally lauded—ask for a tour of the cellar. *Celeb alert:* None other than Michael Jackson has dined here on numerous occasions and considers The Forge one of his favorite restaurants of all time.

432 Arthur Godfrey Rd. (41st St.), Miami Beach. © **305/538-8533.** Reservations recommended. Main courses $25–$60. AE, DC, MC, V. Sun–Thurs 6pm–midnight; Fri–Sat 6pm–1am.

Shula's Steak House ★★ AMERICAN/STEAK   Climb a sweeping staircase in the Alexander All-Suite Luxury Hotel and go through the glass hallway—designed like an atrium, so exotic flora and fauna beckon from both within and without—and you'll find yourself in this magnificent restaurant that has been acclaimed as one of the greatest steakhouses in all of North America. If you're feeling adventurous, try the 48-ounce club (you can get your name engraved on a gold plaque if you can finish this absolutely *huge* piece of meat) or settle for the 20-ounce Kansas City strip or the 12-ounce filet mignon. Fresh seafood abounds when in season, and the oysters Rockefeller are a particularly good choice. The entertaining staff is very knowledgeable. The restaurant also has the "No Name Lounge," where live piano music, premium spirits, and cigar smoking are available.

There's another branch of Shula's at 7601 NW 154th St. (in Don Shula's Golf Club off the Palmetto Expwy.; © **305/820-8102**) in West Dade.

In the Alexander Hotel, 5225 Collins Ave., Miami Beach. © **305/341-6565.** Reservations recommended. Main courses $23–$78. AE, DISC, MC, V. Daily 11am–3:30pm and 6–11pm. Free valet parking.

EXPENSIVE

Christine Lee's ★★ CHINESE   This Cantonese restaurant is a 35-year-old Miami staple that serves excellent but overpriced Chinese-style dishes featuring steak, shrimp, and lobster sauce, as well as a good rendition of steak kew, a

Cantonese dish with oyster sauce and hot bean paste. Considering the dearth of good Chinese restaurants in Miami, this is a good choice if you absolutely *must* satisfy your cravings for Chinese, but it will definitely cost you more than it should.

17082 Collins Ave. (1 block south of the Rascal House, in the RK strip mall, directly on Collins Ave.), Sunny Isles. ⓒ 305/947-1717. Reservations recommended. Main courses $8–$32. AE, DISC, MC, V. Daily 11:30am–3pm and 4–10:30pm (not open for lunch May–Sept).

Crystal Café ★★★ CONTINENTAL/NEW WORLD   Although there is no shortage of trendy, swanky, sceney restaurants in the South Beach and Miami Beach areas, what *is* lacking is that charming, cozy, local gourmet restaurant where the chef/owner seems to know everybody's name. Enter Crystal Café, the missing link in the chain of food establishments that prides itself more on the celebrity clientele than the stellar cuisine. This place dares to be different—and not in a postmodern minimalistic decor-cuisine kind of way, either. Not only is the food spectacular, but the ambience is also extremely inviting and romantic and one that you will want to revisit. Chef/owner Klime is a mastermind of exquisite culinary preparation and attention to detail, from his drool-worthy goat cheese terrine appetizer to his masterful filet mignon. The shrimp cake appetizer is the size of a bread plate and rests on top of a small mound of lightly sautéed watercress and mushrooms. Surrounding the delicately breaded disk are concentric circles of beautiful sauces. The veal Marsala is served in a luscious brown sauce thickened not with heavy cream or flour, but with delicate vegetable broth and a hearty mix of mushrooms. The osso buco is a masterpiece. The wine list is award winning and recognized by experts from all over the world as one of the best. And it's constantly evolving. So is the menu. And I could go on. Words really can't do Crystal Café the justice it deserves. When you go, however, ask for Chef Klime. He will be more than happy to say hello and explain his philosophy that has made his restaurant one of Miami's tastiest standouts.

726 41st St., Miami Beach. ⓒ 305/673-8266. Reservations recommended on weekends. Main courses $13–$28. AE, DC, DISC, MC, V. Sun and Tues–Thurs 5–10pm; Fri–Sat 5–11pm.

MODERATE

Cafe Prima Pasta ★★ ITALIAN   Once a small unknown trattoria on a very trafficky, tacky street, Cafe Prima Pasta has expanded into a place to be for amazing Italian food and quite a bit of fanfare. Because there was always a massive wait that spilled out onto the street, the cafe has expanded to include ample outdoor seating that is set back from the street noise and traffic thanks to some creative landscaping. The pasta here is homemade and the kitchen's choice ingredients include prize worthy ripe, juicy tomatoes, imported olive oil that would cost you a boatload if you bought a bottle in the store, fresh, drippy mozzarella, and fish that tastes as if it had just been caught right out back. The zesty, spicy garlic and oil that is brought out as dip for the bread is something you may want to keep with you during the course of your meal as it doubles as extra seasoning for your food, not that it's necessary. Though tables are packed in a bit, the atmosphere still manages to be romantic. Because of the chef's fancy for garlic, this is a three Altoid restaurant, so be prepared to pop a few or request that they go light on the stuff.

414 71st St. (half a block east of the Byron movie theater), Miami Beach. ⓒ 305/867-0106. Reservations not accepted (except for parties of 6 or more). Main courses $9–$19; pastas $12–$19. V, MC. Mon–Thurs noon–midnight; Fri noon–1am; Sat 1pm–1am; Sun 5pm–midnight.

Cafe Ragazzi ✦✦ ITALIAN   This diminutive Italian cafe, with its rustic decor and a swift, knowledgeable waitstaff, enjoys great success for its tasty, simple pastas. The spicy puttanesca sauce with a subtle hint of fish is perfectly prepared. Also recommended is the salmon with radicchio. You can choose from many decent salads and carpacci, too. Lunch specials are a real steal at $7, including soup, salad, and daily pasta. Unlike Cafe Prima Pasta (see above), Cafe Ragazzi is light on sceniness—people come here for the food only. Nevertheless, you can still expect to wait on weekend nights.

9500 Harding Ave. (on the corner of 95th St.), Surfside. ✆ 305/866-4495. Reservations accepted for 3 or more. Main courses $9–$18. MC, V. Mon–Fri 11:30am–3pm; daily 5–11:30pm.

Wolfie Cohen's Rascal House ✦ DELI   Although Jerry's Famous Deli on South Beach has taken away some of the Rascal House's younger patrons, the retro fabulous vibe at Wolfie's is inimitable. Open since 1954 and still going strong, this historic, nostalgic culinary extravaganza is one of Miami Beach's greatest traditions. Scooch into one of the vinyl booths, practically antique relics of the days when Frank Sinatra and his Rat Pack used to dine here after performances, and review the huge menu that's loaded with authentic Jewish staples. Consider the classic corned beef sandwich, stuffed cabbage, brisket, or potato pancakes. Make sure to warm up to the servers, many of whom have been here since day one, and they will provide you with a coveted wax paper bag (a culinary souvenir, if you will) so you can take home your uneaten Danish and rolls. There is another Wolfie's in Boca Raton, at 2006 NW Executive Center Circle (✆ **561/982-8899**).

17190 Collins Ave. (at 163rd St.), Sunny Isles. ✆ **305/947-4581**. Main courses $8–$30. AE, MC, V. Sun–Thurs 6:30am–1am; Fri–Sat 6:30am–2am.

INEXPENSIVE
Sheldon's Drugs ✦ *Value* AMERICAN   This typical old-fashioned drugstore counter was a favorite breakfast spot of Isaac Bashevis Singer. Consider stopping into this historic site for a good piece of pie and a side of history. According to legend, the author was sitting at Sheldon's eating a bagel and eggs when his wife got the call in 1978 that he had won the Nobel Prize for Literature. The menu hasn't changed much since then. You can get eggs and oatmeal and a good tuna melt. A blue-plate special might be generic spaghetti and meatballs or grilled frankfurters. The food is pretty basic, but you can't beat the prices.

9501 Harding Ave., Surfside. ✆ **305/866-6251**. Main courses $4–$8; soups and sandwiches $2–$7. AE, DISC, MC, V. Mon–Sat 7am–7pm; Sun 7am–4pm.

NORTH MIAMI BEACH
Although there aren't many hotels in North Dade, the population in the winter months explodes due to the onslaught of seasonal residents from the Northeast. A number of exclusive condominiums and country clubs, including William's Island, Turnberry, and the Jockey Club, breed a demanding clientele, many of whom dine out nightly. That's good news for visitors, who can find superior service and cuisine at value prices.

For a map of the restaurants in this section, see the "Where to Stay & Dine in Miami Beach, Surfside, Bal Harbour, Sunny Isles & North Beach" map on p. 75.

VERY EXPENSIVE
Chef Allen's ✦✦✦ NEW WORLD CUISINE   If anyone deserves to have a restaurant named after him, it's chef Allen Susser, winner of the esteemed James

Beard Award for Best American Chef in the Southeast—the Academy Award of cuisine—and practically every other form of praise and honor awarded by the most discriminating palates. Chef Allen, the man, is royalty around here. Chef Allen, the restaurant, is his province, and foodies are his disciples. His platform? New World Cuisine and the harmony of exotic tropical fruits, spices, and vegetables. It is under Chef Allen's magic that ordinary Key limes and mangos reappear in the form of succulent salsas and sauces. A traditional antipasto is transformed into a Caribbean one, with papaya-pineapple barbeque shrimp, jerk calamari, and charred rare tuna. Whole yellowtail in coconut milk and curry sauce is a particularly spectacular entree. Unlike other restaurants where location is key, Chef Allen's, located in the rear of a strip mall, could be in the desert and hordes of people would still make the trek.

19088 NE 29th Ave. (at Biscayne Blvd.), North Miami Beach. (C) **305/935-2900.** Reservations recommended. Main courses $25–$40. AE, DC, MC, V. Sun–Thurs 6–10pm; Fri–Sat 6–11pm.

Prime Grill ⋆ KOSHER STEAKHOUSE   The only thing that's not entirely kosher about this place is the fact that it serves sushi in addition to the steaks it's known for. This glatt kosher New York import has opened in the heavily Jewish neighborhood of Aventura to rave reviews not only from gourmands but from mothers and grandmothers of the single children they're so desperate to marry off. Upscale with a sleek, sophisticated interior, this 12,000-square-foot waterfront restaurant has an executive chef formerly of New York's legendary Windows on the World cooking up kosher New York rib steaks, T-bones, and Delmonico cuts that are hand selected from the restaurant's private aging room. All steaks are served with béarnaise and red wine shallot sauce and tobacco onion rings. Wait, tobacco onion rings? Since when is tobacco kosher? Anyway, if you're not into meat, there are several excellent fish dishes such as the oak grilled tuna mignon. Side dishes are a la carte and include excellent garlic mashed potatoes and creamed spinach. And single people beware: some of the waitstaff has been known to try to play matchmaker.

3599 NE 207th St., North Miami Beach. (C) **305/692-9392.** Reservations recommended. Main courses $19–$34. AE, DC, MC, V. Sun–Thurs 5–11pm; Sunday brunch 11:30am–3pm.

EXPENSIVE

The Fish Joint ⋆⋆ SEAFOOD   People jonesing for an out-of-this-world high that won't get them arrested can usually be found lining up at this small neighborhood seafood spot where the frills are on the fish and not the decor. Industrial kitsch is the best description of The Fish Joint's interior, which tends to be on the loud side, but you don't go here for the decor: Simple, fresh fish is the draw, prepared in a multitude of ways, including the Chilean sea bass in sweet and sour glaze or the grouper oreganato. If you like shrimp, order the shrimp cocktail—the crustaceans are absolutely Jurassic-sized! As an added touch, every meal comes with irresistible potato pancakes rather than your average boring baked potato. No matter what you order, however, you're guaranteed to experience a high of sorts thanks to the stellar quality of this one-of-a-kind fish joint.

2570 NE Miami Gardens Dr., North Miami Beach. (C) **305/936-8333.** Main courses $17–$24. AE, DC, MC, V. Sun–Thurs 5–10pm; Fri–Sat 5–11pm.

Lagoon ⋆ SEAFOOD/CONTINENTAL   This old bayfront fish house has been around since 1936. Major road construction nearby should have guaranteed its doom years ago, but the excellent view and incredible specials make it a worthwhile stop. If you can disregard the somewhat dirty bathrooms and nonchalant service, you'll find the best-priced juicy Maine lobsters around.

Yes, it's true! Lobster lovers can get two 1¼ pounders for $26. Try them broiled with a light buttery-seasoned coating. This dish is not only inexpensive but incredibly succulent, too. Side dishes include fresh vegetables, like broccoli or asparagus, as well as a huge baked potato, stuffed or plain.

488 Sunny Isles Blvd. (163rd St.), North Miami Beach. ℂ 305/947-6661. Reservations accepted. Main courses $20–$47; appetizers $10–$14. AE, MC, V. Daily 4:30–10pm. Happy hour daily 4:30–6pm.

DOWNTOWN

Downtown Miami is a large, sprawling area divided by the Brickell Bridge into two distinct areas: Brickell Avenue and the bayfront area near Biscayne Boulevard. You shouldn't walk from one to the other—it's quite a distance and unsafe at night. Convenient Metromover stops do adjoin the areas, so for a quarter, it's better to hop on the scenic sky tram (even though it's closed after midnight).

For a map of the restaurants in this section, see the "Where to Stay & Dine in Key Biscayne, Downtown Miami, West Miami, Airport Area, North Dade, Little Havana, Coral Gables & Coconut Grove" map on p. 77.

VERY EXPENSIVE

Azul ★★★ GLOBAL FUSION   If there were an epicurean version of the Academy Awards, this restaurant would win best director, hands down. Executive chef Michelle Bernstein, Miami's wunderkind in the kitchen, creates a tour de force of international cuisine, inspired by Caribbean, French, Argentine, Asian, and even American flavors. Like a stunning designer gown, the restaurant's decor, with its waterfront view, high ceilings, walls burnished in copper, and silk-covered chairs, is complemented by sparkling jewels—in this case, the food. The hamachi carpaccio appetizer is a sumptuous arrangement of yellowtail (imported from Japan), shaved fennel, mixed greens, and cucumber. Entrees, or "Plates of Resistance" as they're called here, include braised langoustine open-faced ravioli; ginger-lemon-grass–glazed Chilean sea bass served with black rice, kimchi, and Napa cabbage; and chicken with red Thai curry. Desserts range from fruity to chocolatey and shouldn't be skipped. If you can't afford dinner here, consider the chef's bargain lunch special. "Michelle's Way" is a $25, three-course lunch that will undoubtedly give you incentive to save your pennies for a future dinner here.

At the Mandarin Oriental, 500 Brickell Key Dr., Miami. ℂ 305/913-8254. Reservations strongly recommended. Main courses $24–$38. AE, DC, DISC, MC, V. Mon–Fri noon–3pm; Mon–Sat 7–11pm.

Capital Grille ★★ STEAK   This place reeks of power. Seated among wine cellars filled with high-end classics, the dark wood paneling, pristine white tablecloths, chandeliers, and marble floors all contribute to the clubby atmosphere. For an appetizer, start with the lobster and crab cakes. If you're not in the mood for beef or lobster, try the pan-seared red snapper and asparagus covered with Hollandaise. The wine cellars you're surrounded by are filled with about 5,000 bottles of wine—too extensive and rare to list. While some people prefer the more stalwart style and service of Morton's up the block (see below), others find Capital to be a bit livelier. The food's pretty much the same between the two, though I find the steaks at Morton's to be a notch better; however, the atmosphere at the Capital Grille is *much* more inviting. Complimentary valet parking here as opposed to Morton's, which charges a fee, is another reason to visit this carnivorous capital.

444 Brickell Ave., Miami. ℂ 305/374-4500. Reservations recommended. Main courses $21–$35. AE, DC, DISC, MC, V. Mon–Fri 11:30am–3pm; Mon–Thurs 5–10:30pm; Fri 5–11pm; Sat 6–11pm; Sun 5–10pm.

Morton's of Chicago ⭐ STEAK   A private, clublike ambience, with dark wood, leather booths, and tablecloths, makes Morton's of Chicago the preferred spot for major business transactions and quiet, romantic dinners. A vast menu includes a wide variety of excellent steaks and an award-winning menu consisting of shrimp Alexander, oysters on the half shell, sea scallops with apricot chutney, swordfish medallions with béarnaise sauce, and a dense, hot Godiva chocolate cake that's out of this world. Private dining rooms are perfect to carry on clandestine conversations and romantic liaisons. The open kitchen is probably the only thing here that's not private. At lunchtime, the power is tangible as business deals are sliced and diced as often as the steak is. At night, the scene is more elegant, attracting older sophisticates and pre- and post-theater crowds.

1200 Brickell Ave., Miami. ✆ **305/400-9990.** Reservations recommended. Main courses $30–$35. AE, DC, MC, V. Mon–Fri 11:30am–11pm; Sat 5:30–11pm; Sun 5–10pm.

Ola ⭐⭐ NUEVO LATINO   Star chef Douglas Rodriguez singelhandedly created the nouveau Latino and Cubano cuisine in Miami when he founded Lincoln Road's Yuca restaurant in 1989. From there, he skyrocketed to fame (and left Yuca to rot in mediocrity) and became co-owner and executive chef at New York City's lauded Patria (leaving Miami restaurant goers to wallow in their sorrows). But now Rodriguez is back in full force with Ola, a massive modern space serving Spanish tapas and ceviches as well as Rodriguez's very own inimitable culinary concoctions. For those who are addicted to the low carb craze, you'll find several items on the menu tailored to your diet. But why bother? Latin food is about flavor and carbs, so indulge here (like your wallet will have to).

5061 Biscayne Blvd., Miami. ✆ **305/758-9195.** Reservations recommended. Main courses $24–$40. AE, DC, MC, V. Mon–Thurs 5:30–11pm; Fri–Sat 5:30pm–midnight.

Porcao ⭐⭐ BRAZILIAN   The name sounds eerily like "pork out," which is what you'll be doing at this exceptional Brazilian *churrascaria* (a Brazilian-style restaurant devoted mostly to meat—it's the Portuguese translation of steakhouse). For about $37, you can feast on salads and meats *after* you sample the unlimited gourmet buffet, which includes such fillers as pickled quail eggs, marinated onions, and an entire pig. Do not stuff yourself here, as the next step is the meaty part: Choose as much lamb, filet mignon, chicken hearts, and steaks as you like, grilled, skewered, and sliced right at your table. Side dishes also come with the meal, including beans and rice and fried yucca.

801 Brickell Bay Dr., Miami. ✆ **305/373-2777.** Reservations accepted. Prix fixe $37 per person, all you can eat. AE, DC, MC, V. Daily noon–midnight.

EXPENSIVE

Big Fish ⭐⭐ *Finds* SEAFOOD/ITALIAN   This scenic seafood shack on the Miami River is a real catch—if you can find it. Hard to locate, but well worth the search, Big Fish's remote location keeps many people biting. In fact, it added some Italian options to its all-seafood menu in the hopes of luring more people, and that worked, too. Big Fish has a sweeping view of the Miami skyline and some of the freshest catch around; the pasta served with it is only a starchy diversion. But the spectacular setting may be the real draw, right there on the Miami River where freighters, fishing boats, dinghies, and sometimes yachts slink by to the amusement of the faithful diners who no longer have to fish around for a charming, serene seafood restaurant. However, you should beware of Friday nights, when Big Fish turns into a big happy hour scene.

55 SW Miami Ave. Rd. ⓒ 305/373-1770. Main courses $15–$28. AE, DC, MC, V. Mon–Thu noon–11pm; Fri–Sat noon–midnight. Cross the Brickell Ave. Bridge heading south and take the 1st right on SW 5th St. The road narrows under a bridge. The restaurant is just on the other side.

MODERATE

Joe's Seafood 🔍 *Finds* SEAFOOD   A good catch on the banks of the Miami River, Joe's Seafood (not to be confused with Joe's Stone Crab) has a great waterfront setting and a fairly simple, yet tasty menu of fresh fish cooked in a number of ways—grilled, broiled, fried, or, the best in my opinion, in garlic or green sauce. Meals are quite the deal here, all coming with green salad or grouper soup and yellow rice or french fries. The complimentary fish spread appetizer is also a nice touch. Because of this, not to mention the great, gritty ambience that takes you away from neon, neo-Miami in favor of the old seafaring days, there's usually a wait for a table.

400–404 NW N. River Dr., Miami. ⓒ 305/381-9329. Reservations recommended. Main courses $14–$23. AE, DC, DISC, MC, V. Sun–Thurs 11am–10pm; Fri–Sat 11am–11pm.

Perricone's Marketplace 🔍 ITALIAN   A large selection of groceries and wine, plus an outdoor porch and patio for dining, makes this one of the most welcoming spots downtown. Its rustic setting in the midst of downtown is a fantastic respite from city life. Sundays offer buffet brunches and all-you-can-eat dinners, too. But it's most popular weekdays at noon, when the suits show up for delectable sandwiches, quick and delicious pastas, and hearty salads.

15 SE 10th St. (corner of S. Miami Ave.), Miami. ⓒ 305/374-9693. Sandwiches $5.95 and up; pastas $13 and up. AE, MC, V. Sun and Mon 7am–10pm; Tues–Sat 7am–11pm.

Soyka Restaurant & Café 🔍 AMERICAN   Brought to us by the same man who owns the News and Van Dyke Cafes in South Beach, Soyka is a much-needed addition (though it's easy to miss) to the seedy area known as the Biscayne Corridor. The motif inside is industrial chic, reminiscent of a souped-up warehouse you might find in New York. Lunches focus on burgers, sandwiches, and wood-fired oven pizzas. Dinners include simple fare such as an excellent, massive Cobb salad or more elaborate dishes such as the delicious turkey Salisbury steak. The bar area offers a few comfy couches and bar stools and tables on which to dine, if you prefer not to sit in the open dining room. A children's menu is available for both lunch and dinner. A lively crowd of bohemian Design District types, professionals, and singles gathers here for a taste of urban life. On weekends, the place is packed and very loud. Do not expect an after-dinner stroll around the neighborhood—it's still too dangerous for pedestrian traffic. Instead, head over the causeway to South Beach and stroll there.

5556 NE 4th Court (Design District, off Biscayne Blvd. and 55th St.), Miami. ⓒ 305/759-3117. Reservations recommended for 8 or more. Main courses $8–$26. AE, MC, V. Sun–Thurs 11am–11pm (bar open until midnight); Fri–Sat 11am–midnight (bar open until 1am). Happy hour Mon–Fri 4–7pm.

INEXPENSIVE

Andiamo Brick Oven Pizza 🔍 PIZZA   Leave it to visionary Mark Soyka (News Cafe, Van Dyke Cafe, Soyka) to turn a retro-style 1960s car wash into one of the city's best pizza places. The brick-oven pizzas are to die for, whether you choose the simple Andiamo pie (tomato sauce, mozzarella, and basil) or the more designer combos of pancetta and caramelized onions; hot and sweet sausage with broccoli rabe; or portobello mushrooms with truffle oil and goat cheese. Pizzas come in three sizes—10-inch, 13-inch, and 16-inch. And while the pizza is undeniably delicious here, the most talked about aspect of Andiamo is the fact that while you're washing down slice after slice, for a fee, you can get your car washed and detailed at Leo's, the space's original and still-existing occupant, out back, killing two birds with one, uh, slice.

5600 Biscayne Blvd., Miami. ℭ **305/762-5751.** Main courses $3–$15. MC, V. Sun–Thurs 11am–11pm; Fri–Sat 11am–midnight.

Latin American Cafeteria ★★ CUBAN   The name may sound a bit generic, but this no-frills indoor-outdoor cafeteria has the best Cuban sandwiches in the entire city. They're big enough for lunch and a doggie-bagged dinner, too. Service is fast, prices are cheap, but be forewarned: English is truly a second language at this chain, so have patience—it's worth it.

9796 Coral Way, Miami. ℭ **305/226-2393.** Main courses $5–$9. AE, MC, V. Daily 7:30am–11pm.

PS 14 ★★ SANDWICHES   Don't be deterred by the sketchy neighborhood in which this, the best sandwich shop in town, is located. In a few years, it's going to be too hot to touch. In the meantime, this tiny cafe churns out hot—and cold—sandwiches, so fresh that even the lazy folks from the *Miami Herald* find themselves heading over here to pick up lunch. And who wouldn't want to pick up a fresh baked foccaccia sandwich with Tandoori chicken and herbs grown in PS 14's back yard garden? Or an Italian prosciutto sandwich with mozzarella cheese topped with a spicy salsa spread? Each sandwich is a meal and a half, and you can create just about anything here. All the meats and cheeses are fresh and the condiments home made. A kitschy interior reminiscent of a '50s diner is a great little spot, but the garden patio, weather permitting, is even better. Because hot spot I/O (p. 154) is located next door, PS 14 is open all night on weekends to absorb the alcohol consumed by club kids on a bender.

28 NE 14th St., Miami. ℭ **305/358-3600.** Sandwiches $5–$7. AE, DC, MC, V. Sun–Wed 10am–6pm; Thurs–Sat 24 hr.

S&S Restaurant AMERICAN/DINER FARE   This tiny chrome-and-linoleum-counter restaurant in the middle of downtown looks like a truck stop. But locals have been coming back since it opened in 1938. Expect a wait at lunchtime while the mostly male clientele, from lawyers to linemen, waits patiently for huge quantities of old-fashioned fast food. Although the neighborhood has become pretty undesirable, the food—basic diner fare with some excellent stews and soups—hasn't changed in years. In addition to cheap breakfasts, the diner serves up some of the best comfort food in Miami.

1757 NE 2nd Ave., Miami. ℭ **305/373-4291.** Main courses $5–$11. No credit cards. Mon–Fri 6am–4pm; Sat–Sun 6am–2 or 2:30pm (later on Heat game nights).

Tobacco Road AMERICAN   Miami's oldest bar is a bluesy Route 66–inspired institution favored by barflies, professionals, and anyone else who wishes to indulge in good and greasy bar fare—chicken wings, nachos, and so on—for a reasonable price in a down-home, gritty-but-charming atmosphere. The burgers are also good—particularly the Death Burger, a deliciously unhealthy combo of choice sirloin topped with grilled onions, jalapeños, and pepper jack cheese—bring on the Tums! Also a live music venue, the Road, as it is known by locals, is well traveled, especially during Friday's happy hour and Tuesday's lobster night, when 100 1¼-pound lobsters go for only $11 apiece.

626 S. Miami Ave. ℭ **305/374-1198.** www.tobacco-road.com. Main courses $7–$10 and $12–$15 for nightly specials. AE, DC, MC, V. Mon–Sat 11:30am–5am; Sun noon–5am. Cover charge $5 or $6 Fri–Sat night.

LITTLE HAVANA

The main artery of Little Havana is a busy commercial strip called Southwest 8th Street, or Calle Ocho. Auto-body shops, cigar factories, and furniture stores line this street, and on every corner there seems to be a pass-through window serving superstrong Cuban coffee and snacks. In addition, many of the Cuban, Dominican, Nicaraguan, Peruvian, and other Latin American immigrants have opened full-scale restaurants ranging from intimate candlelit establishments to bustling stand-up lunch counters.

For a map of the restaurants in this section, see the "Where to Stay & Dine in Key Biscayne, Downtown Miami, West Miami, Airport Area, North Dade, Little Havana, Coral Gables & Coconut Grove" map on p. 77.

EXPENSIVE

Casa Juancho ★★ SPANISH   A generous taste of Spain comes to Miami in the form of the cavernous Casa Juancho, which looks like it escaped from a production of *Don Quixote*. The numerous dining rooms are decorated with traditional Spanish furnishings and enlivened nightly by strolling Spanish musicians who tend to be annoying and expect tips—do not encourage them to play at your table; you'll hear them loud and clear from other tables, trust me. Try not to be frustrated with the older staff that doesn't speak English or respond quickly to your subtle glance—the food's worth the frustration. Your best bet is to order lots of *tapas,* small dishes of Spanish finger food. Some of the best include mixed seafood vinaigrette, fresh shrimp in hot garlic sauce, and fried calamari rings. A few entrees stand out, like roast suckling pig, baby eels in garlic and olive oil, and Iberian-style snapper.

2436 SW 8th St. (just east of SW 27th Ave.), Little Havana. ✆ **305/642-2452.** Reservations recommended, but not accepted on Fri–Sat after 8pm. Main courses $15–$34; tapas $6–$10. AE, DC, DISC, MC, V. Sun–Thurs noon–midnight; Fri–Sat noon–1am.

MODERATE

Hy-Vong ★★ VIETNAMESE   A must in Little Havana, expect to wait hours for a table, and don't even think of mumbling a complaint. Vietnamese cuisine combines the best of Asian and French cooking with spectacular results. Food at Hy-Vong is elegantly simple and superspicy. Appetizers include small, tightly packed Vietnamese spring rolls and kimchi, a spicy, fermented cabbage (which they ran out of on my last visit here because I got there too late—get there early!). Star entrees include pastry-enclosed chicken with watercress cream-cheese sauce and fish in tangy mango sauce. Unfortunately, service here is not at all friendly or stellar—in fact it borders on abysmal, but once you finally do get your food, all will be forgotten.

Enjoy the wait with a traditional Vietnamese beer and lots of company. Outside this tiny storefront restaurant, you'll meet interesting students, musicians, and foodies who come for the large, delicious portions.

3458 SW 8th St. (between 34th and 35th aves.), Little Havana. ✆ **305/446-3674.** Reservations accepted for parties of 5 or more. Main courses $7–$19. AE, DISC, MC, V. Sun–Thurs 6–11pm; Fri–Sat 6–11:30pm. Closed Mon and 2 weeks in Aug.

INEXPENSIVE

Versailles ★★ CUBAN   Versailles is the meeting place of Miami's Cuban power brokers, who meet daily over *cafe con leche* to discuss the future of the exiles' fate. A glorified diner, the place sparkles with glass, chandeliers, murals, and mirrors meant to evoke the French palace. There's nothing fancy here—nothing French, either—just straightforward food from the home country. The menu is a veritable survey of Cuban cooking and includes specialties such as *Moors and Christians* (flavorful black beans with white rice), *ropa vieja* (shredded beef stew), and fried whole fish. Versailles is the place to come for mucho helpings of Cuban kitsch. With its late hours, it's also the perfect place to come after spending your night in Little Havana.

3555 SW 8th St., Little Havana. ℂ 305/444-0240. Soup and salad $2–$10; main courses $5–$20. DC, DISC, MC, V. Mon–Thurs 8am–2am; Fri 8am–3am; Sat 8am–4:30am; Sun 9am–1am.

KEY BISCAYNE

Key Biscayne has some of the world's nicest beaches, hotels, and parks, yet it is not known for great food. Locals, or "Key rats" as they're known, tend to go off-island for meals or takeout, but here are some of the best on-the-island choices.

For a map of the restaurants in this section, see the "Where to Stay & Dine in Key Biscayne, Downtown Miami, West Miami, Airport Area, North Dade, Little Havana, Coral Gables & Coconut Grove" map on p. 77.

EXPENSIVE

Rusty Pelican ⭐ SEAFOOD The Pelican's private tropical walkway leads over a lush waterfall into one of the most romantic dining rooms in the city, located right on beautiful blue-green Biscayne Bay. The restaurant's windows look out over the water onto the sparkling stalagmites of Miami's magnificent downtown. Inside, quiet wicker paddle fans whirl overhead and saltwater fish swim in pretty table-side aquariums. The restaurant's surf-and-turf menu features conservatively prepared prime steaks, veal, shrimp, and lobster. The food is good, but the atmosphere—the reason why you're here—is even better, especially at sunset, when the view over the city is magical.

3201 Rickenbacker Causeway, Key Biscayne. ℂ 305/361-3818. Reservations recommended. Main courses $16–$30. AE, DC, MC, V. Daily 11:30am–4pm; Sun–Thurs 5–11pm; Fri–Sat 5pm–midnight.

INEXPENSIVE

Bayside Seafood Hut ⭐ *Finds* SEAFOOD Known by locals as "the Hut," this ramshackle restaurant and bar is a laid-back outdoor Tiki hut and terrace that serves pretty good sandwiches and fish platters on paper plates. A blackboard lists the latest catches, which can be prepared blackened, fried, broiled, or in a garlic sauce. The fish dip is wonderfully smoky and moist, if a little heavy on mayonnaise. Local fishers and yachties share this rustic outpost with equal enthusiasm and loyalty. A completely new air-conditioned area for those who can't stand the heat is a welcome addition, as are the new deck and spruced-up decor. But behind it all, it's nothing fancier than a hut—if it was anything else, it wouldn't be nearly as appealing.

3501 Rickenbacker Causeway, Key Biscayne. ℂ 305/361-0808. Reservations accepted for 15 or more. Appetizers, salads, and sandwiches $5–$15; platters $7–$13. AE, MC, V. Daily 10am until closing (which varies).

Jimbo's *Finds* SEAFOOD Locals like to keep quiet about Jimbo's, a ramshackle seafood shack that started as a gathering spot for fishermen and has since become the quintessential South Florida watering hole, snack bar, and hangout for those in the know. If ever Miami had a backwoods, this was it, right down to the smoldering garbage can, stray dogs, and chickens. Do *not* get dressed up to come here—you will get dirty. Go to the bathroom before you get here, too, because the Porta-Potties are absolutely rancid. Grab yourself a dollar can of beer (there's only beer, water, and soda, but you are allowed to bring your own choice of drink if you want) from the cooler and take in the view of the tropical lagoon where they shot *Flipper.* You may even see a manatee or two. Vacant shacks that served as backdrops for films such as *True Lies* surround this hidden enclave, which attracts everyone from shrimpers and politicians to well-oiled beach bums. Oddly enough, there's even a bocce court here, and the owner, Jimbo, may challenge you to a game. Play if you must, but word has it he never loses. Jimbo's smoked fish—marlin or salmon—is the best in town, but be forewarned: There are no utensils or napkins. When I asked for some, the woman said, "Lady, this is a place where you eat with your hands." I couldn't have said it better.

Off the Rickenbacker Causeway at Sewerline Rd., Virginia Key. ☎ **305/361-7026**. Smoked fish about $8 a pound No credit cards. Daily 6am–6:30pm, weekends until 7:30pm. Head south on the main road toward Key Biscayne, make a left just after the MAST Academy (there will be a sign that says VIRGINIA KEY), tell the person in the toll booth you're going to Jimbo's, and he'll point you in the right direction.

COCONUT GROVE

Coconut Grove was long known as the artists' haven of Miami, but the rush of developers trying to cash in on the laid-back charm of this old settlement has turned it into something of an overgrown mall. Still, there are several great dining spots both in and out of the confines of Mayfair or CocoWalk.

For a map of the restaurants in this section, see the "Where to Stay & Dine in Key Biscayne, Downtown Miami, West Miami, Airport Area, North Dade, Little Havana, Coral Gables & Coconut Grove" map on p. 77.

VERY EXPENSIVE

Baleen ★★★ SEAFOOD/MEDITERRANEAN While the prices aren't lean, the cuisine here is worth every pricey, precious penny. Oversize crab cakes, oak-smoked diver scallops, and steakhouse-quality meats are among Baleen's excellent offerings. The lobster bisque is the best on Biscayne Bay. Everything here is a la carte, so order wisely, as it tends to add up quicker than you can put your fork down. The restaurant's spectacular waterfront setting makes Baleen a true knockout. Request one of the few tables that are actually on the water's edge; lit with Tiki torches and an illuminated backdrop of Biscayne Bay, Baleen is the kind of restaurant that you'd expect a reality show like *The Bachelor* to use as the place where the happy couple expresses their love for each other.

4 Grove Isle Dr. (in the Grove Isle Hotel), Coconut Grove. ☎ **305/858-8300**. Reservations recommended. Main courses $18–$46. AE, DC, MC, V. Sun–Wed 7am–10pm; Thurs–Sat 7am–11pm.

Bice ★★ ITALIAN Upon entering the dining room here, you feel as if you're sailing on a grand ocean liner, with several cozy tables and booths, high ceilings, and a glorious view of the hotel's sprawling waterfall and pool area. Knowledgeable and friendly servers complement the comprehensive Italian menu. Every appetizer sounds so good that it's almost impossible to decide. Beef carpaccio is a delight with hearts of palm and reggiano cheese; a colorful grilled vegetable pyramid consists of gargantuan portions of meaty portobello mushrooms, fresh asparagus, and peppers with bursts of mouthwatering goat cheese lying within; Maryland crab cakes with the perfect hint of lemon are exceptional. For main courses, the pastas, homemade and extremely fresh, are eclipsed by a heavenly slab of Nebraska filet mignon with peppercorn sauce and a tower of french fries and onion rings. The veal chop is also sublime. For dessert, the crème brûlée and coffee gelato are delicious. Unlike many chichi restaurants, especially those found within swanky hotels, all dishes at Bice are generous in portion—huge actually—and the only thing stuffy about dining here is how you'll feel after indulging.

2669 S. Bayshore Dr. (in the Wyndham Grand Bay Hotel), Coconut Grove. ☎ **305/860-0960**. Reservations recommended. Main courses $12–$37. AE, MC, V. Daily 7am–noon; Mon–Fri noon–3pm; Mon–Sat 6–10pm.

EXPENSIVE

Anokha ★★★ INDIAN   This is the best Indian restaurant in Miami. Anokha's motto is "A guest is equal to God and should be treated as such," and they do stick to it. The food here is from the gods, with fantastic tandooris, curries, and stews. The restaurant's location at the end of a quiet stretch of Coconut Grove is especially enticing because it prevents the throngs of pedestrians from overtaking what some people consider a diamond in the rough.

3195 Commodore Plaza (between Main Hwy. and Grand Ave.), Coconut Grove. ⓒ 786/552-1030. Main courses $12–$40. AE, DC, MC, V. Sun and Tues–Wed 6–10:30 pm; Thurs–Sat 6–11:30 pm; closed Mon.

Le Bouchon du Grove ★★ FRENCH   This very authentic, exceptional bistro is French right down to the waitstaff, who may only speak French to you, forgetting that they are in the heart of Coconut Grove, USA. But it matters not. The food, prepared by an animated French (what else) chef, is superb. An excellent starter is the wonderful *gratinée Lyonnaise* (traditional French onion soup). Fish is brought in fresh daily; try the Chilean sea bass when in season *(filet de loup poele)*. Though it is slightly heavy on the oil, it is delivered with succulent artichokes, tomato confit, and seasoned roasted garlic that is a gastronomic triumph. The *carre d'agneau roti* (roasted rack of lamb with Provence herbs) is served warm and tender, with an excellent amount of seasoning. There is also an excellent selection of pricey but doable French and American red and white wines.

3430 Main Hwy., Coconut Grove. ⓒ 305/448-6060. Reservations recommended. Main courses $18–$26. AE, MC, V. Mon–Fri 10am–3pm; Mon–Thurs 5–11pm; Fri 5pm–midnight; Sat 8am–3pm and 5pm–midnight; Sun 8am–3pm and 5–11pm.

INEXPENSIVE

Cafe Tu Tu Tango ★ SPANISH/INTERNATIONAL   This restaurant in the bustling CocoWalk is designed to look like a disheveled artist's loft. Dozens of original paintings—some only half-finished—hang on the walls and on studio easels. Seating is either inside, among the clutter, or outdoors, overlooking the Grove's main drag. Flamenco and other Latin-inspired tunes complement a menu with a decidedly Spanish flair. Hummus spread on rosemary flat bread and baked goat cheese in marinara sauce are two good starters. Tapas items include roast duck with dried cranberries, toasted pine nuts, and goat cheese, plus Cajun chicken egg rolls filled with corn, cheddar cheese, and tomato salsa. Pastas, ribs, fish, and pizzas round out the eclectic offerings, and several visits have proved each consistently good. Try the sweet, potent sangria and enjoy the warm, lively atmosphere from a seat with a view.

3015 Grand Ave. (on the 2nd floor of CocoWalk), Coconut Grove. ⓒ 305/529-2222. Reservations not accepted. Tapas $3–$9.50. AE, MC, V. Sun–Wed 11:30am–midnight; Thurs 11:30am–1am; Fri–Sat 11:30am–2am.

CORAL GABLES & ENVIRONS

Coral Gables is a foodie's paradise—a city in which you certainly won't go hungry. What Starbucks is to most major cities, excellent gourmet and ethnic restaurants are to Coral Gables, where there's a restaurant on every corner, and everywhere in between.

For a map of the restaurants in this section, see the "Where to Stay & Dine in Key Biscayne, Downtown Miami, West Miami, Airport Area, North Dade, Little Havana, Coral Gables & Coconut Grove" map on p. 77.

VERY EXPENSIVE

Christy's ★★ STEAK/AMERICAN   Power is palpable at this elegant English-style restaurant where an ex-president could be sitting at one table and a rock star at another. But Christy's is the kind of place where conversations are at a hush and no one seems to care whom they're sitting next to. The selling point here, rather, is the corn-fed beef and calves' liver, not to mention the broiled lamb chops, prime rib of beef with horseradish sauce, teriyaki marinated filet mignon, and perfectly tossed Caesar salad. Baked sweet potatoes and a sublime blackout cake are also yours for the taking. For a little drama, order the cruise-ship-esque baked Alaska. It livens up the staid place. Just like a fine wine or the typical Christy's customer, the meat here is aged a long time. A landmark since 1978, Christy's has thrived amid the comings and goings of neighboring nouveau Coral Gables restaurants. Located on a nondescript corner, you know you've arrived at the right place if you can count the Rolls Royces parked out front.

3101 Ponce de León Blvd., Coral Gables. Ⓒ 305/446-1400. Reservations recommended. Main courses $20–$37. AE, DC, MC, V. Mon–Thurs 11:30am–10pm; Fri 11:30am–11pm; Sat 5–11pm; Sun 5–10pm.

Norman's ⋆⋆⋆ NEW WORLD CUISINE   *Gourmet* magazine called Norman's the best restaurant in South Florida, but many disagree: They think it's the best restaurant in the entire United States. Gifted chef and cookbook author Norman van Aken takes New World Cuisine (which, along with chef Allen Susser, he helped create) to another plateau with dishes that have landed him on such shows as the Discovery Channel's *Great Chefs of the South* and on the wish lists of gourmands everywhere. The open kitchen invites you to marvel at the mastery that lands on your plate in the form of pan-roasted swordfish with black-bean *muneta;* stuffed baby bell pepper in cumin-scented tomato broth with avocado *crema;* chargrilled New York strip steak with chimichurri sabayon, *pommes frites,* and Creole mustard–spiced caramelized red onions; plantain-crusted dolphin; or chicken and tiny shrimp paella with garbanzo beans and chorizo mojo, to name a few.

The staff is adoring and professional and the atmosphere is tasteful without being too formal. The portions are realistic, but still, be careful not to overdo it. You'll want to try some of the funky, fantastic desserts.

21 Almeria Ave. (between Douglas and Ponce de León), Coral Gables. Ⓒ 305/446-6767. Reservations highly recommended. Main courses $22–$38. AE, DC, MC, V. Mon–Thurs 6–10pm; Fri–Sat 6–10:30pm; closed Sun. Bar opens at 5:30pm.

EXPENSIVE

Caffe Abbracci ⋆⋆ ITALIAN   You'll understand why this restaurant's name means "hugs" in Italian the moment you enter the dark, romantic enclave: Your appetite will be embraced by the savory scents of fantastic Italian cuisine wafting through the restaurant. The homemade black and red ravioli filled with lobster in pink sauce, risotto with porcini and portobello mushrooms, and the house specialty—grilled veal chop topped with tricolor salad—are irresistible and perhaps the culinary equivalent of a warm, embracing hug. A cozy bar and lounge was added recently to further encourage the warm and fuzzy feelings.

318 Aragon Ave. (1 block north of Miracle Mile, between Salzedo St. and Le Jeune Rd.), Coral Gables. Ⓒ 305/441-0700. Reservations recommended for dinner. Main courses $15–$30; pastas $15–$20. AE, DC, MC, V. Mon–Fri 11:30am–3pm; Sun–Thurs 6–11:30pm; Fri–Sat 6pm–12:30am.

MODERATE

Brasserie Les Halles ⋆⋆ FRENCH   Known especially for its fine steaks and delicious salads, this very welcome addition to the Coral Gables dining scene became popular as soon as it opened in 1997 and has since continued to do a brisk business. The modest and moderately priced menu is particularly welcome in an area of overpriced, stuffy restaurants. For starters, try the mussels in white-wine sauce and the escargot. For a main course, the duck confit is an unusual and rich choice. Pieces of duck meat wrapped in duck fat are slow-cooked and served on salad frissé with baby potatoes with garlic. Service by the young French staff is polite but a bit slow. The tables tend to be a little too close, although there is a lovely private balcony space overlooking the long, thin dining room where large groups can gather.

2415 Ponce de León Blvd. (at Miracle Mile), Coral Gables. ✆ **305/461-1099**. Reservations recommended on weekends. Main courses $13–$26. AE, DC, DISC, MC, V. Daily 11:30am–midnight.

House of India ✿ INDIAN House of India's curries, kormas, and kabobs are very good, but the restaurant's well-priced all-you-can-eat lunch buffet is unsurpassed. All the favorites are on display, including tandoori chicken, naan, various meat and vegetarian curries, as well as rice and dal (lentils). This place isn't fancy and could use a good scrub-down (in fact, I've heard it described as a "greasy spoon"), but the service is excellent and the food is good enough to keep you from staring at your surroundings.

22 Merrick Way (near Douglas and Coral Way, 1 block north of Miracle Mile), Coral Gables. ✆ **305/444-2348**. Reservations recommended. Main courses $8–$17. AE, DC, DISC, MC, V. Daily 11:30am–3pm; Sun–Thurs 5–10pm; Fri–Sat 5–11pm.

John Martin's ✿ IRISH PUB Forest green and dark wood give way to a very intimate publike atmosphere in which local businesspeople and barflies alike come to hoist a pint or two. The menu offers some tasty British specialties (not necessarily an oxymoron!), such as bangers and mash and shepherd's pie as well as Irish lamb stew and corned beef and cabbage.

Of course, to wash it down, you'll want to try one of the ales on tap or one of the more than 20 single-malt scotches. The crowd is upscale and chatty, as is the young waitstaff. Check out happy hour on weeknights, plus the Sunday brunch with loads of hand-carved meats and seafood.

253 Miracle Mile, Coral Gables. ✆ **305/445-3777**. Reservations recommended on weekends. Main courses $9–$20; sandwiches and salads $5–$16. AE, DC, DISC, MC, V. Sun–Thurs 11:30am–midnight; Fri–Sat 11:30am–2am.

Ortanique on the Mile ✿✿ NEW WORLD CARIBBEAN You'll be greeted as you walk in by soft spiderlike lights and canopied mosquito netting that will make you wonder whether you're on a secluded island or inside one of King Tut's temples. Chef Cindy Hutson has truly perfected her tantalizing New World Caribbean menu that also graces the tables of her two other Ortaniques in D.C. and Vegas. For starters, an absolute must is the pumpkin bisque with a hint of pepper sherry. For those who absolutely refuse to eat foie gras (goose liver), Chef Hutson makes it worth trying again thanks to the jerk spices in which she marinates the love it or leave it delicacy. Afterward, move on to the tropical mango salad with fresh marinated Sable hearts of palm, julienne mango, baby field greens, toasted Caribbean candied pecans, and passion-fruit vinaigrette. For an entree, I recommend the pan-sautéed Bahamian black grouper marinated in teriyaki and sesame oil. It's served with an ortanique (an orange-like fruit) orange liqueur sauce and topped with steamed seasoned chayote, zucchini, and carrots on a lemon-orange boniato–sweet plantain mash. For dessert, try the chocolate mango tower—layers of brownie, chocolate mango mousse, meringue, and sponge cake, accompanied by mango sorbet and tropical-fruit salsa. Entrees may not be cheap, but they're a lot less than airfare to the islands, from where most, if not all, the ingredients used here hail.

278 Miracle Mile (next to Actor's Playhouse), Coral Gables. © **305/446-7710.** Reservations requested. Main courses $19–$36. AE, DC, MC, V. Mon–Tues 6–10pm; Wed–Sat 6–11pm; Sun 5:30–9:30pm.

INEXPENSIVE

Miss Saigon Bistro 🟊🟊 VIETNAMESE   Unlike Andrew Lloyd Webber's bombastic Broadway show, this Miss Saigon is small, quiet, and not at all flashy. Servers at this family-run restaurant—among them, Rick, the owners' son—will graciously offer to recommend dishes or even to custom-make something for you, and if you're lucky, he may even sing you an aria with a voice ironically tailored to Webber shows. The menu is varied and reasonably priced and the portions are huge—large enough to share. Noodle dishes and soup bowls are hearty and flavorful; caramelized prawns are fantastic, as is the whole snapper with lemon grass and ginger sauce. Despite the fact that there are few tables inside and a hungry crowd usually gathers outside in the street, they will not rush you through your meal, which is worth savoring. There is also a new, much larger location at 9503 S. Dixie Hwy., in South Miami's Pinecrest (© **305/661-2911**).

148 Giralda Ave. (at Ponce de León and 37th Ave.), Coral Gables. © **305/446-8006.** Main courses $9–$18. AE, DC, DISC, MC, V. Mon–Fri 11:30am–3pm; Mon, Wed, Thurs, Sun 5:30–10pm; Tues 6:30–10pm; Fri–Sat 5:30–11pm.

SOUTH MIAMI & WEST MIAMI

Though mostly residential, these areas nonetheless have several eating establishments worth the drive.

EXPENSIVE

Tropical Chinese 🟊🟊 CHINESE   This strip-mall restaurant, way out there in West Miami–Dade, is hailed as the best Chinese restaurant in the city. While the food is indeed very good—certainly more interesting than at your typical beef-and-broccoli shop—it still seems somewhat overpriced. Garlic spinach and prawns in a clay pot is delicious with the perfect mix of garlic cloves, mushrooms, and fresh spinach, but it's not cheap at $17. And unlike most Chinese restaurants, the dishes here are not large enough to share. Sunday-afternoon dim sum is extremely popular, and lines often snake around the shopping center.

7991 Bird Rd., West Miami. © **305/262-7576.** Reservations highly recommended on the weekends. Main courses $10–$25. AE, DC, MC, V. Mon–Fri 11:30am–10:30pm; Sat 11am–11:30pm; Sun 10:30am–10pm. Take U.S. 1 to Bird Rd. and go west on Bird, all the way down to 78th Ave. The restaurant is between 78th and 79th on Bird Rd. on the north side of the road.

INEXPENSIVE

Crepe Maker Café 🟊 *Kids* CREPES/FRENCH   Create your own delicious crepes at this little French cafe. You can choose from ham, tuna, black olives, red peppers, capers, artichoke hearts, and pine nuts. Some of the best combinations include a Philly cheese steak with mushrooms and a classic cordon bleu. Delicious dessert crepes have ice cream, strawberries, peaches, walnuts, and pineapples. Enjoy your crepe fresh off the griddle at the counter or on a bar stool. The soups are also delicious. Kids can run around in a small play area, too.

8269 SW 124th St., South Miami. © **305/233-4458** or 305/233-1113. Crepes $1.50–$8.50. AE, DC, MC, V. Sun–Thurs 11:30am–9:30pm; Fri–Sat 11:30am–10:30pm. Take U.S. 1 south to 124th St. and make a left. Restaurant is on the north side of the street, across from the park.

El Toro Taco Family Restaurant 🟊🟊🟊 *Finds* MEXICAN   Until I discovered this Mexican oasis in the midst of South Florida farmland, I'd never had good enough reason to leave my quasi-cosmopolitan confines in Miami for rural Homestead way down south. This 96-seat family-run restaurant has put major miles on my car since I first stumbled upon it a few years ago when I was lost and very hungry. Fabulous, and I mean fabulous, Mexican fare, from the usual tacos, enchiladas, and burritos drenched with the freshest and zestiest salsa this side of Baja, is what you'll find here in abundance. It may sound odd to travel from a big city with tons of restaurants to farm country for Mexican food, but trust me, it's so cheap and delicious, it's worth the trip.

1 S. Krome Ave., Homestead. ☎ **305/245-8182**. Main courses $1.75–$12. DISC, MC, V. Tues–Sun 10am–9pm (until 10pm Fri–Sat). Take 836 W (Dolphin Expwy.) toward Miami International Airport. Take Florida Tpk. S ramp toward Florida City/Key West. Take U.S. 41/SW 8th St. exit (#25) and turn left onto SW 8th St. Take SW 8th St. to Krome Ave. (⅕ mile) and turn left onto Krome Ave.

Kon Chau ⭐ CHINESE/DIM SUM   Don't be put off by the rather unappealing shopping center in which this cheap dim sum place is located. If you want fancy plastic chopsticks and fancy prices, go up the block to Tropical Chinese. If you want delicious dim sum at ridiculously low prices, Kon Chau is where you'll find it. A simple checklist allows you to choose as much of whatever you want, from savory steamed shrimp dumplings to airy pork buns, for as little as $1 apiece, all day long. They also have regular dishes if you don't want dim sum.

8376 Bird Rd., West Miami. ☎ **305/553-7799**. Items $1 and up. MC, V. Mon–Sat 11am–9:45pm; Sun 10am–9:30pm. Take Bird Rd. west to 83rd St. Restaurant is between 83rd and 84th sts. on the south side of the road, in a Dunkin' Donuts shopping center.

Shorty's ⭐ BARBECUE   A Miami tradition since 1951, this honky-tonk of a log cabin is still serving some of the best ribs and chicken in South Florida. People line up for the smoke-flavored, slow-cooked meat that's so tender it seems to fall off the bone. The secret, however, is to ask for your order with sweet sauce. The regular stuff tastes bland and bottled. All the side dishes, including the coleslaw, corn on the cob, and baked beans, look commercial, but are necessary to complete the experience. This is a jeans and T-shirt kind of place, but you may want to wear an elastic waistband, as overeating is not uncommon.

9200 S. Dixie Hwy. (between U.S. 1 and Dadeland Blvd.), South Miami. ☎ **305/670-7732**. Main courses $5–$9. DISC, MC, V. Sun–Thurs 11am–10pm; Fri–Sat 11am–11pm.

The Tea Room at Cauley Square ⭐ ENGLISH TEA   Do stop in for a spot of tea at this recently rebuilt tearoom in historic Cauley Square off U.S. 1. The little lace-curtained room is an unusual sight in this heavily industrial area better known for its warehouses than its doilies.

Try one of the simple sandwiches, such as the turkey club with potato salad and a small lettuce garnish, or onion soup full of rich brown broth and stringy cheese. The Ambrosia with finger sandwiches is an interesting choice, a blend of pineapple, mandarin oranges, miniature marshmallows, and sour cream served with finger sandwiches or banana nut bread. Daily specials, such as spinach and mushroom quiche, and delectable desserts are a must before beginning your explorations of the old antiques and art shops in this little enclave of civility down south. Oh, and remember to put your pinky up while sipping your tea.

12310 SW 224th St. (at Cauley Sq.), South Miami. ☎ **305/258-0044**. Sandwiches and salads $7–$12; soups $3–$4. AE, DISC, MC, V. Daily 11am–4pm. Take 836 W (Dolphin Expwy.) toward Miami International Airport. Take Palmetto Expwy. S. ramp toward Coral Way. Merge onto 826 S. Follow signs to Florida Tpk. toward Homestead. Take Tpk. south and exit at Caribbean Blvd. (#12). Go about a mile on Caribbean Blvd. and turn left on S. Dixie Hwy. and then right at SW 224th St. Then turn left onto Old Dixie Hwy. and take a slight right onto SW 224th St. The restaurant is at Cauley Square Center.

5

What to See & Do in Miami

If there's one thing Miami doesn't have, it's an identity crisis. In fact, it's the city's vibrant, multifaceted personality that attracts millions each year, from all over the world. South Beach may be on the top of many Miami to-do lists, but the rest of the city, a fascinating assemblage of multicultural neighborhoods, should not be overlooked or neglected. Once considered "God's Waiting Room," the Magic City now attracts an eclectic mix of old and young, celebs and plebes, American and international, and geek and chic with an equally varied roster of activities.

For starters, Miami boasts some of the most natural beauty there is, with blinding blue waters, fine, sandy beaches, and lush tropical parks. The city's man-made brilliance, in the form of Crayola-colored architecture, never seems to fade in Miami's unique Art Deco District. For cultural variation, you can also experience the tastes, sounds, and rhythms of Cuba in Little Havana.

As in any metropolis, however, there are areas that aren't as great as others. Downtown Miami, for instance, is in the throes of a major, albeit slow, renaissance, in which the sketchier, warehouse sections of the city are being transformed into hubs of all things hip. In contrast to this development, however, are the still poverty-stricken areas of downtown such as Overtown, Liberty City, and Little Haiti (though Overtown is striving to transform itself into the Overtown Historic Village, showcasing its landmarks such as the famous Lyric Theater and the home of DA Dorsey, Miami's first African American millionaire). While it's obvious to advise you to exercise caution when exploring the less-traveled parts of the city, we would also be remiss in telling you to bypass them completely.

Lose yourself in the city's nature and its neighborhoods, and, best of all, its people—a sassy collection of artists and intellectuals, beach bums and international transplants, dolled-up drag queens and bodies beautiful. No wonder celebrities love to vacation here—the spotlight is on the city and its residents. And unlike most stars, Miami is always ready for its close-up. With so much to do and see, Miami is a virtual amusement park that's bound to entertain all those who pass through its palm-lined gates.

A "Miami Area Attractions & Beaches" map is in this chapter. For a map of South Beach's attractions, see the "South Beach" map on p. 65 of chapter 4.

1 Miami's Beaches

Perhaps Miami's most popular attraction is its incredible 35-mile stretch of beachfront, which runs from the tip of South Beach north to Sunny Isles and circles Key Biscayne and the numerous other pristine islands dotting the

Miami Area Attractions & Beaches

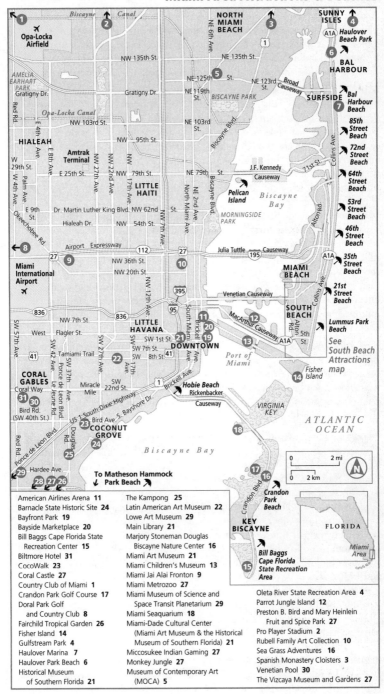

American Airlines Arena 11
Barnacle State Historic Site 24
Bayfront Park 19
Bayside Marketplace 20
Bill Baggs Cape Florida State
 Recreation Center 15
Biltmore Hotel 31
CocoWalk 23
Coral Castle 27
Country Club of Miami 1
Crandon Park Golf Course 17
Doral Park Golf
 and Country Club 8
Fairchild Tropical Garden 26
Fisher Island 14
Gulfstream Park 4
Haulover Marina 7
Haulover Park Beach 6
Historical Museum
 of Southern Florida 21

The Kampong 25
Latin American Art Museum 22
Lowe Art Museum 29
Main Library 21
Marjory Stoneman Douglas
 Biscayne Nature Center 16
Miami Art Museum 21
Miami Children's Museum 13
Miami Jai Alai Fronton 9
Miami Metrozoo 27
Miami Museum of Science and
 Space Transit Planetarium 29
Miami Seaquarium 18
Miami-Dade Cultural Center
 (Miami Art Museum & the Historical
 Museum of Southern Florida) 21
Miccosukee Indian Gaming 27
Monkey Jungle 27
Museum of Contemporary Art
 (MOCA) 5

Oleta River State Recreation Area 4
Parrot Jungle Island 12
Preston B. Bird and Mary Heinlein
 Fruit and Spice Park 27
Pro Player Stadium 2
Rubell Family Art Collection 10
Sea Grass Adventures 16
Spanish Monastery Cloisters 3
Venetian Pool 30
The Vizcaya Museum and Gardens 27

Atlantic. The characteristics of Miami's many beaches are as varied as the city's population: There are beaches for swimming, socializing, or serenity; for family, seniors, or gay singles; some to make you forget you're in the city, others darkened by huge condominiums. Whatever type of beach vacation you're looking for, you'll find it in one of Miami's two distinct beach areas: Miami Beach and Key Biscayne.

MIAMI BEACH'S BEACHES Collins Avenue fronts more than a dozen miles of white-sand beach and blue-green waters from 1st to 192nd streets. Although most of this stretch is lined with a solid wall of hotels and condos, beach access is plentiful. There are lots of public beaches here, wide and well maintained, complete with lifeguards, bathroom facilities, concession stands, and metered parking (bring lots of quarters). Except for a thin strip close to the water, most of the sand is hard-packed—the result of a $10 million Army Corps of Engineers Beach Rebuilding Project meant to protect buildings from the effects of eroding sand.

In general, the beaches on this barrier island (all on the eastern, ocean side of the island) become less crowded the farther north you go. A wooden boardwalk runs along the hotel side of the beach from 21st to 46th streets—about 1½ miles—offering a terrific sun-and-surf experience without getting sand in your shoes. Aside from "The Best Beaches," listed below, Miami's lifeguard-protected public beaches include 21st Street, at the beginning of the boardwalk; 35th Street, popular with an older crowd; 46th Street, next to the Fontainebleau Hilton; 53rd Street, a narrower, more sedate beach; 64th Street, one of the quietest strips around; and 72nd Street, a local old-timers' spot.

KEY BISCAYNE'S BEACHES If Miami Beach doesn't provide the privacy you're looking for, try Virginia Key and Key Biscayne. Crossing the Rickenbacker Causeway ($1 toll), however, can be a lengthy process, especially on weekends, when beach bums and tan-o-rexics flock to the Key. The 5 miles of public beach there, however, are blessed with softer sand and are less developed and more laid-back than the hotel-laden strips to the north.

2 The Art Deco District (South Beach)

"You know what they used to say? 'Who's Art?'" recalls Art Deco revivalist Dona Zemo, "You'd say, 'This is an Art Deco building,' and they'd say, 'Really, who is Art?' These people thought 'Art Deco' was some guy's name."

How things have changed. This guy Art has become one of the most popular Florida attractions since, well, that mouse Mickey. The district is roughly bounded by the Atlantic Ocean on the east, Alton Road on the west, 6th Street to the south, and Dade Boulevard (along the Collins Canal) to the north.

Simply put, Art Deco is a style of architecture that, in its heyday of the 1920s and 1930s, used to be considered ultramodern. Today, fans of the style consider it retro-fabulous. And while some people may not consider the style fabulous, it's undoubtedly retro. According to the experts, Art Deco made its debut in 1925 in an exposition in Paris in which it set a stylistic tone, with buildings based on early neoclassical styles with the application of exotic motifs like flora, fauna, and fountains based on geometric patterns. In Miami, Art Deco is marked by the pastel-hued buildings that line South Beach and Miami Beach. But it's a lot more than just color. If you look carefully, you will see the intricacies and impressive craftsmanship that went into each building back in the day—which, in Miami's case, was the '20s, '30s, and '40s, and now, thanks to intensive restoration, today.

(Finds Walking by Design

The Miami Design Preservation League offers several tours of Miami Beach's historic architecture, which all leave from the Art Deco Welcome Center, located at 1001 Ocean Dr. in Miami Beach. A self-guided audio tour (available 7 days a week, from 10am–4pm) turns the streets into a virtual outdoor museum, taking you through Miami Beach's Art Deco district at your own leisure, with tours in several languages for just $10 per person. Guided tours conducted by local historians and architects offer an in-depth look at the structures and their history. The 90-minute Ocean Drive and Beyond tour (offered every Wed and Sat at 10:30am) takes you through the district, pointing out the differences between Mediterranean Revival and Art Deco for $15 per person. If you're not blinded by neon, the Thursday night Art Deco District Up-to-Date tour (leaving at 6:30pm) will whisk you around for 90 minutes, making note of how certain local hot spots were architecturally famous way before the likes of Madonna and co. entered the scene. The cost is $15. For more information on tours or reservations, call ℭ 305/672-2014.

Most of the finest examples of the whimsical Art Deco style are concentrated along three parallel streets—Ocean Drive, Collins Avenue, and Washington Avenue—from about 6th to 23rd streets.

After years of neglect and calls for the wholesale demolition of its buildings, South Beach got a new lease on life in 1979. Under the leadership of Barbara Baer Capitman, a dedicated crusader for the Art Deco region, and the Miami Design Preservation League, founded by Baer Capitman and five friends, an area made up of an estimated 800 buildings was granted a listing on the National Register of Historic Places. Designers then began highlighting long-lost architectural details with soft sherbet shades of peach, periwinkle, turquoise, and purple. Developers soon moved in, and the full-scale refurbishment of the area's hotels was under way.

Not everyone was pleased, though. Former Miami Beach commissioner Abe Resnick said, "I love old buildings. But these Art Deco buildings are 40, 50 years old. They aren't historic. They aren't special. We shouldn't be forced to keep them." But Miami Beach kept those buildings, and Resnick lost his seat on the commission.

Today, hundreds of new establishments—hotels, restaurants, and nightclubs—have renovated, or are in the process of renovating, these older, historical buildings and are moving in, making South Beach on the cutting edge of Miami's cultural and nightlife scene.

EXPLORING THE AREA

If you're touring this unique neighborhood on your own, start at the **Art Deco Welcome Center,** 1001 Ocean Dr. (ℭ **305/531-3484**), which is run by the Miami Design Preservation League. The only beachside building across from the Clevelander Hotel and bar, the center gives away lots of informational material, including maps and pamphlets, and runs guided tours about the neighborhood. Art Deco books (including *The Art Deco Guide,* an informative compendium of all the buildings here), T-shirts, postcards, mugs, and other paraphernalia are for sale. It's open daily from 10am to 7:30pm.

3 Miami's Museum & Art Scene

Miami has never been known as a cultural mecca as far as museums are concerned. Though several exhibition spaces have made forays into collecting nationally acclaimed work, limited support and political infighting have made it a difficult proposition. Recently, however, things have changed as museums such as the Wolfsonian, the Museum of Contemporary Art, the Bass Museum of Art, and the Miami Art Museum have gotten on the bandwagon, boasting collections and exhibitions high on the list of art aficionados. It's now safe to say that world-class exhibitions start here. Listed below are the most lauded museums that have become a part of the city's cultural heritage, and as such, are as diverse as the city itself. For gallery lovers, see "Specialized Tours" in section 6 of this chapter for scheduled gallery walks.

IN SOUTH BEACH

Work continues to proceed on the **Collins Park Cultural Center,** which comprises a trio of arts buildings on Collins Park and Park Avenue (off Collins Ave.), bounded by 21st to 23rd streets—the newly expanded Bass Museum of Art (see below), the new Arquitectonica-designed home of the Miami City Ballet, and the Miami Beach Regional Library, an ultramodern building designed by architect Robert A. M. Stern, expected to open in spring 2004, which will have a special focus on the arts. The Library Café will be located on the library's first floor, serving coffee and pastries and exuding that cafe society ambience. Collins Park, the former site of the Miami Beach Library, will return to its original incarnation as an open space extending to the Atlantic, but it will also be the site of large sculpture installations and cultural activities planned jointly by the organizations that share the space.

Bass Museum of Art ✦✦✦ The Bass Museum of Art has expanded and received a dramatically new look, rendering it Miami's most progressive art museum. World-renowned Japanese architect Arata Isozaki designed the magnificent new facility, which has triple the former exhibition space, and added an outdoor sculpture terrace, a museum cafe and courtyard, and a museum shop, among other improvements. In addition to providing space in which to show the permanent collection, exhibitions of a scale and quality not previously seen in Miami will now be featured at the Bass. The museum's permanent collection includes European paintings from the 15th through the early 20th centuries with special emphasis on Northern European art of the Renaissance and baroque periods, including Dutch and Flemish masters such as Bol, Flinck, Rubens, and Jordaens. Past exhibitions have included the works of Picasso, Frida Kahlo, and Francois Marie Banier. The museum also has a lab, The New Information Workshop, making it possible for all aspiring artists to create their own masterpieces on computers for free or a nominal charge.

2121 Park Ave. (1 block west of Collins Ave.), South Beach. ✆ **305/673-7530.** www.bassmuseum.org. Admission $6 adults, $4 students and seniors, free for children 6 and under. Free 2nd Thurs of the month 6–9pm. Tues–Wed and Fri–Sat 10am–5pm; Thurs 10am–9pm; Sun 11am–5pm. Closed Mon.

Holocaust Memorial ✦✦✦ This heart-wrenching memorial is hard to miss and would be a shame to overlook. The powerful centerpiece, Kenneth Triester's *Sculpture of Love & Anguish,* depicts victims of the concentration camps crawling up a giant, yearning hand, stretching up to the sky, marked with an Auschwitz number tattoo. Along the reflecting pool is the story of the Holocaust, told in cut marble slabs. Inside the center of the memorial is a tableau that is one of the most solemn and moving tributes to the millions of Jews who lost their lives in the Holocaust I've seen. You can walk through an open hallway lined with photographs and the names of concentration camps and their victims. From the street, you'll see the outstretched arm, but do stop and tour the sculpture at ground level.

1933 Meridian Ave. (at Dade Blvd.), South Beach. © 305/538-1663. www.holocaustmmb.org. Free admission. Daily 9am–9pm.

Latin American Art Museum   In addition to the permanent collection of contemporary artists from Spain and Latin America, this 3,500-square-foot museum hosts monthly exhibitions of works from Latin America and the Caribbean Basin. Usually, the exhibitions focus on a theme, such as international women or surrealism. It's not a major attraction, but worth a stop if you're interested in Latin American art. On the same block, you'll find great design stores and a few other galleries.

2206 SW 8th St., Little Havana. © 305/644-1127. Free admission (though donation suggested). Tues–Fri 11am–5pm; Sat 11am–4pm. 2nd Friday of every month 6:30–10pm. Closed major holidays.

Lowe Art Museum 🎨🎨   Located on the University of Miami campus, the Lowe Art Museum has a dazzling collection of 8,000 works that include American paintings, Latin American art, Navajo and Pueblo Indian textiles, and Renaissance and baroque art. Traveling exhibits such as *Rolling Stone* magazine's photo collection also stop here. For the most part, the Lowe is known for its collection of Greek and Roman antiquities, and, as compared to the more modern MOCA, Bass, and Miami Art Museum, features mostly European and international art hailing back to ancient times.

University of Miami, 1301 Stanford Dr. (at Ponce de León Blvd.), Coral Gables. © 305/284-3603. www.lowemuseum.org. Admission $5 adults, $3 seniors and student with ID. Donation day is 1st Tues of the month. Tues, Wed, Fri, and Sat 10am–5pm; Thurs noon–7pm; Sun noon–5pm.

Miami Art Museum at the Miami–Dade Cultural Center 🎨🎨🎨   The Miami Art Museum (MAM) features an eclectic mix of modern and contemporary works by such artists as Eric Fischl, Max Beckmann, Jim Dine, and Stuart Davis. Rotating exhibitions span the ages and styles, and often focus on Latin American or Caribbean artists. There are also fantastic themed exhibits such as the Andy Warhol exhibit, which featured all-night films by the artist, make-your-own pop art, cocktail hours, and parties with local DJs. JAM at MAM is the museum's popular happy hour, which takes place the third Thursday of the month and is tied in to a particular exhibit. Almost as artistic as the works inside the museum is the composite sketch of the people—young and old—who attend these events.

The Miami–Dade Cultural Center, where the museum is housed, is a fortresslike complex designed by Phillip Johnson. In addition to the acclaimed Miami Art Museum, the center houses the main branch of the Miami–Dade Public Library, which sometimes features art and cultural exhibits, and the Historical Museum of Southern Florida, which highlights the fascinating history of the area. Unfortunately, the plaza onto which the complex opens is home to many of downtown Miami's homeless population, which makes it a bit off-putting but not dangerous.

101 W. Flagler St., Miami. © 305/375-3000. www.miamiartmuseum.org. Admission $5 adults, $2.50 seniors and students, free for children under 12. Tues–Fri 10am–5pm; 3rd Thurs of each month 10am–9pm; Sat–Sun noon–5pm. Closed Mon and major holidays. From I-95 south, exit at Orange Bowl–NW 8th St. and continue south to NW 2nd St.; turn left at NW 2nd St. and go 1½ blocks to NW 2nd Ave.; turn right.

Miami Children's Museum ★★ *Kids*   This brand new museum, located across the MacArthur Causeway from Parrot Jungle Island, is a modern, albeit odd looking, 56,500-square-foot facility that includes 12 galleries, classrooms, a parent/teacher resource center, a Kid Smart educational gift shop, a 200-seat auditorium, and Subway restaurant. The museum offers hundreds of bilingual, interactive exhibits as well as programs and classes and learning materials related to arts, culture, community, and communication. Even as an adult, I have to say I was tempted to participate in some kids-only activities and exhibitions, such as the miniature Bank of America and Publix Supermarket, and a re-creation of the NBC 6 television studio. There's also a re-creation of a Carnival Cruise ship and even a port stop in a re-created Brazil. Perhaps the coolest thing of all is the World Music Studio in which aspiring Britneys, Justins, and Lenny Kravitzes can lay down a few tracks and play instruments.

980 MacArthur Causeway, Miami Beach. ✆ 305/373-5437. www.miamichildrensmuseum.org. Admission $8 adults and children, $4 for city residents. Daily 10am–6pm.

Miami Museum of Science and Space Transit Planetarium ★★ *Kids*   The Museum of Science features more than 140 hands-on exhibits that explore the mysteries of the universe. Live demonstrations and collections of rare natural history specimens make a visit here fun and informative. Many of the demos involve audience participation, which can be lots of fun for willing and able kids and adults alike. There is also the Wildlife Center, with more than 175 live reptiles and birds of prey. The adjacent Space Transit Planetarium projects astronomy and laser shows as well as interactive demonstrations of upcoming computer technology and cyberspace features. Call or visit their website for a list of upcoming exhibits and laser shows.

3280 S. Miami Ave. (just south of the Rickenbacker Causeway), Coconut Grove. ✆ 305/646-4200 for general information. www.miamisci.org. Admission $10 adults, $8 seniors and students, $6 children 3–12, free for children 2 and under; laser shows $7 adults, $4 seniors and children 3–12. $2 off admission for museum ticket holders. Call for laser show times. After 4:30pm, ticket prices are half price. 10% discount for AAA members. Ticket prices include entrance to all museum galleries, planetarium shows, and the Wildlife Center. Museum of Science, daily 10am–6pm; call for planetarium show times (last show is at 4pm weekdays and 5pm on weekends). Closed on Thanksgiving and Christmas Day.

Museum of Contemporary Art (MOCA) ★★★   MOCA boasts an impressive collection of internationally acclaimed art with a local flavor. It is also known for its forward thinking and ability to discover and highlight new artists. A high-tech screening facility allows for film presentations to complement the exhibitions. You can see works by Jasper Johns, Roy Lichtenstein, Larry Rivers, Duane Michaels, and Claes Oldenberg, plus there are special exhibitions by such artists as Yoko Ono, Sigmar Polke, John Baldessari, and Goya. Guided tours are offered in English, Spanish, French, Creole, Portuguese, German, and Italian.

770 NE 125th St., North Miami. ✆ 305/893-6211. Fax 305/891-1472. www.mocanomi.org. Admission $5 adults, $3 seniors and students with ID, free for children 12 and under, Tues by donation. Tues–Sat 11am–5pm; Sun noon–5pm. Closed Mon and major holidays.

Rubell Family Art Collection ★★★ *Finds*   This impressive collection, owned by the Miami hotelier family, the Rubells, is housed in a two-story 40,000-square-foot former Drug Enforcement Agency warehouse in a sketchy area north of downtown Miami. The building looks like a fortress, which is fitting: Inside is a priceless collection of more than a thousand works of contemporary art, by the likes of Keith Haring, Damien Hirst, Julian Schnabel, Jean-Michel Basquiat, Paul McCarthy, Charles Ray, and Cindy Sherman. But be forewarned:

Some of the art is extremely graphic and may be off-putting to some. The gallery changes exhibitions twice yearly and there is a seasonal program of lectures, artists' talks, and performances by prominent artists.

95 NW 29th St. (on the corner of NW 1st Ave. near the Design District), Miami. (C) **305/573-6090.** Admission $5 adults, $2 students and seniors. Wed–Sun 10am–6pm.

Sanford L. Ziff Jewish Museum of Florida ✿
Chronicling over 230 years of Jewish heritage and experiences in Florida, the Jewish Museum presents a fascinating look at religion and culture through films, lectures, and exhibits such as "Mosaic: Jewish Life in Florida," which features over 500 photos and artifacts documenting the Jewish experience in Florida since 1763. The museum also delves into the Jewish roots of Latin America. The museum is housed in a former synagogue.

301 Washington Ave., South Beach. (C) **305/672-5044.** www.jewishmuseum.com. Admission $5 adults, $4 seniors and students, $10 families. Free admission Sat. Tues–Sun 10am–5pm. Closed Mon and Jewish holidays.

Wolfsonian-Florida International University ✿✿✿ (Finds)
Mitchell Wolfson Jr., heir to a family fortune built on movie theaters, was known as an eccentric, but I'd call him a pack rat. A premier collector of propaganda and advertising art, Wolfson was spending so much money storing his booty that he decided to buy the warehouse that was housing it. It ultimately held more than 70,000 of his items, from controversial Nazi propaganda to King Farouk of Egypt's match collection. Thrown in the eclectic mix are also zany works from great modernists such as Charles Eames and Marcel Duchamp. He then gave this incredibly diverse collection to Florida International University. The former 1927 storage facility has been transformed into a museum that is the envy of curators around the world. The museum is unquestionably fascinating and hosts lectures and rather swinging events surrounding particular exhibits.

1001 Washington Ave., South Beach. (C) **305/531-1001.** www.wolfsonian.org. Admission $5 adults, $3.50 seniors, students with ID, and children 6–12. Mon, Tues, Fri, and Sat 11am–6pm; Thurs 11am–9pm; Sun noon–5pm.

4 Historic Homes & Sites

South Beach's well-touted Art Deco District is but one of many colorful neighborhoods that can boast dazzling architecture. The rediscovery of the entire Biscayne Corridor (from downtown to about 80th St. and Biscayne Blvd.) has given light to a host of ancillary neighborhoods on either side that are filled with Mediterranean-style homes and Frank Lloyd Wright gems. Coral Gables is home to many large and beautiful homes, mansions, and churches that reflect architecture from the 1920s, 1930s, and 1940s. Some of the homes, or portions of their structures, have been created from coral rock and shells. The Biltmore Hotel is also filled with history. See p. 84 for information on touring the hotel.

Barnacle State Historic Site ✿✿
The former home of naval architect and early settler Ralph Middleton Munroe is now a museum in the heart of Coconut Grove. It's the oldest house in Miami and it rests on its original foundation, which sits on 5 acres of hardwood and landscaped lawns. The house's quiet surroundings, wide porches, and period furnishings illustrate how Miami's first snowbird lived in the days before condo-mania and luxury hotels. Enthusiastic and knowledgeable state park employees offer a wealth of historical information to those interested in quiet, low-tech attractions like this one. Call for details on

the fabulous monthly moonlight concerts during which folk, blues, or classical music is presented and picnicking is encouraged.

3485 Main Hwy. (1 block south of Commodore Plaza), Coconut Grove. ✆ 305/448-9445. Fax 305/448-7484. Admission $1. Concerts $5, free for children under 10. Fri–Mon 9am–4pm. Tours Fri–Mon at 10am, 11:30am, 1pm, and 2:30pm. From downtown Miami, take U.S. 1 south to 27th Ave., make a left, and continue to S. Bayshore Dr.; then make a right, follow to the intersection of Main Hwy., and turn left.

Coral Castle ★★ *Finds* There's plenty of competition, but Coral Castle is probably the strangest attraction in Florida. In 1923, the story goes, a 26-year-old crazed Latvian, suffering from unrequited love of a 16-year-old who left him at the altar, immigrated to South Miami and spent the next 25 years of his life carving huge boulders into a prehistoric-looking roofless "castle." It seems impossible that one rather short man could have done all this, but there are scores of affidavits on display from neighbors who swear it happened. Apparently, experts have studied this phenomenon to help figure out how the Great Pyramids and Stonehenge were built. Rocker Billy Idol was said to have been inspired by this place to write his song "Sweet 16." An interesting 25-minute audio tour guides you through the spot, now in the National Register of Historic Places. Although Coral Castle is overpriced and undermaintained, it's worth a visit when in the area, which is about 37 miles from Miami.

28655 S. Dixie Hwy., Homestead. ✆ 305/248-6345. www.coralcastle.com. Admission $9.75 adults, $6.50 seniors, $5 children 7–12. Daily 7am–8pm. Take 836 West (Dolphin Expwy.) toward Miami International Airport. Merge onto 826 South (Palmetto Expwy.) and take it to the Florida Turnpike toward Homestead. Take the 288th St. exit (#5) and then take a right on South Dixie Hwy., a left on SW 157th Ave., and then a sharp left back onto South Dixie Hwy. Coral Castle is on the left side of the street.

Spanish Monastery Cloisters ★★★ *Finds* Did you know that the alleged oldest building in the Western Hemisphere dates from 1133 and is located in Miami? The Spanish Monastery Cloisters were first erected in Segovia, Spain for St. Bernard de Clairvaux, an influential church figure. Centuries later, newspaper magnate William Randolph Hearst purchased and brought them to America in pieces. The carefully numbered stones were quarantined for years until they were finally reassembled on the present site in 1954. It has often been used as a backdrop for weddings, movies, and commercials and is a very popular tourist attraction.

16711 W. Dixie Hwy. (at NE 167th St.), North Miami Beach. ✆ 305/945-1461. www.spanishmonastery.com. Admission $5 adults, $2.50 seniors and students with ID, $2 children 3–12. Mon–Sat 9am–5pm; Sun 1–5pm. Call ahead because the monastery closes for special events without being announced.

Venetian Pool ★★★ *Kids* Miami's most beautiful and unusual swimming pool, dating from 1924, is hidden behind pastel stucco walls and is honored with a listing in the National Register of Historic Places. Underground artesian wells feed the free-form lagoon, which is shaded by three-story Spanish porticos and features both fountains and waterfalls. It can be cold in the winter months. During summer, the pool's 800,000 gallons of water are drained and refilled nightly thanks to an underground aquifer, ensuring a cool, *clean* swim. Visitors are free to swim and sunbathe here, just as Esther Williams and Johnny Weissmuller did decades ago. For a modest fee, you or your children can learn to swim during special summer programs.

2701 DeSoto Blvd. (at Toledo St.), Coral Gables. ✆ 305/460-5356. www.venetianpool.com. Admission and hours vary seasonally. Nov–Mar $6 for those 13 and older, $3 children under 13; Apr–Oct $9 for those 13 and older, $5 children under 13. Children must be 3 years old and provide proof of age with birth certificate, or 38 in. tall to enter. Hours are at least 11am–4:30pm but are often longer. Call for more information.

The Vizcaya Museum and Gardens ✦✦✦   Sometimes referred to as the "Hearst Castle of the East," this magnificent villa is more Gatsby-esque than anything else you'll find in Miami. It was built in 1916 as a winter retreat for James Deering, co-founder and former vice president of International Harvester. The industrialist was fascinated by 16th-century art and architecture and his ornate mansion, which took 1,000 artisans 5 years to build, became a celebration of that period. If you love antiques, this place is a dream come true, packed with European relics and works of art from the 16th to the 19th centuries. Most of the original furnishings, including dishes and paintings, are still intact. You will see very early versions of a telephone switchboard, central vacuum cleaning system, elevators, and fire sprinklers. A free guided tour of the 34 furnished rooms on the first floor takes about 45 minutes. The second floor, which consists mostly of bedrooms, is open to tour on your own. The spectacularly opulent villa wraps itself around a central courtyard. Outside, lush formal gardens, accented with statuary, balustrades, and decorative urns, front an enormous swath of Biscayne Bay. Definitely take the tour of the rooms, but immediately thereafter, you will want to wander and get lost in the resplendent gardens.

3251 S. Miami Ave. (just south of Rickenbacker Causeway), North Coconut Grove. ✆ 305/250-9133. www.vizcayamuseum.com. Admission $12 adults, $5 children 6–12, free for children 5 and under. Villa daily 9:30am–5pm (ticket booth closes at 4:30pm); gardens daily 9:30am–5:30pm.

5 Nature Preserves, Parks & Gardens

The Miami area is a great place for outdoors types, with beaches, parks, nature preserves, and gardens galore. For information on South Florida's two national parks, the Everglades and Biscayne National Park, see chapter 7.

At the historic **Bill Baggs Cape Florida State Park** ✦, 1200 Crandon Blvd. (✆ 305/361-5811), at the southern tip of Key Biscayne about 20 minutes from downtown Miami, you can explore the unfettered wilds and enjoy some of the most secluded beaches in Miami. There's also a historic lighthouse that was built in 1825, which is the oldest lighthouse in South Florida. The lighthouse was damaged during the Second Seminole War (1836) and again in 1861 during the Civil War. Out of commission for a while, in 1978 the U.S. Coast Guard restored it to working lighthouse condition. A rental shack leases bikes, hydrobikes, kayaks, and many more water toys. It's a great place to picnic, and a newly constructed restaurant serves homemade Latin food, including great fish soups and sandwiches. Just be careful that the raccoons don't get your lunch—the furry black-eyed beasts are everywhere. Wildlife aside, however, Bill Baggs has been consistently rated as one of the top 10 beaches in the U.S. for its 1¼ miles of wide, sandy beaches and its secluded, serene atmosphere. Admission is $5 per car with up to eight people (or $3 for a car with only one person; $1 to enter by foot or bicycle). Open daily from 8am to sunset. Tours of the lighthouse are available every Thursday through Monday at 10am and 1pm. Arrive at least half an hour early to sign up—there is only room for 10 people on each. Take I-95 to the Rickenbacker Causeway and take that all the way to the end.

Fairchild Tropical Garden ✦✦✦, at 10901 Old Cutler Rd. in Coral Gables (✆ 305/667-1651; www.ftg.org), is the largest of its kind in the continental United States. A veritable rainforest of both rare and exotic plants, as well as 11 lakes and countless meadows, are spread across 83 acres. Palmettos, vine pergola, palm glades, and other unique species create a scenic, lush environment. More than 100 species of birds have been spotted at the garden (ask for a checklist at the front gate), and it's home to a variety of animals. You should not miss the 30-minute narrated tram tour (tours leave on the hour 10am–3pm weekdays and 10am–4pm on weekends) to learn about the various flowers and trees on the grounds. There is also a museum, a cafe, a picnic area, and a gift shop with fantastic books on gardening, cooking, and edible gifts. The 2-acre rainforest exhibit, Windows to the Tropics, will save you a trip to the Amazon. Expect to spend a minimum of 2 hours here. Admission is $10 for adults, $9 for seniors, $5 for children 3 to 12, and is free for children under 3. Open daily, except December 25, from 9:30am to 4:30pm. Take I-95 south to U.S. 1, turn left onto Le Jeune Road, and follow it straight to the traffic circle; from there, take Old Cutler Road 2 miles to the park.

Located on Biscayne Bay in Coconut Grove (4013 Douglas Rd.; www.ntbg. org/kampong.html), the **Kampong** ★★ is a 7-acre botanical garden featuring a stunning array of flowering trees and tropical fruit trees including mango, avocado, and pomelos. In the early 1900s, noted plant explorer David Fairchild traveled the world seeking rare plants of economic and aesthetic value that might be cultivated in the United States. In 1928, he and his wife, Marian (daughter of Alexander Graham Bell), built a two-story residence here (listed on the National Register of Historic Places) amid some of his collections, borrowing the Malaysian word *kampong* for his home in a garden. In the 1960s, the Fairchilds sold the Kampong to Catherine Hauberg Sweeney, who donated the property to the National Tropical Botanical Garden to promote and preserve this South Florida treasure. It's a must-see for those interested in horticulture. Admission and tours are by appointment only, from Monday to Friday. For tour information, call ℂ **305/442-7169** from 9am to 5pm Monday through Friday. Admission is $10 a person. Take U.S. 1 to Douglas Road (SW 37th Ave.). Go east on Douglas Road for about a mile. The Kampong will be on your left.

Named after the late champion of the Everglades, the **Marjory Stoneman Douglas Biscayne Nature Center** ★, 6767 Crandon Blvd., Key Biscayne (ℂ **305/361-6767;** www.biscaynenaturecenter.org), is housed in a brand-new $4 million facility and offers hands-on marine exploration, hikes through coastal hammocks, bike trips, and beach walks. Local environmentalists and historians lead intriguing trips through the local habitat. Call to reserve a spot on a regularly scheduled weekend tour or program. Be sure to wear comfortable closed-toe shoes for hikes through wet or rocky terrain. Open daily 10am to 4pm. Admission to park is $4 per person; admission to nature center is free. Call for weekend programs. To get there, take I-95 to the Rickenbacker Causeway Exit (#1) and take the causeway all the way until it becomes Crandon Boulevard. The center is on the east side of the street (the Atlantic Ocean side). Driving time is about 25 minutes from downtown Miami.

Because so many people are so focused on the beach itself, the **Miami Beach Botanical Garden,** 2000 Convention Center Dr., Miami Beach (ℂ **305/ 673-7256**), remains, for the most part, a secret garden. The lush, tropical 4½-acre garden is a fabulous, all-natural retreat from the hustle and bustle of the silicone-enhanced city. Open Tuesday through Sunday from 9am to 5pm; admission is free.

The **Oleta River State Recreation Area** ★★, 3400 NE 163rd St., North Miami (ℂ **305/919-1846**), consists of 993 acres—the largest urban park in the state—on Biscayne Bay. The beauty of the Oleta River combined with the fact that you're essentially in the middle of a city makes this park especially worth visiting. With miles of bicycle and canoe trails, a sandy swimming beach, shaded picnic pavilions, and a fishing pier, Oleta River State Recreation Area offers visitors an outstanding outdoor recreational experience cloistered from the confines of the big city. There are 14 cabins on the premises, sleeping four people and featuring air conditioning. The cost is $51 per night and guests are required to bring their own linens. Bathrooms and showers are outside, and a fire circle with grill is available for cooking. For reservations, call © **800/326-3521.** Open daily from 8am to sunset. Admission for pedestrians and cyclists is $1 per person. By car: driver plus car costs $3; driver plus one to seven passengers and car costs $5. Take 1-95 to exit 17 (S.R. 826 E.) and go all the way east until just before the causeway. The park entrance is on your right. Driving time from downtown Miami is about a half-hour.

A testament to Miami's unusual climate, the **Preston B. Bird and Mary Heinlein Fruit and Spice Park** ✷, 24801 SW 187th Ave., Homestead (© **305/ 247-5727**), harbors rare fruit trees that cannot survive elsewhere in the country. If a volunteer is available, you'll learn some fascinating things about this 30-acre living plant museum, where the most exotic varieties of fruits and spices—ackee, mango, Ugli fruits, carambola, and breadfruit—grow on strange-looking trees with unpronounceable names. There are also original coral rock buildings dating back to 1912. The Strawberry Folk Festival in February and an art festival here in January are among the park's most popular—and populated—events.

The best part? You're free to take anything that *naturally* falls to the ground. You'll also find samples of interesting fruits and jellies made from the park's bounty as well as exotic ingredients and cookbooks in the gift store.

Admission to the spice park is $5 for adults and $1.50 for children under 12. It's open daily from 10am to 5pm; closed on Christmas. Tours are included in the price of admission and are offered at 11am, 1:30pm, and 3pm. Take U.S. 1 south, turn right on SW 248th Street, and go straight for 5 miles to SW 187th Avenue. The drive from Miami should take 45 minutes to an hour.

6 Sightseeing Cruises & Organized Tours

BOAT & CRUISE-SHIP TOURS

You don't need a boating license or a zillion-dollar yacht to explore Miami by boat. Thanks to several enterprising companies, boat tours are easy to find, affordable, and are an excellent way to see the city from a more liquid perspective.

⟮Moments Venice in Miami

You don't have to endure jet lag and time zone differences to enjoy the beauty of Italy. Located just off Miami Beach, Florida's own Venetian Islands (NE 15th St. and Dade Blvd.) were joined together in 1926 by a bascule bridge known as the Venetian Causeway. A series of 12 bridges connecting the Venetian Islands and stretching between Miami and Miami Beach feature octagonal concrete entrance towers, which give you a great view of the water. The oldest causeway in metropolitan Miami, the Venetian is rickety in a charming way, featuring fantastic views of the city and the mammoth cruise ships docked at the port, not to mention a glimpse of some of Miami's most beautiful waterfront homes. Bikers and joggers especially love the Venetian causeway because of limited traffic and beautiful scenery.

Fast Cats Ferry Service   Finally, a ferry that goes from Miami to Key West. It's about time. The PurrSeavearance may be a cheesy name for a luxury $7.5 million catamaran, but the trip is hardly so. The 102-foot boat can hold up to 149 passengers and will make the 4 hour cruise (driving only takes 3 hr., but with traffic it can take up to 5) four times a week starting at $69 each way. VIP tickets cost $98 and include preferential seating. Food and alcoholic beverages are available but not included in the price.

1635 N. Bayshore Dr., Sealine Marina, Downtown. (C) 305/400-6446. www.fastcats.org. Round-trip $110–$212. Tours leave Miami Thurs–Sun at 7:30am and push off from Key West at 5:30pm.

Heritage Miami II Topsail Schooner   This relaxing ride aboard Miami's only tall ship is a fun way to see the city, since it's on a schooner (as opposed to the other tour company's cruising boats), which gives you more of a feel of the water. The 2-hour cruise passes by Villa Vizcaya, Coconut Grove, and Key Biscayne and puts you in sight of Miami's spectacular skyline and island homes. Call to make sure the ship is running on schedule. On Friday, Saturday, and Sunday evenings, there are 1-hour tours to see the lights of the city for $15 per person.

Bayside Marketplace Marina, 401 Biscayne Blvd., Downtown. (C) 305/442-9697. Fax 305/442-0119. Tickets for day tours $20 adults, $15 children 12 and under. Sept–May only. Tours leave daily at 1:30, 4, and 6:30pm and Fri–Sun also at 9, 10, and 11pm.

Miami Duck Tours   Hands down, this is the corniest, kookiest tour in the entire city. In fact, the company prefers to call these tours the "Quackiest" way to visit Miami and the Beaches. Whatever you call it, it's weird. The *Watson Willy* is the first of several planned Miami Duck Tours "vesicles," not a body party, but a hybrid name that means part vessel, part vehicle (technical name: Hydra Terra Amphibious Vehicle). Each "vesicle" seats 49 guests, plus a captain and tour guide and leaves from Watson Island behind Parrot Jungle Island, traveling through downtown Miami and South Beach. If you're image conscious, you may want to reconsider traveling down Ocean Drive in a duck. That's right, a duck, which is what the "vesicle" looks like. After driving the streets in the duck, you'll end up cruising Biscayne Bay, past all the swanky houses. Embarrassing or downright hilarious, Miami Duck Tours is definitely something unique.

Bayside Marketplace (on land), 401 Biscayne Blvd., Downtown, (C) 877/DUCK-TIX. www.ducktoursmiami. com. Tickets $24 adults, $21 seniors and military, $17 children 12 and under.

SIGHTSEEING TOURS

While there are several sightseeing tour operators in Miami, most, unfortunately, either don't speak English or are just plain shoddy. The following is the one we'd recommend:

Miami Nice Excursion Travel and Service ⭐   Pick your destination, and the Miami Nice tours will take you to the Everglades, Fort Lauderdale, South Beach, the Seaquarium, Key West, Cape Canaveral, or wherever else you desire. The best trip for first-timers is the City Tour, a comprehensive tour of the entire city and its various neighborhoods. If you've got the time, you will definitely want to add on a side trip to the Everglades and/or Key West (though I suggest exploring the Everglades on your own). Included in most Miami trips is a fairly comprehensive city tour narrated by a knowledgeable guide. The company is one of the oldest in town.

18801 Collins Ave., Miami Beach. (C) 305/949-9180. www.miaminicetours.com. Tours $32–$115 adults, $29–$100 children 3–9. Mon–Sat 7am–10pm. Closed Sun. Call ahead for directions to various pickup areas.

SPECIALIZED TOURS

In addition to those listed below, a great option for seeing the city is to take a tour led by **Dr. Paul George.** Dr. George is a history teacher at Miami–Dade Community College and a historian at the Historical Museum of Southern Florida. He also happens to be "Mr. Miami." There's a set calendar of tours (including the Murder, Mystery, and Mayhem Bus Tour detailed below), and all of them are fascinating to South Florida buffs. Tours focus on neighborhoods, such as Little Havana, Brickell Avenue, or Key Biscayne, and on themes, such as Miami cemeteries and the Miami River. The often long-winded discussions can be a bit much for those who just want a quick look around, but Dr. George certainly knows his stuff. The cost is $17 to $37; reservations are required (✆ **305/ 375-1621**). Tours leave from the Historical Museum at 101 W. Flagler St., Downtown. Call for a schedule.

Biltmore Hotel Tour ✮✮✮ *Value*   Take advantage of these free Sunday walking tours to enjoy the hotel's beautiful grounds. The Biltmore is chock-full of history and mystery, including a few ghosts; go out there and see for yourself. In addition, there are also free weekly fireside sessions that are open to the public and presented by Miami Storytellers. Learn about the hotel's early days and rich stories of the city's past. These wonderful sessions are held in the main lobby by the fireplace and are accompanied by a glass of champagne. Call ahead to confirm.

1200 Anastasia Ave., Coral Gables. ✆ **305/445-1926**. www.biltmorehotel.com. Free admission. Tours depart on Sun at 1:30, 2:30, and 3:30pm. Storytelling sessions are held every Thurs at 7:30pm.

Eco-Adventure Tours ✮✮✮   For the eco-conscious traveler, the Miami–Dade Parks and Recreation Department offers guided nature, adventure, and historic tours involving biking, canoeing, snorkeling, hiking, and bird watching all over the city. Contact them for more information.

✆ **305/365-3018**. www.miamidade.gov/parks.

Herencia Hispana Tour   For those looking to immerse themselves in Miami's rich Latin-American culture, the Herencia Hispana Tour is the ideal way to explore it all. Hop on a bus and zoom past such hotbeds of Latin activity as downtown's Flagler Street, the unavoidable Elián González house, the Latin American Art Museum, and Little Havana's Domino Park and Tower Theater, among others. Not just a sightseeing tour, this one includes two very knowledgeable, albeit corny, guides who know just when to infuse a necessary dose of humor into a segment of history that some people may not consider so amusing.

Tours depart at 9, 9:30, and 10am every Sat in Oct from the Steven P. Clark Government Center, 111 NW 1st St. ✆ **305/884-7567**. Tours (which are in Spanish or English, but you must specify which one you require) are free, but advanced reservations are required.

Miami Design Preservation League ✮✮   On Thursday evenings and Saturday mornings, the Design Preservation League sponsors walking tours that offer a fascinating inside look at the city's historic Art Deco District. Tour-goers meet for a 1½-hour walk through some of America's most exuberantly "architectured" buildings. The league led the fight to designate this area a National Historic District and is proud to share the splendid locale with visitors. Also, see p. 123 for more information.

Art Deco Welcome Center, 1001 Ocean Dr., South Beach. ✆ **305/672-2014**. www.mdpl.org. Walking tours $15 per person. Tours leave Wed and Sat at 10:30am and Thurs at 6:30pm. Self-guided audio tours also available daily for $10. No reservations necessary but arrive 15 min. early. Call ahead for updated schedules.

Murder, Mystery, and Mayhem Bus Tour ★★★   Visit the past by video and bus to Miami-Dade's most celebrated crimes and criminals from the 1800s to the present. From the murder spree of the Ashley Gang to the most notorious murders and crimes of our century, including the murder of designer Gianni Versace, historian Paul George conducts a most fascinating 3-hour tour of scandalous proportions.

Held twice a year, usually in Apr and Oct; leaves from the Dade Cultural Center, 101 W. Flagler St., Miami. Tickets $37. Advance reservations required; call ℂ 305/375-1621.

7 Watersports

There are many ways to get well acquainted with Miami's wet look. Choose your own adventure from the suggestions listed below.

BOATING

Private rental outfits include **Boat Rental Plus,** 2400 Collins Ave., Miami Beach (ℂ **305/534-4307**), where 50-horsepower, 18-foot powerboats rent for some of the best prices on the beach. There's a 2-hour minimum and rates go from $99 to $449, including taxes and gas. They also have great specials on Sundays. Cruising is permitted only in and around Biscayne Bay (ocean access is prohibited) and renters must be 21 to rent a boat. The rental office is at 23rd Street, on the inland waterway in Miami Beach. It's open daily from 10am to sunset. If you want a specific type of boat, call ahead to reserve. Otherwise, show up and take what's available.

   Club Nautico of Coconut Grove, 2560 S. Bayshore Dr. (ℂ **305/858-6258;** www.clubnauticomiami.com), rents high-quality powerboats for fishing, water-skiing, diving, and cruising in the bay or ocean. All boats are Coast Guard equipped, with VHF radios and safety gear. Rates start at $299 for 4 hours and $419 for 8 hours. Club Nautico is open daily from 8am to 6pm (weather permitting). Other locations include the Crandon Park Marina, 4000 Crandon Blvd., Key Biscayne (ℂ **305/361-9217**), with the same rates and hours as the Coconut Grove location; and the Miami Beach Marina, Pier E, 300 Alton Rd., South Beach (ℂ **305/673-2502**), where rates start at $299 for 4 hours and $399 for 8 hours. Nautico on Miami Beach is open daily from 9am to 5pm. For money-saving coupons, log on to www.boatrent.com.

JET SKIS/WAVERUNNERS

Don't miss a chance to tour the islands on the back of your own powerful watercraft. Bravery is, however, a prerequisite, as Miami's waterways are full of speeding jet skiers and boaters who think they're in the Indy 500. Many beachfront concessionaires rent a variety of these popular (and loud) water scooters. The latest models are fast and smooth. Try **Tony's Jet Ski Rentals,** 3501 Rickenbacker Causeway, Key Biscayne (ℂ **305/937-0302**), one of the city's largest rental shops, located on a private beach in the Miami Marine Stadium lagoon. There are three models available accommodating up to three people. Rates range from $45 for a half-hour to $80 for a full hour, depending on the number of riders. Tony's is open daily from 10:30am to 6:30pm.

KAYAKING

The laid-back **Urban Trails Kayak Company** rents boats at 3400 NE 163rd St. in Oleta River Park (ℂ **305/947-1302;** www.urbantrails.com). The outfitters here give interested explorers a map to take with them and quick instructions on how to work the paddles and boats. They also operate very scenic 4-hour guided tours through rivers with mangroves and islands as your destination—less than 10 people on the tour costs $45 per person; more than 10 people costs $35 per person. These must be booked in advance. Rates are $8 an hour, $20 for up to 4 hours, and $25 for the whole day. Tandems (for two people) are $12 an hour, $30 for up to 4 hours, and $35 for the day. To keep the kayaks overnight is an extra $10. They also rent mountain bikes. Open daily from 9am to 5pm in the winter and 9am to 6pm in the summer.

SAILING

You can rent sailboats and catamarans through the beachfront concessions desk of several top resorts, such as the Doral Golf Resort and Spa (p. 81).

Sailboats of Key Biscayne Rentals and Sailing School, in the Crandon Marina (next to Sundays on the Bay), 4000 Crandon Blvd., Key Biscayne (© 305/361-0328 days, 305/279-7424 evenings), can also get you out on the water. A 22-foot sailboat rents for $35 an hour or $110 for a half day and $175 for a full day. A Cat-25 or J24 is available for $35 an hour, $110 for a half day, and $175 for a full day. If you've always had a dream to win the America's Cup but can't sail, the able teachers at Sailboats will get you started. They offer a 10-hour course over 5 days for $300 for one person or $400 for you and a buddy.

SCUBA DIVING & SNORKELING

In 1981, the U.S. government began a wide-scale project designed to increase the number of habitats available to marine organisms. One of the program's major accomplishments has been the creation of nearby artificial reefs, which have attracted all kinds of tropical plants, fish, and animals. In addition, Biscayne National Park (see the park's section in chapter 7, beginning on p. 233) offers a protected marine environment just south of downtown.

Several dive shops around the city offer organized weekend outings, either to the reefs or to one of over a dozen old shipwrecks around Miami's shores. Check "Divers" in the Yellow Pages for rental equipment and for a full list of undersea tour operators.

Diver's Paradise of Key Biscayne, 4000 Crandon Blvd. (© 305/361-3483), offers one dive expedition per day during the week and two per day on the weekends to the more than 30 wrecks and artificial reefs off the coast of Miami Beach and Key Biscayne. You can take a 3-day certification course for $399, which includes all the dives and gear. If you already have your C-card, a dive trip costs about $90 if you need equipment and $45 if you bring your own gear. It's open Tuesday through Friday from 10am to 6pm and Saturday and Sunday from 8am to 6pm. Call ahead for times and locations of dives. For snorkeling, they will also set you up with equipment and maps on where to see the best underwater sights. Rental for mask, fins, and snorkel is $45.

South Beach Divers, 850 Washington Ave., Miami Beach (© 305/531-6110; www.southbeachdivers.com), will also be happy to tell you where to go under the sea and will provide you with scuba rental equipment as well for $40. You can rent snorkel gear for $15. They also do dive trips to Key Largo three times a week and do dives off Miami on Sundays at $100 for a two-tank dive.

WINDSURFING

Many hotels rent windsurfers to their guests, but if yours doesn't have a watersports concession stand, head for Key Biscayne. **Sailboards Miami,** Rickenbacker Causeway, Key Biscayne (© 305/361-SAIL; www.sailboardsmiami.com), operates out of two big yellow trucks on Windsurfer Beach, the most popular (though our pick for best is Hobie Beach) windsurfing spot in the city. For those who've never ridden a board but want to try it, they offer a 2-hour lesson for $69 that's guaranteed to turn you into a wave warrior or you get your money back. After that, you can rent a board for $25 to $30 an hour. If you want to make a day of it, a 10-hour prepaid card costs $180. These cards require you to prepay, but they also reduce the price by about $70 for the day. You can use the card year-round, until the time on it runs out. Open Tuesday through Sunday from 10am to 5:30pm. Make your first right after the tollbooth (at the beginning of the causeway—you can't miss it) to find the outfitters. They also rent kayaks.

8 More Ways to Play, Indoors & Out

BIKING

The cement promenade on the southern tip of South Beach is a great place to ride. Biking up the beach (on either the beach or along the beach on a cement pathway—which is a lot easier!) is great for surf, sun, sand, exercise, and people-watching—just be sure to keep your eyes on the road, as the scenery can be most distracting. Most of the big beach hotels rent bicycles, as does the **Miami Beach Bicycle Center,** 601 5th St., South Beach (© **305/674-0150**), which charges $8 per hour or $20 for up to 24 hours. It's open Monday through Saturday from 10am to 7pm, Sunday from 10am to 5pm.

Bikers can also enjoy more than 130 miles of paved paths throughout Miami. The beautiful and quiet streets of Coral Gables and Coconut Grove (several bike trails are spread throughout these neighborhoods) are great for bicyclists, where old trees form canopies over wide, flat roads lined with grand homes and quaint street markers.

The terrain in Key Biscayne is perfect for biking, especially along the park and beach roads. If you don't mind the sound of cars whooshing by your bike lane, **Rickenbacker Causeway** is also fantastic, since it is one of the only bikeable inclines in Miami from which you get fantastic elevated views of the city and waterways. However, be warned that this is a grueling ride, especially going up the causeway. **Key Cycling,** 61 Harbor Dr., Key Biscayne (© **305/361-0061**), rents mountain bikes for $5 an hour or $15 a day, with a 2-hour minimum. It's open Tuesday through Friday from 10am to 7pm, Monday and Saturday from 10am to 6pm, and Sunday from 10am to 3pm.

If you want to avoid the traffic altogether, head out to **Shark Valley** in the Everglades National Park—one of South Florida's most scenic bicycle trails and a favorite haunt of city-weary locals. For more information on Shark Valley and the Everglades, see chapter 7.

For a decent list of trail suggestions throughout South Florida, visit www.geocities.com/floutdoorzone/bike.html. *Biking note:* Children under the age of 16 are required by Florida law to wear a helmet, which can be purchased at any bike store or retail outlet selling biking supplies.

FISHING

Fishing licenses are required in Florida. If you go out with one of the fishing charter boats listed below, you are automatically accredited because the companies are. If you go out on your own, however, you must have a Florida fishing license, which costs $17 for Florida residents and $32 for nonresidents. Call © **888/FISH-FLO** or visit www.wildlifelicense.com for more information.

Some of the best surf casting in the city can be had at **Haulover Beach Park** at Collins Avenue and 105th Street, where there's a bait-and-tackle shop right on the pier. **South Pointe Park,** at the southern tip of Miami Beach, is another popular fishing spot and features a long pier, comfortable benches, and a great view of the ships passing through Government Cut, the deep channel made when the port of Miami was dug.

You can also do some deep-sea fishing in the Miami area. One bargain outfitter, the **Kelley Fishing Fleet,** at the Haulover Marina, 10800 Collins Ave. (at 108th St.), Miami Beach (© **305/945-3801**), has half-day, full-day, and night fishing aboard diesel-powered "party boats." The fleet's emphasis on drifting is geared toward trolling and bottom fishing for snapper, sailfish, and mackerel. Half-day and night fishing trips are $31 for adults and $22 for children up to 10 years old; full-day trips are $49 for adults and $39 for children; prices are $5 cheaper if you have your own rod. Daily departures are scheduled at 9am, and 1:45 and 8pm; reservations are recommended.

Also at the Haulover Marina is the charter boat *Helen C* (10800 Collins Ave.; © **305/947-4081;** www.fishmiamibeach.com). Although there's no shortage of private charter boats here, Capt. Dawn Mergelsberg is a good pick, since she puts individuals together to get a full boat. Her *Helen* is a twin-engine 55-footer, equipped for big-game "monster" fish like marlin, tuna, dolphin fish, shark, and sailfish. The cost is $100 per person. Private, full-day trips are available for groups of six people per vessel and cost $900; half days are $500. Group rates and specials are also available. Sailings are scheduled for 8am to noon and 1 to 5pm daily; call for reservations. Children are welcome.

Key Biscayne offers deep-sea fishing to those willing to get their hands dirty and pay a bundle. The competition among the boats is fierce, but the prices are basically the same no matter which you choose. The going rate is about $400 to $450 for a half day and $600 to $700 for a full day of fishing. These rates are usually for a party of up to six, and the boats supply you with rods and bait as well as instruction for first-timers. Some will also take you out to the Upper Keys if the fish aren't biting in Miami.

You might also consider the following boats, all of which sail out of the Key Biscayne marina and are in relatively good shape and nicer than most out there: *Sunny Boy* (© **305/361-2217**), *Top Hatt* (© **305/361-2528**), and *L & H* (© **305/361-9318**). Call for reservations.

Bridge fishing in Biscayne Bay is also popular in Miami; you'll see people with poles over almost every waterway. But look carefully for signs telling you whether it's legal to do so wherever you are: Some bridges forbid fishing.

GAMBLING

Although gambling is technically illegal in Miami, there are plenty of loopholes that allow all kinds of wagering. Gamblers can try their luck at offshore casinos or on shore at bingo, jai alai, card rooms, horse tracks, dog races, and Native-American reservations.

Especially popular is **Miccosukee Indian Gaming,** 500 SW 177th Ave. (off S.R. 41, in West Miami on the outskirts of the Everglades; © **800/741-4600** or 305/222-4600), where a touch of Vegas meets west Miami. This tacky casino isn't Caesar's Palace, but you can play tab slots, high-speed bingo (watch out for the serious blue-haired players who will scoff if you make too much noise or if you win before they do), and even poker (with a $10 maximum pot). With more than 85,000 square feet of playing space, the complex even offers overnight accommodations for those who can't get enough of the thrill and don't want to make the approximately 1-hour trip back to downtown Miami. Take the Florida Turnpike south toward Florida City/Key West. Take the SW 8th Street exit

(#25) and turn left onto SW 8th Street. Drive for about 3½ miles and then turn left onto Krome Avenue, and left again at 177th Street; you can't miss it.

Recently, many of Miami's sketchier gambling-cruise operators have been shut down. The classiest and most legit gambling cruise still in business is the *Casino Princesa,* which docks behind the Hard Rock Cafe in Bayside Marketplace. This 200-foot $15 million yacht has more than 200 slot machines, 32 tables, a restaurant, and four lounges in 10,000 square feet of gaming space on two decks. It's also a major bargain (unless, of course, you lose) at $10 per person. Ships sail for 5 hours from 12:30 to 5:30pm and 7:30pm to 12:30am daily. They will also pick you up at your hotel. Call 🕐 **305/379-5825** or visit www.casinoprincesa.com for updated schedules. You must be 21 or older to sail.

GOLF

There are more than 50 private and public golf courses in the Miami area. Contact the **Greater Miami Convention and Visitor's Bureau** (🕐 **800/933-8448;** www.miamiandbeaches.com) for a list of courses and costs.

The best hotel courses in Miami are found at the **Doral Golf Resort and Spa** (p. 81), home of the legendary Blue Monster course as well as the Gold Course, designed by Raymond Floyd; the Great White Shark Course; and the Silver Course, refinished by Jerry Pate.

Other hotels with excellent golf courses include the **Turnberry Isle Resort & Club** (p. 83), with two Robert Trent Jones Sr.–designed courses for guests and members, and the **Biltmore Hotel** 🎯🎯 (p. 84), which is my pick for best public golf course because of its modest greens fees and an 18-hole par-71 course located on the hotel's spectacular grounds. It must be good: Despite his penchant for privacy, former President Bill Clinton prefers teeing off at this course over any other in Miami!

Otherwise, the following represent some of the area's best public courses. **Crandon Park Golf Course,** formerly known as the Links, 6700 Crandon Blvd., Key Biscayne (🕐 **305/361-9129**), is the number-one-ranked municipal course in the state and one of the top five in the country. The park is situated on 200 bayfront acres and offers a pro shop, rentals, lessons, carts, and a lighted driving range. The course is open daily from dawn to dusk; greens fees (including cart) are $137 per person during the winter and $58 per person during the summer. Special twilight rates are also available.

One of the most popular courses among real enthusiasts is the **Doral Park Golf and Country Club,** 5001 NW 104th Ave., West Miami (🕐 **305/ 591-8800**); it's not related to the Doral Hotel or spa. Call to book in advance since this challenging, semi-private 18-holer is extremely popular with locals. The course is open from 6:30am to 6pm during the winter and until 7pm during the summer. Cart and greens fees vary, so call 🕐 **305/592-2000** ext. 2104 for information.

Known as one of the best in the city, the **Country Club of Miami,** 6801 Miami Gardens Dr., at NW 68th Avenue, North Miami (🕐 **305/829-8456**), has three 18-hole courses of varying degrees of difficulty. You'll encounter lush fairways, rolling greens, and some history to boot. The west course, designed in 1961 by Robert Trent Jones Sr. and updated in the 1990s by the PGA, was where Jack Nicklaus played his first professional tournament and Lee Trevino won his first professional championship. The course is open daily from 7am to sunset. Cart and greens fees are $38 to $71 per person during the winter, and $20 to $34 per person during the summer. Special twilight rates are available.

> **Tips** **Par for the Course**
>
> You can get information about most Florida courses, including current greens fees, and reserve tee times, through **Tee Times USA**, P.O. Box 641, Flagler Beach, FL 32136 (② **800/374-8633**, 888/Golf-Flo, or 386/439-0001; fax 386/439-0099; www.teetimesusa.com). This company also publishes a vacation guide that includes many stay-and-play golf packages.

Golfers looking for some cheap practice time will appreciate **Haulover Beach Park,** 10800 Collins Ave., Miami Beach (② **305/940-6719**), in a pretty bayside location. The longest hole on this par-27 course is 125 yards. It's open daily from 7:30am to 6pm during the winter, and until 7:30pm during the summer. Greens fees are $6.40 per person during the winter and summer. Handcarts cost $1.90.

IN-LINE SKATING
Miami's consistently flat terrain makes in-line skating a breeze. Lincoln Road, for example, is a virtual skating rink as bladers compete with bikers and walkers for a slab of slate. But the city's heavy traffic and construction do make it tough to find long routes suitable for blading.

Because of the popularity of blading and skateboarding, the city has passed a law prohibiting skating on the west side (the cafe-lined strip) of Ocean Drive in the evenings as well as a law that all bladers must skate slowly and safely. Also, if you're going to partake in the sport, remember to keep a pair of sandals or sneakers with you, since many area shops won't allow you inside with skates on.

Despite all the rules, you can still have fun, and the following rental outfit can help chart an interesting course for you and supply you with all the necessary gear. In South Beach, **Fritz's Skate Shop,** 730 Lincoln Rd. Mall (② **305/ 532-1954**), rents top-quality skates, including safety pads, for $8 per hour, $24 per day, and $34 overnight. They provide free lessons at 10:30am on Sundays when you rent equipment, or they can hook you up with an instructor for private lessons. The shop also stocks lots of gear and clothing.

SWIMMING
There is no shortage of water in the Miami area. See the Venetian Pool listing (p. 124) and the "Miami's Beaches" section earlier in this chapter for descriptions of good swimming options.

TENNIS
Hundreds of tennis courts in South Florida are open to the public for a minimal fee. Most courts operate on a first-come, first-served basis and are open from sunrise to sunset. For information and directions, call the **City of Miami Beach Recreation, Culture, and Parks Department** (② **305/673-7730**) or the **City of Miami Parks and Recreation Department** (② **305/575-5256**).

Of the 590 public tennis courts throughout Miami, the three hard courts and seven clay courts at the **Key Biscayne Tennis Association,** 6702 Crandon Blvd. (② **305/361-5263**), are the best and most beautiful. Because of this, they often get crowded on weekends. You'll play on the same courts as Lendl, Graf, Evert, McEnroe, and other greats; this is also the venue for one of the world's biggest annual tennis events, the Nasdaq 100 Open. There's a pleasant, if limited, pro shop, plus many good pros. Only four courts are lit at night, but if you reserve

> **Tips A Fisherman's Friend**
>
> The Biscayne Bay area is prime tarpon fishing country and a pretty good spot for a lot of other trophy sportfish: snook, bonefish, dolphin fish, swordfish, and sailfish. For a fee, local guides are happy to show you the hot spots and make sure you reel one in. One such guide is **Capt. David Parsons** (© 305/968-9603), who owns a great 28-foot boat, *Hakuna Matada.* He knows where the fish are biting and will take you from Biscayne Bay to the Atlantic Ocean in search of the best catch of the day for $550 for four people (swordfish can be caught at nighttime only; those trips run at $600), including rods, gear, and bait. All you bring is food/drink. Capt. Parsons also leads trips to Bimini for those who want to explore the fishing in the Bahamas.

at least 24 to 48 hours in advance, you can usually take your pick. They cost $6 per person per hour. The courts are open Monday through Friday from 8am to 9pm, Saturday and Sunday until 6pm.

Other courts are pretty run of the mill and can be found in most neighborhoods. I do, however, recommend the **Miami Beach public courts at Flamingo Park,** 1001 12th St. in South Beach (© 305/673-7761), where there are 19 clay courts that cost $4 per person an hour for Miami Beach residents and $8 per person an hour for nonresidents. It's first-come, first-served. Open 8am to 9pm Monday through Friday, 8am to 8pm Saturday and Sunday.

Hotels with the best tennis facilities are the Biltmore, Turnberry Isle Resort and Spa, the Doral Resort and Spa, and the Inn and Spa at Fisher Island. See "Where to Stay in Miami" in chapter 4 for information about these accommodations.

9 Spectator Sports

Check the *Miami Herald*'s sports section for a daily listing of local events and the paper's Friday "Weekend" section for comprehensive coverage and in-depth reports. For last-minute tickets, call the venue directly, since many season ticket holders sell singles and return unused tickets. Expensive tickets are available from brokers or individuals listed in the classified sections of the local papers. Some tickets are also available through **Ticketmaster** (© 305/358-5885).

BASEBALL

The 2003 World Champion **Florida Marlins** shocked the sports world in 1997 when they became the youngest expansion team to win a World Series, but then floundered as their star players were sold off by former owner Wayne Huizenga. They shocked the sports world again in 2003 by winning the World Series and turned many of Miami's apathetic sports fans into major league ball fans. If you're interested in catching a game, be warned: The summer heat in Miami can be unbearable, even in the evenings.

Home games are held at the **Pro Player Stadium,** NW 199th St., North Miami Beach (© 305/623-6200). Tickets cost from $4 to $50. Box office hours are Monday to Friday from 8:30am to 5:30pm and before games; tickets are also available through Ticketmaster. The team currently holds spring training in Melbourne, Florida.

BASKETBALL

The **Miami Heat** (© 786/777-1000), no longer led by celebrity coach Pat Riley, made their NBA debut in November 1988 and their games remain one of Miami's hottest tickets. Courtside seats are full of visiting celebrities from Puff Daddy to Madonna. The season lasts from October to April, with most games beginning at 7:30pm. They play in the brand-new waterfront **American Airlines Arena,** located downtown on Biscayne Boulevard. Tickets are $14 to $100 or much more. Box office hours are Monday through Friday from 10am to 5pm (until 8pm on game nights); tickets are also available through Ticketmaster (© **305/358-5885**).

FOOTBALL

Miami's golden boys are the **Miami Dolphins,** the city's most recognizable team, followed by thousands of "dolfans." The team plays at least eight home games during the season, between September and December, at **Pro Player Stadium,** 2269 NW 199th St., North Miami Beach (© **305/620-2578**). Tickets cost between $20 and much, much more. The box office is open Monday through Friday from 8:30am to 5:30pm; tickets are also available through Ticketmaster (© **305/358-5885**).

HORSE RACING

Located on the Dade–Broward County border in Hallandale (just north of North Miami Beach/Aventura) is **Gulfstream Park,** at U.S. 1 and Hallandale Beach Boulevard (© **305/931-7223;** www.gulfstreampark.com), South Florida's very own version of the Kentucky Derby, albeit not nearly as sceney. This horse track is a haven for serious gamblers and voyeurs alike. Large purses and important races are commonplace at this sprawling suburban course, and the track is typically crowded, especially during its amusing and entertaining concert series from January to April, which features has-beens and one-hit wonders such as Cindy Lauper, REO Speedwagon, and Bryan Adams on the front lawn for just $5. Call for schedules. Admission is $3 to the grandstand weekdays and $5 weekends and $5 to the clubhouse; parking is free. Children under 17 are free. January through March, post times are 1:30pm on weekdays and 1pm on weekends. Closed Tuesdays.

ICE HOCKEY

The young **Florida Panthers** (© **954/835-7000**) have already made history. In the 1994–95 season, they played in the Stanley Cup finals, and they have amassed a legion of fans who love them. Much to the disappointment of Miamians, they moved to a new venue in Sunrise, the next county north of Miami-Dade, more than an hour from downtown Miami. Call for directions and ticket information.

JAI ALAI

Jai alai, sort of a Spanish-style indoor lacrosse, was introduced to Miami in 1924 and is regularly played in two Miami-area frontons (the buildings in which jai alai is played). Although the sport has roots stemming from ancient Egypt, the game, as it's now played, was invented by Basque peasants in the Pyrenees Mountains during the 17th century.

Players use woven baskets, called *cestas,* to hurl balls, called *pelotas,* at speeds that sometimes exceed 170 mph. Spectators, who are protected behind a wall of

Jai Alai Explained

Jai alai originated in the Basque country of northern Spain, where players used to use church walls as their courts. The game looks very much like lacrosse, actually, with rules very similar to handball or tennis and is played on a court with numbered lines. What makes the game totally unique, however, is the requirement that the ball must be returned in one continuous motion. The server must bounce the ball behind the serving line and with the basket, must hurl the ball to the front wall, with the aim being that, upon rebound, the ball will bounce between lines four and seven. If it doesn't, it is an under- or overserve and the other team receives a point.

glass, place bets on the evening's players. The Florida Gaming Corporation owns the jai alai operations throughout the state, making betting on this sport as legal as buying a lottery ticket.

The **Miami Jai Alai Fronton,** 3500 NW 37th Ave., at NW 35th Street (© **305/633-6400**), is America's oldest fronton, dating from 1926. It schedules 13 games per night, which typically last 10 to 20 minutes, but can occasionally go much longer. Admission is $1 to the grandstand, $5 to the clubhouse. There are year-round games. On Wednesdays, Thursdays, and Sundays, there are matinees only that run from noon to 5:30pm. Fridays, Saturdays, and Mondays, there are matinees in addition to evening games from 7pm to midnight. The fronton is closed on Tuesdays. See p. 245 for information on **Dania Jai Alai.**

10 Cruises & Other Caribbean Getaways

Cruising has come a long way since the days of bingo, shuffleboard, and even the delusional *Love Boat.* Whether you prefer megaships with rock-climbing walls or a smaller, less elaborate ship that just sails you to your destination, a floating vacation can be a very enticing option for people traveling to South Florida. The proximity to the Caribbean makes 3-, 4-, 6-, 7-, or 9-day cruises an excellent diversion from the hustle and bustle of the big city.

If you want to catch a weekend in the Caribbean while you're in South Florida but aren't enthralled with the idea of boat travel, there are a number of air packages available as well. Travel to Cuba is severely restricted from Miami (or anywhere in the United States) for all but those who have obtained licenses from the U.S. State Department (see details at www.destinationcuba.com/whocanvisit.htm), although many people choose to go there from Mexico, Jamaica, or the Bahamas.

The following sections aren't intended to be detailed descriptions of the cruising and package options available out of Miami and the Keys—that would fill up an entire book on its own—but they will give you a good overview of the cruising and package picture. At press time, there were deep discounts on all cruise lines, with prices as low as, and sometimes lower than, $50 a day, so be sure to check carefully and get the best deal out there.

CRUISES

The Port of Miami is the world's busiest cruise-ship port, with a passenger load of close to three million annually. The popularity of these cruises shows no sign of tapering off, and the trend in ships is toward bigger, more luxurious liners. Usually all-inclusive, cruises offer value and simplicity compared to other vacation options. Most of the Caribbean-bound cruise ships sail weekly out of the Port of Miami. They are relatively inexpensive, can be booked without advance notice, and make for an excellent excursion.

The Port of Miami is very close to downtown Miami, but the most popular pre- and postcruise destination in Miami is South Beach (about a 10-min. ride from the port), because of its proximity to the port and the fact that it's a relatively small (and walkable) area full of nightlife, beaches, hotels, and restaurants (see the South Beach sections of this book). If you're just looking for a quick overnight stay, your best bet may be one of the downtown-area hotels, which are closest to the port. The only two in the immediate area that I'd recommend, however, are The Hotel Inter-Continental Miami (p. 79), which is literally up the block from the port, or the Biscayne Bay Marriott, located about 5 minutes away. For food and shopping, Bayside Marketplace (p. 142) is within walking distance of the port. For other restaurants in this area, check the downtown dining section of chapter 4, beginning on p. 104. Cabs are abundant at the port. A ride to the airport should cost about $25 and a ride to South Beach should be about $10.

All the shorter cruises (3 and 4 days) are well equipped for gambling. Their casinos open as soon as the ship clears U.S. waters—typically 45 minutes after leaving port. Usually, four full-size meals are served daily, with portions so huge they're impossible to finish. Games, movies, and other onboard activities ensure you're always busy. Passengers can board up to 2 hours before departure for meals, games, and cocktails.

There are dozens of cruises from which to choose—from 1-day excursions to a trip around the world. You can get a full list of options from the **Metro-Dade Seaport Department,** 1015 N. America Way, Miami, FL 33132 (© **305/ 371-7678**). It's open Monday through Friday from 8am to 5pm.

The cruise lines and ships listed below offer 3-, 4-, and 7-night cruises to the Caribbean, Key West, and other longer itineraries that often change. If you want more information, contact the individual line, or, for Bahamas cruises, call the **Bahamas Tourist Office,** 1200 S. Pine Island, Suite 750, Plantation, FL 33234 (© **954/236-9292;** www.bahamas.com). All passengers must travel with a passport or proof of citizenship for reentry into the United States.

For detailed information on Caribbean cruises, pick up a copy of *Frommer's Caribbean Cruises & Ports of Call.*

You can also contact the various cruise lines directly, at: **Carnival Cruise Lines** (© **800/327-9501** or 305/599-2200; www.carnival.com); **Cunard** (© **800/528-6273** or 305/463-3000; www.cunardline.com); **Norwegian Cruise Line (NCL)** (© **800/327-7030** or 305/436-0866; www.ncl.com); **Royal Caribbean International (RCI)** (© **800/327-6700** or 305/539-6000; www.royalcaribbean.com).

FLIGHTS & WEEKEND PACKAGES

For those who want a quick getaway to the Caribbean without the experience of cruising, many airlines and hotels team up to offer extremely affordable weekend packages.

For example, the Bahamas' most entertaining and family-friendly resort, the **Atlantis** on Paradise Island (© **888/528-7155;** www.atlantis.com), is a tropical theme park offering extensive water sports plus an active casino. Reasonably priced 3-day packages start at about $390, depending on departure date. (It's generally cheaper to fly midweek.) Flights on **Continental Airlines** (© **800/ 786-7202**) depart at least twice daily from Miami International. You can also choose to stay in the company's other luxurious resorts: the **Paradise Beach Resort** or the **Ocean Club.** Book package deals through **Paradise Island Vacations** (© **800/722-7466**).

Other groups that arrange competitively priced packages include **American Flyaway Vacations,** operated by American Airlines (© **800/321-2121**); **Bahamas Air** (© **800/222-4262**); and **Chalks Ocean Airways** (© **305/ 371-8628**). Call for rates, since they vary dramatically throughout the year and also depend on what type of accommodations you choose. Keep your eye on the travel section of the *Miami Herald,* as well, as special deals and packages are almost always advertised.

11 Animal Parks

For a tropical climate, Miami's got a lot of nontropical animals to see, and we're not talking about the motorists on I-95. Everything from dolphins and alligators to lions, tigers, and bears call Miami home (most in parks, some in nature).

Miami Metrozoo *Kids* This 290-acre, sparsely landscaped complex (it was devastated by Hurricane Andrew) is quite a distance from Miami proper and the beaches—about 45 minutes—but worth the trip. Isolated and never really crowded, it's also completely cageless—animals are kept at bay by cleverly designed moats. This is a fantastic spot to take younger kids (the older ones seem bored and unstimulated here); there's a wonderful petting zoo and play area, and the zoo offers several daily programs designed to educate and entertain. Mufasa and Simba (of Disney fame) were modeled on a couple of Metrozoo's lions. Other residents include two rare white Bengal tigers, a Komodo dragon, rare koala bears, a number of kangaroos, and an African meerkat. The air-conditioned Zoofari Monorail tour offers visitors a nice overview of the park. An Andean Condor exhibit opened in 2000, and the zoo is always upgrading its facilities, including the impressive aviary. *Note:* The distance between animal habitats can be great, so you'll be doing *a lot* of walking here. Also, because the zoo can be miserably hot during summer months, plan these visits in the early morning or late afternoon. Expect to spend about 3 hours here.

12400 SW 152nd St., South Miami. © 305/251-0400. www.miamimetrozoo.com. Admission $12 adults, $7 children 3–12. Daily 9:30am–5:30pm (ticket booth closes at 4pm). Free parking. From U.S. 1 south, turn right on SW 152nd St. and follow signs about 3 miles to the entrance.

Miami Seaquarium *Kids Overrated* If you've been to Orlando's SeaWorld, you may be disappointed with Miami's version, which is considerably smaller and not as well maintained. It's hardly a sprawling seaquarium, but you will want to arrive early to enjoy the effects of its mild splash. You'll need at least 3 hours to tour the 35-acre oceanarium and see all four daily shows starring a number of showy ocean mammals. You can cut your visit to 2 hours if you limit your shows to the better, albeit corny, Flipper Show and Killer Whale Show. The highly regarded Water and Dolphin Exploration Program (WADE) allows visitors to touch and swim with dolphins in the Flipper Lagoon. The program costs

$140 per person participating, $32 per observer, and is offered twice daily, at noon and 3:30pm, 7 days a week. Children must be at least 52 inches tall to participate. Reservations are necessary for this program. Call ✆ **305/365-2501** in advance for reservations.

4400 Rickenbacker Causeway (south side), en route to Key Biscayne. ✆ **305/361-5705**. www. miamiseaquarium.com. Admission $25 adults, $20 children 3–9, free for children under 3. Daily 9:30am–6pm (ticket booth closes at 4pm).

Monkey Jungle ✦ *(Overrated)*   Personally, I think this place is disgusting. It reeks, the monkeys are either sleeping or in heat, and it's really far from the city, even farther than the zoo. But if primates are your thing and you'd rather pass on the zoo, you'll be in paradise. You'll see rare Brazilian golden lion tamarins and Asian macaques. There are no cages to restrain the antics of the monkeys as they swing, chatter, and play their way into your heart. Screened-in trails wind through acres of "jungle," and daily shows feature the talents of the park's most progressive pupils. People who go here are not monkeying around—many of the park's frequent visitors are scientists and anthropologists. In fact, an interesting archaeological exhibition excavated from a Monkey Jungle sinkhole displays 10,000 year old artifacts including human teeth and animal bones. A somewhat amusing attraction here, if you can call it that, is the Wild Monkey Swimming Pool, a show in which you get to watch Sea Monkeys diving for food. If you can stand the humidity, the smell, and the bugs (flies, mosquitoes, and so on), expect to spend about 2 hours here. The park's website sometimes offers downloadable discount coupons, so if you have Internet access, take a look before you visit.

14805 SW 216th St., South Miami. ✆ **305/235-1611**. www.monkeyjungle.com. Admission $16 adults, $13 seniors and active-duty military, $9.95 children 4–12. Daily 9:30am–5pm (tickets sold until 4pm). Take U.S. 1 south to SW 216th St., or from Florida Turnpike, take exit 11 and follow the signs.

Parrot Jungle Island ✦ *(Kids)*   This Miami institution took flight from its lush, natural South Miami environment and headed north in the winter of 2003 to a new, overly fabricated, disappointing $46 million home on Watson Island, along the MacArthur Causeway near Miami Beach. While the island doubles as a protected bird sanctuary, the jungle's former digs in the heart of South Miami in a circa-1900 coral rock structure were a lot more charming and kitschier. The new, overpriced 18.6-acre park features an Everglades exhibit, a petting zoo, and several theaters, jungle trails, and aviaries. Watch your heads because flying above are hundreds of parrots, macaws, peacocks, cockatoos, and flamingos. But it's not all a loss. Be sure to check out the Crocosaurus, a 20-foot long saltwater crocodile who hangs out in the park's Serpentarium, which also houses the park's reptile and amphibian collection. Also a pleasant surprise here is the Ichimura Japanese Garden. Continuous shows star roller-skating cockatoos, card-playing macaws, and numerous stunt-happy parrots. There are also tortoises, iguanas, and a rare albino alligator on exhibit. The park's website sometimes offers downloadable discount coupons, so if you have Internet access, take a look before you visit, because you definitely won't want to pay full price for this park. If you do get your money's worth and see all the shows and exhibits, expect to spend upwards of 4 hours here.

1111 Parrot Jungle Trail, Watson Island (on the north side of MacArthur Causeway/I-395). ✆ **305/372-3822**. www.parrotjungle.com. Admission $24 adults, $22 seniors and military, $19 children 3–10. Parking an additional $6 per vehicle. Daily 10am–6pm. From I-95, take I-395 East (MacArthur Causeway), make a right on Parrot Jungle Trail which is the first exit after the bridge. Follow the road around and under the causeway to the parking garage on the left-hand side.

Sea Grass Adventures ⚡ *Value* *Kids*   Even better than the Seaquarium is Sea Grass Adventures, in which a naturalist from the Marjory Stoneman Douglas Biscayne Nature Center will introduce ($10 per person) kids and adults to an amazing variety of creatures that live in the sea grass beds of the Bear Cut Nature Preserve near Crandon Beach on Key Biscayne. Not just a walking tour, you will be able to wade in the water with your guide and catch an assortment of sea life in nets provided by the guides. At the end of the program, participants gather on the beach while the guide explains what everyone's just caught, passing the creatures around in miniature viewing tanks. Call for available dates, times, and reservations.

Marjory Stoneman Douglas Biscayne Nature Center, 6767 Crandon Blvd., Key Biscayne. ⓒ 305/361-6767. The center is free. Daily 10am–4pm.

12 Shopping

Miami is one of the world's premier shopping cities; more than 10 million visitors came here last year and they spent in excess of $13 billion. People come to Miami from all over—from Latin America to Hong Kong—in search of some products that are all-American (such as, Levi's, Nikes, and so on).

So if you're not into sunbathing and outdoor activities, or you just can't take the heat, you'll be in good company in one of Miami's many malls—and you are not likely to emerge empty-handed. In addition to the strip malls, Miami offers a choice of megamalls, from the upscale Village of Merrick Park and the mammoth Aventura Mall to the ritzy Bal Harbour Shops and touristy, yet scenic, Bayside Marketplace (just to name a few).

Miami also offers more unique shopping spots, such as the up and coming area near downtown known as the Biscayne Corridor, where funky boutiques dare to defy the Gap, and Little Havana, where you can buy hand-rolled cigars and *guayabera* shirts.

You may want to order the Greater Miami Convention and Visitors Bureau's "Shop Miami: A Guide to a Tropical Shopping Adventure." Although it is limited to details on the bureau's paying members, it provides some good advice and otherwise unpublished discount offers. The glossy little pamphlet is printed in English, Spanish, and Portuguese and provides information about transportation from hotels, translation services, and shipping. Call ⓒ **800/283-2707** or 305/539-3000 for more information.

THE SHOPPING SCENE

Below you'll find descriptions of some of the more popular retail areas, where many stores are conveniently clustered together to make browsing easier.

As a general rule, shop hours are Monday through Saturday from 10am to 6pm and Sunday from noon to 5pm. Many stores stay open late (until 9pm or so) one night of the week (usually Thurs). Shops in Coconut Grove are open until 9pm Sunday through Thursday and even later on Friday and Saturday nights. South Beach's stores also stay open later—as late as midnight. Department stores and shopping malls also keep longer hours, with most staying open from 10am to 9 or 10pm Monday through Saturday, and noon to 6pm on Sunday. With all these variations, call ahead to specific stores to find out what their hours are.

The 6.5% state and local sales tax is added to the price of all nonfood purchases. Food and beverage in hotels and restaurants are taxed via the resort tax, which is 3% in Miami/South Beach and Bal Harbour, 4% in Surfside, and 2% in the rest of Miami–Dade County.

SHOPPING AREAS

Most of Miami's shopping happens at the many megamalls scattered from one end of the county to the other; however, there is also some excellent boutique shopping and browsing to be done in the following areas (see "The Neighborhoods in Brief" in chapter 4 for more information):

AVENTURA   On Biscayne Boulevard between Miami Gardens Drive and the county line at Hallandale Beach Boulevard is a 2-mile stretch of major retail stores including Best Buy, Borders, Circuit City, Linens N' Things, Marshall's, Sports Authority, and more. Also here is the mammoth Aventura Mall, housing a fabulous collection of shops and restaurants.

CALLE OCHO   For a taste of Little Havana, take a walk down 8th Street between SW 27th Avenue and SW 12th Avenue, where you'll find some lively street life and many shops selling cigars, baked goods, shoes, furniture, and record stores specializing in Latin music. For help, take your Spanish dictionary.

COCONUT GROVE   Downtown Coconut Grove, centered on Main Highway and Grand Avenue and branching onto the adjoining streets, is one of Miami's most pedestrian-friendly zones. The Grove's wide sidewalks, lined with cafes and boutiques, can provide hours of browsing pleasure. Coconut Grove is best known for its chain stores (Gap, Banana Republic, and so on) and some funky holdovers from the days when the Grove was a bit more bohemian, plus excellent sidewalk cafes centered on CocoWalk and the Streets of Mayfair.

MIRACLE MILE (CORAL GABLES)   Actually only a half-mile long, this central shopping street was an integral part of George Merrick's original city plan. Today, the strip still enjoys popularity, especially for its bridal stores, ladies' shops, haberdashers, and gift shops. Recently, newer chain stores, like Barnes & Noble, Old Navy, and Starbucks, have been appearing on the Mile. The hyper upscale Village of **Merrick Park,** a mammoth, 850,000-square-foot upscale outdoor shopping complex between Ponce de León Boulevard and Le Jeune Road, just off the Mile, opened in the fall of 2002 with Nordstrom, Neiman Marcus, Armani, Gucci, Jimmy Choo, and Yves St. Laurent on board, to name a few.

DOWNTOWN MIAMI   If you're looking for discounts on all types of goods—especially watches, fabric, buttons, lace, shoes, luggage, and leather—Flagler Street, just west of Biscayne Boulevard, is the best place to start. I wouldn't necessarily recommend buying expensive items here, as many stores seem to be on the shady side and do not understand the word *warranty.* However, you can still have fun here as long as you are a savvy shopper and don't mind haggling with people who may not have the firmest grasp on the English language. Most signs are printed in English, Spanish, and Portuguese; however, many shopkeepers may not be entirely fluent in English. Most recently, the developers responsible for Coconut Grove's CocoWalk shopping and entertainment complex broke ground on Mary Brickell Village, a 192,000-square-foot urban entertainment center west of Brickell Avenue and straddling South Miami Avenue between 9th and 10th streets downtown. The $80 million complex (slated to open in the beginning of 2005) will consist of a slew of trendy restaurants, boutiques, and, of course, the "required" Starbucks—a sure sign that a neighborhood has been revitalized.

BISCAYNE CORRIDOR   ⚓   Amidst the ramshackle old motels of yesteryear exist several funky, kitschy, and arty boutiques along the stretch of Biscayne Boulevard from 50th Street to about 79th Street known as the Biscayne Corridor.

Everything from hand painted tank tops to expensive Juicy Couture sweat suits can be found here, but it's not just about fashion. Several furniture stores selling antiques and modern pieces exist along here as well, so look carefully as you may find something here that would cause the appraisers on Antiques Road Show to lose their wigs.

SOUTH BEACH ⭐   Slowly but surely South Beach has come into its own as far as shopping is concerned. While the requisite stores—Gap, Banana Republic, and others—have anchored here, several higher-end stores have also opened on the southern blocks of Collins Avenue, which has become the Madison Avenue of Miami. For the hippest clothing boutiques (including Armani Exchange, Ralph Lauren, Versace, Benetton, Levi's, Barneys Co-Op, Diesel, Guess?, Club Monaco, Kenneth Cole, and Nicole Miller, among others), stroll along this pretty strip of the Art Deco District.

For those who are interested in a little more fun with their shopping, consider South Beach's legendary Lincoln Road. This pedestrian mall, originally designed in 1957 by Morris Lapidus, recently underwent a multimillion-dollar renovation, restoring it to its former glory. Here, shoppers find an array of clothing, books, tchotchkes, and art as well as a menagerie of sidewalk cafes flanked on one end by a multiplex movie theater, and at the other, the Atlantic Ocean.

SHOPPING A TO Z

BooksYou can find local branches of **Barnes & Noble** at 152 Miracle Mile (© 305/446-4152), 5701 Sunset Dr. (© 305/662-4770), 18711 NE Biscayne Blvd. (© 305/935-9770), 7710 N. Kendall (© 305/598-7292), and 12405 N. Kendall Dr. (© 305/598-7727). **Borders** can be found at 9205 S. Dixie Hwy. (© 305/665-8800), 11401 NW 12th St. (© 305/597-8866), 3390 Mary St. (© 305/447-1655), 19925 Biscayne Blvd. (© 305/935-0027), and 8811 SW 107th Ave. (© 305/271-7457).

Books & Books   A dedicated following turns out to browse at this warm and wonderful little independent shop. Enjoy the upstairs antiquarian room, which specializes in art books and first editions. If that's not enough intellectual stimulation for you, the shop hosts free lectures from noted authors, experts, and personalities almost nightly, from Monica Lewinsky to Martin Amis. At another location (933 Lincoln Rd., South Beach; © **305/532-3222**), you'll rub elbows with tanned and buffed South Beach bookworms sipping cappuccinos at the Russian Bear Cafe inside the store. This branch stocks a large selection of gay literature and also features lectures. 265 Aragon Ave., Coral Gables. © **305/442-4408.** www.booksandbooks.com.

Kafka's Cyberkafe   Check your e-mail and surf the Web while you sip a latte or snack on a sandwich or pastry with friendly neighborhood regulars. This popular used bookstore also stocks a wide range of foreign and domestic magazines and caters to an international-youth-hostel-type crowd. 1464 Washington Ave., South Beach. © **305/673-9669.**

CIGARS

Although it is illegal to bring Cuban cigars into the United States, somehow, forbidden *Cohibas* show up at every dinner party and nightclub in town. Not that I condone it, but if you hang around the cigar smokers in town, no doubt one will be able to tell you where you can get some of the highly prized contraband. Be careful, however, of counterfeits, which are typically Dominican cigars posing as Cubans. Cuban cigars are illegal and unless you go down a sketchy alley to buy one from a dealer (think of it as shady as a drug deal), you are going to be smoking Dominican ones.

The stores listed below sell excellent hand-rolled cigars made with domestic- and foreign-grown tobacco. Many of the *viejos* (old men) got their training in Cuba working for the government-owned factories in the heyday of Cuban cigars.

La Gloria Cubana Cigar   This tiny storefront shop employs about 45 veteran Cuban rollers who sit all day rolling the very popular torpedoes and other criti- cally acclaimed blends. They're usually back-ordered, but it's worth stopping in: They will sell you a box and show you around. 1106 SW 8th St., Little Havana. ℂ 305/858-4162.

Mike's Cigars Distributor's Inc. *Finds*   Mike's may have abandoned its old digs for a bigger, newer location, but it's one of the oldest and best smoke shops in town. Since 1950, Mike's has been selling the best from Honduras, the Dominican Republic, and Jamaica, as well as the very hot local brand, La Glo- ria Cubana. Many say it has the best prices, too. Mike's has the biggest selection of cigars in town and the employees speak English. 1030 Kane Concourse (at 96th St.), Bay Harbor Island. ℂ 305/866-2277. www.mikescigars.com.

COSMETICS, FRAGRANCES, BEAUTY PRODUCTS & A SALON

Brownes & Co. Apothecary *Finds*   Designed to look like an old-fashioned apothecary, this recently expanded beauty emporium combines the best selec- tion of makeup and hair products—MAC, Shu Uemura, Kiehl's, Stila, Molton Brown, Francois Nars, and Dr. Hauschka, just to name a few—with lots of deli- cious-smelling bath and body stuff, plus a full-service beauty salon. Feel free to browse and sample here, as perfume-spritzing salespeople won't bother you. If you do need help, the staff is a collection of experts when it comes to beauty and hair products. Upstairs is the Browne's Beauty Lounge, in which you can get fab- ulously coiffed, colored, buffed, and waxed by the experts at the store's renowned salon, Some Like It Hot. For those of you looking for that J-Lo glow, she shops here, so ask one of the staff to point you in the right direction. 841 Lin- coln Rd., South Beach. ℂ 305/532-8703. www.brownesbeauty.com.

FASHION: CLOTHING & ACCESSORIES

Miami didn't become a fashion capital until—believe it or not—the pastel-hued, Armani-clad cops on *Miami Vice* had their close-ups on the tube. Before that, Miami was all about old men in white patent leather shoes and well-tanned women in bikinis. How things have changed! Miami is now a fashion mecca in its own right, with some of the same high-end stores you'd find on Rue de Fauborg St. Honore in Paris or Bond Street in London. You'll find all the chichi labels, including Prada and Gucci, right here at the posh Bal Harbour Shops. For funkier frocks, South Beach is the place, where designers such as Cynthia Rowley, Betsey Johnson, and Giorgio Armani compete for window shoppers with local up-and-coming designers, some of whom design for drag queens and club kids only. The strip on Collins Avenue between 7th and 10th streets has become quite upscale, including such shops as Armani Exchange and Nicole Miller, along with the inescapable Gap and Banana Republic. Of course, there's also more mainstream (and affordable) shopping in the plethora of malls and outdoor shopping and entertainment complexes that are sprinkled throughout the city (see the section on malls below).

UNISEX

Barneys Co-Op   Finally, an outpost of posh Barneys New York opens on South Beach, only this time, it's more "affordable." Hooey. If you think a T-shirt for $150 is affordable, then this store is for you. Otherwise, Barneys Co-Op is always great for browsing and marveling over the fashion victims who actually do pay such absurd prices for a cotton T-shirt. 832 Collins Ave., South Beach. ℂ 305/421-2010.

Base USA   A beautiful store featuring one-of-a-kind clothing made in St. Vincent that's light, breezy, fashionable, and, of course, pricey. Keep on the lookout for excellent sales. 939 Lincoln Rd., South Beach. ℂ 305/531-4982.

En Avance   If you couldn't get into Mynt or Opium last night, consider plunking down some major pocket change for the au courant labels that En Avance is known for. One outfit bought here and the doormen have no ground to stand on when it comes to high-fashion dress codes. 734 Lincoln Rd., South Beach. ℂ 305/534-0337.

Island Life   Part of music mogul Chris Blackwell's empire, Island sells everything you'd need to wear in a tropical resort town: batik sarongs, sandals, sundresses, bathing suits, cropped tops, and more. Many of the unique styles are created on the premises by a team of young, innovative designers. 1332 Ocean Dr., South Beach. ℂ 305/673-6300.

M-80   Independent designers found a showcase at M-80, an eclectic, hipster vintage and mod clothing store just outside the Design District, where everything from kooky T-shirts, toys, accessories, as well as independent label CDs can be found. 21 NW 36th St., Design District. ℂ 305/573-2122.

Sasparilla   Vintage Pucci, Gucci, and Fiorucci can be found at Sasparilla if you have the patience to comb through the racks. Leather wares, accessories, bags, belts, and even cool vintage T-shirts are all here at insanely vintage prices. 1630 Pennsylvania Ave., South Beach. ℂ 305/532-6611.

Women's

Belinda's Designs   This German designer makes some of the most beautiful and intricate teddies, nightgowns, and wedding dresses. The styles are a little too Stevie Nicks for me, but the creations are absolutely worth admiring. The prices are appropriately high. 917 Washington Ave., South Beach. ℂ 305/532-0068.

Chroma   Before fashion designers become too big for their britches, they sell their fabulous wares at Chroma, which is known for its fashion forward collection of women's clothing from up-and-coming designers. Save whatever you buy here, because one day it may garner lots of money in its vintage status. 920 Lincoln Rd., South Beach. ℂ 305/695-8808.

HiHo Batik   Hand painted tank tops, adorable accessories, and funky jewelry including Hello Kitty is what you'll discover in this tiny Biscayne Corridor storefront. 6909 Biscayne Blvd., Miami. ℂ 305/754-8890.

Intermix   Pretty young things can get all dolled up thanks to Intermix's fun assortment of hip women's fashions, from Stella McCartney's pricey rhinestone T-shirts to the latest jeans worn by everyone at the MTV Awards. 634 Collins Ave., South Beach. ℂ 305/531-5950.

La Perla   The only store in Florida that specializes in superluxurious Italian intimate apparel. Of course, you could fly to Milan for the price of a few bras and a nightgown, but you can't find better quality. 342 San Lorenzo Ave., Coral Gables. ℂ 305/864-2070.

Merenda Boutique Yet another funky boutique hits the Biscayne Corridor, this time with labels like paperscissors&cloth, James Perse, Frankie B., and Ella Moss. 1071 NE 79th St., Miami. ℂ 305/754-3545.

Place Vendome For cheap and funky club clothes from zebra-print pants to bright, shiny tops. Two locations: 934 Lincoln Rd., South Beach ℂ 305/673-4005, and Aventura Mall, North Miami Beach ℂ 305/932-8931.

Rebel Fashionable and funky clothing for mom and daughter is what you'll find in this fabulous Biscayne Corridor boutique that carries labels not found anywhere else. Super friendly help is a bonus, too. 6669 Biscayne Blvd., Miami. ℂ 305/758-2369.

Sage Sage has imports from Australia that are *much* cooler than Nicole Kidman and Russell Crowe combined. Dresses, tops, pants, and accessories, all from down under, definitely make a statement in Miami, where people are always down with cool clothes. 1665 Michigan Ave., South Beach. ℂ 305/538-2242.

Scoop Here's the real scoop: This Shore Club Hotel boutique hails from New York City and is the shop of choice for celebs like Cameron Diaz, who just walks in and doesn't have to ask the price of the latest from Diane Von Furstenberg, Helmut Lang, Marc Jacobs, Paul Smith, Malo, and Jimmy Choo. The Shore Club Hotel, 1901 Collins Ave. ℂ 305/532-5929.

Steam on Sunset Inc. *CSI: Miami* star David Caruso and his wife prove that they know a little something about clothing at their ultra hip store on Sunset Drive in South Miami. Among the designers here are Jiwon Park, D-Squared, Antique Boutique, and others, but the most fun here is found in the store's design itself—one dressing room is a circus tent and the other is an elevator cage. Who knew Caruso was so hip? 5830 Sunset Dr., South Miami. ℂ 305/669-9991.

Men's

Giorgio's European Clothing One of the finest custom men's stores in Miami, Giorgio's features an extensive line of Italian suits and all the latest by Canelli. 350 Miracle Mile, Coral Gables. ℂ 305/448-4302.

La Casa de las Guayaberas *Finds* Miami's premier purveyor of the traditional yet retro-hip Cuban shirt known as the *guayabera*—a loose-fitting, pleated, button-down shirt—was founded by Ramon Puig, who emigrated to Miami over 40 years ago. He still uses the same scissors he did back then, only now he's joined by a team of seamstresses who hand-sew 20 shirts a day in all colors and styles. Prices range from $15 to $375. 5840 SW 8th St., Little Havana. ℂ 305/266-9683.

Yo Yo Skateboarders, hjp-hoppers, and graffiti artists love this funky shop for its cool vintage T-shirts and x-treme clothing and accessories. 742 NE 79th St., Miami. ℂ 305754-4279.

ACCESSORIES

Me & Ro Jewelery This store carries fun and funky baubles (not cheap) as seen on Debra Messing, Sarah Jessica Parker, and Julia Roberts. The Shore Club Hotel, 1901 Collins Ave., South Beach. ℂ 305/672-3566.

SEE This fantastic eyewear store features an enormous selection of stylish specs all priced between $169 and $239, including your prescription. The staff is patient and knowledgeable. 921 Lincoln Rd., South Beach. ℂ 305/672-6622.

Simons and Green Fantastic sterling silver jewelry, leather goods, and other assorted high-end tchotchkes and gift items are what you'll find in this quaint mainstay on South Miami's Sunset Drive. 5843 Sunset Dr., South Miami. ℂ 305/667-1692.

THRIFT STORES/RESALE SHOPS

The Children's Exchange *(Kids)*   Selling everything from layettes to overalls, this pleasant little shop is chock-full of good Florida-style stuff for kids to wear to the beach and in the heat. 1415 Sunset Dr., Coral Gables. $\textcircled{C}$ 305/666-6235.

Douglas Gardens Jewish Home and Hospital Thrift Shop   Prices here are no longer the major bargain they once were, but for housewares and books, you can do all right. Call to see if they are offering any specials for seniors or students. 5713 NW 27th Ave., North Miami Beach. $\textcircled{C}$ 305/638-1900.

Rags to Riches   This is an old-time consignment shop where you might find some decent rags, and maybe even some riches. Though not as upscale as it used to be, this place is still a good spot for costume jewelry and shoes. 12577 Biscayne Blvd., North Miami. $\textcircled{C}$ 305/891-8981.

Red White & Blue Thrift Store *(Finds)*   Miami's best-kept secret is this mammoth thrift store that is meticulously organized and well stocked. You've got to search for great stuff, but it is there. There are especially good deals on children's clothes and housewares. 12640 NE 6th Ave., North Miami. $\textcircled{C}$ 305/893-1104.

MUSIC STORES

Blue Note Records *(Finds)*   Here for more than 18 years, Blue Note is music to the ears of music fanatics with a good selection of hard-to-find progressive and underground music. There are new, used, and discounted CDs and old vinyl, too. Call to find out about performances; some great names show up occasionally. A second location features jazz and LPs only. 16401 NE 15th Ave., North Miami Beach. $\textcircled{C}$ 305/940-3394. For jazz/LPs: 2299 NE 164th St., North Miami Beach $\textcircled{C}$ 305/354-4563. www.bluenoterecords.com.

Casino Records Inc.   The young, hip salespeople here speak English and tend to be music buffs. This store has the largest selection of Latin music in Miami, including pop icons such as Willy Chirino, Gloria Estefan, Albita, and local boy Nil Lara. Their slogan translates to: "If we don't have it, forget it." Believe me, they've got it. 1208 SW 8th St., Little Havana. $\textcircled{C}$ 305/856-6888.

Yesterday and Today Records *(Finds)*   This is Miami's most unique and wellstocked store for vinyl—you know, the audio dinosaur that went out with the Victrola? Y & T, as it's known, is a collector's heaven, featuring every genre of music imaginable on every format. Chances are, you could find some eight-track tapes, too. 7902 NW 36th St., Miami. $\textcircled{C}$ 305/468-0311.

13 Miami After Dark

With all the hype, you'd expect Miami to have long outlived its 15 minutes of fame by now. But you'd be wrong. Miami's nightlife, in South Beach *and,* slowly but surely, downtown, is hotter than ever before—and still getting hotter.

Practically every club in the area has installed closely guarded velvet ropes to create an air of exclusivity. Don't be fooled or intimidated by them—*anyone* can go clubbing in the Magic City, and throughout this chapter, I've provided tips to ensure you gain entry to the venue you want to go to.

South Beach is certainly Miami's uncontested nocturnal nucleus, but more and more diverse areas, such as the Design District, South Miami, and even Little Havana, are increasingly providing fun alternatives without the ludicrous cover charges, "fashionably late" hours of operation (things don't typically get started on South Beach until after 11pm), the lack of sufficient self-parking, and outrageous drink prices that come standard in South Beach.

And while South Beach dances to a more electronic beat, other parts of Miami dance to a Latin beat—from salsa and merengue to tango and cha cha. However, if you're looking for a less frenetic good time, Miami's bar scene offers something for everyone, from haute hotel bars to sleek, loungey watering holes.

Parts of downtown Miami, such as the Biscayne Corridor, the Miami River, and the Design District, are in the throes of a trendy makeover a la New York City's Meatpacking District, in which, slowly but surely, cool lounges, bars, and clubs are popping up and providing the "in" and arty crowds with another, newer, more urban-chic nocturnal pasture.

But if the possibility of a celebrity sighting in one of the city's lounges, bars, or clubs doesn't fulfill your cultural needs, Miami also offers a variety of first-rate diversions in theater, music, and dance, including a world-class ballet (under the aegis of Edward Villella), a recognized symphony, and a talented opera company.

For up-to-date listing information, and to make sure the club of the moment hasn't expired, check the *Miami Herald's* "Weekend" section, which runs on Friday, or the more comprehensive listings in *New Times,* Miami's free alternative weekly, available each Wednesday, or visit www.miami.citysearch.com online.

BARS & LOUNGES

There are countless bars and lounges in and around Miami (most require proof that you are over 21 to enter), with the highest concentration on trendy South Beach. The selection listed here is a mere sample. Keep in mind that many of the popular bars—and the easiest to get into—are in hotels (with a few notable exceptions—see below). For a clubbier scene, if you don't mind making your way through hordes of inebriated club kids, a stroll on Washington Avenue will provide you with ample insight into what's hot and what's not. Just hold onto your bags. It's not dangerous, but, occasionally, a few shady types manage to slip into the crowd. Another very important tip when in a club: *Never put your drink down out of your sight*—there have been unfortunate incidents in which drinks have been spiked with illegal chemical substances. For a less hard-core, more collegiate nightlife, head to Coconut Grove. Oh, yes, and when going out in South Beach, make sure to take a so-called disco nap, as things don't get going until at least 11pm. If you go earlier, be prepared to face an empty bar or club. Off of South Beach and in hotel bars in general, the hours are fashionably earlier, with the action starting as early as, say, 7pm.

Automatic Slim's This is *the* bar where Ozzie and Harriet types become more like Ozzy and Sharon. As South Beach's most popular, unpretentious bar, Automatic Slim's is indeed a slim space of bar, but it packs people in thanks to an exhaustive list of cheap(er) drinks, lack of attitude, great rock music, and a decor that can only be described as white trash chic. 1216 Washington Ave., South Beach. ℂ 305/695-0795. No cover.

Blue A very laid-back, very locals scene set to a sultry soundtrack of deep soul and house music has Miami's hipsters feeling the blues here on a nightly basis from 10pm to 5am. Before you whip out the St. John's Wort, dive into this so-not-trendy-it's-trendy lounge, in which the pervasive color blue will actually heighten your spirits as an eclectic haze of models, locals, and lounge lizards gather to commiserate in their dreaded trendy status. 222 Española Way (between Washington and Collins aves.), South Beach. ℂ 305/534-1009. No cover.

Clevelander If wet T-shirt contests and a fraternity party atmosphere are your thing, then this Ocean Drive mainstay is your kind of place. Popular with tourists and locals who like to pretend they're tourists, the Clevelander attracts a lively, sporty, adults-only crowd (the burly bouncers *will* confiscate fake IDs) who have no interest in being part of a scene, but, rather, taking in the very revealing scenery. A great time to check out the Clevelander is on a weekend afternoon, when beach Barbies and Kens line the bar for a post-tanning beer or frozen cocktail. 1020 Ocean Dr., South Beach. © 305/531-3485. No cover.

Grass Restaurant and Lounge   Though Grass is truly a restaurant, it's also one of the city's biggest nocturnal hotspots and has one of the most oppressive door policies in town. Regardless, the place is uber cool, with its chickee hut decor and its lounge-spinning DJs. The best way for you to get into Grass is by making a dinner reservation and dressing as if you were going up for inspection before Vogue Magazine's Cruella De Vil of Fashion, Anna Wintour. 28 NE 40th St., Design District. © 305/573-3355.

Mac's Club Deuce   Standing on its own amidst an oasis of trendiness, Mac's Club Deuce is the quintessential dive bar, with cheap drinks and a cast of characters ranging from your typical barfly to your atypical drag queen. It's got a well-stocked jukebox, friendly bartenders, a pool table, and best of all, it's an insomniac's dream, open daily from 8am to 5am. 222 14th St., South Beach. © 305/673-9537.

Mynt   This hyper-stylish, hip lounge is reminiscent of a space-age cafeteria. A massive 6,000-square-foot place, Mynt is nothing more than a huge living room in which models, celebrities, and assorted hangers-on bask in the green glow to the beats of very loud lounge and dance music. If you want to dance—or move, for that matter, this is not the place in which to do so. It's all about striking a pose in here. And unless you know the person at the door, be prepared to be ridiculed, emasculated, and socially shattered as you may be forced to wait outside upwards of an hour. If that's the case, forget it; it's not worth it. Wait next door at the Greek place if you want a celebrity sighting, since you'll have a better chance seeing people from there than actually waiting in the melee at the door or inside. 1921 Collins Ave., South Beach. © 786/276-6132. Cover $10–20.

Nerve Lounge   There's nothing nervy about this lounge slash dance club whose owner is nightlife legend Rudolph Piper, best known for his stint at the pre-hip Meatpacking District club Mars in the late '80s. Nerve has several amusing nights, including South Beach Coyotes on Tuesdays, where women writhe atop the bar a la Britney Spears, and a Saturday night hip-hop night that's not for the timid. No cover, little attitude, and a mixed crowd of gays and straights who care more about music than about the scene explain the reason for naming the club Nerve in a city where most places are only about seeing and being seen. 247 23rd St., South Beach. © 305/695-8697.

The Purdy Lounge   With the exception of a wall of lava lamps, Purdy is not unlike your best friend's basement, featuring a pool table and a slew of board games such as Operation to keep the attention-deficit disordered from getting bored. Because it's a no-nonsense bar with relatively cheap cocktails (by South Beach standards), Purdy gets away with not having to have a star DJ or fancy bass-heavy Bose sound system. A CD player somehow does the trick, although lately, in order to keep up with the Joneses, Purdy has been employing some disc-spinning DJs. With no cover and no attitude, a line is inevitable (it gets crowded inside), so be prepared to wait. Saturday night has become the preferred night for locals, while Friday night's happy hour draws a young professional crowd on the prowl. 1811 Purdy Ave./Sunset Harbor, South Beach. © 305/531-4622.

Rok Bar   Larger than life rocker Tommy Lee has assembled a motley Miami crew at this paradox of a bar that combines down 'n' dirty rock and roll with the swank comforts of a chic lounge. The place is claustrophobic with limited seating (unless you're Pamela Anderson, forget about scoring a table), high priced drinks, and an oxymoronic soundtrack of Lynyrd Skynyrd, Michael Jackson, and Kid Rock. 1905 Collins Ave., South Beach. © 305/538-7171. No cover.

Rose Bar at the Delano   If every rose has its thorn, the thorn at this painfully chic hotel bar is the excruciatingly high-priced cocktails. Otherwise, the crowd here is full of the so-called glitterati, fabulatti, and other assorted poseurs who view life through (Italian-made) rose-colored glasses. 1685 Collins Ave., South Beach. © 305/672-2000.

Segafredo Espresso   Although Segafredo is technically a cafe, it has become an integral part of Miami's nightlife in terms of its status as command central for Euros who miss that very special brand of European cafe society. Not in the mood for a club or bar but want to hear great music, sip a few cocktails, snack on some delicious sandwiches and pizza, and sit outside and people watch? This is the place. European lounge music, tons of outdoor tables around a fountain on a prime corner of Lincoln Road, and always a mob scene make 'Fredo one of my—and many other Miamians'—favorite nocturnal diversions. 1040 Lincoln Rd., South Beach. © 305/673-0047.

Skybar at the Shore Club   Skybar lives up to its name in terms of loftiness; something this place has perfected better than anyone else, whether at its original L.A. location at the Mondrian, or at the sprawling South Beach location at the Shore Club. If you're not a hotel guest, not Beyonce, not on the "list," or you're a guy with several other guys and no girls, fugghedabout it. For those of you who can't get in, the Skybar is basically the entire backyard area of the Shore Club, consisting of several areas including the Moroccan themed garden area, the hip-hop themed indoor Red Room, the Sand Bar by the beach, and the Rum Bar by the pool. Popular on any given night, Sky Bar is yet another brilliant example of how hotelier Ian Schrager has managed to control the hipsters in a most Pavlovian way. At the Shore Club, 1901 Collins Ave., South Beach. © 305/695-3100.

Taverna Opa   Although this Greek taverna (also located in Hollywood and Ft. Lauderdale) calls itself a restaurant, I consider it more of a raucous dance club that just happens to serve excellent Greek food. How many restaurants do you know of that allow patrons to dance suggestively with waiters on tables,

---

Moments **Stargazing**

The most popular places for celebrity sightings include Mynt, Opium Garden, Skybar, poolside at the Shore Club or the Delano, and, when it comes to J-Lo, somewhere on the beach around 20th Street. Miami Heat basketball games are also star magnets.

---

throw napkins in the air as if they were confetti, and guzzle ouzo straight from the bottle, all to the tune of some very loud, jazzed up Greek dance music? Get here early, as the place is always packed—and I mean packed as in Standing Room Only. Although there is an outdoor bar, the real fun and scenery is indoors in the dining room where the tables double as dance floors and some very animated characters channel their best Zorbas. Be prepared for a big fat Greek hangover the next day. 36 Ocean Dr., South Beach. ✆ 305/673-6730.

Vino   Nobody can figure out why this place opened in frat-ridden Coconut Grove, which is why Vino is moving to South Beach (probably in September of 2004, with an expected address on 16th Street) after a year in the quasi college town, but nonetheless, Vino is the city's *only* bona fide wine bar with a collection of over 300 bottles and 60 wines by the glass. Decorated as if it came straight out of a West Elm catalogue, this chic, Manhattan-esque wine bar is known for many things, especially the fact that it's a chill lounge in which the 30 and over set can hang out, have audible conversations, sip wine, and even enjoy cheeses, fondues, and delicious desserts. Vino also has a monthly wine tasting event with experts hailing from particular regions from around the world. 3315 Rice St., Coconut Grove. ✆ 305/445-5888. (New address and phone number not available at press time.)

DANCE CLUBS, LIVE MUSIC, THE GAY & LESBIAN SCENE & LATIN CLUBS
DANCE CLUBS

Clubs are as much a cottage industry in Miami as is, say, cheese in Wisconsin. Clubland, as it is known, is not just a nocturnal theme park but a way of life for some. On any given night in Miami, there's something going on—no excuses are needed to throw a party here. Short of throwing a glammy event for the grand opening of a new gas station, Miami is very party hearty, celebrating everything from the fact that it's Tuesday night to the debut of a hot new DJ. Within this very bizarre after-dark community, a very colorful assortment of characters emerge, from your (a)typical nine-to-fivers to shady characters who have reinvented themselves as hot shots on the club circuit. While this scene of seeing and being seen may not be your cup of Absolut, it's certainly never boring.

The club music played on Miami's ever-evolving social circuit is good enough to get even the most rhythmically challenged wallflowers dancing. To keep things fresh in Clubland, local promoters throw one-nighters, which are essentially parties with various themes or motifs, from funk to fashion. Because these change so often, we can't possibly list them here. Word of mouth, local advertising, and listings in the free weekly *New Times,* www.miami.citysearch.com, or the "Weekend" section of the *Miami Herald* are the best ways to find out about these ever-changing events.

Before you get all decked out to hit the town as soon as the sun sets, consider the fact that Miami is a very late town. Things generally don't get started here before 11pm. The Catch-22 is that if you don't arrive on South Beach early enough, you may find yourself driving around aimlessly for parking, as it is very limited outside of absurd $20 valet charges. Municipal lots fill up quickly, so your best bet is to arrive on South Beach somewhat early and kill time by strolling around, having something to eat, or sipping a cocktail in a hotel bar. Another advantage of arriving a bit earlier than the crowds is that some clubs don't charge a cover before 11pm or midnight, which could save you a wad of cash over time. Most clubs are open every night of the week, though some are

Tips Ground Rules: Stepping Out in Miami

- Nightlife on South Beach doesn't really get going until after 11pm. As a result, you may want to consider taking what is known as a disco nap so that you'll be fully charged until the wee hours.
- If you're unsure of what to wear out on South Beach, your safest bet will be anything black.
- Do *not* try to tip the doormen manning the velvet ropes. That will only make you look desperate and you'll find yourself standing outside for what will seem like an ungodly amount of time. Instead, try to land your name on the ever-present guest lists by calling the club early in the day yourself, or, better yet, having the concierge at your hotel do it for you. Concierges have connections. If you don't have connections and you find yourself without a concierge, then act assertive, not surly, at the velvet rope, and your patience will usually be rewarded with admittance. If all else fails—for men, especially—surround yourself with a few leggy model types and you'll be noticed quicker.
- If you are a man going out with a group of men, unless you're going to a gay bar, you will most likely not get into any South Beach hot spot unless you are with women.
- Finally, have fun. It may look like serious business when you're on the outside, but once you're in, it's another story. Attacking Clubland with a sense of humor is the best approach to a successful, memorable evening out.

only open Thursday to Sunday and others are only open Monday though Saturday. Call ahead to get the most up-to-date information possible: Things change very quickly around here, and a call in advance can help you make sure that the dance club you're planning to go to hasn't become a video arcade. Cover charges are very haphazard, too. If you're not on the ubiquitous guest list (ask your concierge to put you on the list—he or she usually has the ability to do so, which won't help you with the wait to get in, but will eliminate the cover charge), you may have to fork over a ridiculous $20 to walk past the ropes. Don't fret, though. There are many clubs and bars that have no cover charge—they just make up for it by charging $13 for a martini!

Bongo's Cuban Café   Gloria Estefan's latest hit in the restaurant business pays homage to the sites, sounds, and cuisine of pre-Castro Cuba. Bongo's is a mammoth restaurant attached to the American Airlines Arena in downtown Miami. On Friday and Saturday after 11:30pm, it's transformed from a friendly family restaurant into the city's hottest 21-and-over salsa nightclub. Cover charges can be hefty, but consider it your ticket to what happens to be an astounding show of some of the best salsa dancers in the city. Prepare yourself for standing room only. Open Fridays from 11pm and Saturdays from 11:30pm. At the American Airlines Arena, 601 Biscayne Blvd., Downtown Miami. © 786/777-2100. Cover Fri, ladies free, guys $10; Sat $20 for all.

Club Space ⊛   Clubland hits the mainland with this cavernous downtown warehouse of a club. With over 30,000 square feet of dance space, you can spin around a la Stevie Nicks (albeit to a techno beat) without having to worry about banging into someone. On Saturday and Sunday nights, the party usually extends to the next morning, sometimes as late 10am. It's quite a sight to see club kids rushing off to work straight from Space on a Monday morning. Known as the venue of choice for world-renowned DJs, Club Space sometimes charges ludicrous admission fees to cover their hefty price tags. *Note:* Club Space doesn't really get going until around 3 am. Call for more information, as it doesn't have a concrete schedule. 34 NE 11th St., Miami. ⓒ 305/372-9378. Cover $0–$20.

crobar ⭐   Still haunted by the ghost of clubs past, the space formerly known as the Cameo Theatre is now possessed by the mod, millennial, industrial spirit that is crobar. With its intense, dance-heavy sound system, an industrially chic ambience, and crowds big enough to scare away any memories of a sadly abandoned Cameo, this Chicago import has raised the bar on South Beach nightlife with crazy theme nights (the monthly Sex Night is particularly, uh, stimulating), top-name DJs, and the occasional celebrity appearance. On Sunday, the club hosts an extremely popular gay night known as Anthem (p. 157). Open Thursday through Monday from 10pm to 5am. 1445 Washington Ave., South Beach. ⓒ 305/531-8225. www.crobarmiami.com. Cover Thurs, Sun, Mon $20; Fri–Sat $25.

I/O   Although I'd like to call this new warehouse-y club "ghetto fabulous," I don't want to give out mixed messages. I/O is the club for that funky, arty/hipster set that listens to music by the likes of Belle and Sebastian and other groups that your Britney-loving sister probably never heard of. The club is composed of three areas—a bar area in which Japanese anime is played, a dance area where live music is performed and cool kids do their best breakdancing (or whatever they're calling it these days), and an outdoor bar area, which is cool during winter months but brutally hot in the summer. The best nights here are Thursday night's Latin-flavored Fuacata! (see the "Buenos Noche" box on p. 157) and Saturday night's Pop Life, an homage to the Depeche Mode era of New Wave. 30 NE 14th St., Downtown Miami. ⓒ 305/358-8007. Cover $5–$10.

Mansion   Housed in the space formerly known as Level, this latest nocturnal venture from the same team behind the utterly addictive Opium Garden (see below) is a massive, multi-leveled lounge that, according to the owners and promoters, is entirely "VIP," meaning you best know someone to get in or else you'll be amongst the masses outside and not even close to the manse. Live DJs, models, and celebrities galore—ubiquitous Paris Hilton, Tara Reid, Shannen Doherty, N*Sync, and more, not to mention high ceilings, wood floors, brick walls, and a decidedly non-smoky interior make this Mansion, despite its cheesy name, a must of the list of see and be scenesters. Open Tuesday through Sunday from 11pm to 5am. 1235 Washington Ave., South Beach. ⓒ 305/531-5535. Cover varies from $10–$40.

Nikki Beach Club *Finds*   What the Playboy Mansion is to L.A., the Nikki Beach Club is to South Beach. This place is the product of local nightlife royalty Tommy Pooch and Eric Omores. Half-naked ladies and men actually venture into the daylight on Sundays (around 4pm, which is ungodly in this town) to see, be seen, and, at times, be obscene. At night, it's very Brady-Bunch-goes-to-Hawaii–seeming, with a sexy Tiki hut/Polynesian theme style, albeit rated R. The Sunday-afternoon beach party is almost legendary and worth a glimpse—that is, if you can get in. This is not your equal-opportunity beach club. Egos are easily shattered, as surly doormen are known to reject those who don't drive up in a Ferrari. Also located within this bastion of hedonism is the super-hot

Pearl, a mod-ish, 380-seat, orange-hued restaurant and lounge that features a Continental menu created by Nikki chef Brian Rutherford. But you'd do better to forget the food and go for the eye candy. 101 Ocean Dr., South Beach. ✆ 305/538-1111. Cover $10–$20.

Opium Garden   Housed in the massive, open-air space, Opium Garden is a highly addictive nocturnal habit for those looking for a combination of sexy dance music, scantily clad dancers, celebrities such as J-Lo, Janet Jackson, Lenny Kravitz, and P. Diddy, and, for the masochists out there, an oppressive door policy in which two sets of velvet ropes are set up to keep those deemed unworthy out of this see-and-be-sceney den of inequity. Opium has a sushi restaurant (decent) and an ultra VIP, celeb-saturated lounge, Prive, whose own separate door policy makes the aforementioned seem like a romp in the sand. 136 Collins Ave., South Beach. ✆ 305/531-5535. Cover $20.

Rumi   Named after a 13th-century Sufi mystic, South Beach's first upscale supper club is command central for hipsters hailing from all coasts. Designed by hot NYC designers Nancy Mah and Scott Kester, Rumi is an urbane oasis of reds, tans, and chocolates, reminiscent of the golden age of supper clubs of the '30s and '40s. This bi-level space features intimate lounge areas as well as private and public dining rooms, in which haute Floribbean cuisine is served until around 11pm, when the tables conspicuously disappear and give way to a neo-Zen-like stamping ground for South Beach's chic elite. Make sure to check out the queen-size Murphy bed that snaps down from the wall to make room for late-night lounging. As long as you can get past the velvet ropes (by either looking pretty, being on the guest list, or just getting the doorman on a good day), there is no cover to bask in this bastion of South Beach scene-dom. 330 Lincoln Rd., South Beach. ✆ 305/672-4353. www.rumimiami.com.

SoHo Lounge *(Finds*   This multi-leveled, multi-faceted Design District club is tons of fun if you are into either '80s music or electroclash. Cheap drinks, a sprawling outdoor patio, and several different nooks, crannies, bars, and dance areas are available for perusal. The best area in the entire club is the two-story dance floor in which a big screen shows everything from Tronn to anime. Music ranges from the '80s greatest hits to more obscure music from Europe. One of the best venues in town for live music, SoHo Lounge has hosted the likes of Peaches and Electro-cute, and if those names don't ring a bell, consider going to SoHo to become acquainted with them. 175 NE 36th St., Design District. ✆ 305/576-1988. Cover $0–$10.

LIVE MUSIC

Unfortunately, Miami's live music scene is not thriving. Instead of local bands garnering devoted fans, local DJs are more admired, skyrocketing much more

---

Rock 'n' Bowl

Inspired by the alcohol-free rave dance parties of the '90s, Rave Bowling at **Cloverleaf Lanes,** 17601 NW 2nd Ave., North Dade (✆ **305/652-4197**), keeps teens off the streets, but in the gutters. Low lighting, glow-in-the-dark pins, and loud music keep things rolling every Friday and Saturday night from 8:30pm until 2am. Games are $4.25 each or $22 an hour; shoes are an extra $2.

easily to fame—thanks to the city's lauded dance-club scene. However, there are still several places that strive to bring Miami up to speed as far as live music is concerned. You just have to look—and listen—for it a bit more carefully. The following is a list of places you can, from time to time, catch some live acts, be it a DJ or an aspiring Nirvana.

Churchill's Hideaway *Finds* British expatriate Dave Daniels couldn't live in Miami without a true English-style pub, so he opened Churchill's Hideaway, the city's premier space for live rock music. Filthy and located in a rather unsavory neighborhood, Churchill's is committed to promoting and extending the lifeline of the lagging local music scene. A fun no-frills crowd hangs out here. Bring earplugs with you, as it is deafening once the music starts. Monday is open mic night while Wednesday is reserved for ladies' wrestling. 5501 NE 2nd Ave., Little Haiti. ℂ 305/757-1807. www.churchillspub.com. Cover $0–$6.

Jazid *Finds* Smoky, sultry, and illuminated by flickering candelabras, Jazid is the kind of place where you'd expect to hear Sade's "Smooth Operator" on constant rotation. Instead, however, you'll hear live jazz (sometimes on acid), soul, and funk. Past surprise performers at Jazid include former Smashing Pumpkin's front man Billy Corgan. An eclectic mix of mellow folk convenes here for a much necessary respite from the surrounding Washington Avenue mayhem. 1342 Washington Ave., South Beach. ℂ 305/673-9372. Cover $10.

Tobacco Road Al Capone used to hang out here when it was a speakeasy. Now, locals flock here to see local bands perform, as well as national acts such as George Clinton and the P-Funk All-Stars, Koko Taylor, and the Radiators. Tobacco Road (the proud owner of Miami's very first liquor license) is small and gritty and meant to be that way. Escape the smoke and sweat in the backyard patio, where air is a welcome commodity. The downright cheap nightly specials, such as the $11 lobster on Tuesday, are quite good and are served until 2am; the bar is open until 5am. 626 S. Miami Ave. (over the Miami Ave. Bridge near Brickell Ave.), Downtown. ℂ 305/374-1198. Cover $5–$10 Thurs–Sat.

Upstairs at the Van Dyke Cafe *Finds* The cafe's jazz bar, located on the second floor, resembles a classy speakeasy in which local jazz performers play to an intimate, enthusiastic crowd of mostly adults and sophisticated young things, who often huddle at the small tables until the wee hours. 846 Lincoln Rd., Miami Beach. ℂ 305/534-3600. Cover Sun–Thurs $5, Fri–Sat $10 for a seat; no cover at the bar.

THE GAY & LESBIAN SCENE

Miami and the beaches have long been host to what is called a "first-tier" gay community. Similar to the Big Apple, the Bay Area, or LaLa land, Miami has had a large alternative community since the days when Anita Bryant used her citrus power to boycott the rise in political activism in the early '70s. Well, things have changed and Miami–Dade now has a gay-rights ordinance.

Newcomers intending to party in any bar, whether downtown or certainly on the beach, will want to check ahead for the schedule, as all clubs must have a gay or lesbian night to pay their rent. Miami Beach, in fact, is a capital of the gay circuit party scene, rivaling San Francisco, Palm Springs, and even the mighty Sydney, Australia, for tourist dollars. However, ever since South Beach got bit by the hip-hop bug, many of Miami's gays have been crossing county lines into Fort Lauderdale, where there are surprisingly many more gay establishments.

Anthem   Sunday nights at crobar sing the gay anthem with this hyperpopular one-nighter featuring Miami's own superstar DJ Abel. 1445 Washington Ave., South Beach. ℂ **877/CRO-SOBE** or 305/531-5027. Cover $20.

Cactus Bar & Grill   Somewhere, over the causeway, there is life beyond South Beach—that is, for Miami's gay society. Housed in a large two-story space, Cactus attracts a mix of unpretentious, professional, and very attractive men and women. There's something for everyone here, whether it's the indoor pool tables, the outdoor swimming pool, or drinks that are considerably cheaper than on South Beach. Friday evening happy hours and Sunday afternoon Tea Dances are a virtual cattle call, attracting hordes of folks looking to quench their thirst for fun at Miami's sprawling urban oasis. 2401 Biscayne Blvd., Downtown. ℂ **305/438-0662.**

O-Zone   This is the zone of choice for gay men with an aversion to South Beach's cruisy, scene-heavy vibes. It's known for a heavily Latin crowd (mixed with a few college boys from nearby University of Miami) and fantastic, outlandish drag shows on the weekends. 6620 SW 57th Ave. (Red Rd.), South Miami. ℂ **305/667-2888.** No cover for men on Sat; other nights $5–$10.

Score   There's a reason this Lincoln Road hotbed of gay social activity is called Score. In addition to the huge pick-up scene, Score offers a multitude of bars, dance floors, loungelike areas, and outdoor tables in case you need to come up for air. Sunday afternoon Tea Dances are legendary here. 727 Lincoln Rd., South Beach. ℂ **305/535-1111.**

Twist   One of the most popular bars (and hideaways) on South Beach, this recently expanded bar (which is literally right across the street from the police station) has a casual yet lively local atmosphere. 1057 Washington Ave., South Beach. ℂ **305/538-9478.**

LATIN CLUBS

Considering that Hispanics make up a large part of Miami's population and that there's a huge influx of Spanish-speaking visitors, it's no surprise that there are some great Latin nightclubs in the city.

Plus, with the meteoric rise of the international music scene based in Miami, many international stars come through the offices of MTV Latino, SONY International, and a multitude of Latin TV studios based in Miami—and they're all looking for a good club scene on weekends. Most of the Anglo clubs also reserve at least 1 night a week for Latin rhythms.

Moments **Buenos Noche**

Formerly the premier Little Havana dancing and live music hootenanny, **Fuacata** (pronounced Fwa-*ka*-ta) has moved downtown. A fusion of music and dance presented in a combination of Latin, funk, hip-hop, and reggae rhythms using turntables and electronic samplers plus wind, string, and other instruments (very multimedia), Fuacata takes place at I/O (30 NE 14th St.; ℂ **305/358-8007**) and packs in a very large, very hip crowd. Created by popular Miami DJ Le Spam, along with two others, Fuacata has been critically acclaimed, and has garnered publicity in such national publications as the *New York Times, Billboard Magazine, Entertainment Weekly,* and *Rolling Stone.*

Casa Panza *Finds* This *casa* is one of Little Havana's liveliest and most popular nightspots. Every Tuesday, Thursday, and Saturday night, Casa Panza, in the heart of Little Havana, becomes the House of Flamenco, with shows at 8 and 11pm. You can either enjoy a flamenco show or strap on your own dancing shoes and participate in the celebration. Enjoy a fantastic Spanish meal before the show, or just a glass of sangria before you start stomping. Open until 4am, Casa Panza is a hot spot for young Latin club kids, and, occasionally, a few older folks who are so taken by the music and the scene that they've failed to realize that it's well past their bedtime. 1620 SW 8th St. (Calle Ocho), Little Havana. ℂ 305/643-5343.

Hoy Como Ayer Formerly known as Cafe Nostalgia, the Little Havana hang-out dedicated to reminiscing about Old Cuba, Hoy Como Ayer is like the Brady Bunch of Latin hangouts—while it was extremely popular with old timers in its Cafe Nostalgia incarnation, it is now experiencing a resurgence among the younger generation, seeking their own brand of Nostalgia. Its Thursday night party, Fuacata (slang for "Pow!"), is a magnet for artsy Latin hipsters, featuring classic Cuban music mixed in with modern DJ-spun sound effects. Open Thurs-day to Sunday from 9pm to 4am. 2212 SW 8th St. (Calle Ocho), Little Havana. ℂ 305/541-2631. Cover $10 Thurs–Sun.

La Covacha *Finds* This hut, located virtually in the middle of nowhere (West Miami), is the hottest Latin joint in the entire city. Sunday features the best in Latin rock, with local and international acts. But the shack is really jumping on weekend nights when the place is open until 5am. Friday is *the* night here, so much so that the owners had to place a red velvet rope out front to maintain some semblance of order. It's an amusing sight—a velvet rope guarding a shack—but once you get in, you'll understand the need for it. Do not wear silk here, as you *will* sweat. 10730 NW 25th St. (at NW 107th Ave.), West Miami. ℂ 305/594-3717. Cover $0–$10.

Mango's Tropical Café Claustrophobic types do not want to go near Mango's. Ever. One of the most popular spots on Ocean Drive, this outdoor enclave of Latin liveliness shakes with the intensity of a Richter-busting earth-quake. Welcome and *bienvenido*, Mango's is *Cabaret*, Latin style. Nightly live Brazilian and other Latin music, not to mention scantily clad male and female dancers, draw huge gawking crowds in from the sidewalk. But pay attention to the music if you can: Incognito international musicians often lose their anonymity and jam with the house band on stage. Open daily from 11am to 5am. 900 Ocean Dr., South Beach. ℂ 305/673-4422. Cover $5–$15.

THE PERFORMING ARTS

Highbrows and culture vultures complain that there is a dearth of decent cultural offerings in Miami. What do locals tell them? Go back to New York! In all seri-ousness, however, in recent years Miami's performing arts scene has improved greatly. The city's Broadway Series features Tony Award–winning shows (the tour-ing versions, of course), which aren't always Broadway caliber, but they are usu-ally pretty good and not nearly as pricey. Local arts groups such as the Miami Light Project, a not-for-profit cultural organization that presents live perform-ances by innovative dance, music, and theater artists, have had huge success in attracting big-name artists such as Nina Simone and Philip Glass to Miami. In addition, a burgeoning bohemian movement in Little Havana has given way to performance spaces that have become nightclubs in their own right.

The Rhythm Is Gonna Get You

Are you feeling shy about hitting a Latin club because you fear your two left feet will stand out? Then take a few lessons from one of the following dance companies or dance teachers. They offer individual and group lessons to dancers of any origin who are willing to learn. These folks have made it their mission to teach merengue and flamenco to non-Latinos and Latino left-foots, and are among the most reliable, consistent, and popular ones in Miami. So what are you waiting for?

Thursday and Friday nights at **Bongo's Cuban Café** (American Airlines Arena, 601 Biscayne Blvd., Downtown; © **786/777-2100**) are an amazing showcase of some of the city's best salsa dancers, but amateurs need not be intimidated thanks to the instructors at Latin Groove Dance Studios, who are on hand to help you with your two left feet.

At **Ballet Flamenco La Rosa** (in the Performing Arts Network building, 13126 W. Dixie Hwy., North Miami; © **305/899-7730**), you can learn to flamenco, salsa, or merengue. This is the only professional flamenco company in the area. If you're feeling shy, $50 will buy you a private lesson; otherwise, it's $10 for a group lesson.

Nobody salsas like **Luz Pinto** (© **305/868-9418**), and she also knows how to teach the basics with patience and humor. She charges between $40 and $55 for a private lesson for up to four people and $10 per person for a group lesson. A good introduction is her multi-level group class at 7pm Sunday evenings at the PAN building. Although she teaches everything from ballroom to merengue, her specialty is Casino-style salsa, popularized in the 1950s in Cuba, Luz's homeland. A mix between disco and country square dancing, Casino-style salsa is all the rage in Latin clubs in town. Good students may be able to convince Luz, for an extra fee, to chaperone a trip to a nightclub to show off their moves. Ask her for more information.

Angel Arroya has been teaching salsa to the clueless out of his home (at 16467 NE 27th Ave., North Miami Beach; © **305/949-7799**) for the past 10 years. Just $10 will buy you an hour's time in his "school." He traditionally teaches Monday and Wednesday nights, but call ahead to check for any schedule changes.

THEATER

The **Actors' Playhouse** (*Kids*), a musical theater at the newly restored Miracle Theater at 280 Miracle Mile, Coral Gables (© **305/444-9293;** www.actors playhouse.org), is a grand 1948 Art Deco movie palace with a 600-seat main theater and a smaller theater/rehearsal hall that hosts a number of excellent musicals for children throughout the year. In addition to these two rooms, the Playhouse recently added a 300-seat children's balcony theater. Tickets run from $27 to $40.

The **Coconut Grove Playhouse,** 3500 Main Hwy., Coconut Grove (© **305/ 442-4000;** www.cgplayhouse.org), is also a former movie house, built in 1927 in an ornate Spanish rococo style. Today, this respected venue is known for its original and innovative staging of both international and local dramas and musicals. The house's second, more intimate Encore Room is well suited to alternative and experimental productions. Tickets run from $35 to $45.

The **Gables Stage** at the Biltmore Hotel (p. 84), Anastasia Avenue, Coral Gables (© **305/445-1119**), stages at least one Shakespearean play, one classic, and one contemporary piece a year. This well-regarded theater usually tries to secure the rights to a national or local premiere as well. Tickets cost $35; $15 and $32, respectively, for students and seniors.

The **Jerry Herman Ring Theatre** is on the main campus of the University of Miami in Coral Gables (© **305/284-3355**). The University's Department of Theater Arts uses this stage for advanced-student productions of comedies, dramas, and musicals. Faculty and guest actors are regularly featured, as are contemporary works by local playwrights. Performances are usually scheduled Tuesday through Saturday during the academic year. In the summer, don't miss "Summer Shorts," a selection of superb one-acts. Tickets sell for $14 to $16.

The **New Theater,** 4120 Laguna St., Coral Gables (© **305/443-5909**), prides itself on showing world-renowned works from America and Europe. As the name implies, you'll find mostly contemporary plays, with a few classics thrown in for variety. Performances are staged Thursday through Sunday year-round. Tickets are $35 on Thursdays, $40 on Fridays and Saturdays, and $35 to $40 on Sundays. If tickets are available on the day of the performance—and they usually are—students pay half price.

CLASSICAL MUSIC

In addition to a number of local orchestras and operas (see below), which regularly offer quality music and world-renowned guest artists, each year brings a slew of classical music special events and touring artists to Miami. The **Concert Association of Florida (CAF)** (© **877/433-3200**) produces one of the most important and longest-running series. Known for more than a quarter of a century for its high-caliber, star-packed schedules, CAF regularly arranges the best "serious" music concerts for the city. Season after season, the schedules are punctuated by world-renowned dance companies and seasoned virtuosi like Itzhak Perlman, Andre Watts, and Kathleen Battle. Since CAF does not have its own space, performances are usually scheduled in the Miami–Dade County Auditorium or the Jackie Gleason Theater of the Performing Arts (see the "Major Venues" section below). The season lasts October through April, and ticket prices range from $20 to $70.

Florida Philharmonic Orchestra   South Florida's premier symphony orchestra, under the direction of James Judd, presents a full season of classical and pops programs interspersed with several children's and contemporary popular music performances. The Philharmonic performs downtown in the Gusman Center for the Performing Arts and at the Miami–Dade County Auditorium (see the "Major Venues" section below). 4120 Leguna St., Coral Gables. © 800/226-1812. Tickets $15–$60. When extra tickets are available, students are admitted free on day of performance.

Miami Chamber Symphony   This professional orchestra is a small, subscription-series orchestra that's not affiliated with any major arts organizations and is therefore an inexpensive alternative to the high-priced classical venues. Renowned international soloists perform regularly. The season runs October to

May, and most concerts are held in the Gusman Concert Hall, on the University of Miami campus. 5690 N. Kendall Dr., Kendall. © 305/284-6477. Tickets $12–$30.

New World Symphony   This organization, led by artistic director Michael Tilson Thomas, is a stepping stone for gifted young musicians seeking professional careers. The orchestra specializes in ambitious, innovative, energetic performances and often features renowned guest soloists and conductors. The symphony's season lasts from October to May, during which time there are many free concerts. 541 Lincoln Rd., South Beach. © 305/673-3331. www.nws.org. Tickets free–$58. Rush tickets (remaining tickets sold 1 hr. before performance) $20. Students $10 (1 hr. before concerts; limited seating).

OPERA

Florida Grand Opera   Around for over 60 years, this company regularly features singers from top houses in both America and Europe. All productions are sung in their original language and staged with projected English supertitles. Tickets become scarce when Placido Domingo or Luciano Pavarotti (who made his American debut here in 1965) comes to town. The opera's season runs roughly from November to April, with five performances each week. A new multimillion-dollar headquarters for the opera is scheduled to open in mid-2004; until then, performances take place at the Miami–Dade County Auditorium and the Broward Center for the Performing Arts, about 40 minutes from downtown Miami. Box office: 1200 Coral Way, Southwest Miami. © 800/741-1010. www.fgo.org. Tickets $19–$145. Student discounts available.

DANCE

Several local dance companies train and perform in the Greater Miami area. In addition, top traveling troupes regularly stop at the venues listed below. Keep your eyes open for special events and guest artists.

Ballet Flamenco La Rosa   For a taste of local Latin flavor, see this lively troupe perform impressive flamenco and other styles of Latin dance on Miami stages. (They also teach Latin dancing—see the "The Rhythm Is Gonna Get You" box above.) 13126 W. Dixie Hwy., North Miami. © 305/899-7729. Tickets $25 at door, $20 in advance, $18 for students and seniors.

Miami City Ballet   This artistically acclaimed and innovative company, directed by Edward Villella, features a repertoire of more than 60 ballets, many by George Balanchine, and has had more than 20 world premieres. The company moved into a new $7.5 million headquarters in January 2000—the Ophelia and Juan Jr. Roca Center at the Collins Park Cultural Center in Miami Beach. This three-story center features eight rehearsal rooms, a ballet school, a boutique, and ticket offices. The City Ballet season runs from September to April. Ophelia and Juan Jr. Roca Center, Collins Ave. and 22nd St., South Beach. © 305/929-7000 or 305/929-7010 for box office. Tickets $17–$50.

MAJOR VENUES

The **Colony Theater,** on Lincoln Road in South Beach (© 305/674-1040), which has become an architectural showpiece of the Art Deco District, is presently closed for a $4.3 million renovation that will add wing and fly space, improve access for those with disabilities, and restore the lobby to its original Art Deco look.

At the **Miami–Dade County Auditorium,** West Flagler Street at 29th Avenue, Southwest Miami (© 305/547-5414), performers gripe about the lack of space, but for patrons, this 2,430-seat auditorium is the only Miami space in which you can hear the opera—for now. A multimillion-dollar performing arts center downtown has been in the works for years (see below). For now, though, the Miami–Dade County Auditorium is home to the city's Florida Grand Opera, and it also stages productions by the Concert Association of Florida, many programs in Spanish, and a variety of other shows.

At the 1,700-seat **Gusman Center for the Performing Arts,** 174 E. Flagler St., downtown Miami (© **305/372-0925**), seating is tight, and so is funding, but the sound is superb. In addition to hosting the Florida Philharmonic Orchestra and the Miami Film Festival, the elegant Gusman Center features pop concerts, plays, film screenings, and special events. The auditorium was built as the Olympia Theater in 1926, and its ornate palace interior is typical of that era, complete with fancy columns, a huge pipe organ, and twinkling "stars" on the ceiling.

Not to be confused with the Gusman Center (above), the **Gusman Concert Hall,** 1314 Miller Dr. at 14th Street, Coral Gables (© **305/284-6477**), is a roomy 600-seat hall that gives a stage to the Miami Chamber Symphony and a varied program of university recitals.

The elegant **Jackie Gleason Theater of the Performing Arts,** located in South Beach at Washington Avenue and 17th Street (© **305/673-7300;** www.gleasontheater.com), is the home of the Miami Beach Broadway Series, which has recently presented Rent, Phantom of the Opera, and Les Misérables. This 2,705-seat hall also hosts other big-budget Broadway shows, classical music concerts, and dance performances.

At press time, the city granted a budget in excess of $200 million for its official Performing Arts Center. Planned are a 2,400-seat ballet/opera house and a 2,000-seat concert hall for the Florida Philharmonic Orchestra, Florida Grand Opera, New World Symphony, Miami City Ballet, and a major concert series. Designed by world-renowned architect Cesar Pelli, it will be the focal point of a planned Arts, Media, and Entertainment District in mid-Miami. The complex will be wrapped in limestone, slate, decorative stone, stainless steel, glass curtain walls, and tropical landscaping, and is slated to be complete in mid-2006. For more information, check out their website at www.pacfmiami.org.

CINEMAS

In addition to the annual Miami Film Festival in February and other, smaller film events, Miami has nearly as many multiplex cinemas as it does palm trees. And for good reason. When it rains in Miami, what else is there to do besides go to the movies, a museum, or the mall? But if 40 screens of Jurassic Park III isn't your idea of a day at the movies, consider the following artsy theaters, known for playing lots of subtitled, foreign films as well as those that get bumped off the big screen by the Jurassic Parks of the celluloid world.

The **Bill Cosford Cinema,** at the University of Miami, is located on the second floor of the memorial building off Campo Sano Avenue (© **305/284-4861**). This well-endowed little theater was recently revamped and boasts high-tech projectors, new air-conditioning, and a new decor. It sponsors independent films as well as lectures by visiting filmmakers and movie stars. Andy Garcia and Antonio Banderas are a few of the big names this theater has attracted. It also hosts the African American Film Festival, a Student Film Festival, and collaborations with the Fort Lauderdale Festival (a very small film festival). Admission is $6, seniors $3.

6

The Keys & the Dry Tortugas

The drive from Miami to the Keys is a slow descent into an unusual but breathtaking American ecosystem: On either side of you, for miles ahead, lies nothing but emerald waters. (On weekends, however, you will also see plenty of traffic.) Strung out across the Atlantic Ocean like loose strands of cultured pearls, more than 400 islands make up this 150-mile-long chain of the Keys.

Despite the usually calm landscape, these rocky islands can be treacherous, as a series of tropical storms, hurricanes, and tornadoes reminded residents in the summer and fall of 1998, when millions of dollars of damage was inflicted. The exposed coast has always posed dangers to those on land as well as at sea.

When Spanish explorers Juan Ponce de León and Antonio de Herrera sailed amid these craggy, dangerous rocks in 1513, they and their men dubbed the string of islands "Los Martires" (The Martyrs), because they thought the rocks looked like men suffering in the surf. It wasn't until the early 1800s that rugged and ambitious pioneers, who amassed great wealth by salvaging cargo from ships sunk nearby, settled the larger islands (legend has it that these shipwrecks were sometimes caused by the "wreckers," who occasionally removed navigational markers from the shallows to lure unwitting captains aground). At the height of the salvaging mania (in the 1830s), Key West boasted the highest per capita income in the country.

However, wars, fires, hurricanes, mosquitoes, and the Depression took their toll on these resilient islands in the early part of the 20th century, causing wild swings between fortune and poverty. In 1938, the spectacular Overseas Highway (U.S. 1) was finally completed atop the ruins of Henry Flagler's railroad (which was destroyed by a hurricane in 1935, leaving only bits and pieces still found today), opening the region to tourists, who had never before been able to drive to this sea-bound destination. These days, the highway connects more than 30 of the populated islands in the Keys. The hundreds of small, undeveloped islands that surround these "mainline" keys are known locally as the "backcountry" and are home to dozens of exotic animals and plants. Therein lie some of the most renowned outdoor sporting opportunities, from bonefishing to spear fishing and—at appropriate times of the year—diving for lobsters. To get to the backcountry, you must take to the water—a vital part of any trip to the Keys. Whether you fish, snorkel, dive, or just cruise, include some time on a boat in your itinerary; otherwise, you haven't truly seen the Keys.

Of course, people go to the Keys for the peaceful waters and the year-round warmth, but the sea and the teeming life beneath it are the main attractions here: Countless species of brilliantly colored fish can be found swimming above the ocean's floor, and you'll discover a stunning abundance of tropical and exotic plants, birds, and reptiles.

The warm, shallow waters (waters are deeper and rougher on the eastern/Atlantic side of the Keys) nurture living coral that supports a complex, delicate ecosystem of plants and animals—sponges, anemones, jellyfish, crabs, rays, sharks, turtles, snails, lobsters, and thousands of types of fish. This vibrant underwater habitat thrives on one of the only living tropical reefs in the entire North American continent. As a result, anglers, divers, snorkelers, and watersports enthusiasts of all kinds come to explore.

Heavy traffic has taken its toll on this fragile ecoscape, but conservation efforts are underway (traffic laws are strictly enforced on Deer Key, for example, due to deer crossings that have been contained thanks to newly installed fences). In fact, environmental efforts in the Keys exceed those in many other high-traffic visitor destinations.

Although the atmosphere throughout the Keys is that of a laid-back beach town, don't expect to find many impressive beaches here, especially after the damaging effects of the tropical storms and hurricanes in 1998. Beaches are mostly found in a few private resorts, though there are some small, sandy beaches in John Pennekamp Coral Reef State Park, Bahia Honda State Park, and in Key West. One great exception is Sombrero Beach in Marathon (p. 168), which is well maintained by Monroe County and is larger and considerably nicer than other beaches in the Keys. Sombrero Beach features a beachfront park, picnic facilities, a playground, and a protected cove for children at the west end of the beach.

The Keys are divided into three sections, both geographically and in this chapter. The Upper and Middle Keys are closest to the Florida mainland, so they are popular with weekend warriors who come by boat or car to fish or relax in towns like Key Largo, Islamorada, and Marathon. Further on, just beyond the impressive Seven-Mile Bridge (which actually measures only 6½ miles), are the Lower Keys, a small, unspoiled swath of islands teeming with wildlife. Here, in the protected regions of the Lower Keys, is where you're most likely to catch sight of the area's many endangered animals—with patience, you may spot the rare eagle, egret, or Key deer. You should also keep an eye out for alligators, turtles, rabbits, and a huge variety of birds.

Key West, the most renowned—and last—island in the Lower Keys, is literally at the end of the road. The southernmost point in the continental United States (made famous by the Nobel Prize–winning Ernest Hemingway), this tiny island is the most popular destination in the Florida Keys, overrun with cruise-ship passengers and day-trippers, as well as franchises and T-shirt shops. More than 1.6 million visitors pass through each year. Still, this "Conch Republic" has a tightly knit community of permanent residents who cling fiercely to their live-and-let-live attitude—an atmosphere that has made Key West famously popular with painters, writers, and free spirits.

The last section in this chapter is devoted to the Dry Tortugas, a National Park, located 68 nautical miles from Key West.

EXPLORING THE KEYS BY CAR

After you have gotten off the Florida Turnpike and landed on U.S. 1, which is also known as the Overseas Highway (see "Getting There," under "Essentials," below), you'll have no trouble negotiating these narrow islands, since it is the only main road connecting the Keys. The scenic, lazy drive from Miami can be very enjoyable if you have the patience to linger and explore the diverse towns

The Florida Keys

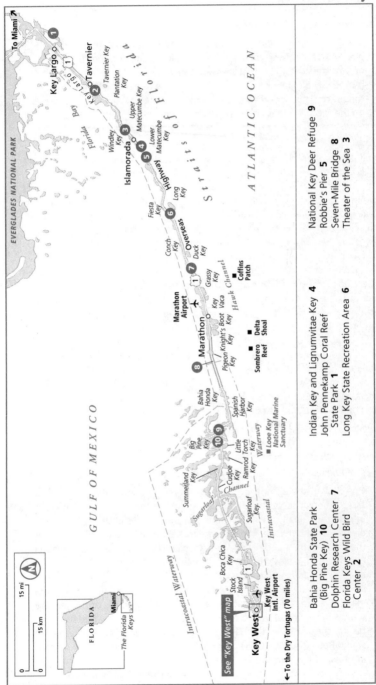

Bahia Honda State Park
(Big Pine Key) **10**
Dolphin Research Center **7**
Florida Keys Wild Bird
Center **2**

Indian Key and Lignumvitae Key **4**
John Pennekamp Coral Reef
State Park **1**
Long Key State Recreation Area **6**

National Key Deer Refuge **9**
Robbie's Pier **5**
Seven-Mile Bridge **8**
Theater of the Sea **3**

Tips **Don't Be Fooled**

Avoid the many "Tourist Information Centers" that dot the main highway. Most are private companies hired to lure visitors to specific lodgings or outfitters (anything that says FREE DISNEY TICKETS or something like that is probably a scam or time share racket). You're better off sticking with the official, not-for-profit centers (the legit ones usually don't advertise on the turnpike) that are extremely well located and staffed.

---

and islands along the way. If you have the time, I recommend allowing at least 2 days to work your way down to Key West and 3 or more days once there.

Most of U.S. 1 is a narrow, two-lane highway, with some wider passing zones along the way. The speed limit is usually 55 mph (35–45 mph on Big Pine Key and in some commercial areas). Despite the protestations of island residents, there has been talk of expanding the highway, but plans have not been finalized. Even on the narrow road, you can usually get from downtown Miami to Key Largo in just over an hour. If you're determined to drive straight through to Key West, allow at least 3½ hours. Weekend travel is another matter entirely: When the roads are jammed with travelers from the mainland, the trip could take upward of 5 to 6 hours (when there's an accident, traffic is at an absolute standstill). If at all possible, I strongly urge you to avoid driving anywhere in the Keys on Friday afternoons or Sunday evenings.

To find an address in the Keys, don't bother looking for building numbers; most addresses (except in Key West and parts of Marathon) are delineated by mile markers (MM), small green signs on the roadside that announce the distance from Key West. The markers start at number 127, just south of the Florida mainland. The zero marker is in Key West, at the corner of Whitehead and Fleming Streets. Addresses in this chapter are accompanied by a mile marker (MM) designation when appropriate.

Moments **No Place Like Homestead**

On its own, there's not much to the waterfront shack that is **Alabama Jack's.** The bar serves beer and wine only, and the restaurant specializes in delicious, albeit, greasy bar fare. But this quintessential Old Floridian dive, located between Homestead and Key Largo, is a colorful must on the drive south, especially on Sundays, when bikers mix with line dancers and Southern belles who look as if they just got off the *Hee Haw* set in all their fabulous frill. Hordes of Harley-Davidson bikers, local Miamians, barflies, and anglers flock here with much devotion, and the views of the mangroves are spectacular. Live country music resurrects the legendary sounds of Johnny Cash and co. Pull up a bar stool, order a cold one, and take in the sights—in the bay and at the bar. To get there, pick up Card Sound Road (the old Rte. 1) a few miles after you pass Homestead, heading toward Key Largo. Alabama Jack's is on the right side and can't be missed (5800 Card Sound Rd., Homestead; ✆ **305/248-8741**).

---

1 The Upper & Middle Keys: Key Largo★★ to Marathon ★

58 miles SW of Miami

The Upper Keys are a popular, year-round refuge for South Floridians, who take advantage of the islands' proximity to the mainland. This is the fishing and diving capital of America, and the swarms of outfitters and billboards never let you forget it.

Key Largo, once called Rock Harbor but renamed to capitalize on the success of the 1948 Humphrey Bogart film (which wasn't actually filmed there), is the largest key and is more developed than its neighbors to the south. Dozens of chain hotels, restaurants, and tourist-information centers service the many water enthusiasts who come to explore the nation's first underwater state park, **John Pennekamp Coral Reef State Park,** and its adjacent marine sanctuary. **Islamorada,** the unofficial capital of the Upper Keys, offers the area's best atmosphere, food, fishing, entertainment, and lodging. It's an unofficial "party capital" for mainlanders seeking a quick tropical excursion. Here (Islamorada is actually composed of four islands), nature lovers can enjoy walking trails, historic explorations, and big-purse fishing tournaments. For a more tranquil, quieter, less party-hearty Keys experience, all other Keys besides Key West and Islamorada are better choices. **Marathon,** smack in the middle of the Florida Keys, is one of the most populated keys and is known as the heart of the Keys. It is part fishing village, part tourist center, and part nature preserve. This area's highly developed infrastructure includes resort hotels, a commercial airport, and a highway that expands to four lanes.

ESSENTIALS

GETTING THERE   From Miami International Airport (there is also an airport in Marathon), take Le Jeune Road (Northwest 42nd Ave.) to Route 836 west. Follow signs to the Florida Turnpike south (about 7 miles). The turnpike extension connects with U.S. 1 in Florida City. Continue south on U.S. 1. For a scenic option, weather permitting, take Card Sound Road south of Florida City, a backcountry drive that reconnects with U.S. 1 in upper Key Largo. The view from the Card Sound Bridge is spectacular and well worth the $1 toll.

If you're coming from Florida's west coast, take Alligator Alley to the Miami exit and then turn south onto the turnpike extension. The turnpike ends in Florida City, at which time you will be dumped directly onto the one-lane road, U.S. 1, that leads to the Keys. Have plenty of quarters (at least $10 worth, round-trip) for the tolls.

Greyhound (© **800/231-2222;** www.greyhound.com) has three buses leaving Miami for Key West every day, which also stop in Key Largo, Tavenier, Islamorada, Marathon, Big Pine Key, Cudjoe Key, Sugarloaf, and Big Coppit on their way south. Prices range up from about $13 to $32 one way and take between an hour and 40 minutes to 4 hours and 40 minutes, depending on how far south you're going. Seats fill quickly in season, so come early. It's first-come, first-served.

VISITOR INFORMATION   Make sure you get your information from official, not-for-profit centers. The **Key Largo Chamber of Commerce,** U.S. 1 at MM 106, Key Largo, FL 33037 (© **800/822-1088** or 305/451-1414; fax 305/451-4726; www.keylargo.org), runs an excellent facility, with free direct-dial phones and plenty of brochures. Headquartered in a handsome clapboard house, the chamber operates as an information clearinghouse for all of the Keys and is open daily from 9am to 6pm.

The **Islamorada Chamber of Commerce,** housed in an actual little red caboose, U.S. 1 at MM 82.5, P.O. Box 915, Islamorada, FL 33036 (© **800/ 322-5397** or 305/664-4503; fax 305/664-4289; www.islamoradachamber. com), also offers maps and literature on the Upper Keys.

You can't miss the big blue visitor center at MM 53.5, the **Greater Marathon Chamber of Commerce,** 12222 Overseas Hwy., Marathon, FL 33050 (© **800/ 262-7284** or 305/743-5417; fax 305/289-0183; www.floridakeysmarathon.com). Here, you can receive free information on local events, festivals, shows, attractions, dining, and lodging.

OUTDOOR SIGHTS & ACTIVITIES

Anne's Beach (at MM 73.5, on Lower Matecumbe Key, at the southwest end of Islamorada) is really more of a picnic spot than a full-fledged beach, but die-hard suntanners still congregate on this lovely but tiny strip of coarse sand that was damaged beyond recognition during the series of storms in 1998. Plans are in place to reconstruct the boardwalk and huts, but at press time, work had not yet started.

A better choice for real beaching is **Sombrero Beach** in Marathon at the end of Sombrero Beach Road (near MM 50). This wide swath of uncluttered beachfront actually benefited from Hurricane George in September 1998, with generous deposits of extra sand and a face-lift courtesy of the Monroe County Tourist Development Council. More than 90 feet of sand is dotted with palms, Australian Pines, and Royal Poincianas as well as with barbecue grills, clean bathrooms, and some brand-new Tiki huts for relaxing in the shade.

If you are interested in seeing the Keys in their natural state, before modern development, you must venture off the highway and take to the water. Two backcountry islands that offer a glimpse of the "real" Keys are **Indian Key** and **Lignumvitae Key** . Visitors come to these to relax and enjoy the islands' colorful birds and lush hammocks (elevated pieces of land above a marsh).

Named for the lignum vitae ("wood of life") trees found there, **Lignumvitae Key** supports a virgin tropical forest, the kind that once thrived on most of the Upper Keys. Over the years, human settlers imported "exotic" plants and animals to the Keys, irrevocably changing the botanical makeup of many backcountry islands and threatening much of the indigenous wildlife. Over the past 25 years, however, the Florida Department of Natural Resources has successfully removed most of the exotic vegetation from this key, leaving this 280-acre site much as it existed in the 18th century. The island also holds the Matheson House, a historic house built in 1919 that has survived numerous hurricanes. You can go inside the house, but this is interesting only if you have a hankering for coral rock, which the house is made out of. It's now a museum dedicated to the history, nature, and topography of the area. More interesting is actually seeing the area via the Botanical Gardens, which surround the house and are a state preserve. Lignumvitae Key has a visitor center at MM 88.5 (© **305/664-2540**).

Indian Key, a much smaller island on the Atlantic side of Islamorada, was occupied by Native Americans for thousands of years before European settlers arrived. The 10-acre historic site was also the original seat of Dade County before the Civil War. Interestingly, from an archaeological standpoint, you can see the ruins of the previous settlement and tour the lush grounds on well-marked trails (off Indian Key Fill, Overseas Highway, MM 79). To get information about Indian Key, call the Florida Park Service at © **305/664-4815** or check out www.abfla.com/parks/IndianKey/indiankey.html.

If you want to see both islands, plan to spend at least half a day. To get there, you can rent your own powerboat at **Robbie's Rent-A-Boat,** U.S. 1 at MM 77.5 on the bay side (p. 171), on Islamorada. It's then a $1 admission fee to each island, which includes an informative hour-long guided tour by park rangers. This is a good option if you are a confident boater.

However, I also recommend taking Robbie's **ferry service.** A visit to one island costs $15, $10 for kids 12 and under, which includes the $1 park admission; trips to both islands cost $25 per person. (If you have time for only one island, make it Lignumvitae.) Not only is the ferry more economical, but it's easier to enjoy the natural beauty of the islands when you aren't negotiating the shallow reefs along the way. The runabouts, which carry up to six people, depart from Robbie's Pier Thursday through Monday at 9am and 1pm for Indian Key, and at 10am and 2pm for Lignumvitae Key. In the busy season, you may need to book as early as 2 days before departure. Call ☎ **305/664-4815** for information from the park service, or ☎ **305/664-9814** for Robbie's.

Crane Point Hammock ★★ *Finds* *Kids*   Crane Point Hammock is a little-known but worthwhile stop, especially for those interested in the rich botanical and archaeological history of the Keys. This privately owned 64-acre nature area is considered one of the most important historical sites in the Keys. It contains what is probably the last virgin thatch palm hammock in North America, as well as a rainforest exhibit and an archaeological dig site with pre-Columbian and prehistoric Bahamian artifacts.

Also headquarters for the Florida Keys Land and Sea Trust, the hammock's impressive nature museum has simple, informative displays of the Keys' wildlife, including a walk-through replica of a coral-reef cave and life-size dioramas with tropical birds and Key deer. Here, kids can participate in art projects, see 6-foot-long iguanas, climb through a scaled-down pirate ship, and touch a variety of indigenous aquatic and landlubbing creatures.

5550 Overseas Hwy. (MM 50), Marathon. ☎ 305/743-9100. www.cranepoint.org. Admission $7.50 adults, $6 seniors over 64, $4 students, free for children under 6. Mon–Sat 9am–5pm; Sun noon–5pm.

Pigeon Key ★★   At the curve of the old bridge on Pigeon Key is an intriguing historical site that has been under renovation since late 1993. This 5-mile-long island was once the camp for the crew that built the old railway in the early part of the 20th century, and later served as housing for the bridge builders. From here, your vista includes both the vestiges of Henry Flagler's old Seven-Mile Bridge as well as the one on which traffic presently soars, many old wooden cottages, and a truly tranquil stretch of lush foliage and sea. If you miss the shuttle tour from the Pigeon Key Visitor Center or would rather walk or bike to the site, it's about 2½ miles. Either way, you may want to bring a picnic to enjoy after a brief self-guided walking tour of the Key and museum visit to what has become an homage to Flagler's railroad, featuring artifacts and photographs of the old bridge. There is also an informative 28-minute video of the island's history offered every hour starting at 10am. Parking is available at the Knight's Key end of the bridge, at MM 48, or at the visitor center at MM 47, on the ocean side.

East end of the Seven-Mile Bridge near MM 47, Marathon. ☎ 305/743-5999. www.pigeonkey.org. Admission $8.50 adults, $5 for children under 13. Price includes shuttle transportation from the visitor center. Daily 10am–3pm; shuttle tours run every hr. 10am–4pm.

Seven-Mile Bridge ★★★   A stop at the Seven-Mile Bridge is a rewarding and relaxing break from the drive south. Built alongside the ruins of oil magnate Henry Flagler's incredible Overseas Railroad, the "new" bridge (between MMs

---

Fun Fact Bridge Mix

The Seven-Mile Bridge is the longest fragmented (unconnected pieces) bridge in the world. Completed in 1985, it was constructed parallel to the original bridge, part of Henry Flagler's Florida East Coast Railroad, which served as the original link to the Lower Keys. Some people may recognize the remnants of the old bridge from the Arnold Schwarzenegger film *True Lies*. Others fearfully contemplate whether a wrong turn would lead them to the old bridge instead of the new one. Not to worry: The old bridge is closed to cars and has been transformed into the world's longest fishing pier.

---

40 and 47) is considered an architectural feat. The wide-arched span, completed in 1985 at a cost of more than $45 million, is impressive, and its apex is the highest point in the Keys. The new bridge and its now-defunct neighbor provide an excellent vantage point from which to view the stunning waters of the Keys. In the daytime, you may want to walk, jog, or bike along the scenic 4-mile stretch of old bridge, or join local anglers, who catch barracuda, yellowtail, and dolphin (the fish, not the mammal) on what is known as "the longest fishing pier in the world." Parking is available on both sides of the bridge.

Between MMs 40 and 47 on U.S. 1. ✆ 305/289-0025.

VISITING WITH THE ANIMALS

Dolphin Research Center ★★★ *Kids*   If you've always wanted to touch, swim, or play with dolphins, this is the place to do it. Of the three such centers in the continental United States (all located in the Keys), the Dolphin Research Center is the most organized and informative. Although some people argue that training dolphins is cruel and selfish, this is one of the most respected of the institutions that study and protect the mammals. Knowledgeable trainers at the Dolphin Research Center will also tell you that the dolphins need stimulation and enjoy human contact. They certainly seem to. They nuzzle and seem to smile and kiss the lucky few who get to swim with them in the daily program. The "family" of 15 dolphins swims in a 90,000-square-foot natural saltwater pool carved out of the shoreline.

If you can't get into the swim program, you can still watch the frequent shows, sign up for a class in hand signals, or feed the dolphins from docks. Because the Dolphin Encounter swimming program is the most popular, reservations must be made in advance (call more than a month in advance to make sure you get in). The cost is $155 per person. If you're not brave enough to swim with the dolphins or you have a child under 12 (not permitted to swim with dolphins), try the Dolphin Splash program, in which participants stand on an elevated platform from which they can "meet and greet" the dolphins. A height requirement of 44 inches is enforced, and an adult must hold up children under the required height. Cost for this program is $80 per person; free for children under 3.

U.S. 1 at MM 59 (on the bay side), Marathon. ✆ 305/289-1121. www.dolphins.org. Educational walking tours 5 times daily: 10 and 11am, and 12:30, 2, and 3:30pm. Admission $18 adults, $15 seniors, $12 children 4–12, free for children 3 and under. Daily 9am–4pm.

Florida Keys Wild Bird Center ★   Wander through lush canopies of mangroves on narrow wooden walkways to see some of the Keys' most famous residents—the large variety of native birds, including broad-wing hawks, great blue and white herons, roseate spoonbills, white ibis, cattle egrets, and a number of pelicans. This not-for-profit center operates as a hospital for the many birds that have been injured by accident or disease. In 2002, the World Parrot Mission was established here, focusing on caring for parrots and educating the public about the birds. Visit at feeding time, usually about 3:30pm, when you can watch the dedicated staff feed the hundreds of hungry birds.

U.S. 1 at MM 93.6, Bayside, Tavernier. © 305/852-4486. www.fkwbc.org. Donations suggested. Daily 8:30am–6pm.

Robbie's Pier ★★★ *(Value* One of the best and definitely one of the cheapest attractions in the Upper Keys is the famed Robbie's Pier. Here, the fierce steely tarpons, a prized catch for backcountry anglers, have been gathering for the past 20 years. You may recognize these prehistoric-looking giants that grow up to 200 pounds; many are displayed as trophies and mounted on local restaurant walls. To see them live, head to Robbie's Pier, where tens and sometimes hundreds of these behemoths circle the shallow waters waiting for you to feed them. Robbie's Pier also offers ranger-led boat tours and guided kayak tours to Indian Key, where you can go snorkeling or just bask in the glory of your surroundings.

U.S. 1 at MM 77.5, Islamorada. © 305/664-9814. Admission $1. Bucket of fish $2. Daily 8am–5pm. Look for the Hungry Tarpon restaurant sign on the right after the Indian Key channel.

Theater of the Sea ★ *(Kids* Established in 1946, the Theater of the Sea is one of the world's oldest marine zoos. Recently refurbished, the park's dolphin and sea lion shows are entertaining and informative, especially for children, who can also see sharks, sea turtles, and tropical fish. If you want to swim with dolphins and you haven't booked well in advance, this is the place you may be able to get into with just a few hours', or days', notice as opposed to the more rigid Dolphin Research Center (see above) in Marathon. (While the Dolphin Research Center is a legitimate, scientific establishment, this is more of a theme parky attraction. That's not to say the dolphins are mistreated, but it's just not as, say, educational and professional as it is at the Dolphin Research Center.) Theater of the Sea also permits you to swim with the sea lions and stingrays. Children under 5 are not permitted to participate. There are also twice daily 4-hour adventure and snorkel cruises, $65 for adults and $40 for children 3–12, in which you can learn about the history and ecology of the marine environment. The facility also serves as a haven for dozens of stray cats that have free run of the grounds and gift shop.

U.S. 1 at MM 84.5, Islamorada. © 305/664-2431. www.theaterofthesea.com. Admission $20 adults, $12 children 3–12. Dolphin swim $140; sea lion swim $95; stingray swim $45 per person. Reservations a must. Daily 10am–5pm (ticket office closes at 4pm).

TWO EXCEPTIONAL STATE PARKS

One of the best places to discover the diverse ecosystem of the Upper Keys is in its most famous park, **John Pennekamp Coral Reef State Park** ★★★, located on U.S. 1 at MM 102.5, in Key Largo (© **305/451-1202;** www.pennekamp park.com). Named for a former *Miami Herald* editor and conservationist, the 188-square-mile park is the nation's first undersea preserve: It's a sanctuary for part of the only living coral reef in the continental United States. The original plans for Everglades National Park included this part of the reef within its boundaries, but opposition from local homeowners made its inclusion politically impossible.

Because the water is extremely shallow, the 40 species of coral and more than 650 species of fish here are particularly accessible to divers, snorkelers, and glass-bottomed-boat passengers. To experience this park, visitors must get in the water—you can't see the reef from the shore. Your first stop should be the visitor center, which is full of educational fish tanks and a mammoth 30,000-gallon saltwater aquarium that re-creates a reef ecosystem. At the adjacent dive shop, you can rent snorkeling and diving equipment and join one of the boat trips that depart for the reef throughout the day. Visitors can also rent motorboats, sailboats, windsurfers, and canoes. The 2-hour glass-bottomed-boat tour is the best way to see the coral reefs if you don't want to get wet. Watch for the lobsters and other sea life residing in the fairly shallow ridge walls beneath the coastal waters. **But remember:** These are protected waters, so you can't remove anything from the water.

Canoeing around the park's narrow mangrove channels and tidal creeks is also popular. You can go on your own in a rented canoe or, in winter, sign up for a tour led by a local naturalist. Hikers have two short trails from which to choose: a boardwalk through the mangroves and a dirt trail through a tropical hardwood hammock. Ranger-led walks are usually scheduled daily from the end of November to April. Phone ℂ **305/451-1202** for schedule information and reservations.

Park admission is $2.50 per vehicle for one occupant; for two or more, it is $5 per vehicle, plus 50¢ per passenger; $1.50 per pedestrian or bicyclist. On busy weekend days, there's often a line of cars to get into the park. On your way into the park, ask the ranger for a map. Glass-bottomed-boat tours cost $20 for adults and $12 for children 11 and under. Snorkeling tours are $27 for adults and $22 for children 17 and under, including equipment. Sailing and snorkeling tours are $32 for adults, $27 for children 17 and under, including equipment. Canoes rent for $10 per hour. For experienced boaters only, four different-sized reef boats (powerboats) rent for $38 to $50 per hour, with cheaper half-day and full-day rates available; call ℂ **305/451-6325** for more information. A $400 deposit (and up depending on boat size, starting at a 22-ft. boat) is required. The park's boat rental is open daily from 8am to 5pm—the last boat rented is at 3pm; phone for tour and dive times. Reservations are recommended for all of the above. Also, see below for more options on diving, fishing, and snorkeling these reefs.

Long Key State Recreation Area ★★★, U.S. 1 at MM 68, Long Key (ℂ **305/664-4815;** www.abfla.com/parks/LongKey/longkey.html), is one of the best places in the Middle Keys for hiking, camping, snorkeling, and canoeing. This 965-acre site is situated atop the remains of an ancient coral reef. At the entrance gate, ask for a free flyer describing the local trails and wildlife.

There are three nature trails that can be explored via foot or canoe: The Golden Orb Trail is a 40-minute walk through mostly just plants; the Layton Trail is a 15-minute walk along the bay; and the Long Key Canoe Trail glides along a shallow-water lagoon. Campsites are located along the Atlantic Ocean and the swimming, snorkeling, and saltwater fishing (license required) are top notch here. Educational programs on the aforementioned are available, too, for novices. Snorkeling is shallow and on the shoreline of the Atlantic Ocean. The nearest place to rent snorkeling equipment is Holiday Isle, 84001 U.S. 1, Islamorada (ℂ **800/327-7070**).

The park's excellent 1½-mile canoe trail is also short and sweet, allowing visitors to loop around the mangroves in about an hour. You can rent canoes at the trail head for about $4 per hour. Long Key is also a great spot to stop for a picnic if you get hungry on your way to Key West.

The 10 "Keymandments"

The Keys have always attracted independent spirits, from Ernest Hemingway and Tennessee Williams to Jimmy Buffett, Zane Grey, and local hero Mel Fisher. Writers, artists, and free thinkers have long drifted down here to escape.

Although you'll generally find a very laid-back and tolerant code of behavior in the Keys, some rules do exist. Be sure to respect the 10 "Keymandments" while you're here, or suffer the consequences.

- Don't anchor on a reef. (Reefs are alive.)
- Don't feed the animals. (They'll want to follow you home, and you can't keep them.)
- Don't trash our place (or we'll send Bubba to trash yours).
- Don't touch the coral. (After all, you don't even know them. Some pose a mild risk of injury as well.)
- Don't speed (especially on Big Pine Key, where deer reside and tar-and-feathering is still practiced).
- Don't catch more fish than you can eat. (Better yet, let them go. Some of them support schools.)
- Don't collect conch. (This species is protected by Bubba.)
- Don't disturb the bird nests. (They find it very annoying.)
- Don't damage the sea grass. (And don't even think about making a skirt out of it.)
- Don't drink and drive on land or sea. (There's absolutely nothing funny about it.)

Railroad builder Henry Flagler created the Long Key Fishing Club here in 1906, and the waters surrounding the park are still popular with game fishers. In summer, sea turtles lumber onto the protected coast to lay their eggs, all lined up on the coast. It's a big event, and educational programs are available to view this phenomenon.

Admission is $3.25 per car plus 50¢ per person (except for the Layton Trail, which is free). Open daily from 8am to sunset.

WATERSPORTS FROM A TO Z

There are literally hundreds of outfitters in the Keys who will arrange all kinds of water activities, from cave dives to parasailing. If those recommended below are booked up or unreachable, ask the local chamber of commerce for a list of qualified members.

BOATING   In addition to the rental shops in the state parks, you will find dozens of outfitters along U.S. 1 offering a range of runabouts and skiffs for boaters of any experience level. **Captain Pip's,** U.S. 1 at MM 47.5, Marathon (© **800/707-1692** or 305/743-4403), rents 18- to 24-foot motorboats with 90- to 225-horsepower engines for $130 to $250 per day. Overnight accommodations are available and include a free boat rental; 2-night minimum $220 to $255; weekly $1,190 to $1,890. Rooms are Key West comfortable and charming, with ceiling fans, tile floors, and pine paneling. But the best part about it is that every room comes with an 18- to 21-foot boat for your use during your stay.

Robbie's Rent-a-Boat, U.S. 1 at MM 77.5, Islamorada (② **305/664-9814**), rents 14- to 27-foot motorboats with engines ranging from 15 to 200 horsepower. Boat rentals are $70 to $205 for a half day and $90 to $295 for a full day.

CANOEING & KAYAKING I can think of no better way to explore the uninhabited, shallow backcountry on the Gulf side of the Keys than by kayak or canoe, since you can reach places big boats just can't get to because of their large draft. Sometimes manatees will even cuddle up to the boats, thinking them another friendly species.

Many area hotels rent kayaks and canoes to guests, as do the outfitters listed here. **Florida Bay Outfitters,** U.S. 1 at MM 104, Key Largo (② **305/451-3018**), rents canoes and sea kayaks for use in and around John Pennekamp Coral Reef State Park for $25 to $45 for a half day and $40 to $60 for a whole day. At **Coral Reef Park Co.,** on U.S. 1 at MM 102.5, Key Largo (② **305/451-1621**), you can rent canoes and kayaks for $8 per hour, $28 for a half day; most canoes are sit-on-tops. **Florida Keys Kayak and Sail**, U.S. 1 at MM 75.5, Islamorada (② **305/664-4878**), at Robbie's Pier, offers back country tours, botanical preserve tours of Lignumvitae Key, historical site tours of Indian Key, and sunset tours through the mangrove tunnels and saltwater flats. Tour rates are from $39 to $49; rental rates range from $15 per hour to $45 per day for single kayak and $20 per hour to $60 per day for double kayak. **Reflections Nature Tours** (② **305/872-4668**) is a small mobile company that specializes in kayak, hiking, and bike tours through the lower Keys. Guided kayak tours cost $50 per person for a 3-hour tour; guided bike tours cost $35 per person for a 2-hour tour; and guided walking tours cost $13 per person for an hour tour. All tours are by appointment only.

DIVING & SNORKELING Located just 6 miles off Key Largo is a U.S. Navy Landing Ship Dock, the latest artificial wreck site to hit the Keys—or, rather, to be submerged 130 feet *below* the Keys.

The **Florida Keys Dive Center,** on U.S. 1 at MM 90.5, Tavernier (② **305/852-4599**), takes snorkelers and divers to the reefs of John Pennekamp Coral Reef State Park and environs every day. PADI (Professional Association of Diving Instructors) training courses are also available for the uninitiated. While some people have complained that employees are rude here, others disagree. We suggest you decide for yourselves. Tours leave at 8am and 12:30pm and cost $30 per person to snorkel (plus $9 rental fee for mask, snorkel, and fins) and $60 per person to dive (plus an extra $20 if you need to rent all the gear).

At **Hall's Dive Center & Career Institute,** U.S. 1 at MM 48.5, Marathon (② **305/743-5929**), snorkelers and divers can choose to dive at Looe Key, Sombrero Reef, Delta Shoal, Content Key, and Coffins Patch. Tours are scheduled daily at 9am and 1pm. You will spend 1 hour at each of two sites per tour. If you mention this book, you will get a special discounted rate ($5–$10 off) of $35 per person to snorkel (additional gear is $11) and $45 per person to dive (tanks are $8.50 each).

With **SNUBA Tours of Key Largo** (② 305/451-6391; www.pennekamp.com/sw/snuba.htm), you can dive down to 20 feet attached to a comfortable breathing apparatus that really gives you the feeling of scuba diving without having to be certified. You can tour shallow coral reefs teeming with hundreds of colorful fish and plant life, from sea turtles to moray eels. Reservations are required; call to find out where and when to meet. A 2- to 3-hour underwater tour (typically 1–4pm) costs $85, including all equipment. If you have never dived before, you may require a 1-hour lesson in the pool, which costs an additional $45.

FISHING   Robbie's Partyboats & Charters, on U.S. 1 at MM 84.5, Isla-morada (© **305/664-8070** or 305/664-4196), located at the south end of the Holiday Isle Docks (see the Holiday Isle Resort in "Where to Stay," later in this chapter), offers day and night deep-sea and reef-fishing trips aboard a 65-foot party boat. Big-game fishing charters are also available, and "splits" are arranged for solo fishers. Party-boat fishing costs $25 for a half-day morning tour (rod and reel rental is $3); it's $15 extra if you want to go back out on an afternoon tour. Charters run $400 for a half day, $600 for a full day; splits begin at $65 per person. Phone for information and reservations.

Bud n' Mary's Fishing Marina, on U.S. 1 at MM 79.8, Islamorada (© **800/742-7945** or 305/664-2461), one of the largest marinas between Miami and Key West, is packed with sailors offering guided backcountry fishing charters. This is the place to go if you want to stalk tarpon, bonefish, and snapper. If the seas are not too rough, deep-sea and coral fishing trips can also be arranged. Charters cost $500 to $550 for a half day, $750 to $800 for a full day, and splits begin at $125 per person.

The Bounty Hunter, 15th Street at Burdine's Marina, Marathon (© **305/743-2446**), offers full- and half-day outings. For 28 years, Captain Brock Hook's huge sign has boasted, NO FISH, NO PAY: You're guaranteed to catch something, or your money back! Choose your prey from shark, barracuda, sailfish, or whatever else is running. Prices are $400 for a half day, $500 for three-quarters of a day, and $600 for a full day. Rates are for groups of no more than six people.

WHERE TO STAY

U.S. 1 is lined with chain hotels in all price ranges. In the Upper Keys, the best moderately priced option is the **Ramada Limited Resort & Casino** (© **800/THE-KEYS** or 305/451-3939) at MM 100, off of U.S. 1 in Key Largo, which has three pools and a casino boat and is just 3 miles from John Pennekamp Coral Reef State Park. Another good option in the Upper Keys is **Islamorada Days Inn,** U.S. 1 at MM 82.5 (© **800/DAYS-INN** or 305/664-3681). In the Mid-dle Keys, the **Wellesley Inn** at 13351 Overseas Hwy., MM 54 in Marathon (© **305/743-8550**), also offers reasonably priced ocean-side rooms.

Since the real beauty of the Keys lies mostly beyond the highways, there is no better way to see this area than by boat. Why not stay in a floating hotel? Espe-cially if you're traveling with a group, houseboats can be economical. To rent a houseboat, call Ruth and Michael Sullivan at **Smilin' Island Houseboat Rentals** (MM 99.5), Key Largo (© **305/451-1930**). Rates are from $750 to $1,350 for 3 nights. Boats accommodate up to six people.

For land options, consider the recommendations below.

Acquaint Yourself

Fans of stone crabs can get further acquainted with those seasonal crus-taceans thanks to Keys Fisheries' 3-hour tours aboard 40- to 50-foot ves-sels, which leave from Marathon. The tour includes views of fishermen as they collect crabs from traps and process their claws. The $425 tour cost includes up to six passengers and up to 6 pounds of fresh claws iced for travel or prepared at a dockside restaurant. Stone crab season is from October 15 to May 15. Call © **305/743-4353** or check the Web at www.keysfisheries.com for more information.

VERY EXPENSIVE

Cheeca Lodge & Spa ★★★ *Kids*   Luxurious and relaxing Cheeca has been hosting celebrities, royalty, and politicians since its opening in 1949. Guests now enjoy the luxury of the Cheeca's freshly renovated and remodeled rooms. Each of the 203 units offers all the amenities of a world-class resort in a very laid-back setting. You may not feel compelled to leave the sprawling grounds, but it's good to know that the hotel is conveniently situated near the best restaurants and nightlife. Located on 27 acres of beachfront property (the 1,100-ft. palm-lined beach is truly idyllic) with gorgeous beachfront bungalows that have private gardens and balconies, this rambling resort is known for its excellent sports facilities, including one of the only golf courses in the Upper Keys. All rooms are spacious and have small balconies. The nicer ones overlook the ocean and have large marble bathrooms. Rooms by the golf course have showers, not bathtubs, and overlook man-made lagoons. The Atlantic's Edge restaurant is one of the best in the Upper Keys (p. 181). In addition to all the sporty amenities, Cheeca also has a state-of-the-art Avanyu health spa and Tropical Island Fitness Studio. Additionally, children 6 to 12 can have their own customized vacation with Camp Cheeca's organized activities and events. A $35 daily resort fee may seem steep at first, but it includes tennis (courts, racquets, balls), golf (green fees, club rental, balls), fishing rods (bait extra), pool floats, beach cabanas, kayaks and paddle boats (subject to availability), fitness studio, valet parking, high-speed Internet (DSL), spa exercise classes, Starbucks in-room coffee, in-room bottled spring water, housekeeping gratuity, local and toll-free calls, Internet station, daily newspaper, and unlimited fax services.

U.S. 1 at MM 82 (P.O. Box 527), Islamorada, FL 33036. © **800/327-2888** or 305/664-4651. Fax 305/664-2893. www.cheeca.com. 202 units. Winter $149–$650 double, $219–$1,600 suite; off-season $129–$475 double, $189–$1,225 suite. AE, DC, DISC, MC, V. **Amenities:** 2 restaurants; 2 lounges (1 poolside); 3 outdoor heated pools; kids' pool; 9-hole, par-3 golf course; 6 lighted hard tennis courts; access to nearby health club; Jacuzzi; 5 hot tubs; watersports equipment rental; bike rental; children's nature programs; concierge; tour desk; car-rental desk; limited room service; in-room massage; babysitting; laundry services; dry cleaning; nature trails. *In room:* A/C, TV/VCR, dataport, kitchenette (in suites), minibar, coffeemaker, hair dryer, CD player.

Hawk's Cay Resort ★★★ *Kids*   Located on its own 60-acre island in the Middle Keys, this resort has a relaxed and casual island atmosphere. If it's recreation you're looking for, Hawk's Cay is far superior to the more luxurious Cheeca Lodge. It offers an impressive array of activities—sailing, fishing, snorkeling, and water-skiing to name a few—and the unique opportunity to swim in a special pool reserved for swimming with dolphins. (You'll need to reserve a spot well in advance for the dolphins—there's a waiting list.) The rooms are large and newly renovated, with island-style furniture, and each opens onto a private balcony with ocean or tropical views (pricing varies depending on the view). The large bathrooms are well appointed and have granite countertops. There are also some hyper posh villas—295 of them—with full kitchen, washer/dryer, and living rooms with water or garden views modeled after the kitschy 1950s concept of the "boatel." The 7,000-square-foot Indies Spa offers stellar treatments and a blissful Eucalyptus steam room that'll clear even the most stubborn of sinuses. The clubhouse has an exercise room, whirlpool, and steam room. In addition to a lagoon and several pools for families, the resort boasts a secluded pool for adults only. Organized children's activities, including special marine- and ecologically inspired programs, will keep your little ones busy while you relax.

61 Hawk's Cay Blvd. at MM 61, Duck Key, FL 33050. © **888/814-9104** or 305/743-7000. Fax 305/743-5215. www.hawkscay.com. 176 units. Winter $260–$410 double, $460–$1,100 suite; off-season $220–$340

double, $380–$1,000 suite. Packages available. AE, DC, DISC, MC, V. **Amenities:** 3 restaurants; lounge; out-door heated pool; adults-only private pool; 18-hole putting course; nearby golf course (transportation available); 8 tennis courts (6 hard, 2 clay, 2 lighted); small exercise room; Jacuzzi; watersports equipment rental; bike rental; children's programs ($25–$35 per child); game room; concierge; limited room service; in-room massage. *In room:* A/C, TV/VCR, fridge, coffeemaker, hair dryer, iron.

EXPENSIVE

Casa Morada ★★★ *Finds*   The closest thing you'll come to a boutique hotel in the Florida Keys, Casa Morada is the brainchild of a trio of seasoned New York City women with major experience in the hotel business—Ian Schrager Hotels, of all places—but no longer in the mood to deal with the brutal winters. This 16-suite hotel is tucked away off a sleepy street and radiates serenity and style in an area where serenity is aplenty but style elusive. Originally built in the 1950s, Casa Morada sits on 1.7 acres of prime bayfront land, which was upgraded with gorgeous landscaping, limestone grotto, freshwater pool, waterside terrace for breakfast, lunch, and poolside beverage service, and bocce ball court. Each of the cool rooms features either a private garden or terrace—request the one with the open air Jacuzzi that faces the bay. While the decor is decidedly island, think St. Barts rather than, say, Gilligan's. Although the hotel doesn't have a restaurant, a complimentary breakfast is served daily, and if you order out from one of the area's excellent restaurants, the hotel will re-plate the food on Casa Morada china. Because of the boutiquey nature of the hotel, expect a young crowd of hipsters. Free use of bikes, bocce, and board games as well as arrangements for snorkeling, diving, and fishing are available, but families with kids should avoid Casa Morada at all costs, since it's such an adult-oriented place and is so quiet, with few distractions for kids.

136 Madeira Rd., Islamorada, FL 33036. ⓒ **888/881-3030** or 305/664-0044. Fax 305/664-0674. www.casamorada.com. 16 units. Winter $199–$419; off-season $179–$349. Rates include continental breakfast. AE, DISC, MC, V. From U.S. 1 S, at MM 82.2, turn right onto Madeira Rd., and continue to the end of the street. Hotel is on your right. **Amenities:** Freshwater pool; complimentary bike use, bocce ball, snorkeling, diving, fishing. *In Room:* A/C, TV, DVD, mini-bar, hair dryer, safe, CD player.

Jules' Undersea Lodge ★★★ *Finds*   Staying here is certainly an experience of a lifetime—if you're brave enough to take the plunge. Originally built as a research lab in the 1970s, this small underwater compartment (which rests on pillars on the ocean floor) now operates as a two-room hotel. As expensive as it is unusual, Jules' is most popular with diving honeymooners. To get inside, guests swim 21 feet under the structure and pop up into the unit through a 4-by-6-foot "moon pool" that gurgles soothingly all night long. The 30-foot-deep underwater suite consists of two separate bedrooms that share a common living area. Room service will deliver your meals, daily newspapers, even a late-night pizza in waterproof containers at no extra charge.

51 Shoreland Dr., Key Largo, FL 33037. ⓒ **305/451-2353.** Fax 305/451-4789. www.jul.com. 2 units. $295–$395 per person. Rates include breakfast and dinner as well as all equipment and unlimited scuba diving in the lagoon for certified divers. Packages available. AE, DISC, MC, V. From U.S. 1 S, at MM 103.2, turn left onto Transylvania Ave., across from the Central Plaza shopping mall. **Amenities:** Entertainment center; dining area. *In room:* A/C, kitchenette.

The Moorings ★★★ *Finds*   Staying at The Moorings is more like staying at a secluded beach house than at a hotel. You'll never see another soul on this 18-acre resort, a former coconut plantation, if you choose not to. There isn't even maid service unless you request it. The romantic whitewashed units, from cozy cottages to three-bedroom houses, are spacious and modestly decorated. All have full kitchens (though there are two restaurants within walking distance), and most have washers and dryers. Some have CD players and VCRs, too; ask when you book. The real reason to come to this resort is to relax on the more than 1,000-foot beach (one of the only real beaches around). There are a hard tennis court, a few kayaks and windsurfers, but absolutely no motorized water vehicles in the waters surrounding the hotel, making it completely quiet and tranquil. There is no room service or restaurant (although Morada Bay across the street is excellent). This is a place for people who like each other a lot. Leave the kids at home unless they are extremely well behaved and not easily bored.

123 Beach Rd. near MM 81.5 on the ocean side, Islamorada, FL 33036. ℂ 305/664-4708. Fax 305/664-4242. www.themooringsvillage.com. 18 cottages. Winter daily $200–$225 small cottages, $375 1-bedroom house, $3,325–$7,875 weekly oceanfront house; off-season daily $185–$200 small cottages, $350 1-bedroom house, $2,625–$6,650 weekly oceanfront house. 2-night minimum for smaller cottages; 1-week minimum for larger cottages. MC, V. **Amenities:** Large outdoor heated pool; tennis court; watersports equipment rental. *In room:* A/C, TV, kitchen, coffeemaker, hair dryer.

MODERATE

Banana Bay Resort & Marina ★★ *Finds*   It doesn't look like much from the sign-cluttered Overseas Highway, but when you enter the lush grounds of Banana Bay, you will realize you're in one of the most bucolic and best-run properties in the Upper Keys. Built in the early 1950s as a place for fishermen to stay during extended fishing trips, the resort is a beachfront maze of two-story buildings hidden among banyans and palms. The rooms are moderately sized, and many have private balconies where you can enjoy your complimentary coffee and newspaper every morning. Recent additions to the hotel include a recreational activity area with horseshoe pits, a bocce court, picnic areas with barbecue grills, and a giant lawn chessboard. The hotel's kitschy restaurant serves three meals a day, indoors or poolside. The hotel also offers bike rentals in addition to boats, wave-runners, kayaks, day sailing dinghies, and bait and tackle rentals. Another surprising amenity is Pretty Joe Rock, the hotel's private island, which is available for long weekends and weekly rentals. The island has a Keys style two-bedroom, two-bathroom cottage that's ideal for romantic escapes. This resort is family friendly, but if you're looking for an adults-only resort, there's also a Banana Bay Resort in Key West (ℂ 305/296-6925) that doesn't allow children.

U.S. 1 at MM 49.5, Marathon, FL 33050. ℂ 800/BANANA-1 or 305/743-3500. Fax 305/743-2670. www.bananabay.com. 60 units. Winter $135–$225 double; off-season $95–$175 double. Rates include continental breakfast. 3- and 7-night honeymoon and wedding packages available. AE, DC, DISC, MC, V. **Amenities:** Restaurant; 3 bars; pool; tennis courts; health club; Jacuzzi; watersports rental; self-service laundromat; small beach and snorkel area; charter fishing; sailing and diving. *In room:* A/C, TV, dataport, fridge, hair dryer, iron.

Conch Key Cottages ★ *Finds*   Here's your chance to play castaway in the Keys. Occupying its own private microisland just off U.S. 1, Conch Key Cottages is a comfortable hideaway run by live-in owners Ron Wilson and Wayne Byrnes, who are constantly fixing and adding to their unique property. This is a place to get away from it all; the cottages aren't located close to much, except maybe one or two interesting eateries. The cabins, which were built at different times over the past 40 years, overlook their own stretch of natural, but very small, private beach and have a screened-in porch, cozy bedroom, bathroom, hammock, barbecue grill, and a two-person kayak. Request one of the two-bedroom cottages—especially if you are traveling with the family. They are the most spacious and are well designed, practically tailor-made for couples or families. On the other side of the pool are a handful of efficiency apartments (all with fully equipped kitchens) that are similarly outfitted but enjoy no beach frontage.

Near U.S. 1 at MM 62.3, Marathon, FL 33050. ℂ **800/330-1577** or 305/289-1377. Fax 305/743-8207. www.conchkeycottages.com. 12 cottages. Dec 15–Sept 8 $110–$288; Sept 9–Dec 14 $74–$215. DISC, MC, V. **Amenities:** Pool; complimentary kayaks; laundry facilities. *In room:* A/C, TV, kitchen, coffeemaker, no phone.

Faro Blanco Marine Resort ★

Spanning both sides of the Overseas Highway and all on waterfront property, this huge, two-shore marina and hotel complex offers something for every taste. Free-standing camp-style cottages with a small bedroom are the resort's least-expensive accommodations, but they are in dire need of rehabilitation, which, thankfully, began at the writing of this book. Old appliances and a musty odor make them the least-desirable units on the property. The houseboats are the best choice and value. Permanently tethered (so tightly moored, you hardly move at all, even in the roughest weather) in a tranquil marina, these white rectangular boats look like floating mobile homes and are uniformly clean, fresh, and recommendable, with four hotel rooms to each boat. They have colonial American-style furnishings, fully equipped kitchenettes, front and back porches, and water, water everywhere. The resort's condos have three bedrooms, two bathrooms, and terraces. Finally, there are two unusual rental units located in a lighthouse on the pier, also under renovation at the time of this writing. Circular staircases, unusually shaped immaculate rooms and showers, and nautical decor make it a unique place to stay, but some guests might find it claustrophobic.

1996 Overseas Hwy., U.S. 1 at MM 48.5, Marathon, FL 33050. ℂ **800/759-3276** or 305/743-9018. Fax 305/866-5235. www.spottswood.com/faroblanco/indexsmall.htm. 123 units, 31 houseboats with 4 units each. Winter $89–$150 cottage, $109–$200 houseboat, $185 lighthouse, $267–$327 condo; off-season $79–$119 cottage, $99–$178 houseboat, $145 lighthouse, $215–$263 condo. AE, DISC, MC, V. **Amenities:** 4 restaurants; 2 lounges; Olympic-size pool; fully equipped dive shop; barbecue and picnic areas; playground. *In room:* A/C, TV.

Holiday Isle Resort

A huge resort complex encompassing five restaurants, several lounges, Tiki huts, a large marina, many retail shops, and four distinct (if not distinctive) hotels, the Holiday Isle is one of the biggest resorts in the Keys, but in this case, when it comes to clean, attractive rooms, size definitely doesn't matter. It attracts a spring-break kind of crowd year-round, a crowd that tends not to care about the room itself and one that has no qualms cramming an entire fraternity into a single room for budget reasons. Its famous Tiki Bar claims to have invented the rum runner drink (151-proof rum, blackberry brandy, banana liqueur, grenadine, and lime juice), and there's no reason to doubt it. It's the Tiki Bar that brings the people, really. Hordes of partiers are attracted to the resort's nonstop merrymaking, live music, and beachfront bars. As a result, some of the accommodations can be noisy. Rooms tend to be bare-bones budget and despite ocean views, they're pretty awful and need a good scrub down—especially the rooms that lead out onto the filthy, sandy Tiki bar. Even the nicest rooms, if you can call them nice, could use a good cleaning. El Captain and Harbor Lights, two of the least-expensive hotels on the property, are both austere. Like the other hotels here, rooms could use a thorough rehab. Howard Johnson, another Holiday Isle property, is a little farther from the action and a tad more civilized in case you should have one too many rum runners and can't drive further to a nicer hotel.

U.S. 1 at MM 84, Islamorada, FL 33036. ℂ **800/327-7070** or 305/664-2321. Fax 305/664-2703. www. holidayisle.com. 178 units. Winter $130–$290 double, $290–$420 suite; off-season $110–$240 double, $240–$410 suite. AE, DISC, MC, V. **Amenities:** 5 restaurants; 12 bars; 3 outdoor heated pools; kids' pool; Jacuzzi; kids' programs; watersports equipment/rentals; laundry facilities. *In room:* A/C, TV, fridge, hair dryer.

Kona Kai Resort & Gallery ★★   Unique to the Upper Keys, this little haven, with just 11 units, is both casual and elegant. Quaint rooms and complete suites dot the lushly landscaped 2-acre property, which boasts a large variety of native vegetation like palms, bougainvillea, and ferns, plus an impressive collection of fruit-bearing trees, such as carambola, passion fruit, banana, Key lime, guava, and coconut, which you can sample. An orchid house has over 250 beautiful flowers. Lounge chairs, hammocks, a Jacuzzi, and a compact beach are available for those who just want to relax (no phones in the rooms make relaxing imperative), while the owners will organize excursions to the Everglades, the backcountry, or wherever for the more adventurous. All the rooms are very private and simply furnished; bathroom amenities are fabulous, with lotions, soaps, and shampoos made from tropical fruits. For meals, you'll need to visit a nearby restaurant—there are three within walking distance and several more a short drive away. Smoking is not permitted in the rooms. An art gallery featuring work by American and international painters, photographers, and sculptors doubles as the property's office and lobby. Even if you are not staying here, stop in to see the artwork.

97802 Overseas Hwy. (U.S. 1 at MM 97.8), Key Largo, FL 33037. ☎ **800/365-7829** or 305/852-7200. Fax 305/852-4629. www.konakairesort.com. 11 units. Winter $149–$259 double, $177–$748 1- to 2-bedroom suite; off-season $159–$192 double, $192–$561 1- to 2-bedroom suite. AE, DISC, MC, V. Closed Sept. Children under 16 not permitted. **Amenities:** Heated pool; tennis court; spa; Jacuzzi; watersports equipment rental; concierge; in-room massage and facials; boat ramp/dockage. *In room:* A/C, TV, VCR, fridge, hair dryer; kitchen, CD player (suites only).

Lime Tree Bay Resort Motel ★   The Lime Tree Bay Resort is the only hotel in the tiny town of Layton (pop. 183). Midway between Islamorada and Marathon, the hotel is only steps from Long Key State Recreation Area. It's situated on a very pretty piece of waterfront graced with hundreds of mature palm trees and lots of other tropical foliage. It prides itself on its promise of no hustle, no valets, and, most amusingly, no bartenders in Hawaiian shirts! Motel rooms and efficiencies have tiny bathrooms with standing showers but are clean and well maintained. The best deal is the two-bedroom bayview cottage. The large living area with new fixtures and furnishings leads out to a large private deck where you can enjoy a view of the Gulf from your hammock. A full kitchen and two full bathrooms make it a comfortable space for six people. Fifteen efficiencies and suites have kitchenettes. Pretty cool in its own right is the Zane Grey suite (named after the famous author and screenwriter who lived right around the corner), a two-bedroom one-bath suite with the best views and a second story location with private stairs.

U.S. 1 at MM 68.5 in Layton, Long Key, FL 33001. ☎ **800/723-4519** or 305/664-4740. Fax 305/664-0750. www.limetreebayresort.com. 30 units. Winter $109–$265 double; off-season $89–$215 double. AE, DC, DISC, MC, V. **Amenities:** Restaurant; small outdoor pool; tennis court; Jacuzzi; watersports equipment rental. *In room:* A/C, TV, dataport, kitchenette (in some units).

INEXPENSIVE

Ragged Edge Resort ★★   This small oceanfront property's Tahitian-style 11 units are spread out along more than half a dozen gorgeous, grassy waterfront acres. All are immaculately clean and comfortable, and most are outfitted with full kitchens and tasteful furnishings. There's no bar, restaurant, or staff to speak of, but the retreat's affable owner, Jackie Barnes, is happy to lend you bicycles or offer good advice on the area's offerings. A large dock attracts boaters and a good variety of local and migratory birds. An outdoor, heated freshwater pool is a bonus for those months when the temperature gets a bit chilly—for Florida anyway.

243 Treasure Harbor Rd. (near MM 86.5), Islamorada, FL 33036. ✆ **800/436-2023** or 305/852-5389. www.ragged-edge.com. 11 units. Winter $79–$199; off-season $49–$142. AE, MC, V. **Amenities:** Outdoor pool; free use of bikes; laundromat. *In room:* A/C, kitchen (most units), fridge, coffeemaker.

CAMPING

John Pennekamp Coral Reef State Park ★★   One of Florida's best parks (p. 171), Pennekamp offers 47 well-separated campsites, half of which are available by advance reservation, the rest distributed on a first-come, first-served basis. The tent sites are small but well equipped with bathrooms, hot water, and showers. Note that the local environment provides fertile breeding grounds for insects, particularly in the late summer, so bring insect repellant or you will be sorry. Two man-made beaches and a small lagoon nearby attract many large wading birds. Reservations are held until 5pm, and the park must be notified of late arrival by phone on the check-in date. Pennekamp opens at 8am and closes around sundown.

U.S. 1 at MM 102.5 (P.O. Box 487), Key Largo, FL 33037. ✆ **305/451-1202.** www.pennekamppark.com. 47 campsites. Reservations can be made in advance by calling Reserve America (✆ 800/326-3521). $24 (without electricity) to $26 (with electricity) per site. Park entry $4 per vehicle (50¢ for each additional person). Yearly permits and passes available. AE, DISC, MC, V. No pets.

Long Key State Park ★   The Upper Keys' other main state park is more secluded than its northern neighbor—and more popular. All sites are located ocean-side and surrounded by narrow rows of trees and nearby toilet and bathroom facilities. Reserve well in advance, especially in winter.

U.S. 1 at MM 67.5 (P.O. Box 776), Long Key, FL 33001. ✆ **305/664-4815.** www.floridastateparks.org/longkey/default.asp. 60 oceanfront sites. $24–$26 per site for 1–4 people. $3.25 per vehicle. AE, DISC, MC, V. No pets.

WHERE TO DINE

Although not known as a culinary hot spot (though always improving), the Upper and Middle Keys do offer some excellent restaurants, most of which specialize in seafood. Often, visitors (especially those who fish) take advantage of accommodations that have kitchen facilities and cook their own meals. Some restaurants will even clean and cook your catch, for a fee.

VERY EXPENSIVE

Atlantic's Edge ★★★ SEAFOOD/REGIONAL   Ask for a table by the oceanfront window to feel really privileged at this restaurant, the most elegant in the Keys. Although the service and food are generally first rate, don't get dressed up—a sports coat for men will be fine but isn't necessary. You can choose from an innovative, varied menu, which offers several choices of fresh fish, steak, chicken, and pastas. The crab cakes, made with stone crab when in season, are the very best in the Keys; served on a warm salad of baby greens with a mild sauce of red peppers, they're the stuff cravings are made of. Other excellent dishes include a Thai-spiced fresh baby snapper and the vegetarian angel-hair pasta with mushrooms, asparagus, and peppers in a rich broth. Service can sometimes be less than efficient but is always courteous and professional.

In the Cheeca Lodge, U.S. 1 at MM 82, Islamorada. ✆ **305/664-4651.** Reservations recommended. Main courses $20–$36. AE, DC, DISC, MC, V. Daily 6–10pm.

Kaiyo ★★★ JAPANESE/SUSHI   This funky, colorful restaurant looks out of place in an area where most restaurants are housed in shanty shacks, and its exquisite, modern sushi and Japanese cuisine is a first for Islamorada, but the food is so good, people from all over South Florida plan trips around a meal at

Kaiyo. The brainchild of Chef Dawn Sieber, former executive chef at Cheeca Lodge, Kaiyo isn't your typical sushi restaurant, but one that fuses Florida's fine ingredients with some of the freshest raw fish this side of Tokyo. Signature sushi rolls such as the Spicy Volcano Conch roll and the Key Lime Lobster roll are outstanding, as are the farm raised raw oysters and farmed baby conch tempura. A hip, modern interior is an amusing contrast to the casually dressed, Key-ed up diners, and service here is of five star caliber—something not typically found in the laid back Keys. Before you say how you came to the Keys not for trendy sushi, but for fresh fish and conch fritters, do have a meal at Kaiyo. It *will* change the way you view Keys cuisine.

81701 Old Highway, U.S. 1 at MM 82, Islamorada. ⓒ 305/664-5556. Reservations recommended. Main courses $12–$15; sushi $4.50–$12. AE, DC, MC, V. Mon–Sat noon–10pm.

EXPENSIVE

Barracuda Grill ⭐⭐ SEAFOOD   Owned by Lance Hill and his wife, Jan (a former sous chef at Little Palm Island; p. 187), this small, casual spot serves excellent seafood, steaks, and chops, but unfortunately, it's open only for dinner. Some of the favorite dishes are the Caicos Gold Conch and Mangrove Snapper and Mango. Try the Tipsy Olives appetizer, marinated in gin or vodka, to kick-start your meal. For fans of spicy food, try the red-hot calamari. Decorated with barracuda-themed art, the restaurant also features a well-priced American wine list with lots of California vintages.

U.S. 1 at MM 49.5 (bay side), Marathon. ⓒ 305/743-3314. www.barracudagrill.com. Main courses $10–$26. AE, MC, V. Mon–Sat 6–10pm.

Marker 88 ⭐⭐⭐ SEAFOOD/REGIONAL   An institution in the Upper Keys, Marker 88 has been pleasing locals and visitors for dinner since it opened in the early 1970s. Chef-owner Andre Mueller fuses tropical fruit and fish with such items as crab-meat stuffing, asparagus, tomatoes, lemons, olives, capers, and mushrooms to make the most delectable and innovative seafood dishes around. Taking full advantage of his island location, Andre offers dozens of seafood selections, including Keys lobster, Bahamas conch, Florida Bay stone crabs, Gulf Coast shrimp, and an impressive variety of fish from around the country. After you've figured out what kind of seafood to have, you can choose from a dozen styles of preparation. The Keys' standard style is meunière, which is a subtle, tasty sauce of lemon and parsley. Although everything looks tempting, don't overorder—portions are huge. The waitresses, who are pleasant enough, require a bit of patience, but the food—not to mention the spectacular Gulf views from the outdoor bar and tables—is worth it.

U.S. 1 at MM 88 (bay side), Islamorada. ⓒ 305/852-9315. Reservations suggested. Main courses $14–$33. AE, DC, DISC, MC, V. Tues–Sun 5–11pm. Closed in Sept.

MODERATE

Green Turtle Inn ⭐ SEAFOOD   The Green Turtle Inn was established in 1947 as a place where anglers and travelers to and from Key West could stop for local delicacies made from sea turtles harvested in local waters. It has become the quintessential Keys eatery, with a friendly, local flavor and delicious and *different* fare, such as turtle steaks, soups, and chowders. Alligator steak is also popular and, yes, it does taste like chicken. Campy house pianist Tina Martin has become somewhat of a local celebrity, but it's really the Turtle Chowder for which the Inn has become best known. The restaurant also has a cannery so you can take some of the chowder to your friends, who won't believe how good it is until they taste it for themselves.

U.S. 1 at MM 81.5, Islamorada. ✆ **305/664-9031.** Main courses $12–$22. AE, DISC, MC, V. Noon–10pm
Tues–Sun.

Lorelei Restaurant and Cabana Bar ✿ SEAFOOD/BAR FOOD   Don't
resist the siren call of the enormous, sparkling roadside mermaid—you won't be
dashed onto the rocks. This big old fish house and bar is a great place for a snack,
a meal, or a beer. Excellent views of the bay remind you that you are in a very
primitive, pristine form of civilization. Inside, a good-value menu focuses mainly
on seafood. When in season, lobsters are the way to go. For $20, you can get a
good-size tail—at least a 1 pounder—prepared any way you like. Other fare
includes the standard clam chowder, fried shrimp, and doughy conch fritters. Salads and soups are hearty and satisfying. For those tired of fish, the menu also offers
a few beef selections. The outside bar has live music every evening, and you can
order snacks and light meals from a limited menu that is satisfying and well priced.

U.S. 1 at MM 82, Islamorada. ✆ **305/664-4656.** Reservations not usually required. Main courses $12–$24.
AE, DC, DISC, MC, V. Daily 7am–10:30pm. Outside bar serves breakfast 7–11am; lunch/appetizer menu
11am–9pm. Bar closes at midnight.

INEXPENSIVE

Calypso's Seafood Grill ✿ SEAFOOD   The awning still bears the name of
the former restaurant, Demar's, but the food here is all Todd Lollis's, an inspired
young chef who looks like he might be more comfortable at a Grateful Dead
concert than in a kitchen, but who turns out inventive seafood dishes in a casual
and rustic waterside setting. If it's available, try the butter-pecan sauce over
whatever fish is freshest. Don't miss the white-wine sangria, full of tangy oranges
and limes and topped with a dash of cinnamon. The prices are surprisingly reasonable, but the service can be a little more laid-back than you're used to. The
toughest part is finding the place. From the south, turn right at the blinking yellow lights near MM 99.5 to Ocean Bay Drive and then turn right. Look for the
blue vinyl-sided building on the left.

1 Seagate Blvd. (near MM 99.5), Key Largo. ✆ **305/451-0600.** Main courses $9–$18. MC, V. Wed–Mon
11:30am–10pm; Fri–Sat until 11pm.

Islamorada Fish Company ✿✿ SEAFOOD   Pick up a cooler of stone crab
claws in season (mid-Oct to Apr), or try the great fried-fish sandwiches, served
with melted American cheese, fried onions, and coleslaw. A few hundred yards
up the road (at MM 81.6) is Islamorada Fish Company Restaurant & Bakery,
the newer establishment, which looks like an average diner but has a selection of
fantastic seafood and pastas. It's also the place for breakfast. Locals gather for
politics and gossip as well as delicious grits, oatmeal, omelets, and homemade
pastries. Keep your eyes open while dining outside—the last time I was here,
there were baby manatees floating around, waiting for their close-ups.

U.S. 1 at MM 81.5 (up the street from Cheeca Lodge), Islamorada. ✆ **800/258-2559** or 305/664-9271.
www.islamoradafishco.com. Reservations not accepted. Main courses $8–$27; appetizers $4–$7. DISC, MC,
V. Sun–Thurs 11am–9pm; Fri–Sat 11am–10pm.

Time Out Barbecue ✿✿ BARBECUE   This barbecue joint serves up hot and
hearty old-fashioned barbecue that is among the best around. According to management, the secret is in the slow cooking—more than 10 hours for the melt-in-
your-mouth soft pork sandwich. Topped off with delicious, not-too-creamy
coleslaw and sweet baked beans, any of the many offerings are worth a stop. You
can grab a seat at the picnic table on the grassy lawn next to the Trading Post.

U.S. 1 at MM 81.5 (ocean side). ✆ **305/664-8911.** Sandwiches $4.25–$6; rib and chicken platters to share
$7–$15. MC, V. Daily 11am–10pm.

THE UPPER & MIDDLE KEYS AFTER DARK

Nightlife in the Upper Keys tends to start before the sun goes down, often at noon, since most people—visitors and locals alike—are on vacation. Also, many anglers and sports-minded folk go to bed early.

Hog Heaven opened in the early 1990s, the joint venture of some young locals tired of tourist traps. Located at MM 85.3, just off the main road on the ocean side in Islamorada (© **305/664-9669**), it's a welcome respite from the neon-colored cocktail circuit. This whitewashed biker bar offers a waterside view and diversions that include big-screen TVs and video games. The food isn't bad, either. The atmosphere is cliquish since most patrons are regulars, so start up a game of pool to break the ice. Open from 11am to 4am daily.

No trip to the Keys is complete without a stop at the **Tiki Bar at the Holiday Isle Resort,** U.S. 1 at MM 84, Islamorada (© **800/327-7070** or 305/664-2321). Hundreds of revelers visit this ocean-side spot for drinks and dancing at any time of day, but the live rock music starts at 8:30pm. (See "Where to Stay," earlier.) The thatched-roof Tiki Bar draws a high-energy but laid-back mix of thirsty people, all in pursuit of a good time. In the afternoon and early evening (when everyone is either sunburned, drunk, or just happy to be dancing to live reggae), head for **Kokomo's,** just next door. Kokomo's often closes at 7:30pm on weekends (5:30pm on weekdays), so get there early. For information, call the Holiday Isle Resort.

Locals and tourists mingle at the outdoor cabana bar at **Lorelei** (see "Where to Dine," above). Most evenings after 5pm, you'll find local bands playing on a thatched-roof stage—mainly rock 'n' roll, reggae, and sometimes blues.

Woody's Saloon and Restaurant, on U.S. 1 at MM 82, Islamorada (© **305/664-4335**), is a lively, wacky, loud, gritty, raunchy, local legend of a place serving up mediocre pizzas, buck naked strippers, and live bands almost every night. The house band, Big Dick and the Extenders, showcases a 300-pound Native American who does a lewd, rude, and crude routine of jokes and songs starting at 9pm, Tuesday through Sunday. He is a legend. By the way, don't think you're lucky if you are offered the front table: It's the target seat for Big Dick's haranguing. Avoid the lame karaoke performance on Sunday and Monday evenings. There's a small cover charge most nights. Drink specials, contests, and the legendary Big Dick keep this place packed until 4am almost every night. *Note:* This place is not for the faint of heart (or tact!), but more for those of the Howard Stern school of nightlife.

For a more subdued atmosphere, try the handsome stained-glass and mahogany-wood bar and club at **Zane Grey's** (on the second floor of World Wide Sportsman at MM 81.5). Outside, enjoy a view of the calm waters of the bay; inside, soak up the history of some real longtime anglers. It is open from 11am to 11pm, and later on weekends. Call to find out who is playing on weekends (© **305/664-4244**), when there is live entertainment and no cover charge.

2 The Lower Keys: Big Pine Key to Coppitt Key

128 miles SW of Miami

Unlike their neighbors to the north and south, the Lower Keys (including Big Pine, Sugarloaf, and Summerland) are devoid of rowdy spring-break crowds, boast few T-shirt and trinket shops, and have almost no late-night bars. What they do offer are the very best opportunities to enjoy the vast natural resources on land and water that make the area so rich. Stay overnight in the Lower Keys, rent a boat, and explore the reefs—it might be the most memorable part of your trip.

ESSENTIALS

GETTING THERE   See "Essentials" for the Upper and Middle Keys (p. 167) and continue south on U.S. 1. The Lower Keys start at the end of the Seven-Mile Bridge. There are also airports in Marathon and Key West.

VISITOR INFORMATION   The **Big Pine and Lower Keys Chamber of Commerce,** ocean side of U.S. 1 at MM 31 (P.O. Box 430511), Big Pine Key, FL 33043 (© **800/872-3722** or 305/872-2411; fax 305/872-0752; www.lower keyschamber.com), is open Monday through Friday from 9am to 5pm and Saturday from 9am to 3pm. The pleasant staff will help with anything a traveler may need. Call, write, or stop in for a comprehensive, detailed information packet.

WHAT TO SEE & DO

Once the centerpiece (these days, it's Big Pine Key) of the Lower Keys and still a great asset is **Bahia Honda State Park** ⚡, U.S. 1 at MM 37.5, Big Pine Key (© **305/872-2353;** www.bahiahondapark.com), which, even after the violent storms of 1998, has one of the most beautiful coastlines in South Florida. Bahia Honda (pronounced *Bah*-ya) is a great place for hiking, bird-watching, swimming, snorkeling, and fishing. The 524-acre park encompasses a wide variety of ecosystems, including coastal mangroves, beach dunes, and tropical hammocks. There are miles of trails packed with unusual plants and animals and a small, white beach. Shaded seaside picnic areas are fitted with tables and grills. Although the beach is never wider than 5 feet even at low tide, this is the Lower Keys' best beach area.

True to its name (Spanish for "deep bay"), the park has relatively deep waters close to shore, and they are perfect for snorkeling and diving. Easy offshore snorkeling here gives even novices a chance to lie suspended in warm water and simply observe diverse marine life passing by. Or else head to the stunning reefs at Looe Key, where the coral and fish are more vibrant than anywhere else in the United States. Snorkeling trips go from the Bahia Honda concessions to Looe Key National Marine Sanctuary (4 miles offshore). They depart twice daily March through September and cost $28 for adults, $23 for youths 6 to 14, and are free for children 5 and under. Call © **305/872-3210** for a schedule.

Admission to the park is $5 per vehicle (plus 50¢ per person), $1.50 per pedestrian or bicyclist, free for children 5 and under. If you are alone in a car, you'll pay only $2.50. Open daily from 8am to sunset.

The most famous residents of the Lower Keys are the tiny Key deer. Of the estimated 300 existing in the world, two-thirds live on Big Pine Key's **National Key Deer Refuge** ⚡ which recently expanded with the acquisition of 20 acres of beach and waterfront property. To get your bearings, stop by the rangers' office at the Winn-Dixie Shopping Plaza near MM 30.5 off U.S. 1. They'll give you an informative brochure and map of the area. The refuge is open Monday through Friday from 8am to 5pm.

If the office is closed, head out to the Blue Hole, a former rock quarry now filled with the fresh water that's vital to the deer's survival. To get there, turn right at Big Pine Key's only traffic light onto Key Deer Boulevard (take the left fork immediately after the turn) and continue 1½ miles to the observation-site parking lot, on your left. The half-mile **Watson Hammock Trail,** about a third of a mile past the Blue Hole, is the refuge's only marked footpath. Try coming out to the footpath in the early morning or late evening to catch a glimpse of these gentle, dog-size deer. There is an observation deck there from which you can watch and photograph the protected species. They are more active in cool hours and in cooler times of the year. Refuge lands are open daily from half an hour before sunrise to half an hour after sunset. Don't be surprised to see a lazy alligator warming itself in the sun, particularly in outlying areas around the Blue Hole. If you do see a gator, do not go near it, do not touch it, and do not provoke it. Keep your distance; and if you must get a photo, use a zoom lens. Also, whatever you do, do not feed the deer—it will threaten their survival. Call the **park office** (© 305/872-2239) to find out about the infrequent free tours of the refuge, scheduled throughout the year.

OUTDOOR PURSUITS

BICYCLING If you have your own bike, or your lodging offers a rental (many do), the Lower Keys are a great place to get off busy U.S. 1 to explore the beautiful back roads. On Big Pine Key, cruise along Key Deer Boulevard (at MM 30). Those with fat tires can ride into the National Key Deer Refuge.

BIRD-WATCHING Bring your birding books. A stopping point for migratory birds on the Eastern Flyway, the Lower Keys are populated with many West Indian bird species, especially during spring and fall. The small, vegetated islands of the Keys are the only nesting sites in the United States for the great white heron and the white-crowned pigeon. They're also some of the very few breeding places for the reddish egret, the roseate spoonbill, the mangrove cuckoo, and the black-whiskered vireo. Look for them on Bahia Honda Key and the many uninhabited islands nearby.

BOATING Dozens of shops rent powerboats for fishing and reef exploring. Most also rent tackle, sell bait, and have charter captains available. For instance, **Jaybird's Powerboats,** U.S. 1 at MM 33, Big Pine Key (© **305/872-8500**), is an excellent option, but they rent for full days only. Prices start at $155 for a 19-footer.

CANOEING & KAYAKING The Overseas Highway (U.S. 1) touches on only a few dozen of the many hundreds of islands that make up the Keys. To really see the Lower Keys, rent a kayak or canoe—perfect for these shallow waters. **Reflections Kayak Nature Tours,** operating out of Parmer's Resort, on U.S. 1 at MM 28.5, Little Torch Key (© **305/872-4668**), offers fully outfitted backcountry wildlife tours, either on your own or with an expert. The expert, Mike Wedeking, a former U.S. Forest Service guide, keeps up an engaging discussion describing the area's fish, sponges, coral, osprey, hawks, eagles, alligators, raccoons, and deer. The 3-hour tours cost $49 per person and include spring water, fresh fruit, granola bars, and use of binoculars. Bring a towel and sea sandals or sneakers.

FISHING A day spent fishing, either in the shallow backcountry or in the deep sea, is a great way to ensure yourself a fresh fish dinner, or you can release your catch and just appreciate the challenge. Whichever you choose, **Larry Threlkeld's Strike Zone Charters,** U.S. 1 at MM 29.5, Big Pine Key (© **305/ 872-9863**), is the charter service to call. Prices for fishing boats start at $450 for a half day and $595 for a full day. If you have enough anglers to share the price, it isn't too steep. They may also be able to match you with other interested visitors.

HIKING You can hike throughout the flat, marshy Keys, on both marked trails and meandering coastlines. The best places to trek through nature are **Bahia Honda State Park** at MM 29.5 and **National Key Deer Refuge** at MM 30 (for more information on both, see "What to See & Do," above). Bahia Honda Park has a free brochure describing an excellent self-guided tour along the Silver Palm Nature Trail. You'll traverse hammocks, mangroves, and sand dunes and cross a lagoon. The walk (which is less than a mile) explores a great cross-section of the natural habitat in the Lower Keys and can be done in under half an hour.

SNORKELING & DIVING   Snorkelers and divers should not miss the Keys' most dramatic reefs at the **Looe Key National Marine Sanctuary.** Here, you'll see more than 150 varieties of hard and soft coral—some, centuries old—as well as every type of tropical fish, including gold and blue parrotfish, moray eels, barracudas, French angels, and tarpon. **Looe Key Dive Center,** U.S. 1 at MM 27.5, Ramrod Key (*©* **305/872-2215**), offers a mind-blowing 5-hour tour aboard a 45-foot catamaran with two shallow 1-hour dives for snorkelers and scuba divers. Snorkelers pay $25, and divers with their own equipment pay $40; on Wednesdays and Saturdays you can do a fascinating dive to the *Adolphus Busch Sr.,* a shipwreck sunk off Looe Key in 100 feet of water, for $45. Good-quality rentals are available. (See "What to See & Do," above, for other diving options.)

WHERE TO STAY

There are a number of cheap, fairly unappealing fish shacks along the highway for those who want bare-bones accommodations. So far, there are no national hotel chains in the Lower Keys. For information on lodging in cabins or trailers at local campgrounds, see "Camping," below.

VERY EXPENSIVE

Little Palm Island ✦✦✦   This exclusive island escape—host to presidents and royalty—is not just a place to stay while in the Lower Keys; it is a destination all its own. Built on a private 5-acre island, it's accessible only by boat. Guests stay in thatched-roof duplexes amid lush foliage and flowering tropical plants. Many villas have ocean views and private sun decks with rope hammocks. Inside, the romantic suites have all the comforts and conveniences of a luxurious contemporary beach cottage, but without telephones, TVs, or alarm clocks. As if its location weren't idyllic enough, a new full-service spa recently opened on the island. Note that on the breezeless south side of the island, mosquitoes can be a problem, even in the winter. (So bring spray and lightweight, long-sleeved clothing.) Known for its innovative and pricey food, Little Palm also hosts visitors just for dinner or lunch. If you are staying on the island, opt for the full American plan, which includes three meals a day for about $140 per person. If you pay a la carte, you could spend that much just on dinner. At these prices, Little Palm appeals to those who aren't keeping track.

Launch is at the ocean side of U.S. 1 at MM 28.5, Little Torch Key, FL 33042. *©* 800/343-8567 or 305/872-2524. Fax 305/872-4843. www.littlepalmisland.com. 28 bungalows, 2 deluxe suites. Winter $795–$1,695 per couple; off-season $695–$1,595 per couple. Rates include transportation to and from the island and unlimited (nonmotorized) watersports. Meal plans include 2 meals daily for $125 per person per day, 3 meals at $140 per person. AE, DC, DISC, MC, V. No children under 16. **Amenities:** Restaurant; bar; 2 pools (1 outdoor with small waterfall, 1 indoor); health club and spa; extensive watersports equipment/rental; concierge; courtesy van from Key West or Marathon airport; ferry service to and from the mainland; limited room service; in-room massage; laundry services; dry cleaning; jogging trail. *In room:* A/C, dataport, minibar, coffeemaker, hair dryer, Jacuzzi. No phone.

INEXPENSIVE

Parmer's Resort ✦   Parmer's, a fixture here for more than 20 years, is well known for its charming hospitality and helpful staff. This downscale resort offers modest but comfortable cottages, each of them unique. Some are waterfront, many have kitchenettes, and others are just a bedroom. Room no. 26, aka Wahoo, a one-bedroom efficiency, is especially nice, with a small sitting area that faces the water. Room no. 6, a small efficiency, has a kitchenette and an especially large bathroom. The rooms have been recently updated—and are consistently very clean. Many can be combined to accommodate large families. The hotel's waterfront location, not to mention that it's only a half-hour from lively Key West, almost makes up for the fact that you must pay extra for maid service.

565 Barry Ave. (P.O. Box 430665), near MM 28.5, Little Torch Key, FL 33043. (C) **305/872-2157.** Fax 305/872-2014. www.parmersresort.com. 45 units. Winter $85–$150 double, from $105 efficiency; off-season $65–$105 double, from $85 efficiency. Rates include continental breakfast. AE, DISC, MC, V. From U.S. 1, turn right onto Barry Ave. Resort is ½ mile down on the right. **Amenities:** Heated pool; bike rental; kayak rentals; coin-op washers and dryers; boat ramp. *In room:* A/C, TV.

CAMPING

Bahia Honda State Park ★★★ ((C) **800/326-3521;** www.abfla.com/parks/ BahiaHonda/bahiahonda.html) offers some of the best camping in the Keys. It is as loaded with facilities and activities as it is with campers. However, don't be discouraged by its popularity—this park encompasses more than 500 acres of land, 80 campsites spread throughout three areas, and six spacious and comfortable cabin units (fitting six people each) that were reconstructed between 2000 and 2001. Cabins hold up to eight guests and come complete with linens, kitchenettes, and utensils as well as a wraparound terrace, barbecue pit, and rocking chairs.

For one to four people, camping here costs about $25 per site without electricity and $26 with electricity. Depending on the season, cabin prices change: Prices range from $50 to $110. Additional people (over four) cost $6 each. MasterCard and Visa are accepted.

Another excellent value can be found at the **KOA Sugarloaf Key Resort** ★★, near MM 20. This ocean-side facility has 200 fully equipped sites, with water, electricity, and sewer, which rent for about $85 a night (no-hookup sites cost about $45). Or pitch a tent on the 5 acres of lush waterfront property. This site is especially nice because of its private beaches and access to diving, snorkeling, and boating; and its grounds are nice and well maintained. The resort also rents travel trailers. The 25-foot Dutchman sleeps six and is equipped with eating and cooking utensils. It costs about $120 a day. More luxurious trailers go for $180 a day. All major credit cards are accepted. For details, write them at P.O. Box 420469, Summerland Key, FL 33042 ((C) **800/562-7731** or 305/745-3549; fax 305/745-9889; www.koa.com).

WHERE TO DINE

There aren't many fine-dining options in the Lower Keys, with the exception of the Dining Room at Little Palm Island Resort, MM 285, Little Torch Key ((C) **305/ 872-2551**), in which you'll be wowed with gourmet French Caribbean fare that looks like a meal but eats like a vacation. You need to take a ferry to this chichi private resort island, on which you can indulge in the exquisite ocean-side restaurant, even if you're not staying over (see above for the resort's full review). If you don't have the chance to get there, try the following, worth a stop for those passing through.

MODERATE

Mangrove Mama's Restaurant SEAFOOD/CARIBBEAN   As the dedicated locals who come daily for happy hour will tell you, this is a true Lower Keys institution and a dive (the restaurant is a shack that used to have a gas pump as well as a grill) in the best sense of the word. Guests share the property with some miniature horses (out back) and stray cats. A handful of simple tables, inside and out, are shaded by banana trees and palm fronds. Fish is the menu's mainstay, although soups, salads, sandwiches, and omelets are also good. Grilled teriyaki chicken and club sandwiches are tasty alternatives to fish, as are meat-less chef's salads and spicy barbecued baby back ribs.

U.S. 1 at MM 20, Sugarloaf Key. © **305/745-3030**. Main courses $10–$20; lunch $6–$9; brunch $5–$7. MC, V. Daily 11am–3pm and 5:30-10pm.

Monte's SEAFOOD   Certainly nobody goes to this restaurant/fish market for its atmosphere: Plastic place settings rest on plastic-covered picnic-style tables in a screen-enclosed dining patio. But Monte's doesn't need great atmosphere, since it has survived for more than 20 years on its very good and incredibly fresh food. The day's catch may include shark, tuna, lobsters, stone crabs, or shrimp.

U.S. 1 at MM 25, Summerland Key. © **305/745-3731**. Main courses $13–$17; lunch $6–$10. No credit cards. Mon–Sat 9am–10pm; Sun 10am–9pm.

INEXPENSIVE

Coco's Kitchen ⋒ CUBAN/AMERICAN   This tiny storefront has been dishing out black beans, rice, and shredded beef to fans of Cuban cuisine for more than 10 years. The owners, who are actually from Nicaragua, cook not only superior Cuban food but also some local specialties, Italian food, and Caribbean food. Specialties include fried shrimp, whole fried yellowtail, and Cuban-style roast pork (available only on Sat). The best bet is the daily special, which may be roasted pork or fresh grouper, served with rice and beans or salad and crispy fries. Top off the huge, cheap meal with a rich caramel-soaked flan.

283 Key Deer Blvd. (in the Winn-Dixie Shopping Center), Big Pine Key. © **305/872-4495**. Main courses $6–$15; breakfast $2–$5. MC, V. Mon–Sat 7am–7:30pm. Turn right at the traffic light near MM 30.5. Stay in the left lane.

No Name Pub PUB FOOD/PIZZA   This funky old bar out in the boonies serves snacks and sandwiches until 11pm on most nights, and drinks until mid-night. Pizzas are tasty—thick-crusted and supercheesy. Try one topped with local shrimp, or consider a bowl of chili with all the fixings—hearty and cheap. Everything is served on paper plates. Locals hang out at the rustic bar, one of the Florida Keys' oldest, drinking beer and listening to a jukebox heavy with 1980s selections. The decor, if you can call it that, is basic—the walls and ceilings are plastered with thousands of autographed dollar bills.

¼ mile south of No Name Bridge on N. Watson Blvd., Big Pine Key. © **305/872-9115**. Pizzas $6–$18; subs $5. MC, V. 11am–11pm. Turn right at Big Pine's only traffic light (near MM 30.5) onto Key Deer Blvd. Turn right on Watson Blvd. At stop sign, turn left. Look for a small wooden sign on the left marking the spot.

THE LOWER KEYS AFTER DARK

Although the mellow islands of the Lower Keys aren't exactly known for wild nightlife, there are some friendly bars and restaurants where locals and tourists gather to hang out and drink.

One of the most scenic is **Sandbar** (© **305/872-9989**), a wide-open breezy wooden house built on slender stilts and overlooking a wide channel on Barry Avenue (near MM 28.5). It attracts an odd mix of bikers and blue-hairs daily from 11am to 10pm and is a great place to overhear local gossip and colorful metaphors. Pool tables are the main attraction, but there's also live music some nights. The drinks are reasonably priced and the food isn't too bad, either. For another fun bar scene, see **No Name Pub,** listed above in "Where to Dine."

3 Key West ★★★

159 miles SW of Miami

There are two schools of thought on Key West—one is that it has become way too commercial, and the other is that it's still a place where one can go and not worry about being prim, proper, or even well groomed. I think it's a bizarre fusion of both—a fascinating look at small-town America in which people truly live by the (off)beat of their own drum, albeit one with a Gap and Banana Republic—but not yet a Starbuck's—thrown in to bring you back to some reality. The locals, or "conchs" (pronounced *conks*), and the developers here have been at odds for years. This once low-key island has been thoroughly commercialized—there's a Hard Rock Cafe smack in the middle of Duval Street and thousands of cruise-ship passengers descend on Mallory Square each day. It's definitely not the seedy town Hemingway and his cronies once called their own. Or is it?

Laid-back Key West still exists, but it's now found in different places: the backyard of a popular guesthouse, for example, or an art gallery, a secret garden, a clothing optional bar, or the hip hangouts of Bahama Village. Fortunately there are plenty of these, and Key West's greatest historic charm is found just off the beaten path. Don't be afraid to explore these residential areas, as conchs are notoriously friendly. In fact, exploring the side streets always seems to yield a new discovery of some sort. Of course, there are always the calm waters of the Atlantic and the Gulf of Mexico all around.

The heart of town offers party people a good time—that is, if your idea of a good time is the smell of stale beer, loud music, and hardly shy revelers. Here, you'll find good restaurants, fun bars, live music, rickshaw rides, and lots of shopping. Key West is still very gay-centric, except during the time of spring break. Same-sex couples walking hand in hand are the norm here, and if you're not open minded and would prefer to avoid this scene, just look for the ubiquitous rainbow flag hanging outside of gay establishments and you'll know what to expect. For the most part, however, the scene is extremely mixed and colorful. If partying isn't your thing, then avoid Duval Street (the Bourbon St. of South Florida) at all costs. Instead, take in the scenery at a dockside bar or ocean-side Jacuzzi. Whatever you do, don't bother with a watch or tie—this is the home of the perennial vacation.

ESSENTIALS

GETTING THERE   For directions by car, see "Essentials" for the Upper and Middle Keys (p. 167) and continue south on U.S. 1. When entering Key West, stay in the far-right lane onto North Roosevelt Boulevard, which becomes Truman Avenue in Old Town. Continue for a few blocks and you will find yourself on **Duval Street** ★, in the heart of the city. If you stay to the left, you'll also reach the city center after passing the airport and the remnants of historic houseboat row, where a motley collection of boats once made up one of Key West's most interesting neighborhoods.

Several regional airlines fly nonstop (about 55 min.) from Miami to Key West; fares are about $120 to $300 round-trip. **American Eagle, Continental, Delta,** and **US Airways Express** land at **Key West International Airport,** South Roosevelt Boulevard (© **305/296-5439**), on the southeastern corner of the island.

Greyhound (© **800/231-2222;** www.greyhound.com) has buses leaving Miami for Key West every day for about $30 to $32 one-way and $57 to $60 round-trip. Seats fill up in season, so come early. The ride takes about 4½ hours.

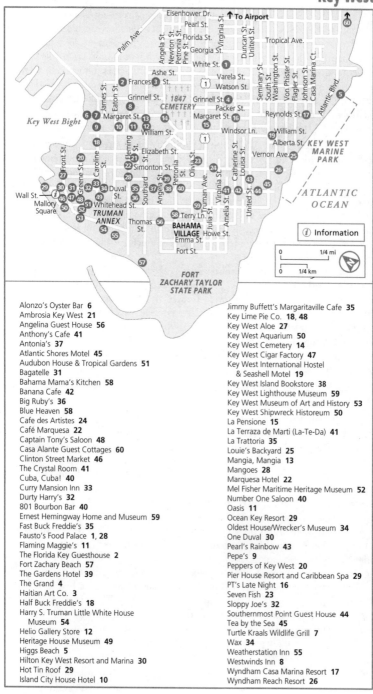

Alonzo's Oyster Bar **6**
Ambrosia Key West **21**
Angelina Guest House **56**
Anthony's Cafe **41**
Antonia's **37**
Atlantic Shores Motel **45**
Audubon House & Tropical Gardens **51**
Bagatelle **31**
Bahama Mama's Kitchen **58**
Banana Cafe **42**
Big Ruby's **36**
Blue Heaven **58**
Cafe des Artistes **24**
Café Marquesa **22**
Captain Tony's Saloon **48**
Casa Alante Guest Cottages **60**
Clinton Street Market **46**
The Crystal Room **41**
Cuba, Cuba! **40**
Curry Mansion Inn **33**
Durty Harry's **32**
801 Bourbon Bar **40**
Ernest Hemingway Home and Museum **59**
Fast Buck Freddie's **35**
Fausto's Food Palace **1, 28**
Flaming Maggie's **11**
The Florida Key Guesthouse **2**
Fort Zachary Beach **57**
The Gardens Hotel **39**
The Grand **4**
Haitian Art Co. **3**
Half Buck Freddie's **18**
Harry S. Truman Little White House
　　Museum **54**
Helio Gallery Store **12**
Heritage House Museum **49**
Higgs Beach **5**
Hilton Key West Resort and Marina **30**
Hot Tin Roof **29**
Island City House Hotel **10**

Jimmy Buffett's Margaritaville Cafe **35**
Key Lime Pie Co. **18, 48**
Key West Aloe **27**
Key West Aquarium **50**
Key West Cemetery **14**
Key West Cigar Factory **47**
Key West International Hostel
　　& Seashell Motel **19**
Key West Island Bookstore **38**
Key West Lighthouse Museum **59**
Key West Museum of Art and History **53**
Key West Shipwreck Historeum **50**
La Pensione **15**
La Terraza de Marti (La-Te-Da) **41**
La Trattoria **35**
Louie's Backyard **25**
Mangia, Mangia **13**
Mangoes **28**
Marquesa Hotel **22**
Mel Fisher Maritime Heritage Museum **52**
Number One Saloon **40**
Oasis **11**
Ocean Key Resort **29**
Oldest House/Wrecker's Museum **34**
One Duval **30**
Pearl's Rainbow **43**
Pepe's **9**
Peppers of Key West **20**
Pier House Resort and Caribbean Spa **29**
PT's Late Night **16**
Seven Fish **23**
Sloppy Joe's **32**
Southernmost Point Guest House **44**
Tea by the Sea **45**
Turtle Kraals Wildlife Grill **7**
Wax **34**
Weatherstation Inn **55**
Westwinds Inn **8**
Wyndham Casa Marina Resort **17**
Wyndham Reach Resort **26**

There's also, finally, a ferry that goes from Miami (from downtown's Sealine Marina) to Key West. It's about time. **Fast Cats'** PurrSeavearance (© **786/ 205-8683**; www.fastcats.org) may be a cheesy name for a luxury $7.5 million catamaran, but the trip is hardly so. The 102-foot boat can hold up to 149 passengers and will make the 4½-hour cruise (driving only takes 3 hours, but with traffic, it can take up to 5) four times a week starting at $65 each way. VIP tickets cost $98 and include preferential seating. Food and alcoholic beverages are available but not included in the price. Tours leave Miami Thursday through Sunday at 7:30am and push off from Key West on Sundays at 5:30pm.

GETTING AROUND   With limited parking, narrow streets, and congested traffic, driving in Old Town Key West is more of a pain than a convenience. Unless you're staying in one of the more remote accommodations, consider trading in the car for a bicycle. The island is small and as flat as a board, which makes it easy to negotiate, especially away from the crowded downtown area. Many tourists also choose to cruise by moped, an option that can make navigating the streets risky, especially since there are no helmet laws in Key West. So be careful and spend the extra few bucks to rent a helmet; hundreds of visitors are seriously injured each year.

Rates for simple one-speed cruisers start at about $8 per day (from $40 per week). Mopeds start at about $12 for 2 hours, $25 per day, and $100 per week. The best shops include **The Bicycle Center** at 523 Truman Ave. (© **305/ 294-4556**); the **Moped Hospital,** 601 Truman Ave. (© **305/296-3344**); and **Tropical Bicycles & Scooter Rentals** at 1300 Duval St. (© **305/294-8136**). **The Bike Shop,** 1110 Truman Ave. (© **305/294-1073**), rents cruisers for $8 per day and $40 per week. A $150 deposit is required.

PARKING   Parking in Key West's Old Town is particularly limited, but there is a well-placed **municipal parking lot** at Simonton and Angela streets, just behind the firehouse and police station. If you have brought a car, you may want to stash it here while you enjoy the very walkable downtown part of Key West.

VISITOR INFORMATION   The **Key West Chamber of Commerce,** 402 Wall St., Key West, FL 33040 (© **800/527-8539** or 305/294-2587; www. keywestchamber.com), offers both general and specialized information. The lobby is open daily from 8:30am to 6pm; phones are answered from 8am to 8pm. The **Key West Visitor Center** is the area's best for information on accommodations, goings-on, and restaurants; the number is © **800/LAST-KEY.** It's open weekdays from 8am to 5:30pm and weekends from 8:30am to 5pm. Gay travelers will want to call the **Key West Business Guild** (© **305/294-4603**), which represents more than 50 guesthouses and B&Bs in town, as well as many other gay-owned businesses (ask for its color brochure) or **Good Times Travel** (© **305/294-0980**), which will set up lodging and package tours on the island.

While you're in one of the above offices, be sure to pick up a free copy of Sharon Wells' Walking & Biking Guide to Historic Key West. Though I still couldn't find all the spots I wanted to in the Key West Cemetery (p. 195) while using her guide, it was helpful for historical descriptions throughout town (and it's free). She also leads guided walking tours around the island. Contact her (© **305/294-8380;** www.seekeywest.com) for more information.

ORIENTATION   A mere 2-by-4-mile island, Key West is simple to navigate, even though there is no real order to the arrangement of streets and avenues. As you enter town on U.S. 1 (also called Roosevelt Blvd.), you will see most of the moderately priced chain hotels and fast-food restaurants. The better restaurants, shops, and outfitters are crammed onto Duval Street, the main thoroughfare of Key West's Old Town. Surrounding streets contain many inns and lodges in picturesque Victorian/Bahamian homes. On the southern side of the island is the coral beach area and some of the larger resort hotels.

The area called Bahama Village has only recently become known to tourists. With several newly opened, trendy restaurants and guesthouses, this hippie-ish neighborhood, complete with street-roaming chickens and cats, is the most urban and rough you'll find in the Keys. You might see a few seedy drug dealings on street corners, but it's nothing to be overly concerned with: It looks worse than it is and resident business owners tend to keep a vigilant eye on the neighborhood. The area is actually quite funky and should be a welcome diversion from the Duvalian mainstream.

SEEING THE SIGHTS

Before shelling out big bucks for any of the dozens of worthwhile attractions in Key West, I recommend getting an overview on either of the two comprehensive island tours, **The Conch Tour Train** or the **Old Town Trolley** (see "Organized Tours," below). There are simply too many attractions and historic houses to list. I've highlighted my favorites below but encourage you to seek out others.

Audubon House & Tropical Gardens ✦✦ This well-preserved home, dating from the early 19th century, stands as a prime example of early Key West architecture. Named after renowned painter and bird expert John James Audubon, who was said to have visited the house in 1832, the graceful two-story home is a peaceful retreat from the bustle of Old Town. Included in the price of admission is a self-guided audio tour that lasts about half an hour and spotlights rare Audubon prints, gorgeous antiques, historical photos, and lush tropical gardens. With voices of several characters from the house's past, the tour never gets boring—although it is at times a bit hokey. Even if you don't want to spend the time and money to explore the grounds and home, check out the impressive gift shop, which sells a variety of fine mementos at reasonable prices.

205 Whitehead St. (between Greene and Caroline sts.). ✆ **305/294-2116**. www.audubonhouse.com. Admission $9 adults, $5 children 6–12. Daily 9:30am–5pm (last admission at 4:30pm). Discounts for students and AAA and AARP members.

East Martello Museum and Gallery Adjacent to the airport, the East Martello Museum is located in a Civil War–era brick fort that itself is worth a visit. The museum contains a bizarre variety of exhibits that collectively do a thorough job of interpreting the city's intriguing past. Historical artifacts include model ships, a deep-sea diver's wooden air pump, a crude raft from a Cuban "boat lift," a supposedly haunted doll, a Key West–style children's playhouse from 1918, and a horse-drawn hearse. Exhibits illustrate the Keys' history of salvaging, sponging, and cigar making. After seeing the galleries (should take about 45 min. to an hour), climb a steep spiral staircase to the top of a lookout tower for good views over the island and ocean. A member of the Key West Art and Historical Society, East Martello has two cousins: the Key West Museum of Art and History, 281 Front St. (✆ 305/295-6616) and the Key West Lighthouse Museum (see below).

3501 S. Roosevelt Blvd. ✆ **305/296-3913**. www.kwahs.com/martello.htm. Admission $6 adults, $4 seniors, $3 children 8–12, free for children 7 and under. Daily 9:30am–4:30pm (last admission is at 4pm).

Ernest Hemingway Home and Museum ✦ Hemingway's particularly handsome stone Spanish Colonial house, built in 1851, was one of the first on the island to be fitted with indoor plumbing and a built-in fireplace, and it contains the first swimming pool built on Key West (look for the penny he pressed into the cement near the pool). The author owned the home from 1931 until his death in 1961, and he lived there with about 50 cats, whose descendants, including the famed six-toed cats, still roam the premises. It was during those years that the Nobel Prize winner wrote some of his most famous works, including *For Whom the Bell Tolls, A Farewell to Arms,* and *The Snows of Kilimanjaro.* Fans may want to take the optional half-hour tour, where you'll see rooms of his house with glass cabinets that store certain artifacts, books, and pieces of mail addressed to him as well as his study. It's interesting (to an extent) and included in the price of admission. If you don't take the tour or have no literary interest in Hemingway, the admission price is really a waste of money, except for the house's lovely architecture and garden. If you're feline phobic, beware: There are cats everywhere.

907 Whitehead St. (between Truman Ave. and Olivia St.). ℂ **305/294-1136.** Fax 305/294-2755. www. hemingwayhome.com. Admission $10 adults, $6 children. Daily 9am–5pm. Limited parking.

Harry S Truman Little White House Museum ★★   President Harry Truman used to refer to the White House as the "Great White Jail." On temporary leave from the big house, Truman discovered the serenity of Key West and made his escape to what became known as the Little White House, which is open to the public for touring. The house is fully restored, and the exhibits document Truman's time in the Keys. Tours are every 15 minutes and last between 45 and 50 minutes. For fans of all things Oval Office–related, there's a presidential gift shop on the premises.

> **Impressions**
>
> *I've a notion to move the capitol to Key West and just stay.*
> —President Harry S Truman

111 Front St. ℂ **305/294-9911.** www.trumanlittlewhitehouse.com. Admission $10 adults, $5 children under 12. Daily 9am–4:30pm.

Heritage House Museum ★ *Finds*   For a glimpse into one of the oldest houses in Key West, check out the Heritage House Museum, the former 1834 home of Jesse Porter, a Key West preservationist who hosted the likes of Robert Frost, Tennessee Williams, Gloria Swanson, and Tallulah Bankhead in his home cum salon. Furnished with 19th-century antiques, the house is a fascinating look at 19th- and early-20th-century Key West. Guided tours are informative and entertaining, sort of like an antique version of an *E! True Hollywood Story.*

410 Caroline St. ℂ **305/296-3573** for tour reservations. www.heritagehousemuseum.org. Free admission. Mon–Sat 10am–4pm.

Key West Aquarium ★★ *Kids*   The oldest attraction on the island, the Key West Aquarium is a modest but fascinating exhibit. A long hallway of eye-level displays showcases dozens of varieties of fish and crustaceans. You'll see delicate sea horses swaying in the backlit tanks. Kids can touch sea cucumbers and sea anemones in a shallow tank in the entryway. If you can, catch one of the free guided tours, where you can witness the dramatic feeding frenzy of the sharks, tarpon, barracudas, stingrays, and turtles. Expect to spend about 1 to 1½ hours here.

1 Whitehead St. (at Mallory Sq.). ℂ **305/296-2051.** www.keywestaquarium.com. Admission $9 adults, $4.50 children 4–12, free for children under 4. Tickets are good for 2 consecutive days. Look for discount coupons at local hotels, at Duval St. kiosks, and from trolley and train tours. Daily 10am–6pm; tours at 11am and 1, 3, and 4pm.

Key West Cemetery ★★★ *Finds*   This funky, picturesque cemetery is the epitome of the quirky Key West image, as irreverent as it is humorous. Many tombs are stacked several high, condominium style—the rocky soil made digging 6 feet under nearly impossible for early settlers. Headstones reflect residents' lighthearted attitudes toward life and death. I TOLD YOU I WAS SICK is one of the more famous epitaphs, as is the tongue-in-cheek widow's inscription AT LEAST I KNOW WHERE HE'S SLEEPING TONIGHT. Pick up a copy of Sharon Wells' Walking & Biking Guide to Historic Key West (p. 192). Though some of the inscriptions are hard to find, even with the free walking tour guide, it's fun to walk through.

Entrance at the corner of Margaret and Angela sts. Free admission. Daily dawn–dusk.

Key West Lighthouse Museum ★   When the Key West Lighthouse opened in 1848, it signaled the end of a profitable era for the pirate salvagers who looted reef-stricken ships. The story of this and other Keys lighthouses is illustrated in a small museum that was formerly the keeper's quarters. It's worth mustering the energy to climb the 88 claustrophobic steps to the top, where you'll be rewarded with magnificent panoramic views of Key West and the ocean.

938 Whitehead St. ✆ 305/294-0012. Admission $8 adults, $6 seniors and locals, $4 children 7–12, free for children 6 and under. Daily 9:30am–4:30pm.

Going, Going, Gone: Where to Catch the Famous Key West Sunset

A tradition in Key West, the Sunset Celebration can be relaxing or overwhelming, depending on your vantage point. If you're in town, you must check out this ritual at least once. Every evening, locals and visitors gather at the docks behind Mallory Square (at the westernmost end of Whitehead St.) to celebrate the day gone by. Secure a spot on the docks early to experience the carnival of portrait artists, acrobats, food vendors, animal acts, and other performers trading on the island's bohemian image. But the carnival atmosphere isn't for everyone: In season, the crowd can be overwhelming, especially when the cruise ships are in port. Also, hold onto your bags and wallets as the tight crowds make Mallory Square at sunset prime pickpocketing territory.

A more refined choice is the Hilton's **Sunset Deck** (✆ 305/294-4000), a luxurious second-floor bar on Front Street, right next door to Mallory Square. From the civilized calm of a casual bar, you can look down on the mayhem with a drink in hand.

Also near the Mallory madness is the **Ocean Key Resort**'s bar. This long open-air pier serves up drinks and decent bar food against a dramatic pink- and yellow-streaked sky. It's located at the very tip of Duval Street (✆ 800/328-9815 or 305/296-7701).

For the very best potent cocktails and great bar food on an outside patio or enclosed lounge, try **Pier House Resort and Caribbean Spa's Havana Docks** at 1 Duval St. (✆ 305/296-4600). There's usually live music and a lively gathering of visitors enjoying this island's bounty. The bar is right on the water and is a prime sunset-viewing spot.

Key West's Shipwreck Historeum   You'll see more impressive artifacts at nearby Mel Fisher's museum, but for the morbidly curious, shipwrecks should rank right up there with car wrecks. For those of you who can't help but look, this museum is the place to be for everything you ever wanted to know about shipwrecks and more. See movies, artifacts, and a real-life wrecker, who will be more than happy to indulge your curiosity about the wrecking industry that pre-occupied the early pioneers of Key West. Depending on your level of interest, you can expect to spend up to 2 hours here.

1 Whitehead St. (at Mallory Sq.). (C) **305/292-8990.** Fax 305/292-5536. Admission $9 adults, $4 children 4–12. Shows daily every half-hour 9:45am–4:45pm.

Mel Fisher Maritime Heritage Museum ★★   This museum honors local hero Mel Fisher, whose death in 1998 was mourned throughout South Florida, and who, along with a crew of other salvagers, found a multimillion-dollar treas-ure trove in 1985 aboard the wreck of the Spanish galleon *Nuestra Señora de Atocha.* If you're into diving, pirates, and sunken treasures, check out this small, informative museum, full of doubloons, pieces of eight, emeralds, and solid-gold bars (one of them you can lift!). A 1700 English merchant slave ship, the only tangible evidence of the transatlantic slave trade, is on view on the museum's sec-ond floor. A dated but informative film provides a good background for Fisher's incredible story. An exhibition telling the story of over 1,400 African slaves cap-tured in Cuban waters and brought to Key West for sanctuary is the museum's latest, most fascinating one to date.

200 Greene St. (C) **305/294-2633.** www.melfisher.org. Admission $7.50 adults, $3.75 children 6–12, free for children 5 and under. Daily 9:30am–5pm. Take U.S. 1 to Whitehead St. and turn left on Greene.

Oldest House/Wrecker's Museum ★   Dating from 1829, this old New England Bahama House has survived pirates, hurricanes, fires, warfare, and eco-nomic ups and downs. The 1½-story home was designed by a ship's carpenter and incorporates many features from maritime architecture, including portholes and a ship's hatch designed for ventilation before the advent of air-conditioning. Especially interesting is the detached kitchen building outfitted with a brick "beehive" oven and vintage cooking utensils. Although not a must-see on the Key West tour, history and architecture buffs will appreciate the finely preserved details and the glimpse of a slower, easier time in the island's life.

322 Duval St. (C) **305/294-9502.** Admission $5 adults, $1 children 6–12, free for children 5 and under. Daily 10am–4pm.

ORGANIZED TOURS
BY TROLLEY-BUS & TRAM   Yes, it's more than a bit hokey to sit on this 60-foot tram of yellow cars, but it's worth it—at least once. The city's whole story is packed into a neat, 90-minute package on the **Conch Tour Train,** which covers the island and all its rich, raunchy history. Operating since 1958, the trains are open-air, which can make the ride uncomfortable in bad weather. The "train's" engine is a propane-powered Jeep disguised as a locomotive. Tours depart from both Mallory Square and the Welcome Center, near where U.S. 1 becomes North Roosevelt Boulevard, on the less-developed side of the island. For more information, contact the **Conch** at (C) **305/294-5161** or www.conch tourtrain.com. The cost is $20 for adults, $10 for children 4 to 12, and free for children 3 and under. Daily departures are every half-hour from 9am to 4:30pm.

The **Old Town Trolley** is the choice in bad weather or if you are staying at one of the many hotels on its route. Humorous drivers maintain a running

Moments A Great Escape

Many people complain that Key West's quirky, quaint panache has been lost to the vulture of capitalism, evidenced by the glut of T-shirt shops and tacky bars. But that's not entirely so. For a quiet respite, visit the Key West Botanical Gardens, a little-known slice of serenity tucked between the Aqueduct Authority plant and the Key West Golf Course. The 11-acre gardens—maintained by volunteers and funded by donations—contain the last hardwood hammock in Key West, plus a colorful representation of wildflowers, butterflies, and birds. A genetically cloned tree is the latest addition to the gardens. Although the gardens received a terrible blow from the storms of 1998, the calm remains within them. Located at Botanical Garden Way and College Road, Stock Island. Free admission. Open daily from 8am to sunset. Follow College Road; then turn right just past Bayshore Manor.

commentary as the enclosed tram loops around the island's streets past all the major sights. Trolleys depart from Mallory Square and other points around the island, including many area hotels. For details, call © **305/296-6688** or visit www.trolleytours.com. Tours are $20 for adults, $10 for children 4 to 12, and free for children 3 and under. Departures are daily every half-hour (though not always on the half-hour) from 9am to 4:30pm. Whichever you choose, these historic trivia-packed tours are well worth the price of admission.

BY AIR Proclaimed by the mayor as "the official air force of the Conch Republic," **Island Airplane Tours,** at Key West Airport, 3469 S. Roosevelt Blvd. (© **305/294-8687**), offers windy rides in its open-cockpit 1940 Waco biplanes that take you over the reefs and around the islands. Thrill seekers—and only they—will also enjoy a spin in the company's S2-B aerobatics airplane, which does loops, rolls, and sideways figure-eights. Company owner Fred Cabanas was "decorated" in 1991, after he spotted a Cuban airman defecting to the United States in a Russian-built MIG fighter. Sightseeing flights cost $50 to $200, depending on the duration.

BY BOAT The catamaran *The Pride of Key West* and *Fireball,* a glass bottom boat, both at Zero Duval St. (© **305/296-6293;** fax 305/294-8704), depart on both day (noon and 2pm) coral-reef tours and evening sunset cruises (call for times). Reef trips cost $25 per person; sunset cruises are $30 per person. Kids 5 through 12 sail all cruises for $13.

Schooner *Western Union* (© **305/292-9830**) was built in 1939 and served as a cable-repair vessel until it was designated the flagship of the city of Key West and began day, sunset, and charter sailings. Sunset sailings are especially memorable and include entertainment, cocktails, and a cannon fire. Prices vary.

M/V *Heritage* (© **305/295-8687**) is Key West's newest water attraction, a 45-foot custom-designed schooner that offers 1-hour tours of Key West's historic harbor. Sites of interest on this tour include Fort Zachary Taylor, a Civil War–era fortification; the Truman Naval Station; the Key West National Wildlife Preserve; and Mallory Square. Tours are fully narrated to highlight the island's connection to pirates, wreckers, spongers, fishermen, and the U.S. Navy and Coast Guard. Tours depart daily at 9 and 11am and 1, 3, and 5pm from the Hilton Marina, 245 Front St. The cost is $12 per person.

Literary Key West

Counting Ernest Hemingway and Tennessee Williams among your denizens would give any city the right to call itself a literary mecca. But over the years, tiny Key West has been home—or at least home away from home—to dozens of literary types who are drawn to some combination of its gentle pace, tropical atmosphere, and lighthearted mood (not to mention its lingering reputation for an oft-ribald lifestyle). Writers have long known that more than a few muses prowl the tree-laden streets of Key West.

Robert Frost first visited Key West in 1934 and wintered here for the remainder of his life. In the early 20th century, writers like John Dewey, Archibald MacLeish, John Dos Passos, Wallace Stevens, and S. J. Perelman were drawn to the island.

Even as Key West boomed and busted and boomed again, and despite the island's growing popularity with world travelers, writers continued to move to Key West or visit with such regularity that they were deemed honorary "conchs." Novelists Phil Caputo, Tom McGuane, Jim Harrison, John Hershey, Alison Lurie, and Robert Stone were among these.

Of course, one of Key West's favorite sons also earned a spot in the annals of local literary history. Famous for his good-time, tropical-laced

OTHER TOURS   Sharon Wells (© **305/294-8380;** www.seekeywest.com) leads a slew of great tours throughout the island, focusing on things as diverse as literature, architecture, and places that have a connection to the island's gay and lesbian culture.

For a lively look at Key West, try a tour of the island's five **most famous pubs.** It starts daily at 2:30pm, lasts 1½ hours, costs $21, and includes four drinks. Another fun tour is the 1-mile, 90-minute **nightly ghost tour,** leaving at 8pm from the Holiday Inn La Concha, 430 Duval St. Cost is $18 for adults and $10 for children under 12. This spooky and interesting tour gives participants insight into many old island legends. The Key West Tour Association offers both tours.

Since the early 1940s, Key West has been a haven for gay luminaries such as Tennessee Williams and Broadway legend Jerry Herman. A new **tour of Gay Key West,** created by the Key West Business Guild, showcases the history, contributions, and landmarks associated with the island's flourishing gay and lesbian culture. Highlights of the tour include Williams' house, the art gallery owned by Key West's first gay mayor, and a variety of guesthouses whose gay owners fueled the island's architectural restoration movement. The 70-minute tours take place every Saturday at 11am, starting and ending at 511 South St. The cost is $20. Call © **305/294-4603** for more information.

OUTDOOR PURSUITS

BICYCLING & MOPEDING   A popular mode of transportation for locals and visitors, bikes and mopeds are available at many rental outlets in the city (p. 192). Escape the hectic downtown scene and explore the island's scenic side music, Jimmy Buffett was also a surprisingly well-received novelist in the 1990s. Although Buffett now makes the infinitely ritzier Palm Beach his Florida home, his presence is still felt in virtually every corner of Key West.

But it is Nobel Prize winner and avid outdoorsman Ernest Hemingway who is most identified with Key West. Much of the island has changed since he lived here from 1931 to 1961. Even the famous Sloppy Joe's bar, which Hemingway frequented mostly from 1933 to 1937, has changed locations (reportedly without closing—customers supposedly picked up their drinks and whatever else from the bar they could carry and brought it all down the block to the new location, and service resumed with barely a blink!). Fortunately, The Ernest Hemingway Home and Museum (p. 193) has been lovingly preserved. But perhaps to get the best feel for what Hemingway loved most about Key West, visit the docks at Garrison Bight. It is from there that Hemingway and his many famous (and infamous) friends and contemporaries departed for Caribbean ports of call and for sport upon the sea.

Key West pays homage to its literary legacy with the annual January Key West Literary Seminar. For information, call ℂ **888/293-9291** or visit www.keywestliteraryseminar.org.

streets by heading away from Duval Street toward South Roosevelt Boulevard and the beachside enclaves along the way.

BEACHES   Unlike the rest of the Keys, you'll actually find a few small beaches here, although they don't compare with the state's wide natural wonders up the coast: A narrow, rocky beach is typical of the Key's beaches. Here are your options: **Smathers Beach,** off South Roosevelt Boulevard west of the airport; **Higgs Beach,** along Atlantic Boulevard between White Street and Reynolds Road; and **Fort Zachary Beach,** located off the western end of Southard Boulevard.

A magnet for partying teenagers, **Smathers Beach** is Key West's largest and most overpopulated beach. Despite the number of rowdy teens, the beach is actually quite clean and it looks lovely since its renovation in the spring of 2000. If you go early enough in the morning, you may notice some people sleeping on the beach from the night before.

Higgs Beach is a favorite among Key West's gay crowds, but what many people don't know is that beneath the sand is an unmarked cemetery of African slaves who died while waiting for freedom. Higgs has a playground and tennis courts and is near the minute Rest Beach, which is actually hidden by the White Street Pier.

Although there is an entrance fee ($3.75 per car, plus more for each passenger), I recommend the beach at **Fort Zachary,** since it also includes a great historical fort, a Civil War museum, and a large picnic area with tables, barbecue grills, bathrooms, and showers. Plus, large trees scattered across 87 acres provide shade for those who are reluctant to bake in the sun. Hurricane George damaged the vulnerable point in 1998, but replanting of native vegetation has made it even better than before.

Parrotheads on Parade

For Jimmy Buffett fans, or Parrotheads as they're also known, there's **Trails of Margaritaville** (© 305/292-2040), an amusing 90-minute walking tour providing fans with an officially sanctioned peek at the stamping grounds of Buffett's carefree days in Key West back in the 1970s. Decked out in full Parrothead regalia—Hawaiian shirts and parrot hats—the informative and often hilarious guides lead you past the hangouts and other high points of Buffett's Key West, spinning yarns about the musician and Key West in general. *Note:* If you're not a huge fan of Jimmy Buffett's, you might want to skip this tour as the price is relatively steep and you probably won't be as interested in these things as die hard fans are or have as much fun as them, either. The tour departs daily at 4pm from **Captain Tony's Saloon** (428 Greene St.), where Buffett used to hang out and perform, and ends at, you guessed it, Margaritaville Cafe on Duval Street. Tour tickets are $18 for adults, $15 for locals with ID, and $10 for children ages 6 through 10. Bring cash or traveler's checks; no credit cards accepted. Reservations are required at least 2 days in advance.

DIVING   One of the area's largest scuba schools, **Dive Key West Inc.,** 3128 N. Roosevelt Blvd. (© **800/426-0707** or 305/296-3823; fax 305/296-0609; www.divekeywest.com), offers instruction on all levels and its dive boats take participants to scuba and snorkel sites on nearby reefs.

Key West Marine Park (© **305/294-3100**), the newest dive park along the island's Atlantic shore, incorporates no-motor "swim only" lanes marked by buoys, providing swimmers and snorkelers a safe way to explore the waters around Key West. The park's boundaries stretch from the foot of Duval Street to Higgs Beach.

Wreck dives and night dives are two of the special offerings of **Lost Reef Adventures,** 261 Margaret St. (© **800/952-2749** or 305/296-9737). Regularly scheduled runs and private charters can be arranged. Phone for departure information.

Also see **Mosquito Coast Outfitters,** under "Kayaking," below.

FISHING   As any angler will tell you, there's no fishing like Keys fishing. Key West has it all: bonefish, tarpon, dolphin, tuna, grouper, cobia, and more. Sharks, too.

Step aboard a small exposed skiff for an incredibly diverse day of fishing. In the morning, you can head offshore for sailfish or dolphin (the fish, not the mammal), and then by afternoon, get closer to land for a shot at tarpon, permit, grouper, or snapper. Here in Key West, you can probably pick up more cobia— one of the best fighting and eating fish around—than anywhere else in the world. For a real fight, ask your skipper to go for the tarpon—the greatest fighting fish there is, famous for its dramatic "tail walk" on the water after it's hooked. Shark fishing is also popular.

You'll find plenty of competition among the charter-fishing boats in and around Mallory Square. You can negotiate a good deal at **Charter Boat Row,** 1801 N. Roosevelt Ave. (across from the Shell station), home to more than 30 charter-fishing and party boats. Just show up to arrange your outing, or call **Garrison Bite Marina** (© **305/292-8167**) for details.

> **Tips Reel Deals**
>
> When looking for the best deals on fishing excursions, know that the bookers from the kiosks in town generally take 20% of a captain's fee in addition to an extra monthly fee. You can usually save yourself money by booking directly with a captain or going straight to one of the docks.

The advantage of the smaller, more expensive charter boats is that you can call the shots. They'll take you where you want to go, to fish for what you want to catch. These "light tackles" are also easier to maneuver, which means you can go to backcountry spots for tarpon and bonefish, as well as out to the open ocean for tuna and dolphin. You'll really be able to feel the fish, and you'll get some good fights. Larger boats, for up to six or seven people, are cheaper and are best for kingfish, billfish, and sailfish. Consider Capt. Vinnie Argiro's **Heavy Hitters Charters** (© 305/745-6665) if you want a light-tackle experience. For a larger boat, try Capt. Henry Otto's 44-foot *Sunday,* docked at the Hyatt in Key West (© **305/294-7052**).

The huge commercial party boats are more for sightseeing than serious angling, though you can get lucky and get a few bites at one of the fishing holes. One especially good deal is the *Gulfstream III* (© 305/296-8494), an all-day charter that goes out daily from 9:30am to 4:30pm. You'll pay $35, plus $3 for a rod and reel. It's $25 for kids under 12. This 65-foot party boat usually has at least 30 other anglers. Bring your own cooler or buy snacks on the boat. Beer and wine are allowed.

Serious anglers should consider the light-tackle boats that leave from **Ocean-side Marina** (© **305/294-4676**) on Stock Island, at 5950 Peninsula Ave., 1½ miles off U.S. 1. It's a 20-minute drive from Old Town on the Atlantic side. There are more than 30 light-tackle guides, which range from flatbed, backcountry skiffs to 28-foot open boats. There are also a few larger charters and a party boat that goes to the Dry Tortugas. Call for details.

For a light-tackle outing with a very colorful Key West flair, call **Capt. Bruce Cronin** at © 305/294-4929 or **Capt. Kenny Harris** at © 305/294-8843, two of the more famous (and pricey) captains working these docks for over 20 years. You'll pay from $650 for a full day, usually about 8am to 4pm, and from $450 for half a day.

GOLF A relative newcomer in terms of local recreation, golf is gaining in popularity here as it is in many visitor destinations. The area's only public golf club is **Key West Golf Club** (© 305/294-5232), an 18-hole course located at the entrance to the island of Key West at MM 4.5 (turn onto College Rd. to the course entrance). Designed by Rees Jones, the course has plenty of mangroves and water hazards on its 6,526 yards. It's open to the public and has a new pro shop. Call ahead for tee-time reservations. Rates are $140 per player, including cart.

KAYAKING Mosquito Coast Outfitters, housed in a woodsy wine bar at 1017 Duval St. (© **305/294-7178**), operates a first-rate kayaking and snorkeling tour every day as long as the weather is mild. The tours depart at 9am sharp (and return around 3pm) and cost $55 per person. Included in the price are snacks, soft drinks, and a guided tour of the mangrove-studded islands of Sugar Key or

Geiger Key just north of Key West. The tour is primarily for kayaking, but you will have the opportunity to get in the water for snorkeling if you're interested.

SHOPPING

You'll find all kinds of unique gifts and souvenirs in Key West, from coconut postcards to Key lime pies. On Duval Street, T-shirt shops outnumber almost any other business. If you must get a wearable memento, be careful of unscrupulous salespeople. Despite efforts to curtail the practice, many shops have been known to rip off unwitting shoppers. It pays to check the prices and the exchange rate before signing any sales slips. You are entitled to a written estimate of any T-shirt work before you pay for it.

At Mallory Square is the **Clinton Street Market,** an overly air-conditioned mall of kiosks and stalls designed for the many cruise-ship passengers who never venture beyond this super-commercial zone. Amid the dreck are some delicious coffee and candy shops and some high-priced hats and shoes. There's also a free and clean restroom.

Once the main industry of Key West, cigar making is enjoying renewed success at the handful of factories that survived the slow years. Stroll through "**Cigar Alley**" (while on Green St., go 2 blocks west and you'll hit Cigar Alley, also known as Pirate's Alley), where you will find *viejitos* (little old men) rolling fat stogies just as they used to do in their homeland across the Florida Straits. Stop at the **Conch Republic Cigar Factory,** at 512 Greene St. (© **305/295-9036**), for an excellent selection of imported and locally rolled smokes, including the famous El Hemingway. Remember, buying or selling Cuban-made cigars is illegal. Shops advertising "Cuban Cigars" are usually referring to domestic cigars made from tobacco grown from seeds that were brought from Cuba decades ago. To be fair, though, many premium cigars today are grown from Cuban seed tobacco—only it is grown in Latin America and the Caribbean, not Cuba.

If you are looking for local or Caribbean art, you will find nearly a dozen galleries and shops clustered on Duval Street between Catherine and Fleming streets. You'll also find some excellent shops scattered on the side streets. One worth seeking out is the **Haitian Art Co.,** 600 Frances St. (© **305/296-8932**), where you can browse through room upon room of original paintings from well-known and obscure Haitian artists in a range of prices from a few dollars to a few thousand. Also, check out **Cuba, Cuba!** at 814 Duval St. (© **305/295-9442**), where you'll find paintings, sculpture, and photos by Cuban artists as well as books and art from the island.

A favorite stop in the Keys is the deliciously fragrant **Key West Aloe** at 524 Front St., between Simonton and Duval streets (© **305/294-5592**). Since 1971, this shop has been selling a simple line of bath products, including lotions, shampoos, and soothing balms for those who want a reminder of the tropical breezes once they're back home. At the main shop (open until 8pm), you can find great gift baskets, tropical perfumes, and candies and cookies, too. In addition to frangipani, vanilla, and hibiscus scents, sample Key West for Men, a unique and alluringly musky bestseller.

For foodies, the **Key Lime Pie Co.** (© **305/294-6567**) is so popular for its pies, cookies, and pretty much anything you can think of made with Key lime (candles, soaps, lotions) that there are two on the tiny island. One is at 701 Caroline St. and the other is at 424 Greene St. From sweet to spicy, **Peppers of Key West** (© **305/295-9333**) at 602 Greene St. is a hot-sauce-lover's heaven, with hundreds of variations of sauce, from brutally spicy to mild. Grab a seat at the tasting bar and be prepared to let your taste buds sizzle.

Literature and music buffs will appreciate the many bookshops and record stores on the island. **Key West Island Bookstore** (© **305/294-2904**) at 513 Fleming St. carries new, used, and rare books and specializes in fiction by residents of the Keys, including Hemingway, Tennessee Williams, Shel Silverstein, Ann Beattie, Richard Wilbur, and John Hersey. It's open daily from 10am to 9pm. **Flaming Maggie's** (© **305/294-3931**) at 830 Fleming St. carries a wide selection of gay books. It's open Monday through Saturday from 10am to 6pm.

For anything else, from bed linens to candlesticks to clothing, go to downtown's oldest and most renowned department store, **Fast Buck Freddie's,** at 500 Duval St. (© **305/294-2007**). For the same merchandise at reduced prices, try **Half Buck Freddie's** ⚘, 726 Caroline St. (© **305/294-2007**), where you can shop for out-of-season bargains and "rejects" from the main store.

Also check out **KW Light Gallery,** 534 Fleming St. (© **305/294-0566**), for high-quality contemporary photography as well as historic images and other artworks that relate to the Keys or exemplify the concept of light and its varied interpretations. Open Thursday through Tuesday 10am to 6pm (summer hours are 10am–4pm).

WHERE TO STAY

You'll find a wide variety of places to stay in Key West, from resorts with all the amenities to seaside motels, quaint bed-and-breakfasts, and clothing-optional guesthouses. Unless you're in town during Key West's most popular holidays— Fantasy Fest (around Halloween), where Mardi Gras meets South Florida for the NC-17 set, Hemingway Days (in July), where Papa is seemingly and eerily alive and well, and Christmas and New Year's—or for a big fishing tournament (many are held from Oct–Dec) or boat-racing tourney, you can almost always find a place to stay at the last minute. However, you may want to book early, especially in winter, when prime properties fill up and many require 2- or 3-night minimum stays. Prices at these times are also extremely high. Finding a decent room for under $100 a night is a real trick.

Another suggestion, and my recommendation, is to call **Vacation Key West** (© **800/595-5397** or 305/295-9500; www.vacationkw.com), which is a wholesaler that offers discounts of 20% to 30% and is skilled at finding last-minute deals. They represent mostly larger hotels and motels but can also place visitors in guesthouses. The phones are answered weekdays from 9am to 6pm and Saturday from 11am to 2pm. The **Key West Innkeepers Association,** P.O. Box 6172, Key West, FL 33041 (© **800/492-1911** or 305/292-3600), can also help find lodging in any price range from its dozens of members and affiliates.

Gay travelers will want to call the **Key West Business Guild** (© **305/294-4603**), which represents more than 50 guesthouses and B&Bs in town, as well as many other gay-owned businesses. Be advised that most gay guesthouses have a clothing-optional policy. One of the most elegant and popular ones is **Big Ruby's** (© **800/477-7829** or 305/296-2323; rates start at $145 for a double during peak season and $85 during the off season) at 409 Applerouth Lane (a little alley just off Duval St.). A low cluster of buildings surrounds a lushly landscaped courtyard where a hearty breakfast is served each morning and wine is poured at dusk. The mostly male guests hang out by a good-size pool, tanning in the buff. Also popular is **Oasis** at 823 Fleming St. (© **305/296-2131;** rates are $169–$229 in winter and $109–$169 in summer), which is superclean and friendly, with a central location and a 14-seat hot tub.

Another luxurious property is **The Florida Key Guesthouse** at 412 Frances St. (© **305/296-4719;** rates are $225 in season and $125 during the off season), which is more romantic and traditionally decorated and welcomes many lesbian travelers as well. *Out and About* gave it a five-star rating. For women only, **Pearl's Rainbow,** 525 United St. (© **800/74-WOMYN** or 305/292-1450), is a large, fairly well-maintained guesthouse with lots of privacy and amenities, including two pools and two hot tubs. Rates in season range from $109 to $229.

VERY EXPENSIVE

The Gardens Hotel ★★★ *(Finds*   At last, the true garden of Eden has been located and it's on Angela Street in Key West. Once a private residence, The Gardens Hotel (whose main house is listed in the National Register of Historic Places) is hidden amidst the exotic Peggy Mills tropical botanical gardens. What lies behind the gardens is a luxurious, Bahamian-style hideaway featuring 17 luxuriously appointed accommodations including two suites; two historic rooms in the main house; 12 garden and courtyard rooms in the backyard, as carriage house-type rooms, not attached to the house; and one uber secluded cottage. I stayed in one of the courtyard rooms and didn't want to leave, even though the hotel is within walking distance of frenetic Duval Street. A gorgeous freeform swimming pool is right in the middle of the courtyard, and a Tiki bar is right there to serve up whatever libation you desire. The Jacuzzi is hidden behind beautiful landscaping. The rooms are resplendent, with Aveda products, Jacuzzi bathtubs, hardwood floors, brass and iron beds, marble bathrooms, and a sense of serenity that words can't describe. Winding brick pathways leading to secluded seating areas in the private gardens make for an idyllic romantic getaway that's the quintessence of paradise.

526 Angela St., Key West, FL 33040. © **800/526-2664** or 305/294-2661. Fax 305/292-1007. 17 units. Winter $685 master suite, $265 historic rooms, $575 carriage house suite, $315 garden rooms, $355 courtyard rooms, $465 cottage; off-season $485–$595 master suite, $155–$215 historic rooms, $385–$495 carriage house suite, $175–$245 garden rooms, $215–$285 courtyard rooms, $295–$395 cottage. Rates include continental breakfast. AE, DC, MC, V. **Amenities:** Pool, bar. *In room:* A/C, TV, hair dryer, safe.

Hilton Key West Resort and Marina ★★   Ideally situated at the very end of Duval Street in the middle of all of Old Town's action, the Hilton Key West Resort and Marina is a prime spot from which to enjoy sunsets as well as that hard-to-find quietly elegant ambience that's so lacking in most big resorts in Key West. The rooms are large and well appointed, with all the modern conveniences. Choose a suite in the main building if you want a large Jacuzzi in your living room. Otherwise, the marina building has great views. The secluded beach is great for an escape from the Duval Street frenzy. For just $10 per person (children under 18 free), you can also enjoy the hotel's private Sunset Key (see below) beach that is reachable only by the hotel's launch at the marina. Bistro 245, the elegant indoor dining room, offers ample breakfasts and a huge Sunday brunch.

Hilton's gorgeous **Sunset Key Guest Cottages** ★★★, with whitewashed interiors, picture windows, and fabulous views, are located 300 feet offshore on Sunset Key and are accessible only by private launch. Check in at the Hilton and take a 10-minute cruise to the island, where there are no cars, only a gourmet grocery, restaurant, bar, and free-form tropical pool with whirlpool jets. Sunset guests also have access to all watersports at the Hilton. Cottages are equipped with full kitchens, high-tech entertainment centers, and one, two, or three massive bedrooms.

245 Front St. (at the end of Duval St.), Key West, FL 33040. © **800/221-2424** or 305/294-4000. Fax 305/294-4086. www.keywestresort.hilton.com. 215 units. Winter $299–$525 double, $375–$800 suite; off-season $195–$425 double, $300–$800 suite. 37 Sunset Key Cottages, up to 5 people: winter $575–$1,825; off-season $325–$1,095. Private chef: $75 per person plus additional chef/hotel fees, tax, and gratuities.

AE, DC, DISC, MC, V. Self-parking $7, valet parking $10. **Amenities:** 2 restaurants; pool bar; outdoor heated pool; health club; Jacuzzi; watersports equipment/rental; bike rental; game room; concierge; business center; limited room service; in-room massage; self-service laundry; dry cleaning; full-service marina. *In room:* A/C, TV, dataport, minibar, coffeemaker, hair dryer, iron.

Ocean Key Resort 𝒢   You can't beat the location of this 100-room resort, located at Zero Duval Street, at the foot of Mallory Square, the epicenter of the sunset ritual. The rooms here are huge and are luxuriously appointed, with living and dining areas, oversize Jacuzzis, and overlooking either the Gulf of Mexico, the Key West Harbor, or Mallory Square and Duval Street. Ocean Key also features a Gulf-side heated swimming pool and the lively, renowned Sunset Pier where guests can wind the day down with cocktails and live tunes (make sure to check out Raven, one of the Pier's most incredible singers). If you want to go big, book the two-bedroom suite—it's 1,200 square feet and has a full kitchen, three beds, and a large private balcony. Classic Key West decor adorns the rooms and the property, from tile floors to hand painted furniture and pastel art. The hotel's restaurant, Hot Tin Roof (p. ###), is one of Key West's best.

Zero Duval St. (near Mallory Docks), Key West, FL 33040. ✆ **800/328-9815** or 305/296-7701. Fax 305/292-2198. www.oceankey.com. 100 units. Winter $245–$410 double, $559–$1,049 suite; off-season $200–$355 double, $339–$749 suite. AE, DC, MC, V. **Amenities:** 2 restaurants; 3 bars; heated swimming pool; watersports equipment/rentals; moped/bike rental; concierge; room service; in-room massage; babysitting; laundry services; private beach. *In room:* A/C, TV, dataport, minibar, coffeemaker, hair dryer, iron.

Pier House Resort and Caribbean Spa 𝒢   If you're looking for something a bit more intimate than the Wyndham Reach (see below), Pier House is an ideal choice. Its location—at the foot of Duval Street and just steps from Mallory Docks—is the envy of every hotel on the island. Set back from the busy street, on a short strip of beach, this hotel is a welcome oasis of calm. The accommodations here vary tremendously, from relatively simple business-style rooms to romantic guest quarters complete with integrated stereo systems and whirlpool tubs. Their best waterfront suites and rooms have recently been renovated. Although every accommodation has either a balcony or a patio, not all overlook the water. My favorites, in the two-story spa building, don't have any view at all. But what they lack in scenery, they make up for in opulence; each well-appointed spa room has a sitting area and a huge Jacuzzi bathroom that opens to the bedroom area.

1 Duval St. (near Mallory Docks), Key West, FL 33040. ✆ **800/327-8340** or 305/296-4600. Fax 305/296-9085. www.pierhouse.com. 142 units. Winter $245–$410 double; off-season $200–$355 double. AE, DC, MC, V. **Amenities:** 3 restaurants; 3 bars; heated swimming pool; full-service spa and fitness center; 2 Jacuzzis; sauna; watersports equipment/rentals; moped/bike rental; concierge; limited room service; in-room massage; babysitting; laundry services; private beach. *In room:* A/C, TV, dataport, minibar, coffeemaker, hair dryer, iron.

Wyndham Reach Resort 𝒢𝒢   Unlike Wyndham's Casa Marina resort, the Reach is better suited to adults only and not families. The location here can be either a highlight or a drawback; it's a 5-minute walk away from the center of the Duval Street action. Supported by stilts that leave the entire ground floor for car parking, the hotel offers four floors of rooms designed around atriums. The wonderful guest rooms are large and feature tile floors and sturdy wicker furnishings. Each has a vanity area separate from the bathroom. The rooms are so nice, you can easily forgive the small closets and diminutive dressers. All have sliding glass doors that open onto balconies, and some have ocean views. There's also a private pier for fishing and tanning. The protected waters are tame and shallow. For steak lovers, there's Shula's on the Beach, a Keys sibling to Miami's lauded Shula's Steak House (p. 100).

1435 Simonton St., Key West, FL 33040. ℂ 800/874-4118, or 800/996-3426 for reservations. Fax 305/296-2830. www.wyndham.com/hotels/EYWRR/main.wnt. 150 units. Winter $269–$469 double; off-season $169–$369 double. AE, DC, DISC, MC, V. **Amenities:** 2 restaurants; bar; outdoor heated swimming pool; nearby tennis and golf; health club and spa; watersports equipment/rental; bike rental; concierge; tour desk; business center; salon; 24-hr. room service; in-room massage; babysitting; dry cleaning. *In room:* A/C, TV, dataport, minibar, fridge, coffeemaker, hair dryer, iron.

EXPENSIVE

Curry Mansion Inn ★★ *Finds*   This wonderfully charismatic inn is the former home of the island's first millionaire, a once penniless Bahamian immigrant who made a fortune as a pirate. Owned today by innkeepers Al and Edith Amsterdam, the Curry Mansion is now on the National Register of Historic Places, but you won't feel like you're staying in a museum, but rather in a wonderfully warm home. Rooms are very sparsely decorated, with white wicker furniture, four-poster wooden beds, and pink walls, in which Key West minimalism meets Victorian. The dining room is reminiscent of a Victorian dollhouse, with rich wood floors and furnishings and elegant table settings. Every morning there's a delicious European-style breakfast buffet, and at night, cocktail parties. There's also a really nice patio out back, on which, from time to time, there's live entertainment.

511 Caroline St., Key West, FL 33040. ℂ 800/253-3466 or 305/294-5349. Fax 305/294-4093. www.currymansion.com. 28 units. Winter $180–$325 double; off-season $145–$245 double. Rates include European breakfast buffet. AE, DC, MC, V. No children under 12. **Amenities:** Dining room; swimming pool; bike rental; concierge. *In room:* A/C, TV, minibar.

Island City House Hotel ★★   A small resort unto itself, the Island City House consists of three separate and unique buildings that share a common junglelike patio and pool. All rooms here are suites. The first building, unimaginatively called the Island City House building, is a historic three-story wooden structure with wraparound verandas that allow guests to walk around the entire edifice on any floor. The warmly dressed, old-fashioned interiors here include wood floors and many antique furnishings. Many rooms have full-size kitchens. The tile bathrooms could use more counter space, and the room lighting isn't always perfect, but eccentricities are part of this hotel's charm.

The unpainted wooden Cigar House has particularly large bedrooms, similar in ambience to those in the Island City House. The Arch House is the least appealing of the three buildings, but still recommended. Built of Dade County pine, the Arch House's cozy bedrooms are furnished in wicker and rattan and come with small kitchens and bathrooms.

411 William St., Key West, FL 33040. ℂ 800/634-8230 or 305/294-5702. Fax 305/294-1289. www.islandcityhouse.com. 24 units. Winter $180–$240 1-bedroom suite, $285–$325 2-bedroom suite; off-season $120–$185 1-bedroom suite, $195–$220 2-bedroom suite. Rates include breakfast. AE, DC, DISC, MC, V. **Amenities:** Outdoor heated pool; access to nearby health club; Jacuzzi; bike rental; concierge; in-room massage; babysitting; laundry service and self-service laundromat; dry cleaning. *In room:* A/C, TV, kitchen, coffeemaker, hair dryer.

Marquesa Hotel ★★★ *Finds*   The Marquesa offers the charm of a small historic hotel coupled with the amenities of a large resort. It encompasses four buildings, two swimming pools, and a three-stage waterfall that cascades into a lily pond. Two of the hotel's houses are luxuriously restored Victorian homes whose rooms are outfitted with extraplush antiques and oversized contemporary furniture. The rooms in the two other, newly constructed buildings are even more opulent; many have four-poster wrought-iron beds with bright floral spreads. The green-marble bathrooms in the new building are lush and spacious; those in the older building are also nice, but not nearly as huge and luxe. The decor is simple, elegant, and spotless. The hotel also boasts one of Key West's most elegant restaurants, Cafe Marquesa.

600 Fleming St. (at Simonton St.), Key West, FL 33040. © **800/869-4631** or 305/292-1919. Fax 305/294-2121. www.marquesa.com. 27 units. Winter $275–$410 double; off-season $170–$285 double. AE, DC, MC, V. No children under 12. **Amenities:** Restaurant; 2 outdoor swimming pools (1 is heated); access to nearby health club; bike rental; concierge; limited room service. *In room:* A/C, TV, dataport, minibar, hair dryer, iron, safe, CD player.

Weatherstation Inn ⊛ *Finds* Originally built in 1912 as a weather station, this beautifully restored and meticulously maintained two-story, Renaissance-style inn is located just 2 blocks from Duval Street. It's situated on the tropical grounds of the former Old Navy Yard, now an exclusive and very private gated community. Harry Truman, Eisenhower, and JFK all visited the station. Spacious and uncluttered, each room is uniquely furnished to complement the interior architecture: hardwood floors, tall sash windows, and high ceilings. The large, modern bathrooms are especially appealing. Enjoy a complimentary continental breakfast by the pool among the flowers. The staff is friendly and accommodating.

57 Front St., Key West, FL 33040. © **800/815-2707** or 305/294-7277. Fax 305/294-0544. www.weather stationinn.com. 8 units. Winter $195–$315 double; off-season $150–$215 double. Rates include continental breakfast. AE, DISC, MC, V. **Amenities:** Outdoor pool; concierge. *In room:* A/C, TV/VCR, hair dryer.

MODERATE

Ambrosia Key West ⊛⊛ *Finds* Although Key West is a tiny island, it's amazing to discover that even after visiting here countless times a year, every time I go back, I discover yet another hidden treasure. Ambrosia is one of them, a private compound situated on 2 acres of lush landscaping just a block away from Duval Street. Three tropical lagoon-style pools, suites, townhouses, and a stand-alone cottage are all spread out on the grounds. Townhouses have full living rooms, complete kitchens, and spiral staircases leading to master suites with vaulted ceilings and private decks. The cottage, overlooking a dip pool, is a perfect family retreat, featuring two bedrooms, two bathrooms, a living room, and a full kitchen. All rooms and suites feature private entrances, most with French doors opening up onto a variety of intimate outdoor spaces, including private verandas, patios, and gardens with sculptures, fountains, and pools. Fantastic service bolstered by the philosophy that it's better to have high occupancy than high rates explains why Ambrosia has a 90% year-round occupancy—a record in seasonal Key West.

622 Fleming St., Key West, FL 33040. © **800/535-9838** or 305/296-9838. Fax 305/296-2425. www.ambrosia keywest.com. 19 units. Winter $169–$499; off-season $120–$289. Rates include breakfast. AE, DISC, MC, V. Off- and on-street parking. Pets accepted. **Amenities:** 3 outdoor heated pools; hot tub. *In room:* A/C, TV, fridge, coffeemaker, hair dryer, iron, CD player, kitchens in some.

Casa Alante Guest Cottages ⊛⊛ *Finds* If you drive too fast on South Roosevelt Boulevard, you will miss Casa Alante, a hidden treasure situated on an acre of property amidst gardens, an orchid terrace, and mahogany trees. A bed-and-breakfast owned by a former Austrian baroness, Casa Alante features 10 charming units with names like Manatee, Dolphin, and Hemingway Cat, each with its own mailbox shaped in the form of whatever the room is named after. All units have full kitchens and private terraces, and, best of all, all rooms have fill-in-the-blank menus on which guests fill out their choices for breakfast, which is decorated on trays with tropical flowers and delivered to your porch front. Each unit is unique, ranging from large efficiencies and one-bedroom suites to a fabulous loft apartment. In addition to the lush gardens and small pool, there are five chickens that call Casa Alante home, so prepare to hear the clucking at an early-ish hour.

1435 S. Roosevelt Blvd., Key West, FL 33040. © 800/688-3942 or 305/293-0702. Fax 305/292-8699. www.casaalante.com. 10 units. Winter $125–$260; off-season $80–$195. Rates include breakfast. AE, DC, DISC, MC, V. Private parking. Pets accepted. **Amenities:** Outdoor heated pool; free bikes; laundry facilities. *In room:* A/C, TV, CD player, kitchen, fridge, coffeemaker, hair dryer, CD player.

Doubletree Grand Key Resort ★ *Finds*   If you don't mind staying on the quiet "other" side of the island, a 10-minute cab ride away from Duval Street, the Doubletree Grand Key Resort is an excellent choice, not to mention value. An ecologically conscious resort, the hotel has been renovated with ecosensitive materials as well as an interior created to conserve energy, reduce waste, and pre-serve the area's natural resources. Rooms are clean and comfortable, with some looking out onto the spacious pool area, which is surrounded by an unsightly empty lot of mangroves and marshes. The newest addition to the hotel is a wel-come one—a Beach Club located off property at Smathers Beach, where the hotel has established a hut with chairs, towels, and umbrellas. Watersports are also available here, as is a free shuttle to transport guests back and forth. The hotel's restaurant is also very good; but for excitement, look elsewhere.

3990 S. Roosevelt Blvd., Key West, FL 33040. © 888/310-1540 or 305/293-1818. Fax 305/296-6962. www. doubletreekeywest.com. 216 units. Winter $159–$259 double, $199–$475 suite; off-season $89–$139 double, $115–$299 suite. Rates include continental breakfast. AE, DISC, MC, V. Free parking. **Amenities:** Restaurant; Tiki bar and lounge; pool; concierge; meeting rooms; limited room service. *In room:* A/C, TV/Web TV, dataport, minibar, coffeemaker, hair dryer, iron, safe, Sony PlayStation.

La Pensione ★★   This classic bed-and-breakfast, located in the 1891 home of a former cigar executive, distinguishes itself from other similar inns by its extreme attention to details. The friendly and knowledgeable staff treats the stunning home and its guests with extraordinary care. The comfortable rooms all have air-conditioning, ceiling fans, king-size beds, and private bathrooms. Many also have French doors opening onto spacious verandas. Although the rooms have no tele-visions, the distractions of Duval Street, only steps away, should keep you ade-quately occupied during your visit. Breakfast, which includes made-to-order Belgian waffles, fresh fruit, and a variety of breads or muffins, can be taken on the wraparound porch or at the communal dining table.

809 Truman Ave. (between Windsor and Margaret sts.), Key West, FL 33040. © 800/893-1193 or 305/ 292-9923. Fax 305/296-6509. www.lapensione.com. 9 units. Winter $168–$178 double; off-season $108–$118 double. Rates include breakfast. 10% discount for readers who mention this book. AE, DC, DISC, MC, V. No chil-dren accepted. **Amenities:** Outdoor pool; access to nearby health club; bike rental. *In room:* A/C.

Southernmost Point Guest House ★★ *Finds* *Kids*   One of the few inns that actually welcome children and pets, this romantic and historic guesthouse is a real find. The antiseptically clean rooms are not as fancy as the house's ornate 1885 exterior, but each is unique and includes some combination of basic beds and couches and a hodgepodge of furnishings, including futon couches and high-back wicker chairs. Room no. 5 is best; situated upstairs, it has a private porch, an ocean view, and windows that let in lots of light. Every room has fresh flowers, a refrig-erator, wine, and a full decanter of sherry. Mona Santiago, the hotel's kind, laid-back owner, provides chairs and towels that can be brought to the beach, which is just a block away. Guests can help themselves to free wine as they soak in the 14-seat hot tub. Kids will enjoy the backyard swings and the pet rabbits.

1327 Duval St., Key West, FL 33040. © 305/294-0715. Fax 305/296-0641. www.southernmostpoint.com. 6 units. Winter $115–$175 double, $235–$265 suite; off-season $79–$110 double, $155–$165 suite. Rates include breakfast. AE, MC, V. Pets accepted, $5 in summer, $10 in winter. **Amenities:** Garden pool; hot tub; laundry facilities; barbecue grills. *In room:* A/C, TV/VCR, fridge, coffeemaker, hair dryer, iron.

Westwinds Inn ⭐ A close second to staying in your own private, 19th-century clapboard, tin-roofed house is this tranquil inn located just 4 blocks from Duval Street in the historic Seaport district. Lush landscaping—banana stalks, mango, and Spanish Lime trees—keeps the inn extremely private and secluded, and at times, you do feel as if you're alone. And that's not a scary thing; it's absolutely fabulous. Two pools, one heated in the winter, are offset by alcoves, fountains, and the extremely well-maintained whitewashed inn, which is actually composed of five separate houses. Rooms are Key West comfortable, with wicker furnishings and fans, and all have private bathrooms. Families are welcome, but children under 12 are not. All rooms are nonsmoking.

914 Eaton St., Key West, FL 33040. ℂ **800/788-4150** or 305/296-4440. Fax 305/293-0931. www.westwindskeywest.com. 19 units. Winter $135–$175 double, $195 suite; off-season $80–$145 double, $130–$165 suite. Rates include continental breakfast. DISC, MC, V. **Amenities:** 2 pools (1 heated); bike rental; self-service laundry. *In room:* A/C (some rooms have TVs and kitchenettes).

INEXPENSIVE

Angelina Guest House ⭐⭐ This former bordello and gambling hall turned youth hostel–type guesthouse is about the cheapest in town and conveniently located near a hot, hippie restaurant called Blue Heaven (see "Where to Dine," below), one of the best restaurants in town. Though the neighborhood is definitely urban, it is generally safe and is full of character. The rooms are all furnished differently in a modest style, recently upgraded with new decor. Only three rooms do not have private bathrooms. Two rooms have full kitchens, and one has a microwave and small refrigerator; there are no televisions or telephones. A gorgeous lagoon-style heated pool with waterfall and tropical landscaping was an excellent addition. Even better are the poolside hammocks—get out there early, they go quickly! Even though the Angelina is sparse (perfect for the bohemian types who don't mind a little grit), it's a great place to crash if you are on the cheap.

302 Angela St. (at the corner of Thomas St.), Key West, FL 33040. ℂ **888/303-4480** or 305/294-4480. Fax 305/272-0681. www.angelinaguesthouse.com. 14 units. Winter $79–$149 double; off-season $59–$99 double. Rates include continental breakfast. DISC, MC, V. **Amenities:** Outdoor heated pool; concierge. *In room:* A/C, hair dryer, iron, no phone.

The Grand ⭐⭐ *(Finds)* Don't expect cabbies or locals to know about this well-kept secret, located in a modest residential section of Old Town, about 5 blocks from Duval Street. It's got almost everything you could want, including a very moderate price tag. Proprietor Elizabeth Rose goes out of her way to provide any and all services for her appreciative guests. All rooms have private bathrooms, air-conditioning, and private entrances. Room no. 2 on the backside of the house is the best deal; it's small and there is no closet or dresser, just hooks on the walls, but it has a porch and the most privacy. Suites are a real steal, too. The large two-room units come with a complete kitchen. This place is undoubtedly the best bargain in town.

1116 Grinnell St. (between Virginia and Catherine sts.), Key West, FL 33040. ℂ **888/947-2630** or 305/294-0590. Fax 305/294-0477. www.thegrandguesthouse.com. 11 units. Winter $98–$138 double, $148–$188 suite; off-season $78–$98 double, $108–$118 suite. Rates include continental breakfast. AE, DISC, MC, V. **Amenities:** Bike/scooter rental; concierge. *In room:* A/C, TV, fridge.

Key West International Hostel & Seashell Motel This well-run, affordable hostel is a 3-minute walk to the beach and to Old Town. Very busy with European backpackers, it's a great place to meet people. The dorm rooms are dark, grimy, and sparse, but livable if you're desperate for a cheap room. The higher-priced motel rooms are a good deal, especially those equipped with full kitchens. Amenities include a pool table under a Tiki roof, and bicycle rentals for $8 per day. There's also cheap food available for breakfast, lunch, and dinner, as well as discounted prices for snorkeling, diving, and sunset cruises.

718 South St., Key West, FL 33040. ✆ **800/51-HOSTEL** or 305/296-5719. Fax 305/296-0672. www. keywesthostel.com. 96 units, 10 private rooms, 1 2-bedroom suite with Jacuzzi. Year-round members $20, nonmembers $23. Motel units $75–$105 in season; $55–$85 off-season. MC, V. Free parking. **Amenities:** Bike rental; kitchen. *In room:* A/C, TV, fridge, coffeemaker, hair dryer. Dorm rooms have only A/C.

WHERE TO DINE

With its share of the usual drive-through fast-food franchises (mostly up on Roosevelt Blvd.) and Duval Street succumbing to the lure of a Hard Rock Cafe, you might be surprised to learn that, over the years, an upscale and high-quality dining scene has begun to thrive in Key West. Wander Old Town or the newly spruced-up Bahama Village and browse menus after you have exhausted my list of picks below.

If you don't feel like venturing out, call **We Deliver** (✆ **305/293-0078**), a service that will bring you anything you want from any of the area's restaurants or stores for a small fee ($3–$6). We Deliver operates between 3 and 11pm. If you are staying in a condominium or efficiency, you may want to stock your refrigerator with groceries, beer, wine, and snacks from the area's oldest grocer, **Fausto's Food Palace.** Open since 1926, there are now two locations: 1105 White St. and 522 Fleming St. The Fleming Street location will deliver (✆ **305/ 294-5221** or 305/296-5663). Fausto's has a $25 delivery minimum.

VERY EXPENSIVE

Cafe des Artistes ★★★ FRENCH   Open for nearly 2 decades, the Cafe des Artistes' impressive longevity is the result of its winning combination of food and atmosphere. The fact that it was once part of a hotel built in 1935 by Al Capone's bookkeeper adds to its allure, but it's really the food that people come for. Traditional French meals benefit from a subtle tropical twist. Start with the duck-liver pâté, made with fresh truffles and old cognac, or Maryland crab meat served with an artichoke heart and herbed-tomato confit. Ask about the escargot du jour. Nouvelle and traditional French entrees include lobster flambé with mango and basil, and wine-basted lamb chops rubbed with rosemary and ginger.

1007 Simonton St. (near Truman Ave.). ✆ **305/294-7100**. Reservations recommended. Main courses $25–$38. AE, MC, V. Daily 6–11pm.

Café Marquesa ★★★ CONTEMPORARY AMERICAN   If you're looking for fabulous dining (and service) in Key West, this is the place. The intimate, 50-seat restaurant is something to look at, but it's really the food that you'll want to admire. Specialties include peppercorn-dusted, seared yellowfin tuna with saffron risotto; grilled Florida lobster tail and diver sea scallops with Thai basil sauce, black Thai rice, and Asian vegetables; and an almost perfect feta and pine nut-crusted rack of lamb with rosemary demi-glace, creamy polenta, and eggplant caponata. If you're looking to splurge, financially and gastronomically, this is the place.

In the Marquesa Hotel, 600 Fleming St. ✆ **305/292-1919**. Reservations highly recommended. Main courses $20–$36. AE, DC, MC, V. Daily 7–11pm summer; 6–11pm winter. No smoking.

Hot Tin Roof ★★★ FUSION   Ever hear of Conch Fusion Cuisine? Neither did I until I experienced it first hand—or mouth, rather—at Hot Tin Roof,

Ocean Key Resort's chichi restaurant where CIA graduate Jesse Van Rossum takes South American, Asian, French, and Keys cuisine and transforms it into a palatable experience unlike any other in this part of the world. Featuring vibrant colors, the 3,000-square-foot space features both indoor seating and outdoor deck seating overlooking the Key West Harbor. Live jazz/fusion adds to the already stunning environment here . . . it's the epitome of casual elegance. Signature dishes here include an irresistible lobster and roasted corn quesadilla, seafood paella, and a chocolate lava cake that makes this tin roof very hot, to say the least, especially for Key West.

In the Ocean Key Resort, Zero Duval St. ℂ **305/296-7701.** Reservations highly recommended. Main courses $18–$35. AE, DC, MC, V. Daily 7:30–11am and 5–10pm.

Louie's Backyard ⭐⭐ CARIBBEAN   Nestled amid blooming bougainvillea on a lush slice of the Gulf, Louie's remains one of the most romantic restaurants on earth. Famed chef Norman Van Aiken of Norman's in Miami brought his talents farther south and started what has become one of the finest dining spots in the Keys. As a result, this is one of the hardest places to score a reservation: Either call way in advance or hope that your hotel concierge has some pull. After dinner, sit at the dockside bar and watch the waves crash, almost touching your feet, while enjoying a cocktail at sunset. You can't go wrong with the fresh catch of the day, or any seafood dish, for that matter. The weekend brunches are also great. Even if you can't stay for dinner, go for lunch; this is one dining experience you won't want to miss.

700 Waddell Ave. ℂ **305/294-1061.** Reservations highly recommended. Main courses $25–$30; lunch $8–$15. AE, DC, MC, V. Daily 11:30am–3pm and 6–10:30pm.

One Duval ⭐⭐⭐ CARIBBEAN   The waterfront setting of this restaurant at the Pier House Resort is beautiful, but you may be too distracted to notice the views when you taste the food, which executive chef Will Greenwood describes as New Calypso Harvest. One of the best restaurants in Key West, One Duval blends the ingredients of the Caribbean and Florida with an innovative twist. For starters, the crab meat stuffed in phyllo dough is outstanding, not to mention filling, and the goat-cheese soufflé is rich and incredibly hedonistic. For main courses, the smoked cured pork chop with Captain Morgan spiced rum sauce is a best bet, as is the ponzu marinated yellowfin tuna tartare and avocado mousse timbale served in a macadamia-nut cilantro jus. The Key lime pie with meringue is a must have. Service is friendly and hyperprofessional, and it's not the kind of restaurant they rush you out of. Eat first, then sit back and digest the views. You don't want to miss any of what this fine restaurant has to offer.

One Duval St. ℂ **305/296-4600.** Reservations highly recommended. Main courses $25–$30. AE, DC, MC, V. Daily 6–10:30pm.

EXPENSIVE
Antonia's ⭐⭐ REGIONAL ITALIAN   The food is great, but the atmosphere is a bit fussy for Key West. If you don't have a reservation in season, don't bother. Still, if you are organized and don't mind paying high prices for dishes that go for much less elsewhere, try this old favorite. From the perfectly seasoned homemade focaccia to an exemplary crème brûlée, this elegant little standout is amazingly consistent. The menu includes a small selection of classics, such as *zuppa di pesce,* rack of lamb in a rosemary sauce, and veal Marsala. However, the way to go is with the nightly specials. You can't go wrong with any of the handmade pastas.

And the owners, Antonia Berto and Phillip Smith, travel to Italy every year to research recipes, so you can be sure you're getting an authentic taste of Italy in small-town Key West.

615 Duval St. ✆ **305/294-6565.** Fax 305/294-3888. Reservations suggested. Main courses $20–$28; pastas $13–$18. AE, DC, MC, V. Daily 6–11pm.

Bagatelle ★★★ SEAFOOD/TROPICAL   Reserve a seat at the elegant second-floor veranda overlooking Duval Street's mayhem. From the calm above, you may want to start your meal with the excellent herb-and-garlic–stuffed whole artichoke or the sashimi-like seared tuna rolled in black peppercorns. Also recommended is a lightly creamy garlic-herb pasta topped with Gulf shrimp, Florida lobster, and mushrooms. The best chicken and beef dishes are given a tropical treatment: grilled with papaya, ginger, and soy.

115 Duval St. ✆ **305/296-6609.** Reservations recommended. Main courses $14–$21; lunch $5–$10. AE, DISC, MC, V. Sun–Thurs 11:30am–10pm; Fri–Sat 11:30am–11pm.

La Trattoria ★ ITALIAN   Have a true Italian feast in a relaxed atmosphere. Each dish here is prepared and presented according to old Italian tradition and is cooked to order. The antipasti are scrumptious. Try the delicious baked bread-crumb–stuffed mushroom caps; they're firm yet tender. The stuffed eggplant with ricotta and roasted peppers is light and flavorful. Or have the seafood salad of shrimp, calamari, and mussels, fish-market fresh and tasty. The pasta dishes are also great: Try the *penne Venezia,* with mushrooms, sun-dried tomatoes, and crab meat, or the cannelloni stuffed with veal and spinach. For dessert, don't skip the homemade tiramisu; it's light yet full-flavored. The dining room is spacious but still intimate, and the waiters are friendly and informative. Before you leave, be sure to visit Virgilio's, the restaurant's very own cocktail lounge with live jazz until 2am.

524 Duval St. ✆ **305/296-1075.** Pasta $10–$17; main courses $17–$22. AE, DC, DISC, MC, V. Daily 5:30–11pm.

Mangoes ★★★ FLORIBBEAN   This restaurant's large brick patio, shaded by overgrown banyan trees, is so alluring to passersby that it's packed almost every night of the week. Many people don't realize how pricey the meals can be here because, upon first glance, it looks like a casual Duval Street cafe, but both its prices and cuisine are a notch above casual. Appetizers include conch chowder laced with sherry, lobster dumplings with tangy Key-lime sauce, and grilled shrimp cocktail with spicy mango chutney. Spicy sausage with black beans and rice, crispy curried chicken, and local snapper with passion-fruit sauce are typical among the entrees, but the Garlic and Lime Pinks—a half pound of Key West pink shrimp seasoned and grilled with a roasted garlic and Key lime glaze—are the menu's best offering by far. The Cuban Coffee Pork is definitely a different take on roast pork, rubbed with Cuban coffee and grilled with a vanilla-bean butter sauce and banana–black currant chutney. Even though it is right on tourist-laden Duval Street, Mangoes enjoys a good reputation among locals and stands out from the rest of the greasy bar fare found there.

700 Duval St. (at Angela St.). ✆ **305/292-4606.** Reservations recommended for parties of 6 or more. Main courses $12–$26; pizzas $10–$13; lunch $7–$14. AE, DC, DISC, MC, V. Daily 11am–midnight; pizza until 1am.

Seven Fish ★★★ *(Finds* SEAFOOD   Simple, good food is Seven Fish's motto, but this hidden little secret is much more than simple. One of the most popular locals' restaurants, Seven Fish is a chic seafood spot serving some of the best fish dishes on the entire island. Crab and shitake mushroom pasta, seafood pasta, sea scallops, fish of the day, and gnocchi with blue cheese and sautéed fish are among the dishes to choose from. Try the tropical shrimp salsa for appetizer and for dessert, do not miss the Key lime cake over tart lime curd with fresh berries. Be sure to make reservations well in advance here; seating is limited.

632 Olivia St. ✆ **305/296-2777.** Main courses $12–$23. AE, MC, V. Wed–Mon 6–10pm.

MODERATE

Alonzo's Oyster Bar ✿ SEAFOOD
Alonzo's Oyster Bar offers good seafood in a casual setting. It's located on the ground floor of the A&B Lobster House at the end of Front Street in the marina. To start off your meal, try the steamed beer shrimp—tantalizingly fresh jumbo shrimp in a garlic, Old Bay, beer, and cayenne-pepper sauce. A house specialty is white clam chili, a delicious mix of tender clams, white beans, and potatoes served with a dollop of sour cream. An excellent entree is the pan-fried lobster cakes, served with sweet-corn mashed potatoes, chipotle gravy, and roasted-corn salsa. Alonzo's is the casual section of the A&B Lobster House; if you want to dress up, go upstairs for their "fine dining." The staff is cheerful and informative, and the service is very good.

231 Margaret St. ✆ **305/294-5880.** Appetizers $5–$8; main courses $11–$17. MC, V. Daily 11am–11pm.

Banana Café ✿✿✿ (Finds) FRENCH
Although neither as elaborate as Café des Artistes nor quite as casual as Blue Heaven, Banana Café is open for three meals a day and benefits from a French country cafe look and feel. It's an upscale local eatery that's been discovered by savvy visitors on the less-congested end of Duval Street and kept its loyal clientele with affordable prices and delightful, light preparations. Banana Café's crepes are legendary on the island for breakfast or lunch, and fresh quality ingredients and a French-themed menu bring daytime diners back for the casual, classy, tropical-influenced dinner menu. Every Thursday night, there's live jazz.

1211 Duval St. ✆ **305/294-7227.** Main courses $4.80–$23; breakfast and lunch $2–$8.50. AE, DC, MC, V. Daily 8am–11pm.

Blue Heaven ✿✿ (Finds) SEAFOOD/AMERICAN/NATURAL
This little hippie-run gallery and restaurant has become the place to be in Key West—and with good reason. Be prepared to wait in line. The food here is some of the best in town, especially for breakfast. You can enjoy homemade granola, huge tropical-fruit pancakes, and seafood Benedict. Dinners are just as good and run the gamut from fresh-caught fish dishes to Jamaican-style jerk chicken, curried soups, and vegetarian stews. But if you're a neat freak, don't bother. Some people are put off by the dirt floors and roaming cats and birds, but frankly, it adds to the charm. The building used to be a bordello, where Hemingway was said to hang out watching cockfights. It's still lively here, but not *that* lively!

305 Petronia St. ✆ **305/296-8666.** Main courses $10–$30; lunch $6–$14; breakfast $5–$11. DISC, MC, V. Daily 8–11:30am, noon–3pm, and 6–10:30pm; Sun brunch 8am–1pm. Closed mid-Sept to early Oct.

Mangia, Mangia ✿ (Value) ITALIAN/AMERICAN
Locals appreciate that they can get good, inexpensive food here in a town filled with tourist traps. Off the beaten track, in a little corner storefront, this great Chicago-style pasta place serves some of the best Italian food in the Keys. The family-run restaurant offers superb homemade pastas of every description, including one of the tastiest marinaras around. The simple grilled chicken breast brushed with olive oil and sprinkled with pepper is another good choice, as is the Picadillo Pasta—black-bean pasta shells smothered in a Cuban-inspired sauce with meat, tomatoes, olives, capers, and spices. You wouldn't know it from the glossy glass-front room, but

there's a fantastic little outdoor patio dotted with twinkling pepper lights and lots of plants. You can relax out back with a glass of one of their excellent wines—they're said to have the largest selection in the Keys—or homemade beer while you wait for your table.

900 Southard St. (at Margaret St.). ℂ 305/294-2469. Reservations not accepted. Main courses $9–$15. AE, MC, V. Daily 5:30–10pm.

Pepe's *(Finds* AMERICAN   This old dive has been serving good, basic food for nearly a century. Steaks and Apalachicola Bay oysters are the big draw for regulars who appreciate the rustic barroom setting and historic photos on the walls. Look for original scenes of Key West in 1909, when Pepe's first opened. If the weather is nice, choose a seat on the patio under a stunning mahogany tree. Burgers, fish sandwiches, and standard chili satisfy hearty eaters. Buttery sautéed mushrooms and rich mashed potatoes are the best comfort food in Key West. There's always a wait, so stop by early for breakfast, when you can get old-fashioned chipped beef on toast and all the usual egg dishes. In the evening, there are reasonably priced cocktails on the deck.

806 Caroline St. (between Margaret and Williams sts.). ℂ 305/294-7192. Main courses $13–$22; breakfast $2–$9; lunch $5–$9. DISC, MC, V. Daily 6:30am–10:30pm.

Turtle Kraals Wildlife Grill ✪ *(Finds* *(Kids* SOUTHWESTERN/SEAFOOD You'll join lots of locals in this out-of-the-way converted warehouse with indoor and dockside seating that serves innovative seafood at great prices. Try the twin lobster tails stuffed with mango and crab meat or any of the big quesadillas or fajitas. Kids will like the wildlife exhibits and the very cheesy menu. Blues bands play most nights.

213 Margaret St. (corner of Caroline St.). ℂ 305/294-2640. Main courses $10–$20. DISC, MC, V. Mon–Thurs 11am–10:30pm; Fri–Sat 11am–11pm; Sun noon–10:30pm. Bar closes at midnight.

INEXPENSIVE

Anthony's Cafe ✪ ITALIAN DELI/ROTISSERIE   Although owned and operated by a Greek import, this rustic Italian-style trattoria is a welcome addition to an area crowded with more expensive and less delicious options. Fragrant roasted chicken and overstuffed sandwiches on fresh baked bread are the best choices. Also good are the many salads and daily specials.

1111 Duval St. (at Amelia St.). ℂ 305/296-8899. Breakfast $2–$5; sandwiches and salads $5.50–$7 with a side; hot plates $8–$13. Cash only. Daily 8am–10pm.

Bahama Mama's Kitchen ✪ BAHAMIAN   Sit outside under an umbrella and enjoy the authentic Bahamian dishes made from recipes that have been handed down through owner Corey's family for the past 150 years. Prepared fresh daily, all dishes are created with their special "Bahamian" seasonings. Try the coconut shrimp butterflied, soaked in coconut oil, battered with egg, and then rolled in fresh shredded coconut and deep-fried. The fresh catch of the day comes blackened, broiled, or fried and is served with island plantains, shrimp hash cakes, and crab rice. The service is good and the staff is friendly.

In the Bahama Village Market, 324 Petronia St. ℂ 305/294-3355. Appetizers $4–$7; main courses $9–$13. MC, V. Daily 11am–10pm.

Naked Lunch *(Finds* AMERICAN   To be honest, I have never eaten here. I did, however, have the dubious pleasure of stumbling upon this alley restaurant during Fantasy Fest and discovered that Naked Lunch is Key West's first clothing-optional restaurant. All walks of life come in here, mostly nude. If you're into nude dining, do write and let me know how the food was. 4 Charles St. ℂ **305/296-4565**. Main courses $5–$10. Daily 11am–2am.

PT's Late Night ★ *(Finds* AMERICAN   This place is worth knowing about not only because it's one of the only places in town serving food past 10pm, but also because it happens to serve good food at extremely reasonable prices. PT's is more like a sports bar than a restaurant, and service can be a bit slow and brusque, but you'll enjoy their heaping plates of nachos, sizzling fajitas served with all the trimmings, and superfresh salads—so big they can be a meal in themselves. 920 Caroline St. (at the corner of Margaret St.). ℂ **305/296-4245**. Main courses $6.95–$15. DISC, MC, V. Daily 11am–4am.

KEY WEST AFTER DARK

Duval Street is the Bourbon Street of Florida. Amid the T-shirt shops and clothing boutiques, you'll find bar after bar serving neon-colored frozen drinks to revelers who bounce from one to the next from noon till dawn. Bands and crowds vary from night to night and season to season. Your best bet is to start at Truman Avenue and head up Duval to check them out for yourself. Cover charges are rare, except in gay clubs (see the "The Gay Scene" section below), so stop into a dozen and see which you like. For the most part, Key West is a late-night town, and bars and clubs don't close until around 3 or 4am.

Captain Tony's Saloon   Just around the corner from Duval's beaten path, this smoky old wooden bar is about as authentic as you'll find. It comes complete with old-time regulars who remember the island before cruise ships docked here; they say Hemingway drank, caroused, and even wrote here. The owner, Capt. Tony Tarracino, a former controversial Key West mayor—"immortalized" in Jimmy Buffett's "Last Mango in Paradise"—has recently capitalized on the success of this once-quaint tavern by franchising the place. 428 Greene St. ℂ **305/294-1838**.

Durty Harry's   This large complex features live rock bands almost every night. You can wander to one of the many outdoor bars or head up to Upstairs at Rick's, an indoor/outdoor dance club that gets going late. For the more racy singles or couples, there is also the Red Garter, a pocket-size strip club. The hawker outside reminds couples, in case they've forgotten, that "the family that strips together sticks together." 208 Duval St. ℂ **305/296-4890**.

Sloppy Joe's   You'll have to stop in here just to say you did. Scholars and drunks debate whether this is the same Sloppy Joe's that Hemingway wrote about, but there's no argument that this classic bar's early-20th-century wooden ceiling and cracked-tile floors are Key West originals. There's live music nightly as well as a cigar room and martini bar. 201 Duval St. ℂ **305/294-5717**, ext. 10. www.sloppyjoes.com.

THE GAY SCENE

Key West's bohemian live-and-let-live atmosphere extends to its thriving and quirky gay community. Since Tennessee Williams and before, Key West has provided the perfect backdrop to a gay scene unlike that of many large urban areas. Seamlessly blended with the prevailing culture, there is no "gay ghetto" in Key West, where alternative lifestyles are embraced and even celebrated.

Although restaurants and businesses welcome visitors without discrimination, nightlife *is* inevitably nightlife. In Key West, the best music and dancing can be found at the predominantly gay clubs. While many of the area's other hot spots are geared toward tourists who like to imbibe, the gay clubs are for those who want to rave, gay or not. Covers vary, but are rarely more than $10.

Two adjacent popular late-night spots are the **801 Bourbon Bar/Number One Saloon** (801 Duval St. and 514 Petronia St.; © **305/294-9349** for both), featuring great drag and lots more disco. A mostly male clientele frequents this hot spot from 9pm until 4am. Another Duval Street favorite is **Aqua,** at 711 Duval St. (© **305/292-8500**), where you might catch drag queens belting out torch songs or judges voting on the best package in the wet jockey shorts contest.

Sunday nights are fun at two local spots. **Tea by the Sea,** on the pier at the Atlantic Shores Motel (510 South St.; © **800/520-3559**), attracts a faithful following of regulars and visitors alike. The clothing-optional pool is always an attraction. Show up after 7:30pm. Better known around town as La-Te-Da, **La Terraza de Martí,** the former Key West home of Cuban exile José Martí, at 1125 Duval St. (© **305/296-6706**), is a great spot to gather poolside for the best martini in town—but don't bother with the food. Just upstairs from there is **The Crystal Room** (© **305/296-6706**), with a high-caliber cabaret performance featuring the popular Randy Roberts in the winter.

4 The Dry Tortugas ★★

70 miles W of Key West

Few people realize that the Florida Keys don't end at Key West, since about 70 miles west of there is a chain of seven small islands known as the Dry Tortugas. As long as you have come this far, you might wish to visit them, especially if you're into bird-watching, which is their primary draw.

Ponce de León, who discovered this far-flung cluster of coral keys in 1513, named them "Las Tortugas" because of the many sea turtles, which still flock to the area during the nesting season in the warm summer months. Oceanic charts later carried the preface "dry" to warn mariners that fresh water was unavailable here. Modern intervention has made drinking water available, but little else.

These undeveloped islands make a great day trip for travelers interested in seeing the natural anomalies of the Florida Keys—especially the birds. The Dry Tortugas are nesting grounds and roosting sites for thousands of tropical and subtropical oceanic birds. Visitors will also find a historical fort, good fishing, and terrific snorkeling around shallow reefs.

GETTING THERE
BY BOAT   The **Yankee Fleet,** based in Key West (© **800/634-0939** or 305/ 294-7009; www.yankeefleet.com/KeyWest.cfm), offers day trips from Key West for sightseeing, snorkeling, or both. Cruises leave daily for the 3-hour journey at 7:30am from the Land's End Marina at Margaret Street and travel to Garden Key. Breakfast is served on board. Once on the island, you can join a guided tour of Fort Jefferson or explore it on your own. Boats return to Key West by 7pm. Tours cost $119 per person, including breakfast, lunch, dinner, and snorkeling equipment; $79 for children 16 and under; $109 for seniors, students, and military personnel. Phone for reservations.

The **Sunny Days Catamarans' "Fast Cat"** (© **800/236-7937** or 305/292-6100) is faster, quieter, and more high-tech than the loud Yankee fleet, as well as a better value. Included in the $95 round-trip adult fare ($65 for children) is a continental breakfast and a buffet lunch with cold cuts, fresh veggies, fruits, salads, unlimited sodas and water, plus an island tour and a snorkeling excursion to a shipwreck in 5 to 20 feet of water. The high-speed power cat leaves Key West for Garden Key at 8am and returns by 6pm.

BY PLANE   Seaplanes of Key West, based at Key West Airport (✆ **800/ 950-2-FLY** or 305/294-0709; www.seaplanesofkeywest.com), offers daily excursions. Weather permitting, flights depart at 8 and 10am, noon, and 2pm. The 40-minute trip at about 500 feet offers a great introduction to the Dry Tortugas. Fares, which include snorkeling equipment and a cooler for use on the island, start at $179 for adults, $129 for kids 12 and under, and $99 for kids 6 and under for a half day; and $305 for adults, $225 for kids 12 and under, and $170 for kids 6 and under for a full day. Bring a bathing suit, snorkeling equipment, and some snacks to enjoy on these remote and beautiful islands. If you want to stay overnight at Fort Jefferson, it costs $329 for adults, $235 for kids 12 and under, and $179 for kids 6 and under.

EXPLORING THE DRY TORTUGAS

Of the seven islands that make up the Dry Tortugas, Garden Key is the most visited, because it is where Fort Jefferson and the visitor center are located. Loggerhead Key, Middle Key, and East Key are open only during the day and are for hiking. Bush Key is for the birds—literally! It's a nesting area for birds only, though it is open from October to January for special excursions. Hospital and Long Keys are closed to the public.

Fort Jefferson, a huge six-sided 19th-century fortress, is built almost at the water's edge of Garden Key, giving the appearance that it floats in the middle of the sea. The monumental structure is surrounded by formidable 8-foot-thick walls that rise up from the sand to a height of nearly 50 feet. Impressive archways, stonework, and parapets make this 150-year-old monument a grand sight. With the invention of the rifled cannon, the fort's masonry construction became obsolete and the building was never completed. For 10 years, however, from 1863 to 1873, Fort Jefferson served as a prison, a kind of "Alcatraz East." Among its prisoners were four of the "Lincoln Conspirators," including Samuel A. Mudd, the doctor who set the broken leg of fugitive assassin John Wilkes Booth. In 1935, Fort Jefferson became a national monument administered by the National Park Service. Today, however, Fort Jefferson is struggling to resist erosion from the salt and sea as iron used in gun openings and shutters in the fort's walls has accelerated the deterioration and the structure's openings need to be rebricked. As a result, the National Park Service has identified the Fort as the recipient of a $15 million face-lift, a project that may take up to a decade to complete. "We are probably going to be replacing this brick the way it was originally constructed," said Michael Jester, facility manager for the Everglades and Dry Tortugas national parks. "It's a very manual project. Bricks are placed one at a time in the wall. We can't do it any better or faster." For more information about Fort Jefferson and the Dry Tortugas, call the **Everglades National Park Service** at ✆ **305/242-7700** or visit www.fortjefferson.com. Fort Jefferson is open during daylight hours on Garden Key, and there is a self-guided trail that interprets the history of human presence in the Dry Tortugas while leading visitors through the fort.

OUTDOOR PURSUITS

BIRD-WATCHING   Bring your binoculars and your bird books: Bird-watching is *the* reason to visit this little cluster of tropical islands. The Dry Tortugas, uniquely situated in the middle of the migration flyway between North and South America, serve as an important rest stop for the more than 200 winged varieties that pass through here annually. The season peaks from mid-March to mid-May, when thousands of birds show up, but many species from the West Indies can be found here year-round.

DIVING & SNORKELING   The warm, clear, shallow waters of the Dry Tortugas produce optimum conditions for snorkeling and scuba diving. Four endangered species of sea turtles—the green, leatherback, Atlantic ridley, and hawksbill—can be found here, along with myriad marine species. The region just outside the seawall of Fort Jefferson is excellent for underwater touring; an abundant variety of fish, coral, and more live in just 3 or 4 feet of water.

FISHING   Fishing for snapper, tarpon, grouper, and other fish used to be popular here until July 2001, when a federal law closed off all fishing in a 90-square-mile tract of open ocean called The Tortugas North and a 61-square-mile tract of open ocean called The Tortugas South, which basically prohibits all fishing in order to preserve the dwindling population of fish (a result of commercial fishermen and environmental factors). Instead, head to Key West.

CAMPING

The rustic beauty of tiny Garden Key (the only island of the Dry Tortugas where campers are allowed to pitch their tents) is a camper's dream. Don't worry about sharing your site with noisy RVs or motor homes; they can't get here. The abundance of birds doesn't make it quiet, but camping here—a stone's throw from the water—is as picturesque as it gets. Picnic tables, cooking grills, and toilets are provided, but there are no showers. All supplies must be packed in and out. Sites are $3 per person per night and are available on a first-come, first-served basis. With only 10 sites, they book up fast. For more information, call the **National Park Service** at © 305/242-7700.

7

The Everglades & Biscayne National Park

President Harry S. Truman once declared the Everglades "an irreplaceable primitive area." And while those words don't exactly do the Everglades and its surrounding Biscayne National Park justice, he clarified, saying, "Here are no lofty peaks seeking the sky, no mighty glaciers or rushing streams wearing away the uplifted land. Here is land, tranquil in its quiet beauty, serving not as the source of water, but as the last receiver of it. To its natural abundance we owe the spectacular plant and animal life that distinguishes this place from all others in our country."

There's no better reality show than the one that exists in the Everglades, really. Up close and personal views of alligators, crocodiles, and bona fide wildlife—not the kind you'd find on, say, South Beach, after midnight— make for a very interesting, photo opportunistic experience even the Crocodile Hunter would find hard to mimic on his show.

Tourists who come to South Florida really shouldn't leave the area without taking time to see some of the wild plant and animal life in the swampy Everglades and the underwater treasures of Biscayne National Park.

1 A Glimpse of Everglades National Park ★★

35 miles SW of Miami

Before going, my conception of the Everglades was that it was one big swamp swarming with ominous creatures. For someone who'd rather endure an endless series of root canals than audition for a role on *Survivor* (the closest I'd ever been to nature was sleep-away camp), the Everglades may as well have been the *Never*glades. That is, until I finally decided to venture there. To my surprise, and contrary to popular belief, the Everglades isn't really a swamp at all, but one of the country's most fascinating natural resources.

For first-timers or those with dubious athletic skills, the best way to see the 'glades is probably via airboats, which actually aren't allowed in the park proper, but cut through the saw grass on the park's outskirts, taking you past countless birds, alligators, crocodiles, deer, and raccoons. A walk on one of the park's many trails will provide you with a different vantage point: up-close interaction with an assortment of tame wildlife. But the absolute best way to see the 'glades is via canoe, where you can get incredibly close to nature. Whichever method you choose, I guarantee you will marvel at the sheer beauty of the Everglades. Despite the multitude of mosquito bites (the bugs seem to be immune to repellent—wear long pants and cover your arms, if possible), an Everglades experience will definitely contribute to a newfound appreciation for Florida's natural (and beautiful) wonderland.

Everglades National Park

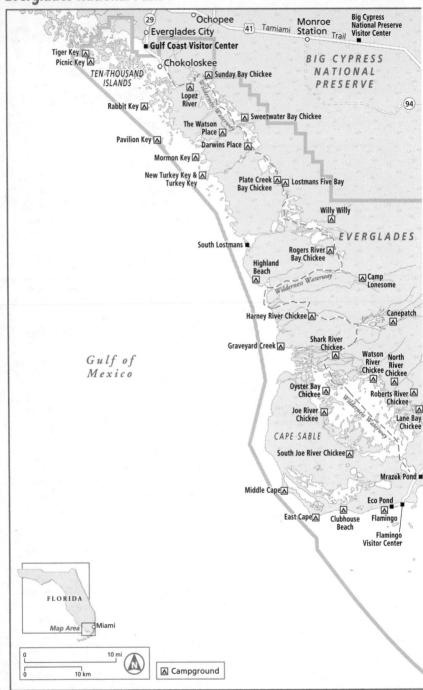

Tiger Key
Picnic Key
TEN THOUSAND ISLANDS

29
Ochopee
Everglades City
Gulf Coast Visitor Center
Chokoloskee

Tamiami
41
Monroe Station
Trail

Big Cypress National Preserve Visitor Center

BIG CYPRESS NATIONAL PRESERVE

Sunday Bay Chickee

Lopez River

Rabbit Key

94

The Watson Place
Darwins Place

Sweetwater Bay Chickee

Pavilion Key

Mormon Key

New Turkey Key & Turkey Key

Plate Creek Bay Chickee
Lostmans Five Bay

EVERGLADES

Willy Willy

South Lostmans

Rogers River Bay Chickee

Highland Beach

Wilderness Waterway
Camp Lonesome

Harney River Chickee

Canepatch

Graveyard Creek

Shark River Chickee

Watson River Chickee
North River Chickee

Gulf of Mexico

Oyster Bay Chickee

Roberts River Chickee

Joe River Chickee

Lane Bay Chickee

CAPE SABLE

South Joe River Chickee

Mrazek Pond

Middle Cape

Eco Pond
Flamingo

East Cape
Clubhouse Beach

Flamingo Visitor Center

FLORIDA

Map Area
Miami

0   10 mi
0   10 km

N

△ Campground

220

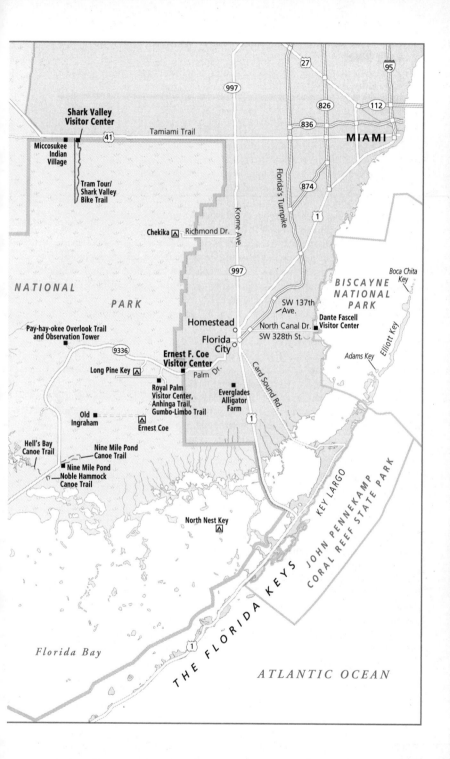

Shark Valley
Visitor Center

Miccosukee
Indian
Village

Tamiami Trail

41

Tram Tour/
Shark Valley
Bike Trail

997

27

826

112

836

MIAMI

Florida's Turnpike

874

1

Chekika △ Richmond Dr.

Krome Ave.

997

SW 137th
Ave.

Boca Chita
Key

BISCAYNE
NATIONAL
PARK

Dante Fascell
Visitor Center

Elliott Key

NATIONAL

PARK

Pay-hay-okee Overlook Trail
and Observation Tower

Homestead

North Canal Dr.
SW 328th St.

Adams Key

9336

Florida
City

Ernest F. Coe
Visitor Center

Long Pine Key △

Palm Dr.

Royal Palm
Visitor Center,
Anhinga Trail,
Gumbo-Limbo Trail

Everglades
Alligator
Farm

Card Sound Rd.

Old
Ingraham

△
Ernest Coe

1

Hell's Bay
Canoe Trail

Nine Mile Pond
Canoe Trail

Nine Mile Pond
Noble Hammock
Canoe Trail

North Nest Key
△

KEY LARGO

JOHN PENNEKAMP
CORAL REEF STATE PARK

Florida Bay

THE FLORIDA KEYS

1

ATLANTIC OCEAN

221

Lazy River

It takes a month for 1 gallon of water to move through Everglades National Park.

This vast and unusual ecosystem is actually a shallow, 40-mile-wide, slow-moving river. Rarely more than knee-deep, the water is the lifeblood of this wilderness, and the subtle shifts in water level dictate the life cycle of the native plants and animals. In 1947, 1.5 million acres—less than 20% of the Everglades' wilderness—were established as Everglades National Park. At that time, few lawmakers understood how neighboring ecosystems relate to each other. Consequently, the park is heavily affected by surrounding territories and is at the butt end of every environmental insult that occurs upstream in Miami.

While there has been a marked decrease in the indigenous wildlife here, Everglades National Park nevertheless remains one of the few places where you can see dozens of endangered species in their natural habitat, including the swallowtail butterfly, American crocodile, leatherback turtle, southern bald eagle, West Indian manatee, and Florida panther.

Take your time on the trails, and a hypnotic beauty begins to unfold. Follow the rustling of a bush, and you might see a small green tree frog or tiny brown anole lizard, with its bright-red–spotted throat. Crane your neck to see around a bend and discover a delicate, brightly painted mule-ear orchid.

The slow and subtle splendor of this exotic land may not be immediately appealing to kids raised on video games and rapid-fire commercials, but they'll certainly remember the experience and thank you for it later. Meanwhile, you'll find plenty of dramatic fun around the park, such as airboat rides, alligator wrestling, and biking, to keep the kids satisfied for at least a day.

JUST THE FACTS

GETTING THERE & ACCESS POINTS   Although the Everglades may seem overwhelmingly large and unapproachable, it's easy to get to the park's two main areas—the northern section, which is accessible via Shark Valley and Everglades City, or the southern section, accessible through the Ernest F. Coe Visitor Center, near Homestead and Florida City.

Northern Entrances   A popular day trip for Miamians, **Shark Valley,** a 15-mile paved loop road, with an observation tower in the middle of the loop, overlooking the pulsating heart of the Everglades, is the easiest and most scenic way to explore the Everglades. Just 25 miles west of the Florida Turnpike, Shark Valley is best reached via the Tamiami Trail, South Florida's pre-turnpike, two-lane road, which cuts across the southern part of the state along the park's northern border. Roadside attractions (boat rides and alligator farms, for example) along the Trail are operated by the Miccosukee Indian Village and are fun and worth a quick stop. An excellent tram tour (leaving from the Shark Valley Visitor Center) goes deep into the park along a trail that's also terrific for biking. This is also the best way to reach the park's only accommodation (and full-service outfitters), the Flamingo Lodge. Shark Valley is about an hour's drive from Miami.

A little less than 10 miles west along the Tamiami Trail from Shark Valley, you'll discover the **Big Cypress National Preserve,** in which stretches of vibrant green cypress and pine trees make for a fabulous Kodak moment. If you pick up State Road 29 and head south from the Tamiami Trail, you'll hit a modified version of civilization in the form of Everglades City (where the Everglades meet the Gulf of Mexico) and see another entrance to the park and the **Gulf Coast Visitor Center.** From Miami to Shark Valley: Go west on I-395 to State Road 821 south (the Florida Tpk.). Take the U.S. 41/SW 8th Street (Tamiami Trail) exit. The Shark Valley entrance is just 25 miles west. To get to Everglades City, continue west on the Tamiami Trail and head south on State Road 29. Everglades City is approximately a 2½-hour drive from Miami, but because it is scenic, it may take longer if you stop or slow down to view your surroundings.

Southern Entrance—via Homestead & Florida City   If you're in a rush to hit the 'glades and don't care about the scenic route, this is your best bet. Just southeast of Homestead and Florida City, off of State Road 9336, the southern access to the park will bring you directly to the Ernest F. Coe Visitor Center. Right inside the park, 4 miles beyond the Ernest F. Coe Visitor Center, is the Royal Palm Visitor Center, which is the starting point for the two most popular walking trails—Gumbo Limbo and Anhinga, on which you will witness a plethora of birds and wildlife roaming freely, unperturbed by their human voyeurs. If you go 13 miles west of the Ernest F. Coe Visitor Center, you will hit the Pa-hay-okee Overlook Trail, which is worth a trek across the boardwalk to reach the observation tower, over which vultures and hawks hover protectively amidst a resplendent, picturesque, bird's-eye view of the Everglades. From Miami to the southern entrance: Go west on I-395 to State Road 821 south (Florida Tpk.). The Turnpike will end in Florida City. Take your first right turn through the center of town (you can't miss it) and follow the signs to the park entrance on State Road 9336. The Ernest F. Coe Visitor Center is about 1½ hours from Miami.

VISITOR CENTERS & INFORMATION   General inquiries and specific questions should be directed to **Everglades National Park Headquarters,** 40001 S.R. 9336, Homestead, FL 33034 (© **305/242-7700**). Ask for a copy of *Parks and Preserves,* a free newspaper that's filled with up-to-date information about goings-on in the Everglades. Headquarters is staffed by helpful phone operators daily from 8:30am to 4:30pm. You can also try www.nps.gov/ever/visit/index.htm.

Note that all hours listed are for the high season, generally November through May. During the slow summer months, many offices and outfitters keep abbreviated hours. Always call ahead to confirm hours of operation.

Thirty-eight miles from the main entrance, at the park's southern access, is the **Flamingo Visitor Center,** which offers natural-history exhibits and information on Flamingo's visitor services.

Especially since its recent expansion, the **Ernest F. Coe Visitor Center,** located at the Park Headquarters' entrance, west of Homestead and Florida City, is the best place for gathering information for your trip. In addition to information on tours and boat rentals, and free brochures outlining trails, wildlife, and activities, you will also find state-of-the-art educational displays, films, and interactive exhibits. A gift shop sells postcards, film, unusual gift items, an impressive selection of books about the Everglades, and a supply of your most important gear: insect repellent. The shop is open from 8am to 5pm daily.

The **Royal Palm Visitor Center,** a small nature museum located 3 miles past the park's main entrance, is a smaller information center. The museum is not great (there are displays with recorded messages interpreting the park's ecosystem), but the center is the departure point for the popular Anhinga and Gumbo Limbo Trails. Open daily from 8am to 4pm.

Knowledgeable rangers, who provide brochures and personal insight into the park's activities, also staff the **Shark Valley Visitor Center,** at the park's northern entrance, and the **Flamingo Visitor Center.** Both are open daily from 8:30am to 5pm.

ENTRANCE FEES, PERMITS & REGULATIONS   Permits and passes can be purchased only at the main park, Chekika, or Shark Valley entrance station.

Even if you are just visiting the park for an afternoon, you'll need to buy a 7-day permit, which costs $10 per vehicle. Pedestrians and cyclists are charged $5 each.

An Everglades Park Pass, valid for a year's worth of unlimited admissions, is available for $25. You may also purchase a 12-month National Parks Pass for $50, which is valid for entrance into any U.S. national park. U.S. citizens aged 62 and older pay only $10 for a Golden Age Passport—that's valid for life. A Golden Access Passport is available free to U.S. citizens with disabilities.

Permits are required for campers to stay overnight either in the backcountry or in the primitive campsites. See "Camping in the Everglades," on p. 229.

Those who want to fish without a charter captain must obtain a standard State of Florida saltwater fishing license. These are available in the park at Flamingo Lodge or at any tackle shop or sporting goods store nearby. Nonresidents will pay $17 for a 7-day license or $7 for 3 days. Florida residents can get a fishing license good for the whole year for $14. Snook and crawfish licenses must be purchased separately at a cost of $2.

Charter captains carry vessel licenses that cover all paying passengers, but ask to be sure. Freshwater fishing licenses are available at various bait-and-tackle shops outside the park at the same rates as those offered inside the park. A good one nearby is **Don's Bait & Tackle,** located at 30710 S. Federal Hwy., in Homestead right on U.S. 1 (© **305/247-6616**). *Note:* Most of the area's freshwater fishing, limited to murky canals and artificial lakes near housing developments, is hardly worth the trouble when so much good saltwater fishing is available.

SEASONS   There are two distinct seasons in the Everglades: high season and mosquito season. High season is also dry season and lasts from late November to May. Despite the bizarre cold and wet weather patterns that El Niño brought in 1998, most winters here are warm, sunny, and breezy—a good combination for keeping the bugs away. This is the best time to visit because low water levels attract the largest variety of wading birds and their predators. As the dry season wanes, wildlife follows the receding water; and by the end of May, the only living things you are sure to spot will cause you to itch. The worst, called "no-see-ums," are not even swattable. If you choose to visit during the buggy season, be vigilant in applying bug spray.

Also, realize that many establishments and operators either close or curtail offerings in the summer, so always call ahead to check schedules.

RANGER PROGRAMS   More than 50 ranger programs, free with admission, are offered each month during high season and give visitors an opportunity to gain an expert's perspective. Ranger-led walks and talks are offered year-round from the Royal Palm Visitor Center, west of the main entrance, and at the Flamingo and Gulf Coast Visitor Centers, as well as the Shark Valley Visitor Center during the winter months. Park rangers tend to be helpful, well informed, and good-humored. Some programs occur regularly, such as Royal Palm Visitor Center's Glade Glimpses, a walking tour during which rangers point out flora and fauna and discuss issues affecting the Everglades' survival. These tours are scheduled at 12:30pm daily. The Anhinga Ambles, a similar program that takes place on the Anhinga Trail, starts at 10:30am or 3:30pm daily.

Since times, programs, and locations vary from month to month, check a schedule, available at any of the visitor centers (see above).

SAFETY There are many dangers inherent in this vast wilderness area. *Always* let someone know your itinerary before you set out on an extended hike. It's mandatory that you file an itinerary when camping overnight in the backcountry (which you can do when you apply for your overnight permit at either the Flamingo Visitor Center or the Gulf Coast Visitor Center). When you're on the water, watch for weather changes; severe thunderstorms and high winds often develop rapidly. Swimming is not recommended because of the presence of alligators, sharks, and barracudas. Watch out for the region's four indigenous poisonous snakes: diamondback and pygmy rattlesnakes, coral snakes (identifiable by their colorful rings), and water moccasins (which swim on the surface of the water). Again, bring insect repellent to ward off mosquitoes and biting flies. First aid is available from park rangers. The nearest hospital is in Homestead, 10 miles from the park's main entrance.

SEEING THE HIGHLIGHTS

Shark Valley, a 15-mile paved road (ideal for biking) through the Everglades, provides a fine introduction to the wonder of the Everglades, but don't plan on spending more than a few hours there. Bicycling or taking a guided tram tour (p. 229) are fantastic ways to see the park's highlights.

If you want to see a greater array of plant and animal life, make sure that you venture into the park through the main entrance, pick up a trail map, and dedicate at least a day to exploring from there.

Stop first along the Anhinga and Gumbo Limbo trails, which start right next to one another, 3 miles from the park's main entrance. These trails provide a thorough introduction to Everglades flora and fauna and are highly recommended to first-time visitors. Each of them is a ½-mile round-trip. **Gumbo Limbo Trail** (my pick for best walking trail in the Everglades) meanders through a gorgeous shaded, junglelike hammock of gumbo limbo trees, royal palms, ferns, orchids, air plants, and a general blanket of vegetation, though it doesn't put you in close contact with much wildlife. **Anhinga Trail** is one of the most popular trails in the park because of its abundance of wildlife: There's more water and wildlife in this area of the park than in most parts of the Everglades, especially during dry season. Alligators, lizards, turtles, river otters, herons, egrets, and other animals abound, making this one of the best trails for seeing wildlife. Arrive early to spot the widest selection of exotic birds, like the Anhinga bird, the Trail's namesake, a large black fishing bird so accustomed to humans that many of them build their nests in plain view. Take your time—at least an hour is recommended for each trail. Both are wheelchair accessible. If you treat the trails and modern boardwalk as pathways to get through quickly, rather than destinations to experience and savor slowly, you'll miss out on the still beauty and hidden treasures that await.

If you want to get closer to nature, a few hours in a canoe along any of the trails allows paddlers the chance to sense the park's fluid motion and to become a part of the ecosphere. Visitors who choose this option end up feeling more like explorers than merely observers. (See "Sports & Outdoor Activities," below.)

No matter which option you choose (and there are many), I strongly recommend staying for the 7pm program, available during high season at the Long Pine Key Amphitheater. This talk and slide show, given by one of the park's rangers, will give you a detailed overview of the park's history, natural resources, wildlife, and threats to its survival.

SPORTS & OUTDOOR ACTIVITIES

BIKING   The relatively flat 38-mile-long paved Main Park Road is great for biking because of the multitude of hardwood hammocks (treelike islands or dense stands of hardwood trees that grow only a few inches above land) and a dwarf cypress forest (stunted and thinly distributed cypress trees, which grow in poor soil on drier land), but Shark Valley is the best biking trail by far. Expect to spend 2 to 3 hours along either.

If the park isn't flooded from excess rain (which it often is, especially in spring), Shark Valley in Everglades National Park is South Florida's most scenic bicycle trail. Many locals haul their bikes out to the 'glades for a relaxing day of wilderness-trail riding. You'll share the flat, paved road only with other bikers and a menagerie of wildlife. (Don't be surprised to see a gator lounging in the sun or a deer munching on some grass. Otters, turtles, alligators, and snakes are common companions in the Shark Valley area.) There are no shortcuts, so if you become tired or are unable to complete the entire 15-mile trip, turn around and return on the same road. Allow 2 to 3 hours to bike the entire loop.

Those who love to mountain bike, and who prefer solitude, might check out the **Southern Glades Trail,** a 14-mile-long unpaved trail opened in late 1998 that is lined with native trees and teeming with wildlife such as deer, alligators, and the occasional snake. The remote trail runs along the C-111 canal, off State Road 9336 and Southwest 217th Street.

You can rent bikes at the Flamingo Lodge, Marina, and Outpost Resort (see "Where to Stay," below) for $17 per 24 hours, $14 per full day, $8.50 per half day (any 4-hr. period), and $3 per hour. A $50 deposit is required for each rental. Rentals can be picked up from 7am and the bikes have to be returned by 5pm. Bicycles are also available from Shark Valley Tram Tours, at the park's Shark Valley entrance (© **305/221-8455**), for $5.25 per hour; rentals can be picked up anytime between 8:30am and 3pm and must be returned by 4pm.

BIRD-WATCHING   More than 350 species of birds make their homes in the Everglades. Tropical birds from the Caribbean and temperate species from North America can be found here, along with exotics that have blown in from more distant regions. Eco and Mrazek ponds, located near Flamingo, are two of the best places for birding, especially in early morning or late afternoon in the dry winter months. Pick up a free birding checklist from a visitor center (see "Just the Facts," on p. 222), and ask there what's been spotted in recent days.

CANOEING   Canoeing through the Everglades may be one of the most serene, surprisingly diverse adventures you'll ever have. From a canoe (where you're incredibly close to the water level), your vantage point is priceless. Canoers in the 'glades can coexist with the gators and birds there in a way no one else can; they behave as if you are part of the ecosystem—something that can't happen on an airboat. A ranger-guided boat tour is your best bet and costs $20, plus a required deposit. As always, a ranger will help you understand the surroundings and give you an education on what you're seeing.

Everglades National Park's longest "trails" are designed for boat and canoe travel, and many are marked as clearly as walking trails. The **Noble Hammock Canoe Trail,** a 2-mile loop, takes 1 to 2 hours and is recommended for beginning canoers. The **Hell's Bay Canoe Trail,** a 3- to 6-mile course for hardier paddlers, takes 2 to 6 hours, depending on how far you choose to go. Park rangers can recommend other trails that best suit your abilities, time limitations, and interests.

You can rent a canoe at the Flamingo Lodge, Marina, and Outpost Resort (p. 229) for $50 for 24 hours, $40 per full day (any 8-hr. period), $30 per half day (any 4-hr. period), and $12 per hour. Skiffs, kayaks, and tandem kayaks are also available. The concessionaire will shuttle your party to the trail head of your choice and pick you up afterward. Rental facilities are open daily from 6am to 8pm.

Overnight canoe rentals are available for $50 to $60. During ideal weather conditions (stay away during bug season!), you can paddle right out to the Gulf and camp on the beach. However, Gulf waters at beach sites can be extremely rough, and people in small watercraft such as a canoe should exercise caution.

You can also take a canoe tour from the Parks Docks on Chokoloskee Causeway on State Road 29, ½ mile south of the traffic circle at the ranger station in Everglades City. Call Everglades National Park Boat Tours at (C) **800/445-7724.**

FISHING   About one-third of Everglades National Park is open water. Freshwater fishing is popular in brackish **Nine-Mile Pond** (25 miles from the main entrance) and other spots along the Main Park Road, but because of the high mercury levels found in the Everglades, freshwater fishers are warned not to eat their catch. Before casting, check in at a visitor center, as many of the park's lakes are preserved for observation only. Fishing licenses are required (see "Just the Facts" on p. 222 for more information).

Saltwater anglers will find snapper and sea trout plentiful. Charter boats and guides are available at Flamingo Lodge, Marina, and Outpost Resort (p. 229). Phone for information and reservations.

MOTORBOATING   Motorboating around the Everglades seems like a great way to see plants and animals in remote habitats, and, indeed, is an interesting and fulfilling experience as you throttle into nature. However, environmentalists are taking stock of the damage motorboats (especially airboats) inflict on the delicate ecosystem. If you choose to motor, remember that most of the areas near land are "no wake" zones and that, for the protection of nesting birds, landing is prohibited on most of the little mangrove islands. Motorboating is allowed in certain areas such as Florida Bay, the backcountry toward Everglades City, and the Ten Thousand Islands area. In all the freshwater lakes, however, motorboats are prohibited if they're above 5 horsepower. There's a long list of restrictions and restricted areas, so get a copy of the park's boating rules from National Park Headquarters before setting out (see "Just the Facts," earlier).

The Everglades' only marina—accommodating about 50 boats with electric and water hookups—is the Flamingo Lodge, Marina, and Outpost Resort, in Flamingo. The well-marked channel to the Flamingo is accessible to boats with a maximum 4-foot draft and is open year-round. Reservations can be made through the marina store ((C) **239/695-3101,** ext. 304). Skiffs with 15-horsepower motors are available for rent. These low-power boats cost $90 per day, $65 per half day (any 5-hr. period), and $22 per hour. A $125 deposit is required.

ORGANIZED TOURS
AIRBOAT TOURS   Shallow-draft, fan-powered airboats were invented in the Everglades by frog hunters who were tired of poling through the brushes. Airboats cut through the saw grass and are sort of like hydraulic boats in which at high enough speeds, the boat actually lifts above the saw grass and into the air. And even though airboats are the most efficient (not to mention fast and fun!) way to get around, they are not permitted in the park (these shallow-bottom runabouts tend to inflict severe damage on animals and plants). Just outside the boundaries of the Everglades, however, you'll find a number of outfitters offering rides (consider bringing earplugs; these high-speed boats are loud).

One of the best airboat outfitters is **Gator Park,** 12 miles west of the Florida Turnpike at 24050 SW 8th St. (© **305/559-2255**), which, despite its touristy name, happens to be one of the most informative and entertaining around, not to mention one of the only airboat tour operators that gives out free earplugs. Request, if you can, Rick, the best tour guide there, who deserves a medal for getting out into the water and poking around a massive alligator even though he's not really supposed to. After the boat ride, there's a free interactive wildlife show that features alligator wrestling and several other frightening acts involving scorpions. Take note of the gorgeous peacocks that live in the trees here. Admission for the boat ride and show is $15. Kids under 6 ride free. Airboats depart every 20 minutes, so there's no worrying about missing the boat. Open daily 9am to 7pm.

Another one we recommend is **Coopertown Airboat Tours** (© **305/226-6048**), located about 11 miles west of Florida's Turnpike on the Tamiami Trail (US41). Here, the super-friendly staff has helped the company garner the title of "Florida's Best" by the *Miami Herald* for 40 years in a row. You never know what you're going to see, but with great guides, you're sure to see *something* of interest on the 9-mile roundtrip, 40-minute tours. There's also a restaurant and a small gator farm on the premises. Airboat rides cost $14 for anyone over 12, $8 for children 7 to 11, and are free for those 6 and under. Open daily from 8am to 6pm (tours leave frequently).

Airboat rides are also offered at the **Miccosukee Indian Village,** just west of the Shark Valley entrance on U.S. 41/the Tamiami Trail and MM 70 (© **305/223-8380**). The price is $10. However, *be warned and advised:* We are not recommending this particular outfit over others—they are merely the ones closest to the Shark Valley entrance. As always, the quality of your tour is only going to be as good as the quality of your tour guide, and, unfortunately, we have gotten some complaints about the Miccosukee tours.

The **Everglades Alligator Farm,** 4 miles south of Palm Drive on Southwest 192nd Avenue (© **305/247-2628**), offers half-hour guided airboat tours from 9am until 6pm daily. The price, which includes admission to the park, is $17 for adults, $10 for children 4 to 11, and free for children 3 and under. Prices are less for admission without the airboat ride. Another reputable company is **Captain Doug's,** located 35 miles south of Naples and 1 mile past the bridge in Everglades City (© **800/282-9194**).

CANOE TOURS A fabulous way to explore the Everglades Backcountry is via canoe. Slink through the mangroves, across saw grass prairies, or even walk the sands of the unfettered 10,000 Islands. Expert guides will lead you in the right direction. Contact **North American Canoe Tours** (© **239/695-3299**) at the Ivey House B&B (p. 231).

ECO TOURS Although it's fascinating to explore on your own, it would be a shame for you to tour the Everglades without a clue as to what you're seeing. It's a lot more than saw grass and alligators in the 'glades backcountry, which is why **Everglades Rentals and Eco Adventures** (© **239/695-3299**), located within the Ivey House B & B (p. 231), is there to help guide, explain, entertain, and clear up key issues like the differences between alligators and crocodiles or swamps and the Florida Everglades.

MOTORBOAT TOURS Both Florida Bay and backcountry tours are offered at the Flamingo Lodge, Marina, and Outpost Resort (p. 229). Florida Bay tours cruise nearby estuaries and sandbars, while six-passenger backcountry boats visit smaller sloughs. Passengers can expect to see birds and a variety of other animals (I once saw a raccoon and some wild pigs). Both are available in 1½- and 2-hour versions that cost $12 or $18 for adults, $7 or $12 for children ages 6 through 13, free for those under 6. Tours depart throughout the day, and reservations are recommended. There are also charter-fishing and sightseeing boats that can be booked through the resort's main reservation number (✆ **239/695-3101**).

TRAM TOURS   At the park's Shark Valley entrance, open-air tram buses take visitors on 2-hour naturalist-led tours that delve 7½ miles into the wilderness and make up the best quick introduction you can get to the Everglades. At the trail's midsection, passengers can disembark and climb a 65-foot observation tower that offers good views of the 'glades, though the tower on the Pa-hay-okee trail is better. Visitors will see plenty of wildlife and endless acres of saw grass. Tours run December through April daily on the hour between 9am and 4pm and May through November at 9:30 and 11am and 1 and 3pm, and are sometimes stalled by flooding or particularly heavy mosquito infestation. Reservations are recommended from December to March. The cost is $12 for adults, $7.25 for children 12 and under, and $11 for seniors. For further information, contact **Shark Valley Tram Tours** at ✆ **305/221-8455.**

WHERE TO STAY

The only lodging in the park proper is the Flamingo Lodge, a fairly priced and very recommendable option. However, there are a few hotels just outside the park that are even cheaper. A $45 million casino hotel (✆ **877/242-6464;** www. miccosukee.com) was built adjacent to the Miccosukee bingo and gaming hall on the northern edge of the park. And although bugs can be a major nuisance, especially in the warm months, camping (the best way to fully experience South Florida's wilderness) is really the way to go in this very primitive environment.

LODGING IN EVERGLADES NATIONAL PARK

Flamingo Lodge, Marina, and Outpost Resort ★★   The Flamingo Lodge is the only lodging actually located within the boundaries of Everglades National Park. This woodsy, sprawling complex offers rooms (overlooking the Florida Bay) in either a two-story simple motel or the lodge. Either option feels very much like being at summer camp, with a few more amenities. Rooms are your standard, cookie-cutter, motel-style rooms, with functional bathrooms. No luxury here, but it's nonetheless a comfort for those who'd rather not experience the great outdoors while they sleep. More interesting than the actual motel, however, are the visitors who crop up on the lawn—alligators, raccoons, and other nomadic creatures. The hotel is open year-round, although the restaurant (p. 233) closes in the summer.

1 Flamingo Lodge Hwy., Flamingo, FL 33034. ✆ **800/600-3813** or 239/695-3101. Fax 239/695-3921. www.flamingolodge.com. 97 units. Winter $79–$95 double, $89–$105 triple, $99–$115 quad, $110–$145 suite, $99–$135 cottage; off-season $68 double, $78 triple, $88 quad, $102 suite, $92 cottage. Rates for cottages or suites are for 1–4 people. Children under 17 stay free. AE, DC, DISC, MC. Take Florida Tpk. south to Florida City; exit on U.S. 1. At 4-way intersection, turn right onto Palm Dr.; continue for 3 miles and turn left at Robert Is Here fruit stand. Turn right at the 3-way intersection. The park entrance is 3 miles ahead. Continue for about 38 miles more to reach lodge. **Amenities:** Waterside bar and restaurant; freshwater swimming pool; bike, canoe, and kayak rentals; marina with boat tours; boat rentals; houseboat and fishing charters; coin-op washers and dryers; convenience store. *In room:* A/C, TV in standard rooms and suites but not in cottages, kitchen in cottages and suites only.

CAMPING IN THE EVERGLADES

Campgrounds are available year-round in Flamingo and Long Pine Key. Both have drinking water, picnic tables, charcoal grills, bathrooms, and tent and trailer pads, and welcome RVs (Flamingo allows up to 40-ft. vehicles while Long Pine Key accepts up to 60 footers), though there are no electrical hookups.

Flamingo has cold-water showers; Long Pine Key does not have showers or hookups for showers. Private ground fires are not permitted, but supervised campfire programs are conducted during winter months. Long Pine Key and Flamingo are popular and require reservations in advance. Reservations for Flamingo and Long Pine may be made through the National Park Reservations Service at © **800/365-CAMP** or online (from 10am–10pm) at www.nps.gov/ ever/visit/camping.htm. Campsites are $14 per night with a 14-day consecutive stay limit, 30 days a year maximum.

Camping is also available in the **backcountry** (those remote areas accessible only by boat, foot, or canoe—basically most of the park) year-round on a first-come, first-served basis. Campers must register with park rangers/get a free permit (see the section on "Safety," on p. 225) in person or by telephone no less than 24 hours before the start of their trip. For more information, contact the Gulf Coast Visitor Center (© **239/695-3311**) or the Flamingo Visitor Center (© **239/695-2945**), which are the only two places that give out these permits. Once you have one, camping sites cost $14 (with a maximum of 8 people per site) or $28 for a group site (maximum of 15 people). Campers can use only designated campsites, which are plentiful and well marked on visitor maps.

Many backcountry sites are *chickee huts*—covered wooden platforms (with toilets) on stilts. They're accessible only by canoe and can accommodate free-standing tents (without stakes). Ground sites are located along interior bays and rivers, and beach camping is also popular. In summer especially, mosquito repellent is necessary gear.

LODGING IN EVERGLADES CITY

Since Everglades City is 35 miles southeast of Naples and 83 miles west of Miami, many people choose to explore this western entrance to Everglades National Park, located off the Tamiami Trail, on State Road 29. An annual seafood festival held the first weekend in February is a major event that draws hordes of people. Everglades City (the gateway to the Ten Thousand Islands), where the 'glades meet the Gulf of Mexico, is the closest thing you'll get to civilization in South Florida's swampy frontier, with a few tourist traps—er, shops, a restaurant, and two bed-and-breakfasts (see below).

Everglades Vacation Rentals and Day Spa ★★★ *Finds*   This very cute bed-and-breakfast is right on the money, as far as kitsch is concerned—it's a fabulous retreat from the lush greenery of the swampy Everglades to the even more lush greenery of money. Located in a building that was formerly the first bank established, in 1923, in Collier County, money is this place's premise, but it won't cost you too much to stay here. Rooms such as the Trust Room, the Checking Department, and the Stocks and Bond Rooms, all with bathrooms, are clean and comfortable and are located on the floor where banking used to be done until 1962. Perhaps the best things about the place, besides the congenial service, are that breakfast is served in the bank's fully restored vault and that original artifacts from the bank are still visible, such as the 3,000-pound cannonball safe. Unlike a real bank, however, the knowledgeable staff at the inn is happy to give free advice on what to do in the area. A new day spa on the premises provides all the necessary pampering after a long day exploring the swamps.

201 W. Broadway, Everglades City, FL 34139. © **239/695-3151**. Spa 239/695-1006. Fax 239/695-3335. www.banksoftheeverglades.com. 7 units. $100–$125. Rates include continental breakfast delivered to your door. AE, DISC, MC, V. **Amenities:** Free use of bikes; Everglades excursions available. *In room:* A/C, TV.

Ivey House B&B ★★ *Finds*   Housed in what used to be a recreational center for the men who built the Tamiami Trail, the Ivey House offers three types of accommodations. In the original house, there are 10 small rooms that share communal bathrooms (one each for women and men). There are no televisions or phones in the rooms. One private cottage consists of two bedrooms, a full kitchen, a private bathroom, and a screened-in porch. The Ivey's newer inn (opened in 2001) adds 18 rooms (with private bathrooms, TVs, and phones) that face a courtyard with a screened-in shallow "conversation" pool. During the summer, however, the mosquitoes are out in full force and a trip to the pool could leave you with multiple bites as it did me (screens or not). Bring bug spray!

Owners Sandee and David Harraden are extremely knowledgeable about the Everglades, and usually the guests are as well. A living-room area offers guests the opportunity to mingle. A full hot breakfast is included in the price from 6:30 to 11am. Boxed lunches, stored in a cooler so you can bring them along for your Everglades excursions, are offered for $9.50 each. Dinners may be available by the time you go. Call to get more information. The Ivey House is closed in September and there's a 2-night minimum in February when the Everglades Seafood Festival is going on. *Note:* There is no smoking in any of the buildings.

107 Camellia St., Everglades City, FL 34139. ℂ **239/695-3299.** Fax 239/695-4155. www.iveyhouse.com. 28 units. Winter $70–$175 main houses, $125–$175 cottage (2-night minimum); off-season $50–$125 main house, cottages closed in the off season. MC, V. **Amenities:** Restaurant; small pool; free use of bikes; Everglades excursions available. *In room:* A/C (all rooms), TV, kitchen (cottage only), fridge (inn and cottage).

Rod & Gun Lodge ★   This rustic, old white clapboard house has plenty of history and all kinds of activities for sports enthusiasts, including a swimming pool, bicycle rentals, tennis center, and nearby boat rentals and private fishing guides. Sitting on the banks of the sleepy Barron River, the Rod & Gun Lodge was originally built as a private residence nearly 170 years ago, but Barron Collier turned it into a cozy hunting lodge in the 1920s. President Herbert Hoover vacationed here after his 1928 election victory, and President Harry S. Truman flew in to sign Everglades National Park into existence in 1947 and stayed over as well. Other guests have included President Richard Nixon, Burt Reynolds, and Mick Jagger. The public rooms are beautifully paneled and hung with tarpon, wild boar, deer antlers, and other trophies. Guest rooms in this single-story building are unfussy but perfectly comfortable. Out by the swimming pool and riverbank, a screened veranda with ceiling fans offers a pleasant place for a libation. The excellent seafood restaurant serves breakfast, lunch, and dinner. The entire property is nonsmoking. *Note:* No credit cards are accepted.

Riverside Dr. and Broadway (P.O. Box 190), Everglades City, FL 34139. ℂ **239/695-2101.** 17 units, all with bathroom and porches looking out on the river. Winter $110 double. No credit cards. Closed after July 4 for the summer. **Amenities:** Restaurant; pool; tennis courts; bicycle rentals. *In room:* A/C, TV.

NEARBY IN HOMESTEAD & FLORIDA CITY

Homestead and Florida City, two adjacent towns that were almost blown off the map by Hurricane Andrew in 1992, have come back better than before. Located about 10 miles from the park's main entrance, along U.S. 1, 35 miles south of Miami, these somewhat rural towns offer several budget lodging options, including a handful of chain hotels. There is a **Days Inn** (ℂ **305/245-1260**) in Homestead and a **Hampton Inn** (ℂ **800/426-7866** or 305/247-8833) right off the turnpike in Florida City. However, the best option is listed below.

Best Western Gateway to the Keys This two-story standard motel offers contemporary style and comfort about 10 miles from the park's main entrance. A decent-size pool and a small spa make it an attractive option to some. Each identical standard room has bright, tropical bedspreads and oversize picture windows. The suites offer convenient extras like a microwave, a coffeemaker, an extra sink, and a small fridge. Clean and conveniently located, the only drawback is that in season, there is often a 3-day minimum stay requirement. You'd do best to call the local reservation line (© **305/246-5100**) instead of the toll-free number—on several occasions, the hotel made an exception to the rule while the central reservation line was not able to do the same.

411 S. Krome Ave. (U.S. 1), Florida City, FL 33034. © 800/528-1234 or 305/246-5100. Fax 305/242-0056. www.bestwestern.com. 114 units. Winter double from $135–$150; off-season double from $109–$124. Rates include continental breakfast. During races and the very high season, there may be a 3-night minimum stay. AE, DC, DISC, MC, V. **Amenities:** Pool; spa; laundry service; dry cleaning. *In room:* A/C, TV, dataport, fridge, coffeemaker, hair dryer.

Evergaldes International Hostel ✹ This is what a hostel *should* be. Sure, I've seen cleaner, more modern ones, but the feeling of comraderie here is what hostels are all about. Located in an old 1930s boarding house, this hostel has dorm rooms as well as doubles (all with shared baths) and a great kitchen plus a washer/dryer, high-speed Internet connection, bike rentals, and a garden (with tents, forts, and an outdoor chess board) to explore. The staff here is amaingly accommodating and friendly, and they run sightseeing/canoe trips to the Everglades as well as offering tons of helpful information.

20 SW 2nd Ave., Florida City, FL 33034. © 800/372-3874 or 305/248-1122. www.evergladeshostel.com. Dorm beds $14, private doubles $35, nonmember fee $3. **Amenities:** Laundry facilities; kitchen; Internet access; bike rentals; tours. *In room:* A/C (in some).

WHERE TO DINE IN & AROUND THE PARK

You won't find fancy nouvelle cuisine in this suburbanized farm country, but there are plenty of fast-food chains along U.S. 1 and a few old favorites worth a taste, listed below.

Here for nearly a quarter of a century, **El Toro Taco Family Restaurant** (p. 114) at 1 S. Krome Ave. (near Mowry Dr. and Campbell Dr.; © **305/245-8182**) opens daily at 9:30am and stays crowded until at least 9pm most days. The fresh grilled meats, tacos, burritos, salsas, guacamole, and stews are all mild and delicious. No matter how big your appetite, it's hard to spend more than $12 per person at this Mexican outpost. Bring your own beer or wine.

Housed in a squat, one-story, windowless stone building that looks something like a medieval fort, the **Capri Restaurant,** 935 N. Krome Ave., Florida City (© **305/247-1542**), has been serving hearty Italian-American fare since 1958. Great pastas and salads complement a full menu (portions are big) of meat and fish dishes. They serve lunch and dinner every day (except Sun) until 9:30pm weekdays and 10:30pm weekends.

The **Miccosukee Restaurant** (© **305/223-8380**), just west of the Shark Valley entrance on the Tamiami Trail (U.S. 41), serves authentic pumpkin bread, fry bread, fish, and not-so-authentic Native American interpretations of tacos and fried chicken. It's worth a stop for brunch, lunch, or dinner.

Near the Miccosukee reservation on 16400 SW 8th St. is **The Pit Bar-B-Q** (© **305/226-2272**), a total pit of a place known for some of the best smoked ribs, barbecue chicken, and cornbread this side of the deep south. Open daily from 11am–8pm.

In Everglades City, **The Oyster House** (© **239/695-2073**) on Chokoloskee Causeway, State Road (the locals call it Highway) 29 South, is a large but homey seafood restaurant with modest prices, excellent service, and a fantastic view of the 10,000 islands. Try their hush puppies.

Once inside the Everglades, you'll want to eat at the only restaurant within the boundaries of this huge park, **The Flamingo Restaurant** (© **239/695-3101**). Located in the Flamingo Lodge (p. 229), this is a very civilized and affordable restaurant. Besides the spectacular view of Florida Bay and numerous Keys from the large, airy dining room, you'll also find fresh fish that is grilled, blackened, or deep-fried. Dinner entrees come with salad or conch chowder, steamed vegetables, black beans, and rice or baked potato. The large menu has something for everyone, including basic and very tasty sandwiches, pastas, burgers, salads, and a kids' menu offering standard choices for less than $6. Prices are surprisingly moderate, with full meals starting at about $11 and going no higher than $22. You may need reservations for dinner, however, especially in season.

2 Biscayne National Park ⟨★

35 miles S of Miami, 21 miles E of Everglades National Park

With only about 500,000 visitors each year (mostly boaters and divers), the unusual Biscayne National Park is one of the least-crowded parks in the country. Perhaps that's because the park is a little more difficult than most to access—more than 95% of its 181,500 acres are underwater.

The park's significance was first formally acknowledged in 1968 when, in an unprecedented move (and against intense pressure from developers), President Lyndon B. Johnson signed a bill to conserve the barrier islands off South Florida's east coast as a national monument—a protected status that's just a rung below national park. After being twice enlarged, once in 1974 and again in 1980, the waters and land surrounding the northernmost coral reef in North America became a full-fledged national park—the largest of its kind in the country.

To be fully appreciated, Biscayne National Park should be thought of more as a preserve than as a destination. I suggest using your time here to explore underwater life, of course, but also to relax.

The park consists of 44 islands, but only a few of them are open to visitors. The most popular one is **Elliott Key,** which has campsites and a visitor center plus freshwater showers (cold water only), restrooms, trails, and a buoyed swim area. It's located about 9 miles from **Convoy Point,** the park's official headquarters on land. During Columbus Day weekend, there is a very popular regatta in which a lively crowd of party people gathers—sometimes in the nude—to celebrate the long weekend. If you'd prefer to rough it a little more, the 29-acre island known as **Boca Chita Key,** once an exclusive haven for yachters, has now become a popular spot for all manner of boaters. Visitors can enjoy camping and tour the island's restored historic buildings, including the county's second-largest lighthouse and a tiny chapel.

The park's small mainland mangrove shoreline and keys are best explored by boat. Its extensive reef system is renowned by divers and snorkelers worldwide.

JUST THE FACTS

GETTING THERE & ACCESS POINTS   Convoy Point, the park's mainland entrance, is located 9 miles east of Homestead. To reach the park from Miami, take the Florida Turnpike to the Tallahassee Road (SW 137th Ave.) exit. Turn left, then left again at North Canal Drive (SW 328th St.) and follow signs to the park. Another option is to rent a speedboat in Miami and cruise south for about an hour and a half. If you're coming from U.S. 1, whether you're heading north or south, turn east at North Canal Drive (SW 328th St.). The entrance is approximately 9 miles away. The rest of the park is accessible only by boat.

Because most of Biscayne National Park is accessible only to boaters, mooring buoys abound, since it is illegal to anchor on coral. When no buoys are available, boaters must anchor on sand or on the new docks surrounding the small harbor off of Boca Chita. Boats can also dock there overnight for $15. Even the most experienced boaters should carry updated nautical charts of the area, which are available at Convoy Point's Dante Fascell Visitor Center. The waters are often murky, making the abundant reefs and sandbars difficult to detect—and there are more interesting ways to spend a day than waiting for the tide to rise. There's a boat launch at adjacent Homestead Bayfront Park and 66 slips on Elliott Key, available free on a first-come, first-served basis.

Transportation to and from the visitor center to Elliot Key costs $26 (plus tax) round-trip per person and takes about an hour. This is a convenient option, ensuring that you don't get lost on some deserted island by boating there yourself. Call © **305/230-1100** for a seasonal schedule.

VISITOR CENTERS & INFORMATION   The **Dante Fascell Visitor Center,** often still referred to by its older name, the **Convoy Point Visitor Center,** 9700 SW 328th St., Homestead, FL 33033-5634, at the park's main entrance (© **305/230-7275;** fax 305/230-1190; www.nps.gov/bisc), is the natural starting point for any venture into the park without a boat. In addition to providing comprehensive information about the park, on request, rangers will show you a short video on the park, its natural surroundings, and what you may see. The center is open daily from 9am to 5pm.

For information on transportation, glass-bottom boat tours, and snorkeling and scuba-diving expeditions, contact the park concessionaire, **Biscayne National Underwater Park, Inc.,** P.O. Box 1270, Homestead, FL 33030 (© **305/230-1100;** fax 305/230-1120; www.nps.gov/bisc). The company is open daily from 8:30am to 5pm.

ENTRANCE FEES & PERMITS   Entering Biscayne National Park is free. There is a $15 per night overnight docking fee at both Boca Chita Key Harbor and Elliott Key Harbor ($7.50 per night for holders of Golden Age or Golden Access Passports), which includes a campsite. Campsites are $10 for those staying without a boat. See p. 224 for information on fishing permits. Backcountry camping permits are free and can be picked up from the Dante Fascell Visitor Center. For information on fees and permits, call the park ranger at © **305/230-1144.**

SEEING THE HIGHLIGHTS

Since the park is primarily underwater, the only way to truly experience it is with snorkel or scuba gear. Beneath the surface of Biscayne National Park, the aquatic universe pulses with multicolored life: Bright parrotfish and angelfish, gently rocking sea fans, and coral labyrinths abound. See the "Snorkeling & Scuba Diving" section below for more information.

Afterward, take a picnic out to Elliott Key and taste the crisp salt air blowing off the Atlantic. Or head to Boca Chita, an intriguing island that was once the private playground of wealthy yachters.

SPORTS & OUTDOOR ACTIVITIES

CANOEING & KAYAKING   Biscayne National Park offers excellent canoeing, both along the coast and across the open water to nearby mangroves and artificial islands that dot the longest uninterrupted shoreline in the state of Florida. Since tides can be strong, only experienced canoeists should attempt to paddle far from shore. If you do plan to go far, first obtain a tide table from the visitor center (see "Just the Facts," above) and paddle with the current. Free ranger-led canoe tours are scheduled the second and fourth Saturdays from January 10 to April 24 from 9am to noon; phone for information. You can rent a canoe at the park's concession stand; rates are $9 an hour. Two person kayaks can be rented for $16 an hour. Call © **305/230-1100** for reservations, information, ranger tours, and boat rentals.

FISHING   Ocean fishing is excellent year-round at Biscayne National Park; many people cast their lines right from the breakwater jetty at Convoy Point. A fishing license is required (see p. 224 for complete information). Bait is not available in Biscayne National Park but is sold in adjacent Homestead Bayfront Park. Stone crabs and Florida lobsters can be found here, but you're allowed to catch these only on the ocean side when they're in season. There are strict limitations on size, season, number, and method of take (including spear fishing) for both fresh- and saltwater fishing. The latest regulations are available at most marinas, bait-and-tackle shops, and the park's visitor centers. Or you can contact the **Florida Fish and Wildlife Conservation Commission,** Bryant Building, 620 S. Meridian St., Tallahassee, FL 32399-1600 (© **850/488-0331**).

HIKING & EXPLORING   Since the majority of this park is underwater, hiking is not the main attraction here, but, nonetheless, there are some interesting sights and trails. At Convoy Point, you can walk along the 370-foot boardwalk and along the ½-mile jetty that serves as a breakwater for the park's harbor. From there, you can usually see brown pelicans, little blue herons, snowy egrets, and a few exotic fish.

Elliott Key is accessible only by boat, but once you're there, you have two good trail options. True to its name, the Loop Trail makes a 1½-mile circle from the bay-side visitor center, through a hardwood hammock and mangroves, to an elevated ocean-side boardwalk. It's likely that you'll see purple and orange land crabs scurrying around the mangrove roots.

Reopened in 1998, Boca Chita Key was once the playground for wealthy tycoons, and it still offers the peaceful beauty that attracted elite anglers from cold climates. Many of the historical buildings are still intact, including an ornamental lighthouse, which was never put into use.

Take advantage of the tours, usually led by a park ranger and available every Sunday in the winter only at 1:30pm. The tour, including the boat trip, takes about 3 hours. The price is $24 for adults, $19 for seniors, and $16 for children under 12. However, call in advance to see if the sea is calm enough for the boat trip—the boats won't run in rough seas. See "Glass-Bottom Boat Tours," below, for information about the daily 10am tours.

SNORKELING & SCUBA DIVING   The clear, warm waters of Biscayne National Park are packed with colorful tropical fish that swim in the offshore reefs. If you don't have your own gear, or don't want to lug it to the park, you can rent or buy snorkeling and scuba gear at the full-service dive shop at Convoy Point. Rates are in line with dive shops on the mainland.

The best way to see the park from underwater is to take a snorkeling or scuba diving tour operated by **Biscayne National Underwater Park, Inc.** (© **305/230-1100;** www.nps.gov/bisc). Snorkeling tours depart at 1:30pm daily, last about 3 hours, and cost $35 per person, including equipment. They also run weekend two-tank dives for certified divers. The price is $54, including two tanks and weights. Make your reservations in advance. The shop is open daily from 9am to 5pm.

Before entering the water, be sure to apply waterproof sunblock—once you begin to explore, it's easy to lose track of time, and the Florida sun is brutal, even during winter.

SWIMMING   You can swim at the protected beaches of Elliott Key, Boca Chita Key, and adjacent Homestead Bayfront Park, but none of these match the width or softness of other South Florida beaches. Check the water conditions before heading into the sea: The strong currents that make this a popular destination for windsurfers and sailors can be dangerous, even for strong swimmers. Homestead Bayfront Park is really just a marina located next to Biscayne National Park, but it does have a beach and picnic facilities as well as fishing areas and a playground. It's located at Convoy Point, 9698 SW 328th St., Homestead (✆ **305/230-3034**).

GLASS-BOTTOM BOAT TOURS

If you prefer not to dive, the best way to see the sights is on a glass-bottom boat tour. **Biscayne National Underwater Park, Inc.** (✆ **305/230-1100;** www.nps. gov/bisc) offers daily trips to view some of the country's most beautiful coral reefs and tropical fish. Boats depart year-round from Convoy Point at 10am and stay out for about 3 hours. At $24 for adults, $19 for seniors, and $16 for children 12 and under, the scenic and informative tours are well worth the price. Boats carry fewer than 50 passengers; reservations are almost always necessary.

WHERE TO STAY

Besides campsites, there are no facilities available for overnight guests to this watery park. Most noncamping visitors come for an afternoon, on their way to the Keys, and stay overnight in nearby Homestead, where there are many national chain hotels and other affordable lodgings (see p. 231 for more information).

CAMPING

Although you won't find hotels or lodges in Biscayne National Park, it does have some of the state's most pristine campsites. Since they are inaccessible by motor vehicle, you'll be sure to avoid the mass of RVs so prevalent in many of the state's other campgrounds. Sites are on Elliott Key and Boca Chita (p. 233) and can be reached only by boat. If you don't have your own, call ✆ **305/230-1100** to arrange a drop-off. Transportation to and from the visitor center costs $26 (plus tax) per person. Boca Chita has only saltwater toilets (no showers or sinks); Elliot Key has freshwater, coldwater showers (and toilets) but is otherwise no less primitive. If you didn't pay for the overnight docking fee, campsites are $10.

With a backcountry permit, available free from the Visitor Center, you can pitch your tent somewhere even more private. Ask for a map at the Visitor Center, and be sure to bring plenty of bug spray. Sites cost $10 a night for up to six persons staying in one or two tents. Backcountry camping is allowed only on Elliot Key, which is a very popular spot (accessible only by boat) for boaters and campers. It is approximately 9 miles from Dante Fascell Visitor Center and offers hiking trails, fresh water, boat slips, showers, and restrooms. While there, don't miss the Old Road, a 7-mile tropical hammock trail that runs the length of Elliott Key. This trail is one of the few places left in the world to see the highly endangered Schaus' swallowtail butterfly, recognizable by its black wings with diagonal yellow bands. They're usually out from late April to July.

8

The Gold Coast:
Hallandale to the Palm Beaches

Named not for the sun-kissed skin of the area's residents but for the gold salvaged from shipwrecks off its coastline, the Gold Coast embraces more than 60 miles of beautiful Atlantic shoreline—from the pristine sands of Jupiter in northern Palm Beach County to the legendary strip of beaches in Fort Lauderdale.

If you haven't visited the cities along Florida's southeastern coast in the last few years, you'll be amazed at how much has changed. Miles of sprawling grassland and empty lots have been replaced with luxurious resorts and high-rise condominiums. Taking advantage of their close proximity to Miami, the cities that make up the Gold Coast have attracted millions looking to escape crowded sidewalks, traffic jams, and the everyday routines of life.

Fortunately, amid all the building, much of the natural treasure of the Gold Coast remains. There are 300 miles of Intracoastal Waterway, not to mention Fort Lauderdale's Venetian-inspired canals. And the unspoiled splendor of the Everglades is just a few miles inland.

The most popular areas in the Gold Coast are Fort Lauderdale, Boca Raton, and Palm Beach. While Fort Lauderdale is a favored beachfront destination, Boca Raton and Palm Beach are better known for their country-club lifestyles and excellent shopping. Farther north is the quietly popular Jupiter, best known for spring training at the Roger Dean Stadium and for its former resident Burt Reynolds. In between these better-traveled destinations are a few things worth stopping for, but not much. Driving north along the coastline is one of the best ways to fully appreciate what the Gold Coast is all about—it's a perspective you certainly won't find in a shopping mall.

Tourists come here by the droves, but they aren't the only people coming; thousands of transplants, fleeing the increasing population influx in Miami and the frigid winters up North, have made this area their home. As a result, there has been a construction boom in the existing cities and even westward, into the swampy areas of the Everglades. More than 20 homes per day are being built in Broward County alone. There has also been a great revitalization of several downtown areas, including Hollywood, Fort Lauderdale, and West Palm Beach. These once-desolate urban centers have been spruced up and now attract more young travelers and families than ever before.

Unfortunately, like its neighbors to the south, the Gold Coast can be prohibitively hot and buggy in the summer. The good news is that bargains are plentiful in the summer months (May–Oct), when many locals take advantage of package deals and uncrowded resorts.

For the purposes of this chapter, the Gold Coast will consist of the towns of Hallandale, Hollywood, Pompano Beach, Fort Lauderdale, Dania, Deerfield, Boca Raton, Delray Beach, Boynton Beach, Jupiter, and the Palm Beaches.

EXPLORING THE GOLD COAST BY CAR

Like most of South Florida, the Gold Coast consists of a mainland and an adjacent strip of barrier islands. You'll have to check the maps to keep track of the many bridges that allow access to the islands where most of the tourist activity is centered. Interstate 95, which runs north-south, is the area's main highway. Farther west is the Florida Turnpike, a toll road that can be worth the expense since the speed limit is higher and it is often less congested than I-95. Also on the mainland is U.S. 1, which generally runs parallel to I-95 (to the east) and is a narrower thoroughfare mostly crowded with strip malls and seedy hotels.

I recommend taking Fla. A1A, a slow ocean-side road that connects the long, thin islands of Florida's whole east coast. Although the road is narrow, it is the most scenic and forces you into the relaxed atmosphere of these resort towns.

1 Broward County: Hallandale & Hollywood ★ to Fort Lauderdale ★★

23 miles N of Miami

Until the 2000 presidential election fiasco, most people had never heard of Broward County. Less exposed than the highly hyped Miami, Broward County is a lot calmer and, according to some, a lot friendlier than the magic city. In fact, a friendly rivalry exists between residents of Miami–Dade County and those of Broward County. Miamians consider themselves more sophisticated and cosmopolitan than their northern neighbors who, in turn, dismiss the alleged sophistication as snobbery and actually prefer their own county's gentler pace.

With more than 23 miles of beachfront and 300 miles of navigable waterways, Broward County is also a great outdoor destination. Scattered amid the shopping malls, condominiums, and tourist traps is a beautiful landscape lined with hundreds of parks, golf courses, tennis courts, and, of course, beaches.

The City of Hallandale Beach is a small, peaceful oceanfront town located just north of Dade County's Aventura. Condos are the predominant landmarks in Hallandale, which is still pretty much a retirement community, although the revamped multimillion-dollar Westin Diplomat Resort (p. 250) is trying to revitalize and liven up the area. Just north of Hallandale is the more energetic, burgeoning, Hollywood.

Like many other small American towns, South Florida's city of Hollywood has been working on redeveloping its downtown area for years. Once a sleepy community wedged between Fort Lauderdale and Miami, Hollywood is now a bustling area of 1.5 million people belonging to an array of ethnic and racial identities: from white and African American, to people of Jamaican, Chinese, and Dominican descent. (*Money* magazine trumpeted the self-described "City of the Future" as having an ethnic makeup that mirrors what America will look like by the year 2022.) In May of 2004, Hard Rock Cafe International debuted its $300 million **Seminole Hard Rock Hotel & Casino** (© **954/327-7625**) at the Seminole Indian Nation reservation land in Hollywood, with a 500-room hotel, a spa, and 130,000-square-foot casino. Starwood Hotels also announced plans

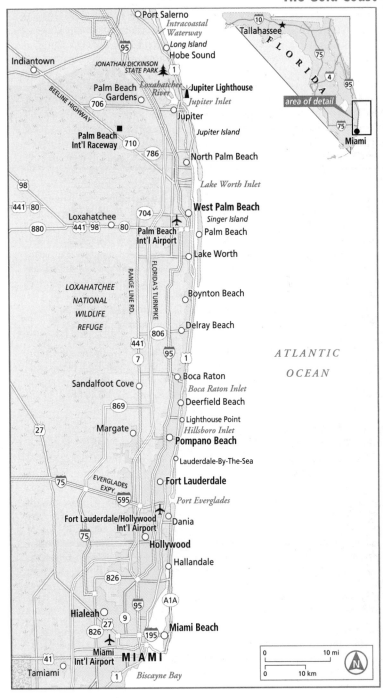

The Gold Coast

Port Salerno
Intracoastal Waterway
Long Island
Hobe Sound
Indiantown
95
JONATHAN DICKINSON STATE PARK
1
BEELINE HIGHWAY
Palm Beach Gardens
Loxahatchee River
706
Jupiter Lighthouse
Jupiter Inlet
Jupiter
Palm Beach Int'l Raceway
710
Jupiter Island
786
North Palm Beach
98
441 80
880
Loxahatchee
441 98 80
704
Lake Worth Inlet
West Palm Beach
Singer Island
Palm Beach Int'l Airport
Palm Beach
Lake Worth
LOXAHATCHEE NATIONAL WILDLIFE REFUGE
RANGE LINE RD.
FLORIDA'S TURNPIKE
Boynton Beach
806
Delray Beach
441
7
95
1
ATLANTIC OCEAN
Sandalfoot Cove
Boca Raton
Boca Raton Inlet
869
Deerfield Beach
Lighthouse Point
Hillsboro Inlet
27
Margate
Pompano Beach
Lauderdale-By-The-Sea
75
EVERGLADES EXPY.
595
Fort Lauderdale
Port Everglades
Fort Lauderdale/Hollywood Int'l Airport
Dania
75
Hollywood
Hallandale
826
Hialeah
95
A1A
27
9
826
195
Miami Beach
Miami Int'l Airport
MIAMI
41
Tamiami
1
Biscayne Bay

10
Tallahassee
75
F L O R I D A
4
95
area of detail
75
• Miami

0   10 mi
0   10 km
N

for a W Fort Lauderdale Hotel, a 346-room boutique hotel originally slated to open in South Beach but instead opening in Fort Lauderdale in December of 2006. This could be exactly what the city needs to kick its slow renaissance up a notch. A spate of redevelopment has made the pedestrian-friendly center along Hollywood Boulevard and Harrison Street, east of Dixie Highway, a popular destination for travelers and locals alike. Some predict Hollywood will be South Florida's next big destination—South Beach without the attitude, traffic jams, and parking nightmares. While the prediction is a dubious one, Hollywood is definitely awakening from its long slumber. Prices are a fraction of other tourist areas, and a quasi-bohemian vibe is apparent in the galleries, clubs, and restaurants that dot the new "strip." Its gritty undercurrent, however, prevents it from becoming too trendy.

Fort Lauderdale, and its well-known strip of beaches, restaurants, bars, and souvenir shops, has also undergone a major transformation. Once famous (or infamous) for the annual mayhem it hosted during spring break, this area is now attracting a more affluent, better-behaved yachting crowd.

In addition to beautiful wide beaches, the city, known as the Venice of America, has more than 300 miles of navigable waterways and innumerable canals, which permit thousands of residents to anchor boats in their backyards. Boating is not just a hobby here; it's a lifestyle. Visitors can easily get on the water, too, by renting a boat or simply hailing a moderately priced water taxi.

Huge cruise ships also take advantage of Florida's deepest harbor, Port Everglades, whose name is somewhat misleading because it is not part of the Florida Everglades. The seaport is actually located on the southeastern coast of the Florida peninsula, near the Fort Lauderdale–Hollywood International Airport on the outskirts of Hollywood and Dania Beach. Port Everglades is the second-busiest cruise-ship base in Florida after Miami and one of the top five in the world. For further information on cruises, see chapter 5, "What to See & Do in Miami," and consult *Frommer's Caribbean Cruises & Ports of Call.*

ESSENTIALS

GETTING THERE   If you're driving from Miami, it's a straight shot north to Hollywood or Fort Lauderdale. Visitors on their way to or from Orlando should take the Florida Turnpike to exit 53, 54, 58, or 62, depending on the location of your accommodations.

The **Fort Lauderdale–Hollywood International Airport** is small, easy to negotiate, and located just 15 minutes from both of the downtown areas it services. But the user-friendliness of this airport may not last much longer: Because of its popularity, the airport is undergoing a $650 million expansion and renovation that may render it just as maddening as any other major metropolitan airport.

Amtrak (© **800/USA-RAIL**) stations are at 200 SW 21st Terrace (Broward Blvd. and I-95), Fort Lauderdale (© **954/587-6692**), and 3001 Hollywood Blvd. (northwest corner of Hollywood Blvd. and I-95), Hollywood (© **954/921-4517**).

VISITOR INFORMATION   The **Greater Fort Lauderdale Convention & Visitors Bureau,** 1850 Eller Dr., Suite 303 (off I-95 and I-595 east), Fort Lauderdale, FL 33316 (© **954/765-4466;** fax 954/765-4467; www.sunny.org), is an excellent resource for area information in English, Spanish, and French. I highly recommend calling them in advance to request a free comprehensive guide covering events, accommodations, and sightseeing in Broward County. In addition,

Fort Lauderdale, Hollywood & Pompano Beach Area

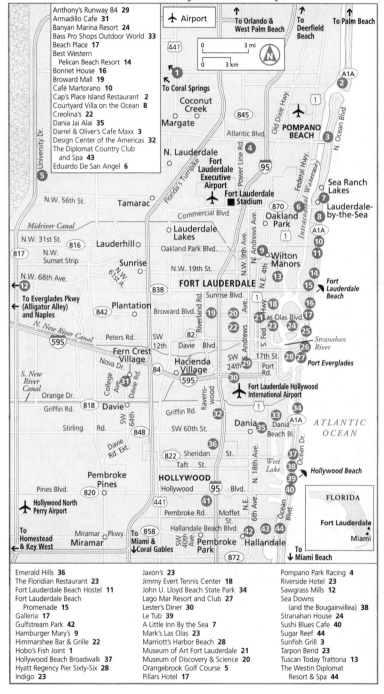

Anthony's Runway 84 **29**
Armadillo Cafe **31**
Banyan Marina Resort **24**
Bass Pro Shops Outdoor World **33**
Beach Place **17**
Best Western
 Pelican Beach Resort **14**
Bonnet House **16**
Broward Mall **19**
Café Martorano **10**
Cap's Place Island Restaurant **2**
Courtyard Villa on the Ocean **8**
Creolina's **22**
Dania Jai Alai **35**
Darrel & Oliver's Cafe Maxx **3**
Design Center of the Americas **32**
The Diplomat Country Club
 and Spa **43**
Eduardo De San Angel **6**

✈ Airport

To Orlando &
West Palm Beach

To
Deerfield
Beach

To Palm Beach

441

0   3 mi
0   3 km

To Coral Springs

Coconut
Creek

Margate

845

Atlantic Blvd.

✈ POMPANO
BEACH

N. Lauderdale

Fort
Lauderdale
Executive
Airport

Fort Lauderdale
■ Stadium

Sea Ranch
Lakes

870

Lauderdale-
by-the-Sea

A1A

N.W. 56th St.

Tamarac

Commercial Blvd.

Oakland
Park

1

Midriver Canal

N.W. 31st St.

Lauderhill

Lauderdale
Lakes

Oakland Park Blvd.

A1A

817   816

N.W.
Sunset Strip

Sunrise

N.W. 19th St.

Wilton
Manors

Fort
Lauderdale
Beach

N.W. 68th Ave.

838

FORT LAUDERDALE

To Everglades Pkwy
← (Alligator Alley)
and Naples

Plantation

Sunrise Blvd.

Broward Blvd.

Las Olas Blvd.

N. New River Canal

842

595

Peters Rd.

SW
12th   Davie   Blvd.

82

*Stranahan
River*

Fern Crest
Village

Nova Dr.

Hacienda
Village

595

17th St.

Port
Rd.

Port Everglades

*S. New
River
Canal*

Orange Dr.

84

SW
24th

Fort Lauderdale Hollywood
✈ International Airport

Griffin Rd.

818   Davie

Griffin Rd.

1

ATLANTIC
OCEAN

Stirling   Rd.

848

SW 60th St.

Dania   A1A
Dania
Beach Bl.

Davie
Rd. Ext.

822   Sheridan   St.

Taft   St.

West
Lake

Hollywood Beach

Pembroke
Pines

Pines Blvd.

HOLLYWOOD

Hollywood   95   Blvd.

820

✈ Hollywood North
Perry Airport

441

Pembroke Rd.   Moffet
St.

FLORIDA

To
Homestead
& Key West

Miramar Pkwy.

Miramar

858
To
Miami &
↓Coral Gables

Hallandale Beach Blvd.

Pembroke   Hallandale
Park

Fort Lauderdale

Miami

To
↓ Miami Beach

872

Emerald Hills **36**
The Floridian Restaurant **23**
Fort Lauderdale Beach Hostel **11**
Fort Lauderdale Beach
 Promenade **15**
Galleria **17**
Gulfstream Park **42**
Hamburger Mary's **9**
Himmarshee Bar & Grille **22**
Hobo's Fish Joint **1**
Hollywood Beach Broadwalk **37**
Hyatt Regency Pier Sixty-Six **28**
Indigo **23**

Jaxon's **23**
Jimmy Evert Tennis Center **18**
John U. Lloyd Beach State Park **34**
Lago Mar Resort and Club **27**
Lester's Diner **30**
Le Tub **39**
A Little Inn By the Sea **7**
Mark's Las Olas **23**
Marriott's Harbor Beach **28**
Museum of Art Fort Lauderdale **21**
Museum of Discovery & Science **20**
Orangebrook Golf Course **5**
Pillars Hotel **17**

Pompano Park Racing **4**
Riverside Hotel **23**
Sawgrass Mills **12**
Sea Downs
 (and the Bougainvillea) **38**
Stranahan House **24**
Sushi Blues Cafe **40**
Sugar Reef **44**
Sunfish Grill **3**
Tarpon Bend **23**
Tuscan Today Trattoria **13**
The Westin Diplomat
 Resort & Spa **44**

once you are in town, you can contact an **information line** (© **954/527-5600;** www.activityline.net) to get easy-to-follow directions, travel advice, and assistance from multilingual operators who staff a round-the-clock help line. Also available for brochures, information, and vacation packages in Fort Lauderdale are operators at Greater Than Ever Fort Lauderdale; © **800/22-SUNNY.**

The **Greater Hollywood Chamber of Commerce,** 330 N. Federal Hwy. (on the corner of U.S. 1 and Taylor St.), Hollywood, FL 33020 (© **954/923-4000;** fax 954/923-8737; www.hollywoodchamber.org), is open Monday through Friday from 9am to 5pm. Here you'll find the lowdown on all of Hollywood's events, attractions, restaurants, hotels, and tours.

BEACHES

The southern part of the Gold Coast, Broward County, has the region's most popular and amenities-laden beaches, which stretch for more than 23 miles. Most do not charge for access, though all are well maintained. Here's a selection of some of the county's best from south to north.

Hollywood Beach, stretching from Sheridan Street to Georgia Street, is a major attraction in the city of Hollywood, a virtual carnival with a motley assortment of young hipsters, big families, and sunburned French Canadians who dodge bicyclers and skaters along the rows of tacky souvenir shops, T-shirt shops, game rooms, snack bars, beer stands, hotels, and even miniature-golf courses. The 3-mile-long Hollywood Beach **Broadwalk,** modeled after Atlantic City's legendary boardwalk, is Hollywood's most popular beachfront pedestrian thoroughfare, a cement promenade that's 30 feet wide and stretches along the shoreline. Popular with runners, skaters, and cruisers, the Broadwalk is also renowned as a hangout for thousands of retirement-age snowbirds who get together for frequent dances and shows at a faded outdoor amphitheater. Despite efforts to clear out a seedy element, the area remains a haven for drunks and scammers, so keep alert.

If you tire of the hectic diversity that defines Hollywood's Broadwalk, enjoy the natural beauty of the beach itself, which is wide and clean. There are lifeguards, showers, bathroom facilities, and public areas for picnics and parties.

The **Fort Lauderdale Beach Promenade,** along the beach, underwent a $26 million renovation, and it looks fantastic. It's especially peaceful in the mornings when there's just a smattering of joggers and walkers; but even at its most crowded on the weekend, the expansive promenade provides room for everyone. Note, however, that the beach is hardly pristine; it is across the street from an uninterrupted stretch of hotels, bars, and retail outlets. Also nearby is a megaretail and dining complex, Beach Place (p. 248), on Fla. A1A, midway between Las Olas Boulevard and Sunrise Boulevard.

Just across the road, on the sand, most days you will find hard-core volleyballers, who always welcome anyone with a good spike, and an inviting ocean welcoming swimmers of any level. The unusually clear waters are under the careful watch of some of Florida's best-looking lifeguards. Freshen up afterward in any of the clean showers and restrooms conveniently located along the strip. Pets have been banned from most of the beach in order to maintain the impressive cleanliness not commonly associated with such highly trafficked public beaches; a designated area for pets exists away from the main sunbathing areas.

Especially on weekends, parking along the ocean-side meters is nearly impossible to find. Try biking, skating, or hitching a ride on the water taxi instead. The strip is located on Fla. A1A, between SE 17th Street and Sunrise Boulevard.

Turtle Trail

In June and July, the John U. Lloyd beach is crawling with nature lovers who come for the spectacular Sea Turtle Awareness Program. Park rangers begin the evening with a lecture and slide show while scouts search the beach for nesting loggerhead sea turtles. If a turtle is located—plenty of them usually are—a beach walk is conducted, where participants can see the turtles nesting and, sometimes, their eggs hatching. The program begins at 9pm on Wednesdays and Fridays from mid-May through mid-July. Call (*C* **954/923-2833** for reservations. Comfortable walking shoes and insect repellent are recommended. The park entrance fee of $3 to $5 per carload applies.

Dania Beach's **John U. Lloyd Beach State Park,** 6503 N. Ocean Dr., Dania (*C* **954/923-2833**), is 251 acres of barrier island between the Atlantic Ocean and the Intracoastal Waterway, from Port Everglades on the north to Dania on the south. Its natural setting contrasts sharply with the urban development of Fort Lauderdale. Lloyd Beach, one of Broward County's most important nesting beaches for sea turtles, produces some 10,000 hatchlings a year. The park's broad, flat beach is popular for swimming and sunning. Self-guided nature trails are great for those who are too restless to sunbathe.

ACTIVE PURSUITS

BOATING   Often called the "yachting capital of the world," Fort Lauderdale provides ample opportunity for visitors to get out on the water, either along the Intracoastal Waterway or on the open ocean. If your hotel doesn't rent boats, try **Aloha Watersports,** Marriott's Harbor Beach Resort, 3030 Holiday Dr., Fort Lauderdale (*C* **954/462-7245**). They will outfit you with a variety of craft, including jet skis, WaveRunners, and catamarans. Rates start at $65 per half-hour for WaveRunners ($15 each additional rider; doubles and triples available), $70 to $125 for sailboats, $60 to $70 for catamarans, $20 per person per hour for ocean kayaks, and $60 per person for a 10- to 12-minute parasailing ride. Aloha also offers Coast Guard classes at 9am daily where adults can obtain their Florida Boaters License for $3.

CRUISES   The **Jungle Queen,** 801 Sea Breeze Blvd. (3 blocks south of Las Olas Blvd. on Fla. A1A), in the Bahia Mar Yacht Center, Fort Lauderdale (*C* **954/462-5596**), a Mississippi River–style steamer, is one of Fort Lauderdale's best-known attractions, cruising up and down the New River. All-you-can-eat 4-hour dinner cruises (departing nightly at 7pm and costing $31 for adults and $17 for children 2–10) and 3-hour sightseeing tours (scheduled daily at 10am and 2pm and costing $14 for adults and $9.25 for children 2–10) take visitors past Millionaires' Row, Old Fort Lauderdale, and the new downtown. They also have a seasonal 8-hour cruise that goes down to Miami (Bayside) leaving Wednesdays and Saturdays at 9:15am and costing $17 for adults and $12 for children.

If you're interested in gambling, several casino-boat companies operate day cruises out of Port Everglades and offer blackjack, slots, and poker. **Discovery Cruise Lines** (*C* **800/937-4477**) has daily cruises to the Bahamas, leaving at 7:45am, where you can gamble, eat, and party for 10 to 12 hours (you have about 3 hr. in the Bahamas to go to the Straw Market or to do even more gambling) for $113 Monday through Thursday and $143 Friday through Sunday. The price includes breakfast, lunch, and dinner, but drinks cost extra.

Sea Escape (© **800/327-2005** or 954/453-3333) also launches daily casino cruises 15 times a week. But theirs don't travel more than a few miles offshore. These trips "to nowhere" are Monday through Sunday from 11am to 4:30pm; Monday through Friday from 7:30pm to 12:30am; and Saturday from 7:30pm to 1:30am. The daytime cruises are free on Mondays but cost $25 in advance for adults ($35 if you pay at the dock) and $13 for kids 2 through 12 (children not allowed on the evening cruises). Evening cruises have the same prices, except on Friday and Saturday, when adults pay $30 in advance, $40 at the dock. The party cruises offer buffet meals and full casinos for $30 to $40 per person. I'd recommend spending an additional $20 for a cabin ($25 per cabin on the evening cruises—though do not expect *Love Boat* luxe here), so you can stretch out and relax between hands. Even though the cruises don't go far from the coast, 5 or 6 hours is a long time to spend at sea, especially if the weather is rough.

FISHING Completed in 1999 at a cost of more than $32 million, the **IGFA (International Game Fish Association) World Fishing Center** at 300 Gulf Stream Way (© **954/922-4212;** www.igfa.org) in Dania Beach is an angler's paradise. One of the highlights of this museum, library, and park is the virtual-reality fishing simulator, which allows visitors to actually reel in their own computer-generated catch. Also included in the 3-acre park are displays of antique fishing gear, record catches, famous anglers, various vessels, and a wetlands lab. To get a list of local captains and guides, call **IGFA headquarters** (© **954/927-2628**) and ask for the librarian. Admission is $6 for adults, $5 for seniors and children between 3 and 16, and free for children under 3. The museum and library are open daily from 10am to 6pm. On the grounds is also **Bass Pro Shops Outdoor World,** a huge multifloor retail complex situated on a 3-acre lake.

GOLF More than 50 golf courses in all price ranges compete for players. Some of the best include **Emerald Hills** at 4100 N. Hills Dr., Hollywood, just west of I-95 between Sterling Road and Sheridan Street. This beauty consistently lands on the "best of" lists of golf writers throughout the country. The 18th hole, on a two-tier green, is the challenging course's signature; it's surrounded by water and is more than a bit rough. The course is pricey—greens fees start at $125 for tee times after 1pm and $150 for tee times before noon Friday through Sunday and $125 before noon, $100 after 1pm Monday through Thursday. Call © **954/ 961-4000** for tee times. **The Diplomat Country Club and Spa,** 501 Diplomat Pkwy., Hallandale Beach (© **954/602-6000;** www.diplomatcountryclub.com), is located across the Intracoastal from the Westin Diplomat Resort and has fabulous golf facilities with 8 acres of lakes and rolling fairways and a fantastic delivery service that brings lunch and drinks straight to your cart. You will pay for the services, however, with greens fees of $189 weekdays, $195 weekends, and 2pm twilights at $95 all week. For one of Broward's best municipal challenges, try the 18-holer at the **Orangebrook Golf Course** at 400 Entrada Dr. in Hollywood (© **954/967-GOLF**). Built in 1937, this is one of the state's oldest courses and one of the area's best bargains. Morning and noon rates range from $29 to $34. After 2pm, you can play for less than $20, including a cart. Men must wear collared shirts to play here, and no spikes are allowed.

SCUBA DIVING In Broward County, the best wreck dive is the *Mercedes I,* a 197-foot freighter that washed up in the backyard of a Palm Beach socialite in 1984 and was sunk for divers the following year off Pompano Beach. The

---

(Fun Fact   Remnants of the Past

Any diving outfit in Jupiter Beach will take you to the spot where the remnants of a shipwreck from a 16th- or 17th-century Spanish galleon lie. Discovered in 1988 by Jupiter lifeguard Peter Leo, who on his morning swim came across an anchor and a cannon, the wreck has since produced 10 more cannons and over 10,000 gold and silver coins. However, should you come across more coins, you won't be able to throw them in your piggy bank—Leo owns the mining rights to the wreck. This is a more historic dive than the *Mercedes I,* since it's an actual wreck and not one that was intentionally submerged for divers.

---

artificial reef, filled with colorful sponges, spiny lobsters, and barracudas, is located 97 feet below the surface, a mile offshore between Oakland Park Boulevard and Sunrise Boulevard. Dozens of reputable dive shops line the beach. Ask at your hotel for a nearby recommendation or contact **Neil Watson's Undersea Adventures,** 1525 S. Andrews Ave., Fort Lauderdale (© **954/462-3400;** www. neilwatson.com).

SPECTATOR SPORTS   Baseball fans can get their fix at the **Fort Lauderdale Stadium,** 5301 NW 12th Ave. (© **954/828-4980**), where the Baltimore Orioles play Spring Training exhibition games starting in early March; call © **954/ 776-1921** for tickets. General admission is $6, a spot in the grandstand $9, $3 for kids 14 and under, and box seats $12. During the season, the Florida Marlins play just south of Hallandale at the **Pro Player Stadium** near the Dade–Broward County line. Call Ticketmaster for tickets (© **305/358-5885**), which range from $4 to $50. Tickets go on sale in January.

   Pompano Park Racing, 1800 SW 3rd St., Pompano Beach (© **954/ 972-2000**), features parimutuel harness racing from October to early August. Both grandstand and clubhouse admission is free.

   Jai alai, a sort of Spanish-style indoor lacrosse, was introduced to Florida in 1924 and still draws big crowds, who bet on the fast-paced action. Broward's only fronton, **Dania Jai Alai,** 301 E. Dania Beach Blvd. at the intersection of Fla. A1A and U.S. 1 (© **954/920-1511**), is a great place to spend an afternoon or evening.

   Wrapped around an artificial lake, **Gulfstream Park,** at U.S. 1 and Hallandale Beach Boulevard, Hallandale (© **954/454-7000**), is pretty and popular. Large purses and important horse races are commonplace at this recently refurbished suburban course, and the track is often crowded. It hosts the Florida Derby each March. Call for schedules. Admission is $3 weekdays, $5 weekends to the grandstand, and always $5 to the clubhouse. Parking is free. From January 3 to April 25, post times are 1:30pm weekdays and 1pm weekends, and the doors open at 11:30am. Many weekends feature live concerts by well-known musicians.

   In the sport of ice hockey, the young Florida Panthers (© **954/835-7000**) have already made history. In the 1994–95 season, they played in the Stanley Cup finals, and the fans love them. They play in Sunrise at the **Office Depot Center** at 2555 NW 137th Way (© **954/835-8000**). Tickets range from $14 to $100. Call for directions and ticket information.

TENNIS   There are hundreds of courts in Broward County, and plenty are accessible to the public. Many are at resorts and hotels. If one's not at yours, try one of these.

Famous as the spot where Chris Evert got in her early serves, the **Jimmy Evert Tennis Center,** 701 NE 12th Ave. (off Sunrise Blvd.), Fort Lauderdale (© **954/ 828-5378**), has 18 lighted clay and 3 hard courts. Her coach and father, James Evert, still teaches young players here, though he is very picky about whom he'll accept. Nonresidents of Fort Lauderdale pay $5 per hour before 4pm and $6 after. Reservations are accepted after 2pm for the following day but cost an extra $3.

SEEING THE SIGHTS

Billie Swamp Safari 🦅   Billie Swamp Safari is an up-close-and-personal view of the Seminole Indians' 2,200-acre Big Cypress Reservation. There are daily tours into reservation wetlands, hardwood hammocks, and areas where wildlife (seemingly strategically placed deer, water buffalo, bison, wild hogs, ornery ostriches, rare birds, and alligators) reside. Tours are provided aboard swamp buggies, customized motorized vehicles specially designed to provide visitors with an elevated view of the frontier while comfortably riding through the wetlands and cypress heads. For the more adventurous, you may want to take a fast-moving airboat ride or trek a nature trail. Airboat rides run about 20 minutes while the swamp buggy tours are about 1-hour-long. A stop at an alligator farm reeks of Disney, but the kids won't care. You can also stay overnight in a native Tiki hut if you're really looking to immerse yourself in the culture.

Big Cypress Reservation, 1½-hr. drive west of Fort Lauderdale. © 800/949-6101. Free admission. Swamp buggy tours $20 adults, $18 seniors 62 and up, $10 children 4–12; airboat tours $12 for all ages. Daily 8:30am–6pm. Airboats depart every 30 min. beginning at 9:30am; last ride at 4:30pm. Swamp buggy tours leave on the hour (except for 4pm) between 11am and 5pm.

Bonnet House ⭐⭐⭐   This historic 35-acre plantation home and estate, accessible by guided tour only, will provide you with a fantastic glimpse of old South Florida. Built in 1921, the sprawling two-story waterfront home (surrounded with formal tropical gardens) is really the backdrop of a love story, which the very chatty volunteer guides will share with you if you ask. Some have actually lunched with the former resident of the house, the late Evelyn Bartlett, the wife of world-acclaimed artist Frederic Clay Bartlett. The worthwhile 1¼-hour tour brings you quirky people, whimsical artwork, lush grounds, and interesting design. Inquire about the literary walks and science workshops, which are offered regularly on the grounds.

900 N. Birch Rd. (1 block west of the ocean, south of Sunrise Blvd.), Fort Lauderdale. © 954/563-5393. www.bonnethouse.org. Admission $10 adults, $9 seniors, $8 students under 18, free for children 6 and under. Call for hours and tour times.

Museum of Art Fort Lauderdale ⭐ *Kids*   A fantastic modern art facility, the Museum of Art Fort Lauderdale features permanent collections including those from William Glackens; the CoBrA Movement in Copenhagen, Brussels, and Amsterdam featuring over 200 paintings; 50 sculptures; 1,200 works on paper from 1948–1951, including the largest repository of Asger Jorn graphics outside the Silkeborg Kunstmuseum in Denmark; a stunning collection of Picasso ceramics; and a contemporary collection of works from over 90 Cuban artists in exile around the world. Traveling exhibits such as Ansel Adams and constant art classes make the Museum a great place to spend a rainy day.

1 E. Las Olas Blvd., Fort Lauderdale. © 954/525-5500. www.museumofart.org. Adults $6, students $3, children under 6 free. Wed–Mon 11am–7pm; Thurs until 9pm.

One If by Land, Taxi If by Sea

Plan to spend at least an afternoon or evening cruising Fort Lauderdale's 300 miles of waterways in the only way you can: by boat. The **Water Bus of Fort Lauderdale** (© 954/467-6677; www.watertaxi.com) is one of the greatest innovations for water lovers since those cool Velcro sandals. A trusty fleet of older port boats serves the dual purpose of transporting and entertaining visitors as they cruise through "The Venice of America." Because of its popularity, the water taxis have welcomed several sleek, 70-passenger "water buses" (featuring indoor and outdoor seating with an atrium-like roof to the fleet.

Taxis operate on demand and also along a fairly regular route, carrying up to 48 passengers to 20 stops. If you stay at a hotel on the route, you can be picked up at your hotel, usually within 15 minutes of calling, and then be shuttled to any of the dozens of restaurants, bars, and attractions on or near the waterfront. If you aren't sure where you want to go, ask one of the personable captains, who can point out historic and fun spots along the way.

Starting daily at 8am, boats run until midnight 7 days a week, depending on the weather. Check their website for exact times of pickup. The cost is $5 for a day pass; $4 for a one-way trip; $10 for a 3-day pass; and $25 for a weeklong pass. Tickets are available on board; no credit cards are accepted.

Museum of Discovery & Science ★★ (Kids)   This museum's high-tech, interactive approach to education proves that science can equal fun. Adults won't feel as if they're in a kiddie museum, either. During the week, school groups meander through the cavernous two-story modern building. Kids 7 and under enjoy navigating their way through the excellent explorations in the "Discovery Center." Florida Ecoscapes is particularly interesting, with a living coral reef, bees, bats, frogs, turtles, and alligators. Most weekend nights, you'll find a diverse crowd ranging from hip high-school kids to 30-somethings enjoying a rock film in the IMAX 3-D theater, which also shows short, science-related, super-size films daily. Out front, see the 52-foot-tall "Great Gravity Clock," located in the museum's atrium, the largest kinetic-energy sculpture in the state. Call for changing exhibits.

401 SW 2nd St., Fort Lauderdale. © 954/467-6637. www.mods.org. Museum admission (includes admission to 1 IMAX film) $14 adults, $13 seniors, $12 children 3–12. Mon–Sat 10am–5pm; Sun noon–6pm. Movie theaters stay open later. From I-95, exit on Broward Blvd. E. Continue to SW 5th Ave.; turn right, garage on right.

Stranahan House ★★★   In a town whose history is younger than many of its residents, visitors may want to take a minute to see Fort Lauderdale's very oldest standing structure and a prime example of classic "Florida Frontier" architecture. Built in 1901 by the "father of Fort Lauderdale," Frank Stranahan, this house once served as a trading post for Seminole trappers, who came here to sell pelts. It's been a post office, town hall, and general store and now is a worthwhile little museum of South Florida pioneer life, containing turn-of-the-last-century furnishings and historical photos of the area. It is also the site of occasional concerts and social functions. Call for details.

335 SE 6th Ave. (Las Olas Blvd. at the New River Tunnel), Fort Lauderdale. ☎ **954/524-4736.** www.stranahanhouse.com. Admission $6 adults, $5 seniors, $3 students and children. Wed–Sat 10am–3pm; Sun 1–3pm. Tours are on the hour; last tour at 3pm. Accessible by water taxi.

SHOPPING & BROWSING

It's all about malls in Broward County. And while most of the best shopping is located within Fort Lauderdale proper, there are other areas in the county also worth browsing.

Dania is known as the Antique Capital of the South because within 1 square mile of Federal Highway, the city has more than 100 dealers selling everything from small collectibles to fine antiques. (If you want to peruse, it's best to park along Federal Highway, on the "row," which is where Federal Highway meets US1.). For more information on "Antique Row," call ☎ **954/924-3627.** Also in Dania is the **Design Center of the Americas (DCOTA),** at the intersection of I-95 and Griffin Road (☎ **954/920-7997;** www.designcenteroftheamericas.com), a 775,000-square-foot full-service interior design center with tons of furniture showrooms featuring everything from ultra mod to classic, designer studios, and, from time to time, fabulous sample sales.

For bargain mavens, there's a strip of "fashion" stores on Hallandale Beach Boulevard's "Schmatta Row," east of Dixie Highway and the railroad tracks, where off-brand shoes, bags, and jewelry are sold at deep discounts. Hollywood Boulevard also offers some interesting shops, with everything from Indonesian artifacts to used and rare books, leather bustiers, and handmade hats. Dozens of shops line the pedestrian-friendly strip just west of Young Circle. The art galleries are clustered along Harrison Street, just east of Dixie Highway.

The area's only beachfront mall, **Beach Place,** is in Fort Lauderdale on Fla. A1A just north of Las Olas Boulevard. The recipient of a $1.6 million face-lift in 2001, this 100,000-square-foot giant sports the usual chains like Sunglass Hut, Limited Express, Banana Republic, and Gap, as well as lots of popular bars and restaurants. While it used to be all the rage with the spring break set, Beach Place is now aiming for a much more upscale clientele, adding many new higher-end stores and restaurants.

Other more traditional malls include the upscale **Galleria,** at Sunrise Boulevard near the Fort Lauderdale Beach, and **Broward Mall,** west of I-95 on Broward Boulevard, in Plantation.

If you are looking for unusual boutiques, especially art galleries, head to quaint **Las Olas Boulevard** ✦ (located west of A1A and a block east of Federal Hwy./U.S. 1, off of SE 8th St.), where there are hundreds of shops with alluring window decorations (like kitchen utensils posing as modern art sculptures) and intriguing merchandise such as mural-size oil paintings.

On the edge of the Arts and Science District is **Las Olas Riverfront,** a retail complex with 260,000 square feet of restaurants, clothing stores, arcades, and a multiplex movie theater.

The Fort Lauderdale Swap Shop, 3291 W. Sunrise Blvd. (☎ **954/791-SWAP**), is one of the world's largest flea markets. I think it's rather schlocky, actually. In addition to endless acres of vendors hawking everything from electronics to underwear, there's a miniature amusement park, a 13-screen drive-in movie theater, weekend concerts, and even a free daily circus complete with elephants, horse shows, high-wire acts, and clowns.

The monster of all outlet malls is **Sawgrass Mills,** 12801 W. Sunrise Blvd., Sunrise (☎ **800-FL-MILLS** or 954/846-2350; fax 954/846-2312). Since the most recent expansion, completed in mid-1999, which added more than 30 new designer outlet stores, this behemoth (shaped like a Florida alligator) now holds more than 300 shops, kiosks, a 24-screen movie theater, and many restaurants and bars, including a Hard Rock Cafe. In late 2004, a $50 million education and amusement center for kids will debut, giving dads and kids something to do while moms shop the day away. The enclosed area covers nearly 2.5 million square feet over 50 acres—there's no way to see it all in a day. To get there, take I-95 to I-595 west to the Flamingo Road exit, turn right, and drive 2 miles to Sunrise Boulevard; you will see the large complex on the left. From the Florida Turnpike, exit Sunrise Boulevard west.

Fishing enthusiasts won't want to miss **Bass Pro Shops Outdoor World** (200 Gulfstream Way, Dania Beach; ℂ **954/929-7710**), a sprawling retail complex just west of I-95, where you can buy anything from yachts to lures.

For those who like to turn an ordinary shopping trip into an extraordinary event, **Activity Planners** (ℂ **954/525-9194**) will do just that, arranging a water taxi, limo, or Town Car for your own private shopping tour through the Greater Ft. Lauderdale area.

WHERE TO STAY

The Fort Lauderdale beach has a hotel or motel on nearly every block, and they range from the run-down to the luxurious. Both the **Howard Johnson** (ℂ **800/ 327-8578** or 954/563-2451), at 700 N. Atlantic Blvd. (on Fla. A1A, south of Sunrise Blvd.), and the **Days Inn** (ℂ **800/329-7466** or 954/563-2521), at 4221 N. Ocean Blvd., offer clean ocean-side rooms starting at about $150. For a more luxurious stay, the **St. Regis Resort, Spa and Residences** (ℂ **954/ 568-4623**), featuring 197 suites, a gourmet restaurant, and a spa, at press time was slated to open in late 2004. And, openen in May 2004, the **Seminole Hard Rock Hotel & Casino,** 1 Seminole Rd. (ℂ **954/327-7625**), a $300 million resort with 500 rooms, a health spa, beach club, and gaming facilities, will undoubtedly bring new life to the Hollywood area.

In Hollywood, where prices are generally cheaper, the **Holiday Inn** at 101 N. Ocean Blvd. (ℂ **954/923-8700**) operates a full-service hotel right on the ocean. With prices starting at around $110 in season and discounts for AAA members, it's a great deal. **Howard Johnson** (ℂ **800/423-9867** or 954/925-1411) has a good location right on the beach at 2501 N. Ocean Dr. (I-95 to Sheridan St. east to Fla. A1A south).

Extended Stay America/Crossland Economy Studios (ℂ **800/398-7829**) has four superclean properties in Fort Lauderdale and offers year-round rates as low as $49 a night and $159 per week. The studios are designed with business travelers in mind. Each includes free local calls, a dataport, a kitchenette, a recliner, and a well-lit desk.

Especially for rentals for a few weeks or months, call **Florida Sunbreak** (ℂ **800-SUNBREAK**). Also, check out the annual list of small lodgings compiled by the **Greater Fort Lauderdale Convention & Visitors Bureau** (ℂ **954/ 765-4466**). It is especially helpful for those looking for privately owned, charming, and affordable lodgings.

VERY EXPENSIVE

Hyatt Regency Pier Sixty-Six ★★   Located on 22 tropical acres on the Intracoastal Waterway, this resort is best known for its world-class marina and its rooftop lounge that spins every 66 minutes. If you experience vertigo after sitting in the revolving lounge, an invigorating body- or skin-care treatment at the hotel's intimate, private, exquisite European Spa LXVI will help relocate your sense of balance. Equally invigorating are the hotel's recreational amenities, which include a sprawling three-pool complex with a 40-person hydrotherapy pool, tennis courts, and an aquatic center complete with every water sport imaginable. The hotel transformed its uber popular California Cafe into Grille 66 and Bar, a classy, upscale steakhouse. After a recent renovation, the tropical-style rooms are spruced up with cherrywood furnishings and bathrooms with marble floors and granite vanities. All rooms have balconies with views of the Intracoastal and the hotel's lushly landscaped gardens. Designer suites come with Jacuzzi, wet bar, living room, dining room, and exceptional views.

2301 SE 17th St. Causeway, Fort Lauderdale, FL 33316. ✆ **800/233-1234** or 954/525-6666. Fax 954/728-3541. www.hyatt.com. 380 units. Winter $209–$219 double; off-season $129–$179 double. Year-round from $1,000 suite. AE, DC, DISC, MC, V. Valet parking $14; self-parking $10 (max) a day. **Amenities:** 5 restaurants; 2 bars; 3 swimming pools; 2 lighted clay tennis courts; spa; watersports equipment/rental; bike rental; concierge; business center; salon; 24-hr. room service; laundry services and self-service laundry; dry cleaning. *In room:* A/C, TV, dataport, minibar, coffeemaker, hair dryer, iron, safe.

Marriott's Harbor Beach 🐾🐾   This resort is loaded with the same amenities as Pier Sixty-Six but with a more secluded setting, located on 16 oceanfront acres just south of Fort Lauderdale's "strip." Everything in this place is huge—from the guest rooms and suites to the 8,000-square-foot swimming pool to the $8 million 24,000-square-foot European spa. Accommodations feature marble, deep crown molding, and newish bathrooms with granite vanities, Italian marble flooring, and wraparound mirrors. A revamped lobby affords sweeping ocean views. All rooms open onto private balconies overlooking either the ocean or the Intracoastal Waterway. The hotel's 3030 Ocean is an excellent seafood restaurant and raw bar; Riva, a Mediterranean-style, oceanfront eatery is also top notch. Return guests include many convention groups and families who enjoy the space and the great location off the beaten strip.

3030 Holiday Dr., Fort Lauderdale, FL 33316. ✆ **800/222-6543** or 954/525-4000. Fax 954/766-6193. www.marriottharborbeach.com. 637 units. Winter $239–$429 double; off-season $179–$219 double. Year-round from $600 suite. AE, DC, DISC, MC, V. Valet parking $18, self-parking $14. From I-95, exit on I-595 east to U.S. 1 N.; proceed to SE 17th St.; make a right and go over the Intracoastal bridge past 3 traffic lights to Holiday Dr.; turn right. **Amenities:** 3 restaurants; 2 bars; outdoor heated pool; 4 clay tennis courts; basketball court; health club; European-style spa; extensive watersports equipment; bike rental; children's center and programs; game room; concierge; tour desk; courtesy car; business center; salon; 24-hr. room service; in-room massage; babysitting; laundry services and self-service laundry. *In room:* A/C, TV, dataport, minibar, coffeemaker, hair dryer, iron, safe, Sony PlayStation.

The Westin Diplomat Resort & Spa   In its day, the Hollywood Diplomat was a swanky affair, an oceanfront playground attending to a host of celebs that included Sinatra and Co. The new Diplomat, which opened in February 2002, was built on the site of the original to the tune of $600 million.

This is a 1,060-room full-service beach resort that's loaded with amenities. The hotel's main building is a 39-story oceanfront tower (with adjacent conference center) surrounded by 8 acres of man-made lakes. A gorgeous bridged, glass-bottomed swimming pool with cascading waterfalls, private cabanas, and a slew of watersports and activities adds a tropical touch. Rooms are a cross between a subtle boutique hotel and an Art Deco throwback, with dark woods, hand-cut marble, and, most impressive, the 10-layer Heavenly Bed, a Westin trademark, with custom-designed pillow-top mattresses and a very cushy down blanket (crank up the A/C!). Dining options are resortlike in quantity and quality. A fine-dining steakhouse is very elegant looking, and several more casual

options are available. A South Beach–style nightclub, Satine, is also on site—
convenient, considering there is no nightlife in the surrounding area unless you
go north to downtown Hollywood or south to South Beach. At press time, construction on Diplomat Landing, the hotel's shopping and entertainment complex across the street, was still ongoing, but a few things such as Nikki Marina,
an offshoot of South Beach's St. Tropez-ish Nikki Beach Club, was already open.

The Diplomat's Country Club and Spa is modeled after an Italian villa, with
60 luxurious guest rooms, yacht slips, a 155-acre golf course, and a world-class
spa and tennis club. The 30,000-square-foot spa has 17 treatment rooms, a spa
pool, a spa menu, and an extensive selection of treatments.

3555 S. Ocean Dr. (Fla. A1A), Hollywood, FL 33019. © 800/327-1212 or 954/602-6000. Fax 954/602-7000.
www.diplomatresort.com. 1,060 units. Winter $255–$295 double, $315–$365 suite; off-season $175–$219
double, $239–$325 suite. AE, DC, DISC, MC, V. Valet parking $16. **Amenities:** 6 restaurants; 3 lounges; 2
pools; golf course; 10 clay tennis courts; health club and spa; watersports equipment/rental; 24-hr. room service. *In room:* A/C, TV/Web TV, fax, dataport, minibar, coffeemaker, hair dryer.

EXPENSIVE

Lago Mar Resort and Club ★★ *Kids*   A charming lobby with a rock fireplace
and saltwater aquarium sets the tone of this utterly inviting resort, a casually elegant piece of Old Florida that occupies its own little island between Lake Mayan
and the Atlantic. Lago Mar guests have access to the broadest and best strip of
beach in the entire city, not to mention the wonderful bougainvillea-lined,
9,000-square-foot swimming lagoon. Lago Mar is very family oriented, with lots
of facilities and supervised activities for children. Service is spectacular. The
rooms and suites have Mediterranean or Key West influences and are well
appointed—but it's likely you won't be spending much time inside. As of January 2002, a full-service spa will offer a wide array of pampering treatments and
steam rooms; and a 1,000-square-foot exercise facility may come in handy after
you indulge in the hotel's northern Italian restaurant, Acquario, which is worth
a visit even if you don't stay here.

1700 S. Ocean Lane, Fort Lauderdale, FL 33316. © 800/524-6627 or 954/523-6511. Fax 954/524-6627.
www.lagomar.com. 212 units. Winter $265 double, from $355 suite; off-season $140–$165 double, from $165
suite. AE, DC, MC, V. Free valet parking. From Federal Hwy. (U.S. 1), turn east onto SE 17th St. Causeway; turn
right onto Mayan Dr.; turn right again onto S. Ocean Dr.; turn left onto Grace Dr.; then left again onto S. Ocean
Lane to the hotel. **Amenities:** 4 restaurants; cocktail lounge; wine room; outdoor pool and lagoon; 2 tennis
courts; exercise room; watersports equipment rental; children's programs during holiday periods; game room;
concierge; tour desk; business center; 24-hr. room service; laundry services; dry cleaning. *In room:* A/C, TV, dataport, kitchenette, coffeemaker in some units, hair dryer.

Pillars Hotel ★★★ *Finds*   It took me a while to discover this hotel and, apparently, that's exactly the point. One of Fort Lauderdale's best-kept secrets, if not
the best, Pillars Hotel transports you from the neon-hued flash and splash of
Fort Lauderdale's strip and takes you to a two-story British Colonial, Caribbean-
style retreat tucked away on the bustling Intracoastal Waterway. Since it has just
23 rooms, you feel as if you have the grand house all to yourself, albeit with
white-tablecloth room service, an Eden-istic courtyard with free-form pool, lush
landscaping, access to a water taxi, and signing privileges at nearby restaurants
and spa. Rooms are luxurious and loaded with amenities such as private-label
bath products, ultra-plush bedding, and, if you're so inclined, a private masseuse
to iron out your personal kinks. Upon arrival, you will be greeted with a welcome cocktail, and there's always free iced tea at the pool in case you're thirsty.
A library area, with a grand piano and over 500 books and videos, is at your

disposal as is pretty much anything you request here. The quintessential Fort Lauderdale retreat, the Pillars is the zenith of Fort Lauderdale accommodations. There are four suites and all rooms are nonsmoking.

111 N. Birch Rd., Fort Lauderdale, FL 33304. ℂ **954/467-9639.** Fax 954/763-2845. www.pillarshotel.com. 23 units. Winter $199–$265 double, $299–$499 suite; off-season $129–$209 double, $199–$409 suite. AE, DC, DISC, MC, V. Complimentary off-street parking. **Amenities:** Waterfront pool; 24-hr. concierge; business services; 24-hr. room service; same-day laundry service; signing privileges at Max's Beach Place restaurant; water-taxi service; preferred rates at beachfront and downtown health clubs. *In room:* AC, TV/VCR, dataport, minibar, hair dryer, iron, safe.

Riverside Hotel 🐾🐾

A touch of New Orleans hits Fort Lauderdale's popular Las Olas Boulevard in the form of this charming, six-story 1936 hotel. There's no beach here, but the hotel is located on the sleepy and scenic New River, capturing the essence of that ever-elusive Old Florida. Guest rooms are a bit nicer than the public areas (outfitted in Mexican tile and wicker furnishings) and are spacious and well maintained. Details like intricately tiled bathrooms and old-style furniture enhance the charm of the otherwise stark building. The best rooms face the New River, but it's hard to see the water past the parking lot and trees. Twelve rooms offer king-size beds with mirrored canopies and flowing drapes. There are also seven elegantly decorated suites with wet bars and French doors that lead to private balconies. The hotel has two restaurants worth trying: Indigo, a fantastic Asian/Indonesian restaurant in the hotel lobby (p. 257), and the Grill Room, for old-world elegance.

620 E. Las Olas Blvd., Fort Lauderdale, FL 33301. ℂ **800/325-3280** or 954/467-0671. Fax 954/462-2148. www.riversidehotel.com. 217 units. Winter $159–$369 suite; off-season $99–$289 suite. Special packages are available. Discount for online bookings. AE, DC, MC, V. Valet parking $8–$10. From I-95, exit onto Broward Blvd.; turn right onto Federal Hwy. (U.S. 1); then left onto Las Olas Blvd. **Amenities:** 2 restaurants; outdoor pool; concierge; secretarial services; limited room service; laundry services; dry cleaning. *In room:* A/C, TV, dataport, minibar, fridge, coffeemaker, hair dryer, iron.

MODERATE

Banyan Marina Resort 🐾🐾

These fabulous waterfront apartments, located on a beautifully landscaped residential island, may have you vowing never to stay in a hotel again. They're intimate, charming, *and* reasonably priced. Built around a stunning 75-year-old banyan tree, the Banyan Marina Resort is located directly on the active canals halfway between Fort Lauderdale's downtown and the beach. When available, you'll choose between one- and two-bedroom apartments, which have been recently renovated. All are comfortable and spacious, with French doors, full kitchens, and living rooms. The best part of staying here, besides your gracious and knowledgeable hosts, Dagmar and Peter Neufeldt, is that the convenient water taxi will find you here and take you anywhere you want to be, day or night. There is a small outdoor heated pool and a marina for those with boats in tow. Since 1998, the Neufeldts have been honored by a local area-enhancing campaign, Broward Beautiful, winning first place for the past 3 years in a row in the category of small multifamily dwellings.

111 Isle of Venice, Fort Lauderdale, FL 33301. ℂ **954/524-4430.** Fax 954/764-4870. www.banyanmarina. com. 10 units. Winter $95–$250 apt; off-season $60–$170 apt. Weekly and monthly rates available. MC, V. Free parking. From I-95, exit Broward Blvd. E.; cross U.S. 1 and turn right on SE 15th Ave. At the first traffic light (Las Olas Blvd.), turn left. Turn left at the 3rd island (Isle of Venice). **Amenities:** Restaurant; pool; dock. *In room:* A/C, TV, dataport, kitchen, coffeemaker, hair dryer.

Best Western Pelican Beach Resort 🐾

Not bad for a Best Western, the brand new (opened in the winter of 2004) Pelican Beach Resort sits on 500 feet of sand, features 180 rooms (including 117 with balconies), and has a sublimely relaxing wraparound oceanfront verandah and sun deck with rocking chairs. What also rocks about this place is the heated outdoor pool complete with lazy river raft ride. On the north end of the property is the older Sun Tower, which has 24 oceanfront rooms and suites. Stick to the newer part, however.

2000 N. Atlantic Blvd., Fort Lauderdale, FL 33301. *C* **800/525-OCEAN** or 954/568-9431. Fax 954/565-2662. www.pelicanbeach.com. 180 units. Winter $180 double, $230 suite; off-season $120 double, $170 suite. Continental breakfast included. AE, DC, MC, V. Free parking. **Amenities:** Restaurant; heated outdoor pool; sun deck. *In room:* A/C, TV, dataport, fridge, microwave, coffeemaker, hair dryer.

Courtyard Villa on the Ocean 🏝🏝 Nestled between a bunch of larger hotels, this small, eight-room historic hotel offers a romantic getaway right on the beach. A remodeling and redecorating included the addition of 18th- and 19th-century antique reproduction furnishings to its charmed setting. Courtyard Villa offers spacious oceanfront efficiencies with private balconies, larger suites overlooking the pool, and full two-bedroom apartments. Rooms are plush, with chenille bedspreads and carved four-poster beds; fully equipped kitchenettes are an added convenience. The tiled bathrooms have strong, hot showers to wash off the beach sand. Room no. 8 is especially nice, with French doors that open to a private balcony overlooking the ocean. Relax in the hotel's unique heated pool/spa or on the second-floor sun deck. You can also swim off the beach to a living reef just 50 feet offshore. Scuba-diving instruction is available on premises.

4312 El Mar Dr., Lauderdale-by-the-Sea, FL 33308. *C* **800/291-3560** or 954/776-1164. Fax 954/491-0768. www.courtyardvilla.com. 10 units. Winter $169 double, $259 2-bedroom; off-season $115 double, $167 2-bedroom. Rates include full breakfast. AE, MC, V. Pets under 35 lb. are accepted with a $200 deposit; must be caged while outside; no pit bulls, Dobermans, or Rottweilers. **Amenities:** Outdoor heated pool; Jacuzzi; free use of bikes; limited room service; scuba instruction; free laptop use with Internet service. *In room:* A/C, TV/VCR, kitchenette, coffeemaker, hair dryer.

INEXPENSIVE

A Little Inn by the Sea 🏝 It's not fancy, but A Little Inn by the Sea sits on a primo piece of oceanfront, and most rooms have private balconies overlooking the ocean. There's also 300 feet of private, palm tree–lined beach, which isn't too shabby either. Rooms are hardly worthy of a spread in an interior design magazine, but the views make up for the lackluster decor. A free breakfast buffet, a rooftop terrace, and a heated freshwater pool are lovely perks.

4546 El Mar Dr., Lauderdale-by-the-Sea, FL 33308. *C* **800/492-0311** or 954/772-2450. Fax 954/938-9354. www.alittleinn.com. 29 units. Winter $119–$149 double, $160–$199 suite; $318 2-bedroom apartment; off-season $79–$109 double, $129–$159 suite; $228–$248 2-bedroom apartment. MC, V. Free parking. **Amenities:** Heated pool; access to nearby tennis court; nearby children's playground; coin laundry. *In room:* A/C, TV.

Fort Lauderdale Beach Hostel For the young, or budget/backpack travelers, this hostel is a great option, offering both dorm beds and private rooms at bargain basement prices. Clean and conveniently located, the hostel is just 654 feet from the ocean, features free parking, free telephones, free self-cook food, a free breakfast buffet, and, if you're lucky, free surfboards or in-line skates lying around for your use.

2115 N. Ocean Blvd., Fort Lauderdale, FL 33305. *C* **954/567-7275.** www.fortlauderdalehostel.com. 12 units. Dorm beds $18 per night, $115 per week; private rooms $59 season, $42 off-season. MC, V. **Amenities:** Free breakfast; Ping-Pong; free Internet access; sun deck; garden. *In room:* A/C, TV, iron.

Sea Downs (and the Bougainvillea) 🏝🏝 This bargain accommodation is often booked months in advance by returning guests who want to be directly on the beach without paying a fortune. The hosts of this superclean 1950s motel, Claudia and Karl Herzog, live on the premises and keep things running smoothly. Renovations completed in 1997 have replaced bathroom fixtures, and many rooms have been redecorated here and at the Herzogs' other even less expensive property next door, the 11-unit Bougainvillea. Guests at both hotels share the Sea Downs' pool.

2900 N. Surf Rd., Hollywood, FL 33019. © **954/923-4968.** Fax 954/923-8747. www.seadowns.com or www.bougainvilleahollywood.com. 12 units. Winter $63–$95 studio, $88–$140 1-bedroom apt; off-season $60–$70 studio, $88–$108 1-bedroom apt. No credit cards. From I-95, exit Sheridan St. E. to Fla. A1A and go south; drive ½ mile to Coolidge St.; turn left. **Amenities:** Freshwater outdoor pool; concierge; laundry facilities. *In room:* A/C, TV, dataport, kitchen, fridge, coffeemaker.

WHERE TO DINE

It took awhile for a more sophisticated, varied Epicurean scene to reach these shores, but Fort Lauderdale, and to some extent Hollywood, finally has several fine restaurants. Increasingly, ethnic options are joining the legions of surf-and-turferies that have dominated the area for so long. **Las Olas Boulevard** has so many eateries that the city has put a moratorium on the opening of new restaurants on the 2-mile-long street.

VERY EXPENSIVE

Café Martorano ★★ ITALIAN   This small storefront eatery doesn't win any awards for decor or location, but when it comes to food that's good enough to feed an entire Italian family, Café Martorano is one of the best, one that has people waiting for a table for upwards of 2 hours as the restaurant accepts no reservations and can get away with it. An almost-offensive sound system (playing disco tunes and Sinatra) has a tendency to turn many a diner off, but you don't go to Café Martorano for an intimate dinner. Eating here is like being in a big, fat, Italian wedding, where eating, drinking, and dancing are paramount. The colossal meatballs are sublime, as are all of the pasta dishes. Ingredients hail from all over Italy, including tomatoes grown in volcanic soil near Salermo, Italy. The menu changes daily, but regulars have the power to request special, off-the-menu items. If you don't ask, you don't get, so open your mouth. Also keep your eyes wide open for celebrities such as Liza Minelli, James Gandolfini, and Steven Van Zandt, among others, who make it a point to stop here for a meal while in town.

3343 E. Oakland Park Blvd., Fort Lauderdale. © **954/561-2554.** Reservations not accepted. Main courses $13–$29. MC, V. Daily 5–11pm.

Darrel & Oliver's Cafe Maxx ★★ FLORIDIAN/NEW WORLD   Despite its bleak location in an unassuming storefront, Darrel & Oliver's Cafe Maxx is one of the best restaurants in Broward County. When it opened in 1984, it was the first restaurant to have an open kitchen, and what a stir that caused! Now, instead of focusing on the kitchen, it's what comes out of it that's a marvel. Consider crispy yucca-scallion Florida grouper with vanilla rum butter, sweet mash, asparagus, and Parisienne vegetables; sweet-onion–crusted yellowtail snapper with Madeira sauce; or a veal chop with truffled mushroom butter and wild mushroom risotto.

2601 E. Atlantic Blvd., Pompano Beach. © **954/782-0606.** Fax 954/782-0648. Reservations recommended. Main courses $18–$39. AE, DC, DISC, MC, V. Mon–Thurs 5:30–10:30pm; Fri–Sat 5:30–11pm; Sun 5:30–10pm. From I-95, exit at Atlantic Blvd. E. The restaurant is 3 lights east of Federal Hwy.

Mark's Las Olas ★★★ NEW WORLD CUISINE   Before star chef Mark Militello hit Las Olas Boulevard, there was really no reason to dine here. However, once he opened the doors to his sleek, modern restaurant, he opened the eyes and mouths of discriminating Fort Lauderdale gourmands to his excellent

New World cuisine. Roasted garlic-stuffed grilled tenderloin of beef with caramelized sweet onion, Swiss chard, marrow toast, and red wine short rib sauce is possibly the best item on the menu. If the kitchen is out of it—they tend to run out quickly—everything else on the menu, from the hot pepper pizza with chorizo to the crab-crusted black grouper with wild mushroom-salsify ragôut, roasted potatoes, and horseradish butter, is delicious. Save room for a chocolate dessert—any one will do.

1032 E. Las Olas Blvd., Fort Lauderdale. ✆ **954/463-1000.** Reservations suggested. Main courses $14–$30. AE, DC, MC, V. Mon–Fri 11:30am–2:30pm; Mon–Thurs 6–10:30pm; Fri–Sat 6–11pm; Sun 6–10pm.

EXPENSIVE

Anthony's Runway 84 ★★★ ITALIAN   Meet Anthony, he's the youthful, gregarious owner of this landmark Fort Lauderdale restaurant whose interior is all about jet setting—albeit circa sometime in the mid to late '70s—and whose bar is crafted out of actual plane fuselage. Once you meet Anthony, he will introduce you to your server, whose name is likely to be Tony. Same goes for the bartender. Although Anthony's isn't necessarily the Tony Danza of restaurants, in which every role played in here is named Tony, it's quite amusing to play count the Tonys while inside. But I digress. The quintessential, convivial Italian (think John Travolta in Saturday Night Fever) vibe in here is conducive to one of the most enjoyable meals you'll ever have in your life. Order individually if you want, but the best way to go is, what else, family style, in which you'll be able to share lots of dishes including mussels marinara, fried clams, roasted red peppers in garlic, shrimp parmigiana, an out of this world rigatoni with cauliflower (although it sounds boring, order it no matter what!), and stellar meat and poultry dishes that frequent fliers to Anthony's rave about each time, as if it were their last meal. For the best pizza, try Anthony's Coal Fired Pizza nearby at 2203 S. Federal Hwy. (✆ **954/462-5555**).

330 S. R. 84, Fort Lauderdale. ✆ **954/467-8484.** Reservations not accepted. Main courses $11–$25. AE, DC, DISC, MC, V. Tues–Thurs and Sun noon–10pm; Fri–Sat 5–11pm.

Armadillo Cafe ★★★ SOUTHWESTERN   The city of Davie may be best known for farmland and rodeos, but it's also celebrated for this outstanding Southwestern restaurant, which attracts city slickers from all over South Florida. The Armadillo recently moved from its strip-mall digs to a much larger space to accommodate all the foodies who flock here in search of porcini-dusted sea bass and lobster quesadillas, among other things. A more casual offshoot, Baby Armadillo Cantina (with the same address, phone number, and hours), offers light meals, lunch, and dinner.

3400 S. University Dr., Davie. ✆ **954/423-9954** or 954/791-4866. Reservations essential. Main courses $17–$29. AE, DC, DISC, MC, V. Mon–Thurs 5–10pm; Fri–Sun 5–11pm.

Eduardo De San Angel ★★★ MEXICAN   Gourmet Mexican is *not* an oxymoron, and for those who don't believe that, take one meal at the sublime Eduardo De San Angel and you'll see how true it is. Chef Eduardo Pria has a masterful way with food as seen in dishes such as Jaibas Rellenas, fresh Florida blue crab, plum tomatoes, onions, jalapeño peppers, and Spanish green olives baked in a shell with melted jack cheese au gratin and mole poblano, herb oil brushed grilled breast of chicken topped with the traditional mole from Puebla, toasted sesame seeds, and sliced avocado. And then there's the roasted poblano pepper filled with fresh Florida blue crab, pickled jalapeño peppers, green olives, and tomatoes over stewed sweet onions baked in a parchment paper pocket.

Fresh flowers and candlelight, not to mention the fact that the restaurant resembles an intimate hacienda, also drive home the fact that this isn't your mom's Old El Paso taco dinner.

2822 E Commercial Blvd., Fort Lauderdale. ℂ **954/772-4731.** Reservations essential. Main courses $18–$29. AE, DC, DISC, MC, V. Mon–Thurs 11:30am–10:30pm; Fri–Sat 5:30–10:30pm.

Himmarshee Bar & Grille ✿ AMERICAN   Located on a popular street of bars frequented by Fort Lauderdale's young professionals, Himmarshee Bar & Grille is known for its cool scene and its cuisine. A mezzanine bar upstairs is ideal for people-watching; outdoor tables, if you can score one, are tight but strategically situated in front of all the street's action. On Friday and Saturday nights, in particular, it's difficult to get a table here. However, if you can deal with cramming into the bar, it's worth a cocktail or two. The wine list is particularly impressive, and the grilled sirloin burger with creamy basil Gorgonzola is a delicious meal in itself for only $7.50. Also try the wasabi-crusted salmon or the pan-roasted Baramundi (Australian sea bass). Check out Side Bar, the restaurant's very Colorado ski-lodgey bar next door featuring live music and a bustling crowd of young hipsters on the prowl.

210 SW 2nd St. (south of Broward Blvd., west of U.S. 1), Fort Lauderdale. ℂ **954/524-1818.** Reservations recommended. Main courses $12–$24. AE, MC, V. Mon–Fri 11:30am–2:30pm; Sun–Thurs 6–10:30pm; Fri–Sat 6–11:30pm.

Hobo's Fish Joint ✿✿ SEAFOOD   Huge portions of extremely fresh fish are prepared in more than a dozen ways at this steakhouse-style restaurant with wood floors and white tablecloths. Despite the fact that it's located away from the ocean in the utterly suburban enclave of Coral Springs, this joint is worth the trip. Some even say it's the best seafood in Broward County. I say it's a tough call between here and the Sunfish Grill (see below). See for yourself with the littleneck clams in garlic bouillon or Chilean sea bass oreganato on a bed of orzo.

10317 Royal Palm Blvd. (at Coral Springs Dr.), Coral Springs. ℂ **954/346-5484.** Reservations for 6 or more. Main courses $17–$27. AE, MC, V. Mon–Thurs 5:30–9:30pm; Fri–Sat 5:30–10:30pm; Sun 5:30–9pm. From I-95, exit at Commercial Blvd., go west to University Dr., turn right and then about a mile up, take a left on Royal Palm Blvd.

Sunfish Grill ✿✿✿ SEAFOOD   Unlike its fellow contemporary seafood restaurants, the Sunfish Grill chooses to focus on fish, not fusion. Chef Anthony Sindaco doesn't want to be a star, either. He'd prefer to leave the spotlight on his fantastic fish dishes, which are possibly the freshest in town thanks to the fact that he buys his fish at local markets and often from well-known local fishermen who appear at his back door with their catches of the day. The shrimp bisque cappuccino is a deliciously rich soup served in a demitasse cup—because it's that rich. Conch fritters are purely spectacular, not full of filler. Chilean sea bass, expertly cooked with roasted fennel, saffron potatoes, and a caramelized-onion broth, is wonderful, but the best thing in my opinion is the seared tuna resting on a bed of mushroom and oxtail ragout with garlic mashed potatoes. It's not your typical Japanese-style seared tuna. It's better. In fact, almost everything is better than at most seafood restaurants at the Sunfish Grill.

2771 E. Atlantic Blvd., Pompano Beach. ℂ **954/788-2434.** Reservations accepted. Main courses $17–$28. AE, MC, V. Mon–Thurs 6–9:30pm; Fri–Sat 6–10:30pm. Closed Sun.

MODERATE

Cap's Place Island Restaurant ✿✿✿ *Finds* SEAFOOD   Opened in 1928 by a bootlegger who ran in the same circles as gangster Meyer Lansky, this barge-turned-restaurant is one of South Florida's best-kept secrets. Although it's no longer a rum-running restaurant and gambling casino, its illustrious past (FDR and Winston Churchill dined here together, too) landed it a coveted spot on the National Register of Historic Places. To get there, you have to take a ferryboat, provided by the restaurant. The ride across the Intracoastal is not long and it definitely adds to the Cap's Place experience. And the food's good, too! Traditional seafood dishes such as Florida or Maine lobster, clams linguine, clams casino, and oysters Rockefeller will take you back to the days when a soprano was thought to be just an opera singer.

2765 NE 28th Court, Lighthouse Point. ✆ 954/941-0418. Reservations accepted. Main courses $20–$25. MC, V. Daily 5:30pm–midnight. To get to Cap's Place motor launch from I-95, exit at Copan's Rd. and go east to U.S. 1 (Federal Hwy.). At NE 24th St., turn right and follow the double lines and signs to the Lighthouse Point Yacht Basin and Marina (8 miles north of Fort Lauderdale). From there, follow a Cap's Place sign pointing you to the shuttle.

Creolina's ★★ CREOLE   You'll find authentic Louisiana Creole cuisine at this small but very popular restaurant, situated along the Riverwalk. Try the shrimp jambalaya with shrimp, sausage, and vegetables in a rich brown Cajun sauce served over rice, or the crayfish étouffée with crayfish tail simmered in a mellow Cajun sauce served over rice. The mashed potatoes are homemade, and the delicious fresh-squeezed lemonade is made daily. There is also a terrific New Orleans Sunday brunch. Ask to sit in sassy Rosie's section.

209 SW 2nd St., Fort Lauderdale. ✆ 954/524-2003. Appetizers $4–$9; main courses $13–$18. AE, MC, V. Mon–Fri 11am–2:30pm; Sun–Mon 5–9pm; Tues–Thurs 5–10pm; Fri–Sat 5–11pm.

Indigo ★★ SOUTHEAST ASIAN/ECLECTIC   It seems a little strange to chow down on Southeast Asian food in an utterly New Orleans–style hotel, but this is South Florida—the wackier, the better. This not-so-traditional meal begins with a basket of pappadams, puffy naan bread, and shrimp-puff bread. Next might be a super-rich grilled vegetable cassoulet au gratin and a fried-rice dish with shallots, corn, and asparagus; or pizzas baked on top of nan covered with such toppings as onions, shiitake mushrooms, goat cheese, spinach, eggplant, garlic, curried tomato, and pine nuts. Particularly good is the meaty soy and portobello mushroom combination wrapped in fluffy puff pastry and served with a delicate broccoli sauce. Sounds like a lot of activity going on in one dish, but like the restaurant itself, somehow it all works.

In the Riverside Hotel, 620 E. Las Olas Blvd., Fort Lauderdale. ✆ 954/467-0671. Reservations accepted for groups of 6 or more. Main courses $12–$22. AE, DC, DISC, MC, V. Daily 7am–9:45pm.

Sugar Reef ★★ FRENCH VIETNAMESE/CARIBBEAN   I could go on about the restaurant's priceless, unobstructed ocean view, but the menu of Mediterranean, Caribbean, and French-Vietnamese dishes is just as outstanding. A pleasant tropical decor is bolstered by the fresh air wafting in from the Atlantic through the open windows. Seafood bouillabaisse in green curry and coconut broth and pork loin Benedict—layers of jerk-spiced pork and hollandaise sauce—are among the restaurant's most popular dishes. The restaurant puts a savory spin on duck, roasted and topped with sweet-chile-and-papaya salsa. This is not a restaurant you'd expect to find on a beach boardwalk, which makes it all the more delightful.

600 N. Surf Rd. (on the Broadwalk just north of Hollywood Blvd.), Hollywood. ✆ 954/922-1119. Reservations accepted for groups of 6 or more. Main courses $10–$24; sandwiches and salads $4–$9. AE, DISC, MC, V. Mon 4–10:30pm; Tues–Thurs 11am–10:30pm; Fri–Sun 11am–11pm (sometimes later in winter).

Sushi Blues Cafe ★ SUSHI   Before Hollywood was "hot," Sushi Blues Cafe was singing the blues—in a good way as the only game in town. Now that the area is bustling, it's singing the blues in an even better way, serving up live music

4 nights a week along with raw fish that's quite good. Garlic and ginger studded tuna steak is also fantastic for those who are bored with sushi. Even better, however, is the fact that for once, a meal at a sushi restaurant in an area where such restaurants are a dime a dozen actually seems like a unique experience.

600 N. Surf Rd. (on the Boardwalk just north of Hollywood Blvd.), Hollywood. ✆ 954/922-1119. Reservations accepted for groups of 6 or more. Sushi rolls $3–$10; main courses $7–$21. AE, DISC, MC, V. Daily 11:30am–2am.

Tarpon Bend ★★ SEAFOOD/AMERICAN   This restaurant is one of the few places where the fishermen still bring the fish to the back door. The oysters from the raw bar are shucked to order and are incredible. Try the house specialty "smoked fish dip"—a kingfish smoked on premises. The steamed clambake, with half a Maine lobster, clams, potatoes, mussels, and corn on the cob is scrumptious and served in its own pot. Also try some of the homemade side dishes. For chocolate lovers, the chocolate brownie sundae is a must. There's live entertainment Wednesday through Saturday and a full bar.

200 SW 2nd St., Fort Lauderdale. ✆ 954/523-3233. Reservations accepted for groups of 6 or more. Main courses $12–$15. AE, MC, V. Mon–Thurs 11:30am–1am; Fri–Sat 11:30am–3am.

Tuscan Today Trattoria ★★ *Finds* ITALIAN   For classic Tuscan food in a charming atmosphere, Tuscan Today is something you should not put off until tomorrow. Inspired by the peasant origins of the original trattoria, the restaurant consistently turns out outstanding pizzas and flavorful meat and fish from a customized wood-burning brick oven imported from Tuscany. A reasonable and excellent wine list provides you with a difficult choice in two affordable price ranges: $19 and $23. Artichokes steamed in white-wine broth provide a flavorful balance between garlic and sun-dried tomatoes. Tagliatelle Arometto St. David is an elaborate name for an elaborate dish of fresh herbs marinated in extra virgin olive oil and lightly tossed with flat semolina pasta, Parmigiano Reggiano cheese, then garnished with diced sweet peppers, olives, and tomatoes. It's outstanding. Grilled thin-crusted pizzas are prepared as the Italians prefer them—light on sauce and cheese but heavy on flavor. For pasta lovers, the powerful but surprisingly light gnocchi with spinach is a good way to go. And if you order a meat or fish entree, be sure to try the rosemary roasted potatoes.

1161 N. Federal Hwy., Fort Lauderdale. ✆ 954/566-1716. Reservations accepted for groups of 6 or more. Main courses $8.95–$15. AE, DC, DISC, MC, V. Sun–Thurs 11am–10pm; Fri–Sat 11am–11pm.

INEXPENSIVE

The Floridian Restaurant ★ *Value* AMERICAN/DINER   The Floridian has been filling South Florida's diner void for over 63 years, serving breakfast, lunch, and dinner, 24/7. It's especially busy on weekend mornings when locals and tourists come in for huge omelets, fresh oatmeal, sausage, and biscuits.

1410 E. Las Olas Blvd., Fort Lauderdale. ✆ 954/463-4041. Fax 954/761-3930. Sandwiches $3–$7; breakfast combos $3.50–$8; hot platters $7–$14. No credit cards. Daily 24 hr.

Hamburger Mary's ★★ AMERICAN   For fans of kitsch, Hamburger Mary's is a place to fawn over and tell your friends about. For one, the check is presented to you in a stiletto heel from Frederick's of Hollywood. Secondly, the hamburgers are fabulous and full of tongue in cheeky names such as Buffy the Hamburger Slayer—a garlic and Swiss burger—Mary's Breast, and Mary Tyler S'mores. Located in the gay-friendly hamlet of Wilton Manors, Mary's is the neon spot on an already colorful neighborhood with its shabby chic decor that consists of lamps made from galvanized steel buckets, beads and feather boas, speakers covered by wigs, and shoes on the ceiling. An outdoor lanai area provides a fabulous setting for events such as Monday night's Martini and a Movie night in which campy classics are shown on a big screen, and Tuesday night's Mary's House of Blues, featuring live jazz and blues and $3 Tarantula Margaritas. On Sundays, live reggae music and $3 Absolut Peppar Bloody Marys bring in the crowds, which are as colorful as the restaurant itself.

2449 Wilton Dr., Wilton Manors. © 954/567-1320. Main courses $6–$10. AE, DC, MC, V. Sun–Thurs 11:30am–11pm; Fri–Sat 11:30am–midnight. Bar stays open 2 hours later.

Jaxon's ★ *Kids* ICE CREAM   South Florida's best and only authentic old-fashioned ice-cream parlor and country store attracts sweet teeth from all over the area looking to satisfy their cravings with an unabridged assortment of homemade ice cream served any which way. Kids love the place because of the candy store in the front of the restaurant, and adults love it for its pre–Ben and Jerry's authenticity. For the calorie-conscious, the sugar-free and fat-free versions are pretty good. Jaxon's most famous everything-but-the-kitchen-sink sundae features countless scoops and endless toppings.

128 S. Federal Hwy., Dania Beach. © 954/923-4445. Sundaes $2.75–$7.95. AE, DISC, MC, V. Mon–Thurs 11:30am–11pm; Fri–Sat 11:30am–midnight; Sun noon–11pm.

Le Tub ★★ *Finds* AMERICAN   Hands down, this is one of the coolest, most unpretentious, quintessential, pre-swanky South Florida restaurants if not one of the coolest restaurants period. Established in 1959 as a Sunoco gas station, Le Tub was eventually closed by the energy crisis of the early '70s. In 1974, the place was purchased by a man who dedicated an entire year to personally transforming the place into this waterfront restaurant, made out of flotsam, jetsam, and ocean bone treasures gathered over 4 years of jogging on Hollywood Beach. But the waterfront location and unique building aren't the only things to marvel at. As you walk in, take note of the hand painted bathtubs and toilet bowls (it's not at all gross; they're used as planters) lining the walkway. Inside the restaurant is a divey bar complete with pool table and jukebox, but outside seating on the deck is the real gem. Le Tub is famous for its burgers, chili, and seafood, but more than the food is the peaceful, easy feeling that exudes from the place.

1100 N. Ocean Dr., Hollywood. © 954/931-9425. Main courses $6–$17. Cash only. Daily 10:30am–4am.

Lester's Diner ★ AMERICAN   Since 1968, Lester's Diner has been serving swarms of hungry South Floridians large portions of great greasy-spoon fare until the wee hours. Try the eggs Benedict and the 14-ounce "cup" of classic coffee, or sample one of Lester's many homemade desserts. The place serves breakfast 24 hours a day and is a Fort Lauderdale institution that attracts locals, after-club crowds, city officials, and a generally motley, friendly crew of hungry people craving no-nonsense food served by seasoned waitresses, whose beehive hairdos only contribute to the campy atmosphere.

250 S.R. 84, Fort Lauderdale. © 954/525-5641. Main courses $5–$12. AE, MC, V. Daily 24 hr.

THE HOLLYWOOD & FORT LAUDERDALE AREA AFTER DARK

Fort Lauderdale no longer mimics the raucous antics of *Animal House* as far as nightlife and partying are concerned. It has gotten hip to the fact that an active nightlife is vital to the city's desires to distract sophisticated, savvy visitors from the magnetic lure of South Beach. And while Fort Lauderdale is no South Beach, it has vastly improved the quality of nightlife throughout the city by welcoming places that wouldn't dare host wet-T-shirt and beer-chugging contests. It also lacks the South Beach attitude, which is part of the attraction.

Hollywood's nightlife seems to be in the throes of an identity crisis, touting itself as the next South Beach, while at the same time hyping its image as an attitude-free nocturnal playground. Here's the real deal: At press time, Hollywood nightlife was barely awake, with the exception of a few bars and one struggling dance club. If you're looking for a quiet night out, it's probably your best bet. But don't come too late—after midnight, the city is absolutely deserted.

For information on clubs and events, pick up a free copy of Fort Lauderdale's weekly newspaper *City Link* or the Fort Lauderdale edition of the *New Times*.

Beach Place   This outdoor shopping and entertainment complex, modeled after Coconut Grove's hugely successful CocoWalk, landed on the legendary "strip" with several franchised bars and restaurants. It's the beachy version of a mall and is popular with a very young set at night. The view overlooking the ocean makes it worth a stop for a drink. Hours vary depending on the establishment. Some places are open until 2 or 3am; others close around 11pm. 17 S. Fort Lauderdale Beach Blvd., Fort Lauderdale. ✆ **954/760-9570.**

The Culture Room   If you consider rock and heavy metal to be culture, visit the Culture Room and bang your head to local bands. Open daily from 8pm to 3am. 3045 N. Federal Hwy. (at the corner of Oakland Park Blvd.), Fort Lauderdale. ✆ **954/ 564-1074.** Cover varies.

Elbo Room   Formerly spring break central, the Elbo Room has actually managed to maintain its rowdy and divey reputation by serving up frequent drink specials and live bands. Open daily from 10am to 2am. 241 S. Atlantic Blvd. on the corner of Las Olas Blvd. and Fla. A1A., Fort Lauderdale. ✆ **954/463-4615.**

Harrison's Wine Gallery   Dark, cozy, and so comfy, it's hard to get up from the big leather couches at Harrison's Wine Gallery, where a hip crowd mulls over, sniffs, and sips from over 100 kinds of vino at reasonable prices such as $30 for a South African merlot or $7 to $10 by the glass. There are also 40 bottled beers. Cheese platters, hummus platters, and panini are also available. Open daily from 4pm to 2am. 1916 Harrison St., Hollywood. ✆ **954/922-0074.**

Karma Lounge   Almost too hip for Fort Lauderdale, Karma Lounge boasts a British resident DJ, which, if you know anything about DJs or club music, is a big deal. Progressive house music is the soundtrack for this glammy, orange and white ultra mod spot that's frequented by the dolled up over-25 set. Open Wednesday though Thursday from 10pm to 3am, Friday and Saturday from 10pm to 4am. 4 West Las Olas Blvd., Fort Lauderdale. ✆ **954/609-6369.** Cover varies.

Mai Kai *(Moments*   Immerse yourself in this fabulous vestige of Polynesian kitsch: hula dancers, fire-eaters, and potent (and sickly sweet) drinks served in coconuts. The food, which draws an ambiguous line between Chinese, Polynesian, and other forms of Asian cuisine, is tasty enough but definitely overpriced. No matter; it's bound to get cold as you watch the hilarious show, which includes everything from Tahitian classics to Polynesian versions of American hits. Trippy and undeniably fun, a trip to Mai Kai is a must. ***Note:*** The cocktails cost almost as much as a meal. Open daily from 5pm until midnight. 3599 N. Federal Hwy. (between Commercial and Oakland Park blvds.), Fort Lauderdale. ✆ **954/563-3272.** Reservations required. Shows (2 nightly) are $9.95 for adults; free for children 12 and under.

O'Hara's   What used to be a mediocre jazz club has turned into a premier venue for excellent, live R&B, pop, and funk music. Two locations: 1905 Hollywood Blvd., Hollywood (✆ **954/925-2555;** 24-hr. Jazz & Blues Hot Line ✆ 954/524-2801); and 722 E. Las Olas Blvd., Fort Lauderdale (✆ **954/524-1764**).

The Parrot   Fort Lauderdale's most famous—and fun—dive bar, The Parrot is a local's and out-of-towner's choice for an evening of beer (16 kinds on tap), bonding, and browsing of the bar's virtual gallery of photos of almost everyone who's ever imbibed here since its opening in 1970. Open Sunday through Thursday from 11am to 2am and Friday and Saturday from 11am to 3am. 911 Sunrise Lane, Fort Lauderdale. ✆ 954/563-1493.

The Poor House   There's nothing poor about this microbrew hangout where excellent live music from local bands starts at midnight and goes on well into the wee hours. A friendly, lively, mixed crowd composes a generational cross section where the gap is bridged by a common love of live music, cold beer, and good times. Open daily from 5pm to 2am. 110 SW 3rd Ave., Fort Lauderdale. ✆ 954/522-5145.

Riverwalk   You'll find this outdoor shopping and entertainment complex located in the heart of downtown Fort Lauderdale on the sleepy yet scenic New River—as a result of its river site, it's got more charm than most such complexes. In fact, if you've got a boat, you can sail here and anchor away until you're ready to move on. A host of bars, restaurants, and shops, not to mention a high-tech virtual reality arcade, The Escape, and a multiplex cinema, are enough to keep you occupied for at least a few hours. On weekends, this place is packed. 400 SW 2nd St. (along the New River from NE 6th Ave. to SW 6th Ave.), Fort Lauderdale.

Rush Street   Known for its ice-cream flavors of martinis, from chocolate to Key lime, Rush Street is a sleek bar, with two dance floors, that attracts a young professional crowd. Open daily from 4pm to 4am. 220 SW 2nd St., Fort Lauderdale. ✆ 954/522-6900.

Shooters   This waterfront bar is quintessential Fort Lauderdale. Inside, you'll find nautical types, families, and young professionals mixed in with a good dose of sunburned tourists enjoying the live reggae, jazz, or Jimmy Buffett–style tunes with the gorgeous backdrop of the bay and marinas all around. Open Monday through Friday from 11:30am to 2am; Saturday from 11:30am to 3am; and Sunday from 10am to 2am. 3033 NE 32nd Ave., Fort Lauderdale. ✆ 954/566-2855.

Where the Boys Are: Gay Fort Lauderdale

While South Beach is a magnet for the so-called circuit boys—gay men who party on a continual, ritualistic basis—Fort Lauderdale has more of a low-key, small-town scene similar to, say, Provincetown. Here, local gay-owned and -operated bars, clubs, and restaurants are the places of choice for those who find South Beach's scene too pretentious, superficial, and drug infested. The Fort Lauderdale neighborhood of Wilton Manors is the hub of gay life, but there is a smattering of gay establishments throughout the city.

    The Copa, located at 2800 S. Federal Hwy. (east on I-595, near the airport; ✆ 954/463-1507), is the hottest gay spot north of South Beach—the granddaddy of Fort Lauderdale's gay club scene. Patrons of **Cathode Ray** call this bar their "Cheers." It's located at 1105 E. Las Olas Blvd. (✆ 954/462-8611). **Georgie's Alibi** is Wilton Manors' most popular gay bar. Find it at 2266 Wilton Dr., Wilton Manors (✆ 954/565-2526). Two great dance clubs are the **Coliseum** (2520 S. Miami Rd.; ✆ 954/832-0100) and **Club 84** (1000 W. S.R. 84; ✆ 954/525-7883).

2 Boca Raton ★★ & Delray Beach ★

26 miles S of Palm Beach, 40 miles N of Miami, 21 miles N of Fort Lauderdale

Boca Raton is one of South Florida's most expensive, well-maintained cities—home to ladies who lunch and SUV-driving yuppies. The city's name literally translates as "rat's mouth," but you'd be hard-pressed to find rodents in this area's fancy digs.

If you're looking for funky, wacky, and eclectic, look elsewhere. Boca is a luxurious resort community and, for some, the only place worth staying in South Florida. Although Jerry Seinfeld's TV parents retired to the fictional Del Boca Vista, Boca's just too pricey to be a retirement community. With minimal nightlife, entertainment in Boca is restricted to leisure sports, excellent dining, and upscale shopping. The city's residents and vacationers happily comply.

Delray Beach, named after a suburb of Detroit, grew up completely separate from its southern neighbor. This sleepy yet starting-to-awaken beachfront community was founded in 1894 by a Midwestern postmaster who sold off 5-acre lots through Michigan newspaper ads. Because of their close proximity, Boca and Delray can easily be explored together. Budget-conscious travelers would do well to eat and sleep in Delray and dip into Boca for sightseeing and beaching only. The 2-mile stretch of beach here is well maintained and crowded, but not mobbed. Delray's "downtown" area is confined to Atlantic Avenue, which is known for casual to chic restaurants, quaint shops, and art galleries. During the day, Delray is definitely asleep, but recently, thanks to the addition of trendy restaurants and bars, nighttime is much more animated, a burgeoning hotbed of hipster activity, young and old. Still, compared to Boca, Delray is much more laid back, hardly as chichi, and more like a cute little beach town than the sprawling, swanky, suburban feel emitted by Boca.

ESSENTIALS

GETTING THERE   Like the rest of the cities on the Gold Coast, Boca Raton and Delray are easily reached from I-95 or the Florida Turnpike. Both the Fort Lauderdale–Hollywood International Airport and the Palm Beach International Airport are about 20 minutes away. Amtrak (© **800/USA-RAIL;** www.amtrak. com) trains make stops in Delray Beach at an unattended station at 345 S. Congress Ave.

VISITOR INFORMATION   Contact or stop by the **Palm Beach County Convention and Visitors Bureau,** 1555 Palm Beach Lakes Blvd., Suite 800, West Palm Beach, FL 33401 (© **800/554-PALM** or 561/233-3000; fax 561/471-3990; www.palmbeachfl.com). They're open Monday through Friday from 8:30am to 5:30pm and have excellent coupons and discounts. On weekdays from 8:30am until at least 4pm, stop by **The Greater Boca Raton Chamber of Commerce** at 1800 N. Dixie Hwy., 4 blocks north of Glades Road (© **561/395-4433;** fax 561/392-3780; www.bocaratonchamber.com), Boca Raton, FL 33432, for information on attractions, accommodations, and events in the area. Also, try the **Greater Delray Beach Chamber of Commerce** (© **561/278-0424;** fax 561/278-0555; www.delraybeach.com) at 64 SE 5th Ave., half a block south of Atlantic Avenue on U.S. 1, Delray Beach, FL 33483; but I recommend the Palm Beach County Convention and Visitors Bureau since it has information on the entire county.

Boca Raton & Delray Beach

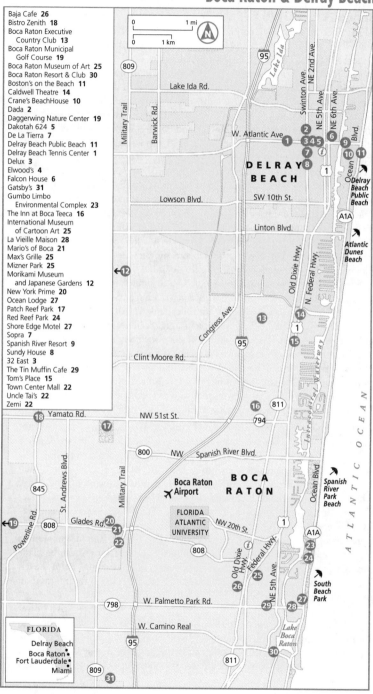

Baja Cafe **26**
Bistro Zenith **18**
Boca Raton Executive
  Country Club **13**
Boca Raton Municipal
  Golf Course **19**
Boca Raton Museum of Art **25**
Boca Raton Resort & Club **30**
Boston's on the Beach **11**
Caldwell Theatre **14**
Crane's BeachHouse **10**
Dada **2**
Daggerwing Nature Center **19**
Dakotah 624 **5**
De La Tierra **7**
Delray Beach Public Beach **11**
Delray Beach Tennis Center **1**
Delux **3**
Elwood's **4**
Falcon House **6**
Gatsby's **31**
Gumbo Limbo
  Environmental Complex **23**
The Inn at Boca Teeca **16**
International Museum
  of Cartoon Art **25**
La Vieille Maison **28**
Mario's of Boca **21**
Max's Grille **25**
Mizner Park **25**
Morikami Museum
  and Japanese Gardens **12**
New York Prime **20**
Ocean Lodge **27**
Patch Reef Park **17**
Red Reef Park **24**
Shore Edge Motel **27**
Sopra **7**
Spanish River Resort **9**
Sundy House **8**
32 East **3**
The Tin Muffin Cafe **29**
Tom's Place **15**
Town Center Mall **22**
Uncle Tai's **22**
Zemi **22**

BEACHES & ACTIVE PURSUITS

BEACHES   Thankfully, Florida had the foresight to set aside some of its most beautiful coastal areas for the public's enjoyment. Many of the area's best beaches are located in state parks and are free to pedestrians and bikers, though most do charge for parking. Among the beaches I recommend are Delray Beach's **Atlantic Dunes Beach,** 1600 S. Ocean Blvd., a 7-acre developed beach with lifeguards, restrooms, changing rooms, and a family park area; Boca Raton's **South Beach Park,** 400 N. Ocean Blvd., with 1,670 feet of beach, 25 acres, lifeguards, picnic areas, restrooms, showers, and 955 feet of developed beach south of the Boca Inlet, for an admission charge of $15 on weekdays and $17 on weekends. The two beaches below are also very popular.

The **Delray Beach Public Beach,** on Ocean Boulevard at the east end of Atlantic Avenue, is one of the area's most popular hangouts. Weekends especially attract a young and good-looking crowd of active locals and tourists. Regular volleyball, Frisbee, and paddleball games make for good entertainment. Refreshments, snack shops, bars, and restaurants are just across the street. Families enjoy the protection of lifeguards on the clean, wide beach. Gentle waters make it a good swimming beach, too. Restrooms and showers are available, and there's limited parking at meters along Ocean Boulevard.

Spanish River Park Beach, on North Ocean Boulevard (Fla. A1A), 2 miles north of Palmetto Park Road in Boca Raton, is a huge 95-acre oceanfront park with a ½-mile-long beach complete with lifeguards as well as a large grassy area, making it one of the best choices for picnicking. Facilities include picnic tables, grills, restrooms, showers, and a bi-level 40-foot observation tower. You can walk through tunnels under the highway to access nature trails that wind through fertile grasslands. Volleyball nets are ocean-side and always have at least one serious game going on. The park is open from 8am to 8pm. Admission is $16 for vehicles on weekdays and $18 on weekends and major holidays. Also, read about Red Reef Park under "Scuba Diving & Snorkeling," below.

GOLF   This area has plenty of good courses. The best ones, that are not located in a gated community, are found at the **Boca Raton Resort & Club** (p. 267) and **The Inn at Boca Teeca** (p. 268). Another great place to swing your clubs is at the **Deer Creek Golf Club** in Deerfield Beach, 2801 Country Club Blvd., Deerfield Beach (© **954/421-5550**), a 300-plus-yard driving range where a large bucket of balls costs $7 and a small one costs $4. Rates at the Deer Creek Golf Club are seasonal and range from $45 to $125. However, from May to October or November, about a dozen private courses open their greens to visitors staying in Palm Beach County hotels. This "Golf-A-Round" program is free or severely discounted (carts are additional), and reservations can be made through most major hotels. Ask at your hotel, or contact the **Palm Beach County Convention and Visitors Bureau** (© **561/471-3995**) for information on which clubs are available for play.

The semiprivate, 18-hole, par-61 course at the **Boca Raton Executive Country Club,** 7601 E. Country Club Blvd. (© **561/997-9410**), is usually open to the public and is an excellent choice for those looking to improve their game in a professional setting. A driving range is on the property as well as a restaurant and a pro shop, where you can rent clubs. If you like, take lessons from a PGA pro. Greens fees are $20 per person.

The **Boca Raton Municipal Golf Course,** 8111 Golf Course Rd. (© **561/ 483-6100**), is the area's best public golf course. There's an 18-hole, par-72 course covering approximately 6,200 yards as well as a 9-hole, par-30 course. There's a snack bar and a pro shop where clubs can be rented. Greens fees are $11 to $14 for 9 holes and $19 to $25 for 18 holes. Ask for special summer discount fees.

SCUBA DIVING & SNORKELING   **Moray Bend,** a 58-foot dive spot located about ¾ mile off Boca Inlet, is the area's most popular. It's home to three moray eels that are used to being fed by scuba divers. The reef is accessible by boat from **Force E Dive Center,** 877 E. Palmetto Park Rd., Boca Raton (*℃* **561/368-0555**). Phone for dive times. Dives cost $40 to $45 per person.

Red Reef Park, 1400 N. Ocean Park Blvd. (*℃* **561/393-7974**), a fully developed 67-acre oceanfront park in Boca Raton, has good swimming and year-round lifeguard protection. There's snorkeling for beginners around the rocks and reefs that lie just off the beach in 2 to 6 feet of water. The park also has restrooms and a small picnic area with grills and tables. Located ½ mile north of Palmetto Park Road, it is open daily from 8am to 10pm. You pay only if you drive in. It's $10 per car during the week or $12 on weekends.

TENNIS   The snazzy **Delray Beach Tennis Center,** 201 W. Atlantic Ave. (*℃* **561/243-7360;** www.delraytennis.com), has 14 lighted clay courts and 5 hard courts available by the hour. Phone for rates and reservations.

The 17 public lighted hard courts at **Patch Reef Park,** 2000 NW 51st St. (*℃* **561/997-0881;** www.ci.boca-raton.fl.us/parks/Patchreef.cfm), are available by reservation. The fee for nonresidents is $5.75 per person per hour. Courts are available Monday through Saturday from 7:30am to 10pm and Sunday from 7:30am to dusk; you can phone ahead to see if a court is available. To reach the park from I-95, exit at Yamato Road West and continue past Military Trail to the park.

SEEING THE SIGHTS

Boca Raton Museum of Art 🏛🏛   In addition to a relatively small but well-chosen permanent collection that's strongest in 19th-century European oils (Degas, Klee, Matisse, Picasso, Seurat), the museum stages a wide variety of excellent temporary exhibitions by local and international artists. Lectures and films are offered on a fairly regular basis, so call ahead for details.

Mizner Park, 501 Plaza Real, Boca Raton. *℃* 561/392-2500. www.bocamuseum.org. Admission $8 adults, $6 seniors, $4 students, free for children under 12. Additional fees may apply for special exhibits and performances. Free on Wed except during special exhibitions. Tues, Thurs, and Sat 10am–5pm; Wed and Fri 10am–9pm; Sun noon–5pm. Closed Mon.

Daggerwing Nature Center 🏛   Seen enough snowbirds? Head over to this 39-acre swampy splendor where birds of another feather reside, including herons, egrets, woodpeckers, and warblers. The park's trails come complete with a soundtrack provided by songbirds hovering above (watch your head). The park's Night Hikes will take you on a nocturnal wake-up call for owls at 6pm. Bring a flashlight.

S. County Regional Park, 11200 Park Access Rd., Boca Raton. *℃* 561/488-9953. Free admission. Tues–Fri 1–4:30pm; Sat 9am–4:30pm. Call for tour and activity schedule.

Gumbo Limbo Environmental Complex 🏛🏛🏛   If manicured lawns and golf courses aren't your idea of communing with nature, then head to Gumbo Limbo. Named for an indigenous hardwood tree with continuously shedding bronze bark, the 20-acre complex protects one of the few surviving coastal hammocks, or forest islands, in South Florida. Visitors can walk through the hammock on a ½-mile-long elevated boardwalk that ends at a 40-foot observation tower, from which you can see the Atlantic Ocean, the Intracoastal Waterway, and much of Boca Raton. From mid-April to September, sea turtles come ashore here to lay their eggs.

1801 N. Ocean Blvd. (on Fla. A1A between Spanish River Blvd. and Palmetto Park Rd.), Boca Raton. ℂ 561/338-1473. Fax 561/338-1483. Free admission. Mon–Sat 9am–4pm; Sun noon–4pm.

Morikami Museum and Japanese Gardens ★★★   Slip off your shoes and enter into a serene Japanese garden that dates from 1905, when an entrepreneurial farmer, Jo Sakai, came to Boca Raton to build a tropical agricultural community. The Yamato Colony, as it was known, was short-lived; by the 1920s only one tenacious colonist remained: George Sukeji Morikami. But Morikami was quite successful, eventually running one of the largest pineapple plantations in the area. The 200-acre Morikami Museum and Japanese Gardens (a stroll through the garden is actually ⅞ mile), which opened to the public in 1977, was Morikami's gift to Palm Beach County and the State of Florida. The park section, dedicated to the preservation of Japanese culture, is constructed to appeal to all the senses. An artificial waterfall that cascades into a koi- and carp-filled moat; a small rock garden for meditation; and a large bonsai collection that includes miniature maple, buttonwood, juniper, and Australian pine trees are all worth contemplation. There's also a cafe with a Japanese- and Asian-inspired menu if you want to stay for lunch.

4000 Morikami Park Rd., Delray Beach. ℂ 561/495-0233. www.morikami.org. Museum $9 adults, $8 seniors, $6 children 6–18, free for members and children 5 and under. Museum Tues–Sun 10am–5pm; gardens Tues–Sat 10am–5pm. Closed major holidays.

SHOPPING & BROWSING

Even if you don't plan to buy anything, a trip to Boca Raton's **Mizner Park** is essential for capturing the essence of the city. Like Main Street in a small town, Mizner is the place to see and be seen, where Rolls-Royces and Ferraris are parked curbside, freshly coifed women sit amidst shopping bags at outdoor cafes, and young movers and shakers make evening plans on their constantly buzzing cellphones. Beyond the human scenery, however, Mizner Park is scenic in its own right with beautiful landscaping. It's really an outdoor mall, with 45 specialty shops, seven good restaurants, and a multiplex. Each shop front faces a grassy island with blue and green gazebos, potted plants, and garden benches. Mizner Park is located on Federal Highway (between Palmetto Park Rd. and Glades Rd.; ℂ 561/362-0606).

Boca's **Town Center Mall,** located on the south side of Glades Road, just west of I-95, has seven huge department stores, including Nordstrom, Bloomingdale's, Burdines, Lord & Taylor, and Saks Fifth Avenue. Add to that the hundreds of specialty shops, an extensive food court, and a range of other restaurants, and you have the area's most comprehensive shopping center.

A lifeless, overrated area, but good enough for a quick stroll, is the more artsy community of Delray Beach, known by many as Pineapple Grove. Here, along Atlantic Avenue, especially east of Swinton Avenue, you'll find a few antiques shops, clothing stores, and art galleries shaded by palm trees and colorful awnings. Pick up the "Downtown Delray Beach" map and guide at almost any of the stores on this strip, or call ℭ **561/278-0424** for more information.

WHERE TO STAY

A number of national chain hotels worth considering include a moderately priced **Holiday Inn Highland Beach Oceanside** at 2809 S. Ocean Blvd., on Fla. A1A, southeast of Linton Boulevard (ℭ **800/234-6835** or 561/278-6241). Although you won't find rows of cheap hotels as in Fort Lauderdale and Hollywood, a handful of mom-and-pop motels have survived along Fla. A1A between the towering condominiums of Delray Beach. Look along the beach just south of Atlantic Boulevard. Especially noteworthy is the pleasant little two-story, shingle-roofed **Bermuda Inn** at 64 S. Ocean Blvd. (ℭ **561/276-5288**).

Even more economical options can be found in Deerfield Beach, Boca's neighbor, south of the county line. A number of beachfront efficiencies offer great deals, even in the winter months. Try the **Panther Motel and Apartments** at 715 S. A1A (ℭ **954/427-0700**). This clean and convenient motel has rates starting as low as $40, although in season you may have to book for a week at a time. Weekly rates in season start at $457.

VERY EXPENSIVE

Boca Raton Resort & Club ★★ (Kids)   This famous and often-photographed property shows that Boca's country-club lifestyle is alive and well. Built in 1926 by Addison Mizner, the posh resort now comprises three oddly matched buildings: the original, more traditional building; the somewhat drab, pink 27-story Tower; and the more modern, airier Beach Club, which is accessible by a water shuttle. Everything at this resort, which straddles the Intracoastal Waterway and encompasses over 350 acres of land, is fully at your fingertips but may sometimes require a little effort to reach it. The amenities here cannot be beat. The resort features two 18-hole championship golf courses, a $10 million Tennis and Fitness Center, indoor basketball and racquetball courts, a 25-slip marina with full fishing and boating facilities, and a private beach with various watersports equipment for rent. With a choice of 10 places to dine, five pools to swim in, and an excellent children's program, the resort is ideal for families. Upon check-in, see if Harry the bellman is available to take you to your room—he's been at the resort for over 46 years and has a photographic memory of the hotel's previous guests, from Joseph Cotton and Charlton Heston to Bill Gates, who became a partner in the hotel after spending enough time there.

501 E. Camino Real (P.O. Box 5025), Boca Raton, FL 33431. ℭ **800/327-0101** or 561/395-3000. Fax 561/447-3183. www.bocaresort.com. 963 units, 120 golf villas. Winter $400–$750 double; off-season $230–$460 double. Reasonable seasonal packages available. AE, DC, DISC, MC, V. From I-95 N., exit onto Palmetto Park Rd. E. Turn right onto Federal Hwy. (U.S. 1), and then left onto Camino Real to the resort. **Amenities:** 8 restaurants; 6 bars; 5 pools; 2 18-hole championship golf courses; 34 clay tennis courts; indoor basketball court; 4 indoor racquetball courts; 3 fitness centers; Mediterranean spa; watersports equipment/rental; extensive children's programs; concierge; business center; 24-hr. room service; laundry; 25-slip marina with full fishing and boating. *In room:* A/C, TV, minibar, hair dryer.

Sundy House ★★★   One of the few properties in South Florida that hasn't given way to the faux Mediterranean, Mizner-style of architecture, Sundy House is the oldest residence in Delray Beach and is a bona fide 1902 Queen Anne house that has been restored to its full Victorian glory—on the outside, at least.

Inside, however, the four one- and two-bedroom apartments are in a style that is best described as Caribbean funky, adorned in brilliant colors and with state-of-the-art audio visual equipment, full modern kitchens, and laundry facilities. Six new guest rooms known as The Stables are equestrian chic, with more rustic appointments, including dark woods and wooden floors. And while the rooms here are comfortable and gorgeous in their own rights, it's the surrounding property of the Sundy House that garners the most oohs and aahs. Set on an acre of lush gardens, the Sundy House is surrounded by over 5,000 species of exotic plants, gently flowing streams, and colorful parrots, making an escape here seem more like something you'd find in Hawaii rather than South Florida. And going along with the whole nature theme is the hotel's swimming pond, literally that, in which guests can swim with the fish (in a good way!). The hotel's restaurant, De La Tierra, is equally awe-inspiring, with star chef Johnny Vinczencz, of South Beach's Hotel Astor fame, crafting exquisite new Florida cuisine, oftentimes using fresh fruits and herbs straight from Sundy House's botanical gardens. One of South Florida's best kept secrets (though not for much longer), Sundy House is paradise rediscovered.

106 S. Swinton Ave., Delray Beach, FL 33444. ℂ **877/439-9601** or 561/272-5678. Fax 561/272-1115. www.sundyhouse.com. 11 units. Winter $250–$500 1- or 2-bedroom or cottage; off-season $175–$500 1- or 2-bedroom or cottage. AE, DC, DISC, MC, V. **Amenities:** Restaurant; bar; swimming pond; limited room service. *In room:* A/C, TV, kitchen, minibar, coffeemaker, hair dryer, safe, DVD player, CD player, washer/dryer.

EXPENSIVE

Crane's BeachHouse ★★ If you can't afford your own South Florida beach house—and why bother with all the maintenance anyway?—Crane's Beach-House, meticulously run and maintained by husband and wife Cheryl and Michael Crane, is a haven away from home, located just 1 block from the beach and right in the middle of historic Delray Beach. Even better, it's well known for its incredible housekeeping service in which everything is *always* super fresh and immaculate. But that aside, the main draws here are the whimsical, tropical suites in which every piece of furniture and bric-a-brac is completely original and oftentimes crafted by local artists. Although each room has its own design theme—Hawaii, Amazon, Anacapri, and Capetown, for instance—the beds are all the same in that they are downright heavenly. Lush gardens, a Tiki bar, and swimming pool leave you with little reason to flee the premises, but when you do, you'll want to return as quickly as possible.

82 Gleason St., Delray Beach, FL 33483. ℂ **866/372-7263** or 561/278-1700. Fax 561/278-7826. www.cranesbeachhouse.com. 27 units. Winter $170–$445 suite; off-season $125–$275 suite. AE, DC, DISC, V. Free parking. **Amenities:** 2 small outdoor pools. *In room:* A/C, TV, VCR, dataport, full kitchen, minibar, coffeemaker, hair dryer, iron, safe.

MODERATE

The Inn at Boca Teeca ★★★ For over 3 decades, this inn has been attracting golf fanatics who could care less about the small but comfortable rooms because they're too busy out on the superb 27-hole golf course at the Inn's Boca Teeca Country Club, open only to members and guests of the Inn. For the golf widow(er)s, however, most of the rooms in this three-story building have balconies or patios from which to watch or signal their significant others that it's time for dinner.

5800 NW 2nd Ave., Boca Raton, FL 33487. ℂ **561/994-0400.** Fax 561/998-8279. 46 units. Winter double $140 and up; off-season double $80–$120. AE, DC, MC, V. **Amenities:** Restaurant; small pool; golf course; 6 tennis courts; fitness center. *In room:* A/C, TV.

INEXPENSIVE

Ocean Lodge ✦   Situated around a small heated pool and sun deck, this two-story motel is a particularly well-kept accommodation in an area of run-down or overpriced options. The large rooms offer furnishings and decor that are clean but a bit impersonal. A recent renovation that added modern Formica and floral wallpaper lifts this a notch above a basic motel. Ask for a room in the back, since the street noise can be a bit loud, especially in season. The bonus is that you are across the street from the ocean and in one of Florida's most upscale resort towns.

531 N. Ocean Blvd. (just north of Palmetto Park Rd. on Fla. A1A), Boca Raton, FL 33432. ℂ **800/STAY-BOCA** or 561/395-7772. Fax 561/395-0554. 18 units. Winter $99–$125 double; off-season $75–$99 double. AE, MC, V. **Amenities:** Pool. *In room:* A/C, TV.

Shore Edge Motel   Another relic of the 1950s, this motel has been recently spiffed up with new landscaping and some redecorating and is a good choice, especially because of its location—across the street from a public beach, just north of downtown Boca Raton. It's the quintessential South Florida motel: a small, pink, single-story structure surrounding a modest swimming pool and courtyard. Although the rooms are on the small side, they're very neat and clean. The higher-priced accommodations are larger and come with full kitchens.

425 N. Ocean Blvd. (on Fla. A1A, north of Palmetto Park Rd.), Boca Raton, FL 33432. ℂ **561/395-4491.** Fax 561/347-8759. 16 units. Winter $85–$99 double; off-season $55–$65 double. AE, MC, V. **Amenities:** Pool. *In room:* A/C, TV.

WHERE TO DINE

Boca Raton, and its surrounding area, is the kind of place where you discuss dinner plans at the breakfast table. Nightlife in Boca means going out to a restaurant. But who cares? These are some of the best restaurants in South Florida.

VERY EXPENSIVE

La Vieille Maison ✦✦✦ FRENCH   The luxurious setting and a Mediterranean-inspired home filled with a variety of antique French furnishings and paintings gives you the feeling of walking into a small château. Culinarily speaking, however, this place is a castle. Begin with lobster bisque, gratin of escargot with fennel and pistachio nuts, or pan-seared foie gras—each is equally delectable. It's difficult to choose from the many enticing entrees, which range from red snapper in black- and green-olive potato crust to medallions of beef, lamb, and venison over three sauces. You'll surely have to try at least a few of the gorgeous cheeses the server offers after your main course—the most extensive selection I've seen in this country. The lemon crepe soufflé with raspberry sauce is the dessert of choice—remember to order it early.

770 E. Palmetto Park Rd., Boca Raton. ℂ **561/391-6701** or 561/737-5677. Reservations recommended. Main courses $18–$50; fixed-price dinners $42 and $68. AE, DC, DISC, MC, V. Daily 6–9:30pm (call for seating times).

New York Prime ✦ STEAKHOUSE   This South Florida outpost of a South Carolina–based chain is the prime spot for carnivores looking to satisfy their cravings for big, succulent steaks. Fish dishes are also available, including lobsters ranging from 3 to 13 pounds. But the price of excess does not come cheap. In fact, the restaurant brazenly states its case on the menu: "We strive to be the Mercedes of steak houses by offering the very best . . . but you can't drive a Mercedes for the same price as a Buick." Cute motto, but in terms of consistency, New York Prime is a Pinto. On one night the food and service is exquisite, while on another, it's abysmal. Take your chances, though, because if you do hit it on a good night, you won't be disappointed.

2350 Executive Center Dr., Boca Raton. ✆ 561/998-3881. Reservations recommended. Main courses $23–$64. AE, MC, V. Daily 5–11pm.

EXPENSIVE

De La Tierra ★★★ FLORIBBEAN   Although chef Johnny Vinczenz left, this restaurant remains a stunning experience that combines elegant indoor dining and lush tropical outdoor settings with gastronomic wizardry that's a product of the fresh fruits, vegetables, and spices grown on the hotel's 5 acre farm. Each dish is prepared with a palpable, edible precision. Consider the following: smoked tomato soup is served with tiny grilled brie sandwiches and cilantro sour cream; leg of duck confit cakes are served with mango coleslaw; calamari is breaded with blue cornmeal, fried crispy, and plated with chipotle lime vinaigrette, red chili aioli, and tropical fruit salsa; diver scallops are caramelized and served with truffle braised oyster mushrooms, corn broth, caviar, and microgreens; slightly smoked salmon is served with chive potato latkes, papaya/apple chutney, and dill shallot sour cream; and chicken is marinated in pesto and served with mushroom risotto, truffled roasted chicken broth, baby carrots, and broccoli rapini. Save room for dessert, which includes a phenomenal American blueberry cobbler and mango and jackfruit shortcake. A decadent Sunday brunch buffet makes the day before going back to work infinitely more bearable. De La Tierra may mean "of the earth," but in my book, it's from the gods.

106 South Swinton Ave., Delray Beach. ✆ 561/272-5678. Reservations essential. Main courses $14–$26. AE, DC, DISC, MC, V. Daily 11:30am–2:30pm and 6–10pm; Sunday brunch 10:30am–2:30pm.

Max's Grille ★★ AMERICAN   Max's Grille is a very popular, very good option in Mizner Park, but you will inevitably wait to be seated. With a large exhibition kitchen that occupies the entire back wall of the restaurant, those lucky enough to score a table can watch as their yellowfin tuna steak or filet mignon is seared on a flaming oak grill. There's also a large selection of chicken, meatloaf, pastas, and main-course salads.

404 Plaza Real, in Mizner Park, Boca Raton. ✆ 561/368-0080. Reservations accepted for 6 or more. Main courses $14–$26; pastas $11–$17. AE, DC, DISC, MC, V. Lunch Mon–Sat 11:30am–3pm. Dinner Mon–Thurs 5–10:30pm, Fri–Sat 5–11pm. Sun brunch/dinner 11:30am–10pm.

Sopra ★ ITALIAN   This cavernous, sleek restaurant is a hotbed of activity that's reminiscent of China Grill on South Beach (p. 88). There's a loud and buzzing ambience here, and the restaurant is full of young professionals and young at heart types. Sopra, by the way, means "above," which aptly describes the attitude it has toward other restaurants. Although Sopra loftily considers itself above the rest, it's not always the case when it comes to the food. The vibe and prices, yes, but the food, no. Linguine with clam sauce is $28 and is something you could probably make at home if you watched Molto Mario on the Food Network. The veal chop, however, is a standout and much more worth its $32 price tag than the absurdly priced linguine. Over 250 bottles of wine are available here, which, in conjunction with the flattering lighting, sleek decor, and hip crowd, earn Sopra its star in my book. As for the food, well, Sopra needs to rise a bit more above.

110 E. Atlantic Ave., Delray Beach. ✆ 561/247-7077. Reservations suggested. Main courses $14–$34. AE, MC, V. Sun–Thurs 5–11pm; Fri–Sat 5pm–midnight.

32 East ★★ NEW AMERICAN   The menu changes every day at this very popular people-watching outpost of tasty, contemporary American food that has finally added a little hip to the Delray Beach dining scene. Among the standouts are Crispy Key West shrimp in lemon mint butter with endives and spicy melon coulis; Oregon porcini, corn, and lobster risotto with herb salad in a Vidalia vinaigrette; and mesquite grilled skirt steak and treviso on fontina polenta with horseradish gremolata. A hip ambience abuzz with activity makes 32 East a popular hangout spot for the cocktail set.

32 E. Atlantic Ave., Delray Beach. © 561/276-7868. Reservations recommended. Main courses $10–$16. AE, DC, MC, V. Sun–Thurs 5:30–10pm; Fri–Sat 5:30–11pm; bar until 2am.

Uncle Tai's ★★★ CHINESE   Not your average egg roll and lo mein kind of place, Uncle Tai's, Boca's best upscale Chinese restaurant, offers a savory spin on classics such as garlic chicken and duck with plum sauce. A family-run restaurant, Uncle Tai's is the product of Wen Dah Tai, a man who studied with the master chefs in China, Japan, and the Philippines. Tai wants to make sure you will emerge from his restaurant fully satisfied, and will even go the extra mile to discourage you from ordering a dish that's less suited to Western palates, having been created for the restaurant's many Chinese diners.

5250 Town Center Circle (between Glades and Palmetto Park roads), Boca Raton. © 561/368-8806. Reservations suggested. Main courses $12–$32. AE, DISC, MC, V. Sun–Thurs 11:30am–2:30pm and 5–10pm; Fri–Sat 11:30am–2:30pm and 5–10:30pm.

Zemi ★★★ NEW AMERICAN   Possibly the best privately owned restaurant to be attached to a mall, Zemi is a sleek and chic neo-American restaurant that's a favorite with the ladies-who-lunch set, the Boca scenesters, and foodies alike. Chef Michael Schwartz, formerly of South Beach's Nemo, is responsible for the fabulous fare, not to mention a loyal clientele that will schlep to wherever Schwartz goes. Chile-crusted shrimp with manchego cheese, roasted garlic, sundried tomatoes, lemon oil, and cilantro; grilled pork T-bone in a pear-ginger compote; and the marinated, grilled skirt steak with vegetable hash and crispy onions are all so good that even the size-two set of mall rats would be happy to go up a half size for a taste.

5050 Town Center Circle, in the Boca Center, Boca Raton. © 561/391-7177. Reservations strongly recommended. Main courses $18–$28. AE, DC, DISC, MC, V. Lunch Mon–Fri 11:30am–2:30pm. Dinner Mon–Thurs and Sun 6–10pm, Fri–Sat 6–11pm.

MODERATE

Bistro Zenith ★ NEW AMERICAN   At the height of innovative cuisine, Bistro Zenith's consistently changing menu keeps local foodies coming back for its tasty offerings of traditional American dishes graced with Asian, Mediterranean, or Southwestern influences served in a high-tech atmosphere. During its Southwestern phase, Zenith hit a new high with a fantastic Grand Canyon chicken with red beans, ancho chili sauce, rice, corn tortillas, and Tex-Mex–corn and cilantro oil.

Regency Court, 3011 Yamato Rd., Boca Raton. © 561/997-2570. Reservations recommended. Main courses $9–$15. AE, MC, V. Lunch Mon–Fri 11:30am–2:30pm. Dinner Sun–Thurs 5:30–10pm, Fri–Sat 5:30–11pm.

Mario's of Boca ★ ITALIAN   This extremely popular, bustling Italian bistro (which moved into new digs in the spring of 2003) keeps Boca's biggest mouths busy with massive portions of great homemade Italian food. The garlic rolls and the pizza are especially worth piping down for. If you're really hungry, there's an all-you-can-eat buffet 7 days a week.

1901 N Military Trail (at the Holiday Inn, opposite from Kings Market), Boca Raton. ℂ **561/392-5595.** Reservations not accepted. Main courses under $15. AE, MC, V. Daily breakfast 7–10:30am; Mon–Thurs 11:30am–10pm; Fri–Sat 11:30am–11pm; Sun noon–9:30pm.

INEXPENSIVE

Baja Cafe 🐸 MEXICAN   A jeans and T-shirt kind of place with wooden tables, Baja Cafe serves fantastic Mexican food at even better prices. It's located right by the Florida East Coast Railway tracks, so don't be surprised if you feel a little rattling. Live music and entertainment in the evening make this place a hot spot for an unpretentious crowd.

201 NW 1st Ave., Boca Raton. ℂ **561/394-5449.** No reservations. Main courses $6–$10. No credit cards. Mon–Thurs 11:30am–10pm; Fri–Sat 11:30am–11pm; Sun 5–10pm.

The Tin Muffin Cafe 🐸 BAKERY/SANDWICH SHOP   Popular with the downtown lunch crowd, this excellent storefront bakery keeps them lining up for big sandwiches on fresh bread, plus muffins, quiches, and good homemade soups like split-pea or lentil. The curried-chicken sandwich is stuffed with oversize chunks of only white meat doused in a creamy curry dressing and fruit. There are a few cafe tables inside and even one outside on a tiny patio. Be warned, however, that service is forgivably slow and parking is a nightmare. Try parking a few blocks away at a meter on the street.

364 E. Palmetto Park Rd. (between Federal Hwy. and the Intracoastal Bridge), Boca Raton. ℂ 561/392-9446. Sandwiches and salads $6.50–$11. No credit cards. Mon–Fri 11am–5pm; Sat 11am–4pm.

Tom's Place 🐸🐸 *(Finds* BARBECUE   There are two important factors in a successful barbecue: the cooking and the sauce. Tom and Helen Wright's no-nonsense shack wins on both counts, offering flawlessly grilled meats paired with well-spiced sauces. Beef, chicken, pork, and fish are served soul-food style, with your choice of two sides such as rice with gravy, collard greens, black-eyed peas, coleslaw, or mashed potatoes. Signed celebrity photographs decorate the walls.

7251 N. Federal Hwy., Boca Raton. ℂ 561/997-0920. Reservations not accepted. Main courses $8–$15; sandwiches $5–$6; early-bird special $7.95. AE, MC, V. Tues–Thurs 11:30am–10:30pm; Fri 11:30am–10pm; Sat noon–10pm.

BOCA RATON & DELRAY BEACH AFTER DARK
THE BAR, CLUB & MUSIC SCENE

Atlantic Avenue in Delray Beach has finally gotten quite hip to nightlife and is now lined by sleek and chic restaurants, lounges, and bars that attract the Palm Beach County "in crowd," along with a few randoms such as the Elvis of New Age, aka Yanni, who has a house nearby. Although it's hardly South Beach or Fort Lauderdale's Las Olas and Riverfront, Atlantic Avenue holds its own as far as a vibrant nightlife is concerned. In Boca Raton, Mizner Park is the nucleus of a makeshift nightlife, with restaurants masking themselves as nightclubs or, at the very least, very sceney bars, such as Gigi's Tavern, 346 Plaza Real, in Mizner Park (ℂ **561/368-4488**), and Mark's Mizner Park, 334 Plaza Real (ℂ **561/395-0770**).

Boston's on the Beach   This is a family restaurant with a somewhat lively bar scene. It's a good choice for postsunbathing, supercasual happy hours Monday through Friday from 4 to 8pm, or live reggae on Monday. With two decks overlooking the ocean, Boston's is an ideal place to mellow out and take in the scenery. Open daily from 7am to 2am. 40 S. Ocean Blvd., Delray Beach. ℂ 561/278-3364.

Dada   Located in a two-story, 1924 house, Dada is a nocturnal outpost of food, drink, music, art, culture, and history. In other words, this is the place you can expect to find neo bohemian, arty types lingering in their black glasses and berets on one of the living room's cozy couches listening to music, poetry, or dissertations on the latest in life. Live music, great food, a bar, an outdoor patio area, and a very eclectic crowd makes Dada the coolest hangout in Delray. Open daily from 5:30pm to 2am. 52 N. Swinton Ave., Delray Beach. © 561/330-DADA.

Dakotah 624   Creative cocktails such as the Kissing Cousin (Southern Comfort, Fris vodka, lime juice, and triple sec) and its own line of cigars attract a hip, young clientele to this vaguely Southwestern-style bar on the beach. Open Monday through Wednesday from 4pm to midnight, Thursday 4pm to 1am, Friday and Saturday from 4pm to 2am, and Sunday from 4 to 11pm. 270 E. Atlantic Ave., Delray Beach. © 561/274-6244.

Delux   No Doubt's Gwen Stefani partied at Delux, requesting the DJ to play reggae. Believe it or not, this red hued dance club on Atlantic Avenue is cooler than some of South Beach's big shot dance clubs thanks to a soundtrack of sexy house music, bedlike seating, and a beautiful crowd in which someone as striking as Stefani can actually blend in without being noticed—at least for a second anyway. Open Wednesday through Sunday from 7pm to 2am. 16 E. Atlantic Ave., Delray Beach. © 561/279-4792.

Elwood's   Over the train tracks just a few feet from the sleek and chic bars and restaurants on Atlantic Avenue is this fabulous blues-themed biker bar housed in a former gas station and garage. No fancy martinis here, just cold beer and good tunes. Open Monday through Friday from 5pm to 2am, Saturday from 11am to 2am, and Sunday from 11am to midnight. 301 E. Atlantic Ave., Delray Beach. © 561/272-7427.

Falcon House   A cozy wine and tapas bar located on a side street off the Atlantic Avenue bustle, Falcon House is reminiscent of a bar you'd expect to find in Napa Valley, with an impressive selection of wines and a well heeled, hip crowd. Falcon House is a haven for those who are over the whole hip-hop loungey scene that's found on Atlantic. Open Monday through Saturday from 5pm to 2am. 116 NE 6th Ave., Delray Beach. © 561/243-9499.

Gatsby's   This always-busy bar is singles central, featuring big-screen TVs, microbrews, and martinis. Thursday-night college nights are especially popular, as are Friday happy hours. Open Monday, Tuesday, and Thursday from 4pm to 2am, Wednesday from 4pm until 3am; Friday from 4pm to 4am, Saturday from 6pm to 4am, and Sunday from 4pm to 3am. 5970 SW 18th St., Boca Raton. © 561/393-3900.

THE PERFORMING ARTS

For details on upcoming events, check the *Boca News* or the *Sun-Sentinel,* or call the **Palm Beach County Cultural Council** information line at © 800/882-ARTS. During business hours, a staffer can give details on current performances. After hours, a recorded message describes the week's events.

The **Florida Symphonic Pops,** a 70-piece professional orchestra, performs jazz, swing, rock, big band, and classical music throughout Boca Raton. For nearly 50 years, this ever-growing musical force has entertained audiences of every age. Call © 561/393-7677 for a schedule of concerts.

Boca's best theater company is the **Caldwell Theatre,** and it's worth checking out. Located in a strip shopping center at 7873 N. Federal Hwy., this equity showcase does well-known dramas, comedies, classics, off-Broadway hits, and new works throughout the year. Prices are reasonable (usually $29–$38). Full-time students with ID will be especially interested in the little-advertised "Student

Rush." When available, tickets are sold for $5 to those who arrive at least an hour in advance. Call ℭ **561/241-7432** for details.

3 Palm Beach ★★ & West Palm Beach ★

65 miles N of Miami, 193 miles E of Tampa, 45 miles N of Fort Lauderdale

Palm Beach County encompasses cities from Boca Raton in the south to Jupiter and Tequesta in the north. But it is Palm Beach, the small island town across the Intracoastal Waterway, which has been the traditional winter home of America's aristocracy—the Kennedys, the Rockefellers, the Pulitzers, the Trumps, titled socialites, and plenty of CEOs. For a real-time perspective on what it means to put on the ritz, there is no better place than Palm Beach, where teenagers cruise around in their parents' Rolls-Royces and socialites, seen only in society publications, seem to jump out of the glossy pages and into an even glossier, glitzier real life. It's really something to be seen, despite the fact that some may consider it all over the top and, frankly, obscene. But it is not only a city of upscale resorts and chic boutiques. In fact, Palm Beach holds some surprises, from a world-class art museum to one of the top bird-watching areas in the state.

Across the water from Palm Beach proper, or the "island" as locals call it, is downtown West Palm Beach, which is where everybody else lives. Clematis Street is the area's nightlife hub, with a great selection of bars, clubs, and restaurants. City Place is West Palm's version of Mizner Park; shops, restaurants, and other entertainment options liven up this once-dead area of West Palm. In addition to good beaching, boating, and diving, you'll find great golf and tennis throughout the county.

Note: Palm Beach's population swells from 20,000 in the summer to 40,000 in the winter. Book early if you plan to visit during the winter months.

ESSENTIALS

GETTING THERE If you're driving up or down the Florida coast, you'll probably reach the Palm Beach area by way of I-95. Exit at Belvedere Road or Okeechobee Boulevard and head east to reach the most central part of Palm Beach.

Visitors on their way to or from Orlando or Miami should take the Florida Turnpike, a toll road with a speed limit of 65 mph. Tolls are pricey, though; you may pay upward of $9 from Orlando and $4 from Miami. If you're coming from Florida's west coast, you can take either State Route 70, which runs north of Lake Okeechobee to Fort Pierce, or State Route 80, which runs south of the lake to Palm Beach.

All major **airlines** fly to the Palm Beach International Airport, at Congress Avenue and Belvedere Road (ℭ **561/471-7400**). **Amtrak** (ℭ **800/USA-RAIL;** www.amtrak.com) has a terminal in West Palm Beach, at 201 S. Tamarind Ave. (ℭ **561/832-6169**).

GETTING AROUND Although a car is almost a necessity in this area, a recently revamped public transportation system is extremely convenient for getting to some attractions in both West Palm and Palm Beach. **Palm Tran** underwent a major expansion in late 1996, increasing service to 32 routes and more than 140 buses. The fare is $1 for adults and 50¢ for children ages 3 to 18, seniors, and riders with disabilities. Free route maps are available by calling ℭ **561/233-4-BUS.** Information operators are available from 6am to 7pm, except Sunday.

In downtown West Palm, free shuttles from City Place to Clematis Street operate Monday through Friday from 9am until 4pm, with plans to expand

Palm Beach & West Palm Beach

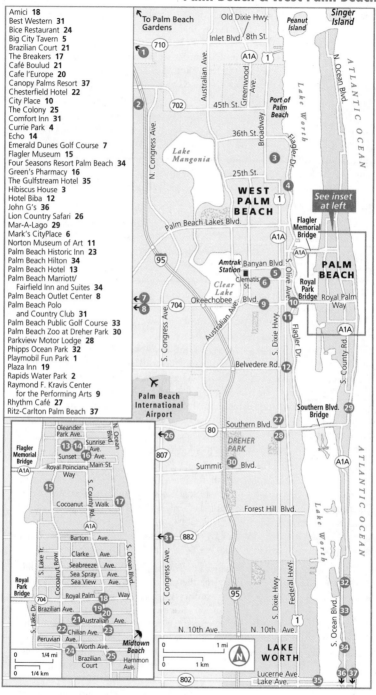

operations to evenings and weekends, too. Allegedly, the shuttles come every 5 minutes, but I'd count on them taking longer. Look for the bubble-gum–pink minibuses throughout downtown. Call ✆ **561/833-8873** for more details.

For a more nostalgic route, consider the stately wicker chariots that run in the downtown area, especially on weekends and during special events. Rates vary according to the time of day but average $1 to $2 per block, plus a per-person charge of $1. Call ✆ **561/835-8922** for pickup or information.

VISITOR INFORMATION   The **Palm Beach County Convention and Visitors Bureau,** 1555 Palm Beach Lakes Blvd., Suite 204, West Palm Beach, FL 33401 (✆ **800/554-PALM** or 561/471-3995; www.palmbeachfl.com), distributes an informative brochure and will answer questions about visiting the Palm Beaches. Ask for a map as well as a copy of its "Arts and Attractions Calendar," a day-to-day guide to art, music, stage, and other events in the county.

BEACHES & ACTIVE PURSUITS

BEACHES   Public beaches are a rare commodity here in Palm Beach. Most of the island's best beaches are fronted by private estates and are inaccessible to the general public. However, there are a few notable exceptions, including **Midtown Beach,** east of Worth Avenue, on Ocean Boulevard, between Royal Palm Way and Gulfstream Road, which boasts more than 100 feet of undeveloped beach. This newly widened sandy coast is now a centerpiece and a natural oasis in a town dominated by commercial glitz. There are no restrooms or concessions here, although a lifeguard is on duty until sundown. About 1½ miles north of there, near Dunbar Street, is a popular hangout for locals, who prefer it to Midtown Beach because of the relaxed and serene atmosphere. Parking is available at meters along Fla. A1A. At the south end of Palm Beach, there's a less-popular but better-equipped beach at **Phipps Ocean Park.** On Ocean Boulevard, between the Southern Boulevard and Lake Avenue Causeways, is a large and lively public beach encompassing more than 1,300 feet of groomed and guarded oceanfront. With picnic and recreation areas, as well as plenty of parking, the area is especially good for families.

BIKING   Rent anything from an English single-speed to a full-tilt mountain bike at the **Palm Beach Bicycle Trail Shop,** 223 Sunrise Ave. (✆ **561/659-4583**). The rates are $8 an hour, $20 a half day (9am–5pm), or $26 for 24 hours and include a basket and lock (not that a lock is necessary in this fortress of a town). The most scenic route is called the Lake Trail, running the length of the island along the Intracoastal Waterway. On it, you'll see some of the most magnificent mansions and grounds and will enjoy the views of downtown West Palm Beach as well as some great wildlife.

GOLF   There's good golfing in the Palm Beaches, but many of the private-club courses are maintained exclusively for the use of their members. Ask at your hotel, or contact the **Palm Beach County Convention and Visitors Bureau** (✆ **561/471-3995**) for information on which clubs are currently available for play. In the off season, some private courses open their greens to visitors staying in a Palm Beach County hotel. This "Golf-A-Round" program offers free greens fees (carts are additional); reservations can be made through most major hotels.

The best hotel for golf in the area is the **PGA National Resort & Spa** (p. 295; ✆ **800/633-9150**), which features a whopping 90 holes of golf.

One of the state's best courses open to the public is **Emerald Dunes Golf Course** ⛳, 2100 Emerald Dunes Dr. in West Palm Beach (✆ **561/687-1700**). Designed by Tom Fazio, this dramatic 7,006-yard, par-72 course was voted

The Sport of Kings

The posh **Palm Beach Polo and Country Club** is one of the world's premier polo grounds and hosts some of the sport's top-rated players. Even if you're not a sports fan, you must attend a match at this field, which is actually on the mainland in an area called Wellington. Rest assured, however, that the spectators, and many of the players, are pure Palm Beach. After all, a day at the pony grounds is one of the only good reasons to leave Palm Beach proper. Don't worry, you need not be a Vanderbilt or a Kennedy to attend—matches are open to the public and are surprisingly affordable.

Even if you haven't a clue as to how the game is played, you can spend your time people-watching. Stargazers have spotted Prince Charles, Sylvester Stallone, Tommy Lee Jones, Bo Derek, and Ivana Trump, among others, in recent years. Dozens of lesser-known royalty, and just plain old characters, keep box seats or chalets right on the grounds.

Dress is casual; a navy or tweed blazer over jeans or khakis is a standard for men, while neat-looking jeans or a pantsuit is the norm for women. On warmer days, shorts and, of course, a polo shirt are fine, too.

General admission is $6 to $10; box seats cost $10 to $36. Matches are held throughout the week. Schedules vary, but the big names usually compete on Sunday at 3:30pm from January to April.

The fields are located at 11809 Polo Club Rd., Wellington, 10 miles west of the Forest Hill Boulevard exit of I-95. Call © **561/793-1440** for tickets and a detailed schedule of events.

"One of the Best 10 You Can Play" by *Golf* magazine. It is located just off the Florida Turnpike at Okeechobee Boulevard. Bookings are taken up to 30 days ahead. Fees start at $130, including carts.

The **Palm Beach Public Golf Course,** 2345 S. Ocean Blvd. (© **561/547-0598**), a popular public 18-hole course, is a par-54. The course opens at 8am and runs on a first-come, first-served basis. Club rentals are available. Greens fees start at $22 per person.

SCUBA DIVING   Year-round warm waters, barrier reefs, and plenty of wrecks make South Florida one of the world's most popular places for diving. One of the best-known artificial reefs in this area is a vintage Rolls-Royce Silver Shadow, which was sunk offshore in 1985. Nature has taken its toll, however, and divers can no longer sit in the car, which has been ravaged by time and saltwater.

Call either of the following outfitters for gear and excursions: **Ocean Sports Scuba Center,** 1736 S. Congress Ave., West Palm Beach (© **561/641-1144**) or **Jim Abernaethy's Scuba Adventures,** at 2116 Avenue B. in Riviera Beach (© **561/691-5808**).

TENNIS   There are hundreds of tennis courts in Palm Beach County. Wherever you are staying, you are bound to be within walking distance of one. In addition to the many hotel tennis courts (see "Where to Stay," below), you can play at **Currie Park,** 2400 N. Flagler Dr., West Palm Beach (© **561/835-7025**), a public park with three lighted hard courts. They are free and available on a first-come, first-served basis.

WATERSPORTS   Call the **Seaside Activities Station** (*© 561/835-8922*) to arrange sailboat, jet ski, bicycle, kayak, water-ski, and parasail rentals.

SEEING THE SIGHTS

Flagler Museum ★★★   The Gilded Age is preserved in this luxurious mansion commissioned by Standard Oil tycoon Henry Flagler as a wedding present to his third wife. *Whitehall,* also known as the "Taj Mahal of North America," is a classically columned Edwardian-style mansion containing 55 rooms, including a Louis XIV music room and art gallery, a Louis XV ballroom, and 14 guest suites outfitted with original antique European furnishings. Out back, climb aboard "The Rambler," Mr. Flagler's private restored railroad car. Allow at least 1½ hours to tour the stunning grounds and interior. School and group tours are available, but, for the most part, this is a self-guided museum.

One Whitehall Way (at Cocoanut Row and Whitehall Way), Palm Beach. *©* 561/655-2833. www.flagler.org. Admission $10 adults, $3 children 6–12. Tues–Sat 10am–5pm; Sun noon–5pm.

Norton Museum of Art ★★★   Since a 1997 expansion doubled the Norton's space, the museum has gained even more prominence in the art world. It is world famous for its prestigious permanent collection and top temporary exhibitions. The museum's major collections are divided geographically. The American galleries contain major works by Edward Hopper, Georgia O'Keeffe, and Jackson Pollock. The French collection contains Impressionist and post-Impressionist paintings by Cézanne, Degas, Gauguin, Matisse, Monet, Picasso, Pissarro, and Renoir. And the Chinese collection contains more then 200 bronzes, jades, and ceramics, as well as a collection of monumental Buddhist sculptures. Allow about 2 hours to see this museum, depending on your level of interest. Recent exhibitions in 2004 include JFK and Art, featuring the various and sometimes complicated responses of American and European artists to John Fitzgerald Kennedy, and The Beatles, an exhibition of photographer Harry Benson's shots of the fab four from 1964 to 1970.

1451 S. Olive Ave., West Palm Beach. *©* 561/832-5196. Fax 561/659-4689. www.norton.org. Admission $8 adults, $3 13–21, free for children 12 and under. Mon–Sat 10am–5pm; Sun 1–5pm. Closed Mon (May–Oct) and all major holidays. Take I-95 to exit 52 (Okeechobee Blvd. E.). Travel east on Okeechobee to Dixie Hwy.; then south ½ mile to the Norton. Parking may be accessed through entrances on Dixie Hwy. and S. Olive Ave.

Playmobil Fun Park ★★ *Kids*   In a child's mind, it doesn't get any better than this. The 17,000-square-foot Playmobil Fun Park is housed in a replica castle and loaded with themed areas for imaginative play: a medieval village, a Western town, a fantasy dollhouse, and more. Plus, there are two water-filled tables on which kids can play with the Playmobil boats. Tech-minded kids could get bored, but toddlers (and up to age 5 or so) will love this place. You *could* spend hours here and not spend a penny, but parents beware: Everything is available for purchase.

8031 N. Military Trail, Palm Beach Gardens. *©* 800/351-8697 or 561/691-9880. Fax 561/691-9517. www.playmobil.com. Admission $1. Mon–Sat 10am–6pm; Sun noon–5pm. From I-95, go north to Palm Beach Lakes Blvd.; then west to Military Trail. Turn left, and the park is about a mile down on the right.

NATURE PRESERVES & ATTRACTIONS

Lion Country Safari ★★ *Kids*   More than 1,300 animals on this 500-acre preserve (the nation's first cageless drive-through safari) are divided into their

Unreal Estate

No trip to Palm Beach is complete without at least a glimpse of Mar-A-Lago, the stately residence of Donald Trump, the 21st century's answer to Jay Gatsby. In 1985, Trump purchased Mar-A-Lago, the former estate of cereal heiress Marjorie Merriweather Post, for what was considered a meager $8 million (for a fully furnished beachfront property of this stature, it was a relative bargain, actually), to the great consternation of locals, who feared that he would turn the place into a casino. Instead, Trump, who sometime resides in a portion of the palace, opened the house to the public—for a price, of course—as a tony country club (membership fee: $100,000).

While there are currently no tours open to the public, you can glimpse the gorgeous manse as you cross the bridge from West Palm Beach into Palm Beach. 1100 S. Ocean Blvd., Palm Beach.

indigenous regions, from the East African preserve of the Serengeti to the American West. Elephants, lions, wildebeest, ostriches, American bison, buffalo, watusi, pink flamingos, and many other more unusual species roam the preserve. When I visited, most of the lions were asleep; when they are awake, they travel freely throughout the cageless grassy landscape (this can be very scary). In fact, you're the one who's confined in your own car without an escort (no convertibles allowed). You're given a detailed informational pamphlet with photos and descriptions and are instructed to obey the 15 mph speed limit—unless you see the rhinos charge (a rare occasion), in which case you're encouraged to floor it. To drive the loop takes just over an hour, though you could make a day of just watching the chimpanzees play on their secluded islands or the calming and graceful giraffes. Included in the admission price is Safari World, an amusement park with paddleboats, a carousel, miniature golf, and a nursery for baby animals born in the preserve. Picnics are encouraged, and camping is available (call for reservations). The best time to go is late afternoon right before the park closes, when they herd up all the animals; plus, it's much cooler then, so the lions are more active. Though some may consider this a tourist trap, I had a great time. Plus, it's way cheaper than flying to Africa for a real safari.

Southern Blvd. W. at S.R. 80, West Palm Beach. © 561/793-1084, or 561/793-9797 for camping reservations. www.lioncountrysafari.com. Admission $18 adults, $16 seniors, $14 children 3–9, free for children under 3. Van rental $8 per hr. Daily 9:30am–5:30pm (last vehicle admitted at 4:30pm). From I-95, exit on Southern Blvd. Go west for about 18 miles.

Palm Beach Zoo at Dreher Park ⊛   If you want animals, go to Lion Country Safari. Unlike big-city zoos, this intimate 23-acre park is more like a stroll in the park than an all-day excursion. It features about 500 animals representing more than 100 different species. A special monkey exhibit and petting zoo are favorites with kids. Stroller and wagon rental are available. Allow at least 2 hours to see all of the sights here. The Zoo's newest attraction is the Tropics of the Americas, a 3-acre jungle path and complex that will immerse zoo guests into the animals, plants, and culture of a New World Rainforest. Visitors will encounter many rare animals such as jaguars, monkeys, giant anteaters, tapirs, bats, birds, snakes, and more.

1301 Summit Blvd. (east of I-95 between Southern Blvd. and Forest Hill Blvd.). © **561/547-WILD.** Fax 561/585-6085. www.palmbeachzoo.org. Admission $7.50 adults, $6 seniors, $5 children 3–12, free for children under 3. Daily 9am–5pm. Closed Thanksgiving.

Rapids Water Park ⚡ *Kids*   It may not be on the same grand scale as the theme parks in Orlando, but Rapids is a great way to cool off on a hot day. There are 12 acres of water rides, including a children's area and miniature golf course. The newest ride is the Superbowl, which is a tubeless water ride that spins and swirls before dumping you into the pool below.

6566 N. Military Trail, West Palm Beach (1 mile west of I-95 on Military between 45th St. [exit 54] and Blue Heron Blvd. [exit 55] in West Palm Beach). © **561/842-8756.** www.rapidswaterpark.com. Admission $26 plus tax per person; free for ages 2 and under. Parking $5. Mid-Mar to Sept Mon–Fri 10am–5pm; Sat–Sun 10am–6pm.

SHOPPING & BROWSING

No matter what your budget is, be sure to take a stroll down Worth Avenue, "the Rodeo Drive of the South" and a window-shopper's dream. Between South Ocean Boulevard and Cocoanut Row, there are more than 200 boutiques, posh shops, art galleries, and upscale restaurants. If you want to fit in, dress as if you were going to an elegant luncheon and not to the mall down the street.

Despite the presence of the usual suspects (**Gucci, Chanel, Armani, Hermès, Louis Vuitton,** among others), Worth Avenue is not impervious to the mainstream. **Victoria's Secret, Limited Express,** and several other chains have sneaked in here, too, but so have a good number of unique boutiques. **History Buff,** 32 Via Mizner (© **561/366-8255**), is a virtual museum, selling every genre of original historical autographs, some dating back to the 1600s, as well as vintage signed photos, first-edition books, and memorabilia. A similar store is **Treasures Gallery,** at 217 Worth Ave. (© **561/835-1891**), an autograph gallery with a priceless collection of John Hancocks, including those of Joe DiMaggio, Mickey Mantle, Andrew Jackson, Abraham Lincoln, Howard Hughes, and hundreds more, all displayed in beautiful frames. For privileged feet, **Stubbs & Wooton,** 4 Via Parigi (© **561/655-4105**), sells velvet slippers that are a favorite of the loofahed locals. **The Purple Turtle,** 150 Worth Ave. (© **561/655-1625**), in the Esplanade shopping promenade, sells designer clothes for infants, including Baby Dior and Baby Armani. For rare and estate jewelry, **Richter's of Palm Beach,** 224 Worth Ave. (© **561/655-0774**), has been specializing in priceless gems since 1893. Just off Worth Avenue, at 374 S. County Rd., is the **Church Mouse** (© **561/659-2154**), a great consignment/thrift shop with antique furnishings and tableware as well as lots of good castaway clothing and shoes, all reasonably priced. This shop usually closes for 2 months during the summer. Call to be sure.

City Place, Okeechobee Rd. (at 1-95), West Palm Beach (© **561/820-9716**), is a $550 million, Mediterranean-style shopping, dining, and entertainment complex that's responsible for revitalizing what was once a lifeless downtown West Palm Beach. Among the 78 mostly chain stores are **Macy's, FAO Schwarz, Benetton,** which has an in-line skating track inside, **Armani Exchange, Pottery Barn,** and **SEE** eyewear. Restaurants include a Ghirardelli ice-cream shop, Legal Seafoods, City Cellar Wine Bar and Grill, and Cheesecake Factory. Best of all is the Muvico Parisian, a 20-screen movie theater where you can wine and dine while watching a feature.

Elsewhere, Downtown West Palm Beach has a scant number of interesting boutiques along Clematis Street. In addition to a large and well-organized bookstore, **Clematis Street Books,** at 206 Clematis (© **561/832-2302**), there are a few used-record stores, clothing shops, and several art galleries.

The **Palm Beach Outlet Center,** at 5700 Okeechobee Blvd. (3 miles west of I-95), West Palm Beach, is the most elegant outlet mall I have ever seen. Upscale clothing, luggage, and shoes are offered at bargain prices in lushly decorated surroundings. The fully enclosed mall also sports a food court.

As if there weren't enough shopping malls in South Florida, enter the newest one, **The Mall at Wellington Green** (10300 W. Forest Hill Blvd., Wellington; ℂ **561/227-6900**), featuring 140 specialty stores and department stores such as Nordstrom, Lord & Taylor, and Dillard's.

WHERE TO STAY

The island of Palm Beach is the epitome of *Lifestyles of the Rich and Famous,* oozing with glitz, glamour, and the occasional scandal. Royalty and celebrities come to winter here, and there are plenty of lavishly priced options to accommodate them. Happily, there are also a few special inns that offer reasonably priced rooms in elegant settings. But the more modest places to lay your straw hat are mostly surrounding the island.

A few of the larger hotel chains operating in Palm Beach include the **Palm Beach Marriott/Fairfield Inn and Suites,** at 2870 S. Ocean Blvd. (ℂ **800/228-2800** or 561/582-2581), which is across the street from the beach. Also beachside is the pricey **Palm Beach Hilton,** at 2842 S. Ocean Blvd. (ℂ **800/433-1718** or 561/586-6542). An excellent and affordable alternative right in the middle of Palm Beach's commercial section is a condominium that operates as a hotel, too: the **Palm Beach Hotel,** at 235 Sunrise Ave. (between County Rd. and Bradley Place, across the street from the Publix supermarket; ℂ **561/659-7794**). With winter prices starting at about $105, this clean and comfortable accommodation is a great option for those looking for the rare bargain in Palm Beach.

In West Palm Beach, the chain hotels are mostly located on the main arteries close to the highways and a short drive from the activities in downtown. They include a **Best Western,** 1800 Palm Beach Lakes Blvd. (ℂ **800/331-9569** or 561/683-8810), and, just down the road, a **Comfort Inn,** 1901 Palm Lakes Blvd. (ℂ **800/221-2222** or 561/689-6100). Farther south is the **Parkview Motor Lodge,** 4710 S. Dixie Hwy., just south of Southern Boulevard (ℂ **561/833-4644**). This 28-room, single-story motel is the best of the many motels along Dixie Highway (U.S. 1). With rates starting at $50 for a room with television, air-conditioning, and telephone, you can't ask for more.

For other options, contact **Palm Beach Accommodations** at ℂ **800/543-SWIM.**

VERY EXPENSIVE

Brazilian Court ★★★   This elegant, old-world Palm Beach Mediterranean-style hotel dates from the 1920s and almost looks like a Beverly Hills bungalow. No two rooms are the same as far as decor, but all are elegant and luxurious with Mahogany crown molding, Provence-style wood shutters, imported fabrics, individual climate controls, and stunning bathrooms adorned in limestone with Ultra Air Jet baths and frameless shower enclosures. Service is doting, though a bit aloof—you won't always be received by smiling faces, but you will get whatever you want. There's even room service exclusively for pets (you know the type: held hostage in Mummy's Gucci bag). A large hotel by Palm Beach standards (The Breakers notwithstanding), Brazilian Court is sprawled over half a block and features fountains and private courtyards. Celebrity stylist Frederick Fekkai wisely set up shop here as the hotel's premier beauty salon and spa. With the most recent addition of Café Boulud (which provides stellar 24-hr. room service), the hauter than thou product of one of the world's most renowned chefs, Daniel Boulud, Brazilian Court has replaced the haute cuisine Italian mainstay, Bice Restaurant (p. 288), as Palm Beach's number one place to see and be seen.

301 Australian Ave., Palm Beach, FL 33480. ℂ 800/552-0335 or 561/655-7740. Fax 561/655-0801. www.thebraziliancourt.com. 103 units. Winter $335–$525 double, $550–$875 suite; off-season $165–$315 double, $350–$525 suite. Special packages available. AE, DC, DISC, MC, V. **Amenities:** Restaurant; private dining room (up to 12); bar (see "The Palm Beaches After Dark," later in this chapter); heated outdoor pool; exercise room; spa treatments; concierge; salon; 24-hr. room service; library. *In room:* A/C, TV, minibar, coffeemaker, hair dryer, iron.

The Breakers ★★★ *Kids*   This 140-acre beachfront hotel is what Palm Beach is all about. Elaborate, stately, and resplendent in all its Italian-Renaissance–style glory, it's where old money mixes with new money, and the Old World gives way, albeit reluctantly, to a bit of modernity (note the hotel's recent elimination of the jackets-required rule). The Breakers consists of a seven-story building with a frescoed lobby and long, majestic hallways reminiscent of a palace. If you can afford it, The Flagler Club is the Breakers' exclusive, hyper luxe hotel within a hotel, featuring private entry, 28 rooms, butlers, concierges, doting service, and tea, cocktails, hors d'oeuvres, and deserts all day and night. Chief Concierge Bernard Nicole is a delight, not to mention a wealth of knowledge on local lore. The indulgent Oceanfront Spa and Beach Club features a spectacular oceanview fitness center (makes workouts a lot less grueling), four oceanfront pools, cabanas, and saunas. Treatments at the sublime Spa at The Breakers are aplenty, filling up a 16-page book. Ask for one upon arrival and marvel at the spa-portunities. Rooms were modernized a bit, but remain elegant, not sterile, with plush furnishings, huge bathrooms, and views of the ocean or the hotel's magnificently manicured grounds. A revamp of Florida's oldest existing golf course, led by Brian Silva, transformed The Breakers Ocean Course into a 6,200-yard, championship-level par 70. For those who need a few lessons before hitting the greens, The Todd Anderson Golf Academy will assist in finding your zone with world class instruction by PGA members and apprentices trained to teach the ways of the man rated as one of America's 50 Greatest Golf Teachers. For more information on the Academy, check out www.tagolf.com or call ℂ **561/659-8474.** While daddy and mommy are out playing golf, send the kids to the hotel's Family Entertainment Center, a fabulous 6,160-square-foot space filled with video games, skee ball, air hockey, board games, a children's movie room, computers and Xbox games, and several supervised camps. I have to say that despite the magnificence of the hotel's adult side, the kids' area was most impressive. Each of the resort's five restaurants holds their own, especially the oceanfront Seafood Bar and signature French restaurant L'Escalier, but do not miss the incredibly decadent Sunday brunch in The Circle, the magnificent dining room with hand painted ceilings and to die for ocean views. Not tampering with its historic characteristics too much, the Breakers has finally completed a $145 million renovation, freshening up and ridding 160 rooms of that stale smell that's been there since about 1945.

1 S. County Rd., Palm Beach, FL 33480. ℂ 800/833-3141, 888/BREAKERS, or 561/655-6611. Fax 561/659-8403. www.thebreakers.com. 560 units. Winter $420–$675 double, $700–$3,000 suite; off-season $270–$425 double, $500–$1,950 suite. Special packages available. AE, DC, DISC, MC, V. Valet parking $17. From I-95, exit Okeechobee Blvd. E., head east to S. County Rd., and turn left. **Amenities:** 5 restaurants; 3 bars; 4 outdoor pools; golf course; 14 tennis courts; health club and spa; watersports equipment (including scuba and sailing); bike rental; children's programs; game rooms; concierge; business center; shopping arcade; salon; 24-hr. room service; in-room massage; babysitting; laundry services; dry cleaning; croquet; shuffleboard; beach volleyball courts. *In room:* A/C, TV, dataport, minibar, hair dryer, iron, CD player, Sony PlayStation.

Four Seasons Resort Palm Beach ★★ *Kids*   Built in 1989 at the edge of Palm Beach's downtown district, this elegant resort has quickly gained accolades from around the world. An incredibly hospitable staff works hard to be sure this beachfront gem lives up to its reputation. The elegant marble lobby is replete with hand-carved European furnishings, grand oil paintings, tapestries, and dramatic flower arrangements—though I did feel like I was in a museum, unable to touch anything. The rooms are spacious with private balconies and lavish bathrooms with color TVs. The full-service spa is excellent, and you will be remiss if you go without experiencing the incredible oceanview massage at the poolside cabanas. The main dining room, known simply as The Restaurant, serves one of the best dinners (Southeastern regional cuisine) in Palm Beach. Executive Chef Hubert Des Marais is one of *Food & Wine* magazine's Ten Best New Chefs. Two other less-formal restaurants, including a pool bar and grill, round out the dining options. Known for many things, but not necessarily as a kid friendly hotel, the Four Seasons has decided to cater a bit more to their future customers by adding a game room complete with Xbox video games, a pool table, and large-screen TV. Meanwhile, parents can entertain themselves at the new Champagne Bar.

2800 S. Ocean Blvd., Palm Beach, FL 33480. ⓒ 800/432-2335 or 561/582-2800. Fax 561/547-1557. www. fourseasons.com. 210 units. Winter $395–$695 double, from $1,500 suite; off-season $275–$595 double, from $870 suite. AE, DC, DISC, MC, V. Valet parking $18. From I-95, take 6th Ave. exit east and turn left onto Dixie Hwy. Turn east onto Lake Ave. and north onto S. Ocean Blvd., and the hotel is just ahead on your right. Pets under 20 lb. accepted. **Amenities:** 3 restaurants; lounge; outdoor heated pool; 3 tennis courts; spa; watersports rentals; bike rental; children's programs; concierge; business center; salon; 24-hr. room service; in-room massage; babysitting; laundry services; dry cleaning; cooking classes weekly. *In room:* A/C, TV/VCR, dataport, minibar, fridge, hair dryer, iron, safe.

Ritz-Carlton Palm Beach ★★★   If The Breakers is too mammoth for your tastes, consider the Ritz-Carlton. A lot warmer than the Four Seasons, the Ritz, though hyperluxurious, manages to lack pretension. Located on a beautiful beach in a tiny town about 8 miles from Palm Beach's shopping and dining area, the Ritz-Carlton's location is a plus for those who seek privacy but may be a drawback for those interested in the activity of "town." It is so discreet, in fact, that Palm Beach's luminaries often escape here for a rare weekend or night of anonymity. The hotel's French 18th- and 19th-century antique furnishings give no hint that the property is not yet even 10 years old. Each room has a private balcony and at least a glimpse of the ocean below. All are spacious, while the large marble bathrooms are extremely inviting. The elegant dining room serves continental-style dinners in ornate surroundings. Other restaurants on the property include a grill, for dinner only; a casual restaurant, open all day; and a poolside cafe and bar. Cocktails are also served in the lobby lounge, where you can often find live entertainment. Afternoon tea is served daily but is best Wednesday through Saturday when a jazz trio entertains.

100 S. Ocean Blvd., Manalpan, FL 33462. ⓒ 800/241-3333 or 561/533-6000. Fax 561/540-4999. www. ritzcarlton.com. 270 units. Winter $395–$820 double, $3,150 suite; off-season $285–$725 double, $2,700 suite. AE, DISC, MC, V. Valet parking $15. From I-95, take exit 45, heading east. After 1 mile, turn left onto Federal Hwy. (U.S. 1). Continue north for about a mile and turn right onto Ocean Ave. Cross the Intracoastal Waterway; turn right onto Fla. A1A. **Amenities:** 4 restaurants; bar; outdoor pool; health club; Jacuzzi; sauna; watersports equipment/rental; bike rental; children's center/programs; concierge; business center; salon; 24-hr. room service; in-room massage; laundry services; dry cleaning. *In room:* A/C, TV, dataport, minibar, hair dryer, iron, safe.

EXPENSIVE

Chesterfield Hotel ★★★   Reminiscent of an English country manor, the Chesterfield Hotel in all its flowery, Laura Ashley–inspired glory is a magnificent, charming hotel with exceptional service to rival that of the Ritz. Warm and inviting, the Chesterfield is one of the only places in South Florida in which the idea of a fireplace (there's one in the hotel's library) doesn't seem ridiculous. Traditional English tea is served every afternoon, with fresh-baked scones, petit fours, and sandwiches. Rooms are decorated with bright fabrics and wallpaper and antiques. The roomy marble bathrooms are stocked with an array of luxurious toiletries. A small heated pool and courtyard are nice, and the beach is only 3 blocks away, but the real action is inside. At night, the hotel's retroelegant Leopard Lounge (see "The Palm Beaches After Dark," later in this chapter) serves decent continental cuisine but is better as a later-night hangout for live music, schmoozing, and staring at the local cognoscenti.

363 Cocoanut Row, Palm Beach, FL 33480. ✆ **800/243-7871** or 561/659-5800. Fax 561/659-6707. www.redcarnationhotels.com. 65 units. Winter $309–$350 double; off-season $139–$230 double. Rollaway bed $15 extra. Packages available. AE, DC, DISC, MC, V. Free valet parking. From I-95, exit onto Okeechobee Blvd. E., cross the Intracoastal Waterway, and turn right onto Cocoanut Row. **Amenities:** Restaurant; lounge; small heated swimming pool; access to nearby health club; Jacuzzi; bike rental; concierge; business center; 24-hr. room service; in-room massage; babysitting; dry cleaning. *In room:* A/C, TV, VCR on request, dataport, hair dryer, iron, safe.

Plaza Inn ★★   This three-story, family-run bed-and-breakfast–style inn located 1 block from the beach is as understated and luxurious as the guests it hosts. From the simple and elegant flower arrangements in the marble lobby to the well-worn period antiques haphazardly placed throughout, the Plaza Inn, whose exterior was renovated in 2001, has the look of studied nonchalance. The courtyard, with its waterfalls and pool, and the intimate piano bar are just two examples of the inn's infinite charms. A small staff is remarkably hospitable and knowledgeable about the island's inner workings. Each uniquely decorated room is dressed with quality furnishings, several with carved four-poster beds, hand-crocheted spreads, and lace curtains. The bathrooms, renovated in 2000, are lovely if quite small, and the wall-mounted air conditioners can be noisy when they are needed in the warm months. Choose a corner room or one overlooking the small pool deck for the best light. It's a tough call to decide which is better—the Plaza Inn or the Chesterfield, but the Plaza, unlike the Chesterfield, does include a full breakfast in the price of the room.

215 Brazilian Ave., Palm Beach, FL 33480. ✆ **800/233-2632** or 561/832-8666. Fax 561/835-8776. www.plazainnpalmbeach.com. 48 units. Winter $245–$305 double, $310–$395 suite; off-season $125–$165 double, $170–$205 suite. Rates include breakfast. AE, MC, V. From I-95, exit onto Okeechobee Blvd. E. and cross the Intracoastal Waterway. Turn right onto Cocoanut Row; then left onto Brazilian Ave. Small pets permitted. **Amenities:** Restaurant; lounge; heated outdoor pool; exercise room; Jacuzzi; access to nearby health club ($15 per day); bike rental; concierge; secretarial services; limited room service; in-room massage; babysitting; laundry services; dry cleaning. *In room:* A/C, TV, dataport, fridge, coffeemaker, hair dryer on request.

MODERATE

The Colony ★★   The sign outside of this Palm Beach mainstay should read ROXANNE PULITZER SLEPT HERE. She did, actually, for quite a while after her 7-week marriage went bust. For years, The Colony has been a favorite hangout—hideout, perhaps—for assorted old timers, socialites, and mysterious luminaries. Beyond that, The Colony is a Georgian-style hotel known for its attentive staff, floral-decorated rooms, and, unfortunately, really small bathrooms. The 39 suites and apartments, not to mention the seven two-bedroom villas with Jacuzzis, are much more lavish—and lavishly priced.

155 Hammon Ave., Palm Beach, FL 33480. ✆ **800/521-5525** or 561/655-5430. Fax 561/659-8104. www.thecolonypalmbeach.com. 85 units, 7 villas. Winter $290–$450 double, $475–$695 suite; off-season $130–$275 double, $290–$495 suite. AE, DC, MC, V. From I-95, exit onto Okeechobee Blvd. E. and cross the Intracoastal

Waterway. Turn right on S. County Rd.; then left onto Hammon Ave. **Amenities:** Restaurant; bar; heated Florida-shaped pool; spa; concierge; limited seasonal room service. *In room:* A/C, TV, dataport, hair dryer, iron.

Palm Beach Historic Inn ★★   Built in 1923, the Palm Beach Historic Inn is an area landmark located within a block's walking distance of the beach (on which chairs and towels are provided for guests of the hotel), Worth Avenue, and several good restaurants. The small lobby is filled with antiques, books, magazines, and an old-fashioned umbrella stand, all of which add to the homey feel of this intimate bed-and-breakfast. In your room, wine, fruit, snacks, tea, and cookies ensure that you won't go hungry—never mind the excellent continental breakfast that is brought to you daily. All the rooms are on the second floor, are uniquely decorated, and feature hardwood floors, down comforters, Egyptian cotton linens, fluffy bathrobes, and plenty of good-smelling toiletries. Gone are the frills, floral prints, sheer curtains, and plethora of lace that once made this inn feel like staying at your grandmother's house. What you'll find here, thanks to new innkeepers who took over in July 2001, is a casual elegance that's comfortable for everyone. In addition, a baby grand piano and guitars for the musically inclined, as well as videotapes to keep the kids entertained, have been added to the hotel's amenities.

365 S. County Rd., Palm Beach, FL 33480. ℂ **561/832-4009.** Fax 561/832-6255. www.palmbeachhistoric inn.com. 13 units. Winter $150–$185 double, $250–$375 suite; off-season $85–$105 double, $150–$175 suite. Rates include continental breakfast. Children stay free in parent's room. AE, MC, V. Small pets accepted. No smoking. *In room:* A/C, TV/VCR, fridge, hair dryer, iron.

INEXPENSIVE

Canopy Palms Resort ★   A cross between Key West and South Beach, the Canopy Palms Resort has become a bona fide hot spot thanks to HBO, which has filmed scenes for a never released show, *Blue Hotel,* here. A hotbed of hipsters hailing from Boca Raton and Palm Beach, the Canopy Palms Resort is a few notches above a beachside motel thanks to its beachfront location and pool that doubles as a swinging spot for the hotel's now legendary "Locals Go Loco" Sunday afternoon pool parties. Rooms are decorated in funky, outlandish zebra prints, pastels, and Ikea-esqe furniture and accessories. But, alas, the focal point of the hotel is its poolside Tiki bar, the appropriately titled Wet Bar, where, among others, porn stars Ron Jeremy and Jenna Jameson have been known to make an appearance or two. This is not necessarily a place you'd want to take the kids, but if you are a kid at heart looking for a wild time, Canopy Palms is worth seeking shade under.

3800 North Ocean Dr., Singer Island, FL 33431. ℂ **800/765-5502** or 561/848-5502. Fax 561/863-6560. www.canopypalmsresort.com. 125 units. Winter $99–$149 double, $239 suite; off-season $95–$135 double, $200 suite. AE, DC, DISC, V. **Amenities:** Restaurant; pool; tennis court; spa and fitness center; concierge; room service; putting green; driving cage. *In room:* A/C, TV, dataport, minibar, coffeemaker, hair dryer, iron, safe.

The Gulfstream Hotel ★   Just over the bridge from glitzy, glammy Palm Beach is Lake Worth, not exactly a hotbed of activity, but this sleepy enclave is nonetheless peaceful and very popular with people looking for no frills relaxation. The Gulfstream Hotel is the only game in town, a historic property on the Intracoastal Waterway, whose rooms are comfortable but nothing to look at. The pool here is functional, but again, nothing to look at. The lobby of the hotel is perhaps the most appealing, reminiscent of an old, deep South hotel with high ceilings, paddle fans, and free cookies at the check-in desk. The restaurant is the focal point of activity, a comfortable wood-floored dining room serving excellent seafood, meat, and pasta dishes, that transforms itself into a veritable disco on Fridays and Saturdays—the only form of nightlife in town. If you're looking to experience the Palm Beaches casually and comfortably without feeling like you have to get decked out to walk out of your hotel room, the Gulfstream is a great option, not to mention a bargain in comparison to the ritzier hotels over the bridge.

1 Lake Ave., Lake Worth, FL 33460. ✆ **888/540-0669** or 561/540-6000. Fax 561/582-6904. www.thegulf streamhotel.com. 106 units. Winter $149 double, $259-$339 suite; off-season $99 double, $259–$339 suite. AE, DC, DISC, V. Free self-parking. **Amenities:** Restaurant; bar; pool bar; outdoor pool; concierge; limited room service. *In room:* A/C, TV, dataport, coffeemaker, hair dryer, iron.

Hibiscus House ★★ *Finds*   Inexpensive bed-and-breakfasts are rare in Southeast Florida, making the Hibiscus House, one of the area's firsts, a true find. Located a few miles from the coast in a quiet residential neighborhood, this 1920s-era B&B is filled with handsome antiques and tapestries in luxurious fabrics. Every room has its own private terrace or balcony. The Red Room has a fabulous new bathroom with Jacuzzi. The backyard, a peaceful retreat, has been transformed into a tropical garden, complete with heated swimming pool and lounge chairs. Also, there are plenty of pretty areas for guests to enjoy inside; one little sitting room is wrapped in glass and is stocked with playing cards and board games. *Beware:* Breakfast portions are enormous. The gourmet creations are as filling as they are beautiful. Ask for any special requests in advance; owners Raleigh Hill and Colin Rayer will be happy to oblige.

501 30th St., West Palm Beach, FL 33407. ✆ **800/203-4927** or 561/863-5633. Fax 561/863-5633. www. hibiscushouse.com. 8 units. Winter $100–$175 double; off-season $85–$150 double. Rates include breakfast. AE, DC, DISC, MC, V. From I-95, exit onto Palm Beach Lakes Blvd. E. and continue 4 miles. Turn left onto Flagler Dr. and continue for about 20 blocks. Then turn left onto 30th St. Pets accepted. **Amenities:** Heated pool; concierge. *In room:* A/C, TV, hair dryer.

Hotel Biba ★★ *Finds*   As West Palm Beach came into its own as far as nightlife is concerned, it was only a matter of time before a hip boutique hotel made its appearance in the historic El Cid neighborhood, located 1 mile from City Place and nightlife-heavy Clematis Street. The very cool Hotel Biba answers the call for an inexpensive, chic hotel that young hipsters can call their own. A word of advice, however: The hotel is not exactly soundproof. Rooms may be cloistered by fence and gardens, but they are still extremely close to a major thoroughfare. Try to ask for one that's on the quieter Belvedere Road as opposed to those facing South Olive Avenue. Housed in a renovated Colonial-style 1940s motor lodge, Biba has been remarkably updated on the inside by de rigueur designer Barbara Hulanicki and features a sleek and chic lobby with the requisite hip hotel bar, the Biba Bar; a gorgeously landscaped outdoor pool area with Asian gardens; and a reflection pond. Rooms are equally fabulous, with private patios, mosaic-tile floors, custom-made mahogany furniture, Egyptian cotton linens, down pillows, exquisite bathroom products, and high-tech amenities. The bold color schemes mix nicely with the high-fashion crowd that convenes here.

320 Belvedere Rd., West Palm Beach, FL 33405. ✆ **561/832-0094.** Fax 561/833-7848. www.hotelbiba.com. 43 units. Year-round rates $99–$135 double, $140–$179 suite. **Amenities:** Restaurant; lounge; outdoor pool; concierge. *In room:* A/C, TV, dataport, hair dryer, CD player.

WHERE TO DINE

Palm Beach has some of the area's swankiest restaurants. Thanks to the development of downtown West Palm Beach, however, there is also a great selection of trendier, less expensive spots. Dress here is slightly more formal than in most other areas of Florida: Men wear blazers, and women generally put on modest dresses or chic suits when they dine out, even in the oppressively hot days of summer.

In addition to the below listings, you may also want to check out City Place's new **Coach Schnellenberger's Original Steakhouse & Sports Theater** (700 S. Rosemary Ave., West Palm Beach; ✆ **561/833-1400**), which features an exhibition kitchen, a mesquite-burning grill, beef aged and cut on the premises, rotisserie chicken, lobster and fresh fish, and hand-spun ice cream in a sports fanatic-friendly environment.

VERY EXPENSIVE

Café Boulud ★★★ FRENCH   Snowbird socialites rejoiced over the opening of star chef Daniel Boulud's eponymous restaurant in the Brazilian Court hotel. Non-socialites just said, "Figures, another restaurant where we can't even afford a bread crumb." If you're out to splurge, Boulud is ideal, with an exquisite menu divided into four sections—La Tradition (French and American classics), La Saison (sea-sonal dishes), Le Potager (dishes inspired by the vegetable market), and Le Voyage (world cuisine). Grilled Colorado lamb with wilted romaine lettuce, Greek yogurt, coriander, and cumin is spectacular and almost worth all $38 you'll pay for it. The chickpea fries at $6 are a bargain, but too bad you'll be frowned upon if you snag a coveted table and just order those. If you don't ever plan to get to Daniel, Boulud's New York City standout, then save your pennies for Café Boulud. If you couldn't care less about star chefs, stuffy socialites, and frou frou cuisine, don't even bother.

Brazilian Court, 301 Australian Ave., Palm Beach. ℂ 561/655-6060. Reservations essential. Main courses $17–$38. AE, DC, MC, V. Daily 9am–10pm.

Cafe l'Europe ★★★ CONTINENTAL   One of Palm Beach's finest and most popular, this award-winning, romantic, luxurious, and formal restaurant gives you good reason to get dressed up. The enticing appetizers, served by a superb staff, might include Chinese spring rolls, baked goat-cheese salad with raspberry-walnut dressing, poached salmon, or chilled gazpacho with avocado. Main courses run the gamut from sautéed potato-crusted Florida snapper to lamb chops to roast Cornish game hen. Seafood dishes and steaks in sumptuous but light sauces are always exceptional.

331 S. County Rd. (at the corner of Brazilian Ave.), Palm Beach. ℂ 561/655-4020. Reservations recom-mended. Main courses $18–$34. AE, DC, DISC, MC, V. Tues–Sat noon–3pm; Tues–Sun 6–10pm.

Echo ★★ ASIAN   Don't think that because this hyper-stylish, New York-ish restaurant is located by the overly commercial City Place that it's either com-mercial or affordable. When I ate here with a group of eight, we ordered a sushi platter that ended up costing $300. Outrageous! The ridiculously expensive sushi is, indeed, delicious, as is the Peking Duck and pretty much every Thai, Vietnamese, Indonesian, Japanese, and Chinese dish, but there are other places to go for that. Instead, check out the groovy bar area, have a few cocktails, and share a few pieces of sushi to get the vibe without breaking the bank and hear-ing those echoes in your empty wallet.

230 Sunrise Ave., Palm Beach. ℂ 561/802-4222. Reservations essential. Main courses $25–$50. AE, DC, MC, V. Tues–Sun 5:30–9:30pm.

Mark's CityPlace ★★★ NEW AMERICAN   Star chef Mark Militello of Mark's Las Olas and South Beach fame has traveled on his high-speed culinary meteor and landed at West Palm's bustling entertainment and dining complex to the delight of foodies in Palm Beach. A Militello specialty, pizza, is cooked in wood-burning ovens, which churn out trendy versions of the thin-crusted clas-sic, such as shrimp, pesto, fontina cheese, and sun-dried tomatoes. The sushi bar here is, frankly, out of place, since this is not a sushi restaurant. Entrees range from risotto with wild mushroom and truffle oil to an outstanding black-pep-percorn–crusted, seared yellowfin tuna. For dessert, try the double-chocolate bread pudding with white-chocolate-chip ice cream.

700 S. Rosemary Ave., West Palm Beach. (✆ 561/514-0770. Reservations recommended. Main courses $17–$38. AE, DC, MC, V. Mon–Thurs 5–11pm; Fri–Sat 5pm–midnight; Sun 5–10:30pm.

Tsunami ✰✰✰ SUSHI   If you're a sushi lover, this place is worth every precious penny you'll pay. One of West Palm's hot spots, Tsunami is reminiscent of a New York City eatery, the kind whose reservation book reads like *The Hollywood Reporter*, but instead of celebrities, this place caters to the chichi crowds of Palm Beach who actually cross the bridge to get here for some of the freshest fish this side of Japan.

651 Okeechobee Blvd., West Palm Beach. (✆ 561/835-9696. Reservations required. Main courses $6–$75. AE, DISC, MC, V. Sun–Wed 5–10pm;.Thurs–Sat 5–11:30pm.

EXPENSIVE

Amici ✰ *Overrated* ITALIAN   This is one of those restaurants in which the scene is tastier than the cuisine. An upper-crusty Palm Beach set tends to convene here and consistently rave about what can only be considered above-average, overpriced Italian food. The best item on the entire menu is gnocchi with white truffle oil, fontina cheese, and spinach. Everything else is fairly standard: grilled sandwiches, pastas with rustic sauces, pizzas, grilled shrimp, and fish. Despite its less-than-stellar food, it's always crowded and very noisy.

288 S. County Rd. (at Royal Palm Way), Palm Beach. (✆ 561/832-0201. Reservations strongly recommended on weekends. Main courses $18–$27; pastas and pizzas $8–$19. AE, DC, MC, V. Mon–Thurs 11:30am–3pm and 5:30–10:30pm; Fri–Sat 11:30am–3pm and 5:30–11pm; Sun 5:30–10:30pm.

Bice Restaurant ✰✰ ITALIAN   Bice's Northern Italian cuisine far surpasses that of Amici's, but as far as atmosphere is concerned, the air in here is a bit haughty, bordering on rude. Servers and diners alike seem to have noticeable attitudes, but you'll forget all that with one bite of the juicy veal cutlet with tomato salad or the *pasta e fagioli* (pasta with beans).

313½ Worth Ave., Palm Beach. (✆ 561/835-1600. Reservations essential. Main courses $20–$32. AE, DC, MC, V. Daily noon–10pm.

MODERATE

Big City Tavern ✰✰ AMERICAN   If the Palm Beach–proper dining scene is too stuffy for you, head over the bridge to Clematis Street, downtown West Palm's hub of urban chic, where you will find this yuppie enclave of brick and pressed tin in which people-watching is at a premium. Despite its all-American appearance, Big City Tavern offers a varied menu, including coconut shrimp tempura with a salmon inside-out sushi roll and a delicious bowl of littleneck clams in wine broth with roasted garlic and escarole. On weekends, the Tavern is mobbed, so be prepared for a long wait that's best spent at the action-packed bar.

224 Clematis St., West Palm Beach. (✆ 561/659-1853. Reservations suggested. Main courses $7.95–$28. AE, MC, V. Daily 10:30am–2pm; Sun–Tues 5:30–10:30pm; Wed–Sat 5:30pm–midnight.

Rhythm Café ✰ *Finds* ECLECTIC AMERICAN   This funky hole-in-the-wall is where those in the know come to eat some of West Palm Beach's most laid-back gourmet food. On the handwritten, photocopied menu (which changes daily), you'll always find a fish specialty accompanied by a hefty dose of greens and garnishes. Also reliably outstanding is the sautéed medallion of beef tenderloin, served on a bed of arugula with a tangy rosemary vinaigrette. Salads and soups are a great bargain, since portions are relatively large and the display usually spectacular. The kitschy decor of this tiny cafe comes complete with vinyl tablecloths and a changing display of paintings by local amateurs. Young, handsome waiters are attentive but not solicitous. The old drugstore where the restaurant recently relocated features an original 1950s lunch counter and stools.

3800 S. Dixie Hwy., West Palm Beach. ℭ 561/833-3406. Reservations recommended on weekends. Main courses $12–$31. AE, DISC, MC, V. Tues–Sat 6–10pm; Sun (Dec–Mar) 5:30–9pm; closed in early Sept. From I-95, exit east on Southern Blvd. Go 1 block north of Southern Blvd.; restaurant on the right.

INEXPENSIVE
Green's Pharmacy ✯ *Value* AMERICAN   This neighborhood corner pharmacy offers one of the best meal deals in Palm Beach. Both breakfast and lunch are served coffee-shop style either at a Formica bar or at plain tables placed on a black-and-white checkerboard floor. Breakfast specials include eggs and omelets served with home fries and bacon, sausage, or corned-beef hash. At lunch, the grill serves burgers and sandwiches, as well as ice-cream sodas and milkshakes to a loyal crowd of pastel-clad Palm Beachers.

151 N. County Rd., Palm Beach. ℭ 561/832-0304. Fax 561/832-6502. Breakfast $2–$5; burgers and sandwiches $3–$6; soups and salads $2–$7. AE, DISC, MC, V. Mon–Sat 7am–5pm; Sun 7am–3pm.

John G's ✯ AMERICAN   This coffee shop is the most popular in the county. For decades, John G's has been attracting huge breakfast crowds; lines run out the door (on weekends, all the way down the block). Stop in for some good, greasy-spoon–style food served in heaping portions right on the beachfront. This place is known for fresh and tasty fish and chips and its selection of creative omelets and grill specials.

10 S. Ocean Blvd., Lake Worth. ℭ 561/585-9860. www.johngs.com. Reservations not accepted. Breakfast $3–$8.50; lunch $5–$14. No credit cards. Daily 7am–3pm. From the Florida Tpk., take the Lake Worth exit and head toward the ocean.

THE PALM BEACHES AFTER DARK
THE BAR, CAFE & MUSIC SCENE
A decade-old project to revitalize downtown West Palm Beach has finally become a reality, with **Clematis Street** at its heart. Artist lofts, sidewalk cafes, bars, restaurants, consignment shops, and galleries dot the street from Flagler Drive to Rosemary Avenue, creating a hot spot for a night out, especially on weekends, when yuppies mingle with stylish Euros and disheveled artists. Every Thursday night is a mob scene of 20- and 30-somethings who come out for "Clematis by Night." Each week features a different rock, blues, or reggae band plus an art show. Vendors sell food and drinks, and the street's bars and restaurants are packed. It is a bit raucous at times, but fun. Minors unaccompanied by their guardians are not permitted in the downtown area around Clematis Street after 10pm on weeknights and after 11pm on weekend nights. Otherwise, most of the nightspots listed below are open until about 3 or 4am.

Over the bridge, it's a completely different world. Palm Beach is much quieter and better known for its rather private society balls and estate parties. With the exception of some restaurants that are more of a scene (such as **Amici;** see above or **Ta-boo;** see below), Palm Beach nightlife is more likely to entail sipping port at one of the finer hotels like The Breakers, The Colony, the Ritz-Carlton, the Four Seasons, or the Chesterfield.

West Palm Beach
E. R. Bradley's   What used to be a swank saloon on the island of Palm Beach is now a very casual, friendly indoor/outdoor bar in downtown West Palm, attracting a mixed crowd. The later-night bar scene is a real draw. If you are hungry, try the "crab bomb," Maryland lump crabmeat baked in a light cream

sauce with steamed vegetables. Open Sunday through Wednesday from 8am to 3am and Thursday through Saturday from 8am to 4am. 104 Clematis St. ✆ 561/833-3520.

Level 2 Nightclub   With its techno, Latin, and hip-hop music and VIP rooms, this West Palm club seems like it belongs in the velvet-roped world of South Beach. Open Tuesday through Saturday from 10pm to 4am. 313 Clematis St. ✆ 561/833-1444. Cover $7. No cover before midnight.

Liquid Room   Former South Beach hot spot Liquid may have evaporated (and subsequently reopened by name alone, in a new space that's not nearly as haute as the original) from the scene, but this Clematis Street location is flowing with Palm Beach club kids who revel in the fact that they finally have a chic, celebrity-saturated dance club to call their own. Open Thursday and Friday from 10pm to 3am and Saturday from 10pm to 4am. 313 Clematis St. ✆ 561/655-2332. Cover $10.

Monkey Club   This tacky yet trendy Caribbean-inspired dance club is 7,500 square feet of wall-to-wall, well-dressed revelers. Theme nights are popular here, from ladies' nights to the classier version of the wet-T-shirt contest—the Miss Hawaiian Tropic Model Search. Open Thursday through Saturday from 9pm to 3am.219 Clematis St. ✆ 561/833-6500. Cover $0–$10.

Respectable Street Café   This is one of the premier live music venues in South Florida. In addition to the requisite DJs, this grungy bar features an impressive lineup of alternative music acts. The cafe's plain store-front exterior belies its funky, high-ceilinged interior decorated with large black booths, psychedelic wall murals, and a large checkerboard-tile dance floor. Open Wednesday and Thursday 9pm to 3am; Friday and Saturday from 9pm to 4am. 518 Clematis St. ✆ 561/832-9999. Cover varies $5–$20.

Palm Beach

The Leopard Lounge *Finds*   *The Flintstones* meets *Dynasty* at this spotty lounge in the Chesterfield Hotel, in which the carpeting, tablecloths, and wait-staff's waistcoats are all in leopard print. There's live music every night from Cole Porter to swing. The crowd's a bit older here, but younger couples and a celebrity or two often find their way here, which makes for an amusing scene. Open daily from 6pm to 1:30am. 363 Cocoanut Row. ✆ 561/659-5800.

Ta-boo   Ta-boo is reminiscent of an upscale TGI Fridays (with food that's about on the same level)—one that caters to a well-heeled crowd—with lots of greenery, a fireplace, and a somewhat cheesy Southwestern decor. But make no mistake, Ta-boo is not about the food: This stellar after-dinner spot is where bejeweled socialites spill out of fancy cars to show off their best Swarovski and salsa. Just find somewhere else to eat first. Open for lunch daily 11:30am to 5pm, Sunday through Thursday from 5 to 10pm and Friday and Saturday from 5 until 11pm. 221 Worth Ave., Palm Beach. ✆ 561/835-3500.

GAMBLING

The *Palm Beach Princess* (✆ 800/841-7447 or 561/845-7447) is a small cruise ship (421 ft.) offering reasonably priced casino gambling cruises out of the Port of Palm Beach (U.S. 1 between 45th St. and Blue Heron Blvd.) every day and evening. Choose from craps, roulette, poker, blackjack, and slots. Cruises include a large buffet with average food like spaghetti and meatballs, chicken, Greek salad, and vegetables; best is the prime rib at the carving board. Cruises sail daily between 11am and 4:30pm and 6:30 and 11:45pm. Friday and Saturday evening cruises go from 6:30pm to 12:30am. Sunday cruises sail from 11am to

5pm and 6:30 to 11:30pm. Prices during the week are $30 per person; on weekends, it's $40 per person. If your birthday is in the month you plan to sail, you'll pay $25 weekdays, $35 weekends. Florida residents, AARP, and AAA discounts are available.

THE PERFORMING ARTS

With a number of dedicated patrons and enthusiastic supporters of the arts, this area happily boasts many good venues for those craving culture. Check the *Palm Beach Post* or the *Palm Beach Daily News* for up-to-date listings and reviews.

The **Raymond F. Kravis Center for the Performing Arts,** 701 Okeechobee Blvd., West Palm Beach (© **561/832-7469;** www.kravis.org), is the area's largest and most active performance space. With a huge curved-glass facade and more than 2,500 seats in two lushly decorated indoor spaces, plus a new outdoor amphitheater, The Kravis, as it is known, stages more than 300 performances each year. Phone or check their website for a current schedule of Palm Beach's best music, dance, and theater.

4 Jupiter ✦ & Northern Palm Beach County ✦

20 miles N of Palm Beach, 81 miles N of Miami, 60 miles N of Fort Lauderdale

While Burt Reynolds is Jupiter's hometown hero (and Celine Dion just built a sprawling manse there, too), the true stars of quaint Jupiter are the beautiful beaches. In the springtime, you can also catch a glimpse of the St. Louis Cardinals and the Montreal Expos during their spring training seasons. North Palm Beach County's other towns—Tequesta, Juno Beach, North Palm Beach, Palm Beach Gardens, and Singer Island—are inviting for tourists who want to enjoy the many outdoor activities that make this area so popular with retirees, seasonal residents, and families.

ESSENTIALS

GETTING THERE   The quickest route from West Palm Beach to Jupiter is on the Florida Turnpike or the sometimes-congested I-95. You can also take a slower but more scenic coastal route, U.S. 1 or Fla. A1A. Since Jupiter is so close to Palm Beach, it's easy to fly into the **Palm Beach International Airport** (© **561/471-7420**) and rent a car there. The drive should take less than half an hour.

VISITOR INFORMATION   A **Visitor Information Center** is located between I-95 and the Florida Turnpike at 8020 Indiantown Rd. in Jupiter (© **561/575-4636;** www.jupiterfloridausa.com) and is open from 8:30am to 5:30pm Monday through Friday.

BEACHES & ACTIVE PURSUITS

BASEBALL   The **Roger Dean Stadium,** 4751 Main St. (© **561/775-1818**), hosts spring training for both the St. Louis Cardinals and the Montreal Expos, along with minor-league action from Florida's state league, the Hammerheads. Tickets range in price from $6 to $18. Call for schedules and specific ticket information.

BEACHES   The farther north you head from populated Palm Beach, the more peaceful and pristine the coast becomes. Just a few miles north of the bustle, castles and condominiums give way to wide open space and public parkland. There are dozens of recommendable spots. Following are a few of the best.

John D. MacArthur Beach is a spectacular beach that preserves the natural heritage of the subtropical coastal habitat that once covered Southeast Florida. This state park has a remarkable 4,000-square-foot Nature Center with exhibits, displays, and a video interpreting the barrier island's plant and animal communities. Dominating a large portion of Singer Island, the barrier island just north of Palm Beach, this beach has lengthy frontage on both the Atlantic Ocean and Lake Worth Cove. The beach is great for hiking, swimming, and sunning. Bathrooms and showers are available. To reach the park from the mainland, cross the Intracoastal Waterway on Blue Heron Boulevard and turn north on Ocean Boulevard.

Jupiter Inlet meets the ocean at **Dubois Park,** a 29-acre beach that is popular with families. The shallow waters and sandy shore are perfect for kids, while adults can play in the rougher swells of the lifeguarded inlet. A footbridge leads to **Ocean Beach,** an area popular with windsurfers and surfers. There's a short fishing pier and plenty of trees shading barbecue grills and picnic tables. Visitors can also explore the Dubois Pioneer Home, a small house situated atop a shell mound built by the Jaega Indians. Made from cypress, the home was built in 1898 by Harry Dubois, a citrus worker, as a wedding gift to his wife Susan, whose pictures are still in the house. You will see an original butter churn and pump sewing machine in the living room, and the dining room and bedroom are almost straight out of *Little House on the Prairie.* The park entrance is on Dubois Road, about a mile south of the junction of U.S. 1 and Fla. A1A.

BIKING   Rent a bike from **Raleigh Bicycles of Jupiter,** at 103 U.S. 1, Unit F1 (© **561/746-0585**). Prices for cruisers are $17 per day and $50 per week. For all terrain bikes, prices are $19 per day and $70 per week. Bike enthusiasts will enjoy exploring this flat and uncluttered area. North Palm Beach has hundreds of miles of smooth, paved roads. Loggerhead Park in Juno Beach or Fla. A1A along the ocean also has great trails for starters. You'll find many more scenic routes over the bridges and west of the highway.

CANOEING   You can rent a boat at several outlets throughout northern Palm Beach County, including **Canoe Outfitters,** 9060 W. Indiantown Rd. (west of I-95), North Jupiter (© **561/746-7053**), which provides access to one of the area's most beautiful natural waterways. Canoers start at Riverbend Park along an 8-mile stretch of Intracoastal Waterway, where the lush foliage supports dozens of exotic birds and reptiles. Keep your eyes open for the gators, who love to sunbathe on the shallow shores of the river. You'll end up, exhausted, at Jonathan Dickinson Park about 5 or 6 hours later. A pamphlet describing local flora and fauna is available for $1. Trips run Thursday through Monday and cost $40 for two people in a double canoe. Guided trips are also available for $35 per person.

CRUISES   Several sightseeing cruises offer tours of the magnificent waterways that make up northern Palm Beach County. Water taxis conduct daily narrated tours through the scenic waters. One interesting excursion that will take you past the mansions of the rich and famous, and possibly past the manatees swimming off the port of Palm Beach, departs from **Panama Hatties** at PGA Boulevard and the Intracoastal Waterway. Prices are $17 for adults, $15 for seniors, and $9 for children under 12 for the 1½-hour ride. Call © **561/775-2628.** The *Manatee Queen,* 1065 N. Ocean Blvd. (at the Crab House), Jupiter (© **561/744-2191**), is a 40-foot catamaran with bench seating for up to 49 people. Two-hour tours of Jupiter Island depart daily at 2:30pm, passing Burt Reynolds's and Perry Como's former mansions, among other spots of historical and natural interest. They also have a daily sunset cruise from 5 to 6:30pm. Reservations are highly recommended, especially in season; call for the current schedule of offerings. Prices are $20 for adults and $13 for children ages 6 through 12. Bring your own lunch or purchase chips and sodas at the mini–snack bar.

FISHING Before you leave, send for an information-packed fishing kit with details on fish camps, charters, and tournament and tide schedules distributed by the **West Palm Beach Fishing Club** (✆ **561/832-6780**). The cost is $10 and well worth it. Allow at least 4 weeks for delivery.

Once in town, several outfitters along U.S. 1 and Fla. A1A have vessels and equipment for rent if your hotel doesn't. One of the most complete facilities is the **Sailfish Marina & Resort,** 98 Lake Dr. (off Blue Heron Blvd.), Palm Beach Shores (✆ **561/844-1724**). Call for equipment, bait, guided trips, or boat rentals.

GOLF Even if you're not lucky enough to be staying at the **PGA National Resort & Spa,** you may still be able to play on their award-winning courses. If you or someone in your group is a member of another golf or country club, have the head pro write a note on club letterhead to Jackie Rogers at PGA (see "Where to Stay," below) to request a play date. Be sure the pro includes his PGA number and contact information. Allow at least 2 weeks for a response. Also, ask about the Golf-A-Round program, where selected private clubs open to non-members for free or discounted rates. Contact the **Palm Beach County Convention and Visitors Bureau** (✆ **561/471-3995**) for details.

Plenty of other great courses dot the area, including the **Golf Club of Jupiter,** 1800 Central Blvd., Jupiter (✆ **561/747-6262**), where a well-respected 18-hole, par-70 course is situated on more than 6,200 yards featuring narrow fairways and fast greens. Fees are $56 until noon, $45 after noon, and $25 after 2pm, and include a mandatory cart. The course borders I-95.

HIKING In an area that's not particularly known for extraordinary natural diversity, **Blowing Rocks Preserve** has a terrific hiking trail along a dramatic limestone outcropping. You won't find hills or scenic vistas, but you will see Florida's unique and varied tropical ecosystem. The well-marked mile-long trail passes oceanfront dunes, coastal strands, mangrove wetlands, and a coastal hammock. The preserve, owned and managed by The Nature Conservancy, also protects an important habitat for West Indian manatees and loggerhead turtles. Located along South Beach Drive (Fla. A1A), north of the Jupiter inlet, the preserve is about a 10-minute drive northeast of Jupiter. Free guided tours are available Fridays at 1pm and Sundays at 11am, and no reservations are necessary. From U.S. 1, head east on S.R. 707 and cross the Intracoastal Waterway to the park. Admission is $3 for adults; kids 12 and under are free. For more information, contact The Nature Conservancy, 574 South Beach Rd., Hobe Sound, FL 33455 (✆ **561/744-6668**).

SCUBA DIVING & SNORKELING Year-round warm, clear waters make northern Palm Beach County great for both diving and snorkeling. The closest coral reef is located ¼ mile from shore and can easily be reached by boat. Three popular wrecks are clustered near each other, less than a mile offshore of the Lake Worth Inlet at about 90 feet. The best wreck, however, is the 16th- or 17th-century Spanish galleon discovered by lifeguard Peter Leo just off Jupiter Beach (see p. 245 for more information). If your hotel doesn't offer dive trips, call the **South Florida Dive Headquarters,** 101 N Riverside Dr., Pampono Beach (✆ **800/771-DIVE** or 954/783-2299); or **Seafari Dive and Surf,** 75 E. Indiantown Rd., Suite 603, Jupiter (✆ **561/747-6115**).

TENNIS In addition to the many hotel tennis courts (see "Where to Stay," below), you can swing a racquet at a number of local clubs. The **Jupiter Bay Tennis Club,** 353 U.S. 1, Jupiter (✆ **561/744-9424**), has seven clay courts (three lighted) and charges $12 per person per day. Reservations are highly recommended.

Discovering a Remarkable Natural World

North Palm Beach is well known for the giant sea turtles that lay their eggs on the county's beaches from May to August. These endangered marine animals return here annually, from as far away as South America, to lay their clutches of about 115 eggs each. Nurtured by the warm sand, but targeted by birds and other predators, only about one or two babies from each nest survive to maturity.

Many environmentalists recommend that visitors take part in an organized turtle-watching program (rather than going on their own) to minimize disturbance to the turtles. The Jupiter Beach Resort (see "Where to Stay," below) and the Marinelife Center of Juno Beach (see below) both sponsor free guided expeditions to the egg-laying sites from May to August. Phone for times and reservations.

Just south of Jupiter, in Juno Beach, is the **Marinelife Center of Juno Beach,** in Loggerhead Park, 14200 U.S. 1, Juno Beach (© **561/627-8280**). Combining a science museum and nature trail, the small Marinelife Center is dedicated to the coastal ecology of northern Palm Beach County. Hands-on exhibits teach visitors about wetlands and beach areas, as well as offshore coral reefs and the local sea life. Visitors are encouraged to walk the center's sand-dune nature trails, all of which are marked with interpretive signs. This is one place in which you're guaranteed to see live sea turtles year-round. During high breeding season (June–July), the center conducts narrative walks along a nearby beach. Reservations are a must. The booking list opens on May 1 and is usually full by midmonth. Admission to the center is free, though donations are accepted. Open Monday through Saturday from 10am to 4pm and Sunday from noon to 3pm.

More economical options are available at relatively well-maintained municipal courts. Call for locations and hours (© **561/966-6600**). Many are available free on a first-come, first-served basis.

A HISTORIC LIGHTHOUSE

Jupiter Inlet Lighthouse ✸   Completed in 1860, this redbrick structure is the oldest extant building in Palm Beach County. Still owned and maintained by the U.S. Coast Guard, the lighthouse is now home to a small historical museum, located at its base. The Florida History Museum sponsors tours of the lighthouse, enabling visitors to explore the cramped interior, which is filled with artifacts and photographs illustrating the rich history of the area. A 15-minute video explains the various shipwrecks, Indian wars, and other events that helped shape this region. Helpful volunteers are eager to tell colorful stories to highlight the 1-hour tour.

500 S.R. 707, Jupiter. © **561/747-8380.** Admission $6. Sat–Wed 10am–4pm (last tour departs at 3:15pm). Children must be 4 ft. or taller to climb. No open-backed shoes.

SHOPPING

Northern Palm Beach County may not have the glitzy boutiques of Worth Avenue, but it does have an impressive indoor mall, the **Gardens of the Palm**

Beaches, at 3101 PGA Blvd., where you can find large department stores including **Bloomingdale's, Burdines, Macy's,** and **Saks Fifth Avenue,** as well as more than 100 specialty shops. A large, diverse food court and fine sit-down restaurants in this 1.3-million-square-foot facility make this shopping excursion an all-day affair. Call © **561/775-7750** for store information.

WHERE TO STAY

The northern part of Palm Beach County is much more laid-back and less touristy than the rest of the Gold Coast. Here, there are relatively few fancy hotels or attractions.

VERY EXPENSIVE

Jupiter Beach Resort ⟨★★⟩ The only resort located directly on Jupiter's beach, this unpretentious retreat is popular with families and seems a world away from the more luxurious resorts just a few miles to the south. The lobby and public areas have a Caribbean motif, accented with green marble, arched doorways, and chandeliers. The simple and elegant guest rooms are furnished in a comfortable island style, and every room has a private balcony with ocean or sunset views looking out over the uncluttered beachfront. A thorough refurbishing in the mid-1990s is responsible for the resort's increasing popularity. In fact, it is so popular that it is being gradually converted into a time-share property. Excursions are available to top-rated golf courses in the area.

5 N. A1A, Jupiter, FL 33477. © 800/228-8810 or 561/746-2511. Fax 561/747-3304. www.jupiterbeach resort.com. 153 units. Winter $219–$389 double, $389–$479 suite, penthouse suite $900–$1,200; off-season $129–$179 double, $179–$219 suite, penthouse suite $600–$850. AE, DC, DISC, MC, V. Valet parking $5. From I-95, take exit 59A, going east to the end of Indiantown Rd. at A1A. Jupiter Beach Resort is at this intersection on the ocean. **Amenities:** 2 restaurants; 2 bars; outdoor heated pool; tennis court; exercise room; extensive watersports equipment/rental; bike rental; children's programs; concierge; business center; limited room service; in-room massage; dry cleaning. *In room:* A/C, TV, VCR and DVD (for a $10 additional charge), dataport, minibar, coffeemaker, iron. Suites have kitchenettes.

PGA National Resort & Spa ⟨★★★⟩ This rambling resort, the national headquarters of the PGA, is a premier golf vacation spot—but its top-rated Mediterranean spa could be a destination in itself. With five 18-hole courses on more than 2,300 acres, golfers and other sports-minded travelers will find plenty to keep them occupied—croquet, tennis, sailing, a health and fitness center, and the sublime spa. Constant updating has kept the grounds and buildings in like-new condition. The par-72 Champion Course, redesigned in 1990 by Jack Nicklaus, is the resort's most valuable asset. More than 100 sand bunkers and plenty of water on 6,400-square-foot greens keep golfers of all levels alert. Watch out for hole 16. Rooms are spacious and comfortable, bordering on residential, with immense bathrooms. Club cottages are especially nice, offering great privacy and serenity. This is not a beach resort, however. Six outdoor therapy pools known as "Waters of the World" are surrounded by mineral pools, which are so sublime, they make the ocean look like a kiddie pool. Don Shula's award-winning steakhouse and restaurant is the hotel's best and most popular restaurant.

400 Ave. of the Champions, Palm Beach Gardens, FL 33418. © 800/633-9150 or 561/627-2000. Fax 561/ 225-2595. www.pga-resorts.com. 339 units, 59 club cottages. Winter $299–$339 double, $369–$829 suite; off-season $144–$169 double, $174–$659 suite. Children 16 and under stay free in parent's room. Special packages available. AE, DC, DISC, MC, V. From I-95, take exit 57B (PGA Blvd.) going west and continue for approximately 2 miles to the resort entrance on the left. **Amenities:** 7 restaurants and lounges; 9 swimming pools; 5 18-hole tournament courses plus the PGA National's Academy of Golf; 19 clay tennis courts; Mediterranean spa; watersports equipment/rentals; concierge; car-rental desk; salon; limited room service; babysitting; laundry; aerobics studio; 5 tournament croquet lawns; 5 indoor racquetball courts. *In room:* A/C, TV, dataport, minibar, hair dryer, safe.

MODERATE/INEXPENSIVE

Baron's Landing Motel & Apartments ☆ *Value*   This charming family-run inn is a perfect little beach getaway. It's not elegant, but it is cozy. The single-story motel fronting the Intracoastal Waterway is often full in winter with snow-birds who dock their boats at the hotel's marina for weeks or months at a time. Nearly all rooms, which are situated around a small pool, have small kitch-enettes. Each unit has a funky mix of used furniture, and some have pullout sofas. Bathrooms have been remodeled. Considering that you're a few blocks from some of the most expensive real estate in the country, this is a good deal. Dock rentals are available.

18125 Ocean Blvd. (Fla. A1A at the corner of Clemens St.), Jupiter, FL 33477. ℂ 561/746-8757. 8 units. Winter $75–$125 double, $1,350–$1,700 monthly; off-season $45–$75 double, $700–$900 monthly. No credit cards. **Amenities:** Small pool. *In room:* A/C, TV, fax, dataport, kitchen, fridge, coffeemaker, iron.

WHERE TO DINE

In addition to all the national fast-food joints that line Indiantown Road and U.S. 1, you'll find a number of touristy fish restaurants serving battered and fried everything. There are only a few really exceptional eateries in North Palm Beach and Jupiter. Try those listed below for guaranteed good food at reasonable prices.

MODERATE

Capt. Charlie's Reef Grill ☆☆ SEAFOOD/CARIBBEAN   The trick here is to arrive early, ahead of the crowd of local foodies who come for the more than a dozen daily local-catch specials prepared in dozens of styles. Imaginative appe-tizers include Caribbean chili, a rich chunky stew filled with fresh seafood; and a tuna spring roll big enough for two. The enormous Cuban crab cake is moist and perfectly browned without tasting fried and is served with homemade mango chutney and black beans and rice. Sit at the bar to watch the hectic kitchen turn out perfect dishes on the 14-burner stove. Somehow, the pleasant waitresses keep their cool even when the place is packed. In addition to the terrific seafood, this little dive offers an extensive, affordable wine and beer selection—more than 30 of each from around the world.

12846 U.S. 1 (behind O'Brian's and French Connection), Juno Beach. ℂ 561/624-9924. Reservations not accepted. Main courses $9.95–$22. MC, V. Sun–Fri 11:30am–3pm and 5–9:30pm.

Nick's Tomato Pie ☆ ITALIAN   A fun, family restaurant, Nick's is a popular attraction that's known to bring folks even from Miami for a piece of this pie. With a huge menu of pastas, pizzas, fish, chicken, and beef, this cheery (and noisy) spot has something for everyone. On Saturday night, you'll see lots of couples on dates and some families leaving with takeout bags left over from the impossibly generous portions. The homemade sausage is a delicious treat, served with sautéed onions and peppers. The *pollo Marsala,* too, is good and authentic.

1697 W. Indiantown Rd. (1 mile east of I-95, exit 59A), Jupiter. ℂ 561/744-8935. Reservations accepted for groups of 6 or more. Main courses $12–$20; pastas $10–$15. AE, DC, DISC, MC, V. Mon–Thurs and Sun 5–9:30pm; Fri–Sat 5–10:30pm.

Sinclair's Ocean Grill & Rotisserie ☆☆ CARIBBEAN   As close to upscale as Jupiter gets, Sinclair's is the Jupiter Beach Resort's excellent restaurant over-looking the pool and featuring fresh, locally caught fish as well as an excellent filet mignon. Especially popular are the Sunday brunches.

Jupiter Beach Resort, 5 N. Fla. A1A. ℂ 561/745-7120. Reservations recommended. Main courses $18–$27. AE, MC, V. Daily 6:30am–2pm and 8–10pm.

The Treasure Coast:
Stuart to Sebastian

The area north of Palm Beach is known as the Treasure Coast for the same reason that the area from Fort Lauderdale to Palm Beach is known as the Gold Coast—it was the site of a number of shipwrecks that date back over 300 years, which led to the discovery of priceless treasures in the water (some historians believe that treasures from these sunken vessels *still* lie buried deep beneath the ocean floor).

The difference, however, is that while the Gold Coast is a bit, well, tarnished as far as development is concerned, the Treasure Coast remains, for the most part, an unspoiled, quiet natural jewel. Miles of uninterrupted beaches and aquamarine waters attract swimmers, boaters, divers, anglers, and sun worshippers who love to dip, dive, and surf. If you love the great outdoors and prefer a more understated environment than hyperdeveloped Miami and Fort Lauderdale, the Treasure Coast is a real find.

For hundreds of years, Florida's east coast was a popular stopover for European explorers, many of whom arrived from Spain to fill coffers with gold and silver. Rough weather and poor navigation often took a toll on their ships, but in 1715, a violent hurricane stunned the northeast coast and sank an entire fleet of Spanish ships laden with gold. Although Spanish salvagers worked for years to collect the lost treasure, much of it remained buried beneath the shifting sand. Workers hired to excavate the area in the 1950s

and 1960s discovered centuries-old coins under their tractors.

Today, you can still see shipwrecks and incredible barrier reefs in St. Lucie County, which can be reached from the beaches of Fort Pierce and Hutchinson Island. On these same beaches, you'll also find an occasional treasure hunter trolling the sand with a metal detector, alongside swimmers and sunbathers who come to enjoy the stretches of beach that extend into the horizon. The sea, especially around Sebastian Inlet, is a mecca for surfers, who find some of the largest swells in the state.

Along with the pleasures of the talcum-powder sands, the Treasure Coast also offers good shopping, sporting, and numerous other opportunities to take a reprieve from the hubbub of the rat race. Visitors to this part of South Florida should not miss the extensive array of wildlife, which includes the endangered West Indian manatee, loggerhead and leatherback turtles, tropical fish, alligators, deer, and exotic birds. For sports enthusiasts, there are boundless sporting opportunities here—from golf and tennis to polo, motorcar racing, the New York Mets during their spring training, and the best freshwater fishing around.

The downtown areas of the Treasure Coast have been experiencing a rebirth in the past few years, along with the influx of unprecedented numbers of new residents. Fortunately, the area's growth has occurred at a reasonable pace so that the neighborhoods have been able to retain their small-town feel. The result is a batch of freshly spruced-up accommodations, shops, and restaurants from Stuart to Sebastian.

Southern Martin County's well-to-do Hobe Sound, in particular, is a Treasure Coast hot spot with its pristine beaches, Banyan tree–canopied streetscapes, one-of-a-kind antiques shops, and art galleries. Hobe Sound rests at the front door of the Gold Coast and the back door of the Treasure Coast, and it has immediate access to the Atlantic Ocean and the Intracoastal Waterway. Real estate here is at a premium, with million-dollar waterfront mansions lining the shores.

For the purposes of this chapter, the Treasure Coast runs roughly from Hobe Sound in the south to the Sebastian Inlet in the north, encompassing some of Martin, St. Lucie, and Indian River Counties and all of Hutchinson Island.

TREASURE COAST ESSENTIALS
GETTING THERE
Since virtually every town described in this chapter runs along a straight route along the Atlantic Ocean, I've given all directions below.

BY PLANE   The **Palm Beach International Airport** (© 561/471-7420), located about 35 miles south of Stuart, is the closest gateway to this region if you're flying. See the "Getting There" section on Palm Beach, on p. 274, in chapter 8 for complete information. If you are traveling to the northern part of the Treasure Coast, **Melbourne International Airport,** off U.S. 1 in Melbourne (© 321/723-6227), is less than 25 miles north of Sebastian and about 35 miles north of Vero Beach.

BY CAR   If you're driving up or down the Florida coast, you'll probably reach the Treasure Coast via I-95. If you are heading to Stuart or Jensen Beach, take exit 61 (Rte. 76/Tanner Hwy.) or 62 (Rte. 714); to Port St. Lucie or Fort Pierce, take exit 63 or 64 (Okeechobee Rd.); to Vero Beach, take exit 68 (S.R. 60); to Sebastian, take exit 69 (County Rd.).

You can also take the Florida Turnpike; this toll road is the fastest (but not the most scenic) route, especially if you're coming from Orlando. If you are heading to Stuart or Jensen Beach, take exit 133; to Fort Pierce, take exit 152 (Okeechobee Rd.); to Port St. Lucie, take exit 142 or 152; to Vero Beach, take exit 193 (S.R. 60); to Sebastian, take exit 193 to State Route 60 east and connect to I-95 north.

If you are staying in Hutchinson Island, which runs almost the entire length of the Treasure Coast, you should check with your hotel or see the listings below to find the best route to take.

Finally, if you're coming directly from the west coast, you'll probably take State Route 70, which runs north of Lake Okeechobee to Fort Pierce, located just up the road from Stuart.

BY RAIL   **Amtrak** (© 800/USA-RAIL; www.amtrak.com) stops in West Palm Beach at 201 S. Tamarind Ave., and in Okeechobee at 801 N. Parrot Ave., off U.S. 441 north.

BY BUS   **Greyhound** buses (© 800/231-2222; www.greyhound.com) service the area with terminals in Stuart, at 1308 S. Federal Hwy.; in Fort Pierce, at 7005 Okeechobee Rd. (© 772/461-3299); and in Vero Beach, at U.S. 1 and State Route 60 (© 772/562-6588).

The Treasure Coast

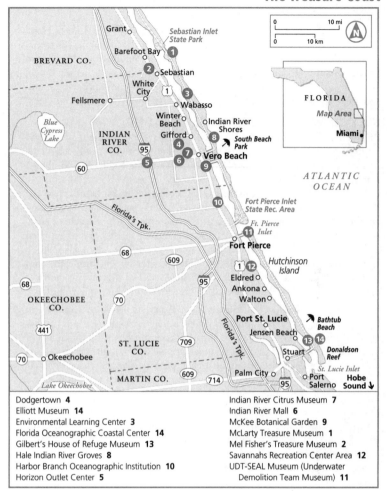

Dodgertown **4**
Elliott Museum **14**
Environmental Learning Center **3**
Florida Oceanographic Coastal Center **14**
Gilbert's House of Refuge Museum **13**
Hale Indian River Groves **8**
Harbor Branch Oceanographic Institution **10**
Horizon Outlet Center **5**

Indian River Citrus Museum **7**
Indian River Mall **6**
McKee Botanical Garden **9**
McLarty Treasure Museum **1**
Mel Fisher's Treasure Museum **2**
Savannahs Recreation Center Area **12**
UDT-SEAL Museum (Underwater
    Demolition Team Museum) **11**

GETTING AROUND

A car is a necessity in this large and rural region. Although heavy traffic is not usually a problem here, on the smaller coastal roads, like A1A, expect to travel at a slow pace, usually between 25 and 40 mph.

1 Hobe Sound ⟨★★★⟩, Stuart (North Hutchinson Island ⟨★★⟩) & Jensen Beach

Once just a stretch of pineapple plantations, the towns of Martin County, which include Hobe Sound, Stuart, and Jensen Beach, still retain much of their rural character. Dotted between citrus groves and mangroves are modest homes and an occasional high-rise condominium. Although the area is definitely still seasonal (with a distinct rise in street and pedestrian traffic beginning after the Christmas holidays), the atmosphere is pure small town. Even in historic downtown Stuart, the result of a successful, ongoing restoration, expect the storefronts to be dark and the streets abandoned after 10pm.

ESSENTIALS

The **Stuart/Martin County Chamber of Commerce,** 1650 S. Kanner Hwy., Stuart, FL 34994 (© **800/524-9704** or 772/287-1088; fax 772/220-3437; www.goodnature.org), is the region's main source for information. The **Jensen Beach Chamber of Commerce,** 1901 NE Jensen Beach Blvd., Jensen Beach, FL 34957 (© **772/334-3444;** fax 772/334-0817; www.jensenchamber.com), also offers visitors information about its simple beachfront town.

BACK TO NATURE: THE BEACHES & BEYOND

BEACHES   Hutchinson Island, located in Stuart, is one of the most popular beach destinations of the Treasure Coast, located just north of Palm Beach on the Atlantic Ocean. Some 70 miles of excellent beaches and laid-back, Old Florida ambience make for an idyllic frozen-cocktail-on-the-beach resort vacation.

The best of them is **Bathtub Beach,** on North Hutchinson Island. Here, the calm waters are protected by coral reefs, and visitors can explore the region on dune and river trails. Pick a secluded spot on the wide stretch of beach, or enjoy marked nature trails across the street. Facilities include showers and toilets open during the day. To reach Bathtub Beach from the northern tip of Hutchinson Island, head east on Ocean Boulevard (Stuart Causeway) and turn right onto MacArthur Boulevard. The beach is about a mile ahead on your left, just north of the Hutchinson Island Marriott Beach Resort and Marina. Parking is plentiful.

CANOEING   **Jonathan Dickinson State Park** (see "Wildlife Exploration: From Gators to Manatees to Turtles," below) is the most popular area for canoeing. The route winds through a variety of botanical habitats. You'll see lots of birds and the occasional manatee. Canoes cost $6 per hour and can be rented through the concession located in the back of the park. The concession (© **561/746-1466**) is open Monday through Friday from 9am to 5pm and Saturday and Sunday from 8am to 5pm.

FISHING   Several independent charter captains operate on Hutchinson Island and Jensen Beach. One of the largest operators is the **Sailfish Marina,** 3565 SE St. Lucie Blvd., in Stuart (© **772/221-9456**), which maintains half a dozen charter boats for fishing excursions year-round. Also on-site are a bait-and-tackle shop and a knowledgeable, helpful staff. Other reputable charter operators include **Hungry Bear Adventures, Inc.,** docked at Indian River Plantation Marriott Resort, 4730-1 SE Teri Place in Stuart (© **772/285-7552;** www.hungrybear.net); and **Bone Shaker Sportfishing,** 3585 SE St. Lucie Blvd., in Stuart (© **772/286-5504;** veejay4842@aol.com).

GOLF   Try the **Champions Club at Summerfield,** on U.S. 1, south of Cove Road in Stuart (© **772/283-1500**), a somewhat challenging championship course designed by Tom Fazio. This rural course, the best in the area, offers great glimpses of wildlife amid the wetlands. Winter greens fees are around $65, and carts are mandatory. Reservations are a must and are taken 4 days in advance.

SCUBA DIVING & SNORKELING   Three popular artificial reefs off Hutchinson Island provide excellent scenery for both novice and experienced divers. The **USS *Rankin*** lies 7 miles east-northeast of the St. Lucie Inlet. The Rankin is a 459-foot ship that lays on its port side in 80 feet of water. This ship was used in World War II for troop transportation and was sunk in 1988. Deck hatches on the wreck are open and allow exploration. Inside, there are thousands of Atlantic Spiny oysters, and a cannon is attached to the bow. The 58-foot-deep **Donaldson Reef** consists of a cluster of steel tanks and barrels sunk in 58 feet of water to create the artificial reef. It's located due east of the Gilbert's House of

Wildlife Exploration: From Gators to Manatees to Turtles

One of the most scenic areas on this stretch of the coast is **Jonathan Dickinson State Park** ⚶, 12 miles south of Stuart at 16450 S. Federal Hwy. (U.S. 1), Hobe Sound (𝄢 **772/546-2771**). The park intentionally receives less maintenance than other, more meticulously maintained parks so that it will resemble the rough-around-the-edges, wilderness-like environment of hundreds of years ago, before Europeans started chopping, dredging, and "improving" the area. Dozens of species of Florida's unique wildlife, including alligators and manatees, live on the park's more than 11,300 acres. Bird-watchers will also be delighted by glimpses of rare and endangered species such as the bald Eagle, the Florida scrub-jay, and the Florida sandhill crane, which still call this park home. You can rent canoes from the concession stand to explore the Loxahatchee River on your own. Admission is $4 per car of up to eight adults. Day hikers, bikers, and walkers pay $1 each. The park is open from 8am until sundown. See "Where to Stay," below, for details on camping.

Close to Jonathan Dickinson State Park is **Hobe Sound Wildlife Refuge,** on North Beach Road off State Route 708, at the north end of Jupiter Island (𝄢 **772/546-6141**). This is one of the best places to see sea turtles that nest on the shore in the summer months, especially in June and July. Because it's home to a large variety of other plant and animal species, the park is worth visiting at other times of year as well. Admission is $4 per car, and the preserve is open daily from sunrise to sunset. Exact times are posted at each entrance and change seasonally.

For turtle walks on Hutchinson Island, call 𝄢 **877/375-4386.** These walks take place from May 22 to July 22 at 9pm, Friday and Saturday. Reservations are necessary and should be made well in advance, as walks are limited to 50 people. Reservations are accepted as of May 1.

Refuge Museum (see below). The **Ernst Reef,** made from old tires, is a 60-foot dive located 4½ miles east-southeast of the St. Lucie inlet. Local dive shops have "tips" on the best spots and rules and regulations for safe diving.

SEEING THE SIGHTS

Balloons Over Florida ⚶⚶⚶ *(Finds)* For a lofty view of Martin County's wildlife, take a hot-air balloon ride above the animals' natural habitat. Two fully licensed and insured balloons and pilots will take a maximum of four people up, up, and away for about an hour, depending on wind and weather conditions. After you've landed, drink in the sights over a glass of complimentary champagne and a continental breakfast.

Tours begin at approximately 6:30am from a takeoff point to be determined. 𝄢 **772/334-9393.** $175 per person, including continental breakfast and champagne.

Elliott Museum ⚶⚶ A treasure trove of wacky artifacts that really personify Americana, the Elliott Museum is a rich tribute to inventors, sports heroes, and collectors. The museum was created by the son of turn-of-the-20th-century inventor Sterling Elliott to display the genius of the American spirit. Among the bizarre things you'll see here are displays of an apothecary, ice-cream parlor, barbershop, other old-fashioned commercial enterprises, and an authentic hand-carved miniature circus. Sports fans will appreciate the baseball memorabilia—a half-million dollars' worth—including an autographed item from every player in the Baseball Hall of Fame.

A gallery of patents and models of machines, invented by the museum's founder, Harmon Parker Elliott, and his son, provides an intriguing glimpse into the business of tinkering. Their collection of restored antique cars is also impressive. Expect to spend at least an hour seeing the highlights.

825 NE Ocean Blvd. (north of Indian River Plantation Resort), Hutchinson Island, Stuart. ⓒ 772/225-1961. Admission $6 adults, $2 children 6–13, free for children 5 and under. Mon–Sat 10am–4pm.

Florida Oceanographic Coastal Center ★★   This is a nature lover's Disney World. Opened by the South Florida Oceanographic Society in late 1994, this 44-acre site (surrounded by coastal hammock and mangroves) is its own little ecosystem and serves as an outdoor classroom, teaching visitors about the region's flora and fauna. The modest main building houses saltwater tanks and wet and dry "discovery tables" with small indigenous animals. The incredibly eager staff of volunteers encourages visitors to wander the lush, well-marked nature trails.

890 NE Ocean Blvd. (across the street from the Elliott Museum), Hutchinson Island, Stuart. ⓒ 772/225-0505. www.fosusa.org. Admission $6 adults, $3 children 3–12, free for children under 3. Mon–Sat 10am–5pm; Sun noon–4pm.

Gilbert's House of Refuge Museum ★   Gilbert's, the oldest structure in Martin County, dates from 1875, when it functioned as one of 10 rescue centers for shipwrecked sailors. After undergoing a thorough rehabilitation to its original condition along the rocky shores, the house now displays marine artifacts and turn-of-the-20th-century lifesaving equipment and photographs and is worth a quick visit to get a feel for the area's early days.

301 SE MacArthur Blvd. (south of Indian River Plantation resort), Hutchinson Island, Stuart. ⓒ 772/225-1875. Admission $4 adults, $2 children 6–13, free for children 5 and under. Daily 10am–4pm.

A BOAT TOUR

The *Loxahatchee Queen* ★★★, a 35-foot, 44-passenger pontoon boat (ⓒ 772/746-1466) in Jonathan Dickinson State Park in Hobe Sound, makes daily tours of the area's otherwise inaccessible backwater, where curious alligators, manatees, eagles, and tortoises often peek out to see who's in their yard. Try to catch the 2-hour tour, given Wednesday through Sunday as the tide permits, when it includes a stop at Trapper Nelson's home. Known as the "Wildman of Loxahatchee," Nelson lived in primitive conditions on a remote stretch of the water in a log cabin he built himself, which is preserved for visitors to see. Tours leave four times daily at 9 and 11am and 1 and 3pm and cost $12 for adults, $7 for children 6 to 12, and free for children 5 and under. See the "Wildlife Exploration: From Gators to Manatees to Turtles" box on p. 301 for more information on the park.

SHOPPING

Downtown Stuart's historic district, along Flagler Avenue between Confusion Corner and St. Lucie Avenue, offers shoppers diversity and quality in a small old-town setting. Shops offer a range of goods: antique bric-a-brac, old lamps and fixtures, books, gourmet foods, furnishings, and souvenirs. For bargains, check out the **B & A Flea Market** (© 772/288-4915), the Treasure Coast's oldest and largest flea market.

WHERE TO STAY

Although the area boasts some beautiful beaches, the bulk of the hotel scene is downtown, where the nicer (and more reasonably priced) accommodations can be found among the shops and restaurants. There are, however, a few excellent beachfront hotels and inns. One of the bigger hotel chains in the area is the **Holiday Inn.** Its recently renovated, stunning beachfront property is at 3793 NE Ocean Blvd., on Hutchinson Island in Jensen Beach (© **800/992-4747** or 772/225-3000). Rates in season range from $150 to $209. Holiday Inn also has a downtown location at 1209 S. Federal Hwy. (© **772/287-6200**). This simple two-story building on a busy main road is kept in very good shape and is convenient to Stuart's downtown historic district. Rates range from $129 to $149. *Note:* In 2002, a 2% tax was added on accommodations in the Stuart-Hutchinson Island area.

VERY EXPENSIVE

Hutchinson Island Marriott Beach Resort and Marina ✦✦✦ *Kids*   This sprawling 200-acre compound offers many diversions for active (or not-so-active) vacationers, and families in particular. This is definitely Hutchinson Island's best resort, occupying the lush grounds of a former pineapple plantation. Activities include tennis, golfing, boating, sport fishing (especially for sailfish), scuba diving, and other watersports.

Some rooms overlook the Intracoastal and the resort's marina, while others face the ocean or the gardens. All are generously sized and have fully equipped kitchens. In the summer months, be sure to sign up for a "turtle watch," so you can observe turtles crawling onto the sand to lay their eggs. Another great activity, offered at an extra cost, is a sightseeing cruise along the St. Lucie and Indian rivers.

555 NE Ocean Blvd., Hutchinson Island, Stuart, FL 34996. © 800/775-5936 or 772/225-3700. Fax 772/225-0003. www.marriott.com. 298 units. Winter $179–$259 double, $265–$399 suite; off-season $99–$109 double, $129–$299 suite. AE, MC, V. From downtown Stuart, take E. Ocean Blvd. over 2 bridges to NE Ocean Blvd.; turn right. Pets accepted with a $50 deposit. **Amenities:** Restaurant; coffee shop; lounge; 4 large pools; 18-hole golf course; 13 tennis courts; fitness center and spa; extensive watersports; bike rental; children's programs; game room; concierge; on-property transportation; limited room service; babysitting; laundry services; dry cleaning. *In room:* A/C, TV, dataport, kitchenette, minibar, coffeemaker, hair dryer, iron.

CAMPING

There are comfortable campsites (rustic cabins or sites for your tent or camper) in **Jonathan Dickinson State Park** in Hobe Sound (see the "Wildlife Exploration: From Gators to Manatees to Turtles" box on p. 301). The River Camp area of the park offers the benefit of the nearby Loxahatchee River, while the Pine Grove site has beautiful shade trees. There are concession areas for daytime snacks and 135 campsites with showers, clean restrooms, water, optional electricity, and an open-fire pit for cooking. Overnight rates in the winter are $18 without electricity, $20 with electricity. In the summer, rates are about $14 for four people.

For a more cushy camping experience, reserve a wood-sided cabin with a furnished kitchen, a bathroom with shower, heat and air-conditioning, and an outdoor grill. Bring your own linens. Cabins rent for $85 (one bed and a pullout couch), $95 (two beds and a pullout couch), and up a night and sleep four people comfortably, six if your group is really into togetherness. Call © 772/546-2771 Monday through Friday from 9am to 5pm, well in advance, to reserve a spot. A $50 key deposit is required.

WHERE TO DINE
EXPENSIVE

The Courtyard Grill ✸✸ CONTINENTAL   Although this restaurant faces railroad tracks and a station that was never fully built, The Courtyard Grill is the quintessence of charm, with a warm and inviting vibe reminiscent of a place where no railroad would ever go. Old school fare such as clams casino and escargot are juxtaposed with nouveau cuisine such as duck stuffed ravioli, but the old standards like Dover sole are best. An impressive wine list, a gorgeous garden room, and homemade deserts assure you that you're on the right track as far as fine food in Hobe Sound is concerned, train or no train.

11970 SE Dixie Hwy., Hobe Sound. © 772/546-2900. Reservations accepted. Main courses $11–$18. MC, V. Mon–Fri 11am–3pm; daily 5:30–9:30pm.

11 Maple Street ✸✸✸ AMERICAN   The most highly rated restaurant in Jensen Beach, 11 Maple Street occupies a cozy, converted, old house. Dining is both indoors and out, in any one of a series of cozy dining rooms or on a covered patio surrounded by gardens. Interesting dishes not typically found in these parts of Florida include the wood grilled venison with French green lentils, broccoli rabe, caramelized turnip, hazelnut and white bean puree with grilled tomato sauce; and the braised Moulard duck leg with wood grilled Oregon quail, Tuscan cabbage, butternut squash, and chestnut tart with a balsamic pear reduction. The restaurant also uses organically grown produce from its own garden (when available) and poultry and meats that are farm raised and free of chemical additives.

11 Maple St., Jensen Beach. © 772/334-7714. Reservations recommended. Main courses $18–$30. MC, V. Wed–Sun 6–10pm. Head east on Jensen Beach Blvd. and turn right after the railroad tracks.

Flagler Grill ✸✸ AMERICAN/FLORIDA REGIONAL   In the heart of historic downtown, this seemingly out-of-place Manhattan-style bistro serves up classics with a twist. The dishes are not so unusual as to alienate the conservative pink-shirted golfers who frequent the place, yet they're fresh and light enough to quench the appetites of the more adventurous—for example, Maryland jumbo lump crab meat and rock shrimp cake served with a Key-lime aioli and spicy Cajun aioli. For main courses, the grilled double-stuffed pork chop filled with pecan-apple corn bread stuffing with cranberry-orange chutney, fresh vegetables, and smashed garlic potatoes gives literal meaning to the term "comfort food." The menu changes every few weeks, so see what your server recommends. It's hard to go wrong with any of the many salads, pastas, fishes, or delectable beef choices. The desserts, too, are worth the calories. Ask the bartender to make you the Big Apple martini—apple vodka, apple schnapps, and a wedge of apple— dessert with a kick! No smoking is allowed in the restaurant or bar.

47 SW Flagler Ave. (just before the Roosevelt Bridge), downtown Stuart. © 772/221-9517. Reservations strongly suggested in season. Main courses $18–$28. AE, DC, DISC, MC, V. Winter daily 5–10pm; off-season Tues–Sat 5:30–9:30pm. Lounge and bar open to 11:30pm. Special sunset menu offered from 5–6pm.

Rottie's ✸✸ SEAFOOD   Ocean views and fabulous seafood make you forget the name of this romantic Jensen Beach eatery. It's expensive, yes, but worth it. Try the pan seared Florida snapper and the jumbo lump crab cakes, and share an appetizer of sautéed calamari and mussels, which is super heavy on the garlic. Live music almost nightly and a lively Tiki bar help set the mood for a delightful dining experience here.

10900 S. Ocean Dr., Jensen Beach. © 772/229-7575. Main courses $25–$35. AE, DC, DISC, MC, V. Sun, Tues, Thurs 11:30am–2:30pm and 5:30–10pm; Fri–Sat 5:30–11pm.

MODERATE

Black Marlin ⭐ FLORIDA REGIONAL   Although it sports the look and feel of a dank English pub, the Black Marlin offers full Floridian flavor. The salmon BLT is typical of the dishes here—grilled salmon on a toasted bun topped with bacon, lettuce, tomato, and coleslaw. Designer pizzas are topped with shrimp, roasted red peppers, and the like; and main dishes, all of which are served with vegetables and potatoes, include a lobster tail with honey-mustard sauce, and a charcoal-grilled chicken breast served on radicchio with caramelized onions.

53 W. Osceola St., downtown Stuart. ℂ 772/286-3126. Reservations not accepted. Salads and sandwiches $4–$8; full meals $9–$24. AE, MC, V. Mon–Thurs 5–10pm; Fri–Sat 5–11pm (the bar is open later).

Conchy Joe's Seafood ⭐⭐ *(Finds* SEAFOOD   Known for fresh seafood and Old Florida hospitality, Conchy Joe's enjoys an excellent reputation that's far bigger than the restaurant itself. Shorts and flip-flops are the attire of choice here, and dining is either indoors, at red-and-white cloth-covered tables, or on a covered patio overlooking the St. Lucie River. The restaurant features a wide variety of freshly shucked shellfish and daily-catch selections that are baked, broiled, or fried, and the conch chowder is sublime. Beer is the drink of choice here, though other beverages and a full bar are available. Conchy Joe's has been the most active place in Jensen Beach since it opened in 1983. The large bar is especially popular at night and during weekday happy hours.

3945 NE Indian River Dr. (½ mile from the Jensen Beach Causeway), Jensen Beach. ℂ 772/334-1130. Reservations not accepted. Main courses $12–$20. AE, DISC, MC, V. Daily 11:30am–2:30pm and 5–10pm.

INEXPENSIVE

Harry and the Natives ⭐⭐ AMERICAN   When you dine at this wild and wacky, kitschy old Florida institution (to which both Harleys and Bentleys flock), you'll get decent bar fare—try the venison burger—with a fabulous dish of local color and humor (sometimes very un-PC humor) on the side. The menu itself is hilarious, especially "Acceptibles: Visa, Mastercard, our gift certificates, cash, oceanfront homes, table dancing, honeydripping and dishwashing." No offense to our Canadian friends, but the menu also kiddingly has a "Canadian Breakfast—(no tip) $20." Hilarious. The food ranges from eggs, omelets, and banana pancakes to the "President Bush Omelet—$1,000,000,000 Profits go to the Palm Beach County Election Supervisor to buy more butterfly ballots, voting machines and incompetent help." I don't want to spoil it all for you, so just make sure to read the entire menu. Okay, one more thing and I promise I'll stop: On the menu where it lists its locations, Harry and the Natives claims to be in Maui, Beverly Hills, Aspen, Tahiti, Bali, Monte Carlo, and Your Backyard. You gotta love it. There's live music Wednesday, Friday, and Saturday. Make sure you request that the band play the Harry and the Natives theme song.

11910 S. Federal Hwy., Hobe Sound. ℂ 772/546-3061. Main courses $5–$10. MC, V. Daily 6:30am–2:30am.

Nature's Way Cafe ⭐ HEALTH FOOD   This lovely dining room has dozens of little tables, a few bar stools, and some sidewalk seating, too. A sort of health-food deli, Nature's Way excels in serving quick and nutritious meals such as huge salads, vegetarian sandwiches, and frozen yogurts. Try some of the homemade baked goods. Sit outside on quaint Osceola Street or ask them to pack your lunch for you to take to the beach.

25 SW Osceola St., in the Post Office Arcade, Stuart. ℂ 772/220-7306. Sandwiches and salads $4–$7; juices and shakes $1–$3. No credit cards. Mon–Fri 10am–4pm; Sat 11am–3pm.

STUART & JENSEN BEACH AFTER DARK

The nightlife on the Treasure Coast may as well be called Night*dead,* because there really isn't any! This is not a place to come if you are looking for active nightlife. That said, Stuart and Jensen Beach are the closest you get to nightlife in the entire region, where local restaurants serve as the centers of after-dark happenings. "Night" ends pretty early here, even on the weekends. The bar at the Black Marlin (see "Where to Dine," above) is popular with locals and out-of-towners alike.

No list of Jensen nightlife would be complete without mention of Conchy Joe's Seafood (see "Where to Dine," above), one of the region's most active spots. Inside, locals chug beer and watch a large-screen TV, while outside on the waterfront patio, live bands perform a few nights a week for a raucous crowd of dancers. Happy hours, weekdays from 3 to 6pm, draw large crowds with low-priced drinks and snacks. There is no cover.

The centerpiece of Stuart's slowly expanding cultural offerings is the newly restored **Lyric Theater** at 59 SW Flagler Ave. (© **772/286-7827**). This beautiful 1920s-era, 600-seat theater hosts a variety of shows, readings, concerts, and films throughout the year.

2 Port St. Lucie & Fort Pierce

Port St. Lucie and Fort Pierce (two Old Florida towns, reminiscent of pre-Neon, pre-condo-maniacal Florida, which are sleepy, different worlds when compared to the Gold Coast and Miami) thrive on sport fishing. A seemingly endless row of piers juts out along the Intracoastal Waterway and the Fort Pierce Inlet for both river and ocean runs. Here visitors can also dive, snorkel, beachcomb, and sunbathe in an area that has been left untouched by the overdevelopment that has altered its neighbors to the south and north.

Most sightseeing takes place along the main beach road (the strip across from the Ocean/A1A). Driving along Fla. A1A on Hutchinson Island, you'll discover several secluded beach clubs interspersed with 1950s-style homes, a few small inns, grungy raw bars, and a few high-rise condominiums. Much of this island is government owned and kept undeveloped for the public's enjoyment.

ESSENTIALS

The **St. Lucie County Chamber of Commerce,** 2200 Virginia Ave., Fort Pierce, FL 34982 (© **772/595-9999;** www.stluciechamber.org), is the region's main source of information. There's another branch at 1626 SE Port St. Lucie Blvd., in Port St. Lucie. Both spots are open Monday through Friday from 9am to 5pm.

BEACHES & NATURE PRESERVES

North Hutchinson Island's beaches are the most pristine in this area. You won't find restaurants, hotels, or shopping; instead, spend your time swimming, surfing, fishing, and diving. Most of the beaches along this stretch of the Atlantic Ocean are private, but thankfully, the state has set aside some of the best areas for the public.

Fort Pierce Inlet State Recreation Area (© **772/468-3985**) is a stunning 340-acre park with almost 4,000 feet of sandy shores that were once the training ground for the original navy frogmen. A short nature trail leads through a canopy of live oaks, cabbage palms, sea grapes, and strangler figs. The western side of the area has swamps of red mangroves that are home to fiddler crabs, osprey, and a multitude of wading birds. Jack Island State Preserve, in the State

Recreation Area, is popular with bird-watchers and offers hiking and nature trails. Jutting out into the Indian River, the mangrove-covered peninsula contains several marked trails, varying in distance from a ½ mile to over 4 miles. The trails go through mangrove forests and lead to a short observation tower.

The best beach in the recreation area, called Jetty Park, lies in the northern part of the state recreation area. Families enjoy the picnic areas and barbecue grills. There are restrooms and outdoor showers, and lifeguards look after swimmers.

The park is located at 905 Shorewinds Dr., north of Fort Pierce Inlet. To get there from I-95, take exit 66 east (Rte. 68) and turn left onto U.S. 1 north; in about 2 miles, you will see signs to Fla. A1A and the North Bridge Causeway. Turn right on A1A and cross over to North Hutchinson Island. Admission is $3.25 per vehicle, and the park is open daily from 8am to sunset.

SPECTATOR SPORTS & OUTDOOR PURSUITS

BASEBALL   The **New York Mets** hold spring training in Port St. Lucie from late February to the end of March at the **Thomas J. White Stadium,** 525 NW Peacock Blvd. (© 772/871-2115). Tickets for spring training exhibition games and practices cost $3 to $15. From April to August, their farm team, the Port St. Lucie Mets, plays home games in the stadium.

FISHING   The **Fort Pierce City Marina,** 1 Ave. A, Fort Pierce (© 772/464-1245), has more than a dozen charter captains who keep their motors running for anglers anxious to catch a few. Brochures available at the marina list all the privately owned charter operators, who organize trips on an as-desired basis. The price usually starts at $150 per person for half-day tours, depending on the season.

GOLF   The most notable courses in Port St. Lucie are at the **PGA Golf Club at the Reserve** (© 772/467-1300), at 1916 Perfect Dr. The club's first of three 18-hole public golf courses opened in January 1996 and was designed by Tom Fazio; another course was designed by Pete Dye. The South Course, a classic Old Florida–style course, is set on wetlands, offers views of native wildlife, and is the most popular. The center also offers lessons for amateurs. The club is open from 7am to 6pm daily. Greens fees are usually $89, but after 2pm they go down to $35. Reserve at least 9 days in advance.

SEEING THE SIGHTS

Harbor Branch Oceanographic Institution ★★   Harbor Branch is a working nonprofit scientific institute that studies oceanic resources and welcomes visitors on regularly scheduled tours. The first stop is the J. Seward Johnson Marine Education Center, which houses institute-built submersibles that are used to conduct marine research at depths of up to 3,000 feet. A video details current research projects, and several large aquariums simulate the environments of the Indian River Lagoon and a saltwater reef. Tourists are then shuttled by minibus to the Aqua-Culture Farming Center, a research facility that contains shallow tanks growing seaweed and other oceanic plants. The 90-minute Lagoon Wildlife Tour, on a pontoon boat, examines the Indian River Lagoon and is a fascinating tour. The bus tour of the 600-acre campus is $10 and leaves Monday through Saturday at 10am, noon, and 2pm. The boat tours are Monday through Saturday at 10am and 1 and 3pm and cost $17 for adults, $12 for children 6 to 12.

5600 U.S. 1 N., Fort Pierce. © 772/465-2400. www.hboi.edu. Admission $10 adults, $6 children 6–12, free for children 5 and under. Mon–Fri 8am–5pm; visitor center gift shop Mon–Sat 9am–5pm. Arrive at least 20 min. before tour.

Savannahs Recreation Area ★★★ *Finds* A 550-acre former reservoir, Savannahs is one of the most interesting places in these parts—it's a veritable wilderness, with botanical gardens, nature trails, campsites, a petting zoo, and scenery reminiscent of the Florida Everglades, but in a much more contained environment.

1400 E. Midway Rd., Fort Pierce. © 772/464-7855. Admission $1 per car. Daily 8am–6pm.

UDT-SEAL Museum (Underwater Demolition Team Museum) Florida is full of unique museums, but none is more curious than the UDT-SEAL Museum, an interesting tribute to the secret forces of the U.S. Navy frogmen and their successors, the SEAL teams. Chronological displays trace the history of these clandestine divers and detail their most important achievements. The best exhibits are those of the intricately detailed equipment used by the navy's most elite members. Expect to spend about an hour here, depending on your interests.

3300 N. S.R. A1A, Fort Pierce. © 772/595-5845. Admission $5 adults, $2 children 6–12, free for children 5 and under. Mon–Sat 10am–4pm; Sun noon–4pm. Closed Mon in off season.

WHERE TO STAY

The Port St. Lucie mainland is pretty run-down, but there are a number of inexpensive hotel options on scenic Hutchinson Island that are both charming and well priced. Probably the best option is the **Hampton Inn** (© **800/426-7866** or 772/460-9855), 2831 Reynolds Dr., which is relatively new and beautifully maintained. However, if you want to be closer to the water, try the **Days Inn Hutchinson Island,** 1920 Seaway Dr. (© **800/325-2525** or 772/461-8737), a small motel that sits along the Intracoastal inlet and is simple but very well kept.

Budget travelers will be glad to know about the **Edgewater Motel and Apartments,** 1160 Seaway Dr. (next door to and under the same ownership as the Dockside–Harborlight Inn and Resort), Fort Pierce (© **800/286-1745** or 772/468-3555). Motel rooms start at less than $70 in high season, and efficiencies are also available from $80. Guests can enjoy a private pool, shuffleboard courts, and a nearby fishing pier.

EXPENSIVE

Club Med–Sandpiper ★★ *Kids* A former Hilton Hotel, the 400-acre, all inclusive Sandpiper resort was purchased by Club Med in 1985 and marketed to Europeans looking for a Florida getaway. They come in droves (Americans, too) with all the kids and nannies for a sunny, active vacation with lavish meals, from buffets to sit-downs, for a reasonable prepaid price. Thanks to tailored programs for kids—there's Baby Club Med, Petit Club Med, Mini Club Med, and Junior's Club Med—the resort is all about families with kids. Rooms are so-so and retro, but not in a cool way. The drawback is that guests are 20 minutes from the nearest beach. The buildings could use a major overhaul, but there are plenty of diversions on the grounds, such as golf and tennis, and water-skiing, sailing, and boating on the Indian River, and even a circus school!

4500 SE Pine Valley, Port St. Lucie, FL 34952. © 800/CLUB-MED or 772/398-5100. Fax 772/398-5101. www. clubmed.com. 338 units. Winter $800–$1700 per week. Off-season $700–$1,000 per week. The prices include accommodations, all meals, unlimited wine, beer, and soft drinks with lunch and dinner, sports equipment, sports instruction, and nightly entertainment. If you have requested it, transport from your city of departure to the village, as well as transfers to and from the village, is included. AE, MC, V. Open from Apr–Oct. From U.S. 1 S., turn left onto Westmoreland Blvd. Make another left onto Pine Valley Rd.; the resort entrance is straight ahead. **Amenities:** 2 restaurants; bar; 4 pools; 3 golf courses; 19 tennis courts (9 are lighted); fitness center; watersports equipment; game rooms; coin-op washers and dryers. *In room:* A/C, TV, hair dryer.

MODERATE

Dockside–Harborlight Inn and Resort ⚡ Fronting the Intracoastal Water-way, the Harborlight is a great choice for boating and fishing enthusiasts, offer-ing 15 boat slips and two private fishing piers. The hotel itself carries on the nautical theme with pierlike wooden stairs and rope railings. While not exactly captain's quarters, the rooms (straight out of Rooms to Go, albeit with a bit of a nautical flair, with wood headboards and wicker) are attractive enough. Higher-priced rooms have either waterfront balconies or small kitchenettes.

1160 Seaway Dr., South Hutchinson Island, FL 34949. ℂ 800/286-1745 or 772/468-3555. Fax 772/489-9848. www.docksideinn.com. 64 units. Winter $65 standard rooms, $79–$130 efficiencies; off-season $49–$89 standard rooms and efficiencies. AE, DC, DISC, MC, V. From I-95, exit at 66A east to U.S. 1 north to Seaway Dr. **Amenities:** 2 outdoor heated pools; self-service laundry; 5 lighted fishing docks; boat dockage; grilling areas. *In room:* A/C, TV, dataport, kitchenette (in higher-priced rooms), minibar, coffeemaker.

Villa Nina Island Inn ⚡⚡ *Finds*   This is a very private inn in a simple but new home on 8 acres of the river's edge. Although privacy is paramount at Villa Nina, silence isn't necessarily deafening here, as it's more serene than quiet. In fact, the atmosphere is rather cheery and extremely romantic. Innkeepers Nina and Glenn Rappaport live in the main house and have built riverfront rooms along the back, each with a private entrance and either a fully equipped kitchen or a kitchenette. Riverfront rooms are very homey, with comfortable beds and pri-vate bathrooms. Enjoy breakfast poolside or delivered to your room (you may also opt out of breakfast for a $10 nightly savings). Possibly the best deal—and best room—in the Inn is the Grand View Suite, with high ceilings, a massive sit-ting area, sweeping views of the river and pool, floor-to-ceiling windows, break-fast nook, and marble shower, all for $165 off season and $195 during high season. Smoking is not permitted anywhere in the inn. On this stunning 8-acre property, you can use canoes and rowboats for river rides. A nearby shipwreck site makes for an excellent diving excursion.

3851 N. S.R. A1A, North Hutchinson Island, FL 34949. ℂ and fax 772/467-8673. www.villanina.com. 5 units. Year-round $113–$240. DISC, MC, V. **Amenities:** Outdoor heated pool; canoe, diving gear, and snorkel rental; bike rental; free laundry facilities; private beach access. *In room:* A/C, TV, kitchen or kitchenette, mini-bar (in most rooms), fridge, coffeemaker.

WHERE TO DINE

There are a number of good seafood restaurants in the Fort Pierce and St. Lucie area, but it's also easy to drive to Stuart for more diverse dining options. See sec-tion 1 of this chapter for recommendations in Stuart.

MODERATE

Archie's Seabreeze ⚡ AMERICAN   A haven for the Harley crowd, Archie's Seabreeze is a 50-year-old landmark on Ft. Pierce's South Beach. Although it's best known for its rough-and-tumble looking crowds and very raucous nightlife, this dive bar slash restaurant happens to boast one of the best hamburgers, if not the best, in the entire Treasure Coast. Greasy bar fare (fried foods galore) aside, Archie's is best known for its very colorful regulars and ambience in which *Easy Rider* meets *Cocoon* with a little bit of *American Pie* thrown in to lower the median age. Bottom line: Archie's Seabreeze is the place to go if you're not look-ing for gourmet fare, just fun.

401 S. Ocean Dr., Fort Pierce. ℂ 772/460-3888. Main courses $6–$10. No credit cards. Daily 10am–2am.

Le Brittany's ⚡⚡ FRENCH   Strip mall dining never tasted as good as this French Continental find in which seafood is paramount and prix fixe bargains make haute cuisine an accessible reality. Try the smoked salmon, duck pâté, Dover sole, and Grand Marnier. Chef Denis Floch and his wife Francoise definitely know their French food.

899 Prima Vista Blvd., Port St. Lucie. ✆ 772/871-2231. Reservations accepted. Main courses $12–$20. MC, V. Wed–Sun 4:30–9pm.

Mangrove Mattie's ★★ SEAFOOD   A rustic restaurant on the Fort Pierce Inlet, Mangrove Mattie's is the best place for outdoor dining, with its priceless location—right on the inlet, affording panoramic views of the Atlantic—and excellent fresh seafood. Weekday happy hours (4–7pm) are especially popular, thanks to the view and the free buffet.

1640 Seaway Dr., Fort Pierce. ✆ 772/466-1044. Reservations accepted. Main courses $11–$18. AE, DISC, MC, V. Daily 11:30am–10pm.

Theo Thudpucker's Raw Bar and Seafood Restaurant ★ SEAFOOD Located in a little building by the beach and wallpapered with maps and newspapers, Thudpucker's is a straightforward chowder bar. There's not much more to the dining room than one long bar and a few simple tables. Chowder and stews, often made with sherry and half-and-half, make excellent starters or light meals. The most recommendable (and filling) dinner dishes are sautéed scallops, deviled crabs, and deep-fried Okeechobee catfish.

2025 Seaway Dr., Fort Pierce. ✆ 772/465-1078. Reservations not accepted. Main courses $12–$29. MC, V. Mon–Thurs 11:30am–9:30pm; Fri–Sat 11:30am–11pm; Sun 1–9:30pm.

PORT ST. LUCIE/FORT PIERCE AFTER DARK

ArtWalk, a monthly event to showcase the downtown galleries, restaurants, and shops of Fort Pierce, takes place the second Wednesday of every month from 5 to 8pm and costs $5 per person, beginning in front of downtown's Sunrise Theater (✆ 772/466-3880). All galleries are usually open to the public for this event, and they supply free beverages and cheese. The **Friday Fest Street Festival** occurs on the first Friday of every month at the Historic Downtown Riverfront in Fort Pierce and is free of charge, featuring live music and refreshments for sale. The **St. Lucie Blues Club,** 338 Port St. Lucie Blvd. (✆ 772/873-1111), features live jazz, blues, and rock music Tuesday through Sunday nights. Reservations are recommended.

3 Vero Beach ★ & Sebastian ★★

Old Florida is thriving in these remote and tranquil villages. Vero Beach, known for its exclusive and affluent winter population, and Sebastian, known as one of the last remaining fishing villages, are located at the northern tip of the Treasure Coast region in Indian River County. These two beach towns are populated with folks who knew Miami and Fort Lauderdale in the days before massive high-rises and overcrowding. They appreciate the area's small-town feel, and that's exactly the area's appeal for visitors: a laid-back, relaxed atmosphere, friendly people, and friendlier prices.

A crowd of well-tanned surfers from all over the state descends on the region, especially the Sebastian Inlet, to catch some of the state's biggest waves. Other watersports enthusiasts enjoy the area's fine diving and windsurfing. Anglers are also in heaven here, and in spring, baseball buffs can catch some action from the L.A. Dodgers as they train in exhibition games.

ESSENTIALS

The **Indian River County Tourist Council,** 1216 21st St., Vero Beach, FL 32961 (© **772/567-3491;** fax 772/778-3181; www.vero-beach.fl.us/chamber), will send visitors an incredibly detailed information packet on the entire county (which includes Vero Beach and Sebastian), with a full-color map of the area, a comprehensive listing of upcoming events, a hotel guide, and more.

BEACHES & OUTDOOR ACTIVITIES

BEACHES   You'll find plenty of free and open beachfront along the coast—most are uncrowded and are open from 7am until 10pm.

South Beach Park, on South Ocean Drive, at the end of Marigold Lane, is a busy, developed, lifeguarded beach with picnic tables, restrooms, and showers. It's known as one of the best swimming beaches in Vero Beach and attracts a young crowd that plays volleyball and Frisbee in a tranquil setting. A nicely laid-out nature walk takes you into beautiful secluded trails.

At the very north tip of the island, **Sebastian Inlet State Park** ✿ has flat, sandy beaches with lots of facilities, including kayak, paddleboat, and canoe rentals; a well-stocked surf shop (there's supposedly some of the hottest surfing on the East Coast on the north jetty in this park); picnic tables; and a snack shop. The winds seem to stir up the surf with no jetty to stop their swells, to the delight of surfers and boarders, who get here early to catch the big waves. At press time, the park was readying itself for the arrival of cozy cabins ranging from 1,150 to 1,600 square feet and featuring high tech amenities such as Internet access as well as woodsy ones such as rocking chairs, porches, and fireplaces. Call © **321/ 984-4852** for rental fees and more information. Campers enjoy fully equipped sites in a woody area. Admission to the Sebastian Inlet State Park, 9700 S. Fla. A1A, Melbourne, is $5 per car and $1 for those who walk or bike in.

FISHING   Capt. Jack Jackson works 7 days a week out of **Vero's Tackle and Sport-Shop,** 57–59 Royal Palm Point (© **772/567-6550**), taking anglers on his 25-foot boat for private river excursions (all equipment is provided). Half-day jaunts on the Indian River cost $250 for one or two people (the minimum required for a charter), tackle, rigs, and everything included; $50 extra for a third person. You can either bring your own food and drinks or purchase food from the shop.

Many other charters, guides, party boats, and tackle shops operate in this area. Consult your hotel for suggestions, or call the **Vero Beach Chamber of Commerce** (© 772/567-3491) for a list of local operators. You can also contact **Captain Hiram's** (© 772/589-4345; www.hirams.com), a restaurant/bar/hotel/marina that houses many charter fishing boats.

GOLF   Hard-core golfers insist that of the dozens of courses in the area, only a handful are worth their plot of grass.

Set on rolling hills with uncluttered views of sand dunes and sky, the **Sandridge Golf Club** (© 772/770-5000), at 5300 73rd St., Vero Beach, offers two par-72 18-holers. The Dunes is a long course with rolling fairways, and the newer Lakes course has lots of water. Both charge $38, including a cart. Weekends the cost is $32 after noon. A small snack bar sells drinks and sandwiches. Reservations are recommended and are taken 2 days in advance.

Although less challenging, the **Sebastian Municipal Golf Course** (© 772/ 589-6800), at 1010 E. Airport Dr., is a good 18-hole par-72. It's scenic, well maintained, and a relative bargain. Greens fees are $35 per player with a cart, and about half that if you want to play nine holes after 1:30pm.

Also, see "Dodgertown," below.

TENNIS   Many of the tennis courts around Vero Beach and Sebastian are at hotels and resorts, which do not allow nonguests to use their courts. Instead, try **Riverside Racket Complex,** 350 Dahlia Lane, at Royal Palm Boulevard at the east end of Barber Bridge in Vero Beach (℃ **772/231-4787**). This popular park has 10 hard courts (6 lighted) that can be rented for $3.20 per person per hour if you are a county resident and $4.30 if not, and two racquetball courts, also with reasonable rates. Reservations are accepted up to 24 hours in advance. Nature trails are also on the premises.

SEEING THE SIGHTS

Environmental Learning Center ★★ (Kids)
The Indian River is not really a river at all, but a large brackish lagoon that's home to a greater variety of species than any other estuary in North America—it has thousands of species of plants, animals, fish, and birds, including 36 species on the endangered list. The privately funded Environmental Learning Center was created to protect the local habitat and educate visitors about the Indian River area's environment. Situated on 51 island acres, the center features a 600-foot boardwalk through the mangroves and dozens of hands-on exhibits that are geared to both children and adults. There are live touch-tanks, exhibits, and microscopes for viewing the smallest sea life up close. The best thing to do here is join one of the center's interpretive canoe trips, offered by reservation only ($10 for adults, $5 for children ages 6 through 12).

255 Live Oak Dr. (just off the 510 Causeway), Wabasso Island (a 51-acre island sitting in the middle of the Indian River Lagoon). ℃ 772/589-5050. www.elcweb.org. Free admission. Tues–Fri 10am–4pm; Sat 9am–noon; Sun 1–4pm.

Indian River Citrus Museum
The tiny Indian River Citrus Museum exhibits artifacts relating to the history of the citrus industry, from its initial boom in the late 1800s to the present; a small grove displays several varieties. The gift shop sells citrus-themed gift items, along with, of course, ready-to-ship fruit.

2140 14th Ave., Vero Beach. ℃ 772/770-2263. Admission $1 donation. Tues–Fri 10am–4pm.

McKee Botanical Garden ★★
This impressive 18-acre attraction was originally opened in 1932 and featured a virtual jungle of orchids, exotic and native trees, monkeys, and birds. After years of neglect, it was placed on the National Register of Historic Places in 1998. It underwent a top-to-bottom overhaul that was completed in February 2000, and you can now again experience the full charms of this little Eden.

350 U.S. 1, Vero Beach. ℃ 772/794-0601. Fax 772/794-0602. www.mckeegarden.org. Admission $6 adults, $5 seniors, $3.50 children 5–12. Tues–Sat 10am–5pm; Sun noon–5pm.

McLarty Treasure Museum ★
If you're unconvinced about why this area is called the Treasure Coast, then this is a must-see. Erected on the actual site of a salvaging camp from a 1715 shipwreck, this quaint little museum is full of interesting history. It may not have the vast treasures of the nearby Mel Fisher museum (see below), but it does offer a very engaging 45-minute video describing the many aspects of treasure hunting. You'll also see household items salvaged from the Spanish fleet and dioramas of life in the 18th century.

13180 N. Fla. A1A, Sebastian Inlet State Recreation Area, Vero Beach. ℃ 772/589-2147. Admission $1, free for children under 6. Daily 10am–4:30pm.

Mel Fisher's Treasure Museum ★★   This museum (where you can see millions of dollars of treasures from the doomed Spanish fleet that went down in 1715) is truly priceless. Although not as extensive as the museum in Key West (p. 196), this exhibit includes gold coins, bars, and Spanish artifacts that are worth a look. Also, the preservation lab shows how the goods are extricated, cleaned, and preserved.

1322 U.S. 1, Sebastian. © 772/589-9874. www.melfisher.com. Admission $6.50 adults, $5 seniors over 55, $2 children 6–12, free for children 5 and under. Mon–Sat 10am–5pm; Sun noon–5pm.

DODGERTOWN

Vero is the winter home of the **Los Angeles Dodgers** (at least for the time being; there's been talk of a move), and the town hosts the team in grand style. The 450-acre compound, Dodgertown, at 3901 26th St. (© 772/569-4900), encompasses Spring Training Camp, two golf courses, a conference center, a country club, a movie theater, a recreation room, citrus groves, and a residential community. It is a city unto its own for baseball fanatics and retirees. You can watch afternoon exhibition games during the winter (usually between mid-Feb and the end of Mar) in the comfortable 6,500-seat outdoor stadium. Even if the game sells out, you can sprawl on the lawn for just $8 (the stadium has never turned away an eager fan). Even when spring training is over, you can still catch a game; the Dodgers' farm team, the Vero Beach Dodgers, has a full season of minor-league baseball in summer.

Admission to the complex is free; tickets to games are $15 for a reserved seat, and the complex is open daily from 9am to 5pm; game time is usually 1pm. From I-95, take the exit for State Route 60 east to 43rd Avenue and turn left; continue to 26th Street and turn right.

SHOPPING

Ocean Boulevard and Cardinal Drive are Vero's two main shopping streets. Both are near the beach and are lined with specialty boutiques, including antiques and home-decorating shops.

If you want to send fruit back home, the local source is **Hale Indian River Groves,** 615 Beachland Blvd. (© 800/562-4502; www.halegroves.com), a shipper of local citrus and jams since 1947, with four locations in Vero Beach. The grove is closed 2 to 3 months a year, usually from summer through early fall, depending on the crops; the season generally runs from November to Easter.

The **Horizon Outlet Center,** at State Route 60 and I-95, Vero Beach (© 877/GO-OUTLET or 772/770-6171), contains more than 80 discount stores selling name-brand shoes, kitchenware, clothing, and more. The center is open Monday through Saturday from 9am to 8pm and Sunday from 11am to 6pm.

Indian River Mall (© 772/770-6255), 6200 20th St. (S.R. 60, about 5 miles east of I-95), is a monster mall with all the big national chains (Gap, Structure, and Victoria's Secret) as well as several department stores. It's open Monday through Saturday from 10am to 9pm and Sunday from noon to 6pm.

WHERE TO STAY

You can choose from accommodations on the mainland or on the beach. As you might expect, the beachfront accommodations are a bit more expensive—but, I think, worth it. A great spot to know, especially if you are planning to fish, is the **Key West Inn at Captain Hiram's** (1580 US Highway 1, Sebastian FL; © 772-388-8588; www.hirams.com; see "Fishing," above, and also "Vero Beach & Sebastian After Dark," below), where there are 70 rooms available adjacent to the restaurant and overlooking the water.

Comfortable and inexpensive chain options near the Vero Beach Outlet Center off State Route 60 include a **Holiday Inn Express** (ⓒ 800/465-4329 or 772/567-2500) and a **Hampton Inn** (ⓒ **800/426-7866** or 772/770-4299). Rates for both run between $70 and $80 and include breakfast and free local calls.

EXPENSIVE

Disney's Vero Beach Resort ★★★ *(Kids)*   Situated on the tip of 71 acres of pristine beaches, this Disney timeshare resort is reminiscent of a turn-of-the-last-century Florida beach community. The resort offers exciting children's programs, such as canoe adventures, poolside miniature golf, turtle walks, campfire tales, a trip to a working cattle ranch, and stargazing from a powerful telescope. The best part is a large pool designed like a lagoon with a two-story winding slide that elicits squeals of delight from kids and adults alike. The beach is also an attractive option. Rooms are bright and spacious, many with balconies. The resort offers reservation-only Disney character breakfasts on select days and is less than 2 hours away from Walt Disney World.

9250 Island Grove Terrace, Vero Beach, FL 32963. ⓒ **800/359-8000** or 772/234-2000. Fax 772/234-2030. http://dvc.disney.go.com/disneyvacationclub/intro. 112 units, 60 cottages. Winter from $305 oceanview double, from $380 and up for villas, from $960 cottages (sleep up to 12); off-season from $180 oceanview double, from $250 villas, from $700 cottages. AE, MC, V. From I-95 take exit 69 (512 going east); turn right onto County Rd. 510 heading east. Turn right again onto S. Fla. A1A. **Amenities:** 2 restaurants; bar; large pool; miniature golf; 2 lighted tennis courts; health club; Jacuzzi; sauna; watersports equipment/rental; extensive children's programs; game room and sports areas; concierge; tour desk; business center; room service; babysitting; laundry service; dry cleaning. *In room:* A/C, TV, minibar, fridge, coffeemaker, microwave.

MODERATE

Driftwood Resort ★★ *(Finds)*   Originally planned in the 1930s as a private estate by eccentric entrepreneur Waldo Sexton, the Driftwood was opened to the public in the late '30s after several travelers stopped by to inquire about renting a room here, since it was the largest property in Vero Beach and people assumed it was an attraction or, at least, a hotel. All of the guest rooms were renovated in 2000, and each is unique. Some feature terra-cotta–tiled floors and lighter furniture, while others have a more rustic feel with hardwoods and antiques. Some of the rooms contain Jacuzzis, and all are equipped with full kitchens. Two of the best rooms at the Driftwood are the Captain's Quarters, which overlook the ocean with a private staircase to the pool, and the town house located in the breezeway building, featuring a spiral staircase as well as living room and bedroom views of the ocean. The resort is listed on the National Register of Historic Places and, to say the least, has lots of quirky charm.

3150 Ocean Dr., Vero Beach, FL 32963. ⓒ **772/231-0550.** Fax 772/234-1981. www.thedriftwood.com. 100 units. Winter $130–$160 double; off-season $79–$120 double. AE, DISC, MC, V. **Amenities:** 2 outdoor heated pools; dry cleaning service. *In room:* A/C, TV, kitchen (in most 1-bedroom and all 2-bedroom units), coffeemaker, Jacuzzi in some rooms.

Islander Inn ★   This is one of the most comfortable and welcoming inns in the area. Well located in downtown Vero Beach, this small, quaint Key-West-meets-Old-Florida–style motel is just a short walk to the beach, restaurants, and shops. Every breezy guest room has a small refrigerator, either a king-size bed or two double beds, paddle fans, wicker furniture, and vaulted ceilings, and opens onto a pretty courtyard and sparkling pool. Efficiencies have full kitchens.

3101 Ocean Dr., Vero Beach, FL 32963. ⓒ **800/952-5886** or 772/231-4431. 16 units. Winter $105–$120 double; off-season $72–$99 double. Efficiencies cost $10 extra. AE, MC, V. **Amenities:** Cafe; pool. *In room:* A/C, TV, fridge.

INEXPENSIVE

Davis House Inn ★★ Each of the dozen rooms in this contemporary three-story B&B has a private entrance. The rooms are large and clean, although somewhat plain, and each has a king-size bed, a pullout sofa, and a small kitchenette, making the rooms popular with long-term guests. The bathrooms are equally ample and have plenty of counter space. Guests will find a large wooden deck for sunbathing and a sunny second-floor breakfast room. The inn is a bit out of the way but is within walking distance of some nearby restaurants; the beach is a 10-minute drive away.

607 Davis St., Sebastian, FL 32958. ✆ 772/589-4114. Fax 772/589-1722. www.davishouseinn.com. 12 units. Winter $69–$79 double; off-season $50–$69 double. 7-night min. in Feb. Weekly and monthly rates available. AE, DISC, MC, V. From I-95, take exit 69, heading east to Indian River Dr. and turn left. Go 1¼ miles to Davis St.; turn left. **Amenities:** Coin-op washers and dryers. *In room:* A/C, TV.

Sea Turtle Inn & Azalea Lane Apartments ★ This two-part nonsmoking property offers the best value on the beach (just 2 blocks from the ocean). The 1950s motel and an adjacent apartment building have been fully renovated and outfitted with understated but efficient furnishings. You won't find any fancy amenities (or even a phone, for that matter, unless you request one), but its price and location make up for what it lacks in frills. The properties share a small pool and sun deck. Book early, especially in season, since it fills up quickly with long-term visitors.

835 Azalea Lane, Vero Beach, FL 32963. ✆ 772/234-0788. Fax 772/234-0717. www.vero-beach.fl.us/ seaturtle. 20 units. Winter $69–$109 double; off-season $59–$89 double. Weekly and monthly rates available. MC, V. From I-95, go east on S.R. 60 (about 10 miles to Cardinal Dr.; turn right onto Azalea Lane). **Amenities:** Small pool; bike rental; laundry facilities. *In room:* A/C, TV, small fridge, coffeemaker.

CAMPING

The Vero Beach and Sebastian area of the Treasure Coast area is popular with campers, who can choose from nearly a dozen camping locations throughout. If you aren't camping at the scenic and very popular **Sebastian Inlet** (see "Beaches," on p. 311), then try the **Vero Beach KOA RV Park,** 8850 U.S. 1, Wabasso (✆ **772/589-5665**). This 120-site campground is 2 miles from the ocean and the Intracoastal Waterway and ¼ mile from the Indian River, a big draw for fishing fanatics. There's access to running water and electricity, as well as showers, a shop, and hookups for RVs. Rates are $30 per site and $25 for tents. To get there, take I-95 to exit 69 east; at U.S. 1, turn left.

WHERE TO DINE
EXPENSIVE

Chez Yannick ★★★ FRENCH/CONTINENTAL Excellent cooking, a comprehensive wine list, and white-glove service complement the crystal and gilded decor at this French standout, complete with fireplaces, a piano player, and steeped in old world charm. Excellent starters include a succulent sliced duckling breast, cream of lobster soup, and hearts-of-palm salad with a slightly spicy vinaigrette. Some items, like lobster and shrimp in a cognac-dill sauce, are available as either an appetizer or an entree. Other main courses include beef tenderloin stuffed with Gorgonzola cheese and sautéed soft-shell crabs. Desserts might include profiteroles with ice cream and chocolate or raspberry sauce, crème caramel, chocolate-mousse pie, or raspberry sorbet.

1605 S. Ocean Dr., Vero Beach. ✆ 772/234-4115. Reservations recommended. Main courses $15–$30; fixed-price dinner $19–$21 available in the off season. AE, MC, V. Mon–Sat open at 6pm; closing time varies based on last reservation.

MODERATE

Black Pearl Brasserie and Grill ★★ CONTINENTAL   This sophisticated brasserie may seem out of place in this beachy town, but it happens to be one of Vero Beach's trendiest spots. The restaurant's small list of appetizers includes salads, chilled sweet-potato vichyssoise, crispy fried-chicken fingers with mango dipping sauce, and grilled oysters with tangy barbecue sauce. Equally creative main courses are uniformly good. Don't miss their signature dish, an onion-crusted mahimahi with caramel-citrus glaze; the herb-crusted tilapia with roasted tomato beurre blanc is also fab. All fruits and vegetables used here come from local markets, farms, and groves. Both this original, unassuming restaurant and its newer counterpart, The **Black Pearl Riverfront,** at 4445 N. Fla. A1A (✆ 772/234-4426), serve fantastically fresh and inventive food. The riverfront location is more formal and serves only dinner, starting at 5pm.

2855 Ocean Dr., Vero Beach. ✆ 772/234-7426. Fax 772/234-9074. Reservations recommended. Main courses $12–$21. AE, DC, DISC, MC, V. Mon–Sun 11:30am–10pm; Sun brunch 10:30am–2pm.

Ocean Grill ★★ Finds STEAK/SEAFOOD   The Ocean Grill attracts its faithful devotees with its simple but rich cooking and its stunning locale, right on the ocean's edge; ask for a table along the wall of windows that open onto the sea. Built over 60 years ago by Vero Beach eccentric Waldo Sexton, the restaurant was once an officers club for residents of the nearby naval airbase during World War II. Try stone crab claws when they are in season, or the house shrimp scampi baked in butter and herbs and served with a tangy mustard sauce, or any of the big servings of meats. All fish can be prepared Cajun style, wood grilled, or deep fried. I especially recommend the Cajun Ribeye—the béarnaise sauce is delightfully jolting on the taste buds. Indian River Crab Cakes make for a memorable meal, deep fried with fresh backfin and claw meat rolled in cracker meal. The restaurant is particularly proud of its roast duckling because the fowl comes from Wisconsin and is high quality. Dinners are uniformly good. The only tacky element of this place is the gift shop.

1050 Sexton Plaza (by the ocean at the end of S.R. 60), Vero Beach. ✆ 772/231-5409. Reservations accepted only for large parties. Main courses $17–$30. AE, DC, DISC, MC, V. Mon–Fri 11:30am–2:30pm and 5:30–10pm; Sat–Sun 5:30–10pm. Closed Thanksgiving, Super Bowl Sunday, and July 4.

INEXPENSIVE

Beachside Restaurant at the Palm Court Resort ★ Value AMERICAN/ DINER   For a great big, cheap American breakfast with an ocean view, this is the place to go. You can get omelets, home fries, cream chipped beef, corned-beef hash, pancakes, Belgian waffles, and even grits. Friendly waitresses also serve lunch and dinner in the comfy wooden booths. The best dishes, like chili, fried chicken, and steaks, are hearty and delicious. No smoking.

3244 Ocean Dr., Vero Beach. ✆ 772/234-4477. Breakfast $2–$5; full dinners $8.95 and up. AE, DC, DISC, MC, V. Mon–Sat 6am–9pm; Sun 6am–1:30pm.

Nino's Cafe ★ ITALIAN   This little beachside cafe looks like a stereotypical pizza joint, complete with fake brick walls, murals of the Italian countryside, and red-and-white checked tablecloths. The atmosphere is pure cheese and so is much of the food—pizza and parmigiana dishes are smothered in the stuff. Still, the thin crust and fresh toppings make the pizza here a cut above the rest. Entrees and pastas are also tasty.

1006 Easter Lily Lane (off Ocean Dr., next to Humiston Park), Vero Beach. ✆ 772/231-9311. Main courses $9–$13. No credit cards. Mon–Thurs 11am–9pm; Fri–Sat 11am–10pm; Sun 4–9pm.

VERO BEACH & SEBASTIAN AFTER DARK

More than half the residents in this area are retirees, so it shouldn't be a surprise that even on weekends, this town retires relatively early. Hotel lounges often have live music and a good bar scene, however, especially in high season, and sometimes stay open as late as 1am, if you're lucky. For beachside drinks, go to the Driftwood Resort (p. 314).

A mostly 30-something and younger crowd goes to **Bombay Louie's** in Vero Beach, at 398 21st St. (© 772/978-0209), where a DJ spins dance music after 9pm Wednesday through Saturday. Vero Beach is also known as an artsy enclave, hosting galleries such as **The Art Works,** 2855 Ocean Dr., Vero Beach (© 772/231-4688), and the **Bottalico Gallery,** 3121 Ocean Dr., Vero Beach (© 772/231-0414). **The Civic Arts Center** at Riverside Park is a hub of culture, including the **Riverside Theatre** (© 772/231-6990), the **Agnes Wahlstrom Youth Playhouse** (© 772/234-8052), and the **Center for the Arts** (© 772/231-0707), known for films and an excellent lecture series.

In Sebastian, you'll find live music every weekend (and daily in season) at **Captain Hiram's,** 1606 N. Indian River Dr. (© **772/589-4345**), a salty outdoor restaurant and bar on the Intracoastal Waterway that locals and tourists love at all hours of the day and night (well, until it closes at 11pm, that is). The feel is tacky Key West, complete with a sand floor and thatched-roof bar.

North of the inlet, head for the tried-and-true **Sebastian Beach Inn** (SBI to locals), 7035 S. Fla. A1A (© **321/728-4311**), for live music on the weekends. Jazz, blues, or sometimes rock 'n' roll starts at 9pm on Friday and Saturday. On Sunday, it's old-style reggae after 2pm. The inn is open daily for drinks from 11am until anywhere from midnight to 2am.

4 A Side Trip Inland: Fishing at Lake Okeechobee ★★★

60 miles SW of West Palm Beach

Many visitors to the Treasure Coast come to fish, and they certainly get their fill of it off the miles of Atlantic shore and on the inland rivers. But if you want to fish freshwater and nothing else, head for "The Lake"—**Lake Okeechobee,** that is. The state's largest, it's chock-full of good eating fish. Only about a 1½-hour drive from the coast, it makes a great day or weekend excursion.

ESSENTIALS

GETTING THERE   From Palm Beach, take I-95 south to Southern Boulevard (U.S. 98 west) in West Palm Beach, which merges with State Route 80 and State Route 441. Follow signs for State Route 80 west through Belle Glade to South Bay. In South Bay, turn right onto U.S. 27 north, which leads directly to Clewiston.

VISITOR INFORMATION   Contact the **Clewiston Chamber of Commerce,** 544 W. Sugarland Hwy., Clewiston, FL 33440 (© **863/983-7979;** www.clewiston.org), for maps, business directories, and the names of numerous fishing guides throughout the area. In addition, you might contact the **Pahokee Chamber of Commerce,** 115 E. Main St., Pahokee, FL 33476 (© **772/924-5579;** fax 772/924-8116; www.pahokee.com); they'll send a complete package of magazines, guides, and accommodations listings.

OUTDOOR PURSUITS

FISHING   See the "Going After the Big One" box, below.

SKY DIVING   Besides fishing, the biggest sport in Clewiston is jumping out of planes, due to the area's limited air traffic and vast areas of flat, undeveloped land. **Air Adventures** (© **800/533-6151** or 863/983-6151) operates a year-round program from the Airglades Airport. If you've never jumped before, you can go on a tandem dive, where you'll be attached to a "jumpmaster." For the first 60 seconds, the two of you free-fall, from about 12,500 feet. Then, a quick pull of the chute turns your rapid descent into a gentle, balletlike cruise to the ground, with time to see the whole majestic lake from a privileged perspective. Dive packages start at $165; group rates start at $150.

WHERE TO STAY

If you aren't camping (see below), book a room at the **Clewiston Inn** ★★, 108 Royal Palm Ave., Clewiston (© **800/749-4466** or 863/983-8151). Built in 1938, this Southern plantation–inspired hotel is the oldest in the Lake Okee-chobee region. Its 52 rooms are simply decorated and nondescript. The lounge area sports a 1945 mural depicting the animals of the region. Double rooms start at $99 a night; suites begin at $129. All have air-conditioning and TVs.

Going After the Big One

Fishing on Lake Okeechobee is a year-round affair, though the fish tend to bite a little better in the winter, perhaps for the benefit of the many snowbirds who flock here (especially in Feb–Mar). RV camps are mobbed almost year-round with fish-frenzied anglers who come down for weeks at a time for a decent catch.

You'll need a fishing license to go out with a rod and reel. It's a simple matter to apply. The chamber of commerce and most fishing shops can sign you up on the spot. The cost for non-Florida residents for 7 days is $17 or $32 for the year.

You can rent, charter, or bring your own boat to Clewiston; just be sure to schedule your trip in advance. You don't want to show up during one of the frequent fishing tournaments only to find you can't get a room, campsite, or fishing boat. All tournaments are held at Roland Martin's marina (see below). For more information on tournaments, log on to their website at www.rolandmartinmarina.com.

There are several marinas where you can rent or charter boats. If it's your first time on the lake, I suggest chartering a boat with a guide who can show you the lake's most fertile spots and help you handle your tackle. **Roland Martin,** 920 E. Del Monte (© 863/983-3151), is the one-stop spot where you can find a guide, tackle, rods, bait, coolers, picnic supplies, and a choice of boats. Rates for a guided fishing tour are $200 for a half day and $300 for a full day for one to two people. You need a fishing license, which is available there for $17. They also have boat rentals: A 16-foot johnboat is $40 for half a day and $60 for a full day with a $40 deposit.

Another reputable boat-rental spot is **Angler's Marina,** 910 Okee-chobee Blvd. (© **800/741-3141** or 863/983-BASS). Rentals for a 14-footer start at $40 for a half day, for a maximum of four people. A full day is $60. If you want a guide, rates start at $150 (for two people) for a half day, though in the summer (June–Oct), when it's slow, you can usually get a cheaper deal.

Another choice, especially if you're here to fish, is **Roland Martin,** 920 E. Del Monte (*©* **800/473-6766** or 863/983-3151), the "Disney of fishing." This RV park (no tent sites) also offers modest motel rooms, efficiencies, condominiums, apartments, or sites for your RV, with two heated pools, gift and marina shops, and a restaurant. The modern complex, dotted with prefab buildings painted in white and gray, is clean and well manicured. Rooms rent for $68 and efficiencies cost $88. Condominiums are about $150 a night with a 3-night minimum. RV sites are about $25 with TV and cable hookup.

CAMPING

During the winter, campers own the Clewiston area. Campsites are jammed with regulars, who come year after year for the simple pleasures of the lake and, of course, the warm weather. Every manner of RV, from simple pop-top Volkswagens to Winnebagos to fully decked-out mobile homes, finds its way to the many campsites along the lake. (Also see Roland Martin, above.)

Okeechobee Landings, U.S. 27 east (*©* **863/983-4144**), is one of the best; it has every conceivable amenity included in the price of a site. More than 250 sites are situated around a small lake, clubhouse, snack bar, pool, Jacuzzi, horseshoe pit, shuffleboard court, and tennis court. Full hookup includes a sewage connection, which is not the case throughout the county. RV spots are sold to regulars, but there are usually some spots available for rental to one-time visitors. Rates start at $25 a day or $150 weekly plus tax, including hookup. Year-round rates for trailer rentals, which sleep two people, start at $32 Sunday through Thursday and from $37 on Friday and Saturday.

WHERE TO DINE

If you aren't frying up your own catch for dinner, you can find a number of good eating spots in town. At the **Clewiston Inn** (see "Where to Stay," above), you can get catfish, beef stroganoff, ham hocks, fried chicken, and liver and onions in a setting as Southern as the food. The dining room is open daily from 6am to 2pm and 5 to 9pm, and entrees cost $9 to $18. **L&L Restaurant,** 265 N. Devils Garden Rd. (*©* **863/983-6666**), is a good Spanish restaurant, with entrees ranging from $8 to $12. **Pinky's On the Green Pub,** Highway 80 (*©* **863/ 983-8464**), is a no-frills diner, with entrees under $8.

10

Southwest Florida

Although there are no adobe houses, cacti, deserts, and, as far as we know, no John Edwards' Crossing Over–esque mystics hawking crystals here, Southwest Florida is definitely the Southwest in terms of serenity, golf, retirees, and expensive homes. While the area, itself, may be staid, and the ride there, through the Everglades, may be the closest thing to adventure you're going to get in terms of this neck of the So Flo woods, it's definitely an area worth exploring.

As primitive as it gets, Alligator Alley (I-75) is the closest thing to a dirt road that South Florida's got. Once a desolate two-lane road connecting Southeast Florida with the Gulf Coast, Alligator Alley is still pretty quiet, but hardly lifeless thanks to the presence of the egrets, wood storks, owls, herons, osprey, red-shouldered hawks, belted kingfishers, and, of course, alligators that call the area behind the fenced in, protected shoulders home. As you go through Alligator Alley, en route to or from Southwest Florida, your cellphone will not work and the only option for refueling will be at the Miccosukee Indian Reservation. Driving through Alligator Alley is like entering a time warp. When you reach the end, you will enter another world, where million-dollar mansions, posh resorts, golf courses, and all signs of the good life juxtapose with nature.

Bordered on the east by the Everglades and on the west by an intriguing island-studded coast, Southwest Florida traces its nature-loving roots to inventor and amateur botanist

Thomas A. Edison, who was so enamored of it that he spent his last 46 winters in Fort Myers. His friend Henry Ford liked it, too, and built his own winter home next door. The world's best tarpon fishing lured President Theodore Roosevelt and his buddies to the 10,000 or so islands dotting this coast. Some of the planet's best shelling helped entice the du Ponts of Delaware to Gasparilla Island, where they founded the Nantucket-like village of Boca Grande. The unspoiled beauty of Sanibel and Captiva islands so entranced Pulitzer Prize–winning political cartoonist J. N. "Ding" Darling that he campaigned to preserve many of those islands in their natural states. And the millionaires who built Naples enacted tough zoning laws that to this day make their town one of the most alluring—and expensive—in Florida.

Southwest Florida International Airport, on the eastern outskirts of Fort Myers, is this region's major airport (see "Essentials," in section 1, below). From here it's only 20 miles to Sanibel Island, 35 miles to Naples, or 46 miles to Marco Island. If you have a car, you can see the area's sights and participate in most of its activities easily from one base of operations.

EXCURSIONS TO THE EVERGLADES & KEY WEST You won't be in Southwest Florida for long before you see advertisements for excursions to the Everglades. Naples is only 36 miles from Everglades City, the "back door" to wild and wonderful Everglades National Park, so it's easy to combine a visit to the national park with your stay in Southwest

Southwest Florida

ATTRACTIONS

Briggs Nature Center **10**
Edison & Ford
  Winter Estates **2**
Fort Myers
  Historical Museum **3**
Koreshan State Historic Site **5**
Lover's Key State Park **7**
Mound Key State
  Archeological Site **6**
Olde Naples **9**
Sanibel Lighthouse **4**
The Shell Factory **1**
Teddy Bear Museum **8**
Tigertail Public Beach **11**

FLORIDA

Fort Myers
Map Area

0   2 mi
0   2 km

Florida. See chapter 7 for full details about the Everglades.

You also can easily make a day trip to Key West from here by air or sea. **Cape Air** (© **800/352-0714;** www. flycapeair.com) shuttles its small planes several times a day between Key West and both Southwest Florida International Airport and the Naples Municipal Airport. The same-day round-trip fare is about $180.

The **Key West Shuttle** (© **888/ 539-2628** or 239/732-7744; www. keywestshuttle.com) runs to Key West from both Fort Myers Beach and Marco Island November through May, departing in the morning, arriving in Key West about midday, and beginning the return voyage about 5pm. That will give you about 5 hours in Key West, so you may want to stay there overnight in order to more thoroughly explore the town. Round-trip fare is about $120 for adults, $90 for children 6 to 12. Contact the shuttle for schedules and reservations.

See chapter 6 for full details about Key West and the rest of the Keys.

1 Fort Myers

148 miles NW of Miami, 142 miles S of Tampa, 42 miles N of Naples

You know how there are two schools of martini drinkers—one whose students consider themselves shaken not stirred purists and the other whose students believe in candy-flavored and -colored cocktails, the brighter and sweeter, the better? The purists usually shudder at the candy cocktailers and vice versa. Now replace those opposing martini camps with fans of technological progress and those who thought things were just fine the way they were, and you're on your way to understanding the dual mindset of historical Fort Meyers. You see, inventor Thomas Alva Edison came here in 1885 to regain his health after years of incessant toil and the death of his first wife. But unlike most new arrivals, he didn't just merge quietly into the population. Rather, his presence turned the city into one big lightbulb: The cows didn't know what hit 'em. Some regret the lightbulb ever making its way into Fort Myers. Others could care less.

Today, however, the debate is moot, and, in fact, the city's prime attractions are the homes Edison and Henry Ford built on the banks of the Caloosahatchee. Edison planted lush tropical gardens around the two homes and royal palms in front of the properties along McGregor Boulevard, once a cow trail leading from town to the docks at Punta Rassa. Had those two never showed up, Fort Myers would probably have been yet another Denny's-lined truck stop. Now lining McGregor Boulevard for miles, the trees give Fort Myers its nickname: The City of Palms.

After you've seen the Edison and Ford homes, you'll want to hightail it to the sands at nearby Fort Myers Beach or on Sanibel or Captiva Islands (see sections 2 and 3, later in this chapter). You also can venture inland and observe incredible numbers of wildlife in their river and swamp habitats, including those at the Babcock Ranch, largest of the surviving cattle producers and now a major game preserve. *Note:* If you're looking for action of the *Girls Gone Wild, MTV Spring Break* kind, this area is *not even close* to where you want to be.

ESSENTIALS

GETTING THERE   This entire region is served by **Southwest Florida International Airport** (© 239/768-1000; www.swfia.com), on Daniels Parkway east of I-75. You can get here on **Air Canada** (© 888/247-2262), **AirTran** (© 800/ 247-8726), **America West** (© 800/235-9292), **American** (© 800/433-7300), **American Trans Air** (© 800/225-2995), **Continental** (© 800/525-0280), **Delta** (© 800/221-1212), **JetBlue** (© 800/538-2583), **LTU International**

(© 800/888-0200), **Midwest Express** (© 800/452-2022), **Northwest/KLM** (© 800/225-2525), **Royal** (© 800/667-7692), **Spirit** (© 800/772-7117), **Sun Country** (© 800/359-5786), **United** (© 800/241-6522), and **US Airways** (© 800/428-4322).

The two baggage-claim areas have information booths (with maps) and free phones to various hotels in the region.

Alamo (© 800/327-9633), **Avis** (© 800/331-1212), **Budget** (© 800/527-0700), **Dollar** (© 800/800-4000), **Enterprise** (© 800/325-8007), **Hertz** (© 800/654-3131), **National** (© 800/CAR-RENT), and **Thrifty** (© 800/367-2277) have rental cars here.

Vans and taxis are available at a booth across the street from the baggage claim. The maximum fares for one to three passengers are $26 to downtown Fort Myers, $38 to Fort Myers Beach, $40 to $47 to Sanibel Island, $60 to Captiva Island, $60 to Naples, and $75 to Marco Island. Each additional passenger pays $8.

Amtrak provides bus connections between Fort Myers and its nearest station, in Tampa (© **800/USA-RAIL;** www.amtrak.com). The Amtrak buses arrive and depart the **Greyhound/Trailways** bus station, 2275 Cleveland Ave. (© **800/ 231-2222;** www.greyhound.com).

VISITOR INFORMATION   For advance information about Fort Myers, Fort Myers Beach, and Sanibel and Captiva islands, contact the **Lee Island Coast Visitor and Convention Bureau,** 2180 W. 1st St., Suite 100, Fort Myers, FL 33901 (© **800/237-6444** or 239/338-3500; fax 239/334-1106; www.lee islandcoast.com).

Volunteers staff information booths in the baggage-claim areas at Southwest Florida International Airport.

Once you're here, the **Greater Fort Myers Chamber of Commerce** (© **800/ 366-3622** from outside Florida, or 239/332-3624; fax 239/332-7276; www.fortmyers.org) has a walk-in visitor center at the corner of Edwards Drive and Lee Street on the downtown waterfront. Open Monday through Friday from 9am to 4:30pm.

There's also an information booth at the Edison and Ford Winter Estates (see "Exploring the Area," below).

GETTING AROUND   **LeeTran** (© **239/275-8726;** www.rideleetran.com) operates public buses. System maps are available from the Greater Fort Myers Chamber of Commerce (see "Visitor Information," above). There's no public bus service to Sanibel and Captiva islands, but you can connect to the Fort Myers Beach trolleys (see "Getting Around," in section 2, later in this chapter).

For a taxi, call **Yellow Cab** (© **239/332-1055**), **Bluebird Taxi** (© **239/ 275-8294**), or **Admiralty Taxi** (© **239/275-7000**).

EXPLORING THE AREA
TOURING THE ESTATES

Edison and Ford Winter Estates ★★   Thomas Edison and his second wife, Mina, brought their family to this Victorian retreat—they called it Seminole Lodge—in 1886 and wintered here until the inventor's death in 1931. Mrs. Edison gave the 14-acre estate to the city of Fort Myers in 1947, and today it's Southwest Florida's top historic attraction. It looks exactly as it did during Edison's lifetime. Costumed actors portraying the Edisons, the Fords, and their friends such as Harvey Firestone give "living history" accounts of how the wealthy lived in those days.

An avid amateur botanist, Edison experimented with the exotic foliage he planted in the lush tropical gardens surrounding the mansion (he turned goldenrod into rubber and used bamboo for light-bulb filaments). Some of his light bulbs dating from the 1920s still burn in the laboratory where he and his staff worked on some of his 1,093 inventions. The monstrous banyan tree that shades the laboratory was 4 feet tall when Harvey S. Firestone presented it to Edison in 1925; today it's the largest banyan in Florida. A museum displays some of Edison's inventions, as well as his unique Model-T Ford, a gift from friend Henry Ford. In 1916, Ford and his wife, Clara, built **Mangoes,** their bungalow-style house, next door, so they could winter with the Edisons. Like Seminole Lodge, Mangoes is furnished as it appeared in the 1920s. The Fords' home is not as interesting as the Edisons', but when you go to the Edison House, you have no choice but to go through the Ford House, too, since the only way to see either one is on a guided tour, which includes both.

Allow an extra hour here to take a scenic ride on the river in a replica of Edison's electric boat *Reliance.*

2350 McGregor Blvd. Ⓒ **239/334-3614** for a recording, or 239/334-7419. www.edison-ford-estate.com. Admission $15 adults, $8.50 children 6–12, free for children 5 and under. Boat rides $4 per person. Homes open Mon–Sat 9am–5:30pm, Sun noon–5:30pm (1½-hr. tours of both homes depart continuously. Last tour daily departs at 4pm). Boat rides Mon–Fri 9am–3pm (weather permitting). Closed Thanksgiving, Christmas Eve, Christmas Day.

OTHER DOWNTOWN ATTRACTIONS

A good way to explore downtown Fort Myers during the winter season is on a leisurely, 2-hour guided walking tour hosted by the **Fort Myers Historical Museum,** 2300 Peck St., at Jackson Street (Ⓒ **239/332-5955;** www.cityft myers.com/attractions/historical.htm). The tours are held on Wednesdays from 10am to noon and cost $5 a head. Reservations are required.

The historical museum itself is housed in the restored Spanish-style depot served by the Atlantic Coast Line from 1924 to 1971. Inside you'll see exhibits depicting the city's history from the ancient Calusa peoples and the Spanish conquistadors to the first settlers, including the remains of a P-39 Aircobra, which helps explain the town's role in training fighter pilots in World War II. Outside stands a replica of an 1800s "cracker" home and the *Esperanza,* the longest and one of the last of the plush Pullman private cars. Admission is $9.50 for adults, $8.50 for seniors, $4 for children 3 to 12, free for kids under 3. Open Tuesday through Saturday from 10am to 5pm and Sunday from noon to 4pm.

The Georgian Revival **Burroughs Home,** 2505 1st St., at Fowler Street (Ⓒ **239/332-6125;** www.cityftmyers.com/Attractions/burroughs.htm), was built on the banks of the Caloosahatchee River in 1901 by cattleman John Murphy and later sold to the Burroughs family. You must take a 30-minute tour; they usually are given from mid-October to mid-May, Tuesday through Friday, on the hour from 11am to 3pm and by appointment off-season, but call ahead any time of year. Admission is $6 for adults, $3 for children 3 to 12, free for children under 3. At press time, the home was under renovation and closed until further notice, so call before you go to make sure it's open.

Playing in the Sand

At the American Sandsculpting Festival, held each November on Fort Myers Beach, sand sculptors from around the world compete for prize money in two competitions, one for amateurs and one for pros.

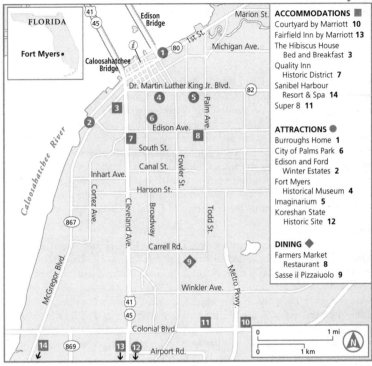

ACCOMMODATIONS ■
Courtyard by Marriott **10**
Fairfield Inn by Marriott **13**
The Hibiscus House
   Bed and Breakfast **3**
Quality Inn
   Historic District **7**
Sanibel Harbour
   Resort & Spa **14**
Super 8 **11**

ATTRACTIONS ●
Burroughs Home **1**
City of Palms Park **6**
Edison and Ford
   Winter Estates **2**
Fort Myers
   Historical Museum **4**
Imaginarium **5**
Koreshan State
   Historic Site **12**

DINING ◆
Farmers Market
   Restaurant **8**
Sasse il Pizzaiuolo **9**

Rather than have the kids go batty on a rainy day, head for the **Imaginarium,** 2000 Cranford Ave., at Martin Luther King Jr. Boulevard (✆ **239/337-3332;** www.cityftmyers.com/Attractions/imaginarium.htm), a hands-on museum in the old city water plant. A host of toylike exhibits explains basic scientific principles such as gravity and the weather. Admission is $7 for adults, $6.50 for seniors, and $4 for children 3 to 12. Open Monday through Saturday from 10am to 5pm, Sunday noon to 5pm. Closed Thanksgiving and Christmas.

A NEARBY HISTORICAL ATTRACTION

Koreshan State Historic Site   Worth a 15-mile drive south of downtown Fort Myers if you're into canoeing or quirky gurus, these 300 acres on the narrow Estero River were home to the Koreshan Unity Movement (pronounced Ko-*resh*-en), a sect led by Chicagoan Cyrus Reed Teed. The Koreshans—who should not be confused with the late, disturbing Branch Davidian leader David Koresh—who believed that humans lived *inside* the earth and—ahead of their time—that women should have equal rights, established a self-sufficient settlement here in 1894. You can visit their garden and several of their buildings, plus view photos from their archives. Canoeists will find marked trails winding down the slow-flowing river to **Mound Key,** an islet made of the shells discarded by the Calusa Indians (see "Canoeing & Kayaking" under "Enjoying the Outdoors," below). There's also a picnic and camping area with 60 wooded sites for tents or RVs. For information, contact the park superintendent at P.O. Box 7, Estero, FL 33928.

U.S. 41 at Corkscrew Rd., Estero (15 miles south of downtown Fort Myers). ℂ **239/992-0311.** www.florida stateparks.org/koreshan/default.asp. Admission $4 per vehicle for up to 8 people, $3 for a single occupant vehicle, $1 pedestrians or bikers; tours $2 adults, $1 children 6–12. Canoes $3 an hr., $15 per day. Camping winter $16; off-season $10. Park daily 8am–sunset; settlement buildings daily 8am–5pm; 1-hr. tours Sat–Sun 1pm. From I-75, take Corkscrew Rd. (exit 19), go 2 miles west, and cross U.S. 41 into the site.

AN OLD-FASHIONED TRAIN RIDE

For those who claim there's little excitement or intrigue to be had in these parts, consider a ride on the **Seminole Gulf Railway** (ℂ **800/736-4853** or 239/ 275-8487; www.semgulf.com), the original railroad that ran between Fort Myers and Naples. Today it chugs on daytime sightseeing trips and evening dinner-murder mystery excursions (think Clue meets Agatha Christie) south to Bonita Springs and north across the river. Call for the schedule and for reservations, which are required for the dinner trips. The trains depart Fort Myers from its Colonial Station, a small coral-colored building on Colonial Boulevard at Metro Parkway. The Bonita Springs station is on Old U.S. 41 at Pennsylvania Avenue.

SHOPPING

A kitschy (read: tacky) tourist attraction, **The Shell Factory and Nature Park,** 5 miles north of the Caloosahatchee River Bridge on U.S. 41 (ℂ **800/282-5805** or 239/995-2141; www.shellfactory.com), not only carries one of the world's largest collections of shells, corals, sponges, and fossils, but also has bumper-boat rides, a light show, a gallery of African art, a small zoo, and two restaurants. Inside the store, entire sections are devoted to shell jewelry and shell lamps, and many items here cost under $10, some under $1. The Shell Factory is good for a rainy day, but if it's sunny, why pay for shells when you can collect them for free on the beach? Open daily from 9am to 9pm.

Outlet shoppers will find a large Levi's store among other major-brand shops at the **Sanibel Tanger Factory Stores,** on the way to the beaches at the junction of Summerlin Road and McGregor Boulevard (ℂ **888/SHOP-333** or 239/ 454-1616; www.tangeroutlet.com). Another Levi's store, plus Brooks Brothers, Donna Karan, Dockers, Fila, Nike, Reebok, Maidenform, Nautica, OshKosh B'Gosh, and many more stores are at the much larger **Miromar Outlets,** on Corkscrew Road at I-75 in Estero (ℂ **239/948-3766;** www.miromar.com), about halfway between Fort Myers and Naples. Both outlet malls are open Monday through Saturday from 10am to 9pm, Sunday from 11am to 6pm.

ENJOYING THE OUTDOORS

CANOEING & KAYAKING   The area's slow-moving rivers and quiet, island-speckled inland waters offer fine canoe and kayak ventures; you'll visit with birds and manatees along the way. Two popular local venues are the winding waterways around Pine Island west of town and the Estero River south of Fort Myers. The Estero River route is an official Florida canoe trail and leads 3½ miles from U.S. 41 to Estero Bay, which is itself a state aquatic preserve (p. 331). Near the mouth of the river lies **Mound Key State Archaeological Park,** one of the largest Calusa shell middens. Scholars believe that this mostly artificial island dates back some 2,000 years and was the capital of the Calusa chief who ruled all of South Florida when the Spanish arrived. There's no park ranger on the key, but signs explain its history.

Koreshan State Historic Site, ½ mile south of the bridge at the intersection of U.S. 41 and Corkscrew Road (ℂ **239/992-0311**), rents canoes (see "A Nearby Historical Attraction," above). Less than a mile from the site, **Estero River Tackle & Canoe Outfitters,** 20991 S. Tamiami Trail (U.S. 41), Estero, at

"Buggy" Rides Through a Mysterious Swamp

One of the easiest and most informative ways to see Southwest Florida's abundant wildlife is on a "swamp buggy" ride with **Babcock Wilderness Adventures** ★★, 8000 S.R. 31, Punta Gorda, about 11 miles northeast of Fort Myers (© **800/500-5583** or 239/338-6367; www. babcockwilderness.com). Experienced naturalists lead 90-minute tours through the Babcock Ranch, the largest contiguous cattle operation east of the Mississippi River and home to countless birds and wildlife as well as domesticated bison and quarter horses.

Unlike most wildlife tours in the region, this one covers five different ecosystems, from open prairie to cypress swamp. Admission is $18 for adults, $9.95 for children 3 to 12. The tours usually leave on the hour between 9am and 3pm November through April, from 9am to noon May through October. Reservations are required, so call ahead. Three-hour off-road bicycle tours cost $35 for adults and $30 for children 10 to 14. Reservations are required at least 3 days in advance.

the Estero River bridge (© **239/992-4050;** www.all-florida.com/swestero.htm), has guided historic and nature tours (call for schedule and prices) and rents canoes and kayaks from 8am to 4pm at prices ranging from $18 to $30 a day. Open daily from 8am to sunset.

In addition to its cruises mentioned below, **Tropic Star Cruises,** based at Knight's Landing marina, 16499 Porto Bello in Bokeelia on Pine Island (© **239/ 283-0015;** www.tropicstarcruises.com), rents kayaks and has guided tours over 18 miles of paddling trails. Rentals cost $35 a day for single-seaters, $45 for doubles. Call for schedule and prices of guided tours. The company also has a ferry service to Cayo Costa State Park, where it rents kayaks (p. 358).

CRUISES **J. C. Boat Cruises** (© 239/334-7474; www.floridatravel. com/jccruises) presents a variety of year-round cruises on the Caloosahatchee River and its tributaries, including lunch and dinner voyages on the stern-wheeler *Captain J. P.* The 3-hour Everglades Jungle Cruise is a good way to observe the area's wildlife, with lots of manatees to be seen from November to April. Once a week, a full-day cruise goes all the way up the Caloosahatchee to Lake Okeechobee and back. The ticket office is at the downtown Fort Myers City Yacht Basin, Edwards Drive at Lee Street, opposite the chamber of commerce. Prices range from $14 to $75 for adults. Schedules change and advance reservations are required, so call ahead.

If you're headed out to Cabbage Key, Cayo Costa State Park, or Boca Grande (see "Nearby Island Hopping," in section 3, later in this chapter, beginning on p. 356), **Tropic Star Cruises** (© **239/283-0015;** www.tropicstarcruises.com) are a faster way to get there from Fort Myers than driving to Captiva Island and taking a boat from there. Tropic Star's all-day nature cruises on Pine Island Sound depart from Knight's Landing marina, 16499 Porto Bello in Bokeelia on Pine Island, daily at 9:30am. They include a stop at Cayo Costa and Cabbage Key and cost $25 for adults, $15 for kids under 12. The company also runs daily ferries to Cayo Costa State Park ($20 for adults, $15 for those under 12) and to

Boca Grande ($30 adults, $15 for those under 12). The ferries take less than 30 minutes to cross the sound. Call for departure times.

Much more luxurious, the sleek, 100-foot-long yacht **Sanibel Harbour Princess** (© 239/466-2128) goes on sunset dinner cruises from its base at Sanibel Harbour Resort & Spa (p. 329). Evening cruises start at $53 for adults, $33 for children 6 though 12, including tax and gratuity. A 2-hour Sunday-brunch cruise costs $33 for adults, $23 for children 6 though 12, including tax and gratuity. Call ahead for departure times and reservations.

GOLF & TENNIS For an excellent rundown of Southwest Florida golf courses, pick up a free copy of **Golfer's Guide,** available at the visitor information centers and many hotel lobbies, or on the Internet at www.golfersguide. com. See "Special-Interest Trips," in chapter 2, for information about subscribing or ordering the current edition. And don't forget that you can call **Tee Times USA** (© 800/374-8633 or 888/465-3356; www.teetimesusa.com) to book starting times at Florida courses.

Although it looks like an exclusive private enclave, the **Fort Myers Country Club,** McGregor Boulevard at Hill Avenue (© 239/936-2457), actually is a municipal course. Designed in 1917 by Donald Ross, it's flat and uninteresting by today's standards, but it's right in town. A steak-and-seafood restaurant now occupies the fine old clubhouse. The city's other municipal course is the more challenging **Eastwood Golf Club,** on Ortiz Avenue between Colonial Boulevard and Dr. Martin Luther King Jr. Boulevard in the eastern suburbs (© 239/ 275-4848). Greens fees at both range from about $25 in summer to $60 during winter. Nonresidents must book tee times at least 24 hours in advance.

Other area courses open to the public include the Tom Fazio–designed **Gateway Golf & Country Club,** on Daniels Parkway east of the airport (© 239/ 561-1010), and the two nationally acclaimed **Pelican's Nest** courses in Bonita Springs (© 239/947-4600).

SPECTATOR SPORTS While many Major League **baseball** teams have jumped around Florida for their **spring training,** the Boston Red Sox and the Minnesota Twins have worked out in Fort Myers for years. The **Boston Red Sox** play at the 6,500-seat City of Palms Park, at Edison Avenue and Broadway (© 877/733-7699 or 239/334-4799; www.redsox.mlb.com). Tickets range from $6 to $21. The **Minnesota Twins** work out at the 7,500-seat William Hammond Stadium in the Lee County Sports Complex on Six Mile Cypress Parkway between Daniels Parkway and Metro Parkway (© 800/338-9467 or 239/768-4200; www.twins.mlb.com). The Twins' minor-league affiliate, the **Fort Myers Miracle** (© 239/768-4210; www.miraclebaseball.com), play in the stadium April through August.

The **Texas Rangers** hold their spring training at **Charlotte County Stadium** (© 817/273-5222; www.rangers.mlb.com), about an hour's drive north of Ft. Myers. To get there from Ft. Myers, take I-75 north to exit 31 and go south on Kings Highway (Fla. 769); then take an immediate right on Veterans Boulevard (Fla. 776) to the stadium on the left.

The **Florida Everblades** (© 239/948-7825; www.floridaeverblades.com) play minor-league professional hockey October through March at TECO Arena, at exit 19 off I-75 in Estero. Tickets range from $8 to $29.

WHERE TO STAY

If you're looking for a stay with personality in Fort Myers proper, you're not going to find it. For that, you'll have to head to Fort Myers Beach (see the next section of this chapter). But if you're looking for bargains and don't mind driving to the beach, Fort Myers has just about every chain hotel imaginable. Most are quite clean and reliable.

As in the rest of southern Florida, room rates here are highest, and reservations essential, during winter, from mid-December to April. Even the chain hotels and motels along U.S. 41 in Fort Myers—most brands are represented along this busy thoroughfare—charge premium rates then. During the off season, however, they drop by as much as 50% or more.

If you can't get a room at the properties mentioned below, the **Lee Island Coast Visitor and Convention Bureau** operates a free reservation service (© **800/ 733-7935**) covering many more accommodations in Fort Myers, Fort Myers Beach, and Sanibel and Captiva islands.

A few blocks from the Edison and Ford homes, the recently renovated and under-new-management inn formerly known as Li-Inn Sleeps is now known as **The Hibiscus House Bed and Breakfast,** 2135 McGregor Blvd., at Clifford Street (© **239/332-2651;** fax 239/332-8922; www.cyberstreet.com/users/ li-inn/li-inn.html), and is a must-stay for B&B fans, with five comfortable rooms, each with private bathroom, in a charming wooden house built a century ago in North Fort Myers. The building, full of antiques and collectibles, was later split in two, floated across the river, and nailed back together. The inn's new owner brings 20 plus years of culinary experience (as the former owner of haute caterer A Moveable Feast in New York's tony Hamptons). Renovations here include new linens, new paint, the addition of a television and a dining area reminiscent of a Tuscan trattoria. Rates range from $100 to $130 in winter, $85 to $115 off-season, including full breakfast.

Chain hotels in the area include **Courtyard by Marriott** (4455 Metro Pkwy., at the corner of Colonial Blvd.; © **800/321-2211** or 239/275-8600; www. Marriott.com), **Fairfield Inn by Marriott** (7090 Cypress Terrace, off U.S. 41 a block south of Daniels Pkwy.; © **800/228-2800** or 239/437-5600; www. Marriott.com), and **Super 8** (2717 Colonial Blvd.; © **800/800-8000** or 239/ 275-3500; www.super8.com).

Many business travelers opt for the Art Deco **Quality Inn Historic District,** 2431 Cleveland Ave. (U.S. 41), at Edison Ave. (© **800/998-0466** or 239/ 332-3232). Its location, a 2-block walk to the Boston Red Sox training facility and a short drive to the Edison and Ford homes, is a plus for vacationers, too. Minor-league hopefuls stay here during baseball spring training, so you could meet a future major-leaguer.

All hotel bills in Southwest Florida are subject to a 9% tax.

The only campground with tent sites near here is at **Koreshan State Historic Site** (p. 325).

Sanibel Harbour Resort & Spa ⭐⭐⭐ 𝘒𝘪𝘥𝘴   This secluded, sports-oriented resort overlooks San Carlos Bay and Sanibel Island (a complimentary shuttle takes guests to the island's beaches and to a bike-rental shop three times a day). The main hotel and the boutique-style **Inn at Sanibel Harbour** are both modern and luxurious throughout. All of the hotel rooms (refurbished in 2003) and most of the condominium apartments have wonderful water and island views from their balconies, including spectacular sunsets over Sanibel. A large, attractive pool and sunning complex sit by the water, but don't be disappointed by the quality of the beach here—this is the bay and not the Gulf, after all, so stay over on the islands if a great beach is among your top priorities. The spa here has just been enhanced and features over 60 sublime treatments, including the unique

Caloosa Experience, where couples and small groups can perform their own treatements, and the BETAR bed, one of only 16 such systems in the world, an incredible and almost indescribable use of energy wave impulses through music and natural sound rhythms, which bathe the body in sound waves to create a state of total relaxation.

If tennis is your game, the resort has 8 clay courts and a 5,000-seat stadium that has hosted Davis Cup matches. And although the resort is romantic, it's also fabulous for kids, thanks to its outstanding Kids Klub. The program is packed with fun-filled, educational adventures featuring different themes each day. Designed for kids ages 5 through 12, the Kids Klub operates 7 days a week from 10am to 4pm (night programs are added on the weekends). Souvenirs, prizes, and lunch are included in the $34 daily fee.

17260 Harbour Pointe Rd., Fort Myers, FL 33908. ℂ 800/767-7777 or 239/466-4000. Fax 239/466-2150. www.sanibel-resort.com. 401 units, including 54 condo apts. Winter $329–$459 double, $389–$519 suite, $469–$689 condo apt; off-season $169–$310 double, $219–$379 suite, $299–$449 condo apt. $12 per unit per day resort benefits fee. Packages available. AE, DC, DISC, MC, V. Free self-parking; valet parking $10. Take the last exit off Summerlin Rd. before the Sanibel Causeway toll plaza. **Amenities:** 3 restaurants; 2 bars; 6 heated outdoor pools; 8 clay tennis courts; health club and spa; watersports equipment/rentals; concierge; children's programs; activities desk; business center; 24-hr. room service; laundry service; dry cleaning. *In room:* A/C, TV, high-speed Internet access, kitchen (condos only), minibar (main building only), fridge, coffeemaker, hair dryer, iron, safe.

WHERE TO DINE

Fort Myers's main commercial strip, Cleveland Avenue (U.S. 41), has most national fast-food and family chain restaurants, especially near College Parkway.

Farmers Market Restaurant ★★ *(Finds* SOUTHERN   Cabbage, okra, green beans, and tomatoes at the retail Farmers Market next door provide the fodder for some of the best country-style cooking in Florida at this plain and simple restaurant frequented by everyone from business executives to truck drivers. Specialties are beef and pork barbecue from the tin smokehouse out by Edison Avenue, plus other Southern favorites like country-fried steak, fried chicken livers and gizzards, and smoked ham hocks with a bowl of lima beans. Yankees can order fried chicken, roast beef, or pork chops, and they can have hash browns instead of grits with their big breakfast. But forget about Southern Comfort: No alcohol is served, nor is smoking permitted.

2736 Edison Ave. (at Cranford Ave.). ℂ 239/334-1687. Breakfast $3–$7.50; sandwiches $3–$6; meals $7.50. No credit cards. Mon–Sat 6am–8pm; Sun 6am–7pm.

Sasse il Pizzaiuolo ★★ *(Finds* CONTINENTAL/ITALIAN   In a small shopping strip north of the Edison Mall, this informal, often-noisy spot offers one of the area's most unusual and reasonably priced dining experiences. Aromas waft from the wood-fired oven in the open kitchen, from which come enormous slabs of pizzalike bread (served with seasoned olive oil for dipping). The selections change daily, although you can usually count on braised lamb shank served over polenta, and veal scallopini stuffed with prosciutto, roasted peppers, and mozzarella. It's all of a quality rarely found at these prices, and the portions are so huge that most patrons carry home doggie bags. Note that reservations are not accepted (and preference is sometimes given to regulars), so be prepared to wait for a table, especially on weekends. We have gotten complaints about the service here, though we've never had a bad experience.

3651 Evans Ave., in Carrell Corner shopping center (between Carrell Rd. and Winkler Ave.). ℂ 239/ 278-5544. Reservations not accepted. Main courses $8–$18. No credit cards. Tues–Fri 11:30am–1:15pm; Wed–Sat 5:30–8:15pm.

FORT MYERS AFTER DARK

For the most part, Fort Myers shuts down after dark and the pay-per-view on your hotel room's television may just be your best bet for entertainment. But there are some activities that happen when the sun goes down around here. For entertainment ideas and schedules, consult the daily *News-Press* (www.news-press.com), especially Friday's "Gulf Coasting" section. Also be on the lookout for *Happenings,* a tabloid-size entertainment guide distributed free at the visitor information offices and in some hotel lobbies. Tickets for most events are available from **Ticketmaster** (© **239/334-3309**).

The city's showcase performing-arts venue is the **Barbara B. Mann Performing Arts Hall** 𝕬, 8099 College Pkwy., at Summerlin Road (© **800/440-7469** or 239/481-4849 for tickets; www.bbmannpah.com), on the campus of Edison Community College. It features world-famous performers and Broadway plays.

Originally a downtown vaudeville playhouse, the 1908-vintage **Arcade Theater,** 2267 1st St., between Bay and Hendry streets (© **239/332-4488**), presents a variety of performances.

2 Fort Myers Beach 𝕬 𝕬

13 miles S of Fort Myers, 28 miles N of Naples, 12 miles E of Sanibel Island

Often overshadowed by trendy Sanibel and Captiva Islands to the north and ritzy Naples to the south, down-to-earth Fort Myers Beach, which occupies all of skinny Estero Island, offers just as much sun and sand as its affluent neighbors, both a half-hour drive away, but at more moderate prices. In fact, if you're looking for that Jimmy Buffet style of slacking, Fort Myers Beach is where it's at.

Droves of families and young singles flock to the busy intersection of San Carlos Boulevard and Estero Boulevard, an area so packed with bars, beach-apparel shops, restaurants, and motels that the locals call it "Times Square." That Coney Island image certainly doesn't apply to the rest of Estero Island, where old-fashioned beach cottages, manicured condominiums, and quiet motels beckon couples and families in search of more sedate vacations. In fact, promoters of the southern end of the island say that they're not in Fort Myers Beach; they're on Estero Island. It's their way of distinguishing their part of town from congested Times Square.

Narrow Matanzas Pass leads into broad Estero Bay, which separates the island from the mainland. While the pass is the area's largest commercial fishing port (when they say "fresh off the boat" here, they aren't kidding), the bay is an official state aquatic preserve inhabited by a host of birds as well as manatees, dolphins, and other sea life. Nature cruises go forth onto this lovely protected bay, which is dotted with islands.

A few miles south of Fort Myers Beach, a chain of pristine barrier islands includes unspoiled **Lover's Key,** a state park where a tractor-pulled tram runs through a mangrove forest to one of Florida's best beaches. Many people seem to feel the need to prove that they belong on Lover's Key, so beware of where you walk or park your car, and don't be surprised if you see steamy windows.

ESSENTIALS

GETTING THERE   See section 1 on Fort Myers, beginning on p. 322, for information about Southwest Florida International Airport, car-rental firms, Amtrak's trains, and Greyhound/Trailways bus service to the area.

VISITOR INFORMATION   You can get advance information from the Lee Island Coast Visitor and Convention Bureau (p. 323) and from the **Fort Myers**

Beach Chamber of Commerce, 17200 San Carlos Blvd., Fort Myers Beach, FL 33931 (© **800/782-9283** or 239/454-7500; fax 239/454-7910; www. fmbchamber.com), which provides free information, sells a detailed street map for $2, and operates a visitor welcome center on the mainland portion of San Carlos Boulevard just south of Summerlin Road. The chamber is open Monday through Friday from 8am to 5pm, Saturday from 10am to 5pm, and Sunday from 11am to 5pm.

GETTING AROUND   Estero Island is absolutely inundated with traffic during the peak winter months, but you can get around on the **Beach Trolley,** which operates every 15 minutes daily from 7am to 9:30pm along the full length of Estero Boulevard from Bowditch Regional Park at the north end south to Lover's Key. It operates year-round. During the winter, the **Beach Park & Ride Trolley** runs daily from 6:30am to 9:30pm between Summerlin Square Shopping Center, on the mainland at Summerlin Road and San Carlos Boulevard, to Bowditch Regional Park. Rides on both trolleys cost 25¢ per person. Ask your hotel staff or call **LeeTran** (© **239/275-8726;** www.rideleetran.com) for more information.

For a cab, call **Local Motion Taxi** (© **239/463-4111**).

There are no bike paths per se here, although many folks ride along the paved shoulders of Estero Boulevard. A variety of rental bikes, scooters, and in-line skates are available at **Fun Rentals,** 1901 Estero Blvd. at Ohio Avenue (© **239/463-8844**). Charges start at $40 a day for one-passenger scooters, $14 a day for bikes.

HITTING THE BEACH

A prime attraction for both beachgoers and nature lovers is the gorgeous **Lover's Key State Park** ★★★, 8700 Estero Blvd. (© **239/463-4588;** www.florida stateparks.org/loverskey/default.asp), on the totally preserved Lover's Key, south of Estero Island. Although the highway runs down the center of the island, access to this unspoiled beach from the parking lot is restricted to footpaths or a tractor-pulled tram through a bird-filled forest of mangroves. The beach itself is known for its multitude of shells. There are bathhouses with outdoor showers, and a snack shop here. The park is open daily from 8am to sunset. Admission is $4 per vehicle with two to eight occupants, $2 for vehicles with a single occupant, and $1 for pedestrians and bicyclists. No alcohol is allowed, nor are pets permitted on the beach or in the water (you must keep them on a leash elsewhere in the park).

On Estero Island, **Lynn Hall Memorial Park** features a fishing pier and beach in the middle of Times Square. It has changing rooms, restrooms, and one of the few public parking lots in the area; the meter costs 75¢ per hour, but keep it fed—there's a $32 fine if your time runs out. At the island's north end, **Bowditch Regional Park** has picnic tables, cold-water showers, and changing rooms. It has parking only for drivers with disabilities permits, but it's the turn-around point for the Beach Connection Trolley.

Several beach locations are hotbeds of parasailing, jet skis, sailboats, and other beach activities. **Times Square,** at the intersection of San Carlos Boulevard and Estero Boulevard, and the **Best Western Beach Resort,** about ¼ mile north, are popular spots on Estero's busy north end. Other hotbeds are **Diamond Head All Suite Beach Resort** (see "Where to Stay," below), just south of Times Square, and the **Junkanoo Beach Bar** in the middle beach area (see "Fort Myers Beach After Dark," later in this chapter). Down south, activities are centered at the **Outrigger Beach Resort** (see "Where to Stay," below).

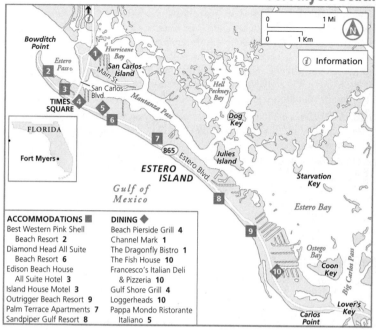

ACCOMMODATIONS ■
Best Western Pink Shell
  Beach Resort **2**
Diamond Head All Suite
  Beach Resort **6**
Edison Beach House
  All Suite Hotel **3**
Island House Motel **3**
Outrigger Beach Resort **9**
Palm Terrace Apartments **7**
Sandpiper Gulf Resort **8**

DINING ◆
Beach Pierside Grill **4**
Channel Mark **1**
The Dragonfly Bistro **1**
The Fish House **10**
Francesco's Italian Deli
  & Pizzeria **10**
Gulf Shore Grill **4**
Loggerheads **10**
Pappa Mondo Ristorante
  Italiano **5**

ENJOYING THE OUTDOORS

BOATING & BOAT RENTALS Powerboats are available from the **Mid Island Marina** (© 239/765-4371), the **Fort Myers Beach Marina** (© 239/463-9552), the **Fish Tale Marina** (© 239/463-3600), and **Salty Sam's Marina** (© 239/463-7333). **Dockside Boat Rentals** (© 239/765-4433) rents them at the Best Western Pink Shell Beach Resort on Estero Island's northern end. Boats cost about $125 for half a day, $200 for a full day.

CRUISES A good way to get out on the water and see some of this area's wildlife is on a nature cruise aboard the *Island Princess* (© **239/765-4433**), an open-air pontoon boat based at the Best Western Pink Shell Beach Resort marina on the north end of the island (see "Where to Stay," below). The boat usually goes on 1½-hour nature cruises Monday through Saturday afternoons. Prices are $13 for adults, $7 for children 6 though 12. The *Island Princess* also has bay fishing trips departing at 9am on Monday, Wednesday, Friday, and Saturday ($25 adults, $23 children 6 though 12) and shelling trips at 9am on Tuesday and Thursday ($25 adults, $12 children 6 though 12). Call ahead for reservations, which are required, and to learn what time the afternoon nature cruises depart.

FISHING You can surf-cast, throw your line off the pier at Times Square, or venture offshore on a number of charter-fishing boats here. The staff at **Getaway Marina,** 18400 San Carlos Blvd., about ½ mile north of the Sky Bridge (© **239/466-3600**), is very adept at matching clients with skilled charter-boat skippers. Expect to spend about $60 a day for a full day's fishing for up to six persons and $37 for a half day.

No reservations are required on "party boats" that take groups out. Operating year-round, the *Great Getaway* and *Great Getaway II* (✆ 239/466-3600) sail from the Getaway Marina, about ½ mile north of the bridge. The *Island Lady* (✆ 239/482-2005) is docked at Fisherman's Wharf, virtually under the San Carlos Island end of the Skyway Bridge. They all depart between 8 and 9:30am; charge between $30 and $50 per person, depending on the length of the voyage; and have air-conditioned lounges with bars. Call for details and reservations.

SCUBA DIVING & SNORKELING   Scuba diving is available at **Seahorse Scuba,** 15600 San Carlos Blvd. (✆ 239/454-3111). Two-tank dives start at $69. In business since 1989, the company also teaches diver-certification courses.

The live-aboard dive boat *Ultimate Getaway,* based at Getaway Marina, 18400 San Carlos Blvd. (✆ 239/466-3600; fax 239/644-7529; www.ultimate getaway.net), makes 4-day voyages to the Dry Tortugas (70 miles west of Key West). This 100-foot vessel carries a maximum of 20 divers and is equipped with a dive platform, chase boat, and TV/VCR. Trips cost about $500 per person, including meals, beer, air, and weights, but bring your own regulator, mask, and fins. Reservations are essential.

WHERE TO STAY

The hostelries recommended below are removed from the crowds of Times Square, but three chain motels offer comfortable accommodations right in the center of the action: **Ramada Inn** (✆ 800/544-4592 or 239/463-6158), **Days Inn** (✆ 800/544-4592 or 239/463-9759), and **Howard Johnson Inn** (✆ 800/ 544-4592 or 239/463-9231). The mid-rise **Best Western Beach Resort** (✆ 800/336-4045 or 239/463-6000) is ¼ mile north, just far enough to escape the noise but still have a lively beach.

Sunstream Resorts, 6640 Estero Blvd., Fort Myers Beach, FL 33931 (✆ 800/ 625-4111; fax 239/463-3060; www.sunstream.com), manages three "condo-minium hotels" here, including the plush **Casa Playa,** 510 Estero Blvd. (✆ 800/ 569-4876 or 239/765-0510; www.casaplayaresort.com), and the **Lover's Key Beach Club & Resort,** 8771 Estero Blvd. (✆ 877/798-4879 or 239/765-1040; www.loverskey.com), both of which opened in 2000. The latter is on the north end of Lover's Key. The 60 spacious apartments in the older, 16-story **Pointe Estero Island Resort,** 6640 Estero Blvd. (✆ 239/765-1155), all have whirlpool bathtubs and screened balconies with gorgeous Gulf or bay views. The less expensive **Santa Maria,** 7317 Estero Blvd. (✆ 239/765-6700), is on the bay side of the island.

For information about rate seasons, see the "Where to Stay" portion of the "Fort Myers" section, beginning on p. 328.

For campers, the somewhat-cramped **Red Coconut RV Resort,** 3001 Estero Blvd. (✆ 239/463-7200; fax 239/463-2609; www.redcoconut.com), has sites for RVs and tents both on the Gulf side of the road and right on the beach. They start at $40 a night during winter and are $25 off-season.

EXPENSIVE

Best Western Pink Shell Beach Resort ⭐   Not to be confused with the nearby Best Western Beach Resort, this popular, family-oriented establishment fronts 12 acres of the Gulf and the Matanzas Pass from its perch on Estero's quiet northern end. It has efficiencies, suites, and one- and two-bedroom fully equipped apartments in three mid-rise, Gulf-front buildings with lovely views of Sanibel Island from screened balconies. The standard efficiencies are the least-expensive units here. Old-Florida–style cottages on stilts are pure kitsch. Rooms underwent a thorough renovation in 2001 and are still in pretty good shape. For a more luxurious stay, choose one of the beachfront White Sand Villas. More oceanfront villas—Captiva Villas—should be completed in 2005. Sailboats and nature and sightseeing cruises pick up guests at the bay-side marina, which rents boats and bikes. The scenic Hungry Pelican Cafe, on a covered deck overlooking the channel, is a great spot for breakfast or lunch.

275 Estero Blvd., Fort Myers Beach, FL 33931. © 800/554-5454 or 239/463-6181. Fax 239/463-1229. www.pinkshell.com. 234 units. Winter $205–$515 condo or cottage; off-season $145–$500 condo or cottage. Packages and weekly rates available. AE, DC, DISC, MC, V. **Amenities:** Restaurant; bar; 4 heated outdoor pools; lighted tennis courts; watersports equipment rental; bike rental; babysitting; laundry service; coin-op washers and dryers. *In room:* A/C, TV, dataport, kitchen, fridge, coffeemaker, hair dryer, iron, safe, microwave.

Diamond Head All Suite Beach Resort ⭐   This luxurious, 12-story, beachside building sports large, comfortable one-bedroom apartments. Sliding-glass doors lead from both the living quarters and the bedroom to screened balconies. The beachfront apartments are the most appealing, but every unit has a view (spectacular from the upper floors). All rooms were renovated and feature 700-square-foot, private screened-in balconies, sleeper sofas, two televisions, and kitchen areas. There's a full-service restaurant indoors, and Cabana's Beach Bar provides libation and light lunches beside the pool. Evidence of some nightlife is available at the hotel's lounge, which has live music during the winter season. If it's summer, however, you're on your own.

2000 Estero Blvd. (at Palm Ave.), Fort Myers Beach, FL 33931. © 888/765-5002 or 239/765-7654. Fax 239/765-1694. www.diamondheadfl.com. 124 units. Winter $165–$335 double; off-season $119–$210 double. AE, DISC, MC, V. **Amenities:** 2 restaurants; 2 bars; heated outdoor pool; exercise room; Jacuzzi; watersports equipment rental; children's programs; game room; limited room service; laundry service; coin-op washers and dryers. *In room:* A/C, TV, dataport, kitchen, fridge, coffeemaker, hair dryer, iron, microwave.

Edison Beach House All Suite Hotel ⭐⭐   No standardized list of amenities does justice to this hyper, almost obsessive compulsively clean, intimate, five-story, nonsmoking beachside inn, for when owner Larry Yax built it in 1999, he equipped every unit as if he were going to live in it. Each of the light and airy units has a balcony, a ceiling fan, a fully equipped kitchen (look for your complimentary bag of popcorn in the microwave oven), a writing desk stocked with office supplies, and a linen closet packed with extra towels. Most of the bathrooms also have a combo washer-dryer. The freshly laundered bedspreads provided each new guest are but one example of the premium Larry puts on cleanliness. The beachfront units have the best view, but much more romantic are the "A" suites, whose queen-size beds are almost surrounded by windows formed by a turret on one corner of the building—as in, you fall asleep and wake up to a panoramic view spanning from Gulf to bay.

830 Estero Blvd., Fort Myers Beach, FL 33931. © 800/399-2511 or 239/463-1530. Fax 239/765-9430. www.edisonbeachhouse.com. 24 units. Winter $145–$325 double; off-season $95–$175 double. AE, DISC, MC, V. **Amenities:** Heated outdoor pool; laundry service. *In room:* A/C, TV, dataport, kitchen, coffeemaker, hair dryer, iron.

MODERATE

Outrigger Beach Resort   Well known for its beachside Tiki bar, this clean, pleasant motel has been owned and operated by the same family since 1965. Their "garden efficiencies" in the original building have the feel of small cottages, with excellent ventilation through both front and rear windows and doors opening to backyard decks. Other buildings here are two-story blocks containing motel-style rooms and efficiencies, which have views of the large parking lot. The beachside bar is one of the best places in Fort Myers Beach to watch the sun set.

6200 Estero Blvd., Fort Myers Beach, FL 33931. ℂ **800/749-3131** or 239/463-3131. Fax 239/463-6577. www.outriggerfmb.com. 144 units. Winter $120–$215 double; off-season $85–$185 double. AE, MC, V. **Amenities:** Restaurant; bar; heated outdoor pool; small exercise room; game room; coin-op washers and dryers. *In room:* A/C, TV, dataport, kitchen (in efficiencies only), fridge, coffeemaker (in efficiencies only), hair dryer, safe.

Sandpiper Gulf Resort   Reminiscent of a private condo right on Fort Myers Beach, the Sandpiper Gulf Resort is composed of two low-rise buildings, both of which have front-row access to the beach and to two tropical garden court-yards in case the sand should get too hot. Suites are the beachfront apartments you always wanted to own but could never afford, although they could benefit from a little remodeling and updating (they are a bit reminiscent of a beachy keen Holiday Inn circa 1975). Shuffleboard courts are delightfully retro, as are the guests (who tend to be on the AARP side).

5550 Estero Blvd., Fort Myers Beach, FL 33931. ℂ **800/584-1449** or 239/463-5721. Fax 239/765-0039. www. sandpipergulfresort.com. 63 units. Winter $160–$225 double; off-season $90–$125 double. $8 additional person. AE, DC, DISC, MC, V. **Amenities:** 2 heated pools; Jacuzzi. *In room:* A/C, TV, dataport, kitchen, coffeemaker.

INEXPENSIVE

Island House Motel ⭐ *Value*   Sitting on stilts in the Old Florida fashion, but with modern furnishings, Ken and Sylvia Lachapelle's clapboard-sided Island House Motel enjoys a quiet location along a bay-side channel, directly across the boulevard from the Best Western Beach Resort and within walking distance of busy Times Square. Four of their units have screened porches; all have kitchens and ceiling fans. Ken and Sylvia maintain an open-air lounge with a small library beneath one of the units. They also provide free beach chairs and bikes. Book as early as possible for February and March. The Lachapelles also operate the three-story **Edgewater Inn,** less than a block away at 781 Estero Blvd. (same phone, fax, and website). The two one-bedroom and four two-bedroom apart-ments there all have screened lanais. They are available on a weekly basis during winter and for 3-day minimum stays off-season.

701 Estero Blvd., Fort Myers Beach, FL 33931. ℂ **800/951-9975** or 239/463-9282. Fax 239/463-2080. www.edgewaterfmb.com. 5 units. Winter $119–$139 double; off-season $59–$79 double. Rates include local phone calls. Weekly rates available. MC, V. **Amenities:** Heated outdoor pool; access to nearby health club; coin-op washers and dryers; bicycles lent for free. *In room:* A/C, TV, kitchen, coffeemaker, hair dryer, iron.

Palm Terrace Apartments ⭐ *Value*   Many European guests stay in these comfortable, well-maintained apartments about midway down the beach. In fact, between them, husband-and-wife owners Deborah Bowers and Peter Piazza speak fluent German and French and passable Italian. Their smaller, less-expen-sive units are on the ground level, with sliding-glass doors opening to a grassy yard, but even these units have cooking facilities including microwave ovens. Most units are upstairs, with screened porches or decks overlooking a courtyard with a heated swimming pool, a shuffleboard court, and a charcoal grill for bar-becuing. Public access to the beach is across Estero Boulevard. There's no daily maid service, but you'll have an ample supply of clean linens.

3333 Estero Blvd., Fort Myers Beach, FL 33931. ℂ **800/320-5783** or 239/765-5783. Fax 239/765-5783. www.palm-terrace.com. 9 units. Winter $93–$140 double; off-season $52–$86 double. 3-day minimum stay required in winter. Weekly rates available. AE, DISC, MC, V. **Amenities:** Heated outdoor pool; access to nearby health club; coin-op washers and dryers. *In room:* A/C, TV/VCR, dataport, kitchen, coffeemaker.

WHERE TO DINE

The busy area around Times Square has fast-food joints to augment several local restaurants catering to the beach crowds. The pick is the moderately priced

Beach Pierside Grill, directly on the beach at the foot of Lynn Hall Memorial Pier (℗ **239/765-7800**), a lively pub with bright-blond wood trim and vivid fabric colors reminiscent of establishments in Miami's South Beach. It all opens onto a large beachside patio with dining at umbrella tables, outstanding sunsets, and live bands playing at night. The reasonably priced fare is a catch-all of conch fritters, shrimp and fish baskets, burgers, and seafood main courses. They take reservations—a plus in this busy area. Food is served daily from 11am to 11pm.

EXPENSIVE

The Dragonfly Bistro ⭐⭐ AMERICAN   Chef Preston Dishman (what better name for a chef?), graduate of New York City's French Culinary Institute, set his sights on this sleek restaurant after working at New York's famed Le Bernadin restaurant, and Fort Myers couldn't be luckier. Rich red banquettes contribute to the coolness of the restaurant, but the menu, which changes with the seasons, even though Florida doesn't really experience seasons, is cooler and richer. Everything but the sorbet is made from scratch here. Salivate over local hand-picked jumbo lump crab salad with aged cheddar and corn blini with tomato vinaigrette, and crisp bacon; seared fresh Maine sea scallops with roasted cauliflower, Yukon gold potatoes, sweet garlic greens, and mustard butter; and chargrilled prime steak with Yukon gold fries and caramelized onion aioli.

19051 San Carlos Blvd., Fort Myers Beach. ℗ **239/765-8200.** Reservations recommended. Main courses $21–$27. AE, DC, MC, V. Mon–Sat 7:30–9am; Sun 7:30–10am; Mon–Fri 11:15am–3pm, Sat 11:15am–4pm; Mon–Sat 5pm until "the customers stop coming in the door."

MODERATE

Channel Mark ⭐⭐ SEAFOOD   Maryland-style crab cakes, delicately seasoned with Old Bay spice in true Maryland fashion, are enough to make this the beach's best place for seafood. Nestled by the "Little Bridge" leading onto San Carlos Island's northern end, every table here looks out on a maze of channel markers on Hurricane Bay. A dock with palms growing through it makes this a tranquil place for a waterside lunch. At night, a relaxed tropical ambience is ideal for kindling romance. The adjacent lounge offers the same menu and has live entertainment on weekends.

19001 San Carlos Blvd. (at the north end of San Carlos Island). ℗ **239/463-9127.** Reservations recommended on major holidays; not accepted other times. Main courses $10–$21. AE, DISC, MC, V. Sun–Thurs 11am–10pm; Fri–Sat 11am–11pm.

Gulf Shore Grill SEAFOOD/AMERICAN   On the southern fringes of Times Square, this old clapboard building offers splendid views of the Gulf and the beach. It began life in the 1920s as the Crescent Beach Casino and has seen various incarnations as a bathhouse, gambling casino, dance hall, and rooming house. These days, an extensive salad bar accompanies traditional Florida-style main courses such as baked grouper imperial, grilled mahimahi, and shrimp wrapped in bacon and coated with honey. This is one of the best breakfast spots on the beach, with choices ranging from biscuits under sausage gravy to eggs served on a muffin under Alaskan crab meat and a charon sauce. The kitchen also provides the pub fare for **The Cottage Bar,** an open-air drinking establishment next door (open daily 11am–2am).

1270 Estero Blvd. (on the beach at Ave. A). ℗ **239/765-5440.** Reservations recommended for dinner. Main courses $13–$25; breakfast $4–$11; sandwiches and burgers $6–$13. AE, DISC, MC, V. Daily 8am–3pm and 5–10pm.

Loggerheads SEAFOOD/AMERICAN   The motto "The Local's Nest" accurately describes this friendly storefront restaurant, the best bet on the island's south end. Charter-boat captains and other locals congregate around a big square bar on one side of the knotty-pine–accented dining room. The menu offers a wide range of appetizers, big salads, sandwiches, burgers, and main course options from both land and sea. Grouper prepared in a number of satisfying if not spectacular ways leads the main courses, but you can also order traditionally fried, grilled, broiled, or blackened seafood plus pastas, steaks, ribs, and jerk chicken.

In Santini Marina Plaza, 7205 Estero Blvd. (at Lennel Rd.). ☎ **239/463-4644.** Reservations recommended on weekends. Main courses $12–$18; sandwiches and burgers $7–$8. AE, DISC, MC, V. Sun–Thurs 11am–11pm; Fri–Sat 11am–midnight.

Pappa Mondo Ristorante Italiano ★★ *Value* NORTHERN ITALIAN Pasquale Riso (he's the chef) and Andrea Mazzonetto hail from Italy, and the fare they present in their attractive dining room—or out on their roadside patio—is authentic old-country cooking. They make everything from scratch— you can watch them producing pasta at a big machine behind a large picture window. Especially tasty is the ravioli, either ricotta-and-cheese topped with butter and sage sauce, or stuffed with veal and served with a light cream sauce tinged with balsamic vinegar.

1821 Estero Blvd. (at Ohio Ave.). ☎ **239/765-9660.** Reservations recommended. Main courses $11–$16. AE, MC, V. Daily 3:30–10pm. Closed Christmas.

INEXPENSIVE

The Fish House SEAFOOD   You'll find the beach's least-expensive outdoor dining at the dockside tables of this no-frills friendly pub. You'll also see charter-boat skippers slaking their thirst at a large wooden bar occupying about half the open-air but screened dining room. Go for the fried or grilled grouper and other fish the captains have just landed. Sandwiches are available all day, including a tasty grouper version.

7225 Estero Blvd. (at Fish Tale Marina, behind Santini Marina Plaza). ☎ **239/765-6766.** Main courses $7–$20; sandwiches $6.50–$9. AE, DISC, MC, V. Winter daily 11am–11pm; off-season daily 11am–10pm. Closed Thanksgiving, Christmas.

Francesco's Italian Deli & Pizzeria ★ ITALIAN   Wonderful aromas of baking pizzas, cannoli, breads, cookies, and fabulous calzones waft from this New York–style Italian deli. Order at the counter over a chiller packed with fresh deli meats, Italian sausage, and cheeses; then devour your goodies at tables inside or out on the covered walkway, or take them to the beach for a picnic. You can also take "heat-and-eat" meals of spaghetti, lasagna, eggplant parmigiana, manicotti, and ravioli to your hotel or condominium oven. Shelves are loaded with Italian wines, pastas, butter cookies, and anisette toast.

In Santini Marina Plaza, 7205 Estero Blvd. (at Lennel Rd.). ☎ **239/463-5634.** Subs and sandwiches $5.50–$8; pizzas $12–$14; ready-to-cook meals $9–$11. No credit cards. Mon–Sat 8am–7pm.

FORT MYERS BEACH AFTER DARK

To find out what's going on while you're here, pick up copies of the daily *News-Press* (www.news-press.com) and of the *Beach Bulletin* and the *Fort Myers Beach Observer,* two local tabloid newspapers. They're available at the chamber of commerce (p. 332).

The area around Times Square is always active, every day during winter and on weekends off-season. In the very heart of Times Square, at the foot of Lynn

Hall Memorial Pier, the **Beach Pierside Grill,** 1000 Estero Blvd. (© **239/ 765-7800**), has live entertainment on its beachside patio. Facing due west, **Jimmy's Beach Bar,** in the Days Inn at 1130 Estero Blvd. (© **239/463-9759**), has live music nightly for the "best sunsets on the island" (actually, you can say that of all the beachside establishments here). It's not directly on the beach, but locals in the know head for the rooftop bar at **The Beached Whale,** 1249 Estero Blvd. (© **239/463-5505**), which supplies free chicken wings during their nightly happy hour. Rock and reggae music is played downstairs for nighttime dancing.

Away from the crowds in the "middle beach" area, the **Junkanoo Beach Bar,** under Anthony's on the Gulf, 3040 Estero Blvd. (© **239/463-2600**), attracts a more affluent crowd for its bohemian-style parties that run from 11:30am to 1:30am daily. Live bands here specialize in reggae and other island music. The menu offers inexpensive subs, sandwiches, burgers, and pizzas, and a concessionaire rents beach cabanas and watersports toys, making it a good place for a lively day at the beach.

On Sunday afternoons, revelers jam the docks for the famous outdoor reggae parties at **The Bridge Waterfront Restaurant,** 708 Fisherman's Wharf (© **239/ 765-0050**), which is under the Sky Bridge on San Carlos Island.

3 Sanibel & Captiva Islands ★★★

14 miles W of Fort Myers, 40 miles N of Naples

Sanibel and Captiva are Florida's unfussy cousins. Au natural is how they prefer to be so that you can appreciate their natural beauty. They don't need lip gloss and eye shadow to make them pretty. Leave the Tammy Faye makeup for Miami and Orlando. Here you will find none of the neon signs, amusement parks, and high-rise condominiums that clutter most beach resorts in the state. Indeed, Sanibel's main drag, Periwinkle Way, runs under a canopy of whispery pines and gnarled oaks so thick they almost obscure the small signs for chic shops and restaurants. This wooded ambience is the work of local voters, who have saved their trees and tropical foliage, limited the size and appearance of signs, and permitted no building higher than the tallest palm and no WaveRunner or other noisy beach toy within 300 yards of their gorgeous, shell-strewn beaches. And although they haven't yet banned cacophonous cellphones, don't be surprised if they eventually do. It's *that* peaceful.

Nevertheless, the islands still have wildlife: More than half of the two islands is preserved in its natural state as wildlife refuges. Here you can ride, walk, bike, canoe, or kayak through the J. N. ("Ding") Darling National Wildlife Refuge, one of Florida's best.

Legend says that Ponce de León named the larger of these two barrier islands "San Ybel," after Queen Isabella of Spain. Another legend claims that Captiva's name comes from the captured women kept here by the infamous pirate Jose Gaspar. The modern era of the islands dates from 1892, when a few farmers settled on the islands. One of them, Clarence Chadwick, started an unsuccessful Key lime and copra plantation on Captiva; many of his towering coconut palms still stand, adding to that skinny island's tropical luster.

ESSENTIALS

GETTING THERE   See "Getting There," in section 1 of this chapter, for information about air, train, bus, and rental-car services. The Amoco station at 1015 Periwinkle Way, at Causeway Road, is the Sanibel agent for **Enterprise Rent-a-Car** (© **800/325-8007** or 239/395-2880).

VISITOR INFORMATION   The Sanibel & Captiva Islands Chamber of Commerce, 1159 Causeway Rd., Sanibel Island, FL 33957 (© **239/472-1080;** fax 239/472-1070; www.sanibel-captiva.org), maintains a visitor center on Causeway Road as you drive onto Sanibel from Fort Myers. The chamber gives away an island guide and sells a detailed street map for $3. Other books are for sale, including comprehensive shelling guides and a helpful collection of menus from the islands' restaurants. There are phones for making hotel and condominium reservations (check the brochure racks for discounts during summer and Dec). Open Monday through Saturday from 9am to 7pm, Sunday from 10am to 5pm.

GETTING AROUND   Neither Sanibel nor Captiva has public transportation. **No parking** is permitted on any street or road on Sanibel. Free beach parking is available on the Sanibel Causeway. Other municipal lots either are reserved for local residents or have a 75¢ hourly fee. Accordingly, many residents and visitors get around by bicycle (see "More Ways to Enjoy the Outdoors," below).

   If you need a cab, call **Sanibel Taxi** (© **239/472-4160**).

PARKS & NATURE PRESERVES

Named for the *Des Moines Register* cartoonist who was a frequent visitor here and who started the federal Duck Stamp program, the outstanding **J. N. ("Ding") Darling National Wildlife Refuge** ✶✶✶, on Sanibel-Captiva Road, is home to alligators, raccoons, otters, and hundreds of species of birds. Occupying more than half of Sanibel Island, this 6,000-plus-acre area of mangrove swamps, winding waterways, and uplands has a 2-mile boardwalk nature trail and a 5-mile, one-way **Wildlife Drive.** The visitor center shows brief videos about the refuge's inhabitants every half-hour and sells a map keyed to numbered stops along the Wildlife Drive. The best times for viewing the wildlife are early morning, late afternoon, and at low tide (tables are posted at the visitor center and are available at the chamber of commerce). Mosquitoes and "no-see-ums" (tiny, biting sand flies) are especially prevalent at dawn and dusk, so bring repellent.

   Admission to the visitor center is free. The Wildlife Drive costs $5 per vehicle, $1 for hikers and bicyclists (free to holders of current federal Duck Stamps and National Park Service access passports). The visitor center is open from November to April, daily from 9am to 5pm; off-season, daily from 9am to 4pm. The center is open on federal holidays January through May, closed on holidays the rest of the year. The Wildlife Drive is open year-round, Saturday through Thursday from 1 hour after sunrise to 1 hour before sunset.

   For more information, contact the refuge at 1 Wildlife Dr., Sanibel Island, FL 33957 (© **239/472-1100**).

   You'll get a lot more from your visit by taking a naturalist-narrated tram tour given by **Tarpon Bay Recreation,** at the north end of Tarpon Bay Road (© **239/ 472-8900;** www.dingdarlingsociety.org). The tours last 2 hours and cost $10 for adults, $5 for children 12 and under. Schedules are seasonal, so call ahead.

   Tarpon Bay Recreation also offers a variety of guided **canoe and kayak tours,** with an emphasis on the historical, cultural, and environmental aspects of the refuge (call for the schedule and reservations, which are required). It also rents canoes, kayaks, and small boats with electric trolling motors (see "More Ways to Enjoy the Outdoors," below).

   A short drive from the visitor center, the nonprofit **Sanibel/Captiva Conservation Foundation,** 3333 Sanibel-Captiva Rd. (© **239/472-2329;** www.sccf. org), maintains a nature center, a native plant nursery, and 4½ miles of nature

ACCOMMODATIONS ■
Beachview Cottages **33**
Buttonwood Cottages **22**
Captiva Island Inn
  Bed & Breakfast **5**
Casa Ybel Resort **31**
Gulf Breeze Cottages **29**
Island Inn **32**
Jensen's On the Gulf **5**
Palm View Motel **28**

Sanibel Inn **27**
Sanibel's Seaside Inn **25**
Song of the Sea **26**
South Seas Resort **1**
Sundial Beach Resort **32**
Tarpon Tale Inn **24**
'Tween Waters Inn **6**

ATTRACTIONS ●
Bailey-Matthews
  Shell Museum **10**
J.N. (Ding) Darling
  National Wildlife
  Refuge **8**
Sanibel Historical Village
  & Museum **14**
Sanibel Lighthouse **23**
Sanibel/Captiva
  Conservation
  Foundation **9**
Tarpon Bay Recreation **11**

DINING ◆
The Bubble Room **2**
Captiva Sunshine Cafe **2**
Grandma Dot's
  Seaside Saloon **20**
The Green Flash **4**
Hungry Heron **13**
Jacaranda **18**
Jerry's Family
  Restaurant **16**
The Lazy Flamingo II **19**
Lighthouse Cafe **21**
Mad Hatter **7**
McT's Shrimp House
  & Tavern **17**
Morgan's Forest **30**
Mucky Duck **3**
R.C. Otter's Island Eats **2**
Sanibel Cafe **15**
The Timbers Restaurant
  & Fish Market **12**

trails on 1,100 acres of wetlands along the Sanibel River. You can learn more about the islands' unusual ecosystems through environmental workshops, guided 1½-hour trail walks, beach walks, and a 2-hour natural-history boat cruise (call for seasonal schedules and reservations). Various items are for sale, including native plants and publications about the islands' birds and other wildlife. Admission is $3 for adults, free for children 16 and under. The nature center is open from November 15 to April 14, Monday through Friday from 8:30am to 4pm, Saturday from 10am to 3pm; off-season, Monday through Friday from 8:30am to 3pm.

Also nearby, the **Clinic for the Rehabilitation of Wildlife (C.R.O.W.),** 3883 Sanibel-Captiva Rd. (© **239/472-3644;** www.crowclinic.org), is dedicated to the care of sick, injured, or orphaned wildlife. Tours of the facility usually take place year-round Monday through Friday at 11am, but call to make sure. Tours cost $3 per person.

(**Fun Fact Did You Know?**

Captiva Island was the inspiration for the best-selling book, *A Gift from the Sea,* written by Anne Morrow Lindbergh, wife of the famous flyer. She described in detail the stunning island but never revealed its name.

HITTING THE BEACH: SHELLING & SEA LIFE

BEACHES   Sanibel has four public beach–access areas with metered parking: the eastern point around **Sanibel Lighthouse,** which has a fishing pier; **Gulf-side City Park,** at the end of Algiers Lane, off Casa Ybel Road; **Tarpon Bay Road Beach,** at the south end of Tarpon Bay Road; and **Bowman's Beach,** off Sanibel-Captiva Road. **Turner Beach,** at Blind Pass between Sanibel and Captiva, is highly popular at sunset since it faces due west; there's a small free parking lot on the Captiva side, but parking on the Sanibel side is limited to holders of local permits. All except Tarpon Bay Road Beach have restrooms. *Be fore-warned:* Although nude bathing is illegal, the end of Bowman's Beach near Blind Pass often sees more than its share of bare straight and gay bodies.

Another popular beach on Captiva is at the end of Andy Rosse Lane in front of the Mucky Duck Restaurant. It's the one place here where you can rent motorized watersports equipment (see "More Ways to Enjoy the Outdoors," below), but you'll have to use the Mucky Duck's restrooms if you need to go. There's limited free parking just north of here, at the end of Captiva Drive (go past the entrance to South Seas Resort to the end of the road).

SHELLING   Sanibel and Captiva are famous for their seashells, and local residents and visitors alike can be seen in the "Sanibel stoop" or the "Captiva crouch" while searching for some 200 species.

Only if you're a hard core shell fanatic should you check out the **Bailey-Matthews Shell Museum** ★★, 3075 Sanibel-Captiva Rd. (© **888/679-6450** or 239/395-2233; www.shellmuseum.org), the only museum in the United States devoted solely to saltwater, freshwater, and land shells (yes, snails are included). If you don't get shell-shocked over the stuff, then stick to the beaches. This, however, is a far cry from the ubiquitous, tourist trappy shell factories you will see throughout the state. Shells from as far away as South Africa surround a 6-foot globe in the middle of the main exhibit hall, thus showing their geographic origins. A spinning wheel–shaped case identifies shells likely to wash up on Sanibel. Other exhibits are devoted to shells in tribal art, fossil shells found in Florida, medicinal qualities of various mollusks, the endangered Florida tree snail, and "sailor's Valentines"—shell craft made by natives of Barbados for sailors to bring home to their loved ones. The upstairs library attracts serious malacologists—for the uninitiated, those who study mollusks—and a shop purveys clever shell-themed gifts. The museum is open Tuesday through Sunday from 10am to 4pm; admission is $6 adults, $3 children 8 to 16, free for children under 8.

The months from February to April, or after any storm, are the prime times of the year to look for whelks, olives, scallops, sand dollars, conch, and many other varieties of shells. Low tide is the best time of day. The shells can be sharp, so wear Aqua Socks or old running shoes whenever you go walking on the beach.

With so many residents and visitors scouring Sanibel, you may have better luck finding that rare shell on the adjacent shoals and nearby islands, such as Upper Captiva and Cayo Costa (see "Nearby Island Hopping," later in this chapter). **Captiva Cruises** ★★ (© **239/472-5300;** www.captivacruises.com) has shelling trips from the South Seas Resort on Captiva daily at 9am and noon. They cost $35 for adults, $18 for children. Reservations are required. Captiva Cruises also has popular dolphin-watching and wildlife cruises, with narration by a naturalist from the Sanibel-Captiva Conservation Foundation, daily from 4 to 5:30pm. These cost $20 for adults, $10 for kids. All of Captiva Cruises' boats are air-conditioned and have restrooms and snack bars.

Tips **Don't Take Live Shells**

Florida law prohibits taking live shells (those with living creatures inside them) from the beaches, and federal regulations prevent them from being removed from the J. N. ("Ding") Darling National Wildlife Refuge.

At least 15 charter-boat skippers also offer to take guests on shelling expeditions to these less-explored areas. Their half-day rates are about $200 for up to four people, so get up a group to go. Several operate from the **'Tween Waters Inn Marina** (✆ **239/472-5161**) on Captiva, including **Capt. Mike Fuery** (✆ **239/466-3649**). Others are based at **Jensen's Twin Palms Marina,** on Captiva (✆ **239/472-5800**), and at the **Sanibel Marina,** on North Yachtsman Drive, off Periwinkle Way east of Causeway Boulevard (✆ **239/472-2723**). They all distribute brochures at the chamber of commerce visitor center (p. 340) and are listed in the free tourist publications found there.

MORE WAYS TO ENJOY THE OUTDOORS

BICYCLING, WALKING, JOGGING & IN-LINE SKATING   Paved bicycle paths follow alongside most major roads, including the entire length of Periwinkle Way and along Sanibel-Captiva Road to Blind Pass, making Sanibel a paradise for cyclists, walkers, joggers, and in-line skaters. And you can walk or bike the 5-mile, one-way nature trail through the J. N. ("Ding") Darling National Wildlife Refuge.

The chamber of commerce visitor center has bike maps, as do Sanibel's rental firms: **Finnimore's Cycle Shop,** 2353 Periwinkle Way (✆ 239/472-5577); **The Bike Rental,** 2330 Palm Ridge Rd. (✆ 239/472-2241); **Billy's Rentals,** 1470 Periwinkle Way (✆ 239/472-5248); **Boats, Bikes & Beach Stuff,** 2427 Periwinkle Way (✆ 239/472-8717); and **Tarpon Bay Recreation,** at the north end of Tarpon Bay Road (✆ 239/472-8900). On Captiva, **Jim's Bike & Skate Rentals** on Andy Rosse Lane (✆ 239/472-1296) rents bikes and beach equipment. Bike rates range from $7 for up to 4 hours to $15 a day for basic models. Both Finnimore's and Jim's also rent in-line skates.

There are no bike paths on Captiva, where trees alongside the narrow roads can make for dangerous riding.

BOATING & FISHING   On Sanibel, rental boats and charter-fishing excursions are available from **The Boat House** at the Sanibel Marina, on North Yachtsman Drive (✆ **239/472-2531**), off Periwinkle Way east of Causeway Road. **Tarpon Bay Recreation,** at the north end of Tarpon Bay Road (✆ **239/ 472-8900**), rents boats with electric trolling motors and tackle for fishing.

On Captiva, check with **Sweet Water Rentals** at the 'Tween Waters Inn Marina (✆ **239/472-6376**), **Jensen's Twin Palms Marina** (✆ **239/472-5800**), and **McCarthy's Marina** (✆ **239/472-5200**), all on Captiva Road. Rental boats cost about $125 for half a day, $200 for a full day.

Many **charter-fishing captains** are docked at these marinas. Half-day rates are about $300 for up to four people. The skippers leave free brochures at the chamber of commerce visitor center (p. 340), and they're also listed in the free tourist publications found there.

CANOEING & KAYAKING   As noted under "Parks & Nature Preserves," above, **Tarpon Bay Recreation** (✆ **239/472-8900;** www.tarponbay.com) has guided canoe and kayak trips in the J. N. ("Ding") Darling National Wildlife Refuge. Do-it-yourselfers can rent canoes and kayaks here. They cost $20 for the first 2 hours, $5 for each additional hour. **Captiva Kayak Co./WildSide Adventures,** based at McCarthy's Marina (℃ **877/395-2925** or 239/395-2925), rents canoes and kayaks on Captiva, as does **'Tween Waters Inn Marina** (℃ **239/ 472-5161**).

Naturalist, avid environmentalist, and former Sanibel mayor Mark "Bird" Westall of **Canoe Adventures** ✿✿ (℃ **239/472-5218;** fax 239/472-6833) takes visitors on guided canoe trips through the wildlife refuge and on the Sanibel River. His excursions are timed for low tide and cost $45 for adults, $25 for children under 18. He will tailor shorter trips to accommodate children or anyone else not up to 2½ to 3 hours in a canoe. Naturalist **Brian Houston** leads kayaking trips from 'Tween Waters Inn Marina on Captiva, but make your reservations at Tarpon Bay Recreation on Sanibel (℃ **239/472-8900**). Brian also charges $45 per person. **Captiva Kayak Co./WildSide Adventures,** based at McCarthy's Marina on Captiva (℃ **877/395-2925** or 239/395-2925), has both day and night back-bay ecology trips for $35 for adults, $25 for teenagers, $20 for children (add $10 to each price for night trips). They will customize tours, including camping on Cayo Costa (see "Nearby Island Hopping," later in this chapter) for advanced kayakers. Reservations are essential with all these operators.

GOLF & TENNIS   Golfers may view a gallery of wild animals while playing the 5,600-yard, par-70, 18-hole course at the **Dunes Golf and Tennis Club,** 949 Sandcastle Rd., Sanibel (℃ **239/472-2535;** www.dunesgolfsanibel.com), whose back nine runs across a wildlife preserve. Call a day in advance for seasonal greens fees and a tee time. The Dunes also has seven tennis courts.

You can also play nine water-bordered holes at **Beachview Golf Club,** 1100 Par View Dr. (℃ **239/472-2626**). The **South Seas Resort** has tennis courts and a nine-hole golf course, but they're for guests only.

Don't Take the Bait

If you plan on fishing, keep the following information in mind:

- Fees start at $200 for a half day (4-hour) trip; 6-hour and 8-hour trips are also available.
- The guide will provide the boat, license, fishing gear, equipment, and bait.
- Many guides will clean and filet the catches and recommend places that will mount the big ones.
- Licensed guides are required to know CPR and first aid and are periodically retested.
- Virtually all guides have ship-to-shore radios on their boat in the event of emergency.
- If a meal is planned at a restaurant after the trip, usually the client buys the guide's lunch.
- Clients usually tip guides after a successful fishing experience, ranging from $20 to $50 per trip.

SAILING   If you want to learn how to sail, noted yachties Steve and Doris Colgate have a branch of their **Offshore Sailing School** at the South Seas Resort (© **888/454-9002** or 239/472-5111, ext. 7141; www.offshore-sailing.com). You can either learn to sail or polish your skills here. Clinics ranging from half a day to a full week are available. Also ask about their popular women-only, father/son, and mother/daughter programs.

Also based on Captiva, two sailboats take guests out on the waters of Pine Island Sound: the *Adventure* (© **239/472-5300**) and the *New Moon* (© **239/ 395-1782**). They cost $95 per hour with a 2-hour minimum. Reservations are required.

Do-it-yourselfers can rent small sailboats from **Captiva Kayak Co./WildSide Adventures,** based at McCarthy's Marina (© **877/395-2925** or 239/395-2925). Prices range from $25 to $55 an hour, depending on the size of the craft.

WATERSPORTS   Sanibel may prohibit motorized watersports equipment on its beaches, but Captiva doesn't. **Yolo Watersports** (© **239/472-9656**) offers parasailing and WaveRunner rentals on the beach in front of the Mucky Duck Restaurant, at the Gulf end of Andy Rosse Lane on Captiva.

MORE TO SEE & DO

Worth a brief stop after you've done everything else here, the **Sanibel Historical Village & Museum,** 950 Dunlop Rd. (© **239/472-4648**), includes the 1913-vintage Rutland home and the 1926 versions of Bailey's General Store (complete with Red Crown gasoline pumps), the post office, and Miss Charlotta's Tea Room. Displays highlight the islands' prehistoric Calusa tribal era, as well as old photos from pioneer days, turn-of-the-20th-century clothing, and a variety of other memorabilia. Open November through May, Wednesday through Saturday from 10am to 4pm; from June to mid-August, Wednesday through Saturday from 10am to 1pm. Admission is by $3 donation.

At the east end of Periwinkle Way, the **Sanibel Lighthouse** has marked the entrance to San Carlos Bay since 1884. The lightkeepers used to live in the cottages at the base of the 94-foot tower. The now-automatic lighthouse makes for a lovely Kodak moment a la the Leaning Tower of Pisa, but it isn't open to visitors, though the grounds and beach are.

The best way to get the lay of the land and learn all about the islands' history is on a 2-hour **Sanibel Island Eco-History Trolley Tour,** staged by Adventures in Paradise (© **239/472-8443;** www.adventureinparadiseinc.com). Tours depart the chamber of commerce (p. 340) Monday through Saturday at 10:30am and 1pm and cost $30 for adults, $15 for children, and are free for kids 3 and under. Call for reservations.

In addition to its other trips, **Captiva Cruises** (© **239/472-5300;** www. captivacruises.com) goes out daily on sunset cruises from the South Seas Resort on Captiva. These cost $18 for adults, $10 for children ages 6 through 12. Call for daily departure times and reservations.

SHOPPING

You can burn up a rainy day and lots of credit at Sanibel's numerous upscale boutiques carrying expensive jewelry, apparel, and gifts. Many are in **Periwinkle Place** and **Tahitian Gardens,** the main shopping centers along Periwinkle Way. The larger Periwinkle Place sports mostly high-end men's and women's clothiers, while Tahitian Gardens has some excellent gift shops, including **The Cheshire Cat** (© **239/482-8697**), offering nature toys and other unique items for kids.

More than a dozen Sanibel galleries feature original works of art; pick up a gallery guide at the chamber of commerce visitor center (p. 340). On Captiva, the treehouselike **Jungle Drums,** on Andy Rosse Lane (✆ **239/395-2266**), has the area's most unique collection of wildlife art.

Founded in 1899, **Bailey's General Store** is still going strong at the corner of Periwinkle Way and Tarpon Bay Road (✆ **239/472-1516**), with a supermarket, deli, salad bar, hardware store, beach shop, shoe repair, and Western Union all under one roof.

Bailey's General Store is open daily from 7am to 9pm. Most other shops are open Monday through Saturday from 9am to 6pm, Sunday from noon to 5pm.

WHERE TO STAY

Sanibel & Captiva Central Reservations, Inc. (✆ **800/325-1352** or 239/472-0457; fax 239/472-2178; www.sanibel-captivarent.com), and **1-800-SANIBEL** (✆ **800/726-4235** or 239/472-1800; fax 239/395-9690; www.1-800-sanibel.com) are reservations services that will book you into most condominiums and cottages here.

In general, Sanibel and Captiva room and condominium rates are highest during the shelling season, February through April. January is usually somewhat less expensive. But note that most rates fall drastically during the off season. Don't hesitate to ask for a discount or special deal then. Since most properties on the islands are geared to 1-week vacations, you can also save by purchasing a package deal if you're staying for 7 nights or longer.

The islands' sole campground, the **Periwinkle Trailer Park,** 1119 Periwinkle Way, Sanibel Island (✆ **239/472-1433**), is so popular it doesn't even advertise. No other camping is permitted on either Sanibel or Captiva.

SANIBEL ISLAND
Very Expensive

Casa Ybel Resort ✦✦✦   One of the best resorts on Sanibel, this all-condo property sits on 23 acres of beachfront property beside the beach on the historic site of the island's first beachfront hotel, the Thistle Lodge. The present-day Casa Ybel's turn-of-the-20th-century central building houses a restaurant of that name, where both guests and nonguests can enjoy wonderful cuisine—butter poached lobster tail, pan steamed Maine lobster, crackling coconut prawns with Thai orange chili sauce—and magnificent Gulf views. There are also 14 miles of seashell studded white sand. This is bliss. Reflecting Thistle Lodge, the swimming pool in front of the restaurant is one of Florida's most picturesque. In four-story, gray buildings on the island's most beautifully landscaped grounds, the spacious one- and two-bedroom condominiums all have screened porches (complete with outdoor gas grills facing the Gulf). With upstairs bedrooms, the town house–style units provide more privacy than most condominiums on Sanibel.

2255 W. Gulf Dr., Sanibel Island, FL 33957. ✆ **800/276-4753** or 239/472-3145. Fax 239/472-2109. www.casaybelresort.com. 114 units. Winter $315–$495 condo; off-season $220–$315 condo. Packages and weekly rates available. AE, DISC, MC, V. **Amenities:** Restaurant; bar; heated outdoor pool; tennis courts; Jacuzzi; watersports equipment rental; bike rental; children's programs; concierge; massage; babysitting; laundry service. *In room:* A/C, TV, kitchen, coffeemaker, hair dryer, iron.

Sanibel Inn ✦ *Kids*   A back-to-nature theme prevails at this beachside inn, in both the room decor and the grounds planted with native Florida foliage specifically designed to attract butterflies and hummingbirds. In fact, back-to-nature children's programs make this a great choice for ecofriendly families. Kids can go on shell safaris, nature walks, and dolphin watches. The hotel rooms and fully equipped two-bedroom, two-bathroom condominium apartments (the latter are some of Sanibel's most luxurious) are blah as far as decor, but they're spacious and clean. Even better, all units have screened porches to keep the relentless mosquitoes out.

937 E. Gulf Dr., Sanibel Island, FL 33957. © **800/237-1491** or 239/472-3181. Fax 239/472-5234. www.sanibel inn.com. 94 units. Winter $329–$539 double; off-season $175–$275 double. Packages available. AE, DC, DISC, MC, V. **Amenities:** Restaurant; bar; heated outdoor pool; tennis courts; access to nearby health club; water-sports equipment rental; bike rental; children's programs; limited room service; babysitting; laundry service. *In room:* A/C, TV, dataport, kitchen, fridge, coffeemaker, hair dryer, iron.

Sanibel's Seaside Inn ★★
This comfortable and friendly Key West–style establishment enjoys a tranquil location near the island's southeastern tip. The duplex, 1960s-style cottages are spacious, brightly furnished one-bedroom apartments, but if you can do without a kitchen, the choice units here are the beachfront hotel rooms, whose screened porches face the Gulf. All units have ceiling fans and open-air balconies or decks. No smoking indoors. Guests also receive special privileges at the nearby Dunes Golf and Tennis Club.

541 E. Gulf Dr., Sanibel Island, FL 33957. © **800/831-7384** or 239/472-1400. Fax 239/472-6518. www.seasideinn.com. 32 units. Winter $239–$539 double; off-season $169–$279 double. Rates include continental breakfast. Packages available. AE, DC, DISC, MC, V. **Amenities:** Heated outdoor pool; access to nearby health club; free use of bikes; babysitting; coin-op washers and dryers. *In room:* A/C, TV/VCR, dataport, kitchen (some units), fridge, coffeemaker, hair dryer, iron.

Song of the Sea ★★
Popular with Europeans, this beachside inn offers motel-like efficiencies and one-bedroom suites with plantation-style shutters behind sliding-glass doors opening to screened porches. Don't expect a lot of extra space in the suites, whose bedrooms are barely large enough to hold their king-size beds, but the decor is quite lovely. Furnished in French country-style, the rooms feature Thomasville pine furniture, light-washed oak tables and chairs, and natural pine Bahamian shutters on patio doors and windows. A pathway leads next door to the Sanibel Inn (see above), where guests can use the facilities. An extensive continental breakfast is served in the public building and eaten at umbrella tables on a brick patio. Guests get discounts on the facilities at the Sundial Beach Resort (see below).

863 E. Gulf Dr., Sanibel Island, FL 33957. © **800/231-1045** or 239/472-2220. Fax 239/472-8569. www.songofthesea.com. 30 units. Winter $299–$399 double; off-season $159–$229 double. Rates include continental breakfast. Packages available. AE, DC, DISC, MC, V. **Amenities:** Heated outdoor pool; access to nearby health club; Jacuzzi; free use of bikes; babysitting; coin-op washers and dryers. *In room:* A/C, TV, fax, dataport, kitchen, fridge, coffeemaker, hair dryer, iron, safe.

Sundial Beach Resort ★★ (Kids)
The largest resort on Sanibel, this condominium complex lacks intimacy but has lots to keep families occupied (they even provide jogging strollers so you don't have to schlep your own), from a palm-studded, beachside pool area to a complimentary marine biology program and a small ecology center with a touch tank. The one-, two-, and three-bedroom condominiums are housed in two- and three-story buildings (as high as they get on Sanibel) and have screened balconies overlooking the beach or tropically landscaped gardens. Rooms are pleasantly decorated in a Golden Girls kind of way. Among several dining options here, the award-winning **Windows on the Water** dining room offers glorious Gulf views at breakfast, lunch, and dinner; master chefs put on a show as they prepare delicious steak, chicken, and seafood dishes right by your table in **Noopie's Japanese Seafood & Steakhouse,** where dinner reservations are required (© **239/395-6014**). Overlooking

the pool and the Gulf, the relaxing Beaches Grill & Bar is popular at sunset and has entertainment nightly.

1451 Middle Gulf Dr., Sanibel Island, FL 33957. ℭ 800/237-4184 or 239/481-3636. Fax 239/481-4947. www.sundialresort.com. 270 units. Winter $349–$519 condo apt; off-season $179–$429 condo apt. Packages available. AE, DC, DISC, MC, V. **Amenities:** 4 restaurants; 2 bars; 5 heated outdoor pools; 12 tennis courts; exercise room; Jacuzzi; watersports equipment rental; bike rental; children's programs; game room; concierge; activities desk; business center; limited room service; massage; babysitting; laundry service; coin-op washers and dryers. *In room:* A/C, TV/VCR, kitchen, coffeemaker, hair dryer, iron.

Moderate

Island Inn ★★   It's difficult to get accommodations here during the peak winter season, but it's worth trying, because this classic beach resort situated on 550 feet of Gulf beach has been in business for more than a century. Its original central building houses a bright, genteel dining room, a spacious lounge, and a library brightly furnished with old-style bentwood and wicker sofas and chairs. This is the kind of place where guests dress for dinner—jackets and collared shirts required, ties recommended for men at dinner—and seating is assigned (some guests have had the same table for years). Don't oversleep and miss the sticky buns they serve at breakfast. You will thank me for this later (although your wasteline won't). This main building looks out over a sandy, South Pacific–like yard to the Gulf. The private cottages aren't luxurious, but they certainly are private and give off that beach house vibe. Motel rooms (with or without kitchens) are fine, but I say go for the cottage. Most rooms also have screened porches or balconies.

3111 W. Gulf Dr., Sanibel Island, FL 33957. ℭ 800/851-5088 or 239/472-1561. Fax 239/472-0051. www.islandinnsanibel.com. 57 units, including 9 cottages. Winter (including breakfast and dinner). $175–$490 double; off-season (no meals) $115–$260 double. AE, DISC, MC, V. **Amenities:** Restaurant (seasonal); bar; small heated outdoor pool; tennis court; croquet area; coin-op washers and dryers. *In room:* A/C, TV, kitchen (some units), fridge, coffeemaker, hair dryer, iron.

Tarpon Tale Inn ★ *Finds*   Owners Dawn and Joe Ramsey preside over this low-slung gray building in Sanibel's Old Town, the island's first settlement where the ferries from Fort Myers used to dock near the lighthouse. White walls and tile floors make their comfortable units bright; French doors lead to gardens dense with seagrape, palm, and ficus trees, which provide privacy for a large outdoor hot tub. Three of their five units (which are attached yet completely private bungalows hidden amidst palms, bougainvillea, hibiscus, ferns, sea grape, gumbo limbo, and key lime) have separate bedrooms, while two other "deluxe studios" actually are two-bedroom suites. All units have shower-only bathrooms. Continental breakfast makings are delivered the night before. Smoking is not permitted inside the inn's rooms. There is no daily maid service, though towels and linens are exchanged every three days or as needed.

367 Periwinkle Way, Sanibel Island, FL 33957. ℭ 888/345-0939 or 239/472-0939. Fax 239/472-6202. www.tarpontale.com. 5 units. $99–$159 double (depending on which room and length of stay). Rates include continental breakfast. AE, DC, DISC, MC, V. Some pets accepted for a fee; call first. **Amenities:** Jacuzzi; free use of bikes; free use of beach chairs and umbrellas; coin-op washers and dryers; free local calls. *In room:* A/C, TV/VCR, kitchen w/stove and microwave, coffeemaker, hair dryer and iron on request, CD player, no phone (though guest phones are in common room and laundry room).

Inexpensive

Palm View Motel   In a quiet residential area less than a block from the Holiday Inn Beach Resort and Morgan's Forest restaurant, this little property is one of Sanibel's few inexpensive motels. The best choices here are the spacious, well-ventilated one- and two-bedroom apartments, but even the smaller efficiencies have kitchens and separate living and sleeping areas. There's a hot tub in the backyard plus fire pits and barbecues, and pets are allowed. A 2001 renovation included a remodeling of the suites, new brick walkways, major plantings, outdoor retreats, gardens, and water effects.

706 Donax St., Sanibel Island, FL 33957. ⓒ 239/472-1606. Fax 239/472-6733. www.palmviewsanibel.com. 5 units. Winter $145–$185 efficiency and apts; off-season $85–$135 efficiency and apts. Weekly rates available. MC, V. Pets accepted ($10 per day). **Amenities:** Jacuzzi; free guest laundry; free bike, beach chair, and umbrella lending. *In room:* A/C, TV/VCR, kitchen, coffeemaker, hair dryer, iron, microwave.

CAPTIVA ISLAND

Captiva Island Inn Bed & Breakfast ⓖ   This B&B complex sits virtually surrounded by restaurants, art galleries, and boutiques along Captiva's block-long commercial street. That can make it a bit too busy for some eyes and ears, but it has its charms. Two suites in the Key West–style main building open to porches overlooking the lane, while four Dutch clapboard cottages sit out back on the fringes of a gravel parking lot (you get just enough yard here for hammocks and a gas grill). The ceiling in one Martha's Vineyard-esque cottage that once housed aviator Charles Lindbergh has clouds painted against a blue sky. It and the rest of the units have ceiling fans, kitchens, large bathrooms, queen-size sofa beds in their living rooms, cool tile floors, and designer bed linens (including down comforters for the occasional chilly night). Some rooms have only showers in their bathrooms. Guests also get free use of bicycles and towels and chairs for the beach (a block away) and get a complimentary full breakfast at the **Keylime Bistro,** which has good American-style food and superb Key lime cheesecake and is open from 8am to 10pm daily.

11509 Andy Rosse Lane (P.O. Box 848), Captiva Island, FL 33924. ⓒ 800/454-9898 or 239/395-0882. Fax 239/395-0862. www.captivaislandinn.com. 12 units, 1 5-bedroom, 5-bathroom house. Winter $190–$300 double; off-season $99–$150 double. Rates include full breakfast. AE, DISC, MC, V. **Amenities:** Access to nearby spa; free use of bikes. *In room:* A/C, TV, fridge, coffeemaker.

South Seas Resort ⓖ (Kids)   Formerly Clarence Chadwick's 330-acre copra plantation, this exclusive establishment is the premier property on these two islands. It's one of the best choices in southern Florida for serious tennis buffs; its Gulf-side golf course is one of the most picturesque nine-holers anywhere; and its two marinas host scuba-dive operators. The resort occupies all of Captiva's northern third, making it ideal if you want to step from your luxury house or condominium right onto 2½ miles of gorgeous beach. The resort is so spread out along the shore that a free trolley shuttles back and forth through the mangrove forests.

Food is excellent here, but service isn't so great. After losing her bathing suit in the pool restroom, it took three phone calls for one guest to finally receive an answer. Even worse, the hotel asked for a credit card to mail the bathing suit back to her home. Not exactly five star service.

Most accommodations are so-called villas (actually condominium apartments), but there is a great variety of offerings, including luxury homes with private pools and their own tennis courts (many are occupied exclusively by their owners; watch for famous folks wandering about). The name "Oceanfront Villa" is a bit deceiving considering some of them barely have beach or water views (other than a smidge if you're willing to crane your neck). Furniture is, for lack of a better word, ugly. With three bedrooms or more, some units are ideal for families or couples who want to share the cost of a vacation. The least-expensive (and least-inspired) units are the "Harbourside" hotel rooms at the yacht basin and marina near the island's northern tip, the jumping-off point for Captiva

Cruises and Steve and Doris Colgate's Offshore Sailing School. Next up are the "Bayside Villas" and "Beachside Villas"—condominium apartments in three-story buildings near the main-gate area and its shops and restaurants. Whatever type of living space you choose, by all means inquire about package deals, which can result in significant savings for stays of 3 nights or more.

Outside the main gate, Chadwick's Shopping Center includes restaurants, high-fashion boutiques, jewelry stores, and gift shops, all open to the public, but the resort's no-cash, charge-to-your-room policy prevents gate-crashers from entering the resort proper.

P.O. Box 194, Captiva Island, FL 33924. (*C*) **800/CAPTIVA** or 239/472-5111. Fax 239/481-4947. www. south-seas-resort.com. 660 units. Winter $260–$370 double, $350–$1,800 condo or house; off-season $169–$240 double, $165–$1,300 condo or house. $8 per person per day added to room bills, 18%–20% to food and bar bills, in lieu of tipping. Packages available. AE, DC, DISC, MC, V. **Amenities:** 3 restaurants; 2 bars; 18 heated outdoor pools; 9-hole golf course; 18 tennis courts; health club; Jacuzzis; watersports equipment rental; bike rental; children's programs; game room; concierge; activities desk; business center; shopping arcade; salon; limited room service; massage; babysitting; laundry service; coin-op washers and dryers. *In room:* A/C, TV, dataport, kitchen (larger units only), coffeemaker, hair dryer, iron.

'Tween Waters Inn ★★   Wedged between the Gulf beach and the bay on the narrowest part of Captiva, this venerable establishment was the regular haunt of cartoonist J. N. ("Ding") Darling. Anne Morrow Lindbergh also dined here often while writing *A Gift from the Sea.* Just as Darling preserved the islands' wildlife, the 'Tween Waters has saved the cottages he stayed in. Situated in a sandy palm grove, these pink shiplap buildings have been upgraded but still capture Old Florida. Some face the Gulf, others, the bay. Themed to honor their famous guests, they range in size from the bay-side honeymoon cottage with barely enough room for its king-size bed and a tiny kitchen to a three-bedroom, two-bathroom house. The spacious hotel rooms and apartments are in three modern buildings on stilts; they all have screened balconies facing the Gulf or the bay.

The Old Captiva House restaurant appears very much as it did in Ding Darling's days (note his cartoons adorning the dining room walls), and The Canoe & The Kayak restaurant provides inexpensive lunches on its bay-side deck. The popular Crow's Nest Lounge has live entertainment and provides snacks and light evening meals from 9pm to 1am.

Charter captains dock at the full-service marina.

15951 Captiva Rd., Captiva Island, FL 33924. (*C*) **800/223-5865** or 239/472-5161. Fax 239/472-0249. www.tween-waters.com. 138 units. Winter $245–$285 double, $250–$585 suite, $290–$650 cottage; off-season $155–$230 double, $210–$440 suite, $210–$460 cottage. Rates include continental breakfast. Packages available. AE, DC, MC, V. Pets accepted in some units ($15 per day). **Amenities:** 2 restaurants; 2 bars; outdoor pool; 3 tennis courts; exercise room; massage room; Jacuzzi; watersports equipment rentals; bike rentals; coin-op washers and dryers. *In room:* A/C, TV, dataport, kitchen (suites and cottages), fridge, coffeemaker, hair dryer, iron (suites only), safe.

COTTAGES

The islands have several Old Florida–style cottages that offer charming and often less-expensive alternatives to hotels and condominiums. Some of the best are members of the **Sanibel-Captiva Small Inns & Cottages Association.** You can contact the association (via its website only) at www.sanibelsmallinns.com for a complete listing of properties.

Sitting between two condominium complexes off Middle Gulf Drive, **Gulf Breeze Cottages** ★★, 1081 Shell Basket Lane, Sanibel Island, FL 33957 ((*C*) **800/388-2842** or 239/472-1626; www.gbreeze.com), is a collection of clapboard cottages separated from the beach by a lawn with covered picnic area and outdoor shower. One two-story building is divided into four efficiencies (the pick is no. 7, with a two-way view of the Gulf from its big picture windows). Rates are $215 to $350 a day in winter, $115 to $230 a day off-season.

With only one monstrous mansion standing between them and a narrow bay beach near Sanibel Lighthouse, **Buttonwood Cottages** ✮, 1234 Buttonwood Lane, Sanibel Island, FL 33957 (© **887/395-COTTAGE** or 239/395-9061; fax 239/395-2620; www.buttonwoodcottages.com), are less expensive options at $125 to $220 a day in winter, $75 to $160 off-season. Remodeled and equipped with many modern amenities, the five units occupy two long cottages built on stilts. Four of them have screened porches, with two overlooking a lushly tropical backyard sporting two hammocks and two hot tubs. The Lighthouse Cafe (see "Where to Dine," below) is around the corner.

Barely updated since the 1950s are the 32 pink clapboard structures at **Beachview Cottages,** 3325 W. Gulf Dr., Sanibel Island, FL 33957 (© **800/ 860-0532** or 239/472-1202; fax 239/472-4720; www.beachviewsanibel.com). None of the cottages has a phone, and some have shower-only bathrooms. There's a heated outdoor swimming pool here. Winter rates are $155 to $265 a day, off-season $85 to $170 a day.

On Captiva, **Jensen's On the Gulf,** 15300 Captiva Dr., Captiva Island, FL 33924 (© **239/472-4684;** www.jensen-captiva.com), has cottages as well as homes, apartments, and studios ranging from $250 to $600 a day in winter, $150 to $450 a day off-season. **Jensen's Twin Palm Resort & Marina,** P.O. Box 191, Captiva Island, FL 33924 (© **239/472-5800;** same website), on the bay side near the Andy Rosse Lane dining district, has cottages ranging from $120 to $190 a day during winter, from $105 to $130 a day off-season.

WHERE TO DINE

No restaurant can survive on these affluent islands without serving good food, so you're assured of getting a fine meal wherever you go. Oddly, only a handful of restaurants offer dining with water views.

SANIBEL ISLAND

Much of the "help" on this affluent island dines at **Jerry's Family Restaurant,** 1700 Periwinkle Way at Casa Ybel Road (© **239/472-9300**), which offers wholesome and inexpensive diner fare (ingredients come fresh from the adjacent Jerry's Supermarket). Both the restaurant and the supermarket are open daily from 6am to 11pm. Breakfast is served from 6am to 4pm, and you can usually get a table quickly here (which can't be said of Sanibel's other popular breakfast spots).

You'll find very reasonably priced pub fare at Sanibel's sports bars, such as **The Lazy Flamingo II** (see below) and **Sanibel Grill,** 703 Tarpon Bay Rd., near Palm Ridge Road (© **239/472-3128**), which actually serves as the bar for Timbers, the fine seafood restaurant next door (see below).

For picnics at Sanibel's beaches or on a canoe, the deli and bakery in **Bailey's General Store,** at Periwinkle Way and Tarpon Bay Road (© **239/472-1516**), carries a gourmet selection of breads, cheeses, and meats. **Huxter's Deli and Market,** 1203 Periwinkle Way, east of Donax Street (© **239/472-6988**), has sandwich fixings and "beach box" lunches to go.

Very Expensive

Mad Hatter ✮✮ ECLECTIC   One of Sanibel's best choices for a romantic special dinner, this New American Gulf-front restaurant has only 12 tables, but each has a view that's perfect at sunset. The ever-changing eclectic menu features flavors from around the world, such as Thai-style peanut sauce over a seared, sesame-encrusted yellowfin tuna steak. The jumbo shrimp Wellington is a fascinating twist on the classic beef dish, and the stuffed crab served with a lobster velouté is another winner.

6467 Sanibel-Captiva Rd., at Blind Pass. ☏ **239/472-0033**. Reservations highly recommended. Main courses $26–$34. AE, MC, V. Dec 15–Jan 31 daily 5–9pm; Feb 1–Easter, Sun–Mon 5–9:30pm, Tues–Sat 11:30am–2pm and 5–9:30pm; Easter–May 31 daily 5–9:30pm; June 1–Dec 14 Mon–Sat 5–9:30pm. Closed Sept after Labor Day.

Moderate

Jacaranda SEAFOOD/PASTA/STEAKS   With live music nightly, the Patio Lounge attracts an affluent over-40 crowd to this friendly and casual restaurant named for the purple-flowered jacaranda tree. Although the Jacaranda is best known as a local gathering spot, it has received several dining awards. Fresh fish is well prepared here, or you can choose certified Angus steaks or prime rib. The linguine with a dozen littleneck clams tossed in a piquant red or white clam sauce is consistently excellent. For dessert, the gooey turtle pie—ice cream, caramel, fudge sauce, chopped nuts, and whipped cream—will send you away stuffed.

1223 Periwinkle Way (east of Donax St.). ☏ **239/472-1771**. Reservations recommended. Main courses $12–$30. AE, MC, V. Daily 5–10pm. Lounge daily 4pm–12:30am. Closed Christmas.

McT's Shrimp House & Tavern SEAFOOD   Shrimp reigns at this casual Old Florida–style establishment, where you'll see a line outside at 4pm waiting for the early-bird specials served to the first 100 persons in the door. Everyone else gets to view the daily catch displayed in a chiller case, including the night's shrimp ready for the chef to prepare in one of at least a dozen ways, from steamed to fried in a coconut-and-almond batter. There are also grouper and swordfish, plus steaks and chicken for the land-minded, but stick to the shrimp here (see below for the Timbers Restaurant & Fish Market, which does a much better job of cooking fish). McT's Tavern offers an extensive choice of appetizers and light dinners. All you can eat peel-and-eat shrimp and stone crabs are available nightly, though if it's not stone crab season (Oct–May) the crab will likely be frozen.

1523 Periwinkle Way (at Fitzhugh St.). ☏ **239/472-3161**. Main courses $13–$22; early-bird specials $10. AE, DC, DISC, MC, V. Shrimp House daily 4:45–10pm. McT's Tavern daily 4pm–midnight. Closed Thanksgiving, Christmas.

Morgan's Forest (Kids) SEAFOOD   The kids will love dining in this miniature jungle patterned after the Rainforest Cafes elsewhere. Parents, on the other hand, will suffer for the love of the children. Almost hidden among all the foliage are mechanical but lifelike moving jaguars, monkeys, birds, and a huge python entangled in vines above the bar. Squawking bird sounds, strobe-lightning bolts followed by claps of thunder, and an occasional faux fog rolling across the floor are as pleasant as the sound of fingernails to a chalkboard. The owner of Fort Myers Beach's excellent Channel Mark restaurant is in charge here, which means that at least the food makes up for the harassing ambience. The fine crab cakes are the pick of a menu otherwise accented with South- and Central-American seasonings. Obviously, there's a children's menu.

1231 Middle Gulf Dr., adjacent to the Holiday Inn Beach Resort. ☏ **239/472-3351**. Main courses $14–$23. AE, DC, DISC, MC, V. Mon–Sat 7–11am and 5–10pm; Sun 7am–noon and 5–10pm.

⌒Tips   Deals on Meals

Local restaurants often run advertisements containing discount coupons in the "Sanibel-Captiva Shopper's Guide," a free publication available at the chamber of commerce visitor center.

The Timbers Restaurant & Fish Market ★★ SEAFOOD/STEAK   This casual upstairs restaurant, with bamboo railings, oversized canvas umbrellas, and paintings of tropical scenes through faux windows, consistently is Sanibel's best place for fresh fish and aged beef hot off the charcoal grill. It's true what they say—"We serve it fresh or we don't serve it at all." In the fish market out front, you can view the catch and have the chef charcoal-grill or blacken it to order. The steaks, cut on the premises, are the island's best. You can order a drink from the adjoining Sanibel Grill sports bar and wait for a table outside on the shopping center's porch.

703 Tarpon Bay Rd. (between Periwinkle Way and Palm Ridge Rd.). © **239/472-3128.** Main courses $15–$23; early birds get $2.50 off regular price. AE, MC, V. Winter daily 4:30–9:30pm; off-season daily 5–9:30pm.

Inexpensive

Grandma Dot's Seaside Saloon SEAFOOD   One of Sanibel's most popular lunch spots, this open-air but screened cafe on the docks of Sanibel Marina offers excellent salads (try the seafood Caesar) and fine sandwiches plus a few main courses led by broiled grouper in a sauce of lemon, dill, butter, and white wine.

At Sanibel Marina, 634 N. Yachtsman Dr. © **239/472-8138.** Reservations not accepted. Main courses $6–$23; salads and sandwiches $6–$12. MC, V. Daily 11:30am–7:30pm.

Hungry Heron ★★ *(Kids* AMERICAN   This tropically decorated eatery is Sanibel's most popular family restaurant. There's something for everyone on the huge, tabloid-size menu—from hot and cold appetizers and overstuffed "sea-wiches" to pasta and steamed shellfish. And if the 280 regular items aren't enough, there's a list of nightly specials. Seafood, steaks, and stir-fries from a sizzling skillet are popular with local residents, who bring the kids here for fun and a children's menu. An all-you-can-eat breakfast buffet on Saturday and Sunday mornings is an excellent value.

In Palm Ridge Place, 2330 Palm Ridge Rd. (at Periwinkle Way). © **239/395-2300.** Reservations not accepted, but call for preferred seating. Main courses $9–$18; sandwiches, burgers, and snacks $6–$11; weekend breakfast buffet $9 adults, $5 children under 10. AE, DISC, MC, V. Mon–Fri 11am–9pm; Sat–Sun 7:30am–9pm (breakfast buffet to 11am Sat, to noon Sun).

The Lazy Flamingo II *(Value* SEAFOOD/PUB FARE   The Lazy Flamingo is a down-homey type place where the food is consistently good. Locals and visitors become repeat customers who flock here for reasonably priced food, a wide choice of beers iced down in a huge box behind the bar, and sports TVs. Some of that beer is used to steam shrimp and a finger-stinging collection of oysters, clams, and spices known as "The Pot." Best pick, however, is grouper from the charcoals, as either a main course or a sandwich. The flamingo-pink menu also has an array of sandwiches, burgers, fish platters, and very spicy "Dead Parrot Wings." Fillet your own catch, and the chef will cook it to order for you. Happy-hour prices prevail whenever football games are on the TVs. A sister institution, the **Lazy Flamingo I,** 6520-C Pine Ave., at Sanibel-Captiva Road, a ¼ mile south of Blind Pass (© **239/472-5353**), has the same menu and hours.

1036 Periwinkle Way, west of Causeway Blvd. © **239/472-6939.** Reservations not accepted. Main courses $11–$15; sandwiches and snacks $5–$9. Cook your catch $8. AE, DISC, MC, V. Daily 11:30am–1am.

Lighthouse Cafe ★ *(Value* AMERICAN   This casual storefront establishment dishes up breakfast omelets that are meals in themselves, especially the ocean frittata containing delicately seasoned scallops, crab meat, shrimp, broccoli, and fresh mushrooms, and crowned with an artichoke heart and creamy Alfredo sauce. Seafood Benedict is one of the more decadent offerings. For the light(er) eater, a slew of creative sandwiches are served after 11am. Reasonably priced cafe-style dinners are served during winter only. For the best pancakes ever, the Lighthouse Cafe has cornered the market, using a special recipe that draws up to 700 people a day in season. For just $3.95, you can go nuts on malted blueberry or banana pancakes, or pretend to be healthy with granola nut wholewheat hot cakes with sliced bananas.

In Seahorse Shops, 362 Periwinkle Way (at Buttonwood Lane, east of Causeway Rd.). ℂ **239/472-0303.** Call ahead to get on waiting list. Main courses $10–$15; breakfast $3.50–$7.50; sandwiches and salads $4.50–$8.50. MC, V. Mid-Dec to Easter daily 7am–3pm and 5–9pm; Easter to mid-Dec daily 7am–3pm.

Sanibel Cafe ⭐ *Value* AMERICAN   Seashells are the not-so original theme at Lynda and Ken Boyce's pleasant cafe, whose tables are museum-like glass cases containing delicate fossilized specimens from the Miocene and Pliocene epochs. Fresh-squeezed orange and grapefruit juice, Danish Havarti omelets, and homemade muffins and biscuits highlight the breakfast menu (eggs Benedict and fruit-filled waffles are served until closing). Lunch features specialty sandwiches; shrimp, Greek, and chicken-and-grape salads made with a very light, fat-free dressing; and a limited list of main courses such as grilled or blackened chicken breast. At dinner, they add homemade meatloaf, crunchy grouper, and certified Angus steaks. Fatten up on Lynda's homemade red-raspberry jam, apple or cherry crisps, and terrific Key lime pie.

In the Tahitian Gardens Shops, 2007 Periwinkle Way. ℂ **239/472-5323.** Call ahead for preferred seating. Main courses $7.50–$17; breakfast $3.50–$9; salads, sandwiches, and burgers $4.50–$13. MC, V. Daily 7am–9pm.

CAPTIVA ISLAND

Big deli sandwiches and picnic fare are available at the **Captiva Island Store,** Captiva Road at Andy Rosse Lane (ℂ **239/472-2374**), and the gourmet-oriented **C. W.'s Market and Deli,** at the entrance to the South Seas Resort (ℂ **239/472-5111**). The beach is a block from these stores.

Also, see the review for the Captiva Island Inn Bed & Breakfast on p. 349 for information on the **Keylime Bistro.**

The Bubble Room ⭐⭐⭐ *Kids* STEAK/SEAFOOD   Imagine Walt Disney on acid and you'll understand where the Bubble Room is coming from. The kitschiest restaurant you'll probably ever find, the Bubble Room's tongue-in-cheeky American cuisine is complemented by a decor that's filled with Christmas and Hollywood memorabilia from the '30s, '40s, and '50s. Distracting, to say the least—but in a very good way—The Bubble Room makes it hard to decide which is cooler, the Henny Young-One boneless breast of young chicken, the prime ribs Weissmuller, or the thousands of movie stills, puppets, antique jukeboxes, or toy trains. *Note:* We've gotten complaints about the "awful" food here (others recommend the diagonally opposite **Keylime Bistro**—see p. 349—instead), but we still think The Bubble Room is fun, with good (though admittedly not fabulous) food and a great atmosphere.

15001 Captiva Rd. (at Andy Rosse Lane). ℂ **239/472-5558.** www.bubbleroomrestaurant.com. Reservations not accepted, but call for preferred seating. Main courses $17–$30. AE, DC, DISC, MC, V. Daily 11:30am–2:30pm and 5–10pm. Closed Christmas.

The Cabbage Key Restaurant ⭐⭐⭐ AMERICAN   You can only get here by boat, but there are constant shuttles from Captiva, so get on one and experience the true meaning of cheeseburgers in paradise. Jimmy Buffet allegedly wrote his famous song here, and when you get here, you'll understand why. The cheeseburgers rock, the setting is sublime, and there are no fried foods or microwave in sight. It's a place rich in history—and in money: there are thousands of dollar bills here, signed and stuck to the walls and ceiling with masking tape.

Intracoastal Water Marker 60, North Fort Myers. © **239/283-22781**. Main courses $5–$15. Mon–Sat 7:30–9am, Sun 7:30–10am; Mon–Fri 11:15am–3pm, Sat 11:15am–4pm; Mon–Sat 6–8:30pm, Sun 6–7pm.

Captiva Sunshine Cafe ⋇ ECLECTIC   This friendly, open-kitchen cafe has only 12 tables—five of them inside, seven on the shopping center's porch—but the food is worth the claustrophobia. Everything except the bread is prepared on the premises; all of it is available for takeout. Specialties are steak, fish, and shrimp from a wood-fired grill. The portions are as big as the prices are high here; in fact, appetizers such as black beans and rice can make a meal for lighter appetites. Various desserts are offered daily; the apple crisp is a winner.

In Captiva Village Square, Captiva Rd. at Laika Lane. © **239/472-6200**. Reservations recommended. Main courses $23–$33; burgers $10. AE, MC, V. Daily 11:30am–3:30pm and 5–9pm.

The Green Flash ⋇ SEAFOOD   You can't miss this restaurant, which sits at the infamous "curve" where Captiva Road takes a sharp turn to the north. You won't see the real "green flash" as the sun sets here, because this modern building looks eastward across Pine Island Sound, but it does make for a nice view at lunch. And seeing the full moon turn the sound into glistening silver is worth having at least an evening drink here. The overall quality of the cuisine here is very good, and the prices are very reasonable for Captiva. Start with oysters Rockefeller or shrimp bisque. Both are house specialties, as is the garlicky grouper "café de Paris" and salmon with a dill-accented béarnaise sauce.

15183 Captiva Rd. © **239/472-3337**. Reservations recommended. Main courses $13–$22. AE, DC, DISC, MC, V. Daily 11:30am–3:30pm and 5:30–9:30pm (bar open 11:30am–9:30pm).

Mucky Duck ⋇ SEAFOOD/PUB FARE   A Captiva institution since 1976, this lively, British-style pub, named after a pub of the same name in Shakespeare's Stratford-Upon-Avon in the U.K., is the only place on either island here where you can dine right by the beach. If you don't get a real seat with this great view, the humorous staff will gladly roll a fake window over to appease you. The menu offers a selection of fresh seafood items, plus English fish and chips, steak-and-sausage pie, and a ploughman's lunch. There's also a vegetarian platter. No smoking is allowed inside. You can't make a reservation, but you can order drinks, listen to live music (Mon–Sat), and bide your wait at beachside picnic tables out front (come early for sunset).

Andy Rosse Lane (on the Gulf). © **239/472-3434**. Reservations not accepted. Lunch $5.50–$11; dinner main courses $13–$19. AE, DC, DISC, MC, V. Mon–Sat 11am–2:30pm and 5–9:30pm.

R. C. Otter's Island Eats ⋇⋇ *Value* AMERICAN   Occupying an old clapboard-sided island cottage, this Key West–style cafe brings informality and good, inexpensive food to Captiva. In contrast to the island's 15 or so formal haute-cuisine restaurants, you can dine here in your bare feet and not spend a fortune for an excellent breakfast, snack, lunch, or full meal. The tables are covered with wrapping paper, and rolls of paper towels substitute for napkins. The choice seats are under ceiling fans on the front porch or beneath umbrellas on the brick patio. In hot weather, you can opt for the air-conditioned dining room, whose walls are adorned with the works of local artists. The wide-ranging menu includes salads, hot dogs, burgers, sandwiches, stir-fries, meatloaf, country-fried steak, broiled fish, and soft-shell crabs, plus delicious nightly specials.

The island's best breakfasts are equally varied, from bacon and eggs to a seafood quesadilla. Musicians perform out in the yard every day, and you could find yourself dancing on the front porch.

11506 Andy Rosse Lane. (C) 239/395-1142. Reservations not accepted, but call for preferred seating. Main courses $10–$20; breakfast $6–$12; salads, sandwiches, and burgers $6–$12. AE, DISC, MC, V. Daily 7:30am–10pm (breakfast to 11:30am).

SANIBEL & CAPTIVA ISLANDS AFTER DARK

You won't find glitzy nightclubs on these family-oriented islands, but night owls do have some fun places to roost at the resorts and restaurants mentioned above. Here's a brief recap:

ON SANIBEL   The Sundial Beach Resort's **Beaches Bar & Grill,** 1451 Middle Gulf Dr. (© 239/472-4151), features entertainers during dinner, then live bands for dancing from 9pm on. The **Patio Lounge,** in the Jacaranda, 1223 Periwinkle Way (© 239/472-1771), attracts an affluent crowd of middle-agers and seniors to its live music every evening. **McT's Tavern,** 1523 Periwinkle Way (© 239/ 472-3161), has darts, video games, and a large-screen TV for sports fans. The **Sanibel Grill,** 703 Tarpon Bay Rd. (© 239/472-4453), and the two **Lazy Flamingo** branches (see "Where to Dine," above) are other popular sports bars.

The Pirate Players, a group of professional actors, perform Broadway dramas and comedies from November to April in Sanibel's state-of-the-art, 150-seat **J. Howard Wood Theatre,** 2200 Periwinkle Way (© 239/472-4109). The **Old Schoolhouse Theater,** 1905 Periwinkle Way (© 239/472-6862; www.old schoolhousetheater.com), complements its neighbor by offering Broadway musicals and revues from December to April. Call for the current schedule and prices.

ON CAPTIVA   Local songwriters perform their works nightly at **R. C. Otter's Island Eats,** 11500 Andy Rosse Lane (© 239/395-1142). The **Crow's Nest Lounge,** in the 'Tween Waters Inn, on Captiva Road (© 239/472-5161), is Captiva's top nightspot for dancing. **Chadwick's Lounge,** at the entrance to the South Seas Resort (© 239/472-5111), has a large dance floor and music from 9pm on.

NEARBY ISLAND HOPPING

Sanibel and Captiva are jumping-off points for island-hopping boat trips to barrier islands and keys teeming with ancient legends and Robinson Crusoe–style beaches. You don't have to get completely lost out there, however, because several islets have comfortable inns and restaurants. The trip across shallow Pine Island Sound is itself a sightseeing adventure, with playful dolphins surfing on the boats' wakes and a variety of cormorants, egrets, frigate birds, and (in winter) rare white pelicans flying above or lounging on sandbars between meals.

Captiva Cruises (© 239/472-5300; www.captivacruises.com) has daily trips from the South Seas Resort on Captiva. One vessel goes daily to Cabbage Key, departing at 10:30am and returning at 3:30pm. It stops at Useppa Island going and coming Tuesday through Sunday. During the winter months, another goes to Boca Grande by way of Cayo Costa State Park, departing Tuesday through Saturday at 10:30am and returning at 4pm. These day trips cost $28 for adults, $15 for children ages 6 through 12 to Cabbage Key or Useppa; $35 for adults, $18 for children ages 6 through 12 to Boca Grande or Cayo Costa. Reservations are required.

From Pine Island off Fort Myers, you can take **Tropic Star Cruises'** daily ferry service (© 239/283-0015; www.tropicstarcruises.com) to Cayo Costa (p. 358).

Fun Fact **Where Chocolate Grows on Trees**

From December through February, the area's Black Sapote trees bear a most interesting fruit. Known as the "chocolate pudding fruit," it is round with thin olive-green skin and has a mass of glossy, chocolate-colored pulp that's soft, sweet, and mild, very much like pudding. It is also a tasty and healthy dessert, a delicious pie filling, or an exotic tropical beverage when mixed with pineapple juice. The **Sunburst Tropical Fruit Company** (© 239/283-1200), on Pine Island, has the fruit for sale so you needn't go picking in the trees.

CABBAGE KEY ★★
You never know who's going to get off a boat at 100-acre Cabbage Key and walk unannounced into the funky **Cabbage Key Inn** ★★, a rustic house built in 1938 by the son and daughter-in-law of mystery novelist Mary Roberts Rinehart. Ernest Hemingway liked to hang out here in the early days, and novelist John D. MacDonald was a frequent guest 30 years later. Today, you could find yourself rubbing elbows at the bar with the likes of Walter Cronkite, Ted Koppel, Sean Connery, or Julia Roberts. Singer and avid yachtie Jimmy Buffett likes Cabbage Key so much that it inspired his hit song "Cheeseburger in Paradise."

A path leads from the tiny marina across a lawn dotted with coconut palms to this white clapboard house that sits atop an ancient Calusa shell mound. Guests dine in the comfort of two screened porches and seek libations in the Rineharts' library-turned-bar, its pine-paneled walls now plastered with dollar bills left by visitors. The straight-back chairs and painted wooden tables show their age, but that's part of Cabbage Key's laid-back, don't-give-a-you-know-what charm.

In addition to the famous thick, juicy cheeseburgers so loved by Jimmy Buffett (and erroneously thought by the misinformed to have hailed from Key West), the house specialties are fresh broiled fish and shrimp steamed in beer. Lunches range from $5 to $10; main courses at dinner, $15 to $25.

Most visitors come out here for the day, but if you want to stay overnight, the Cabbage Key Inn has six rooms and six cottages. The more expensive cottages, four of which have kitchens, are preferable to the rooms. Although the units have private bathrooms and air conditioners, they are very basic by today's standards, and some of their original 1920s furnishings have seen better days. Service for overnight guests can leave a lot to be desired, and there's no place on the islet to buy snacks or sundries. If you do decide to rough it, rates are $89 single or double for rooms, $145 to $239 for cottages. For information or reservations, contact Cabbage Key Inn, P.O. Box 200, Pineland, FL 33945 (© **239/283-2278;** fax 239/283-1384; www.cabbage-key.com).

Captiva Cruises (© 239/472-5300; www.captivacruises.com) goes to Cabbage Key daily from Captiva Island, charging $28 for adults, $15 for children ages 6 through 12 (reservations are required). You can also get here from Pine Island via **Tropic Star Cruises** (© **239/283-0015;** www.tropicstarcruises.com), which depart from Knight's Landing marina daily (p. 327). Fares are $25 for adults, $15 for children under 7. Call for departure times. You can also get here from Pine Island with **Island Charters** (© **800/340-3321** or 239/283-1113).

Fishing with the Bushes

Former President George Bush, present President George W. Bush, Florida Governor Jeb Bush—indeed, the entire Bush clan—like to retreat to **Boca Grande** ✿✿ for a little rest and relaxation every now and then. And well they should, for this charming village on Gasparilla Island is a head-of-state's kind of place. The du Ponts, the Astors, the Morgans, the Vanderbilts, and other moneyed folk started coming here in the 1920s and still turn the island into a Florida version of Nantucket during their winter "social season." In addition to the warm weather, the lure was then, and still is, some of the world's best tarpon fishing. Descendants of the watermen who were here first still guide the rich and famous. They live in modest homes on streets named Dam-If-I-Know, Dam-If-I-Care, and Dam-If-I-Will. You can see their backyards full of boats and fishnets, but high hedges hide the manicured "beachfronter" mansions over by the Gulf.

You can explore the little village in a few hours on foot or on a bike rented from **Island Bike 'n' Beach,** 333 Park Ave. (© 941/964-0711). The pink-brick **Railroad Depot,** at the corner of Park Avenue and 4th Street, has been restored to the turn-of-the-20th-century grandeur it enjoyed when the rich arrived by train. It now houses a cluster of upscale boutiques and the **Loose Caboose** restaurant and ice-cream parlor (© 941/964-0440), where movie stars have been seen satiating their sweet

CAYO COSTA ✿✿✿

Short of Tom Hanks in *Castaway,* you can't get any more deserted than at **Cayo Costa State Park** ✿✿✿ (pronounced *Kay*-oh *Cos*-tah), which occupies a 2,132-acre, completely unspoiled barrier island with miles of white-sand beaches, pine forests, mangrove swamps, oak-palm hammocks, and grasslands. Other than natural wildlife, the only permanent residents here are park rangers.

Day-trippers can bring their own supplies and use a picnic area with pavilions. A free tram carries visitors from the sound-side dock to the Gulf beach. The state maintains 12 very basic cabins and a primitive campground on the northern end of the island near Johnson Shoals, where the shelling is spectacular. Cabins cost $20 a day, and campsites are $13 a day year-round. For camping or cabin reservations, call © 800/326-3521 or go to www.reserveamerica. com. There's running water on the island but no electricity.

The park is open daily from 8am to sundown. There's a $1-per-person honor-system admission fee for day visitors. You can rent single-seat kayaks for $35 a day, $45 a day for two-seaters; for reservations, call the *Tropic Star* on Pine Island (© 239/283-0015; www.tropicstarcruises.com).

For more information contact **Cayo Costa State Park,** P.O. Box 1150, Boca Grande, FL 33921 (© 941/964-0375; www.floridastateparks.org/cayocosta). Office hours are Monday through Friday from 8am to 5pm.

UPPER (NORTH) CAPTIVA

Cut off by a pass from Captiva, its northern barrier-island sibling is occupied by the upscale resort of **North Captiva Island Club,** P.O. Box 1000, Pineland, FL teeth. **Banyan Street** (actually 2nd St.) is canopied with tangled banyan trees and is one of the prettiest places for a stroll. The **Johann Fust Community Library,** at Gasparilla Road and 10th Street (© 941/964-2488), contains the extraordinary **Du Pont Shell Collection,** gathered by Henry Francis du Pont during nearly 50 years of combing the island's beaches. At the island's south end, **Boca Grande Lighthouse Museum and Visitor's Center** (© 941/964-0060) occupies the wood-frame lighthouse that began marking the pass into Charlotte Harbor in 1890. Exhibits explain the island's history, its tarpon fishing, and its wildlife and seashells. The white-sand beaches of **Gasparilla Island State Recreation Area** (© 941/964-0375; www.floridastateparks.org/gasparillaisland) trim the lighthouse.

Captiva Cruises (© 239/472-5300) has daily trips here during the winter season (see "Nearby Island Hopping, above"). The fare is $35 for adults, $18 for children under 7, and reservations are required. *Tropic Star* cruises (© 239/283-0015; www.tropicstarcruises.com) come here daily from Pine Island off Fort Myers (p. 327). Fares are $25 for adults and $15 for children ages 6 through 12. Call for departure times.

For more information, contact the **Boca Grande Area Chamber of Commerce,** 5800 Gasparilla Rd. (P.O. Box 704), Boca Grande, FL 33921 (© 941/964-0568; fax 941/964-0620; www.bocagrandechamber.com).

33945 (© **800/576-7343** or 239/395-1001; fax 239/472-5836; www.north captiva.com). Despite the development, however, about 750 of the island's 1,000 acres are included in a state preserve. The club rents accommodations ranging from efficiencies to luxury homes. There's scheduled water-taxi service from **Jensen's Twin Palms Marina** on Captiva (© **239/472-5800**), or you can get here from Matson Marine on Pine Island with **Island Charters** (© **800/ 340-3321** or 239/283-1113). Both charge $25 per person round-trip.

USEPPA ISLAND

Useppa was a refuge of President Theodore Roosevelt and his tarpon-loving industrialist friends at the turn of the 20th century. New York advertising magnate Barron G. Collier bought the island in 1906 and built a lovely wooden home overlooking Pine Island Sound. His mansion is now the **Collier Inn,** where day-trippers and overnight guests can partake of lunches and seafood dinners in a country-club ambience. They can also visit the **Useppa Museum,** which explains the island's history and displays 4,000-year-old Calusa artifacts. Admission is by $2 donation.

The Collier Inn is the centerpiece of the **Useppa Island Club,** an exclusive development with more than 100 luxury homes, all in the clapboard-sided, tin-roofed style of Old Florida. For information, rates, and reservations, contact **Collier Inn & Cottages,** P.O. Box 640, Bokeelia, FL 33922 (© **888/735-6335** or 239/283-1061; fax 239/283-0290; www.useppa.com).

Bokeeli-huh?

In Spanish, it means "little mouth," but in terms of traveling through Southwest Florida, *Bokeelia* means heaven. Located west of Fort Myers on the northern tip of Charlotte Harbor, Bokeelia joins Pine Island and St. James City as peaceful places where they've yet to pave paradise and put up a Starbucks. The Bokeelia Tarpoon Inn, 8241 Main St. (© **866/TARPON2** or 239/283-8961), is located in the historic Poe Johnson House, whose lineage dates back to 1914. Revamped without ruining its historic charm, the six room inn features pine floors and walls, a fireplace, Indonesian wicker furniture, and spacious rooms with louvered shutters and plush queen-size beds. Because the waters around here are swimming with tarpon, among other fish, the inn has a fly-tying room where a local fisherman demonstrates the finer points of fly-fishing. The inn will also arrange for boat charters. Complimentary breakfast, wine, and hors d'oeuvres, as well as the stunning views of Boca Grande and Charlotte Harbor leave you with no reason to leave this little, unfettered piece of Starbucks-free paradise.

4 Naples ★★★

42 miles S of Fort Myers, 106 miles W of Miami, 185 miles S of Tampa

Ah, sleepy, swanky Naples. A place that may have defined the meaning of R&R, considering the fact that there's not much to do here besides linger on the beach, play golf, and dream that this isn't just a vacation but a way of life, Naples is easily Southwest Florida's most sophisticated city. And while Naples has its requisite waterfront mansions, sprawling country club fairways, and a thoroughfare of pricey boutiques and restaurants, it's not nearly as upper crusty as, say, Palm Beach or Beverly Hills. Although the people are indeed very Ralph Lauren upper crusty types, heavy on the starch, the snobbery factor and upper tax bracket lockjaw is conspicuously absent here, unlike how people usually characterize the east coast of Florida, which is just as monied, but nowhere near as friendly or laid back.

Don't even think of thumbing your nose at the long-bearded man dressed in ratty shorts and a Hawaiian T-shirt until you make sure he doesn't hop into a Bentley or zillion-dollar yacht. Therein lies the beauty of Naples. People are wealthy here, but have no need to flaunt it. What they do flaunt are St. Tropez tans and a general joie de vivre. And leave the kids at home. Even though there's a zoo and a teddy bear museum here, it's not a place where the little ones will have fun. Your relaxation *will* be disturbed when little Johnny and Jane start tugging at your shirt whining of boredom. Naples is a romantic spot for couples; it's not a swinging singles scene whatsoever. In fact, this is the kind of city where the young singles need to try out for reality shows in order to find a mate. But you never know if the Mr. or Ms. Howell sitting at the bar is recently divorced and looking for a companion to share their wealth. The median age in Naples can't be much lower than 45, but Naples itself isn't a spring chicken, either.

Naples was born in 1886, when a group of 12 Kentuckians and Ohioans bought 8,700 acres fronted by a gorgeous beach, laid out a town, and started selling lots. They built a pier and the 16-room Naples Hotel, whose first guest

Naples

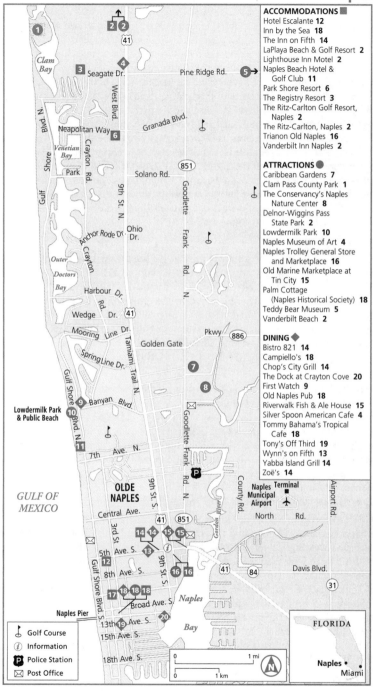

ACCOMMODATIONS ■
Hotel Escalante **12**
Inn by the Sea **18**
The Inn on Fifth **14**
LaPlaya Beach & Golf Resort **2**
Lighthouse Inn Motel **2**
Naples Beach Hotel &
  Golf Club **11**
Park Shore Resort **6**
The Registry Resort **3**
The Ritz-Carlton Golf Resort,
  Naples **2**
The Ritz-Carlton, Naples **2**
Trianon Old Naples **16**
Vanderbilt Inn Naples **2**

ATTRACTIONS ●
Caribbean Gardens **7**
Clam Pass County Park **1**
The Conservancy's Naples
  Nature Center **8**
Delnor-Wiggins Pass
  State Park **2**
Lowdermilk Park **10**
Naples Museum of Art **4**
Naples Trolley General Store
  and Marketplace **16**
Old Marine Marketplace at
  Tin City **15**
Palm Cottage
  (Naples Historical Society) **18**
Teddy Bear Museum **5**
Vanderbilt Beach **2**

DINING ◆
Bistro 821 **14**
Campiello's **18**
Chop's City Grill **14**
The Dock at Crayton Cove **20**
First Watch **9**
Old Naples Pub **18**
Riverwalk Fish & Ale House **15**
Silver Spoon American Cafe **4**
Tommy Bahama's Tropical
  Cafe **18**
Tony's Off Third **19**
Wynn's on Fifth **13**
Yabba Island Grill **14**
Zoë's **14**

Clam Bay
Seagate Dr.
Pine Ridge Rd.
West Blvd.
Granada Blvd.
Neapolitan Way
Venetian Bay Park
Solano Rd.
Gulf Shore Blvd. N.
Crayton Rd.
9th St. N.
Goodlette Frank Rd. N.
Ohio Dr.
Anchor Rode Dr.
Outer Doctors Bay
Harbour Dr.
Wedge Dr.
Mooring Line Dr.
Spring Line Dr.
Golden Gate Pkwy
Banyan Blvd.
Lowdermilk Park & Public Beach
7th Ave. N.

GULF OF MEXICO

OLDE NAPLES
Central Ave.
3rd St.
5th Ave. S.
8th Ave. S.
13th Ave. S.
15th Ave. S.
18th Ave. S.
9th St. S.
Gulf Shore Blvd. S.
Broad Ave. S.
Naples Pier
Naples Bay
Gordon River
County Rd.
Naples Municipal Airport
North Rd.
Airport Rd.
Davis Blvd.
Tamiami Trail N.
Naples Terminal

♪ Golf Course
ⓘ Information
🅿 Police Station
✉ Post Office

0   1 mi
0   1 km

FLORIDA
Naples ●
Miami

was President Grover Cleveland's sister Rose. She and other notables soon built a line of beach homes known as "Millionaires' Row." Today that area is known as Olde Naples and is carefully protected by its modern residents. Despite a recent building boom that has expanded the city to the north and east, the original settlement still retains the air of that time a century ago.

Although high-rise buildings now line the beaches north of the old town, the newer sections of Naples still have their charm, thanks to Ohio manufacturer Henry B. Watkins Sr. In 1946, Watkins and his partners bought the old hotel and all the town's undeveloped land and laid out the Naples Plan, which created the very wealthy but environmentally conscious city you see today.

About 4 miles north of Olde Naples, Vanderbilt Beach has a more traditional beach-resort character than the historic district. Lined with a mix of two-story, 1960s-style motels and high-rise hotels and condominiums, the main beach here sits like an island of development between two preserved areas: Delnor-Wiggins Pass State Park to the north, and a county reserve fronting the expensive Pelican Bay golf-course community to the south.

ESSENTIALS

GETTING THERE Most visitors arrive at the **Southwest Florida International Airport,** 35 miles north of Naples in Fort Myers (p. 320). **Naples Municipal Airport,** on North Road off Airport-Pulling Road (© 239/643-6875; www.flynaples.com), is served by the commuter arms of **American** (© 800/433-7300) and **United/US Airways** (© 800/428-4322), which means you'll have to change planes in Miami, Tampa, or Orlando. Taxis await all flights outside the small terminal building. **Avis** (© 800/331-1212), **Budget** (© 800/527-0700), **Hertz** (© 800/654-3131), and **National** (© 800/CAR-RENT) have booths at the airport. **Enterprise** (© 800/325-8007) is in town.

VISITOR INFORMATION The most comprehensive source of information is the **Naples Area Chamber of Commerce,** which maintains a visitor center at 895 5th Ave. S. (at U.S. 41), Naples, FL 34102 (© **239/262-6141;** fax 239/435-9910; www.napleschamber.org). The center has a host of free information and phones for making hotel reservations, and it sells a detailed street map for $2. By mail, it will send you a free list of accommodations and other basic information, or you can order a complete Naples vacation packet for $8 ($12 to Canada and other countries) and the street map for $5. The visitor center is open Monday through Saturday from 9am to 5pm.

GETTING AROUND The **Naples Trolley** (© **239/262-7300;** www.naplestrolleytours.com) clangs around 25 stops between the Naples Trolley General Store and Welcome Center, 1010 6th Ave. S. at 10th Street South (2 blocks west of Tin City in Olde Naples), and Vanderbilt Beach Monday through Saturday from 8:30am to 5:15pm and Sunday from 10:15am to 5:15pm. Daily fares are $17 for adults, $7 for children 4 to 12, free for children under 4, with free reboarding. Schedules are available in brochure racks in the lobbies of most hotels and motels. The drivers provide narration, so the entire loop makes a good 2-hour sightseeing tour.

For taxis, call **Yellow Cab** (© **239/262-1312**), **Checker Cab** (© **239/455-5555**), **Maxi Taxi** (© **239/262-8977**), or **Naples Taxi** (© **239/775-0505**).

HITTING THE BEACH

Unlike many Florida cities where you have to drive over to a barrier island to reach the beach, this city's beach is right in Olde Naples. And rather than being fronted by tall condominium buildings, here, the mansions along Millionaires'

Row form the backdrop. Access to the gorgeous white sand is at the Gulf end of each avenue, although parking in the neighborhood can be brutal. Try the metered lots on 12th Avenue South near the **Naples Pier,** the town's most popular beaching spot (see "Exploring the Town," below), where there are also restrooms and a food concession. Families gather on the beach north of the pier, while local, bored teens aimlessly congregate on the south side.

Also popular, the very Norman Rockwellian **Lowdermilk Park,** on Millionaires' Row at Gulf Shore Boulevard and North Banyan Boulevard, has a pavilion, restrooms, showers, a refreshment counter, professional-quality volleyball courts (the area's best players practice here), a duck pond, and picnic tables. There's also metered parking, so bring quarters. A few blocks farther north is another metered parking lot with beach access beside the Naples Beach Hotel & Golf Resort, 851 Gulf Shore Blvd. N., at Golf Drive.

Nature lovers head to the Pelican Bay development north of the historic district and the popular **Clam Pass County Park** ★★ (© **239/353-0404**). A free tram takes you along a 3,000-foot boardwalk winding through mangrove swamps and across a back bay to a beach of fine white sand. It's a strange sight, what with high-rise condominiums standing beyond the mangrove-bordered backwaters, but this actually is a miniature wilderness. Some 6 miles of canoe and kayak trails—with multitudes of birds and an occasional alligator—run from Clam Pass into the winding streams. The beach pavilion here has a bar—drinking is a sport in Naples—restrooms with foot showers only, picnic tables, and beach equipment rentals, including one- and two-person kayaks and 12-foot canoes. Entry is from a metered parking lot beside The Registry Resort at the end of Seagate Drive. There's a $4-per-vehicle parking fee. You can push, but not ride, bicycles on the boardwalk.

At Vanderbilt Beach, about 4 miles north of Olde Naples, the **Delnor-Wiggins Pass State Park** ★★★, at the west end of Bluebill Avenue–111th Avenue North (© **239/597-6196;** www.floridastateparks.org/delnor-wiggins), has been listed among America's top 10 stretches of sand. It has bathhouses, a boat ramp, and the area's best picnic facilities. A concessionaire sells hot dogs, sandwiches, and ice cream and rents beach chairs, umbrellas, kayaks, canoes, and snorkeling gear. Fish viewing is great over a small reef under 12 feet of water about 150 feet offshore. Fishing from the beach is excellent here, too. Rangers provide nature tours throughout the year, with the most interesting during the Loggerhead turtle nesting season from June to October (call or check the website for the schedule). People nesting season is in the winter, when most Naples residents are at their winter homes. Naples is *very* seasonal.

The area is open daily from 8am to sunset. Admission is $2 per vehicle with one occupant, $5 for vehicles with two to eight occupants, and $1 for pedestrians and bikers. To get here from Olde Naples, go north on U.S. 41 about 4 miles and take a left on 111th Avenue, which turns into Bluebill Avenue before reaching the beach. Note that 111th Avenue is known as Immokalee Road east of U.S. 41.

OTHER OUTDOOR ACTIVITIES

BOATING   Powerboat and WaveRunner rentals are available from **Club Nautico,** at the Boat Haven Marina, 1484 E. Tamiami Trail (© **239/417-3474**), on the east bank of the Gordon River behind Kelly's Fish House; and from **Port-O-Call Marina,** also behind Kelly's Fish House (© **239/774-0479**).

CRUISES   The Gordon River and Naples Bay from the U.S. 41 bridge on 5th Avenue South to the Gulf are prime territory for sightseeing, dolphin-watching, and sunset cruises. Day Star Charters is a great outfit featuring the double-decked *Double Sunshine* (© 239/263-4949), which sallies forth onto the river and bay daily from Tin City, where it has a ticket office. The 1½-hour cruises usually leave at 10am, noon, 2pm, and an hour before sunset. They cost $23 for adults and $12 for children under 12.

The *Sweet Liberty* (© 239/793-3525; www.sweetliberty.com), a 53-foot sailing catamaran, makes 3-hour morning shelling cruises to Keewaydin Island. The vessel then spends the afternoon on 2-hour sightseeing cruises (you'll usually see dolphins playing in the river on this one) and 2-hour sunset cruises on Naples Bay before docking at Boat Haven Marina on the east side of the Gordon River Bridge. Shelling cruises cost $35 for adults, $15 for children 12 and under; sightseeing and sunset cruises cost $25 for adults, $15 for children 12 and under.

For a good deal more luxury, the 83-foot *Naples Princess* (© 800/728-2970 or 239/649-2275; www.naplesprincesscruises.com) has narrated breakfast, lunch, and sunset dinner cruises from Port-O-Call Marina, on the eastern shore of the Gordon River. With extensive buffets, the sightseeing, lunch, sunset, and dinner cruises are good values at $24, $30, $31, and $44 to $50 per person, respectively. Call for schedules and reservations.

FISHING The locals like to fish from the **Naples Pier** (see "Exploring the Town," below). The pier has tables on which to clean your catch, but watch out for the ever-present pelicans, which are master thieves. You can buy tackle and bait from the local marinas (see "Boating," above). The pier is open around the clock, and admission is free. No fishing license is required.

The least expensive way for singles, couples, and small families to fish without paying for an entire boat is on the 45-foot *Lady Brett* (© 239/263-4949), which makes two daily half-day trips from Tin City for $50 for adults, $45 for kids under 12. Rod, reel, bait, and fishing license are included, but bring your own drinks and lunch. Its sister boat, the *Captain Paul,* goes on half-day backcountry fishing trips, departing daily at 9am. These cost $45 for adults, $40 for children 12 and under.

A number of charter boats are based at the marinas mentioned under "Boating," above; call or visit them for booking information and prices.

GOLF Naples has an extraordinary number of fine golf courses for a city its size. Most are out in the suburbs, but not the flat but challenging 18 holes at the **Naples Beach Hotel & Golf Club** 🏌🏌 (p. 369), which are right in the middle of town. Nonguests can play here, but call ahead for a tee time.

Two of the best-known courses are **Lely Flamingo Island Club** 🏌🏌 and the **Lely Mustang Golf Club,** both on U.S. 41 between Naples and Marco Island (© 800/388-GOLF or 239/793-2223). Robert Trent Jones Sr. designed the Lely Flamingo course, and its hourglass fairways and fingerlike bunkers present many challenges. Designed by Lee Trevino, the Lely Mustang course is more forgiving but still fun. Former PGA Tour player Paul Trittler has his golf school at these courses. You'll pay a price here in winter, when 18-hole fees are about $135 at Lely Flamingo and $150 at Lely Mustang, including cart and range balls, but they drop progressively after Easter to about $40 and $50, respectively, in the muggy summer months.

Boyne South, on U.S. 41 between Fla. 931 and Fla. 92 (© 239/732-5108), is another winner, with lots of wildlife inhabiting its many lakes (a 16-ft. alligator reportedly resides near the 17th hole). There are a driving range, practice facility, and restaurant; instruction is available. Wintertime fees are about $70, but in the off season they drop to $45 or less. Tee times are taken up to 4 days in advance.

Another local favorite is the player-friendly **Hibiscus Golf Club,** ½ mile east of U.S. 41 off Rattlesnake Hammock Road in East Naples (© **239/774-0088**). A pro shop and teaching professional are available. Fees are about $70 in winter, cart included, dropping to about $30 in summer.

At the intersection of Vanderbilt Beach and Airport-Pulling Roads, the Greg Norman–designed 27 championship holes at the **Tiburón Golf Club** ★★, 2620 Tiburón Dr. (© **877/WCI-PLAY** or 239/594-2040), play like a British Open course—but without the thick-thatch rough. Fees reach $200 in winter but drop as low as $70 in summer. The course is home to the **Rick Smith Golf Academy** (© **877/464-6531** or 239/593-1111) and The Ritz-Carlton Golf Resort, Naples (p. 371).

The area also has several other courses worth playing, most described in the Naples–Fort Myers edition of the *Golfer's Guide* available at the chamber of commerce visitor center (or check the magazine's website at www.golfersguide. com). On the Web, www.naplesgolf.com is also a good source of information about area courses.

SCUBA DIVING   Kevin Sweeney's **SCUBAdventures,** 971 Creech Rd., at Tamiami Trail (© **239/434-7477;** www.scubadventureslc.com), which also has a base on Marco Island (see section 5, later in this chapter), takes divers into the Gulf, teaches diver-certification courses, and rents watersports equipment.

TENNIS   In Olde Naples, the city's **Cambier Park Tennis Center** ★★, 755 8th Ave. S., at 9th Street South (© **239/213-3060;** www.cambiertennis.com), is one of the country's finest municipal facilities. In fact, it matches those found at many luxury resorts. Play on its 12 lighted clay courts costs $25 an hour. Book at the pro shop upstairs in the modern building, which has restrooms but no showers. The shop is open Monday through Friday from 8am to 9pm, Saturday and Sunday from 8am to 5pm.

WATERSPORTS   **Naples Watersports,** 550 Port A Call Way (© **239/774-0479**), will hook you up with WaveRunners, jet skis, and all requisite water toys. Hobie Cats and windsurfers can also be rented on the beach at the **Naples Beach Hotel & Golf Club,** 851 Gulf Shore Blvd. N. (© **239/261-2222**), and at **Clam Pass County Park,** at the end of Seagate Drive (© **239/353-0404**). See p. 363 for more about Clam Pass.

EXPLORING THE TOWN
OLDE NAPLES ★★★
Its history may go back only to 1886, but the beach skirting **Olde Naples** still has the charm of that Victorian era. The heart of the district lies south of 5th Avenue South (that's where U.S. 41 takes a 45-degree turn). The town docks are on the bay side, the stunning **Naples Beach** along the Gulf. Laid out on a grid, the tree-lined streets run between many houses, some dating from the town's beginning, and along Millionaires' Row between Gulf Shore Boulevard and the beach. With these gorgeous homes virtually hidden in the palms and casuarinas, Naples Beach seems a century removed from the high-rise condominiums found farther north.

The **Naples Pier,** at the Gulf end of 12th Avenue South, is a focal point of the neighborhood. Built in 1888 to let steamers land potential real-estate customers, the original 600-foot-long, T-shaped structure was destroyed by hurricanes and damaged by fire. Local residents have rebuilt it because they like strolling its length to catch fantastic Gulf sunsets—and to get a glimpse of Millionaires' Row from the Gulf side. The pier is now a state historic site. It's open 24 hours a day, but parking in the nearby lots is restricted between 11pm and 7am.

Nearby, **Palm Cottage,** 137 12th Ave. S., between 1st Street and Gordon Drive (*C* **239/261-8164**), was built in 1885 by one of Naples's founders, *Louisville Courier-Journal* publisher Walter Haldeman, as a winter retreat for his chief editorial writer. After World War II, its socialite owners hosted many galas attended by Hollywood stars such as Hedy Lamarr, Gary Cooper, and Robert Montgomery. One of the few remaining Southwest Florida houses built of tabby mortar (made by burning shells), Palm Cottage today is the home of the Naples Historical Society, which maintains it as a museum filled with authentic furniture, paintings, photographs, and other memorabilia. Tours are given during winter, Monday through Friday from 1 to 3:30pm. Adult admission is $5, free for children 12 and under.

Near the Gordon River Bridge on 5th Avenue South, the old corrugated waterfront warehouses are now a cheesy shopping-and-dining complex known as the **Old Marine Marketplace at Tin City,** which tourists throng to and local residents assiduously avoid during the winter months. It does, however, look cool from the outside.

MUSEUMS & ZOOS

Caribbean Gardens 🐾 *(Kids)*   The only zoo in Florida to have rare, Indochinese tigers and a supporting cast of lions, leopards, spotted hyenas, and African wild dogs, Caribbean Gardens is an oasis of animal activity. In addition to the standard caged animals, the zoo also has boat rides, primate islands, a large display of flora, and close encounters with kangaroos, alligators, and pythons. You can see them on a boat safari that slinks through spectacular lush tropical gardens and the islands of Lake Victoria, the place here where monkeys, lemurs, and apes call home. Everyone gets to handle some of the animals and reptiles at the "Scales & Tails" area. The Safari Canyon presentation is a cool multimedia presentation that combines video, music, and live animals that swim, leap, stalk, and slither around the natural rock-work theater that's only a splash away from the audience. You will easily fill 3 to 4 hours here. If you have kids with you, perhaps you may want to break the zoo up into several days of sightseeing so that you have something to do with them when they get antsy from swimming at the beach or pool. Should all this animal activity make you hungry, a Subway branch sells sandwiches, and there are picnic facilities on the premises.

1590 Goodlette-Frank Rd. (at Fleischmann Blvd.). *C* **239/262-5409**. www.caribbeangardens.com. Admission $16 adults, $10 children 4–15, free for children 3 and under. Daily 9:30am–5:30pm. Closed Easter, Thanksgiving, Christmas.

Naples Museum of Art ★★   If anything's a sign of the emerging sophistication of a sleepy seaside town, it's the appearance of this three-story, 30,000-square-foot art museum, attached to the Naples Philharmonic Center for the Arts. The first full-scale art museum in Southwest Florida, the Naples Museum of Art features an impressive 15 different galleries, highlighting paintings, sculptures, and drawings, with major permanent collections concentrating on both the American Modern and Ancient Chinese genres. Touring shows and exhibitions bring a welcome element of eclecticism to the museum, whose very structure, including a 90-foot by 45-foot glass dome and 14-foot entrance gates, is a dramatic work of art on its own. Tuesdays through Saturdays October through May, there are free guided tours at 11am and 2pm.

5833 Pelican Bay Blvd. (at West Blvd.). © **239/597-1900.** www.thephil.org. Admission $6 adults, $3 students. Tues–Sat 10am–4pm; Sun noon–4pm. Closed Mon, Memorial Day, July 4, Thanksgiving Day, Christmas Eve, Christmas Day, New Year's Eve, New Year's Day, and Aug 1–Labor Day.

Teddy Bear Museum *Kids* Another family favorite, this entertaining museum contains 3,000-plus examples of stuffed bears from around the world. They're displayed descending from the rafters in hot-air balloons, attending board meetings, sipping afternoon tea, and even doing bear things like hibernating. On Saturday mornings at 10:30, you can even stuff your own bear, although I'd personally rather stuff my face at breakfast somewhere. Unless you are a rabid bear fan or have kids, however, a trip to this museum is not unlike one to, say, Toys "R" Us.

2511 Pine Ridge Rd. (at Airport-Pulling Rd.). © **800/365-2327** or 239/598-2711. www.teddymuseum.com. Admission $8 adults, $6 seniors, $3 children 4–12, free for children under 4. Tues–Sat 10am–5pm. Closed New Year's Day, July 4, Thanksgiving, Christmas.

A NATURE PRESERVE

You can experience Southwest Florida's abundant natural life—and we don't mean those without silicone—without leaving town at **The Conservancy's Naples Nature Center** 🐾, 14th Avenue North, east of Goodlette-Frank Road (© **239/262-0304;** www.conservancy.org), one of two preserves operated by The Conservancy of Southwest Florida (see the Briggs Nature Center on p. 378). There are nature trails and an aviary with bald eagles and other birds. You can take 45-minute guided boat rides on the hour, between 10am and 3pm, weather permitting. The naturalist guides will explain the vegetation along the upper reaches of the Gordon River, which isn't all that interesting unless you're a vegetation fanatic, but what is interesting is the wildlife—including an occasional monkey escapee from Caribbean Gardens next door (see "Museums & Zoos," above). You can also rent canoes and kayaks and see the area by yourself. An excellent nature store carries gift items. Admission fees of $7.50 for adults and $2 for children 3 to 12 (free for children under 3) include the boat rides. Canoes and kayaks cost $15 for 2 hours, $7.50 for each additional hour. The center is open year-round Monday through Saturday from 9am to 4:30pm, and from February through April, it's also open from 1 to 5pm on Sundays. Closed July 4, Labor Day, Thanksgiving, Christmas Eve, and Christmas Day.

SHOPPING

A 2-block stretch of **3rd Street South** 🐾🐾, at Broad Avenue, aspires to be the Rodeo Drive of Naples, but with the conspicuous absence of Gucci, Prada, and Tiffany and Co., remains just an ordinary, albeit lovely, pricey place for window shopping. This glitzy collection of jewelers, clothiers, and art galleries may be too rich for many wallets, but the window-shopping here is unmatched. Be sure to pick up a free brochure from the chamber of commerce visitor center (p. 362); it lists the merchants and has a map of the area.

Nearby, the **5th Avenue South** 🐾 shopping area, between 3rd and 9th streets south, has seen a renaissance in recent years and is now Naples's hottest wining and dining spot, complete with requisite Starbucks, though the avenue is longer and a bit less chic than 3rd Street South, with stockbrokerages and real-estate offices thrown into the mix of boutiques and antiques dealers.

Also in Olde Naples, the very rustic, very tacky **Old Marine Marketplace at Tin City,** 1200 5th Ave. S., at the Gordon River (© **239/262-4200**), has 50 boutiques selling everything from souvenirs to avant-garde resort wear and imported statuary. There are more boutiques in the **Dockside Boardwalk,** a half block west on 6th Avenue South.

Even the malls in Naples have their charms. And if it rains, you will definitely want to go to the mall since there's not much to do otherwise. The **Village at Venetian Bay,** 4200 Gulf Shore Blvd., at Park Shore Drive (© **239/643-0835**), evokes images of its Italian namesake, with 50 canal-side shops featuring high-fashion men's and women's clothiers and fine-art galleries. Ornate Mediter-ranean architecture and a tropical waterfall highlight the open-air **Waterside Shops at Pelican Bay,** Seagate Drive at North Tamiami Trail (U.S. 41; © **239/598-1605**), where the anchor stores are Saks Fifth Avenue and Jacobson's. There's also a huge Barnes & Noble bookstore across Seagate Drive.

Discount shoppers can head to **Prime Outlets Naples,** on Fla. 951, about a mile south of U.S. 41 on the way to Marco Island (© **888/545-7196** or 239/775-8083; www.primeoutlets.com). The 43 shops are open from 10am to 8pm Monday through Saturday and 11am to 6pm on Sunday.

WHERE TO STAY

Branches of most chain hotels sit along U.S. 41, but these tend to be of higher quality and better value than their counterparts elsewhere in Southwest Florida.

One of the most reasonably priced of the town's many condominium com-plexes, **Park Shore Resort,** 600 Neapolitan Way, Naples, FL 34103 (© **800/548-2077** or 239/263-2222; fax 239/263-0946; www.parkshorefl.com), has 156 attractive one- and two-bedroom condominiums surrounding an artificial lagoon with waterfalls cascading on its own island. Guests can walk across a bridge to the artificial island, where they can swim in the heated pool, barbecue on gas grills, or order a meal from the restaurant or a drink from the bar. There's also once-a-day (11am) complimentary transport to the beach (to return from the beach, make a reservation at the front desk to catch a ride back at 2pm). The condo-miniums range from $145 to $260 in winter but drop to $99 to $119 off-season.

One of the biggest condominium-rental agents here is **Bluebill Properties,** 26201 Hickory Blvd., Bonita Springs, FL 33923 (© **800/237-2010** or 239/992-6620; www.naplesvacation.com).

I have organized the accommodations below geographically: in Olde Naples and north of the historic district, including Vanderbilt Beach.

IN OLDE NAPLES
Very Expensive

Hotel Escalante ★★ On the western end of the 5th Avenue shopping dis-trict and 2 blocks from the beach, this romantic boutique hotel is perfect for couples who want convenience, no crowds, and a bit of pampering. The closest thing to Italy that you'll find in Naples, *Florida,* this 71-room Mediterranean villa–style hotel is only blocks away from the beach and worlds away from the hustle and bustle of the real world, ensconced in 4 acres of lush, private gardens with over 300 species of plants, walkways of old brick from Chicago, and foun-tains from France. The large rooms and spacious one-bedroom suites are in eight one- and two-story buildings spread out over most of a city block. The cottage-like suites have private patios opening to the lush courtyards. All units are luxu-riously appointed, and the bathrooms have two hand basins, ample vanity space, and big shower heads (the majority have walk-in showers as opposed to tubs). Special services include lunch served on the beach, a day spa with facials and massage, an evening wine reception, and an honor bar and complimentary cookies in the library. Although there's no on-site restaurant, the hotel will be happy to suggest one of the 15 restaurants located within walking distance.

290 5th Ave. S., Naples, FL 34102. ℂ **877/GULF-INN** or 239/659-3466. Fax 239/262-8748. www.hotel escalante.com. 71 units. Winter $195–$655; off-season $165–$400. Rates include continental breakfast. AE, DC, DISC, MC, V. **Amenities:** Bar; heated outdoor pool; exercise room; day spa; Jacuzzi; sauna; 24-hr. room service; massage; laundry service. *In room:* A/C, TV, dataport, minibar, fridge, coffeemaker, hair dryer, iron.

The Inn on Fifth ✦

This former bank building still exudes that old money, old world European charm, but it's hardly stuffy. Located ideally on the closest thing to "happening" Fifth Avenue South, The Inn features 87 large guest rooms elegantly decorated with rich, warm tones—the antithesis of Florida decor, frankly. French doors opening to a balcony or terrace may not reveal the ocean, but you will see either the lovely pool or "action" on the Avenue. The one drawback of this place is that it's six blocks away from the beach, but that's hardly a big deal. McCable's Irish Pub downstairs is a hotbed of activity, featuring live music, a fabulous beer selection, and a youngish contingency of revelers. The Inn on Fifth is extremely relaxing, although the hotel's concierge could use a few lessons in service, being no help whatsoever when my car ran out of gas out front. That aside, it's a charming, quiet (although the third floor rooms facing the street can get a tad bit noisy between the hours of 8 and 11pm), ideally located spot that's perfect for those looking for a quiet, romantic stay with little or no fuss.

699 Fifth Ave. S., Naples, FL 34102. ℂ **888/403-8778** or 239-403-8777. Fax 239/403-8778. www.naplesinn.com. 87 units. Winter $250–$300; off-season $130–$180. Rates include continental breakfast. AE, DC, DISC, MC, V. **Amenities:** Restaurant; bar; heated outdoor pool; fitness center; spa/salon; Jacuzzi; concierge; business services; room service; laundry service. *In room:* A/C, TV, dataport, coffeemaker, hair dryer, iron, safe.

Naples Beach Hotel & Golf Club ✦✦✦ *Kids*

In contrast to The Ritz-Carlton, Naples, and The Registry Resort (see below for both), which could be anywhere, this beachy keen retro-resort definitely belongs in Olde Naples. In fact, the beachside setting on Millionaires' Row couldn't be better for carrying on the friendly and relaxed Old Florida ambience installed by Henry B. Watkins half a century ago and carried on by his family today. This is also Southwest Florida's only resort with its own 18-hole golf course, tennis center, and full-service spa right on the premises. And did we mention that it has managed to remain impervious to the sterile minimalism that has invaded most hotels today? The hotel does not look luxurious, but there are certainly aspects of luxury that are quite visible and palpable. The spa, golf club, and a restaurant are in a stunning new building across Gulf Shore Boulevard from reception. Since the hotel predates the city's strict historic-district zoning laws, it also has Olde Naples's only restaurants and bar directly on the beach. Of these, the **Sunset Beach Bar** is one of the region's most famous beachside open-air bars and is always crammed as the sun sets over the Gulf and when live bands perform on Sunday afternoons during the winter season. Facing the Gulf, the semicircular Everglades Dining Room emphasizes traditional Florida cuisine, offers a reasonably priced breakfast buffet to guests and nonguests alike, and has live entertainment and dancing Tuesday through Saturday night in winter. Complimentary afternoon tea and cookies are served in the lobby lounge, and guests can hang shopping lists on their doorknobs at night for the staff to deliver breakfast goodies from the Seminole Store, which sells inexpensive pastries, pizzas, salads, and sandwiches.

Rooms and suites are in several buildings spread over lush gardens hung with more than 5,000 orchids. The least expensive are in the Florida Wing, a two-story relic from 1948, whose recently updated rooms and suites open to a long, rail-ing-enclosed porch with views across a manicured lawn to the swimming pool by the Gulf. Units in the Tower are over the main dining room and directly across the boulevard from the golf course, tennis center, and spa. The Watkins Wing houses the most spacious suites here. Rooms in the Penthouse Wing, removed from the action at the north end of the property, directly face the beach and are the best choice for couples, especially during holidays and the summer, when many families stay here (the clientele is mostly couples at other times).

851 Gulf Shore Blvd., Naples, FL 33940. © 800/237-7600 or 239/261-2222. Fax 239/261-7380. www.naplesbeachhotel.com. 318 units. Winter $165–$320 double, $330–$525 suite; off-season $135–$225 double, $250–$310 suite. Packages available. AE, DC, DISC, MC, V. **Amenities:** 4 restaurants; 2 bars; heated Olympic-size outdoor pool; 18-hole golf course; 6 tennis courts; full-service spa; watersports equipment rental; bike rental, children's programs; game room; concierge; activities desk; salon; room service; massage; babysitting; laundry service. In room: A/C, TV, dataport, fridge, hair dryer, iron, safe.

Expensive

Trianon Old Naples ☆   Located in a quiet (read: no activity) residential neigh-borhood, this elegant Mediterranean-style building, with a classical European interior, offers convenience and comfort without a lot of frills. The spacious rooms are equipped with Ritz-Carlton–quality furniture, including mahogany armoires, chairs, and writing desks. All have seating areas and extra-large bath-rooms. Some units have balconies large enough for chairs, but others are for standing only. There's no restaurant here, but continental breakfast is served on silver in a refined lounge, where coffee and tea are available all day, and the staff will arrange for meals to be delivered from local restaurants. Champagne and port are served at a wine bar in the evenings.

955 7th Ave. S., Naples, FL 34102. © 877/482-5228 or 239/437-9600. Fax 239/261-0025. www.trianon.com. 58 units. Winter $120–$215 double, suite $210–$300; off-season $99–$125 double, suite $175–$210. Rates include continental breakfast. AE, DC, DISC, MC, V. **Amenities:** Heated outdoor pool; laundry service. In room: A/C, TV, dataport, fridge (in some units), coffeemaker, hair dryer, iron, safe.

Moderate

Inn by the Sea ☆   Listed in the National Register of Historic Places, this uber charming bed-and-breakfast, 2 blocks from the beach in the heart of Olde Naples, was built in 1937 as a boardinghouse by Alice Bowling, one of Naples's first schoolteachers and a grocer and entrepreneur to boot. The Federal-style house still has much of its original pine floors and pine or cypress ceilings and woodwork. With windows on three sides, the Sanibel on the ground floor is the lightest and airiest unit here, while the Bokeelia suite is the most romantic, with its bed set at an angle in one corner. For those looking for an even more natural setting, the one-bedroom cottage in the garden is a splendid choice. Bikes, beach chairs, and towels are provided; in season, guests are served oranges from the backyard tree. You'll have to do without a phone or TV in your room here; how-ever, there is a TV in the common living space area.

287 11th Ave. S., Naples, FL 34102. © 800/584-1268 or 239/649-4124. Fax 239/434-2842. www.innbythesea-bb.com. 5 units, 1 1-bedroom cottage. Winter $149–$189 double; off-season $94–$114 double. Rates include extended continental breakfast. AE, DISC, MC, V. Children 10 and under not accepted. **Amenities:** Access to nearby health club; free use of bikes. In room: A/C, hair dryer, no phone.

LaPlaya Beach & Golf Resort ☆☆   There is certainly no dearth of beach resorts in Naples, but what is conspicuously missing—that is until now—has been a more intimate beach resort, directly on the beach, in which you don't feel underdressed or socially inappropriate when walking through the lobby in a bathing suit cover-up. Located on pristine Vanderbilt Beach, LaPlaya Beach & Golf Resort has filled the void with plush, beautifully decorated rooms overlooking the Gulf and bay (all have a private balcony), a spectacular 4,500-square-foot spa, and a sprawling, scenic, and challenging Bob Cupp–designed golf club and the David Leadbetter Golf Academy for the novices. But let's get back to the rooms for a minute. The French country decor and goose down pillows are hardly what you'd expect at a beach resort, but there's the rub! You'll find none of that cookie-cutter, as-seen-in-*Martha-Stewart-Living* stuff here. Bathrooms are spacious and luxurious, decked out in marble and overflowing with phenomenal bath products that are tempting to take home. Everything at this resort has a distinct personality, especially the impressive staff that will go to any lengths to accommodate you without being overly doting. The house restaurant also happens to be Baleen, a la the acclaimed Miami restaurant at the Grove Isle Resort. Executive Chef Jeffrey Bowles works his culinary magic on local seafood to produce a mesmerizing dining experience.

9891 Gulf Shore Dr., Naples, FL 34108. © **800/237-6883** or 239/597-3123. Fax 239/597-6278. www.laplaya resort.com. 189 units. Winter $395–$695 double; off-season $159–$359 double; suites $495–$1,500 year round. AE, DC, DISC, MC, V. Valet parking only: $15. **Amenities:** Restaurant; bar; 4 outdoor pools; pool bar; golf course; spa; watersports equipment/rentals (parasailing, kayaking, paddle boats, jet skis); concierge; room service. *In room:* A/C, TV, dataport, minibar, coffeemaker, hair dryer, iron, safe, CD player.

NORTH OF OLDE NAPLES
Very Expensive

The Registry Resort & Club ⭐   This sports-minded luxury high-rise is not directly on the beach: Guests must ride the free Clam Pass County Park shuttle along a 3,000-foot boardwalk through mangroves to the Gulf (see "A Nature Preserve," on p. 378). Once there, they can charge lounge chairs, cabanas, watersports equipment rentals, and drinks to their rooms. To compensate for the lack of a beachside setting, the resort recently installed a big outdoor complex with two swimming pools with water slide and waterfall. Plus, there is a 15-court tennis center, one of the main draws here. Inside its architecturally nondescript modern tower, the Registry radiates a more relaxed ambience than the traditional Ritz-Carlton, but none of the Old Florida charm of its other chief rival, the Naples Beach Hotel & Golf Club (see above). Dining here is at least on a par with The Ritz-Carlton, with the magnificent **Lafite** dining room offering some of the city's finest French cuisine (open nightly during winter; only Fri–Sat evenings off-season). As for nightlife (and, yes, there is some semblance of it here), the hotel's Luna—one of the city's few and far between dance clubs—is an ultra-mod haute spot reminiscent of South Beach. There's a full-service spa here, too, but treatment rooms are on the cramped side.

475 Seagate Dr., Naples, FL 34103. © **800/247-9810** or 239/597-3232. Fax 239/597-3147. www.registry hotels.com. 474 units. Winter $395–$475 double, $460–$715 suite; off-season $160–$395 double, $205–$450 suite. $12-per-day resort amenities fee. Packages available. AE, DC, DISC, MC, V. From Olde Naples, go about 1½ miles north on U.S. 41 and turn left on Seagate Dr. Hotel is on right. **Amenities:** 6 restaurants; 4 bars; 5 heated outdoor pools; access to golf course; 15 tennis courts; health club; spa; Jacuzzi; sauna; watersports equipment rentals; bike rental; children's programs; game room; concierge; business center; salon; 24-hr. room service; massage; babysitting; laundry service. *In room:* A/C, TV, fax, dataport, minibar, kitchen (some suites), coffeemaker, hair dryer, iron, safe.

The Ritz-Carlton Golf Resort, Naples ⭐⭐⭐   This Mediterranean-style resort opened in 2001 at the 36-hole (two 18-hole courses), Greg Norman–designed Tiburón Golf Club, in an exclusive residential enclave at the intersection of Vanderbilt Beach and Airport-Pulling roads. This is a golf-lover's version of its sister resort, The Ritz-Carlton, Naples (see below), and guests here can use the spa, beach, and other facilities at its older sibling, a 5-minute drive away. Each of the spacious, luxuriously appointed guest units here has a private balcony overlooking the gorgeously landscaped course.

2600 Tiburón Dr., Naples, FL 34109. © **888/856-4372** or 239/593-2000. Fax 239/254-3300. www.ritz carlton.com. 295 units. Winter $479–$729 double, $829–$1,649 suite; off-season $229–$489 double, $389–$1,099 suite. Packages available. AE, DC, DISC, MC, V. From Olde Naples, go north 3½ miles on U.S. 41. Turn right on Vanderbilt Beach Rd. (C.R. 862), to Airport-Pulling Rd. Hotel is on left. **Amenities:** 2 restaurants; 2 bars; heated outdoor pool; 36-hole golf course; 4 tennis courts; health club; Jacuzzi; sauna; bike rentals; children's programs; game room (billiards, cards); concierge; business center; 24-hr. room service; massage; babysitting; laundry service; concierge-level rooms. *In room:* A/C, TV, dataport, minibar, hair dryer, iron, safe.

The Ritz-Carlton, Naples ☆☆☆ This opulent 14-story Mediterranean-style hotel, one of Florida's finest, is a favorite among affluent guests who like standard Ritz-Carlton amenities such as imported marble floors, antique art, Oriental rugs, Waterford crystal chandeliers, British-style afternoon tea, and a staff that starts fawning over you from the moment you arrive. Still, it lacks the wonderful, unfabricated Old Florida charm of the Naples Beach Hotel & Golf Club (see above). Nor is it as close to the beach, for guests must walk through a narrow mangrove forest to reach the sands. The beach here is part of a public park, but the hotel has staff out there to answer phones, deliver drinks and snacks, and rent cabanas, boats, and other toys (only towels, chairs, and ice water are complimentary). The plush, fully equipped guest rooms and suites overlook the Gulf, but not all have balconies. The **Dining Room,** the hotel's signature restaurant, prepares seafood with an Asian flair, while the wood-paneled **Grill Room** is a beef emporium reminiscent of a British private club. Together, they serve some of Naples's finest and most expensive cuisine. A $50 million, 51,000-square-foot full-service spa offers a host of pampering treatments. Guests here can play the golf course and use the other amenities at The Ritz-Carlton Golf Resort, Naples as well (see above).

280 Vanderbilt Beach Rd., Naples, FL 34108. © **888/856-4372** or 239/598-3300. Fax 239/598-6690. www. ritzcarlton.com. 463 units. Winter $449–$899 double, $769–$969 suite; off-season $200–$439 double, $365–$625 suite. AE, DC, DISC, MC, V. Valet parking $18; self-parking $10 in winter, free off-season. From Olde Naples, go north 3½ miles on U.S. 41. Turn left on Vanderbilt Beach Rd. (C.R. 862), to hotel on left. **Amenities:** 5 restaurants; 2 bars; 5 heated outdoor pools; access to golf course; 4 tennis courts; spa; Jacuzzi; sauna; watersports equipment rental; bike rental; children's programs; game room; concierge; business center; salon; 24-hr. room service; massage; babysitting; laundry service. *In room:* A/C, TV, dataport, minibar, hair dryer, iron.

Expensive

Vanderbilt Inn Naples ☆ Beach casual decor in the accommodations and public areas sets the tempo for a casual, fun vacation at this two-story motel right on Vanderbilt Beach, where you can go parasailing and rent boats and watersports equipment. Nature lovers can walk along the beach and into Delnor-Wiggins Pass State Park next door (p. 363). The 16 efficiencies (with kitchens) on the ends of the building open to the beach. About half of the standard motel-style rooms face a magnificently landscaped courtyard with a kidney-shaped swimming pool surrounded by a brick terrace, while the other, less-expensive units open to parking lots. Although the rooms are entered from exterior walkways, their big windows are darkly tinted to provide privacy. A thatch-roof bar and full-service outdoor restaurant serve lunches and dinners by the beach and draw a crowd for sunset happy hour. The indoor dining room, Splash, serves breakfast and dinner. Another restaurant turns lively when bands play on Friday and Saturday nights. Kids 12 and under dine free when accompanied by adults here.

11000 Gulf Shore Dr., Naples, FL 34108. ℂ **800/643-8654** or 239/597-3151. Fax 239/597-3099. www.
vanderbiltinn.com. 147 units. Winter $145–$350 double; off-season $110–$220 double. Weekly rates available. AE, DC, DISC, MC, V. From Olde Naples, go 4 miles north on U.S. 41; take a left on 111th Ave. (which
becomes Bluebill Ave.) to hotel on left. **Amenities:** 2 restaurants; 2 bars; heated outdoor pool; Jacuzzi; watersports equipment rental; business center. *In room:* A/C, TV, dataport, fridge, coffeemaker (efficiencies only),
microwave (efficiencies only), safe.

Inexpensive

Lighthouse Inn Motel   A relic from decades gone by, Judy and Buzz Dugan's
no-frills but spotlessly clean motel sits across the street from other more expensive
Gulf-side properties on Vanderbilt Beach and within walking distance of The Ritz-
Carlton, Naples. The efficiencies and apartments are simple, with cinder-block
walls and small kitchens. The one kitchenless room has a small fridge and coffeemaker, but note: No unit has a telephone, and four of them have shower-only
bathrooms. Most guests take advantage of weekly and monthly rates in winter,
when it's heavily booked. The Dugans also operate Buzz's Lighthouse Cafe next
door, a pleasant place for an inexpensive dockside breakfast, lunch, or dinner.

9140 Gulf Shore Dr. N., Naples, FL 34108. ℂ **239/597-3345.** Fax 239/597-5541. 15 units. Winter $105 double,
$110 efficiency, $120 apt; off-season $49 double, $59 efficiency, $69 apt. MC, V. From Olde Naples, go 3½ miles
north on U.S. 41; take a left on Vanderbilt Beach Rd. (C.R. 862). Turn right on Gulf Shore Dr. to hotel on right.
Amenities: Restaurant; bar; heated outdoor pool. *In room:* A/C, TV, kitchen, fridge, coffeemaker, no phone.

WHERE TO DINE

Naples's beaches are ideal for picnics. In Olde Naples, you can get freshly baked
breads and pastries, prepackaged gourmet sandwiches, and fruit plates at **Tony's
Off Third,** 1300 3rd St. S. (ℂ **239/262-7999**). **Wynn's on Fifth,** 745 5th Ave.
S. (ℂ **239/261-0901**), between 8th Street and Park Street South, has high-quality deli items, prepackaged sandwiches, salads, takeout meals, and gourmet pastries at very reasonable prices. Both have a few sidewalk tables and are fine places
for coffee or a snack while window-shopping on 3rd and 5th avenues South.

IN OLDE NAPLES
Expensive

Campiello's ⊛ ITALIAN   It's not about the homemade pasta at this see and
be scene spot in Naples, where the open air bar is command central for local
Naples luminaries and suntanned socialites and, par for the Naples course, the
martini menu is impressive, featuring over 20 creative concoctions. Daily specials
are the most interesting here, created by chef Andrew Wicklander, including fabulous wood oven pizzas and delicious pastas that you've never heard of before.

1177 Third St. (at Broad Ave.). ℂ 239/435-1166. Reservations recommended. Main courses $10–$15. AE,
DC, DISC, MC, V. Daily 11:30am–2:30pm; Sun–Thurs 5–10:30pm; Fri–Sat 5–11pm.

Chop's City Grill ⊛⊛ STEAKS/SEAFOOD   The smell of steak and money
waft through this urbane bistro that's more Miami hip than Naples nautical.
Aged, top-quality steaks and lamb chops are the house specialties, either chargrilled to perfection and served with thick onion rings and mashed potatoes, or
peppered and served with a blackberry and cabernet-wine sauce. Fresh fish from
the grill is another good choice. Asian influences appear here, too, such as deel-
ish Mongolian beef, sea scallops "shocked" in a wok with Thai curry sauce and
served over noodles with wild mushrooms and stir-fried vegetables.

837 5th Ave. S. (between 8th and 9th sts. S.). ℂ 239/262-4677. Reservations recommended. Main courses
$15–$30. AE, DC, DISC, MC, V. Sun–Thurs 5–10pm; Fri–Sat 5–11pm.

Zoë's ⊛⊛ ECLECTIC   This dimly lit mod-ish bistro draws a lively crowd of
young professionals who preen at the big bar to one side or at a raised, English

pub–style drinking table (you can dine at the table, too, which is handy if you're traveling alone since you're sure to get into conversations with your fellow guests). The eclectic menu changes every week or so to take advantage of fresh produce. Meatloaf, macaroni and cheese, and pot roast are regulars. They sound on the menu like those your mother made, but they're seasoned as lively as Zoë's patrons. If they're offered, opt for the homemade veal meatloaf, the pecan-crusted sea bass or the seared, sesame-coated yellowfin tuna served with a cucumber relish, a horseradish-tinged mayonnaise drizzle, and spicy soba noodles. Zoë's turns into a Saturday Night Fever-esque disco (with $5 cover charge) on Friday and Saturday nights.

720 5th Ave. S. (between 7th and 8th sts. S.). ℰ 239/261-1221. Reservations recommended. Main courses $15–$34. AE, MC, V. Sun–Thurs 5–10pm; Fri–Sat 5–10:30pm (music and dancing Fri–Sat 11pm–2am).

Moderate

Bistro 821 ✷ FUSION   This South Beachy bistro is an excellent choice for Mediterranean-influenced fusion cuisine. Although the quarters are too close for private conversations, small spotlights hanging from the ceiling romantically illuminate each table. The house specialty is rotisserie chicken, and a daily risotto leads a menu featuring penne pasta in a vodka sauce, and a seasonal vegetable plate with herb couscous. But in my opinion, the best dish on the menu is the rock lobster satay, with a spicy ginger and lime dipping sauce, farfalle with Alaskan King crab meat, artichoke, tomato, and a mustard cream sauce and seafood risotto. Dishes are huge, but you can order either full or half portions. There's sidewalk dining here, too.

821 5th Ave. S. (between 8th and 9th sts. S.). ℰ **239/261-5821.** Reservations recommended. Main courses $13–$26. AE, DC, MC, V. Daily 5–10pm.

The Dock at Crayton Cove ✷ *Value* SEAFOOD   Located right on the City Dock, this locals hangout is the best place in town for a super casual open-air meal or a cool drink while watching the boats go back and forth across Naples Bay. Servers are friendly and conversational, which, depending on how you look at it, can be a good or not so good thing. The chow ranges from hearty chowders by the mug to seafood with a Floribbean fare, with Jamaican-style jerk shrimp thrown in for spice; main courses are moderately priced. Grilled seafood Caesar salad and a good selection of sandwiches, hot dogs, and other pub-style fare also appear on the menu. "Margarita madness" happy hour and a half-price raw bar (don't miss the steamed mussels with French bread for dipping the garlic sauce) run daily from 9:30 to 11:30pm. The "Great Dock Canoe Race" draws thousands on the second Saturday in May.

12th Ave. S. (at the City Dock in Olde Naples). ℰ **239/263-9940.** Reservations not accepted. Main courses $11–$26; sandwiches $9–$13. AE, DISC, MC, V. Daily 11am–midnight.

Tommy Bahama's Tropical Cafe ✷✷ CARIBBEAN   You walk through a thatch gateway into this lively, island-style watering hole or upscale Margaritaville, if you will—an incongruous sight in the middle of the staid 3rd Street South shopping enclave. Diners, if not in Tommy Bahama's Indiana Jones meets Florida threads, look as if they've stepped right out of a Ralph Lauren or Abercrombie and Fitch catalog and gather on a large front patio under shade trees, where a musician performs, or inside, where a large back-wall mural creates a Polynesian scene. An open kitchen and service bar are on one side of the dining room, a real bar dispensing drinks on the other. In between, round-backed cane chairs and classic ceiling fans add to the exotic mood. Although the Jamaican pork, salmon St. Croix, and other Caribbean-style cuisine don't quite live up to the ambience, you'll have too much fun here to care whether or not it's gourmet—and the huge portions will satisfy any appetite. They don't appear on the dinner menu, but sandwiches are served if you ask for them (the meal-size grouper sandwich is a bargain at $10).

1220 3rd St. S. (between 12th and 13th aves. S.). ✆ **239/643-6889**. Reservations recommended. Main courses $17–$27; sandwiches $8–$14. AE, MC, V. Daily 11am–10pm.

Yabba Island Grill ★ *Value* CARIBBEAN Perhaps the noisiest, most crowded spot on Fifth Avenue, Yabba Island Grill attempts to channel the Caribbean with loud music, a massive bar, and a tropical decor and does a very decent job doing it. The food here makes as loud a statement as Yabba's pastel color scheme, with most items providing a riot of flavors from across the Caribbean. And if the party hearty crowd that convenes here isn't enough to entice you, consider the St. Croix Sizzler, a terrific combination of small lobster tail, a chunk of mahimahi, and mussels over a bed of peppers, onions, and a sweet mango-curry sauce. Also worthy of a repeat: the Monsoon salad consisting of grilled chicken breast, hearts of palm, candied pecans, and mushrooms under a warm bacon-and-berry vinaigrette and topped with crispy onion rings. If you're looking for a peaceful and quiet meal, get here super early—in fact, at 4:30pm, right when they open, before all the antsy vacationers looking for some action start piling in.

711 5th Ave. S. (between 8th St. S. and Park Ave. S.). ✆ **239/262-5787**. Reservations recommended. Main courses $10–$24; sandwiches $8–$10. AE, DISC, MC, V. Daily 4:30–11pm (bar to 2am Fri–Sat).

Inexpensive

Cheeburger Cheeburger ★★ *Value* Though this is a chain restaurant, with no decor to speak of, if you're hankering after a good, no, make that great, burger with a side of fries or onion rings and a milkshake, this is definitely the place to go. Choose the size burger you want (from 5 oz. to a pound!) and any of more than a dozen toppings, and enjoy (there are also salads for those who want to be healthy).

505 5th Ave. S. (between 5th and 6th sts.). ✆ **239/435-9796**. Burgers $4.25–$10.30. Daily 11am–9pm.

First Watch *Value* AMERICAN Just like its siblings elsewhere in Florida, this diner is a favorite local haunt for breakfast, late brunch, or a mid-day meal. You may have to wait for a table, but once seated, a young staff will provide quick and friendly service. The menu leans heavily on healthy selections, but you can get your cholesterol from a sizzling skillet of fried eggs served over layers of potatoes, vegetables, and melted cheese. Lunch features large salads, sandwiches, and quesadillas. In addition to the dining room, there's more seating at umbrella tables in the shopping center's courtyard.

In Gulf Shore Sq., 1400 Gulf Shore Blvd. (at Banyan Rd.). ✆ **239/434-0005**. Most items $3.50–$8. AE, DISC, MC, V. Daily 7am–2:30pm. Closed Christmas.

Old Naples Pub ★★ *Value* AMERICAN/PUB FARE You would never guess that the person sitting next to you at the bar here is a mogul of some sort, so relaxed is this small, somewhat-cramped pub in the middle of the fabulous 3rd Street South shops. Diners fortunately find more room at tables on the shopping center's patio. The menu features very good pub fare (and at extraordinarily inexpensive prices for Olde Naples), including homemade soups, nachos, burgers, and sandwiches ranging from charcoal-grilled bratwurst to fried grouper. Only six main courses are offered: platters with New York strip steak, grilled tuna, the catch of the day, fried grouper or clam strips, and baby back ribs. Best bets are the chicken salad with grapes and walnuts, and the burgers, steaks, and fish from the charcoal grill. You can catch live entertainment here nightly during winter, Wednesday through Saturday off-season.

255 13th Ave. S. (between 3rd and 4th sts. S.). ☎ **239/649-8200.** Main courses $11–$15; salads, sandwiches, and burgers $5–$9. AE, DISC, MC, V. Mon–Sat 11am–10pm; Sun noon–9pm.

North of Olde Naples

Silver Spoon American Cafe *Value* AMERICAN/ITALIAN/SOUTHWEST
Even though this member of the American Cafe chain is in the Waterside Shops complex and immediately screams TGI Friday's, it happens to be one of Naples's best dining bargains and is a perfect spot for lunch. While hardly gourmet, the food here is high quality chain restaurant cuisine. Thick sandwiches are served with french fries, spicy pecan rice, or black beans. The tomato-basil soup is worth a try, and the bruschetta appetizer—served on toasted French bread—is nearly a full meal in itself. Gourmet pizzas and pasta dishes also are popular, especially with the after-theater crowds from the nearby Philharmonic Center for the Arts. The less-expensive main courses, such as Cajun or herb-grilled chicken, are both tasty and an excellent value. Shoppers love to do lunch here, so come early or be prepared for a wait.

In the Waterside Shops at Pelican Bay, 5395 N. Tamiami Trail (at Seagate Dr.). ☎ **239/591-2123.** Reservations not accepted, but call ahead for preferred seating. Main courses $9.50–$15; pizza and pasta $8–$12; soups, salads, and sandwiches $7–$9. AE, DC, DISC, MC, V. Sun–Thurs 11am–10pm; Fri–Sat 11am–11pm. From Olde Naples, go north on U.S. 41 and left on Seagate Dr. right into shopping center. Go right at dead end to restaurant on left.

NAPLES AFTER DARK

For entertainment ideas, check the *Naples Daily News* (www.naplesnews.com), especially the "Neapolitan" section in Friday's edition.

PERFORMING ARTS   Known locally as "The Phil," the impressive **Philharmonic Center for the Arts** ☆☆, 5833 Pelican Bay Blvd., at West Boulevard (☎ **800/597-1900** or 239/597-1900; www.thephil.org), is the home of the Naples Philharmonic, but its year-round schedule is filled with cultural events, concerts by celebrated artists and internationally known orchestras, and Broadway plays and shows aimed at children and families. Call or check the website for its seasonal calendar.

A fine local theater group, the **Naples Players,** holds their winter-season performances in the new Sugden Community Theatre, 701 5th Ave. S. (☎ **239/263-7990;** www.naples.net/presents/theatre). Tickets can be hard to come by, so call well in advance.

THE CLUB & BAR SCENE   Remember: Naples is not South Beach nor does it portend to be. It does, however, realize that some people like to party well past the early bird hours and, as a result, there are a few good spots here to get your groove on. The restaurants and bistros along 5th Avenue South are popular watering holes, especially for young professional singles who make this their "meat market" on Friday nights. **Zoë's,** 720 5th Ave. S. (☎ **239/261-1221;** see "Where to Dine," above), turns into a high-energy nightclub Friday and Saturday from 10:30pm to 2am. Nearby, **McCabe's Irish Pub,** 699 5th Ave. S. (☎ **239/403-7170**), features traditional Irish music nightly. For a lot of camp with your cabaret, the **Ridgway Bar and Grill,** 3rd Street South and 13th Avenue (☎ **239/262-5500**), is a hot spot thanks to pianist Jim Badger, whose bawdy shows bring in crowds of all ages (under 18 not recommended).

In the 3rd Street South shopping area, **Old Naples Pub,** 255 13th Ave. S. (☎ **239/649-8200**), has live music nightly during winter, Wednesday through Saturday nights off-season. See "Where to Dine," above.

The touristy **Old Marine Marketplace at Tin City,** comprised of the restored waterfront warehouses on 5th Avenue South on the west side of the Gordon River, comes alive during the winter when visitors flock to its shops and the **Riverwalk Fish & Ale House** (✆ **239/262-2734**), which has live entertainment during the season.

Some of the hotels mentioned earlier in this section have entertainment throughout the year. The beachside "chickee hut" bar at the **Naples Beach Hotel & Golf Club** (✆ **239/261-2222**) is always popular, has live entertainment many nights, and is *the* place to go on Sunday afternoon and early evening. So is the beachside bar at the **Vanderbilt Inn Naples** (✆ **239/597-3151**).

5 Marco Island

15 miles SE of Naples, 53 miles S of Fort Myers, 100 miles W of Miami

Marco Island is reminiscent of a sleepy, albeit swanky, beachfront retirement community. When the sun goes down, you can hear a pin drop, though. There is absolutely no life after dark here, but still Captain William Collier would hardly recognize Marco Island if he were to come back from the grave today. No relation to Collier County founder Barron Collier, the captain settled his family on the north end of this island, the largest of Florida's Ten Thousand Islands, back in 1871. He traded pelts with the Native Americans, caught and smoked fish to sell to Key West and Cuba, and charged fishermen and other guests $2 a day for a room in his home. A few turn-of-the-20th-century buildings still stand here, but Captain Collier would be shocked to come across the high-rise bridge to the island and see it now sliced by man-made canals and virtually covered by resorts, condominiums, shops, restaurants, and winter homes. These are the products of an extensive real-estate development begun in 1965, which means that Marco lacks any of the charm found in Naples and on Sanibel and Captiva islands. Much of the sales effort here was aimed at the northeastern states, so the island smacks more of New York and Massachusetts than of the laid-back Midwestern style of its neighbors.

Marco's only real attractions are its crescent-shaped beach and access to the nearby waterways running through a maze of small islands, its excellent boating and fishing, and the island's proximity to thousands of acres of wildlife preserves.

ESSENTIALS

GETTING THERE   See p. 320 and 362 for information about the **Southwest Florida International Airport** and the **Naples Municipal Airport,** respectively, and about Amtrak's train service and Greyhound/Trailways buses (p. 323 and 323) to those cities.

VISITOR INFORMATION   The **Marco Island Area Chamber of Commerce,** 1102 N. Collier Blvd., Marco Island, FL 34145 (✆ **800/788-6272** or 239/394-7549; fax 239/394-3061; www.marcoislandchamber.org), provides free information about the island. A message board and a phone are located outside for making hotel reservations even when the office is closed. The chamber is open Monday through Friday from 9am to 5pm and Saturday from 10am to 3pm during winter.

GETTING AROUND   **Marco Island Trolley Tours** (✆ **239/394-1600**) makes four complete loops around the island and into the wacky, shacky fishing village of Goodland from 10am to 3:15pm Monday through Saturday. The conductors sell tickets and render an informative narration about the island's history. Daily fare is $17 for adults, $7 for children 11 and under, with free reboarding. The entire loop takes about 1 hour and 45 minutes.

Enterprise Rent-a-Car (© 800/325-8007 or 239/642-4488) has an office here. For a cab, call **A-Action Taxi** (© 239/394-4400), **Classic Taxi** (© 239/394-1888), or **A-Okay Taxi** (© 239/394-1113).

Depending on the type, rental bicycles cost $5 an hour to $65 a week at **Scootertown,** 845 Bald Eagle Dr. (© 239/394-8400), north of North Collier Boulevard near Olde Marco. Scooters cost about $50 for 24 hours.

HITTING THE BEACH & OTHER OUTDOOR ACTIVITIES

BEACHES The sugar-white Crescent Beach curves for 3½ miles down the entire western shore of Marco Island. Its southern 2 miles are fronted by an unending row of high-rise condominiums and hotels, but the northern 1½ miles are preserved in **Tigertail Public Beach** (© 239/642-8414). There are restrooms, cold-water outdoor showers, a children's playground, a watersports rental concessionaire, and a snack bar. The park is at the end of Hernando Drive. It's open daily from dawn to dusk. There's no admission charge to the beach, but parking in the lot costs $3 per vehicle.

The beaches in front of the Marriott, Hilton, and Radisson resorts have parasailing, windsurfing, and other watersports activities, all for a fee.

If you're not staying at the big resorts, Collier County maintains a $3-per-vehicle parking lot and access to the developed beach on the southern end of the island, on Swallow Avenue at South Collier Boulevard.

OUTDOOR ACTIVITIES **Marco River Marina,** 951 Bald Eagle Dr. (© 239/394-2502; www.marcoriver.com), is the center for boat rentals, fishing, and cruises. Operating from a booth on the marina's dock, **Sunshine Tours** (© 239/642-5415; www.sunshinetoursmarcoisland.com) will book offshore fishing charters and arrange back-bay fishing ($47 adults, $37 kids under 10), shelling excursions to the small islands ($37 adults, $27 children under 10), sunset cruises ($30 adults, $15 children under 10), and dinner cruises ($49 per person). The back-bay fishing trips go at high tide, the shelling trips at low tide, so call for the schedule and reservations.

SCUBAdventures has a base at 845 Bald Eagle Dr. (© 239/389-7889) in Olde Marco. Two-tank dives range from $65 to $85 depending on distance offshore.

Naples's Lely and Boyne South golf courses are a short drive away (see "Other Outdoor Activities," in section 4, earlier in this chapter). The closest public courses are the **Marco Shores Golf Club,** 1450 Mainsail Dr. (© 239/394-2581), and **Marriott's Golf Club at Marco** (© 239/353-7061), both in the marshlands off Fla. 951 north of the island. A sign at the Marriott's course ominously warns: PLEASE DON'T DISTURB THE ALLIGATORS. Fees range from about $120 in winter down to $75 in summer.

A NATURE PRESERVE

Operated by The Conservancy and part of the Rookery Bay National Estuarine Research Reserve, the **Briggs Nature Center** 🎣, on Shell Island Road, off Fla. 951 between U.S. 41 and Marco Island (© 239/775-8569; www.conservancy. org), has a ½-mile boardwalk through a pristine example of Florida's disappearing scrublands, home to the threatened scrub jays and gopher tortoises. Rangers lead a variety of nature excursions (call for the seasonal schedule), and there is a self-guided canoe trail, with canoes for rent Tuesday through Saturday mornings (you must return them by 1pm) at $13 for the first 2 hours, $5 for each additional hour. The center is open Monday through Saturday from 9am to 4:30pm.

Admission to the boardwalk is $4 for adults, $2 for children 3 to 12, free for children under 3. For more information, contact **The Conservancy of Southwest Florida,** 1450 Merrihue Dr., Naples, FL 34102 (© **239/262-0304;** fax 239/262-0672; www.conservancy.org).

WHERE TO STAY

There are no chain hotels on Marco Island other than the large Marriott, Hilton, and Radisson properties listed below, which stand in a row along Crescent Beach on the island's southwestern corner. **Century 21 First Southern Trust** (© **800/ 523-0069** or 239/394-7653; fax 239/394-8048; www.c21marco.com) is one of the largest agents representing rental property owners.

As elsewhere in South Florida, the high season here is from mid-December to mid-April. Rates drop precipitously in the off season.

Boat House Motel *Value*   One of the best bargains in these parts, this pleasant little motel is a throwback to the '50s and sits beside the Marco River in Olde Marco, on the island's northern end. The rooms are in an old school two-story, lime-green-and-white building that ends at a wooden dock with a small heated swimming pool, lounge furniture, picnic tables, and barbecue grills. Two rooms on the end have their own decks, and all open to tiny courtyards. Bright paint, ceiling fans, and louvered shutters add a tropical ambience throughout. The one-bedroom condominiums next door open to a riverside dock, upon which is built a two-bedroom cottage named "The Gazebo," whose peaked roof is supported by umbrella-like spokes from a central pole. There's a heated waterfront pool, too.

1180 Edington Place, Marco Island, FL 34148. © **800/528-6345** or 239/642-2400. Fax 239/642-2435. www.theboathousemotel.com. 25 units. Winter $99–$155 double, $170–$260 apt or cottage; off-season $63–$130 double, $125–$220 apt or cottage. MC, V. Pets accepted ($15 fee plus $5 per day). **Amenities:** Heated outdoor pool; coin-op washers and dryers. *In room:* A/C, TV, fridge, iron.

Marco Beach Ocean Resort *★★*   Making up for the lack of a Ritz-y resort on Marco Island is this posh, all suite stay and full service spa in which a dress code (no T-shirts, shorts, tank tops, or casual hats allowed in the lobby and jackets required at the resort's excellent Italian restaurant, Sale e Pepe) is loosely enforced. Suites here are definitely comfortable, complete with full kitchens and patios overlooking the Gulf. Although the marble lobby is mausoleum-like with little or no activity (could it be the no-shorts rule?), it is a sight to see. Neither golf nor tennis courts are on the premises, but the concierge can arrange both at nearby clubs and courses. Surprisingly, the pool here is nothing to speak of, small and nondescript, but the beach is what really matters. Pristine and private, the Marco Beach Ocean Resort features beach service all day long and, thankfully, there's no dress code on the beach.

480 S. Collier Blvd., Marco Island, FL 34145. © **800/260-5089** or 239/393-1400. Fax 239/393-1401. www.marcoresort.com. 103 units. Winter $479–$579 double, $589–$859 2-bedroom suite; off-season $219–$309 double, $389–$449 2-bedroom suite. Valet parking $15 (no self-parking). AE, DC, DISC, MC, V. **Amenities:** 4 restaurants; 2 bars; heated outdoor pool; golf and tennis at nearby facilities; fitness center; spa; Jacuzzi; sauna; watersports equipment rental; concierge; business center; sundry shop; limited room service; massage; laundry service. *In room:* A/C, TV, dataport, full kitchen, minibar, fridge, coffeemaker, hair dryer, iron, safe.

Marco Island Hilton Beach Resort *★★*   About half the size of the nearby Marco Island Marriott Resort & Golf Club (see below) but nevertheless a group-oriented hotel, this 11-story beachside tower overlooks the Gulf and a courtyard with a multiangled swimming pool wrapped around four coconut palms. The spacious units have curved balconies angled to give water views. One-bedroom units have cooking facilities. One kitchen here serves two outlets: the elegant

Sandcastles for dinner and the adjacent Paradise Cafe for casual breakfasts, lunches, and dinners. The Beach Club by the pool serves lunches, snacks, and drinks. Sandcastles Lounge has a piano bar with nightly entertainment.

560 S. Collier Blvd., Marco Island, FL 34145. © 800/HILTONS or 239/394-5000. Fax 239/394-8410. www.marcoisland.hilton.com. 298 units. Winter $199–$359 double; off-season $89–$189 double. $9 per unit per day resort amenities fee (includes local calls). Packages available. AE, DC, DISC, MC, V. Free parking. **Amenities:** 2 restaurants; 2 bars; heated outdoor pool; 3 tennis courts; exercise room; Jacuzzi; sauna; watersports equipment rental; children's programs; game room; concierge; activities desk; business center; salon; limited room service; massage; babysitting; laundry service; concierge-level rooms. In room: A/C, TV, dataport, kitchen (suites only), minibar, fridge, coffeemaker, hair dryer, iron, safe.

Marco Island Marriott Resort & Golf Club ★★ Kids

Marco Island is far from Disney World, so if you plan to bring your kids while you experience the utmost in R&R, the sprawling Marco Island Marriott will make sure they're entertained with a summer camp's worth of activities, from watersports and Everglades excursions to bingo, Frisbee, and dive-in movies (watch from the pool). Parents can play, too, or they can opt for the hotel's convenient nanny service (it's one of the few North American resorts to have won the National Parenting Center's seal of approval). A $55 million renovation has spruced up the 735 guest rooms and 8 restaurants and lounges and added a par-72 golf course located 7 minutes away as well as a 24,000-square-foot Balinese spa. Luxuriously furnished and decorated, the spacious accommodations range from hotel rooms to two-bedroom suites. All have balconies or patios with indirect views of the Gulf. If you don't want to be bored during your Marco Island stay (something which can be a common affliction after too much laying out at the pool or beach), definitely stay here, where there actually are things to do off—and on—the beach.

400 S. Collier Blvd., Marco Island, FL 34145. © 800/438-4373 or 239/394-2511. Fax 239/642-2672. www.marcomarriottresort.com. 797 units. Winter $275–$385 double, from $520 suite; off-season $149–$340 double, from $320 suite. Packages available. AE, DC, DISC, MC, V. Valet parking $11; free self-parking. **Amenities:** 5 restaurants; 4 bars; 3 heated outdoor pools; golf course; 1 tennis court; exercise room; Jacuzzi; watersports equipment rental; children's programs; game room; concierge; activities desk; car-rental desk; business center; shopping arcade; salon; limited room service; massage; babysitting; laundry service; concierge-level rooms. In room: A/C, TV, dataport, minibar, fridge, coffeemaker, hair dryer, iron, safe.

Olde Marco Inn & Suites ★★★

Considered by many to be one of Florida's most romantic seaside resorts, the Victorian-style Olde Marco Inn & Suites dates from 1883 when Captain Bill Collier built it on the Calusa Indian Grounds. With views of the Gulf of Mexico and an unfettered beach, one would think the Old Marco Inn hasn't changed a lick since the 1800s. Not so. Maintaining its historic charm, the Inn has been remodeled and updated featuring 51 new one- and two-bedroom, two-bathroom suites decorated with a tropical flair and featuring a complimentary bottle of the inn's private label wine. Six penthouses on the fifth floor overlooking the Gulf are worth the splurge, ranging in size from 1,300 to 6,000 square feet. Lush gardens almost make you feel as if you're not even close to the beach, but when you walk out of the hotel's backyard, alas, the Gulf! In addition to the stellar service, which includes the hotel's "Funcierge" team that will plan any activity from jet-skiing, ecotours, and golfing, one of the area's nicest restaurants, Cafe De Marco, offers fine seafood inside or out. For further relaxation, a spa and fitness center are also available. But the best amenity of the hotel, hands down, is the private 38-foot catamaran that sails guests to serene, unspoiled beaches on and around Marco Island. These trips are complimentary and include beach chairs and towels. While on the boat, keep your eyes open for manatees. Evening cruises with wine, beer, soft drinks, and appetizers are also available, but at a nominal fee. Couples looking for a first, second, or third honeymoon should stay here, without question.

100 Palm St., Marco Island, FL 34145. ℂ **877/475-3466.** Fax 239/394-4485. www.oldmarco.com. 329 units. Winter $189–$489 1-bedroom, $259–$519 2-bedroom; off-season $99–$309 1-bedroom, $129–$339 2-bedroom. Penthouses $600–$2,500. AE, DC, DISC, MC, V. **Amenities:** Restaurant; bar; outdoor pool; fitness center; full-service spa; concierge; limited room service. *In room:* A/C, TV, VCR, dataport, kitchenette, minibar, hair dryer, iron, safe.

WHERE TO DINE

Cafe de Marco 𝒜𝒜 SEAFOOD Purveyor of some of the island's finest cuisine, this homelike establishment at the Marco Village shops was originally constructed as housing for maids at Captain William Collier's Olde Marco Inn. The chef specializes in excellent treatments of fresh seafood, from your choice of shrimp or fresh baked fish with mushrooms, seasoned shallots, and garlic butter to his own luscious creation of seafood and vegetables combined in a lobster sauce and served over linguine. If your waistline can stand it, finish with a Cafe Puff, an almond praline ice-cream ball rolled in chocolate cookie crumbs, placed in a puff pastry shell, and served with whipped cream. Early-bird specials here are a very good value. You can dine inside or on a screened patio.

244 Palm St., Olde Marco. ℂ **239/394-6262.** Reservations recommended. Main courses $16–$30; early-bird specials $13. Minimum charge $13 per adult, $4.50 per child. AE, MC, V. Winter daily 5–10pm; off-season Mon–Sat 5–10pm. Early-bird specials 5–6pm.

Kahuna Restaurant AMERICAN With fanciful Hawaiian themes highlighted by a small steaming volcano and a big mural of porpoises playing underwater on one wall, Kahuna is the least-expensive choice here. You can sit outside in the shopping center's parking lot or inside at colored booths and round tables under ceiling fans. The burgers are some of Marco's best (there's a condiment bar with a variety of fixings). Main courses include several fried seafood selections, baked crab cakes, and charcoal-grilled tuna, but your best bet should be a nightly special such as salmon in a light dill sauce. Don't expect gourmet dining here, but the quality is good for the price.

1035 N. Collier Blvd., in Town Center Mall (at Bald Eagle Dr.). ℂ **239/394-4300.** Reservations not accepted. Main courses $8.50–$15; sandwiches and burgers $3.50–$7.50; breakfast $3–$8. MC, V. Winter daily 8:30am–9pm; off-season daily 11:30am–9pm.

Kretch's 𝒜𝒜 *Value* SEAFOOD/CONTINENTAL Noted pastry chef Bruce Kretschmer rules this shopping-center roost, Marco's best all-around restaurant. Bruce has created a sinfully rich seafood strudel by combining shrimp, crab, scallops, cheeses, cream, and broccoli in a flaky Bavarian pastry and serving it all under a lobster sauce. It's available in appetizer or main course–size portions. Cholesterol counters can choose from broiled or charcoal-grilled fish, shrimp, Florida lobster tail, steaks, or lamb chops. Bruce's popular "Mexican Friday" lunches feature delicious tacos and other inexpensive south-of-the-border selections. Sunday is home-cooking night during winter, with chicken and dumplings, Yankee pot roast, and braised lamb shanks.

527 Bald Eagle Dr. (south of N. Collier Blvd.). ℂ **239/394-3433.** Reservations recommended in winter. Main courses $14–$25. DISC, MC, V. Mon–Fri 11am–3pm and 5–9pm; Sat–Sun 5–9pm. Closed Sun off-season and Easter, July 4, Thanksgiving, Christmas Eve, Christmas Day.

Snook Inn SEAFOOD The choice dinner seats at this Old Florida establishment are in an enclosed dock right beside the scenic Marco River, but for lunch or libation (they make fabulous Bloody Marys with pickled okra), head to the dockside Chickee Bar, a fun place anytime but especially at sunset. A new garden courtyard isn't a bad place to be, either, as long as it's not mosquito season, in which case, avoid all outdoor areas unless you've bathed in Off. Live entertainment is featured out there both day and night during the winter season, nightly the rest of the year. Although seafood is the specialty, tasty steaks, chicken, burgers, and sandwiches are among the choices. Even the sandwiches come with a trip to the salad bar at dinner, making them a fine bargain. Bring a filet of that fish you caught today and the chef will cook it for you. Call A-Okay Taxi (see "Essentials," above) for a free ride from anywhere on Marco Island to Snook Inn.

1215 Bald Eagle Dr. (at Palm St.), Olde Marco. © 239/394-3313. Reservations not accepted. Main courses $12–$21; sandwiches $8–$10; cook-your-catch $11. AE, DC, DISC, MC, V. Daily 11am–4pm and 4:30–10pm. Closed Thanksgiving, Christmas.

MARCO ISLAND AFTER DARK

Marco Island nightlife is an oxymoron. When the sun sets, so does everything else here, for the most part. With the exception of the island's movie theater and a few hotel bars, there's not much doing here after dark. A drive to Naples is necessary for those looking to burn the midnight oil.

To find out what's going on, check the *Naples Daily News* (www.naplesnews. com), especially the "Neapolitan" section in Friday's edition and its weekly "The Marco Islander" section, available at the chamber of commerce (p. 362).

It's not after dark, but one of the biggest parties in Florida takes place every Sunday afternoon at **Stan's Idle Hour Seafood Restaurant,** on County Road 892 in Goodland (© 239/394-3041), where owner Stan Gober—an Ernest Hemingway look-alike—plays host and fires up the barbecue grills; bands crank up country music for dancing the "Buzzard Lope"; and men compete to see who has the best legs. Stan's Goodland Mullet Festival, always the weekend before the Super Bowl, is the mother of all parties.

Marco Island's much tamer but nevertheless entertaining version is the **Snook Inn** (see the "Where to Dine" section, above), where bands play out in the dockside Chickee Bar.

Much more sedate are the lounges in the **Marriott** and **Hilton** resorts (see "Where to Stay," above), which provide pianists every evening.

It seems like everyone turns out for free outdoor entertainment at the **Mission San Marco Plaza** shopping center, South Collier Boulevard at Winterberry Drive, every Tuesday night year-round, and at the **Town Center Mall,** at North Collier Boulevard and Bald Eagle Drive, every Thursday night.

11

The Tampa Bay Area

San Francisco isn't the country's only Bay Area. In fact, when some people hear the word "Tampa," they typically think of Busch Gardens and never even mention the Bay Area. They'd be missing out: Tampa Bay is a stunning, picturesque city, and while it may not have a red bridge, it does have an array of colors reflecting off of the sparkling waters. If you haven't had a chance to explore Florida's Bay Area, do so now. There's so much more to the Tampa Bay area than beer and amusement parks. Sure, you can chug as much Busch Beer here as you want, but you can also do (and see, and eat, and experience) much more here.

Florida's very own city by the bay, Tampa is a scenic spot. It's also got its own vibrant culture with roots firmly implanted in Cuban and American history. Many families visiting Orlando's theme parks eventually drive an hour west on I-4 to another major theme park, Busch Gardens in Tampa. But this area shouldn't be a mere side trip from Disney World, for Florida's west-central coast is an exciting destination unto itself.

The city of Tampa is the commercial center of Florida's west coast—a growing seaport and center of banking and high-tech manufacturing. You can come downtown during the day to see the sea life at the Florida Aquarium and stroll through the Henry B. Plant Museum, housed in an ornate, Moorish-style hotel built more than a century ago to lure tourists to the city. A short trolley ride will take you from downtown Tampa to Ybor City, the historic Cuban enclave, which is now a bustling, often rowdy, nightlife and dining hot spot.

Two bridges and a causeway will whisk you west across Old Tampa Bay to St. Petersburg, Pinellas Park, Clearwater, Dunedin, Tarpon Springs, and other cities on the Pinellas Peninsula, one of Florida's most densely packed urban areas. Over here on the bay front, photo-ready downtown St. Petersburg is famous for wintering seniors, a shopping and dining complex built on a pier, and, surprisingly, the world's largest collection of Salvador Dalí's surrealist paintings.

Keep driving west and you'll come to a line of barrier islands where St. Pete Beach, Clearwater Beach, and other Gulf-side communities boast 28 miles of sunshine, surf, and white sand.

Heading south, I-275 will take you across the mouth of Tampa Bay to Sarasota and another chain of barrier islands that stretches 42 miles along the coast south of Tampa Bay. One of Florida's cultural centers, affluent Sarasota is the gateway to St. Armands and Longboat keys, two playgrounds of the rich and famous, and to Lido and Siesta keys, both attractive to families of more modest means.

1 Tampa

200 miles SW of Jacksonville, 85 miles SW of Orlando, 254 miles NW of Miami

Even if you stay on the beaches 20 miles to the west, you should consider driving into Tampa for a mild taste of metropolis. If you have children in tow, they may *demand* that you go into the city so they can ride the rides and see the animals at Busch Gardens. Once there, you can also educate them (and yourself) at the Florida Aquarium and the city's other fine museums. Additionally, historic Ybor City has the bay area's liveliest and hottest nightlife.

Tampa was once a sleepy little port when Cuban immigrants founded Ybor City's cigar industry in the 1880s. A few years later, Henry B. Plant put Tampa on the tourist map by building a railroad that ran into town and constructing the bulbous minarets over his garish Tampa Bay Hotel, now a museum named in his honor. During the Spanish-American War, Teddy Roosevelt trained his Rough Riders here and walked the Ybor City streets with Cuban revolutionary José Martí. A land boom in the 1920s gave the city its charming, Victorian-style Hyde Park suburb, now a gentrified redoubt for the baby boomers just across the Hillsborough River from downtown.

Today's downtown skyline is the product of the 1980s and 1990s booms, when banks built skyscrapers and the city put up an expansive convention center, a performing-arts center, and the St. Pete Times Forum (formerly the Ice Palace), a 20,000-seat bay-front arena that is home to professional hockey's Tampa Bay Lightning. The renaissance hasn't been as rapid as planned, given the recent economic recession, but it is continuing into the 21st century with redevelopment of the seaport area east of downtown. There the existing Florida Aquarium and the Garrison Seaport Center (a major home port for cruise ships bound for Mexico and the Caribbean) are being joined by office buildings, apartment complexes, and a major shopping-and-dining center known as Channelside (in the Channel District) at Garrison Seaport.

You won't want to spend your entire Florida vacation in Tampa, but everything it offers adds up to a fast-paced, modern city on the go.

ESSENTIALS

GETTING THERE   **Tampa International Airport** (© 813/870-8770; www.tampaairport.com), 5 miles northwest of downtown Tampa, is the major air gateway to this area (**St. Petersburg–Clearwater International Airport** has limited service; see section 2, "St. Petersburg," later in this chapter). Most major and many no-frills airlines serve Tampa International, including **Air Canada** (© 800/268-7240 in Canada, or 800/776-3000 in the U.S.), **AirTran** (© 800/247-8726), **America West** (© 800/235-9292), **American** (© 800/433-7300), **British Airways** (© 800/247-9297), **Continental** (© 800/525-0280), **Delta** (© 800/221-1212), **JetBlue** (© 800/538-2583), **Lufthansa** (© 800/824-6200), **MetroJet** (© 800/428-4322), **Midway** (© 800/446-4392), **Midwest Express** (© 800/452-2022), **Northwest** (© 800/225-2525), **Southwest** (© 800/435-9792), **Spirit** (© 800/722-7117), **United** (© 800/241-6522), and **US Airways** (© 800/428-4322).

    Alamo (© 800/327-9633), **Avis** (© 800/331-1212), **Budget** (© 800/527-0700), **Dollar** (© 800/800-4000), **Enterprise** (© 800/325-8007), **Hertz** (© 800/654-3131), **National** (© 800/227-7368), and **Thrifty** (© 800/367-2277) all have rental-car operations here.

    The Limo/SuperShuttle (© **800/282-6817** or 727/527-1111; www.supershuttle.com) operates van services between the airport and hotels throughout the Tampa Bay area. Fares for one person range from $13 to $33 round-trip, depending on your destination. **Taxis** are plentiful at the airport; the ride to downtown Tampa takes about 15 minutes and costs $11 to $19.

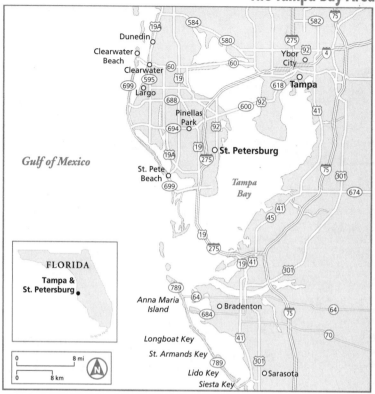

Amtrak trains arrive downtown at the **Tampa Amtrak Station,** 601 Nebraska Ave. N. (© **800/872-7245;** www.amtrak.com).

VISITOR INFORMATION   Contact the **Tampa Bay Convention & Visitors Bureau,** 400 N. Tampa St., Tampa, FL 33602-4706 (© **800/448-2672,** 800/368-2672, or 813/223-2752; www.visittampabay.com), for advance information. If you're downtown, you can head to the bureau's **visitor information center** at 400 N. Tampa St. (Channelside), Suite 2800 (© **813/223-1111**). It's open Monday through Saturday from 9:30am to 5:30pm.

Operated by the Ybor City Chamber of Commerce, the **Centro Ybor Museum and Visitor Information Center,** in Centro Ybor, 1514½ E. 8th Ave. (between 15th and 16th sts. E.), Tampa, FL 33605 (© **813/248-3712;** www.ybor.org), distributes information and has exhibits about the area's history. A 7-minute video will help get you oriented with this area—an 8-block stretch of Seventh Avenue. The center is open Monday through Saturday from 10am to 6pm, Sunday from noon to 6pm.

GETTING AROUND   Like most other Florida destinations, it's virtually impossible to see Tampa's major sights and enjoy its best restaurants without a car. You can get around downtown via the free **Uptown-Downtown Connector Trolley,** which runs north-south between Harbor Island and the city's North Terminal bus station on Marion Street at I-275. The trolleys run every 10 minutes from 6am to 6pm Monday through Friday. Southbound they follow Tampa

Tampa & St. Petersburg

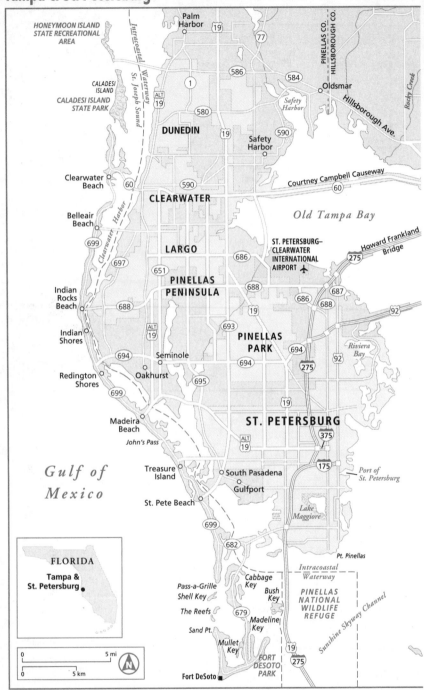

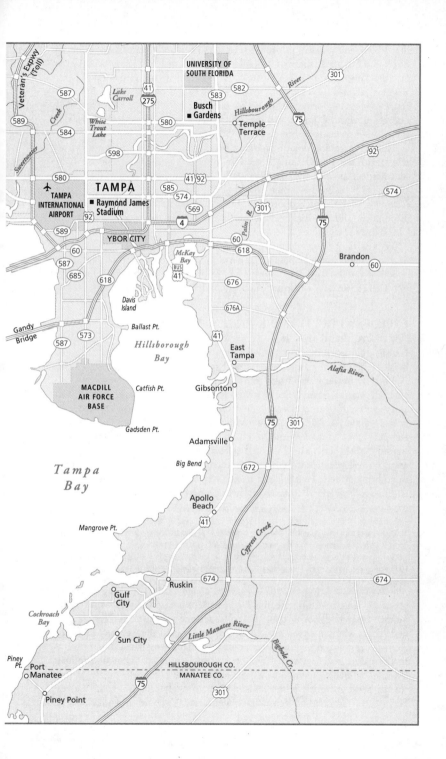

Street between Tyler and Whiting streets, and Franklin Street between Whiting Street and Harbor Island. Northbound trolleys follow Florida Avenue from the St. Pete Times Forum to Cass Street. It's operated by the Hillsborough Area Regional Transit/HARTline (© **813/254-4278;** www.hartline.org), the area's transportation authority, which also provides scheduled **bus service** ($1.25–$3) between downtown Tampa and the suburbs. Pick up a route map at the visitor information center (see above).

The transportation situation has gotten somewhat better, not to mention nostalgic, with the **TECO Line Street Car System,** a new 2⅖-mile but old-fashioned streetcar system, complete with overhead power lines, that hauls passengers between downtown and Ybor City via the St. Pete Times Forum, Channelside, Garrison Seaport, and the Florida Aquarium. The cars run every 30 minutes, and one-way fares are $1.25. Check with the visitor center or call HARTline for schedules.

Taxis in Tampa don't normally cruise the streets for fares, but they do line up at public places, such as hotels, the performing-arts center, and bus and train depots. If you need a taxi, call **Tampa Bay Cab** (© **813/251-5555**), **Yellow Cab** (© **813/253-0121**), or **United Cab** (© **813/253-2424**). Fares are $1 at flag fall, plus $1.50 for each mile.

EXPLORING THE THEME & ANIMAL PARKS

Adventure Island *Kids* If the summer heat gets to you before one of Tampa's famous thunderstorms brings late-afternoon relief, you can take a waterlogged break at this 25-acre outdoor water theme park near Busch Gardens Tampa Bay (see below). You can also frolic here during the cooler days of spring and fall, when the water is heated. The Key West Rapids, Tampa Typhoon, Gulf Scream, and other exciting water rides will drench the teens, while other, calmer rides are geared toward younger kids. Wahoo Run plunges up to five riders more than 15 feet per second as the half-enclosed tunnel corkscrews more than 600 feet to a waiting splash pool. There are also places to picnic and sunbathe, a games arcade, a volleyball complex, and an outdoor cafe. Although some people tend to go barefoot here, I suggest you make sure you bring and wear your shoes at all times as it gets kind of nasty out there after a while.

10001 Malcolm McKinley Dr. (between Busch Blvd. and Bougainvillea Ave.). © 813/987-5600. www.4adventure.com. Admission at least $30 adults, $28 children 3–9, plus tax; free for children 2 and under. Combination tickets with Busch Gardens Tampa Bay (1 day each) $65 adults, $55 children 3–9, free for children under 3. Website sometimes offers discounts. Parking $5. Mid-Mar to Labor Day daily 10am–5pm; Sept–Oct Fri–Sun 10am–5pm (extended hours in summer and on holidays). Closed Nov to late Feb. Take exit 50 off I-275 and go east on Busch Blvd. for 2 miles. Turn left onto McKinley Dr. (N. 40th St.) and entry is on right.

Busch Gardens Tampa Bay *Kids* Although its heart-stopping thrill rides get much of the ink, this venerable theme park (it predates Disney World) ranks among the largest zoos in the country. It's a don't-miss attraction for children and adults, who can see, in person, all those wild beasts they've watched on the *Animal Planet*—and they'll get better views of them here than at Disney's Animal Kingdom in Orlando (p. 496). Busch Gardens has several thousand animals living in naturalistic environments that help carry out the park's overall African theme. Most authentic is the 80-acre plain, strongly reminiscent of the real Serengeti of Tanzania and Kenya, upon which zebras, giraffes, and other animals graze. Unlike the animals on the real Serengeti, however, the grazing animals have nothing to fear from lions, hyenas, crocodiles, and other predators, which are confined to enclosures—as are hippos and elephants.

Tips If You Need Another Day

Once you're inside Busch Gardens Tampa Bay and decide you really need more time to see it all, check to see if the park has (frequently offered) **Next-Day Tickets,** which let you back in the next day for about $16 per person.

Also, if you're going to Orlando, Busch Gardens Tampa Bay is included in the five-park version of the **FlexTicket,** a 14-day pass that also gives admission to Universal Studios Florida, SeaWorld, Islands of Adventure, and Wet 'n' Wild for $210 for adults and $176 for children 3 to 9.

The park has eight areas, each of which has its own theme, animals, live entertainment, thrill rides, kiddie attractions, dining, and shopping. A Skyride cable car soars over the park, offering a bird's-eye view of it all. Turn left after the main gate and head to **Morocco,** a walled city with exotic architecture, craft demonstrations, a sultan's tent with snake charmers, and an exhibit featuring alligators and turtles. The Moorish-style Moroccan Palace Theater features an ice show, which many families consider to be the park's best entertainment for both adults and children. Here you can also attend a song-and-dance show in the Marrakech Theater. Overlooking it all is the Crown Colony Restaurant, the park's largest.

After watching the snake charmers, walk eastward past Anheuser-Busch's fabled Clydesdale horses to **Egypt,** where you can visit King Tut's tomb with its replicas of the real treasures and listen to comedian Martin Short narrate "Akbar's Adventure Tours," a wacky simulator that "transports" one and all across Egypt via camel, biplane, and mine car. The whole room moves on this ride, which lasts only 5 minutes—much less time than the usual wait to get inside. Youngsters can dig for their own ancient treasures in a sand area. Adults and kids 54 inches or taller can ride Montu, the tallest and longest inverted roller coaster in the world with seven upside-down loops. Your feet dangle loose on Montu, so make sure your shoes are tied tightly and your lunch has had time to digest.

From Egypt, walk to the **Edge of Africa,** the most unique of the park's eight areas, and the home of most of the large animals. Go immediately to the Expedition Africa Gift Shop and see if you can get on one of the park's zoologist-led wildlife tours (see the "How to See Busch Gardens" box, below).

Next stop is **Nairobi,** the most beautiful part of the park, where you can see gorillas and chimpanzees in the Myombe Reserve in a lush area that replicates their natural rainforest habitat. Nairobi also has a baby animal nursery, a petting zoo, turtle and reptile displays, an elephant exhibit (alas, the magnificent creatures seem to be bored to the point of madness), and Curiosity Caverns, where bats, reptiles, and small mammals that are active in the dark are kept in cages (it's the most traditional zoolike area here). The entry to Rhino Rally, the park's safari adventure, is at the western end of Nairobi.

Next, head to **The Congo,** highlighted by rare white Bengal tigers that live on Claw Island. The Congo is also home to two roller coasters: Kumba, the largest and fastest roller coaster in the southeastern United States (54-in. minimum height); and The Python (48-in. minimum), which twists and turns for 1,200 feet. You will get drenched—and refreshed on a hot day—by riding the Congo River Rapids, where you're turned loose in round boats that float down the swiftly flowing "river" (42-in. minimum). There are bumper cars and kiddie rides here, too.

Tampa

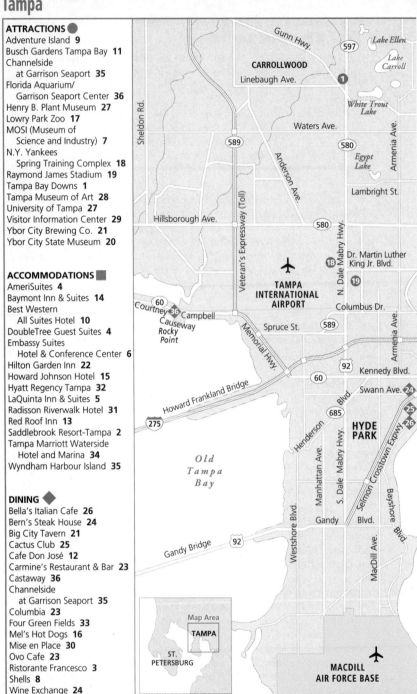

⌒*Tips* How to See Busch Gardens

You can save a few dollars and avoid waiting in long lines by buying your tickets to Busch Gardens Tampa Bay at the privately owned **Tampa Bay Visitor Information Center,** opposite the park at 3601 E. Busch Blvd., at North Ednam Place (© **813/985-3601;** www.home town.aol.com\tpabayinfoctr). Owner Jim Boggs worked for the park for 13 years and gives expert advice on how to get the most out of your visit. He sells slightly-discounted tickets (buying here will also save you from standing in line to buy tickets at the parks) to Busch Gardens, Adventure Island, and other attractions, and he will book hotel rooms and car rentals for you, often at a discount. The center is open Monday through Saturday from 10am to 5:30pm, Sunday from 10am to 2pm, except Christmas.

Arrive early and allow at least a day to see the park. Try not to come when it's raining, since some rides may not be operating. Bring comfortable shoes; and, remember, you will get wet on some of the rides, so wear or bring appropriate clothing (shops near the rides sell plastic ponchos for $5 or $6, but they're cheaper in the outside world). There are lockers throughout the park where you can stash your gear.

As soon as you're through the turnstiles, pick up a copy of a park map and the day's activity schedule, which tells what's showing and when at the 14 entertainment venues in the park. Then take a few minutes to carefully plan your time—it's a big park with lots to see and do.

Although you'll get close to Busch Garden's predators, hippos, and elephants in their glass-walled enclosures, the only way to mingle with the grazers is on a tour. The best is a **VIP Animal Adventure Tour,** on which you'll roam the plains in the company of a zoologist. These 2-hour excursions cost a pricey $100 per person (in addition to the park's entry fee) and usually leave about 1:30pm daily. The tours can fill up fast, and you can't call ahead for reservations, so as soon as you enter the park, go to the Expedition Africa Gift Shop, opposite the Crown Colony Restaurant in the Edge of Africa, to reserve a spot. Another (though less attractive) alternative is the 30-minute, zoologist-led **Serengeti Safari Special Tours,** in which you ride out among the grazers on the back of a flatbed truck. These are worth an extra $30 per person regardless of age. You can make reservations for the morning tour at the Expedition Africa Gift Shop, but the midday and afternoon tours are first-come, first-served. Note that children under 5 are not allowed on either tour.

From The Congo, walk south into **Stanleyville,** a prototype African village, with a shopping bazaar, orangutans living on an island, and the Stanleyville Theater, usually featuring shows for children. Two more water rides are here: the Tanganyika Tidal Wave (48-in. minimum height), where you'll come to a very damp end and the Stanley Falls Flume (an aqua version of a roller coaster). Also here, serving ribs and chicken, the picnic-style Stanleyville Smokehouse has some of the best chow in the park.

Up next is **Land of the Dragons,** the most entertaining area for small children. They can spend an entire day enjoying a variety of play elements in a fairy-tale setting, plus just-for-kids rides. The area is dominated by Dumphrey, a whimsical dragon who interacts with visitors and guides children around a three-story treehouse with winding stairways, tall towers, stepping stones, illuminated water geysers, and an echo chamber.

The next stop is **Bird Gardens,** the park's original core, offering rich foliage, lagoons, and a free-flight aviary for hundreds of exotic birds, including golden and American bald eagles. Be sure to see the Florida flamingos and Australian koalas while you're here.

Then you're off to take a break at the **Hospitality House,** which offers piano entertainment and free samples of Anheuser-Busch's famous beers. You must be 21 to imbibe (there's a limit of two free mugs per seating), but soft drinks are also available.

If your stomach can take another hair-raising ride, try **Gwazi** (48-in. minimum), an adrenaline-pumping attraction where a pair of old-fashioned wooden roller coasters (named the Lion and the Tiger) start simultaneously and whiz within a few feet of each other six times as they roar along at 50 mph and rise to 90 feet. In Gwazi's "Water Wars," participants shoot water-filled balloons at each other with big slingshots. It's a soaking way to end your visit.

If you want to experience the park's fifth and final roller coaster, head to **Timbuktu** and climb aboard the **Scorpion,** a high-speed number with a 60-foot drop and 360-degree loop (42-in. height minimum).

Added attractions include a $325, 6-hour zookeeper-for-a-day program, the devotion of 26 acres of its 65-acre Serengeti Plain to free-roaming white rhinos, and a 4-D multisensory R.L. Stine film in a new theater.

You can exchange foreign currency in the park, and interpreters are available.

Note: You can get to Busch Gardens from Orlando via shuttle buses, which pick up at area hotels between 8:00 and 10:15am for the 1½- to 2-hour ride, with return trips starting at 5pm and continuing until the park closes. Round-trip fares are $5 per person. Call ✆ **800/511-2450** for schedules, pickup locations, and reservations.

3000 E. Busch Blvd. (at McKinley Dr./N. 40th St.). ✆ **888/800-5447** or 813/987-5283. www.buschgardens.com. **Note:** Admission and hours vary so call ahead, check website, or get brochure at visitor centers. Admission single day ticket $54 adults, $45 children 3–9, plus tax; free for children 2 and under. Daily 10am–6pm (extended hours to 7 and 8pm in summer and on holidays). Parking $8. Take I-275 north of downtown to Busch Blvd. (exit 50) and go east 2 miles. From I-75, take Fowler Ave. (exit 54) and follow the signs west.

Florida Aquarium 🌟🌟 *Kids*   See more than 5,000 aquatic animals and plants that call Florida home at this entertaining and informative attraction. The exhibits follow a drop of water from the pristine springs of the Florida Wetlands Gallery, through a mangrove forest in the Bays and Beaches Gallery, and out onto the Coral Reefs, where an impressive 43-foot-wide, 14-foot-tall panoramic window lets you look out to schools of fish and lots of sharks and stingrays. Also worth visiting are the "Explore a Shore" playground to educate the kids, a deep-water exhibit, and a tank housing moray eels. You can also go out on the bay to look for birds and sea life on 90-minute Dolphin Quest cruises in the *Bay Spirit,* a 64-foot diesel-powered catamaran. The aquarium also offers a **Dive with the Sharks** program (✆ **813/367-4005**) that gives certified scuba divers the chance to swim with blacktip reef, sand tiger, and nurse sharks for 30 minutes. The $150 price tag includes a souvenir photo and T-shirt.

Fun Fact **Step Right Up . . . Lobster Boy Slept Here**

If you're looking for a true attraction, not of the animatronic, electronic, or supersonic ilk, deviate off the beaten path from Tampa and head straight to the little seaside town of Gibsonton. Best known as "Freaktown, USA," this town of 7,000 residents boasts the country's largest concentration of carnies (people who make their livings by working in traveling circuses and sideshows). Today, these people, once proudly known as "professional freaks," primarily work as ticket takers, clowns, acrobats, and animal trainers, but over fifty years ago, some of them were better known as "The Bearded Lady," "The Blockhead," "The Hermaphrodite," and "The Three Legged Man." At one point in this colorful town's history, the police chief was an 8-foot, 4-inch giant while the fire chief was a dwarf. Gibsonton is also where Lobster Boy (the frequent Jerry Springer Show guest who was born with a genetic condition that caused his fingers and toes to fuse into two digit claws) called home. Surprisingly, the town wasn't very pleased with his penchant for self-exploitation and appearing on trash television. Although the sideshow stars are, for the most part, gone from Gibsonton (thanks to advanced depilatory techniques, the Bearded Lady is now clean shaven), if you're lucky you may stumble upon a bona fide barker who'll invite you to step right up to his mobile home so he can regale you with tales of the sideshow days of yore.

701 Channelside Dr. © 813/273-4000. www.flaquarium.net. Admission $16 adults, $14 seniors, $11 children 3–11, free for children under 3. Dolphin Quest $19 adults, $18 seniors, $14 children 3–11, free for children under 3. Combination aquarium admission and Dolphin Quest $30 adults, $26 seniors, $20 children 3–11, free for children under 3. Website sometimes offers discounts. Parking $4. Daily 9:30am–5pm. Dolphin Quest Mon–Fri 2pm; Sat–Sun 1 and 3pm. Closed Thanksgiving, Christmas.

Lowry Park Zoo ★ *Kids*   The opportunity to watch 3,000-pound manatees, Komodo dragons, Persian leopards, and rare red pandas makes this a worthwhile, albeit not entirely necessary, excursion after the kids have seen the plains of Africa at Busch Gardens. With lots of greenery, bubbling brooks, and cascading waterfalls, this 24-acre zoo displays animals in settings similar to their natural habitats. Other major exhibits include a Florida wildlife display, an Asian Domain, a Primate World, an Aquatic Center, a free-flight aviary with a birds-of-prey show, a hands-on Discovery Center, and an endangered-species carousel ride. The new Wallaroo Station has kids' rides, a small water park, a kangaroo walk-about, and a petting zoo. Lowry Park has one of Florida's three manatee hospital and rehabilitation centers. It's also a sanctuary for Florida panthers and red wolves.

1101 W. Sligh Ave. © 813/935-8552, or 813/932-0245 for recorded information. www.lowryparkzoo.com. Admission $12 adults, $11 seniors, $8 children 3–11, free for children 2 and under. Daily 9:30am–5pm. Closed Thanksgiving, Christmas. Take I-275 to Sligh Ave. (exit 48) and follow the signs.

VISITING THE MUSEUMS

Henry B. Plant Museum   Originally built in 1891 by railroad tycoon Henry B. Plant as the super-chi chi 511-room Tampa Bay Hotel, this ornate building alone is worth a short trip across the river from downtown to the University of Tampa campus. Its 13 silver minarets and distinctive Moorish architecture, modeled after the Alhambra in Spain, make this National Historic Landmark a focal point of the Tampa skyline. Although the building is the highlight of a visit, don't skip its contents: art and furnishings from Europe and the Orient; and exhibits that explain the history of the original railroad resort, Florida's early tourist industry, and the hotel's role as a staging point for Theodore Roosevelt's Rough Riders during the Spanish-American War.

401 W. Kennedy Blvd. (between Hyde Park and Magnolia aves.). ⓒ 813/254-1891. www.plantmuseum. com. Free admission; suggested donation $5 adults, $2 children 12 and under. Tues–Sat 10am–4pm; Sun noon–4pm. Closed Thanksgiving, Christmas Eve, and Christmas Day. Take Kennedy Blvd. (Fla. 60) across the Hillsborough River.

MOSI (Museum of Science and Industry) ★★ *Kids*   A great place to take the kids, MOSI is the largest science center in the Southeast and has more than 450 interactive exhibits. You can step into the Gulf Hurricane and experience 74 mph winds or explore the human body in The Amazing You. If your heart is up to it, you can ride a bicycle across a 98-foot-long cable suspended 30 feet above the lobby (don't worry: you'll be harnessed to the bike). You can also watch stunning movies in Florida's first IMAX dome theater or take a 5-minute ride in a flight simulator ($3.50 additional charge). Outside, trails wind through a 47-acre nature preserve with a butterfly garden.

4801 E. Fowler Ave. (at N. 50th St.). ⓒ 813/987-6100. www.mosi.org. Admission $15 adults, $13 seniors, $12 children 2–12, free for children under 2. Admission includes IMAX movies. Daily 9am–5pm or later. From downtown, take I-275 north to the Fowler Ave. E. exit (#51). Take this 2 miles east to museum on right.

Tampa Museum of Art   Located on the east bank of the Hillsborough River, next to the round NationsBank building (locals facetiously call it the "Beer Can"), this fine-arts complex offers eight galleries with changing exhibits ranging from classical antiquities to contemporary Florida art. There's also a 7-acre riverfront park and sculpture garden. Call or check the website for the schedule of temporary exhibits. If you only have time allotted for one art museum on this trip, skip this one and head to St. Petersburg for the more innovative Salvador Dali Museum.

600 N. Ashley Dr. (at Twiggs St.), downtown. ⓒ 813/274-8130. www.tampamuseum.com. Admission $7 adults, $6 seniors, $3 children 6–18 and students with ID cards, free for children under 6, by donation Thurs 5–8pm and Sat 10am–noon. Tues–Sat 10am–5pm; Thurs 10am–8pm; Sun 11am–5pm. Parking 90¢ per hour. Take I-275 to exit 44 (Ashley Dr.).

YBOR CITY

Northeast of downtown, the city's historic Latin district takes its name from Don Vicente Martinez Ybor (*Eeee*-bore), a Spanish cigar maker who arrived here

A Free Attraction

The Tampa Electric Company is a hot spot, not just because it provides the juice that makes the city tick, but because the waters surrounding the plant are a haven for manatees who revel in the fact that the water here is warm—manatees need to be in water at least 68°F, and the Electric Company's water is at least that warm. The **Manatee Viewing Center** (ⓒ 813/228-4289; www.tampaelectric.com) is open from November 1 to April 15 from 10am to 5pm for viewing the manatees.

in 1886 via Cuba and Key West. Soon his and other Tampa factories were producing more than 300,000 hand-rolled stogies a day.

It may not be the cigar capital of the world anymore, but Ybor is still smokin' as the happening part of Tampa and it's one of the best places in Florida to buy hand-rolled cigars. It's not on a par with New Orleans's Bourbon Street, Washington's Georgetown, or Miami's South Beach, but good food and great music dominate the scene, especially on weekends when the streets bustle until 4am (note to claustrophobes: avoid it at all costs on weekends). Live-music offerings run the gamut from jazz and blues to rock.

At the heart of it all is **Centro Ybor,** a dining-shopping-entertainment complex sprawling between 7th and 8th avenues and 16th and 17th streets (© **813/ 242-4660;** www.thecentroybor.com). Here you'll find a multiscreen cinema, a comedy club, several restaurants, and a large open-air bar. The Ybor City Chamber of Commerce has its visitor center here (see "Essentials," earlier in this chapter), and the Ybor City State Museum's gift shop is here as well (see below).

Check with the visitor center about **walking tours** of the historic district. **Ybor City Ghost Walks** (© 813/242-4660) will take you to the spookier parts of the area beginning at 4pm Thursday and Saturday. They cost $10 per person, last 75 minutes, and are by reservation only.

Even if you're not a cigar smoker, you'll enjoy a stroll through the **Ybor City State Museum** ★, 1818 9th Ave., between 18th and 19th streets (© **813/ 247-6323;** www.ybormuseum.org), housed in the former Ferlita Bakery (1896–1973). You can take a self-guided tour around the museum to see a collection of cigar labels, cigar memorabilia, and works by local artisans. Admission is $2 per person. Depending on the availability of volunteer docents, admission includes a 15-minute guided tour of **La Casita,** a renovated cigar worker's cottage adjacent to the museum; it's furnished as it was at the turn of the last century. The museum is open daily from 9am to 5pm, but the best time to visit is between 11am and 3pm, when you have the best chance for the guided tour of La Casita. Better yet, plan to catch the cigar-rolling demonstrations (ongoing; no specific schedule) Friday through Sunday from 10am to 3pm.

Housed in a 100-year-old, three-story former cigar factory, **Ybor City Brewing Company,** 2205 N. 20th St., facing Palm Avenue, produces Ybor Gold and other brews, none with preservatives.

Like any area with trendy bars and restaurants, things are always changing, going out of business, and opening, so you may want to check with www.ybor times.com for the latest in what's hot in Ybor City.

ORGANIZED TOURS

Swiss Chalet Tours, 3601 E. Busch Blvd. (© **813/985-3601;** www.hometown. aol.com\tpabayinfoctr), opposite Busch Gardens in the privately run Tampa Bay Visitor Information Center (see the "How to See Busch Gardens" box, above), operates guided bus tours of Tampa, Ybor City, and environs. The 4-hour tours of Tampa are given from 10am to 3pm daily, with a stop for lunch at the Columbia Restaurant in Ybor City. They cost $45 for adults and $40 for children 12 and under. The full-day tours (10am–5pm) of both Tampa and St. Petersburg give a good overview of the two cities and the beaches; these cost $70 for adults and $65 for children 12 and under. Reservations are required at least 24 hours in advance; passengers are picked up at major hotels and various other points in the Tampa/St. Petersburg area. The company can also book bus tours to Orlando, Sarasota, Bradenton, and other regional destinations (call for schedules, prices, and reservations).

OUTDOOR ACTIVITIES & SPECTATOR SPORTS

BIKING, IN-LINE SKATING & JOGGING   Bayshore Boulevard, a 7-mile-long promenade, is famous for its sidewalk right on the shores of Hillsborough Bay and is a favorite for runners, joggers, walkers, and in-line skaters. The route goes from the western edge of downtown in a southward direction, passing stately old homes in Hyde Park, a few high-rise condominiums, retirement communities, and houses of worship, ending at Ballast Point Park. The view from the promenade across the bay to the downtown skyline is unmatched here (Bayshore Blvd. is also great for a drive).

> ### Cruise Control
> The **Port of Tampa** (℃ 800/741-2297 or 813/905-7678; www.tampaport.com) is home to four cruise lines and a changing cast of ships that travel the Caribbean and Latin America. At press time, the players were Celebrity Cruise Line, Royal Caribbean Cruise Lines, Holland America Cruise Lines, and Carnival Cruise Line.

FISHING   For charters, try **Captain Jim's Inshore Sportfishing Charters,** 512 Palm Ave., Palm Harbor (℃ 727/439-9017; www.captainhud.com) , which offers private sport-fishing trips for tarpon, redfish, trout, and snook. Rates are $300 to $450 for two anglers. Call for schedule and required reservations.

GOLF   Tampa has three municipal golf courses where you can play for about $30 to $35, a relative pittance when compared with fees at the privately owned courses here and elsewhere in Florida. The **Babe Zaharias Municipal Golf Course,** 11412 Forest Hills Dr., north of Lowry Park (℃ 813/631-4374), is an 18-hole, par-70 course with a pro shop, putting greens, and a driving range. It is the shortest of the municipal courses, but its small greens and narrow fairways present ample challenges. Water provides obstacles on 12 of the 18 holes at **Rocky Point Golf Course,** 4151 Dana Shores Dr. (℃ 813/673-4316), located between the airport and the bay. It's a par-71 course with a pro shop, a practice range, and putting greens. On the Hillsborough River in north Tampa, the **Rogers Park Golf Course,** 7910 N. 30th St. (℃ 813/673-4396), is an 18-hole, par-72 championship course with a lighted driving and practice range. All the courses are open daily from 7am to dusk, and lessons and club rentals are available.

You can book starting times and get information about these and the area's other courses by calling **Tee Times USA** (℃ 800/374-8633; www.teetimesusa.com).

If you want to do some serious work on your game, the **Arnold Palmer Golf Academy World Headquarters** is at Saddlebrook Resort, 5700 Saddlebrook Way, Wesley Chapel, 12 miles north of Tampa (℃ 800/729-8383 or 813/973-1111; www.saddlebrookresort.com). Half-day and hourly instruction is available as well as 2-, 3-, and 5-day programs for adults and juniors. You have to stay at the resort or enroll in the golf program to play at Saddlebrook. See p. 402 for more information about the resort.

For course information online, go to **www.golf.com** and **www.floridagolfing. com**, or call the **Florida Sports Foundation** (℃ 850/488-8347) or **Florida Golfing** (℃ 866/833-2663).

SPECTATOR SPORTS   National Football League fans can catch the Super Bowl champ **Tampa Bay Buccaneers** at the modern, 66,000-seat Raymond James Stadium, 4201 N. Dale Mabry Hwy., at Dr. Martin Luther King Jr. Boulevard (℃ 813/879-2827; www.buccaneers.com) August through December. Single-game tickets (starting at $30) are very hard to come by.

The National Hockey League's **Tampa Bay Lightning,** winners of the 2004 Stanley Cup, play in the St. Pete Times Forum, beginning in October (© **813/ 301-6500;** www.tampabaylightning.com). You can usually get single-game tickets ($8–$155) on game day.

New York Yankees fans can watch the Bronx Bombers during baseball spring training from mid-February to the end of March at Legends Field (© **813/ 879-2244** or 813/875-7753; www.yankees.mlb.com), opposite Raymond James Stadium. This scaled-down replica of Yankee Stadium is the largest spring-training facility in Florida, with a 10,000-seat capacity. Tickets are $10 to $16. The club's minor-league team, the **Tampa Yankees** (same phone and website), plays at Legends Field April through August.

The only thoroughbred racecourse on Florida's west coast, **Tampa Bay Downs,** 11225 Racetrack Rd., Oldsmar (© **800/200-4434** in Florida, or 813/855-4401; www.tampadowns.com), is the home of the Tampa Bay Derby. Races are held from December to May ($2 general admission, $3 clubhouse), and the track presents simulcasts year-round. Call for post times.

TENNIS   Players at all levels can sharpen their games at the **Hopman Tennis Program,** at the Saddlebrook Resort (p. 402). You must be a member or a guest to play here.

SHOPPING

Hyde Park and Ybor City are two areas of Tampa worth some window shopping, perhaps sandwiched around lunch at one of their fine restaurants (see "Where to Dine," later in this chapter).

On the mall front, the newest player in town is the upscale **International Plaza** (© **813/342-3790;** www.shopinternationalplaza.com) near Tampa International Airport, where the headliners include Neiman Marcus, Nordstrom, and Lord & Taylor.

CIGARS   Ybor City is no longer a major producer of hand-rolled cigars, but you can still watch artisans making stogies at the **Gonzalez y Martinez Cigar Factory,** 2025 7th Ave., in the Columbia Restaurant building (© **813/247- 2469**). Gonzalez and Martinez are recent arrivals from Cuba and don't speak English, but the staff does at the adjoining **Columbia Cigar Store** (it's best to enter here). Rollers are on duty Monday through Saturday from 10am to 6pm.

You can stock up on fine domestic and imported cigars at **El Sol,** 1728 E. 7th Ave. (© **813/247-5554**), the city's oldest cigar store; **King Corona Cigar Factory,** 1523 E. 7th Ave. (© **813/241-9109**); and **Metropolitan Cigars & Wine,** 2014 E. 7th Ave. (© **813/248-3304**).

SHOPPING CENTERS   Old Hyde Park Village, 1507 W. Swann Ave., at South Dakota Avenue (© **813/251-3500;** www.oldhydeparkvillage.com), is a terrific alternative to cookie-cutter suburban malls. Walk around little shops in the sunshine and check out Hyde Park, one of the city's oldest and most historic neighborhoods at the same time. The cluster of 50 upscale shops and boutiques is set in a village layout. The selection includes Williams-Sonoma, Pottery Barn, Restoration Hardware, Brooks Brothers, Crabtree & Evelyn, and Godiva, to name a few. There's a free parking garage on South Oregon Avenue behind Jacobson's department store. Most shops are open Monday through Saturday from 10am to 7pm and Sundays from noon to 5pm. There's a farmers' market (at Swan and Dakota avenues) every Saturday from 9am to 2pm offering local produce, seafood, and assorted tchotchkes.

Fun Fact   Did You Know?

Tampa used to be called Tanpa. No, this is not a spelling error. In the early days, when the place was an Indian fishing village, that's what it was called. Loosely translated, *Tanpa* means "land by the water." Early explorers had illegibly written Tanpa on the maps. It wasn't until 1539, when gold-searching explorers put the town on their map, that the name was mistakenly changed to Tampa.

The centerpiece of the downtown seaport renovation, the massive mall known as **Channelside at Garrison Seaport,** on Channelside Drive between the Garrison Seaport and the Florida Aquarium (© **813/223-4250;** www.channelside.com), has stores, restaurants, a dance club, a games arcade, and a multiscreen cinema with an IMAX screen.

In Ybor City, the new **Centro Ybor,** on 7th Avenue East at 16th Street (© **813/242-4660;** www.centroybor.com), is primarily a dining and entertainment complex, but you'll find a few national stores here such as American Eagle, Birkenstock, Urban Outfitters, and Victoria's Secret.

WHERE TO STAY

We've organized the accommodations listings below into three geographic areas: near Busch Gardens, downtown, and Ybor City. If you're going to Busch Gardens, Adventure Island, Lowry Park Zoo, and the Museum of Science and Industry (MOSI), the motels near Busch Gardens are much more convenient than those downtown, about 7 miles to the south. The downtown hotels are geared to business travelers, but staying there will put you near the Florida Aquarium, the Tampa Museum of Art, the Henry B. Plant Museum, the Tampa Bay Performing Arts Center, scenic Bayshore Boulevard, and the dining and shopping opportunities in the Channelside and Hyde Park districts. Staying in Ybor City will put you within walking distance of numerous restaurants and the city's hottest nightspots.

The Westshore area, near the bay, west of downtown and south of Tampa International Airport, is another commercial center, with a wide range of national chain hotels catering to business travelers and conventioneers. It's not far from Raymond James Stadium and the New York Yankees' spring-training complex. Check with your favorite chain for a Westshore-Airport location.

Room rates at most hotels in Tampa vary little from season to season. This is especially true downtown, where the hotels do a brisk convention business year-round. Hillsborough County adds 12% tax to your hotel room bill.

NEAR BUSCH GARDENS

The nearest chain motel to the park is **Howard Johnson Hotel Near Busch Gardens Maingate,** 4139 E. Busch Blvd. (© **800/4061411** or 813/988-9191), an older property that was extensively renovated in 1999. It's 1½ blocks east of the main entrance. A bit farther away, the 500-room **Embassy Suites Hotel and Conference Center,** 3705 Spectrum Blvd., facing Fowler Avenue (© **800/362-2779** or 813/977-7066; fax 813/977-7933), is the plushest and most expensive establishment near the park. Almost across the avenue stands **LaQuinta Inn & Suites,** 3701 E. Fowler Ave. (© **800/687-6667** or 813/910-7500; fax 813/910-7600). Side-by-side, just south of Fowler Avenue, are

---

Tips **Discount Packages**

Many Tampa hotels combine tickets to major attractions such as Busch Gardens in their packages, so always ask about special deals.

---

editions of **AmeriSuites,** 11408 N. 30th St. (© **800/833-1516** or 813/979-1922; fax 813/979-1926), and **DoubleTree Guest Suites,** 11310 N. 30th St. (© **800/222-8733** or 813/971-7690; fax 813/972-5525).

Baymont Inn & Suites *(Value)*   Fake banana trees and a parrot cage welcome guests to the terra-cotta–floored lobby of this comfortable and convenient member of the small chain of cost-conscious but amenity-rich motels. All rooms are spacious and have ceiling fans and desks. Rooms with king beds also have recliners; business rooms sport dataport phones and extralarge desks; and the suites have refrigerators and microwave ovens. Outside, a courtyard with an unheated swimming pool has plenty of space for sunning. There's no restaurant on the premises, but plenty are within walking distance.

9202 N. 30th St. (at Busch Blvd.), Tampa, FL 33612. © **800/428-3438** or 813/930-6900. Fax 813/930-0563. www.baymontinns.com. 146 units. Winter $89–$119 double; off-season $79–$99 double. Rates include continental breakfast and local phone calls. AE, DC, DISC, MC, V. **Amenities:** Outdoor pool; game room; coin-op washers and dryers. *In room:* A/C, TV, dataport, fridge, coffeemaker, hair dryer, iron.

Best Western All Suites Hotel *(Value)*   This three-story all-suites hotel is the most beachlike vacation venue you'll find close to the park. Whimsical signs lead you around a lush tropical courtyard with heated pool, hot tub, and a lively, sports-oriented Tiki bar. They pride themselves on being "so close" to Busch Gardens that "the parrots escape to our trees," hence the hotel's nickname "that parrot place." The bar can get noisy before closing at 9pm, and ground-level units are musty, so ask for an upstairs suite away from the action. Suite living rooms are well equipped and separate bedrooms have narrow screened patios or balconies. Great for kids, 11 "family suites" have bunk beds in addition to a queen-size bed for parents.

Behind Busch Gardens, 3001 University Center Dr. (faces N. 30th St. between Busch Blvd. and Fowler Ave.), Tampa, FL 33612. © **800/786-7446** or 813/971-8930. Fax 813/971-8935. www.thatparrotplace.com. 150 units. Winter $99–$159 suite for 2; off-season $79–$99 suite for 2. Rates include hot and cold breakfast buffet. AE, DC, DISC, MC, V. **Amenities:** Restaurant (breakfast and dinner only); bar; heated outdoor pool; access to nearby health club; Jacuzzi; game room; limited room service; laundry service; coin-op washers and dryers. *In room:* A/C, TV, dataport, fridge, coffeemaker, hair dryer, iron.

DOWNTOWN TAMPA

Hyatt Regency Tampa   Just off the Franklin Street pedestrian mall, and in the heart of the business district, the Hyatt has lost its place as downtown's premier hotel to the newer Tampa Marriott Waterside (see below), but still attracts a mostly corporate crowd. The spacious, recently renovated contemporary rooms lack balconies, and the higher office towers that now surround the hotel restrict views from the windows. Office workers congregate at the Avanzare restaurant for inexpensive light lunches.

2 Tampa City Center (corner of Tampa and E. Jackson sts.), Tampa, FL 33602. © **800/233-1234** or 813/225-1234. Fax 813/273-0234. www.tamparegency.hyatt.com. 521 units. $249–$274 double. Weekend packages available in summer. AE, DC, DISC, MC, V. Valet parking $12. **Amenities:** 2 restaurants; bar; heated outdoor pool; exercise room; Jacuzzi; concierge; business center; limited room service; laundry service; coin-op washers and dryers; concierge-level rooms. *In room:* A/C, TV, dataport, coffeemaker, hair dryer, iron.

Radisson Riverwalk Hotel ★ Set on the east bank of the Hillsborough River, this six-story hotel was completely remodeled in 1998. Half the rooms face west and have lovely views from their (unlighted) balconies of the Arabesque minarets atop the Henry B. Plant Museum and University of Tampa across the river—quite a scene at sunset. They cost more but are more preferable to units on the east side of the building, which face downtown's skyscrapers and don't have balconies. Rooms here are clean and of a moderate size, but are tired and impersonal, decorated in Drexel Heritage furniture, as is common with any chain hotel of this size. Beside the river, the Ashley Drive Grill serves indoor-outdoor breakfasts and lunches, then turns to fine dining in the evenings. The Boulanger bakery and deli, open from 5am to midnight, purveys fresh pastries, soups, sandwiches, and snacks. Unless you're on business or are intent on staying downtown to be close to an attraction such as the performing arts center or the aquarium, there's not much here to entice a mainstream traveler.

200 N. Ashley Dr. (at Jackson St.), Tampa, FL 33602. © **800/333-3333** or 813/223-2222. Fax 813/221-5929. www.radisson.com/tampafl_riverwalk. 282 units. Winter $219–$239 double; off-season $129–$179 double. AE, DC, DISC, MC, V. Valet parking $10, self-parking $7. **Amenities:** 2 restaurants; bar; heated outdoor pool; exercise room; access to nearby health club; sauna; concierge; limited room service; laundry service; coin-op washers and dryers; concierge-level rooms. *In room:* A/C, TV, dataport, coffeemaker, hair dryer, iron.

Tampa Marriott Waterside Hotel and Marina ★★ This luxurious 22-story hotel occupies downtown's most strategic location in the area's emerging Channel District—beside the river and between the Tampa Convention Center and the St. Pete Times Forum. Opening onto a riverfront promenade, the towering, three-story lobby is large enough to accommodate the many convention-eers drawn to the two neighboring venues and the hotel's own 50,000 square feet of meeting space. The third floor has a fully equipped spa, modern exercise facility, and outdoor heated pool. About half of the guest quarters have balconies overlooking the bay or city (choice views are high up on the south side). Although spacious, the regular rooms are dwarfed by the 720-square-foot suites. For those interested in boating the bay, there's also a 32-slip marina.

700 S. Florida Ave. (at St. Pete Times Forum Dr.), Tampa, FL 33602. © **800/228-9290** or 813/221-4900. Fax 813/221-0923. www.marriott.com. 717 units. $215–$285 double. AE, DC, DISC, MC, V. Weekend rates available. Valet parking $14; no self-parking. **Amenities:** 3 restaurants; 3 bars; heated outdoor pool; health club; spa; Jacuzzi; concierge; activities desk; car-rental desk; business center; salon; limited room service; massage; babysitting; laundry service; coin-op washers and dryers; concierge-level rooms. *In room:* A/C, TV, fax, dataport (with high-speed Internet), fridge, coffeemaker, hair dryer, iron.

Wyndham Harbour Island ★★★ Close enough to downtown but still worlds away on its own 177-acre island, this tropical-flaired Wyndham insists that you're here on vacation and not stuck in some insipid downtown convention hotel. Rooms overlook the harbor and are hyper-comfortable with pillow-top mattresses and large bathrooms with Golden Door products. Luna di Mare is the hotel's exquisite Italian restaurant, overlooking the water and offering an extensive wine list, seafood, and chops. Guest privileges at the Harbour Island Athletic Club include full workout facilities, tennis courts, racquetball courts, and a full service spa. Stroll the boardwalk to fully appreciate your surroundings.

725 S. Harbour Island Blvd., Tampa, FL 33602. © **877/999-3223** or 813/229-5000. Fax 813/229-5322. www.wyndham.com/hotels/TPAHI/main.wnt. 299 units. $209–$289 double, $495–$895 suite. AE, DC, DISC, MC, V. Weekend rates available. Valet parking $12; no self-parking. **Amenities:** Restaurant; 3 bars; heated outdoor pool; access to nearby health club; access to spa; Jacuzzi; concierge; activities desk; car-rental desk; business center; salon; limited room service; massage; babysitting; laundry service. *In room:* A/C, TV, fax, high-speed Internet, coffeemaker, hair dryer, iron.

YBOR CITY

Hilton Garden Inn ★   This modern, four-story hotel stands just 2 blocks north of the heart of Ybor City's dining and entertainment district. A one-story brick structure in front houses the bright lobby, a comfy relaxation area with fireplace, a dining area providing cooked and continental breakfasts, and a small 24-hour pantry selling beer, wine, soft drinks, and frozen dinners. You can heat up the dinners in your comfortable guest room's microwave oven or store them in your fridge. Since Hilton's "Garden" hotels are aimed primarily at business travelers (they compete with Marriott's Courtyards), your room will also have a large desk and two phones. If you opt for a suite, you'll have a separate living room and a larger bathroom than in the regular units.

1700 E. 9th Ave. (between 17th and 18th sts.), Tampa, FL 33605. ✆ **800/445-8667** or 813/769-9267. Fax 813/769-3299. www.hiltongardeninn.com. 95 units. $129–$250 double. AE, DC, DISC, MC, V. **Amenities:** Restaurant (breakfast only); heated outdoor pool; exercise room; Jacuzzi; business center; laundry service; coin-op washers and dryers. *In room:* A/C, TV, dataport (with high-speed Internet), fridge, coffeemaker, hair dryer, iron.

A NEARBY SPA & SPORTS RESORT

Saddlebrook Resort–Tampa ★★ *Kids*   Set on 480 rolling acres of priceless countryside, Saddlebrook is off the beaten path (30 min. north of Tampa International Airport) and is a landlocked condominium development. If you're interested in spas, tennis, golf, or all of the above, we recommend this resort, which offers complete spa treatments, the Hopman Tennis Program (Jennifer Capriati pitches a tent here), and the Arnold Palmer Golf Academy (see "Outdoor Activities & Spectator Sports," earlier in this chapter). In this condominium development, you'll stay in hotel rooms or one-, two-, or three-bedroom suites. Much more appealing than the rooms, the suites have kitchens and a patio or balcony overlooking lagoons, cypress and palm trees, and the resort's two 18-hole championship golf courses. There are also shops, restaurants, a stunning pool, and an excellent kids club with supervised activities and theme-oriented activities.

5700 Saddlebrook Way, Wesley Chapel, FL 33543. ✆ **800/729-8383** or 813/973-1111. Fax 813/973-4504. www.saddlebrookresort.com. 800 units. Winter $200–$327 per person; off-season $130–$180 per person. Rates include breakfast and dinner. Packages available. AE, DC, DISC, MC, V. Valet parking $10; free self-parking. Take I-75 north to Fla. 54 (exit 58); go 1 mile east to resort. **Amenities:** 3 restaurants; 2 bars; heated outdoor pool; 2 golf courses; 45 grass, clay, and hard tennis courts; health club; spa; Jacuzzi; sauna; bike rental; children's activities program; concierge; activities desk; car-rental desk; business center; limited room service; massage; laundry service; coin-op washers and dryers. *In room:* A/C, TV, dataport, kitchen, minibar, fridge, coffeemaker, hair dryer, iron.

WHERE TO DINE

As with the hotels, we have organized the restaurants that follow by geographic area: near Busch Gardens, in or near Hyde Park (across the Hillsborough River from downtown), and in Ybor City. Although Ybor City is better known, Tampa's trendiest dining scene is along South Howard Avenue—"SoHo" to the locals—between West Kennedy Boulevard and the bay in affluent Hyde Park.

NEAR BUSCH GARDENS

You'll find the national fast food and family restaurants east of I-275 on Busch Boulevard and Fowler Avenue.

Moderate

Cafe Don José SPANISH/AMERICAN   It's not nearly on a par with the Columbia in Ybor City (see below), but this Spanish-themed restaurant is

Amish Country South?

Twelve miles east of Tampa, you'll find **Behind the Fence,** 1400 Viola Dr. at Country Side Street (𝄐 **813/685-8201**), a fabulous and secluded country-style B&B in Brandon, Florida. Innkeeper Larry Yoss, raised in an Amish home in Ohio, brought his heritage to Florida by encouraging traveling artisans to hang out in the inn's backyard where they'd demonstrate their skills in soap-making, candle dipping, basket weaving, looming, and open-hearth cooking. This became a yearly August to September weekend trip into the past, which is often carried over to Christmas, during which time Behind the Fence re-creates itself as an homage to Christmas in the 1800s (though it's a great place to stay at any time of the year). The inn itself is as charming as it sounds, with a porch overlooking a pool, breakfasts including Amish sweet rolls, and three guest rooms in the main house usually rented by friends and families because they share a single bathroom. The two cottage rooms by the pool are stunning and have their own facilities including clawfoot tubs. Rates are Amishly reasonable, from $79 to $89.

among the best there is within a short drive of Busch Gardens. High-back chairs, dark wood floors, and Spanish posters and paintings set an appropriate scene for the house specialties of traditional paella (allow 30 min. for preparation) and Valencia-style rice dishes. Don José also offers non-Spanish fare such as red snapper baked in parchment.

11009 N. 56th St. (in Sherwood Forest Shopping Center, ¼ mile south of Fowler Ave.). 𝄐 **813/985-2392.** Main courses $13–$59. AE, DC, MC, V. Mon–Fri 11:30am–4:30pm and 5–10pm; Sat 5–9pm.

Ristorante Francesco 𝄐 NORTHERN ITALIAN Gregarious owner Francesco "Frankie" Murchesini patrols the tables in the hottest dining spot in North Tampa (as witnessed by the photos of famous patrons adorning the walls). When not playing his harmonica to celebrate someone's birthday, Frankie's making sure everyone is enjoying his delicious *cernia portofino* (scrumptious grouper in a brandy sauce with shrimp) and other Northern-Italian dishes. His sister makes the pasta, which shows up in more traditional fare such as seafood over linguini with a choice of marinara or white-wine sauce. Be sure to start with half a Caesar salad.

In La Place Village Shopping Center, 1441 E. Fletcher Ave. (between 14th and 15th sts.). 𝄐 **813/971-3649.** www.ristorantefrancesco.com. Reservations recommended. Main courses $10–$27. AE, DC, DISC, MC. V. Mon–Fri 11:30am–2:30pm and 5:30–10pm; Sat 5:30–10pm; Sun 5–9pm.

Shells 𝄐 *Value* SEAFOOD You'll see Shells restaurants in many parts of Florida, and with good reason, for this casual, award-winning chain consistently provides excellent value. They all have virtually identical menus, prices, and hours. Particularly good are the spicy Jack Daniel's buffalo shrimp and scallop appetizers. Main courses range from the usual fried seafood platters to pastas and charcoal-grilled shrimp, fish, steaks, and chicken.

11010 N. 30th St. (between Busch Blvd. and Fowler Ave.). 𝄐 **813/977-8456.** Main courses $9–$20 (most $10–$12). AE, DISC, MC, V. Sun–Thurs 11:30am–10pm; Fri–Sat 11:30am–11pm.

Inexpensive

Mel's Hot Dogs *(Kids* AMERICAN   Catering to everyone from businesspeople on a lunch break to hungry families craving inexpensive all-beef hot dogs, Mel Lohn's red-and-white cottage offers everything from "bagel-dogs" to bacon/cheddar Reuben-style hot dogs. All choices are served on a poppy-seed bun and can be ordered with french fries and a choice of coleslaw or baked beans. Even the decor is dedicated to wieners: The walls and windows are lined with hot-dog memorabilia, and there's usually a wiener-mobile parked out front. And just in case hot-dog mania hasn't won you over, there are a few alternative choices (chicken, beef and veggie burgers, and terrific onion rings).

4136 E. Busch Blvd., at 42nd St. *(C)* 813/985-8000. Most items $4–$9. No credit cards (but they have an ATM machine on premises). Sun–Thurs 11am–8pm; Fri–Sat 11am–9pm.

HYDE PARK
Expensive

Bern's Steak House *(★★* STEAKHOUSE   The exterior of this famous steakhouse looks like a factory. Inside, however, some say it looks like a brothel with eight ornate dining rooms with themes such as Rhône, Burgundy, and Irish Rebellion. However you perceive the decor, this is a carnivore's paradise, one to which I actually drove from Miami and back just for dinner. At Bern's, you order and pay for expertly charcoal-grilled steaks of perfectly aged beef according to the thickness and weight (the 60-oz., 3-in.-thick Porterhouse can feed four adults). The phone book–size wine list—one of the restaurant's most famous attributes—offers more than 7,000 selections, with many available by the glass. Ask your server for a sampling before you purchase a bottle.

Upstairs, the restaurant's other most famous attribute—the dessert quarters—have 50 romantic booths paneled in aged California redwood, which can privately seat from 2 to 12 guests each. All of these little chambers are equipped with phones for placing your order and closed-circuit TVs for watching and listening to a resident pianist. The dessert menu offers almost 100 selections, plus some 1,400 after-dinner drinks. It's possible to reserve a booth for dessert only, but preference is given to those who dine.

The big secret here is that steak sandwiches are available at the bar but are not mentioned on the menu. Smaller versions of the chargrilled steaks served in the dining rooms, they come with a choice of french fries or crispy onion rings. Add a salad and you have a terrific meal for about half the price of the least-expensive main course. **Sidebern's,** 2208 W. Morrison Ave. (at S. Howard Ave.), *(C)* **813/ 258-2233,** is the restaurant's New American offshoot, which is also quite good, but choose the original, because missing Bern's would be like seeing the remake of *Psycho* without ever seeing the original.

1208 S. Howard Ave. (at Marjory Ave.). *(C)* 813/251-2421. www.bernssteakhouse.com. Reservations recommended. Main courses $17–$59; sandwiches $9–$12. AE, DC, DISC, MC, V. Daily 5–11pm. Closed Christmas. Valet parking $5.

Moderate

Castaway *(★★* SEAFOOD   Gorgeous ocean views compete with stellar seafood at Castaway, where crab legs, coconut shrimp, and fresh daily catches reel in a steady crowd of locals and visitors alike. Insist on sitting outside on the deck and try to time your meal around sundown, because the vantage point for sunsets here is the kind that makes developers drool and diners delight in the fact that this Castaway isn't going anywhere anytime soon.

7720 Courtney Campbell Causeway. *(C)* 813/281-0770. Reservations recommended. Main courses $13–$40 AE, DC, DISC, MC, V. Mon–Sat 11:30am–10:30pm, Sun brunch 10:30am–2:30pm, Sun dinner 4–10pm.

Dining on the Bay

One of the newest additions to Tampa's dining scene is the 180-foot-long *StarShip Dining Yacht* (© **877/744-7999** or 813/223-7999; www.starshipdining.com), which makes 2-hour lunch and dinner cruises from the Channelside out onto Tampa Bay. The ship's four dining rooms serve exceptional cruise fare. A house band plays during dinner and then moves to the top deck for dancing under the stars. Lunch cruises cost $40 per person with a meal, $16 for sightseers. Dinner cruises cost $70. There's also a Sunday brunch for $40. Call for the schedule.

Mise en Place ✦✦ ECLECTIC   Look around at all those happy, stylish people soaking up the trendy ambience, and you'll know why chef Marty Blitz and his wife, Maryann, have been among the culinary darlings of Tampa since 1986. They present the freshest of ingredients, with a creative, award-winning menu that changes weekly. Main courses often include fascinating choices such as grainy mustard pecan crusted rack of lamb with bourbon shallot demi glace, cayenne onion rings, and tarragon white cheddar grits or Creole-style mahimahi served with chili cheese grits and a ragout of black-eyed peas, andouille sausage, and rock shrimp.

In Grand Central Place, 442 W. Kennedy Blvd. (at S. Magnolia Ave., opposite the University of Tampa). © 813/254-5373. www.miseonline.com. Reservations recommended. Main courses $15–$26; tasting menu $48. AE, DC, DISC, MC, V. Tues–Thurs 11:30am–2:30pm and 5:30–10pm; Fri 11:30am–2:30pm and 5:30–11pm; Sat 5–11pm.

Wine Exchange ✦✦ MEDITERRANEAN   This Tampa hotspot is an oenophile's dream come true, in which each dish is paired with a particular wine available by the bottle or glass. While the menu is rather simple, featuring pizzas, pastas, salads, and sandwiches, the daily specials are more elaborate, including grilled Delmonico steak, blackened pork tenderloin, or dijon-crusted salmon. The outdoor patio is a great place to sit, that is, if there's room. There's almost always a wait at this buzzworthy eatery.

1611 W. Swan Ave. © 813/254-9463. Reservations not accepted. Main courses $10–$22. AE, DC, DISC, MC, V. Mon–Fri 11:30am–10pm; Sat 11am–11 pm, Sun 11am–9 pm; brunch on Sat and Sun 11am–3pm.

Inexpensive
Bella's Italian Cafe ✦ (Value) ITALIAN   Creative dishes and very reasonable prices make this sophisticated yet informal cafe one of SoHo's most popular neighborhood hangouts. Although you can order the wood-fired pizzas and homemade pasta under traditional Bolognese or Alfredo sauces, the stars here feature the tasty likes of blackened chicken in a creamy tomato sauce over fettuccine, or shrimp and scallops in a roasted tomato sauce over bow-tie pasta. Finish with the house version of tiramisu. Local professionals flock to the friendly bar during two-for-one happy hours nightly from 4 to 7pm and from 11pm until closing. The open kitchen provides only appetizers, salads, pizzas, and desserts after 11pm.

1413 S. Howard Ave. (at Mississippi Ave.). 813/254-3355. Reservations not accepted. Main courses $7–$15; pizza $7.50–$9.50. AE, DC, DISC, MC, V. Mon–Tues 11:30am–11:30pm; Wed–Thurs 11:30am–12:30am; Fri 11am–1:30am; Sat 4pm–1:30am; Sun 4–11:30pm.

Four Green Fields IRISH/AMERICAN   Just across the bridge from the downtown convention center, this thatched-roof Irish pub may be surrounded by palm trees instead of potato fields, but it still offers the ambience and tastes of Ireland. Staffed by Irish immigrants, the large room with a square bar in the center smells of Bass and Harp ales. The Gaelic stew is predictably bland, but the salads and sandwiches are passable. The live Irish music Thursday through Saturday nights and on Sunday afternoon draws a fun crowd ranging from post-college to early retirees.

205 W. Platt St. (between Parker St. and Plant Ave.). ℂ 813/254-4444. www.fourgreenfields.com. Reservations accepted. Main courses $9.50–$15; sandwiches $6–$7. AE, MC, V. Daily 11am–3am.

YBOR CITY
Moderate
Big City Tavern ⚘ NEW AMERICAN   Although this restaurant is a chain, located in West Palm Beach and Fort Lauderdale, Ybor City's Big City Tavern take the prize for best decor, housed in a converted ballroom and featuring columns, floor to ceiling windows, and wrought-iron balconies. The food's pretty good, too, especially the roasted duck with mango and basil risotto, and the bar scene is a people watching paradise as a youngish, well heeled, hip clientele gathers to trade tales of life in the big city.

1600 E. 8th Ave. ℂ 813/247-3000. Reservations recommended. Main courses $11–$20. AE, MC, V. Sun–Thurs 11:30am–1am; Fri–Sat 11:30am–2am.

Columbia ⚘⚘⚘ SPANISH   Dating from 1905, this hand-painted tile building occupies an entire city block in the heart of Ybor City. Tourists flock here to soak up the ambience, and so do the locals because it's so much fun to clap along during fire-belching Spanish flamenco floor shows Monday through Saturday evenings ($6 per person additional charge). You can't help coming back time after time for the famous Spanish bean soup and original "1905" salad. The *paella a la valenciana* is outstanding, with more than a dozen ingredients from Gulf grouper and Gulf pink shrimp to calamari, mussels, clams, chicken, and pork. One of our favorites is *boliche* (eye of round stuffed with chorizo), accompanied by plantains and black beans and rice. All entrees come with a crispy hunk of Cuban bread with butter. Lighter appetites can choose from a limited menu of tapas, including "Cuban caviar" (actually a spicy black-bean dip). The decor throughout is graced with hand-painted tiles, wrought-iron chandeliers, dark woods, rich red fabrics, and stained-glass windows. You can breathe your own fumes in the Cigar Bar.

2117 E. 7th Ave. (between 21st and 22nd sts.). ℂ 813/248-4961. www.columbiarestaurant.com. Reservations recommended. Main courses $14–$28. AE, DC, DISC, MC, V. Mon–Thurs 11am–10pm; Fri–Sat 11am–11pm; Sun noon–9pm.

Inexpensive
Carmine's Restaurant & Bar ⚘ CUBAN/ITALIAN/AMERICAN   Bright blue poles hold up an ancient pressed-tin ceiling above this noisy corner cafe. It's

---

The Hub of Tampa's Bar Scene
Ybor City and Bern's Steak House are command central for the boozy sophisticates of Tampa, but if you go downtown, you'll find the true hub of Tampa's bar scene in the form of, well, The Hub, 719 N. Franklin St. (ℂ 813/229-1553), a classic dive bar in which judges, lawyers, and the over-21 set shake and stir over stiff libations and a fabulous jukebox.

(*Tips* **Careful Where You Park**

Parking can be scarce during nighttime in Ybor City, and the area has seen an occasional robbery late at night. Play it safe and use the municipal parking lots behind the shops on 8th Avenue East or the new parking garages near Centro Ybor, on 7th Avenue East at 16th Street.

---

not the cleanest joint in town, but a great variety of loyal local patrons gather here for genuine Cuban sandwiches—smoked ham, roast pork, Genoa salami, Swiss cheese, pickles, salad dressing, mustard, lettuce, and tomato on crispy Cuban bread. There's a vegetarian version, too, and the combination half-sandwich and choice of black beans and rice or a bowl of Spanish soup made with sausages, potatoes, and garbanzo beans all make a hearty meal for just $7 at lunch, $8 at dinner. Main courses are led by Cuban-style roast pork, thin-cut pork chops with mushroom sauce, spaghetti with a blue-crab tomato sauce, and a few seafood and chicken platters.

1802 E. 7th Ave. (at 18th St.). (*C*) 813/248-3834. Reservations not accepted. Main courses $7–$17; sandwiches $4–$8. No credit cards. Mon–Tues 11am–11pm; Wed–Thurs 11am–1am; Fri–Sat 11am–3am; Sun 11am–6pm.

TAMPA AFTER DARK

The Tampa/Hillsborough Arts Council maintains an **Artsline** ((*C*) **813/229-2787**), a 24-hour information service providing the latest on current and upcoming cultural events. Racks in many restaurants and bars have copies of *Weekly Planet* (**www.weeklyplanet.com**), *Focus,* and *Accent on Tampa Bay,* three free publications detailing what's going on in the entire bay area. And you can also check the "BayLife" and "Friday Extra" sections of *The Tampa Tribune* (**www.tampa trib.com**) and the Thursday "Weekend" section of the *St. Petersburg Times* (**www.sptimes.com**). The visitor center usually has copies of the week's newspaper sections (see "Essentials," earlier in this chapter).

THE CLUB & MUSIC SCENE Ybor City is Tampa's favorite nighttime venue by far. All you have to do is stroll along 7th Avenue East between 15th and 20th streets, and you'll hear music blaring out of the clubs. The avenue is packed with people, a majority of them high schoolers and early 20-somethings, on Friday and Saturday from 9pm to 3am, but you'll also find something going on Tuesday through Thursday, and even on Sundays. The clubs change names and character frequently, so you don't need names, addresses, or phone numbers; your ears will guide you along 7th Avenue East. With all of the sidewalk seating, it is easy to judge what the clientele is like in any given place and make your choice from there.

The center of the action these days is **Centro Ybor,** on 7th Avenue East at 16th Street ((*C*) **813/242-4660;** www.thecentroybor.com), the district's large dining-and-entertainment complex. The restaurants and pubs in this family-oriented center tend to be considerably tamer than many of those along 7th Avenue, at least on nonweekend nights. You don't have to pay to listen to live music in the center's patio on weekend afternoons.

THE PERFORMING ARTS With a prime downtown location on 9 acres along the east bank of the Hillsborough River, the huge **Tampa Bay Performing Arts Center** (*★*), 1010 N. MacInnes Place next to the Tampa Museum of Art

(© **800/955-1045** or 813/229-7827; www.tampacenter.com), is the largest performing-arts venue south of the Kennedy Center in Washington, D.C. Accordingly, this four-theater complex is the focal point of Tampa's performing-arts scene, presenting a wide range of Broadway plays, classical and pop concerts, operas, cabarets, improv, and special events.

A sightseeing attraction in its own right, the restored **Tampa Theatre,** 711 Franklin St. (© **813/274-8286;** www.tampatheatre.org), between Zack and Polk streets, dates from 1926 and is on the National Register of Historic Places. It presents a varied program of classic, foreign, and alternative films, as well as concerts and special events. (And it's said to be haunted!)

The 66,321-seat **Raymond James Stadium,** 4201 N. Dale Mabry Hwy. (© **813/673-4300;** www.raymondjames.com/stadium), is sometimes the site of headliner concerts. The **USF Sun Dome,** 4202 E. Fowler Ave. (© **813/974-3111;** www.sundome.org), on the University of South Florida campus, hosts major concerts by touring pop stars, rock bands, jazz groups, and other contemporary artists.

Bars featuring live music include **Whiskey Joe's,** 2500 N. Rocky Point Dr. (© **813/281-0557**), a bayfront shack with plenty of visual and audible color; Ybor City's **Twilight,** 1507 E. 7th Ave. (© **813/247-4225**), an industrial-chic soundstage for the likes of local bands and national bands such as Seven Mary Three; and **Skipper's Smokehouse,** 910 Skipper Rd. (© **813/971-0666**), a Key West–style former smokehouse turned blues, jazz, zydeco, ska, and reggae hot spot.

Ticketmaster (© **813/287-8844**) sells tickets to most events and shows.

2 St. Petersburg ⋆

20 miles SW of Tampa, 289 miles NW of Miami, 84 miles SW of Orlando

On the western shore of the bay, St. Petersburg stands in contrast to Tampa, much like San Francisco compares to Oakland in California. Whereas Tampa is the area's business, industrial, and shipping center, St. Petersburg was conceived and built a century ago primarily for tourists and wintering snowbirds. Here you'll find one of the most picturesque and pleasant downtowns of any city in Florida, with a waterfront promenade and the famous, inverted pyramid-shaped Pier offering great views across the bay, plus quality museums, interesting shops, and a few good restaurants. Thanks to an urban redevelopment program, St. Pete has awoken from its slumber and is starting to actually resemble a city that could be considered "hip," with renewed, restored streetscapes full of punk'd out skateboarders, clubs, bars, and a vibrancy that goes well beyond the excitement surrounding Bingo night at the "adult" communities in town.

Away from downtown, the city pretty much consists of strip malls dividing residential neighborhoods, but plan at least to have a look around the charming bay-front area. If you don't do anything else, go out on The Pier and take a pleasant stroll along Bayshore Drive.

Fun Fact Sunny Days

St. Petersburg is listed in the Guinness Book of World Records as the city with the longest number of days of consecutive sunshine—768 to be exact. From February 9, 1967 to March 17, 1969, the city experienced not a drop of rain, no clouds, just pure, unadulterated, tanning-friendly sunshine!

Downtown St. Petersburg

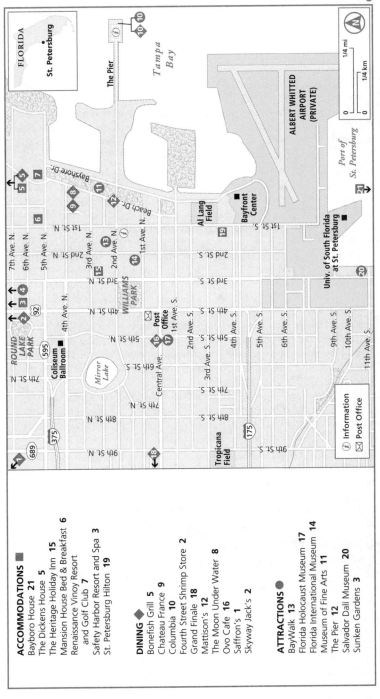

FLORIDA

St. Petersburg

Tampa Bay

The Pier

ALBERT WHITTED AIRPORT (PRIVATE)

Port of St. Petersburg

Al Lang Field

Bayfront Center

Univ. of South Florida at St. Petersburg

WILLIAMS PARK

Post Office

Coliseum Ballroom

ROUND LAKE PARK

Mirror Lake

Tropicana Field

Bayshore Dr.

Beach Dr.

1st St. N.
2nd St. N.
3rd St. N.
4th Ave. N.
5th St. N.
6th St. N.
7th St. N.
8th St. N.
9th St. N.

7th Ave. N.
6th Ave. N.
5th Ave. N.
3rd Ave. N.
2nd Ave. N.
1st Ave. N.

1st Ave. S.
2nd Ave. S.
3rd Ave. S.
4th Ave. S.
5th Ave. S.
6th Ave. S.
9th Ave. S.
10th Ave. S.
11th Ave. S.

Central Ave.
1st St. S.
2nd St. S.
3rd St. S.
4th St. S.
5th St. S.
6th St. S.
7th St. S.
8th St. S.
9th St. S.

ⓘ Information
⊠ Post Office

0   1/4 mi
0   1/4 km

ACCOMMODATIONS ■
Bayboro House **21**
The Dickens House **5**
The Heritage Holiday Inn **15**
Mansion House Bed & Breakfast **6**
Renaissance Vinoy Resort
    and Golf Club **7**
Safety Harbor Resort and Spa **3**
St. Petersburg Hilton **19**

DINING ◆
Bonefish Grill **5**
Chateau France **9**
Columbia **10**
Fourth Street Shrimp Store **2**
Grand Finale **18**
Mattison's **12**
The Moon Under Water **8**
Ovo Cafe **16**
Saffron's **1**
Skyway Jack's **2**

ATTRACTIONS ●
BayWalk **13**
Florida Holocaust Museum **17**
Florida International Museum **14**
Museum of Fine Arts **11**
The Pier **12**
Salvador Dalí Museum **20**
Sunken Gardens **3**

ESSENTIALS

GETTING THERE   **Tampa International Airport,** approximately 16 miles northeast of St. Petersburg, is the prime gateway for the area (see "Essentials," in section 1, earlier in this chapter). The primary carrier at **St. Petersburg–Clearwater International Airport,** on Roosevelt Boulevard (Fla. 686) about 10 miles north of downtown St. Petersburg (© 727/453-7800; www.fly2pie.com), is **American Trans Air (ATA),** © 800/435-9282, www.ata.com. The Canadian carrier **Air Transat** (© 877/872-6728; www.airtransat.com) flies here during the winter months. **Amtrak** (© 800/USA-RAIL; www.amtrak.com) has bus connections from its Tampa station to downtown St. Petersburg (see "Getting There," in section 1, above).

VISITOR INFORMATION   For advance information about St. Petersburg and the beaches (see section 3, later in this chapter), contact the **St. Petersburg/Clearwater Area Convention & Visitors Bureau,** 14450 46th St. N., Clearwater, FL 34622 (© 800/345-6710, or 727/464-7200 for hotel reservations; fax 727/464-7222; www.floridasbeach.com for information specific to the beaches).

When you arrive, you can head to the **St. Petersburg Area Chamber of Commerce,** 100 2nd Ave. N. (at 1st St.), St. Petersburg, FL 33701 (© 727/821-4069; fax 727/895-6326; www.stpete.com). Across the street from the Bay-Walk shopping-and-dining complex, this downtown main office and visitor center is open Monday through Friday from 8am to 5pm, Saturday from 10am to 4pm, and Sunday from noon to 4pm. Ask for a copy of the chamber's visitor guide, which lists hotels, motels, condominiums, and other accommodations.

Also downtown, there are **walk-in information centers** on the first level of The Pier and in the lobby of the Florida International Museum (see "Seeing the Top Attractions," below).

The chamber also operates the **Suncoast Welcome Center** (© 727/573-1449), on Ulmerton Road at exit 31B southbound off I-275 (there's no exit here for northbound traffic). The center is open daily from 9am to 5pm except New Year's Day, Easter, Thanksgiving, and Christmas.

GETTING AROUND   The **Pinellas Suncoast Transit Authority/PSTA** (© 727/530-9911; www.psta.net) operates regular bus service throughout St. Petersburg and the rest of the Pinellas Peninsula. Rides cost $1.25 for adults, 60¢ for seniors, and 75¢ for students.

If you need a cab, call **Yellow Cab** (© 727/821-7777) or **Independent Cab** (© 727/327-3444). Fares are $2 at flag fall, plus $1.60 for each additional mile.

SEEING THE TOP ATTRACTIONS

Florida Holocaust Museum 𝔸   This thought-provoking museum (the fourth-largest Holocaust museum in the U.S.) has exhibits about the Holocaust (Jewish life before the Holocaust, the rise of the Nazi party, the world's response, and so on), including a boxcar used to transport human cargo to the Auschwitz death camp in Poland and a 2nd-floor gallery of art relating to the Holocaust. Its main focus, however, is to promote tolerance and understanding in the present. It was founded by Walter P. Loebenberg, a local businessman who escaped Nazi Germany in 1939 and fought with the U.S. Army in World War II.

55 5th St. S. (between Central Ave. and 1st Ave. S.). © 800/960-7448 or 727/820-0100. www.flholocaust museum.org. Admission $8 adults, $7 seniors and colleges students, $3 children 6–18, free for kids under 6. Mon–Fri 10am–5pm; Sat–Sun noon–5pm (last admission at 4pm). Closed Easter, Rosh Hashanah, Yom Kippur, Thanksgiving, and Christmas.

Fun Fact **Open-Air Mail**

St. Petersburg residents don't have to go inside to get mail out of their boxes at St. Petersburg's open-air **Post Office,** at the corner of 1st Avenue North and 4th Street North. Built in 1917, this granite, arcaded Spanish Colonial structure is a popular local landmark and is often photographed by those enchanted by its charm.

Florida International Museum ★★   Housed in the former Maas Brothers Department Store, long an area landmark, this excellent museum attracted 600,000 visitors from around the world when it opened its first exhibition in 1995, and the success has continued. Its outstanding exhibit on the Cuban Missile Crisis was such a smash hit that it's now permanent—and well worth seeing even if the two temporary exhibits don't catch your fancy. On the other hand, they very well could, since the museum is associated with—and gets some of its staff on loan from—the Smithsonian Institution in Washington, D.C. Call to see what's scheduled during your visit. Allow at least 3 hours to tour all three exhibitions. There's an excellent museum store here as well.

100 2nd St. N. (between 1st and 2nd aves. N.). © **800/777-9882** or 727/822-3693. www.floridamuseum. org. Admission to all exhibits $10 adults, $8 seniors, $5 children 6–18, free for children under 6. Mon–Sat 10am–5pm; Sun noon–5pm (last entry 4pm daily).

Museum of Fine Arts ★★   Resembling a Mediterranean villa on the waterfront, this museum houses an excellent permanent collection of European, American, pre-Colombian, and Far Eastern art, with works by such artists as Fragonard, Monet, Renoir, Cézanne, and Gauguin. Other highlights include period rooms with antiques and historical furnishings, plus a gallery of Steuben crystal, a new decorative-arts gallery, and world-class rotating exhibits. The best way to see it all is on a guided tour, which takes about 1 hour. Ask about classical-music performances from October to April.

255 Beach Dr. NE (at 3rd Ave. N.). © 727/896-2667. www.fine-arts.org. Admission $8 adults, $7 seniors 65 and older, $4 students older than 6 with ID, free for children under 6 (special exhibits cost more). Admission includes guided tour. Tues–Sat 10am–5pm; Sun 1–5pm. Guided tours Tues–Sat 11am, 1, 2, and 3pm; Sun 1 and 2pm (no additional charge). Closed New Year's Day, Martin Luther King Jr. Day, Thanksgiving, and Christmas.

The Pier ★ *Kids*   The Pier is a festive waterfront dining-and-shopping complex overlooking Tampa Bay. Originally built as a railroad pier in 1889, today it's capped by a spaceshiplike inverted pyramid offering five levels of shops, three restaurants, a tourist information desk, an observation deck, catwalks for fishing, boat docks, miniature golf, boat and watersports rentals, sightseeing boats, and a food court, plus an aquarium. Cruise boats often operate from The Pier during the winter months, and you can rent fishing gear and drop your line into the bay year-round. There's valet parking at the end of the pier, or you can park on land and ride a free trolley out to the complex.

800 2nd Ave. NE. © 727/821-6443. www.stpete-pier.com. Free admission to all the public areas and decks; donations welcome at the Pier Aquarium. Valet parking $6; self-parking $3. Pier Mon–Thurs 10am–9pm; Fri–Sat 10am–10pm; Sun 11am–7pm. Aquarium Mon–Sat 10am–8pm; Sun 11am–6pm.

Salvador Dalí Museum ★★★   This starkly modern museum houses the world's most comprehensive (and most valuable, at $125 million) collection of works by the renowned Spanish surrealist—and for art lovers is reason enough

---

Tips **Car Smarts**

You can spend a small fortune in a parking garage or in feeding the meters in St. Petersburg, but you can cut costs substantially by parking at The Pier ($3 all day) and taking The Looper, the city's trolley service, which operates between The Pier and all major downtown attractions.

---

to visit downtown St. Petersburg. Housing 6 of the artist's Masterworks, the museum was given 3 stars by the Michelin Guide—the highest-ranked museum in the entire South. It includes oil paintings, watercolors, drawings, and more than 1,000 graphics, plus posters, photos, sculptures, objets d'art, and a 5,000-volume library on Dalí and surrealism. Reynolds Morse, an Ohio plastics engineer, and his wife, Eleanore, discovered the Catalonian artist and began collecting his works in 1943. They moved the collection here in 1980 and are credited with introducing the seemingly normal city to the kind of skewed perception usually reserved for much larger metropolises. Make sure to take one of the free docent-led tours to get the most out of the museum and its artwork.

1000 3rd St. S. (near 11th Ave. S.). ℅ 727/823-3767. www.salvadordalimuseum.org. Admission $13 adults, $11 seniors, $7 students 10 and older and children 5–9, free for children 4 and under, Thurs between 5–8pm $5 for all. Mon–Wed and Fri–Sat 9:30am–5:30pm; Thurs 9:30am–8pm; Sun noon–5:30pm. Closed Thanksgiving, Christmas.

Sunken Gardens   Dating from 1935, this former tourist attraction is now operated as a 7-acre botanical garden by the City of St. Petersburg. It contains a vast array of 5,000 plants, flowers, and trees; plus a butterfly aviary; a display of snakes, spiders, and scorpions; and a rainforest information center. There's also a daily wildlife show. Call for a schedule of exhibits and tours.

1825 4th St. N. (between 18th and 19th aves. NE). ℅ 727/551-3100. www.stpete.org/fun/parks/sunken.htm. Admission $7 adults, $5 seniors, $3 children 3–16, free for children 2 and under. Mon–Sat 10am–4:30pm; Sun noon–4:30pm.

ORGANIZED TOURS

The only organized tours of St. Petersburg—and they are pretty good ones—are with **Duck Tours of Tampa Bay** (℅ 727/432-3825; www.ducktoursoftampa bay.com), which has 1-hour, 20-minute tours of downtown and the nearby waterways using reconditioned World War II amphibious "Ducks." The vehicles depart from The Pier daily from 11am to 5pm. The narrated tours cost $19 for adults, $17 for seniors, and $9.95 for children 3 to 12, plus tax. Kids under 3 ride free. The same company has tours of Tampa. *Note:* As this book went to press, an insurance issue had temporarily suspended operations of Duck Tours. Check with them to see if they're back up and running before making any plans.

OUTDOOR ACTIVITIES & SPECTATOR SPORTS

You can get information about the city's parks and leisure activities on the Internet at **www.stpete.com/leisure.htm**.

BIKING, IN-LINE SKATING & HIKING   With miles of flat terrain, the St. Petersburg area is ideal for bikers, in-line skaters, and hikers. The **Pinellas Trail** is especially good, since it follows an abandoned railroad bed 47 miles from St. Petersburg north to Tarpon Springs (℅ 727/464-8201; www.pinellascounty.org/trailgd/default.htm). The **St. Pete trail head** is on 34th Street South (U.S. 19) between 8th and Fairfield avenues south. It's packed on the weekends. Free strip maps of the trail are available at the St. Petersburg Area Chamber of Commerce (see "Visitor Information," above). The 2½-mile-long **Friendship TrailBridge** (www.friendshiptrail.org/index.html), linking Tampa and St. Petersburg, is another popular venue for hikers, bikers, bicyclists, anglers, and in-line skaters, but be careful going up and down the steep center span, especially if you're on skates.

GOLF   One of the nation's top 50 municipal courses, the **Mangrove Bay Golf Course** ★★, 875 62nd Ave. NE (✆ 727/893-7800), hugs the inlets of Old Tampa Bay and offers 18-hole, par-72 play. Facilities include a driving range; lessons and golf-club rental are also available. Fees are about $30 in winter, slightly lower off-season.

In Largo, the **Bardmoor Golf & Tennis Club,** 8001 Cumberland Rd. (✆ 727/392-1234), is often the venue for major tournaments. Lakes punctuate 17 of the 18 holes on this par-72 championship course. Lessons and rental clubs are available, as is a Tom Fazio–designed practice range. Call the clubhouse for seasonal greens fees. The course is open daily from 7am to dusk.

Call **Tee Times USA** (✆ 800/374-8633; www.teetimesusa.com) to reserve times at these and other area courses.

For course information online, go to www.golf.com and www.floridagolfing.com, or call the **Florida Sports Foundation** (✆ 850/488-8347) or **Florida Golfing** (✆ 866/833-2663).

SAILING   Both Steve and Doris Colgate's **Offshore Sailing School** (✆ 888/454-8002 or 239/454-1700; www.offshore-sailing.com) and the **Annapolis Sailing School** (✆ 800/638-9192 or 727/867-8102; www.annapolissailing.com) have operations here. Various courses lasting from 2 days to a week are offered. Contact the schools for prices and schedules.

SPECTATOR SPORTS   St. Petersburg has always been a baseball town, and **Tropicana Field,** a 45,000-seat domed stadium alongside I-175 between 9th and 16th streets (✆ 727/825-3100), is the home of the American League **Tampa Bay Devil Rays** (✆ 888/326-7297 or 727/825-3137; www.devilrays.mlb.com). The baseball season runs April through October. Single-game tickets are $3 to $75 and usually are available on game days. Call or check the website for the schedule. The Devil Rays move outdoors to **Florida Power Park at Al Lang Field,** on 2nd Avenue South at 1st Street South, for their spring-training workouts and games from mid-February to the end of March.

The **Philadelphia Phillies** now play their spring-training season in new digs in Clearwater (**Bright House Networks Field;** 601 Old Coachman Rd.; ✆ 727/442-8496). Their minor-league affiliate, the **Clearwater Phillies** (✆ 727/441-8638; www.clearwaterphillies.com; $7–$13), plays in the stadium April through August. The **Toronto Blue Jays** do their spring thing at Grant Field, 373 Douglas Ave. in Dunedin (✆ 800/707-8269 or 813/733-9302; www.bluejays.mlb.com; $13–$15), which also is home to their minor-league affiliate, the **Dunedin Blue Jays** (✆ 727/733-9302; www.dunedinbluejays.com), April through August.

TENNIS   You can learn to play or hone your game at the **Phil Green Tennis Academy** at Safety Harbor Resort and Spa (p. 418).

SHOPPING

The Pier, at the end of 2nd Avenue Northeast (see "Seeing the Top Attractions," earlier in this chapter), houses more than a dozen boutiques and crafts shops; but nearby Beach Drive, running along the waterfront, is one of the most fashionable

Ancient Burial Mounds & Manatees

Drive north of St. Petersburg for an hour on congested U.S. 19, and you'll come to one of Florida's original tourist attractions, the famous Weeki Wachee Springs (℡ **877/469-3354** or 352/596-2062; www.weeki wachee.com). "Mermaids" have been putting on acrobatic swimming shows here every day since 1947. It's a sight to see them doing their dances in waters that come from one of America's most prolific fresh-water springs, pouring some 170 million gallons of 72°F (22°C) water a day into the river. There's more than mermaids here; you can take a Wilderness River Cruise across the Weeki Wachee River and send the kids on the flume ride at Buccaneer Bay, the water-park part of the attraction. Admission is $20 for adults, $16 for children 3 to 10. Kids under 3 get in free (reduced prices are available when Buccaneer Bay is closed). Weeki Wachee Springs is open Monday through Thursday from 10am to 3pm and Friday through Sunday from 10am to 4pm. Buccaneer Bay water park is only open Fridays from 10am to 4pm and Saturday and Sunday from 10am to 5pm.

You can also rent canoes on the Weeki Wachee River for $33 a day (℡ **352/597-0360**).

From Weeki Wachee, travel 21 miles north to the **Homosassa Springs Wildlife State Park,** 4150 S. Suncoast Blvd. (U.S. 19) in Homosassa Springs (℡ **352/628-5343**; www.floridastateparks.org/homosassasprings). The highlight here is a floating observatory where visitors can "walk" under-water and watch manatees in a rehabilitation facility, as well as thou-sands of fresh- and saltwater fish. You'll also see deer, a bear, bobcats, otters, egrets, and flamingos along unspoiled nature trails. The park is open daily from 9am to 5:30pm (last ticket sold at 4pm). Admission is $9 for adults and $5 for children 3 to 12 and includes a 20-minute narrated boat ride. Kids under 3 get in free.

About 7 miles north of Homosassa Springs, more than 300 **manatees** spend the winter in Crystal River, and you can **swim or snorkel** with them ★★ in the warm-water natural spring of Kings Bay. **American Pro Diving Center,** 821 SE Hwy. 19, Crystal River, FL 34429 (℡ **800/291-3483**

downtown strolling and shopping venues. Here you'll find the **Glass Canvas Gallery,** at 4th Avenue Northeast (℡ **727/821-6767**), featuring a dazzling array of glass sculpture, tableware, art, and craft items by 250 local, national, and international artists. Also at 4th Avenue Northeast is **P. Buckley Moss** (℡ **727/ 894-2899**), a museum-grade store carrying the works of the individualistic artist best known for her portrayal of the Amish and the Mennonites. The works include paintings, graphics, figurines, and collector dolls. **Red Cloud,** between 1st and 2nd avenues (℡ **727/821-5824**), is an oasis for Native-American crafts, including jewelry, headdresses, and art.

Downtown's new commercial showplace is **BayWalk** (℡ **727/895-9277;** www.stpete.org/baywalk.htm), an open-air shopping, dining, and entertain-ment complex bordered by 1st and 2nd streets and 2nd and 3rd avenues North. It has a branch of Ann Taylor and some small boutiques.

or 352/563-0041; fax 352/563-5230; www.americanprodive.com), offers daily swimming and snorkel tours. Early mornings are the best time to see the manatees, so try to take the 6:30am departure. The trips range from about $30 to $50 per person. Call for the schedule and reservations. American Pro Diving also rents cottages on the Homosassa River.

Also check out the **Weedon Island Preserve**, 4801 37th St. South (℃ 727/893-2627), located in the upper Tampa Bay waters of Pinellas County, on the western shore of the entrance to Old Tampa Bay and directly west of Port Tampa. The island was named for Dr. Leslie Weedon, a renowned authority on yellow fever, who acquired the 1,250-acre island in 1898 in what is now north St. Petersburg. Weedon had a fascination with Indian culture, and developed a weekend retreat on the island, from which he began excavations that first revealed the importance of the site as an Indian burial mound. A Smithsonian expedition to the island in 1923 to 1924 further documented the importance of the site, which is now managed as a county preserve. Weedon Island also housed a dance club and movie studio in the 1920s, and was the site of the bay area's first airport in 1930. Today it's home to an assortment of fish, snakes, raccoons, and dolphins. Rent a canoe to explore, and find yourself easily "becoming one" with nature.

Baseball fans won't want to miss the **Ted Williams Museum & Hitters Hall of Fame**, 2455 N. Citrus Hills Blvd., off C.R. 486 west of Hernando (℃ 352/527-6566; www.twmuseum.com). Built in the shape of a baseball diamond, the museum holds the great hitter's personal memorabilia, including his two Triple Crown batting titles. It's open Tuesday through Sunday from 10am to 4pm. Admission is $5 for adults, $1 for children.

For more information about the area, contact the **Citrus County Chamber of Commerce**, 28 NW Hwy. 19, Crystal River, FL 34428 (℃ 352/795-3149; fax 352/795-4260; www.citruscountychamber.com). The chamber's visitor center is open Monday through Friday from 8:30am to 4:30pm, Saturday from 9am to 1pm.

Haslam's Book Store, 2025 Central Ave. (℃ 727/822-8616; www.haslams.com), is one of our favorite places to browse. Dating from 1933, its collection has grown to more than 350,000 volumes, making it Florida's largest bookstore. (As an added perk, it, too, is said to be haunted.)

Central Avenue is another shopping area, featuring the **Gas Plant Antique Arcade**, between 12th and 13th streets (℃ 727/895-0368), the largest antiques mall on Florida's west coast, with more than 100 dealers displaying their wares. (Downtown has several antiques-and-collectibles dealers; get a list and map from the chamber of commerce.) The **Florida Craftsmen Gallery**, at 5th Street (℃ 727/821-7391; www.floridacraftsmen.net), is a showcase for the works of more than 150 Florida artisans and craftspeople specializing in jewelry, ceramics, woodwork, fiber works, glassware, paper creations, and metalwork.

WHERE TO STAY

The **St. Petersburg/Clearwater Area Convention & Visitors Bureau** (see "Essentials," earlier in this chapter) operates a free **reservations service** (© **800/ 345-6710**), through which you can book rooms at most hotels and motels in St. Petersburg and at the beaches. The bureau also publishes a brochure that lists members of its Superior Small Lodgings program; all establishments have fewer than 50 rooms and have been inspected and certified for cleanliness and value.

Other than the Renaissance Vinoy Resort and Golf Club (see below), the only chain hotel downtown is the **St. Petersburg Hilton,** 333 1st St. S., between 3rd and 4th avenues South (© **800/445-8667** or 727/894-5000; fax 727/823-4797; www.stpetehilton.com), a 15-story business and convention hotel within steps of the Salvador Dalí Museum, Florida Power Park at Al Lang Field, and the Bayfront Center's theaters. Otherwise, views from the upper-floor rooms are its main draw for casual travelers.

Note: Sales and hotel taxes will add 11% to your bill.

VERY EXPENSIVE

Renaissance Vinoy Resort and Golf Club ✸✸✸   For the swankiest digs in the area, the Renaissance Vinoy is it. Built as the grand Vinoy Park in 1925, this elegant Spanish-style establishment that has hosted everyone from Jimmy Stewart to Bill Clinton, reopened in 1992 and landed on the National Register of Historic Places after a total and meticulous $93 million restoration that made it once again the city's finest hotel. Dominating the northern part of downtown, it overlooks Tampa Bay and is within walking distance of The Pier, Central Avenue, museums, and other attractions. All the guest rooms, many of which enjoy lovely views of the bay front, offer the utmost in comfort and elegance and include three phones, an additional TV in the bathroom, and bath scales. Some rooms in the original building have standing-room-only balconies; so if you need enough room to sit outside, request a balconied unit in the new Tower wing (some of these have whirlpool tubs, too). Overlooking the bay, the Mediterranean-style **Marchand's Grill** is the city's most elegant dining room and serves some of the best steaks and chops in town. The Vinoy also has an 18-hole golf course, which has undergone a total greens renovation and detailing and 12 tennis courts.

501 5th Ave. NE (at Beach Dr.), St. Petersburg, FL 33701. © **800/468-3571** or 727/894-1000. Fax 727/822-2785. www.renaissancehotels.com. 360 units. Winter $299–$429 double; off-season $199–$369 double. Packages available. AE, DC, DISC, MC, V. Valet parking $13; self-parking $9. **Amenities:** 4 restaurants; 2 bars; 2 heated outdoor pools (connected by a waterfall); golf course; 12 tennis courts; health club and spa; Jacuzzi; concierge; activities desk; car-rental desk; business center; salon; 24-hr. room service; massage; laundry service; coin-operated washers and dryers; concierge-level rooms. *In room:* A/C, TV, dataport, minibar, coffeemaker, hair dryer, iron.

MODERATE

Bayboro House ✸✸ *(Finds)*   A huge departure from the area's monstrous resorts, this four room Victorian mansion, located along the shore of Tampa Bay, is a well-kept secret preserved by innkeepers Antonia and Gordon Powers, who managed to preserve the home's early 1900s ambiance with heart-of-pine flooring, wooden mantelpiece, fireplace, and 1926 player piano. Each of the rooms has a private bath and other modern amenities. The Charles Harvey room has a bay window and four-poster Jenny Lind bed. The Audubon Suite has a kitchen, living room, and wing chairs tucked into an alcove, and the Williams Room has a fabulous view of the bay. The last room, the Sarah Armistead room, has twin beds. Wine and cheese is served every afternoon in the parlor or on the veranda and features the inn's own citrus wine, bottled at the Florida Orange Groves, Inc. and Winery. The house has a large front porch, complete with rocking chairs and a swing, and the Florida room, where breakfast is served, is a sunny room in which even those who have awoken on the wrong side of the bed can't help but smile.

1719 Beach Dr. SE., St. Petersburg, FL 33701. © **877/823-4955.** Fax 727/823-2341. www.bayborohouse bandb.com. 8 units. Winter $159–$189 double, $219–$239 suite; off season $149 double, $189 suite. MC, V. **Amenities:** Complimentary breakfast, wine, soda. *In room:* A/C, TV/VCR.

The Dickens House ★★★
No relation to British author Charles Dickens, this Dickens House once belonged to Henry and Sadie Dickens, early St. Pete settlers who built this, their home, in 1912 in the heart of the city's growing northeast residential district. Purchased in 1995 by mural artist Ed Caldwell, a graduate of the prestigious Rhode Island School of Design, The Dickens House has been restored to its original Craftsman-style architecture that was promoted by Sears, Roebuck in their famous catalogue. The charming inn has five guest rooms with three on the second floor and two on the third. The Cracker Suite has a custom-made bent willow bed, and the Orange Blossom Room, the smallest but cutest room in the house, has a Jenny Lind bed and a tiny bath that just happens to have a whirlpool. My personal fave, however, is the second floor Cottage Suite, which resembles a Victorian-age beach cottage with white wicker, sea grass carpet, roll up awnings, and nightstands displaying shells. The Dickens Room isn't too shabby, either, with a two-person shower and a four-poster cherry canopy bed—tres romantic. All rooms have Egyptian cotton linens, fridges, and high-speed Internet access, which is a definite dichotomy when compared to your surroundings. Complimentary breakfasts are served on the veranda, and every afternoon in the Arts and Crafts living room, complimentary wine, soft drinks, and snacks are served.

335 8th Ave. NE St. Petersburg, FL 33701. © **800/381-2022** or 727/822-4814. Fax 727/823-1644. www.dickenshouse.com. 5 units. Winter $120–$210 double; $96–$168 off season. AE, DC, DISC, MC, V. **Amenities:** Library, laundry service. *In room:* A/C, TV, dataport, coffeemaker, hair dryer, iron.

The Heritage Holiday Inn ★
When it comes to Holiday Inns, most people complain about the old, musty decor, or lack thereof. This hotel has that feel, to be sure, but it also has soom non-Holiday Inn-like qualities that may appeal to some (though the rooms are still pretty basic). No ordinary Holiday Inn, the Heritage dates from the early 1920s, and although significantly updated, it still retains the ambience of an old-fashioned hotel, with tall double-hung windows and hardwood floors that creak as you walk down the long central hallway. A lovely sweeping veranda, French doors, and a tropical courtyard help attract an eclectic clientele, from business travelers to seniors.

234 3rd Ave. N. (between 2nd and 3rd sts.), St. Petersburg, FL 33701. © **800/283-7829** or 727/822-4814. Fax 727/823-1644. www.sixcontinentshotels.com. 71 units. $100–$150 double. AE, DC, DISC, MC, V. **Amenities:** Restaurant; bar; heated outdoor pool; Jacuzzi; limited room service; laundry service. *In room:* A/C, TV, dataport, coffeemaker, hair dryer, iron.

Mansion House Bed & Breakfast ★★
Mirror images of each other, these two houses separated by a landscaped courtyard were built between 1901 and 1912. The comfortable living room in the main house, which has 6 of the 10 units here, opens to a sunroom, off which a small screened porch provides mosquito-free lounging and the only place where guests can smoke. Both houses have upstairs front parlors with TVs, VCRs, and libraries. Tall, old-fashioned windows let lots of light into the attractive guest rooms. The pick of the litter is

the "Pembroke" room, upstairs over the carriage house. It has a four-poster bed with mosquito netting, and its residents have their own whirlpool in an outdoor, screened hut. The brick courtyard garden between the two houses (there's a heated swimming pool and Jacuzzi out there) is a popular spot for weddings, receptions, and other functions.

105 5th Ave. NE (at 1st St. NE.), St. Petersburg, FL 33701. ✆ **800/274-7520** or 727/821-9391. Fax 727/821-6909. www.mansionbandb.com. 10 units (all with bathroom). $99–$220 double. Rates include full breakfast. AE, DC, DISC, MC, V. **Amenities:** Heated outdoor pool; access to nearby health club; Jacuzzi; bicycle rentals; laundry service. *In room:* A/C, TV, dataport, hair dryer.

A NEARBY SPA

Safety Harbor Resort and Spa *★★* *Value*   Hernando de Soto thought he had found Ponce de León's fabled Fountain of Youth when, in 1539, he happened upon five mineral springs in what is now Safety Harbor on the western shore of Old Tampa Bay (see the "Tampa & St. Petersburg" map on p. 386). You may not recover your youth at this venerable spa, which has been in operation since 1926 and got a face lift in 1998, but you will be rejuvenated with such services as massage and hydrotherapy and a full menu of fitness classes from boxing to yoga. The mineral springs enable it to offer acclaimed water-fitness programs, and this is a good place to work on your games at the Quinzi Golf Academy and the Phil Green Tennis Academy (see "Outdoor Activities & Spectator Sports" on p. 412). This sprawling complex of beige stucco buildings with Spanish-tile roofs and lame, old fogie-style rooms, sits on 22 waterfront acres in the sleepy town of Safety Harbor, north of St. Petersburg. The grounds of the place make up for what the rooms lack. Moss-draped Safety Harbor has a charming small-town ambience, with a number of shops and restaurants just outside the spa's entrance. Given the reasonable off-season room rates and special packages available, this is one of Florida's better spa values.

105 N. Bayshore Dr., Safety Harbor, FL 34695. ✆ **888/237-8772** or 727/726-1161. Fax 727/724-7749. www. safetyharborspa.com. 193 units. Winter $205–$235 double; off-season $175–$205 double. Packages available. AE, DC, DISC, MC, V. Valet parking $10; free self-parking. Pets accepted ($35-per-night charge). **Amenities:** 2 restaurants; bar; heated indoor and outdoor pools; golf course; 9 tennis courts; full-service spa; bicycle rentals; concierge; activities desk; car-rental desk; business center; limited room service; laundry service; coinop washers and dryers. *In room:* A/C, TV, dataport (with high-speed Internet), coffeemaker, hair dryer, iron.

WHERE TO DINE

Don't overlook the food court at **The Pier,** where the inexpensive chow is accompanied by a very rich, but quite free, view of the bay. Among The Pier's restaurants is a branch of Tampa's famous **Columbia** (✆ **727/822-8000;** p. 406).

EXPENSIVE

Chateau France *★★* CLASSICAL FRENCH   Chef Antoine Louro provides St. Petersburg's most romantic setting in this charming pink Victorian house built in 1910. He specializes in French classics such as homemade paté, Dover sole meunière, filet mignon au poivre, coq au vin, orange duck, and a rich seafood bouillabaisse. Fresh baby vegetables, Gruyère-cheese potatoes, and Antoine's special Eiffel Tower salad accompany all main courses. The wine list is excellent, as are the bananas flambé and crêpes suzette.

136 4th Ave. N. (between Bayshore Dr. and 1st St. N.). ✆ **727/894-7163.** Reservations recommended. Main courses $20–$38. AE, DC, DISC, MC, V. Daily 5–11pm.

Saffron's *★★* CARIBBEAN   It may be a bit odd to hear reggae music emanating from this historic building, but once you enter the building, beckoned by the savory scents of jerk chicken, curried goat, conch fritters, roasted pork, and grilled steaks, you'll think you're somewhere floating in the Caribbean and immediately thirst for an ice cold Red Stripe beer and an encore of your favorite Bob Marley tune. Don't expect much in the way of decor—Saffron's looks like it could have been a Denny's with its booths and blasé tables, but when it comes to food and entertainment, Denny's has nothing on Saffron's.

1700 Park St. North. ✆ 727/345-6400. Reservations recommended. Main courses $13–$32. MC, V. Mon–Fri 11am–5:30pm; Mon–Thurs 5:30–9pm, Fri 5:30–9:30pm, Sat 4–9:30pm; late-night menu Fri–Sat 9:30pm–1:30am; Sun brunch 10:30am–4pm.

MODERATE

Bonefish Grill ⭐ SEAFOOD   Although this noisy seafood spot has become part of the Outback Steakhouse family, it hardly resembles a chain with its fresh fish dishes served in massive portions not to mention a very happening martini bar. Swordfish with spinach and feta cheese is a favorite, but feel free to mix and match from a choice of five fish and three sauces. The rock shrimp appetizer is delicious—South Beach's swank sushi spot to the stars, Nobu, has the same dish for about five times the price. Because of this, expect long lines.

5901 4th St. North St. Petersburg. ✆ 727/521-3434. Main courses $13–$18. AE, MC, V. Mon–Thurs 4–10:30pm; Fri–Sat 4–11:30pm; Sun 4–10pm.

Mattison's AMERICAN   Chef Paul Mattison's cozy bistro near the bay is a hit with business travelers as well as locals, thanks to a menu brimming with seafood (crab-stuffed salmon, grouper piccata, and basil-pesto crusted Idaho trout) and red meat (veal medallions with prosciutto and Parmesan butter, grilled rib-eye with roasted onions and cabernet sauce, and rack of lamb with rosemary paste and stewed veggies). There's also a small vegetarian menu that includes a grilled portobello stack with brie and roasted tomatoes and penne pasta tossed with spinach, shiitake mushrooms, veggies, and tomatoes.

111 2nd Ave. NE (between Beach Dr. and 1st St. in The Plaza Tower in the Republic Bank bldg.). ✆ 727/ 895-2200. www.mattisons.com. Reservations recommended. Main courses $10–$29. AE, DC, DISC, MC, V. Mon–Thurs 11am–10pm; Fri–Sat 11am–11pm.

INEXPENSIVE

Fourth Street Shrimp Store ⭐⭐ *Value* SEAFOOD   If you're anywhere in the area, don't miss at least driving by to see the colorful, cartoonlike mural on the outside of this eclectic and casual establishment just north of downtown. On first impression, it looks like graffiti, but it's actually a gigantic drawing of people eating. Inside, it gets even better, with paraphernalia and murals on two walls making the main dining room seem like a warehouse with windows that look out on an early-19th-century seaport (one painted sailor permanently peers in to see what you're eating). You'll pass a seafood market counter when you enter, from which comes the fresh namesake shrimp, the star here. You can also pick from grouper, clam strips, catfish, or oysters fried, broiled, or steamed, all served in heaping portions. This is the best and certainly the most interesting bargain in town. There's also limited outdoor seating.

1006 4th St. N. (at 10th Ave. N.). ✆ 727/822-0325. Main courses $5–$14; sandwiches $2.50–$7. MC, V. Daily 11am–9pm.

The Moon Under Water ⭐ ASIAN/MIDDLE EASTERN/AMERICAN Tables on the veranda or sidewalk in front of this pub are a great place to take a break during your downtown stroll. The British Raj rules supreme inside the darkly paneled dining room with its slowly twirling ceiling fans and plethora of colonial artifacts, including obligatory pith helmets. Your taste buds are in for a treat here, because the bill of fare covers a number of former British outposts, including America (burgers and Philly cheese steaks), but the emphasis here is on mild, medium, or blazing-hot Indian curries—with a recommended Irish, British, or Australian beer to slake the resulting thirst. For lighter fare, consider Mideastern tabbouleh. There's also live music on weekend evenings.

332 Beach Dr. NE (between 3rd and 4th aves.). © 727/896-6160. Main courses $7.50–$17; sandwiches and salads $6–$8. AE, DC, DISC, MC, V. Sun–Thurs 11:30am–11pm; Fri–Sat 11:30am–midnight. Closed New Year's Day, Thanksgiving, Christmas.

Ovo Cafè ★ INTERNATIONAL   This cafe, popular with the business set by day and the club crowd on weekend nights, features a mélange of sophisticated offerings. Pirogies and pasta pillows come with taste-tempting sauces and fillings, and there are several creative salads and unusual individual-size pizzas. Strawberries or blackberries and a splash of liqueur cover the thick waffles. Portions are substantial, but be careful of the strictly a la carte pricing here. The big bar dispenses a wide variety of martinis, plus some unusual liqueur drinks.

515 Central Ave. © 727/895-5515. Reservations strongly recommended Fri–Sat. Main courses $10–$15; sandwiches $7–$8.50; pizza $8.50–$10. AE, DC, DISC, MC, V. Mon–Tues 11am–3pm; Wed–Thurs 11am–10pm; Fri–Sat 11am–1am.

Skyway Jack's ★ BREAKFAST   This is the restaurant that Cracker Barrel aspires to be, a down home, country kitchen with kitsch *and* outstanding breakfast fare. Start the day off with eggs Florentine, stuffed French toast, even sweetbreads and eggs, or go old school with eggs, grits, hash browns, and biscuits 'n' gravy. For early risers or late night partiers, Skyway Jack's greases its griddle starting at 5am.

2795 34th St. South. © 727/867-1907. Main dishes $2.75–$6.50. No credit cards (but there's an ATM on premises). Daily 5am–3pm.

ST. PETERSBURG AFTER DARK

Good sources of nightlife information are the Thursday "Weekend" section of the *St. Petersburg Times* (www.sptimes.com), the "BayLife" and "Friday Extra" sections of the *Tampa Tribune* (www.tampatrib.com), and the *Weekly Planet* (www.weeklyplanet.com), a tabloid available at the visitor information offices and in many hotel and restaurant lobbies.

The heart of downtown's nighttime scene is **BayWalk** (© 727/895-9277; www.stpete.org/baywalk.htm), downtown's new shopping-dining-entertainment complex bordered by 1st and 2nd streets and 2nd and 3rd avenues North. There, a 20-screen cinema and several restaurants and bars will keep you busy.

THE BAR, CLUB & MUSIC SCENE   Ever since St. Pete started coming into its own as far as the hipster quotient is concerned, cool bars started appearing as quickly as Madonna changes her accent. Among them, **A Taste for Wine**, 241 Central Ave., (© 727/895-1623), is an upscale spot with polished woods and a granite bar offering terrific by-the-glass vintages, appetizers, and a gorgeous outdoor balcony; the **Haymarket Pub**, 8308 4th St. North, (© 727/577-9621), is the gay-friendly Cheers of St. Pete where audible conversation and reasonably priced drinks aren't implausible demands; **Janus Landing,** 200 1st Ave. North (© 727/896-1244), is a fantastic outdoor concert venue and bar where mostly alternative and rock bands perform; **Ringside Cafe,** 2742 4th St. North (© 727/894-8465), is a laid back jazz and blues bar; and **Martini Bar**, 131 2nd Ave. North, (© 727/895-8558), where a crowd that looks as if it stepped off the set of *Sex and the City* or *Friends* convenes for some serious seeing and being seen.

A historic attraction as well as an entertainment venue, the Moorish-style **Coliseum Ballroom,** 535 4th Ave. N. (© **727/892-5202;** www.stpete.org/coliseum.htm), has been hosting dancing, big bands, boxing, and other events since 1924 (it even made an appearance in the 1985 movie *Cocoon*). Come out and watch the town's many seniors doing the jitterbug just like it was 1945 again! Call for the schedule and prices.

PERFORMING ARTS VENUES The **Bayfront Center,** 400 1st St. S. (© **727/892-5767,** or 727/892-5700 for recorded information), houses the 8,100-seat Bayfront Arena (www.stpete.org/bayfront.htm) and the 2,000-seat Mahaffey Theater (www.stpete.org/mahaffey.htm). The schedule includes a variety of concerts, Broadway shows, big bands, ice shows, and circus performances. **Ticketmaster** (© **813/287-8844**) sells tickets to most events and shows.

Tropicana Field, 1 Stadium Dr. (© **727/825-3100;** www.stpete.org/dome.htm), has a capacity of 50,000 for major concerts, but it also hosts a variety of smaller events when the Devil Rays aren't playing baseball.

3 St. Pete & Clearwater Beaches 𝓐𝓐

If you're looking for sun and sand, you'll find plenty of both on the 28 miles of slim barrier islands that skirt the Gulf shore of the Pinellas Peninsula. With some one million visitors coming here every year, don't be surprised if you have lots of company. But you'll also discover quieter neighborhoods geared to families, and some of the nation's finest beaches, some of which are protected from development by parks and nature preserves.

At the southern end of the strip, St. Pete Beach is the granddaddy of the area's resorts: Visitors started coming here a century ago, and they haven't quit. Today, St. Pete Beach is heavily developed and often overcrowded during the winter season. If you like high-rises and mile-a-minute action, St. Pete Beach is for you. But even here, Pass-a-Grille, on the island's southern end, is a quiet residential enclave with eclectic shops and a fine, though crowded, public beach.

A more gentle lifestyle begins just to the north on the 3½-mile-long Treasure Island. From there, you cross famous John's Pass to Sand Key, a 12-mile-long island occupied by primarily residential Madeira Beach, Redington Shores, Indian Shores, Indian Rocks Beach, and Belleair Beach. Finally the road crosses a soaring bridge to Clearwater Beach, whose silky sands attract active families and couples.

If you like your great outdoors unfettered by development, the jewels here are Fort Desoto Park, south of St. Pete Beach at the mouth of Tampa Bay, and Caladesi Island State Park, north of Clearwater Beach. They are consistently rated among America's top beaches. Sand Key Park, looking at Clearwater Beach from the southern shores of Little Pass, which separates Clearwater Beach from Belleair Beach, is one of Florida's finest local beach parks.

ESSENTIALS

GETTING THERE See "Getting There," in section 1, on p. 384, for information about getting to the beaches.

VISITOR INFORMATION See "Visitor Information," in section 2 (p. 410), for the St. Petersburg/Clearwater Area Convention & Visitors Bureau and the St. Petersburg Area Chamber of Commerce. The bureau's website at www.floridasbeach.com has information specific to the beaches.

Once you're here, you can get beach information at the **Gulf Beaches of Tampa Bay Chamber of Commerce,** 6990 Gulf Blvd. (at 70th Ave.), St. Pete Beach, FL 33706 (© **800/944-1847** or 727/360-6957; fax 727/360-2233; www.gulfbeaches-tampabay.com). The chamber is open Monday through Friday from 9am to 5pm.

For advance information about Clearwater Beach, contact the **Clearwater Regional Chamber of Commerce,** 1130 Cleveland St., Clearwater, FL 33755 (© **727/461-0011;** fax 727/449-2889; www.clearwaterflorida.org). You can also walk into the **Clearwater Visitor Information Center,** on Causeway Boulevard in the lobby of the Clearwater Beach Marina Building (© **727/ 462-6531**). It's open Monday through Saturday from 9am to 5pm, Sunday from 1 to 5pm.

GETTING AROUND   The **Pinellas Suncoast Transit Authority/PSTA** (© **727/530-9911**) operates motorized trolley service along Gulf Boulevard (Fla. 699) between the Hurricane restaurant (p. 432) in St. Pete Beach and the Sheraton Sand Key Resort (this entire trip, one way, takes about an hour), where it connects with the **Jolly Trolley** (© **727/445-1200**), which continues on Gulf Boulevard through Clearwater Beach. The PSTA trolley runs daily, every 20 minutes between 5am and 10pm, to midnight on Friday and Saturday. Rides cost $1.25, or you can buy a daily pass for $3. One-ride fares on the Jolly Trolley are 50¢ per person, 25¢ for seniors. Call the trolleys for schedules, or pick up printed copies at the Gulf Beaches of Tampa Bay Chamber of Commerce (p. 422).

Along the beach, the major cab company is **BATS Taxi** (© **727/367-3702**). Fares are $2 at flag fall, plus 20¢ for each ½ mile.

HITTING THE BEACH

This entire stretch of coast is one long beach, but since hotels, condominiums, and private homes occupy much of it, you may want to sun and swim at one of the area's public parks. The very best are described below, but there's also the fine **Pass-a-Grille Public Beach,** on the southern end of St. Pete Beach, where you can watch the boats going in and out of Pass-a-Grille Channel and quench your thirst at the Hurricane restaurant (p. 432). This and all other Pinellas County public beaches have metered parking lots, so bring a supply of quarters. There are public restrooms along the beach.

Sand Key Park ⊛, on the northern tip of Sand Key facing Clearwater Beach, sports a wide beach and gentle surf and is relatively off the beaten path in this commercial area. It's great to go out for a morning walk or jog here. The park is open from 8am to dark and has restrooms. Admission is free, but the parking lot has meters. For more information, call © **727/464-3347.**

Clearwater Public Beach (also known as Pier 60) has beach volleyball, watersports rentals, lifeguards, restrooms, showers, and concessions. The swimming is excellent, and there is a fishing pier with a bait-and-tackle shop, plus a children's playground. Gated municipal parking lots here cost $1 per hour or $7 a day. The lots are right across the street from the Clearwater Beach Marina, a prime base for boating, cruises, and other waterborne activities (see "Outdoor Activities," below). A somewhat-less-crowded spot in Clearwater Beach is at the Gulf end of Bay Esplanade.

CALADESI ISLAND STATE PARK ⊛⊛⊛

Occupying a 3½-mile-long island north of Clearwater Beach, **Caladesi Island State Park** boasts one of Florida's top beaches—a lovely, relatively secluded stretch with fine, soft sand edged in sea grass and palmettos. Dolphins often

St. Pete & Clearwater Beaches

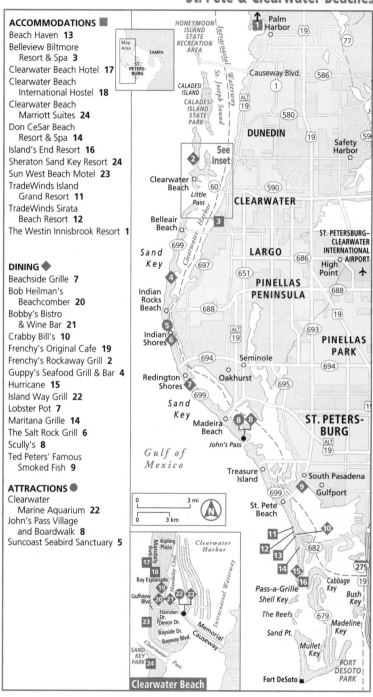

ACCOMMODATIONS ■
Beach Haven **13**
Belleview Biltmore
    Resort & Spa **3**
Clearwater Beach Hotel **17**
Clearwater Beach
    International Hostel **18**
Clearwater Beach
    Marriott Suites **24**
Don CeSar Beach
    Resort & Spa **14**
Island's End Resort **16**
Sheraton Sand Key Resort **24**
Sun West Beach Motel **23**
TradeWinds Island
    Grand Resort **11**
TradeWinds Sirata
    Beach Resort **12**
The Westin Innisbrook Resort **1**

DINING ◆
Beachside Grille **7**
Bob Heilman's
    Beachcomber **20**
Bobby's Bistro
    & Wine Bar **21**
Crabby Bill's **10**
Frenchy's Original Cafe **19**
Frenchy's Rockaway Grill **2**
Guppy's Seafood Grill & Bar **4**
Hurricane **15**
Island Way Grill **22**
Lobster Pot **7**
Maritana Grille **14**
The Salt Rock Grill **6**
Scully's **8**
Ted Peters' Famous
    Smoked Fish **9**

ATTRACTIONS ●
Clearwater
    Marine Aquarium **22**
John's Pass Village
    and Boardwalk **8**
Suncoast Seabird Sanctuary **5**

cavort in the waters offshore. In the park itself is a nature trail, where you might see one of the rattlesnakes, raccoons, armadillos, or rabbits that live here. A concession stand, a ranger station, and bathhouses (with restrooms and showers) are available. Caladesi Island is accessible only by ferry from **Honeymoon Island State Recreation Area,** which is connected by Causeway Boulevard (Fla. 586) to Dunedin, north of Clearwater.

You'll first have to pay the admission to Honeymoon Island: $5 per vehicle with two to eight occupants, $2 per single-occupant vehicle, $1 for pedestrians and bicyclists. Beginning daily at 10am, the ferry (© 727/734-5263) departs Honeymoon Island every hour. Round-trip rides cost $8 for adults, $4.50 for kids.

Neither Caladesi nor Honeymoon allows camping, but pets are permitted in the inland parts of the island and on South Beach (bring a leash and use it at all times).

The two parks are open daily from 8am to sunset and are administered by Gulf Islands Geopark, 1 Causeway Blvd., Dunedin, FL 34698 (© 727/469-5918; www.floridastateparks.org/caladesiisland and www.floridastateparks.org/honeymoonisland).

To really get to know the islands, go with Linda Taylor of **It's Our Nature, Inc.** (© 888/535-7448 or 727/441-2599; www.itsournature.com), on one of her guided walks of Honeymoon and Caladesi . They last about 2 hours and cost $15 for adults, $8 for children, plus park admission and ferry fare. Call for reservations, which are required, and for information about other guided walks and nature experiences.

FORT DESOTO PARK

South of St. Pete Beach at the very mouth of Tampa Bay, **Fort Desoto Park** encompasses all of Mullet Key, set aside by Pinellas County as a 900-acre bird, animal, and plant sanctuary. Besides the stunning white-sugar sand, it is best known for a Spanish-American War–era fort, which has a museum (open daily 9am–4pm). Other diversions include great fishing from piers, large playgrounds for kids, and 4 miles of trails winding through the park for in-line skaters, bicyclists, and joggers. Park rangers conduct nature and history tours, and you can rent canoes and kayaks to explore the winding mangrove channels along the island's bay side. The park has changing rooms and restrooms.

Sitting by itself on a heavily forested island, the park's **campground** is one of Florida's most picturesque (many sites are beside the bay). It's such great camping that the 233 tent and RV sites usually are sold out, especially on weekends, so it's best to reserve well in advance. But, there are a few catches: You must appear in person no more than 30 days in advance at the campground office, at 631 Chestnut St. in Clearwater, or at 150 5th St. N. in downtown St. Petersburg. You must pay when you make your reservation in cash or by traveler's check (no credit cards or personal checks). And, you must reserve for at least 2 nights, but you can stay no more than 14 nights in any 30-day period. Sites cost $33 a night January through July, $28 a night the rest of the year. All sites have water and electricity hookups.

Admission to the park is free. It's open daily from 8am to dusk, although campers and persons fishing from the piers can stay later. To get here, take the Pinellas Byway (50¢ toll) east from St. Pete Beach and follow Fla. 679 (35¢ toll) and the signs south to the park. For more information, contact the park at 3500 Pinellas Byway, Tierra Verde, FL 33715 (© 727/582-2267; www.fortdesoto.com).

OUTDOOR ACTIVITIES

BOATING, FISHING & OTHER WATERSPORTS   You can indulge in parasailing, boating, deep-sea fishing, wave running, sightseeing, dolphin watching, water-skiing, and just about any other waterborne diversion your heart could desire in the St. Pete and Clearwater Beaches area. All you have to do is head to one of two beach locations: **Hubbard's Marina,** at John's Pass Village and Boardwalk (✆ **800/755-0677** or 727/393-1947; www.hubbards marina.com), in Madeira Beach on the southern tip of Sand Key; or **Clearwater Beach Marina,** at Coronado Drive and Causeway Boulevard (✆ **800/772-4479** or 727/461-3133), which is at the beach end of the causeway leading to downtown Clearwater. Agents in booths there will give you the schedules and prices (expect to pay $35–$45 for a half day of fishing on a large party boat, $65–$70 for a full day), answer any questions you have, and make reservations if necessary. Go in the early morning to set up the day's activities, or in the afternoon to book the next day's.

CRUISES   The top nature cruise here is the **Sea Life Safari** ★★ (✆ **888/239-9414** or 727/441-1790; www.cmaquarium.org), operated by the Clearwater Marine Aquarium (p. 426). These 2½-hour safaris are available at 11am, 1:30, and 4pm, and are more like field trips than pleasure cruises. Aquarium biologists go along to explain what they pull up in trawl nets (don't worry: They throw it all back). You'll also see birds and other wildlife on a visit to a bird sanctuary islet. Dolphin sightings are likely, too. The cruises are well worth $19 for adults, $12 for kids 3 to 12. You can combine the cruise with aquarium admission and save $3. Call for the schedule and to reserve. Also ask about sunset nature cruises from mid-April to mid-October.

Hubbard's Sea Adventures, based at John's Pass Village and Boardwalk in Madeira Beach (✆ **800/755-0677** or 727/393-1947; www.hubbardsmarina. com), offers a 2-hour dolphin watch and sightseeing cruise. It costs $12 for adults, $6 for kids 11 and under. There's also a 3-hour shelling tour ($20 for adults, $10 for kids), but the best outings are cruises to fascinating **Egmont Key State Park** ★ on historic Egmont Key at the mouth of Tampa Bay (www.florida stateparks.org/egmontkey). This uninhabited island is the site of a lighthouse, of now-crumbling Fort Dade (built in 1900 during the Spanish-American War but abandoned long ago), and of threatened gopher tortoises. Sea turtles also come ashore here to nest. You can go snorkeling and shelling here, so bring your swimsuit (snorkeling gear is available). The half-day cruises leave from St. Pete Beach Tuesday through Sunday and cost $35 for adults, $25 for children.

Another popular cruise target is lovely **Shell Key,** one of Florida's last completely undeveloped barrier islands. Shell Key is great for bird-watchers, who could spot a remarkable 88 different species, including some of North America's rarest shorebirds. Hubbard's Shell Key beachcombing trips usually depart at 9am Monday through Saturday, for $20 adults, $10 kids 12 and under. You can rent beach chairs, umbrellas, snorkeling gear, and other equipment once you get there. Call to confirm the schedule and make reservations, which are recommended.

You can also get there on the **Shell Key Shuttle,** Merry Pier, on Pass-a-Grille Way at the eastern end of 8th Avenue in southern St. Pete Beach (✆ **727/360-1348;** www.shellkeyshuttle.com). Boats leave daily at 10am, noon, and 2pm. Prices are $14 for adults, $7 for children 12 and under. The ride takes 15 minutes, and you can return on any shuttle you wish.

The most unusual outings here are with **Captain Memo's Pirate Cruise,** at Clearwater Beach Marina (© 727/446-2587; www.captmemo.com), which sails the *Pirate's Ransom,* a reproduction of a pirate ship with a pirate crew, on 2-hour daytime cruises, as well as sunset and evening champagne cruises ($30–$32 adults, $25 seniors and children 13–17, $20 kids under 13).

Two paddle-wheel riverboats operate here: The *Show Queen* has lunch, sunset dinner, and Sunday-brunch cruises from Clearwater Beach Marina (© **800/ 772-4479** or 727/461-3113; www.showqueen.com). The *Starlite Princess* does likewise from 3400 Pasadena Ave. S. (© **800/444-4814** or 727/462-2628; www.starlitecruises.com), at the eastern side of the Corey Causeway linking St. Pete Beach to the mainland. Call for prices, schedules, and reservations.

SCUBA DIVING   You can dive on reefs and wrecks with **Dive Clearwater,** P.O. Box 3594, Clearwater, FL 33767 (© **800/875-3483** or 727/443-6731; www.diveclearwater.com), which also operates the live-aboard boat *Plunger V.* Call for schedule and prices.

ATTRACTIONS ON LAND

Clearwater Marine Aquarium ★★ *(Kids)*   This little jewel of an aquarium on Clearwater Harbor is very low-key and friendly; it's dedicated to the rescue and rehabilitation of marine mammals and sea turtles. Exhibits include otters, sea turtles, sharks, stingrays, mangroves, and sea grass.

249 Windward Passage, Clearwater Beach. © 888/239-9414 or 727/441-1790. www.cmaquarium.org. Admission $8.75 adults, $6.25 children 3–11, free for children 2 and under. Mon–Fri 9am–5pm; Sat 9am–4pm; Sun 11am–4pm. The aquarium is off the causeway between Clearwater and Clearwater Beach; follow the signs.

John's Pass Village and Boardwalk   Casual and charming, albeit too touristy, this Old Florida, turn of the century fishing village on John's Pass consists of a string of simple wooden structures topped by tin roofs and connected by a 1,000-foot boardwalk. Most of the buildings have been converted into shops, art galleries, restaurants, and saloons. The focal point is the boardwalk and marina, where many watersports are available for visitors (see "Outdoor Activities," above). If you don't go out on the water, this is a great place to have an alfresco lunch—**Scully's** (© **727/393-7749**) is the best restaurant here—and watch the boats go in and out of the pass.

12901 Gulf Blvd. (at John's Pass), Madeira Beach. © 800/944-1847 or 727/394-0756. www.johnspass.com. Free admission. Shops and activities daily 9am–6pm or later.

Suncoast Seabird Sanctuary ★   At any one time, there are usually more than 500 sea and land birds living at this sanctuary, from cormorants, white herons, and birds of prey to the ubiquitous brown pelican. The nation's largest wild-bird hospital, dedicated to the rescue, repair, recuperation, and release of sick and injured wild birds, is also here.

18328 Gulf Blvd., Indian Shores. © 727/391-6211. www.seabirdsanctuary.org. Free admission, donations welcome. Daily 9am–sunset. Free tours Wed and Sun 2pm.

SHOPPING

John's Pass Village and Boardwalk, on John's Pass in Madeira Beach (see "Attractions on Land," above), has an unremarkable collection of beach souvenir shops, but the atmosphere makes it worth a stroll. The pick of the lot is the **Bronze Lady** (© **727/398-5994;** www.bronzelady2000.com), featuring a collection of works by the late comedian-artist Red Skelton, best known for his numerous clown paintings. The shops are open daily from 9am to 6pm or later.

If you're in the market for one-of-a-kind hand-hammered jewelry, try **Evander Preston Contemporary Jewelry,** 106 8th Ave., Pass-a-Grille (℡ **727/367-7894**), a unique gallery/workshop housed in a 75-year-old building in Pass-a-Grille's 1-block-long 8th Avenue business district. Check out the golden miniature train with diamond headlight (it's not for sale). Open Monday through Saturday from 10am to 5:30pm. There's also a branch in the TradeWinds Island Grand Resort (see "Where to Stay," below).

Among the shops in St. Pete Beach's Corey Landings Area, the town's original business strip along 75th Street east of Gulf Boulevard, **The Shell Store** (℡ **727/360-0586**) specializes in corals and shells, with an on-premises mini-museum illustrating how they live and grow. There's a good selection of shell home decorations, shell hobbyist supplies, shell art, planters, and jewelry. The store is open Monday through Saturday from 9:30am to 5pm.

WHERE TO STAY

St. Pete Beach and Clearwater Beach have national chain hotels and motels of every name and description. You can also use the St. Petersburg/Clearwater Convention & Visitors Bureau's free **reservations service** (℡ **800/345-6710**) to book rooms at most of them. The **St. Petersburg Area Chamber of Commerce** lists a wide range of hotels, motels, condominiums, and other accommodations in its annual visitor guide (see p. 410 for more information on them), and it publishes a brochure listing all members of its Superior Small Lodgings program.

As is the case throughout Florida, there are more short- and long-term rental condominiums here than there are hotel rooms. Many of them are in high-rise buildings right on the beach. Among local rental agents, **JC Resort Management,** 17200 Gulf Blvd., North Redington Beach, FL 33708 (℡ **800/535-7776** or 727/397-0441; fax 727/397-8894; www.jcresort.com), has many from which to choose.

ST. PETE BEACH
Very Expensive

Don CeSar Beach Resort & Spa ★★★ *Kids*   This Moorish-style "Pink Palace" was built to be a grand hotel (it's on the National Register of Historic Places), but its scheduled 1928 opening was derailed when Florida real estate went bust. The federal government used it as a rest-and-recreation center for soldiers during World War II and as an office building until 1967. Developer William Bowman Jr. bought it in 1972 and restored it to its intended, Gatsby-esque glory. Today it appeals to a wide range of clientele, from groups to families, from honeymooning couples to locals taking treatments in the full-service spa. Sitting majestically on 7½ acres of beachfront, the landmark sports a lobby of classic high windows and archways, crystal chandeliers, marble floors, and original artwork. A newly designed pool deck with rich Brazilian Ippa wood is surrounded by fresh new landscaping including Canary Island Date Palms and tree-formed Oleander as well as a whirlpool ensconced in a lovely garden. Extensively renovated in 2000, some of the 275 rooms under the minarets of the original building may seem rather small by today's standards, but they have high windows and offer views of the Gulf or Boca Ciega Bay. Some but not all of them have balconies. If you want more room but less charm, the resort has 70 spacious luxury condominiums in The Don CeSar Beach House, a midrise building ¾ mile to the north (there's 24-hr. complimentary transportation between the two). An excellent kids program features supervised activities such as nighttime pizza parties, hermit crab races, and T-shirt decorating. Most amusing, however, are the hotel's etiquette classes offering kids and adults instruction on which fork to use first, and, most importantly, when and when not to use that irksome cellphone.

3400 Gulf Blvd. (at 34th Ave./Pinellas Byway), St. Pete Beach, FL 33706. ℰ 866/728-2206 or 727/360-1881. Fax 727/367-6952. www.doncesar.com. 347 units. Winter $234–$428 double, $334–$1,731 suite; off-season $212–$350 double, $269–$1,445 suite. $10 per person per day resort fee. Packages available. AE, DC, DISC, MC, V. Valet parking $10; free self-parking. **Amenities:** 4 restaurants; 3 bars; 2 heated outdoor pools; exercise room; spa; Jacuzzi; watersports equipment rental; children's programs; game room; concierge; business center; shopping arcade; salon; 24-hr. room service; massage; babysitting; laundry service; coin-op washers and dryers. *In room:* A/C, TV, dataport, minibar, hair dryer, iron.

Expensive

TradeWinds Island Grand Resort ★★ (Kids)   Don't be dismayed by the outward appearance of this six- and seven-story, concrete-and-steel monstrosity, for underneath and beside it runs a maze of brick walkways, patios, and lily ponds connected by ¼ mile of streams. Many of the guest units, which look out on the Gulf or the 18 acres of grounds, have up-to-date kitchens or kitchenettes, and most have private balconies. Choice units (all renovated a bit too brightly in oranges and pastel blues) directly face the Gulf, but note that like its sister property, the TradeWinds Sirata Beach Resort (see below), this hotel has a great variety of accommodations; so consult with the reservation clerk when booking. Although the resort draws large meetings and conventions, it's a big hit with families, too, especially Europeans, all of whom appreciate the children's program, ice-cream parlor, Pizza Hut outlet, and summer packages. One of the four heated swimming pools is reserved for adults, and there's lots more to keep grown-ups busy, such as the libation offered by a unique Florida cracker-house–style beachside bar floating on one of the lily ponds and the live entertainment nightly in another pub.

5500 Gulf Blvd. (at 55th Ave.), St. Pete Beach, FL 33706. ℰ 800/360-4016 or 727/363-2212. Fax 727/363-2222. www.justletgo.com. 585 units. Winter $219–$385 double; off-season $189–$326 double. Resort amenities fee of $12 per day per unit covers most activities. Packages available summer and fall. AE, DC, DISC, MC, V. Valet parking $6; free self-parking. **Amenities:** 4 restaurants; 4 bars; 4 heated outdoor pools; 4 tennis courts; health club; Jacuzzi; sauna; watersports equipment rental; children's programs; concierge; car-rental desk; business center; salon; limited room service; massage; babysitting; laundry service; coin-op washers and dryers. *In room:* A/C, TV, dataport, kitchen, fridge, coffeemaker, hair dryer, iron, microwave.

TradeWinds Sirata Beach Resort ★   A ton of money was spent a few years ago to completely renovate this older property and bring it up to second-tier status here, almost on a par with its sister hotel, the TradeWinds Island Grand Resort, but well below the Don CeSar Beach Resort & Spa. A yellow-and-green Old Florida–style facade now disguises the eight-story main building, which houses hotel rooms and one-bedroom suites upstairs (upper-level units have nice views) and a convention center. Some guest rooms in this two-story building face the courtyard, but the choice quarters here are its Gulf-side rooms, the only units with patios or balconies opening directly onto the beach. The most spacious units are efficiencies and one-bedroom suites in two long, two-story buildings; they all have kitchenettes, but they look out primarily on parking lots.

5300 Gulf Blvd. (at 53rd Ave.), St. Pete Beach, FL 33706. ℰ 800/360-4016 or 727/363-2212. Fax 727/363-2222. www.justletgo.com. 380 units, including 170 suites. Winter $199–$385 double; off-season $159–$327 double. Resort amenities fee of $12 per day per unit covers most activities. AE, DC, DISC, MC, V. **Amenities:** 2 restaurants; 2 bars; 3 heated outdoor pools; exercise room; Jacuzzi; watersports equipment rental; game room; concierge; business center; limited room service; babysitting; laundry service; coin-op washers and dryers. *In room:* A/C, TV, dataport, kitchen, fridge, coffeemaker, hair dryer, iron.

Moderate

Island's End Resort ★★★ *Value*   A wonderful respite from the maddening crowd, and a great bargain to boot, this little all-cottage hideaway sits right on the southern tip of St. Pete Beach, smack-dab on Pass-a-Grille, where the Gulf of Mexico meets Tampa Bay. You can step from the six contemporary cottages right onto the beach. And since the island curves sharply here, nothing blocks your view of the emerald bay. Strong currents run through the pass, but you can safely swim in the Gulf or grab a brilliant sunset at the Pass-a-Grille public beach, just one door removed. Linked to each other by boardwalks, the comfortable one- or three-bedroom cottages have dining areas, living rooms, VCRs, and fully equipped kitchens. You will love the one monstrous unit with two living rooms (one can be converted to sleeping quarters), two bathrooms (one with a whirlpool tub and separate shower), and its own private bay-side swimming pool. Maid service is available on request.

1 Pass-a-Grille Way (at 1st Ave.), St. Pete Beach, FL 33706. ☎ **727/360-5023.** Fax 727/367-7890. www.islandsend.com. 6 units. Winter $115–$235 cottage; off-season $100–$235 cottage. Weekly rates available. Complimentary breakfast served Tues, Thurs, and Sat. MC, V. **Amenities:** Coin-op washers and dryers. *In room:* A/C, TV, kitchen, coffeemaker, hair dryer, iron.

Inexpensive

Beach Haven ★ *Value*   Nestled on the beach between two high-rise condominiums, these low-slung, pink-with-white-trim structures look from the outside like the early 1950s motel they once were. But Jone and Millard Gamble, who used to own this motel and still have the charming Island's End Resort (see above), replaced the innards and installed bright tile floors, vertical blinds, pastel tropical furniture, and many modern amenities, including VCRs and refrigerators. Five of the original quarters remain as motel rooms (with shower-only bathrooms), but the others are linked to make 12 one-bedroom units and one two-bedroom unit, all with kitchens. The top choice is the one-bedroom suite with sliding-glass doors opening to a tiled patio beside an outdoor heated pool. There's also a sunning deck with lounge furniture by the beach. You don't get maid service on Sunday or holidays, and the rooms and bathrooms are 1950s smallish; but every unit here is bright, airy, and comfortable.

4980 Gulf Blvd. (at 50th Ave.), St. Pete Beach, FL 33706. ☎ **727/367-8642.** Fax 727/360-8202. www.beach havenvillas.com. 18 units. Winter $90–$150 double; off-season $68–$122 double. AE, DISC, MC, V. **Amenities:** Heated outdoor pool; coin-op washers and dryers; concierge-level rooms. *In room:* A/C, TV, dataport, kitchen, coffeemaker, hair dryer, iron.

CLEARWATER BEACH
Moderate

Clearwater Beach Hotel ★   Besides the idyllic beach location, you'll enjoy easy access to many nearby shops and restaurants from this Old Florida–style structure, built in 1986 to replace an old wooden hotel. The resort has been owned and operated by the same family since the 1950s and attracts a mixed clientele. Directly on the Gulf, the complex consists of the six-story main building and two contemporary motel-style wings. Some rooms have balconies, and the efficiencies in the wings have kitchenettes. Offering French cuisine, the formal dining room is romantic at sunset and offers great views of the Gulf, while the nautically themed lounge has entertainment nightly. A bar provides snacks and libations beside an outdoor heated swimming pool.

500 Mandalay Ave. (at Baymont St.), Clearwater Beach, FL 33767. ☎ **800/292-2295** or 727/441-2425. Fax 727/449-2083. www.clearwaterbeachhotel.com. 157 units. Winter $145–$169 double; off-season $125–$169 double. AE, DC, MC, V. Free valet parking. **Amenities:** Restaurant; bar; heated outdoor pool; access to nearby

health club; concierge; limited room service; laundry service. *In room:* A/C, TV, kitchen (efficiencies only), fridge, coffeemaker.

Clearwater Beach Marriott Suites on Sand Key ★ *(Kids)*   You'll see the beauty of Sand Key Island from the suites in this boomerang-shaped, 10-story, all-suites hotel located across the boulevard from the Sheraton Sand Key Resort (see below). Although the resort sits on the bay and not the Gulf, it has a large swimming pool complex next to the water, and the beach and beautiful Sand Key Park are short walks or trolley rides away. The resort has a good children's program, and the whole family will enjoy exploring the adjacent boardwalk with 25 shops and restaurants, including a branch of Ybor City's excellent Columbia (p. 406). Each suite has a bedroom with a balcony offering water views, as well as a complete living room with a sofa bed, a wet bar, and an entertainment unit. The heated swimming pool with cascading waterfalls is gorgeous and reminiscent of an exotic resort in Mexico, Hawaii, or even Las Vegas.

1201 Gulf Blvd., Clearwater Beach, FL 33767. © **800/228-9290** or 727/596-1100. Fax 727/595-4292. www.clearwaterbeachmarriottsuites.com. 220 units. Winter $199–$239 suite; off-season $189–$229 suite. Packages available. AE, DC, DISC, MC, V. **Amenities:** 2 restaurants; 2 bars; heated outdoor pool; golf course; exercise room; Jacuzzi; sauna; children's programs; game room; car-rental desk; business center; shopping arcade; limited room service; massage; babysitting; laundry service; coin-op washers and dryers. *In room:* A/C, TV, dataport, minibar, coffeemaker, hair dryer, iron.

Sheraton Sand Key Resort ★   Away from the honky-tonk of Clearwater, this nine-story Spanish-look hotel on 10 acres next to Sand Key Park is a big favorite with watersports enthusiasts and groups. It's only a 150-yard walk across the broad beach in front of the hotel to the water's edge. The moderately spacious guest rooms here all have traditional dark wood furniture and balconies or patios with views of the Gulf or the bay. The exercise room here is on the top floor, rendering great workout views.

1160 Gulf Blvd., Clearwater Beach, FL 33767. © **800/325-3535** or 727/595-1611. Fax 727/596-1117. www.sheratonsandkey.com. 390 units. Winter $165–$336 double; off-season $165–$259 double. AE, DC, DISC, MC, V. **Amenities:** 2 restaurants; 2 bars; 24-hr. convenience store; heated outdoor pool; 3 tennis courts; exercise room; Jacuzzi; sauna; watersports equipment rental; children's programs (summer only); game room; concierge; business center; limited room service; babysitting; laundry service; concierge-level rooms. *In room:* A/C, TV, dataport, coffeemaker, hair dryer, iron.

Inexpensive

Sun West Beach Motel *(Value)*   Sitting among several small motels, a 2-block walk from the beach, Scott and Judy Barrows's simple one-story establishment

---

(**Tips** **Cheap Bunks for the Young at Heart**

The young and young at heart can find an inexpensive bed at **Clearwater Beach International Hostel,** 606 Bay Esplanade (© and fax **727/443-1211;** www.clearwaterbeachhostel.com), in a predominately residential neighborhood a short walk north of the busy beach area. There's a swimming pool, communal kitchen, TV lounge with hundreds of videos to watch, canoes and other toys to borrow, and bicycles to rent. The hostel's 33 dorm beds rent for $13 a night, while four private rooms range from $34 to $57. MasterCard and Visa credit cards are accepted. Reservations are strongly advised during the winter and summer months. The hostel is affiliated with both Hostelling International and American Youth Hostels.

dates from 1954, but it's well maintained, overlooks the bay, and has a fishing/boating dock and a heated bay-side pool and sun deck. All units, which face the bay, the pool, or the sun deck, have tropical-style furnishings, which make the place seem more modern than it is. The four motel rooms have small refrigerators, the 10 efficiencies have kitchens, and a few suites have separate bedrooms. The biggest and best unit is the Bayside Suite, which has vaulted ceilings, a steam room in its bathroom, and a fully equipped kitchen.

409 Hamden Dr. (at Bayside Dr.), Clearwater Beach, FL 33767. ✆ 727/442-5008. Fax 727/461-1395. 15 units. Winter $63–$99 double; off-season $42–$70 double. MC, V. **Amenities:** Heated outdoor pool; access to nearby health club; coin-op washers and dryers. *In room:* A/C, TV, kitchen (some units), fridge, coffeemaker.

TWO NEARBY GOLF RESORTS

Belleview Biltmore Resort & Spa 🌟   The Gulf Coast's oldest operating tourist hotel, this gabled clapboard structure was built in 1896 by Henry B. Plant as the Hotel Belleview to attract customers to his Orange Belt Railroad. Sited on a bluff overlooking the bay, it's the largest occupied wooden structure in the world. Today it attracts mostly groups and serious golfers (guests can play at the adjoining Belleview Country Club, an 18-hole, par-72 championship course), but there's no denying its Victorian charm and old-fashioned ambience—once you get past the out-of-place glass-and-steel foyer added by more recent owners. Historic tours are given daily ($5 adults, $3 kids 12–17). The creaky hallways lead to several shops and a museum explaining the hotel's history. The hotel provides complimentary shuttle service to the country club and to Clearwater Beach and features a new beach club on nearby Sand Key.

25 Belleview Blvd., Clearwater, FL 33756. ✆ 800/237-8947 or 727/373-3000. Fax 727/441-4173 or 727/443-6361. www.belleviewbiltmore.com. 240 units. Winter $95–$139 double, $150–$302 suite; off-season $93–$120 double; $141–$302 suite. AE, DC, DISC, MC, V. Valet parking $5; free self-parking. Resort is 1 mile south of downtown on Belleview Blvd., off Alt. U.S. 19. **Amenities:** Restaurant; 2 bars; heated indoor and outdoor pools; golf course; 4 clay tennis courts; health club; Jacuzzi; sauna; concierge; business center; shopping arcade; salon; limited room service; babysitting; laundry service. *In room:* A/C, TV, coffeemaker, hair dryer, iron.

The Westin Innisbrook Resort 🌟🌟   *Golf Digest, Golf,* and other magazines pick this as one of the country's best places to play (provided you stay here, of course). Situated off U.S. 19 between Palm Harbor and Tarpon Springs, this 1,000-acre, all-condominium resort has 90 holes on championship courses that are more like the rolling links of the Carolinas than the usually flat courses found in Florida. Some golf magazines think the **Copperhead course** 🌟🌟, former home of the annual JCPenney Classic, is number one in Florida. If you want to learn, Innisbrook has the largest resort-owned and -operated golf school in North America, and it boasts a tennis center with instruction, too. It's similar to the sports-oriented Saddlebrook Resort near Tampa (p. 402), except that the courses are more challenging here and you're much closer to the beach. A free shuttle runs around the property, and another goes to the beach three times a day. Ranging in size from suites to two-bedroom models, the quarters are privately owned condos spread all over the premises. The focal points are the golf and tennis clubhouses, all of which have restaurants and bars: This place is not for serious beachgoers.

36750 U.S. 19 N., Palm Harbor, FL 34684. ✆ 877/752-1480 or 727/942-2000. Fax 727/942-5576. www. westin-innisbrook.com. 700 units. Winter $229–$485 suite; off-season $145–$289 suite. Golf packages available. AE, DC, DISC, MC, V. **Amenities:** 7 restaurants; 7 bars; heated outdoor pools; 4 golf courses; 15 tennis courts; health club; Jacuzzis; sauna; children's programs; concierge; activities desk; car-rental desk; limited room service; massage; babysitting; laundry service; coin-op washers and dryers. *In room:* A/C, TV, dataport, minibar, kitchen, coffeemaker, hair dryer, iron.

WHERE TO DINE

We have grouped the restaurants by their geographic location: St. Pete Beach, including Pass-a-Grille; Indian Rocks Beach, including Madeira Beach, Redington Beach, North Redington Beach, Redington Shores, and Indian Shores; and, finally, Clearwater Beach.

ST. PETE BEACH

Crabby Bill's *Kids* SEAFOOD   This member of a small local chain sits right on the beach in the heart of the hotel district. There's an open-air rooftop bar, but big glass windows enclose the large dining room. They offer fine water views from picnic tables equipped with rolls of paper towels and buckets of saltine crackers, the better with which to eat the blue, Alaskan, snow, and stone crabs that are the big draws here. The crustaceans fall into the moderate price category or higher, depending on the market, but most other main courses, such as fried fish or shrimp, are inexpensive—and they aren't overcooked or overbreaded. The creamy smoked fish spread is a delicious appetizer, and you'll get enough to whet the appetites of at least two people. This is a very good place to feed the entire family.

5300 Gulf Blvd. (at 53rd Ave.), St. Pete Beach. © 727/360-8858. Main courses $10–$24, market price for lobster and stone crab claws; sandwiches $5.50–$8. AE, MC, V. Mon–Thurs 11:30am–10pm; Fri–Sat 11:30am–11pm; Sun noon–10pm.

Hurricane SEAFOOD   A longtime institution, across the street from Pass-a-Grille Public Beach, this three-level gray Victorian building with white gingerbread trim is a great place to toast the sunset, especially at the rooftop bar. It's more beach pub than restaurant; but the grouper sandwiches are excellent, and there's always fresh fish to be fried, broiled, or blackened, and shrimp and crab to be steamed. Downstairs you can dine inside the knotty-pine–paneled dining room or on the sidewalk terrace, where bathers from across Gulf Way are welcome (there's a walk-up bar for beach libation). The second-floor dining area also has seating on a wraparound veranda. You must be at least 21 years old to go up to the Hurricane Watch rooftop bar or to join the revelry when the second level turns into Stormy's Nightclub at 10pm Wednesday through Saturday.

807 Gulf Way (at 9th Ave.), Pass-a-Grille. © 727/360-9558. www.thehurricane.com. Main courses $9–$18; sandwiches $5–$9. AE, MC, V. Daily 8am–1am.

Maritana Grille ⚲⚲ SEAFOOD/FLORIBBEAN   If you're not staying in the Don CeSar Resort, consider eating there, at this bastion of fabulous, Floribbean cuisine that's known for elegant dinners of steaks and seafood, but even better known for its spectacular Sunday brunch in which the food goes on as much as Celine Dion's heart goes on in her overplayed theme to *Titanic*. The dining room is adorned with 1,500 gallons of salt-water aquariums and Florida fish. A specialty that's one of the most innovative dishes I've ever had is the orange habanero BBQ Gulf fish with warm pineapple, vanilla bean stew, glazed banana, and rum pepper paint. The chef's table is a dégustation that takes place in the kitchen, at a private table at which guests are able to interact directly with and observe the chef in action. Bill Clinton dined here, and we all know his penchant for bountiful, good food (McDonald's fetish notwithstanding).

At the Don CeSar Resort, 3400 Gulf Blvd. (at 9th Ave.), St. Pete Beach. © 727/360-1882. Reservations recommended. Main courses $27–$38. AE, MC, V. Sun–Thurs, 5:30 -10pm; Fri–Sat 5:30-11pm.

Ted Peters' Famous Smoked Fish ⚲ *Value* SEAFOOD   This open-air eatery is an institution in these parts: Ted's has been around since the '50s. Some folks bring the fish they caught for the staff to smoke ($1.50 a pound), others figure fishing is a waste of time and come right to Ted's table for mullet, mackerel, salmon, and other fish slowly cooked over red oak. Enjoy the smell and sip a cold one while you wait for your order.

1530 Pasadena Ave. (just across St. Pete Beach Causeway), Pasadena. ℂ 727/381-7931. Main courses $8–$18. No credit cards. Wed–Mon 11am–7:30pm.

INDIAN ROCKS BEACH AREA

Guppy's Seafood Grill & Bar ⚡⚡ SEAFOOD   Locals also love this small bar and grill across from Indian Rocks Public Beach because they know they'll always get terrific chow (it's associated with the excellent Lobster Pot; see below). You won't soon forget the salmon coated with potatoes and lightly fried, then baked with a creamy leek and garlic sauce; it's fattening, yes, but also a bargain at $10. Another good choice is lightly cooked tuna finished with a peppercorn sauce. The atmosphere is casual beach friendly, with a fun bar in the middle of it all. Try the delicious upside-down apple-walnut pie topped with ice cream. You can dine outside on a patio beside the main road.

1701 Gulf Blvd. (at 17th Ave.), Indian Rocks Beach. ℂ 727/593-2032. Main courses $10–$18; sandwiches $6–$7. AE, DC, DISC, MC, V. Sun–Thurs 11:30am–10:30pm; Fri–Sat 11:30am–11pm.

Lobster Pot ⚡⚡⚡ SEAFOOD/STEAKS   Step into this weathered-looking restaurant near the beach and experience some of the finest seafood in the area. The prices are high, but the variety of Maine lobster dishes is amazing. The lobster cardinal is a blend of meat, cream, and cognac baked to succulent perfection, and the bouillabaisse is as authentic as any you'd find in the south of France. In addition to lobster, there's a wide selection of grouper, snapper, salmon, swordfish, shrimp, scallops, crab, Dover sole, and steaks, most prepared with elaborate sauces. The children's menu here is definitely out of the ordinary: It features half a Maine lobster and a petite filet mignon.

17814 Gulf Blvd. (at 178th Ave.), Redington Shores. ℂ 727/391-8592. www.lobsterpotrestaurant.com. Reservations recommended. Main courses $16–$40. AE, DC, MC, V. Daily 4:30–10pm.

The Salt Rock Grill ⚡⚡ SEAFOOD/STEAKS   Affluent professionals and the so-called beautiful people pack this waterfront restaurant, making it *the* place to see and be seen on the beaches. The big urbane dining room is built on three levels, thus affording every table a view over the creeklike waterway out back. And in warm, fair weather you can dine out by the dock or slake your thirst at the lively Tiki bar (bands play out here Sat–Sun during the summer). Anything from the wood-fired grill is excellent. Thick, aged steaks are the house specialties. Pan-seared peppered tuna and salmon cooked on a cedar board lead the seafoods. You can avoid spending a fortune by showing up in time for the early-bird specials or by ordering the meatloaf topped with mashed potatoes and onion straws ($9) or the half-pound sirloin steak ($11).

19325 Gulf Blvd. (north of 193rd Ave.), Indian Shores. ℂ 727/593-7625. www.saltrockgrill.com. Reservations strongly advised. Main courses $8–$36 (early-bird specials $8–$10). AE, DC, DISC, MC, V. Sun–Thurs 4–10pm; Fri–Sat 4–11pm (early-bird specials daily 4–5:30pm). Tiki bar open Sat 2pm–midnight (or later); Sun 2–10pm.

CLEARWATER BEACH

Bobby's Bistro & Wine Bar ⚡ AMERICAN   Son of Bob Heilman's Beachcomber, this chic bistro draws a more urbane crowd than its parent. A wine-cellar theme is amply justified by the real thing: a walk-in closet with several thousand bottles kept at a constant 55°F (12°C). Walk through and pick your vintage, then listen to jazz while you dine inside at tall, bar-height tables or outside on a covered patio. The chef specializes in gourmet pizzas on homemade

The Sponge Capital of the World ⍟

One of Florida's most fascinating small towns and a fine day trip from Tampa, St. Petersburg, or the beaches (it's 30 miles north of St. Petersburg, 23 miles west of Tampa, and 13 miles north of Clearwater), **Tarpon Springs** calls itself "the Sponge Capital of the World." Greek immigrants from the Dodecanese Islands settled here in the late 19th century to harvest sponges, which grew in abundance offshore. By the 1930s, Tarpon Springs was producing more sponges than any other place in the world. A blight ruined the business in the 1940s, but the descendants of those early immigrants stayed on. Today they compose about a third of the population, making Tarpon Springs a center of transplanted Greek culture.

Sponges still arrive at the historic **Sponge Docks,** on Dodecanese Boulevard. With a lively, carnival-like atmosphere, the docks are a great place to spend an afternoon or early evening, poking your head into shops selling sponges and other souvenirs while Greek music comes from the dozen or so family restaurants purveying authentic Aegean cuisine. You can also venture offshore from here, because booths on the docks hawk sightseeing and fishing cruises. Make your reservations as soon as you get here; then go sightseeing ashore or grab a meal at one of the multitudinous Greek restaurants and bakeries facing the dock while waiting for the next boat to shove off.

You also can visit the tin-roofed **Spongeorama** (510 Dodecanese Blvd.; no phone; open daily 10am–5pm), a museum dedicated to sponges and sponge divers that sells a wide variety of sponges (they'll

focaccia crust (as a tasty appetizer), plus charcoal-grilled lamb chops, filet mignon, fresh fish, and monstrous pork chops with caramelized Granny Smith apples and a Mount Vernon mustard sauce. Everything's served a la carte here, so watch your credit card. On the other hand, there's a less expensive sandwich menu featuring the likes of bronzed grouper and chicken with a spicy Jack cheese.

447 Mandalay Ave. (at Papaya St., behind Bob Heilman's Beachcomber). ✆ 727/446-9463. Reservations recommended. Main courses $8–$22; sandwiches and pizzas $6–$10. AE, DC, DISC, MC, V. Sun–Thurs 5–11pm; Fri–Sat 5pm–midnight, bar later.

Bob Heilman's Beachcomber ⍟ AMERICAN In a row of restaurants, bars, and T-shirt shops, this establishment has been popular with the locals since 1948. Each dining room here is unique: Large models of sailing crafts create a nautical theme in one, a pianist makes music in a second, works of art create a gallery in the third, and booths and a fireplace make for a cozy fourth. The menu presents a variety of well-prepared fresh seafood and beef, veal, and lamb selections. If you tire of fruits-of-the-sea, the "back to the farm" fried chicken—from an original 1910 Heilman family recipe—is incredible. The Beachcomber shares valet parking and an extensive wine collection with Bobby's Bistro & Wine Bar (see below).

447 Mandalay Ave. (at Papaya St.). ✆ 727/442-4144. Reservations recommended. Main courses $13–$29. AE, DC, DISC, MC, V. Mon–Sat 11:30am–11pm; Sun noon–10pm.

Frenchy's Original Cafe SEAFOOD Popular with locals and visitors in the know since 1981, this casual pub makes the best grouper sandwiches in the area ship your purchase home) and shows a 30-minute video several times a day about sponge diving. Admission is free. A scuba diver feeds sharks three times a day in the **Konger Tarpon Springs Aquarium** (850 Dodecanese Blvd.; ☎ **727/938-5378;** open Mon–Sat 10am–5pm, Sun noon–5pm), at the western end of the boulevard. Admission is $4.75 adults, $4 seniors, $2.75 for children 3 to 11, free for kids under 3.

South of the docks, the **Downtown Historic District** sports turn-of-the-last-century commercial buildings along Tarpon Avenue and Pinellas Avenue (Alt. U.S. 19). On Tarpon Avenue west of Pinellas Avenue, you'll come to the Victorian homes overlooking **Spring Bayou.** This creek-side area makes for a delightfully picturesque stroll.

The **Tarpon Springs Chamber of Commerce,** 11 E. Orange St., Tarpon Springs, FL 34689 (☎ **727/937-6109;** fax 727/937-2879; www.tarponsprings.com), has an information office on Dodecanese Boulevard at the Sponge Docks, which is open Tuesday through Sunday from 10:30am to 4:30pm.

To get to Tarpon Springs from Tampa or St. Petersburg, take U.S. 19 north and turn left on Tarpon Avenue (C.R. 582). From Clearwater Beach, take Alt. U.S. 19 north through Dunedin. The center of the historic downtown district is at the intersection of Pinellas Avenue (Alt. U.S. 19) and Tarpon Avenue. To reach the Sponge Docks, go 10 blocks north on Pinellas Avenue and turn left at Pappas' Restaurant onto Dodecanese Boulevard.

and has all the awards to prove it. The sandwiches are fresh, thick, juicy, and delicious. The atmosphere is pure Florida casual style. There can be a wait during winter and on weekends year-round. For a similarly relaxed setting, directly on the beach, **Frenchy's Rockaway Grill,** at 7 Rockaway St. (☎ **727/446-4844;** www.frenchysonline.com/rockaway.html), has a wonderful outdoor setting, and it keeps a charcoal grill going to cook fresh fish.

41 Baymont St. ☎ **727/446-3607.** www.frenchysonline.com/original.html. Sandwiches and burgers $5–$7.50. AE, MC, V. Mon–Thurs 11:30am–11pm; Fri–Sat 11:30am–midnight; Sun noon–11pm.

Island Way Grill ☆☆ SEAFOOD Not your ordinary waterfront seafood shanty, the glass-encased and wood-enhanced sleek Island Way Grill serves whatever the fishermen catch that day, but prepare it in their open kitchen, Pan Asian-style. Everything here is delicious, from cooked fish to sushi. The wine list is also superb. Sit outside on the patio and then hang out at the outdoor bar, where the fabulous people like members and owners of the Tampa Bay Buccaneers hang out, talk shop, and scope the scene.

20 Island Way. ☎ **727/461-6617.** Main courses $21–$30. AE, MC, V. Sun–Thurs 4–10pm; Fri–Sat 4–11pm.

THE BEACHES AFTER DARK
If you haven't already found it during your sightseeing and shopping excursions, the restored fishing community of **John's Pass Village and Boardwalk,** on Gulf Boulevard at John's Pass in Madeira Beach, has plenty of restaurants, bars, and

shops to keep you occupied after the sun sets. Elsewhere, the nightlife scene at the beach revolves around rocking bars that pump out music until 2am. All of the places listed in this section are bars that have live music.

Pass-a-Grille has the popular, always-lively lounge at **Hurricane,** on Gulf Way at 9th Avenue, opposite the public beach (p. 432).

Up on the northern tip of Treasure Island, **Gators on the Pass** (© 727/367-8951) claims to have the world's longest waterfront bar, with a huge deck overlooking the waters of John's Pass. The complex also includes a nonsmoking sports bar and a three-story tower with a top-level observation deck for panoramic views of the Gulf of Mexico. There's live music, from acoustic and blues to rock, most nights.

In Clearwater Beach, the **Palm Pavilion Grill & Bar,** on the beach at 18 Bay Esplanade (© 727/446-2742), has live music Tuesday through Sunday nights during winter and on weekends in the off-season. Nearby, **Frenchy's Rockaway Grill,** at 7 Rockaway St. (© 727/446-4844; www.frenchysonline.com/rock away.html), is another popular hangout.

If you're into laughs, **Coconuts Comedy Club,** at the Howard Johnson motel, Gulf Boulevard at 61st Avenue in St. Pete Beach (© 727/360-5653), has an ever-changing program of live stand-up funny men and women. Call for the schedule, performers, and prices.

For a more highbrow evening, go to the Clearwater mainland and the 2,200-seat **Ruth Eckerd Hall,** 1111 McMullen-Booth Rd. (© 727/791-7400; www.rutheckerdhall.com), which hosts a varied program of Broadway shows, ballet, drama, symphonic works, popular music, jazz, and country music.

4 Sarasota ★★★

52 miles S of Tampa, 150 miles SW of Orlando, 225 miles NW of Miami

Far enough away from Tampa Bay to have an identity very much its own, Sarasota is, surprisingly, one of Florida's cultural centers. In fact, many retirees spend their winters here because there's so much to keep them entertained and stimulated, including the Van Wezel Performing Arts Hall and the FSU Center for the Performing Arts, home of the annual Asolo Theatre Festival. Sarasota also has an extensive array of first-class resorts, restaurants, and upscale boutiques.

Offshore, more than 40 miles of gloriously white beaches fringe a chain of long, narrow barrier islands stretching from Tampa Bay to Sarasota. To the south, **Siesta Key** is a residential enclave popular with artisans and writers and is home to Siesta Village, this area's funky, laid-back, and often-noisy beach hangout. Shielded from the Gulf by **Lido Key,** which has a string of affordable hotels attractive to family vacationers, **St. Armands Key** sports one of Florida's ritziest shopping and dining districts, while adjacent **Longboat Key** is one of the country's swankiest islands.

ESSENTIALS

GETTING THERE   You probably will get a less-expensive airfare by flying into **Tampa International Airport,** an hour's drive north of Sarasota (p. 384), and you could save even more since Tampa's rental-car agencies usually offer some of the best deals in Florida. If you don't rent a car, **Sarasota-Tampa Express** (© 800/326-2800 or 941/727-1344) provides bus connections for $22 for adults, $11 for children 3 to 12. Call in advance for schedule and pickup locations.

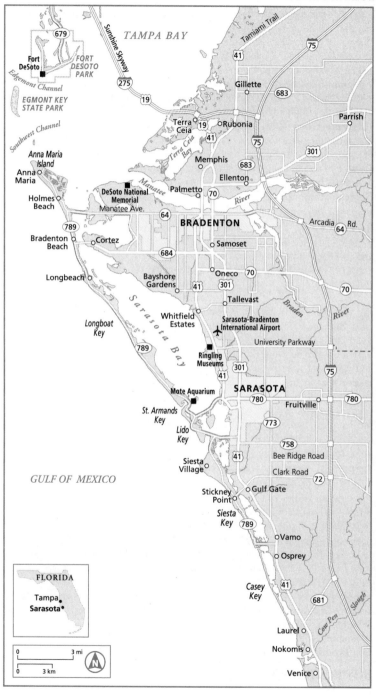

If you decide to fly directly here, **Sarasota-Bradenton International Airport** (© **941/359-2770;** www.srq-airport.com), north of downtown, off University Parkway between U.S. 41 and U.S. 301, is served by **American Trans Air** (© 800/225-2995), **Continental** (© 800/525-0280), **Delta** (© 800/221-1212), **Northwest** (© 800/225-2525), and **US Airways** (© 800/428-4322).

Alamo (© 800/327-9633), **Avis** (© 800/331-1212), **Budget** (© 800/527-0700), **Dollar** (© 800/800-4000), **Hertz** (© 800/654-3131), and **National** (© 800/227-7368) all have car-rental offices here.

Diplomat Taxi (© **941/355-5155**) has a monopoly on service from the airport to hotels in Sarasota and Bradenton. Look for the cabs at the west end of the terminal outside baggage claim. Fares range from about $10 to downtown Sarasota to $35 to Longboat Key or Anna Maria Island.

Amtrak has bus connections to Sarasota from its Tampa station (© **800/872-7245;** www.amtrak.com).

VISITOR INFORMATION   Contact the **Sarasota Convention and Visitors Bureau,** 655 N. Tamiami Trail (U.S. 41), Sarasota, FL 34236 (© **800/522-9799** or 941/957-1877; fax 941/951-2956; www.sarasotafl.org). The bureau and its helpful visitor center are in a blue pagoda-shaped building on Tamiami Trail (U.S. 41) at 6th Street. They're open Monday through Saturday from 9am to 5pm, Sunday from 11am to 3pm, closed holidays.

You can get a packet of advance information about Bradenton and surrounding Manatee County from the **Greater Bradenton Area Convention and Visitors Bureau,** P.O. Box 1000, Bradenton, FL 34206 (© **800/462-6283** or 941/729-9177; fax 941/729-1820; www.floridaislandbeaches.org).

If you're driving from the north via I-75, you can get off at U.S. 301 (exit 224) and head west if you want to go to the **Manatee County Tourist Information Center** (© **941/729-7040**), where volunteers are on hand to answer your questions and sell you excellent road maps for less than you'll pay elsewhere. It's open daily from 8:30am to 5pm except Easter Sunday, Thanksgiving, the day after Thanksgiving, and Christmas Day. The office also has an information kiosk at **Prime Outlets,** across I-75, which is open Monday through Saturday from 10am to 6pm and Sundays from 11am to 6pm.

GETTING AROUND   Operated by the Sarasota County Area Transit, or SCAT (© **941/861-1234;** www.co.sarasota.fl.us/public_works_scat/scat.asp), the **Sarasota Trolley** runs every 20 minutes from 9am to 5pm Monday through Friday, every 40 minutes on Saturday. The Scenic Loop Trolley operates from Island Park, Bayfront at Ringling Boulevard, through downtown Sarasota, north to the FSU Ringling Center for the Cultural Arts, and out to St. Armands and Lido Keys (but not to Siesta or Longboat keys). The Main Street Trolley goes from Island Park through downtown and eastward along Main Street. Fares are $1 on the Scenic Loop, 25¢ on the Main Street line, or you can buy a daily pass to both lines for $2. SCAT also operates regularly scheduled bus service. The Sarasota Convention and Visitors Bureau distributes route maps (see "Visitor Information," above).

Sarasota taxi companies include **Diplomat Taxi** (© **941/355-5155**), **Green Cab Taxi** (© **941/922-6666**), and **Yellow Cab of Sarasota** (© **941/955-3341**).

HITTING THE BEACH

Many of the area's 40-plus miles of beaches are occupied by hotels and condominium complexes, but there are excellent public beaches as well. The area's most popular is **Siesta Key Public Beach,** with a picnic area, a 700-car parking lot, crowds of families, and quartz sand reminiscent of the blazingly white beaches in Northwest Florida. There's also beach access at **Siesta Village,** which has a plethora of casual restaurants and pubs with outdoor seating (see "Where to Dine," later in this chapter). The more secluded and quiet **Turtle Beach** is at Siesta Key's south end. It has shelters, boat ramps, picnic tables, and volleyball nets. Both beaches have bathroom facilities.

Unless you're staying on Longboat Key, you won't be able to hit the beach there, since luxury homes and condos block access to the Gulf. However, do drive the length of Longboat Key and admire the luxurious residences. Then, take a right off St. Armands Circle onto Lido Key and **North Lido Beach.** The south end of the island is occupied by **South Lido Beach Park,** with plenty of shade, making it a good spot for picnics and walks.

OUTDOOR ACTIVITIES & SPECTATOR SPORTS

BICYCLING & IN-LINE SKATING   The flat terrain in this area makes for good in-line skating and for fine, though not challenging, bike riding. You can bike and skate from downtown Sarasota to Lido and Longboat keys, since paved walkways/bike paths run alongside the John Ringling Causeway and then up Longboat Key. **Siesta Sports Rentals,** 6551 Midnight Pass Rd., in the South-bridge Mall just south of Stickney Point Bridge on Siesta Key (© **941/346-1797;** www.siestasportsrentals.com), rents bikes of various sizes (including stroller attachments for kids), plus motor scooters, in-line skates, kayaks, and beach chairs and umbrellas. Bike rentals range from about $14 a day to $50 a week, while scooters go for $15 an hour, $50 a day, or $175 a week. The shop is open daily from 9am to 5pm.

BOAT RENTALS   **All Watersports,** in the Boatyard Shopping Village, on the mainland end of Stickney Point Bridge (© **941/921-2754**), rents personal watercraft such as jet skis, speedboats, runabouts, and bow riders. At the island end of the bridge, **C. B.'s Saltwater Outfitters,** 1249 Stickney Point Rd. (© **941/349-4400**), and **Dockside Marine,** 1265 Old Stickney Point Rd. (© **941/349-8880**), both rent runabouts, pontoon boats, and other craft. Bait and tackle are available at the marinas.

CRUISES   The area's best nature cruises go forth from Mote Aquarium (see the "Exploring the Area" section below).

That paddle-wheeler you see going up and down the bay is the *Seafood Shack Showboat,* operated by the Seafood Shack restaurant, 4110 127th St. W., in Cortez (© **800/299-5048** or 941/794-5048). It has afternoon cruises to Sarasota Bay, Tampa Bay, and as far away as the Sunshine Skyway. Prices are $16 for adults, $15 for seniors, and $8 for children 4 to 10. The *Showboat* goes to a different destination each day, and its schedule is seasonal, so call a day ahead for the schedule. Reservations are not accepted.

FISHING   Charter fishing boats dock at most marinas here. Check out **www.sarasotaboating.com** for a list. In downtown Sarasota, the **Flying Fish Fleet,** at Marina Jack's Marina, U.S. 41 at Island Park Circle (© **941/366-3373;** www.flyingfishfleet.com), offers party-boat charter-fishing excursions, with bait and tackle furnished. Prices for half-day trips are $35 adults, $30 seniors, and $25 kids 4 to 12. All-day voyages cost $55, $50, and $45, respectively. Call for the schedule. Charter boats also line up along the dock here.

GOLF   The **Bobby Jones Golf Complex** ⛳, 1000 Circus Blvd. (© **941/365-4653**), is Sarasota's only municipal facility, but it has two 18-hole championship layouts—the American (par-71) and British (par-72) courses—and the 9-hole

Gillespie executive course (par-30). Tee times are assigned 3 days in advance. Greens fees range from $25 to $35, including cart rental.

The semiprivate **Rolling Green Golf Club,** 4501 Tuttle Ave. (© **941/355-6620**), is an 18-hole, par-72 course. Facilities include a driving range, rental clubs, and lessons. Tee times are assigned 2 days in advance. Prices, including cart, are about $50 in winter and $30 off-season. Also semiprivate, the **Sarasota Golf Club,** 7820 N. Leewynn Dr. (© **941/371-2431**), is an 18-hole, par-72 course. Facilities include a driving range, lessons, club rentals, a restaurant, a lounge, and a golf shop. Fees, including cart, are about $65 in winter, $45 off-season.

If you have reciprocal privileges, **University Park Country Club,** west of I-75 on University Parkway (© **941/359-9999**), is Sarasota's only nationally ranked course. Fees, including cart, are about $55 year-round.

Bradenton is home to the well-known **David Leadbetter Golf Academy,** 1414 69th Ave., at U.S. 41 (© **800/872-6425** or 941/755-1000; www.leadbetter.com), a part of the Nick Bollettieri Sports Academy (see "Tennis," below). Presided over by one of golf's leading instructors, this facility offers practice tee instruction, video analysis, scoring strategy, and more.

For course information online, go to www.golf.com or www.floridagolfing.com, or call the **Florida Sports Foundation** (© **850/488-8347**) or **Florida Golfing** (© **866/833-2663**).

KAYAKING   Based at Mote Aquarium (see "Exploring the Area," below), **Sarasota Bay Explorers** ★★ (© **941/388-4200;** www.sarasotabayexplorers. com) uses a 38-foot pontoon boat to ferry novice and experienced kayakers and their craft to a marine sanctuary, where everyone paddles through tunnels formed by mangroves. The paddling is easy and the waters are shallow. Experienced naturalists serve as guides. Wear swimsuits and tennis shoes or rubber-soled booties, and bring a towel and lunch. The 3-hour trips cost $50 for adults, $40 for children 5 to 17, and are free for kids under 5 (seats are provided for the youngsters). Reservations are required.

SAILING   Take a leisurely cruise on the waters of Sarasota Bay and the Gulf of Mexico aboard the 41-foot, 12-passenger sailboat *Enterprise,* docked at Marina Jack's Marina, U.S. 41 at Island Park Circle (© **888/232-7768** or 941/951-1833; www.sarasotaboating.com/sailingcharters.html). Cruises range from 3 hours for $45 per person to 4 hours for $55 a head, while 2-hour sunset cruises cost $35 per person. Departure times vary, and reservations are required. **Siesta Key Sailing,** 1219 Southport Dr. (© **941/346-7245;** www.siestakey sailing.com), charges the same for similar cruises in a 42-foot Morgan Outlander sloop. Reservations are essential. Call for rates.

You can also get to historic Egmont Key, 3 miles off the northern end of Anna Maria Island at the mouth of Tampa Bay (p 425), on a 30-foot sloop-rigged sail-boat with **Spice Sailing Charters** (© **941/778-3240**), based at the Galati Yacht Basin on Bay Boulevard on northern Anna Maria Island. The company also has sunset cruises. Rates start at $30 per person. Call for schedule and reservations, which are required.

SPECTATOR SPORTS   **Ed Smith Stadium,** 2700 12th St., at Tuttle Avenue, east of downtown Sarasota (© **941/954-4464**), is the winter home of the **Cincinnati Reds** (© **941/955-6501;** www.cincinnatireds.com), who hold spring training here in February and March. Game tickets are $5 to $12. From April to August, the stadium is home to the **Sarasota Red Sox** (© **941/365-4460,** ext. 2300; www.sarasox.com), a Class A minor-league affiliate of the Boston Red Sox. Tickets are $4 and $5.

The **Pittsburgh Pirates** (© **941/748-4610;** www.pirateball.com) do their February-through-March spring training at 6,562-seat McKechnie Field, 9th Street West and 17th Avenue West, south of downtown Bradenton. Tickets are $6 to $9.

The **Sarasota Polo Club,** 8201 Polo Club Lane, Sarasota (© **941/907-0000**), at Lakewood Ranch, a planned community midway between Sarasota and Bradenton, is the site of weekly polo matches from mid-December to early April, on Sunday afternoons. General admission is $6, free for children under 13. Call for the schedule of matches.

TENNIS   The **Nick Bollettieri Sports Academy,** 5500 34th St. W. in Bradenton (© **800/872-6425** or 941/755-1000; www.bollettieri.com), is one of the world's largest tennis training facilities, with more than 70 championship grass, clay, and hard courts and a pro shop. It's open year-round, and reservations are required for all activities.

WATERSPORTS   You'll find watersports activities in front of the major hotels out on the keys (see "Where to Stay," beginning on p. 445). **Siesta Sports Rentals,** 6551 Midnight Pass Rd. on Siesta Key (© **813/346-1797;** www.siesta sportsrentals.com), rents kayaks and sailboats, plus beach chairs and umbrellas.

EXPLORING THE AREA
IN SARASOTA

Art Center Sarasota   In addition to the marvelous John and Mable Ringling Museum of Art (see below), Sarasota is home to more than 40 art galleries and exhibition spaces, all open to the public year-round. A convenient artistic starting point is this downtown community art center, next to the Sarasota Convention and Visitors Bureau. It contains three galleries and a small sculpture garden, presenting the area's largest display of art by national and local artists, from paintings and pottery to sculpture, cartoons, jewelry, and enamelware. There are also art demonstrations and special events.

707 N. Tamiami Trail (at 6th St.). © 941/365-2032. www.artsarasota.org. Free admission ($2 suggested donation). Tues–Sat 10am–4pm; Sun noon–4pm.

Florida Ever-Glides, Inc. 🛵🛵   Ride the future (and get some history at the same time) when you take a tour with this great company, the first in the U.S. to offer historic and scenic guided tours using Segway Human Transporters, you know, those cool electric scooter-type things you've seen on TV (and saw George Bush, Jr. fall off of). The friendly staffers here will have you up, riding, and comfortable (I swear) in a matter of minutes, with orientation, training, and as many practice runs as you need before you start off on your 2-hour 9am or 2pm tour of Downtown Sarasota and the Bayfront, including the vintage 1920s Towles Court Artist Colony.

200 S. Washington Blvd., #11 (on the corner of Adams Lane). © 941/363-9556. Fax 941/363-9557. www.floridaever-glides.com. $59 per person. AE, DISC, MC, V. Daily 8am–5pm.

FSU Ringling Center for the Cultural Arts 🛵🛵🛵   By far the top attraction here, this 66-acre site is where showman and circus legend John Ringling and his wife, Mable, collected art and built houses on a grand scale. Now under the aegis of Florida State University, **The John and Mable Ringling Museum of Art** is the state's official art museum. It's filled with more than 500 years of European and American art, including one of the world's most important collections of grand 17th-century baroque paintings as well as collections of decorative arts and traveling exhibits. The old-master collection also includes five world-renowned tapestry cartoons by Peter Paul Rubens and his studio.

(Tips **How to See the Ringling Museums**

It's best to visit the FSU Ringling Center for the Cultural Arts on a week-day when the center offers adult guided tours and school tours of the art museum, house, and circus museum, which are included in the price of admission. Call ahead or check at the information desk as soon as you arrive for tour times. In between, explore the gardens and have lunch at The Banyan Cafe.

Built in 1924 and 1925 at a cost of $1.5 million and modeled after a Venet-ian palace, the Ringlings' spectacular 32-room palatial, bay-front, four-story winter residence **Ca'd'Zan** ("House of John" in the Venetian dialect) has been recently restored. An 8,000-square-foot terrace leads down to the dock at which Mable Ringling moored her Venetian gondola. Don't miss a tour of this house to see the period furniture and stunning architecture and artwork; in fact, I'd make it the first stop on your Ringling itinerary.

The **Ringling Museum of the Circus** is devoted to circus memorabilia (which is, in a way, more fascinating than the circus itself) including parade wagons, calliopes, costumes, and colorful posters. The grounds also include a classical courtyard, a rose garden, a museum shop, and the historic **Asolo The-ater,** a 19th-century Italian court playhouse, which the Ringlings moved here in the 1950s. It's now the centerpiece of the Florida State University Center for the Performing Arts. You'll need most of a day to see everything here.

5401 Bay Shore Rd. at N. Tamiami Trail (U.S. 41). (941/359-5700, or 941/351-1660 for recorded informa-tion. www.ringling.org. Admission $15 adults, $12 seniors, $5 out-of-state students, free for Florida students and all children 12 and under. Daily 10am–5:30pm. Closed New Year's Day, Thanksgiving, and Christmas. From downtown, take U.S. 41 north to University Pkwy. and follow signs to museum.

G. Wiz (Gulfcoast Wonder & Imagination Zone)   This hands-on, state-of-the-art science center has two floors of fun exhibits that cover the physical, earth, and health sciences. In June 2002, G. Wiz opened its three-year ExploraZone exhibit, which features annually rotating interactive exhibits from San Fran-cisco's renowned Exploratorium. The 35 exhibits have themes ranging from sound and music to mathematics and motion, color and optics, sight and illu-sion, and others.

1001 Blvd. of the Arts (in the Blivas Science and Technology Center, 1 block west of U.S. 41). (**941/ 9061851.** www.gwiz.org. Admission $7 adults, $6 seniors, $5 kids 2 and over; free 5–8pm the 1st Wed of the month. Tues–Sat 10am–5pm; Sun noon–5pm.

Marie Selby Botanical Gardens ✶✶   A must-see for serious plant lovers and a should-see for those looking for good photo ops, this peaceful retreat on the bay, just south of downtown, is said to be the only botanical garden in the world specializing in the preservation, study, and research of epiphytes, that is, "air plants" such as orchids. It's home to more than 20,000 exotic plants, includ-ing more than 6,000 orchids, as well as a bamboo pavilion, a butterfly and hum-mingbird garden, a medicinal plant garden, a waterfall garden, a cactus and succulent garden, a fernery, a hibiscus garden, a palm grove, two tropical food gardens, and a native shore-plant community. Selby's home and the Payne Man-sion (both on the National Registry) are also located here.

811 S. Palm Ave. (south of U.S. 41). (941/366-5731. www.selby.org. Admission $12 adults, $6 children 6–11, free for children 5 and under accompanied by an adult. Daily 10am–5pm. Closed Christmas.

Sarasota Classic Car Museum   There's more to this museum than its 90-plus classic and "muscle" autos, from Rolls-Royces and Pierce Arrows to the four cars used personally by circus czar John Ringling. Also here are more than 1,200 antique music boxes and several of Thomas Edison's early phonographs, including a 1909 diamond-tipped-needle model. Check out the Penny Arcade with antique games (with original prices), and grab a cone at the ice-cream and sandwich shop. In operation since 1953, this is now a nonprofit museum dedicated to preserving antique automobiles.

5500 N. Tamiami Trail (at University Pkwy.). © 941/355-6228. www.sarasotacarmuseum.org. Admission $8.50 adults, $7.65 seniors, $5.75 children 13–17, $4 children 6–12, free for children under 6. Daily 9am–6pm. Take U.S. 41 north of downtown; museum is 2 blocks west of the airport.

ON ST. ARMANDS KEY

Mote Aquarium ★★ *Kids*   Kids get to touch cool stuff like a stingray (minus the stinger, of course) and watch sharks in the shark tank at this excellent aquarium. Part of the noted Mote Marine Laboratory complex, it is more broad-based than Tampa's Florida Aquarium, which concentrates primarily on local sea life. The kids won't believe all the sea-horse babies that come from the dad's pouch (one of Mother Nature's strange-but-true surprises), and they surely will gawk at a 35-foot-long deceased giant squid (it was 45 ft. long when alive). They can see manatees in the Marine Mammal Center, a block's walk from the aquarium. There are also many research-in-progress exhibits. Start by watching the aquarium's 12-minute film on the feeding habits of sharks; then allow at least 90 minutes to take in everything on land. Add another 2 hours to take a narrated sea-life encounter cruise with **The Sarasota Bay Explorers** (© 727/388-4200; www.sarasotabayexplorers.com). These fun and informative cruises visit a deserted island, and the guides throw out nets and bring up sea life for inspection. It's a good idea to make reservations for the cruise a day in advance. This company has unusual kayaking adventures, too (p. 440).

1600 Ken Thompson Pkwy. (on City Island). © 800/691-6683 or 941/388-2541. www.mote.org. Admission $12 adults, $8 children 4–12, free for children under 4. Nature cruises $24 adults, $20 children 4–12, free for kids under 4. Combination aquarium-cruise tickets $30 adults, $25 children. Daily 10am–5pm. Nature cruises daily 11am, and 1:30 and 4pm. From St. Armands Circle, go north toward Longboat Key; turn right just before the Lido-Longboat bridge.

IN & NEAR BRADENTON

DeSoto National Memorial   Nestled on the Manatee River, west of downtown, this park attracts history buffs by re-creating the look and atmosphere of the period when Spanish explorer Hernando de Soto landed here in 1539. It includes a restoration of de Soto's original campsite and a scenic half-mile nature trail that circles a mangrove jungle and leads to the ruins of one of the first settlements in the area. Start by watching a 21-minute film about de Soto in America. From December to March, park employees dress in 16th-century costumes and portray the way the early settlers lived, including demonstrations of cooking and the firing of an arquebus, one of the world's earliest firearms.

DeSoto Memorial Hwy. (north end of 75th St. W.). © 941/792-0458. www.nps.gov/deso. Free admission. Daily 9am–5pm. Take Manatee Ave. (Fla. 64) west to 75th St. W. and turn right; follow the road to its end and the entrance to the park.

(*Fun Fact* **Soto's Sara**

Legend has it that Sarasota was named after the explorer Hernando de Soto's daughter, Sara—hence, Sara-sota.

Milky-White Stallions

Horse lovers are drawn to the famous **Lipizzaner Stallions,** which do their spectacular leaps at the Ottomar Herrmann training grounds, 32755 Singletary Rd., Myakka City (© **941/322-1501**), from late December to March (they tour the country the rest of the year). Members of a now-rare breed, the parents of these milky-white stallions were brought here from Austria in the 1960s by Colonel Ottomar Herrmann. Their *haute école* performances are straight from Vienna's famous Spanish Riding School. Call for schedule and directions. Admission is by donation.

Gamble Plantation ☆   Situated northeast of downtown Bradenton, this is the oldest structure on the southwestern coast of Florida, and a fine example of an antebellum plantation home—something that's quite rare in Florida—over a 6-year period in the late 1840s by Major Robert Gamble, it was constructed primarily of "tabby mortar" (a mixture of oyster shells, sand, molasses, and water), with 10 rooms, verandas on three sides, 18 exterior columns, and eight fireplaces. Maintained as a state historic site, it includes a fine collection of 19th-century furnishings. Entrance to the house is by tour only, although you can explore the grounds on your own. The Prime Outlets Ellenton is a 5-minute drive from here via U.S. 301, so you can combine a plantation visit with some bargain hunting (see p. 445 for more information).

3708 Patten Ave. (U.S. 301), Ellenton. © 941/723-4536. www.floridastateparks.org/gambleplantation. Free admission. Tours $4 adults, $2 children 6–12, free for children under 6. Thurs–Mon 9am–4:30pm; 30-min. guided house tour 9:30 and 10:30am, and 1, 2, 3, and 4pm. Take U.S. 301 north of downtown to Ellenton; the site is on the left, just east of Ellenton-Gillette Rd. (Fla. 683).

Solomon's Castle ☆☆   This attraction gets the vote and the award for the Weirdest and Wackiest (and boy, are there many) of Florida category. Howard Solomon, in 1974, began building what has become a 60-foot-tall, 12,000-square-foot castle in a Manatee County swamp. Solomon, a metal and wood sculptor by trade, built the huge structure (where he now lives) out of 22-by-34-inch offset aluminum printing plates discarded by a local newspaper. He and other tour guides (though try to get a tour led by him, or at least meet him and talk to him about his work) lead guests on a pun-filled tour of the castle, which is decked out with some of his smaller artistic creations, mostly made of other people's "trash," including a chair made out of 86 beer cans, an elephant pieced together with seven oil drums, a unicorn fashioned out of coat hangers, and about 80 stained-glass windows. Howard is continually building new things—you never know what you'll find. If that's not enough to tempt you, you can have lunch in the restaurant, which is in a Spanish galleon that Howard built in his spare time. You *have* to experience this to believe it. Seriously.

4533 Solomon Road, Ona. © 863/494-6007. www.solomonscastle.com. Admission $10 adults, $4 kids under 12. Tours Tues–Sun 11am–4pm, Oct–June. Closed all Mondays and the months of July, Aug, and Sep. Take Hwy. 64 east of I-75 29 miles to Hwy. 665, go south nine miles and turn left at the sign to the castle.

South Florida Museum and Parker Manatee Aquarium *Kids*   The star at this downtown complex is "Snooty," the oldest manatee born in captivity (1948) and Manatee County's official mascot. Snooty and his pal "Mo" live in the Parker Manatee Aquarium. The South Florida Museum tells the story of Florida's history, from prehistoric times to the present, including a Native American collection with life-size dioramas and a Spanish courtyard containing replicas of 16th-century buildings. (Fire recently damaged the museum's Bishop Planetarium, which is now closed.)

201 10th St. W. (on the riverfront, at Barcarrota Blvd.). © 941/746-4131. www.southfloridamuseum.org. Admission $9.50 adults, $7.50 seniors, $6 students with ID, $5 children 5–12, free for children 4 and under. Jan–Apr and July Mon–Sat 10am–5pm; Sun noon–5pm. Rest of year Tues–Sat 10am–5pm; Sun noon–5pm. Closed New Year's Day, Thanksgiving, and Christmas. From U.S. 41, take Manatee Ave. west to 10th St. W. and turn right.

SHOPPING

Visitors come from all over the world to shop at **St. Armands Circle** ✦✦, on St. Armands Key. Wander around this outdoor circle of more than 150 international boutiques, gift shops, galleries, restaurants, and nightspots, all surrounded by lush landscaping, patios, and antiques. Pick up a map at the Sarasota Convention and Visitors Bureau (p. 438). Many shops here are comparable to those in Palm Beach and on Naples's Third Avenue South, so check your credit-card limits—or resort to some great window shopping. We love to browse through **Global Navigator** (© 813/388-4514), a travel-equipment and apparel shop that reminds us of Banana Republic when it carried really cool stuff (open daily 10am–10pm).

For discount shopping, the focal point of this area is the **Prime Outlets Ellenton,** on U.S. 301 at exit 43 off I-75 in Ellenton (© **941/723-1150;** www.primeoutlets.com), about a 15-minute drive northeast of downtown Bradenton (turn left at the 1st stoplight east of I-75). This Spanish-style outdoor center has more than 100 factory and outlet stores. Shops are open Monday through Saturday from 10am to 9pm and Sunday from 11am to 6pm.

Anna Maria Island and Holmes Beach have jewelry, clothing, antique, and specialty shops along or near Gulf Drive. Our favorites include **Fur Kids & U2,** which sells gifts and gear for pets and their people (© **941/778-4460**), **Ginny's Antiques & Art** (© **941/779-1773**), **Island Gallery West,** featuring 2-D and 3-D art (© **941/778-6648**), and **The Museum Shoppe,** which stocks English and American antiques as well as maritime art (© **941/779-0273**).

WHERE TO STAY

The beaches here are virtually lined with condominiums, many of which are actually all-condominium projects operated as hotels. Among the rental agencies requiring stays of less than a month are **Argus Property Management,** 2477 Stickney Point Rd., Sarasota, FL 34231 (© **941/927-6464;** fax 941/927-6767; www.argusmgmt.com), and **Florida Vacation Accommodations,** 4030 Gulf of Mexico Dr., Longboat Key, FL 34228 (© **800/237-9505** or 941/364-9505; fax 941/364-1830; www.vacationinfl.com).

The hotels below are organized by geographic region: in downtown Sarasota, on Lido Key, on Longboat Key, and on Siesta Key. The high season is from January to April. The hotel tax here is 10%.

Tips **Finding the Elusive Parking Space**

Parking on or near St. Armands Circle can be scarce, and if you *can* find a spot, on-street parking is limited to 3 hours. Your best bets are the free, unrestricted lots on Adams Drive at Monroe and Madison drives.

DOWNTOWN SARASOTA

Most visitors stay out at the beaches, but cost-conscious travelers will find some good deals on the mainland, such as the **Best Western Midtown,** 1425 S. Tamiami Trail (U.S. 41), at Prospect St. (© **800/722-8227** or 941/955-9841; fax 941/954-8948; www.bwmidtown.com). This older but well-maintained motel is 2 miles in either direction from the main causeways leading to the keys. Winter rates are $119 for a double room, dropping to $79 off season.

Downtown's top hotel before the opening of the new Ritz-Carlton (see below), the **Hyatt Sarasota,** 1000 Blvd. of the Arts (© **800/233-1234** or 941/953-1234; fax 941/952-1987; www.sarasota.hyatt.com), is adjacent to the Civic Center and the Van Wezel Performing Arts Hall and within walking distance of downtown shops and restaurants.

Most other national chain motels are near the airport, including a **Comfort Inn** (© **800/228-5150** or 941/355-7091), a **Days Inn** (© **800/329-7466** or 941/355-9271), and a **Hampton Inn** (© **800/336-9335** or 941/351-7734). All of recent vintage and thoroughly modern, they stand side-by-side on Tamiami Trail (U.S. 41) near the FSU Ringling Center for the Cultural Arts and the Asolo Center for the Performing Arts.

The Cypress ★★★ A throwback to the 1940s, The Cypress is a two-story, tin-roofed inn tucked away amidst giant mango trees and hovering palms, among other lush forms of vegetation. Best of all, it overlooks the bay. You can't get much better than this, with antiques, a grand piano, and rooms with private baths, queen sized beds, hardwood floors, ceiling fans, and Oriental rugs. The best room is the Essie Leigh Key West Room with its own side entrance, a front porch view of the bay, a brass and pewter bed, antique oak chest, and Spanish pine side tables. Other rooms are distinctly Victorian meets Ralph Lauren, some with French doors and others with neoclassical twists.

621 Gulfstream Ave. South Sarasota, FL 34236. © 941/955-4683. www.cypressbb.com. 4 units. Winter $210–$230 double; off-season $150–$180 double. AE, DISC, MC, V. *In room:* A/C, TV.

The Ritz-Carlton Sarasota ★★★ Downtown's swankiest digs opened in late 2001, just north of the Ringling Causeway and across a narrow creek from the Sarasota Quay shopping-and-dining complex (p. 455). The Ritz occupies the bottom 10 floors of an 18-story Mediterranean-style building (the top floors are private residencies). It sits perpendicular to the bay, so most of the spacious guest units have views looking across the water to the keys and the Gulf. The rooms are luxuriously appointed in typical Ritz-Carlton fashion, including marble bathrooms. The hotel's four restaurants are led by Vernona, offering Mediterranean-influenced cuisine, while the Bay View Bar & Grill offers casual dining both indoors and out. The elegantly appointed lobby opens to a bay-side courtyard with a heated pool. There is no beach on site, but a shuttle will take you to Lido Key, where the hotel debuted its own private beach club in January, 2004. There's also a full-service spa and fitness center on site.

1111 Ritz-Carlton Dr. (at Tamiami Trail/U.S. 41), Sarasota, FL 34236. © 800/241-3333 or 941/309-2000. Fax 941/309-2100. www.ritzcarlton.com. 266 units. Winter $395–$695 double; off-season $215–$535 double. AE, DC, DISC, MC, V. **Amenities:** 4 restaurants; 3 bars; outdoor pool; golf course; 3 tennis courts; health club; Jacuzzi; sauna; children's programs; concierge; activities desk; car-rental desk; business center; 24-hr. room service; massage; babysitting; laundry service; concierge-level rooms. *In room:* A/C, TV, dataport, minibar, hair dryer, iron, safe.

The Villa at Raintree Gardens ★★★ (Value High trees that mist sprays to alleviate the brutal summer heat hover over orchids that line this charming 18-room (2 guestroom) former turn-of-the-century fishing lodge turned inn that's expertly run by innkeepers Raymond Nick and Elizabeth Sanford. Located within the orchid garden is a free form pool built from black lava and green river stones. A screened in whirlpool bath and thermal spa is surrounded by lush greenery. Nearby is a pool you won't want to swim in, brimming with a family of koi and waterlillies, where heron love to hang out. Bold colors bring the rooms to life, as do the motley collection of antiques that fill them. The two guest rooms with queen sized beds and private baths are distinctly and uniquely furnished and are as different as Bill and Roger Clinton. A giant dictionary on a stand in the entry hallway adds to the character of this stunning home. A made-from scratch breakfast includes herb sautéed potatoes and eggs Benedict with Key Lime-infused hollandaise sauce. If you're in the market for a quiet, romantic getaway, The Villa at Raintree Gardens is the closest thing you'll get to Eden in these parts.

1758 Vamo Dr., Sarasota, FL 34236. (C) **800/862-8583**. Fax 941/966-6977. 2 units. Winter $115 double; off-season $85 double. MC, V. **Amenities:** Heated pool, whirpool spa, bicycles. *In Room:* A/C, in-room massage.

ON LIDO KEY

The Helmsley Sandcastle ⭐   Set on 600 feet of a private, white-sand beach on the Gulf of Mexico and only minutes from the upscale St. Armands Circle, the rooms here are nothing special, though they are large and most have great views of the water. With an incredibly friendly staff and a nice resorty feel, stay here if you want to relax in a perfectly fine location without dealing with the stuffiness of a fancier hotel.

1540 Ben Franklin Dr., Sarasota, FL 34236. (C) **800/225-2181** or 941/388-2181. Fax 941/388-2655. www. helmsleyhotels.com. 179 units. Winter $169–$279 double; off-season $109–$189 double. AE, DC, DISC, MC, V. **Amenities:** 3 restaurants; poolside bar; 2 outdoor heated pools; nearby golf and tennis; business center. *In room:* A/C, TV, fridge, coffeemaker, hair dryer, iron.

Holiday Inn Lido Beach   Conveniently located at the north end of Lido, this modern seven-story hotel is within walking distance of St. Armands Circle. Unfortunately, the beach across the street (you'll have to dodge the traffic) isn't the best stretch of sand here. The motel-style bedrooms have balconies that face the Gulf or the bay, and the rooftop restaurant and lounge offer panoramic views of the Gulf of Mexico.

233 Ben Franklin Dr. (at Thoreau Dr.), Sarasota, FL 34236. (C) **800/465-4329**, 800/892-9174, or 941/388-5555. Fax 941/388-4321. www.lidobeach.net. 135 units. Winter $127–$279 double; off-season $135–$199 double. AE, DC, MC, V. **Amenities:** Restaurant; 2 bars; heated outdoor pool; access to nearby health club; exercise room; watersports equipment rental; bike rental; limited room service; babysitting; laundry service; coin-op washers and dryers; concierge-level rooms. *In room:* A/C, TV, dataport, fridge, coffeemaker, hair dryer, iron.

ON LONGBOAT KEY

Colony Beach & Tennis Resort ⭐⭐   Sitting 3 miles north of St. Armands Circle, this beachside facility is consistently rated one of the nation's finest tennis resorts. The beachside Colony Restaurant and swimming pool date from 1952 when this was a beach club, but today's accommodations are in modern, luxurious one- and two-bedroom condominium apartments complete with living rooms, dining areas, fully equipped kitchenettes, sun balconies, whirlpool tubs, and steam showers. The choice accommodations are three private cottages right on the superb beach (they also are the most expensive units). The condominiums are built around a 21-court tennis center, where a staff of professionals conducts highly acclaimed programs for both adults and children. The beachside Colony Restaurant offers fine continental cuisine for lunch and dinner (jackets requested for men at dinner).

1620 Gulf of Mexico Dr., Longboat Key, FL 34228. ℂ 800/282-1138 or 941/383-6464. Fax 941/383-7549. www.colonybeachresort.com. 235 units. Winter $275–$1,150 suite; off-season $195–$975 suite. Packages available. AE, DC, DISC, MC, V. **Amenities:** 2 restaurants; 2 bars; heated outdoor pool; 21 clay and hard tennis courts; health club; Jacuzzi; sauna; watersports equipment rental; bike rental; children's programs; game room; concierge; activities desk; car-rental desk; business center; salon; limited room service; massage; babysitting; laundry service; coin-op washers and dryers. *In room:* A/C, TV, kitchen, coffeemaker, hair dryer, iron.

Holiday Inn Hotel & Suites ⭐ *Kids*   Longboat Key's only family-oriented beachside motel is built around an indoor courtyard with a swimming pool, a whirlpool, a games area, and the island's only fast-food outlets (Pizza Hut, Nathan's Famous Hot Dogs, Mrs. Field's Cookies, and Seattle's Best Coffee). In addition, there's a restaurant with an adjacent clubby bar plus a beachside snack bar. The enclosed area makes this a good respite on rainy days, during a cool snap, or when it's stiflingly hot outside. Extensively refurbished in 1999, most of the contemporary rooms and suites open to walkways overlooking the inside pool area; accordingly, the more expensive units with patios or balconies facing the beach are preferable.

4949 Gulf of Mexico Dr., Longboat Key, FL 34228. ℂ 800/465-4436 or 941/383-3771. Fax 941/383-7871. www.hilongboat.com. 146 units. Winter $206–$289 double; off-season $165–$289 double. AE, DC, DISC, MC, V. **Amenities:** 2 restaurants; convenience food court; 2 bars; heated indoor and outdoor pools; clay tennis courts; exercise room; Jacuzzi; sauna; watersports equipment rental; bike rental; children's programs; game room; concierge; limited room service; babysitting; laundry service; coin-op washers and dryers. *In room:* A/C, TV, dataport, fridge, coffeemaker, hair dryer, iron, safe, Nintendo.

The Resort at Longboat Key Club ⭐⭐   Part of a real-estate development on 410 acres at the southern end of Longboat Key, this award-winning condo-minium resort pampers the country-club set with upscale restaurants and a vari-ety of recreational activities in a lush tropical setting. The spacious and luxurious rooms and suites have private balconies overlooking the Gulf of Mexico, a lagoon, or golf-course fairways. All have custom-designed furnishings and neo-classical decor, and all but 20 have full kitchens. Among several dining options here, the Gulf-side Sands Pointe Restaurant has the feel of an informal but ele-gant supper club, serving classical Italian cuisine in a romantic setting by the Gulf, while the adjacent lounge offers casual dining and live entertainment. Other choices are in the clubhouses at the resort's two golf courses and two ten-nis centers (all with instruction).

301 Gulf of Mexico Dr. (P.O. Box 15000), Longboat Key, FL 34228. ℂ 800/237-5545 or 941/383-8821. Fax 941/383-0359. www.longboatkeyclub.com. 232 units. Winter $295–$435 double, $350–$1,120 suite; off-sea-son $225–$290 double, $285–$555 suite. Packages available. AE, DISC, MC, V. From St. Armands Key, take Gulf of Mexico Dr. north; take 1st left after bridge. **Amenities:** 5 restaurants; bars; heated outdoor pool; 2 golf courses (45 holes); 38 tennis courts; health club with spa treatments; Jacuzzi; sauna; watersports equipment rental; bike rental; children's programs; concierge; activities desk; salon; limited room service; mas-sage; babysitting; laundry service. *In room:* A/C, TV, dataport, kitchen, coffeemaker, hair dryer, iron.

ON SIESTA KEY

Captiva Beach Resort ⭐ *Value*   Owners Robert and Jane Ispaso have sub-stantially upgraded and improved this older property in the Stickney Point busi-ness district, about half a block from the beach on a narrow, closely packed circle populated by other small motels. They pride themselves on being throwbacks to the 1950s, and it's said that if someone says good morning to you at this place, even if you are in the worst mood, hung over or anti social, if you don't respond, it's considered rude. So if you're looking for a place where people keep to them-selves, this isn't it. Every one of the comfortable, sparkling-clean units here has some form of cooking facility, and some have separate living rooms with sleeper sofas. These are older buildings, so you'll find window air conditioners mounted through the walls, and shower-only bathrooms in some units. It's very popular with longer-term guests during winter. You'll get fresh towels daily but maid service only once a week. This and the circle's other motels share a common pool area, and guests get complimentary use of beach towels, chairs, and umbrellas. Several restaurants are a short walk away.

6772 Sara Sea Circle, Siesta Key, FL 34242. ℭ **800/349-4131** or 941/349-4131. Fax 941/349-8141. www.captivabeachresort.com. 20 units. Winter $135–$215 double, $225–$305 bungalows and suites; off-season $90–$170 double, $160–$180 bungalows and suites. Weekly and monthly rates available. AE, DISC, MC, V. **Amenities:** Heated outdoor pool; coin-op washers and dryers. *In room:* A/C, TV, kitchen, coffeemaker, hair dryer.

Turtle Beach Resort ★★★ On Siesta Key's south end, 2½ miles south of the Stickney Point Bridge, this intimate little bay-side charmer is one of Florida's most romantic retreats. It began life years ago as a ramshackle fishing camp, but owners Gail and Dave Rubinfeld renovated the five original clapboard cottages and added five more in a modern building. The complex is tightly packed; and although some units are very close to a small bay-side swimming pool, heavy tropical foliage provides a reasonable degree of privacy, and high wooden fences surround each unit's private outdoor hot tub. Sitting right on the bay, the two choice units also have one-way mirror walls, allowing guests to look out at the water in complete privacy, while passersby see only reflections of themselves. The cottages are done in various styles such as Caribbean and Nantucket, and have at least one bedroom each. Although they can accommodate small families, they are better suited as a terrific escape for couples. There's no restaurant on the grounds, but Ophelia's on the Bay is a seafood restaurant next door, once the old fishing camp's dining room, and all units have kitchens. Guests can use fishing poles, rowboats, kayaks, canoes, and paddle boats for free. Smoking is not allowed inside the units.

9049 Midnight Pass Rd., Sarasota, FL 34242. ℭ **941/349-4554.** Fax 941/312-9034. www.turtlebeachresort.com. 10 units. Winter $265–$370 double; off-season $180–$230 double. Weekly rates available. AE, DISC, MC, V. Pets accepted at an extra charge. **Amenities:** Outdoor pool; Jacuzzi; free watersports equipment. *In room:* A/C, TV, kitchen, coffeemaker, hair dryer, iron.

WHERE TO DINE

The restaurants below are organized geographically: in downtown Sarasota, in Southside Village (the city's hottest new dining scene), on St. Armands Key (next to Lido Key), on Longboat Key, and on Siesta Key.

IN DOWNTOWN SARASOTA

Downtown's best breakfast spot is the local branch of **First Watch,** 1395 Main St., at Central and Pineapple avenues (ℭ **941/954-1395**). Like its siblings in Naples (see "Where to Dine," in section 4 of chapter 10) and elsewhere, First Watch offers a wide variety of inexpensive breakfast and lunch fare. It's open daily from 7:30am to 2:30pm. If the wait's too long, walk south along Central Avenue; this block has several coffeehouses and cafes with sidewalk seating.

The local **Shells** seafood restaurant is at 7253 S. Tamiami Trail (U.S. 41), south of downtown in the vicinity of the Sarasota Square Mall (ℭ **941/924-2568**). (See p. 403 for details about this inexpensive chain.) You'll also find most of the national chain fast-food and family restaurants nearby along U.S. 41.

Bijou Cafe ★★ INTERNATIONAL Chef Jean-Pierre Knaggs prepares award-winning cuisines from around the world in his cafe, a former gas station, in the heart of the theater district. Although the more casual Michael's on East (see below) bistro draws a hefty after-theater crowd, this is the best place to dine within walking distance of the downtown entertainment venues. Jean-Pierre artfully presents the likes of prime veal Louisville (with crushed pecans and bourbon-pear sauce), pan-seared crab cakes served under a rémoulade and over a bed of fresh greens, and gently simmered lamb shanks with rosemary and garlic. His outstanding wine list has won accolades from *Wine Spectator* magazine.

1287 1st St. (at Pineapple Ave.). ✆ 941/366-8111. Reservations recommended. Main courses $17–$30. AE, DC, MC, V. Mon–Sat 11:30am–2pm and daily 5–9:30pm. Closed Sun June–Dec. Free valet parking nightly in winter, on weekends off season.

Marina Jack SEAFOOD/CONTINENTAL   Overlooking the waterfront with a wraparound 270-degree view of Sarasota Bay and Siesta and Lido keys, this establishment has spectacular water vistas and a carefree "on vacation" attitude, especially on the open-air raw-bar deck, which often is packed all afternoon on weekends and at sunset every day. The food is good but not the best in town, so come here for a relaxing, fun time. You may have to wait for a table or bar stool down on the deck, but be sure to make reservations if you want to have a meal in the upstairs dining room. Fresh local seafood is the star both upstairs and down—grilled grouper is your best bet. The downstairs lounge and raw bar also serves sandwiches and burgers.

In Island Park, Bayfront at Central Ave. ✆ 941/365-4232. Reservations recommended in dining room. Dining room main courses $16–$35. Deck main courses $14–$17; sandwiches and salads $8–$11; Sun brunch $12–$24. AE, DISC, MC, V. Daily 11:30am–2am. Closed Christmas.

Michael's on East ★★ CREATIVE INTERNATIONAL   At the rear of the Midtown Plaza shopping center on U.S. 41 south of downtown, Michael Klauber's chic bistro is one of the top places here for fine dining and is the locals' favorite after-theater haunt. Huge cut-glass walls create three intimate dining areas, one a piano bar for pre- or after-dinner drinks. Prepared with fresh ingredients and a creative flair, the offerings here will tempt your taste buds. House specialties are the Dungeness crab cakes, pan-seared Chilean sea bass with couscous and artichoke hearts in a thyme-accented tomato coulis, and grilled duck breast with Bermuda onion, shiitake fondue, and pecan risotto.

1212 East Ave. S. (between Bahia and Prospect sts.). ✆ 941/366-0007. Reservations recommended. Main courses $18–$36. AE, DC, DISC, MC, V. Winter Mon–Fri 11:30am–2pm, Sat 5:30–10pm, Sun 6–10pm; off-season Mon–Fri 11:30am–2pm, Mon–Sat 6–10pm. Complimentary valet parking.

Morel ★★ NEW AMERICAN   A warm, sophisticated, bistro-like ambiance and innovative menu created by chef/owner Fredy Mayer has made Morel one of Sarasota's hottest and hautest restaurants. Among the excellent fare, I recommend the potato and leek latkes with house smoked salmon; grilled veal chop in tomato basil coulis; and glazed Chilean sea bass.

3809 S. Tuttle Ave. ✆ 941/927-8716. Reservations recommended. Main courses $11–$30. AE, MC, V. Tue–Sat 4:30–9:30pm

Patrick's AMERICAN/PUB FARE   With a semicircular facade, this up-scale, polished-oak and brass-rail sports bar offers wide-windowed views of downtown's main intersection. The menu offers very good pub fare: steaks and chops, burgers, seafood, pastas, small pizzas, salads, sandwiches, and omelets. Other entrees include broiled salmon with dill-hollandaise sauce, sesame chicken, and veal done three ways—piccata, Française, or Marsala. There's a good happy hour here Monday through Friday between 5 and 7pm.

1400 Main St. (at Pineapple Ave.). ✆ 941/952-1170. Main courses $14–$21; sandwiches and burgers $7–$9. AE, DC, DISC, MC, V. Daily 11am–midnight; Sun brunch 11am–3pm. Closed Christmas.

Yoder's ⭐ Ⓥ*alue* AMISH/AMERICAN   Just 3 miles east of downtown is an award-winning, value eatery operated by an Amish family (Sarasota and Bradenton have sizable Amish communities and several other Amish restaurants). Evoking the Pennsylvania Dutch country, the simple dining room displays handcrafts, photos, and paintings celebrating the Amish way. The menu emphasizes plain, made-from-scratch cooking such as home-style meatloaf, Southern fried chicken, country-smoked ham, and fried filet of flounder. Burgers, salads, soups, and sandwiches are also available. Leave room for Mrs. Yoder's traditional shoofly and other homemade pies, one of the restaurant's biggest draws. *Note:* Alcohol is neither served nor allowed here, so don't even think about sneaking in a flask.

3434 Bahia Vista St. (west of Beneva Rd.). Ⓒ 941/955-7771. Main courses $6.25–$9.50; breakfast $2.50–$7; sandwiches, burgers, and salads $3.25–$8. No credit cards (ATM on premises). Mon–Sat 6am–8pm.

Zoria ⭐⭐⭐ ECLECTIC   Sleek and stylish, Zoria is a trend setter in terms of Sarasota's innovative cuisine scene, with such interesting menu items as duck breast with French lentils, crispy pancetta, turnips, and cherry marmalade; pepper-crusted broken arrow ranch antelope, foie gras with rosemary poached pea and onion jam; duck foie gras, fig jam, pear puree, and 8-year balsamic; and, my favorite—from the bar menu, which also happens to be exquisite and much cheaper—a ground beef burger with rosemary, roasted garlic, and goat cheese on focaccia bread.

1991 Main St. Ⓒ 941/955-4497. www.zoria.net. Reservations recommended. Main courses $18–$31. AE, DC, MC, V. Mon–Sat 5–10pm; Sun 5–9pm.

IN SOUTHSIDE VILLAGE

Sarasota's hottest dining area is **Southside Village,** centered on South Osprey Avenue between Hyde Park and Hillview streets, about 15 blocks south of downtown. Here you'll find several hip restaurants, including Fred's and Pacific Rim (see below). The village landmark is **Morton's Gourmet Market** ⭐, 1924 S. Osprey Ave. (Ⓒ **941/955-9856**), which offers a multitude of deli items, specialty sandwiches, a ton of fresh salads, freshly baked pastries and desserts, and cooked meals dispensed from a cafeteria-style steam table, which you can dine on picnic-fashion on sidewalk tables outside. Most ready-to-go items cost less than $7. Open Monday through Saturday from 8am to 8pm, Sunday from 10am to 5pm.

Fred's ⭐ CONTINENTAL   A popular hangout for the 20- and 30-something sets, especially on Friday nights, Fred's is the quintessential neighborhood brasserie serving an eclectic mix of American, European, Asian, and Latin influences in a stunning setting reminiscent of a sleek New York City bistro with copper ceilings and black and white checked floor. The food is essentially comfort food—rib-eye with mashed potatoes and penne pasta with chicken—and is pretty inconsistent, but what is consistent is the scene here, especially in the restaurant's cigar-friendly Tasting Room, which is abuzz with activity late into the night.

1923 S. Osprey Ave. Ⓒ 941/364-5811. Reservations recommended. Main courses $15–$30. AE, DC, MC, V. Mon–Thurs 11am–10pm; Fri–Sat 11am–1am; Sun 9am–10pm.

Pacific Rim ⭐ Ⓥ*alue* JAPANESE/THAI   Sarasotans love this chic and very casual restaurant for exceptional cuisine at economical prices. Japanese influence is felt at the authentic sushi bar along one side of the dining room, while Thai spices make a strong impact on the regular menu. The chargrilled shrimp with Thai curry and coconut-milk sauce is especially tasty, as is the combination of chicken and vegetables stir-fried in the wok. Here you can select your meat and vegetables separately from the sauce and the chefs will combine them on the grill, on the wok, or in the bowl (as in rice dishes).

In Hillview Centre, 1859 Hillview St. (between Osprey Ave. and Laurent Place). © 941/330-8071. Main courses $7.50–$15. AE, DISC, MC, V. Mon–Thurs 11:30am–2pm and 5–9pm; Fri 11:30am–2pm and 5–10pm; Sat 5–10pm.

ON ST. ARMANDS KEY

While the locals are hanging out in Southside Village, part-year residents and visitors flock to St. Armands Circle. Plan to spend at least one evening here, since the nighttime scene is like a fair, with everyone strolling around the circle, poking heads into a few stores that stay open after dark, and window-shopping the others. It's fun and safe, so come early and plan to stay late. See "Shopping," earlier in this chapter, for parking tips.

The circle has a branch of Tampa's famous **Columbia** (p. 406) between John Ringling Boulevard and John Ringling Parkway (© **941/388-3987**). The Spanish food is excellent, there's outdoor seating, and the Patio Lounge is one of the liveliest spots here for evening entertainment Thursday through Sunday. Like its sibling in Naples (p. 374), the local edition of **Tommy Bahama's Tropical Cafe,** 300 John Ringling Blvd. (© **941/388-2446**), draws a lively crowd of young professionals to its moderately priced seafood. It's upstairs over Tommy Bahama's clothing store.

At night, you may wish to forgo an expensive dessert and wander over to the local branch of **Kilwin's,** 312 John Ringling Blvd. (© **941/388-3200**), for some gourmet chocolate, Mackinac Island fudge, or ice cream or yogurt in a homemade waffle cone. Enjoy your sweets on one of the sidewalk park benches—everyone else does.

Blue Dolphin Cafe *Value* AMERICAN/DINER   On the John Ringling Boulevard spoke of St. Armands Circle, this informal diner is the affluent area's best inexpensive place to have breakfast, and the owners, Jill and Rob Ball, are a font of free information, too. They serve standard breakfast fare as well as fresh crab or lobster benedict, raspberry pancakes, and pecan-peach waffles. Lunchtime highlights are homemade soups and grouper sandwiches. You can order breakfast anytime. The Blue Dolphin is open for dinner on Friday nights during the winter season, offering the likes of flaky-crust chicken potpie, slow-roasted prime rib, and spicy crab cakes.

470 John Ringling Blvd. (1 block off St. Armands Circle). © 941/388-3566. Breakfast $4.50–$10; sandwiches, burgers, and salads $5–$10. AE, DC, DISC, MC, V. Daily 7am–3pm.

Café L'Europe *★★★* CONTINENTAL   One of Sarasota's most lauded restaurants, Café L'Europe has been the recipient of countless awards and praises for its continental cuisine that fuses French, Caribbean, and Spanish influences into what the chef prefers to call New European Cuisine. An elegant ambiance renders the restaurant a place to celebrate special occasions, whether over the classic Dover sole or an updated version of sweetbreads—crispy sweetbreads, this time, with mixed lettuces, poached pear, and mustard sauce. Sea bass, steamed in papillote, with spinach, zucchini, roasted garlic, fingerling potatoes, dill, and tomatoes matched with one of the restaurant's many vintages is a sublime choice as well. Service, as to be expected in a restaurant of this caliber, is outstanding.

431 St. Armands Circle (at John Ringling Blvd.). © 941/388-4415. Reservations recommended. Main courses $10–$30. AE, DC, MC, V. Daily 11am–10:30pm.

Hemingway's ✪ FLORIDIAN/CARIBBEAN   For a casual spot with an eclectic Floribbean menu and a large bar with a friendly, laid-back Key West ambience, take the elevator or climb the winding stairs to this second-floor hideaway. Hemingway's is a charming and comfortable combination of good food and Old Florida tradition. You can dine inside or on one of two second-floor balconies.

325 John Ringling Blvd. (½ block off St. Armands Circle). ℂ 941/388-3948. Reservations recommended on weekends. Main courses $16–$22. AE, DC, DISC, MC, V. Sun–Thurs 11:30am–10pm; Fri–Sat 11:30am–11pm.

Hungry Fox AMERICAN   This upstairs restaurant is the only place on St. Armands Circle offering three inexpensive meals a day year-round. It's not much to look at inside, with marble-look tables and plastic lawn chairs, so wait for a table out on the veranda, especially next to the railing where you can oversee all the action down below. Breakfast, which is served until noon, offers everything from lox and bagels to Virginia ham and eggs. Sandwiches and salads appear at lunch, followed by steaks, chicken, pastas, and spicy jambalaya for dinner. Most items are a good value for the price, but stay away from anything cooked in the deep fryer if you're concerned about your cholesterol.

419 St. Armands Circle (above Cha Cha Coconuts). ℂ 941/388-2222. Main courses $11–$17; sandwiches, burgers, and salads $4.50–$9; breakfast $4.50–$10. AE, DISC, MC, V. Mon–Sat 8am–9pm; Sun 8am–2:30pm.

ON LONGBOAT KEY

Euphemia Haye/The Haye Loft ✪✪✪ INTERNATIONAL   This area's most extraordinary restaurant, the romantically lighted Euphemia Haye is best known for Chef Raymond Arpke's crispy roast duck filled with bread stuffing and accompanied by a tangy fruit sauce. His prime strip steak rolled in cracked peppercorns and served with an orange, brandy, and butter sauce is another winner, as are his shrimp in a delightful curry and coconut cream sauce. If all this sounds sweet, wait until you go upstairs to The Haye Loft, his casual dessert bar. Up here you can take your pick from fabulous pies topped with thick whipped cream or Ben & Jerry's ice cream. You can also sample the kitchen's offerings, for the loft has its own light-fare menu, including soups, appetizers, small pizzas, and sandwiches. If you're lucky, the night's special sandwich will be steak topped with Raymond's peppercorn sauce. Served open-face and garnished with a field-greens salad, it's a meal for about $10. Add a glass of superb wine and a slice of pie a la mode, and you've had a wonderful dinner for under $20.

5540 Gulf of Mexico Dr. (at Gulfbay Rd.). ℂ 941/383-3633. www.euphemiahaye.com. Reservations recommended downstairs, not accepted in The Haye Loft. Main courses $18–$39; sandwiches, pizzas, and salads $7–$12. DC, DISC, MC, V. Restaurant Sun–Thurs 5–10pm; Fri–Sat 5–10:30pm. The Haye Loft daily 6pm–midnight.

Moore's Stone Crab SEAFOOD   Located in Longbeach, the old fishing village on the north end of Longboat Key, this popular bay-front restaurant began in 1967 as an offshoot of a family seafood business established 40 years earlier. From the outside, in fact, it still looks a little like a packing house, but the view of the bay dotted with mangrove islands makes a fine complement to stone crabs fresh from the family's own traps from October 15 to May 15. Otherwise, the menu offers an incredibly large variety of seafood, most of it fried or broiled. Sandwiches and salads are served all day.

800 Broadway (at Bayside Dr.). ℂ 941/383-1748. Main courses $15–$23; stone crab market price (as much as $40–$45 in season, from mid-Oct to mid May); sandwiches and salads $7–$13. AE, DISC, MC, V. Winter daily 11:30am–9:30pm; off-season Mon–Fri 4:30–9:30pm; Sat–Sun 11:30am–9:30pm.

ON SIESTA KEY

Ocean Boulevard, which runs through **Siesta Village,** the area's funky, laid-back beach hangout, is virtually lined with restaurants and pubs. Most have outdoor seating and bars, which attract the beach crowd during the day. At night, rock-and-roll bands draw teenagers and college students to this lively scene.

Blasé Café ★★ *Finds* INTERNATIONAL   Tongue in cheeky, to say the least, this restaurant doesn't take itself seriously, hence the ironic and oxymoronic name. One of Florida's most unusual restaurants, Ralph and Cindy Cole's super-casual establishment has tables indoors and a few under the cover of the Village Corner shopping center's walkway, but most are alfresco, on a wooden deck built around a palm tree in the center's asphalt parking lot. Never mind the cars pulling in and out virtually next to your chair: Ralph's food is so good that it draws droves of locals, who don't mind waiting for an umbrella table. This is Siesta Key's best breakfast spot, offering Italian- and Louisiana-flavored frittatas as well as plain old bacon and eggs. Lunch sees burgers, big salads, and platters such as chicken Alfredo and Florentine crepes with shrimp. At night, Ralph puts forth the likes of pan-seared sushi-quality yellowfin tuna with tangy wasabi and pickled ginger. You can while away the rest of the evening in the wine bar, where the Coles have installed the original bar from the Don CeSar Beach Resort & Spa in St. Pete Beach. There's also live music in there on weekends.

In Village Corner, 5263 Ocean Blvd. (at Calle Miramar), Siesta Village. ✆ 941/349-9822. Reservations recommended. Main courses $10–$23; breakfast and lunch $5–$9. MC, V. Mon–Thurs 8:30am–9:30pm; Fri–Sat 8:30am–10pm. Closed Mon June–Nov.

Turtles AMERICAN   With tropical overtones and breathtaking water vistas across from Turtle Beach, this informal restaurant on Little Sarasota Bay has tables indoors and on an outside deck. Unique seafood offerings include snapper New Orleans and potato-encrusted mahimahi. You can't go wrong ordering grouper grilled, broiled, blackened, or fried. There's also a selection of pastas on the menu. The economical early-bird specials offer several choices ranging from a medium-sized portion of mahimahi to spicy Szechuan shrimp.

8875 Midnight Pass Rd. (at Turtle Beach Rd.). ✆ 941/346-2207. Main courses $11–$20; salads and sandwiches $7–$15; early-bird specials $9–$11. AE, DISC, MC, V. Mon–Sat 11:30am–9:30pm; Sun 10am–9pm. Early-bird specials daily 4–6pm.

SARASOTA AFTER DARK

The cultural capital of Florida's west coast, Sarasota is home to a host of performing arts, especially during the winter season. To get the latest update on what's happening any time of year, call the city's 24-hour **Artsline** (✆ **941/365-2787**). Also check the "Ticket" section in Friday's *Herald-Tribune* (www.newscoast.com), the local daily newspaper; the Sarasota Convention and Visitors Bureau usually has copies (p. 438).

THE PERFORMING ARTS   Located at the FSU Ringling Center for the Cultural Arts (p. 441), the Florida State University Center for the Performing Arts, 5555 N. Tamiami Trail (U.S. 41; ✆ **800/361-8388** or 941/351-8000; www.asolo.org), presents the winter-through-spring **Asolo Theatre Festival** ★★★. This annual program of ballet and Broadway-style musicals and drama is one of the state's finest. In addition to the Asolo Theatre, a 19th-century Italian court playhouse moved here from Asolo, Italy, in the 1950s by the Ringlings, the center uses the 487-seat Harold E. and Ethel M. Mertz Theatre, originally constructed in Scotland in 1900 and transferred piece by piece to Sarasota in 1987.

The 161-seat Asolo Conservatory Theatre was later added as a smaller venue for experimental and alternative offerings. The complex is under the direction of Florida State University (FSU).

The city's other prime venue is the lavender, seashell-shaped **Van Wezel Performing Arts Hall** ★★★, 777 N. Tamiami Trail (U.S. 41), at 9th Street (✆ **800/826-9303** or 941/953-3368; www.vanwezel.org). Recently renovated, it offers excellent visual and acoustic conditions and a wide range of year-round programming, including touring Broadway shows and visiting orchestras and dance troupes. It and the FSU Center host performances by the **Florida West Coast Symphony** (✆ **941/953-4252;** www.fwcs.org), the **Jazz Club of Sarasota** (✆ **941/366-1552** or 941/316-9207; www.jazzclubsarasota.com), the **Sarasota Pops** (✆ **941/795-7677**), and the **Sarasota Ballet** (✆ **800/361-8388** or 941/351-8000; www.sarasotaballet.org).

Downtown Sarasota's theater district is home to the **Florida Studio Theatre,** 1241 N. Palm Ave., at Cocoanut Avenue (✆ **941/366-9000;** www.fst2000.org), which has contemporary performances from December to August, including a New Play Festival in May. Built in 1926 as the Edwards Theater, **The Opera House,** 61 N. Pineapple Ave., between Main and 1st Streets (✆ **941/366-8450;** www.sarasotaopera.org), presents classical operas (in their original languages) as well as highbrow concerts. Next door to The Opera House, the **Golden Apple Dinner Theatre,** 25 N. Pineapple Ave. (✆ **941/366-5454**), presents cocktails, dinner, and a professional Broadway-style show year-round. The professional, nonequity **Theatre Works,** 1247 1st St., at Cocoanut Avenue (✆ **941/952-9170**), presents musical revues and other works year-round.

THE CLUB & MUSIC SCENE   You can find plenty of music to dance to on the mainland at **Sarasota Quay,** the downtown waterfront dining-shopping-entertainment complex on Tamiami Trail (U.S. 41), a block north of John Ringling Causeway. Just walk around this brick building and your ears will take you to the action. The laser sound-and-light crowd gathers at **In Extremis** (✆ **941/954-2008**), where a high-energy DJ spins Top 40 tunes for 20-somethings. Michael's Mediterranean Grill turns into **Anthony's After Dark** rocking disco at 10:30pm. An older but still energetic crowd dances to contemporary jazz at the **Downunder Jazz Bar** (✆ **941/951-2467**). In Siesta Key Village, **The Old Salty Dog**, 5023 Ocean Blvd. (✆ **941/349-0158**), offers a fabulous selection of British ales and a lovely outdoor patio.

Over on St. Armands Circle, the Patio Lounge in the **Columbia** restaurant (✆ **941/388-3987**) is one of the liveliest spots along the beach strip, featuring live, high-energy dance music Tuesday through Sunday evenings. And on Siesta Key, the pubs and restaurants along Ocean Boulevard in Siesta Village have noisy rock-and-roll bands entertaining a mostly young crowd, but you can retire to the pleasant confines of the wine bar at **Blasé Café** (✆ **941/349-9822**) for live jazz. See "Where to Dine," above, for more about these two restaurants.

12

Walt Disney World & Orlando

by Laura Lea Miller

When Disney first opened the gates to the Magic Kingdom in 1971, few could have imagined the transformation of the surrounding area that would take place over the next thirty or so years. Orlando has evolved into an international vacation destination, offering an incredible array of recreational activities, shopping and dining experiences, world-class accommodations, all set in the middle of the natural beauty of Florida.

Walt Disney World (WDW) now has four major theme parks of its own, dozens of smaller attractions, tens of thousands of hotel rooms, scores of restaurants, an array of bars and clubs, and to top it all off—two cruise ships.

When Universal Orlando (which now consists of two theme parks and three resorts), SeaWorld, and some of the smaller players add their share, well, it can really get quite overwhelming.

Most of you don't have unlimited time and money, so it's my job to provide you with the resources to save on both. Later in this chapter, you'll find the best deals on hotels, restaurants, attractions, and more. These tips will make your vacation both easier to plan as well as more enjoyable and affordable to carry out.

Note: For a more in-depth look at WDW, check out *Frommer's Walt Disney World® & Orlando.*

1 Essentials

GETTING THERE

BY PLANE   Over 37 scheduled airlines and several more charter companies serve the more than 26 million Orlando passengers who arrive at **Orlando International Airport** (© **407/825-2001;** www.orlandoairports.net) each year. The best fares to Orlando are for travel during the months of November, December, and January, excluding holidays.

Delta (© 800/221-1212; www.delta.com) provides nearly 20% of the flights to and from Orlando International Airport, offering service from roughly 150 cities. Other carriers include **Air Canada** (© 888/247-2262; www.aircanada.ca), **America West** (© 800/235-9292; www.americawest.com), **American** (© 800/433-7300; www.americanair.com), **British Airways** (© 800/247-9297; www.british-airways.com), **Continental** (© 800/525-0280; www.continental.com), **JetBlue Airways** (© 800/538-2583; www.jetblue.com), **Northwest** (© 800/225-2525; www.nwa.com), **Southwest Airlines** (© 800/435-9792; www.southwest.com), **United Airlines** (© 800-241-6522; www.united.com), and **US Airways** (© 800/428-4322; www.usairways.com).

Located only 25 miles from Walt Disney World, Orlando International is extremely easy to navigate and conveniently located to the city's tourist areas. For those of you who don't wish to rent a car **Mears Transportation** (© **407/423-5566;** www.mearstransportation.com) provides shuttle service to and from the airport with vans running 24 hours a day and departing every 15 to 25 minutes. Round-trip fares are $25 to $29 adults and $18 to $21 children ages 4 to 11 (actual price depends on the location you're going to); children 3 and under ride free.

BY CAR   From Atlanta, take I-75 south to the Florida Turnpike to I-4 west. From the Northeast, take I-95 south to I-4 west. From Chicago, take I-65 south to Nashville, I-24 south to I-75, and then south to the Florida Turnpike to I-4 west. From Dallas, take I-20 east to I-49, then south to I-10, east to I-75, and south to the Florida Turnpike to I-4 west.

BY TRAIN   **Amtrak** trains (✆ **800/872-7245;** www.amtrak.com) pull into stations both in downtown Orlando (23 miles from Walt Disney World) and Kissimmee (15 miles from Disney). There are also stops in Winter Park (10 miles north of downtown) and Sanford (23 miles northeast of downtown Orlando). The Sanford stop is the terminal for Amtrak's Auto Train as well.

PACKAGE TOURS

Finding a vacation package to Orlando is easy; it's making a selection that can be difficult as each package offers a variety of services and options. To make the best choice, you need to determine exactly what it is that you are looking for ahead of time, whether it is airline tickets, car-rental reservations, resort reservations, park tickets, or all of the above.

If you're planning on spending the majority of your time at Walt Disney World, contact the **Walt Disney World Central Reservations Office (CRO)** at ✆ **407/934-7639** or www.disneyworld.com for a wide assortment of packages.

Universal Orlando packages can be booked at ✆ **888/322-5537.** You can also get information online at **www.universalorlando.com**.

For **SeaWorld,** call ✆ **800/423-8368** or go to **www.seaworld.com** for information.

The major airlines also offer Orlando packages. **Delta** (✆ **800/872-7786;** www.deltavacations.com), **Continental Airlines Vacations** (✆ **800/301-3800;** www.coolvacations.com), **American Airlines Vacations** (✆ **800/321-2121;** www.americanair.com) and **United Vacations** (✆ **888/854-3899;** www.united vacations.com) are just a few of the many available options.

American Express Travel (✆ **800/732-1991;** http://travel.americanexpress. com/travel) offers packages that include special deals for their cardholders.

The **American Automobile Association,** better known as **AAA** (✆ **800/836-2582;** www.aaa.com), also offers a wide variety of vacation packages, and special amenities and savings are available for AAA members.

VISITOR INFORMATION

The **Orlando/Orange County Convention & Visitors Bureau,** 8723 International Dr., Suite 101, Orlando, FL 32819 (✆ **407/363-5872;** www.orlandoinfo. com), can answer questions and send maps and brochures, such as the *Official Visitors Guide* and *Official Accommodations Guide*. The packet should reach you in a couple of weeks and also include the "Magicard," which is good for up to $500 in discounts on rooms, car rentals, attractions, and more. If you don't mind using an automated recording system, you can order by calling ✆ **800/643-9492.**

For information about **Walt Disney World**—including vacation brochures and videos—contact Walt Disney World, Box 10000, Lake Buena Vista, FL 32830-1000 (✆ **407/934-7639** or 407/824-2222; www.disneyworld.com).

Orlando

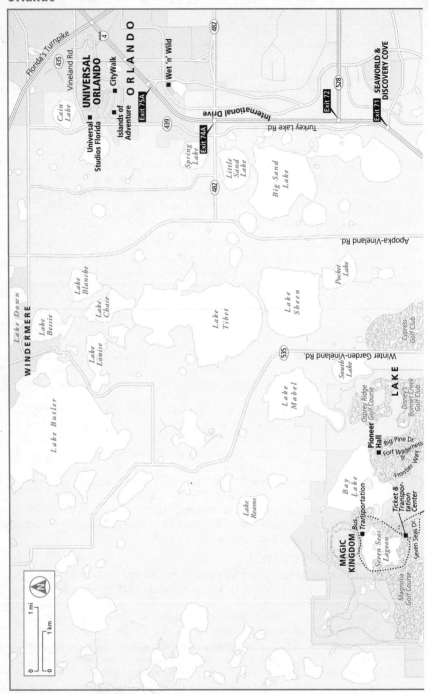

Florida's Turnpike

435

Vineland Rd.

4

UNIVERSAL
ORLANDO

CityWalk

O R L A N D O

Wet 'n' Wild

482

Universal
Studios Florida

Islands of
Adventure

Exit 75A

439

Cain
Lake

Exit 74A

Spring
Lake

International Drive

Turkey Lake Rd.

Exit 72

528

Exit 71

SEAWORLD &
DISCOVERY COVE

Little
Sand
Lake

Big Sand
Lake

482

Apopka-Vineland Rd.

Lake
Down

WINDERMERE

Lake
Bessie

Lake
Louise

Lake
Blanche

Lake
Chase

Lake
Tibet

Lake
Sheen

Pocket
Lake

Winter Garden-Vineland Rd.

535

Cypress
Golf Club

Lake Butler

Lake
Mabel

South
Lake

Osprey Ridge
Golf Course

Disney's
Bonnet Creek
Golf Club

L A K E

Pioneer
Hall

Big Pine Dr.

Fort Wilderness
Tr.

Frontier Way

Lake
Reams

Bay
Lake

Ticket &
Transportation
Center

MAGIC
KINGDOM

Bus.
Transportation

Seven Seas
Lagoon

Seven Seas Dr.

Magnolia
Golf Course

N

1 mi

1 km

0

0

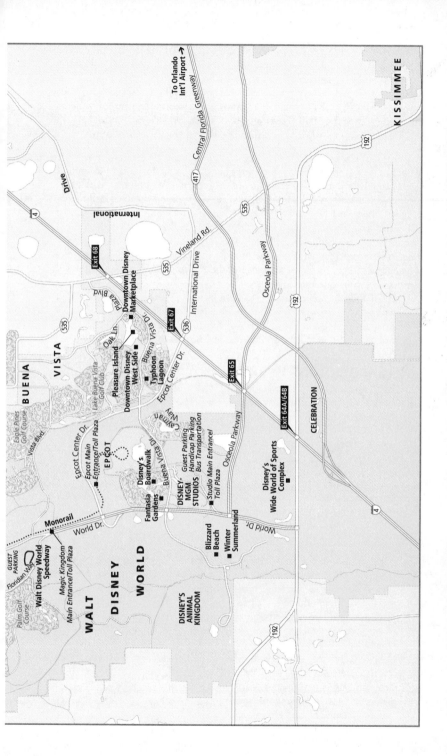

To Orlando Int'l Airport →

KISSIMMEE

Central Florida Greenway

417

535

Vineland Rd.

International Drive

Osceola Parkway

192

192

4

CELEBRATION

Exit 68

Exit 67

Exit 65

Exit 64A/64B

Downtown Disney Marketplace

Buena Vista Dr.

Epcot Center Dr.

Oak Ln.

Pleasure Island

Downtown Disney West Side

Typhoon Lagoon

BUENA VISTA

Lake Buena Vista Golf Club

Vista Blvd.

Eagle Pines Golf Course

Epcot Center Dr.

Epcot Main Entrance/Toll Plaza

EPCOT

Carman Way

Buena Vista Dr.

Disney's Boardwalk

Fantasia Gardens

DISNEY-MGM STUDIOS

Guest Parking
Handicap Parking
Bus Transportation

Studio Main Entrance/Toll Plaza

Osceola Parkway

Disney's Wide World of Sports Complex

World Dr.

Blizzard Beach

Winter Summerland

Monorail

World Dr.

GUEST PARKING

Floridan Way

Palm Golf Course

Walt Disney World Speedway

Magic Kingdom Main Entrance/Toll Plaza

WALT DISNEY WORLD

DISNEY'S ANIMAL KINGDOM

535

Plaza Blvd.

International

Drive

4

535

536

459

The website is an especially good bet; Disney just revamped it and it is now easier to navigate and provides more detailed information than ever before on both the parks and the resorts.

For information about **Universal Orlando,** call ✆ **800/837-2273** or 407/363-8000; surf the Internet to **www.universalorlando.com**, or write to Universal Orlando, 1000 Universal Studios Plaza, Orlando, FL 32819.

You can obtain SeaWorld information online at **www.seaworld.com**.

CITY LAYOUT

Interstate 4 (I-4) will take you everywhere you want to go in and around Orlando, with several exits along the way to get you to Walt Disney World, Sea-World, and Universal Studios Orlando, not to mention the areas of International Drive (or I-Drive), Lake Buena Vista, and Kissimmee. *Note:* I-4 can be woefully congested. It's best to use it during non-peak hours, when the tourists and locals aren't rushing to and from Orlando and the parks. There are many alternate routes that will allow you to avoid the highway completely, and I recommend you get a detailed road map of the area to check out what routes will work best with your touring plans.

The Florida Turnpike crosses I-4 and links to I-75 to the north. U.S. 192, a major east-west highway, runs along Kissimmee's major motel area to U.S. 27, where it crosses I-4 near the Disney World entrance. The Bee Line Expressway goes east from I-4 past Orlando International Airport to Cape Canaveral.

NEIGHBORHOODS IN BRIEF

Walt Disney World Located southwest of the city of Orlando, WDW encompasses over 47 square miles and includes four major theme parks, two smaller water parks, several resorts, and a plethora of restaurants and shops including the Downtown Disney Marketplace, the entertainment district of Pleasure Island and Disney Westside, not to mention the Wide World of Sports Complex, and Disney Quest.

Lake Buena Vista Lake Buena Vista actually encompasses all of WDW, but also includes much of the area bordering the resort. Here you can find the "official" (but not Disney-owned) hotels located on Hotel Plaza Boulevard. The area along 535, or Apopka-Vineland as it is also known, is home to many a resort and restaurant. Though the region is bustling, many of the resorts, restaurants, and shops are set far off the main thoroughfare to maintain a quieter atmosphere.

Celebration What else would you expect from Disney, the original creators of this 4,900-acre community, but a picture-perfect town. This area offers not only beautiful homes, but also a charming collection of shops, restaurants, and even its own hotel.

Downtown Disney This is really not a neighborhood as much as it is the area encompassing Disney's two nighttime entertainment districts, Pleasure Island and West Side, as well as its shopping complex, the Downtown Disney Marketplace. Full of clubs, entertainment venues, unique restaurants, and shopping experiences, you can celebrate New Year's Eve here every night, shop till you drop, or tempt your taste buds.

Kissimmee Thanks to a million dollar "Rebeautivacation" project, the neighborhood that was the region's tourist hotspot B.D. (Before Disney) has come back to life with the addition of extra wide sidewalks, colorful (and plentiful) streetlamps, landscaping, and location markers. Even U.S. 192 itself has been improved to handle traffic more easily and safely. Kissimmee is home to a variety of budget and moderate resorts and hotels, a plentitude of restaurants, and a handful of minor attractions.

International Drive Area (Hwy. 536) Known as **I-Drive,** this busy tourist zone is home to more than 100 resorts and hotels, countless restaurants, attractions both big and small, shopping, entertainment, and even it's own transportation

system—the I Ride Trolley. There is literally something here for everybody. The areas north of Sand Lake Road are the most congested with T-shirt shops and tourist traps, and until you get south of the intersection at S.R. 528 (aka the Beeline Expwy.), the driving is slow going at best.

Downtown Orlando The downtown area is actually northeast of Walt Disney World on I-4. It offers restaurants, hotels, theaters, museums, the Orlando Science Center, nightclubs and more.

2 Getting Around

In a city that thrives on tourists, you won't find it difficult to get from point A to point B—especially if you have a car—but the going can be slow at times. If you're traveling outside or between the tourist areas, try to avoid the 7-day-a-week rush hour (7–9am and 4–6pm). Rush hours are bad anywhere, but commuter traffic here only compounds the tourist traffic.

ON INTERNATIONAL DRIVE   Traffic on I-Drive can be absolutely infuriating, compounded exponentially if you are visiting at one of the busier times of year (the two weeks surrounding the Easter holiday being among the busiest). Its extremely high concentration of hotels, restaurants, shops, and attractions, not to mention the numerous traffic lights and alcoves located along the way make driving very slow going. The two ways to conquer the traffic of I-Drive are to travel by foot (while points of interest can be reasonably close together, keep in mind that safety can be a factor when walking here) and the **I-Ride Trolley** (© **407/248-9590;** www.iridetrolley.com), which stops about every 2 blocks from one end of I-Drive to the other. The trolley runs from 8am to 10:30pm (75¢ adults, 25¢ seniors, and children under 12 ride for free; *exact change is required*). Unlimited passes for between one and fourteen days are available as well and the cost averages out to about a dollar a day. It really is a fun way to get around the area.

BY THE DISNEY TRANSPORTATION SYSTEM   If you plan to stay at and spend most of your time in Disney, there's an extensive, free transportation network that runs throughout the WDW property.

Disney resorts and official hotels offer unlimited free transportation via bus, monorail, ferry, or water taxi to all WDW properties throughout the day and, at times, well into the evening.

The system is free, saving you money on a rental car, insurance, and gas, as well as theme-park parking fees. The drawback, however, is that you're at the mercy of the Disney departure schedules and routes, which can often be slow and sometimes *very* indirect. A copy of the "WDW Transportation Guide Map" is available inside Disney's new shopping and dining guide. Ask for the guide at Guest Services desks inside any of the Disney resorts and themeparks.

BY SHUTTLE Mears Transportation operates vans and buses that go to all of the theme parks, as well as the Kennedy Space Center and Busch Gardens (yes, in Tampa), among others. Rates vary according to destination. Call ② 407/ 423-5566 for rates.

BY TAXI Taxis gather at the major resorts, and smaller properties will be happy to call a cab for you. **Yellow Cab** (② 407/699-9999) and **Ace Metro** (② 407/855-0564) are both good choices, though you should keep in mind that taxis are expensive and charges may run as much as $3.25 for the first mile and $1.75 per mile thereafter.

FAST FACTS: Walt Disney World & Orlando

Babysitters Many Orlando hotels, including all of Disney's resorts, offer babysitting services, usually from an outside service such as **Kids Night Out** (② **800/696/8105** or 407/828-0920; www.kidsniteout.com), or **All About Kids** (② **800/728-6506** or 407/812-9300; www.all-about-kids.com). Childcare rates usually run somewhere between $10 and $15 per hour for the first child and $1 per additional child, per hour. Several Orlando resorts have good child-care facilities with counselor-supervised activity programs right on the premises (The Disney resorts' programs are only for kids age 4–12 and cost $10 per hour). Reservations are a good idea (② **407/939-3463**).

Business Hours Theme park operating hours vary depending on the time of year, even on the day of the week. While most open at 8 or 9am and close at 6 or 7pm, you should call or check a park's website for its most current schedule before arriving. Other businesses are generally open from 9am to 5pm, Monday through Friday.

Doctors & Dentists There are basic first-aid centers in all of the theme parks. There's also a 24-hour, toll-free number for the **Poison Control Center** (② **800/282-3171**). To find a dentist, call **Dental Referral Service** at ② **800/235-4111** or go online to www.dentalreferral.com.

Disney offers in-room medical service 24 hours a day (② **407/238-2000**). **Doctors on Call Service** (② **407/399-3627**) makes house and room calls in most of the Orlando area. **Centra-Care** lists several walk-in clinics in the Yellow Pages, including ones on International Drive (② **407/370-4881**), and at Lake Buena Vista near Disney (② **407/934-2273**).

Emergencies Dial ② **911** for police, fire departments, and ambulance.

Hospitals **Sand Lake Hospital**, 9400 Turkey Lake Rd. (② **407/351-8550**), is about 2 miles south of Sand Lake Road. From the WDW area, take I-4 east to the Sand Lake Road exit and make a left on Turkey Lake Road. The hospital is 2 miles up on your right. To avoid the highway, take Palm Parkway (off of Apopka-Vineland near Hotel Plaza Blvd.), it turns into Turkey Lake road. The hospital is 2 miles up on your left. **Celebration Health** (② **407/ 303-4000**), located in the near-Disney town of Celebration, is at 400 Celebration Place. From I-4, take the U.S. 192 exit. At the first traffic light, turn right onto Celebration Avenue. At the first stop sign, take another right.

Kennels The theme parks board pets for $6 per day. WDW also offers overnight boarding ($11 for the general public or $9 for Disney resort guests) at the Transportation and Ticket Center's kennel near the Polynesian

Resort. Universal Orlando's resorts all welcome pets, which can stay with you right in your room.

Lost Children Every theme park has a designated spot for parents to reunite with lost children. Ask a park employee or check at guest services for details.

Pharmacies **Walgreens**, 7650 W. Sand Lake Road (© **407/345-9497**), operates a 24-hour pharmacy. Other locations can be found near Universal Orlando and Kissimmee by logging on to **www.walgreens.com**.There are scores of others located throughout the area as well, all listed in the Yellow Pages.

Post Office The post office most convenient to Disney and Universal is at 10450 Turkey Lake Road (© **800/275-8777**). It's open Monday through Friday from 9am to 4:30pm and Saturdays from 9am to noon.

Taxes A 6.5% to 7% sales tax (depending on which local county you happen to be in) is charged on all goods with the exception of most edible grocery-store items and medicines. Hotels add another 2% to 5% in resort taxes to your bill, so the total tax on accommodations can run you up to 12%.

Telephone If you're making a local call in Orlando, even to someone just across the street, *you must dial the 407 area code followed by the number you wish to call,* for a total of 10 digits.

Weather Call © **321/255-0212** for the local weather forecast or check out the Weather Channel at **www.weather.com** for the most up-to-date information.

3 Where to Stay

There are more than 110,000 rooms in the Orlando area, with hundreds, sometimes thousands added annually. While the economy has been soft since the second half of 2001, occupancy can be high, so it's a smart idea to book as far ahead as possible, especially if you're coming during peak season, generally around the holidays and in the summer. The lowest rates are usually available September through November (excluding the week of Thanksgiving) and January through April (excluding the weeks of spring break).

WALT DISNEY WORLD CENTRAL RESERVATIONS OFFICE

To reserve a room or book packages at Disney's resorts, villas, campgrounds, and official hotels, contact the **Walt Disney World Central Reservations Office (CRO)**, P.O. Box 10000, Lake Buena Vista, FL 32830-1000 (© **407/934-7639;** www.disneyworld.com).

Both can recommend accommodations suited to your price range and specific needs, such as proximity to your favorite park or those with supervised child-care centers. The people who answer the telephones can be very helpful and knowledgeable but usually won't volunteer information about a better deal or a special *unless you ask.*

DISNEY RESORTS
VERY EXPENSIVE

Disney's BoardWalk Inn & Villas ★★★   Romantics and families alike will enjoy staying at this plush 1940s-style "seaside" resort. Here you will find an array of clubs, restaurants, shops, and carnival style entertainment located on the ¼-mile boardwalk situated directly behind the resort and overlooking the water. The Cape Cod–style rooms comfortably sleep four, and some have balconies. The priciest rooms overlook the boardwalk or pool; the less expensive face the parking lot but are sheltered from the boardwalk noise. Hang onto your swimsuit if you hit the pool's famous—or infamous, depending on how you look at it—200-foot "keister coaster" water slide. The BoardWalk's villas range from studios to villas that can comfortably sleep up to 12 people and offer all of the comforts of home.

2101 N. Epcot Resorts Blvd. (off Buena Vista Dr.; P.O. Box 10000), Lake Buena Vista, FL 32830-1000. © 407/ 934-7639 or 407/939-5100. Fax 407/934-5150. www.disneyworld.com. 372 units. 520 villas, $289–$675 double; $289–$1,915 villa. Extra person $25. Children 17 and under stay free in parent's room. AE, DC, DISC, MC, V. Free self-parking; $6 valet. Take I-4 to the Hwy. 536/Epcot Center Dr. exit and follow the signs. Pets $9 a night. **Amenities:** 4 restaurants; grill; 2 lounges; 3 clubs; 2 outdoor heated pools; kids' pool; 2 lighted tennis courts; health club; Jacuzzi; bike and sporting equipment rentals; children's activity center; playground; arcade; concierge; WDW Transportation System; transportation to non-Disney parks for a fee; business center; shopping arcade; 24-hr. room service; babysitting; guest laundry; nonsmoking rooms; concierge-level rooms. *In room:* A/C, TV, dataport, fridge ($10 a night at the Inn), hair dryer, iron, safe.

Disney's Grand Floridian Resort & Spa ★★★ *(Finds)*

From the moment you step into the opulent five-story domed lobby, you'll feel as if you've slipped back to an era when a guy named Gatsby was at the top of his game. High tea is served in the afternoon; later, a small band plays music from the 1940s. The Grand Floridian is the romantic choice for couples, especially honeymooners. Spend the day luxuriating in the first-class spa and health club—the best in WDW. The Victorian-style rooms sleep at least four; virtually all overlook a garden, pool, courtyard, or the Seven Seas Lagoon. Located directly on the monorail system, it makes for a quick trip to the Magic Kingdom.

4401 Floridian Way (P.O. Box 10000), Lake Buena Vista, FL 32830-1000. © 407/934-7639 or 407/824-3000. Fax 407/824-3186. www.disneyworld.com. 900 units. $339–$840 double; $885–$2,450 suite. Extra person $25. Children 17 and under stay free in parent's room. AE, DC, DISC, MC, V. Free parking; $6 valet. Take I-4 to the Hwy. 536/Epcot Center Dr. exit and follow the signs. Pets $9 a night. **Amenities:** 5 restaurants; grill; 3 lounges; heated outdoor pool; kids' pool; 2 lighted tennis courts; health club; spa; watersports equipment; children's center; arcade; concierge; car-rental desk; WDW Transportation System; transportation to non-Disney parks for a fee; business center; shopping arcade; salon; 24-hr. room service; babysitting; guest laundry; valet; nonsmoking rooms; concierge-level rooms. *In room:* A/C, TV, dataport, minibar, fridge ($10 a night), hair dryer, iron, safe.

Disney's Polynesian Resort ★ *(Kids)*

Just south of the Magic Kingdom, the 25-acre Polynesian is the third resort on the monorail line. Its extensive play areas and themed swimming pools make it a good choice for those traveling with kids. Public areas have canvas cabanas, hammocks, and big swings overlooking a 200-acre lagoon. Lush landscaping gives it a true island feel. Rooms are average size, and all but a few can accommodate up to five people.

1600 Seven Seas Dr. (P.O. Box 10000), Lake Buena Vista, FL 32830-1000. © 407/934-7639 or 407/824-2000. Fax 407/824-3174. www.disneyworld.com. 853 units. $299–$560 double; $390–$675 concierge-level; $680–$2,490 suite. Extra person $25. Children 17 and under stay free in parent's room. AE, DC, DISC, MC, V. Free parking; $6 valet. Take I-4 to the Hwy. 536/Epcot Center Dr. exit and follow the signs. Pets $9 a night. **Amenities:** Restaurant; cafe; 2 lounges; d inner show located here; 2 heated outdoor pools; kids' pool; watersports equipment; children's club; arcade; concierge; WDW Transportation System; transportation to non-Disney parks for a fee; shopping arcade; 24-hr. room service; babysitting; guest laundry; nonsmoking rooms; concierge-level rooms. *In room:* A/C, TV, fridge ($10 a night), hair dryer, iron, safe.

Disney's Yacht Club Resort ★★

The Yacht Club is a cut above its sister, the Beach Club, with which it shares a 25-acre lake with white sandy beaches, a first-class swimming area (including a life size shipwreck with waterslides and a sand bottom pool), and magnificent landscaping. The rooms, views, and the atmosphere are all a bit more upscale. It's geared more toward adults and families with older children, although young kids are certainly catered to (this *is* Disney). The theme is turn-of-the-20th-century New England, complete with a lighthouse to help you find your way home. The rooms have space for up to five people, and most have balconies.

1700 Epcot Resorts Blvd. (off Buena Vista Dr.; P.O. Box 10000), Lake Buena Vista, FL 32830-1000. ✆ **407/ 934-7639** or 407/934-7000. Fax 407/924-3450. www.disneyworld.com. 630 units. $289–$510 double; $425–$660 concierge-level; $525–$2,290 suite. Extra person $25. Children 17 and under stay free with paying parent. AE, DC, DISC, MC, V. Free parking; $6 valet. Take I-4 to the Hwy. 536/Epcot Center Dr. exit and follow the signs. Pets $9 a night. **Amenities:** 3 restaurants; grill; lounge; 2 heated outdoor pools; kids' pool; 2 lighted tennis courts; Jacuzzi; watersports equipment; children's center; arcade; concierge; WDW Transportation System; transportation to non-Disney parks for a fee; business center; shopping arcade; salon; 24-hr. room service; babysitting; guest laundry; nonsmoking rooms; concierge-level rooms. *In room:* A/C, TV, dataport, minibar, fridge ($10 a night), coffeemaker, iron, safe.

Walt Disney World Dolphin 👶👶 If Antonio Gaudí and Dr. Seuss had teamed up on an architectural design, they might have created something like this Starwood resort and its adjacent sister, the Walt Disney World Swan. This hotel centers on a 27-story pyramid with two 11-story wings crowned by 56-foot twin dolphin sculptures (the Swan's have—no surprise—45-foot swans). Not as theme-intensive as the other Disney resorts, it's popular with business travelers and those who prefer their accommodations a little less sugary. Rooms comfortably sleep four (the Swan's are a tad smaller). The resort has a grotto pool with waterfalls, water slide, and whirlpools. The Swan and Dolphin share a beach, Body by Jake health club, some restaurants, and other trimmings. Epcot is the nearest park, just a short water taxi ride away. *Tip:* The beach next to the pool offers a great view of Epcot's IllumiNations fireworks.

1500 Epcot Resorts Blvd. (off Buena Vista Dr.; P.O. Box 22653), Lake Buena Vista, FL 32830-2653. ✆ **800/ 227-1500** or 407/934-4000. Fax 407/934-4884. www.swandolphin.com. 1,509 units. $325–$519 double; $485–$3,150 suite. $10 daily resort fee. Extra person $25. Children 17 and under stay free in parent's room. AE, DC, DISC, MC, V. Free parking; valet $9. Take I-4 to the Hwy. 536/Epcot Center Dr. exit and follow the signs. Pets $9 a night. **Amenities:** 4 restaurants; grill; 2 lounges; 4 heated outdoor pools; 4 lighted tennis courts; health club; watersports equipment; children's center; 2 game rooms; concierge; car-rental desk; WDW Transportation System; transportation to non-Disney parks for a fee; shopping arcade; salon; 24-hr. room service; massage; babysitting; guest laundry; nonsmoking rooms; concierge-level rooms. *In room:* A/C, TV, dataport, minibar, hair dryer, iron, safe, Nintendo.

EXPENSIVE

Disney's Animal Kingdom Lodge 👶 The feel of an African game-reserve lodge surrounds you as you enter the lobby with the thatched roof and ornate shield chandeliers overhead. The room layout follows a *kraal* design (a semicircular layout) that overlooks a 30-acre savannah, giving guests an occasional view of birds, giraffes, and other animals that call the savannah home. Typical rooms are a bit smaller than those in Disney's Very Expensive category, making it slightly more crowded for four. The lodge is adjacent to Animal Kingdom, but most everything else on WDW property is quite a distance away. Families will appreciate the animals and activities for kids, while the more relaxed and sedate nature of the resort makes it a good spot for couples as well.

2901 Osceola Pkwy., Bay Lake, FL 32830. ✆ **407/934-7639** or 407/938-3000. Fax 407/939-4799. www. disneyworld.com. 1,293 units. $190–$515 double; $425–$610 concierge; $635–$2,505 suite. Extra person $25. Children 17 and under stay free in parent's room. AE, DC, DISC, MC, V. Free parking; valet $9. Take I-4 to the Hwy. 536/Epcot Center Dr. exit and follow the signs. Pets $9 a night. **Amenities:** 3 restaurants; lounge;

heated outdoor pool; kids' pool; health club; children's center; arcade; concierge; WDW Transportation System; transportation to non-Disney parks for a fee; shopping arcade; limited room service; babysitting; guest laundry; nonsmoking rooms; concierge-level rooms. *In room:* A/C, TV, dataport, fridge ($10 a night), hair dryer, iron, safe.

Disney's Saratoga Springs Resort and Spa   The newest of the Disney vacation club resorts opened in May 2004, and transports guests back in time to the heyday of upstate New York's 19th-century resorts. The small resort town of Saratoga Springs is evoked through lavish gardens, Victorian architecture, bubbling springs, and a country setting. The resort's main pool brings to mind its namesake's natural springs, with "healing" waters spilling over the rocky landscaping. The renowned spa at the now-closed Disney Institute has been incorporated into this resort. Accommodations resemble those of the other Disney vacation properties and range from studios that sleep four to grand villas that can sleep up to 12 people quite comfortably.

Lake Buena Vista, FL. ☎ **407/827-1100** or 407/939-6244. Fax 407/827-1151. www.disneyworld.com. 552 units. $254–$329 studio, $340–$1,310 villas. Extra person $25. Children 17 and under stay free in parent's room. AE, DC, DISC, MC, V. **Amenities:** Restaurant; outdoor pool; kids' pool; watersports equipment; limited grocery delivery available; golf; health club; spa;playground; arcade; WDW Transportation System; transportation to non-Disney parks for a fee; guest laundry; nonsmoking rooms; concierge-level rooms;. *In room:* A/C, TV, dataport, fridge ($10 a night at the Inn), hair dryer, iron, safe.

Disney's Wilderness Lodge 🎖🎖🎖   The surrounding tall timbers, spouting geyser and hot springs, mammoth stone hearth, and bunk beds for the kids give the Wilderness Lodge a old time national-park feel, making it a favorite of families and couples alike. Standard rooms sleep four, and if a view is important to you, those with woods views are the best. The restaurants located at this resort offer some of the most spectacular views in the park. While the nearest park is Magic Kingdom, the resort, in keeping with its theme, is in a fairly remote area.

901 W. Timberline Dr. (on the southwest shore of Bay Lake just east of the Magic Kingdom; P.O. Box 10000), Lake Buena Vista, FL 32830-1000. ☎ **407/934-7639** or 407/938-4300. Fax 407/824-3232. www.disneyworld.com. 909 units. $194–$515 lodge; $350–$475 concierge-level; $720–$1,155 suite; $279–$955 villa. Extra person $25. Children 17 and under stay free in parent's room. AE, DC, DISC, MC, V. Free parking. Take I-4 to the Hwy. 536/Epcot Center Dr. exit and follow the signs. Pets $9 a night. **Amenities:** 2 restaurants; 2 lounges; heated outdoor pool; kids' pool; 2 Jacuzzis; watersports equipment; children's center; arcade; WDW Transportation System; transportation to non-Disney parks for a fee; limited room service; babysitting; guest laundry; nonsmoking rooms; concierge-level rooms. *In room:* A/C, TV, fridge ($10 a night), hair dryer, iron, safe.

MODERATE
Disney's Caribbean Beach Resort 🎖   The Caribbean Beach is a great value for families who don't require over the top frills and amenities. The rooms are grouped into five island "villages" surrounding a large duck-filled lake. The recently refurbished rooms are best, however the bathrooms are still fairly tight. Parrot Cay Island, where the main pool (of 7) is located, replicates a Spanish-style fort complete with a water slide, waterfalls, and cannons. The closest park is Disney–MGM Studios, but it can take up to 45 minutes to get there using the Disney Transportation system.

900 Cayman Way (off Buena Vista Dr.; P.O. Box 10000), Lake Buena Vista, FL 32830-1000. ☎ **407/934-7639** or 407/934-3400. Fax 407/934-3288. www.disneyworld.com. 2,112 units. $133–$209 double. Extra person $15. Children 17 and under stay free in parent's room. AE, DC, DISC, MC, V. Free parking. Take I-4 to the Hwy. 536/Epcot Center Dr. exit and follow the signs. Pets $9 a night. **Amenities:** Restaurant; grill; lounge; large heated outdoor pool and 6 smaller ones in the villages; kids' pool; Jacuzzi; watersports equipment; arcade; WDW Transportation System; transportation to non-Disney parks for a fee; limited room service; babysitting; guest laundry; nonsmoking rooms. *In room:* A/C, TV, fridge ($10 a night), hair dryer, iron, safe.

Disney's Port Orleans Resort ★ *Value*   This resort, resembling turn-of-the-20th-century New Orleans, includes the old Dixie Landings property that was merged into it in 2000. It has the best location, landscaping, and the coziest atmosphere of all resorts in this class. Its Doubloon Lagoon pool is a hit with the kids as it has a water slide curving from out of a dragon's mouth. The rooms are big enough for four, but it makes for a tight fit. Make sure to ask for a recently refurbished room. All 1,080 rooms in the French Quarter side reopened in March 2004 after a large-scale refurbishment. The 2,048 rooms in Riverside will be renovated in phases starting in the summer of 2004. Port Orleans is east of Epcot and Disney–MGM Studios.

2201 Orleans Dr. (off Bonnet Creek Pkwy.; P.O. Box 10000), Lake Buena Vista, FL 32830-1000. ✆ **407/ 934-7639** or 407/934-5000. Fax 407/934-5353. www.disneyworld.com. 3,056 units. $133–$209 double. Extra person $15. Children 17 and under stay free in parent's room. AE, DC, DISC, MC, V. Free parking. Take I-4 to the Hwy. 536/Epcot Center Dr. exit and follow the signs. Pets $9 a night. **Amenities:** 2 restaurants; grill/food court; 2 lounges; 6 heated outdoor pools; 2 kids' pools; Jacuzzi; watersports equipment; 2 arcades; WDW Transportation System; transportation to non-Disney parks for a fee; limited room service; babysitting; guest laundry; nonsmoking rooms. *In room:* A/C, TV, fridge ($10 a night), hair dryer, iron, safe.

INEXPENSIVE

Disney's All-Star Sports Resort *Value*   This resort sports surfing, basketball, football, and tennis themes, which would explain the oversized equipment found throughout the grounds. The main pool is surrounded by shark fins and surfboards, not to mention gigantic waves, to give it an ocean feel. The smaller baseball diamond pool is a homerun as well. As with all of the Disney value resorts, the rooms are on the small side and lack frills. But it is nevertheless a good choice for the budget conscious family—kids love the larger-than-life themes—that wants to stay on Disney property.

Note: Disney has two additional All-Star resorts—the All-Star Movies Resort and the All-Star Music resort—both identical to the Disney's All Star Sports resort where it counts (like room size and layout). The only major difference is the change in theme: one offers musical themes ranging from jazz to Calypso, and the other features movies (of the Disney variety of course). All three of the All Star resorts are located out in the Disney boonies, and the closest park is Animal Kingdom.

1701 W. Buena Vista Dr. (at World Dr. and Osceola Pkwy.; P.O. Box 10000), Lake Buena Vista, FL 32830-1000. ✆ **407/934-7639** or 407/939-5000. Fax 407/939-7333. www.disneyworld.com. 1,920 units. $77–$126 double. Extra person $10. Children 17 and under stay free in parent's room. AE, DC, DISC, MC, V. Free parking. Take I-4 to the Hwy. 536/Epcot Center Dr. exit and follow the signs. Pets $9 a night. **Amenities:** Food court; lounge; 2 heated outdoor pools; kids' pool; arcade; WDW Transportation System; transportation to non-Disney parks for a fee; limited room service; babysitting; guest laundry; nonsmoking rooms. *In room:* A/C, TV, dataport, fridge ($10 a night), safe.

Disney's Pop Century Resort *Value*   Gigantic memorabilia from decades past—remember the 8-track and the Rubik's Cube?—mark the exteriors at Disney's newest value resort. While there might not be a lot of frills, the price is right for families on a budget who want to bunk with Mickey. The rooms and bathrooms—just like Disney's All-Star properties—are tiny, but will work for a family of four with a concerted bit of effort. The resort opened its first phase, covering the 1950s to the 1990s, in December 2003; additional "decades" are scheduled to open in the near future. The resort is closest to the Wide World of Sports Complex.

1050 Century Dr. (off the Oceola Pkwy; P.O. Box 10000), Lake Buena Vista, FL 32830-1000. ✆ **407/938-4000** or 407/939-6000. Fax 407/938-4040. www.disneyworld.com. 2880 units. $77–$126 double. Extra person $10. Children 17 and under stay free in parent's room. AE, DC, DISC, MC, V. Free parking. Take I-4 east to Exit 67,

Hwy. 536/Epcot Center Dr. Follow signs to WDW, then to the resort. Pets $9 a night. **Amenities:** Food court; lounge; 2 heated outdoor pools; kids' pool; arcade; WDW Transportation System; transportation to non-Disney parks for a fee; limited room service; babysitting; guest laundry; nonsmoking rooms. *In room:* A/C, TV, dataport, fridge ($10 a night), safe.

ROUGHING IT, DISNEY-STYLE

Disney's Fort Wilderness Resort & Campground ✪
Pines, cypress trees, and fish-filled lakes and streams surround this woodsy 780-acre camping resort. It is, however, close only to the Magic Kingdom. If you're a true outdoors type, you'll enjoy the breath of fresh air away from the hustle and bustle of the parks. There are 110/220-volt outlets, grills, and comfort stations with showers and restrooms. The wide variety of outdoor recreational activities just adds to the appeal of this resort. It is also the home to the Hoop De Doo Musical Review dinner show (p. 481)—a must for anyone visiting WDW.

Some sites are open to pets—at a cost of $3 per site, *not* per pet—which is cheaper than using the WDW overnight kennel, where you pay $9 per pet. The 408 wilderness cabins (actually trailers) are large enough for six people once you pull down the Murphy beds, and they also have kitchens.

3520 N. Fort Wilderness Trail (P.O. Box 10000), Lake Buena Vista, FL 32830-1000. ✆ **407/934-7639** or 407/824-2900. Fax 407/824-3508. www.disneyworld.com. 784 campsites, 408 wilderness cabins. Campsite $35–$82 double; wilderness cabin $229–$329 double. Extra person $2 for campsite, $5 for cabin. Children 17 and under stay free in parent's room. AE, DC, DISC, MC, V. Free parking. Take I-4 to the Hwy. 536/Epcot Center Dr. exit and follow the signs. **Amenities:** 2 restaurants; grill; lounge; 2 heated outdoor pools; kids' pool; 2 lighted tennis courts; watersports equipment; outdoor activities (fishing, horseback and hay rides, campfires); 2 game rooms; WDW Transportation System; transportation to non-Disney parks for a fee; babysitting; guest laundry; nonsmoking homes. *In room:* outdoor grill; Cabins only: A/C, TV, VCR, kitchen, fridge, coffeemaker, hair dryer.

LAKE BUENA VISTA/OFFICIAL HOTELS

The "official" Disney hotels are located on or around Hotel Plaza Boulevard, on the northeast side of Disney property and adjacent to Downtown Disney. Guests can enjoy some of the perks of staying in a WDW resort (free transportation to the Disney parks being one of them) while staying in a location somewhat more central to the rest of Orlando's offerings. You can reserve a room through Central Reservations Operations (✆ **407/934-7639**), but it's best to call the individual hotel or parent chain to check on the availability of special deals or packages.

EXPENSIVE

Wyndham Palace Resort ✪✪
This is the most upscale of the "official" properties and is popular with both business and leisure travelers. Rooms are comfortable and sleep at least four. Many have balconies or patios; ask for one above the fifth floor with a "recreation view" facing the pools and Downtown Disney. The resort is known for its full-service, European-style spa.

1900 Buena Vista Dr. (just north of Hotel Plaza Blvd.; P.O. Box 22206), Lake Buena Vista, FL 32830. ✆ **800/ 996-3426** or 407/827-2727. Fax 407/827-6034. www.wyndham.com/hotels/MCOPV/main.wnt. 1,014 units. $179–$398 double; $289–$749 suite. $8 daily resort fee. Extra person $20. Children 17 and under stay free in parent's room. AE, DC, DISC, MC, V. Free parking; valet $10. From I-4, take the Hwy. 535/Apopka-Vineland Rd. exit north to Hotel Plaza Blvd. and go left. At 1st stoplight, turn right onto Buena Vista Dr. It's the 1st hotel on the right. **Amenities:** 2 restaurants; grill; 4 lounges; 3 heated outdoor pools; kids' pool; spa; Jacuzzi; sauna; children's center; arcade; concierge; complimentary bus service to WDW parks; transportation to non-Disney parks for a fee; salon; 24-hr. room service; massage; babysitting; guest laundry; valet; nonsmoking rooms; concierge-level rooms. *In room:* A/C, TV w/pay movies, dataport, minibar, coffeemaker, hair dryer, iron.

MODERATE

Note: Accommodations in this category are usually a step above the "moderate" resorts located inside of WDW.

Best Western Lake Buena Vista Hotel *Value*   This 12-acre lakefront hotel has nicer rooms and public areas than you might find in others within the chain. Rooms are in an 18-story tower, and all of them come with balconies. The views improve from the eighth floor up, and guests on the west side have a better chance of seeing something Disney. The hotel's 18th-floor lounge offers an excellent view of the Magic Kingdom's fireworks. You can reserve an oversize room (20% larger) or one with a view of WDW fireworks for $15 more a night.

2000 Hotel Plaza Blvd. (between Buena Vista Dr. and Apopka-Vineland Rd./Hwy. 535), Lake Buena Vista, FL 32830. ⓒ 800/348-3765 or 407/828-2424. Fax 407/828-8933. www.downtowndisneyhotels.com or www.orlandoresorthotel.com. 325 units. $99–$159 for 4 persons; $199–$339 suite. $5 daily resort fee. 5th person $15. AE, DC, DISC, MC, V. Free parking. From I-4, take the Hwy. 535/Apopka-Vineland Rd. exit north to Hotel Plaza Blvd. and go left. It's the 1st hotel on the right. **Amenities:** Restaurant; grill; heated outdoor pool; kids' pool; guest-services desks; complimentary bus service to WDW parks; transportation to non-Disney parks for a fee; limited room service; guest laundry; nonsmoking rooms. *In room:* A/C, TV w/pay movies, coffeemaker, hair dryer, iron, safe, Nintendo.

DoubleTree Guest Suites *★ Kids*   Children have their own check-in desk and theater, and they get a gift upon arrival at this hotel, which is the best of the official hotels for families traveling with little ones. All of the accommodations in this seven-story hotel are two-room suites, large by most standards. There is space to sleep up to six with room to spare. This is the easternmost of the "official" resorts making it the farthest from the Downtown Disney action. Oh, and don't forget the cookies you get at check-in, a tasty tradition at the DoubleTree properties.

2305 Hotel Plaza Blvd. (just west of Apopka-Vineland Rd./Hwy. 535), Lake Buena Vista, FL 32830. ⓒ 800/222-8733 or 407/934-1000. Fax 407/934-1011. www.downtowndisneyhotels.com or www.doubletreeguest-suites.com. 229 units. $119–$249 double. Extra person $20. Children 17 and under stay free in parent's room. AE, DC, DISC, MC, V. Free parking. From I-4, take the Hwy. 535/Apopka-Vineland Rd. exit north to Hotel Plaza Blvd. and go left. It's the 1st hotel on the left. **Amenities:** Restaurant; 2 lounges; heated outdoor pool; kids' pool; 2 lighted tennis courts; arcade; concierge; car-rental desk; complimentary bus service to WDW parks; transportation to non-Disney parks for a fee; limited room service; guest laundry; nonsmoking rooms. *In room:* A/C, TV, dataport, fridge, microwave, coffeemaker, hair dryer, iron, safe.

Holiday Inn in The Walt Disney Resort *Value*   This former Courtyard by Marriott recently changed hands and is very popular with families. The inner and outer glass elevators in the center of the hotel offer a fun ride for everyone. The rooms are what you'd expect of a Holiday Inn and can comfortably fit four. For a great view of the Magic Kingdom's fireworks display, a room on the west side is best, and the higher up the better.

1805 Hotel Plaza Blvd. (between Lake Buena Vista Dr. and Apopka-Vineland Rd./Hwy. 535), Lake Buena Vista, FL 32830. ⓒ 888/782-9722 or 407/828-8888. Fax 407/827-4623. www.downtowndisneyhotels.com or www.holiday-inn.com. 323 units. $86–$199 double. AE, DC, DISC, MC, V. Free parking. From I-4, take the Hwy. 535/Apopka-Vineland Rd. exit north to Hotel Plaza Blvd. and go left. It's the 3rd hotel on left. **Amenities:** Restaurant; 2 lounges; 2 heated outdoor pools; kids' pool; Jacuzzi; arcade; guest-services desk; complimentary bus service to WDW parks; transportation to non-Disney parks for a fee; car-rental desks; limited room service; guest laundry; nonsmoking rooms. *In room:* A/C, TV w/pay movies, coffeemaker, hair dryer, iron, safe, Nintendo

Hotel Royal Plaza *★*   The Plaza is one of the boulevard's original hotels, but renovations over its 25-year history (its most recent makeover was 3 years ago) have kept it in good shape. A favorite with the budget-minded, its hallmark is a friendly staff. The nicely decorated rooms are medium-size and have enough space for five. Poolside rooms have balconies and patios; the tower rooms have separate sitting areas, and some offer whirlpool tubs in the bathrooms. If you want a view from up high, ask for a room facing west and WDW.

1905 Hotel Plaza Blvd. (between Buena Vista Dr. and Apopka-Vineland Rd./Hwy. 535), Lake Buena Vista, FL 32830. ℂ **800/248-7890** or 407/828-2828. Fax 407/827-6338. www.downtowndisneyhotels.com or www. orlandotravel.com/hotels/royal.htm. 394 units. $119–$235 double; $159–$695 suite. $7 daily resort fee. Extra person $15. Children 17 and under stay free in parent's room. AE, DC, DISC, MC, V. Free parking; valet $8. From I-4, take the Hwy. 535/Apopka-Vineland Rd. exit north to Hotel Plaza Blvd. and go left. It's the 2nd hotel on the left. **Amenities:** Restaurant; lounge; heated outdoor pool; whirlpool; 4 lighted tennis courts; fitness center; guest-services desk; complimentary bus service to WDW parks; transportation to non-Disney parks for a fee; limited room service; laundry; nonsmoking rooms. *In room:* A/C, TV w/pay movies and VCR, dataport, minibar, coffeemaker, hair dryer, iron, safe.

OTHER LAKE BUENA VISTA HOTELS

The hotels in this section are within a few minutes' drive of the WDW parks, offering the location but not the privileges of staying at an "official" hotel.

VERY EXPENSIVE

Gaylord Palms ⭐⭐⭐   This is not your run of the mill resort. It could be considered a destination unto itself, offering its own entertainment, fabulous dining, shops, recreational facilities, and to top it off the Canyon Ranch Spa Club for working out the kinks from the day's activities. The 4½-acre octagonal Grand Atrium, topped by a glass dome, surrounds a miniature version of the Castillo de San Marcos, the old fort at St. Augustine. Waterfalls, lush foliage and a rocky landscape complete the feel. The Emerald Bay, a 362-room hotel within the hotel, has the most elegant air about it, while other themed areas include Key West, St. Augustine, and the Everglades. The rooms are spacious, beautifully decorated, and well appointed each with its own balcony overlooking the Florida landscape within. As is befitting a luxury resort, the service is impeccable; yet it's also extremely friendly and welcoming, not standoffish, as is the case at many other resorts of this class.

6000 Osceola Pkwy., Kissimmee, FL 34747. ℂ **877/677-9352** or 407/586-0000. Fax 407/239-4822. www. gaylordpalms.com. 1,406 units. $239–$2700 double. $10 daily resort fee. Extra adult $20. Kids under 18 stay free in parent's room. AE, DC, DISC, MC, V. self-parking (fee); valet $12. Take the I-4 Osceola Pkwy. exit east to the hotel. **Amenities:** 3 restaurants; 4 lounges; 2 outdoor heated pools; fitness center; spa; children's center; concierge; tour desk; car-rental desk; free transportation to Disney parks; transportation to non-Disney parks for a fee; business center; shopping arcade; salon; room service; massage; babysitting; dry cleaning; nonsmoking rooms; concierge-level rooms. *In room:* A/C, TV w/pay movies, high-speed Internet, dataport, coffeemaker, hair dryer, iron, safe, Sony PlayStation.

Hyatt Regency Grand Cypress Resort ⭐⭐⭐ *(Finds)*   A favorite of honeymooners and those seeking a luxurious adult oasis, this getaway's lobby has lush foliage from which macaws wave to passersby. The 18-story atrium has inner and outer glass elevators (ride the outers to the roof for a panoramic rush). The rooms are beautifully decorated and sleep four. The Hyatt shares a top-rated golf club and academy, racquet club, and equestrian center with its sister property, The Villas of Grand Cypress (see below); both offer excellent packages aimed at the sports set. The Hyatt's half-acre, 800,000-gallon pool is one of the best in Orlando and features caves, grottoes, waterfalls, and a 45-foot water slide.

1 N. Jacaranda (off Hwy. 535), Orlando, FL 32836. ℂ **800/233-1234** or 407/239-1234. Fax 407/239-3800. www.grandcypress.com. 750 units. $239–$585 double; $395–$5,750 suite. Optional $10 daily resort fee. Extra person $25. Children 17 and under stay free in parent's room. AE, DC, DISC, MC, V. Free parking; valet $12. Take I-4 to the Hwy. 535/Apopka-Vineland Rd. exit and go north; then turn left at the 2nd light (after the ramp light) onto Hwy. 535. **Amenities:** 4 restaurants; 4 lounges; large heated outdoor pool; 45 holes of golf; 12 tennis courts (5 lighted); 2 racquetball courts; health club; spa; watersports equipment; children's center; arcade; concierge; free Disney shuttle; transportation to non-Disney parks for a fee; car-rental desk; store; salon; 24-hr. room service; in-room massage; babysitting; guest laundry; valet; nonsmoking rooms; concierge-level rooms; equestrian center. *In room:* A/C, TV, dataport, minibar, hair dryer, iron, safe.

The Villas of Grand Cypress ★★★ *(Finds*   If you are willing to splurge—and I mean *splurge*—this is an exceptional place to retreat, with a remote location away from the buzz of the theme parks that's not too far off the beaten path. At its "modest" end, this Mediterranean-inspired resort has junior suites with beds for four, Roman tubs, and patios. Floor plans then progress to elegant one- to four-bedroom villas, all with kitchens, dining rooms, and patios. The beautiful landscaping runs throughout the resort. The resort shares facilities with its sister property, the Hyatt Regency Grand Cypress Resort (see above), but this resort caters primarily to adults.

1 N. Jacaranda (off Hwy. 535), Orlando, FL 32836. ✆ **800/835-7377** or 407/239-4700. Fax 407/239-7219. www.grandcypress.com. 146 villas. $215–$500 club suite; $315–$2,000 villa. $10 daily resort fee. Extra person included. Children 17 and under stay free in parent's room. AE, DC, MC, V. Free self parking. Take I-4 to the Hwy. 535/Apopka-Vineland Rd. exit and go north; then go left at the 2nd light (after the ramp light) onto Hwy. 535. It's on the right. **Amenities:** 2 restaurants; 2 lounges; heated outdoor pool; 45 holes of golf; 12 tennis courts (5 lighted); 2 racquetball courts; health club; spa; watersports equipment; kids' center; arcade; concierge; free Disney shuttle; transportation to non-Disney parks for a fee; car-rental desk; salon; 24-hr. room service; in-room massage; babysitting; guest laundry; equestrian center; nonsmoking rooms; concierge-level rooms. *In room:* A/C, TV, dataport, minibar, hair dryer, iron, safe.

EXPENSIVE

Marriott's Orlando World Center ★★ *(Finds*   Golf, tennis, and spa lovers will find plenty to do at this 230-acre resort, which caters to couples and business travelers but is also very suitable for families. The sports facilities are first-class and the largest of its five pools has water slides and waterfalls. The location, only 2 miles from the Disney parks, is a fabulous plus. The large, comfortable and beautifully decorated rooms sleep four, and the higher poolside floors offer views of Disney.

8701 World Center Dr. (on Hwy. 536 between I-4 and Hwy. 535), Orlando, FL 32821. ✆ **800/621-0638** or 407/239-4200. Fax 407/238-8777. www.marriottHotels.com/MCOWC/. 2,111 units. $189–$410 for up to 5; $425–$2,400 suite. $5 daily resort fee. Children 17 and under stay free in parent's room. AE, DC, DISC, MC, V. Free self-parking; valet $12. Take I-4 to the Hwy. 535/Apopka-Vineland Rd. exit, go south 1½ miles, then right/west on Hwy. 536, and go ⅓ mile. **Amenities:** 4 restaurants; 2 lounges; 3 heated outdoor pools; heated indoor pool; kids' pool; 18-hole golf course; 8 lighted tennis courts; health club; spa; whirlpool; sauna; concierge; car-rental desk; transportation to all theme parks for a fee; business center; salon; 24-hr. room service; massage; babysitting; guest laundry; nonsmoking rooms. *In room:* A/C, TV w/pay movies, dataport, minibar, coffeemaker, hair dryer, iron, safe.

MODERATE

Embassy Suites Lake Buena Vista ★   Set near the end of Palm Parkway, just off Apopka-Vineland, this fun and welcoming all-suite resort is close to all the action, yet still remains a quiet retreat. Each suite sleeps five and includes separate living area (with a pullout sofa) and sleeping quarters. The roomy accommodations make it a great choice for families. Some of the other perks here include a complimentary cooked-to-order breakfast and a daily manager's reception.

8100 Lake Ave., Orlando, FL 32836. ✆ **800/257-8483** or 407/239-1144. Fax 407/238-0230. www.embassy-suitesorlando.com. 333 units. $109–$259. Extra person $15. AE, DC, DISC, MC, V. Free self-parking, Valet $8. From I-4, take the Hwy. 535/Apopka-Vineland Rd. exit east to Palm Pkwy. Follow ½ mile to Lake Ave. on the right. **Amenities:** Restaurant; cafe; lounge; indoor and outdoor heated pools; kids pool and play area; tennis court; basketball court; fitness center; whirlpool and sauna; free shuttle to Disney parks; business center; high-speed Internet access, room service; guest laundry. *In room:* A/C, TV w/pay movies, dataport, fridge, hair dryer, iron, safe, microwave.

Hawthorn Suites Lake Buena Vista ★ *(Value*   One of the features that is most appealing about this property, which opened in summer 2000, is its floor plan. Standard rooms have a living room with pullout sofa, chair, and TV; full kitchen with dining-room table for four; bathroom with vanity; and bedroom with recliner and TV. Two-bedroom units are also available. The atmosphere is friendly, the service is good, and it's just 3 minutes from Hotel Plaza Boulevard.

8303 Palm Pkwy., Orlando, FL 32836. ℂ 800/936-9417, 800/527-1133, or 407/597-5000. Fax 407/597-6000. www.hawthornsuiteslbv.com. 120 units. $99–$179 for 4–6. AE, DC, DISC, MC, V. Free self-parking. From I-4, take the Hwy. 535/Apopka-Vineland Rd. exit east to Palm Pkwy. then right ¼ mile to hotel. **Amenities:** Outdoor heated pool; basketball court; exercise room; Jacuzzi; free shuttle to Disney parks; transportation to non-Disney parks for a fee; guest laundry; nonsmoking rooms. *In room:* A/C, TV w/pay movies, dataport, kitchen, fridge, coffeemaker, hair dryer, iron, microwave.

Holiday Inn Family Suites Resort 🅐🅐 *Finds* *Kids*   This all-suite property is one of the absolute best resorts in the Orlando area for families. Its two-bedroom Kid Suites feature a second bedroom for the kids with either bunk or twin beds and full kitchens. The resort, voted in 2003 as the best Holiday Inn in North America, has themed activity nights (movies, magic, variety shows) and a wide variety of recreational activities including a small mini-golf area, playground, and children's activity center. And it's about to get even better. The property has teamed up with Nickelodeon to transform itself into what will eventually be called The Nickelodeon Family Suites (sometime in 2005); it will remain open while the work is done. Nick character breakfasts, wake up calls from a favorite Nick star, and many other "Nickprovements" will take place. The introduction of the 3-bedroom Kid Suite, offering three bedrooms (room for 9), two bathrooms, and a full kitchen, will only add to the appeal of this resort.

14500 Continental Gateway (off Hwy. 536), Lake Buena Vista, FL 32821. ℂ 877/387-5437 or 407/387-5437 or 866/GO2-NICK. Fax 407/387-1489. www.hifamilysuites.com or www.nickhotel.com. 800 units. $146–$199 suite. AE, DC, DISC, MC, V. Free self-parking. From I-4, take the Hwy. 536/International Dr. exit east 1 mile to the resort. **Amenities:** Restaurant; lounge; several fast-food counters; large lap pool; family swimming pool; fitness center; 2 Jacuzzis; 3 outdoor Ping-Pong tables; 2 shuffleboard courts; game room; mini-golf course; complimentary recreation center for ages 4–12; tour desk; free shuttle to Disney parks; transportation to non-Disney parks for a fee; coin-op washers and dryers. *In room:* A/C, TV w/pay movies and VCR (some with Nintendo), dataport, fridge, coffeemaker, hair dryer, iron, safe, microwave.

Staybridge Suites Lake Buena Vista 🅐🅐   A Summerfield Suites in a previous life, this recent edition to the Staybridge Suites chain is located just off Apopka-Vineland, close to the action of Downtown Disney and the theme parks, as well as many restaurants. Featured are one- and two-bedroom suites, all with full kitchens (the two-bedroom suites have two bathrooms). The suites' separate living areas are larger and more comfortable than similar ones at other all-suite hotels. A unique plus here for those who'd rather not spend time in a supermarket on their vacation is the complimentary grocery shopping service, which allows you to select items for delivery to your room (you don't have to be there, and only the service is free—you still have to pay for the groceries).

8751 Suiteside Dr., Orlando FL 32836. ℂ 800/866-4549 or 407/238-0777. Fax 407/238-2640. www. ichotelsgroup.com. 150 units. $119–$289. Rates include continental breakfast. Rollaway beds and cribs available at no charge. AE, DC, DISC, MC, V. Free self-parking. From I-4, take the exit for 535 (exit #68), turn right; follow to Vinings Way Rd., turn right; the hotel is located on the left. **Amenities:** Deli; convenience store; outdoor heated pool; children's pool; 24-hr. exercise room; Jacuzzi; 24-hr. game room; free shuttle to Disney parks; complimentary grocery delivery service; guest services desk; high-speed Internet access; 24-hr. guest laundry; nonsmoking rooms; accessible suites. *In room:* A/C, TV/VCR, dataport, kitchen, hair dryer, iron, ironing board, safe.

ON U.S. 192/KISSIMMEE

This stretch of highway is within close proximity of the Disney parks, and over the last few years, a revitalization of the area has made it a more friendly and appealing area to stay and play. The hotels and restaurants here generally cater to the budget-conscious traveler.

EXPENSIVE

Celebration Hotel ★★   This hotel is as picture perfect as the town that surrounds it. Its three-story, wood-frame design is straight out of 1920s Florida, as
is its interior. The beautifully decorated rooms have incredibly comfortable beds;
to enjoy a soothing view, ask for a lakefront room. The upscale ambience caters
to adults, especially those seeking a romantic getaway. The only drawback: you'll
have to deal with the traffic on U.S. 192 to get anywhere.

700 Bloom St. © **888/499-3800** or 407/566-6000. Fax 407/566-6001. www.celebrationhotel.com. 115
units. $139–$219 for up to 4; $289–$470 suite. $5 daily resort fee. AE, DC, DISC, MC, V. Free self-parking;
valet $10. Take I-4 to the U.S. 192 exit, go east to the 2nd light, then right on Celebration Ave. and follow the
signs. **Amenities:** Restaurant; lounge; outdoor heated pool; 18-hole golf course; state-of-the-art health-and-
fitness center; spa; concierge; free shuttle to Disney parks; transportation to non-Disney parks for a fee;
nearby shopping district. *In room:* A/C, TV/Nintendo, dataport, hair dryer, iron, safe.

MODERATE

Comfort Suites Maingate East ★/Value   Set back from the main drag, this
fairly new and welcoming hotel is one of the nicest in the area. The lobby and
accommodations—consisting of studio and one-bedroom suites—are bright
and inviting. The main pool and the children's pool, with an umbrella fountain
to keep everyone cool, are open around the clock. For entertainment, Old Town
(a small-scale shopping, dining, and entertainment complex) is next door, and a
great miniature golf course is located just in front of the property.

2775 Florida Plaza Blvd., Kissimmee, FL 34746. © **888/782-9772** or 407/397-7848. Fax 407/396-7045.
www.comfortsuitesfl.com. 198 units. $65–$150 double. Extra person $10. Nonsmoking suites available. Rates
include continental breakfast. Children 17 and under stay free in parent's room. AE, DC, DISC, MC, V. Free self-
parking. From I-4 take the US192 exit east; go 1¾ miles, then right on Florida Plaza Blvd. **Amenities:** Outdoor heated pool; kids pool; fitness center; game room; concierge; free shuttle to Disney, Universal, and
SeaWorld parks; business center; guest laundry. *In room:* A/C, TV, dataport, fridge, coffeemaker, hair dryer, iron,
safe, microwave.

INTERNATIONAL DRIVE AREA

The hotels and resorts listed here are 7 to 10 miles northeast of the Walt Disney
World parks and 1 to 3 miles from Universal Orlando and SeaWorld, which
makes this area the most centrally located for those who want to sample more
than one area. The disadvantages: The northern end of International Drive is
badly congested. The shops, motels, eateries, and attractions along this stretch
can vary greatly in quality (and some are decidedly tacky); as a rule, the closer
you get to the convention center, the better the class of hotels and dining.

VERY EXPENSIVE

Peabody Orlando ★★★ Finds   The five mallards that march into a lobby
fountain every morning at 11am and then back out at 5pm, accompanied by
John Philip Sousa's *King Cotton March,* are just part of the appeal of this serv-
ice-oriented hotel. If your budget allows for a splurge, you won't be disappointed
with a stay here. Primarily a business and convention destination, the Peabody
also appeals to adults looking for a classy hotel that provides top-of-the-line service, amenities, and atmosphere. Rooms sleep up to five, and are tastefully decorated and well appointed. Those on the west side (6th floor and higher) offer a
distant view of Disney and its fireworks displays.

9801 International Dr. (between Bee Line Expwy. and Sand Lake Rd.), Orlando, FL 32819. © **800/732-2639**
or 407/352-4000. Fax 407/354-1424. www.peabodyorlando.com. 891 units. $395–$480 standard room for up
to 3; $520–$1,675 suite. Extra person $20. Children 17 and under stay free in parent's room. AE, DC, DISC,
MC, V. Free self-parking; valet $8. From I-4, take the Sand Lake Rd./Hwy. 482 exit east to International Dr.,
then south. Hotel is on the left across from the Convention Center. **Amenities:** 3 restaurants; deli; 3 lounges;

outdoor heated pool; kids' pool; 4 lighted tennis courts; fitness center; spa; Jacuzzi; concierge; guest-services desk; shuttle to WDW and other parks for a fee; business center; shopping arcade; 24-hr. room service; massage; valet; nonsmoking rooms; concierge-level rooms. *In room:* A/C, TV, dataport, minibar, hair dryer.

Renaissance Orlando Resort at SeaWorld ★★ This resort just goes to show that you should never judge a book by its cover. What appears to be a rather blah looking hotel on the outside, is absolutely beautiful and inviting on the inside, with a glass covered atrium, lush gardens, cascading waterfalls, and an elegant free-flight aviary. The rooms are oversized, providing plenty of space to spread out and relax. You can't beat the location if you are a fan of Sea-World—the park is just across from the hotel.

6677 Sea Harbour Dr., Orlando, FL 32821. ℂ 800/327-6677 or 407/351-5555. Fax 407/351-1991. www. renaissancehotels.com. 778 units. $149–$249 double. Extra person $20. Children 17 and under stay free in parent's room. AE, DC, DISC, MC, V. Free self-parking; valet parking $9. From I-4, the Hwy. 528/Bee Line Expressway exit east to International Dr., then go south to Sea Harbour Dr. and turn right. **Amenities:** 2 restaurants; grill; 3 lounges; outdoor heated pool; kids' pool; 4 lighted tennis courts; health club; spa; 2 Jacuzzis; sauna; arcade; concierge; tour desk; car-rental desk; transportation to all the parks for a fee; business center; shopping arcade; 24-hr. room service; massage; babysitting; guest laundry; valet; nonsmoking rooms. *In room:* A/C, TV w/pay movies, dataport, safe, PlayStation.

MODERATE

AmeriSuites/Universal It's tough to beat the value and roominess of these kitchenette-equipped suites, especially if your goal is to be very close to the Universal theme parks without having to pay the heftier rates that come with staying on park property. The modern, spacious rooms allow you to stretch out more than in standard hotel/motel accommodations and the location is especially convenient if Universal Orlando is your destination of choice.

5895 Caravan Court, Orlando, FL 32819. ℂ 800/833-1516 or 407/351-0627. Fax 407/331-3317. www. amerisuites.com. 151 units. $89–$179 for up to 4. Rates include free buffet breakfast. Children 17 and under stay free in parent's room. AE, DC, DISC, MC, V. Free self-parking. From I-4, take Exit 75B Kirkman Rd., then turn right at the 1st light, Major Blvd., and the next right, Caravan Court. The hotel is on the right. **Amenities:** Outdoor heated pool; exercise room; tour desk; free transportation to all theme parks; guest laundry; valet; nonsmoking rooms. *In room:* A/C, TV/VCR, dataport, kitchenette, coffeemaker, hair dryer, iron, safe.

La Quinta Inn & Suites Convention Center This is one of a handful of upscale, moderately priced motels on Universal Boulevard, which runs parallel to (but isn't as congested as) International Drive. The hotel is aimed at business travelers, but families traveling with kids will find the accommodations most comfortable. King rooms come with a fridge and microwave. There are a limited number of two-room suites offering separate living and sleeping areas.

8504 Universal Blvd., Orlando, FL 32819. ℂ 800/531-5900 or 407/345-1365. Fax 407/345-5586. www. laquinta.com. 185 units. $90–$150 double. Extra person $10. Rates include continental breakfast. Children 18 and under stay free in parent's room. AE, DC, DISC, MC, V. Free self-parking. Take I-4 to the Sand Lake Rd./Hwy. 482 exit, go east toward Universal, then right. **Amenities:** Outdoor heated pool; exercise room; Jacuzzi; transportation to all theme parks for a fee; guest laundry; nonsmoking rooms. *In room:* A/C, TV w/pay movies, dataport, coffeemaker, hair dryer, iron, Nintendo.

INEXPENSIVE

Fairfield Inn International Drive ★ *Value* If you're looking for I-Drive's best value, it's hard to beat the Fairfield. It offers a quiet location off the main drag, earthly rates, and a clean motel in one package. The rooms are very comfortable and there are a number of restaurants within walking distance of the hotel.

8342 Jamaican Court (off International Dr. between the Bee Line Expressway and Sand Lake Rd.), Orlando, FL 32819. ℂ 800/228-2800 or 407/363-1944. Fax 407/363-1944. www.fairfieldinn.com. 135 units. $69–$99 for up to 4. AE, DC, DISC, MC, V. Free self-parking. From I-4, take the Sand Lake Rd./Hwy. 482 exit east 1 block, turn right on I-Dr., then right on Jamaican Court. **Amenities:** Outdoor heated pool; guest-services desk; transportation to the parks for a fee; guest laundry; valet; nonsmoking rooms. *In room:* A/C, TV w/pay movies, dataport, safe.

UNIVERSAL ORLANDO RESORTS

Universal Orlando has three unique and upscale theme properties of its own, all run by the Loews hotel group. Like the Disney resorts, Universal offers its resort guests additional privileges, including preferred access to the Universal parks' rides and attractions—show a room key and you will head right to the front of the lines.

Portofino Bay Hotel ★★   Universal's first hotel has the stature of Disney's Grand Floridian. This romantic, upscale resort is designed to look like the village of Portofino, Italy, complete with a harbor and canals that lead you via boat to the theme parks. The rooms sleep up to five, and have beds with Egyptian-woven sheets and pillows so soft you'll want to take them home. Ask for a view overlooking the piazza and "bay" area. The Portofino doesn't just have swimming pools; its beach pool has a fort with a water slide and the villa pool offers several cabanas with laptop hookups for the perfect mix of business and pleasure. The resort's Mandara Spa features a state-of-the-art fitness center and full-service spa. The drawbacks: There are stairs everywhere you turn, and the sheer size of the resort can make it difficult to find your way around.

5601 Universal Blvd., Orlando FL. 32819. © **888/322-5541** or 407/503-1000. Fax 407/224-7118. www. loewshotels.com/hotels/orlando. 750 units. $259–$390 double; $450–$2,200 suite and villas. Extra person $25. Children 17 and under stay free in parent's room. AE, DC, DISC, MC, V. Self-parking $6; valet $12. From I-4, take the Kirkman Rd./Hwy. 435 exit and follow the signs to Universal. Pets accepted (no fee, though deposit against damage required). **Amenities:** 3 restaurants; deli; 3 lounges; 2 outdoor heated pools (1 for concierge and suite guests only); kids' pool; fitness center; spa; watersports equipment; kids' club; arcade; concierge; tour desk; free water-taxi transportation to Universal Studios, Islands of Adventure, and CityWalk; free shuttle to SeaWorld; transportation to WDW parks for a fee; business center; shopping arcade; 24-hr. room service; babysitting; guest laundry; nonsmoking rooms; concierge-level rooms. *In room:* A/C, TV, hair dryer, iron, safe.

EXPENSIVE

Hard Rock Hotel ★★ *Kids*   You can't get any closer than this to Universal Studios Florida. Opened in 2001, this California mission–style resort sports a rock-and-roll theme and rack rates a shade less expensive than the Portofino (above). The Hard Rock is a cut above some of Disney's comparable properties, including Animal Kingdom Lodge. The rooms are very comfortable. Unfortunately, though the rooms are fairly soundproof, a few notes seep through the walls, so you may want to ask for one that's away from the lobby area. I rate this the most kid-friendly of the Universal resorts because of the atmosphere, the music, the ease of getting around the resort, and the fabulous pool.

5000 Universal Blvd., Orlando, FL 32819. © **800/232-7827** or 407/363-8000. Fax 407/224-7118. www. loewshotels.com/hotels/orlando. 650 units. $209–$359 double; $345–$1,675 suite. Extra person $20. Children 17 and under stay free in parent's room. AE, DC, DISC, MC, V. Self-parking $6; valet $12. From I-4, take the Kirkman Rd./Hwy. 435 exit and follow the signs to Universal. Pets accepted (no fee, though deposit against damage required). **Amenities:** 2 restaurants; grill; 2 lounges; outdoor heated pool; kids' pool; fitness center; kids' club; arcade; concierge; free water-taxi transportation to Universal Studios, Islands of Adventure, and CityWalk; free shuttle to SeaWorld; transportation to WDW parks for a fee; shopping arcade; 24-hr. room service; babysitting; guest laundry; valet, nonsmoking rooms. *In room:* A/C, TV, hair dryer, iron, safe.

PLACES TO STAY ELSEWHERE IN ORLANDO

There are two good reasons to choose accommodations away from all of the hustle and hassle of the attractions: Crowds are thinner and, in some cases, prices are lower. On the flip side, if you're heading to the theme parks, your location off the beaten path means that you'll have to deal with a longer drive and a great deal more traffic.

Westin Grand Bohemian ★★ *(Finds)*   Downtown's hotel jewel, the Grand Bohemian caters almost exclusively to the business and romance crowds, which means—much to the satisfaction of the adult guests here—you'll find almost no children on premises. The "Heavenly Beds" (firm mattresses, down blankets, comforters, and with five pillows) are among the best in Orlando. Upper floors on the east side overlook the pool; those on the north side face downtown. This smoke-free hotel boasts more than 100 pieces of 19th- and 20th-century American fine art adorning its interior.

325 S. Orange Ave. (across from City Hall). © **866/663-0024** or 407/313-9000. Fax 407/313-6001. www.grandbohemianhotel.com. 250 units. $159–$189 for up to 4; $225 and up suite. AE, DC, DISC, MC, V. Valet parking $12. Take I-4 to the Washington St. exit, merge with W. Robinson/Hwy. 526, then south on Orange. The garage is 2 blocks west on Jackson. **Amenities:** Restaurant; lounge; coffee shop; heated outdoor pool and spa; fitness center; concierge; shuttle to the theme parks for a fee; business center; 24-hr. room service; guest laundry and dry cleaning; concierge-level rooms. *In room:* A/C, TV w/pay movies, dataport, minibar, coffeemaker, hair dryer, iron, safe, Nintendo.

4 Where to Dine

Orlando has a diverse array of restaurants: From family style restaurants to five-star dining, there is something for every taste and budget to be found here. Because most visitors spend the majority of their time at Disney, I focus a lot of this section on dining there. But I certainly don't leave out other worthwhile spots in the city, including the better places to eat at Universal's CityWalk, and International Drive.

ARRANGING PRIORITY SEATING AT DISNEY RESTAURANTS
Priority Seating *isn't* a reservation. It's exactly what its name implies: You will get priority over any others waiting for a table at the time you schedule. There may still be a wait, but it will generally be significantly shorter than it would be if you didn't have one. And if you don't use Priority Seating, especially for the most popular restaurants such as Cinderella's Table or Victoria & Albert's, you may miss out all together as these popular restaurants are usually booked well in advance, leaving little or no room at all for the guests who decide to just show up for a table. To arrange for Priority Seating at any WDW restaurant (in the parks or at the resorts), call © **407/939-3463.** You can book as far as 90 days (180 in some cases) in advance of your arrival for most restaurants (which may be necessary during the busier times of year and is essential at some restaurants).

If you're staying on Disney property, you can arrange Priority Seating right at your resort. At Epcot, you can do it at the WorldKey interactive terminals at Guest Relations near Innoventions East, the WorldKey Information Service on the main concourse to the World Showcase, as well as at the restaurant of your choice.

TIPS ON WALT DISNEY WORLD RESTAURANTS
All park restaurants (as well as all restaurants in Florida) are **nonsmoking.**

Magic Kingdom restaurants don't serve alcohol, but those at Animal Kingdom, Epcot, and Disney–MGM Studios do.

Sit-down restaurants in WDW take American Express, Diners Club, Discover, MasterCard, Visa, and the Disney Card.

Unless otherwise noted, *restaurants in the parks require park admission.*

Unless you're using WDW transportation or are a Disney resort guest, there is also an $8 parking fee.

Nearly all WDW restaurants with sit-down or counter service offer children's menus with items ranging anywhere from around $4 to $6.

INSIDE THE WALT DISNEY WORLD THEME PARKS

For the most part, the food offered throughout the parks is fairly decent though, with few exceptions, you won't find Disney's park restaurants winning accolades from *Food & Wine* or *Bon Appétit*. And while the portions are generally on the large side, so are the prices. The following list includes Magic Kingdom, Epcot, Disney–MGM Studios, and Animal Kingdom. You can get information on all Disney restaurants by calling ℂ **407/939-3463** or visiting **www.disneyworld.com**.

EPCOT
World Showcase

The World Showcase has some of the best dining options inside the WDW theme parks, thanks to the cultural cuisine of its 11 nation pavilions. Although many consider a meal here an essential part of the experience, I must point out that the food (as in all the parks) is priced higher than comparable fare in the free world.

The restaurants below are arranged geographically, beginning at the Canada pavilion and proceeding counterclockwise around the World Showcase Lagoon. *Prices are for entrees only* and don't include tax, tip, and beverages.

CANADA   Le Cellier Steakhouse has a castlelike ambience accentuated by vaulted stone arches. Red-meat main events (all Midwest, corn-fed) include the usual range of cuts—filet, porterhouse, prime rib, veal chop, and so on. They do, however, offer some choices in the way of pasta and seafood as well. Lunch runs $10 to $21; dinner is $16 to $27.

UNITED KINGDOM   The Tudor-beamed **Rose & Crown** is a cozy pub suggestive of Victorian England. Visitors from the U.K. flock to this spot, where folk music and saucy servers entertain you as you feast on a short but joyfully traditional menu including prime rib with Yorkshire pudding or fish and chips. The outdoor dining area overlooks the lagoon and is a good place to see the IllumiNations fireworks display. Lunch is $11 to $14; dinner is $14 to $20.

FRANCE   Chefs de France has an Art Nouveau interior agleam with mirrors and brass chandeliers. Three French chefs designed the menu, which is respectable by park standards. The dinner entrees include Mediterranean seafood casserole (grouper, scallops, and shrimp dusted with saffron, then swum in a mild garlic sauce) and a garlicky braised lamb shank. Lunch is $11 to $18; dinner is $15 to $30.

MOROCCO   Of all the Epcot restaurants, **Marrakesh** ⍟ best exemplifies the spirit of the park, yet a lot of guests don't know it's there or ignore it because they're worried that the menu is too exotic. Expect belly dancers to entertain while you feast on options like marinated beef shish kabob, braised chicken with green olives, and a medley of seafood, chicken, and lamb. Most entrees come with couscous. Lunch costs $12 to $18; dinner is $17 to $26.

JAPAN   If you've been to any of the Japanese steakhouse chains, you know what to expect at **Teppanyaki:** Guests sit around large grill tables while white-hatted chefs rapidly dice, slice, stir-fry, and launch the occasional shrimp tail onto your plate with amazing skill. The culinary acrobatics here are a sight to see, the cuisine however, is average. Lunch is $12 to $22; dinner is $13 to $32. The adjoining **Yakitori House** is a bamboo-roofed cafeteria that serves casual fare including noodle dishes and chicken, beef or shrimp brochettes. Meals here are generally under $10.

ITALY **L'Originale Alfredo di Roma,** set inside one of the most beautiful of the world pavilions, is Epcot's most popular restaurant. Singing waiters top off the dining experience here. The menu includes the celebrated namesake fettuccine. For something on the meatier side of the menu, try the veal chops served with chianti-and-truffle sauce, mushrooms, asparagus, and roasted potatoes. If you want a quieter setting, ask for a seat on the veranda. Lunch costs $10 to $25; dinner runs $17 to $38.

GERMANY ⊛ The **Biergarten** simulates a Bavarian village at Oktoberfest, and has a very festive atmosphere. The all-you-can-eat buffet is filled with traditional Bavarian fare (assorted sausages, pork schnitzel, sauerbraten, spaetzle with gravy, sauerkraut, and a large assortment of trimmings). The lunch buffet is $15 for adults, $7 for kids 3 to 11; dinner is $20 for adults, $8 for children. At **Sommerfest,** a cafeteria, you can purchase bratwurst sandwiches with sauerkraut. All items there are under $7.

CHINA When it comes to decor, the **Nine Dragons** shines with carved rosewood furnishings and a dragon-motif ceiling. Some windows overlook the lagoon outside. Portions here are small when compared with those at most Chinese restaurants. Lunch runs $9.50 to $19; dinners go for $13 to $30. If you want something lighter, the open-air **Lotus Blossom Café** sells egg rolls, pork fried rice, and stir-fried chicken and vegetables served over noodles ($4–$6.50).

NORWAY **Akershus** is a re-created 14th-century castle where you can sample a 40-item smorgasbord of *smavarmt* (hot) and *koldtbord* (cold) dishes. The reasonably good entrees usually include such dishes as venison stew, roast pork, gravlax, smoked mackerel, and mustard herring. The lunch buffet costs $14 for adults, $7 for children 4 to 9; the dinner buffet is $20 for adults, $9 for kids. The **Kringla Bakeri og Kafe** sells open-face sandwiches, sugar-sprinkled waffles, and fresh-baked Norwegian pastries. All items there cost under $6.

MEXICO ⊛ It's always night at the **San Angel Inn** ⊛, where candlelit tables set a romantic mood, and the menu delivers reasonably authentic food. A popular choice is the *mole poblano* (chicken brought to life with more than 20 spices, carrots, and a hint of chocolate). Another favorite: *filete motuleno* (grilled beef tenderloin served over black beans, melted cheese, pepper strips, and fried plantains). Lunch runs $9.25 to $18 and dinners around $18 to $24. The **Cantina de San Angel,** a cafeteria with outdoor seating at umbrella tables overlooking the lagoon, offers tacos, burritos, and other items under $8.

Future World

At the Living Seas pavilion, the mood is half the fun at the **Coral Reef,** where the tables circle a 5.6-million-gallon aquarium that has 4,000 denizens of the deep. Tiered seating ensures everyone a good view. Highlights include pan-seared salmon with garlic-pesto mashed potatoes and candied carrots, and Caribbean lobster with summer squash and potatoes. Lunch is $14 to $21; dinner is $16 to $32.

IN THE MAGIC KINGDOM

In addition to the restaurant listed below, there are plenty of fast-food outlets located throughout the park of which Pecos Bill Cafe, Cosmic Ray's Starlight

Cafe, and the Columbia Harbour House are your best choices. That said, you may find that a quiet, sit-down meal is an essential, if brief, getaway from the day's activities.

Fantasyland   Romantics may find it hard to beat the ambience of eating at **Cinderella's Royal Table** ⚐ in Cinderella Castle, the Magic Kingdom's icon. Servers treat you like a lord or lady while fetching you headliners such as spice-crusted salmon, a New York strip, or roasted chicken. Lunch costs $9 to $26; dinner sells for $21 to $26. Don't forget to make Priority Seating arrangements if you want to eat here.

The **Crystal Palace,** named for its glass exterior, is a favorite with the young set because of its all-you-can eat character buffets (where kids and adults can pick and choose from a decent variety of meats, veggies, and desserts). Lunch costs $18 for adults and $10 for children (3–11). Dinner runs $22 for adults and $10 for children (3–11). Priority Seating is a must.

AT DISNEY–MGM STUDIOS

There are more than a dozen places to refuel in this Hollywood-style theme park. The ones listed below are the best of the bunch. Again, Priority Seating is a must.

Modeled after the Los Angeles celebrity haunt where Louella Parsons and Hedda Hopper held court, the **Hollywood Brown Derby** offers a good time and a pricey meal. The Derby's signature dessert, grapefruit cake with cream-cheese icing, is a perfect meal capper. Entrees go for $14 to $19 at lunch; $19 to $27 at dinner.

The **50's Prime Time Cafe** is like going home to mom's kitchen for dinner—back in the 1950s. The atmosphere delivers with black-and-white TV sets showing *My Little Margie* and servers threatening to withhold dessert if you don't eat all your food. Although the desserts are good, the meatloaf and pot roast aren't quite as good as mom used to make. Meals cost $14 to $19 at lunch and dinner.

The best bets at **Mama Melrose's Ristorante Italiano** are the wood-fired and brick-baked specialties including the flat breads (grilled pepperoni, portobello mushroom, and four cheese). Lunch is $12 to $21; dinner is $12 to $22.

Take the above review for the 50's Prime Time Café, give it a science-fiction spin, and welcome to the **Sci-Fi Dine-In Theater Restaurant.** Diners sit in chrome-plated convertibles with the Hollywood hills as a backdrop and are treated to newsreels, cartoons, and "B" horror flicks. The meals here are served with less culinary flair than in other Disney restaurants. Lunches run $11 to $17; dinners are $14 to $19.

IN THE ANIMAL KINGDOM

You'll find only a few options in Animal Kingdom, and most of those are of the grab-and-go style. Nevertheless, there are two spots where you can sit yourself down for a spell.

Expect California fare with an island spin at the **Rainforest Cafe.** Menu offerings tend to be tasty and somewhat creative, but the prices tend to run on the high side for what you get. It is the atmosphere that attracts most guests to this establishment, with the sites and sounds of a tropical rainforest thoroughly surrounding and entertaining you while you dine. Lunch and dinner run anywhere from $10 to $40.

The **Tusker House** offers options such as grilled chicken salad in focaccia bread; rotisserie or fried chicken; and wraps with turkey, chicken and ham. Prices run $7 to $8.

IN THE WALT DISNEY WORLD RESORTS

Most of these restaurants continue the trend of being above market price, but the food generally is a notch (or more) higher than what you find in the theme parks.

VERY EXPENSIVE

Citricos ⚘ NEW FRENCH   The chefs create what the resort calls French, Alsatian, and Provençal cuisine with California and Florida touches. The translation: The oft-changing menu might offer yummy basil-crusted rack of lamb, sautéed halibut with asparagus and shiitake mushrooms, or grilled salmon with roasted fennel and potatoes.

4401 Floridian Way, in Disney's Grand Floridian Resort & Spa. ✆ 407/939-3463. www.disneyworld.com. Priority Seating recommended. Main courses $22–$45. AE, DC, DISC, MC, V. Daily 5:30–10pm Wed–Sun; Chef's Domain (Table) 6 and 8:30pm (Tues–Sat).

Victoria & Albert's ★★★ *(Finds* INTERNATIONAL   It's not often that dinner can be described as "an event," but Disney's most elegant restaurant earns that distinction. Dinner is next to perfect—if the portions seem small, I dare you to make it through all six courses. The setting is exceptionally romantic. The fare changes nightly, but you might find main events such as tamari-glazed bluefin tuna over bok choy stir-fry or Colorado lamb with corn risotto. The dining room is crowned by a domed, chapel-style ceiling; 20 exquisitely appointed tables are lit softly by Victorian lamps; and your servers (always named Victoria and Albert) provide service that will have you begging to take them home.

4401 Floridian Way, in Disney's Grand Floridian Resort & Spa. ✆ 407/939-3463. www.disneyworld.com. Reservations required. Jackets required for men. Not recommended for children. Prix fixe $95 per person, $145 with wine pairing; $125 Chef's Table, $185 with wine. AE, DC, DISC, MC, V. 2 dinner seatings daily Sept–June, 5:45–6:30pm and 9–9:45pm; 1 seating July–Aug 6:45–8pm. Chef's Table 6pm only. Free self- and validated valet parking.

Yachtsman Steakhouse ⚘ SEAFOOD/STEAKS   Even by outside WDW standards, this is a solid steakhouse with a cordial staff. The exhibition kitchen provides a tantalizing peek at steaks, chops, and seafood being seared over oak and hickory. Options range from an 8-ounce filet to a 12-ounce strip to a belly-busting 24-ounce T-bone. The menu also has rack of lamb, salmon, and chicken.

1700 Epcot Resorts Blvd., in Disney's Yacht Club Resort. ✆ 407/939-3463. Priority Seating is recommended. Main courses $20–$50. AE, DC, DISC, MC, V. Daily 5:30–10pm. Free self- and valet parking.

EXPENSIVE

Artist Point ⚘ *(Finds* SEAFOOD/STEAKS   Enjoy a grand view of Disney's Wilderness Lodge in this rustically elegant establishment. Select from a seasonally-changing menu that might include grilled buffalo sirloin with a sweet potato and hazelnut gratin; or a cedar-plank roasted Silver Bay salmon with maple-whiskey glaze. *Note:* Artist Point has a more relaxed atmosphere than some of the busier WDW resort restaurants.

901 W. Timberline Dr., in Disney's Wilderness Lodge. ✆ 407/939-3463 or 407/824-1081. www.disney world.com. Priority Seating recommended. Main courses $23–$34. AE, DC, DISC, MC, V. Daily 5:30–10pm. Free self- and valet parking.

California Grill ⚘⚘ CALIFORNIA   Make your way to the 15th floor of the Contemporary Resort and enjoy views of the Magic Kingdom while you drool over healthy options prepared in an exhibition kitchen. Headliners change often, but might include seared yellowfin tuna served rare with shiitake mushrooms and scallions or roasted pumpkin ravioli. The Grill also has a nice sushi and sashimi menu. This is one of the few spots in WDW that isn't well suited to kids. It can be tough to get a table, so arrange Priority Seating as far ahead as possible.

4600 N. World Dr., at Disney's Contemporary Resort. (C) 407/939-3463 or 407/824-1576. www.disney-world.com. Reservations recommended. Main courses $20–$34; sushi and sashimi $10–$23. AE, DC, DISC, MC, V. Daily 5:30–10pm. Free self-parking.

Jiko—The Cooking Place ⭐ INTERNATIONAL   The Animal Kingdom Lodge's signature restaurant is a nice diversion from the usual Disney fare. Jiko's show kitchen turns out a unique menu of international cuisine with African overtones. Dishes, depending on the season, include broiled buttermilk-curry shrimp, pomegranate-glazed quail, and spicy steamed bass. The muted atmosphere makes this a good place for a relaxing dinner.

2901 Osceola Pkwy., at Disney's Animal Kingdom Lodge. (C) 407/939-3463. www.disneyworld.com. Priority Seating recommended. Main courses $18–$29. AE, DC, DISC, MC, V. Daily 5:30–10pm. Free self-parking.

Hoop De Doo Musical Review ⭐⭐⭐ *(Kids)* AMERICAN   This entertaining dinner show is fun for the entire family. Featuring singing and dancing, sprinkled with a bit of comedy, this review is Disney's most popular dinner show—and with good reason. It's the review's fun factor that earns it a 3-star rating, though the food isn't bad. Dinner consists of country-fried chicken served in a bucket, along with corn on the cob, biscuits, and dessert. It can get a bit expensive if you have a large family, but its entertainment value is well worth the price.

4510 N. Fort Wilderness Trail, at Disney's Fort Wilderness Resort and Campground. (C) 407/WDW-DINE. Reservations required. $49 adult, $25 child (ages 3–11). AE, DC, DISC, MC, V. Shows at 5:00, 7:15, and 9:00pm nightly.

MODERATE

ESPN Club ⭐ AMERICAN   If you are a sports enthusiast, this is *the* place for you. Upon entering you will be surrounded by monitors showing every possible sporting event. The all-American fare includes such choices as "Boo-Yeah" chili, hot wings, and burgers. Sandwiches and salads are available as well. The service is impeccable—never have I had a waiter so quick on his feet. While the food is quite good, it's really the atmosphere that draws the crowds here.

2101 N. Epcot Resorts Blvd. At Disney's BoardWalk. (C) 407/939-1177. www.disneyworld.com. Priority Seating is not available. $8–$15 lunch and dinner. AE, DC, MC, V. Mon–Thurs 11:30am–1:00am; Fri–Sat 11:30am–2:00am. Valet or free self-parking.

'Ohana ⭐ *(Kids)* PACIFIC RIM   Its star is earned on the fun front, but the decibel level here may turn some off. As your luau is being prepared over an 18-foot-wide fire pit, the staff keeps you busy with coconut races, hula lessons, and other shenanigans. Turkey, shrimp, pork, and steak fill out the menu.

1600 Seven Seas Dr., at Disney's Polynesian Resort. (C) 407/939-3463 or 407/824-2000. www.disney-world.com. Priority Seating strongly encouraged. $24 adults, $10 children 3–11. AE, DC, DISC, MC, V. Daily 7:30–11am and 5–10pm. Valet or free self-parking.

DOWNTOWN DISNEY
VERY EXPENSIVE

Fulton's Crab House ⭐ SEAFOOD   Oysters and stone crab claws are the specialties of this fun and fashionable eatery, which is in a replica of a (permanently moored) 19th-century Mississippi riverboat. It's one of the area's best seafood houses, but you might want to bring along some extra cash. The grilled tuna mignon is delicious—it's served rare with lemon grass dipping sauce, steamed bok choy, and a jasmine rice cake.

1670 Buena Vista Dr., aboard the riverboat docked at Downtown Disney. © 407/934-2628. www. levyrestaurants.com. Priority Seating recommended. Main courses $12–$45 at lunch, $17–$45 at dinner. AE, DC, DISC, MC, V. Daily 11:30am–4pm and 5–11pm. Free self-parking; valet parking $6.

MODERATE

Rainforest Cafe ★ CALIFORNIA   Don't arrive starving. Waits here average 2 hours if you fail to call ahead for Priority Seating, although even then you'll wait longer than at Animal Kingdom's Rainforest Cafe (p. 479). The menu can be tasty and creative, though somewhat overpriced. Fun dishes include Mogambo Shrimp (sautéed in olive oil and served with penne pasta), Rumble in the Jungle Turkey Wrap (with romaine, tomatoes, and bacon), and Maya's Mixed Grill (ribs, chicken breast, and shrimp).

Downtown Disney Marketplace; near the smoking volcano. © 407/827-8500. www.rainforest.com. Priority Seating. Main courses $11–$40 at lunch and dinner (most under $25). AE, DISC, MC, V. Sun–Thurs 10:30am–11pm; Fri–Sat 10:30am–midnight. Free self-parking.

Wolfgang Puck Café ★ CALIFORNIA   The wait can be distressing and the sticker prices depressing, but the chefs turn out a mean menu of pizza, sushi, and fu-fu food. Our favorite stop is the sushi bar, an artistic copper-and-terrazzo masterpiece that delivers some of the best sushi in Orlando. Puck's is noisy, making conversation difficult.

1482 Buena Vista Dr., at Disney's West Side. © 407/938-9653. www.wolfgangpuck.com/myrestaurants. Reservations not accepted. Main courses upstairs $26–$38; pizza and sushi $8–$25. AE, DC, DISC, MC, V. Daily 11am–1am. Free self-parking.

ELSEWHERE IN LAKE BUENA VISTA
MODERATE

Pebbles ★★ *Finds* FLORIDIAN   If you want to dine like a gourmet without the hefty price, this is the restaurant for you. This local chain has a reputation for great food and creative appetizers. Its pleasant Key West style is casual and comfortable, and portions are generous and presented with an artistic flair. The delicious Ybor Gold twin filets are seared, and then bathed in the namesake lager and delivered with caramelized onions and three-cheese potatoes.

12551 Apopka-Vineland Rd., in the Crossroads Shopping Center. © 407/827-1111. www.pebbles worldwide.com. Reservations not accepted. Main courses $10–$18. AE, DC, DISC, MC, V. Sun–Thurs noon–11pm; Fri–Sat 11am–11pm. Free self-parking. Take the I-4 Hwy. 535/Apopka-Vineland Rd. exit north to the Crossroads Shopping Center on the right.

The Crab House SEAFOOD   This casual restaurant offers good seafood (as well as other options for land lubbers) at good prices. The all-you-can-eat seafood and salad bar is a great way to sample all the tasty offerings. On the regular menu you will find a variety of fish and shrimp dishes, live Maine lobster, and, of course, crab—every kind from Alaskan and king to Maryland blue. The service is friendly and relatively prompt.

8496 Palm Pkwy., Orlando, FL. 32836. (Just off Apopka-Vineland across and up from Hotel Plaza Blvd.) © 407/239-1888. www.landrysrestaurants.com. Reservations accepted. Entrees $10–$20. AE, DC, DISC, MC, V. Open daily 11:30am–11:00pm. Free self-parking. Take I-4 to exit 68 (535) and turn right, follow past the Crossroads to Palm Pkwy., turn right. The restaurant is back a bit on the right.

INEXPENSIVE

Romano's Macaroni Grill ★ *Value* NORTHERN ITALIAN   Though it's part of a multi-state chain, Romano's has the down-to-earth cheerfulness and friendly service of a mom-and-pop joint. The laidback atmosphere makes it a good place for families or those looking for a casual dinner. The menu offers thin-crust pizzas made in a wood-burning oven and topped with such items as barbecued chicken. The grilled chicken portobello (simmering between smoked mozzarella and spinach orzo pasta) is worth the visit.

12148 Apopka-Vineland Rd. (just north of County Rd. 535/Palm Pkwy.). ☎ **407/239-6676.** www.macaroni grill.com. Main courses $6–$9 at lunch; $8–$17 at dinner (most under $12). AE, DC, DISC, MC, V. Sun–Thurs 11:30am–10pm; Fri–Sat 11:30am–11pm. Free self-parking. Take I-4 Exit 68, Hwy. 535/Apopka-Vineland Rd. north and continue straight when Hwy. 535 goes to the right. Romano's is about 2 blocks on the left.

PLACES TO DINE IN UNIVERSAL ORLANDO

Universal Orlando's CityWalk and its resorts are home to a number of good dining spots.

VERY EXPENSIVE

Emeril's 😊😊 NEW ORLEANS   It's next to impossible to get short-term reservations for dinner here unless you're willing to take your chances with no-shows. If you do get in, you'll find the dynamic, Creole-inspired cuisine is worth the struggle. Best bets are andouille-crusted redfish (a moist white fish with roasted pecan-vegetable relish and meunière sauce) and kosher-salt-and-cracked-black pepper-dusted rib-eye steak with wild mushroom bread pudding and grilled vegetables. The back half of the building is a glass-walled 12,000-bottle aboveground cellar. If you want a show, we recommend one of eight counter seats, where you can watch chefs working their magic; but to get one, reservations are required *excruciatingly* (2–3 months, at least) early.

Note: Lunch costs about half what you'll spend on dinner, and the menu and portions are almost the same. It's also easier to get a midday reservation. No matter when you come, leave the kids at home—this restaurant caters to adults.

6000 Universal Studios Blvd., in CityWalk. ☎ **407/224-2424.** www.emerils.com. Reservations necessary. Main courses $18–$28 at lunch; $18–$45 at dinner. Daily 11:30am–2:30pm and 5:30–10pm (until 11pm Fri–Sat). AE, DISC, MC, V. Parking $8 (free after 6pm). From I-4, take the Kirkman Rd./Hwy. 435 exit and follow the signs to Universal.

EXPENSIVE

Tchoup Chop 😊😊 PACIFIC RIM   Pronounced "chop chop," Emeril Lagasse's second restaurant in Orlando is named for the location of his original restaurant, Tchoupitoulous Street in New Orleans. The exhibition kitchen offers a look at chefs making Polynesian- and Asian-influenced entrees such as Kona coffee glazed duck breast with duck and vegetable chow mein; and grilled rib-eye steak with garlic mashed potatoes, fried Maui onions, teriyaki sauce, and stir-fried vegetables.

6300 Hollywood Way, in Universal's Royal Pacific Hotel. ☎ **407/503-2467.** www.emerils.com. Reservations strongly recommended. Main courses $15–$24. AE, DISC, MC, V. Daily 11:30am–2pm; Sun–Thurs 5:30–10pm; Fri-Sat 5:30–11pm. Valet parking $4. From I-4, take the Kirkman Rd./Hwy. 435 exit, and follow the signs to Universal.

MODERATE

Pastamore Ristorante SOUTHERN ITALIAN   The antipasto primo here is a meal unto itself, and includes bruschetta, eggplant Caponata, melon with prosciutto, grilled portobello mushrooms, Italian cold cuts, olives, plum tomatoes, mozzarella, and more. The menu also has traditional options such as veal Marsala, chicken piccata, shrimp scampi, fettuccine Alfredo, lasagna, and pizza. An open kitchen allows diners a view of the chefs at work. You can also eat in a cafe where lighter fare—breakfast and sandwiches—is served from 8am to 2am.

1000 Universal Studios Plaza, in CityWalk. ☎ **407/363-8000.** www.universalorlando.com. Reservations accepted. Main courses $7–$18. AE, DISC, MC, V. Daily 5pm–midnight. Parking $8 (free after 6pm). From I-4, take the Kirkman Rd./Hwy. 435 exit and follow the signs to Universal.

> ## Value Bring On the Barbecue
>
> I don't normally recommend places too far off the beaten path from the main tourist zones, but **Bubbalou's Bodacious BBQ** ⭐, 1471 Lee Rd., Winter Park (© **407/628-1212**; www.bubbalous.com) serves some of the best barbecue in Florida and is well worth the drive (about 5 min. from Downtown Orlando). Go for the full pork platter that comes with a heaping helping of pork and all the fixin's. The uninitiated should stay away from the "Killer" sauce if they value their taste buds; you might even taste-test the mild sauce before moving up to the hot. Main courses run $4 to $13. It's open Monday through Saturday from 10am to 9pm. To get here, take the I-4 Lee Rd. exit and follow your nose; Bubbalou's is on the left next to a dry cleaner.

PLACES TO DINE IN THE INTERNATIONAL DRIVE AREA

International Drive has one of the area's larger collections of fast-food joints, but the midsection and southern third also have some of this region's better restaurants. International Drive is 10 minutes by car from the Walt Disney World parks.

VERY EXPENSIVE

Atlantis ⭐ SEAFOOD/STEAKS/CHOPS   This intimate dining room has a rich, warm, woody feel, especially in the booths separated by etched-glass panels. Chef's specials such as a Mediterranean seafood medley (Florida lobster, grouper, shrimp, and scallops) frequently complement menu standards such as grilled sea bass or pan-seared duck and rock shrimp. Sunday's champagne brunch is served in the atrium. Themes change, but the menu often has treats such as quail, duck, lamb chops, Cornish hen, clams, mussels, snapper, sea bass, sushi, and much more. Although pricey, it's one of Orlando's more popular brunches.

6677 Sea Harbour Dr., in the Renaissance Orlando Resort. © 407/351-5555. www.renaissancehotels.com. Reservations recommended. Main courses $24–$36; Sun brunch $32 adults, $16 children 3–11. AE, DC, DISC, MC, V. Daily 6–10pm. Free self-parking; valet parking $9. From the I-4 Hwy., take the 417/Central Florida Pkwy., exit and follow the signs to SeaWorld.

Dux ⭐⭐ *Finds* INTERNATIONAL   Named for the Peabody's famous mallards, Dux offers a marvelous and oft-changing menu, as well as impeccable service. If it's there, try the succulent oven-roasted grouper with bok choy, mushrooms, and ginger sauce; or sample the tender veal chop marinated in apple cider and honey and served medium rare. The candle-lit dining room provides a wonderful atmosphere, and Dux is best reserved for a very special night out or a meal on an expense account.

9801 International Dr., in the Peabody Orlando. © 407/345-4550. www.peabodyorlando.com. Reservations recommended. Main courses $26–$45. AE, DC, DISC, MC, V. Mon–Sat 6–10pm. Free self- and validated valet parking. From I-4, take the Sand Lake Rd./Hwy. 528 exit east to International Dr., then south. Hotel is on the left across from the Convention Center.

EXPENSIVE

Ran-Getsu of Tokyo JAPANESE   Its authentic cuisine and sushi bar has made Ran-Getsu a popular haunt for moneyed Asian tourists, though some diners find the prices too high. *Tekka-don,* tender slices of tuna mild enough for first-timers, is a refreshing sushi choice. *Yosenabe* is a bouillabaisse with a savory twist—duck and chicken are added to the seafood mix. A Japanese drum team usually performs at 7:30 and 9pm, Thursday through Saturday.

8400 International Dr., near Orlando Convention Center. © 407/345-0044. www.rangetsu.com. Reservations recommended. Main courses $14–$35 (most under $25); sushi entrees $14–$41 (most under $25). AE, DC, DISC, MC, V. Daily 5–11:30pm. From I-4, take the Sand Lake Rd./Hwy. 528 exit east to International Dr., then south. Restaurant is on the right.

MODERATE

Café TuTu Tango ★ *Finds* INTERNATIONAL/TAPAS   Authentic cuisine and the eclectic atmosphere of a Mediterranean artists loft are the main draws to this interesting eatery. The portions are small, but the tastes are big. The roasted pears on pecan crisps are a must—they are topped with a Spanish blue cheese, a balsamic reduction, and served with arugula. The service is fabulous; your server will be happy to educate you about the menu as well as offer some great suggestions to tempt your taste buds.

8625 International Dr. © 407/248-2222. Reservations accepted but not required. Tapas (small portions) $4–$11. AE, DC, DISC, MC, V. Sun–Thurs 11:30am–11:00pm; Fri–Sat 11:30am–midnight. Free self-parking. From I-4, take exit 74A, Sand Lake Rd./Hwy. 528, east to International Dr., then south. It is on the left.

Ming Court ★ CHINESE   Its diverse menu makes this one of Orlando's most popular Chinese restaurants. The lightly battered, deep-fried chicken breast gets zip from a delicate lemon-tangerine sauce. If you're in the mood for beef, try the grilled filet mignon seasoned Szechuan-style. Portions are sufficient and the service is excellent. The 250- foot, ornately carved dragons that greet you upon approaching its entrance, gives you just a hint of what awaits you inside. The décor has a flair to equal the menu.

9188 International Dr., between Sand Lake Rd. and Bee Line Expressway © 407/351-9988. www.ming-court.com. Reservations recommended. Dim sum mostly $3–$5; main courses $7–$13 at lunch, $13–$36 at dinner. AE, DC, DISC, MC, V. Daily 11am–2:30pm and 4:30–10:30pm. Free self-parking. From I-4, take the Sand Lake Rd./Hwy. 528 exit east to International Dr., then south. It's on the right.

Siam Orchid ★ *Finds* THAI   Tim and Krissnee Martsching grow the mint, chiles, cilantro, lemon grass, and wild lime that go into their entrees. The star attractions include Pad Thai (rice noodles tossed with ground pork, garlic, shrimp, crab claws, crab meat, and crushed peanuts in a tongue-twanging sweet sauce) and Royal Thai (a curry with chicken chunks, potato, and onion in yellow curry sauce). Siam Orchid serves sake, plum wine, and Thai beers from a full bar.

7575 Universal Dr. (between Sand Lake Rd. and Carrier Dr.). © 407/351-0821. Reservations recommended. Main courses $12–$24. AE, DC, DISC, MC, V. Mon–Fri 11am–2pm; daily 5–11pm. Free self-parking. From I-4, take the Sand Lake Rd./Hwy. 528 exit east to Universal, then go north to the restaurant (on the left).

ONLY IN ORLANDO: DINING WITH DISNEY CHARACTERS

Dining with the Disney characters is a treat for almost any Disney fan, but it's a special one for those under the age of 10. The characters will greet, sign autographs, pose for photos, and interact with the entire family. These dining experiences are extremely popular, so make Priority Seating arrangements (© 407/939-3463) as early as possible, and call for schedules. Prices vary, but generally expect breakfast (most serve it) to be $17 to $20 for adults, $9 to $10 for kids 3 to 11; those that serve dinner charge $21 to $24 for adults and $10 to $11 for kids.

Character meals are offered at **Cape May Café** (in Disney's Beach Club Resort), **Chef Mickey's** (at Disney's Contemporary Resort), **Cinderella's Royal Table** (in Cinderella Castle, Magic Kingdom), **Crystal Palace Buffet** (at Crystal Palace, Magic Kingdom), **Donald's Prehistoric Breakfastosaurus** (in Dinoland U.S.A., Animal Kingdom), **Garden Grill** (in The Land Pavilion at Epcot), **Liberty Tree Tavern** (in Liberty Square, in the Magic Kingdom),

'Ohana (at Disney's Polynesian Resort), **Princess Storybook Breakfast** (at Akershus Castle in Epcot's Norway Pavilion), and **1900 Park Fare** (at Disney's Grand Floridian Resort & Spa).

5 Tips for Visiting Walt Disney World Attractions

Walt Disney World, home to the four major theme parks of Magic Kingdom, Epcot, Disney–MGM Studios, and Animal Kingdom, welcomes around 40 million guests in a typical year.

Besides its larger theme parks, Disney has an assortment of other venues, including Downtown Disney (Cirque du Soleil, DisneyQuest, and Pleasure Island), Blizzard Beach, Typhoon Lagoon, just to name a few.

Parking   Cars, light trucks, and vans pay $8. Visitors with disabilities can park in special areas near the entrances; ask the parking-lot attendants or call (©) **407/ 824-4321**. *Don't forget* to write down where you parked (area and row number), because after a long day at the parks, they all start to look and sound alike.

When You Arrive   Grab a park map. It not only tells you where the fun is but where to eat and where to shop as well. Pick up a copy of the daily entertainment schedule too. If you want to see certain shows or parades, you will need to know when to go. Don't forget to arrive early so you get a good seat.

Best Times to Visit   There isn't really an off season in Orlando, but crowds are usually thinner from mid-January to March and from mid-September until the week before Thanksgiving. The busiest days at all theme parks are generally Saturdays and Sundays, when the locals visit. Beyond that, Monday, Thursday, and Saturday are pretty frantic in the Magic Kingdom; Tuesday and Friday are hectic at Epcot; Sunday and Wednesday are crazy at Disney–MGM Studios; and Monday, Tuesday, and Wednesday are a zoo at Animal Kingdom. Major holidays attract scores of visitors: from Christmas to New Year's is a frenzied time and the week preceding and following Easter are out of control busy.

Note: Summer is the worst time to visit, because of the crowds, the heat, and the humidity.

Operating Hours   Park hours vary and are influenced by special events as well as the economy. Call ahead or go to **www.disneyworld.com** to check for operating times otherwise you could find yourself expecting to stay all night when in reality the park closes at 6:00pm. Not only will hours vary from park to park, but from week to week, and even day to day. This can greatly affect your plans in regards to what park you visit, and when so don't just assume, check the schedule ahead of time or once you arrive.

Tickets   There are several options, from 1-day to multiday tickets. The best choices are the 4- and 5-day passes. While they don't always save you money they add the flexibility of moving from park to park and returning on the same or multiple days. The following don't include **6.5% sales tax** unless noted. *Note:* Price hikes are frequent occurrences, so call (© **407/824-4321**) or visit WDW's website (**www.disneyworld.com**) for up-to-the-minute fees.

One-day/one-park tickets, for admission to the Magic Kingdom, Epcot, Animal Kingdom, or Disney–MGM Studios, are $54.75 for adults, $43.75 for children ages 3 to 9.

Four-Day Park Hopper Passes provide unlimited admission to the Magic Kingdom, Epcot, Animal Kingdom, and Disney–MGM Studios for any four days. Prices are $219 for adults and $176 for kids 3 to 9.

> ⌒ *Tips* **Advanced Ticket Purchase Saves Money**
> Purchasing your multi-day Disney tickets ahead of time can result in sub-stantial savings. You can save up to $22 by purchasing tickets for guests ages 10 and over in advance. A 4-Day Park Hopper purchased at the gate would cost $219, but if you buy it before you arrive (through Disney online, a participating Disney Store, or travel agent), it's only $202.

Five-Day Park Hopper Plus Passes also include your choice of two admissions to Typhoon Lagoon, River Country, Blizzard Beach, Pleasure Island, or Disney's Wide World of Sports. They sell for $282 for adults and $226 for kids.

Passes for 6 and 7 days are available as well.

One-day ticket to Typhoon Lagoon or Blizzard Beach is $32 for adults, $26 for children.

One-day ticket to Pleasure Island is $21. Because this is primarily an 18-and-over entertainment complex, there's no bargain price for children.

The **Ultimate Park Hopper,** available only to WDW resort guests and priced according to the length of your stay, can also save you money in the long run.

If you're planning an extended stay or going to visit Walt Disney World more than once during the year, **annual passes** ($379–$499 adults, $322–$424 children) are another great option.

6 The Magic Kingdom

The Magic Kingdom is home to the best known and most recognized symbol of Disney, Cinderella's Castle. Welcoming you as you walk down Main Street U.S.A., it is the center of this enchanting park. The **seven "lands"** surround the castle to form the most magical kingdom on Earth.

MAIN STREET, USA

The gateway to the Kingdom, Main Street resembles a turn-of-the-20th-century American street (okay, so it leads to a 13th-century European castle). Main Street is best left for the end of the day when you're heading back to your hotel.

Right as you enter Main Street, you can board the **Walt Disney World Railroad,** an authentic 1928 steam-powered train for a 15-minute trip clockwise around the perimeter of the park. It's a good way to travel if you're headed to one of its three stations—the park entrance, Frontierland, and Mickey's Toontown Fair—or if you just want to go for a relaxing ride with shorter lines.

ADVENTURELAND

Cross a bridge and stroll through an exotic jungle of foliage, thatched roofs, and totems. Amid dense vines and stands of bamboo, drums are beating and swashbuckling adventures are beginning.

On the 10-minute **Jungle Cruise**, you sail through an African veldt in the Congo, an Amazon rain forest, and the Nile river in Egypt among others. Dozens of animatronic creatures inhabit the hanging vines, cascading waterfalls, and tropical foliage.

The first major ride added to Adventureland since 1971, the **Magic Carpets of Aladdin** ⊛ delights wee ones and some older kids. Its 16 four-passenger carpets circle a giant genie's bottle while the camels spit water at the passengers. The flying carpets spin and move up, down, forward, and back.

In the classic **Pirates of the Caribbean** ✪, the pirates chase "wenches" as your boat passes audio-animatronic figures that include "yo-ho-hoing" pirates raiding a Caribbean town. After a lot of looting and boozing, the pirates pass out. This ride might be a bit scary for kids under 5 due to the unexpected yet small waterfalls and bits of darkness.

The **Enchanted Tiki Room Under New Management** is a very upbeat and enchanting show featuring a slew of tropical birds singing and telling jokes. It is a bit loud on the decibel front, but is otherwise cute and entertaining.

FRONTIERLAND

From Adventureland, step into the wild and woolly past of the American frontier. The landscape is straight out of the Wild West, complete with log cabins and rustic saloons.

The low-key **Big Thunder Mountain Railroad** ✪✪ roller coaster has tight turns and dark descents rather than sudden, steep drops. It's situated in a 200-foot-high, red-stone mountain with 2,780 feet of track through caves and canyons. Your train careens through the ribs of a dinosaur, under a thundering waterfall, past geysers and bubbling mud pots, and over a bottomless volcanic pool. It's tailor-made for kids and grown-ups who want a thrill but aren't quite up to tackling the big coasters. *Note:* You must be 40 inches or taller to ride.

The **Country Bear Jamboree** ✪✪ is a hoot. It's a 15-minute show featuring audio-animatronic bears belting out rollicking country tunes and crooning plaintive love songs.

Based on Disney's 1946 film *Song of the South,* **Splash Mountain** ✪✪✪ takes you flume-style past 26 colorful scenes that include swamps, bayous, caves, and waterfalls. Riders are caught in the schemes of Brer Fox and Brer Bear as they chase the ever-wily Brer Rabbit. Your hollow-log vehicle twists, turns, and splashes, sometimes plummeting in darkness as the ride leads to a 45-degree, 52-foot-long, 40 mph splashdown in a briar-filled pond. *Note:* You must be at least 40 inches tall to ride.

LIBERTY SQUARE

This zone depicts 18th-century America. Thirteen lanterns, symbolizing the colonies, hang from the Liberty Tree, an immense live oak. And you might encounter a fife-and-drum corps on the cobblestone streets.

Every American president is represented by a lifelike audio-animatronic figure in the **Hall of Presidents** ✪. Look closely, and you'll see them fidget and whisper. The show begins with a film, and then the curtain rises on America's leaders. Each president's costume reflects his period's fashion, fabrics, and tailoring techniques.

Once inside the **Haunted Mansion** ✪✪, darkness, spooky music, howling, and screams enhance the ambience. The slow-motion ride has bizarre scenes: a ghostly banquet and ball, a graveyard band, a suit of armor that comes alive, a talking head in a crystal ball, and weird flying objects. At the end, a ghost joins your car. It's a classic that's more amusing than terrifying.

FANTASYLAND

The attractions in this happy land are themed after classics such as *Snow White, Peter Pan,* and *Dumbo.* If your kids are 8 and under, you may want to make this and Mickey's Toontown your primary stops in the Magic Kingdom.

There's not a lot to do at **Cinderella Castle** ✪, but its status as the Magic Kingdom's icon makes it a must (not that you can really miss it, as it stands at

Tips FASTPASS

Don't want to stand in long lines? Disney parks use a reservation system whereby you go to the most popular rides, feed your theme-park ticket into a small ticket-taker machine, and get an assigned time to return. When you reappear at the appointed time, you get into a reasonably short line and then hop aboard. Here's the drill:

Hang onto your ticket stub when you enter, and head to the hottest ride of your choosing. If it's a FASTPASS attraction (they're noted in the guide map you get when you enter) and there's a line, feed your ticket stub into the waist-level ticket taker. Retrieve both your ticket stub and the FASTPASS stub that comes with it. Look at the two times stamped on the FASTPASS. Come back during that 1-hour window and you can enter the ride with almost no wait. In the interim, venture on out and experience another attraction or show.

Note: Early in the day, your window may begin as close as only 40 minutes after you feed the FASTPASS machine, but later in the day it could be hours. Initially, Disney allowed you to do this on only one ride at a time, however now you can get a pass for a second attraction 2 hours after your first assigned time.

185 feet tall). The namesake character appears on occasion, and Cinderella's Royal Table restaurant is located inside.

The elaborate and beautiful **Cinderella's Golden Carousel** ★★ was constructed by Italian carvers in 1917 and refurbished by Disney artists, who added 18 hand-painted scenes from Cinderella on a wooden canopy above the horses. Kids of all ages will enjoy this ride.

Dumbo the Flying Elephant ★ is a very tame kids' ride, in which the Dumbos go around in a circle, gently rising and dipping. If you can stand the lines, and they are usually quite long here, it's very exciting for wee ones.

Built for the 1964 New York World's Fair, **It's a Small World** ★ takes you to countries inhabited by appropriately costumed audio-animatronic dolls singing "It's a small world after all," in tiny doll-like voices. Every adult who has ever ridden this in the past will remember the tune as it can be difficult to get it out of your mind. *Note:* This ride is closed for refurbishment until mid-2005.

Mad Tea Party is a traditional amusement park ride with an *Alice in Wonderland* theme that's always a hit with the younger set. Riders sit in big pastel-hued teacups on saucers that careen around a circular platform while tilting and spinning. Adults may want to ground themselves when they get off as the kids tend to spin as fast as physically possible.

Debuting in 2003, **Mickey's PhilharMagic** ★★★ is by far the most amazing 3-D film I've ever seen. Covering one of the largest screens ever made for a 3-D movie, the production's special effects (similar in style to those in **Jim Henson's Muppet*Vision 3-D,** p. 495) are incredible. Many of Disney's most beloved characters make an appearance to help (or in some cases hinder) the attempts of Donald Duck to retrieve Mickey's magical sorcerer's hat. This is a must see for everyone.

On **Peter Pan's Flight** ⚸ you'll ride in airborne versions of Captain Hook's ship, and take a calm flight over nighttime London to Never-Never Land. You will fly overhead the mermaids, the ticking crocodile, the Lost Boys, Princess Tiger Lilly, Tinker Bell, Hook, and Smee. It's a fun ride for younger kids and Peter Pan fans of all ages.

Though it may still scare kids under 5, contrary to its name, in **Snow White's Scary Adventures** the storyline is bright, and the title heroine appears in pleasant scenes, such as one at a wishing well, and rides off to live happily ever after.

MICKEY'S TOONTOWN FAIR

Where's Mickey? This 2-acre site is a great place for small children to find him and his pals. Toontown offers a chance to meet Disney characters, including Mickey, Minnie, Donald, and Goofy and even have your photo taken with them (if you can make it through the sometimes seemingly endless lines).

The Barnstormer at Goofy's Wiseacre Farm ⚸⚸ is a mini–roller coaster likely inspired by Woody Woodpecker's Nuthouse Coaster at Universal Orlando (p. 501). It looks and feels like a crop duster that flies off-course and through Goofy's barn. The ride has very little in the dip-and-drop department, but a bit of zip on the spin-and-spiral front. (It even gets squeals from adults.) The 60-second corkscrew ride has a 35-inch height minimum.

Donald's Boat (S.S. Miss Daisy) ⚸ offers a lot of interactive fun, and the "waters" around it feature fountains of water snakes and other wet fun things that earn squeals of joy (and relief on hot days).

Mickey's & Minnie's Country Houses ⚸ are separate cottages that offer a lot of visual fun and some marginal interactive areas for youngsters. Mickey's place features garden and garage playgrounds. Minnie's lets kids play in her kitchen, where popcorn goes wild in a microwave and a cake comes to life in the oven as the utensils play melodies.

TOMORROWLAND

In 1994, Tomorrowland was revamped with a more futuristic feel, and recent additions have kept the atmosphere up to date. *Note:* Scheduled to open in late 2004, the family-friendly **Stitch's Great Escape** will recruit riders to help capture the infamous "experiment 626," who is wreaking havoc while loose in the galaxy. Disney animatronics will bring this adventure to life.

On **Buzz Lightyear's Space Ranger Spin** ⚸⚸, join Buzz and try to save the universe while flying your cruiser through a world you'll recognize from the original *Toy Story* movie. Kids enjoy using the dashboard-mounted laser cannons as they spin through the sky (filled with gigantic toys instead of stars). If they're good shots, they can set off sight and sound gags with their lasers. You may be riding this more than once if you have kids.

The cosmic coaster, **Space Mountain** ⚸ usually has *long* lines (if you don't use FASTPASS), even though it's years past its prime. Once aboard a "rocket," you'll climb and dive through the inky, starlit blackness of outer space. The hairpin turns and plunges make it seem as if you're going at breakneck speed, but your car doesn't go any faster than 28 mph. *Note:* Riders must be at least 44 inches tall.

The Timekeeper is hosted by a robot/mad scientist (Robin Williams) and his assistant, 9-EYE, a flying, camera-headed droid that moonlights as a time-machine test pilot. In this jet-speed escapade, the audience hears Mozart as a young prodigy playing for French royalty, watches da Vinci work, and floats in a hot-air balloon over Red Square. It's more for adults than kids.

Younger kids love **Tomorrowland Indy Speedway**, especially if their adult companion lets them drive (without a big person, there's a 52-in. height minimum for driving a lap). Teens and other fast starters find it just too slow—the cars go only 7 mph and are loosely locked into lanes.

PARADES, FIREWORKS & MORE

For up-to-the-moment information, see the entertainment schedule given in the park guide map that you get when entering the park.

Magic Kingdom's first new fireworks display in just over 30 years, **Wishes** ★★★ debuted in October of 2003 to lots of acclaim. It's precise mix of choreographed bursts, music and story is just amazing and has to be experienced to be appreciated. This is absolutely the best way to end your day in the Magic Kingdom. The fireworks go off nightly during peak periods, but only on selected nights the rest of the year.

A 20-minute after-dark display, **SpectroMagic** ★★ combines fiber optics, holographic images, old-fashioned twinkling lights, and a soundtrack featuring classic Disney tunes. The parade runs on a *very limited basis.*

7 Epcot

Epcot is an acronym for Experimental Prototype Community of Tomorrow, and it was Walt Disney's dream for a planned residential community. But, long after his death, it opened in 1982 as Central Florida's second Disney theme park.

The 260-acre park has two sections, **Future World** and **World Showcase**. It's so large that hiking World Showcase from tip to tip (1⅓ miles) can be exhausting. That's why some folks say Epcot really stands for "Every Person Comes Out Tired." Depending on how long you intend to linger at each of the 11 countries in World Showcase, this park can be seen in 1 day, but it's better to do it over 2 to take it all in properly.

FUTURE WORLD

Future World is centered on Epcot's icon, a giant geosphere known as Spaceship Earth. Major corporations sponsor most themed areas, and the focus is on discovery, scientific achievements, and tomorrow's technologies in areas running from energy to undersea exploration. Here are the headliners:

The fountains at the **Imagination** ★★ pavilion are magical—they fire "water snakes" that arch in the air and dare kids to avoid their "bite." The 3-D *Honey I Shrunk the Audience* ★★ show shrinks you, then terrorizes you with giant mice, a cat, and a 5-year-old who gives you a sound shaking. **Journey into Your Imagination** ★ features a park favorite, Figment the dragon.

Innoventions ★ is divided into two sections. House of Innoventions in **Innoventions East** heralds a smart house equipped with a refrigerator that can make your grocery list and a picture frame that can send photos to other smart frames. The exhibits in **Innoventions West** are led by Sega's Video Games of Tomorrow.

The largest of Future World's pavilions, **The Land** ★ looks at our relationships to food and nature. **Living with the Land** ★ is a 13-minute boat ride through a rain forest, an African desert, and the windswept American plains. **Circle of Life** ★ blends spectacular live-action footage with animation in a 15-minute, 70mm motion picture based on *The Lion King* that delivers a cautionary environmental message.

The Living Seas ★ pavilion's 5.7-million-gallon aquarium has a reef and 4,000 sea creatures, such as sharks, barracudas, parrotfish, rays, and dolphins.

A 2½-minute multimedia pre-show about today's ocean technology is followed by a 7-minute film on the formation of the earth and seas as a means to support life. After the films, you enter "hydrolators" for a hokey "descent" to the simulated ocean floor, where you get close-up views through acrylic windows of the denizens in a natural coral-reef habitat.

Get set to blast off to Mars on **Mission: Space** ★★★, Epcot's newest attraction. Sophisticated simulator technology developed in partnership with NASA and Hewlett Packard launch you on an amazing ride through space that feels a lot like the real deal (so some NASA astronauts have claimed, anyway). This one is definitely not for the faint at heart, and has a 44-inch height limit.

Spaceship Earth is the large, silvery geosphere that is Epcot's icon, but all that awaits inside is a bland 15-minute show/ride that takes you through the history of communications.

Test Track ★★ is a marvel that combines GM engineering and Disney Imagineering. The line for this one can be more than an hour long, so consider FASTPASS. Once you're in your six-passenger convertible, the 5-minute ride follows what looks like a real highway and includes a brake test, climb, and tight S-curves. There's also a 12-second burst of speed that reaches 65 mph on the straightaway. *Note:* Riders must be at least 40 inches tall.

Sponsored by Exxon, the **Universe of Energy** ★ pavilion is home to a 32-minute ride, **Ellen's Energy Adventure,** which features comedian Ellen DeGeneres being tutored by Bill Nye the Science Guy to be a *Jeopardy!* contestant. In the process, you learn about energy resources from fossil fuels and take a ride through the dinosaur age.

Housed in a vast geodesic dome fronted by a 75-foot-tall replica of a DNA strand, **Wonders of Life** ★★ offers some of Future World's most engaging shows and attractions. The *Making of Me* is a captivating 15-minute motion picture combining live action (starring Martin Short) with animation and spectacular in-utero photography to create the sweetest introduction imaginable to the facts of life. (Be aware; if your kids are under 8, this show may prompt certain questions about reproduction that you may or may not be ready for.) In **Body Wars,** you're "reduced" to the size of a cell in order to join a medical rescue inside the immune system of a human body. The motion simulator takes you on a wild ride through gale-force winds in the lungs and pounding heart chambers. This one isn't a smart choice for those prone to motion sickness or who generally prefer to be stirred rather than shaken. *Note:* Riders must be at least 40 inches tall. In the hilarious, multimedia **Cranium Command** ★★, you tag along with Buzzy, an audio-animatronic brain-pilot-in-training charged with a seemingly impossible task—controlling the brain of a typical 12-year-old boy. Celebrities play the boy's body parts as he encounters preadolescent traumas such as meeting a girl and having a run-in with the principal. *Note:* This pavilion is only open during busy periods and high season.

WORLD SHOWCASE

This community of 11 miniaturized nations surrounds a 40-acre lagoon at the park's south end. All of these "countries" have indigenous architecture, landscaping, restaurants, and shops. The nations' cultural facets are explored in art exhibits, dance or other live performances, and innovative films. The employees in each pavilion are natives of that country. The World Showcase opens at 11am or noon, so there's time for Future World if you arrive earlier.

Moments A Grand Nightcap

IllumiNations ✹✹ is a blend of fireworks, lasers, and fountains in a display that's signature Disney. The show is worth the crowds that flock to the parking lot when it's over—don't miss it! *Tip:* Stake your claim to the best viewing areas a half-hour before show time (listed in your entertainment schedule). The ones near Showcase Plaza have a head start for the exits. The Rose & Crown Pub in the U.K. pavilion (see earlier), offers a great view of the proceedings.

The architecture in **Canada** ✹✹ ranges from a mansard-roofed replica of Ottawa's 19th-century, French-style Château Laurier (here called Hôtel du Canada) to a British-influenced stone building modeled after a landmark near Niagara Falls. But the highlight is *O Canada!* ✹, a dazzling, 18-minute, 360-degree CircleVision film that shows Canada's scenic splendor, from a dog-sled race to the thundering flight of thousands of snow geese.

Bounded by a serpentine wall that wanders its perimeter, the **China** ✹ pavilion is entered via a triple-arched ceremonial gate inspired by the Temple of Heaven in Beijing, a summer retreat for Chinese emperors. Passing through the gate, you'll see a half-size replica of this ornately embellished red-and-gold circular temple, built in 1420 during the Ming dynasty. Gardens simulate those in Suzhou, with miniature waterfalls, fragrant lotus ponds, bamboo groves, corkscrew willows, and weeping mulberry trees. Outside, the amazing **Dragon Legend Acrobats** provide live thrills.

The **France** pavilion focuses on La Belle Epoque, a period from 1870 to 1910 in which French art, literature, and architecture flourished. It's entered via a replica of the Pont des Arts footbridge over the Seine and leads to a 1/10-scale model of the Eiffel Tower constructed from Gustave Eiffel's original blueprints. The big attraction here is *Impressions du France* ✹✹, an 18-minute film featuring the country's top sights and scenery set to the music of famous French composers.

Enclosed by castle walls and towers, the festive **Germany** pavilion is centered on a cobblestone square with pots of colorful flowers girding a fountain statue of St. George and the Dragon. The adjacent clock tower has glockenspiel figures that herald each hour with quaint melodies. Sixteenth-century facades replicate a merchant's hall in the Black Forest and the town hall in Römerberg Square. Model-train enthusiasts shouldn't miss the detailed **miniature German village** ✹.

One of the prettiest World Showcase pavilions, **Italy**, lures visitors over an arched footbridge to a replica of Venice's pink-and-white Doge's Palace. Other highlights include an 83-foot-tall bell tower, Venetian bridges, and a central piazza enclosing a version of Bernini's Neptune Fountain.

At **Japan** ✹✹, a flaming red *torii* (gate of honor) leads the way to the Goju No To pagoda, inspired by a shrine built at Nara in A.D. 700. In a traditional Japanese garden, cedars, yews, bamboos, willows, and flowering shrubs frame pebbled footpaths, rustic bridges, waterfalls, rock landscaping, and a pond of koi. The Yakitori House is based on the 16th-century Katsura Imperial Villa in Kyoto, considered the crowning achievement of Japanese architecture. Another highlight is the moated **White Heron Castle,** a replica of the Shirasagi-Jo, a 17th-century fortress overlooking the city of Himeji. The drums of **Matsuriza** ✹✹—one of the best performances in the World Showcase—entertain guests daily. There's also a gallery exhibit on **Japanese baseball.**

You'll hear marimbas and mariachi bands (including **Mariachi Cobre**) as you approach the festive **Mexico** ⍟ showcase, fronted by a towering Mayan pyramid modeled on the Aztec temple of Quetzalcoatl (God of Life) and surrounded by dense Yucatán jungle landscaping. Upon entering the pavilion, you'll find yourself in a museum of pre-Colombian art and artifacts. Down a ramp, after you have passed through the local shops, **El Rio del Tiempo (River of Time)** ⍟ offers an 8-minute cruise through Mexico's past and present.

When you enter **Morocco** ⍟⍟, note the imperfections in the mosaic tile in the Koutoubia Minaret, the prayer tower of a 12th-century mosque in Marrakech. They were put there intentionally in accordance with the belief that only Allah is perfect. The **Medina** (old city), entered via a replica of an arched gateway in Fez, leads to Fez House (a traditional Moroccan home) and the narrow, winding streets of the *souk,* a bustling marketplace where all manner of authentic handcrafted merchandise is on display. **Treasures of Morocco** is a daily, 35-minute guided tour (1–5pm) that highlights this country's culture, architecture, and history.

Inside **Norway** ⍟, a *stavekirke* (stave church), styled after the 13th-century Gol Church of Hallingdal, features changing exhibits. A replica of Oslo's 14th-century **Akershus Castle,** next to a cascading woodland waterfall, is the setting for the pavilion's restaurant (p. 478). **Maelstrom** ⍟, a ride in a dragon-headed Viking vessel, traverses fjords before you crash through a gorge into the North Sea, where you're hit by a storm (albeit a relatively calm one). Passengers disembark at a 10th-century Viking village to view the 70mm film *Norway,* which documents Norwegian history.

The **United Kingdom** pavilion beckons you with **Britannia Square,** a formal London-style park complete with copper-roofed gazebo bandstand, a stereotypical red phone booth, and a statue of the Bard. Four centuries of architecture are represented along quaint cobblestone streets. A formal garden with low box hedges in geometric patterns, flagstone paths, and a stone fountain replicates the landscaping of 16th- and 17th-century palaces. *Tip:* Don't miss **The British Invasion** ⍟, a group that impersonates the Beatles daily except Sundays, and pub pianist Pam Brody (Tues, Thurs, Fri, and Sun).

Housed in a Georgian-style structure, the 29-minute **U.S.A.—The American Adventure** ⍟ is a dramatization of U.S. history using video, rousing music, and a cast of audio-animatronic figures, including narrators Mark Twain and Ben Franklin. You'll see Jefferson writing the Declaration of Independence, Matthew Brady photographing a family being divided by the Civil War, the stock market crash of 1929, the attack on Pearl Harbor, and the *Eagle* heading for the moon. Entertainment includes the **Spirit of America Fife & Drum Corps** and **Voices of Liberty,** an a cappella group that sings patriotic songs.

8 Disney–MGM Studios

You'll probably spy the Tower of Terror and the Earful Tower—a water tower outfitted with gigantic mouse ears—before you enter this park, which Disney bills as "the Hollywood that never was and always will be." Once inside, you'll find pulse-quickening rides and movie- and TV-themed shows. Movie sets remember the golden age of Hollywood and street performers dressed as starlets, gossip columnists, and studio execs wander around, interacting with the crowds (you might even get a chance to yell "cut!").

MAJOR ATTRACTIONS & SHOWS

The 35-minute **Disney–MGM Studios Backlot Tour** ⍟ takes you behind the scenes via tram for a look at the vehicles, props, costumes, sets, and special effects used in movies and TV shows. But the real fun begins once you reach **Catastrophe Canyon,** where an earthquake causes canyon walls to rumble. A raging oil fire, massive explosions, torrents of rain, and flash floods threaten you and other riders before you're taken behind the scenes to see how filmmakers use special effects to make such disasters.

Producers adapted the 30-minute **Beauty and the Beast Live on Stage** 🌀 show from the same-name movie. The sets and costumes are lavish, and the production numbers are pretty spectacular. Arrive early to get a good seat.

On **The Great Movie Ride,** film footage and 50 audio-animatronic replicas of movie stars re-create some of the most famous scenes in film. It's 22 minutes of sheer bliss for the cinema buff.

Peek into the world of movie stunts at the 30-minute **Indiana Jones Epic Stunt Spectacular** 🌀🌀🌀, which re-creates major scenes from the Indiana Jones films. Arrive early and sit near the stage for your shot at being an audience participant. Alas, this is a job for adults only.

Kermit and Miss Piggy star in **Jim Henson's Muppet*Vision 3D** 🌀🌀, a must-see film that marries Jim Henson's puppets with Disney audio-animatronics, special-effects, 70mm film, and 3-D technology. The coming-at-you action includes flying Muppets, cream pies, and cannonballs, as well as high winds, fiber-optic fireworks, bubble showers, even an actual spray of water. The 25-minute show runs continuously.

At press time, **Disney** was revamping the **Magic of Disney Animation**, ditching the old but beloved tour hosted by Walter Cronkite and Robin Williams in favor of more interactive options. The new attraction is set to feature characters from Disney's *Mulan* interacting with a live actor and a video on the making of that film. Visitors will also get a chance to watch real animators at work and ask questions about the animation process before attempting their own Disney character drawings while under the supervision of a working animator.

Younger audiences (2–5) love the 20-minute **Playhouse Disney—Live on Stage!,** where they meet characters from *Bear in the Big Blue House, The Book of Pooh,* and others. It encourages preschoolers to dance, sing, and play along with the cast. It happens several times a day. Check your schedule.

Want the best thrill ride WDW has to offer? Then tackle the fast-and-furious **Rock 'n' Roller Coaster** 🌀🌀🌀. You sit in a 24-passenger "stretch limo" with 120 speakers that blare Aerosmith at 32,000 watts as you blast from 0 to 60 mph in 2.8 seconds, then fly into the first gut-tightening inversion at 5Gs. Then you're off on a wild ride through a make-believe California freeway system in the semidarkness. *Note:* Riders must be at least 48 inches tall.

Moments A Nighttime Spectacle

The fireworks, laser lights, and choreography of **Fantasmic!** 🌀★★ make it a spectacular, 25-minute, end-of-day experience. The extravaganza features shooting stars, fireballs, animated fountains, a cast of 50, a giant dragon, a king cobra, and one million gallons of water. And everything is orchestrated by a sorcerer mouse who looks more than remotely familiar. Throughout, musical scores and characters from Disney classics entertain you.

Tip: Make a Priority Seating reservation for the Hollywood Brown Derby, Mama Melrose's Ristorante Italiano, or Hollywood & Vine and, when you do, ask for the Fantasmic! package (pricing depends on restaurant selected; ② 407/939-3463). After dinner you'll get preferred seating at the show.

Cutting-edge when it opened, **Star Tours,** based on the original *Star Wars* trilogy, is now a couple of rungs below the latest technology but is still fun. You board a 40-seat "spacecraft" for an otherworldly journey that greets you with sudden drops, crashes, and oncoming laser blasts as it careens out of control. *Note:* Riders must be at least 40 inches tall.

Disney continues to fine-tune **The Twilight Zone Tower of Terror** 🌟🌟🌟 into a true stomach-lifter. As legend has it, during a violent storm on Halloween night 1939, lightning struck the Hollywood Tower Hotel, causing an entire wing and an elevator full of people to disappear. And you're about to meet them as you star in a special episode of *The Twilight Zone.* The ride now features random drop sequences, allowing for a real sense of unknown, and new visual, audio, and olfactory effects have also been added to make the experience even more frightening. It's definitely a couple of grades above Doctor Doom's Fearfall at Islands of Adventure (p. 502). *Note:* You must be at least 40 inches tall to ride.

Hazy lighting creates an underwater effect in a reef-walled theater and helps set the mood for the charming musical show, **Voyage of the Little Mermaid** 🌟, which combines live performers with puppets, film clips, and more. All the movie's major songs, including the theme, "Under the Sea," are featured. The 17-minute show is a great place to rest and sing along.

Contestants can't win $1 million on **Who Wants to Be a Millionaire—Play It!** 🌟, but they can win points used to buy prizes ranging from collectible pins to a leather jacket or a trip to New York to meet Regis Philbin. Based on Disney-owned ABC TV's game show, the theme-park version features lifelines (such as asking the audience or calling a stranger on two phones set up in the park). Games run continuously in the 600-seat studio. Audience members play along on keypads. The fastest to answer qualifying questions become contestants.

9 Animal Kingdom

Disney's fourth major park combines exotic animals, elaborate landscapes, and a handful of rides to create yet another reason that many guests don't venture outside this World of Disney very often.

Animal Kingdom is a 500-acre park for animals, a conservation venue as much as an attraction, so it's easy for most of the animals to escape your eyes here. Busch Gardens (p. 505) at 335 acres has fewer places for critters to play hide-and-seek, so it's easier to see them there if you're up for the 3-hour round-trip to Tampa. Animal Kingdom wins the battle of the shows with **Tarzan Rocks!** and **Festival of the Lion King,** but Busch wins hands-down the battle of thrill rides with its five roller coasters.

DISCOVERY ISLAND

Like Cinderella Castle in the Magic Kingdom, the 14-story **Tree of Life** 🌟🌟 is the park's central landmark. WDW artisans built the tree, which has 8,000 limbs, 103,000 leaves, and 325 mammals, reptiles, amphibians, bugs, birds, Mickeys, and dinosaurs carved into its trunk, limbs, and roots. Teams of artisans worked for a year creating its sculptures, and it's worth a walk around its roots, especially on the way to see **It's Tough to Be a Bug!** 🌟🌟, a 3-D movie with pretty impressive special effects. Grab your glasses and settle into a creepy-crawly seat. It's not a good one for very young kids (it's dark and loud) or bug haters, but for others it's a fun, sometimes poignant look at life from a smaller perspective. Near the conclusion, a stinkbug truly awakens your senses.

DINOLAND U.S.A.

Enter by passing under "Olden Gate Bridge," a 40-foot Brachiosaurus reassembled from fossils. You'll also find a replica of "Sue," a 67-million-year-old Tyrannosaurus Rex skeleton that was worked on by paleontologist here before being shipped to her new home at Chicago's Field Museum.

Kids love the chance to slip, slither, slide, and slink through **The Boneyard** ✫, a giant playground, where they can discover the real-looking remains of Triceratops, T-Rex, and other vanished giants. It's also a great place for parents to take a break from the pavement pounding of a day in the park.

Dinosaur hurls you through darkness in CTX Rover "time machines" that pass an array of snarling (though somewhat hokey) dinosaurs. Young children may find the dinos and darkness a bit frightening. *Note:* You must be 40 inches or taller to climb aboard.

Disney introduced **Primeval Whirl,** a spinning, free-style twin roller coaster in 2002. You control the action through its wacky maze of curves, peaks, and dippity-do-dahs. This is a modern version of those old carnival roller coasters of the '50s and '60s. *Note:* It carries a 48-inch height minimum.

Phil Collins's soundtrack and a cast of 27 very live performers (tumblers, dancers, and in-line skating daredevils) put on quite a show during the 28-minute **Tarzan Rocks!** ✫. The costumes and music are spectacular, second in Animal Kingdom only to "Festival of the Lion King" (see below).

TriceraTop Spin is a minithrill for youngsters. Dinosaurs attached to arms circle a hub while moving up and down and all around much like Dumbo (p. 489) at the Magic Kingdom.

CAMP MINNIE-MICKEY

Characters and one of the best theme-park shows in town are the main attractions in this small area of Animal Kingdom.

The **Character Greeting Trails** ✫ are a must-do for people traveling with children. A variety of Disney characters, from Winnie the Pooh and Pocahontas to Timon and Baloo, have separate trails where you can meet and mingle. Mickey, Minnie, Goofy, and Pluto also make periodic appearances.

Everyone in the audience comes alive when the music starts at the rousing, 28-minute **Festival of the Lion King** ✫✫✫ in the Lion King Theater. The festival celebrates nature's diversity, with a very talented troupe of singers, dancers, and life-size critters that lead the way to an inspiring sing-along that gets the crowd caught up in the fun. The action is onstage as well as moving around the audience. It is a sight and sound spectacular that shouldn't be missed. Make sure to arrive at least 20 minutes early.

AFRICA

Enter through the town of Harambe, a representation of an African coastal village on the edge of the 21st century. A central marketplace is surrounded by structures built of coral stone and thatched with reed by craftspeople from Africa.

Animal Kingdom doesn't have many rides, so calling **Kilimanjaro Safaris** ✫✫✫ the best may sound like a qualified endorsement. But the animals make it a winner as long as your timing is right. They're scarce at midday most times of year (in cooler months you may get lucky), so *ride this one as close to the park's opening or closing as you can*. Your vehicle is a very large truck that takes you through a simulated African landscape. You might see black rhinos, hippos, crocodiles, antelopes, wildebeests, zebras, or a lion.

Hippos, tapirs, ever-active mole rats, and some other critters are often on the **Pangani Forest Exploration Trail** ★★for your viewing, but the real prize is getting a look at the gorillas. They're not always cooperative, especially in hot weather when they tend to spend most of the day in shady areas out of view. Those who come early, stay late, are patient, or make return visits can be rewarded with a close look at some special creatures.

ASIA

Disney's Imagineers did a good job of creating the mythical kingdom of **Anandapur.** The intricately painted artwork is just another example of the lengths that Disney has gone to transport you from the everyday real world to the places of your imagination.

Kali River Rapids ★ is a good raft ride—slightly better than Congo River Rapids at Busch Gardens in Tampa, but not quite as good as Popeye & Bluto's Bilge-Rat Barges at Islands of Adventure (p. 503). Its churning water mimics real rapids, and some optical illusions will have you wondering if you're about to drop over the falls. You *will* get wet. *Note:* There's a 38-inch height minimum.

With **Maharajah Jungle Trek** ★, Disney keeps its promise to provide up-close views of animals. If you don't show up in the midday heat, you may see Bengal tigers through the thick glass, while nothing but air divides you from dozens of giant fruit bats (wing spans up to 6 ft.) in another habitat.

10 Other WDW Attractions

TYPHOON LAGOON ★★★

A storm-stranded fishing boat—the *Miss Tilly*—sits atop 95-foot-high Mount Mayday and overlooks this Disney water park. Every few minutes the boat blows its stack, shooting a 50-foot geyser into the air. It has several other attractions.

Castaway Creek's rafts and inner tubes glide along a 2,100-foot-long river that circles most of the park and includes a rain forest, caves, and grottoes. At **Water Works,** jets of water spew from shipwrecked boats.

Ketchakiddie Creek is for 2- to 5-year-old guests. An innovative water playground, it has bubbling fountains to frolic in, mini–water slides, a pint-size "white-water" tubing run, spouting whales and squirting seals, rubbery crocodiles to climb on, grottoes to explore, and waterfalls to loll under.

At **Shark Reef,** guests get free equipment and instructions for a 15-minute swim through this very small snorkeling area that includes a simulated reef populated by parrotfish, rays, and small sharks.

Typhoon Lagoon ★★, the park's 2.75-million-gallon wave pool, launches **big breakers** every 90 seconds. A foghorn warns you when, in case you want to head for cover. Young children can wade in the lagoon's more peaceful tidal pools—**Blustery Bay** or **Whitecap Cove.**

Humunga Kowabunga consists of three 214-foot Mount Mayday slides that propel you down the mountain on a serpentine route through waterfalls and bat caves and past nautical wreckage before depositing you into a bubbling catch pool. *Note:* You must be 48 inches or taller to ride this. **White-Water Rides** at Mount Mayday is the setting for three white-water rafting adventures—**Keelhaul Falls, Mayday Falls,** and **Gangplank Falls**—all offering steep drops coursing through caves and passing lush scenery.

Typhoon Lagoon is open from 10am to 5pm, with extended hours during holiday periods and summer (© **407/560-4141;** www.disneyworld.com). A 1-day ticket is $32 for adults, $26 for children 3 to 9.

BLIZZARD BEACH ✦✦✦

This 66-acre "ski resort" in the midst of a tropical lagoon is centered on the 90-foot Mount Gushmore.

Its 2,900-foot-long **Cross Country Creek** is a lazy tube run, but watch out for the cave, where you'll get splashed with melting ice. **Runoff Rapids** offers another tube job. This one lets you career down one of three twisting, turning runs through semidarkness.

Ski-Patrol Training Camp, designed for preteens, features a rope swing, a T-bar hanging over the water, the wet and slippery **Mogul Mania** slide, and an ice-floe walk along slippery floating icebergs.

Snow Stormers has three flumes descending from the top of Mount Gushmore, following a switchback course through slalom-type gates.

Summit Plummet ✦✦ is one of the most breath-defying adventures in any water park. Read every speed, motion, vertical-dip, wedgie, and hold-onto-your-breast-plate warning before hopping on. This starts slow, with a lift ride to the 120-foot summit. But it finishes as the world's fastest body slide—a test of your courage and swimsuit—that virtually goes straight down and has you moving sans vehicle at 60 mph into the catch pool. *Note:* It has a 48-inch height minimum.

Teamboat Springs is this World's longest white-water raft ride, twisting down a 1,200-foot series of rushing waterfalls.

Tike's Peak is a kiddie version of Mount Gushmore. It has short water slides, animals to climb aboard, a snow castle, a squirting ice pond, and a fountain play area for young guests.

Blizzard Beach is open from 10am to 5pm, with extended hours during some holiday periods and summer (✆ **407/560-3400;** www.disneyworld.com). A 1-day ticket is $32 for adults, $26 for children 3 to 9.

MINIATURE GOLF ✦

Hippos, ostriches, and alligators decorate the **Fantasia Gardens** course. This course is a good bet for beginners and kids. Seasoned mini-golfers probably will prefer the second 18-hole course, **Fantasia Fairways,** which is a scaled-down golf course complete with sand traps, water hazards, tricky putting greens, and holes ranging from 40 to 75 feet – this one can be tricky.

Santa Claus and his elves provide the theme for **Winter Summerland,** which offers two more 18-hole courses. The summer course is pure Florida, from sand castles to surfboards to a visit with Santa on the "Winternet."

Tickets are about $10 for adults and $8 for kids 3 to 9. The courses are open from 10am to 10 or 11pm daily. For information about Fantasia Gardens, call ✆ **407/560-4582.** For information on Winter Summerland, call ✆ **407/560-3000.** Find both on the Internet at **www.disneyworld.com.**

---

11 What to See & Do Beyond Disney: Universal Orlando, SeaWorld & Other Orlando Attractions

There are so many attractions in Orlando (over 95) that it's impossible to see half of them unless you're here for a month. The following should help you finish picking your must-see list.

UNIVERSAL STUDIOS FLORIDA

Even with fast-paced, grown-up rides such as Twister, Terminator, and Men in Black Alien Attack, Universal Studios Florida is fun for kids. And as a plus, it's a working motion-picture and TV studio, so occasionally there's filming being done at Nickelodeon's sound stages or elsewhere in the park. **Hanna-Barbera characters** usually are on hand to greet visitors, as is a talented group of actors portraying a wide range of characters.

TICKET PRICES   A **1-day ticket** costs $54.75 for adults, $44.95 for children 3 to 9. A 2-day, two-park unlimited-access pass is $100 for adults, $89 for children 3 to 9; a two-park preferred annual pass will run $169. This includes free parking and has no blackout dates. The two-park annual power pass is less expensive at $99; however, most holidays and a lot of weekends are blacked out and parking is not included.

As with Disney, Universal offers savings on ticket purchases if you purchase them before you leave home. If you buy your tickets online, you can get a 5-day ticket (good for both Universal parks and select CityWalk clubs) for the price of a 2-day ticket ($100 adult, $89 kids ages 3–9). You can pick your tickets up at the front gate of either park or have them sent (for a delivery charge) to your home.

THE FLEXTICKET   The least expensive way to see Universal, SeaWorld, *and* Wet 'n Wild is with a FlexTicket. This pass lets you pay one price for unlimited admission to participating parks during a 14-day period. A four-park pass to Universal Studios Florida, Islands of Adventure, Wet 'n Wild, and SeaWorld is $180 for adults and $146 for children 3 to 9. A five-park pass, which adds Busch Gardens in Tampa, is $215 for adults and $180 for kids. The **FlexTicket** can be ordered through Universal (✆ **800/711-0080** or 407/363-8000; www.universalorlando.com) or the other participating parks.

PARKING   Parking is $8 for cars, light trucks, and vans. Valet is $14.

MAJOR ATTRACTIONS

On *Back to the Future: The Ride* ★★★, you blast through the space-time continuum in a flight simulator built to look like the movie's famous DeLorean car. You twist, turn, dip, and dive—all the while feeling like you're really flying. *Note:* It's bumpy and might not be a good idea if you're prone to dizziness or motion sickness. Riders must be at least 40 inches tall.

Set in a parklike theater-in-the-round, the 25-minute musical, **A Day in the Park with Barney,** stars the Purple One, Baby Bop, and BJ. It uses song, dance, and interactive play to deliver an environmental message. This could be the highlight of the day for preschoolers, though for many adults, it can have serious, brain-eating effects.

Not long after you climb on a San Francisco BART train at **Earthquake—The Big One** ★★, there's an earthquake that's 8.3 on the Richter scale! As you sit helplessly trapped, concrete slabs collapse around you, a propane truck bursts into flames, a runaway train hurtles your way, and the station floods.

Tips **Goodbye Kong, Hello Mummy**

Kongfrontation was part of Universal Studios Florida when it opened in 1990, but the ride closed in September 2002 and was replaced as this book went to press with **Revenge of the Mummy.** The new $40-million indoor roller coaster will rely on speed, pyrotechnics, and robotics for its thrill factors as riders hurtle through Egyptian sets, passageways, and tombs in cars that move forward and in reverse. The 5-minute journey includes encounters with overhead flames and a skeletal warrior that hops aboard.

Soar with E.T. on a mission to save his ailing planet at **E.T. Adventure** 🎯, and you'll pass through the forest and into space aboard a bicycle.

The $45-million *Jaws* 🎯 features a boat ride into a 7-acre, 5-million-gallon lagoon, where a 3-ton, 32-foot-long, mechanical great white shark will attack you. You'll truly feel the heat when a wall of flame surrounds your boat as you char-grill the fish.

Buckle up for **Jimmy Neutron's Nicktoon Blast** 🎯🎯, one of Universal's new rides. Jimmy's Rocket Pod hurtles you through hyperspace thanks to sophisticated computer graphics, state-of-the-art ride technology, animation, and programmable motion-based seats. The attraction also features other popular characters, including SpongeBob SquarePants and Rugrats.

In **Men in Black Alien Attack** 🎯🎯, you board a six-passenger cruiser, buzz the streets of New York, and use your "zapper" to splatter up to 120 bug-eyed targets. You have to contend with return fire and light, noise, and clouds of liquid nitrogen (aka fog) that can spin you out of control. Your laser tag–style gun fires infrared bullets. The 4-minute, $70-million ride relies on 360-degree spins rather than speed for its thrill factor. *Note:* Guests must be at least 42 inches tall for this $70 million ride.

At the **Nickelodeon Studios** 🎯, you'll tour the sound stages where Nick shows are produced. You'll also view concept pilots, visit the kitchen where Gak and green slime are made, and try new Sega video games. This 45-minute behind-the-scenes walking tour is a fun escape from the hustle of the midway. A child volunteer gets slimed, but don't worry—it's only green applesauce or a reasonable facsimile.

Another new ride, **Shrek 4-D** 🎯 is a 20-minute show that can be seen, heard, felt and smelled thanks to motion simulator technology, OgreVision glasses, and special effects, such as water spritzers. The theater's seats are pneumatic air propulsion nodules that can turn and tilt. I expected more from Universal in the seating effects department, but the movie is definitely worthwhile.

James Cameron, who directed T2, supervised the $60 million **Terminator 2: 3-D Battle Across Time** 🎯🎯, which features Arnie and other original cast members (on film). It combines three huge screens with technical effects and live action on stage, including a custom-built Harley and six 8-foot-tall cyberbots. The crisp 3-D effects are among the best in any Orlando park. *Note:* Universal has given this show a PG-13 rating.

Two million cubic feet of air per minute (enough to fill four full-size blimps) create a funnel cloud, five stories tall at **Twister . . . Ride It Out** 🎯🎯. The roar of a freight train, at rock-concert decibel level, fills the theater as cars, trucks, and a cow fly by while the audience watches just 20 feet away. Crowds sometimes applaud when it's all over. *Note:* This show also has a PG-13 rating.

Woody Woodpecker's Nuthouse Coaster 🎯🎯 is a kiddie coaster that will thrill some moms and dads, too. Although only 30 feet at its peak, it offers quick, banked turns. The ride lasts only about 60 seconds and waits can be 30 minutes or more, but few kids will want to miss the experience. *Note:* The coaster has a 36-inch height minimum.

ISLANDS OF ADVENTURE

At 110 acres, Universal's second theme park (opened in 1999) is the same size as its big brother, Universal Studios Florida, but it seems larger. Roller coasters roar above pedestrian walkways and water rides slice through the park. It is, bar none, *the* Orlando theme park for thrill-ride junkies.

A few words of caution: *Nine of the park's 14 major rides have height restrictions.* Many of the same rides may not be suitable for those who are tall enough but are pregnant or have health problems, physical restrictions, heart, neck, or back problems, or a tendency toward motion sickness.

TICKET PRICES See the "Ticket Prices" information for Universal Studios Florida on p. 500.

THE FLEXTICKET See "The FlexTicket" information for Universal Studios Florida on p. 500.

PARKING Parking is $8 for cars, light trucks, and vans. Valet is $14.

MAJOR ATTRACTIONS
Port of Entry
This park gateway has five shops, four restaurants, and the **Island Skipper Tours,** which ferry passengers to **Jurassic Park.**

Seuss Landing
You will feel as if you have jumped right into the pages of a Dr. Seuss classic as you enter Seuss Landing. The main attractions here are aimed at youngsters, however anyone who loved the good Doctor as a child will enjoy the nostalgic fun.

Seuss fans recognize the giant candy-striped hat looming over the entrance to **The Cat in the Hat** ★★, and probably the chaotic journey. Comparable to, but a lot spunkier than It's a Small World at WDW, The Cat in the Hat puts you in a spinning couch that travels through 18 scenes from the famous book, retelling the tale of a day gone very much awry.

One Fish, Two Fish, Red Fish, Blue Fish ★ is a kiddie charmer similar to the Dumbo ride at WDW (including the ridiculously long line). Here, your controls let you move your funky fish up or down 15 feet as you spin around on an arm attached to a hub. Watch out for "squirt posts," which spray unsuspecting riders who don't follow the rhyme (and some who do).

Forget tradition and hop on **Caro-Seuss-El** ★★★. The not-so-normal carousel gives you a chance to ride whimsical characters from Dr. Seuss, including Cowfish, elephant birds, and Mulligatawnies.

The 19-station **If I Ran the Zoo** ★★ interactive play land features flying water snakes and a chance to tickle the toes of a Seussian animal. Kids can also spin wheels, explore caves, fire water cannons, climb, slide, and otherwise burn off excited energy that most adults can't remember ever having.

Marvel Super Hero Island
Thrill junkies love the twisting, turning, stomach-churning rides on this island filled with building-tall murals of Marvel super heroes.

The original web master is the star of the exceptional, special effects–laden **The Amazing Adventures of Spider-Man** ★★★. Passengers wearing 3-D glasses squeal as their 12-passenger cars twist and spin, plunge, and soar through a comic-book universe. There's a simulated 400-foot drop that feels an awful lot like the real thing.

Look! Up in the sky! It's a bird, it's a plane . . . uh, it's you falling 150 feet, if you're courageous enough to climb aboard **Doctor Doom's Fearfall** ★. The screams that can be heard far from the ride's entrance add to the anticipation. You're fired to the top, with feet dangling, and dropped in intervals, leaving your stomach at several levels. The fall isn't quite up to Disney's Tower of Terror (p. 496), but it's still frightful. *Note:* Minimum height is 52 inches.

On the **Incredible Hulk Coaster** ✫✫✫, you're launched from a dark tunnel and hurtled into the lower ozone while accelerating from 0 to 40 mph in 2 seconds. You will spin upside down 128 feet from the ground, feel weightless, and careen through the center of the park. Coaster-lovers will be pleased to know this ride, which lasts 2 minutes and 15 seconds, includes seven inversions and two deep drops. *Note:* Riders must be at least 54 inches tall.

Toon Lagoon

More than 150 life-size cartoon images let you know you've entered an island dedicated to your favorites from the Sunday funnies.

Dudley Do-Right's Ripsaw Falls ✫✫, which lies under Dudley's staid red hat, has a lot more speed and drop than onlookers think. Six-passenger logs launch you into a 75-foot dip at 50 mph. You *will* get wet on this ride. *Note:* Riders must be 44 inches or taller.

The three-story boat, **Me Ship, The Olive** ✫ is family-friendly from bow to stern. Kids can toot whistles, clang bells, or play the organ. Sweet Pea's Playpen is fun for young guests. Adults and kids 6 and up love Cargo Crane, which lets you drench riders on Popeye & Bluto's Bilge-Rat Barges (see below).

Popeye & Bluto's Bilge-Rat Barges ✫✫ are similar to the rafts at WDW's Kali River Rapids (p. 498), but they're faster and bouncier. Adding to the fun, you'll be squirted by water cannons fired from Me Ship, The Olive (above). The rafts bump and dip 14 feet at one point, as you travel a *c-c-cold* white-water course. You will get *soaked!* Riders must be at least 42 inches tall.

Jurassic Park

All of the basics and some of the high-tech wizardry from Stephen Spielberg's wildly successful films are incorporated in this lushly landscaped tropical locale that includes a replica of the visitor center from the *Jurassic Park* movie.

The **Camp Jurassic** ✫✫ play area has everything from lava pits with dino bones to a rain forest. Watch out for the spitters that lurk in dark caves. The multilevel play area has plenty of places for kids to crawl, explore, and spend energy. But keep an eye on young ones: It's easy to get confused in the caverns.

Jurassic Park Discovery Center is an amusing, educational pit stop that offers life-size dinosaur replicas and interactive games. The sequencer lets you combine your DNA with a dinosaur's. "Beasaur" allows you to see and hear as "they" did. The highlight is watching a velociraptor "hatch" in the lab.

On the **Jurassic Park River Adventure** ✫✫, after you enjoy a leisurely raft tour along a faux river, things get dicey. A T-Rex thinks you look like a tasty morsel, and spitters launch "venom" your way. The only way out: an 85-foot plunge in your log-style life raft. It's steep and quick enough to lift your fanny out of the seat. Expect to get wet. *Note:* Guests must be at least 42 inches tall.

The Lost Continent

Universal has created a foreboding mood in this section of the park, whose entrance is marked by menacing stone griffins.

Coaster crazies love **Dueling Dragons** ✫✫✫, an intertwined set of two leg-dangling racers that climb to 125 feet, invert five times, and three times come within 12 inches of each other as the dragons test your bravery and bowels. There's a special (longer!) line for the front seat. *Note:* Riders must be at least 54 inches tall.

The Flying Unicorn ✫✫ is a small roller coaster that travels through a mythical forest with a fast, corkscrew run sure to earn squeals, but probably not at the risk of losing one's lunch. Riders must be at least 36 inches tall.

Those who notice it have fun at **The Mystic Fountain** ✦, a "smart" fountain that especially delights kids. It can "see," "hear," and talk, leading to a lot of kibitzing with those who stand before it and take the time to kibitz back. But be careful: It can squirt you.

The park's best show (given the lack of competition, that's something of a backhanded compliment), **Poseidon's Fury** ✦ has changed a couple of times, but still revolves around a battle between the evil Poseidon, god of the sea, and Zeus, king of the gods. Speaking of revolving, you'll pass through a small room that has a 42-foot vortex where 17,500 gallons of water swirl around you, barrel-roll style, and see the gods hurl fireballs at each other.

SEAWORLD

This 200-acre marine-life park explores the mysteries of the deep by combining conservation awareness with entertainment. Over the years it has expanded by adding more rides, additional entertainment venues, and of course more wildlife. While not as large as its neighbors (Universal and Disney), and won't leave you as thoroughly exhausted as its neighbors can, SeaWorld (✆ **800/327-2424** or 407/351-3600; www.seaworld.com) is a must see for anyone visiting the Orlando area.

TICKET PRICES   A **1-day ticket** costs $53.95 for ages 10 and over, $44.95 for children 3 to 9, plus 6% sales tax. If you purchase tickets online (at home only) at least 7 days in advance from the time of your visit, you can save an additional 10%, making the tickets $49 for an adult and $40.45 for kids 3 to 9.

MULTI-PARK PASSES   For information on the **FlexTicket,** see p. 500. The **Value Ticket** is a 2-day pass good for 1 day at SeaWorld and 1 day at Bush Gardens Tampa Bay. Prices are $89.95 adult and $80.95 kids ages 3 to 9. (This is a savings of up to $18 if tickets are purchased separately).

Multi-day and multi-park **Passports** are also available. These are essentially annual passes, good for either 1 or 2 years, and cover 1, 2, or 3 parks, depending on which level you choose—gold, silver, or platinum. The passes start at $90 and run up to $295. For more information, check **www.seaworld.com**.

PARKING   Parking is $8 for cars, light trucks, and vans. For a few dollars more, you can park close to the entrance in a special designated section.

MAJOR ATTRACTIONS

A lovable sea lion and otter, with a supporting cast of walruses and harbor seals, appear in **Clyde & Seamore Take Pirate Island** ✦, fish-breath comedy with a swashbuckling conservation theme. It's corny, but allot of fun. Just watch out if you enter to close to showtime; the mime entertaining the crowds ahead of time may target you for the audiences amusement.

Taking a cue from Disney Imagineers, SeaWorld created a story to go with its $30 million water coaster, **Journey to Atlantis** ✦✦. But what really matters is the drop—a wild plunge from 60 feet with lugelike curves. *Note:* Riders must be at least 42 inches tall, and pregnant women as well as those with heart, neck, or back problems should not ride.

Atlantic bottlenose dolphins perform flips and high jumps, twirl, swim on their backs, and give rides to trainers at **Key West Dolphin Fest.** The tricks are impressive, but it's like any other dolphin show. If you go, see this before Shamu. He puts these little mammals to shame.

Kraken ✦✦✦, SeaWorld's deepest venture into thrill rides, starts slow but ends with speed. Its floor-less, open-sided 32-passenger trains plant you on a pedestal high above the track. You climb 151 feet, fall 144 feet, hit 65 mph, go underground three times (spraying bystanders with water), and make seven loops during a 4,177-foot-long course. It may be the longest 3 minutes and 39 seconds of your life. *Note:* Kraken has a 54-inch height minimum.

In **Manatees: The Last Generation?** ✦, underwater viewing stations, innovative cinema techniques, and interactive displays combine for a tribute to these gentle marine mammals. While this isn't as good as seeing them in the wild, it's as close as most folks get, and it's a much roomier habitat than the tight quarters their kin have at Epcot's The Living Seas (p. 491).

You are transported by moving sidewalk through Arctic and Antarctic displays at **Penguin Encounter**. You'll get a glimpse of penguins as they preen, socialize, and swim at bullet speed in their 22°F (−5°C) habitat. You'll also see puffins and murres in a similar, separate area. While it gives you a nice view of the penguins (and they are always a hit with the kids) the surroundings about the viewing area leave a bit to be desired.

The 3-acre **Shamu's Happy Harbor** ✦ play area has a four-story net tower with a 35-foot-high crow's nest, water cannons, remote-controlled vehicles, nine slides, a submarine, and a water maze. Most kids relish the freedom of running, jumping and climbing (and, of course, getting wet) after hearing "don't wander too far away from us" all day long.

Everyone comes to SeaWorld to see Shamu and his friends—the stars of the well-choreographed show, **The Shamu Adventure** ✦✦✦. When you hear the warning that Hurricane Shamu is approaching, it's time for those sitting in the first 14 rows to hightail it. Those who don't are drenched with *icy water* as the orcas race around the pool, creating a huge wave that rolls over the edge and into the audience.

SeaWorld has added 220 species to its old Shark Encounter attraction and created **Terrors of the Deep**. The pools out front have small sharks and rays (feeding isn't allowed). The interior aquariums have big eels, poisonous lionfish, menacing barracudas, and bug-eyed pufferfish.

Enveloping guests in the beauty, exhilaration, and danger of a polar expedition, **Wild Arctic** ✦ combines a high-definition adventure film with flight-simulator technology to display breathtaking Arctic panoramas. After a hazardous flight over the frozen north, visitors emerge into an exhibit where you can see a playful polar bear, beluga whales, and walruses. Kids and those prone to motion sickness may find the ride bumpy. There's a separate line if you want to skip the flight.

A prime example of SeaWorld's ongoing expansion is **The Waterfront,** a 5-acre themed seaport village offering a variety of desperately needed restaurants, shops, and shows for all to enjoy.

Tips Shuttle Service

SeaWorld and **Busch Gardens** (p. 496), both owned by Anheuser-Busch, offer round-trip shuttle service ($10 per person) to get you from Orlando to Tampa and back. The 1½- to 2-hour one-way shuttle runs daily and has five pickup locations in Orlando, including at Universal and on International Drive. The schedule allows for about 7 hours at Busch Gardens. The service is free if you have a FlexTicket. Call ℭ **800/221-1339** for details.

DINING AT SEAWORLD

The park offers a trio of entertaining dining experiences. **Dine with Shamu** ($32 adults, $18 kids ages 3–9) offers visitors the experience of seeing Shamu up close (inside an area usually restricted to trainers during normal hours) while enjoying a buffet style meal. **Makahiki Luau** offers both island-style entertainment as well as a luau-style meal. The cost is $43 adults, $28 kids 3 to 9 (theme park admission is *not* required). The new **Sharks Underwater Grill** is an upscale restaurant geared mostly to adults that allows up-close viewing of sharks through a wall of glass. Entrees ($16–$27) are on the pricey side for park dining, but the food is very good and not the usual park blah. The interesting menu features such dishes as coconut-crusted chicken spears, Caribbean seafood ragout, herb crusted tuna, and scallops and shrimp with mango-papaya salsa.

DISCOVERY COVE: A DOLPHIN ENCOUNTER

Anheuser-Busch spent $100 million building SeaWorld's sister park, which debuted in 2000. Prices vary seasonally, but range from $229 to $249 per person (plus 6% sales tax) for ages 6 and up if you want to swim with the dolphins; and $129 to $149 if you will forego the dolphin swim. Double-check prices when you make your reservations (required to enter the park).

The **dolphin encounter** ✸✸✸ stars an amazing group of 28 of these mammals. They do tricks and take guests on brief but thrilling rides. The experience lasts 90 minutes, 35 to 40 minutes of which is spent in the lagoon with a dolphin. The rest is a classroom experience on these remarkable mammals.

Here's what you get for your money, with or without the dolphin encounter:

- A limit of *no more than 1,000 other guests a day.* (The average daily attendance at Disney's Magic Kingdom is 41,000.) This ensures your experience will be more relaxing and private—which is really part of what you are paying for in the first place anyway.
- Lunch, a towel, locker, sunscreen, snorkeling gear including a flotation vest, a souvenir photo, and free parking are also part of the deal.
- Other 9am-to-5:30pm activities include a chance to swim near (but on the other side of Plexiglas from) **barracudas and black-tip sharks.** There are no barriers, however, between you and the gentle rays and brightly colored tropical fish in the 1.3 million-gallon coral reef. The 3,300-foot-long Tropical River is a great place to swim or float in a mild current—it goes through a cave, two waterfalls, and a 100-foot-long, 30-foot-high aviary where you can take a stroll, becoming a human perch. There also are beaches for tanning.
- Seven consecutive days of **unlimited admission** to either SeaWorld *or* Busch Gardens. For an additional $30 per person, you can upgrade this option to 14 days of unlimited admission to both SeaWorld *and* Busch Gardens.

Get more information on Discovery Cove by calling ✆ **877/434-7268** or go to **www.discoverycove.com**. If you want to try it, make a reservation as far in advance as possible. Despite the price, it reaches its capacity almost every day.

12 Other Area Attractions

We've covered the monster parks. Now, we're going to explore some of the best smaller attractions. Many of these require less than a day (or a fortune) to see, so we'll note how much time and money to budget. **Add 6.5% sales tax** to the prices below unless otherwise noted.

IN KISSIMMEE

Kissimmee's tourist strip is 10 to 15 minutes west of Disney.

Gatorland ☆   Founded in 1949 with only a handful of alligators living in huts and pens, Gatorland now houses thousands of alligators and crocodiles on its 70-acre spread. There are three shows. **Gator Wrestlin'** uses the old "put-them-to-sleep" trick, but it's more of an environmental awareness program. **The Gator Jumparoo** is a crowd-pleaser in which some of these big reptiles lunge 4 or 5 feet out of the water to snatch meat from a trainer's hand. And **Jungle Crocs** is a showcase of toothy carnivores. The new **Adventure Tours** program offers a number of hands-on experiences, including a chance to wrangle and doctor alligators with trainers by your side ($190, minimum age 12). Plan to spend around 4 to 5 hours here. It makes for a entertaining afternoon away from the hustle and bustle of the major parks.

14501 S. Orange Blossom Trail (U.S. 441; between Osceola Pkwy. and Hunter's Creek Blvd.). ℂ 800/393-5297 or 407/855-5496. www.gatorland.com. Admission $20 adults, $9.95 children 3–12 (plus tax). Open daily at 9am; closing times vary. Free parking. From I-4, take the Osceola Pkwy. exit east to U.S. 17/92/441 and go left/north. Gatorland is 1½ miles on the right.

ON INTERNATIONAL DRIVE

Like Kissimmee attractions, these are a 10- to 15-minute drive from the Disney area and 5 to 10 minutes from Universal Orlando.

Wet 'n Wild ☆☆   Orlando's favorite non-Disney water park offers 25 acres of fun including: **Fuji Flyer,** a six-story, four-passenger toboggan run through 450 feet of banked curves; **The Surge,** one of the longest (580 ft. of curves) and fastest multipassenger tube rides in the Southeast; and **Black Hole,** a two-person, spaceship-style raft that makes a 500-foot, twisting, turning voyage through darkness (all three require that kids 36–48 in. tall be accompanied by an adult). You also can ride **Raging Rapids,** a simulated white-water run with a waterfall plunge; **Blue Niagara,** a 300-foot-long, six-story loop-and-dipster that also has a plunge (48-in. height minimum); **Knee Ski,** a cable-operated knee-boarding course that's open in warm-weather months only (56-in. height minimum); and **Mach 5,** a trio of twisting, turning flumes. The park also has a large kids' area with mini-versions of the big rides. Plan on a full day here.

In addition to the admission prices below, Wet 'n Wild is part of the multi-day **FlexTicket package** that includes admission to Universal Orlando (which owns this attraction), SeaWorld, and Busch Gardens in Tampa. See "The FlexTicket" on p. 500 for details and prices.

6200 International Dr. (at Universal Blvd.). ℂ 800/992-9453 or 407/351-1800. www.wetnwild.com. Admission $35.09 adults, $29 children 3–9. Hours vary seasonally, weather permitting. You can rent tubes ($4), towels ($2), and lockers ($5); all require an additional $2 deposit refundable upon return. Parking is $6 for cars, light trucks, and vans. From I-4, take the Universal Orlando exit and follow the signs.

ELSEWHERE IN ORLANDO

These attractions are about a 30-minute drive from the Disney area.

Harry P. Leu Gardens *Value*   This 50-acre garden offers a respite from theme-park razzle-dazzle. Paths lead through camphors, oaks, palms, cicadas, and camellias—the latter represented by one of the world's largest collections, 50 species and 2,000 plants that bloom October through March. There's also an extensive rose garden. There are free 20-minute tours of his house, built in 1888. More extensive tours of the house and grounds cost $6 per person. It takes about 2 hours to see everything.

1920 N. Forest Ave. (between Nebraska St. and Corrine Dr.). © **407/246-2620.** www.ci.orlando.fl.us/departments/leu_gardens/. Admission $5 adults, $1 children grades K–12 (free Mon 9am–noon). Daily 9am–5pm; museum tours 10am–3:30pm (closed during July). Free parking. Take I-4 to the Princeton St. exit and go east, then right on Mills Ave. and left on Virginia Dr. Look for the gardens on your left, just after you go around a curve.

Orlando Museum of Art ⭐ This local heavyweight handles some of the most prestigious traveling exhibits in the nation. It hosts special exhibits throughout the year, but even if you miss one it's worth a stop to see the rotating permanent collection of 19th- and 20th-century American art, pre-Columbian art dating from 1200 B.C. to A.D. 1500, and African art. Allow 2 to 3 hours.

2416 N. Mills Ave. (in Loch Haven Park). © **407/896-4231.** www.omart.org. Admission $12 adults, $10.50 seniors and students, $5 children 7–18. Tues–Fri 10am–4pm; Sat–Sun noon–4pm; closed Mondays and major holidays. Free parking. Take the I-4 Princeton St. exit east and follow signs to Loch Haven Park.

Orlando Science Center ⭐⭐ *(Finds)* The four-story center has 10 exhibit halls that explore everything from swamps to the plains of Mars. One of the big attractions is the **Dr. Phillips CineDome,** a 310-seat theater that presents films, planetarium shows, and laser-light displays. **KidsTown** has a pint-size park and construction site. **Science City** includes a power plant, and **123 Math Avenue** uses puzzles and other things to make learning fun. Allow 3 to 4 hours.

777 E. Princeton St. (between Orange and Mills aves., in Loch Haven Park). © **888/672-4386** or **407/514-2000.** www.osc.org. Admission (includes exhibits, Cinedome film, and planetarium show) $15 adults, $14 seniors 55 and older, $10 children 3–11. Tues–Thurs 9am–5pm; Fri–Sat 9am–9pm; Sun noon–5pm. Parking available in a garage across the street for $3.50. Take the I-4 Princeton St. exit east and cross Orange Ave.

BEYOND ORLANDO
Located in neighboring towns, these attractions are about a 45-minute drive from the theme-park zones.

Audubon of Florida—National Center for Birds of Prey ⭐ *(Finds)* In addition to being a rehabilitation center—one of the biggest and most successful in the Southeast—this is a great place to get to know rehabilitated winged wonders that roost here and earn their keep by entertaining the relatively few visitors who come. Allow 2 hours. It's worth the drive.

1101 Audubon Way, Maitland. © **407/644-0190.** www.adoptabird.org. Admission $5 adults, $4 children 3–12. Tues–Sun 10am–4pm, closed Mondays and federal holidays. From Orlando, go north on I-4 to Lee Rd., turn right/east, and at the 1st light (Wymore Rd.) go left, then right/east at the next light (Kennedy Blvd.). Continue ½ mile to East Ave., turn left, and go to the stop sign at Audubon Way. Turn left, and the center is on the right.

Charles Hosmer Morse Museum of American Art ⭐ *(Value)* Louis Comfort Tiffany left a fingerprint on this museum, which has 40 vibrantly colored windows and 21 paintings of his. There are also non-Tiffany windows by Frank Lloyd Wright, paintings by John Singer Sargent and Maxfield Parrish, and photographs by Tiffany and other 19th-century artists. Allow 2 hours.

445 Park Ave. N., Winter Park © **407/645-5311.** www.inusa.com/tour/fl/orlando/morse.htm. Admission $3 adults, $1 children 12–17. Tues–Sat 9:30am–4pm; Sun 1–4pm; open Friday evenings 4-8pm at no charge. Take I-4 to Fairbanks Ave. and exit east to Park Ave., and go left for 4 traffic lights.

13 Staying Active

SPORTS ACTIVITIES
If you want some exercise other than walking the parks, Walt Disney World and the surrounding areas have plenty of recreational options. Most of the following are open to everyone, no matter where you're staying (we note the exceptions below).

BICYCLING   Bike rentals (single and multispeed bikes for adults, tandems, baby seats, and children's bikes including those equipped with training wheels) are available from the **Bike Barn** (℃ **407/824-2742**) at Fort Wilderness Resort and Campground. Rates are $8 per hour, $22 per day (including tax). Fort Wilderness offers good bike trails.

BOATING   With a ton of man-made lakes and lagoons, WDW owns a navy of pleasure boats. **Capt. Jack's** at Downtown Disney rents Water Sprites and canopy boats ($23–$37 per half-hour). For information call ℃ **407/828-2204.**

The **Bike Barn** at Fort Wilderness (℃ **407/824-2742**) rents canoes and paddleboats ($6.50 per half-hour, $12 per hour).

GOLF   Disney operates five 18-hole, par-72 golf courses and one 9-hole, par-36 walking course. The rates are $130 to $175 per 18-hole round for resort guests ($10 more if you're not staying at a·WDW property). For tee times and information, call ℃ **407/824-2270** up to 7 days in advance (up to 30 days for guests of the Disney resort and official properties). Call ℃ **407/934-7639** about golf packages.

The **Grand Cypress Golf Club** (℃ **407/239-1909**; www.grandcypress.com) at the **Hyatt Regency Grand Cypress Resort** (p.470) is one of the best in the country. Its four Jack Nicklaus–designed courses offer 45 challenging holes. The best of the lot is the New Course, an 18-hole tribute to the venerable Old Course at St. Andrews. The courses are open to guests only and greens fees run $115 to $175, depending on the season. Golf packages are available.

Beyond Mickey's shadow, **Golfpac** (℃ **888/848-8941** or 407/260-2288; www.golfpacinc.com) is an organization that packages golf with accommodations and arranges tee times at more than 40 Orlando-area courses. **Tee Times USA** (℃ **888/465-3356;** www.teetimesusa.com) and **Florida Golfing** (℃ **866/833-2663;** www.floridagolfing.com) are reservation services that offer packages and course information.

HORSEBACK RIDING   **Disney's Fort Wilderness** offers 45-minute guided trail rides daily. The cost is $32 per person. Children must be at least 9. Maximum weight limit is 250 pounds. For information, call ℃ **407/824-2832.**

The **Villas of Grand Cypresses' Equestrian Center** (℃ **800/835-7377** or 407/239-1938; www.grandcypress.com) offers 45-minute walk-trot trail rides for $45. A 30-minute private lesson is $55; an hour lesson is $100.

SWIMMING   The **YMCA Aquatic Center** has a full fitness center, racquetball courts, and an indoor Olympic-size pool. Admission is $10 per person, $25 for families. It's at 8422 International Dr. (℃ **407/363-1911**).

TENNIS   There are 26 tennis courts (most of them lighted) scattered throughout the Disney properties. Most are free and open to resort guests only on a first-come, first-served basis. Call ℃ **407/939-7529** to make reservations or for more information. The Racquet Club at the Contemporary Resort ($15 an hour per court) has six clay courts, all lighted for evening play, and offers lessons ($40–$70, depending on duration of lesson).

SPECTATOR SPORTS

BASEBALL   The **Atlanta Braves** play 18 spring-training games at Disney's Wide World of Sports beginning in early March. Tickets are $12 to $20. Call ℃ **407/839-3900** or see **www.atlantabraves.com** for more information. From April to September, the **Orlando Rays,** the Tampa Bay Devil Rays' Class AA Southern League affiliate, play their 70 home games at the same complex. Tickets through **Ticketmaster** (℃ **407/839-3900**) sell for $5 to $8.

BASKETBALL   The **TD Waterhouse Centre,** 600 W. Amelia St., between I-4 and Parramore Avenue, is the home of the **Orlando Magic,** which plays 41 of its regular season games here from October to April. Call ✆ **407/896-2442** or check out **www.nba.com/magic**. Single-game tickets are $25 to $175.

14 Shopping

Some of us get as much pleasure from shopping as from a good meal or show. But if you're going to ring registers in the theme parks, expect to pay top dollar. So plan a day out of the parks and be as savvy here as you are back home.

On International Drive, look for **Pointe Orlando,** 9101 International Dr. (✆ **407/248-2838;** www.pointeorlandofl.com), an open-air complex with three dozen stores including Tommy Hilfiger and Abercombie and Fitch.

There are several factory outlets, but their publicized discounts of 25% to 75% are often a mirage. You can avoid being taken by knowing suggested retail prices, so you can decide whether you're making a killing. **Belz Factory Outlet World,** 5401 W. Oak Ridge Rd. (at the north end of International Dr.; ✆ **407/352-9611;** www.belz.com), and **Orlando Premium Outlets,** 8200 Vineland Ave. (✆ **407/238-7787;** www.PremiumOutlets.com), and **Lake Buena Vista Factory Stores,** 155591 Apopka-Vineland Rd. (✆ **407/238-9301;** www.lbvfs.com), are the better ones, with the Premium Outlets having the best variety and nicest atmosphere to shop in.

Mall at Millenia, 4200 Conroy Rd. (✆ **407/363-3555;** www.mallatmillenia.com), is the new upscale kid on the block (Bloomingdale's, Neiman Marcus, Tiffany), while **Florida Mall,** 8001 S. Orange Blossom Trail (✆ **407/851-6255;** www.shopsimon.com), has Saks, Dillards, and more.

Old-stuff buffs love **Antique Row** on Orange Avenue in downtown Orlando. This collection of two-dozen shops is about as far away as you can get from the manufactured fun of Disney. Headliners include **Flo's Attic** (✆ **407/895-1800**), which sells traditional antiques.

15 Walt Disney World & Orlando After Dark

Central Florida has plenty for night owls to do. Parties last into the wee hours at **Pleasure Island, Downtown Disney, CityWalk,** and other hot spots.

DISNEY DINNER SHOWS

Hoop-Dee-Doo Musical Revue ★ *(Moments)*   As WDW's most popular show, Hoop-Dee-Doo requires Priority Seating reservations, which should be made as early as possible. The reward: You can feast on an all-you-can-eat barbecue. While you stuff yourself silly, performers in 1890s garb lead you in a foot-stomping, hand-clapping high-energy show that includes jokes you haven't heard since second grade.

3520 N. Fort Wilderness Trail (at WDW's Fort Wilderness Resort and Campground). ✆ **407/939-3463.** www.disneyworld.com. Reservations required. Adults $49, kids 3–11 $25, including tax and gratuity. Free parking. Show times 5, 7:15, and 9:30pm daily.

Polynesian Luau *(Moments)*   While not quite as much in demand as the Hoop-Dee-Doo, the Polynesian Resort presents a delightful (and new) 2-hour show that's like a big neighborhood party. **Disney's Spirit of Aloha Dinner Show** features Tahitian, Samoan, and Hawaiian singers, drummers, and dancers who entertain you while you feast on a menu that includes tropical appetizers, Lanai roasted chicken, Polynesian wild rice, South Seas vegetables, dessert, wine, beer and other beverages. It all takes place 5 nights a week in an open-air theater (dress for nighttime weather).

1600 Seven Seas Dr. (at Disney's Polynesian Resort). ✆ 407/939-3463. www.disneyworld.com. Reservations required. Adults $49, kids 3–11 $25, including tax and gratuity. Free parking. Show times 5:15 and 8pm Tues–Sat.

ENTERTAINMENT MECCAS
AT DISNEY

PLEASURE ISLAND   This 6-acre complex has clubs, restaurants, shops, and movie theaters where during the day you can enjoy for free whatever's open (only the restaurants). At night, for one admission price ($20.50 plus tax; ✆ 407/939-2648), you can go club hopping and rock into the wee hours every night of the week. The mood is festive, especially at midnight, when the New Year's Eve party gets started. *Note:* At night, this is primarily an adult venue. Here's the lineup:

Adventurers Club   The most unique of Pleasure Island's clubs, Adventurers occupies a multistory building chock-full of artifacts like 1940s aviation photos, hunting trophies, shrunken heads, Buddhas, and a mounted "yakoose"—a half yak, half moose that occasionally speaks, whether you've been drinking or not. In the Mask Room, the 100 or so masks move their eyes, jeer, and make bizarre pronouncements. Improv comedy takes place throughout the evening in the salon.

BET Soundstage ✮   This club grooves with traditional R&B and the rhyme of hip-hop. If you like the BET Cable Network, you'll love it. Boogie on an expansive dance floor or kick back on the terrace. The club sometimes has concerts for a separate charge. Call ✆ **407/934-7666.**

Mannequins Dance Palace ✮✮   Housed in a vast dance hall with a small-town movie-house facade, Mannequins is supposed to be a converted mannequin warehouse (remember, you're still in Disney World). This high-energy club has a big, rotating dance floor, and its popularity makes it one of the toughest nightspots to get into. It offers three levels of bars and hangout space that are festooned with elaborately costumed mannequins and moving scenery suspended from the overhead rigging. A deejay plays contemporary tunes filtered through speakers that could wake the dead, and there are high-tech lighting effects. You must be 21 to get in, and they're *very* serious about it.

The Pleasure Island Jazz Company   This big, barnlike club features contemporary and traditional live jazz. Most performers are locals, but about once a month there's a big name, such as Kenny Rankin or Maynard Ferguson.

Rock 'n' Roll Beach Club   Live bands play classic rock from the 1960s through the 1990s. There are bars on all three floors. The first level has a dance floor; the others offer arcade-style games, pizza, and more.

Motion   Pleasure Island's newest dance club is a hyperactive joint that features Top-40 tunes and alternative rock, and uses moody blue lighting to halfway convey the sensation that you're dancing the night away in space.

DOWNTOWN DISNEY WEST SIDE

House of Blues   This three-tier, barnlike building may be a little difficult for those with disabilities to maneuver in, but there really isn't a bad seat in the house. The atmosphere is dark, perfect for the oft-featured bluesy sounds that raise the rafters. The dance floor is big enough to boogie without doing the bump with a stranger, and food is served. ✆ **407/934-2583.** www.hob.com. Cover charges vary.

Moments **Not Your Ordinary Circus**

Cirque du Soleil, the famous no-animals circus in Downtown Disney West Side, seems to put all 64 performers onstage at once in the trampoline routine. Trapeze artists, high-wire walkers, an aerial gymnast, a strongman, and two zany clowns cement a show called **La Nouba** ★★★ (it means "live it up") into a five-star, multiact performance.

But, in a world of pricey attractions, this is one of the priciest. There are two ticket categories: $87 for adults and $52 for kids 3 to 9 (including tax) for center of the theater seats; $77 and $47, respectively, to the right and left of the stage. The 90-minute shows are at 6 and 9pm; days rotate. Call ✆ **407/939-7600** or check out **www.cirquedusoleil.com** for details.

CITYWALK

Located between Islands of Adventure and Universal Studios Florida, this 30-acre club-and-restaurant district (✆ **407/363-8000;** www.citywalk.com) is five times larger than Pleasure Island. Alcohol is prominently featured, so an adult should accompany all children and free-flowing peers.

You can walk the district for free or visit individual clubs for the cover charges in the following listings. CityWalk also offers two **party passes.** A pass to all clubs costs $8.95 plus tax. For $12 plus tax, you get a club pass and a movie at Universal Cineplex (✆ **407/354-5998**). *Note:* Daytime parking in the Universal Orlando garages costs $8, but parking is free after 6pm.

Bob Marley—A Tribute to Freedom   This hybrid bar/restaurant has a party atmosphere that makes the food more appealing as the night wears on. Jamaican food is served amid portraits of the original Rastamon. Reggae bands, local and national, perform on a microdot-size stage. The hours are daily from 4pm to 2am. ✆ **407/224-3663.** Cover $5 after 8pm, more on special nights. Must be 21 to enter after 10pm.

CityJazz   The cover includes the **Downbeat Jazz Hall of Fame** (which has memorabilia from Louie Armstrong and other greats) as well as the **Thelonious Monk Institute of Jazz,** a performance venue that's also the site of jazz workshops. The two-story, 10,500-square-foot building has more than 500 pieces of memorabilia representing Dixieland, swing, bebop, and jazz and is open Sunday through Thursday from 8pm to 1am and Friday and Saturday from 7pm to 2am. ✆ **407/224-2189.** Cover $5 (more for special events). Must be 18 to enter.

the groove   This club is Universal's answer to Mannequins at Pleasure Island, though it's not quite as popular and, therefore, has less of a waiting list. There's a high-tech sound system that will blow your hair back and a spacious dance floor in a room gleaming with chrome. A deejay plays tunes most nights, featuring the latest in hip-hop, jazz-fusion, techno, and alternative music. Bands occasionally play the house, too. Open daily from 9pm to 2am. ✆ **407/363-8000.** Cover $5. Must be 21 to get in.

Hard Rock Cafe/Hard Rock Live   The cafe side is the chain's standard—a theme restaurant with memorabilia and other tributes to rock's greats. The difference is that this one has the first concert hall with the Hard Rock name on the door. Call ahead to find out what acts are featured. Tickets for big-name performers sell fast. Hard Rock Cafe is open daily from 11am to midnight. © 407/351-5483; www.hardrock.com. No cover in the cafe; concerts range from $6–$150.

Jimmy Buffett's Margaritaville   Music from the maestro drifts through the building, and live tunes are performed on a small stage inside later in the evening. A Buffett sound-alike also strums on the back porch. Inside, there are three themed bars. If you opt for dinner among the palm trees, go for the true Key West experience. Early in the day that means a cheeseburger; later, it's one of several kinds of fish. Open daily from 11am to 2am.© 407/224-2155. Cover $5 after 10pm.

Latin Quarter   This two-level restaurant/nightclub offers you a chance to absorb the salsa-and-samba culture and cuisine of 21 Latin nations. If you don't know how to move your hips, there's a dance instructor to lend a hand. The music ranges from merengue to Latin rock. The sound system is loud enough to blow you into the next county, but before that happens you can leave on your own to peruse a Latin American art gallery. Open Saturday and Sunday from noon to 2am and Monday through Friday from 5pm to 2am. The restaurant closes at 10pm and the nightclub hours are 10pm to 2am. © 407/224-3663. Cover $5–$10 Thurs–Sat after 10pm.

Motown Cafe Orlando   Try finger food and sandwiches ($8–$16), or just enjoy the canned music of Motown greats like Smokey Robinson and the Supremes. A live band frequently plays. Motown Cafe's hours are Sunday through Thursday from 11:30am to 11pm and Friday and Saturday from 11:30am to 2am. © 407/224-3663. www.motown.com. Cover $5 after 9pm.

Pat O'Brien's *(Overrated)*   Just like the French Quarter, which is home to the original Patty O's, drinking, drinking, and more drinking are the highlights here. Enjoy dueling Baby Grands and a flame-throwing fountain while you suck down the drink of the Big Easy, a Hurricane. Open daily from 4pm to 2am. © 407/363-8000. Cover $5 after 9pm. Must be 21 to enter.

13

Northeast Florida

When driving through the elongated state of Florida, many people make the grave mistake of gunning their engines and jetting through the Northeast part of the state without as much as a single stop beyond the Cracker Barrels, Denny's, and gas stations lining the highways. Thankfully, Juan Ponce de León actually made the *fortunate* mistake of playing accidental tourist and discovering just how magnificent the Northeast part of the state truly is. You would do well to explore in his footsteps.

Northeast Florida traces its roots back to 1513, when the wanderlusty Spaniard Juan Ponce de León, who later undertook a misguided quest for the Fountain of Youth, sighted this coast and landed somewhere between present-day Jacksonville and Cape Canaveral. (He was a bit off course—he meant to land in what is now Bimini—but who can blame a guy who didn't have GPS?) Observing the land's lush foliage, he named it *La Florida,* or "the flowery land." In 1565, the Spanish established a colony at St. Augustine, a city that remains the country's oldest continuous settlement.

Not much, if anything at all, has changed in St. Augustine (in a wonderful way). The streets of the restored Old City look much as they did in Spanish times. But not everything in Northeast Florida is antiquated.

To the south there's the Jetsonian "Space Coast," where rockets blast off from the Kennedy Space Center at Cape Canaveral. In nearby Cocoa Beach you can witness the retro-fabulous phenomenon of surfers riding the rather sizeable waves. And in Daytona Beach, brace yourself for the deafening roar of the stock cars and motorbikes that make this beach town the "World Center of Racing." And don't blink, because you wouldn't want to miss Daytona's other pop cultural phenom, known as the MTV Spring Break bikini crowd.

A far cry from spring breakers on a budget, if you go north along the coast, you'll come to the monied haven of Ponte Vedra Beach, where golf definitely takes precedence over manual labor. Over in Jacksonville, Florida's largest metropolis and a thriving port city and naval base, experience a little taste of so-called city life before retreating back to the beach.

Up near the Georgia border, cross a bridge to Amelia Island, where you'll discover exclusive resorts taking full advantage of 13 miles of beautiful beaches. Amelia's Victorian-era town, Fernandina Beach, is yet another throwback to the past, helping to further render the Northeast region of Florida a fascinating juxtaposition of old, new, and somewhere delightfully in between. However you perceive it, just make sure not to make the mistake of missing it. After all, Ponce de León didn't blow off Bimini for nothing, you know.

1 Cocoa Beach, Cape Canaveral, the Kennedy Space Center & Melbourne ⋆

46 miles SE of Orlando, 186 miles N of Miami, 65 miles S of Daytona

The "Space Coast," the area around Cape Canaveral, was once a sleepy place where city dwellers escaped the crowds from the exploding urban centers of Miami and Jacksonville. But then came the NASA space program. Today, the region produces and accommodates its own crowds, especially hordes of tourists who come to visit the Kennedy Space Center and enjoy the area's 72 miles of beaches (this is, after all, the closest beach to Orlando's mega-attractions) and excellent fishing, surfing, and golfing.

Thanks to NASA, this is also a prime destination for nature lovers. The space agency originally took over much more land than it needed to launch rockets. Rather than sell off the unused portions, it turned them over to the Canaveral National Seashore and the Merritt Island National Wildlife Refuge (www.nbbd.com/godo/minwr), which have preserved these areas in their pristine natural states.

A handful of Caribbean-bound cruise ships also depart from the man-made Port Canaveral, and the number has grown slowly over the years. The south side of the port is lined with seafood restaurants and marinas, which serve as home base for gambling ships and the area's deep-sea charter and group fishing boats.

ESSENTIALS

GETTING THERE   The nearest airport is **Melbourne International Airport** (② 321/723-6227; www.mlbair.com), 22 miles south of Cocoa Beach, which is served by **Continental** (② 800/525-0280; www.continental.com) and **Delta** (② 800/221-1212; www.delta.com). **Orlando International Airport,** about 35 miles to the west, is a much larger hub with many more flight options and generally less expensive fares (p. 456). It's an easy 45-minute drive from the Orlando airport to the beaches via the Bee Line Expressway (Fla. 528, a toll road)—it can take almost that long from the Melbourne airport, where **Avis, Budget, Hertz**, and **National** have car-rental desks. **The Melbourne Airport Shuttle** (② 321/724-1600) will take you from the Melbourne airport to most local destinations for about $10 to $20 per person.

VISITOR INFORMATION   For information about the area, contact the **Florida Space Coast Office of Tourism/Brevard County Tourist Development Council,** 8810 Astronaut Blvd., Suite 102, Cape Canaveral, FL 32920 (② 800/872-1969 or 321/868-1126; www.space-coast.com). The office is in the Sheldon Cove building, on Fla. A1A a block north of Central Boulevard, and is open Monday through Friday from 8am to 5pm.

The office also operates an information booth at the Kennedy Space Center Visitor Complex (see below).

GETTING AROUND   A car is essential in this area. If you're not coming by car, you can rent one at the airport. **Space Coast Area Transit** (② 321/633-1878; www.ridescat.com) operates buses ($1 adults, 50¢ seniors and students), but routes tend to be circuitous and therefore extremely time-consuming.

ATTRACTIONS

In addition to the two attractions below, Brevard College's **Astronaut Memorial Planetarium and Observatory,** 1519 Clearlake Rd., Cocoa Beach (② 321/634-3732; www.brevardcc.edu/planet), south of Fla. 528, has its own International

Hall of Space Explorers, but its big attractions are sound and light shows in the planetarium. Call or check the website for schedules and prices.

Brevard Zoo *(Kids)*   This delightful small-town zoo has more than 500 animals including white rhinos, dingoes, red kangaroos, wallabies, cotton-top tamarins, crocodiles, howler monkeys, bald eagles, red wolves, and river otters. The zoo also offers a 10-minute train tour of the grounds ($2), kayak trips ($3), a new tropical garden inhabited by flying fox bats and muntjac deer, a free-flight aviary, and alligator feedings usually 3 days a week (check the schedule or Internet site below for days and times; they change as the gators' appetites do over the year). There's also a petting zoo where the cute and cuddly critters include fallow deer and Amazon parrots. The zoo's newest attraction is the 10-acre Expedition Africa exhibit, where impala, gazelle, duiker, and Scimitar-horned oryx chill out over the savanna.

8225 N. Wickham Rd., Melbourne (just east of I-95 Exit 73/Wickham Rd.). © 321/254-9453. www.brevard zoo.org. Admission $9 adults, $8 seniors, $6 children 3–12, free for kids under 3. Daily 10am–5pm.

John F. Kennedy Space Center *(★★★)*   Whether you're a space buff or not, you'll appreciate the sheer grandeur of the facilities and technological achievements displayed at NASA's primary space-launch facility. Astronauts departed Earth at this site in 1969 en route to the most famous "small step" in history—humankind's first walk on the moon—and today's space shuttles still regularly lift off from here on their latest missions.

Since all roads other than Fla. 405 and Fla. 3 are closed to the public in the space center, you must begin your visit at the **Kennedy Space Center Visitor Complex.** A bit like a themed amusement park, this privately operated complex has been undergoing an ambitious $130 million renovation and expansion, so check to see that they have not changed their tours and exhibits before going. Call beforehand to see what's happening on the day you intend to be here, and arrive early to plan your visit. You'll need at least 2 hours to see the highlights on the bus tour through the space center, up to 5 hours if you linger at the stops along the way, and a full day to see and do everything here. Buy a copy of the *Official Tour Book;* it's easier to use than the rental cassette tapes, and you can take it home as a colorful souvenir (though some of our readers think you don't need any extra information because the bus tours are narrated and the exhibits have good descriptions).

The visitor complex has real NASA rockets and the actual Mercury Mission Control Room from the 1960s. Exhibits look at early space exploration and where it's going in the new millennium. There are space-related hands-on activities aimed at kids, a daily "Encounter" with a real astronaut, several dining venues, and a shop selling a variety of space memorabilia and souvenirs. IMAX movies shown on 5½-story-high screens are informative and entertaining.

While you could spend your entire day at the visitor complex, you must take a **KSC Tour** to see the actual space center where rockets and shuttles are prepared and launched. Plan to take the bus tour early in your visit (the lines for these are brutal) and be sure to hit the restrooms before boarding the bus—there's only one out on the tour. The buses depart every 10 minutes or so, and you can reboard as you wish. They stop at the LC-39 Observation Gantry, with a dramatic 360-degree view over launch pads where space shuttles blast off; the International Space Station Center, where scientists and engineers prepare additions to the space station now in orbit; and the Apollo/Saturn V Center, which includes artifacts, photos, films, interactive exhibits, and the 363-foot-tall Saturn V, the most

powerful rocket ever launched by the United States. The bus tour was the low point of our recent visit. Though the commentary on the bus itself was interesting, the stops themselves were relatively dull and waiting to board and reboard buses was more than frustrating (though touching a moon rock at the Apollo/Saturn V Center was pretty cool): Stick around the visitor's center if you're short on time.

Don't miss the Astronaut Memorial, a moving black-granite monument that has the names of the U.S. astronauts (the names of those who perished in the recent Columbia tragedy should be up there by the time this book hits the shelves) who have died on missions or while in training. The 60-ton structure rotates on a track that follows the movement of the sun (on clear days, of course), causing the names to stand out above a brilliant reflection of the sky.

On launch days, the center is closed at least part of the day. These aren't good days to see the center, but they're great days to observe history in the making. For $38 adults and $28 for kids 3 through 11, you get a **combined ticket** that

Tips **Out to Launch**

If you'd like to see a shuttle launch at the **Kennedy Space Center,** first call
© **321/867-5000** or check NASA's official website (www.ksc.nasa.gov) for a
schedule of upcoming takeoffs. (However, you should note that since the
Columbia accident, possible takeoffs could be a long way off or policies for
viewing could have changed.) You can buy launch tickets at the Kennedy
Space Center Visitor Complex (© **321/449-4444**) or online at www.ksctickets.
com. (*A word of caution:* Shuttle launches are frequently delayed due to
weather, equipment malfunctions, or other factors, so you might have to
make multiple visits to see one. If you don't have that flexibility, the
launch window may be delayed beyond your going-home date.)

If you can't get into the space center, other good viewing spots are on
the causeways leading to the islands and on U.S. 1 as it skirts the waterfront in Titusville. The **Holiday Inn Riverside–Kennedy Space Center,** on
Washington Avenue (U.S. 1) in Titusville (© **800/465-4329** or 321/269-2121;
www.holidayinnksc.com), also has a clear view of the launch pads across
the Indian River, but area motels raise their rates and often book up during launch periods.

---

entitles you to admission to the center for the shortened operating hours, plus
at least a two-hour excursion to *NASA Parkway* to see the liftoff. You must pick
up tickets, available 5 days before the launch, on site.

An out of this world experience is to do lunch with an astronaut, a once in a
lifetime opportunity that is available every day during lunch hours ($20 adults,
$10 kids 3–11). Some of the greatest astronauts have participated, including
John Glenn, Jim Lovell, Walt Cunningham, Story Musgrave, and Jon McBride.
Call © **321/449-4400** to make a reservation. Seating is limited.

Note: The financially troubled **Astronaut Hall of Fame** in Titusville closed
its doors in fall 2002. Kennedy Space Center acquired many of its exhibits and
added them as a separate attraction at the KSC visitor center ($14 adults and
$9.95 kids 3–11, or $31 adults and $21 kids for a 2-day Maximum Access
Admission to the Center and the Hall of Fame). The new attraction includes
displays, exhibits, and tributes to the heroes of the Mercury, Gemini, and Apollo
space programs. There's also a collection of spacecraft, including a Mercury 7
capsule, a Gemini training capsule, and an Apollo 14 command module. And
in "Simulator Station," guests can experience the pressure of four times the force
of gravity, ride a rover across Mars, and land a Space Shuttle.

NASA Pkwy. (Fla. 405), 6 miles east of Titusville, ½ mile west of Fla. 3. © **321/449-4444** for general information, or 321/449-4444 for guided bus tours and launch reservations. www.kennedyspacecenter.com.
Admission $35 adults, $25 children 3–11. Annual passes $44 adults, $28 children 3–11. Audio tours $5 per
person. All tours and movies free for children under 3. Daily 9am–5:30pm. Shuttle-bus tours daily
9:45am–2:15pm. Closed Christmas and some launch days.

BEACHES & WILDLIFE REFUGES

To the north of the Kennedy Space Center, **Canaveral National Seashore**
✪✪✪ is a protected 13-mile stretch of barrier-island beach backed by cabbage
palms, sea grapes, palmettos, marshes, and Mosquito Lagoon. This is a great area
for watching herons, egrets, ibises, willets, sanderlings, turnstones, terns, and
other birds. You might also glimpse dolphins and manatees in Mosquito Lagoon.
Canoeists can paddle along a marked trail through the marshes of Shipyard

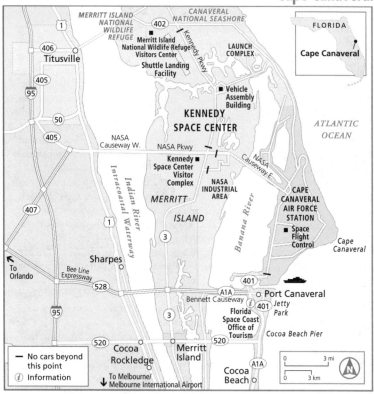

Island, and you can go backcountry camping November through April (permits required—see below).

The main **visitor center** is at 7611 S. Atlantic Ave., New Smyrna Beach, FL 32169 (© **321/867-4077,** or 321/867-0677 for recorded information; www.nps.gov/cana), on Apollo Beach, at the north end of the island. The southern access gate to the island is 8 miles east of Titusville on Fla. 402, just east of Fla. 3. A paved road leads from the gate to undeveloped **Playalinda Beach** ★★★, one of Florida's most beautiful. While it's illegal, nude sunbathing has long been a tradition here (at least for those willing to walk a few miles to the more deserted areas). The beach has toilets but no running water or other amenities, so bring everything you will need. The seashore is open daily from 6am to 8pm during daylight saving time, daily from 6am to 6pm during standard time. Admission fees are $5 per motor vehicle, $3 for pedestrians or bicyclists. National Park Service passports are accepted. Backcountry camping permits cost $10 for up to six people and must be obtained from the New Smyrna Beach visitor center (see above). For advance information, contact the seashore headquarters at 308 Julia St., Titusville, FL 32796 (© **321/867-4077** or 321/267-1110; www.nps.gov/cana).

Its neighbor to the south and west is the 140,000-acre **Merritt Island National Wildlife Refuge** ★★, home to hundreds of species of shorebirds, waterfowl, reptiles, alligators, and mammals, many of them endangered. Stop and pick up a map and other information at the visitor center, on Fla. 402 about

4 miles east of Titusville (it's on the way to Playalinda Beach). The center has a ¼-mile-long boardwalk along the edge of the marsh and has displays showing the animals you may see here. You can see them from the 6-mile-long Black Point Wildlife Drive or one of the nature trails through the hammocks and marshes. The visitor center is open Monday through Friday from 8am to 4:30pm, Saturday from 9am to 5pm (closed Sun Apr–Oct). Admission is free. For more information and a schedule of interpretive programs, contact the refuge at P.O. Box 6504, Titusville, FL 32782 (© **321/861-0667;** www.nbbd. com/godo/minwr).

Note: Those parts of the national seashore near the Kennedy Space Center and all of the refuge close 4 days before a shuttle launch and usually reopen the day after a launch.

Another good beach area is **Lori Wilson Park,** on Atlantic Avenue at Antigua Drive in Cocoa Beach (© **321/868-1123**), which preserves a stretch of beach backed by a forest of live oaks. It's home to a small but interesting nature center, and it has restrooms by the beach. The park is open daily from sunrise to sunset, the nature center, Monday through Friday from 1 to 4pm.

The beach at **Cocoa Beach Pier,** on Meade Avenue east of Fla. A1A (© **321/783-7549**), is a popular spot, especially with surfers, who consider it the East Coast's surfing capital. The rustic pier was built in 1962 and has 842 feet of fishing, shopping, and food and drinks overlooking a wide, sandy beach (see "Where to Dine," below). Because this is not a public park, there are no restrooms other than the ones in the restaurants on the pier.

Jetty Park, 400 E. Jetty Rd. (© **321/783-7111;** www.portcanaveral.org/fun-port/parks.htm), at the south entry to Port Canaveral, has lifeguards, a fishing pier with bait shop, a children's playground, a volleyball court, a horseshoe pit, picnic tables, a snack bar, a grocery store, restrooms and changing facilities, and the area's only campground. From here you can watch the big cruise ships as they enter and leave the port's narrow passage. The park is open daily from 7am to 10pm, and the pier is open 24 hours for fishing. Admission is $3 per car, $7 for RVs. The 150 tent and RV campsites (some of them shady, most with hookups) cost $17 to $26 a night, depending on location and time of year. No pets are allowed.

OUTDOOR ACTIVITIES
ECOTOURS   Funday Discovery Tours (© **321/725-0796;** www.funday tours.com) offers a variety of day trips, including dinner and sunset cruises, airboat and swamp-buggy rides, dolphin-watching cruises, bird-watching expeditions, and personalized tours of the Kennedy Space Center and Merritt Island National Wildlife Refuge. Reservations are required, so call, check the website, or pick up a copy of their list of trips from the visitor center (see "Essentials," above).

FISHING   Head to Port Canaveral for catches such as snapper and grouper. **Jetty Park** (© **321/783-7111**), at the south entry to the port, has a fishing pier equipped with a bait shop (see "Beaches & Wildlife Refuges," above). The south bank of the port is lined with charter boats, and you can go deep-sea fishing on the *Miss Cape Canaveral* (© **321/783-5274** or 321/648-2211 in Orlando; www.misscape.com), one of the party boats based here. All-day voyages departing daily at 8am cost $45 to $60 for adults, $40 to $55 for seniors, $35 to $50 for students 11 to 17, and $25 to $40 for kids 6 to 10.

GOLF   You can read about Northeast Florida's best courses in the free *Golfer's Guide,* available at the tourist information offices and in many hotel lobbies. See p. 35 for information about ordering copies.

In Cocoa Beach, the municipal **Cocoa Beach Country Club,** 500 Tom War-ringer Blvd. (© **321/868-3351**), has 27 holes of golf and 10 lighted tennis courts set on acres of natural woodland, rivers, and lakes. Greens fees are about $40 in winter, dropping to about $35 in summer, including cart.

On Merritt Island south of the Kennedy Space Center, **The Savannahs at Sykes Creek,** 3915 Savannahs Trail (© **321/455-1377**), has 18 holes over 6,636 yards bordered by hardwood forests, lakes, and savannahs inhabited by a host of wildlife. You'll have to hit over a lake to reach the seventh hole. Fees with cart are about $40 in winter, less in summer.

The best nearby course is the Gary Player–designed **Baytree National Golf Club,** 8010 N. Wickham Rd., ½ mile east of I-95 in Melbourne (© **321/259-9060**), where challenging marshy holes are flanked by towering palms. This par-72 course has 7,043 yards with a unique red-shale waste area. Fees are about $90 in winter, dropping to about $50 in summer, including cart.

For course information online, go to **www.golf.com** and **www.florida golfing.com,** or call the **Florida Sports Foundation** (© **850/488-8347**) or **Florida Golfing** (© **866/833-2663**).

SURFING   Rip through some occasionally awesome waves (by Florida's stan-dards, not California's or Hawaii's) at the **Cocoa Beach Pier** area or down south at **Sebastian Inlet.** Get outfitted at Ron Jon Surf Shop (4151 N. Atlantic Ave.; © **321/799-8888;** www.ronjons.com) or learn how to hang five or 10 with **Cocoa Beach Surfing School** ⚐, 150 E. Columbia Lane (© **321/868-1980;** www.cocoabeachsurfingschool.com). They offer equipment and lessons for beginners or pros at area beaches. Be sure to bring along a towel, flip-flops, sun-screen, and a lot of nerve.

WHERE TO STAY

The hotels listed below are all in Cocoa Beach, the closest resort area to the Kennedy Space Center, about a 30-minute drive to the north. For TV and pop culture junkies, Cocoa Beach was where the show *I Dream of Jeannie* took place. Closest to the space center and Port Canaveral is the **Radisson Resort at the Port,** 8701 Astronaut Blvd. (Fla. A1A) in Cape Canaveral (© **800/333-3333** or 321/784-0000; www.Radisson.com). It isn't on the beach, but you can relax in a landscaped courtyard with a waterfall cascading over fake rocks into an out-door heated pool. This comfortable, well-equipped hotel caters to business trav-elers and passengers waiting to board cruise ships (free transportation to the port and free parking while you cruise) departing from nearby Port Canaveral and has a great complimentary breakfast.

The newest chain motels in this area are the **Hampton Inn Cocoa Beach,** 3425 Atlantic Blvd. (© **877/492-3224** or 321/799-4099; www.hamptonin-ncocoabeach.com), and **Courtyard by Marriott,** 3435 Atlantic Blvd. (© **800/ 321-2211** or 321/784-4800; www.marriott.com). Opened in 2000 and 2001, respectively, they stand side-by-side and have access to the beach via a pathway through a condominium complex.

The **Florida Space Coast Office of Tourism** (8810 Astronaut Blvd. #102; Cape Canaveral, FL 32920; © **800/93-OCEAN** or 321/868-1126; www.space-coast.com) publishes a booklet of the area's Superior Small Lodgings.

The area has a plethora of rental condominiums and cottages. **King Rentals Inc.,** 102 W. Central Blvd., Cape Canaveral, FL 32920 (© **888/295-0934** or 321/784-5046; www.kingrentals.com), has a wide selection in its inventory.

Given the proximity of Orlando, the generally warm weather year-round, and business travelers visiting the space complex, there is little if any seasonal fluctuation in room rates here. They are highest weekends, holidays, and during special events, such as space shuttle launches.

Tent and RV camping are available at **Jetty Park** in Port Canaveral (see "Beaches & Wildlife Refuges," above).

You'll pay a 4% hotel tax on top of the Florida 6% sales tax here.

DoubleTree Hotel Cocoa Beach Oceanfront ⭐ This six-story hotel was extensively remodeled and upgraded in 1998, and although not as upscale as the Hilton Cocoa Beach Oceanfront (see below), it's the pick of the full-service beachside hotels here. All rooms have balconies with ocean views and easy chairs, and 10 suites have living rooms with sleeper sofas and separate bedrooms. A charming dining room facing the beach serves decent Mediterranean fare and opens to a bi-level brick patio with water cascading between two heated swimming pools. Conference facilities draw groups.

2080 N. Atlantic Ave., Cocoa Beach, FL 32931. ℂ 800/552-3224 or 321/783-9222. Fax 321/799-3234. www.cocoabeachdoubletree.com. 148 units. $125–$179 double; $185–$275 suite. AE, DC, DISC, MC, V. **Amenities:** Restaurant; bar; 2 heated outdoor pools; exercise room; game room; limited room service; laundry service; coin-op washers and dryers; concierge-level rooms. *In room:* A/C, TV, dataport, coffeemaker, hair dryer, iron.

Hilton Cocoa Beach Oceanfront Instead of balconies or patios from which you can enjoy the fresh air and view down the shore, the rooms at this seven-story Hilton have smallish, sealed-shut windows, and only 16 of them actually face the beach. That and other architectural features make it seem more like a downtown commercial hotel transplanted to a beachside location. Nevertheless, it's one of the few upscale beachfront properties here. No doubt you will run into a crew of name-tagged conventioneers, since it's especially popular with groups. Despite their lack of fresh air, the rooms are spacious and comfortable.

1550 N. Atlantic Ave., Cocoa Beach, FL 32931. ℂ 800/445-8667 or 321/799-0003. Fax 321/799-0344. www.hilton.com. 296 units. $89–$199 double. AE, DC, DISC, MC, V. **Amenities:** Restaurant; 2 bars; heated outdoor pool; exercise room; game room; watersports equipment rentals; business center; limited room service; laundry service; coin-op washers and dryers; concierge-level rooms. *In room:* A/C, TV, dataport, coffeemaker, hair dryer, iron.

The Inn at Cocoa Beach ⭐⭐⭐ Despite having 50 units, an intimate bed-and-breakfast ambience prevails at this seaside inn, far and away the most romantic place to stay in the area (which is why it draws so many couples). The inn began as a beachfront motel but underwent a transformation under current owner Karen Simpler, a skilled interior decorator. She has furnished each unit with an elegant mix of pine, tropical, and French country pieces. Rooms in the three- and four-story buildings are much more spacious and have better sea views from their balconies than the "standard" units in the original two-story motel wing (all but six units here have balconies or patios). The older units open to a courtyard with a swimming pool tucked behind the dunes. Highest on the romance scale are two rooms with Jacuzzi tubs, large showers, and easy chairs facing gas fireplaces. In addition to the complimentary breakfast, guests are treated to evening wine-and-cheese socials and afternoon tea. There's also an honor bar where you can pour your own drinks and a library from which to feed your head.

4300 Ocean Blvd., Cocoa Beach, FL 32932. ℂ 800/343-5307 or 321/799-3460. Fax 321/784-8632. www.theinnatcocoabeach.com. 50 units. $135–$295 double. Rates include continental breakfast and afternoon tea. AE, DISC, MC, V. No children under 12 accepted. **Amenities:** Bar (guests only); heated outdoor pool; sauna; massage; laundry service. *In room:* A/C, TV, dataport.

Riverview Hotel ★★★   Located right on the Intracoastal Waterway in New Smyrna Beach, the Riverview Hotel, a former fishing and hunting shack for sportsmen scoping the Indian River Lagoon, is a spectacularly restored, 18-room hotel featuring a 5,000-foot spa complete with a mineral pool. Every night, there's jazz on the deck and, to boot, a fabulous restaurant, Riverview Charlie's, which some consider to be one of the state's best seafood spots, is on the premises. The owners, Christa and Jim Kelsey used to work at the Faro Blanco Marina Resort in the Florida Keys, so they are well versed in the art of hospitality. Some rooms have private patios or porches and all rooms are immaculate, charming in a Little House on the Prairie Way, and come complete with modern amenities such as cable television. If I had a choice, however, I'd choose the two-bedroom cottage or house with private pool, which are bargains at $175 to $210!

103 Flagler Ave., New Smyrna Beach 32169. ✆ **800/945-7416** or 386/428-5858. Fax 321/423-8927. www.riverviewhotel.com. 18 units. $100–$120 double. Rates include expanded continental breakfast. AE, DISC, MC, V. **Amenities:** Restaurant, heated pool; spa; sauna; massage. *In room:* A/C, TV.

WHERE TO DINE

On the **Cocoa Beach Pier,** at the beach end of Meade Avenue, you'll get a fine view down the coast to accompany the seafood offerings at **Atlantic Ocean Grill** (✆ **321/783-7549**) and the mediocre pub fare at adjacent **Marlins Good Times Bar & Grill** (same phone). The restaurants may not justify spending an entire evening on the pier, but the outdoor, tin-roofed **Boardwalk Tiki Bar** ★, where live music plays most nights, is a prime spot to have a cold one while watching the surfers or a sunset.

Bernard's Surf/Fischer's Seafood Bar & Grill ★ SEAFOOD/STEAKS Photos on the walls testify that many astronauts—and Russian cosmonauts, too—come to these adjoining establishments to celebrate their landings. It all started as Bernard's Surf, which has been serving standard steak-and-seafood fare in a nautically dressed setting since 1948. Bernard's offers house specials such as stone crab claws, Florida lobster tails stuffed with crab, char-grilled red snapper, and a belly-busting platter of shrimp, scallops, grouper, crab cakes, lobster, and oysters. You can even get some Russian Beluga or Sevruga caviar if you so desire. The fresh seafood also finds its way into Fischer's Seafood Bar & Grill, a friendly, *Cheers*-like lounge popular with the locals. Fischer's menu features fried combo platters, shrimp and crab-claw meat sautéed in herb butter, and mussels with a wine sauce over pasta, to mention a few worthy selections. Fischer's also provides sandwiches, burgers, and other pub fare, and it has the same 25¢ happy-hour oysters and spicy wings as a branch of **Rusty's Seafood & Oyster Bar** (see below), also part of this complex.

2 S. Atlantic Ave. (at Minuteman Causeway Rd.), Cocoa Beach. ✆ **321/783-2401**. Reservations recommended in Bernard's, not accepted in Fischer's. Bernard's main courses $14–$55. Fischer's main courses $9–$16; sandwiches and salads $4–$9. AE, DC, DISC, MC, V. Bernard's Mon–Fri 4–10pm; Sat 4–11pm. Fischer's Mon–Fri 11am–10pm; Sat 11am–11pm. Closed Christmas.

The Mango Tree ★★ CONTINENTAL   Gourmet seafood, pastas, and chicken are served in a plantation-home atmosphere with elegant furnishings in this stucco house, the finest dining venue here. Although the ambience borders on Tavern on the Green touristy tacky, the restaurant is, much like Tavern, rather picturesque. Goldfish ponds inside and a waterfall splashing into a Japanese koi pond out in the lush tropical gardens provide pleasing backdrops. Start with finely seasoned Indian River crab cakes, then go on to the chef's expert spin on fresh tuna filets, roast Long Island duckling, beef tips with peppercorn-mushroom sauce, and other excellent dishes drawing their inspiration from the continent.

118 N. Atlantic Ave. (Fla. A1A, between N. 1st and N. 2nd sts.), Cocoa Beach. ⓒ **321/799-0513.** Reservations recommended. Main courses $15–$39. AE, MC, V. Tues–Sun 6–10pm.

Rusty's Seafood & Oyster Bar *Value* SEAFOOD   This lively sports bar beside Port Canaveral's man-made harbor offers inexpensive chow ranging from very spicy seafood gumbo to a pot of seafood that will give two people their fill of steamed oysters, clams, shrimp, crab legs, potatoes, and corn on the cob. Raw or steamed fresh oysters and clams from the raw bar are first rate and a very good value, as is a lunch buffet on weekdays. Seating is available indoors or out, but the inside tables have the best view of fishing boats and cruise liners going in and out of the port. Daily happy hours from 3 to 6pm see beers drafted at 60¢ a mug, and tons of raw or steamed oysters and spicy Buffalo wings go for 25¢ each. It's a busy and sometimes noisy joint, especially on weekend afternoons, but the clientele tends to be somewhat older and better behaved than at some other pubs along the banks of Port Canaveral. There's another **Rusty's** in the Bernard's Surf/Fischer's Seafood Bar & Grill restaurant complex in Cocoa Beach (see above). It has the same menu.

628 Glen Cheek Dr. (south side of the harbor), Port Canaveral. ⓒ **321/783-2033.** Main courses $7–$25; sandwiches and salads $4–$7; lunch buffet $6. AE, DC, DISC, MC, V. Sun–Thurs 11am–11:30pm; Fri–Sat 11am–12:30am (lunch buffet Mon–Fri 11am–2pm).

THE SPACE COAST AFTER DARK

For a rundown of current performances and exhibits, call the **Brevard Cultural Alliance's Arts Line** (ⓒ **321/690-6819**). For live music, walk out on the **Cocoa Beach Pier,** on Meade Avenue at the beach, where **Oh Shuck's Seafood Bar & Grill** (ⓒ **321/783-7549**), **Marlins Good Times Bar & Grill** (ⓒ **321/783-7549**), and the alfresco **Boardwalk Tiki Bar** (same phone as Marlins) have bands on weekends, more often during the summer season. The Tiki bar is a great place to hang out over a cold beer all afternoon and evening.

2 Daytona Beach ★★

54 miles NE of Orlando, 251 miles N of Miami, 78 miles S of Jacksonville

Daytona Beach is a town with many personalities. It is at once the self-proclaimed "World's Most Famous Beach" and "World Center of Racing," a mecca for tattooed motorcyclists and pierced spring-breakers, *and* the home of a surprisingly good art museum. The city and developers are also spending millions of dollars to turn the somewhat seedy beachfront area (complete with the requisite T-shirt and souvenir shops), around the famous Main Street Pier, into Ocean Walk Village, a redevelopment area of shops, entertainment, and resort facilities.

Daytona Beach has been a destination for racing enthusiasts since the early 1900s when "horseless carriages" raced on the hard-packed sand beach. One thing is for sure: Daytonans still love their cars. Recent debate over the environmental impact of unrestricted driving on the beach caused an uproar from citizens who couldn't imagine it any other way. As it worked out, they can still drive on the sand, but not everywhere, and especially not in areas where sea turtles are nesting.

Today, hundreds of thousands of race enthusiasts come to the home of the National Association for Stock Car Auto Racing (NASCAR) for the Daytona 500, the Pepsi 400, and other races throughout the year. The Speedway is also home to DAYTONA USA, a state-of-the-art motor-sports entertainment attraction worth a visit even by nonracing fans.

Be sure to check the "Florida Calendar of Events," in chapter 2, to know when the town belongs to college students during spring break, hundreds of

Daytona Beach

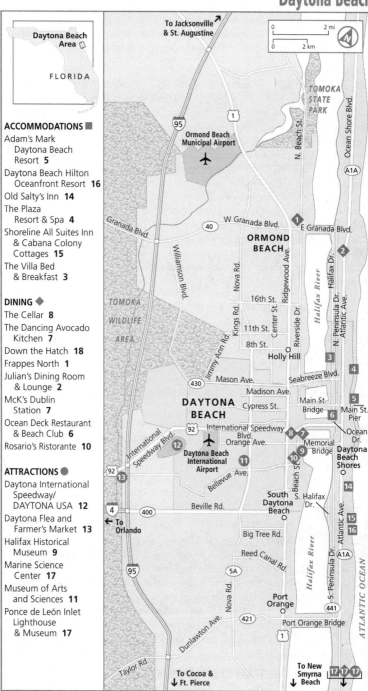

Daytona Beach Area

FLORIDA

ACCOMMODATIONS ■
Adam's Mark
Daytona Beach
Resort **5**
Daytona Beach Hilton
Oceanfront Resort **16**
Old Salty's Inn **14**
The Plaza
Resort & Spa **4**
Shoreline All Suites Inn
& Cabana Colony
Cottages **15**
The Villa Bed
& Breakfast **3**

DINING ◆
The Cellar **8**
The Dancing Avocado
Kitchen **7**
Down the Hatch **18**
Frappes North **1**
Julian's Dining Room
& Lounge **2**
McK's Dublin
Station **7**
Ocean Deck Restaurant
& Beach Club **6**
Rosario's Ristorante **10**

ATTRACTIONS ●
Daytona International
Speedway/
DAYTONA USA **12**
Daytona Flea and
Farmer's Market **13**
Halifax Historical
Museum **9**
Marine Science
Center **17**
Museum of Arts
and Sciences **11**
Ponce de León Inlet
Lighthouse
& Museum **17**

thousands of leather-clad motorcycle buffs during Bike Week (March) and Bike-toberfest (Oct), or racing enthusiasts for big competitions. You can't find a hotel room, drive the highways, or enjoy a peaceful vacation when they're in town.

ESSENTIALS

GETTING THERE　**Continental** (© 800/525-0280) and **Delta** (© 800/221-1212) fly into the small, pleasant, and calm **Daytona Beach International Airport** (© 386/248-8030; http://flydaytonafirst.com), 4 miles inland from the beach on International Speedway Boulevard (U.S. 92), but you usually can find less expensive fares to **Orlando International Airport** (p. 456), about an hour's drive away. **Daytona-Orlando Transit Service (DOTS)** (© 800/231-1965 or 386/257-5411; www.dots-daytonabeach.com) provides van transportation to and from Orlando International Airport. Fares are about $27 for adults one-way, $49 round-trip; fares for children 11 and under are $14 one-way and $28 round-trip. The service brings passengers to the company's terminal at 1034 N. Nova Rd., between 3rd and 4th streets, or to beach hotels for an additional fee.

If you fly into the Daytona airport, rates for the **Daytona Shuttle** (© 386/255-2294) range up to $12 per person, $14 per couple, or $6 per person for parties of three or more. The ride from the airport to most beach hotels via **Yellow Cab Co.** (© 386/255-5555) is between $7 and $18.

Alamo (© 800/327-9622), **Avis** (© 800/831-2847), **Budget** (© 800/527-0700), **Dollar** (© 800/800-4000), **Enterprise** (© 800/325-8007), **Hertz** (© 800/654-3131), and **National** (© 800/227-7368) have booths at the airport. If it suits you, why not rent a Harley? This is Daytona, after all. Contact **Daytona Harley-Davidson** (© 800/307-4464 or 386/258-0638; www.daytona hd.com). Rates are $125 to $135 daily, $600 to $640 weekly.

Amtrak (© 800/872-7245; www.amtrak.com) trains stop at Deland, about 15 miles southwest of Daytona Beach, with connecting bus service from Deland to the beach.

VISITOR INFORMATION　The **Daytona Beach Area Convention & Visitors Bureau,** 126 E. Orange Ave. (P.O. Box 910), Daytona Beach, FL 32115 (© 800/544-0415 or 386/255-0415; www.daytonabeach.com), can help you with information on attractions, accommodations, dining, and events. The office is on the mainland just west of the Memorial Bridge. The information area of the lobby is open daily from 9am to 5pm. The bureau also maintains a branch at DAYTONA USA, 1801 W. International Speedway Blvd. (open daily 9am–7pm), and a kiosk at the airport.

GETTING AROUND　Although Daytona is primarily a driver's town, VOTRAN, Volusia County's public transit system (© 386/761-7700; http://votran.org), runs a **free shuttle** around the Main Street Pier/Ocean Walk Village area and a pay **trolley** along Atlantic Avenue on the beach, Monday through Saturday from noon to midnight. Trolley fares are $1 for adults, 50¢ for seniors and children 6 to 17, and free for kids under 6 riding with an adult. VOTRAN also runs **buses** throughout downtown and the beaches.

For a taxi, call **Yellow Cab** (© 386/255-5555) or **Southern Komfort Cab** (© 386/252-2222).

A VISIT TO THE WORLD CENTER OF RACING

Daytona International Speedway/DAYTONA USA ★★　You don't have to be a racing fan to enjoy a visit to the **Daytona International Speedway,** 4 miles west of the beach. Opened in 1959 with the first Daytona 500, this 480-acre complex is one of the keynotes of the city's fame. The track presents about nine weekends of major racing events annually, featuring stock cars, sports cars, motorcycles, and go-karts, and is used for automobile and motorbike testing and other events many other days of the year. Its grandstands can accommodate more than 150,000 fans. Big events sell out months in advance (tickets to the Daytona 500 in Feb can be gone a year ahead of time), so get your tickets and hotel reservations as early as possible.

Start your visit at the **World Center of Racing Visitors Center,** in the NASCAR office complex at the east end of the speedway. Admission to the center is free, and you can walk out and see the track during nonrace days (there's a small admission to the track during qualifying races leading up to the main events). Entertaining 30-minute guided tram tours of the facility (garage area, pit road, and so on) depart from the visitor center and are well worth taking.

The visitor center houses a large souvenir shop, a snack bar, and the phenomenally popular **DAYTONA USA,** a 60,000-square-foot, state-of-the-art interactive motor-sports entertainment attraction. Here you can learn about the history, color, and excitement of stock car, go-kart, and motorcycle racing in Daytona. In Daytona Dream Laps, one of its newest "rides," you get the feel of what it's like to zoom around the track in a Daytona 500 race from a 32-seat motion simulator. If that doesn't get your stomach churning, hop inside your own 80% scale NASCAR car in Acceleration Alley, buckle up, and roar up to 200 mph in a spectacular simulator that combines motion, video, projection, and sound for the ultimate virtual reality–like racing experience ($5 per ride above the admission price, below). On the milder side, you can participate in a pit stop on a NASCAR Winston Cup stock car, see an actual winning Daytona 500 car still covered in track dust, talk via video with favorite competitors, and play radio or television announcer by calling the finish of a race. An action-packed IMAX film will put you in the winner's seat of a Daytona 500 race.

To really experience what it's like, you can actually make (for $106) three laps around the track in a stock car from May to October with the **Richard Petty Driving Experience Ride-Along Program** (✆ 800/237-3889; www.1800be petty.com). Professional drivers (sorry, none are named Petty) are at the wheel as you see and feel what it's like to travel an average 115 mph.

Allow at least 4 hours to see everything, and bring your video camera.

1801 W. International Speedway Blvd. (U.S. 92, at Bill France Blvd.). ✆ 386/253-7223 for race tickets, 386/253-7223 for information, or 386/947-6404 or 386/947-6800 for DAYTONA USA. www.daytonaintl speedway.com and www.daytonausa.com. Speedway free admission except on race days; tram rides $7. DAYTONA USA admission $16 adults, $13 seniors, $8 children 6–12. Combination DAYTONA USA–tram tour $20 adults, $17 seniors, $14 children 6–12. Tram rides and DAYTONA USA free admission for children under 6. Speedway daily 9am–7pm; trams depart every 30 min. 9:30am–5pm except during races and special events. DAYTONA USA daily 9am–7pm (later during race events). Closed Christmas.

HITTING THE WORLD'S MOST FAMOUS BEACH

The beautiful and hard-packed beach here runs for 24 miles along a skinny peninsula separated from the mainland by the Halifax River. The bustling hub of activity is at the end of Main Street, near the Adam's Mark Daytona Beach Resort, where you'll find the **Main Street Pier,** which was the longest wooden pier on the East Coast until Hurricane Floyd washed away about a third of its 1,006 feet in 1999. Out here you'll find a restaurant, bar, bait shop, beach-toy concessions, a chairlift running its length, and views from the 180-foot-tall Space Needle. Admission as far out as the restaurant and bar is free (at about a third of the way, this is far enough for a good view down the beach), but you'll have to pay $1 to walk beyond that point, and more than that if you fish (see

> **Tips** **Driving on the Beach**
>
> You can drive and park directly on sections of the sand along 18 miles of the beach during daylight hours and at low tide (Hurricane Floyd and other recent storms have greatly reduced the beach's width), but watch for signs warning of sea turtles nesting. There's a $5 per vehicle access fee and 10 mph speed limit. *Watch out for the tides.* If you park on an incoming tide and lose track of time, your vehicle may become an inadvertent rust bucket or artificial reef!

"Outdoor Activities," below). Beginning at the pier, the city's famous ocean-side **Boardwalk** is lined with restaurants, bars, and T-shirt shops, as are the 4 blocks of Main Street nearest the beach. The city's Ocean Walk Village redevelopment project begins here and runs several blocks north.

There's another busy beach area at the end of **Seabreeze Boulevard,** which has a multitude of restaurants, bars, and shops.

Couples seeking greater privacy usually prefer the northern or southern extremities of the beach. **Ponce Inlet,** at the very southern tip of the peninsula, is especially peaceful, since there is little commerce or traffic there to disturb the silence.

OUTDOOR ACTIVITIES

CRUISES   Take a leisurely cruise on the Halifax River aboard the 14-passenger, 25-foot *Fancy,* a replica of an 1890s-style fantail launch. It's operated by **A tiny Cruise Line River Excursions,** 425 S. Beach St., at Halifax Harbor Marina (© 386/226-2343). Captain Jim regales passengers with river lore and points out dolphins (which are more commonly spotted in the mornings), manatees, herons, diving cormorants, pelicans, egrets, osprey, oyster beds, and other natural phenomena during his 2-hour midday cruise. In the afternoon, you can see the man-made estates along the river. Cruises range from $9.50 to $15 for adults, $6 to $8 for children 4 to 12, and free for children 3 and under. Weather permitting, the midday cruises depart year-round (with a brief hiatus during the holidays), Monday through Saturday at 11:30am. The 1-hour tour of riverfront homes is at 2pm and of historic downtown at 3:30pm; there are no Monday cruises in winter months. Call for reservations. Romantic sunset cruises are also available.

FISHING   The easiest and least-expensive way to fish offshore for marlin, sailfish, king mackerel, grouper, red snapper, and more is with the **Critter Fleet,** 4950 S. Peninsula Dr., just past the lighthouse in Ponce Inlet (© 800/338-0850 or 386/767-7676; www.critterfleet.com), which operates two party boats. One goes on all-day trips (about $60 adults, $35 kids under 12), while the other makes morning and afternoon voyages (about $40 adults, $25 kids under 12). The fares include rod, reel, and bait. Call for schedules, prices, and reservations.

Save the cost of a boat and fish with the locals from the **Main Street Pier,** at the ocean end of Main Street near the Adam's Mark Daytona Beach Resort (© 386/253-1212). Admission for anglers is $3.50 for adults, $2 for kids under 12. Bait and fishing gear are available, and no license is required.

GOLF   There are more than 25 courses within 30 minutes of the beach, and most hotels can arrange starting times for you. **Golf Daytona Beach,** 126 E. Orange Ave., Daytona Beach, FL 32114 (© 800/881-7065 or 386/239-7065; fax 386/239-0064), publishes an annual brochure describing the major courses. It's available at the tourist information offices (see "Essentials," above).

For course information online, go to www.golf.com and www.floridagolfing.com, or call the **Florida Sports Foundation** (© 850/488-8347) or **Florida Golfing** (© 866/833-2663).

Two of the nation's top-rated links for women golfers are at the **LPGA International** ★★, 1000 Championship Dr. (© 386/274-5742; www.lpgainternational.com): Those are the Champions course designed by Rees Jones and the Legends course designed by Arthur Hills. Both boast 18 outstanding holes. LPGA International is a center for professional and amateur women golfers (workshops and teaching programs), and the pro shop carries a great selection of ladies' equipment and clothing. Greens fees with a cart are usually about $75, less in summer. *Pssst*—They let guys play here, too!

A Lloyd Clifton–designed course, the centrally located 18-hole, par-72 **Indigo Lakes Golf Course,** 2620 W. International Speedway Blvd. (© 386/254-3607; www.indigolakesgolf.com), has flat fairways and large bunkered Bermuda greens. Fees here are about $65 in winter, including a cart, less in summer.

The semiprivate South Course at **Pelican Bay Country Club,** 550 Sea Duck Dr. (© 386/756-0034; www.pelicanbaygolfclub.com), is one of the area's favorites, with fast greens to test your putting skills. Fees are about $45 with cart in winter, less in summer (no walking allowed). The North Course is for members only.

The city's prime municipal course is the **Daytona Beach Country Club,** 600 Wilder Blvd. (© 386/258-3119), which has 36 holes. Winter fees are about $20 to walk, $30 to share a cart. They drop $3 in summer.

HELICOPTER RIDES   Take a helicopter ride around the Daytona area to see the city from a different point of view. **Air Florida** (© 386/257-6993; www.airfloridahelicopters.com) offers rides starting at $20 (two person minimum), leaving from the Daytona Flea and Farmer's Market (see below).

HORSEBACK RIDING   **Shenandoah Stables,** 1759 Tomoka Farms Rd., off U.S. 92 (© 386/257-1444), offers daily trail rides and lessons. Call for prices and schedules.

SPECTATOR SPORTS   The **Daytona Cubs** (© 386/872-2827; www.daytonacubs.com), a Class A minor-league affiliate of the Chicago Cubs, play baseball April through August at Jackie Robinson Ballpark, on City Island downtown. A game here is a treat, since the park has been restored to its classic 1914 style by the designers of Baltimore's Camden Yards and Cleveland's Jacobs Field. Tickets are $4 to $7.

WATERSPORTS   Watersports equipment, bicycles, beach buggies, and mopeds, can be rented along the Boardwalk, at the ocean end of Main Street (see "Hitting the World's Most Famous Beach," above), and in front of major beachfront hotels.

MUSEUMS & ATTRACTIONS

Halifax Historical Museum ☞   Located on Beach Street, Daytona's original riverfront commercial district on the mainland side of the Halifax River (see "Shopping," below), this local history museum is worth a look just for the 1912 neoclassical architectural details of its home, a former bank (you can see the old vault). A mural of Old Florida wildlife graces one wall, the stained-glass ceiling reflects the sunlight, and across the room an old gold-metal teller's window still stands. The Halifax's eclectic and interesting collection includes tools and household items from the Spanish and British periods, more than 10,000 historic photographs, possessions of past residents (such as a ball gown worn at Lincoln's inauguration), and, of course, model cars. A noteworthy race exhibit opens annually in mid-January as a stage-setter for Race Week.

252 S. Beach St. (just north of Orange Ave.). ℂ 386/255-6976. www.halifaxhistorical.org. Admission $4 adults, $1 children 11 and under; free Sat for children. Tues–Sat 10am–4pm.

Marine Science Center *(Kids* This new center (opened in June 2002) has interior displays (with exhibits on mangroves, mosquitoes, marine mammal bones, shells, artificial reefs, dune habitats, and pollution solutions), a 5,000-gallon aquarium, and offers educational programs and activities. Though the exhibit area is rather small, there's more than enough information for a child to digest at one time. Perhaps the most interesting part of the center is the space reserved for the rehabilitation of endangered and threatened sea turtles (once they're cured, the healthy turtles are set back into nature). You can watch them in any of seven turtle tanks—look for the ones who need life jackets to stay afloat!

100 Lighthouse Dr., Ponce Inlet. ℂ 386/304-5545. www.marinesciencecenter.com. $3 adults, $1 children 5–12, free for children under 5. Tues–Sat 10am–4pm; Sun noon–4pm; closed Mon. See directions for Ponce de León Inlet Lighthouse & Museum (below).

Museum of Arts and Sciences *(★★* An exceptional institution for a town of Daytona's size and reputation (as a culturally devoid, trashy, spring break mecca), this museum is best known for its Cuba: A History of Art exhibit, with paintings acquired in 1956, when Cuban dictator Fulgencio Batista donated his private collection to the city. Among them is a portrait of Eva ("Evita") Perón, said to be the only existing painting completed while she was alive (it hangs near the lobby, not within the Cuban exhibit). The Dow Gallery displays Smithsonian-quality examples of American decorative arts, and the Bouchelle Study Center for the Decorative Arts contains American and European jewelry, furniture, mirrors, and more. Other rooms worth visiting include the Schulte Gallery of Chinese Art; Africa: Life and Ritual, with the largest collection of Ashante gold ornaments (these are stunning) in the United States; and the Center for Florida history, with the skeleton of a 13-foot-tall, 130,000-year-old giant ground sloth. A recent addition is the unique collection of the late Chapman S. Root, a Daytona philanthropist and a founder of the Coca-Cola empire; among the Root memorabilia is the mold for the original Coke bottle as well as many other changing exhibitions (the collection is very large). The Root family's two private railroad cars are also on display. The planetarium presents 30-minute shows of what the night sky will look like on the date of your visit. Even though this is a first-class art museum, except for the skeleton and the model railroads, children are apt to be bored here.

1040 Museum Blvd. (off Nova Rd./Fla. 5A between International Speedway Blvd. and Bellevue Ave.). ℂ 386/255-0285. www.moas.org. Museum $8 adults, $4 children and students with ID, free for children 5 and under. Planetarium shows $3 adults, $2 children and students. Tues–Fri 9am–4pm; Sat–Sun noon–5pm. Planetarium shows Tues–Fri 2pm; Sat–Sun 1 and 3pm. Closed Thanksgiving, Christmas Eve, Christmas Day. Take International Speedway Blvd. west, make a left on Nova Rd. (Fla. 5A), and look for a sign on your right.

Ponce de León Inlet Lighthouse & Museum *(★★* This National Historic Landmark is well worth a stop even if you're not a lighthouse enthusiast. The 175-foot brick-and-granite structure is the second-tallest lighthouse in the United States. (Only the beacon at Cape Hatteras, North Carolina, is taller.) Built in the 1880s, the lighthouse and the graceful Victorian brick buildings surrounding it have been restored (it's one of the only light stations in the United States to have all its original buildings still standing). There are no guided tours, but you can walk through the 12 areas, which feature different exhibits (lighthouse lenses, historical artifacts, and a film of early car racing on the nearby beach), and around the tugboat *F. D. Russell,* now sitting high-and-dry in the sand. Use common sense if you climb the 203 steps to the top of the lighthouse; it's a grinding ascent, but the view from up there is spectacular.

4931 S. Peninsula Dr., Ponce Inlet. (C) 386/761-1821. www.ponceinlet.org. Admission $5 adults, $1.50 children under 12. Memorial Day to Labor Day daily 10am–9pm; rest of year daily 10am–5pm. Follow Atlantic Ave. south, make a right on Beach St., and follow the signs.

Crossing Over Into Cassadaga

If you're in the Daytona Beach/Orlando area, suspend your disbelief for a few hours and make a pit stop in Cassadaga, the tiny century-old community composed completely of psychics and mediums who will be happy to tell you your future, your fortune, or put you in touch with the deceased—for a price, of course.

Should you find the whole concept of psychics and talking to the dead completely kooky and out of whack, consider the history of Cassadaga, which is fascinating in its own right.

Without sounding too much like the intro to the SciFi Channel show *Crossing Over with John Edward,* as a young man from New York, George Colby was told during a séance that he would someday establish a spiritualist community in the South. In 1875, the prophecy came true when Colby was led through the wilderness of Central Florida by his spiritual guide to a 35-acre area that was to become the Cassadaga Spiritualist Camp.

Although it sounds like a bizarre cult, it's not. Consisting of about 57 acres and 55 no-nonsense clapboard houses, Cassadaga caters to those who have chosen to share in a community of like-minded people who happen to believe in the otherworldly. Yes, the people are eccentric, to say the least, but they are all very friendly. Designated a Historic District on the National Register of Historic Places, Cassadaga is the Spiritualist version of Lourdes, to which skeptics and believers alike flock for answers, or at least kicks.

When you get to town, head straight for the **Information Center** (for directions, see below), where you can find out which psychics and mediums are working that day, and make an appointment for a session, which ranges from $25 and up for a palm reading to $50 and up for a session with a medium. A general store, restaurant, hotel, and a few curious shops selling crystals and potions of sorts are there to keep you occupied while you wait for your appointment. Whether you're a believer or not, an hour or two in Cassadaga will make for interesting cocktail conversation.

From Daytona, take I-4 to exit 114. Turn right onto Highway 472 at the end of the exit ramp toward Orange City/Deland. At the traffic light, turn right onto Dr. Martin Luther King Parkway. Turn right at the first light, which is Cassadaga Road. Continue 1½ miles to the intersection with Stevens Street. The Information Center is on the right. For more information, call (C) **386/228-3171** or log on to www.cassadaga.org.

SHOPPING

On the mainland, Daytona Beach's main riverside drag, **Beach Street,** is one of the few areas in town where people actually stroll. The street is wide and inviting, with palms down its median and decorative wrought-iron archways and fancy brickwork overlooking a branch of the Halifax River that separates downtown from City Island, home of municipal offices and the lovingly restored Jackie Robinson Ballpark (see "Spectator Sports," above). Today, Beach Street, between Bay Street and Orange Avenue, offers antiques and collectibles shops, art galleries, clothiers, a magic shop, the local historical museum (see "Museums & Attractions," above) and several good cafes. At 154 S. Beach St., you'll find the home of the **Angell & Phelps Chocolate Factory** (© 386/252-6531; www.angellandphelps.com), which has been making candy for more than 75 years. Come here to watch the goodies being made (and get a free sample!) or just to buy some of the handmade treats.

"Hog" riders will find several shops to their liking along Beach Street, north of International Speedway Boulevard, including the **Harley-Davidson Store,** 290 N. Beach St., at Dr. Mary McLeod Bethune Boulevard (© 386/253-2453), a 20,000-square-foot retail outlet and diner serving breakfast and lunch. It's one of the nation's largest dealerships. In addition to hundreds of gleaming new and used Hogs, you'll find as much fringed leather as you've ever seen in one place.

The **Daytona Flea and Farmer's Market,** on Tomoka Farms Road at the junction of I-95 and U.S. 92, a mile west of the Speedway (© 386/253-3330; www.daytonafleamarket.com), is huge, with 1,000 covered outdoor booths plus 100 antiques and collectibles vendors in an air-conditioned building. Most of the booths feature new (though not necessarily first-rate) wares along the lines of socks, sunglasses, luggage, handbags, jewelry, tools, and the like. It's open year-round Friday through Sunday from 8am to 5pm. Admission and parking are free.

Ocean Walk Shoppes at Ocean Walk Village, 250 N. Atlantic Ave. (© 386/257-5077; www.oceanwalkvillage.com), is a collection of upscale boutiques and restaurants and a 10-screen movie theater.

WHERE TO STAY

Room rates here are among the most affordable in Florida. Some properties have as many as 20 rate periods during the year, but generally they are somewhat higher from the beginning of the races in February all the way to Labor Day. They skyrocket during major events at the Speedway, during bikers' gatherings, and during college spring break (see "Florida Calendar of Events," in chapter 2, beginning on p. 23), when local hotels fill to the bursting point. Even if you can find a room then, there's often a minimum-stay requirement.

Hundreds of hotels and motels line Atlantic Avenue along the beach, many of them family owned and operated. The Daytona Beach Area Convention & Visitors Bureau (see "Essentials," earlier in this chapter) distributes a brochure that lists **Superior Small Lodgings** for Daytona Beach, Deland, and New Smyrna Beach. All of the small motels listed below are members.

If you're going to the races and don't care about staying on the beach, some upper-floor rooms at the new **Hilton Garden Inn Daytona Beach Airport,** 189 Midway Ave. (© 877/944-4001 or 386/944-4000), overlook the international speedway track. Unlike most members of Hilton's Garden Inn chain, this one has a restaurant.

Thousands of rental condominiums line the beaches here. Among the most luxurious is the new, 150-unit condominium hotel **Ocean Walk Resort,** 300 N. Atlantic Ave., Daytona Beach, FL 32118 (© 800/649-3566 or 386/323-4800;

www.oceanwalkresort.com), which is part of the Ocean Walk Village redevelopment. Near the Main Street Pier, it's in the center of the action and has one- and two-bedroom apartments with fully equipped kitchens, washers and dryers, and all of the usual hotel amenities, plus a wondrous computer golf simulator, a "lazy river" in the outdoor pool, an island putting green, and much more—including the gaudiest lobby we've ever seen. One of the largest rental agents is **Peck Realty,** 2340 S. Atlantic Ave., Daytona Beach Shores, FL 32118 (© **800/447-3255** or 386/257-5000; www.peckrealty.com).

In addition to the 6% state sales tax, Volusia County levies a 4% tax on hotel bills.

Adam's Mark Daytona Beach Resort
If you can't get rooms anywhere else—especially during race weeks—this is a decent place to stay. Otherwise, unless you enjoy staying amongst tons of name tagged conventioneers, this hotel is best avoided. Daytona's largest beachfront hotel has extensive on-site meeting facilities, and the city's Ocean Center convention complex is across the street, meaning lots of big groups stay here. It's also in the middle of the beach action, right on the city's Boardwalk and a block north of the busy Main Street Pier. One of Daytona's best-equipped properties, it's designed so every room has an ocean view.

100 N. Atlantic Ave. (Fla. A1A, between Earl St. and Auditorium Blvd.), Daytona Beach, FL 32118. © **800/444-2326** or 386/254-8200. Fax 386/253-0275. www.adamsmark.com. 746 units. $115–$185 double. AE, DC, DISC, MC, V. Valet parking $9; free self-parking. **Amenities:** 3 restaurants; 3 bars; heated outdoor pool; exercise room; Jacuzzi; sauna; watersports equipment rentals; bike rental; game room; concierge; limited room service; massage; babysitting; laundry service; coin-op washers and dryers; concierge-level rooms. *In room:* A/C, TV, dataport, coffeemaker, hair dryer, iron.

Daytona Beach Hilton Oceanfront Resort ★★
Far enough south to escape the maddening crowds at Main Street, the Hilton is among the best choices here. It welcomes you in an elegant terra-cotta–tiled lobby with comfortable seating areas, a fountain, and potted palms. The large guest rooms are grouped in pairs and can be joined to form a suite; only one of each pair has a balcony. Oceanfront rooms are preferable, but all have sea and/or river views. A few also have kitchenettes. The surprisingly good Blue Water lobby restaurant is one of Daytona's most beautiful; patio dining is an option.

2637 S. Atlantic Ave. (Fla. A1A, between Florida Shores Blvd. and Richard's Lane), Daytona Beach, FL 32118. © **800/774-1500** or 386/767-7350. Fax 386/760-3651. www.hilton.com. 214 units. $116–$359 double. AE, DC, DISC, MC, V. **Amenities:** Restaurant; bar; heated outdoor pool; exercise room; Jacuzzi; watersports equipment rentals; game room; salon; limited room service; babysitting; laundry service; coin-op washers and dryers; concierge-level rooms. *In room:* A/C, TV, dataport, kitchen, coffeemaker, hair dryer, iron.

Old Salty's Inn (Value)
The most unusual of the many mom-and-pop beachside motels here, Old Salty's is a lush tropical enclave carrying out a *Gilligan's Island* theme, with old motors, rotting boats, life preservers, and a Jeep lying about. The TV series' main characters are depicted in big murals painted on the buildings. The two-story wings flank a courtyard festooned with palms and banana trees (you can pick one for breakfast). Facing this vista, the bright rooms have microwaves, refrigerators, and front and back windows to let in good ventilation. The choice units have picture windows overlooking the beach. There are gas grills and rocking chairs under a gazebo by a heated beachside swimming pool.

1921 S. Atlantic Ave. (Fla. A1A, at Flamingo Ave.), Daytona Beach Shores, FL 32118. © **800/417-1466** or 386/252-8090. Fax 386/947-9980. www.oldsaltys.com. 19 units. $53–$71 doubles; $63–$93 efficiencies; $75–$121 suites. AE, DISC, MC, V. **Amenities:** Heated outdoor pool; free use of bikes; coin-op washers and dryers. *In room:* A/C, TV, kitchen, fridge, coffeemaker, hair dryer, iron.

The Plaza Resort & Spa ★★
Remodeled in 2000 to the tune of $26 million (the original seven-story hotel was built in the early 20th century), these

elegant adjoining 7- and 13-story buildings now hold some of Daytona Beach's best rooms (in a much more tasteful atmosphere than many of the neighboring hotels)—provided you don't need a large bathroom. The choice units are the corner suites, which have sitting areas and two balconies overlooking the Atlantic; some even have a Jacuzzi. All units have balconies and microwaves (an on-premises convenience store sells frozen dinners). The renovations also saw the opening of the full-service **Ocean Waters Spa** ★★ (© **386/267-1660;** www.oceanwatersspa.com). There are 16 treatment rooms and a soothing menu of facials, massages, and wraps.

600 N. Atlantic Ave. (at Seabreeze Ave.), Daytona Beach, FL 32118. © **800/874-7420** or 386/255-4471. Fax 386/238-7984. www.plazaresortandspa.com. 323 units. $69–$215 doubles; $189–$449 suites. AE, DC, DISC, MC, V. **Amenities:** Restaurant; bar; heated outdoor pool; exercise room; spa; Jacuzzi; watersports equipment rentals; game room; business center; limited room service; massage; babysitting; laundry service; coin-op washers and dryers; concierge-level rooms. In room: A/C, TV, dataport, microwave, fridge, coffeemaker, hair dryer, iron.

Shoreline All Suites Inn & Cabana Colony Cottages ★ *Value* The Shoreline All Suites Inn, built in 1954 but substantially modernized, features one- and two-bedroom suites that occupy two buildings separated by a walkway leading to the beach. Most have small bathrooms with scant vanity space and—shall we say—intimate shower stalls. Every unit has a full kitchen, plus there are barbecue grills on the premises. For a change of scenery, consider the fine little cottage complex at the Shoreline's sister property, the **Cabana Colony Cottages** ★★. All 12 of the cottages were built in 1927 but have been upgraded by the owners. They aren't much bigger than a motel room with a kitchen, but they're light and airy and are attractively furnished with white wicker pieces. The cottages share a heated beachside swimming pool with the Shoreline.

2435 S. Atlantic Ave. (Fla. A1A, at Dundee Rd.), Daytona Beach Shores, FL 32118. © **800/293-0653** or 386/252-1692. Fax 386/239-7068. www.daytonashoreline.com. 30 units, including 12 cottages. $59–$350 suites and cottages. Rates include continental breakfast. Golf packages available. AE, DISC, MC, V. **Amenities:** Heated outdoor pool; coin-op washers and dryers. In room: A/C, TV/VCR, kitchen, coffeemaker.

The Villa Bed & Breakfast ★★★ You'll think you're in Iberia upon entering this 70+-year-old Spanish mansion's great room with its fireplace, baby grand piano, terra-cotta floors, and walls hung with Mediterranean paintings. A sunroom equipped with a TV and VCR, a formal dining room, and a breakfast nook are also located downstairs. The lush backyard surrounds a swimming pool and a covered, four-person Jacuzzi. Upstairs, the nautically themed Christopher Columbus room has a vaulted ceiling and a small balcony overlooking the pool. The largest quarter here is the King Carlos suite, the original master bedroom with a four-poster bed, entertainment system, refrigerator, rooftop deck, dressing area, and bathroom equipped with a four-head shower. The Queen Isabella room has a portrait of the queen over a queen-size bed, and the Marco Polo room has Chinese black-lacquer furniture and Oriental rugs evoking the great explorer's adventures.

801 N. Peninsula Dr. (at Riverview Blvd.), Daytona Beach, FL 32118. © and fax **386/248-2020.** www.thevillabb.com. 4 units (all with bathroom). $100–$250 double. Rates include continental breakfast. AE, MC, V. No children or pets accepted. **Amenities:** Heated outdoor pool; Jacuzzi. In room: A/C, TV, hair dryer, no phone.

WHERE TO DINE

Daytona Beach has a few interesting dining venues, but not many are likely to leave an indelible memory. A profusion of fast-food joints line the major thoroughfares, especially along Atlantic Avenue on the beach and International Speedway Boulevard (U.S. 92) near the racetrack. Restaurants come and go in the Beach Street district on the mainland, and along Main Street and Seabreeze Boulevard on the beach. A casual restaurant serves burgers and chicken wings and lots of suds out on the Main Street Pier.

The local **Shells** seafood restaurant is on the beach at 200 S. Atlantic Ave. (© **386/258-0007;** www.shellsseafood.com), a block north of International Raceway Boulevard. See p. 403 for details about this inexpensive chain.

There are two other outlets of chain restaurants that are worth a special mention here. **Buca di Beppo** (a boisterous, fun, and loud restaurant serving "immigrant southern Italian specialties" family style) is open for dinners only, until 10pm (11pm Fri–Sat). Expect to take home leftovers, as the portions are huge— but don't worry, you'd want to anyway: The food is surprisingly good, especially for a "theme" restaurant (2514 W. International Speedway Blvd.; © **386/253-6523;** www.bucadibeppo.com). **Stonewood Tavern & Grill** (100 S. Atlantic Ave. in Ormond Beach; © **386/671-1200;** www.stonewoodgrill.com) is a casual but upscale restaurant with a nice but dark mahogany interior, good American food, and excellent service. Also only open for dinner, you won't be disappointed with its menu of steaks, seafood, and the like.

AT THE BEACHES

Down the Hatch ⭐ (Value) SEAFOOD   Occupying a 1940s fish camp on the Halifax River, Down the Hatch serves big portions of fresh fish and seafood (note its shrimp boat docked outside). Inexpensive burgers and sandwiches are available, too. The scenic views include boats and shorebirds visible through the big picture windows—you might even see dolphins frolicking. At night, arrive early to catch the sunset over the river, and also to beat the crowd at this very popular place. In summer, light fare is served outside on an awning-covered deck.

4894 Front St., Ponce Inlet. © 386/761-4831. Call ahead for Priority Seating. Main courses $9–$25 (most $10–$16); breakfast $2–$5; burgers and sandwiches $3–$6.50; early-bird menu (served 11am–5pm) $6–$8. AE, MC, V. Daily 8am–10pm. Closed 1st week in Dec. Take Atlantic Ave. south, make a right on Beach St., and follow the signs.

Julian's Dining Room & Lounge ⭐ AMERICAN   This family-owned and -operated restaurant has catered to locals and tourists since 1967, offering a casual atmosphere and friendly service. Unlike most eateries in this area, it specializes in prime Western beef (filet mignons, strip steaks, and T-bones, any of which we recommend), but the seafood is far from second fiddle here. Good choices include broiled snapper, fried or sautéed softshell crab, and king crab au gratin.

88 S. Atlantic Ave., Ormond Beach. © 386/677-6767. www.juliansrest.com. Reservations suggested. Main courses $9–$26. AE, DC, MC, V. Daily 4–11pm. From Daytona Beach, take Atlantic Ave./Fla. A1A north and look for the large A-frame on the left, 2 blocks before Fla. 40.

Ocean Deck Restaurant & Beach Club (Value) SEAFOOD/PUB FARE   Known by spring-breakers, bikers, and other beachgoers as Daytona's best "beach pub" since 1940, the Ocean Deck is also the best restaurant in the busy area around the Main Street Pier. Opening to the sand and surf, the downstairs reggae bar is as sweaty, noisy, and packed as ever (a band plays down there nightly from 9pm–2:30am). The upstairs dining room can be noisy, too, but you can come here for some good food, reasonable prices, and great ocean views. You can choose from a wide range of seafood, chicken, sandwiches, and the best burgers on the beach, but don't pass up the mahimahi (look for "trophy" on the menu), first broiled with peppery Jamaican spices and then finished off on a grill, a bargain at $9. There's valet parking after dark, or you can park free at the lot behind the Ocean Deck's Reggae Republic surf shop, a block away on Atlantic Avenue.

127 S. Ocean Ave. (at Kemp St.). ℂ **386/253-5224.** www.oceandeck.com. Main courses $9–$18; salads and sandwiches $5–$8. AE, DISC, MC, V. Daily 11am–2am (bar to 3am).

ON THE MAINLAND

The Cellar ✹ AMERICAN   An excellent place for ladies who lunch, this tearoom occupies the basement of a Victorian home built in 1907 as President Warren G. Harding's winter home (he spent election eve here in 1920) and now is listed in the National Register of Historic Places. It couldn't be more charming, with low ceilings, backlit reproduction Tiffany windows, fresh flowers everywhere, linen tablecloths and napkins, and china teacups. If you can play the piano, help yourself to the baby grand. A wide-ranging lunch menu offers the likes of the house signature chicken salad as a platter or croissant sandwich, a quiche du jour, crab-cake sandwich, vegetarian lasagna, or chicken potpie. In the warm months, there's outdoor seating at umbrella tables on a covered garden patio.

220 Magnolia Ave. (between Palmetto and Ridgewood aves.). ℂ **386/258-0011.** Soups, salads, and sandwiches $6–$9. AE, DISC, MC, V. Mon–Fri 11am–3pm.

The Dancing Avocado Kitchen ✹ VEGETARIAN   A healthy place to start your day, or have lunch while touring downtown, this store-front establishment purveys a number of vegetarian omelets, burritos, salads, personal-size pizzas, and hot and cold sandwiches such as an avocado Reuben. A few chicken and turkey items are on the menu, but the only red-meat selection is a hamburger. You can dine outside or inside the store with vegetable drawings on its brick walls and ceiling fans suspended from black rafters.

110 S. Beach St. (between Magnolia St. and International Speedway Blvd.). ℂ **386/947-2022.** Breakfast $2.50–$5; sandwiches, salads, and pizzas $4–$8. AE, DC, DISC, MC, V. Mon–Sat 8am–4pm.

Frappes North ✹✹ CREATIVE AMERICAN/FUSION   It's worth the 6-mile drive north to Bobby and Meryl Frappier's sophisticated, hip establishment, at which they provide this area's most entertaining cuisine. Several chic dining rooms—one has beams extending like spokes from a central pole—set the stage for an inventive, ever-changing "Menu of the Moment" fusing a multitude of styles. Ingredients are always fresh, and the herbs come from the restaurant's garden. You may run into treats such as organically groovy chicken with goat cheese, prosciutto, shiitake mushrooms, and Madeira wine sauce or maple-glazed crispy duck. Bobby and Meryl always have at least one vegetarian (though not necessarily nondairy) main course. Lunch is a steal here, with dinner-size main courses at a fraction of dinnertime prices. The restaurant is in a storefront on the mainland stretch of Granada Boulevard, Ormand Beach's main drag.

123 W. Granada Blvd. (Fla. 40; between Ridgewood Ave. and Washington St.), Ormand Beach. ℂ **386/615-4888.** www.frappesnorth.com. Reservations recommended. Main courses $15–$25; lunch $7–$11. AE, MC, V. Mon–Fri 11:30am–2:30pm; Mon–Sat 5–10pm. From the beaches, drive 4 miles north on Fla. A1A to left on Granada Blvd. (Fla. 40); cross Halifax River to restaurant on right.

McK's Dublin Station AMERICAN/IRISH   Worth knowing about because it serves food after midnight, this upscale Irish pub has an eclectic menu. The fare includes club sandwiches, burgers, a mahimahi wrap, and a few main courses of steaks, fish, and chicken. The food isn't exceptional, but it's perfectly acceptable after a few Bass ales. The service is sometimes rushed, but usually pleasant.

218 S. Beach St. (between Magnolia St. and Ivy Lane). ℂ **386/238-3321.** Reservations not accepted. Main courses $6–$15; salads and sandwiches $5–$8. AE, MC, V. Mon–Wed 11am–9pm; Thurs–Sat 11am–10pm (bar open later).

Rosario's Ristorante ⭐ SOUTHERN ITALIAN/TUSCAN   A Victorian boardinghouse with lace curtains on high windows makes an incongruous setting for a lively restaurant. The menu delivers pastas with Bolognese and marinara sauces, but nightly specials are much more intriguing, drawing inspiration from ancient Tuscan recipes. If the mixed grill of squirrel, pheasant, rabbit, and quail in a hunter's sauce doesn't appeal, you can always opt for grouper Livornese. There's also music in the cozy bar Thursday through Saturday nights.

In Live Oak Inn, 448 S. Beach St. (at Loomis Ave.). ℂ **386/258-6066.** Reservations recommended. Main courses $12–$24. MC, V. Tues–Sat 5–10pm.

DAYTONA BEACH AFTER DARK
Check the Friday edition of the Daytona Beach *News-Journal* (www.n-jcenter.com) for its weekly "Go-Do" and the Sunday edition for the "Master Calendar" section, which list upcoming events. Other good sources are *Happenings Magazine* and *Backstage Pass Magazine,* two tabloids available at the visitor center (see "Essentials," earlier in this chapter) and in many hotel lobbies.

There are also ghost tours led by certified ghost hunters. Merging legends with science, you're guaranteed to have a spooky time (at least it's more interesting than most touristy ghost tours). A portion of all proceeds goes to cemetery preservation and restoration, so at least you can feel good about the fee. Tickets are $8 per person, children under 6 are free. Contact **Haunts of Daytona** (ℂ **386/253-6034;** www.hauntsofdaytona.com) for tours and start times.

THE PERFORMING ARTS   The city-operated **Peabody Auditorium,** 600 Auditorium Blvd., between Noble Street and Wild Olive Avenue (box office ℂ **386/254-4545** or 386/671-3460), is Daytona's major venue for serious performance, including concerts by the local Symphony Society (ℂ **386/253-2901**). Professional actors perform Broadway musicals during winter and summer at the **Seaside Music Theater,** 176 N. Beach St., downtown (ℂ **800/854-5592** or 386/252-6200; www.seasidemusictheater.org).

Under the city auspices, the **Oceanfront Bandshell** (ℂ **386/671-3400**), on the boardwalk next to the Adam's Mark Hotel, hosts a series of free big-name concerts every Sunday night from early June to Labor Day. It's also the scene of raucous spring-break concerts.

THE CLUB & BAR SCENE   In addition to the following, the sophisticated **Clocktower Lounge** at the Adam's Mark Daytona Beach Resort (p. 533) is worth a visit.

600 North, 600 North Atlantic (ℂ **904/255-4471**), *is* Baywatch revisited, with buxom bikini babe staffers who have actually been extras on the show, and a year-round spring break vibe with assorted drinking and thong sporting contests.

The **Boot Hill Saloon,** 310 Main St. (ℂ **904/258-9506**), is a bluesy, brew-sy honky tonk especially popular during race and bike weeks. If line dancing is your thang, then scoot your boots over to the **Rockin' Ranch,** 801 S. Nova Rd. (ℂ **904/947-0785**), an uber fun country western bar with live music and even line dancing lessons.

Main Street and **Seabreeze Boulevard** on the beach are happening areas where dozens of bars (and a few topless shows) cater to leather-clad bikers.

A popular beachfront bar for more than 40 years, the **Ocean Deck Restaurant & Beach Club,** 127 S. Ocean Ave. (ℂ **386/253-5224;** see "Where to Dine," above), is packed with a mix of locals and tourists, young and old, who come for live music and cheap drinks. Reggae or ska bands play after 9:30pm.

There's valet parking after dark, or leave your vehicle at Ocean Deck's Reggae Republic surf shop on Atlantic Avenue.

3 St. Augustine: America's First City ⟨★⟨★

105 miles NE of Orlando, 302 miles N of Miami, 39 miles S of Jacksonville

With its 17th-century fort, old city gates, horse-drawn carriages clip-clopping along narrow streets, historic buildings, and reconstructed 18th-century Spanish Quarter, St. Augustine seems more like a picturesque European village than a modern Floridian city. This is, after all, the oldest continuous European settlement in the United States (no, it wasn't Jamestown in 1607 or the Pilgrims at Plymouth Rock in 1620). A group of French Huguenots settled in 1562 near the mouth of the St. Johns River, in present-day Jacksonville. Three years later, a Spanish force under Pedro Menéndez de Avilés arrived on the scene, wiped out the Huguenot men (de Avilés spared their women and children), and established a settlement on the harbor he named "St. Augustín."

The colony survived a succession of attacks by pirates, Indians, and the British over the next 2 centuries. The Treaty of Paris, ending the French and Indian War, ceded the town to Britain in 1763, but the British gave it back 20 years later. The United States took control when it acquired Florida from Spain in 1821.

Tourism is St. Augustine's main industry these days; but despite the daily invasion (with good reason—there are a plethora of interesting attractions), it's an exceptionally charming town, with good restaurants, a small-town nightlife, and shopping bargains. Give yourself 2 days here just to see the highlights, longer to savor this historic gem: St. Augustine is one of those places that actually lives up to most of the sickly sweet and sentimental promotional literature written about it.

ESSENTIALS

GETTING THERE   The Daytona Beach airport (p. 526) is about an hour's drive south of St. Augustine, but services are more frequent—and fares usually lower—at Jacksonville's international airport, about the same distance north (p. 555). Amtrak's nearest train station is in Jacksonville. See "Essentials," in sections 2 and 4 of this chapter, for details.

VISITOR INFORMATION   Before you go, contact the **St. Augustine, Ponte Vedra & The Beaches Visitors and Convention Bureau,** 88 Riberia St., Suite 400, St. Augustine, FL 32084 (✆ **800/653-2489** or 904/829-1711; www.visitoldcity.com), and request the *Visitor's Guide,* detailing attractions, events, restaurants, accommodations, shopping, and more.

The **St. Augustine Visitor Information Center** is at 10 Castillo Dr., at San Marco Avenue, opposite the Castillo de San Marcos National Monument (✆ **904/825-1000**). There are numerous ways to see the city, depending on your interest and time, and this is a good place to make your plans. For $1, you can watch "Struggle to Survive," a 42-minute video about the town's difficult first 14 years (history buffs will enjoy it; otherwise, it's a good way to kill an hour on a rainy day). However, the free 22-minute orientation video is more helpful in planning your visit. Once you've looked through their extensive information and made a plan, you can buy tickets for sightseeing trains and trolleys, which include discount admissions to the attractions (see "Getting Around," below). The center is open daily, from 8:30am to 5:30pm.

(*Tips*) **Where to Park in "St. Aug"**

On-street parking is nonexistent in St. Augustine's historic district, and metered parking lots are difficult to find and are often full. Your best bet is to park in the large lots behind the visitor center on Castillo Drive. The $3 fee is good for 2 consecutive days, so you may leave and return at will. Plus, most of the top historic attractions are within walking distance of the center, as it is virtually across the street from the Old City Gates.

GETTING AROUND   Once you've parked at the visitor center, you can walk or take one of the sightseeing trolleys, trains, or horse-drawn carriages around the historic district. The trolleys and trains follow 7-mile routes, stopping at the visitor center and at or near most attractions between 8:30am and 5pm daily. You can get off at any stop, visit the attraction, and step aboard the next vehicle that comes along. Several vehicles make continuous circuits along the route throughout the day; you won't have to wait more than 20 minutes. If you don't get off at any attractions, it takes about 1 hour and 10 minutes to complete the tour. They don't all go to the same sights, so speak with their agents at the visitor center to pick the right one for you. You can buy tickets there or from the drivers. The companies also sell **discounted tickets** to some attractions.

St. Augustine Historical Sightseeing (© **904/826-4218** or 904/829-3800; operates the green-and-white, open-air buses (and enclosed buses when it rains, a definite advantage). You can park your car at the headquarters (the Authentic Old Jail and the Florida Heritage Museum at the Authentic Old Jail, which are also stops on the tour). The bus tours cost $15 for adults, $5 for kids 6 to 12, free for kids under 6.

St. Augustine Sightseeing Trains (© **800/226-6545** or 904/829-6545; www.redtrains.com) cover all the main sites except the Authentic Old Jail and the Florida Heritage Museum at the Authentic Old Jail, but its red open-air trains are small enough to go down more of the narrow historic-district streets. Tickets are $14 for adults, $5 for kids 6 to 12, free for kids under 6, and are good for 3 consecutive days. The company also sells package tickets for your convenience.

You may also want to see the sights from the back of a horse-drawn carriage. **St. Augustine Transfer Company** (© **904/829-2391;** www.staugustinetransfer. com) has been showing people around town since 1877. The carriages line up on Avenida Menendez, south of Castillo de San Marcos National Monument. Slow-paced, entertainingly driver-narrated 45-minute to 1-hour rides past major landmarks and attractions are offered from 8am to midnight. Private tours and hotel and restaurant pickups are available. Carriage tours cost $20 for adults, $10 for kids 5 to 11, free for kids under 6. Add $3 if you want to take a ride after dark.

For more personalized tours, call **Tour Saint Augustine** (© **800/797-3778** or 904/825-0087), which offers guided walking tours around the historical area. Tours range from $10 per person for 1 hour.

You can also search for old spirits with the nightly **Ghost Tours of St. Augustine** (★★ (© **888/461-1009** or 904/461-1009; www.ghosttoursofstaugustine. com), in which guides in period dress lead you through the historic district or to the St. Augustine Lighthouse; tickets are $10 to $20 per person, depending on the tour you choose, children under 6 free. They also have 1-hour ghost cruises on the river in a 72-foot-tall-mast schooner. They cost $28 per person including soft drinks and snacks. Call for schedule and reservations.

The Sunshine Bus Company (© 904/823-4816) runs public bus routes Monday through Saturday from 6am to 7pm. The north-south line runs between the St. Augustine Airport on U.S. 1 and the historic district via San Marco Avenue and the Greyhound bus terminal on Malaga Street. Rides cost $1 per person. Call for the schedule.

For a taxi, call **Yellow Cab** (© 904/824-6888).

Solano Cycle, 61 San Marco Ave., at Locust Avenue (© 904/825-6766; www.solanocycle.com), 2 blocks north of the visitor center, rents bicycles, mopeds, and scooters. Bikes cost $14 a day; scooters are $56, and mopeds are $38. Open daily from 10am to 6pm.

SEEING THE TOP HISTORIC ATTRACTIONS

St. George Street from King Street north to the Old City Gate (at Orange St.) is the heart of the historic district. Lined with a plethora of restaurants and boutiques selling everything from T-shirts to antiques, these 4 blocks get the lion's share of the town's tourists. You'll have much less company if you poke around the narrow streets of the primarily residential neighborhood south of King Street.

Most of the town's attractions do not have guided tours, but most do have docents on hand to answer questions.

Be sure to drive through the parking lot of the Howard Johnson Express Inn, at 137 San Marco Ave., to see a gorgeous and stately **live oak tree** 🌟🌟 that is at least 600 years old and then continue east to **Magnolia Avenue** 🌟🌟, which is a spectacularly beautiful street with a lovely canopy of old magnolia trees.

Castillo de San Marcos National Monument 🌟

As far as fortresses are concerned, this one's pretty cool. America's oldest and best-preserved masonry fortification took 23 years (1672–95) to build. It is stellar in design, with a double drawbridge entrance (the only way in or out) over a 40-foot dry moat. Diamond-shaped bastions in each corner, which enabled cannons to set up a deadly crossfire, contained domed sentry towers. The seemingly indestructible Castillo was never captured in battle, and its coquina (limestone made from broken sea shells and corals) walls did not crumble when pounded by enemy artillery or violent storms throughout more than 300 years. Today, the old bombproof storerooms surrounding the central plaza house exhibits documenting the history of the fort, a national monument since 1924. You can also tour the vaulted powder magazine, a dank prison cell (supposedly haunted), the chapel, and guard rooms. Then, climb the stairs to get a great view of the Matanzas Bay. A self-guided tour map and brochure are provided at the ticket booth. If available, the 20- to 30-minute ranger talks are well worth attending. There are popular torchlight tours of the fort in winter (call for schedule).

If you like forts, you should also check out **Fort Matanzas,** built on an island in the 1740s to warn St. Augustine of enemy attacks from the south (which were out of reach of the Castillo de San Marcos). For more information, call © 904/471-0116 or visit www.nps.gov/foma. The monument is open daily from 8:30am to 5:30pm, and both admission to the fort and the ferry ride to the island are free, though donations are accepted.

1 E. Castillo Dr. (at San Marco Ave.). © 904/829-6506. www.nps.gov/casa. Admission $5 adults for 7-day pass, $2 children 6–16, free for children under 6 with an adult. Fort daily 8:45am–4:45pm; grounds daily 5:30am–midnight.

St. Augustine

San Sebastian River

Genoply St.
Milton St.
Douglas Ave.
A1A
Dismure St.
May St.
Matanzas Ave.
Dufferin Ave.
Williams St.
Magnolia Ave.
BUS 1 Ballard Ave.
Myrtle Ave. Ocean Ave.
Ponce de Leon Blvd.
San Marco Ave.
Macaris Creek
Old Mission Ave.
Pine St.
Locust St.
Rhode Ave.
Water St.
Mulberry St.
1
Castillo Dr.
Orange St.
5A
Malaga St.
Saragossa St.
Spanish St.
Cuna St.
Matanzas River
Carrera St.
Sevilla St.
Cordova St.
Hypolita St.
Menendez
Valencia St.
207
Treasury St.
Cathedral Pl.
St. Augustine Blvd.
King St.
BUS 1
214
Aviles St.
Charlotte St.
Bay St.
Epworth
Bridge of Lions A1A
To the Beach →
Anastasia Blvd.
Arredondo Inlet Dr.
Artillery Lane
Cadiz St.
Riberia St.
Bridge St.
Granada St.
Weedon St.
Marine St.
St. Francis St.
George St.
Maria Sanchez Lake
Matanzas River
DeHaven St.
Washington St.
Lovet St.
Central Ave.
South St.

St. Augustine

FLORIDA

ⓘ Information

0 — 1/2 mi
0 — 1/2 km
N

Colonial Spanish Quarter and Spanish Quarter Museum ✦✦   If H.G. Wells were alive, he'd think he was witnessing living proof of a bona fide time travel machine when he got a load of this recreated colonial Spanish village, complete with costumed folk doing things they used to do back in the 1700s. Watch as the blacksmiths, carpenters, leatherworkers, and home makers demonstrate their skills and show you what life was like before the Internet. All architecture and landscape have been recreated within this 2-square-block park, which, in my opinion, is infinitely more fun than the museum itself. Do take a 20-minute guided tour of the **DeMesa-Sanchez House** (ca. 1740–60), the only authentic colonial-era structure in the compound (the others are reproductions). If you're into all this recreated history, then do not miss the Old St. Augustine Village Museum (see below), which covers even more history.

33 St. George St. (between Cuna and Orange sts.). ✆ **904/825-6830.** www.historicstaugustine.com. Admission $7 adults, $6 seniors, $4 students 6–18, free for children 5 and under; or $13 per family. Daily 9am–5:30pm (last entry at 4:30pm).

Lightner Museum ✦✦✦   Now *this* is a museum. Henry Flagler's opulent Spanish Renaissance–style Alcazar Hotel, built in 1889, closed during the Depression and stayed vacant until Chicago publishing magnate Otto C. Lightner bought the building in 1948 to house his vast collection of Victoriana. The building is an attraction in itself and makes a gorgeous museum, centering on an open palm courtyard with an arched stone bridge spanning a fishpond. The first floor houses a Victorian village, with shop fronts representing emporia selling period wares. A Victorian Science and Industry Room displays shells, rocks, minerals, and Native American artifacts in beautiful turn-of-the-20th-century cases. Other exhibits include stuffed birds, an Egyptian mummy, steam-engine models, and amazing examples of Victorian glassblowing (yes, it's a strange amalgamation for a museum, but there's sure to be *something* you're interested in). Plan to spend about 90 minutes exploring it all, and be sure to be here at 11am or 2pm, when a room of automated musical instruments erupts in concerts of period music. Check out where the cafe is, too, which is housed in what used to be a stunning indoor pool. The imposing building across King Street was Henry Flagler's rival resort, the Ponce de León Hotel. It now houses **Flagler College,** which runs don't-miss-it 45-minute tours daily (at 10am and 2pm) of its magnificent Tiffany stained-glass windows, ornate Spanish-Renaissance architecture, and gold-leafed Maynard murals ($5 adults, $1 kids under 12; call ✆ **904/823-3378** or visit www.flagler.edu/news_events/tours.html for more information). Across Cordova Street stands another competitor of the day, the 1888-vintage Casa Monica Hotel (p. 549).

75 King St. (at Granada St.). ✆ **904/824-2874.** www.lightnermuseum.org. Admission $8 adults, $2 college students with ID and children 12–18, free for children 11 and under. Daily 9am–5pm (last tour 4pm).

The Oldest House ✦✦   Archaeological surveys indicate that a dwelling stood on this site as early as the beginning of the 17th century. What you see today, called the Gonzáles-Alvarez House (named for two of its prominent owners), evolved from a two-room coquina dwelling built between 1702 and 1727. The rooms are furnished to evoke various historical eras. Admission also entitles you to explore the adjacent **Manucy Museum of St. Augustine History,** where artifacts, maps, and photographs document the town's history from its origins through the Flagler era a century ago. Both are owned and operated by the St. Augustine Historical Society. Allow about 30 minutes here.

14 St. Francis St. (at Charlotte St.). ✆ **904/824-2872.** www.oldcity.com/oldhouse. Admission $6 adults, $5.50 seniors 55 and over, $4 students, free for children under 6; or $12 families. Daily 9am–5pm; tours depart every half-hour (last tour at 4:30pm).

The Oldest Store Museum ★★   The C&F Hamblen General Store, think a prehistoric WalMart, was St. Augustine's one-stop shopping center from 1835 to 1960, and the museum on its premises today replicates the emporium at the turn of the 20th century. On display are more than 100,000 items sold here in that era, many of them gleaned from the store's attic. They include high-button shoes, butter churns, spinning wheels, 1890s bathing suits, barrels of dill pickles (you can purchase one), and medicines that were 90% alcohol. Some 19th-century brand-name products shown here are still available today, among them Hershey's chocolate, Coca-Cola, Ivory soap, and Campbell's soups. It all makes for about 30 minutes of fascinating browsing.

4 Artillery Lane (between St. George and Aviles sts. behind Trinity Episcopal Church). ℂ **904/829-9729.** www.oldcity.com/oldstore. Admission $5 adults, $4.50 seniors over 60, $1.50 children 6–12, free for children 5 and under. Mon–Sat 10am–4pm; Sun noon–4pm.

The Oldest Wooden Schoolhouse in the U.S.A. ★ *Kids*   Excellent photo ops abound here at this Little House in the Prairie meets The Little Rascals old fashioned schoolhouse. One of three structures here dating from the Spanish colonial period of more than 2 centuries ago, this red-cedar and cypress structure is held together by wooden pegs and handmade nails, its hand-wrought beams still intact. The last class was held here in 1864. Today, the old-time classroom is re-created using cheesy animated pupils and teacher, complete with a dunce and a below-stairs "dungeon" for unruly children, which will make your kids count their lucky stars that they weren't in school back then.

14 St. George St. (between Orange and Cuna sts.). ℂ **904/824-0192.** www.oldestschoolhouse.com. Admission $2.75 adults, $2.25 seniors 55 and over, $1.75 children 6–12, free for children 5 and under. Daily 9am–5pm (later during summer).

Old St. Augustine Village Museum ★★   More time travel in St. Augustine is available at this awesome museum recreating life back in the old days. Operated by Daytona Beach's excellent Museum of Arts and Sciences (p. 530), this museum brings to life each period of the city's history, from Spanish colonial times to the early 20th century. The 10 restored homes here—built between 1790 and 1910—are original and on their original building sites. The oldest was owned for a year in the early 19th century by Achille Murat, Napoleon's exiled nephew (original letters from the French emperor are among the many fascinating exhibits). Many of the houses have varying exhibits inside, though since this museum is a work in progress, some are also closed, temporarily, until refurbishments are complete. The reconstructed Star General Store sells preserves and other Victorian-era goods. You'll need 2 hours to see it all, including the 30-minute guided tour. Admission is good all day, so if you miss the start of a tour, you can leave and come back.

250 St. George St. (entry on Bridge St. between St. George and Cordova sts.). ℂ **904/823-9722.** www.old-staug-village.com. Admission $7 adults, $6 seniors, $5 children under 12. Daily 9am–5pm. Guided tours on the hour 10am–3pm except 1pm.

Spanish Military Hospital   Hypochondriacs, doctors, and fans of medicine in general will love this place, but if you're squeamish in hospitals, this one isn't an exception. This clapboard building is a reconstruction of part of a hospital that stood here during the second Spanish colonial period from 1784 to 1821. A 20-minute guided tour will show you what the apothecary, the administrative offices, the patients' ward, and the herbarium probably looked like in 1791. The ward and a collection of actual surgical instruments of the period will enhance your appreciation of modern medicine.

3 Aviles St. (south of King St.). © 904/825-6830. Admission $2.50 adults, $2 seniors, $1.50 children. Mon–Sat 10am–5pm; Sun noon–5pm.

MORE HISTORIC ATTRACTIONS

Authentic Old Jail   It's no Alcatraz, but in a sinister way, this old jail is kind of quaint. This compact prison, a mile north of the visitor center, may be authentic, but it is not particularly historic. It was built in 1890 and served as the county jail until 1953. The sheriff and his wife raised their children upstairs and used the same kitchen facilities to prepare the inmates' meals and their own. Among the "regular" cells, you can also see a maximum-security cell where murderers and horse thieves were confined, a cell housing prisoners condemned to hang (they could see the gallows being constructed from their window), and a grim solitary-confinement cell—with no windows or mattress. A restaurant here serves inexpensive lunch fare.

167 San Marco Ave. (at Williams St.). © 904/829-3800. Admission $5 adults, $4 children 6–12, free for children 5 and under. Daily 8:30am–5pm.

Florida Heritage Museum at the Authentic Old Jail   Compared to the other museums in town, this one isn't so special. After you've seen the Authentic Old Jail, you can spend another 30 minutes wandering through this commercial museum documenting 400 years of Florida's past, focusing on the colorful life of Henry Flagler, the Civil War, and the Seminole Wars. Highlights are an extraordinary collection of toys and dolls, mostly from the 1870s to the 1920s, and a replica of a Spanish galleon filled with weapons, pottery, and treasures complementing display cases filled with actual gold, silver, and jewelry recovered by treasure hunters. A typical wattle-and-daub hut of a Timucuan Indian in a forest setting illustrates the lifestyle of St. Augustine's first residents.

167 San Marco Ave. (at Williams St.). © 904/829-3800. Admission $5 adults, $4 children 6–12, free for children 5 and under. Free admission with purchase of Old Town Trolley Tour. Daily 8:30am–5pm.

Fountain of Youth Archaeological Park *(Overrated)*   Considering that Botox and plastic surgery are the real fountains of youth, why bother? Never mind that Juan Ponce de León never found the Fountain of Youth, this 25-acre archaeological park bills itself as North America's first historic site. Smithsonian Institution archaeological digs have established that a Timucuan Indian village existed on this site some 1,000 years ago, but there's no evidence that Ponce de León visited here during his 1513 voyage of discovery. You can wander around the not-so-interesting grounds yourself, but you'll learn more on a 45-minute guided tour or a planetarium show about 16th-century celestial navigation. *Be warned:* This place could be a secondary dictionary definition for the phrase *tourist trap* (not to mention the water from the fountain smells and tastes *awful*). Nevertheless, the grounds are lovely and the nonfountain exhibits are okay, which is good, because people feel the need to come here, even though it's basically a waste of time.

11 Magnolia Ave. (at Williams St.). © 800/356-8222 or 904/829-3168. Admission $6 adults, $5 seniors, $3 children 6–12, free for children 5 and under. Daily 9am–5pm.

Mission of Nombre de Dios   This serene setting overlooking the Intracoastal Waterway is believed to be the site of the first permanent mission in the United States, founded in 1565. The mission is a popular destination of religious pilgrimages. Whatever your beliefs, it's a beautiful tree-shaded spot, ideal for quiet meditation.

27 Ocean Ave. (east of San Marco Ave.). © 904/824-2809. Free admission; donations appreciated. Daily 8am–5:30pm.

Old Florida Museum ★★ *Kids* For those who can't resist touching things in museums, it's okay to do so here, in fact it's encouraged, so help yourself! This mostly outdoors museum gives you the chance to experience historic Florida, with many hands-on activities (shelling and grinding corn, pumping water, writing with a quill pen, and so on) that kids and parents may enjoy. Showcasing daily living activities, everyday objects (games, weapons, tools, and more), and recreational pastimes, the museum is able to demonstrate how three different eras of people in the area—the native Timucuan Indians, colonial Spaniards, and American pioneers—lived, worked, and played from the 16th to the early 20th century.

254-D San Marco Ave. © 800/813-3208 or 904/824-8874. www.oldfloridamuseum.com. Adults $5, kids 12 and under $3. Daily 10am–5pm.

St. Augustine Lighthouse & Museum ★ Photo op alert! This 165-foot-tall structure, Florida's first official lighthouse, was built in 1875 (with a signature black-and-white spiral stripe and red lantern) to replace the old Spanish lighthouse that had stood at the inlet since 1565. Sitting in a shady grove of live oaks, the lightkeeper's Victorian cottage was destroyed by fire in 1970 but was meticulously restored to its Victorian splendor. Also new is a Victorian-style visitor center that houses a museum explaining the history of the lighthouse and the area. You should be in good physical condition (children must be at least 7 years old *and* 4 ft. tall) to climb the 219 steps to the top of the lighthouse, where you can see as far as 19 nautical miles on a clear day.

81 Lighthouse Ave. (off Fla. A1A east of the Bridge of Lions). © 904/829-0745. www.staugustinelighthouse.com. Admission to museum and tower $6.95 adults, $5.95 seniors, $4.50 children 7–11, free for kids under 7 and all active-duty and retired military personnel. Daily 9am–6pm. Follow Fla. A1A south across Bridge of Lions; take last left before turnoff to Anastasia State Park.

OTHER ENTERTAINING ATTRACTIONS

Marineland If you absolutely can't make it to Sea World, fine. If you can, bypass this schlocky 7-acre beachfront tourist trap. This, the world's first oceanarium (1938), is located 15 minutes south of St. Augustine and is on the National Register of Historic Places. Here you can see dolphins, sea lions, penguins, flamingos, and a myriad of other ocean life or you can snorkel or scuba in the 450,000 gallon oceanarium with some of them, if you make reservations. Though the facility is not presently in spectacular condition, Marineland is still in the process of renovating, rebuilding, and revitalizing back into the modern first-class attraction it was when it first opened.

9600 Ocean Shore Blvd. © 904/460-1275. www.marineland.net. Admission $14 adults, $9 children 3–11. Dolphin encounter $120 (minimum height 50 in.). Scuba diving $65 (need your own equipment); snorkeling $35 (just need a bathing suit). Dolphin touch and feed (includes photo) $20. Wed–Mon 9:30am–4:30pm. South of St. Augustine on A1A.

Ripley's Believe It or Not! Museum *Kids* Another tourist trap, go here only if it's raining outside and you have absolutely nothing to do. This is the original Ripley's museum, housed in an architecturally interesting converted 1887 Moorish Revival residence—complete with battlements, massive chimneys, and rose windows. Like the Ripley's in a dozen other U.S. cities, the exhibits run the gamut, from a Haitian voodoo doll owned by Papa Doc Duvalier to letters carved on a pencil with a chainsaw by Ray "Wild Mountain Man" Murphy.

19 San Marco Ave. (at Castillo Dr.). © 904/824-1606. www.staugustine-ripleys.com. Admission $12.95 adults, $8.95 seniors, $7.95 children 5–12, free for children 4 and under. June 8 to Labor Day daily 9am–9pm; day after Labor Day to June 7 9am–7pm.

St. Augustine Alligator Farm and Zoological Park 𝔸𝔸 *Kids*   If you have gotten over the shock of Steve Irwin aka The Crocodile Hunter's Jacko-esque foible in which he dangled his three month old infant in front of a massive crocodile, then head over to the St. Augustine Alligator Farm and Zoological Park, where gators and crocs are a dime a dozen. In fact, there are more than 2,700 gators and crocodiles—including some rare white ones—on display at this more-than-century-old attraction. In fact, it houses the world's only complete collection of all 22 species of crocodilians, a category that includes alligators, crocodiles, caimans, and gavials. Other creatures living here include geckos, prehensile-tailed skinks, lizards, snakes, tortoises, monkeys, and exotic birds. There are ponds and marshes filled with a variety of ducks, geese, swans, herons, egrets, ibises, wood storks, and other native wading birds as well as a petting zoo with pygmy goats, potbellied pigs, miniature horses, mouflon sheep, and deer. Entertaining (and educational) 20-minute alligator and reptile shows take place hourly throughout the day, and spring through fall you can often see narrated feedings. There's also a stuffed (and famous) giant crocodile from New Guinea named Gomek on display.

999 Anastasia Blvd. (Fla. A1A), east of Bridge of Lions at Old Quarry Rd. ℂ 904/824-3337. www.alligator-farm.com (check for discounts). Admission $16 adults, $9 children 3–10, free for children under 3. Daily 9am–5pm; summer hours 9am–6pm.

HITTING THE BEACH

There are several places to find sand and sea: in **Vilano Beach,** on the north side of St. Augustine Inlet; and in **St. Augustine Beach,** on the south side (the inlet dumps the Matanzas and North rivers into the Atlantic). Be aware, however, that erosion has almost swallowed the beach from the inlet as far south as Old Beach Road in St. Augustine Beach. The U.S. Army Corps of Engineers is reclaiming the sand, but in the meantime, hotels and homes here have rock seawalls instead of sand bordering the sea.

Erosion has made a less noticeable impact on the beautiful **Anastasia State Park** 𝔸𝔸, on Anastasia Boulevard (Fla. A1A) across the Bridge of Lions and just past the Alligator Farm, where the 4 miles of beach (on which you can drive and park) are still backed by picturesque dunes. On its riverside, the area faces a lagoon flanked by tidal marshes. Amenities and activities include shaded picnic areas with grills, restrooms, windsurfing, sailing and canoeing (on a saltwater lagoon), a nature trail, and saltwater fishing (for bluefish, pompano, sea trout, redfish, and flounder—a license is required for out-of-state residents). In summer, you can rent chairs, beach umbrellas, and surfboards. There's good bird-watching here, too, especially in spring and fall; pick up a brochure at the entrance. The 139 wooded campsites are in high demand year-round. They have picnic tables, grills, and electricity. Admission to the park is $5 per vehicle and $1 for bicyclists and pedestrians. Campsites cost $23. For camping reservations, call ℂ **800/326-3521** or go to the website at www.reserveamerica.com. The day-use area is open daily from 8am to sunset. You can bring your pets. For more information, contact Anastasia State Park, 1340A Fla. A1A S., St. Augustine, FL 32084 (ℂ **904/461-2033;** www.floridastateparks.org/anastasia).

All St. Augustine beaches charge a fee of $3 per car at official access points from Memorial Day to Labor Day; the rest of the year you can park free, but there are no lifeguards on duty or toilet facilities on the beach.

Where Golf Is King

Passionate golf fans can easily spend a day at the **World Golf Hall of Fame** ★ (📞 **904/940-4123**), a state-of-the-art museum honoring professional golf, its great players, and the sport's famous supporters (including comedian Bob Hope and singer Dinah Shore). It's the centerpiece of **World Golf Village,** which is a complex of hotels, shops, offices, and 18-hole golf courses (see "Cruises, Fishing, Golf, Sailing & Watersports" below). There's an IMAX screen next door.

Museum admission is $12 adults, $11 seniors and students, $7 children 5 to 12. IMAX movie tickets range from $9 to $14 adults, $6 to $12 seniors and students, $5 to $9 children 5 to 12. Combination tickets to the museum and one IMAX movie cost $17 for adults, $15 seniors and students, $11 children 5 to 12. A round on the putting green costs $7 for adults, $6 seniors and students, and $5 for children 5 to 12. Admission and movies are free for children under 5. The museum is open daily from 10am to 6pm (IMAX movies run until 8pm Fri–Sat).

You don't have to play the real courses, because the village is built around a lake with a "challenge hole" sitting out in the middle, 132 feet from the shoreline. You can hit balls at it or play a round on the nearby putting course. The Walkway of Champions (whose signatures appear in pavement stones) circles the lake and passes a shopping complex whose main tenant is the two-story **Tour Stop** (📞 **904/940-0422**), a purveyor of pricey apparel and equipment.

You can stay at the luxurious **World Golf Village Renaissance Resort,** 500 S. Legacy Trail, St. Augustine, FL 32092 (📞 **888/740-7020** or 904/940-8000; www.worldgolfrenaissance.com).

The village is at exit 95A off I-95. For more information, contact World Golf Village, 21 World Golf Place, St. Augustine, FL 32092 (📞 **904/940-4000**; www.wgv.com).

CRUISES, FISHING, GOLF, SAILING & WATERSPORTS

For additional outdoor options, contact the St. Augustine, Ponte Vedra & The Beaches Visitors and Convention Bureau (p. 538) and ask them to send you a copy of their *Outdoor Recreation Guide.*

CRUISES   The Usina family has been running **St. Augustine Scenic Cruises** (📞 **904/824-1806;** www.scenic-cruise.com) on Matanzas Bay since the turn of the 20th century. They offer 75-minute narrated tours aboard the double-decker *Victory III,* departing from the Municipal Marina just south of the Bridge of Lions. You can sometimes spot dolphins, brown pelicans, cormorants, and kingfishers. Snacks, soft drinks, beer, and wine are sold on board. Departures are normally at 11am and 1, 2:45, and 4:30pm daily except Christmas, with an additional tour at 6:15pm from April 1 to May 21 and Labor Day to October 15; from May 22 to Labor Day there are two additional tours, at 6:45 and 8:30pm. Call ahead—schedules can change during inclement weather. Fares are $12 adults, $8.50 seniors, $7.50 juniors 13 to 18, $5.75 children 4 to 12, free for children under 4. If you're driving, allow time to find parking on the street.

You can also take the free ferry to Fort Matanzas on Rattlesnake Island. There are often dolphins in the water as you make the trip, and the fort is interesting if you have the time. Ferries take off from 8635 Highway A1A (follow A1A south out of St. Augustine for about 15 miles). Call © **904/471-0116** or visit www.nps.gov/foma/ for more information.

FISHING You can fish to your heart's content at **Anastasia State Park** (see "Hitting the Beach," above). You can also cast your line off **St. Johns County Fishing Pier,** on the north end of St. Augustine Beach (© **904/461-0119**). The pier is open 24 hours daily and has a bait shop with rental equipment that is open from 6am to 10pm. Admission is $2 ($1 children under 12) for fishing, 50¢ per person for sightseeing.

For full-day, half-day, and overnight **deep-sea fishing** excursions (for snapper, grouper, porgy, amberjack, sea bass, and other species), contact the **Sea Love Marina,** 250 Vilano Rd. (Fla. A1A north), at the eastern end of the Vilano Beach Bridge (© **904/824-3328;** www.sealovefishing.com). Full-day trips on the party boat *Sea Love II* cost about $50, half-day trips, $35. No license is required, and rod, reel, bait, and tackle are supplied. Bring your own food and drink.

GOLF The area's best golf resorts are in Ponte Vedra Beach—about a half-hour's drive north on Fla. A1A, closer to Jacksonville than St. Augustine (see "Where to Stay," in section 4, later in this chapter, for details).

At World Golf Village, 12 miles north of St. Augustine at exit 95A off I-95 (see the box, "Where Golf Is King," above), **The Slammer & The Squire** and **The King & The Bear** (© **904/940-6088;** www.wgv.com) together offer 36 holes amid a wildlife preserve. Locals say they're not as challenging as their greens fees, about $100 in summer, $165 in winter, including cart. For those not schooled in golf history, the "Slammer" is in honor of Sam Sneed, the "Squire" is for Gene Sarazen, the "King" is Arnold Palmer, and the "Bear" is Jack Nicklaus. Palmer and Nicklaus actually collaborated in designing their course.

Nicklaus also had a hand in the stunning course at the **Ocean Hammock Golf Club** ♠♠ (© **386/477-4600;** www.oceanhammock.com), on Fla. A1A in Palm Coast, about halfway between St. Augustine and Daytona Beach. Opened in late 2000 with six of its holes skirting the beach, it is the first truly ocean-side course built in Florida since the 1920s.

There are only a few courses in St. Augustine, including a rather flat 18 at the **Ponce de León Hotel, Golf & Conference Resort** and the **St. Augustine Shores Golf Club,** 707 Shores Blvd., off U.S. 1 (© **904/794-4653**). The latter is a par-70 course featuring 18 holes, lots of water, a lighted driving range and putting green, and a restaurant and lounge. Greens fees usually are under $30, including cart.

For more course information online, go to www.golf.com and www.floridagolfing.com, or call the **Florida Sports Foundation** (© **850/488-8347**) or **Florida Golfing** (© **866/833-2663**).

SAILING You can spend 4 hours under sail with Captain Paul Kulik on board his *Voyager* (© **904/347-7183;** www.villavoyager.com), a 22-foot-wide trimaran, which departs the Municipal Marina next to the Bridge of Lions. The cruises cost $38 per person, including sandwiches, soft drinks, and beer. The boat can carry a maximum of six guests, so call for reservations and schedule.

WATERSPORTS Jet skis and surfing and windsurfing equipment can be rented at **Surf Station,** 1020 Anastasia Blvd. (Fla. A1A), a block south of the Alligator Farm (© **904/471-9463**); and at **Raging Water Sports,** at the Conch

House Marina Resort, 57 Comares Ave. (© **904/829-5001**), which is off Anastasia Avenue (Fla. A1A) halfway between the Bridge of Lions and the Alligator Farm.

SHOPPING

The winding streets of the historic district are home to dozens of **antiques
stores** and **art galleries** stocked full of original paintings, sculptures, bric-a-brac,
fine furnishings, china, and other treasures. Brick-lined **Aviles Street,** 1 block
from the river, has an especially good mix of shops for browsing, as does **St.
George Street** south of the visitor center and the Uptown area on **San Marco
Avenue** a few blocks north of the center. The **Alcazar Courtyard Shops** at the
Lightner Museum (© **904/824-2874**) have a good selection of antiques shops
(p. 542). The visitor center has lists of art galleries and antiques shops, or you
can contact the **Antique Dealers Association of St. Augustine,** 60 Cuna St.,
St. Augustine, FL 32084 (no phone).

Experience chocolate heaven at **Whetstone Chocolates,** 2 Coke Rd. (Fla.
312), between U.S. 1 and the Mickler O'Connell Bridge (© **904/825-1700**).
Free self-guided tours of the store and factory usually take place Monday through
Saturday from 10am to 5pm, but call to make sure of the factory's schedule.
Whetstone has a retail outlet at 42 St. George St. in the historic district.

Outlet shoppers will find plenty of good hunting 7 miles northwest of downtown on Fla. 16 at I-95 in the **St. Augustine Outlet Mall** (© **904/825-1555;**
www.staugustineoutlets.com), on the west side of I-95; and the enclosed, air-
conditioned **Belz Factory Outlet World** (© **904/826-1311;** www.belz.com),
on the east side of the Interstate. Stores in both malls are open Monday through
Saturday from 9am to 9pm, Sunday from 10am to 6pm.

WHERE TO STAY

There are plenty of moderate and inexpensive motels and hotels in St. Augustine. Most convenient to the historic district is the 40-room **Best Western
Spanish Quarter Inn,** 6 Castillo Dr. (© **800/528-1234** or 904/824-4457;
www.staugustinebestwestern.com), directly across the street from the visitor center. It's completely surrounded by an asphalt parking lot but does have a swimming pool and hot tub.

Almost all accommodations increase their prices on weekends, when the town
is most crowded with visitors, so if you're coming on a weekend expect the
higher end of the listed rates. St. Johns County charges a 9% tax on hotel bills.

HOTELS & MOTELS

Casa Monica Hotel ★★★   This Moorish revival hotel was built in 1888 as a
luxury hotel by Bostonian and YMCA founder Franklin W. Smith. Unfortunately, Smith never really opened it, since the furniture he'd purchased for the
hotel never made it to St. Augustine, thanks to Henry Flagler, who owned the
railroad the furniture was to be shipped on as well as the neighboring—and thus
competing—hotel. In a bind and losing too much money, Smith finally sold the
hotel to Flagler, for 25¢ on the dollar of what he originally spent, and the furniture mysteriously appeared almost immediately! (This Spanish-Moorish–style
building—look for the atmospheric, arched, old-time carriage entrance near the
present garage—was also used as the St. Johns County Courthouse from the
1960s until 1997.)

Now totally restored, it's easily the best hotel in town, with top-notch rooms
and services. Most of the lovely guest quarters are spacious and fully modern
hotel rooms, with Iberian-style armoires, wrought-iron headboards, and tapestry

drapes. "Premium" rooms have sitting areas with sofas and easy chairs. All units have big bathrooms equipped with high-end toiletries and either a large walk-in shower or a combination tub-shower. Much more interesting are the "signature suites" installed in the building's two tile-topped towers and fortresslike central turret. Each of these one- to four-bedroom units is unique. One in the turret has a half-round living room with gun-port windows overlooking the historic district, while a three-story town house model in one of the towers has a huge whirlpool bathroom on its top floor. The 95 Cordova restaurant, which serves regional fare (such as Calypso-spiced mahimahi and sweet and sour rubbed Long Island duckling), has an excellent wine list, great service, and is beautifully decorated. However, though a lot of people swear the food served there is the best in the city, we couldn't find much to our taste. A player piano provides music in the adjoining bar. Guests here can pay $15 a day to use the swimming pools, restaurants, and other facilities at The Serenata Beach Club, an exclusive oceanfront club located ten minutes from the hotel.

95 Cordova St. (at King St.), St. Augustine, FL 32084. ✆ **800/648-1888** or 904/827-1888. Fax 904/819-6065. www.casamonica.com. 138 units. $149–$239 double. Packages available. AE, DC, DISC, MC, V. Valet parking $13; limited free self-parking 2 blocks from hotel. **Amenities:** Restaurant; marketplace; bar; heated (and cooled) outdoor pool; access to nearby health club; exercise room; Jacuzzi; bike rental; children's programs; concierge; business center; limited room service; babysitting; coin-op washers and dryers. *In room:* A/C, TV, dataport (high-speed access), fridge, coffeemaker, hair dryer, iron, safe.

Monterey Inn *(Value)*   For the price, you can't find a better choice than this modest, wrought-iron–trimmed motel overlooking the Matanzas Bay and close to the attractions and nightlife of the Old City. Three generations of the Six family have run this simple two-story motel, and they keep the 1960s building and grounds clean and functional. Rooms are not especially spacious but they are good enough to sleep in after a day on the beach.

16 Avenida Menendez (between Cuna and Hypolita sts.), St. Augustine, FL 32084. ✆ **904/824-4482.** Fax 904/829-8854. www.themontereyinn.com. 59 units. $59–$159 double. AE, DC, DISC, MC, V. **Amenities:** Heated outdoor pool. *In room:* A/C, TV, dataport, hair dryer.

BED-&-BREAKFASTS

St. Augustine has more than two-dozen bed-and-breakfasts in restored historic homes. They all provide free parking, complimentary breakfast, 24-hour refreshments, and plenty of atmosphere (the St. Francis Inn has a spectacular walled courtyard), but most accept neither young children nor guests who smoke (check before booking). Those listed below are in the historic district. For more choices, contact **St. Augustine Historic Inns,** P.O. Box 5268, St. Augustine, FL 33085-5268 (no phone; www.staugustineinns.com), for descriptions of its member properties.

Alexander Homestead 🟊🟊   A restored 1888 Victorian beauty, the four room Alexander Homestead is spectacular, not to mention romantic, and is a popular place for weddings and honeymoons. One room has a Jacuzzi, two have fireplaces, and each have lavender sachets tucked away in drawers, their own private porches, and antiques, many from the family heirloom collection of innkeeper Bonnie Alexander. Gourmet breakfasts include Bonnie's own recipe for baked French toast with almond syrup, and at night, you can have a glass of complimentary brandy to go along with your complimentary chocolate. Even better, coffee is delivered directly to your door in the morning so there's no need to really have to stir yourself too much.

14 Sevilla St., St. Augustine, FL 32084. ✆ **888/292-4147** or 904/826-4147. www.alexanderhomestead.com. 4 units (all with bathroom). $159–$199. Rates include full breakfast. AE, DISC, MC, V. *In room:* A/C, TV.

Tips **A Swashbuckling Hostel**

International travelers on the cheap congregate at the **Pirate Haus Inn & Hostel**, 32 Treasury St., at Charlotte Street (© **904/808-1999; www.piratehaus.com**), smack in the middle of the historic district. Done up in a pirate theme, this Spanish-style building has a communal kitchen, living room, and rooftop terrace. Affiliated with both Hostelling International and American Youth Hostels, the inn has five private rooms (three with their own bathrooms) equipped with either a queen or double bed plus one or two bunk beds. Two other rooms have dormitory-style bunk beds. Rooms cost $42 to $56 a night (higher on some weekends), while dorm beds go for $17 a night. MasterCard and Visa credit cards are accepted. Reservations are advised, especially on weekends. Rates include the hostel's famous all you can eat pancake breakfast.

Bayfront Westcott House Bed & Breakfast Inn ⭐   Overlooking Matanzas Bay, this romantic, two-story, Key West–style wood-frame house offers rare opportunities for an uncluttered view from the porch, the second-story veranda, and a shady courtyard. The rooms—some with bay windows, two-person whirlpool tubs, and working fireplaces—are exquisitely furnished and immaculate. Yours might have authentic Victorian furnishings and a brass bed made up with a white quilt and lace dust ruffle.

146 Avenida Menendez (between Bridge and Francis sts.), St. Augustine, FL 32084. © **800/513-9814** or 904/824-4301. Fax 904/824-4301. www.westcotthouse.com. 9 units (all with bathroom). $129–$229 double. Rates include full breakfast. AE, DISC, MC, V. **Amenities:** Access to nearby health club; Jacuzzi; free bicycles; massage. *In room:* A/C, TV, hair dryer.

Carriage Way Bed and Breakfast ⭐ *Value*   Primarily occupying an 1883 Victorian wood-frame house fronted by roses and hibiscus, this bed-and-breakfast isn't fancy or formal, but it is comfortable, relaxed, and a good value. Rooms in the main house are furnished with simple antique reproductions, including many four-poster beds. One room even retains its original fireplace. A console TV, books, magazines, and games are provided in a homey parlor. For more privacy, two more rooms are down the street in "The Cottage," a one-story clapboard house built in 1885. It has its own living room and kitchen, and both the Miranda and the Ashton rooms have claw-foot bathtubs. Miranda also sports a two-person Jacuzzi, and Ashton has its own small back porch. Special packages can provide you with nice little touches as a gourmet picnic lunch, a horse drawn carriage around the city, and breakfast in bed.

70 Cuna St. (between Cordova and Spanish sts.), St. Augustine, FL 32084. © **800/908-9832** or 904/829-2467. Fax 904/826-1461. www.carriageway.com. 11 units (all with bathroom). $89–$159 double. Rates include full breakfast. AE, DISC, MC, V. **Amenities:** Free use of bikes. *In room:* A/C, dataport.

Casablanca Inn on the Bay ⭐   This 1914 Mediterranean-style white-stucco house on the National Register of Historic Places faces the bay, although only a few of the rooms offer views. The most stunning are the two second-floor suites with bay-front balconies, generously sized hammocks, and private porches. The furnishings—a mix of turn-of-the-20th-century American oak, European, and

Victorian pieces—are of a higher quality than those at many other inns. One modern convenience is a cassette player with a small selection of classical tapes. This may be appreciated, especially if you are in a ground-floor room that unfortunately suffers from the noise of the street and the next-door bar and grill. Breakfast is served alfresco on the porch or in a glass-enclosed conservatory. Six units have neither TVs nor telephones. A porch with rocking chairs is an ideal spot to chill out, read a book, and sip a cocktail.

24 Avenida Menendez (between Hypolita and Treasury sts.), St. Augustine, FL 32084. © 800/826-2626 or 904/829-0928. Fax 904/826-1892. www.casablancainn.com. 20 units (all with bathroom). $99–$229 double. Rates include full breakfast. AE, DISC, MC, V. **Amenities:** Access to nearby health club; free use of bikes. *In room:* A/C, TV (18 units), no phone (6 units).

Kenwood Inn   There's lots of pink here, but what makes this inn so unusual is its relatively large outdoor space, which includes a swimming pool, a lushly landscaped sun deck, and a secluded garden courtyard (complete with a koi pond and neat flower bed under a sprawling pecan tree). The Victorian wood-frame house with graceful verandas has served as a boardinghouse or inn since the late 19th century. Everything from the carpeting to the linens to the china is first class. Rooms are larger and more private than most other accommodations in converted single-family homes. Some rooms have neither televisions nor telephones.

38 Marine St. (at Bridge St.), St. Augustine, FL 32084. © 800/824-8151 or 904/824-2116. Fax 904/824-1689. www.oldcity.com/kenwood. 14 units (all with bathroom). $95–$175 double; bridal suite $225. Rates include continental breakfast. DISC, MC, V. **Amenities:** Outdoor pool; free use of bikes. *In room:* A/C, TV (in some), fax, dataport, kitchen, minibar, fridge, coffeemaker, hair dryer, iron, no phone (in some).

Victorian House *Kids*   This 1897-vintage Victorian bed-and-breakfast features a wraparound porch and an adjoining old store, now dubbed the "Carriage House." The latter is divided into four units, one of which has a kitchenette. What's unusual is that children are welcome to stay in the Carriage House units, all of which have TVs and private entrances. Kids are not welcome to stay in the main house, however, whose rooms lack TVs. Country Victorian antiques adorn all units here, but none of the units have telephones.

11 Cadiz St. (between Aviles and Charlotte sts.), St. Augustine, FL 32084. © 877/703-0432 or 904/824-5214. Fax 904/824-7990. www.victorianhouse-inn.com. 8 units (all with bathroom). $95–$175 double. Rates include full breakfast. AE, DISC, MC, V. **Amenities:** Free bikes. *In room:* A/C, TV (4 units), kitchen (1 unit), no phone.

WHERE TO DINE

In a town with as much tourist traffic as St. Augustine, there are, of course, a fair number of "tourist trap" restaurants. But on the whole, the food in St. Augustine, even at the popular eateries, is fairly priced and of good quality.

The historic district has a branch of Tampa's famous **Columbia** restaurant, at 98 St. George St., at Hypolita Street (© **904/824-3341**). Like the original in Ybor City (p. 406), this one sports Spanish architecture, including intricate tile work and courtyards with fountains.

A1A Ale Works 🐊 SEAFOOD   Anyone who has ever chugged from a beer bong, entered a beer drinking contest, or simply just loves beer must visit the A1A Ale Works, the quintessential brew pub. You can't miss this two-story Victorian-style building on the waterfront opposite the Bridge of Lions. One of the city's most popular and fun watering holes, the noisy downstairs bar offers nightly entertainment, which sometimes filters upstairs into the restaurant. Despite the noise potential, the kitchen turns out a surprisingly good blend of new-world Floribbean, Cuban, Caribbean, and Latino styles, in a nice setting with big windows and outside balcony seating overlooking the river and Bridge of Lions. Most of the seafood is very fresh, and the sauces are made to order. The spicy ahi stick appetizer (sushi-grade tuna, pickled ginger, and sesame seeds wrapped in a wonton skin, cooked rare, served over Caribbean slaw and topped with a wasabi and siracha aioli) is as good as it gets, and you shouldn't leave without trying it. Don't overlook the nightly specials, either, especially the fresh fish. The house brew ranges from a very light lager to a nonalcoholic root beer.

1 King St. (at Avenida Menendez). ⓒ 904/829-2977. Call for preferred seating. Main courses $12–$28; sandwiches $7–$9. AE, DC, DISC, MC, V. Sun–Thurs 11am–10:30pm; Fri–Sat 11am–11pm. Late-night menu served downstairs.

The Bunnery Bakery & Café ⭐ *Value* BAKERY/DELI   If you suffer from attacks of the raging sweet tooth, get thee to the Bunnery. Alluring aromas waft from this bakery and cafe in the heart of the historic district. It's lovely to come here for breakfast or for a fresh pastry and hot cup of latte, cappuccino, or espresso anytime you need a break from sightseeing. At lunch, plop yourself into one of the colorful booths and indulge in soup, salads, burgers, panini, or a croissant stuffed with walnut-and-pineapple chicken salad. Order at the counter; the staff will call your number when it's ready.

121 St. George St. (between Treasury and Hypolita sts.). ⓒ 904/829-6166. Breakfast $3–$7; sandwiches and salads $3.50–$8. No credit cards. Daily 8am–6pm. Closed New Year's Day, Easter, Thanksgiving, Christmas Eve, Christmas.

Gypsy Cab Co. ⭐⭐ *Value* NEW AMERICAN   Billing itself as a temple of "urban cuisine," owner-chef Ned Pollack's high-energy establishment, with gaudy purple neon stripes outside and bright, art-filled dining rooms inside, offers the town's most interesting culinary experience. Ned's creative menu changes daily, although a hearty black-bean soup is a constant winner. If it's available, try the veal with bacon-horseradish cream or the grouper in a tomato-basil sauce. As a capper, we recommend Amaretto cheesecake or Key lime pie. Also worthy of note, the house salad dressing is so good they sell it by the bottle. Lunch is served (Mon–Fri 11am–4pm) in the Gypsy Bar & Grill next door, which has live music Wednesday, Friday, and Saturday evenings (ⓒ **904/ 808-1305**). Taking the concept a little too far, there's also a Gypsy Comedy Club right next door.

828 Anastasia Blvd. (Fla. A1A, at Ingram St., east of the Bridge of Lions). ⓒ 904/824-8244. www.gypsy-cab.com. Reservations not accepted. Main courses $12–$25. AE, DC, DISC, MC, V. Mon–Thurs 4:30–10pm; Fri 4:30–11pm; Sat 11am–11pm; Sun 10:30am–10pm.

La Parisienne ⭐⭐ CONTEMPORARY FRENCH   Somewhat of an accidental tourist in these parts, La Parisienne is a welcome respite from all the nearby Americana. Despite its name, this lovely dining room evokes the French countryside, with a rough-hewn beamed-pine ceiling, lace-curtained windows, and ladder-back chairs. Changing seasonally, the menu always features fresh seafood, and in fall you'll see venison and quail. If they're offered, begin with pan-seared sea scallops in a citrus sauce; then go on to steak au poivre with a Cognac-cream sauce, roast rack of lamb Provençal, or the day's treatment of fresh local fish. A fixed-price, five-course menu offers a choice of meat or seafood appetizers and main courses plus cheeses and dessert. The weekend brunch menu offers beignets, eggs Benedict, and scrambled eggs with smoked salmon.

60 Hypolita St. (between Spanish and Cordova sts.). ⓒ 904/829-0055. www.laparisienne.net. Reservations recommended. Main courses $19–$28; 5-course prix fixe menu $60. AE, DISC, MC, V. Tues–Fri 5–9pm; Sat–Sun 11am–3pm and 5–9pm.

Raintree ⚜ INTERNATIONAL Even if you don't have a full meal at this romantic 1879 Victorian house (about ½ mile north of the historic district), the tempting variety of hot crepes and an exemplary crème brûlée are worth a visit. Sweetness works its way onto the main menu, too, with the likes of cashew-encrusted pork tenderloin mignonettes with a champagne and ruby raspberry sauce. More traditional main courses include beef Wellington and rack of New Zealand lamb. It's all very good, though not as mod as at Gypsy Cab Co. or as expertly prepared as at La Parisienne (see above). The list of more than 300 vintages has won *Wine Spectator* awards. Keep in mind that Raintree is a destination restaurant, which means hordes of people are constantly traipsing through marveling at the lovely old world ambience.

102 San Marco Ave. (at Bernard St.). ℂ 904/824-7211. www.raintreerestaurant.com. Reservations recommended. Main courses $15–$24; dessert bar $5.50. AE, DC, MC, V. Sun–Thurs 6–9:30pm; Fri–Sat 6–10pm. Courtesy car provides transportation from/to downtown hotels.

The Spanish Bakery COLONIAL Occupying a reconstructed 17th-century kitchen building, this little family-operated establishment bakes almond, lemon, and cinnamon cookies, using recipes from the Spanish colonial period, when a lack of refrigeration limited the use of milk and eggs. A couple of these crunchy morsels, eaten at the picnic tables outside, make a fine snack while you're touring the historic district. Or you can have lunch here, choosing from daily specials such as spicy Spanish-style chili over rice.

Rear of 42½ St. George St. (between Cuna and Orange sts.). ℂ 904/471-3046. Reservations not accepted. Lunch specials $5; cookies and rolls 40¢–50¢ each. No credit cards. Daily 9:30am–3pm. Closed Thanksgiving, Christmas.

ST. AUGUSTINE AFTER DARK

Especially on weekends, the Old Town is full of strollers and partiers making the rounds to the dozens of active bars, clubs, and restaurants. For up-to-date details on what's happening in town, check the local daily, the *St. Augustine Record* (www.staugustine.com), or the irreverent *Folio Weekly* (www.folioweekly.com).

The best-looking and rowdiest crowd in town can be found at the **A1A Ale Works** (see "Where to Dine," above). Twenty-something hipsters and middle-aged partiers mingle at this handsome New Orleans–style microbrewery and restaurant. Thursday through Saturday nights, downstairs at the bar, on a crowded window-front stage, you'll find live music, usually light rock and R&B tunes.

Ann O'Malley's, 23 Orange St., near the Old City Gate (ℂ 904/825-4040), is an Irish pub, open until 1am. Besides the selection of ales, stouts, and drafts, this is one of the only spots in town where you can grab a late-night bite.

Also popular with locals, **Mill Top Tavern,** 19½ St. George St., at the Fort (ℂ 904/829-2329), is a warm and rustic tavern housed in a 19th-century mill building (the waterwheel is still outside). Weather permitting, it's an open-air space. There's music here every day from 1pm until 1am.

At **Scarlett O'Hara's,** 70 Hypolita St., at Cordova Street (ℂ 904/824-6535; www.scarlettoharas.net), a catacomb of cozy rooms with working fireplaces in a rambling, 19th-century wood-frame house is the setting for everything from DJs and karaoke to live music. Sporting events are also aired on a large-screen TV.

Across the river, the **Gypsy Bar & Grill,** part of the Gypsy Cab Co. restaurant (see "Where to Dine," above), 828 Anastasia Blvd. (ℂ 904/824-8244), often has live music as well as a next-door comedy club.

You can also take one of the many ghost tours that are offered nightly.

4 Jacksonville

36 miles S of the Georgia border, 134 miles NE of Orlando, 340 miles N of Miami

Once infamous for its smelly paper mills, the sprawling metropolis of Jacksonville—residents call it "Jax," from its airport abbreviation—is now one of the South's insurance and banking capitals. Development was rampant throughout Duval County during the 1990s, with hotels, restaurants, attractions, and clubs springing up, especially in suburban areas near the interstate highways. Nevertheless, there are 20 miles of Atlantic Ocean beaches upon which to sun and swim, many championship golf courses to play, and an abundance of beautiful and historic national and state parks to roam.

Spanning the broad, curving St. Johns River, downtown Jacksonville is a vibrant center of activity during weekdays and on weekend afternoons and evenings, when many locals return to the restaurants and bars of Jacksonville Landing and Southbank Riverwalk, two dining-and-entertainment complexes facing each other across the river that have helped to revitalize downtown.

ESSENTIALS

GETTING THERE   **Jacksonville International Airport,** on the city's north side about 12 miles from downtown (© **904/741-2000;** www.jaxairports.org), is served by **Air Canada** (© 888/247-2262), **AirTran** (© 800/247-8726), **American** (© 800/433-7300), **Continental** (© 800/525-0280), **Delta** (© 800/221-1212), **Midway** (© 800/446-4392), **Northwest** (© 800/225-2525), **Southwest** (© 800/435-9792), **United** (© 800/241-6522), and **Metro Jet** and **US Airways** (© 800/428-4322).

Alamo (© 800/327-9633), **Avis** (© 800/331-1212), **Budget** (© 800/527-0700), **Dollar** (© 800/800-4000), **Enterprise** (© 800/325-8007), **Hertz** (© 800/654-3131), and **National** (© 800/227-7368) have rental-car booths at the airport.

Gator City Taxi (© **904/741-0008** at the airport, or 904/355-8294 elsewhere) provides cab service. Fares for up to four persons are about $20 to downtown, $38 to $45 to beach hotels, $55 to $65 to St. Augustine, and $40 to Amelia Island. **Express Shuttle** (© **904/353-8880**) provides van service to and from hotels and resorts throughout the area. Per-person fares are about $17 to downtown Jacksonville, $22 to $28 to the beaches, $57 to $67 to St. Augustine, and $35 to Amelia Island.

There's an **Amtrak** station in Jacksonville at 3570 Clifford Lane, off U.S. 1, just north of 45th Street (© **800/USA-RAIL;** www.amtrak.com).

VISITOR INFORMATION   Contact the **Jacksonville and the Beaches Convention & Visitors Bureau,** 201 E. Adams St., Jacksonville, FL 32202 (© **800/733-2668** or 904/798-9111; fax 904/789-9103; www.jaxcvb.com), for maps, brochures, calendars, and advice. The bureau is open Monday through Friday from 8am to 5pm. It operates information booths in the upstairs food court of **Jacksonville Landing** (see "Exploring the Area," below). The latter is open Monday through Saturday from 10am to 7pm, Sunday from 12:30 to 5:30pm. The bureau also has a walk-in information office in **Jacksonville Beach** at 403 Beach Blvd., between 3rd and 4th streets (© **904/242-0024**), which is open Monday through Saturday from 10am to 6pm.

GETTING AROUND   You can get around downtown Jacksonville via the **Skyway,** an elevated and completely automated train that runs down Hogan

---

Fun Fact   Once a Cow Town

Although Jacksonville claims to be the capital of Florida's historic "First Coast," the city dates its beginnings from an early-1800s settlement named Cowford, because cattle crossed the St. Johns River here. It changed its name in 1822 to honor General Andrew Jackson, who had forced Spain to cede Florida to the United States 2 years earlier.

Street from the Florida Community College Jacksonville campus through downtown and across the river via the Acosta/Fla. 13 bridge to the Southbank Riverwalk. The Skyway operates Monday through Friday from 6am to 11pm, Saturday from 10am to 11pm, and Sunday only for special events. Skyway rides cost 35¢. **The Trolley** connects with the Skyway and runs east-west through downtown, primarily along Bay Street. It's free and operates Monday through Friday from 6:30am to 7pm and Saturday 8am to 6pm. Get maps and schedules from the convention and visitors bureau or at the visitor information booth at Jacksonville Landing (see above). Both are operated by the **Jacksonville Transportation Authority** (© 904/630-3181; www.jtaonthemove.com), which also provides local bus service.

Otherwise, you're better off having a car if you want to explore this vast area. You can hail a **taxi** downtown if you spot one, although it is usually best to call **Gator City Taxi** (© 904/355-8294) or **Yellow Cab** (© 904/260-1111) for a pickup. Fares are $1.50 when the flag drops, and 25¢ for each ⅓ mile thereafter.

Out at the beaches, the **St. Johns River Ferry** (© 904/241-9969; www.stjohnsferry.com) shuttles vehicles across the river between Mayport, an Old Florida fishing village on the south side, and Fort George on the north shore. The boats run daily. (Times vary, so call for the current schedule.) One-way fare is $2.75 per two-axle private vehicle, 50¢ for pedestrians and bicyclists. Even if you have to wait 30 minutes for the next ferry, the 5-minute ride greatly shortens the trip between the Jacksonville beaches and Amelia Island.

EXPLORING THE AREA

Cummer Museum of Art & Gardens ★★   Built on the grounds of a private Tudor mansion, this modestly sized but impressive museum is worth a visit for anyone who appreciates the visual arts. The permanent collection encompasses works from 2000 B.C. to the present. It's especially rich in American Impressionist paintings and includes an impressive collection of 18th-century porcelain and 18th-century Japanese woodblock prints. Personally, I find the art here a bit boring and too focused on landscapes, but that's my taste. Frankly, and art snobs may gasp at this statement, the actual landscaping of the museum is infinitely more spectacular. Don't miss the stunning Italian and English gardens set on the scenic St. Johns River. The museum hosts temporary and traveling exhibits and sponsors a multitude of activities during the year, so call to see what's happening.

829 Riverside Ave. (between Post and Fisk sts.). © 904/356-6857. www.cummer.org. Admission $6 adults, $4 seniors over 65 and military, $3 students, $1 children under 5; free Tues after 4pm. Tues and Thurs 10am–9pm; Wed and Fri–Sat 10am–5pm; Sun noon–5pm.

Jacksonville Landing   Resembling New York City's South Street Seaport, Boston's Faneuil Hall, Miami's Bayside, and Baltimore's Inner Harbor, this glass-and-steel complex on the north bank of the river serves as the focus of downtown activity. Yeah, you may see a mime or two occasionally, and there's a

Jacksonville

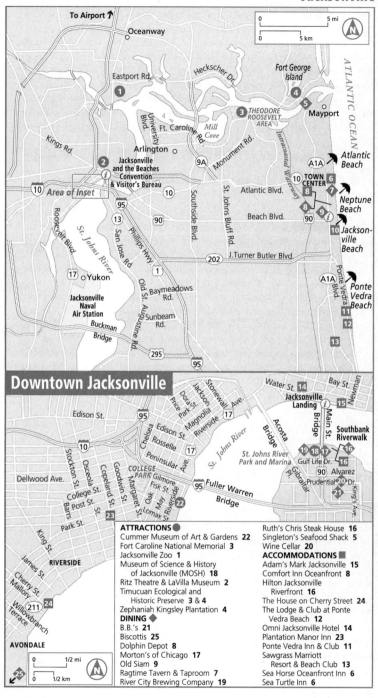

Downtown Jacksonville

ATTRACTIONS ●
Cummer Museum of Art & Gardens **22**
Fort Caroline National Memorial **3**
Jacksonville Zoo **1**
Museum of Science & History
  of Jacksonville (MOSH) **18**
Ritz Theatre & LaVilla Museum **2**
Timucuan Ecological and
  Historic Preserve **3 & 4**
Zephaniah Kingsley Plantation **4**
DINING ◆
B.B.'s **21**
Biscottis **25**
Dolphin Depot **8**
Morton's of Chicago **17**
Old Siam **9**
Ragtime Tavern & Taproom **7**
River City Brewing Company **19**

Ruth's Chris Steak House **16**
Singleton's Seafood Shack **5**
Wine Cellar **20**
ACCOMMODATIONS ■
Adam's Mark Jacksonville **15**
Comfort Inn Oceanfront **8**
Hilton Jacksonville
  Riverfront **16**
The House on Cherry Street **24**
The Lodge & Club at Ponte
  Vedra Beach **12**
Omni Jacksonville Hotel **14**
Plantation Manor Inn **23**
Ponte Vedra Inn & Club **11**
Sawgrass Marriott
  Resort & Beach Club **13**
Sea Horse Oceanfront Inn **6**
Sea Turtle Inn **6**

Hooter's, a Ruby Tuesday, and a Starbuck's, but there's also amazing local live music, good non-chain sushi, Thai and Mexican, too. Unlike in the other cities, this complex is not just for tourists and is command central for many locals looking for a lively day/night out. There are more than 65 stores here, but shopping is secondary to dining and entertainment. You can choose from a half dozen full-service restaurants, plus an inexpensive food court with indoor and outdoor seating overlooking the river. The Landing is the scene of numerous special events, ranging from arts festivals to baseball-card shows, and outdoor rock, blues, country, and jazz concerts on weekends. Call or check the website to find out what's going on during your stay.

2 Independent Dr. (between Main and Pearl sts.), on the St. Johns River. © **904/353-1188**. www.jacksonvillelanding.com. Free admission. Mon–Thurs 10am–8pm; Fri–Sat 10am–9pm; Sun noon–5:30pm; bars and restaurants open later. From I-95, take exit 107 downtown to Main St., go over the Blue Bridge, and turn left at Bay St. Then go 2 blocks and make a left on Laura St., which dead-ends at the Landing. Park on east side of complex.

Jacksonville Zoo ✪ *Kids*   Another city, another zoo. But this isn't just any zoo. Located between downtown and the airport, this environmentally sensitive zoo is well on its way to becoming one of the Southeast's best. While the zoo's Wild Florida area presents local fauna, including black bears, red wolves, Florida panthers, and alligators, the main exhibits feature an extensive and growing collection of lions, rhinos, elephants, antelopes, Nile crocodiles, cheetahs, monkeys, western lowland gorillas, and other African wildlife. You'll enter the 73-acre park through an authentic thatched roof built in 1995 by 24 Zulu craftsmen. Whether you go on foot or by tram, allow at least 3 hours to tour this vast and lush zoo. When you arrive, ask about current animal shows and special events. Strollers and wheelchairs are available for rent. The newest attraction, Range of the Jaguar opened in the spring of 2004 to the tune of $15.4 million. The exhibit focuses on a neotropical rain forest setting that can be found in Central or South America. Although this attraction spotlights the jaguar, you will see other animals here as well, such as golden lion tamarins, tapirs, capybaras, giant river otters, anteaters and a variety of bird, reptile, amphibian, and fish species including the anaconda.

8605 Zoo Pkwy. © **904/757-4462** or 904/757-4463. www.jaxzoo.org. Admission $9.50 adults, $8 seniors, $5 children 3–12, free for children under 3. Daily 9am–5pm. Closed Thanksgiving, Christmas. Take I-95 north to Hecksher Dr. (exit 124A) and follow the signs.

Ritz Theatre & LaVilla Museum   From 1921 to 1971, the Ritz Theatre was the center of cultural life in LaVilla, an African-American neighborhood so vibrant that it was known as the Harlem of the South. Many entertainers played the Ritz before moving on to the Apollo Theater in the real Harlem. Most of LaVilla's small, clapboard "shotgun" houses (so called because you could fire a shotgun through the central hallway and not hit anything) have been torn down in anticipation of urban renewal, but the Ritz has been rebuilt and is once again a center of the city's cultural life. Only the northwest corner of the building, including the Ritz sign, is original, but the new 426-seat theater captures the spirit of vaudevillian times. Off the lobby, LaVilla Museum recounts local African-American history and exhibits the works of black artists.

829 N. Davis St. (between State and Union sts.). © **904/632-5555**. Admission $4 adults, $2 seniors and children 18 and under. Tues–Fri 10am–6pm; Sat 10am–2pm; Sun 2–5pm. From downtown, take Main St. north, turn left (west) on State St. to theater and museum at Davis St.

Southbank Riverwalk *Kids*   Bordering the St. Johns River, directly opposite Jacksonville Landing (see above), this 1¼-mile wooden zigzag boardwalk is usually filled with joggers, tourists, folks sitting on benches, and lovers walking hand-in-hand, all of them watching the riverboats, the shorebirds, and downtown's skyline reflected on the water. At 200 feet in diameter, the **Friendship Fountain** near the west end is the nation's largest self-contained fountain; it's especially beautiful at night when illuminated by 265 colored lights. Nearby, you'll pass military memorials, a small museum dedicated to the city's history, and the **Museum of Science & History of Jacksonville (MOSH),** at Museum Circle and San Marco Boulevard (© **904/396-6674;** www.themosh.org). The latter is an interactive children's museum focusing on science and the history of Northeast Florida. One of its stars is an Allosaurus dinosaur skeleton. It also has a small planetarium, whose shows are included in admission to the museum: $7 adults, $5.50 seniors, $5 children 3 to 12, free for children under 3. Open Monday through Friday from 10am to 5pm, Saturday from 10am to 6pm, and Sunday from 1 to 6pm. The Riverwalk is the scene of special MOSH programs, seafood fests, parties, parades, and arts-and-crafts festivals.

On the south bank of the St. Johns River, flanking Main St. Bridge between San Marco Blvd. and Ferry St. © 904/396-4900. Take I-95 north to Prudential Dr. exit, make a right, and follow signs.

AN UNUSUAL BREED OF NATIONAL PARK

Named after the American Indians who inhabited Central and North Florida some 1,000 years before European settlers arrived, the **Timucuan Ecological and Historic Preserve** offers visitors an opportunity to explore untouched wilderness, historical buildings, and informative exhibits on the area's natural history. Unusual for a national park, this 46,000-acre preserve hasn't been hacked off from the rest of the community and drawn within arbitrary boundaries. The result is a vast, intriguing system of sites joined by rural roads alongside tumbledown fish camps, trailer parks, strip malls, condominiums, and stately old homes.

   Admission to all park facilities is free (though donations are accepted). The visitor centers at Fort Caroline National Memorial and Zephaniah Kingsley Plantation (see below) are open daily from 9am to 5pm except New Year's Day, Thanksgiving, and Christmas. The Theodore Roosevelt Area is open daily from 7am to 5pm during Eastern Standard Time, daily from 7am to 8pm during daylight savings time. Closed Christmas.

SOUTH OF THE RIVER

The preserve's prime attractions are 14 miles northeast of downtown on the south bank of the St. Johns River. Your starting point is the **Fort Caroline National Memorial** ⟨, 12713 Ft. Caroline Rd. (© **904/641-7155;** www.nps.gov/timu), which serves as the preserve's visitor center. This was the site of the 16th-century French Huguenot settlement that was wiped out by the Spanish who landed at St. Augustine. This two-thirds–size replica shows you what the original was like. You can see archaeological artifacts and two well-produced half-hour videos highlighting the area as well.

   The fort sits at the northwestern edge of the 600-acre **Theodore Roosevelt Area,** a beautiful woodland and marshland rich in history that has been undisturbed since the Civil War. On a 2-mile hike along a centuries-old park trail, you'll see a wide variety of birds, wildflowers, and maritime hammock forest. Bring binoculars if you have them, since such birds as endangered wood storks, great and snowy egrets, ospreys, hawks, and painted buntings make their home here in spring and summer. On the ground, you might catch sight of a gray fox or raccoon. You may also want to bring a blanket and picnic basket to spread out under the ancient oak trees that shade the banks of the wide and winding St. Johns River. After the trail crosses Hammock Creek, you're in ancient Timucuan country, where their ancestors lived as far back as 500 B.C. Farther along is the site of a cabin in the wilderness that belonged to the reclusive brothers Willie and Saxon Browne, who lived without the modern conveniences of indoor plumbing or electricity until the last brother's death in 1960.

If you're here on a weekend, take the fascinating 1½-hour guided tour of the fort and Theodore Roosevelt Area, offered every Saturday and Sunday (when weather and staffing permit). Call the fort for details and schedules.

The **Ribault Monument,** on St. Johns Bluff about ½ mile east of the fort, was erected in 1924 to commemorate the arrival in 1562 of French Huguenot Jean Ribault, who died defending Fort Caroline from the Spanish. It's worth a stop for the dramatic view of the area.

To get here from downtown Jacksonville, take Atlantic Boulevard (Fla. 10) east, make a left on Monument Road, and turn right on Fort Caroline Road; the Theodore Roosevelt Area is entered from Mt. Pleasant Road, about 1 mile southeast of the fort; look for the trail head parking sign and follow the narrow dirt road to the parking lot.

NORTH OF THE RIVER

On the north side of the river, history buffs will appreciate the **Zephaniah Kingsley Plantation** ⚓, at 11676 Palmetto Ave. on Fort George Island (© **904/ 251-3537**). A winding 2½-mile dirt road runs under a canopy of dense foliage to the remains of this 19th-century plantation. The National Park Service maintains the well-preserved two-story clapboard residence, kitchen house, barn/carriage house, and remnants of 23 slave cabins built of "tabby mortar"—oyster shell and sand. Exhibits in the main house and kitchen focus on slavery as it existed in the rice-growing areas of Northern Florida, Georgia, and South Carolina. You can see it all on your own, but 40-minute ranger-guided tours are much more informative. They are usually given at 1pm Monday through Friday, 1 and 3pm on weekends, but call to confirm. Also allot some extra time to explore the grounds. A well-stocked book and gift shop will keep you even longer. The plantation is open daily from 9am to 5pm, except Christmas.

To get here from I-95, take Heckscher Drive (Fla. 105) east and follow the signs. From Fort Caroline, take Fla. 9A north over the St. Johns River to Heckscher Drive east. The plantation is about 12 miles east of Fla. 9A, on the left. From the beaches, take Fla. A1A to the St. Johns River Ferry and ride it from Mayport to Fort George; the road to the plantation is a ½ mile east of the ferry landing.

Escaping Intolerance

Zephaniah Kingsley, the white man who from 1817 to 1829 owned the plantation that is now part of the Timucuan Ecological and Historic Preserve, held some seemingly contradictory views on race. Although he owned more than 200 slaves, he believed that "the coloured race were superior to us, physically and morally." He married a Senegalese woman—one of his former slaves—and in 1837 moved his mixed-race family to what is now the Dominican Republic to escape what he called the "spirit of intolerant injustice" in Florida.

HITTING THE BEACH

You can fish, swim, snorkel, sail, sunbathe, or stroll on the sand dunes (at least Mar–Nov, since winter can get downright chilly here). All of these activities are just a 20- to 30-minute drive east of downtown at Jacksonville's four beach communities.

Atlantic Boulevard (Fla. 10) will take you to **Atlantic Beach** and **Neptune Beach.** The boulevard divides the two towns, and where it meets the ocean, you'll come to **Town Center,** a quaint community with a number of shops, restaurants, pubs, and a few inns.

Beach Boulevard (U.S. 90) dead-ends at **Jacksonville Beach,** where you'll find beach concessions, rental shops, and a fishing pier. This is also the most popular local surfing beach.

To the south, J. Turner Butler Boulevard (Fla. 202) leads from I-95 to the boundary between Jacksonville Beach and Ponte Vedra Beach. A right turn there will take you to **Ponte Vedra Beach** (pronounced here as Ponti *Vee*-dra). This ritzy, golf-oriented enclave actually is in St. Johns County (St. Augustine), but it's so much closer to Jacksonville that we've included it in this chapter.

OUTDOOR ACTIVITIES & SPECTATOR SPORTS

CRUISES   **Jacksonville River Cruises** (© 904/396-2333; www.rivercruise. com) operates sightseeing, dinner, and dancing cruises on the stern-wheel paddleboats the *Lady St. Johns* and the *Annabelle Lee.* They usually dock at the Radisson Riverwalk Hotel on the Southbank Riverwalk. Prices are $30 to $45; schedules vary greatly by season, so call ahead or check the website.

FISHING   The least-expensive way to fish for red snapper, grouper, sea bass, small sharks, amberjack, and more, 15 to 30 miles offshore in the Atlantic Ocean, is aboard the *King Neptune,* a 65-foot air-conditioned deep-sea party boat. The full-day trips depart at 7:30am daily from Monty's Marina, 4378 Ocean St. (Fla. A1A), ½ mile south of the Mayport Ferry landing (© **904/ 246-7575**), and return at 4:30pm. Price is $50 per person, including bait and tackle. You don't need a license, but reservations are required.

GOLF   The Jacksonville area offers a great variety of golf courses, some of which are ranked among the top in the country. In Ponte Vedra Beach, the Sawgrass Marriott Resort sits on the most famous course, the **TPC at Sawgrass** ★★★, home of the Players Championship in March. Ranked among the nation's top courses, its island hole is one of the most photographed in the world. Nearby are the Ocean and Lagoon courses at the Ponte Vedra Inn & Club. See "Where to Stay," below, for information about the resorts.

Top courses open to the public include the **Golf Club of Jacksonville,** at 10440 Tournament Lane (© **904/779-0800**), which is managed by the PGA Tour. It's a great bargain, with greens fees ranging from $30 to $45. The semiprivate **Cimarrone,** at 2690 Cimarrone Blvd. (© **904/287-2000**), is a fast and watery course with greens fees ranging from $30 to $65.

Be on the lookout for the free *Golfer's Guide* in visitor centers and hotel lobbies (see "Special-Interest Trips," on p. 35, for information about ordering copies).

For course information online, go to www.golf.com and www.floridagolfing. com, or call the **Florida Sports Foundation** (© **850/488-8347**) or **Florida Golfing** (© **866/833-2663**).

HORSEBACK RIDING   For a scenic ride along the sand and dunes (or lessons), try **Sawgrass Stables,** 23900 Marsh Landing Pkwy., off Fla. A1A in Ponte Vedra Beach (© **904/285-3791**). Call for rates and reservations.

SPECTATOR SPORTS   The 73,000-seat **Alltel Stadium,** 1 Stadium Place, at East Duval and Haines streets (© **904/353-3309** to charge tickets), hosts the annual Florida-Georgia football game every October, and other college football games September through December. It also is the home field of the National Football League's **Jacksonville Jaguars** (© **877/452-4784** or 904/633-2000 for ticket information; www.jaguars.com). One of the stadium's biggest draws is the **Toyota Gator Bowl,** usually on New Year's Day.

Adjacent to the stadium, the 10,600-seat **Jacksonville Veterans Memorial Coliseum,** 1145 E. Adams St. (© **904/630-3900** for information, or 904/353-3309 to charge tickets), hosts National Hockey League exhibition games, college basketball games, ice-skating exhibitions, wrestling matches, and various family shows.

SHOPPING & BROWSING

Jacksonville has plenty of shopping opportunities, including an upscale mall, **The Avenues Mall,** south of town at 10300 Southside Blvd., as well as a number of flea markets, including the **Beach Boulevard Flea and Farmer's Market** on Beach Boulevard (Fla. 90; © **904/645-5961**). More than 600 vendors show up Saturday and Sunday from 9am to 5pm to sell their wares in a partially covered facility. Some booths are open other days of the week as well.

San Marco Square, at San Marco and Atlantic boulevards, south of the river, is a quaint shopping district in the middle of a stunning residential area. Shops in meticulously refashioned Mediterranean-revival buildings sell antiques and home furnishings, in addition to wares such as clothing, books, and records.

Another worthwhile neighborhood to explore is the **Avondale/Riverside** historic district southwest of downtown on St. Johns Avenue between Talbot Avenue and Boone Park, on the north bank of the river. More than 60 boutiques, antiques stores, art galleries, and cafes line the wide, tree-lined avenue.

Nearby, the younger set hangs out at **Five Points,** on Park Street at Avondale Avenue, where used-record stores, vintage clothiers, coffee shops, and funky art galleries stay open late.

Like St. Augustine, Jacksonville is a mecca for chocoholics, particularly **Peterbrooke Chocolatier Production Center,** 1470 San Marco Blvd., on San Marco Square (© **904/398-2489;** www.peterbrooke.com). If you've never tried chocolate-covered popcorn or pretzels, well, this is the place if you're up to the experience. Open Monday through Friday from 10am to 5pm. Peterbrooke also has a retail shop on St. Johns Avenue in Avondale.

WHERE TO STAY

Because Jacksonville hasn't yet made it onto the hip list, there are no boutique hotels in the city—yet. Instead, you have a choice of either a large chain hotel a la Hilton or Omni, or, preferably, much cozier, more charming bed and breakfasts.

We've arranged the accommodations listed below geographically, in and around downtown first, followed by the beach scene. The suburbs have dozens more options to choose from, especially along I-95. Many are clustered south of downtown in the **Southpoint** (exit 101, Turner Butler Blvd./Fla. 202) and **Baymeadows** (exit 101, Baymeadows Rd./Fla. 152) areas. These locales have a multitude of chain restaurants, and you can hop on the highways and zoom to the beach or downtown—although you aren't really at either one if you stay out there.

Rates in the downtown hotels are higher midweek when rooms are in demand by business travelers. Beach accommodations are somewhat less expensive in the cold months from December through March.

Note: Hotel **taxes** in the area tack on an additional 12 to 14%!

IN JACKSONVILLE

Prudential Drive in the Southbank Riverwalk area is home to the **Radisson Riverwalk Hotel** (© 800/333-3333 or 904/396-5100), the **Hampton Inn Central** (© 800/426-7866 or 904/396-7770), and the all-suites **Extended Stay American Downtown** (© 800/398-7829 or 904/396-1777; www.extended stay.com).

Adam's Mark Jacksonville ★★ This 18-story hotel opened its doors in 2001 on a choice location a block east of Jacksonville Landing. It's definitely a convention hotel, with a whopping 110,000 square feet of meeting space, a showy lobby, two big restaurants, and a sports bar, all of which open onto a riverside promenade. Most of the guest rooms are relatively small; in fact, those with two double beds have room for little else, so opt for a king-bed room or a suite. Although none has a balcony, about half have sliding glass doors (be careful!). The swimming pool is on the rooftop, where a Tiki bar serves refreshments in summertime.

225 Coastline Dr., Jacksonville, FL 32202. © 800/444-2326 or 904/358-6800. Fax 904/634-4554. www.adamsmark.com. 966 units. $149–$259. AE, DC, DISC, MC, V. Valet parking $12; self-parking $8. **Amenities:** 2 restaurants; 4 bars; heated outdoor pool; exercise room; Jacuzzi; sauna; concierge; activities desk; business center; limited room service; laundry service; concierge-level rooms. *In room:* A/C, TV, dataport, coffeemaker, hair dryer, iron.

Hilton Jacksonville Riverfront ★ On the Southbank Riverwalk, this 10-story tower is famous for its Elvis Presley Suite, where "the King" purportedly stayed half a dozen times between 1955 and 1976 when this establishment was known as the Jacksonville Hotel. Funny, but it still looks as if it's steeped in the 70s, much like its sister hotel, The Beverly Hilton in California. People don't seem to mind, though. If you can afford its $300-a-night price tag, you will see some of Elvis's million-seller gold records mounted on the walls and can watch some of his movies on the suite's two VCRs. It and the other units have dark-wood furniture and smallish marble-tiled bathrooms. Riverfront rooms have balconies (those on the west end catch traffic noise from the Main St. Bridge). A branch of Ruth's Chris Steak House here offers extraordinarily tender beef.

1201 Riverplace Blvd. (at Main St. on Southbank Riverwalk), Jacksonville, FL 32207. © 800/445-8667 or 904/398-8800. Fax 904/398-9170. www.jacksonvillehilton.com. 292 units. $109–$300 double. AE, DC, DISC, MC, V. Valet parking $10; self-parking $8. **Amenities:** 2 restaurants; 2 bars; heated outdoor pool; exercise room; Jacuzzi; concierge; business center; limited room service; laundry service; concierge-level rooms. *In room:* A/C, TV, dataport, coffeemaker, hair dryer, iron.

The House on Cherry Street ★★ This colonial-style, wood-frame house, on the St. Johns River in the Riverside neighborhood, is ideal for a romantic B&B vacation. French doors open to a delightful screened-in back porch furnished with rocking chairs; it overlooks an expanse of tree-shaded lawn (where guests play croquet) leading to the river (where they play with kayaks and canoes). You might select the Rose or the Duck room, both with canopied four-poster beds and river views. Ducks are rather a theme here, with hundreds of antique decoys on display. All accommodations offer adjacent sitting rooms and ceiling fans and have fresh flowers, books, and magazines. No smoking is permitted inside. This place gets booked up fast, so make reservations as early as possible.

1844 Cherry St. (on the St. Johns River), Jacksonville, FL 32205. (℃ **904/384-1999.** Fax 904/384-5013. www.1bbweb.com/cherry. 4 units (all with bathroom). $75–$105 double. Rates include full breakfast. AE, MC, V. No small children accepted. **Amenities:** Free use of bikes; canoes; kayaks. *In room:* A/C, TV, hair dryer, no phone.

Omni Jacksonville Hotel ⚑   Located directly across the street from the Times-Union Center for the Performing Arts (see "Jacksonville After Dark," later in this chapter) and a block west of Jacksonville Landing, the Omni enjoys a more convenient location than the Hilton across the river. It caters primarily to a corporate clientele that fills the meeting facilities during the week. Most rooms are of moderate size, with the pick being the Florida suites, which have sitting areas with river or city views. The pool is on the rooftop overlooking the river. The reasonably priced Juliette's Restaurant & Bistro provides a locally famous pasta bar. Your pet can stay with you here, for a *$50 nonrefundable* fee.

245 Water St. (between Pearl and Hogan sts.), Jacksonville, FL 32202. (℃ **800/843-6664** or 904/355-6664. Fax 904/791-4809. www.omnihotels.com. 354 units. $139–$219 double. Weekend rates available. AE, DC, DISC, MC, V. Valet and self-parking $12. Pets accepted ($50 fee). **Amenities:** Restaurant; bar; heated outdoor pool; small exercise room; Jacuzzi; concierge; business center; limited room service; laundry service; concierge-level rooms. *In room:* A/C, TV, dataport, minibar, coffeemaker, hair dryer, iron.

Plantation Manor Inn ⚑⚑   The setting for many weddings and special events, this three-story plantation-style bed-and-breakfast in the historic River-side district is blocks from the river, 10 minutes from downtown, and a short drive to Avondale's shopping and dining. Its homey interior, outfitted with a mix of thrift-store antiques, features glossy pine floors and gorgeous cypress panel-ing, wainscoting, and carved moldings. Breakfast, including freshly baked muffins and breads, is served in a lovely dining room with a working fireplace. When the sun is shining, take the morning meal on a brick patio, a delightful setting with ivy-covered walls, flower beds, and garden furnishings under the shade of a massive oak tree. The patio also contains a lap pool and whirlpool spa. On the second floor, you can enjoy a big wraparound porch with seating amid potted geraniums, hibiscus, and bougainvillea. All but one of the rooms here have shower-only bathrooms.

1630 Copeland St. (between Oak and Park sts.), Jacksonville, FL 32204. (℃ **904/384-4630.** Fax 904/387-0960. www.plantationmanorinn.com. 9 units (all with bathroom). $150–$180 double. Rates include full breakfast. AE, DC, MC, V. **Amenities:** Outdoor pool; Jacuzzi. *In room:* A/C, TV, hair dryer, iron.

AT THE BEACHES

A dozen modest hotels line Jacksonville Beach's 1st Street, along the Atlantic Ocean. Completely renovated in 1998, the **Comfort Inn Oceanfront,** 1515 N. 1st St., 2 blocks east of Fla. A1A (℃ **800/654-8776** or 904/241-2311; fax 904/249-3830; www.comfortinnjaxbeach.com), is one of the better values. Its rooms have balconies or screened patios, and guests can enjoy a large pool with four rock waterfalls and a palm-fringed sun deck, a secluded grotto whirlpool, an exercise room, a gift/sundries shop, and a multicourt sand-volleyball park.

If you'd like to rent an old-fashioned cottage or a luxurious condominium in the affluent enclave of Ponte Vedra, contact **Ponte Vedra Club Realty,** 280 Ponte Vedra Blvd., Ponte Vedra Beach, FL 32082 (℃ **800/278-8171** or 904/285-6927; fax 904/285-5218; www.pvclubrealty.com). The company has more than 100 properties in its rental inventory, about 75% of them on the ocean. Its renters get a discount on use of facilities at The Lodge & Club at Ponte Vedra Beach and at the Ponte Vedra Inn & Club (see below).

The Lodge & Club at Ponte Vedra Beach ★★★   Hello, gorgeous! One of Florida's more romantic hotels, this long, two-story Mediterranean-style building sits along the beach, affording every unit an ocean view from its private balcony or patio. The recipient of a recent $4.5 million renovation, all 66 rooms have been fully refreshed and refurbished and are the epitome of high-end luxury. Rooms have considerable charm, with gorgeous artwork on their walls, two-person settees recessed in front of windows looking out to the beach, and huge bathrooms with two-person tubs and separate showers. The "preferred" rooms and all of the suites also have gas fireplaces, and ceiling fans hang from vaulted ceilings in the upstairs units. The suites also come with sleeper sofas and kitchenettes, making them suitable for small families. Some suites have marble faced fireplaces and French doors. Down by the beach, one swimming pool with a hot tub is reserved for couples, while families can use two other pool areas. Guests here have access to all facilities of the Ponte Vedra Inn & Club (see below), including the spa, tennis center, and two golf courses. Restricted to guests of the two properties, the bright Innlet Dining Room serves fine Continental cuisine with an ocean view, and afternoon tea daily in the adjoining lounge, where a pianist performs by the fireplace at night. The poolside Oasis Bar & Grill is open daily during summer, weekends the rest of the year. *Note:* There is a nightly gratuity charge of $12 per room double for the bellman, doorman, chambermaid, and valet parking staff, so *don't double tip.*

607 Ponte Vedra Blvd. (at Corona Rd.), Ponte Vedra Beach, FL 32082. © **800/243-4304** or 904/273-9500. Fax 904/273-0210. www.pvresorts.com. 66 units. Winter $330–$410 double, $460–$510 suite; summer $240–$310 double, $360–$410 suite. Packages available. AE, DC, DISC, MC, V. **Amenities:** 2 restaurants; 2 bars; 3 heated outdoor pools; health club (with lap pool); access to nearby spa; Jacuzzi; sauna; watersports equipment rentals; bike rental; concierge; business center; 24-hr. room service; babysitting; laundry service. *In room:* A/C, TV, fax, dataport, minibar, kitchen (suites only), coffeemaker, hair dryer, iron, safe.

Ponte Vedra Inn & Club ★★   This luxurious 300-acre country club and spa is a great place to pamper yourself between rounds of golf or games of tennis. The inn is ultra elegant from the moment you drive up to its manicured front lawn, which doubles as a putting green. A gorgeous on-premises spa offers oceanview massage, a salon, herbal and seaweed wraps, facials, hydrotherapy, fitness training, and much more. A new three-story building in front of the original 1937 clubhouse contains an expansive lobby downstairs and spacious, upscale guest rooms upstairs. Across the road, the condominiums are in two-story buildings along the beach. They all have furnished patios or balconies and are individually decorated; some have four-poster or sleigh beds. Ceiling fans are among the numerous in-room amenities. The larger units have full kitchens, and microwave ovens and small refrigerators are available upon request. In addition to the inn's two 18-hole golf courses, its excellent tennis center, and fully equipped gym with six-lane Olympic pool, guests can use the three beachside swimming pools and other facilities at the nearby Lodge & Club at Ponte Vedra Beach (see above). The Island House, a lodging favorite of guests since it was originally built in 1972, was razed in order to make way for a new and modern version: This Island House (opened in the winter of 2003) has 28 luxurious rooms and suites, all overlooking the famous Island 9th golf hole and blue lagoons. *Note:* There is a nightly gratuity charge of $12 per room double for the bellman, doorman, chambermaid, and valet parking staff, so *don't double tip.*

200 Ponte Vedra Blvd. (off Fla. A1A), Ponte Vedra Beach, FL 32082. © **800/234-7842** or 904/285-1111. Fax 904/285-2111. www.pvresorts.com. 221 units. Winter $250–$410 double, $460–$620 suite; summer $180–$310 double, $360–$510 suite. Packages available. AE, DC, DISC, MC, V. **Amenities:** 3 restaurants;

3 bars; indoor pool; golf courses; tennis courts; health club and spa; watersports equipment rentals; bike rental; children's programs (summer only); concierge; business center; 24-hr. room service; massage; babysitting; laundry service; coin-op washers and dryers. *In room:* A/C, TV, dataport, kitchen (some units), minibar, coffeemaker, hair dryer, iron.

Sawgrass Marriott Resort & Beach Club ★★

Swingers love this hotel. No, not *that* kind of swinger, but, rather the kind that emulates Tiger Woods. One of the nation's largest golf resorts, this duffer's paradise is virtually surrounded by 99 holes, including the Pete Dye–designed **TPC at Sawgrass** ★★★, home of the annual Players Championship in March. In fact, this course has appeared on every golf critic's "best of" list since it opened in 1980. Overlooking the TPC's picturesque 13th hole, the seven-story hotel sits beside one of the lakes that make the course so challenging. The view augments the gourmet fusion cuisine served in the Augustine Grille, the hotel's signature restaurant. The guest rooms in the hotel are comfortable but of modest size. Best for families are the fully equipped one- and two-bedroom "villa suites" (condominium apartments) on or near a golf course, which offer large furnished patios or balconies. Especially luxurious are the one- to three-bedroom beachfront units, which sport huge kitchens, living rooms with working fireplaces, full dining rooms, and large screened wooden decks. A complimentary shuttle takes guests to the ocean-side Cabana Beach Club for snacks and meals.

1000 PGA Tour Blvd. (off Fla. A1A between U.S. 210 and J. Turner Butler Blvd.), Ponte Vedra Beach, FL 32082. ✆ **800/228-9290** or 904/285-7777. Fax 904/285-0906. www.sawgrassmarriott.com. 508 units. $109–$135 double, $175–$205 suite. Golf packages available. AE, DC, DISC, MC, V. Free self-parking; valet parking $12. **Amenities:** 6 restaurants; 4 bars; 3 outdoor pools (2 heated); 5 golf courses; 17 tennis courts; 2 health clubs; Jacuzzi; watersports equipment rentals; bike rental; children's programs; game room; concierge; activities desk; business center; limited room service; babysitting; laundry service; coin-op washers and dryers; concierge-level rooms. *In room:* A/C, TV, dataport, kitchen (condos only), minibar, coffeemaker, hair dryer, iron.

Sea Horse Oceanfront Inn *Value*

This old-school beachfront motel offers clean, spacious rooms with ocean views from balconies or patios. Families will appreciate the six units here with kitchenettes, not to mention a big beachfront lawn with pool, shuffleboard, picnic tables, and a barbecue grill. And others will enjoy proximity to some of Jacksonville's top nightspots. The pool itself boasts a happening watering hole, The Lemon Bar. If you have a large family or group, consider the vast and lovely third-floor penthouse—it has a big living room and dining area, full kitchen, separate bedroom as well as sofa beds, and a huge balcony furnished with a dining table and chaise lounges. A coffee shop adjoins the motel, and Town Center's restaurants and bars are across the street.

120 Atlantic Blvd. (at beach end of Atlantic Blvd.), Neptune Beach, FL 32266. ✆ **800/881-2330** or 904/246-2175. Fax 904/246-4256. www.seahorseresort.com. 38 units. $109–$119 double; $200–$225 penthouse suite for up to 6. AE, DC, DISC, MC, V. **Amenities:** Bar; heated outdoor pool. *In room:* A/C, TV, dataport, kitchen (6 units).

Sea Turtle Inn ★

Completely gutted and restored in 1999 and 2000, this elegant, eight-story beachfront hotel (whose exterior façade could use some work and updating to match the lovely interior) is much more upscale than the Sea Horse Oceanfront Inn, which it faces across Atlantic Boulevard (despite their shouting-distance proximity, one technically is in Atlantic Beach; the other, in Neptune Beach). The guest units are spacious except for their faux-marble—but somewhat cramped—bathrooms. Choice units on the beachfront have balconies, but the majority of rooms don't face the beach or have balconies. Plantains Restaurant is a fine spot for an alfresco beachside meal, and it has live music on weekends. There's also a lounge in the restaurant and a summertime Tiki bar beside the swimming pool by the beach.

1 Ocean Blvd. (at beach end of Atlantic Blvd.), Atlantic Beach, FL 32233. (© **800/874-6000** or 904/249-7402. Fax 904/247-1517. www.seaturtle.com. 193 units. $99–$349 double. AE, DC, DISC, MC, V. **Amenities:** Restaurant; 2 bars; outdoor pool; access to nearby health club; watersports equipment rentals; limited room service; babysitting; laundry service; coin-op washers and dryers. *In room:* A/C, TV, fax, dataport, minibar, fridge, coffeemaker, hair dryer, iron.

WHERE TO DINE

The convention and visitors bureau's annual guide (p. 555) contains a complete list of restaurants. For more choices, check listings in the "Shorelines" and "Go" sections of Friday's *Florida Times-Union* (**www.jacksonville.com**) and in *FolioWeekly* (**www.folioweekly.com**), the free local alternative paper available at restaurants, hotels, and nightspots all over town. We have concentrated here on restaurants in downtown Jacksonville and at the beaches.

IN DOWNTOWN JACKSONVILLE

Southbank Riverwalk is the city's up-and-coming mecca for eating out. In addition to B.B.'s and the River City Brewing Company, both reviewed below, the area has riverfront branches of **Ruth's Chris Steak House,** in the Hilton Jacksonville Riverfront, 1201 Riverplace Blvd. (© **904/396-6200**); **Morton's of Chicago,** 1510 Riverplace Blvd. (© **904/399-3933**); and the **Wine Cellar,** 1314 Prudential Dr. (© **904/398-8989**), offers very good Continental fare and has a wine list to justify its name.

You will also find a plethora of good cafes and restaurants in the San Marco Square and Avondale neighborhoods, to break up your shopping excursions.

Don't forget that on the north side of the river, **Jacksonville Landing** has several full-service restaurants and an inexpensive food court with outdoor seating (p. 556).

B.B.'s ★★ ECLECTIC   South of the Southbank Riverwalk, this bistro son of Biscottis (see below) is one of the city's hottest restaurants. You'll find local yuppies congregating at the big marble-top bar on one side of the sometimes noisy Art Deco dining room, especially during weekday "wine-downs" featuring beer and wine specials and discounted appetizers (the mozzarella bruschetta is a big hit here and at Biscottis), from 4 to 7pm. There's a small but inventive selection of sandwiches, salads, and individual-size pizzas available all day. Featuring local seafood, the nightly main-course specials run the gamut from roasted sea bass with citrus couscous to seared scallops with lemon grass–scented rice, sun-dried tomatoes, and lobster-flavored butter. Save room for the famous desserts, available for inspection in the chiller case near the open kitchen. Saturday brunch sees the likes of yummy Benedict-style crab cakes and flaming bananas Foster.

1019 Hendricks Ave. (between Prudential Dr. and Home St.). © 904/306-0100. Call for Priority Seating. Main courses $12–$23; sandwiches and salads $5–$8.50; pizzas $6–$8. AE, DC, DISC, MC, V. Mon–Thurs 11am–10:30pm; Fri 11am–midnight; Sat 10am–midnight (Sat brunch 10am–2pm).

Biscottis ★★ (Value) ECLECTIC   This brick-walled little gem in the trendy Avondale neighborhood might easily have come out of New York's East Village. Start your day here (except on Mon) with a pastry and cup of joe. For lunch and dinner, daily specials such as pan-seared tuna or pork loin are always fresh and beautifully presented. The huge and inventive salads are especially good: Try the Oriental version with chicken breast, orange slices, roasted peppers, and creamy sesame dressing. Pizzas, too, are served with wonderfully exotic and delicious toppings—ever try guacamole and black beans on your slice? And by all means, don't leave without sampling the wonderful desserts. On warm days, choose a tiny sidewalk table for great people-watching. *Note:* If the wait's too long here, several other choices ranging from a neighborhood diner to expensive haute cuisine line these 2 blocks of St. Johns Avenue in Avondale.

3556 St. Johns Ave. (between Talbot and Ingleside aves. in Avondale). ✆ **904/387-2060.** Main courses $9–$19; sandwiches and salads $5–$8.50; pizzas $7–$8.50. AE, DC, DISC, MC, V. Mon 11am–10pm; Tues–Thurs 7am–10pm; Fri 7am–midnight; Sat 8am–midnight; Sun 8am–3pm.

River City Brewing Company 🌟🌟 NEW AMERICAN/LOUISIANA
Occupying a prime location on the Southbank Riverwalk, this gorgeous restaurant and microbrewery has dramatic waterfront and skyline views. For an even better vantage point, sit outside on the enormous covered deck. The quality of the cuisine very nearly lives up to the vista, especially the coconut shrimp served with a sweet Mandarin-orange sauce. For a main course, try the Cajun chicken linguine with mushrooms and ham in a spicy cream sauce, or pretzel-encrusted mahimahi with a mustard-cream sauce. While you can easily drop a bundle in the main dining room, you can devise an inexpensive, simpler meal (burgers and such) in the Brew Haus, a large sports bar that opens to the big covered deck and the riverbank. Bands play on the deck weekend evenings. Sunday brunch brings incredible buffets with decadent desserts.

835 Museum Circle (on Southbank Riverwalk). ✆ **904/398-2299.** Main courses $15–$18; sandwiches and salads $5–$11; Sun brunch buffet $22 adults, $16 seniors, $12 children 3–12. AE, DC, DISC, MC, V. Dining room Sun–Thurs 11am–3pm and 5–10pm; Fri–Sat 11am–3pm and 5–11pm; Sun 10:30am–2:30pm and 5–10pm. Pub and deck (light fare) Sun–Thurs 3–10pm (bar to midnight); Fri–Sat 3–11pm (bar to 2am). Closed Christmas. Valet parking available on weekends.

AT THE BEACHES

In addition to the Ragtime Tavern & Taproom (see below), you'll have several dining (and drinking) choices in the brick storefronts of Town Center, the old-time beach village at the end of Atlantic Boulevard. Among the best is the ocean-front **Plantains,** in the Sea Turtle Inn (p. 566).

Dolphin Depot 🌟🌟 LOW COUNTRY CUISINE This restaurant doesn't win any awards for its name, which has little to do with Flipper and friends other than the fact that it's on the beach, but when it comes to ambience and food, it's off the chart, and you'll be the one flipping over it. Housed in a former gas station, the very rustic, antique filled Dolphin Depot provides a low country high with such dishes as shrimp and grits, She-Crab soup, blackened scallops, and five fresh fish choices daily served blackened, casino-style, with horseradish, or Low-Country style with a lemon, artichoke, and herb sauce. Only adding to the restaurant's allure, the staff is Southern-style friendly, and the setting is resplendent.

704 1st St. North. ✆ **904/270-1424.** Reservations recommended. Main courses $12–$26. AE, DC, DISC, MC, V. Mon–Thurs 5:30–10pm; Fri–Sat 5:30pm–midnight; Sun 5:30–9pm.

Old Siam 🌟🌟 THAI The best of several Thai restaurants here, this sophisticated little cafe serves fine cuisine and a good selection of wines to match the fare's spicy yet subtle flavors. The signature dish is a seafood special: shrimp, sea scallops, mussels, squid, and crab claws in a red chile sauce accented with sweet basil. The "number three" spice level (out of six) touches the tongue but does not overwhelm the other seasonings. Standard favorites such as Pad Thai are light and perfectly balanced with sweet and slightly sour fish sauce.

1716 N. 3rd St. (Fla. A1A, in Holiday Plaza shopping center, between 16th and 17th aves. N.), Jacksonville Beach. ✆ **904/247-7763.** www.oldsiam.com. Main courses $10–$23. AE, DISC, MC, V. Mon–Thurs 5–10pm; Fri–Sat 5–11pm; Sun 5–9:30pm.

Ragtime Tavern & Taproom ★★ SEAFOOD/CAJUN   In the heart of Town Center, this lively sister of St. Augustine's A1A Ale Works (p. 552) offers six hand-crafted brews, including a refreshing pilsner known as Dolphin's Breath. You can imbibe at one of two bars on either end of the building. In between, a rabbit warren of dining rooms provides fine enough fare to keep it filled with local professionals right through the cool winter months. Try the conch fritters or the coconut shrimp as an appetizer. For a main course, you can select from seared sesame-coated yellowfin tuna (the best dish here if you like rare fish) or several other treatments of fish, shrimp, chicken, and pastas. Save room for some New Orleans–style beignets for dessert. Also from the Big Easy, po' boy sandwiches are served at all hours. Good local bands play here Thursday through Sunday evenings.

207 Atlantic Blvd. (at 1st Ave.), Atlantic Beach. (✆) **904/241-7877.** Call to get on waiting list. Main courses $12–$22; sandwiches and salads $6–$8. AE, DC, DISC, MC, V. Sun–Thurs 11am–10:30pm; Fri–Sat 11am–11pm (bar open later).

Singleton's Seafood Shack ★★ *Value* SEAFOOD   This rustic fish camp has been serving every imaginable kind of fresh-off-the-boat seafood since 1969. And rustic it is, constructed primarily of unpainted, well-weathered plywood nailed to two-by-fours. Unlike most other fish camps that tend to overwork the deep fryer, the fried standbys such as conch fritters, shrimp, clam strips, oysters, and squid actually retain their seafood taste! (Usually, that means they change the oil before it gets the too-fishy or burnt taste of the last entree.) Singleton's also offers other preparations such as blackened mahimahi and Cajun shrimp. Best bets at lunch are the fried shrimp or oyster po'boy sandwiches covered in crispy onion rings. At dinner your Styrofoam plate will come stacked with a choice of side items such as black beans and rice, marvelous horseradishy coleslaw, fries, and hush puppies. They have a selection of chicken dishes, but stick to seafood.

4728 Ocean St. (Fla. A1A, at St. Johns River Ferry landing), Mayport. (✆) **904/246-4442.** Main courses $10–$18; sandwiches $2–$7. AE, DISC, MC, V. Sun–Thurs 10am–9pm; Fri–Sat 10am–10pm.

JACKSONVILLE AFTER DARK

In addition to the spots recommended below, check the listings in the "Shore-lines" and "Go" sections of Friday's *Florida Times-Union* (**www.jacksonville. com**) and *FolioWeekly* (**www.folioweekly.com**), the free local alternative paper, available at restaurants, at hotels, and all over town. Another source is **www.jax events.com.**

THE PERFORMING ARTS   Jacksonville has plenty of seats for concerts, touring Broadway shows, dance companies, and big-name performers with the 73,000-seat **Alltel Stadium,** at East Duval and Haines streets ((✆) **904/630-3900**); the 10,600-seat **Jacksonville Veterans Memorial Coliseum,** 1145 E. Adams St. ((✆) **904/630-3900** for information or 904/353-3309 to charge tickets); the 3,200-seat **Florida Times-Union Center for the Performing Arts,** 300 Water St., between Hogan and Pearl streets ((✆) **904/630-3900**); and the revitalized **Ritz Theatre** ((✆) **904/632-5555;** p. 558). Call or check the sources above for what's playing.

THE BAR SCENE   You will find several libation options downtown at **Jacksonville Landing** (p. 556), including, if you must, a lively waterfront **Hooters** ((✆) **904/356-5400**), plus free outdoor rock, blues, country, and jazz concerts every Friday and Saturday night except during winter. There's also live music on weekends across the river at the **River City Brewing Company** (see "Where to Dine," above).

Out at Town Center, at the ocean end of Atlantic Boulevard, one of several popular spots is **Ragtime Tavern & Taproom** (see "Where to Dine," above), where local groups play live jazz and blues Wednesday through Sunday nights. Weekends, especially, the place is really jumping and the crowd is young, but it's lively rather than rowdy. Across the street is the **Sun Dog Diner,** at 207 Atlantic Blvd. (© **904/241-8221**), with nightly acoustic music and decent diner food. If these don't fit your mood, walk around Town Center until you find something you like. The **Freebird Café,** 200 N. 1st St. (© **904/246-2473**), is a two-story homage to native Jacksonville band Lynyrd Skynyrd, run by late lead singer Ronnie Van Zant's widow and daughter and featuring live music six nights a week as well as pretty good nouveau Southern cuisine. Music fans of a different genre shouldn't miss **Stella's Piano Café,** 1521 Margaret St. (© **904/353-2900**), a restaurant housed in an old Victorian home with a second floor piano bar.

5 Amelia Island ★★

32 miles NE of Jacksonville, 192 miles NE of Orlando, 372 miles N of Miami

Alas, paradise is found on the northernmost barrier island of Florida. With 13 beautiful miles of beach and a quaint Victorian town, Amelia Island is a charming getaway about a 45-minute drive northeast of downtown Jacksonville. Overall, this skinny barrier island, 18 miles long by 3 miles wide, has more in common with the Low Country of Georgia (across Cumberland Sound from here) and South Carolina. In fact, it's more like St. Simons Island in Georgia or Hilton Head Island in South Carolina than other beach resorts in Florida.

Amelia has five distinct personalities. First is its southern end, an exclusive real-estate development built in a forest of twisted, moss-laden live oaks. Here you will find world-class tennis and golfing at two of Florida's most luxurious resorts. Second is modest **American Beach,** founded in the 1930s so that African Americans would have access to the ocean in this then-segregated part of the country. Today it's a modest, predominately black community tucked away among all that south-end wealth. Third is the island's middle, a traditional beach community with a mix of affordable motels, cottages, condominiums, and a seaside inn. Fourth is the historic bay-side town of **Fernandina Beach** ★★★, which boasts a 50-square-block area of gorgeous Victorian, Queen Anne, and Italianate homes listed in the National Register of Historic Places. And fifth is lovely **Fort Clinch State Park,** which keeps developers from turning the island's northern end into more ritzy resorts.

The town of Fernandina Beach dates from the post–Civil War period, when Union soldiers who had occupied Fort Clinch began returning to the island. In the late 19th century, Amelia's timber, phosphate, and naval-stores industries boomed. Back then, the town was an active seaport, with 14 foreign consuls in residence. You'll see (and occasionally smell) the paper mills that still stand near the small seaport here. The island experienced another economic explosion in the 1970s and 1980s, when real-estate developers built condominiums, cottages, and two big resorts on the island's southern end. In recent years, Fernandina Beach has seen another big boom, this time in bed-and-breakfast establishments.

ESSENTIALS

GETTING THERE The island is served by **Jacksonville International Airport** (p. 555), which is 12 miles north of Jacksonville's downtown and 43 miles from the island. Skirting the Atlantic in places, the scenic drive here from downtown Jacksonville is via Fla. A1A and the St. Johns River Ferry. The fast, four-lane way is via I-95 north and the Buccaneer Trail (Fla. A1A) east.

Amelia Island

ACCOMMODATIONS ■
Amelia Island Plantation **4**
Elizabeth Pointe Lodge **2**
Fairbanks House **12**
Florida House Inn **10**
Hampton Inn & Suites **8**
The Ritz-Carlton
   Amelia Island **3**

ATTRACTIONS ●
Amelia Island Museum of
   History **13**
Fort Clinch State Park **1**

DINING ◆
Beech Street Grill **11**
Brett's Waterway Cafe **7**
Florida House Inn **10**
The Grill **3**
Joe's 2nd Street Bistro **9**
Le Clos **9**
Marina Restaurant **7**

NIGHTLIFE ★
O'Kanes Irish Pub & Eatery **6**
Palace Saloon **5**

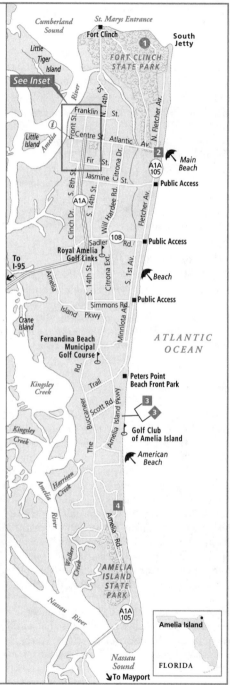

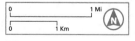

VISITOR INFORMATION   For advance information, contact the **Amelia Island–Fernandina Beach–Yulee Chamber of Commerce,** 102 Centre St. (P.O. Box 472), Fernandina Beach, FL 32035 (✆ **800/226-3542** or 904/277-0717; fax 904/261-6997; www.ameliaisland.org). The chamber's visitor information center, in the rustic train station at the bay end of Centre Street, is open Monday through Friday from 9am to 5pm, Saturday from 10am to 2pm.

GETTING AROUND   There's no public transportation on this 13-mile-long island, so you'll need a vehicle. An informative and entertaining way to tour the historic district is on a 30-minute ride with **Old Towne Carriage Company** (✆ **904/277-1555**), whose horse-drawn carriages leave from the waterfront on Centre Street between 6:30 and 9pm. Advance reservations are essential. Rides cost $15 for adults, $7.50 for kids under 13, with a minimum of $55 per ride. The carriage company closes from November to April when the horses get a much-deserved rest.

Another excellent way to see the town is on a walking tour sponsored by the Amelia Island Museum of History (see the "An Old Jail Turned Historic Museum," section below).

HITTING THE BEACH

Thanks to a reclamation project, the widest beaches here are at the exclusive enclave on the island's southern third. Even if you aren't staying at one of the swanky resorts there, you can enjoy this section of beach at **Peters Point Beach Front Park,** on Fla. A1A, north of the Ritz-Carlton. The park has picnic shelters and restrooms. North of the resort, the beach has public-access points with free parking every ¼ mile or so. The center of activity is **Main Beach,** at the ocean end of Atlantic Avenue (Fla. A1A), with good swimming, restrooms, picnic shelters, showers, a food concession, and a playground. There's also lots of free parking, and this area is popular with families.

The beach at **Fort Clinch State Park** 🐾🐾, which wraps around the island's heavily forested northern end, is backed by rolling dunes and is filled with shells and driftwood. A jetty and pier jutting into Cumberland Sound are popular with anglers. There are showers and changing rooms at the pier. Elsewhere in the park, you might see an alligator—and certainly some of the 170 species of birds that live here—by hiking the Willow Pond nature trail. Rangers lead nature tours on the trail, usually beginning at 10:30am on Saturday. There are also 6 miles of off-road bike trails here. Construction on the remarkably well-preserved **Fort Clinch** began in 1847 on the northern tip of the island and was still underway when Union troops occupied it in 1862. The fort was abandoned shortly after the Civil War, except for a brief reactivation in 1898 during the Spanish-American War. Reenactors gather the first full weekend of each month to re-create how the Union soldiers lived (including wearing their wool underwear, even in summer!) in the fort in 1864. Rangers are on duty at the fort year-round, and they lead candlelight tours on Friday and Saturday evenings during summer, beginning about an hour after sunset. The candlelight tours cost $3 per person. You can arrange guided tours at other times for an extra fee. The park entrance is on Atlantic Avenue near the beach. Entrance fees are $5 per vehicle with up to eight occupants, $1 for pedestrians and bicyclists. Admission to the fort costs $2, free for children under 5. The park is open daily from 8am to sunset, the fort, daily from 9am to 5pm. For a current schedule of tours and events, contact the park at 2601 Atlantic Ave., Fernandina Beach, FL 32034 (✆ **904/ 277-7274;** www.floridastateparks.org/fortclinch).

> (*Fun Fact* **Did You Know?**
> The 1988 film Pippi Longstocking didn't take place in a Scandinavian village, but, rather, right here on Amelia Island. Pippi's house in the film, Villa Villekulla, is now a pink B&B, the Posada San Carlos.

The park also has 62 **campsites,** some behind the dunes at the beach (no shade out there), most in a forest along the sound side. They cost $21 per night with electricity, $19 without, including tax. Pets cost an extra $2 a night. You can reserve a site up to 11 months in advance (a very good idea in summer) by calling © 800/326-3521 or surfing the Web to www.reserveamerica.com.

Pets on leashes are allowed on all the island's public beaches and in Fort Clinch State Park.

OUTDOOR ACTIVITIES
BOATING, FISHING, SAILING & KAYAKING   The **Amelia Island Charter Boat Association,** at Tiger Point Marina on 14th Street north of the historic district (though the boats dock at Centre St.) (© 800/229-1682 or 904/261-2870), can help arrange deep-sea fishing charters, party-boat excursions, and dolphin-watching and sightseeing cruises. Other charter boats also dock at Fernandina Harbor Marina, downtown at the foot of Centre Street.

Windward Sailing School, based at Fernandina Harbor Marina, 3977 1st Ave. (© 904/261-9125; www.windwardsailing.com), will teach you to skipper your boat and also has charters and boat rentals. Call for details and reservations.

You have to be careful in the currents, but the backwaters here are great for kayaking, whether you're a beginner or a pro. However, you'll have to travel just off the island to do it. Ray and Jody Hetchka's **Kayak Amelia** ★★ (© 888/305-2925 or 904/251-0016; www.kayakamelia.com) is based near Talbot Island State Park (technically in Jacksonville) and offers beginner- and advanced-level trips on back bays, creeks, and marshes. Half-day trips go for about $55 per person, all-day costs about $95. Reservations are required.

GOLF   If you're not staying in a resort with a golf course (see "Where to Stay," below, and note that these courses can be extremely expensive), try the new 18-hole **Royal Amelia Golf Links** (© 904/491-8500; www.royalamelia.com), for $95 a person, or the older and less expensive 27-hole **Fernandina Municipal Golf Course** (© 904/277-7370), where prices start at $37 weekdays, $41 weekends.

For course information online, go to www.golf.com and www.floridagolfing.com, or call the **Florida Sports Foundation** (© 850/488-8347) or **Florida Golfing** (© 866/833-2663).

HORSEBACK RIDING   You can go horseback riding on the beach with the **Kelly Seahorse Ranch** (© 904/491-5166; www.kellyranchinc.com), located on the southernmost tip of Amelia Island within the Amelia Island State Park. Cost is $45 per person for a one-hour ride; the ranch is open daily from 8am to 6pm and reservations are required. *Note:* Riders must be age 13 or older and weigh less than 230 pounds. No experience is necessary.

AN OLD JAIL TURNED HISTORIC MUSEUM
Amelia Island Museum of History ★   Housed in the old Nassau County jail, built of brick in 1878, this award-winning local museum explains Amelia Island's fascinating history, from Timucuan Indian times through its possession

by France, Spain, Great Britain, the United States, and the Confederacy (the island changed flags eight times). Only an upstairs photo gallery is open for casual inspection, so plan to take the 1-hour, 15-minute docent-led tour of the newly remodeled ground floor if you want to get the most out of this museum.

The museum also offers excellent **walking tours** of historic Centre Street on Thursday and Friday September through June. These depart at 3pm from the chamber of commerce (see "Essentials," above) and cost $8 for adults, $3 for students. You can't make a reservation; just show up. Longer tours of the entire 50-square-block historic district can be arranged with 24-hour notice; these cost $10 per person, with a minimum of four persons required.

233 S. 3rd St. (between Beech and Cedar sts.). (✆ **904/261-7378.** www.ameliaislandmuseumofhistory.org. Admission by donation. Tours $5 adults, $3 students. Mon–Sat 10am–4pm. Tours Mon–Sat 11am and 2pm.

SHOPPING

Stroll down **Centre Street** in downtown Fernandina Beach, with its vintage storefronts and charming boutiques. Quality antiques shops, consignment shops, and bookstores line the wide boulevard ending at the marina. Be sure to go around the corner and poke your head into the **Island Art Association Gallery,** 18 N. 2nd St. (✆ **904/261-7020**), a co-op exhibiting works by local artists.

On the south end of the island on Fla. A1A, **Palmetto Walk,** under a canopy of live oaks, and the **Village Shops,** at the entrance to the Amelia Island Plantation (✆ **877/624-1854**), are other good shopping bets.

WHERE TO STAY

More than two-dozen of the town's charming Victorian and Queen Anne houses have been restored and turned into B&Bs. For a complete list, contact the chamber of commerce (p. 572) or the **Amelia Island Bed & Breakfast Association** (✆ **888/277-0218;** www.ameliaislandinns.com). You can tour all the B&Bs during an island-wide open house the first weekend in December.

A number of agencies will book vacation properties ranging from affordable cottages to magnificent mansions. Contact **Amelia Island Lodging Systems,** 584 S. Fletcher Ave., Fernandina Beach, FL 32034 (✆ **800/872-8531** or 904/261-4148; www.amelialodgings.com), which even has two lighthouse replicas for rent. *Warning:* Some properties on the website aren't as nice as they seem. Be sure to check very carefully before booking a specific property.

Your best **camping** option here is **Fort Clinch State Park** (see "Hitting the Beach," above).

Note: Rates are subject to a 9% hotel tax.

Amelia Island Plantation 🏆🏆 If you're comparing in terms of *Gone With the Wind's* Tara, this is hardly a plantation, but rather a massive compound that could very easily host several plantations. This huge development occupies 1,350 lush beachfront acres that encompass manicured golf greens as well as a breathtaking coastal wilderness of marshes and lagoons, oceanfront property, miles and miles of lovely bike trails, and much more. The resort is so spread out that a free tram runs around the grounds every 15 minutes. Choose this rustically elegant resort for its natural beauty and its outstanding sports offerings. Most notable are the three consistently top-rated championship golf courses open to resort guests; they comprise 54 holes bordering the ocean, swamps, marshes, and woodlands. The **Long Point** 🏆🏆 course, a mind-blowing beautiful 18-holer, has two par-3s in a row bordering the ocean. Ranked among the nation's top 50 by *Tennis* magazine, the plantation's 23 tennis courts (naturally shaded by a canopy of gorgeous trees) host many professional tournaments, including the annual Bausch & Lomb Championships. A 13,200-square-foot spa has 25 treatment rooms and offers a rejuvenating array of massages, facials, peels, herbal wraps, and hydrotherapies as well as a very small island right near the spa dedicated to Watsu® Massage treatments. Along with the adjoining convention center, the six-story, Mediterranean-style **Amelia Inn & Beach Club** serves as the resort's focal point and holds its 249 spacious, upscale hotel rooms. Traditionally furnished, the rooms boast patios or balconies facing the sea across a row of dunes. All of the inn's rooms are nonsmoking. (***Note:*** Watch out for the minibar. Our bellhop told us that guests get charged [an electronic eye monitors all fridge movement] for moving the contents around, even if you don't eat anything.) The other accommodations here are one- to three-bedroom privately owned condominium apartments (or "villas" in Florida-speak). All but a few have balconies or patios. Each is uniquely decorated with an eclectic mix of high-end furnishings, and all offer living and dining areas (VCRs can be rented) and fully equipped kitchens. The inn's dining room offers exceptional and expensive New American cuisine, with stunning ocean views. An adjoining lounge offers dancing and entertainment. Other restaurants are also on the property. And, really, with all you've got here, why leave?

6800 First Coast Hwy., Amelia Island, FL 32035-3000. © 888/261-6161 or 904/261-6161. Fax 904/277-5945. www.aipfl.com. 249 units, 400 condo apts. $135–$335 double; $185–$945 condo. Packages available. AE, DC, DISC, MC, V. Free self-parking; $12 valet parking. **Amenities:** 4 restaurants; 4 bars; heated indoor pool; 26 outdoor pools; 3 golf courses; 23 tennis courts; health club and spa; Jacuzzi; sauna; watersports equipment rentals; bike rental; Island Hopper (golfcart-like cars to drive around the property) rental; children's programs; nature programs; game room; concierge; business center; shopping arcade; salon; 24-hr. room service; massage and many other spa treatments; babysitting; laundry service. *In room:* A/C, TV, dataport, kitchen (condos only), minibar (Amelia Inn only), coffeemaker, hair dryer, iron, safe.

Elizabeth Pointe Lodge 🏵🏵

You'd swear that this three-story, Nantucket-style shingled beauty, sitting right on the beach, was a lovingly maintained Victorian home—but you'd be wrong. Built in 1991 by B&B gurus David and Susan Caples, it has big-paned windows that look out from the comfy library (with stone fireplace) and dining room to an expansive front porch and the surf beyond. Antiques and reproductions, handmade quilts, and other touches lend the 20 rooms in the main building a turn-of-the-20th-century cottage ambience. They all have oversize bathtubs. Four other rooms are in the Harris Lodge next door, and the two-bedroom, two-bathroom Miller Cottage is also available.

98 S. Fletcher Ave. (just south of Atlantic Ave.), Fernandina Beach, FL 32034. © **800/772-3359** or 904/277-4851. Fax 904/277-6500. www.elizabethpointelodge.com. 24 units, 1 cottage. $165–$250 double; $295 cottage. Rates include buffet breakfast and morning newspaper. Packages available. AE, DISC, MC, V. **Amenities:** Restaurant; bar; access to nearby health club; Jacuzzi; watersports equipment rental; bike rental; 24-hr. room service; laundry service. *In room:* A/C, TV, dataport, hair dryer, iron.

Fairbanks House 🏵🏵

Having all the amenities and almost as much privacy as a first-class hotel in a superbly refurbished 1885 Italianate home, the Fairbanks House is a top B&B choice in the historic district. As gorgeous as it is, it used to be known as "Fairbanks' Folly," because of its pronounced decor. Many rooms and all of the cottages offer private entrances for guests who prefer not to walk through the main house. Room no. 3, in the back of the house on the main floor, is one of the finest rooms, with a private entrance, large sitting room, plush king-size bed, period antiques, porcelain, oil paintings, and fresh flowers. Occupying the entire top floor, the two-bedroom Tower Suite has plenty of room to spread out, plus 360-degree views and its own whirlpool tub. Five other units here have whirlpool tubs. Note that Fairbanks is the only B&B on the island with a swimming pool. No smoking indoors or out. Kids over 12 are welcome.

227 S. 7th St. (between Beech and Cedar sts.), Fernandina Beach, Amelia Island, FL 32034. ✆ **888/891-9882** or 904/277-0500. Fax 904/277-3103. www.fairbankshouse.com. 9 units, 3 detached cottages (all with bathroom). $170–$295 double; $220–$295 cottage. Rates include full breakfast and evening social hour (beverages and hors d'oeuvres). Packages available. AE, DISC, MC, V. **Amenities:** Heated outdoor pool. *In room:* A/C, TV, dataport, kitchen (cottage only), minibar, fridge, coffeemaker, hair dryer, iron.

Florida House Inn 🌟 *Value*   Built near a railroad in 1857, this clapboard Victorian building is Florida's oldest operating hotel. Ulysses S. Grant stayed here, as did Cuban revolutionary José Martí; and the Rockefellers and Carnegies broke bread at the boardinghouse-style dining room that still provides family-style, all-you-can-eat traditional Southern fare. You can rock away on the two gingerbread-trimmed front verandas (Grant made a speech from the upstairs porch) or on a back porch overlooking a brick courtyard shaded by a huge oak tree. The 11 rooms in the original building, all mostly up to modern standards, are loaded with antiques. Most have working fireplaces, and some have claw-foot tubs. Four rooms are in a wing added in 1998; one of these has log-cabin walls, and the others are done country-style. All have fireplaces and whirlpool tubs.

20 S. 3rd St. (between Centre and Ash sts.), Fernandina Beach, FL 32034. ✆ **800/258-3301** or 904/261-3300. Fax 904/277-3831. www.floridahouse.com. 15 units. $99–$219 double. Rates include full breakfast. AE, DISC, MC, V. Dogs accepted ($10 nightly fee). **Amenities:** Restaurant; bar; coin-op washers and dryers. *In room:* A/C, TV, coffeemaker, hair dryer, iron.

Hampton Inn & Suites 🌟🌟   A Hampton Inn that garners two stars, you ask? Believe it or not, it's true. When plans were announced a few years ago to build this four-story hotel in the center of the historic district, they created quite a stir among preservationists. But the all-woman hotel firm of Miriam Taylor & Co. put those fears to rest by designing one of the most unusual Hampton Inns we've ever seen. Although there's only one building, the exterior looks like a row of different structures, all in the styles and sherbet hues of the Victorian storefronts lining Centre Street. Above a curving staircase rising in the two-story Victorian-style lobby, quadrants of an unusual ceiling clock have been painted to represent the 4 centuries of Fernandina Beach's history. Wooden floors taken from an old Jacksonville church, slatted door panels evocative of 19th-century sailing schooners, and many other touches add to the Victorian ambience. About half of the guest rooms are near the top of the romance scale: king beds, gas-burning fireplaces, and two-person whirlpool tubs. (If honeymooning in a Hampton Inn has never crossed your mind, you haven't seen the luxurious, two-room bridal suite here. Admittedly, it's not for most, but some honeymooners, especially those on a second honeymoon, may find virtues.) The standard suites are large enough for families, and the other standard rooms are adequately equipped for business travelers, making this a good choice for everyone. About a third of the units have balconies. Those higher up on the west side have fine views over the river and marshes. The only drawback: Trains slowly rumble by on the west side a few times a day.

19 S. 2nd St. (between Centre and Ash sts.), Fernandina Beach, FL 32034. ✆ **800/426-7866** or 904/491-4911. Fax 904/491-4910. www.hamptoninn.com. 122 units. $109–$189 double. Rates include extensive breakfast buffet. AE, DC, DISC, MC, V. **Amenities:** Outdoor pool; exercise room; Jacuzzi; business center; babysitting; laundry service; coin-op washers and dryers. *In room:* A/C, TV, dataport, fridge, coffeemaker, hair dryer, iron.

The Ritz-Carlton Amelia Island 🌟🌟🌟 *Kids*   Sprawling over 13 acres of stunning beachfront, this member of the world-renowned chain offers slightly glitzier accommodations than its neighbor, the Amelia Island Plantation, but not as much "glamour" as some of its siblings. This could be positive or negative, depending on what you want from a hotel. While some may like that it's perfectly acceptable to walk through the lobby of this Ritz in shorts (it's downright relaxed in this way), other might find the service and surroundings not as polished as they might have expected or experienced in other Ritz-Carlton's. The Ritz-Kids program makes well-heeled families feel just as much at home as the conventioneers who flock here to meet and make use of the extensive recreational facilities, including a beautiful and challenging 18-hole championship golf course. The spacious guest rooms—all with oceanfront or oceanview balconies or patios—have many extra amenities such as scales, cosmetic mirrors, and phones in their marble bathrooms. Concierge-level guests enjoy a lounge with a working fireplace. Leading the hotel's restaurants, **The Grill** offers an ocean view to go along with its exceptional seafood. A gourmet takeout shop sells the oft-requested Ritz dressings, condiments, and sauces, in addition to salads, sandwiches, and decadent desserts.

4750 Amelia Island Pkwy., Fernandina Beach, FL 32034. ✆ **800/241-3333** or 904/277-1100. Fax 904/277-1145. 449 units. $199–$429 double; $269–$579 suite. Golf, tennis, and other packages available. AE, DC, DISC, MC, V. Valet parking $15; no self-parking. **Amenities:** 3 restaurants; 3 bars; heated indoor and outdoor pools; golf course; 9 tennis courts; health club and spa; watersports equipment rentals; bike rental; children's programs; game room; concierge; business center; salon; 24-hr. room service; massage; babysitting; laundry service; concierge-level rooms. *In room:* A/C, TV, dataport, minibar, coffeemaker, hair dryer, iron, safe.

WHERE TO DINE

You'll find several restaurants, pubs, and snack shops along Centre Street, between the bay and 8th Street (Fla. A1A), in Fernandina Beach's old town. Two good dining options stand opposite the Hampton Inn & Suites on South 2nd Street, between Centre and Ash streets: the hip **Joe's 2nd Street Bistro** (✆ **904/321-2558**) and the more formal but still relaxed **Le Clos** (✆ **904/261-8100**). Joe's serves fine international fare in an old store, while Le Clos provides provincial French fare in a charming old house. Both are open for dinner only, and reservations are recommended. Drop by during the day for a look at the menus posted outside each.

And don't forget **The Grill** at the Ritz-Carlton Amelia Island, where great food and impeccable service come at a high price. Lastly, the **Florida House Inn** (see "Where to Stay," above) serves boardinghouse-style, all-you-can-eat lunches and dinners Tuesday through Saturday from 11:30am to 2:30pm ($7 per person) and from 5:30 to 9pm ($13 per person).

Beech Street Grill 🐟🐟 REGIONAL NEW AMERICAN   On par with The Grill in the Ritz-Carlton, the cosmopolitan chic Beech Street Grill pleases all palates with a rich menu of fish, chicken, and meat choices, including seasonal game dishes such as roasted venison loin in a black-currant sauce with sweet-potato-and-onion hash. Nightly fish specialties are always exceptional (some can be pricier than printed menu options). A Parmesan-encrusted red snapper with a mustard-basil sauce is superb. Seared tuna is always perfect, too. The dense and tasty crab cakes and the chewy steamed dumplings are great choices for starters, as is the huge mixed-green salad with mustard-basil vinaigrette, toasted pecans, and blue cheese. Housed in a century-old landmark home and in a newer wing to one side, five dining rooms offer a lively atmosphere. The upstairs features a pianist.

Fun Fact **José Martí Was Here**

Freedom fighter José Martí plotted the Cuban War for Independence (1895–1898) against Spain from his suite in Amelia's Florida House Inn, the state's oldest surviving tourist hotel. An island eavesdropper (with the makings of a modern day tabloid reporter) heard the secret strategies, which led to the demise of the ill-fated revolution.

---

801 Beech St. (at 8th St./Fla. A1A), Fernandina Beach. © **904/277-3662.** Reservations strongly recommended. Main courses $22–$35. AE, DC, DISC, MC, V. Daily 6–10pm.

Brett's Waterway Cafe SEAFOOD/STEAKS   You'll pay for the view, but this friendly waterfront cafe at the foot of Centre Street is the only place in town to dine while watching the boats coming and going on the river—and to sip a drink (they're best known for their excellent martinis) while watching the sun setting westward over the marshes between here and the mainland. In fine weather, you can grab a table outside by the docks. One of the best dishes is shrimp broiled with a sun-dried-tomato cream sauce. The nightly fresh fish specials are well prepared, and there are also steaks and chops. At lunch, try the bacon, lettuce, and fried-green-tomato sandwich.

1 S. Front St. (at Centre St., on the water), Fernandina Beach. © **904/261-2660.** Main courses $15–$26. AE, MC, V. Mon–Sat 11:30am–2:30pm; daily 5:30–9:30pm.

Joe's 2nd Street Bistro ★★★ NEW AMERICAN   In the heart of the Fernandina Beach historic district, you'll find this diminutive restored 1900s home that is full of massive flavor. The island-inspired dining room features a brick fireplace, and upstairs is a private dining room, but I suggest grabbing a table—weather permitting—outside on the covered front porch. Eating here is almost like eating in a chef's home, a quaint and delectable experience to say the least. Try the pecan-breaded breast of duck with wild rice pancakes and red currant sauce, or loin lamb chops with a southwestern-style rub and served over a three bean ragout with roasted tomatoes and tobacco fried onions. Yowza! For dessert, the apple bread pudding kicks that part of your body where perhaps the calories will end up. It rocks. Joe's rocks. Don't miss it. Eat at Joe's.

101 Centre St. (at Front St.), Fernandina Beach. © **904/261-5310.** Reservations recommended. Main courses $14–$26. AE, DC, MC, V. Daily 6–9:30pm.

Marina Restaurant *(Value* AMERICAN   Occupying a brick store built in the 1880s, this quintessential small-town restaurant has been feeding Low Country fare to the locals since 1965. A lot of the seafood here is fried and broiled, but you can order crab-stuffed shrimp or flounder as well as grouper topped with scallops and a garlicky wine sauce. Budgeteers love the $10-and-under list of Southern favorites such as country-fried steak, breaded veal cutlet, grilled pork chops, and fried chicken. Meatloaf with tomato-and-basil gravy, stuffed bell peppers with a Greek-style tomato sauce, and other lunchtime specials come with three fresh country-style vegetables, which are themselves worth the price of the meal. Hearty breakfasts feature eggs, omelets, French toast, and hotcakes.

101 Centre St. (at Front St.), Fernandina Beach. © **904/261-5310.** Main courses $8–$19; breakfast $3–$6; sandwiches $5–$9. DC, MC, V. Daily 7–10am and 11:30am–9pm.

AMELIA ISLAND AFTER DARK

This romantic island goes to bed early. If you tire of the lounges in the island's resorts, check out the **Palace Saloon,** 117 Centre St., at 2nd Street (© **904/261-6320**). It claims to be Florida's oldest watering hole (open since 1878). Complete with a pressed-tin ceiling and a 40-foot-long mahogany bar, it once hosted the Carnegies and the du Ponts. Some nights you'll even find live local blues or rock. It's open daily from 11am until 2am.

Another popular local watering hole, **O'Kane's Irish Pub & Eatery,** 318 Centre St., at 4th Street (© **904/261-1000**), has live music until midnight Monday through Thursday; until 1:30am on weekends.

14

Northwest Florida: The Panhandle

The Florida Panhandle is kind of like the Jan Brady of the state. Consider that Cindy, the cute sister, could represent Orlando and Tampa, with their amusements and attractions, while South and Southwest Florida could be Marcia, the gorgeous sister whom everyone fawns over and talks about. And then there's the misrepresented, misunderstood, underestimated Jan, in this case Northwest Florida, aka the Panhandle, always getting the shaft, even though she's got some great qualities all her own, if only people took the time to discover them. For the Panhandle, this is a particular shame, since it is, undeniably, a dynamic, uncommonly beautiful part of the state.

If you like beaches, you'll love the Panhandle, the land of the two-way sun, which runs east to west along the Gulf of Mexico and, therefore, offers sunrises *and* sunsets. Once and sometimes erroneously still known as the Redneck Riviera (thanks to fans in Georgia, Alabama, and Louisiana)—a refreshing change from the glitz and glamour oozing from Florida's south, the Panhandle, while still rugged in a sexy, Marlboro Man kind of way, has slowly shed that rep with the emergence of upscale residential developments and boutique hotels.

Three other reasons to love this zone: water as turquoise as colored contact lenses, smaller crowds than other Florida beaches, and ghost-white sand that's so talcumlike it squeaks when you walk on it. (The sand in these parts is so brilliantly white, because

over thousands of years, quartz particles were washed downstream from the eroding Appalachian Mountains and pummeled into grains as fine and soft as baby powder before finally landing at its final resting place under towels of the 3 million sunbathers who flock here every year.) Speaking of walking, you can, for some 100 miles of these incomparable sands are protected in state parks and the gorgeous Gulf Islands National Seashore.

Pensacola, Destin, Fort Walton Beach, and Panama City Beach are summertime meccas for families, couples, and singles from the aforementioned adjoining states—a geographic proximity that lends this area the languid charm of the Deep South. Indeed, Southern specialties such as collard greens and cheese grits (in the South it's a two-syllable word, pronounced *gree-its*) appear frequently on menus here.

But there's more to the northwestern Panhandle than beaches and Southern charm. Record catches of grouper, amberjack, snapper, mackerel, cobia, sailfish, wahoo, tuna, and blue marlin have made Destin one of the world's fishing capitals. In the interior near Pensacola, the Blackwater, Shoal, and Yellow rivers teem with bass, bream, catfish, and largemouth bass, and also feature some of Florida's best canoeing and kayaking adventures.

The area is also steeped in history. Rivaling St. Augustine as Florida's oldest town, picturesque Pensacola preserves a heritage derived from Spanish, French, English, and American conquests. Famous for its oysters, Apalachicola saw the invention of the air conditioner, a moment of great historical note for Florida. And Tallahassee, seat of state government since 1824, has a host of 19th-century buildings, including the majestic Old State Capitol, not to mention a cool little town named, yes, Havana, which is one of the Southeast's largest antiques centers.

One note to those traveling the entire state: While "season" in South Florida tends to fall in the winter months, because of the Panhandle's geographic location and tendency to get chilly to downright cold during winter months, their "season" is during the summer, so hotel rates will be higher during that time while it's the opposite down south.

EXPLORING NORTHWEST FLORIDA BY CAR

Both I-10 and U.S. 98 link Tallahassee and Pensacola, some 200 miles apart. The fastest route is I-10, but all you'll see is a huge pine forest divided by two strips of concrete. Plan to take U.S. 98 instead, a scenic excursion in itself. Although it can be traffic-clogged in the beach towns during summer, U.S. 98 has some beautiful stretches out in the country, particularly as it literally skirts the bay east of Apalachicola and the Gulf west of Port St. Joe. It's also lovely along skinny Okaloosa Island and across the high-rise bridge between Fort Walton Beach and Destin. From the bridge you'll see the brilliant hue of the Gulf and immediately understand why they call this the Emerald Coast. If you turn off U.S. 98 onto 30A, a 20-mile drive along the coastline, you will immediately be transported back in time, to the pre-Golden Arch-lined highways of Florida. Along this scenic stretch, you'll not only see sand and surf, but, believe it or not, pine forests, saw palmettos, the Choctawhatchee Bay, and Hogtown Bayou, a magnet for fiery sunsets.

1 Pensacola ★★

191 miles W of Tallahassee, 354 miles W of Jacksonville

A charming blend of Old Spanish brickwork, colonial French balconies reminiscent of New Orleans, and magnificent Victorian mansions built by British and American lumber barons, Pensacola is definitely worthy of its motto, "City of Five Flags," but, today, it's much more than just pretty buildings and a nice vibe. Thanks to the Pensacola Downtown Improvement Board, work has continued to progress on the revitalization of downtown, promoting the full occupancy of once abandoned, 125-year-old buildings and the emergence of downtown businesses, stores, historic theaters, restaurants, bars, and events such as the Florida Springfest, a three day music festival that lures big names like Bonnie Raitt, Trace Adkins, The Allman Brothers, and Jethro Tull, with coverage by VH-1.

A Friendly Feud

Native Americans left pottery shards and artifacts in the coastal dunes in Pensacola centuries before Tristan de Luna arrived with a band of Spanish colonists in 1559. Although his settlement lasted only 2 years, modern Pensacolans claim de Luna made their town the oldest in North America. Pensacola actually dates its permanence from a Spanish colony established here in 1698, however, so St. Augustine wins this friendly feud, having been continuously settled since 1565. France, Great Britain, the United States, and the Confederacy subsequently captured (and in one case recaptured) this strategically important deep-water port.

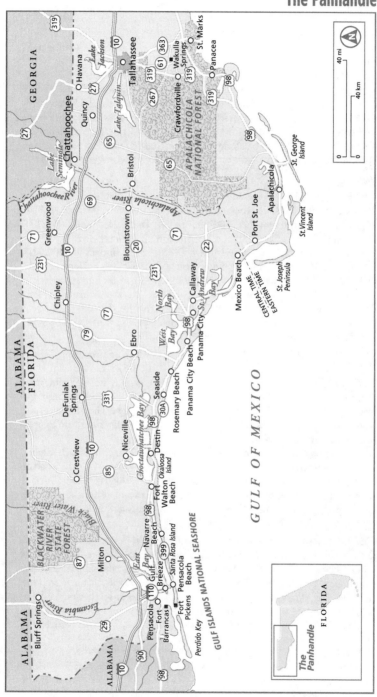

GEORGIA

ALABAMA
FLORIDA

ALABAMA

GULF OF MEXICO

319

Lake Jackson
Havana
Quincy
Chattahoochee
27
27
319
10
Tallahassee
61 363
Wakulla
Springs
St. Marks
319
Panacea
319
319
Crawfordville
267
APALACHICOLA
NATIONAL FOREST
98

Lake Seminole
Chattahoochee River
65
Bristol
65
St. George
Island

Greenwood
71
69
Apalachicola River
Blountstown
20
71
Apalachicola
St. Vincent
Island

231
10
Chipley
231
22
Port St. Joe
St. Joseph
Peninsula

77
Callaway
St. Andrew
Bay
CENTRAL TIME
EASTERN TIME
Mexico Beach

79
Ebro
North Bay
98
Panama City

DeFuniak
Springs
331
West Bay
Panama City Beach

Niceville
98
Seaside
30A
Rosemary Beach
Crestview
10
Destin
85
Okaloosa
Island

Fort
Walton
Beach

Choctawhatchee Bay

BLACKWATER
RIVER
STATE
FOREST

Black Water River
87
Milton
East
Bay
Navarre
Beach
98
Gulf
Breeze
399
Santa Rosa Island
GULF ISLANDS NATIONAL SEASHORE

Escambia River
Bluff Springs
29
Pensacola
110
Fort
Barrancas
Fort
Pickens
Pensacola
Beach

Perdido Key

90
10
98

N

40 mi
40 km
0
0

The
Panhandle
FLORIDA

West of town, the excellent National Museum of Naval Aviation at the U.S. Naval Air Station celebrates the storied past of U.S. Navy and Marine Corps pilots who trained at Pensacola. The Blue Angels, who are based here, demonstrate the high-tech present with thrilling exhibitions of precision flying in the navy's fastest fighters.

Also on the Naval Station, historic Fort Barrancas looks across the bay to Perdido Key and Santa Rosa Island, which reach out like narrow pinchers to form the harbor. Out there, powdery white-sand beaches beckon sun-and-surf lovers to their spectacular Gulf shores, which include Pensacola Beach, a small family-oriented resort, and most of Florida's share of Gulf Islands National Seashore, home of historic Fort Pickens.

ESSENTIALS

GETTING THERE   **Pensacola Regional Airport** (© **850/436-5005;** www. flypensacola.com), on 12th Avenue at Airport Road, is served by **AirTran** (© 800/ 247-8726), **Continental** (© 800/525-0280), **Delta** (© 800/221-1212), **Northwest** (© 800/225-2525), and **US Airways** (© 800/428-4322).

Alamo (© 800/327-9633), **Avis** (© 800/331-1212), **Budget** (© 800/527-0700), **Dollar** (© 800/800-4000), **Enterprise** (© 800/325-8007), **Hertz** (© 800/ 654-3131), and **National** (© 800/227-7368) have rental-car operations here.

Taxis wait outside the modern terminal. Fares are approximately $11 to downtown, $17 to Gulf Breeze, and $22 to Pensacola Beach.

The **Amtrak** transcontinental Sunset Limited stops in Pensacola at 980 E. Heinberg St. (© 800/872-7245; www.amtrak.com).

VISITOR INFORMATION   The **Pensacola Visitor Information Center,** 1401 E. Gregory St., Pensacola, FL 32501 (© **800/874-1234** or 850/434-1234; fax 850/432-8211; www.visitpensacola.com), gives away helpful information about the Greater Pensacola area, including maps of self-guided tours of the historic districts, and sells a detailed street map of the area. The office is at the mainland end of the Pensacola Bay Bridge and is open daily from 8am to 5pm (until 4pm Sat–Sun Oct–Mar).

For information specific to the beach, contact the **Pensacola Beach Chamber of Commerce,** 735 Pensacola Beach Blvd. (P.O. Box 1174), Pensacola Beach, FL 32561 (© **800/635-4803** or 850/932-1500; fax 850/932-1551; www.visitpensacolabeach.com). The chamber's offices and visitor center are on the right as you drive onto Santa Rosa Island across the Bob Sikes Bridge. They're open daily from 9am to 5pm.

GETTING AROUND   To see the historic sights in town, park at the Pensacola visitor center (see above) and take the **Five Flags Trolley** (© **850/436-9383**). The one-way East Bay (Blue) Line runs Monday through Friday from 9am to 4pm between the visitor center and downtown. The Palafox (Red) Line runs Monday through Friday from 7am to 6pm north-south along Palafox Street between the waterfront and North Hill Preservation District. Both pass through Historic Pensacola Village. The 25¢ fare includes a transfer between the two lines. The visitor center has free route maps.

A free Tiki Trolley operates along the full length of Pensacola Beach Memorial Day weekend through Labor Day weekend, Friday and Saturday from 10am to 3am, Sunday from 10am to 10pm.

Both trolleys are operated by **Escambia County Area Transit System (ECAT)** (© **850/595-3228;** www.ecat.pensacola.com), which also runs public

Downtown Pensacola

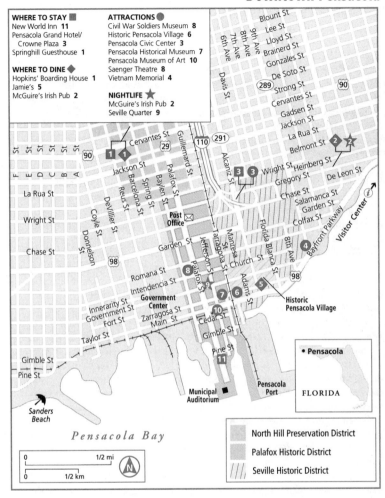

WHERE TO STAY ■
New World Inn **11**
Pensacola Grand Hotel/
  Crowne Plaza **3**
Springhill Guesthouse **1**

WHERE TO DINE ◆
Hopkins' Boarding House **1**
Jamie's **5**
McGuire's Irish Pub **2**

ATTRACTIONS ●
Civil War Soldiers Museum **8**
Historic Pensacola Village **6**
Pensacola Civic Center **3**
Pensacola Historical Museum **7**
Pensacola Museum of Art **10**
Saenger Theatre **8**
Vietnam Memorial **4**

NIGHTLIFE ★
McGuire's Irish Pub **2**
Seville Quarter **9**

North Hill Preservation District
Palafox Historic District
Seville Historic District

Pensacola Bay

buses around town Monday through Saturday ($1; 50¢ seniors)—but not to the beach. Call for schedules.

If you need a cab, call **Airport Express Taxi/City Cab** (✆ **850/478-4477**), Orange Cab (✆ **850/478-0222**), or **Yellow Cab** (✆ **850/433-3333**). Fares are $1.50 at flag fall, plus $1.60 a mile.

You can rent bicycles from **Key Sailing,** 500 Quietwater Beach Rd. (✆ **877/ 932-7272** or 850/932-5520; www.keysailing.com), in Pensacola Beach. Rentals are $10 for 4 hours and $15 for a full day.

TIME Pensacola is in the Central Time zone, 1 hour behind Miami, Orlando, and Tallahassee.

HITTING THE BEACH: GULF ISLANDS NATIONAL SEASHORE & MORE
Stretching eastward 47 miles, from the entrance to Pensacola Bay to Fort Walton Beach, skinny Santa Rosa Island is home to the resorts, condominiums, cottages,

restaurants, and shops of Pensacola Beach, the area's prime vacation spot. This relatively small and low-key resort began life a century ago as the site of a beach pavilion, or "casino" as such facilities were called back then; and the heart of town—at the intersection of Pensacola Beach Boulevard, Via de Luna, and Fort Pickens Road—is still known as Casino Beach. This lively area at the base of the town's water tank sports restaurants, snack bars, a games arcade for kids, a mini-golf course, public restrooms, walk-up beach bars with live bands blaring away, an indoor sports bar, and an outdoor concert pavilion with summertime entertainment. And the shops, restaurants, and bars of Quietwater Boardwalk are just across the road on the bay side of the island. If you want an active beach vacation, it's all here in one compact zone.

One reason Pensacola Beach is so small is that most of Santa Rosa Island is included in the **Gulf Islands National Seashore** ✴✴✴. Jumping from island to island from Mississippi to Florida, this magnificent preserve, possibly the best beach in the entire state, includes 150 miles of undeveloped and federally protected white-sand beach and rolling dunes covered with sea grass and sea oats. Established in 1971, the national seashore is a protected environment for more than 280 species of birds.

The most interesting part of the seashore is **Fort Pickens** (© **850/934-2635**), on the western end of Santa Rosa Island, about 7 miles west of Pensacola Beach. Built in the 1830s to team with Fort Barrancas in guarding Pensacola's harbor entrance, this huge brick structure saw combat during the Civil War, but it's best known as the prison home of Apache medicine man Geronimo from 1886 to 1888. The visitor center has a small museum featuring displays about Geronimo, coastal defenses, and the seashore's ecology. Plan to be here at 2pm, when rangers lead 45-minute tours of the fort (the schedule can change, so call the fort to make sure). Seven-day admission permits (that's the minimum you can get) to the Fort Pickens area are $7 per vehicle, $3 per pedestrian or bicyclist, free for holders of National Park Service passports. The fort and museum are open March through October daily from 9:30am to 5pm, November through February daily from 8:30am to 4pm. Both are closed on Christmas.

The Fort Pickens area has 200 campsites (135 with electricity) in a pine forest on the bay side of Santa Rosa Island. Nature trails lead from the camp through Blackbird Marsh and to the beach. A small store sells provisions. Sites cost $15 a night without power, $20 a night with it, and you have to pay the admission fee to the Fort Pickens area. Golden Age and Golden Access cardholders get a 50% discount. Call © **800/365-2267** for reservations (enter code GUL) or 850/934-2621 for recorded information. You can make reservations up to 5 months in advance.

The national seashore's headquarters are in the 1,378-acre Naval Live Oaks Area, on U.S. 98, a mile east of Gulf Breeze (© **850/934-2600**). This former federal tree plantation is a place of primitive beauty, with nature trails leading through the oaks and pines to picnic areas and a beach. Pick up a map at the headquarters building, which has a small museum and a gorgeous view through the pines to Santa Rosa Sound. Picnic areas and trails are open from 8am to sunset year-round except Christmas. Admission is free. The visitor center is open daily from 8am to 5:30pm.

The national seashore also maintains historic Fort Barrancas on the U.S. Naval Air Station west of town. See the "Pensacola's Other Fort" box on p. 589 for details.

For more information, contact the Gulf Islands National Seashore, 1801 Gulf Breeze Pkwy., Gulf Breeze, FL 32561 (© **850/934-2600;** www.nps.gov/guis).

Florida's Canoe Capital

The little town of Milton, the official "Canoe Capital of Florida" (by an act of the state legislature, no less), is about 20 miles northeast of Pensacola via U.S. 90. It's a well-earned title, because the nearby Blackwater River, Coldwater River, Sweetwater Creek, and Juniper Creek are perfect for canoeing, kayaking, tubing, rafting, and paddleboating.

The Blackwater is considered one of the world's purest sand-bottom rivers. It has remained a primordial, backwoods beauty, thanks chiefly to Florida's largest state forest (183,000 acres of oak, pine, and juniper) and **Blackwater River State Park** ★★, 7720 Deaton Bridge Rd., Holt, FL 32564 (© 850/983-5363; www.floridastateparks.org/blackwaterriver) where you can closely observe plant life and wildlife along nature trails. The park has facilities for fishing, picnicking, and camping. Admission is $3 per day per vehicle, $1 more for extra passengers, pedestrians, or bicyclists. Campsites cost $12 plus $2 per pet with tags and vaccination papers. For camping reservations call © 800/326-3521 or go to the website (www.reserveamerica.com).

Adventures Unlimited, Route 6, Box 283, Milton, FL 32570 (© 800/239-6864 or 850/623-6197; fax 850/626-3124; www.adventuresunlimited.com), is a year-round resort with day and overnight canoeing, kayaking, and rafting expeditions. Special arrangements are made for novices. Canoe trips start at $17 per person (4 miles), kayaking adventures from $22. Inner tubes start at $6. Campsites cost $15 a night, $20 with electricity. The resort also has 14 cottages on the Coldwater River ($49–$129 a night), and bed-and-breakfast accommodations at the Wolfe Creek Old School House Inn (eight rooms, all with bathrooms, $89–$109 double). Two-night minimum stays are required, 3 nights on holidays. Call for schedules and reservations for trips, accommodations, and camping.

Blackwater Canoe Rental, 10274 Pond Rd., Milton, FL 32570 (© 800/967-6789 or 850/623-0235; www.blackwatercanoe.com), also rents canoes, kayaks, floats, tubes, and camping equipment. It has day and overnight camping trips by canoe or kayak, or inner tubes ranging from $11 to $19 per person and overnight excursions ranging from $22 to $33 per person. Tents, sleeping bags, and coolers are available for rent.

OUTDOOR ACTIVITIES

FISHING   Red snapper, grouper, mackerel, tuna, and billfish are abundant off the Panhandle. The easiest way to drop a line into the Gulf is off the new **Pensacola Beach Gulf Fishing Pier,** on Fort Pickens Road in Pensacola Beach (© 850/934-7200; www.fishpensacolabeachpier.com). At 1,471 feet, it's the longest fishing pier on the Gulf coast. The pier is open 24 hours a day year-round. Fees to fish are $6.50 per day for adults, $5.50 for seniors, and $3.50 for children 6 to 12. Bait and equipment cost extra. Observers can watch for $1 per person.

Fishing-charter services are offered at Pensacola by the **Beach Marina Fishing Fleet** (© 877/650-3474 or 850/932-0304) and at Pensacola Beach by **Reel**

Eazy Charters (© 877/733-5329 or 850/932-8824). Expect to pay between $400 and $900 for one to four passengers, depending on the length of your trip. You may be able to save by driving to Destin, where party boats charge less per person (p. 599). Sightseeing and evening cruises here go for $50 to $200 per person.

GOLF   The Pensacola area has its share of Northwest Florida's numerous championship golf courses. Look for free copies of *South Coast Golf Guide,* an annual directory describing all of them, at the visitor information offices and in many hotel lobbies (see "The Active Vacation Planner," in chapter 2, for information about ordering copies). Reasonably priced golf packages can be arranged through many local hotels and motels.

For course information online, go to www.golf.com and www.floridagolfing. com or call the **Florida Sports Foundation** (© 850/488-8347) or **Florida Golfing** (© 866/833-2663).

Among this region's best courses is **Marcus Pointe,** on Marcus Pointe Boulevard off North W Street (© 800/362-7287 or 850/484-9770), which has hosted the Nike Tour, the American Amateur Classic, and the Pensacola Open. *Golf Digest* magazine described this 18-hole course as a "great value," and that's not far off: Greens fees with cart are about $40 to $65, depending on the season.

The Moors, on Avalon Boulevard north of I-10 (© 800/727-1010 or 850/ 995-4653), also has greeted the Nike Tour and is home to the Emerald Coast Classic, a PGA Seniors event. Pot bunkers here make you think you're playing in Scotland. Greens fees are similarly priced. The Moors also has a lodge with eight luxury rooms.

Others worth considering are the **Lost Key Golf Club** on Perdido Key (© 888/256-7853 or 850/492-1300), one of the area's more difficult courses; **Scenic Hills,** on U.S. 90 northwest of town (© 850/476-9611), whose rolling fairways are unique for this mostly flat area; the 36-hole **Tiger Point,** 1255 Country Club Rd. east of Gulf Breeze by Santa Rosa Sound (© 850/932-1330), overlooking the water (the 5th-hole green of the East Course actually sits on an island); **Hidden Creek,** 3070 PGA Blvd., in Navarre between Gulf Breeze and Fort Walton Beach (© 850/939-4604); **Creekside Golf Course,** 2355 W. Michigan Ave. (© 850/944-7969); and **Osceola Municipal Golf Course,** 300 Tonawanda, off Mobile Highway (© 850/456-2761).

In addition, **The Sportsman Golf Resort,** 1 Doug Ford Dr. (© 866/319-2471 or 850/492-1223; www.sportsmanresort.com), on the mainland north of Perdido Key, has accommodations available for visiting golfers. It was the home of the PGA Pensacola Open from 1978 to 1987, when it was known as the Perdido Bay Golf Resort. Greens fees here range from $55 to $65.

WATERSPORTS   Visibility in the waters around Pensacola can range from 30 to 50 feet deep inshore to 100 feet deep 25 miles offshore. Although the bottom is sandy and it's too far north for coral, the battleship USS *Massachusetts,* submerged in 30 feet of water 3 miles offshore, is one of some 35 artificial reefs where you can spot loggerhead turtles and other creatures. There are also good snorkeling sites just off the beach; get a map from the Gulf Islands National Seashore (see "Hitting the Beach: Gulf Islands National Seashore & More," above).

Scuba Shack, 711 S. Palafox St. (© 850/433-4319), offers sales, rentals, classes, and diving and fishing charters on the *Wet Dream,* moored behind the office. **Divers Den,** 512 N. 9th Ave. (© 850/438-0650; www.diversden.com), also provides trips, equipment rental, and PADI instruction. **MBT Divers** (© 850/455-7702; www.mbtdivers.com) has rentals, instruction, and trips to several sites, including the habitats of sea turtles, manta rays, and nurse sharks.

Gulf Breeze Dive Pros, 297B Gulf Breeze Pkwy. (U.S. 98), in Gulf Breeze (© **850/934-8845**), has a menu that includes rentals, all levels of instruction, and diving excursions on the 30-foot *Easy Dive.*

Key Sailing Center, 500 Quietwater Beach Rd., on the Quietwater Beach Boardwalk (© **877/932-7272** or 850/932-5520; www.keysailing.com), and **Radical Rides,** 444 Pensacola Beach Blvd., near the Bob Sikes Bridge (© **850/ 934-9743**), rent Hobie Cats, pontoon boats, WaveRunners, jet skis, and wind-surfing boards.

EXPLORING HISTORIC PENSACOLA

Adjacent to the Historic Pensacola Village, the city's **Vietnam Memorial,** on Bayfront Parkway at 9th Avenue, is known as the "Wall South," since it is a three-quarter–size replica of the national Vietnam Veterans Memorial in Washington, D.C. Look for the "Huey" helicopter atop the wall.

Civil War Soldiers Museum ★   Founded by Dr. Norman Haines Jr., a local physician who started collecting Civil War relics in Sharpsburg, Maryland, when he was growing up, this 4,200 square foot store-front museum in the heart of the Palafox Street business district emphasizes how ordinary soldiers lived during that bloody conflict. The doctor's collection of military medical equipment and treatment methods is especially informative. A 23-minute video tells of Pensacola's role during the Civil War. The museum's bookstore carries more than 600 titles about the war.

108 S. Palafox St. (south of Romana St.). © 850/469-1900. www.cwmuseum.org. Admission $5 adults, $2.50 children 6–12, free for children 5 and under. Tues–Sat 10am–4:30pm. Closed New Year's Day, Thanksgiving, Christmas Eve, Christmas Day.

Historic Pensacola Village ★★★   History buffs as well as those who appreciate delightful architecture will *love* this retro-fabulous old-school village that's comparable to Long Island's Old Bethpage Village Restoration or Virginia's Colonial Williamsburg. Bounded by Government, Taragona, Adams, and Alcanz streets, this original part of Pensacola resembles a shady English colonial town—albeit with Spanish street names—complete with town green and **Christ Church,** built in 1832 and resembling Bruton Parish in Williamsburg, Virginia. Some of Florida's oldest homes, now owned and preserved by the state, are here, and the village has charming boutiques and interesting restaurants. All twenty of the Village's properties are on the National Register as a historic district. During summer, costumed characters go about their daily chores and demonstrate old crafts, and University of Florida archaeologists unearth the old Spanish commanding officer's compound at Zaragosa and Tarragona streets. Among the landmarks you can visit are the **Museum of Industry,** the **Museum of Commerce,** the French Creole–style **Charles Lavalle House,** the elegant **Victorian Dorr House,** the French Colonial–Creole **Quina House,** and **St. Michael's Cemetery** (land was deeded by the king of Spain). The **Julee Cottage Black History Museum,** 204 E. Zaragosa St., is another fascinating site. Built around 1790, this small house was owned by Julee Panton, a freed slave who ran her business, invested in real estate, and loaned money to slaves so they could buy their freedom. Today the museum recalls her life and deeds. Start your tour by buying tickets at **Tivoli House,** 205 E. Zaragosa St., just east of Tarragona Street, where you can get free maps and brochures. Try to take one of the 90-minute guided walking tours of the village, which will take you through Christ Church and other buildings not otherwise open to the public.

Admission to the village includes the **T. T. Wentworth Jr. Florida State Museum,** 330 S. Jefferson St. (© **850/595-5985**), at Church Street downtown, a classic yellow-brick building housing exhibits of Western Florida's history and a special hands-on Discovery Museum for children. The museum's newest exhibition is "La Frontera de Pensacola," a hands-on exhibit highlighting local heritage

205 E. Zaragosa St. (east of Tarragona St.). © 850/595-5985. www.historicpensacola.org. Admission $6 adults, $5 seniors, $2.50 children 4–16, free for children 3 and under. Mon–Fri 10am–4pm; 90-min. guided tours 11am and 1pm. Closed New Year's Day, Thanksgiving, Christmas Eve, Christmas Day, all other state holidays.

National Museum of Naval Aviation 🌟🌟   Given the present world circumstances, this museum should be required attendance for everyone. Yes, it's fascinating, but it also gives you a look into just how much blood, sweat, and tears go into defending this country. The U.S. Navy and Marine Corps have trained at the sprawling U.S. Naval Air Station since they began flying airplanes early in the last century. Celebrating their heroics, this remarkable museum has more than 100 aircraft dating from the 1920s to the space age plus interesting exhibits on subjects such as POWs. There's even a torpedo bomber flown by former President George (the first) Bush during World War II. Both children and adults can sit at the controls of a jet trainer, and the mock-ups of aircraft carrier conning towers and hanger decks are realistic. You can almost feel the tug of gravity while watching the Blue Angels and other naval aviators soaring about the skies in the stunning *Magic of Flight,* one of two IMAX films shown at the museum. If the movie doesn't get your stomach churning, then a 15-minute ride in the museum's flight-motion simulator will. Using high-tech video and real motion, it simulates a high-speed, low-level mission in the navy's F-18 Hornet jet fighter. All guides are retired naval and Marine Corps aviators, which adds a personal touch to the hour-long museum tours. Allow at least half a day here, and save 20 minutes for a Flight Line bus tour of more than 40 aircraft parked outside the museum's restoration hangar.

Radford Blvd., U.S. Naval Air Station. © 850/452-3604. www.naval-air.org. Free admission. IMAX movies $6.50 adults; $6.00 seniors, military, and children 5–13; free for children under 5. Add $3 for second movie. Flight-motion simulator rides $3.50 per person. Daily 9am–5pm. Guided tours daily at 9:30 and 11am, and 1 and 2:30pm. Flight Line bus tours daily every 30 min. 10am–noon and 1–4pm. IMAX movies on the hour daily 10am–4pm. Flight-motion simulator every 15 min. 9am–4:45pm. Closed New Year's Day, Thanksgiving, Christmas. Enter naval station either at the Main Gate at the south end of Navy Blvd. (Fla. 295) or at the Back Gate on Blue Angel Pkwy. (Fla. 173) and follow the signs. No passes are required.

Pensacola Historical Museum   To learn more about Pensacola's diverse, five-flag history, spend 30 to 60 minutes at this local museum in the Arbona Building, a commercial structure built around 1882. An archaeological dig of the Spanish commanding officer's compound across Zaragosa Street has a boardwalk with explanatory signposts. The museum is operated by the Pensacola Historical Society, which has a resource center and library at 117 E. Government St. (© **850/434-5455**).

115 E. Zaragosa St. (between Tarragona and Jefferson sts.). © 850/433-1559. www.pensacolahistory.org. Admission $1. Mon–Sat 10am–4:30pm.

Pensacola Museum of Art 🌟   Housed in what was the city jail from 1906 to 1954, this museum showcases an impressive collection of European and American decorative glass, some African tribal art, and sometimes minor works by Salvador Dalí, John Marin, Ansel Adams, Thomas Hart Benton, Lynda Benglis, Milton Avery, George Rodrigue, Alexander Calder, Pablo Cano, and Rembrandt among others, all displayed in the former cell blocks. They also sponsor cool events such as Art After Dark, in which you are invited to use the

Pensacola's Other Fort

Standing on Taylor Road near the National Museum of Naval Aviation, **Fort Barrancas** 👁👁 (© 850/455-5167) is definitely worth a visit while you're at the naval station. This imposing brick structure sits on a bluff overlooking the deep-water pass into Pensacola Bay. The Spanish built the water battery in 1797. Linked to it by a tunnel, the incredibly intricate brickwork of the fort's upper section was constructed by American troops between 1839 and 1844. Entry is by means of a drawbridge across a dry moat, and an interior scarp gallery goes all the way around the inside of the fort. Meticulously restored and operated by the National Park Service as part of Gulf Islands National Seashore, the fort is open March through October, daily from 9:30am to 4:45pm; November through February, daily from 8:30am to 3:45pm. Ranger-led, 1-hour guided tours are well worth taking. The schedule changes seasonally, so call for the latest information. Admission and the tours are free.

The **Pensacola Lighthouse,** opposite the museum entrance on Radford Boulevard, has guided ships to the harbor entrance since 1825. Except for occasional guided tours (call the Pensacola visitor centers, listed earlier in this chapter, for a schedule), the lighthouse is not open to the public, but you can drive right up to it. The nearby **Lighthouse Point Restaurant** (© 850/452-3251) offers bountiful, all-you-can-eat luncheon buffets and magnificent bay views for about $5.50 per person Monday through Thursday and $6.25 per person on Fridays; it's open Monday through Friday from 10:30am to 2pm (closed Sat–Sun), and reservations are not required.

walls of the museum as your personal canvas in your best display of personal, artistic expression. Call before going to see what's on.

407 S. Jefferson St. (at Main St.). © 850/432-6247. www.pensacolamuseumofart.org. Free admission on Tues; other days $5 adults, $2 students and active-duty military, free for children under 6. Tues–Fri 10am–5pm; Sat–Sun noon–5pm.

HISTORIC DISTRICTS

In addition to Historic Pensacola Village (see above) in the Seville Historic District (see below), the city has two other preservation areas worth a stroll. The Pensacola Visitor Information Center provides free walking-tour maps (see "Essentials," earlier in this chapter) if you're interested.

PALAFOX HISTORIC DISTRICT 👁👁 Running up Palafox Street from the water to Wright Street, the Palafox Historic District is also the downtown business district. Beautiful Spanish Renaissance and Mediterranean-style buildings stand from the early days, including the ornate Saenger Theatre. In 1821, General Andrew Jackson formally accepted Florida into the United States during a ceremony in Plaza Ferdinand VII, now a National Historic Landmark. His statue commemorates the event.

For architecture buffs, this district is a theme park, with the 1902 Theisen Building and its vivid displays of Beaux Arts details, and the 1925 Seanger Theatre, with its terra-cotta ornamentation and grille work on the front façade showcasing it as an elegant gem of the Spanish Baroque style.

The Palafox district is home to the **Pensacola Historical Museum;** the **Pensacola Museum of Art,** in the old city jail; and the **T. T. Wentworth Jr. Florida State Museum** (see "Exploring Historic Pensacola," above).

And, no visit to the Palafox District is complete without visits to the **Hopkins' Boarding House** restaurant, 900 N. Spring St. (© **850/438-3979**), for family-style grub in a turn-of-the-century house (p. 593), and, for boozehounds, **The Palace Oyster Bar,** 130 E. Government St. (© **850/434-6211**), which includes a bar from the old Palace Hotel, where Florida's first liquor license was issued.

NORTH HILL PRESERVATION DISTRICT ☆   Another entry in the National Register of Historic Places, the North Hill Preservation District covers the 50 square blocks north of the Palafox Historic District bounded by Wright, Blount, Palafox, and Reus streets. Descendants of Spanish nobility, timber barons, British merchants, French Creoles, buccaneers, and Civil War soldiers still live in some of the more than 500 homes. They are not open to the public but are a bonanza for anyone interested in architecture. In 1863, Union troops erected a fort in Lee Square, at Palafox and Gadsden streets. It later was dedicated to the Confederacy, complete with a 50-foot-high obelisk and sculpture based on John Elder's painting *After Appomattox.*

A NEARBY ZOO WITH LIONS & TIGERS

The Zoo *Kids*   Situated in a 50-acre forest 15 miles east of Pensacola, this zoo has more than 700 exotic animals—including tigers, lions, rhinos, and lowland gorillas—living in landscaped habitats. Japanese gardens, a giraffe-feeding tower, and a petting farm make for a fun visit. A Safari Line train chugs through a 30-acre wildlife preserve with free-ranging herds, and youngsters also will love riding the wild animals instead of horses on a merry-go-round. The 2003 birth of a Pygmy Hippo and a sable antelope here garnered national attention for the zoo on The Animal Planet cable channel. Set aside about 3 to 4 hours to cover the entire park.

5701 Gulf Breeze Pkwy. (U.S. 98), Gulf Breeze. © 850/932-2229. www.the-zoo.com. Admission $11 adults, $9.95 seniors, $7.95 children 3–11, free for children 2 and under. Train rides $3 per person. Carousel rides $2 per person. Open daily 9am–5pm. Closed Thanksgiving, Christmas Eve, Christmas Day, and New Year's Eve.

SHOPPING

Sightseeing and shopping can be combined in Pensacola's Palafox and Seville Historic Districts, where many shops are housed in renovated centuries-old buildings. The **Quayside Art Gallery,** on Plaza Ferdinand at the corner of Zaragosa and Jefferson streets (© **850/438-2363;** www.quaysidegallery.com), is the largest cooperative gallery in the Southeast. More than 100 artists display their works here, and the friendly staff will direct you to other nearby galleries.

North T Street between West Cervantes Street and West Fairfield Drive has so many antiques dealers and small flea markets that it's known as Antique Alley. Other dealers have booths in the **Ninth Avenue Antique Mall,** 380 N. 9th Ave. between Gregory and Strong streets (© **850/438-3961**). Get a complete list of local antiques dealers from the Pensacola Visitor Information Center (p. 582).

Browsers will enjoy poking through the 400 dealer spaces at the **Flea Market,** on U.S. 98, opposite The Zoo, 15 miles east of Pensacola (© **850/934-1971**). It's open on Saturday and Sunday from 9am to 5pm. Admission is free.

WHERE TO STAY

The Pensacola Visitor Information Center (p. 582) publishes a complete list of rental condominiums and cottages. Among the leading rental agents are **JME Management,** 22-A Via de Luna, Pensacola Beach, FL 32561 (© **800/554-3695;**

Tips When Room Rates Are Lowest

Room rates at all Panhandle beaches are highest from mid-May to mid-August, and premiums are charged at Easter, Memorial Day, July 4, and Labor Day. Hotel or motel reservations are essential during these periods. There's another high-priced peak in March, when thousands of raucous college students invade during spring break. Economical times to visit are April (except Easter) and September—the weather is warm, most establishments are open, and room rates are significantly lower than during summer. The least-expensive rates are available during winter, but many attractions and some restaurants may be closed then.

---

www.jmevacations.com), and **Tristan Realty,** 1020 Fort Pickens Rd., Pensacola Beach, FL 32561 (© **800/445-9931** or 850/932-7363; fax 850/932-8361; www.tristanrealty.com).

The **Fort Pickens Area** of Gulf Islands National Seashore is your best bet here for camping (p. 584).

Escambia County adds 11.5% tax to all hotel and campground bills.

The accommodations listed below are arranged by geographic area: downtown Pensacola and Pensacola Beach. Bear in mind that Pensacola Beach is at least a 15-minute drive from downtown.

DOWNTOWN PENSACOLA

The University Mall complex at I-10 and Davis Highway, about 5 miles north of downtown, has a host of chain motels, and there's an ample supply of inexpensive restaurants on Plantation Road and in the adjacent mall. Another good bet is the 1998-vintage **Hampton Inn Airport,** 2187 Airport Blvd. (© **800/426-7866** or 850/478-1123; fax 850/478-8519). This area is not as congested as that around University Mall. The inn runs a free shuttle to nearby Cordova Mall and its adjacent chain restaurants.

Several of the town's Victorian homes have been turned into luxurious bed-and-breakfasts. Among the best is **Springhill Guesthouse,** 903 N. Spring St. (© **800/475-1956** or 850/438-6887; www.bbonline.com/fl/springhill), whose wraparound porch faces the extraordinary Hopkins' Boarding House across the street (see "Where to Dine," below).

New World Inn   Near the scenic bay and in the historic district, this urban version of a comfortable country inn (it looks more like a concrete fortress) is part of a meeting facility known as New World Landing. Inside, however, is an entirely different—much more pleasing to the eye—story. From the colonial-style lobby, a grand staircase leads to high-ceilinged and spacious rooms and suites artistically decorated with antiques. The rooms depict aspects of Pensacola's rich history: Four of them flaunt Spanish decor, four are très chic French style, four portray Early Americana, and four focus on old England.

600 S. Palafox St. (at Pine St.), Pensacola, FL 32501. © 850/432-4111. Fax 850/432-6836. www.newworld landing.com. 15 units. $75–$95 double; $125–$145 suite. Rates include continental breakfast. AE, MC, V. **Amenities:** Access to nearby health club; laundry service. *In room:* A/C, TV, dataport.

Pensacola Grand Hotel/Crowne Plaza ⭐   Opposite the Civic Center in the Seville Historic District near the southern end of I-110, this unique hotel has turned the historic L&N Railroad Depot into a grand lobby with bar, restaurants, lounges, meeting rooms, and a cozy library. You'll see such turn-of-the-20th-century accouterments as an ornate railroad clock, original oak stair rails, imported marble, ceramic mosaic-tile floors, and old-fashioned carved furniture. An unimpressive 15-story glass-and-steel tower behind the depot holds the rooms and suites, which are popular primarily with business travelers and groups.

200 E. Gregory St. (at Alcanz St.), Pensacola, FL 32501. ℂ 800/348-3336 or 850/433-3336. Fax 850/432-7572. www.pensacolagrandhotel.com. 212 units. $105–$150 double; $260–$425 suite. AE, DC, DISC, MC, V. **Amenities:** Restaurant; bar; outdoor pool; exercise room; business center; limited room service; laundry service; concierge-level rooms. *In room:* A/C, TV, dataport, fridge (suites only), coffeemaker, hair dryer, iron.

PENSACOLA BEACH

Best Western Pensacola Beach Resort   It's a Best Western, yes, but this hotel has a better view than some fancier hotels could ever dream of, right on the Gulf, and it's notable for bright, clean, and extra-spacious accommodations, complete with refrigerators, coffeemakers, microwaves, and wet bars. Outside corridors lead to all rooms. Although none has its own balcony or patio, units facing the beach have great views but higher prices. Two pools and a kids' playground are on the beach, and restaurants are within walking distance.

16 Via de Luna Dr., Pensacola Beach, FL 32561. ℂ 800/934-3301 or 850/934-3300. Fax 850/934-4366. www.pensacolabeach.com/bestwestern. 123 units. Summer $149–$189 double; off-season $79–$149 double. Rates include continental breakfast. Golf packages available. AE, DC, DISC, MC, V. **Amenities:** 2 outdoor pools; watersports equipment rentals; game room. *In room:* A/C, TV, dataport, fridge, microwaves, coffeemaker, hair dryer, iron.

Clarion Suites Resort & Convention Center ★★   This most unusual of Pensacola Beach's resorts resembles a village of tin-roofed, pastel-sided cottages located on the sand dunes and reminiscent of a tony rental community in New York's Hamptons. Pretty swank for Clarion Suites, I'd say. The attractively decorated accommodations are one-bedroom suites with kitchens and two televisions that can accommodate four people. The best units are those directly facing the beach. They have balconies or patios, while the others do not. There are no restaurants in the resort, and if you don't feel like cooking in your suite's kitchen, area eateries are within walking distance. The outdoor pool is lovely, but why use the pool when you're right on this stunning beach?

20 Via de Luna Dr., Pensacola Beach, FL 32561. ℂ 800/874-5303 or 850/932-4300. Fax 850/934-9112. www.clarionsuitesresort.com. 86 units. Summer $119–$199 up to 4 persons; off-season $84–$119 up to 4 persons. Rates include continental breakfast. AE, DC, DISC, MC, V. **Amenities:** Heated outdoor pool; watersports equipment rentals; coin-op washers and dryers. *In room:* A/C, TV, dataport, kitchen, coffeemaker, hair dryer, iron.

The Dunes ★   Although this is a full-service beachfront highrise hotel, there's something oddly impersonal about it and given the choice, I'd stay at the Clarion Suites. The eight-story beachfront tower has spacious rooms, all with Gulf or bay vistas. All rooms have a Gulf-facing balcony, and the penthouse suites have their own whirlpool tubs. The extra-large suites can accommodate small families. The Dunes has a restaurant and bar (both with lovely views of the Gulf), so you don't have to go out for lunch or dinner unless you want to. There's also a jogging trail, a bike path, and an undeveloped dune preserve next door. A Gulf-front pool with waterfall and available golf packages in conjunction with area courses are great diversions.

333 Fort Pickens Rd., Pensacola Beach, FL 32561. ℂ 800/833-8637 or 850/932-3536. Fax 850/932-7088. www.theduneshotel.com. 76 units. Summer $115–$185 double, $140–$365 suite; off-season $85–$115 double, $265–$305 suite. Packages available. AE, DISC, MC, V. **Amenities:** Restaurant; bar; heated outdoor pool; access to nearby health club; watersports equipment rentals; limited room service; laundry service. *In room:* A/C, TV, dataport, coffeemaker, hair dryer, iron.

Five Flags Inn *(Value)*   Sitting between the Holiday Inn Express and The Dunes, this basic but friendly motel looks like a jail from the road and the rooms have cinderblock walls, but if it's location and view you're looking for at a bargain basement rate, flag this hotel. Big picture windows in the rooms overlook the swimming pool (heated Mar–Oct) and the gorgeous white-sand beach, which comes right up to the property. Although the accommodations are small, trust us on this: The rates are a bargain for clean, Gulf-front rooms.

299 Fort Pickens Rd., Pensacola Beach, FL 32561. © 850/932-3586. Fax 850/934-0257. www.fiveflagsinn. com. 49 units. Summer $99 double; off-season $55–$75 double; $20 more for holidays. AE, DC, DISC, MC, V. **Amenities:** Heated outdoor pool. *In room:* A/C, TV, hair dryer, iron.

Hampton Inn Pensacola Beach *(★)*   This pastel, long-and-low (four-story) hotel sits on a sliver of land—600 feet, specifically—between Santa Rosa Sound and the Gulf, next to the action on Casino Beach. The bright lobby opens to a wooden sun deck with beachside swimming pools on either side (one is heated). Half the oversize rooms have balconies overlooking the Gulf; these are more expensive than rooms on the bay side, which have nice views but no outside sitting areas. Their Gilligan's Tiki Bar is directly on the beach and is a fun place to spend some time.

2 Via de Luna, Pensacola Beach, FL 32561. © 800/320-8108 or 850/932-6800. Fax 850/932-6833. www.hamptonbeachresort.com. 181 units. Summer $159–$199 double; off-season $89–$149 double. Rates include continental breakfast and local phone calls. AE, DC, DISC, MC, V. **Amenities:** Bar; 2 outdoor pools; access to nearby health club; exercise room; watersports equipment rentals; laundry service, coin-op washers and dryers. *In room:* A/C, TV, dataport, fridge, coffeemaker, hair dryer, iron.

The Portofino *(★★★)* *(Kids)*   The one and only luxe spot in the area, Portofino is a stunning, Italian-Mediterranean-style 28-acre resort and condo at the quieter, east end of Pensacola Beach. Because it's a residence cum resort, the richly decorated 2 and 3 bedroom suites here are spectacular and very much like luxury apartments, with panoramic views of the Gulf. The spa offers many luxurious treatments while the resort also features an indoor Olympic and 5 heated pools; whirlpool spas, saunas, and steam rooms; a gourmet restaurant; seasonal Kids' Camp; and complimentary shuttle service to Tiger Point, a 36-hole championship golf course.

10 Portofino Dr., Pensacola Beach, FL 32561. © 866/478-3400 or 850/916-5000. Fax 850/916-5010. www.theportofino.com. 150 units. Summer $693–$1,299 two and three bedroom apartments; off season $495–$650 two and three bedroom apartments. AE, DC, DISC, MC, V. **Amenities:** Restaurant; bar; 6 pools; 2 rubico tennis courts; fitness center; kids programs; watersports rentals. *In room:* A/C, TV, dataport, full kitchen, coffeemaker, hair dryer, iron.

WHERE TO DINE
PENSACOLA

Hopkins' Boarding House *(★★★)* *(Value)* SOUTHERN   You haven't had true comfort food until you dine at this extraordinary Victorian boardinghouse founded by Arkie Dell Hopkins in 1949 and now run by her son Ed in the heart of the North Hill Preservation District, where it feels as if you are dining at your own grandma's house. Outside, ancient trees shade a wraparound porch with old-fashioned rocking chairs in which you'll wait the next available place at the large dining tables inside. It's all-you-can-eat family-style, so you could be seated next to a football star, the mayor, or a mechanic, since everyone in town dines here. Platters are piled high with staples of down-home Southern cooking: black-eyed peas, collard greens, and other seasonal vegetables from nearby farms. Tuesday is famous as Fried Chicken Day, and you're likely to be served fried fish on Friday. Yankees should sample the piping-hot grits accompanying each boun- tiful breakfast (slop on some butter or salt and pepper to give them taste but never use sugar on this staple that some Yankees confuse with Cream of Wheat). In true boardinghouse fashion, you'll bus your own dishes and pay on the way out. No alcoholic beverages are served, but the "don't-call-it-sweet-if-you-want- to-be-considered-a-local" iced tea is a sweet treat.

900 N. Spring St. (at Strong St.). ℂ **850/438-3979**. Breakfast $3.50–$8; lunch and dinner full meals $8. No credit cards. Tues–Sun 7–9:30am and 11:15am–2pm; Tues and Fri 5–7:30pm.

Jamie's ★★★ TRADITIONAL FRENCH Occupying a restored Victorian home in Historic Pensacola Village, the town's classiest and most romantic restaurant enhances the dining experience with a stellar ambience augmented by working fireplaces, fabulous antiques, candlelight, and subdued background music. The excellent French Provincial fare includes roast leg of lamb, tourne- dos of beef, and seafood specials. The wine list is also exquisite. This is as fine as Pensacola's cuisine gets.

424 E. Zaragosa St. (between Alcanz and Florida Blanca). ℂ **850/434-2911**. Reservations recommended at both lunch and dinner. Main courses $17–$30. AE, DISC, MC, V. Mon–Sat 11:30am–2pm and 5:30–9pm, sometimes later.

Marina Oyster Barn ★ *Value* SEAFOOD Exuding the ambience of the quickly vanishing Old Florida fish camps, this plain but clean restaurant at the Johnson-Rooks Marina is to seafood what the Hopkins' Boarding House is to grits. It's been a local favorite since 1969, for its view and its down-home–style seafood. Freshly shucked oysters, served raw, steamed, fried, or Rockefeller-style, are the main feature; but the seafood salad here is also first-rate, and the fish, shrimp, and oysters are breaded with cornmeal in true Southern fashion. The daily luncheon specials give you a light meal at a bargain price.

505 Bayou Blvd. (on Bayou Texar). ℂ **850/433-0511**. Main courses $5–$15; sandwiches $2.50–$5.50; lunch specials $3.75–$6.50. AE, DISC, MC, V. Tues–Sat 11am–9pm (lunch specials 11am–2pm). Go east on Cer- vantes St. (U.S. 90) across the Bayou Texar Bridge, then take 1st left on Stanley Ave., and left again to the end of Strong St.

McGuire's Irish Pub ★ STEAKS/SEAFOOD Every day and night is St. Patrick's Day at this lively and popular pub. The menu is delectably Irish, com- plete with corned beef and cabbage, Irish stew, and other such Dublin delicacies. Supersize steaks are the best offerings, however, as are hickory-smoked ribs and chicken. You can also order seafood, including a hearty bouillabaisse with shrimp, red snapper, clams, mussels, and oysters. The big burgers come with a choice of more than 20 toppings, from smoked Gouda cheese to sautéed Vidalia onions. You can watch your ale being brewed in copper kettles and dine in a cel- larlike room with 8,000 bottles of wine on display. More than 125,000 dollar bills line the bar's walls and ceilings. Live music is offered most nights.

600 E. Gregory St. (between 11th and 12th aves.). ℂ **850/433-6789**. www.mcguiresirishpub.com. Main courses $16–$25; snacks, burgers, and sandwiches $8–$12. AE, DC, DISC, MC, V. Daily 11am–midnight, later on weekend.

Skopelos on the Bay ★ SEAFOOD/STEAKS/GREEK If you didn't know any better—or drank too much ouzo, you'd think you were in Santorini. Perched on a bluff overlooking the bay, this family-owned restaurant has been famous hereabouts since 1959 for its great views and creative seafood dishes, such as the scamp Cervantes (scamp is a deepwater fish with white, flaky meat). Other seafood selections range from broiled scallops to Mediterranean-style grouper prepared with a sauce of tomato and roasted eggplant. The menu also features charcoal-grilled steaks and chicken and roast leg of lamb. Befitting the owner's Greek heritage, roast lamb is served with moussaka, dolmades, titopita, and spanakopita. In warm weather, opt for an outside table with a bay view.

670 Scenic Hwy. (U.S. 90 east, at E. Cervantes St.). (C) **850/432-6565.** Reservations recommended. Main courses $15–$35. AE, DISC, MC, V. Tues–Thurs and Sat 5–10:30pm; Fri 11:30am–2:30pm and 5–10:30pm.

PENSACOLA BEACH

Bobaloo's on the Beach ✦ SEAFOOD Waterfront views aside, Bobaloo's is proudest of serving the "largest seafood platter on the beach," in addition to delicious southern cooking such as fried dill pickles, fried crawfish tails, and collard greens. The fishing motif is most apropos, but the best part about the place is that they will cook, fry, boil, or do whatever to any fish caught right there by one of the many charter boats scouting the waters. Live music and a lively crowd make Bobaloo's a great choice for lunch, dinner, or just kicking back with a beer, some fried food, and a phenomenal sunset.

699 Pensacola Beach Blvd. (C) **850/934-3434.** Main courses $3.25–$13. MC, V. Daily 11:30am–1am.

Flounder's Chowder & Ale House ✦✦ SEAFOOD Floundering around for a place where you can get fresh fish cooked any way, and live reggae almost nightly? Then Flounder's Chowder & Ale House is where you need to be, on the boardwalk, overlooking the Santa Rosa Sound, and serving great food for breakfast, brunch, lunch, dinner, or late night snacks. The best of the offerings include the Maine lobster and chargrilled tuna, grouper, and mahimahi. If you're lucky, a big smoker grill outside will be producing more fish and some exceptional ribs. Burgers, salads, and sandwiches are offered all day. The dining room is cool and not at all what you'd expect from a fish house, with stained glass windows imported from a convent, of all places, confessional booth walls straight from a church, and bookshelves contributing to a cozy, Nantucket in the winter kind of feel. But when the weather's warm, you'll definitely want to be outdoors.

800 Quietwater Beach Rd. (at ia de Luna and Fort Pickens Rd.). (C) **850/932-2003.** Reservations not accepted. Main courses $15 21; burgers and sandwiches $8–$10. AE, DC, DISC, MC, V. Sun–Thurs 11am–midnight (to 11pm in inter); Fri–Sat 11am–2am (to 11pm in winter).

PENSACOLA AFTER DARK

For what's hip and happening when the sun goes down, pick up the daily *Pensacola News Journal* (www.pensacolanewsjournal.com), especially its Friday entertainment section. Another good source is the *Pensacola Downtown Crowd* (www.burchellpublishing.com/downtown.asp), a free publication available at the Pensacola Visitor Information Center (p. 582) covering the nightly events going on in downtown Pensacola.

THE PERFORMING ARTS Pensacola has a surprisingly sophisticated array of entertainment choices for such a relatively small city. For a schedule of upcoming events, get a copy of *Vision*, a bimonthly newsletter published by the Arts Council of Northwest Florida ((C) **850/432-9906;** www.artsnwfl.org). Also pick up **Sneak Preview,** a calendar of events at the Pensacola Civic Center and the Saenger Theater. Both publications are available at the Pensacola Visitor Information Center (p. 582). Tickets for all major performances can be purchased from **Ticketmaster** ((C) **800/488-5252** or 850/433-6311; www.ticketmaster.com).

The highlight venue here is the ornate **Saenger Theatre** ✦, 118 S. Palafox St., near Romana Street ((C) **850/444-7686;** www.pensacolasaenger.com), a painstakingly restored masterpiece of Spanish baroque architecture that locals call the

> **Fun Fact** The Last Great Road House ★★★
>
> Sitting precisely on the Florida-Alabama state line on Perdido Key, about 15 miles west of downtown Pensacola, the **Flora-Bama Lounge,** 17401 Perdido Key Dr. (✆ **850/492-0611;** www.florabama.com), is almost a shrine to country music. Billing itself as the "Last Great American Road House," this slapped-together Gulf-side pub is famous for its special jam sessions from noon until way past midnight on Saturday and Sunday. Flora-Bama is the prime sponsor and a key venue for the Frank Brown International Songwriters' Festival during the first week of November. But the wackiest shindig held here has to be the Interstate Mullet Toss and Beach Party (the last weekend in Apr), which defies more in-depth description. The raw oyster bar is popular all the time. Granted, the joint can get a bit rough from time to time, but you won't soon forget the great Gulf views while sipping a cold one at the Deck Bar. The Flora-Bama is open daily from 8:30am to 2:30am.

Grande Dame of Palafox. Presentations include the local opera company and symphony orchestra, Broadway musicals, and touring performers. The 10,000-seat **Pensacola Civic Center,** 201 E. Gregory St., at Alcaniz Street (✆ **850/432-0800;** www.pensacolaciviccenter.com), hosts a variety of concerts, exhibitions, sports events, and conventions. Call ahead for the current schedule.

THE CLUB & BAR SCENE   Pensacola's downtown nighttime entertainment center is **Seville Quarter,** 130 E. Government St., at Jefferson Street (✆ **850/434-6211;** www.rosies.com), in the Seville Historic District. This restored antique-brick complex with New Orleans–style wrought-iron balconies is actually a collection of pubs and restaurants whose names capture the ambience: Rosie O'Grady's Goodtime Emporium, Lili Marlene's Aviator's Pub, Apple Annie's Courtyard, End o' the Alley Bar, Phineas Phogg's Balloon Works (a dance hall, not a balloon shop), and Fast Eddie's Billiard Parlor (which has electronic games, too). The pubs serve libations, food, and live entertainment from Dixieland jazz to country and western. Get a monthly calendar at the information booth next to Rosie O'Grady's. Open daily from 11am to 2am.

Every night is party time at **McGuire's Irish Pub,** the city's popular Irish pub, brewery, and eatery (see "Where to Dine," above). Irish bands appear nightly ...ⁱ~ summer, on Saturday and Sunday the rest of the year.

Beach nightlife centers around **Quietwater Boardwalk,** Via de Luna at Fort Pickens Road (no phone), a shopping/dining complex on Santa Rosa Sound. With the lively beach and reggae bar at **Flounder's Chowder & Ale House** (p. 595) just a few steps away, it's easy to barhop until you find a band to your liking. Across Via de Luna at Casino Beach is **The Dock** (✆ **850/934-3314;** www.thedock.Pensacola.com), which has live bands nightly in summer, on weekends in off-season. And **Sidelines Sports Bar & Restaurant** (✆ **850/934-3660**) has a great game lineup.

2 Destin & Fort Walton Beach ★★

40 miles E of Pensacola, 160 miles W of Tallahassee

Sitting on a round harbor off East Pass, which lets broad and beautiful Choctawhatchee Bay flow into the Gulf of Mexico, Destin, along with Fort

Walton Beach and Okaloosa Island, comprise the Emerald Coast, is justly famous for its fishing fleet, the largest in the state. It's also Northwest Florida's fastest-growing and most upscale vacation destination, with a multitude of high-rise condominiums, the huge Sandestin resort, several golf courses, and some of the Panhandle's best restaurants and lively nightspots. By and large, Destin attracts a more affluent crowd than Fort Walton Beach, its more down-to-earth neighbor.

Although Fort Walton Beach has its own strip of white sand on Okaloosa Island, it is a city whose economy is supported less by tourism than by the sprawling Eglin Air Force Base. Covering more than 700 square miles, Eglin is the world's largest air base and is home to the U.S. Air Force's Armament Museum and the 33rd Tactical Fighter Wing, the "Top Guns" of Operation Desert Storm in 1991.

To the east of Destin, development is picking up steam along the beaches of southern Walton County. Still, this picturesque area has mostly cottages nestled among rolling sand dunes covered with sea oats. Here you'll find Grayton Beach State Park, which sports one of America's finest beaches, and the quaint, albeit Stepford-esque planned village of **Seaside** ☆☆, which served as the set for Jim Carrey's movie *The Truman Show.* Seaside was built on a lovely stretch of beach in the 1980s—but with Victorian architecture that makes it look a century older. The village's Gulf-side honeymoon cottages make for one of Florida's most romantic retreats; and the village has interesting shops and art galleries, a stamp-size, Greek Revival–style post office, and a resident population of artists, writers, and other creative folks, who permit only their own cars in their relatively expensive little enclave. Don't worry; there are parking spaces for tourists on the one main road through Seaside, but you can't drive into the village itself unless you live there. Although I appreciate Seaside for what it is, the last time I was there I couldn't help feeling like the secret had gotten too far out and that Seaside was slowly falling under the weight of commercialism and too much tourism.

ESSENTIALS

GETTING THERE   Flights arriving at and departing from **Okaloosa Regional Airport** (© **850/651-7160;** www.co.okaloosa.fl.us/airport.html) actually use the enormous strips at Eglin Air Force Base. The terminal is on Fla. 85 north of Fort Walton Beach and is served by **Delta** (© 800/221-1212), **Northwest** (© 800/225-2525), and **US Airways** (© 800/428-4322).

Avis (© 800/331-1212), **Budget** (© 800/527-0700), **Hertz** (© 800/654-3131), and **National** (© 800/CAR-RENT) have rental cars at the airport, and **Enterprise** (© 800/325-8007) is in town.

AAA Annie's Shuttle (© **850/978-2450**) provides 24-hour van transportation to and from the airport. Fares for up to three people are based on a zone system: $15 to $18 to Fort Walton Beach, $27 to Destin, and $40 to Sandestin and southern Walton County.

The Sunset Limited transcontinental service on **Amtrak** (© **800/872-7245;** www.amtrak.com) stops at Crestview, 26 miles north of Fort Walton Beach.

VISITOR INFORMATION   For advance information about both Fort Walton Beach and Destin, contact the **Emerald Coast Convention and Visitors Bureau,** P.O. Box 609, Fort Walton Beach, FL 32549 (© **800/322-3319** or 850/651-7122; fax 850/651-7149; www.destin-fwb.com). The bureau shares quarters with the **Okaloosa County Visitors Welcome Center** in a tin-roofed, beachside building on Miracle Strip Parkway (U.S. 98) on Okaloosa Island at the eastern edge of Fort Walton Beach. Stop there for brochures, maps, and other information. The welcome center is open Monday through Friday from 8am to 5pm, Saturday and Sunday from 10am to 4pm.

The **Destin Area Chamber of Commerce,** 4484 Legendary Dr., Destin, FL 32541 (© **850/837-6241;** fax 850/654-5612; www.destinchamber.com), gives away brochures and sells maps of the area. The chamber is in an office complex at the entry to Regatta Bay Golf & Country Club, on U.S. 98, ½ mile east of the Mid-Bay Bridge. It's open Monday through Friday from 9am to 5pm, closed holidays.

For information about the beaches of South Walton, contact the **South Walton Tourist Development Council,** P.O. Box 1248, Santa Rosa Beach, FL 32459 (© **800/822-6877** or 850/267-1216; fax 850/267-3943; www.beachesofsouth walton.com). Its **visitor center** is at the intersection of U.S. 98 and U.S. 331 in Santa Rosa Beach (© **850/267-3511**). Open daily from 8:30am to 5:30pm.

GETTING AROUND   The Okaloosa County Tourist Development Authority (© **850/651-7131**) operates a free **Island Shuttle** trolley during the summer months along the entire length of Santa Rosa Boulevard on Okaloosa Island. The two trolleys run every 30 minutes Sunday through Thursday from 7am to 10pm, Friday and Saturday from 7am to 1am. They also connect the island to the Uptown Bus station, on Eglin Parkway NE on the Fort Walton Beach mainland.

For a cab in Fort Walton Beach, call **Black and Gold Taxi** (© **850/244-7303**) or **Yellow Cab** (© **850/244-3600**). In Destin, call **Destin Taxi** (© **850/654-5700**). Fares are based on a zone system rather than meters, with a $5 minimum. Trips within Fort Walton Beach or Destin should range from $5 to $10.

TIME   The area is in the Central Time zone, 1 hour behind Miami, Orlando, and Jacksonville.

HITTING THE BEACH

DESTIN   Like an oasis in the middle of Destin's rapid development, the 208-acre **Henderson Beach State Park** ⋆⋆, east of Destin Harbor on U.S. 98, allows easy access to swimming, sunning, surf fishing, picnicking, and seabird-watching along its 1½ miles of beach. There are restrooms, outdoor showers, and surf chairs for people with disabilities. The area is open daily from 8am to sunset. Admission is $4 per vehicle with up to 8 occupants, $1 for pedestrians and cyclists. Several good restaurants are just outside the park's western boundary. The park has 60 campsites in a wooded setting. They cost $21, including electricity, and can be reserved up to 11 months in advance. Pets on leashes are allowed in the park, including the beach and campground. For camping reservations call © **800/326-3521** or go to www.reserveamerica.com. For more information, contact the park at 1700 Emerald Coast Pkwy., Destin, FL 32541 (© **850/837-7550;** www.floridastateparks.org/hendersonbeach).

The **James W. Lee Park,** between Destin and Sandestin on Scenic Highway 98, has a long white-sand beach overlooked by covered picnic tables, an ice-cream parlor, and a moderately priced seafood restaurant with great views.

FORT WALTON BEACH   Do your loafing on the white sands of **Okaloosa Island,** joined to the mainland by the high-rise Brooks Bridge over Santa Rosa Sound. Most resort hotels and amusement parks are grouped around the Gulf-arium marine park on U.S. 98, east of the bridge. Here you'll find **The Board-walk,** a collection of tin-roofed beachside buildings that have a games arcade for the kids, a saloon for adults, covered picnic areas, a summertime snack bar, and a seafood restaurant. Just to the east, you can use the restrooms, cold-water showers, and other free facilities at **Beasley Park,** home of the Okaloosa County Visitor Welcome Center.

Tips How to Find a Street Address

Don't worry about getting lost, since most of what you'll want to see and do in Destin and Fort Walton Beach is either on, or no more than a few blocks from, U.S. 98, the area's main east-west drag. Finding a street address is another matter, however, for even many local residents don't fully comprehend the post office's bizarre naming and numbering system along U.S. 98.

In Fort Walton Beach, U.S. 98 is known as "Miracle Strip Parkway," with "southwest" and "southeast" addresses on the mainland and "east" addresses on Okaloosa Island.

In Destin, U.S. 98 is officially known as "Highway 98 East" from the Destin Bridge east to Airport Road, and street numbers get progressively higher as you head east from the bridge. East of Airport Road, however, the post office calls U.S. 98 the "Emerald Coast Parkway"—although locals still say a place is on "98 East." The highway also is known as the Emerald Coast Parkway in Walton County, but the street-numbering system changes completely once you pass the county line.

Adding to the confusion in Destin, "Old Highway 98 East" is a short spur from Airport Road to the western side of Henderson Beach State Park, and "Scenic Highway 98 East" parallels the real U.S. 98 along the beach from the eastern side of Henderson Beach to Sandestin.

In other words, call and ask for directions if you're not sure how to find an establishment here.

Across U.S. 98, the Okaloosa portion of the **Gulf Islands National Seashore** has picnic areas and sailboats for rent on Choctawhatchee Bay, plus access to the Gulf. Admission to this part of the national seashore is free.

SOUTHERN WALTON COUNTY   Sporting the finest stretch of white sand on the Gulf, **Grayton Beach State Park** 🌟🌟🌟, on County Road 30A, also has 356 acres of pine forests surrounding scenic Western Lake. There's a boat ramp and a campground with electric hookups on the lake. Get a leaflet at the main gate for a self-guided tour of the nature trail. Pets are not allowed anywhere in the recreation area. The area is open daily from 8am to sunset. Admission is $4 per vehicle with up to eight occupants, $1 per pedestrian or bicyclist. Campsites cost $19, including electricity. For camping reservations call ℭ **800/326-3521** or go to www.reserveamerica.com. For information, contact the park at 357 Main Park Rd., Santa Rosa Beach, FL 32459 (ℭ **850/231-4210;** www.florida stateparks.org/graytonbeach).

Seaside has free parking along County Road 30A and is a good spot for a day at the beach, a stroll or bike ride around the quaint village, and a tasty meal at one of its restaurants.

OUTDOOR ACTIVITIES
BOATING & BOAT RENTALS   Pontoon boats are highly popular for use on the back bays and Sunday-afternoon floating parties in East Pass. Several companies rent them, including **Adventure Pontoon Rentals** (ℭ 850/837-3041),

B&J Boat Rentals (© 850/243-4488), **East Pass Watersports** (© 850/654-4253), and **Destin Water Toys** (© 850/837-7755), all on Destin Harbor. Expect to pay about $80 for a half day, $125 for a full day. Destin Water Toys also has speedboats for rent ($125–$175 for 4 hr. and $175–$285 for 8 hr.).

CRUISES The *Emerald Magic* (© **850/837-1293;** www.moodysinc.com) and the *Southern Star* (© **888/424-7217** or 850/837-7741) have daily dolphin and sunset cruises June through August and by arrangement the rest of the year. The *Emerald Magic* is operated by Moody's, on U.S. 98 at Destin Harbor (see "Fishing," below), while the *Southern Star* docks in Destin at the Harbor Walk Marina, behind the Lucky Snapper Restaurant. The *Emerald Magic* charges $15 for adults, $7.50 for kids 3 to 12. The *Southern Star* costs $17 for adults, $7 for children 3 to 12, and $14 for seniors.

FISHING Billing itself as the "World's Luckiest Fishing Village," Destin has Florida's largest charter-boat fleet, with more than 140 vessels based at the marinas lining the north shore of Destin Harbor, on U.S. 98 east of the Destin Bridge. Arranging a trip is as easy as walking along the Destin Harbor waterfront, where you will find the booking booths of several agents, such as **Harborwalk Charters** (© **800/242-2824** or 850/837-2343; www.harborwalk fishing.com), **Pelican Charters** (© **850/837-2343**), and **Harbor Cove Charters** (© **850/837-2222**). Rates for private charters range from about $440 to $1,320 per boat, depending on the length of the voyage.

A less-expensive way to try your luck is on a larger group-oriented party boat such as those operated by **Moody's,** at 194 U.S. 98 east on Destin Harbor (© **850/837-1293;** www.moodysinc.com). Moody's charges $35 per person ($30 off-season) for its half-day runs (morning is the best time to fish). Children 8 to 12 and nonfishing sightseers are charged half price.

For additional information on small and large group charters, check out **FishDestin.com** (© **850/837-9401** or 850/585-0049; www.fishdestin.com). And, if you're a die-hard angler, consider coming in October for the **Destin Fishing Rodeo,** a month-long fishing extravaganza (© **850/837-6734;** www. destinfishingrodeo.org).

You don't have to go to sea to fish from the catwalk of the 3,000-foot **Destin Bridge** over East Pass. The marinas and bait shops at Destin Harbor can provide gear, bait, and a fishing license. In Fort Walton Beach, you can cast a line off **Okaloosa Island Fishing Pier,** 1030 Miracle Strip Pkwy. E. (U.S. 98; © **850/ 244-1023**). The pier is open 24 hours a day. Adults pay $6.50 to fish; children 12 and under pay $3.50. Observers pay $1. Bait and equipment rentals are available.

GOLF For advance information on area courses, contact the **Emerald Coast Golf Association,** P.O. Box 304, Destin, FL 32540. Also look for *South Coast Golf Guide,* the free annual directory published in Pensacola (p. 586). Be sure to ask if your choice of accommodations offers golf packages, which can mean significant savings.

For course information online, go to www.golf.com and www.floridagolfing. com, or call the **Florida Sports Foundation** (© **850/488-8347**) or **Florida Golfing** (© **866/833-2663**).

On the mainland, nonresidents are welcome to play at the city-owned **Fort Walton Beach Golf Club,** on Lewis Turner Boulevard (C.R. 189) north of town (© **850/833-9530;** www.fwb.org/golf/index.htm). The club has two 18-hole courses—the **Pines** and the **Oaks** (© **850/833-9528**)—plus a pro shop. Greens fees at both courses are about $35 year-round, including a cart.

In Destin, scenic **Indian Bayou Golf and Country Club,** off Airport Road (© **850/837-6191**), has three nine-hole courses with large greens and wide fairways. They look easy, but watch out for water hazards and strategically placed hidden bunkers! Greens fees, including cart, are about $60.

In southern Walton County, **Sandestin Golf and Beach Resort** on U.S. 98 East (© **850/267-8211** for tee times) is the largest facility here (p. 605). Its 72 holes are spread over three outstanding championship courses. The Baytowne and Links courses overlook Choctawhatchee Bay. Fees for 18 holes are $65 to $125 for resort guests, $85 to $145 for nonguests.

Some of the 18 championship holes at **Emerald Bay Golf Club,** 2 miles east of the Mid-Bay Bridge on U.S. 98 (© **850/837-5197**; www.emeraldbaydestin. com), run along Choctawhatchee Bay; the water adds both beauty and challenges to the otherwise wide and forgiving fairways. Greens fees are about $80 with cart; $65 in winter.

In southern Walton County, the semiprivate **Santa Rosa Golf & Beach Club,** off County Road 30A in Dune Allen Beach (© **850/267-2229**; www. santarosaclub.com), offers a challenging 18-hole course through tall pines looking out to vistas of the Gulf. The club has a pro shop, a beachside restaurant, a lounge, and tennis courts. Fees are about $70 in summer, $50 off-season.

In Niceville, a 20-minute drive north via the Mid-Bay Bridge, nonguests may play golf (four nine-hole courses) or tennis (21 courts) at the **Bluewater Bay Resort** (© **850/897-3241**; www.bwbresort.com), which also has condominiums for rent.

Call ahead for reservations and current fees at all these clubs, and ask about afternoon and early-evening specials.

SAILING   Sailing South (© **850/837-7245**; www.sailingsouth.com), on U.S. 98 at Destin Harbor, has half-day cruises aboard the 72-foot schooner *Daniel Webster Clements.* The 2½-hour afternoon cruises stop for swimming and snorkeling virtually under the Destin Bridge; these cost $35 for adults and $20 for kids under 12. It also offers sunset cruises (same rates and length). The 54-foot schooner *Nathaniel Bowditch* (© **850/650-8787**; www.bowditch sailing.com) will take you on sunset and half-day shelling excursions ($35 adults, $20 kids 12 and under).

SCUBA DIVING & SNORKELING   At least a dozen dive shops are located along the beaches. Considered one of the best, **Scuba Tech Diving Charters** has two locations in Destin: at 301 U.S. 98 E. (© **850/837-2822**; www.scubatech-nwfl.com) and at 10004 U.S. 98 E. (© **850/837-1933**), about ½ mile west of the Sandestin Beach Resort.

WATERSPORTS   Hobie Cats, WaveRunners, jet boats, jet skis, and parasailing are available all along the beach. The largest selection of operators are at the marinas just east of the Destin Bridge, behind Hooter's and Fat Tuesday's pubs, including **Boogies** (© **850/654-4497**) and **Destin Watertoys** (© **888/357-2608** or 850/837-7755; www.destinwatertoys.com).

EXPLORING THE AREA

Eden Gardens State Park   Evoking images from *Gone With the Wind,* the 115 acres of land here house the magnificent 1895 Greek Revival–style Wesley Mansion, which has been lovingly restored and richly furnished with period antiques (the 2nd-largest collection of Louis XVI furniture in the country is here along with a Chippendale nightstand worth about $1 million and original Sears & Roebuck wallpaper in 2 rooms downstairs). Plus, over 95% of the window panes are originals. The house overlooks scenic Choctawhatchee Bay and is surrounded by immense Spanish moss-draped oak trees and the Eden Gardens, resplendent with camellias, azaleas, and other typical Southern flowers. Your visit won't be complete without a guided tour of the house, so avoid coming here on a Tuesday or Wednesday. Picnicking is allowed on the plantation grounds.

181 Eden Gardens Rd. (off C.R. 395), Point Washington. ℂ 850/231-4214. www.floridastateparks.org/eden gardens. Grounds and gardens $3 per vehicle; $1 per pedestrian or bicyclist; mansion tours $3 adults, $1 children 12 and under. Gardens and grounds daily 8am–sunset; 45-min. mansion tours on the hour. Thurs–Mon 10am–3pm. Take County R. 395 north from Hwy. 98. Proceed for a mile and park entrance is on the left.

Florida's Gulfarium *Kids*   The country's second oldest marine park (it opened in 1955) features ongoing 25-minute shows with dolphins, California sea lions, Peruvian penguins, loggerhead turtles, sharks, sting rays, moray eels, and alligators. There are fascinating exhibits, including the Living Sea, with special windows for viewing undersea life. During one of the shows, a scuba diver explains the sea life while swimming among the various creatures. The Spotted Dolphin Encounter is a terrific program in which brave participants receive an up-close and personal hand-to-flipper encounter with two of their Pantropical Spotted dolphins, Kiwi and Daphne. A trainer will guide you through the 40-minute interactive session. If you're not satisfied with seeing a few dolphins and leaving, expect to spend about 3 hours here between all the shows and exhibits.

1010 Miracle Strip Pkwy. (U.S. 98) on Okaloosa Island. ℂ 850/244-5169. www.gulfarium.com. Admission $17 adults, $15 seniors, $10 children 4–11, free for children 3 and under; Dolphin encounter $100. Mid-May to Labor Day daily 9am–6pm (park closes 8pm); Sept to mid-May daily 9am–4pm (park closes 6pm).

Indian Temple Mound and Museum   This ceremonial mound, one of the largest ever discovered, dates from A.D. 1200. The museum showcases part of its collection of more than 6,000 ceramic artifacts from southeastern American Indian tribes, the nation's largest such collection. Exhibits depict the lifestyles of the four tribes that lived in the Choctawhatchee Bay region for 12,000 years.

139 Miracle Strip Pkwy. SE, on the mainland. ℂ 850/833-9595. www.fwb.org/html/fwbmuseum01.htm. Park free; museum $2 adults, $1 children 6–17, free for children 5 and under. Park daily dawn–dusk. Museum Sept–May Mon–Fri 11am–4pm, Sat 9am–4pm; June–Aug Mon–Sat 9am–4:30pm, Sun 12:30–4:30pm.

U.S. Air Force Armament Museum *★*   Although this fascinating museum is not on a par with Pensacola's National Museum of Naval Aviation, you'll love it if you're into warplanes. Located on the world's largest air force base, it traces military developments from World War II through Operation Desert Storm. Reconnaissance, fighter, and bomber planes, including the SR-71 Blackbird spy plane, are on display.

100 Museum Dr., off Eglin Pkwy. (Fla. 85) at Eglin Air Force Base, 5 miles north of downtown. ℂ 850/882-4062. Free admission. Daily 9:30am–4:30pm. Closed federal holidays.

SHOPPING

Silver Sands Factory Stores *★★*, on U.S. 98 between Destin and Sandestin (ℂ 800/510-6255 or 850/864-9771; www.silversandsfactorystores.com), has more than 120 upscale stores such as Liz Claiborne, DKNY, J. Crew, Brooks Brothers, Hartmann luggage, Coach leather, Dooney & Burke, Bose electronics, and so on. Shops are open Monday through Saturday from 10am to 9pm (to 7pm Jan–Feb), Sunday from 10am to 6pm (noon–6pm Jan–Feb). There are electronic games for kids and a sports bar for adults.

Over at the Sandestin Beach Resort on U.S. 98, you can window-shop in **The Market at Sandestin,** where boutiques purvey expensive clothing, gifts, and Godiva chocolates.

WHERE TO STAY

The area has a vast supply of condominiums and cottages for rent. One good-value example is Venus Condos, listed below. The visitor information offices (see the "Visitor Information" section on p. 597) will provide lists of others for rent. The largest rental agent is **Abbott Realty Services**, 3500 Emerald Coast Pkwy., Destin, FL 32541 (© **888/909-6807;** fax 850/654-2937; www.abbott-resorts. com). It publishes a magazine-size annual brochure picturing and describing its many properties throughout the area.

The Flamingo Cottage (© **832/309-5866;** www.flamingocottage.com), on Santa Rosa Beach, is perfect for families or large groups (it can sleep up to 16), with fabulous features such as stone tile throughout the downstairs, 9-foot beaded board ceilings, crown moldings, oak staircase, upgraded light fixtures, and a large master suite with Jacuzzi and private covered balcony. In addition to a large den and kitchen, a laundry room, and an outdoor gas grill, the cottage has four bedrooms and three full bathrooms. Rates are $1,300 to $2,950 per week, depending on the season.

There are several commercial campgrounds here, but the best camping is at **Henderson Beach State Park** in Destin and at **Grayton Beach State Park** in south Walton County (see "Hitting the Beach," earlier in this chapter).

State and local governments add 9% to 11% to all hotel and campground bills.

DESTIN

A former Comfort Inn, the local **Motel 6,** 405 U.S. 98 E. (© **800/466-8356** or 850/837-0007; fax 850/837-5325; www.motel6.com), sitting across the highway from the harbor, has rooms that are generally larger than those at many other members of this cut-rate chain. There's also an outdoor swimming pool on the premises, which makes it a more attractive place to stay.

Best Western SummerPlace Inn   Located just one block from the beach, this four-story, Spanish-motif Best Western is a refreshing change from its cookie cutter siblings, offering innlike rooms and suites decorated with wildlife prints. A few suites have hot tubs in their living rooms. The more expensive Gulf-side units have balconies (those facing the bay do not). Larger units have microwave ovens and refrigerators. Doors open from an indoor pool, a whirlpool, and an exercise room to an outdoor pool, but you'll have to negotiate your way across busy U.S. 98 to reach the Gulf.

14047 Emerald Coast Pkwy. (U.S. 98, at Airport Rd.), Destin, FL 32541. © **888/232-2499** or 850/650-8003. Fax 850/650-8004. www.bestwestern.com/summerplaceinn. 72 units. Summer $119–$179; off-season $49–$99. Rates include continental breakfast and local telephone calls. AE, DISC, MC, V. **Amenities:** Indoor and outdoor pools; exercise room; Jacuzzi; business center; coin-op washers and dryers. *In room:* A/C, TV, dataport, fridge, coffeemaker, hair dryer.

Henderson Park Inn 🏠🏠🏠   This inn is absolutely stunning in an Edith Wharton, Age of Innocence way. At the end of Old U.S. 98 on the undeveloped eastern edge of the Henderson Beach State Park, this shingle-sided, Cape Hatteras–style bed-and-breakfast is the area's most romantic get-away-from-it-all escape (children and pets are not accepted). Individually decorated in a Victorian theme, the rooms have high ceilings, fireplaces, Queen Anne furniture, and Gulf views from private balconies. Most have Jacuzzis and some have canopy beds. The main building (16 rooms are in a separate shingle-sided structure next door) sports a beachside veranda complete with old-fashioned rocking chairs from which you can admire the glorious sunsets. Guests are treated to a

Southern-style buffet breakfast and to beer and wine at the nightly before-dinner social hour in the wonderful Veranda Restaurant (reservations recommended), which opens to the wraparound porch of the main building. Guests are provided with complimentary beach umbrellas and chairs.

2700 Scenic Hwy. 98 E. (P.O. Box 30), Destin, FL 32541. ℂ 800/336-4853 or 850/837-4853. Fax 850/654-0405. www.hendersonparkinn.com. 35 units. Summer $189–$334 double; off-season $95–$189 double. Rates include full breakfast and evening cocktails. Packages and weekly rates available. AE, DISC, MC, V. No children or pets accepted. **Amenities:** Restaurant; bar; heated outdoor pool; Jacuzzi; limited room service; laundry service. *In room:* A/C, TV, dataport, fridge, coffeemaker, hair dryer, iron.

FORT WALTON BEACH

The managers of Venus by the Sea (see below) also run the **Sea Crest Condominiums,** located next door at 895 Santa Rosa Blvd. (ℂ **800/476-1885** or 850/301-9600; fax 850/301-9205; www.seacrestcondos.com). The 112 units in this seven-story building aren't as spacious as those in Venus, but they're considerably more luxurious, and those on the higher floors have great views toward the west. The complex has indoor and outdoor pools (actually one pool; you can swim under a glass partition between them), and it sits next to a county park with a boardwalk leading over the dunes to the beach.

Among chain motels here is the **Hampton Inn Ft. Walton Beach,** 1112 Santa Rosa Blvd. (ℂ **800/426-7866** or 850/301-0906; www.hamptoninnfwb.com). It's adjacent to the Radisson Beach Resort and shares its facilities (see below).

Marina Motel   This family-operated, self-described "fisherman's motel" may look like a shack from the outside, but it has clean, comfortable rooms and apartments directly across U.S. 98 from the magnificent public beach at Beasley Park. A low-slung, brick-fronted motel block holds most of the rooms. Other units are in two-story stucco structures near a marina whose 560-foot pier is home to charter-fishing boats. Two one-bedroom apartments at the end of the complex overlook the marina and bay. All units here have refrigerators and microwaves; 16 have full kitchens. If traffic is too busy to cross U.S. 98 to the beach (there are no nearby overpasses or traffic lights), you can sun at the motel's little bay-side beach or take a dip in its roadside pool.

1345 E. Miracle Strip Pkwy. (U.S. 98), Fort Walton Beach, FL 32548. ℂ 800/237-7021 or 850/244-1129. Fax 850/243-6063. www.marinamotel.net. 38 units. Summer $69–$89 double, $115–$150 apt; off-season $39–$69 double, $65–$99 apt. AE, DC, DISC, MC, V. **Amenities:** Outdoor pool; coin-op washers and dryers. *In room:* A/C, TV, kitchen (efficiencies and apts only), fridge, coffeemaker, iron.

Radisson Beach Resort ⭐ *Kids*   A glass-enclosed elevator climbs a soaring, six-story lean-to atrium lobby to rooms with spectacular Gulf views from their standing-room-only balconies at this resort where you'll never be bored. An Olympic-sized heated pool and lazy river raft ride, fitness center, two lighted tennis courts, a basketball court, beach volleyball, and a pirate ship-shaped playground for kids are just some of the resort's many diversions. Rooms are standard unless you book an Emerald Suite, in which case you'll never leave your bathroom because a large Jacuzzi tub sits directly in front of a floor to ceiling window overlooking the water. Beach lovers are more likely to appreciate the units in an older two-story motel building that have sitting-room patios or balconies facing the Gulf. Other units in the older building open to a lush courtyard surrounding a pool. In the atrium, a tropically adorned cafe serves breakfast, lunch, and dinner, and a bar has nightly entertainment during summer.

1110 Santa Rosa Blvd. (at U.S. 98), Fort Walton Beach, FL 32548. ℂ 800/333-3333 or 850/243-9181. Fax 850/664-7652. www.radisson.com/ftwaltonfl. 287 units. Summer $129–$230 double; off-season $69–$129 double. Packages available. AE, DC, DISC, MC, V. **Amenities:** Restaurant; 2 bars; 3 outdoor pools

(1 children's); 2 lighted hard tennis courts; exercise room; watersports equipment rentals; limited room service; babysitting; laundry service. *In room:* A/C, TV, dataport, coffeemaker, hair dryer, iron.

Ramada Plaza Beach Resort ⭐ This big resort boasts the prettiest outdoor areas in northwest Florida, with waterfalls cascading over lofty rocks and a romantic grotto bar, all surrounded by thick tropical foliage. Although there is another swimming pool, a large sun deck, and a bar out by the beach, this gorgeous courtyard would have even more charm if it weren't cut off from the Gulf by a six-story block of hotel rooms. The guest rooms and the one-bedroom suites in this beachfront building are the best here, with Gulf or courtyard views from balconies or patios. The least-expensive units, in the adjacent building, overlook a parking lot. Though the decor is blasé, the hotel's views make up for that. On-site dining options include a barbecue shack out in the tropical forest. The Boardwalk beach pavilion and restaurants are next door.

1500 E. Miracle Strip Pkwy. (U.S. 98), Fort Walton Beach, FL 32548. © 800/874-8962 or 850/243-9161. Fax 850/243-2391. www.ramadafwb.com. 335 units. Summer $120–$185 double, $280–$350 suite; off-season $70–$195 double, $160–$270 suite. AE, DC, DISC, MC, V. **Amenities:** 3 restaurants; 3 bars; 2 outdoor pools (1 heated); exercise room; Jacuzzi; watersports equipment rentals; children's programs; game room; limited room service; coin-op washers and dryers. *In room:* A/C, TV, dataport, fridge, coffeemaker, hair dryer, iron, safe.

Venus by the Sea ⭐ *Value* Offering considerably more space than a hotel normally would at these rates, this pleasant, three-story enclave on western Okaloosa Island was built in the 1970s and has been well maintained ever since, though the decor is still stuck in the '70s (think retirement home) and should be updated. Each of the one-, two-, and three-bedroom units has a long living/dining/kitchen room, with a rear door leading to a balcony or to a patio opening to a grassy courtyard. The beach is a short walk across the dunes, and you can stroll along the undeveloped beach at an Eglin Air Force Base auxiliary facility about 600 feet away. The same management also operates the new and much more luxurious **Sea Crest Condominiums** next door (see above), and guests here can use the indoor-outdoor pool there.

885 Santa Rosa Blvd., Fort Walton Beach, FL 32548. © 800/476-1885 or 850/301-9600. Fax 850/301-9205. www.venuscondos.com. 45 units. Summer $130–$205 apt; off-season $70–$100 apt. Weekly and monthly rates available. Ask for off-season specials. MC, V. **Amenities:** Outdoor pool; tennis court; coin-op washers and dryers. *In room:* A/C, TV/VCR, kitchen, coffeemaker, iron.

SOUTHERN WALTON COUNTY

If you want to stay near Sandestin Golf and Beach Resort (see below) without paying its prices, there's a modern **Sleep Inn** a mile west at 5000 Emerald Coast Pkwy. (U.S. 98; © 800/627-5337 or 850/654-7022).

Hilton Sandestin Beach & Golf Resort ⭐⭐ *Kids* This all-inclusive, all-suites beachside resort, housed in two adjacent towers, is the top full-service hotel here. It's nicely situated on the grounds of Sandestin Golf and Beach Resort (see the next listing) and shares its golf and tennis facilities. The elegant Elephant Walk restaurant is next door. "Executive suites" in one wing are equipped primarily for business travelers and conventioneers (lots of meeting space here), while the spacious "junior suites" in the old wing are geared toward families, with a special area for children's bunk beds. Parents can send the kids off to a supervised summertime program while pampering themselves at the full-service spa. Miniature golf, three pools, thirteen tennis courts, four championship golf courses, and the stunning private beach make for a very enticing stay.

4000 Sandestin Blvd. S., Destin, FL 32541. © 800/367-1271 or 850/267-9500. Fax 850/267-3076. www.sandestinresort.hilton.com. 598 suites. Summer $260–$395 suite; off-season $160–$335 suite. Golf and tennis packages available. AE, DC, DISC, MC, V. **Amenities:** 2 restaurants; 2 bars; indoor and outdoor pools; golf course; tennis courts; health club, spa; Jacuzzi; watersports equipment rentals; children's programs; game room; concierge; activities desk; car-rental desk; business center; shopping arcade; salon; 24-hr. room service; massage; babysitting; laundry service; coin-op washers and dryers; concierge-level rooms. *In room:* A/C, TV, dataport, minibar, coffeemaker, hair dryer, iron.

Sandestin Golf and Beach Resort ★★★ *Kids* Although it could be mistaken for yet another Stepfordized planned community, this luxurious real-estate development is one of Florida's biggest sports-oriented resorts and is the epitome of the great escape. It sprawls over 2,400 acres complete with a spectacular beach 5 miles west of Destin, plus a marina. It's notable for its 81 holes of championship golf and its tennis clinic (both with instruction available), plus a fully equipped sports spa and health center. An array of handsomely decorated accommodations overlooks the Gulf or Choctawhatchee Bay, the golf fairways, lagoons, or a nature preserve. The hotel rooms and suites are in the Bayside Inn. They all have kitchenettes and balconies, but you'd be wise to opt for one of the much more spacious junior suites or one-, two-, and three-bedroom condominium apartments, which are in high- and midrise buildings either on the Gulf or along the manicured fairways. The privately owned condominiums are individually decorated and come with full kitchen and patio or balcony, and many have washers and dryers. Most amenities are a short walk or bike or free tram ride away, and a tunnel runs under U.S. 98 to connect Sandestin's Gulf and bay areas. Among the relatively limited on-site dining options is the romantic **Elephant Walk** ★★ (© 850/267-4800), located on the Gulf; it serves different, gourmet-quality choices for dinner every evening. On top of Elephant Walk is the **Governor's Attic,** a swanky cigar and cognac kind of place overlooking the Gulf. The coolest, newest addition to this resort cum city is the **Village of Baytowne Wharf,** a 28-acre pedestrian village overlooking the Choctawhatchee Bay, featuring a unique collection of more than two dozen specialty merchants ranging from quaint boutique shops and charming eateries to lively nightclubs. It also features hotel and one-, two- and three-bedroom luxury accommodations surrounding the bay with rates ranging from $89 in the off season to $272 during the summer. Fantastic kids and teens programs include Jolee Island Nature Park, a mile-long trail dotted with weather-beaten, double-wide porch swings, where you can sit and watch the waters of Horseshoe Bayou lap up against the shore or catch the sunset over Choctawhatchee Bay.

9300 Emerald Coast Pkwy. W. (U.S. 98), Destin, FL 32541. © 800/277-0800 or 850/267-8000 in the U.S., or 800/933-7846 in Canada. Fax 850/267-8222. www.sandestin.com. 175 units, 620 condo apts. Summer $155–$210 double, $210–$560 condo apt; off-season $85–$190 double, $105–$395 condo apt. Packages and weekly/monthly rates available. Rates include health club, bicycle, Boogie Board, canoe, and kayak use; 1-hr. tennis daily; discounts on other amenities. AE, DC, DISC, MC, V. **Amenities:** 3 restaurants; 3 bars; 9 heated outdoor pools; 4 golf courses; 18 tennis courts; spa; Jacuzzis; watersports equipment rentals; children's programs; game room; concierge; shopping arcade; salon; limited room service (hotel only); massage; babysitting; laundry service; coin-op washers and dryers. *In room:* A/C, TV, dataport, kitchen, coffeemaker, hair dryer, iron.

SEASIDE

Mayberry meets Metropolitan Home here in this pastel-hued community where life seems like a dreamlike state of mind. If you decide to rent a home or a **romantic honeymoon cottage** ★★ in this quaint village, contact the **Seaside Cottage Rental Agency,** P.O. Box 4730, Seaside, FL 32459 (© **800/277-8696** or 850/231-1320; fax 850/231-2293; www.seasidefl.com). The agency has several hundred cottages in its rental inventory, from one to six bedrooms. The beachside cottages are one of Florida's best getaways for newlyweds or anyone

---

Tips **Luxurious Cottages and Luscious Surroundings at Rosemary Beach**

Rosemary Beach, a newer, smaller, and, I think, better, Seaside-style community, offers a collection of about 300 luxurious Pan-Caribbean-style cottages and carriage houses (studios to six-bedroom cottages), all of which are nonsmoking. This is another pedestrian-friendly community—almost everything on the 107 acres is within a 5-minute walk from the town center—and most of the homes are owned by people who live here part-time and lease to vacationers the rest of the year. The white-sand (and soft as talcum powder) beach here is ridiculously gorgeous though guests can also choose from among 4 pools (1 indoors). Nothing on the architecturally stunning and strikingly planted property here is more than 4 stories, and all the homes telescope in from the beach so everyone can have a (at least partial) view of the gulf. Other amenities include a health club, bike rental, a raquet club, a 2⅓-mile fitness trail, a spa, shops, a town hall and post office, and a few very good restaurants. Cottages were individually designed and decorated, so check online for exactly what yours will have and to see pictures of each of the properties before deciding. Though they all come with full kitchens, washers/dryers, and TV/VCR, some have added amenities such as Jacuzzis or private pools. There is also a B&B on premises (rooms start at $118), and the town is building a full-service hotel. Daily rates are $153 to $968 in spring and fall, $183 to $1,062 in summer, and $143 to $812 during winter. Rosemary Beach is located at the east end of County Road 30-A (© **888/855-1551;** www.rosemary beach.com) just 8 miles east of Seaside.

---

else looking for a romantic escape, though if you want a little more privacy and less action, you might want to choose Rosemary Beach (see above) instead.

Josephine's French Country Inn at Seaside ★★★   With its six large Tuscan columns reminiscent of a Virginia mansion, Josephine's is an elegant and romantic country inn, with mahogany four-poster beds, lace comforters, rich furnishings, and marble bathtubs. Most guest rooms also have fireplaces. Conveniences such as wet bars, microwaves, and small refrigerators are neatly incorporated into the design so they don't conflict with the nostalgic charm. Sumptuous breakfasts are served either in-room (beside the fireplace or on your private veranda) or in the gracious dining room. The Guest House offers four suites, two with Gulf views. Each has a fireplace, kitchen, and full bathroom. Smoking is prohibited inside. With rich mahogany furniture and a wealth of period accouterments, the dining room here is one of the region's finest places for a gourmet dinner. Glowing with candlelight, this intimate room seats only 22 people (by reservation only). Josephine's Maryland-style crab cakes are consistently delicious.

County Rd. 30A (P.O. Box 4767), Seaside, FL 32459. © **800/848-1840** or 850/231-1940. Fax 850/231-2446. www.josephinesinn.com. 9 units (all with bathroom). Year-round $225 double; $275 suite. Rates include gourmet breakfast. Weekly rates available. AE, DISC, MC, V. **Amenities:** Restaurant; bar; free use of bikes. *In room:* A/C, TV, dataport, kitchen (in some suites) fridge, coffeemaker, hair dryer, iron.

⌒ *Tips* Picture Perfect

Designed by renowned architect David Rockwell, the **WaterColor Inn, 34 Goldenrod Circle** (𝒞 **866/426-2656** or 850/534-500; www.watercolorinn. com), is a stunning, 499-acre beachfront boutique hotel. A hyper luxe inn with just 60 rooms, WaterColor Inn is more like being at a private beach house than a hotel. A ground floor library, a circular room with club chairs and overstuffed sofa, and a cocktail lounge opening to the pool deck drive that feeling even further home. Rooms feature a pantry, a walk-in shower room with high windowed views to the beach, and custom Adirondack chairs on the balcony. Six ground floor bungalows sport outside showers enclosed by striped blue and gray tends, lending to a very French Riviera feel a la F. Scott Fitzgerald's *Tender Is the Night*. Rotunda guest rooms in the center tower offer stunning 180-degree views from massive balconies. Access to WaterColor community facilities such as the Tom Fazio–designed Camp Creek Golf Club 6 miles east is another bonus. Five Har-Tru tennis courts are available for players. A Gulf-front beach club complete with pool deck, children's pool, and beach services including complimentary boogie boards, Hobie kayaks, surfing kayaks, beach volleyball, and snorkel equipment as well as a lakefront boat house offering sailboats, canoes, kids' activities, and fishing will keep you from ever wanting to leave this piece of pre-fabbed, fabulous paradise. Rates range from $270 to $480 for a double, $530 for a suite.

WHERE TO DINE

Except for the strip on Okaloosa Island, a plethora of national fast-food and family chain restaurants line U.S. 98.

DESTIN

If you didn't catch a fish to be grilled at Fisherman's Wharf (see below), you can buy one to brag about from **Sexton's Seafood,** 602 Hwy. 98 E., opposite Destin Harbor (𝒞 **850/837-3040**). It's the best market here.

AJ's Seafood & Oyster Bar 𝆕𝆕 SEAFOOD   Jimmy Buffett tunes set the tone at this fun, Tiki-topped establishment on the picturesque Destin Harbor docks, where fishing boats unload their daily catches right into the kitchen. The best items here are grilled or fried fish, but raw or steamed Apalachicola oysters also headline the menu. You can sample a bit of everything with a "run of the kitchen" seafood platter. AJ's is most famous for its topside bar, Club Bimini, featuring live bands (you should have dinner elsewhere if you're not in a partying mood) and open nightly. At lunch, picnic tables on the covered dock make a fine venue with a view across the harbor. Locals love this place and you will, too.

116 Hwy. 98 E., Destin Harbor. 𝒞 850/837-1913. www.ajs-destin.com. Main courses $11–$22; sandwiches and salads $6–$9. AE, DISC, MC, V. Apr–Sept Sun–Thurs 11am–10pm, Fri–Sat 11am–midnight (bar until 4am); off-season daily 11am–9pm.

Back Porch 𝆕 SEAFOOD   This cedar-shingled seafood shack offers glorious beach and Gulf views from its long porch. The popular, casual restaurant originated charcoal-grilled amberjack, which you'll now see on menus throughout Florida. Other fish and seafood, as well as chicken and juicy hamburgers, also come from the coals. Monthly specials feature crab, lobster, and seasonal fish. Come early, order a rum-laden Key Lime Freeze, and enjoy the sunset. The Back Porch sits with a number of other restaurants near the western boundary of the Henderson Beach State Park and is a popular hangout for Frisbee players and sunbathers.

1740 Old Hwy. 98 E. ℭ **850/837-2022.** www.backporchseafood.com. Main courses $12–$20; sandwiches, burgers, and pastas $6.50–$9. AE, DC, DISC, MC, V. Apr–Sept daily 11am–11pm; off-season daily 11am–10pm. From U.S. 98, turn toward the beach at the Hampton Inn.

Callahan's Island Restaurant & Deli ⭐ *Value* AMERICAN/DELI The best place in the area for picnic fare, this family-operated deli offers burgers, excellent Reubens, and other made-to-order sandwiches, pastas, and nightly specials such as charcoal-grilled chicken and grilled pork chops. A long refrigerator case across the rear holds a variety of top-grade cheeses, deli meats, steaks, and chops (choose your own cut, and the chef will chargrill it to order). Tables and booths are set up garden fashion, adding an outdoorsy ambience to this pleasant storefront establishment. Locals like to do lunch here. Breakfast is served only on Saturday mornings.

950 Gulf Shore Dr. (2 blocks south of U.S. 98). ℭ **850/837-6328.** Main courses $8–$16; sandwiches, burgers, and salads $4–$7. DISC, MC, V. Mon–Fri 10am–9pm; Sat 8am–9pm.

Copper Grill ⭐⭐ STEAK An upscale restaurant lit by gas torches, the Copper Grill is a delicious dichotomy of swank and kitsch—check out the zebra prints inside the dining room. Each table has its own DVD player, television screen, and coffeemaker, and, to add to the distraction, there's an open pit grill in the middle of the action. Their Angus beef is top notch, but order the steak fondue—it's absolutely to die for.

11225 Hwy. 98, Destin. ℭ **850/654-6900.** Reservations recommended. Main courses $18–$35. Sun–Thurs 5:30–9:30pm; Fri–Sat 5:30–11pm.

Donut Hole SOUTHERN Available around the clock, breakfasts at this popular spot highlight eggs Benedict, hot fluffy biscuits under sausage gravy, Belgian waffles, and freshly baked doughnuts. Lunch sees fresh deli sandwiches, half-pound burgers, and big salads. The rough-hewn building has booths and counter seating. Be prepared to wait on the deck, especially on weekends. Daily specials such as half a Southern fried chicken with three country-style vegetables and dessert are a bargain. There's another Donut Hole, open daily from 6am to 10pm, on U.S. 98 East in southern Walton County 2½ miles east of the Sandestin Beach Resort (ℭ **850/267-3239**).

635 U.S. 98 E., Destin. ℭ **850/837-8824.** Breakfast $4–$7.50; sandwiches, salads, and burgers $4.50–$7.50; main courses $6.50–$10. No credit cards. Daily 24 hr. Closed 2 weeks before Christmas.

Fisherman's Wharf Seafood House ⭐⭐ SEAFOOD Go fishing, then bring your catch here and the chef will chargrill it at this atmospheric restaurant next to a charter fleet marina (the restaurant hosts most of Destin's fishing competitions). If you struck out fishing, and didn't stop by Sexton's Seafood on

Fun Fact **Building Fences**

Seaside's Urban Code requires that all homes sport white-painted wood picket fences at the street-front and path-front property lines, and that no two fences be the same on any one avenue. Explore all the fences, which range from subdued to downright wacky.

the way here to buy a few filets (see above), you can select from the restaurant's fresh-off-the-boat catch for grilling, broiling, frying, or blackening. Charcoal grilling is the house specialty—the triggerfish filet comes white and flaky but still moist. All main courses include a trip to the salad bar, rice pilaf, baked potato, or roasted vegetables. Although this building dates from 1996, it reminds us of an Old Florida fish camp, with rough-hewn wood walls and double-hung windows looking out to a large harborside deck, a venue during the warmer months for two bars, an oyster bar, live music, and great sunsets.

210D Hwy. 98 E., Destin Harbor. © 850/654-4766. www.fishwharf.com. Main courses $11–$21; sandwiches and burgers $6–$9; cook-your-catch $7 lunch, $10 dinner. AE, DC, DISC, MC, V. Summer daily 11am–11pm (deck bar open later); off-season daily 11am–9pm.

Fudpucker's Beachside Bar and Grill ⭐ AMERICAN   A sprawling, 26,000 square foot complex, Fudpucker's is a beachside burger and beer joint with a twist—or, rather, many twists. For one, there's also a sushi bar. The decor is funky, with antique beer cans, mirrors and what they call "Fud Junk." The Fudburger is the menu's most popular, but an unabridged selection of everything from fried crab to Puckeroni Pizza is available for the taking. Eight different dining rooms, a kids' playground, and game rooms with air hockey and video games are nothing compared to Fudpucker's Gator Beach, the restaurant's very own alligator collection located in the pond underneath the building. Live music and a new addition, Club Key West, make this place one of the area's most popular night spots. **Fudpucker's on the Island**, 108 Santa Rosa Blvd., Fort Walton Beach (© **850/243-3833**), is the original, located on Okaloosa Island.

20001 Emerald Coast Parkway, Destin. © **850/654-4200**. Reservations accepted only for hibachi tables. Main courses $12–$21. AE, DC, DISC, MC, V. Mon–Wed 11am–10pm; Thurs–Sat 11am–4am.

Harbor Docks SEAFOOD/JAPANESE   The harbor views are spectacular from indoors or outdoors at this casual, somewhat-rustic establishment. You can order your fill of fried fish, but specialties such as the daily catch sautéed with artichoke hearts are far more enjoyable. Asian influences include a sushi bar and hibachi table, which are open for dinner, and a few Thai specialties that grace the lunch menu. The bar here is popular with charter-boat skippers, and frequent live entertainment keeps the action going on the outdoor deck at night.

538 U.S. 98 E., Destin Harbor. © **850/837-2506**. Reservations accepted only for hibachi table. Main courses $16–$23; sushi $4.50–$8. AE, DC, DISC, MC, V. Feb–Oct daily 5:30–10:30am and 11am–11pm; Nov–Jan daily 11am–11pm. Sushi bar daily 5–10pm.

Harry T's Boat House ⭐ *Kids* AMERICAN   To honor the memory of trapeze artist "Flying Harry T" Baben, his family opened this lively spot on the ground floor of Destin Harbor's tallest building. Standing guard is the stuffed Stretch, Harry's beloved giraffe. Other decor includes circus memorabilia and relics from the luxury cruise ship *Thracia*, which sank off the Emerald Coast in 1927; Harry T was presented with the ship's salvaged furnishings and fixtures for personally leading the heroic rescue of its 2,000 passengers. The tabloid-style menu offers traditional seafood, steaks, chicken, and pasta dishes. The house specialty are smoke house ribs, which are juicy and full of flavor. Kids eat for 99¢ from 11am to 7pm and Tuesday is kids' night, with a clown, face painting, and balloon animals. The dining room and the downstairs lounge (with live entertainment Thurs, Fri, and Sat nights) enjoy harbor views.

320 U.S. 98 E., Destin Harbor. © **850/654-4800**. www.harryts.com. Main courses $13–$24; soups and salads $3–$12. AE, DISC, MC, V. Summer Mon–Sat 11am–2am, Sun 10am–2am; off-season Mon–Sat 11am–9pm, Sun 10am–9pm. Bar open later. Sun brunch year-round 10am–3pm.

Marina Cafe ★★★ NEW AMERICAN Destin's finest restaurant provides a classy atmosphere with soft candlelight, subdued music, and walls of glass overlooking the harbor. The changing menu always offers nouveau preparations of seafood. Pizzas are topped with the likes of spicy cayenne rock shrimp, roasted corn, and onion marmalade, and pastas might feature fusilli with roast chicken, sun-dried tomatoes, goat cheese, broccoli, pine nuts, and an herb-and-balsamic-vinegar broth. The marine cuisine includes pan-seared redfish with a sausage crust and almond-crusted mahimahi. Try the sautéed spicy lump crab cakes with roasted pepper butter and habanero-tomato relish and my favorite, the chipotle-honey barbecued Gulf shrimp, roasted poblano, onion, and corn quesadilla, with a spicy tomato-mint salsa. Weather permitting, enjoy the outdoor deck for drinks and appetizers.

404 Hwy. 98 E., Destin Harbor. © 850/837-7960. www.marinacafe.com. Reservations recommended. Main courses $15–$29; pizza and pasta $9–$17. AE, DC, DISC, MC, V. Daily 5–11pm. Closed first 3 weeks in Jan.

McGuire's Irish Pub & Brewery STEAKS/SEAFOOD Like Pensacola's original McGuire's (p. 594), this younger sibling sports thousands of dollar bills stuck on the ceilings and walls, plus Notre Dame football schedules, a prominent logo of the Boston Celtics, and other memorabilia recalling Irish-American lore. This is Destin's most popular hangout, and local professionals congregate at the big oak bar in the center of the dining room, especially when the live entertainment starts at 9pm Tuesday through Sunday. You can opt for a table on either side of the bar or on a rooftop deck. Dining here is almost secondary to the see-and-be-seen scene, although the tender chargrilled steaks and giant hamburgers are worthy antidotes to a big appetite.

33 Hwy. 98 E., Destin Harbor (in Harborwalk Center near Destin Bridge). © 850/654-0567. Main courses $16–$25; snacks, burgers, and sandwiches $8–$12. AE, DC, DISC, MC, V. Mon–Sat 11am–midnight; later on weekends.

Rutherford's 465 ★★ NEW AMERICAN An elegant restaurant overlooking Lake Regatta, Rutherford's 465 is an eclectic dining experience thanks to Chef Todd Misener's New American cuisine. Dishes like Ashley Farm's Natural Chicken, grilled breast of chicken with roasted garlic mashed potatoes, asparagus, and cider reduction sauce and a succulent Kansas City Midwestern Bone-in-Strip Loin are outstanding.

465 Regatta Bay Blvd., (inside the Regatta Bay community), Destin. © 850/337-8888. Main courses $18–$35. AE, DC, DISC, MC, V. Tues–Sat 11am–2pm and 6–10pm.

FORT WALTON BEACH

Big City Coffeehouse and Cafe COFFEE/PASTRIES/DELI For a caffeine fix, an inexpensive breakfast or lunch, or afternoon tea, head to Tina and Jim Ivanchukov's bright yellow-and-purple cafe on the mainland near the Brooks Bridge. In addition to offering gourmet coffees, the owners make great salads such as herb-roasted chicken with apples, walnuts, and tarragon dressing (sold by the pound), and sandwiches served on homemade focaccia bread.

201 Miracle Strip Pkwy. SE (U.S. 98). © 850/664-0664. Sandwiches and salads $6.50–$9. MC, V. Mon–Fri 7am–7pm; Sat 8am–5pm; Sun 8am–3pm.

Café Tango ★★ AMERICAN Despite the name, this restaurant has nothing to do with Argentina. Housed in a 50-year-old red, vine-covered cottage, Café Tango is best known for its seafood, steaks and pastas. With only eight tables, the restaurant is so romantic it will make you want to do some sort of after dinner tango, so perhaps that's really why the place is named that way.

14 Vicki St., Santa Rosa Beach. © **850/267-0054**. Reservations recommended. Main courses $15–$27. AE, MC, V. Summer 5–10pm; off-season, call for hours.

Caffè Italia ★★ NORTHERN ITALIAN   Nada Eckhardt is from Croatia, but she met her American husband, Jim, while working at a restaurant named Caffè Italia in northern Italy. The Eckhardts duplicated that establishment in this 1925 Sears Roebuck mail-order house tucked away on the waterfront. You can dine on the patio with a view of the sound through sprawling live oak trees (one table is set romantically under a gazebo) or dine inside, where Nada has installed floral tablecloths and photos from the old country. A limited but fine menu includes excellent pizzas; pasta dishes such as tortellini with tomatoes, chicken, and peas in Alfredo sauce; northern Italian risotto with either aspara-gus or smoked salmon; and meat and seafood dishes to fit the season. Don't expect to make a full meal by ordering only pasta, because meals are served in the authentic Italian fashion, with a small portion of pasta preceding the seafood or meat course. On the other hand, you can quickly fill up on the seasoned, pizza-dough bread sticks served with olive oil for dipping. The cappuccino is absolutely first rate, as are the genuine Italian desserts.

189 Brooks St., on the mainland in the block west of Brooks Bridge. © **850/664-0035**. Reservations rec-ommended. Main courses $15–$18; pizza and pasta $8–$13. AE, DC, DISC, MC, V. Sun and Tues–Fri 11am–10pm; Sat 5–11pm. Closed Thanksgiving, Christmas.

Pandora's Restaurant & Lounge ★ STEAKS/PRIME RIB/SEAFOOD The front part of this unusual restaurant is a beached yacht now housing the main-deck lounge. Below is a beam-ceilinged dining room aglow with lights from copper chandeliers. Try for the private Bob Hope booth, where you can dine below two of the great comedian's golf clubs (he used to come here to raise money for a local air force widows' home). Anything from the charcoal grill is excellent, including the wonderful bacon-wrapped scallops offered as an appe-tizer. Several varieties of freshly caught fish are among the main-course choices, but steaks and prime rib keep the locals coming back for more. The tender beef is cut on the premises and grilled to perfection. The delicious breads and pies are homemade. There's another Pandora's in Grayton Beach at the corner of Fla. 283 and County Road 30A (© 850/231-4102).

1120B Santa Rosa Blvd. © **850/244-8669**. Reservations recommended. Main courses $12–$25. AE, DISC, MC, V. Sun–Thurs 5–10pm; Fri–Sat 5–10:30pm.

Staff's Seafood Restaurant SEAFOOD/STEAKS   Considered the first Emerald Coast restaurant, Staff's started as a hotel in 1913 and moved to this barnlike building in 1931. Among the display of memorabilia are an old-fash-ioned phonograph lamp and a 1914 cash register. Staff's tangy seafood gumbo has gained fame for this casual, historic restaurant. One of the most popular main dishes is the "seafood skillet," sizzling with broiled grouper, shrimp, scallops, and crab drenched in butter and sprinkled with cheese. Main courses are served with baskets of hot, home-baked wheat bread from a secret 70-year-old recipe, a salad, and dessert. A pianist plays at dinner year-round.

24 SW Miracle Strip Pkwy. (U.S. 98), on the mainland. © **850/243-3526**. Main courses $12–$30. AE, DISC, MC, V. Summer daily 5–11pm; off-season Mon–Thurs 5–9pm, Fri–Sat 5–10pm.

SOUTHERN WALTON COUNTY

Criolla's ★★★ (Value) INTERNATIONAL   One of Florida's finest restaurants, Johnny Earles' charming establishment derives its name from the archaic word *criollo*, signifying persons of pure Spanish descent born in the New World. The attractive decor, combining New Orleans with the Caribbean, features potted palms, whirling ceiling fans, and tropical island paintings reminiscent of another era. The menus change seasonally, but many fish dishes carry the wonderful aroma of smoke from a wood-fired grill (the bacon-wrapped swordfish, if available, is always a winner). Be sure to ask about a special four-course, fixed-price dinner, which draws inspiration from such warm spots as the Caribbean, Central America, and Tahiti. It's also worth asking in advance about special events featuring visiting chefs and spotlighting excellent vineyards (the wine cellar here has won awards).

170 E. Scenic Hwy. 30A, ¼ mile east of C.R. 283, Grayton Beach. © 850/267-1267. Reservations recommended. Main courses $19–$32. AE, DISC, MC, V. Jan–Feb and Oct–Dec Tues–Sat 5:30–10pm; Mar–Apr and Sept Mon–Sat 5:30–10pm; May–Aug daily 5:30–10pm.

SEASIDE

Several cafes and sandwich shops in Seaside's Gulf-side shopping complex offer inexpensive snacks to beachgoers.

Bud & Alley's ⭐⭐ SEAFOOD/STEAKS/MEDITERRANEAN In this cracked-crab-and-champagne-loving village, Bud & Alley's (named for a dog and a cat probably now in the ever-after) features spectacular sunsets from the rooftop bar and a menu that changes frequently but always has savory surprises. The offerings feature an infusion of Basque, Italian, Louisianian, and Floridian dishes that might include seafood stew (clams, mussels, scallops, shrimp, and fish in a saffron-fresh fennel sauce) or sautéed heads-on shrimp with garlic, shallots, and cracked pepper. You can dine indoors or out, on the screened porch, or under an open-air gazebo where you'll hear the waves splashing against the white sands. Jazz is usually in the spotlight on weekends. On New Year's Eve, everyone in town and from miles around celebrates at Bud & Alley's. Call ahead to see whether a noted guest chef is cooking or a special wine-tasting dinner is scheduled. Smoking is not permitted.

County Rd. 30A, in the beachside shops. © 850/231-5900. www.budandalleys.com. Reservations recommended. Main courses $18–$29; lunch $7.50–$23. MC, V. Apr–Sept Sun–Thurs 11:30am–3pm and 5:30–9:30pm, Fri–Sat 11:30am–3pm and 5:30–10pm; Oct–Mar Sun–Thurs 5:30–9pm, Fri–Sat 5:30–9:30pm.

DESTIN & FORT WALTON BEACH AFTER DARK

Most resorts spotlight live entertainment during the summer season, including the Radisson Beach Resort and the Ramada Plaza Beach Resort in Fort Walton Beach, and the Sandestin Hilton Beach & Golf Resort and Sandestin Golf and Beach Resort in southern Walton County (see "Where to Stay," earlier in this chapter). It's a good idea to inquire ahead to be sure of what's scheduled, especially during the slow season October through February.

For other ideas and listings of what's happening, pick up a copy of the weekly *Walton Sun* newspaper.

DESTIN Several Destin restaurants offer entertainment nightly during summer, on weekends in the off season. The dockside **AJ's Club Bimini,** 116 U.S. 98 E. (© 850/837-1913), has live reggae under a big thatch-roofed deck. A somewhat older, if not more sober, crowd gathers for entertainment at the big harborside deck at **Fisherman's Wharf,** on U.S. 98 East (© 850/654-4766); **The Deck,** on U.S. 98 East at the Harbor Docks restaurant, overlooking the harbor (© 850/837-2506); and **Harry T's Boat House** (© 850/654-4800), also on the harbor; and for Irish tunes nightly year-round at **McGuire's Irish Pub & Brewery** (© 850/650-0567), in the Harborwalk Shops on U.S. 98 just east of the Destin Bridge. See "Where to Dine," earlier in this chapter, for details about the restaurants. The **Grande Isle Sky Bar,** above Grazti Italian Restaurant, 1771 Old Hwy. 98 (© **850/837-7475**), draws the after-dinner crowd from the Back Porch and other adjacent restaurants.

Twenty-somethings are attracted to the dance club, rowdy saloon, Jimmy Buffett–style reggae bar, and sports TV and billiards parlor all under one roof at the acclaimed **Nightown,** 140 Palmetto St. (© **850/837-6448;** www.nightown. com), near the harbor on the inland side of U.S. 98 East. One admission covers it all. There's live music Friday and Saturday nights and amateur boxing on Tuesdays. Nearby, **Hogs Breath Destin,** 541 Hwy. 98 E. (© **850/837-5991;** www. hogsbreath.com), is another lively pub with bands playing rock, blues, and jazz.

Out toward Sandestin, **Fudpucker's Beachside Bar & Grill,** 20001 Hwy. 98 E. (© **850/654-4200**), opposite the Henderson Beach State Park, offers double the fun with two summertime stages. There's another Fudpucker's at 108 Santa Rosa Blvd. on Okaloosa Island in Fort Walton Beach (© **850/243-3833**).

FORT WALTON BEACH   Country music and dancing fans will find a home at the **Seagull,** on Miracle Strip Parkway (U.S. 98) opposite the Gulfarium (© **850/243-3413**). The generations of air force pilots who have hung out here call it the "Dirty Gull." Its main rival for the country set is the **High Tide Oyster Bar,** at Okaloosa Island off the Brooks Bridge (© **850/244-2624**).

3 Panama City Beach

100 miles E of Pensacola, 100 miles SW of Tallahassee

Panama City Beach, a Spring Break mecca that was once erroneously featured as a bleak, desolate wasteland of sun and strip malls in the Ashley Judd film *Ruby in Paradise,* has long been known as the "Redneck Riviera," since it's a mecca for millions of vacationers from the bordering states of Georgia, Alabama, Mississippi, and Louisiana. It still has a seemingly unending strip of bars, amusement parks, and old-fashioned motels. But this lively and crowded destination (in season) also has luxury resorts and condominiums to go along with its 20-plus miles of sandy beaches, golf courses, fishing, boating, and fresh seafood.

Panama City Beach is the most seasonal resort in Northwest Florida, since many restaurants, attractions, and even some hotels close between October and spring break in March. Spring break is a big deal here; MTV even sets up shop in Panama City Beach for annual beach-party broadcasts.

ESSENTIALS

GETTING THERE   The commuter arms of **Delta** (© 800/221-1212), **Northwest** (© 800/225-2525), and **US Airways** (© 800/428-4322) fly into **Panama City/Bay County International Airport** (© **850/763-6751;** www.pc airport.com), on Lisenby Avenue, north of St. Andrews Boulevard, in Panama City.

Alamo (© 800/327-9633), **Avis** (© 800/331-1212), **Budget** (© 800/527-0700), **Enterprise** (© 800/325-8007), **Hertz** (© 800/654-3131), and **National** (© 800/CAR-RENT) have rental-car offices here.

Taxi fares to the beach are about $25.

The Sunset Limited service on **Amtrak** (© **800/USA-RAIL;** www.amtrak. com) stops at Chipley, 45 miles north of Panama City.

VISITOR INFORMATION   For advance information, contact the **Panama City Beach Convention & Visitors Bureau,** P.O. Box 9473, Panama City Beach, FL 32417 (© **800/722-3224** in the U.S., 800/553-1330 in Canada, or 850/233-6503; fax 850/233-5072; www.800pcbeach.com). It operates a visitor information center in the city hall complex, 17001 Panama City Beach Pkwy. (U.S. 98), at Fla. 79. The center is open daily from 8am to 5pm, closed New Year's Day, Thanksgiving, and Christmas.

GETTING AROUND   The **Bay Town Trolley** (℗ 850/769-0557) runs five times a day Monday through Friday year-round along Thomas Drive and on Front Beach Road as far west as Fla. 79. Rides cost 50¢. Call for the schedule. For taxis, call **Yellow Cab** (℗ 850/763-4691). Fares at the beach are $2.50 to climb aboard and $1.50 per mile, or $5 to $10 for rides within Panama City Beach.

TIME   The Panama City area is in the Central Time zone, 1 hour behind Miami, Orlando, and Tallahassee.

HITTING THE BEACH: ST. ANDREWS STATE PARK

A nearly unbroken strand of fine white sand fronts all 22 miles of Panama City Beach, but the highlight for many is **St. Andrews State Park** ★★★, at the east end of the beach. With more than 1,000 acres of dazzling white sand and dunes, this preserved wilderness demonstrates what the area looked like before motels and condominiums lined the beach. Lacy, golden sea oats sway in the refreshing Gulf breezes, and fragrant rosemary grows wild. Picnic areas are on the Gulf beach and the Grand Lagoon. Restrooms and open-air showers are available for beachgoers. For anglers, there are jetties and a boat ramp. A nature trail reveals wading birds and perhaps an alligator or two. And drive carefully here, for the area is home to foxes, coyotes, and a herd of deer. Overnight camping is permitted (see "Where to Stay," below). A historic turpentine still that's on display was formerly used by lumbermen to make turpentine and rosin, both important for caulking the old wooden ships.

The park's 176 RV and tent **campsites** are among the state's most beautiful, especially the 40 situated in a pine forest right on the shores of Grand Lagoon. They are very popular, so reservations are highly recommended—and absolutely essential in summer (call ℗ 800/326-3521 or go to the website www.reserve america.com). Sites cost $17 to $19 March through September. They drop to $10 to $12 October through February.

Park admission is $5 per car with two to eight occupants, $3 for single-occupant vehicles, and $1 for pedestrians and cyclists. The area is open daily from 8am to sunset. Pets are not allowed in the park. For more information or for camping reservations, contact the park at 4607 State Park Lane, Panama City, FL 32408 (℗ 850/233-5140; www.floridastateparks.org/standrews).

Pristine **Shell Island** ★★, a 7½-mile-long, 1-mile-wide barrier island that's accessible only by boat, sits a few hundred yards across an inlet from St. Andrews State Park. This uninhabited natural preserve is great for shelling and also fun for swimming, suntanning, or just relaxing. Visitors can bring chairs, beach gear, coolers, food, and beverages. The best way to get there is on the park's **Shell Island Shuttle** (℗ 800/227-0132 or 850/234-7245; www.shellislandshuttle. com), which runs every 30 minutes daily from 9am to 5pm in summer, weekends from 10am to 3pm in spring and fall. Fares are $9.50 for adults, $5.50 for children 11 and under, plus admission fees to the state recreation area (see above). A special snorkel package costs $18, including shuttle ride and equipment. Kayak rentals cost $35 a day for a single-seat boat, $45 for a double seater.

Several cruise boats go to Shell Island, including the glass-bottomed *Captain Anderson III,* which cruises there from Captain Anderson's Marina, 5500 N. Lagoon Dr., at Thomas Drive (℗ 850/234-3435). It charges $16 for adults, $10 for kids 12 and under (Mar–Oct).

OUTDOOR ACTIVITIES

BOATING A variety of rental boats are available at the marinas near the Thomas Drive bridge over Grand Lagoon. These include the **Captain Davis Queen Fleet,** based at Captain Anderson's Marina, 5500 N. Lagoon Dr. (℃ **800/ 874-2415,** or 850/234-3435 from nearby states); the **Passport Marina,** 5325 N. Lagoon Dr. (℃ **850/234-5609**); the **Port Lagoon Yacht Basin,** 5201 N. Lagoon Dr. (℃ **850/234-0142**); the **Pirates Cove Marina,** 3901 Thomas Dr. (℃ **850/234-3939**); and the **Treasure Island Marina,** 3605 Thomas Dr. (℃ **850/ 234-6533**).

Many resorts and hotels provide beach toys for their guests' use. WaveRunners, jet boats, inflatables, and other equipment can be rented from **Lagoon Rentals** (℃ **850/234-7245**).

CRUISES You'll have your choice of numerous cruises here, from sailing to visiting the dolphins aboard noisy jet skis. The visitor information center (see above) has information about them all—and discount coupons for many.

Children get a kick out of the make-believe swashbucklers on the *Sea Dragon* (℃ **850/234-7400;** www.piratecruise.net), an 80-foot-long replica of a pirate ship that goes on 2-hour cruises from its dock next to the Treasure Ship on Thomas Drive at Grand Lagoon. The trips cost $16, $14 for seniors, $12 for children 3 to 12, and is free for children under 3. Call for seasonal schedules and reservations.

FISHING The least-expensive way to try your luck fishing is with **Captain Anderson's Deep Sea Fishing,** at Captain Anderson's Marina on Thomas Drive at Grand Lagoon (℃ **800/874-2415** or 850/234-5940; www.captandersons fishing.com/trips.html). The captain's party-boat trips last from 5 to 6 hours, with prices ranging from about $35 to $40 per person, including bait and tackle. Observers can go along for $20 less.

The more expensive charter-fishing boats depart daily from March to November from the marinas mentioned in "Boating," above.

You definitely won't get seasick casting your line from the **M. B. Miller County Pier,** 12213 Front Beach Rd. (℃ **850/233-3039**), or the **Dan Russell Municipal Pier,** 16101 Front Beach Rd. (℃ **850/233-5080**).

GOLF **Bay Point Yacht and Country Club** (p. 620), 3900 Marriott Dr., off Jan Cooley Road (℃ **850-235-6950;** www.baypointgolf.com), offers 36 holes of championship play, including the Bruce Devlin–designed **Lagoon Legends** ★★ course, rated as one of the country's most difficult. Both it and the Club Meadows course have clubhouses, putting greens, driving ranges, clinics, and private instruction. Greens fees with cart start at about $55 in summer and $60 in winter, depending on the day of the week.

The **Edgewater Beach Resort,** 11212 U.S. 98A (℃ **850/235-4044**), also has a nine-hole resort course, and its guests have access to **The Hombre,** 120 Coyote Pass, 3 miles west of the Hathaway Bridge off Panama City Beach Parkway/U.S. 98 (℃ **850/234-3573**), a par-72 championship course that is home to the Nike Panama City Beach Classic. Fifteen of its 18 holes have water hazards (the unforgiving 7th hole sits on an island). Greens fees are about $65 in summer, $60 in winter, including cart.

The course at the semiprivate **Holiday Golf Club,** 100 Fairway Blvd. (℃ **850/ 234-1800**), sports lake-lined fairways and elevated greens. Greens fees with cart are about $45 in summer, $35 in winter. You can play at night on a lighted nine-hole, par-29 executive course.

The least-expensive place to play here is the flat and forgiving **Signal Hill,** 9516 N. Thomas Dr. (© 850/234-3218), where you'll pay about $20 to walk 18 holes in summer, $15 in winter. Add about $10 per person for a cart.

For course information online, go to www.golf.com and www.floridagolfing. com, or call the **Florida Sports Foundation** (© 850/488-8347) or **Florida Golfing** (© 866/833-2663).

SCUBA DIVING & SNORKELING   Although the area is too far north for extensive coral formations, more than 50 artificial reefs and shipwrecks in the Gulf waters off Panama City attract a wide variety of sea life. The largest local operator is **Hydrospace Dive Shop,** 6422 W. Hwy. 98 (© 850/234-3063; www.hydrospace.com). Others include **Panama City Dive Center,** 4823 Thomas Dr. (© 850/235-3390; www.pcdivecenter.com); **Emerald Coast Divers,** 5121 Thomas Dr. (© 800/945-DIVE or 850/233-3355); and **Pete's Scuba Center,** 9007 Front Beach Rd. (© 800/401-DIVE or 850/230-8006). These companies lead dives, teach courses, and take snorkelers to the grass flats off Shell Island.

EXPLORING THE AREA

Gulf World Marine Park *Kids*   This landscaped tropical garden and marine attraction features shows with talented dolphins, sea lions, penguins, and more. Not to be upstaged, parrots perform daily, too. Sea turtles, alligators, and other critters also call Gulf World home. Scuba demonstrations, shark feedings, and underwater shows keep the crowds entertained. The park also has special interactive programs, including trainer for a day ($175 per person), dolphin encounter ($125), and a Meet the Dolphins tour ($6). Allow about 3½ hours to see it all, more if you do one of the encounters.

15412 Front Beach Rd. (at Hill Ave.), Panama City Beach. © 850/234-5271. www.gulfworldmarinepark. com. Admission $20 adults, $14 children 5–11, free for children under 5. Summer daily 9am–4pm; off-season daily 9am–2pm.

Museum of Man in the Sea   Owned by the Institute of Diving, this small museum exhibits relics from the first days of scuba diving, historical displays of the underwater world dating from 1500, and treasures recovered from sunken ships, including Spanish treasure galleons. Hands-on exhibits explain water and air pressure, light refraction, and why diving bells work. Both kids and adults can climb through a submarine and see live sea animals in a pool. Videos and aquariums explain the sea life found in St. Andrews Bay.

17314 Panama City Beach Pkwy. (at Heather Dr., west of Fla. 79), Panama City Beach. © 850/235-4101. Admission $5 adults, $2.50 children 6–16, free for children 5 and under. Daily 9am–5pm. Closed New Year's Day, Thanksgiving, Christmas.

ZooWorld Zoological & Botanical Park ★ *Kids*   Sitting in a pine forest, this educational and entertaining zoo is an active participant in the Species Survival Plan, which helps protect endangered species by employing specific breeding and housing programs. Among the 350 guests here are orangutans and other primates; lions, tigers, and leopards; and alligators and other reptiles. Also included are a walk-through aviary, a bat exhibit, and a petting zoo. The zoo's newest and most precious attraction is The Tilghman Infant Care Facility, a nursery facility that allows you to closely view the baby animals born at ZooWorld.

9008 Front Beach Rd. (near Moylan Dr.), Panama City Beach. © 850/230-1243. Admission $11 adults, $6.95 children 3–11, free for children under 3. Daily 9am–5:30pm (to 4:30pm in winter).

AMUSEMENT PARKS

For that Panama City meets Coney Island vibe, there are two amusement parks at which to kill some time. A 105-foot-high roller coaster is just one of the 30 rides at the **Miracle Strip Amusement Park,** 12000 Front Beach Rd., at Alf Coleman Road (© **850/234-5810;** www.miraclestrippark.com; $5.50 per person, more for rides and shows). Little ones will love the traditional carousel. Nine acres of fun include continuing live entertainment and tons of junk food. The adjoining **Shipwreck Island Water Park** (© **850/234-0368;** www.ship wreckisland.com; $25 for guests over 50 in. tall, $20 for those 35–50 in., free for those under 35 in.) offers a variety of water amusements, including the 1,600-foot-long winding Lazy River for tubing and a daring 35 mph Speed Slide. The Tad Pole Hole is exclusively for young kids. Lounge chairs, umbrellas, and inner tubes are free, and lifeguards are on duty. Combination tickets are available. Both are open weekends from mid-March to Memorial Day, then daily to mid-August, and weekends from then to Labor Day weekend.

SHOPPING

The main branch of **Alvin's Island Tropical Department Store,** 12010 Front Beach Rd. (© **850/234-3048;** www.alvinsisland.com), opposite the James I. Lark Sr. Visitors Information Center, is an attraction in itself. It not only sells a wide range of beach gear and apparel, but also has cages containing colorful parrots, tanks with small sharks, and an enclosure with alligators. The sharks are fed at 11am daily; the gators get theirs at 4pm in summer only. (Only in Florida—live sharks and alligators in a department store!)

WHERE TO STAY

There are scores of motels along the beach here, ranging from small mom-and-pop operations to sizable members of national chains. The annual guide distributed by the Panama City Beach Convention & Visitors Bureau has a complete list (p. 614).

The most modern of the chain motels are the recently renovated **Howard Johnson Resort Hotel,** 9400 S. Thomas Dr. (© **800/654-2000** or 850/234-6521), and the **Four Points by Sheraton,** 9600 S. Thomas Dr. (© **888/625-5144** or 850/234-6511), both part of the redeveloped Boardwalk Beach Resort area, a center of beach action.

Panama City Beach also abounds with condominium complexes, such as the Edgewater Beach Resort listed below. Among the many rental agents are **Coldwell Banker Beach Rental,** 726 Thomas Dr., Panama City Beach, FL 32408 (© **800/621-2462** or 850/235-4075; fax 850/233-2833; www.panamabeach rentals.com); and **Condo World,** 8815A Thomas Dr. (P.O. Box 9456), Panama City Beach, FL 32408 (© **800/232-6636** in the U.S., 800/824-5411 in Canada, or 850/234-5564; fax 850/233-6725; www.condoworld.net).

The best camping is at the lovely sites in **St. Andrews State Park,** one of this area's major attractions (p. 615).

Rates at even the most expensive properties here drop precipitously during winter, when the town rolls up the sidewalks. Bay County adds 3.5% tax to all hotel and campground bills, bringing the total add-on tax (with the county's 6% sales tax) to 9.5%.

Beachcomber by the Sea 🏄 Watercolors by local artist Paul Brent grace every unit in this eight-story all-suites, Spring Breaker-free (they're prohibited, really, I swear!) resort, built and opened in 1998 at the junction of Front Beach

Road and Fla. 79. They also have balconies overlooking a Gulf-side swimming pool and hot tub bordered by a concrete deck accented by areas of palm trees. The well-equipped suites come in two sizes. The larger editions have living rooms with sleeper sofas and bedrooms with either king-size or two double beds. Bathrooms and kitchenettes separate the living rooms and bedrooms. The suites are similar to those at the Flamingo Motel & Tower (see below), except that here they have air conditioners in both the living rooms and the bedrooms. The smaller units are more like motel rooms, but they have microwaves. Two of the smaller units also have whirlpool tubs. There's no restaurant here but several are nearby, and complimentary continental breakfast is available in the lobby each morning.

17101 Front Beach Rd., Panama City Beach, FL 32413. © **888/886-8916** or 850/233-3600. Fax 850/233-3622. www.beachcomberbythesea.com. 96 units. Summer $109–$250; off-season $39–$109. Rates include continental breakfast. Packages available. AE, DISC, MC, V. **Amenities:** Heated outdoor pool; access to nearby health club; Jacuzzi; game room; coin-op washers and dryers. *In room:* A/C, TV, dataport, kitchen, fridge, coffeemaker, hair dryer, iron.

Edgewater Beach Resort ★★ Kids   One of the Panhandle's largest condominium resorts, this sports-oriented, private, gated facility enjoys a beautiful beachfront location and 110 tropically landscaped acres. Units in five Gulf-side towers offer commanding views of the emerald Gulf and gorgeous sunsets from their private balconies. A pedestrian overpass leads across Front Beach Road to low-rise apartments and town homes fringing ponds and the fairways of the resort's nine-hole golf course. A daytime shuttle runs around the resort to swimming pools, whirlpools, the tennis center, and the golf course (guests also get privileges at the 18-hole Hombre Golf Club, ¼ mile north). The Shoppes at Edgewater restaurants are across the road. There are also supervised children's programs and activities, not to mention the gorgeous 11,000 square foot, Polynesian style pool with waterfalls, islands, and a deck that features live entertainment daily from 11am to 4pm.

11212 Front Beach Rd. (P.O. Box 9850), Panama City Beach, FL 32407. © **800/874-8686** or 850/235-4044. Fax 850/235-6899. www.edgewaterbeachresort.com. 500 units. Summer $166–$471 condo; off-season $86–$174 condo. $5-per-day, per-unit amenities fee. Weekly rates and maid service available. AE, DC, DISC, MC, V. **Amenities:** 2 restaurants; 2 bars; 11 heated outdoor pools; 9-hole golf course; 11 tennis courts; health club; Jacuzzi; watersports equipment rentals; children's programs; concierge; car-rental desk; limited room service; babysitting; coin-op washers and dryers. *In room:* A/C, TV, dataport, kitchen, coffeemaker, hair dryer, iron.

Flamingo Motel & Tower ★ Value   The Lancaster family takes great pride in the gorgeous tropical garden surrounding a heated swimming pool and a large sun deck overlooking the Gulf at their well-maintained motel. The brightly decorated rooms have either full kitchens or refrigerators and microwave ovens. They can sleep two to six people, some in separate bedrooms. Kitchenette rooms in a two-story motel block across the road are less appealing but will accommodate six to eight. Budget-conscious families can opt for lower-priced rooms, accommodating two to four. Next door, the seven-story Flamingo Tower contains 49 suites, all sporting living rooms with sofa beds and dining tables; bedrooms with ceiling fans and their own TVs; kitchens; and balconies overlooking the Gulf and a beachside swimming pool and hot tub. These suites have air-conditioning units in their living rooms but not in their bedrooms (the ceiling fans will come in handy during the hot, humid summer months). Some older units have shower-only bathrooms. The Dan Russell fishing pier is only ½ mile away, and Gulf World Marine Park and Shuckums Oyster Pub & Seafood Grill are virtually across the road (see "Exploring the Area," above, and "Where to Dine," below). College spring-breakers are not welcome.

15525 Front Beach Rd., Panama City Beach, FL 32413. ℂ **800/828-0400** or 850/234-2232. Fax 850/234-1292. www.flamingomotel.com. 117 units. Summer $94–$159; off-season $39–$139. AE, DISC, MC, V. **Amenities:** 2 heated outdoor pools; access to nearby health club; Jacuzzi; watersports equipment rental; coin-op washers and dryers. *In room:* A/C, TV, kitchen, fridge, coffeemaker.

Holiday Inn SunSpree Resort 🌟 One building removed from the Edgewater Beach Resort and across the road from the Shoppes at Edgewater, this 15-story establishment is the top full-service Gulf-front hotel here. It's designed in an arch, with all rooms having balconies looking directly down on the beach, where a heated, foot-shaped, lagoon-style swimming pool and wooden sun deck are separated from the beach by a row of palms and Polynesian torches, which are lighted at night. The hotel has won architectural awards for its dramatic lobby with a waterfall and the Fountain of Wishes (the coins go to charity). The attractive, spacious guest rooms feature full-size ice-making refrigerators, microwave ovens, and two spacious vanity areas with their own lavatory sinks. Decor is dramatically different from your typical Holiday Inn and is more reminiscent of a resort in, say, the Caribbean, with its pastel colors and tile floors.

11127 Front Beach Rd., Panama City Beach, FL 32407. ℂ **800/633-0266** or 850/234-1111. Fax 850/235-1907. www.holidayinnsunspree.com. 340 units. Summer $159–$239 double; off-season $75–$139 double. AE, DC, DISC, MC, V. **Amenities:** 2 restaurants; 1 bar; heated outdoor pool; exercise room; Jacuzzi; watersports equipment rentals; game room; concierge; limited room service; babysitting; laundry service; concierge-level rooms. *In room:* A/C, TV, dataport, fridge, coffeemaker, hair dryer, iron, safe.

Marriott's Bay Point Resort Village 🌟🌟 *Value* Not only is this luxurious vacation miniworld ranked among the nation's top golf and tennis resorts, but it's an extraordinarily good value for Florida as well. Although guests pay extra for most activities, its room rates are among the top steals in the state. They would be higher if the property were beside the Gulf; instead, it's the centerpiece of a manicured real-estate development sprawling over 1,100 acres on a wildlife sanctuary bordered by St. Andrews Bay and the Grand Lagoon. Situated beside the lagoon, the luxurious, vivid-coral stucco hotel is surrounded by gardens, palm trees, oaks, and magnolias. From the glamorous three-story lobby, window walls look out to scenic water views and two swimming pools (one in its own glass-enclosed building). Furnished in dark woods, the newly renovated Marriott-esque rooms are spacious and luxurious, and all have balconies or patios. The highlights for duffers are the Lagoon Legends and the Club Meadows golf courses (see Baypoint Yacht and Country Club under "Outdoor Activities," earlier in this chapter). Watersports here are at Grand Lagoon Beach, reached by the hotel's long pier. There's also a free shuttle to the Gulf beaches from here. A fun locals' scene happens here at Teddy's Back Bay Beach Club, a waterfront, open-air beach bar with a tin roof and sprawling docks, which attracts a lively crowd ashore from their WaveRunners, pontoon boats, yachts, and sailboats.

4200 Marriott Dr., Panama City Beach, FL 32408. ℂ **800/874-7105** or 850/236-6000. Fax 850/236-6158. www.marriottbaypoint.com. 356 units. Summer $149–$209 double; off-season $149–$159 double. Packages available. AE, DC, DISC, MC, V. From Thomas Dr., take Magnolia Beach Rd. and bear right on Dellwood Rd. to resort complex. **Amenities:** 2 restaurants; 2 bars; 3 heated outdoor pools; indoor pool; 2 golf courses; 4 tennis courts; health club; Jacuzzi; watersports equipment rental; bike rental; concierge; business center; limited room service; massage; babysitting; laundry service; coin-op washers and dryers; concierge-level rooms. *In room:* A/C, TV, dataport, fridge, coffeemaker, hair dryer, iron.

Sunset Inn This well-maintained establishment, near the east end of the beach, is right on the Gulf but away from the crowds. The spacious beachside rooms accommodate families in one- and two-bedroom apartments with kitchens, while refurbished efficiencies and a new building with tropically furnished one- and two-bedroom condominiums are across the street. The condominiums are the most expensive units here, but the units with patios or balconies right on the beach will better suit sun-and-sand lovers. Some of the older units have shower-only bathrooms. The best part about this motel is the beach—it's quiet, complete with umbrellaed chairs and a sense of peace not necessarily found elsewhere along the strip.

8109 Surf Dr., Panama City Beach, FL 32408. ✆ 850/234-7370. Fax 850/234-7370, ext. 303. www.sunset innfl.com. 62 units. Rooms and efficiencies: spring break and summer $70–$130; spring $55–$95; fall and winter $45–$80. Condos (4–6 people): spring break and summer $140–$165, spring $110–$125, fall and winter $80–$100. Weekly and monthly rates available. AE, DISC, MC, V. **Amenities:** Heated outdoor pool; coin-op washers and dryers. In room: A/C, TV, kitchen, fridge, coffeemaker.

WHERE TO DINE

Except for fast-food joints, there aren't many national-chain family restaurants in Panama City Beach (you'll find those along 15th and 23rd sts. over in Panama City). One local chain worth a meal is the **Montego Bay Seafood House** (ww.montegobaypcb.com), which offers a wide range of fairly inexpensive munchies, sandwiches, burgers, and seafood main courses. Branches are at the "curve" at 4920 Thomas Dr. (✆ **850/234-8686**) and in the Shoppes at Edgewater, Front Beach Drive at 473 Beckrich Rd. (✆ **850/233-6033**).

Pay attention to the restaurant hours here, because some places are closed during the winter months. Even if they're open, many will close early when business is slow. Call ahead to make sure the restaurant you want to go to is open.

Billy's Steamed Seafood Restaurant (Value) SEAFOOD

More a lively raw bar than a restaurant, Billy and Eloise Poole's casual spot has been serving the best crabs in town since 1982. These are hard-shell blue crabs prepared Maryland style: steamed with spicy Old Bay Seasoning. Unlike crab houses in Baltimore, however, Billy and Eloise remove the crab's top shell, clean out the "mustard" (intestines), and cut the crabs in two for you; all you have to do is "pick" the meat. Don't worry, they'll show you. Other steamed morsels include shrimp (also with spicy seasoning), oysters, crabs, and lobster served with corn on the cob and garlic bread. Order anything from the briny deep here, but pass over other items.

3000 Thomas Dr. (between Grand Lagoon and Magnolia Beach Rd.). ✆ 850/235-2349. Main courses $5.50–$18; sandwiches $3.50–$5.50. AE, DISC, MC, V. Daily 11am–9pm.

Boar's Head Restaurant ✿ STEAKS/SEAFOOD

An institution since 1978, this shingle-roofed establishment appears from the road to be a South Seas resort. Inside, its impressive beamed ceiling, stone walls, and fireplaces create a warm, almost–English tavern atmosphere suited to the house specialties: tender, marbled prime rib of beef and perfectly cooked steaks. Beef eaters don't have the Boar's Head to themselves, however, because the coals are also used to give a charred flavor to salmon, grouper, and yellowfin tuna. Other temptations are offered, too, including lobster, shrimp, and scallops in a cream sauce over angel-hair pasta. And venison, quail, and other game dishes find their way here during winter. An extensive wine list has won awards, and a cozy tavern to one side has live music, usually Wednesday through Saturday evenings.

17290 Front Beach Rd. (just west of Fla. 79). ✆ 850/234-6628. www.boarsheadrestaurant.com. Main courses $14–$29. AE, DC, DISC, MC, V. Summer daily 4:30–10pm; off-season Sun–Thurs 4:30–9pm, Fri–Sat 4:30–10pm.

Canopies ✿✿ SEAFOOD/STEAKS

This area's most elegant restaurant and purveyor of its finest cuisine occupies a 1910-vintage gray clapboard house with a magnificent view of St. Andrews Bay. Dining is outside on the patio or on an enclosed veranda, and the dark, cozy bar in the old living room invites before- or after-dinner drinks. The menu changes monthly but always offers the consistently excellent creamy she-crab soup under a flaky croissant dome. Other selections could include sushi-quality yellowfin tuna in a sherry-soy sauce served over a haystack of leeks; a "trio" of tuna, salmon, and grouper with a citrus-butter sauce served with a mandarin-orange salsa and Vidalia-onion mashed potatoes; and sautéed grouper with lump crab meat in a sherry-butter sauce. Forget the crab cakes. Landlubbers can partake of award-winning beef, veal, lamb, pork, and game dishes. White-chocolate mousse is among several wonderful sweet endings.

4423 W. Hwy. 98, Panama City (1 mile east of Hathaway Bridge on U.S. 98). © 850/872-8444. www. canopiespc.com. Reservations recommended. Main courses $18–$26; early-bird specials $11. AE, DC, DISC, MC, V. Daily 5–10pm. Early-bird specials 5–6pm.

Captain Anderson's Restaurant & Waterfront Seafood Market
SEAFOOD 👍 Since 1953, this famous restaurant has been attracting early diners, who come to watch the fishing fleet unload the catch of the day at the busy marina on Grand Lagoon. It's so popular, in fact, that you may have to wait 2 hours for a table during the peak summer months; three bars are there to help you pass the time. The Captain's menu is noted for grilled local fish (grouper, amberjack, and yellowfin tuna), crab-stuffed jumbo shrimp, and a heaped-high seafood platter. The food isn't as interesting as at Hamilton's Seafood Restaurant & Lounge across the road (see below), but the local atmosphere makes it worth a visit while you're here.

5551 N. Lagoon Dr. (at Thomas Dr.). © 850/234-2225. www.captanderson.com. Main courses $11–$37. AE, DC, DISC, MC, V. Summer Mon–Sat 4–10pm; off-season Mon–Sat 4:30–10pm. Closed Nov–Jan.

Hamilton's Seafood Restaurant & Lounge 👍 SEAFOOD Proprietor Steve Stevens continues in the tradition of his noted Mississippi-born, restaurateur father. The attractive blond-wood and knotty-pine restaurant lies on Grand Lagoon. The grilled grouper with shrimp, scallops, and crab is a real treat. Several other dishes are locally unique to Hamilton's, such as spicy snapper étouffée and a Greek-accented shrimp Christo. Mesquite-grilled fish and steaks are also house specialties, and vegetarians can order a coal-fired vegetable kabob served over angel-hair pasta. The Lagoon Saloon makes the wait for a table pass quickly, and you can select from an extensive selection of well-chosen California and French wines.

5711 N. Lagoon Dr. (at Thomas Dr.). © 850/234-1255. www.hamiltonspcbeach.com. Main courses $13–$25. AE, DISC, MC, V. Summer daily 4–10pm; off-season Mon–Thurs 5–9pm, Fri–Sat 5–9:30pm. Closed 1 week in Jan.

SPECIAL DINING EXPERIENCES

You've got to see the **Treasure Ship**, at Treasure Island Marina, 3605 S. Thomas Dr. at Grand Lagoon (© **850/234-8881;** http://thetreasureship.com), to believe it. This amazing 2 acres of ship space claims to be the world's largest land-based Spanish galleon and a reputed replica of the three-masted sailing ships that carried loot from the New World to Spain in the 16th and 17th centuries. You can get anything from an ice-cream cone to peel-it-yourself shrimp to a sophisticated dinner in the restaurant and bar here, which are open daily from 4:30 to 10pm (and sometimes later); closed during the winter months. Call to make sure it's open when you want to go.

Lady Anderson **dinner-dance cruises** are a romantic evening escape; they're available March through October. This modern, three-deck ship boards at Captain Anderson's Marina, 5550 N. Lagoon Dr. (© **800/360-0510** or 850/234-5940; www.ladyanderson.com), Monday through Saturday evenings, with the

That's the motto at **Shuckums Oyster Pub & Seafood Grill,** 15614 Front Beach Rd. at Powell Adams Drive (© **850/235-3214;** www.shuckums.com). Comedian Martin Short made this noisy, lively, and smoky pub famous when he tried unsuccessfully to shuck oysters at its bar during the making of an MTV spring-break special. The original bar where Short tried to shuck is virtually papered over with dollar bills signed by old and young patrons who have been flocking here since 1967. The obvious specialty is fresh Apalachicola oysters, served raw, steamed, or baked with a variety of toppings. Otherwise, the menu consists of pub fare and mediocre seafood main courses. Shuckums is open daily during the summer from 11am to 2am. It closes during the off season at 9pm during the week, at midnight on weekends.

cruises lasting from 7 to 10pm. Buffet dinners are featured, followed by live music for dancing Monday, Wednesday, Friday, and Saturday nights, gospel music on Tuesday and Thursday. Dinner-dance tickets cost $40 for adults, $38 for seniors, $23 for children 6 to 11, and $15 for children 2 to 5. Gospel music cruises go for $35 for adults, $33 for seniors, $23 for children 6 to 11, and $15 for children 2 to 5. Tips are included. Summertime reservations should be made well in advance.

PANAMA CITY & PANAMA CITY BEACH AFTER DARK
THE PERFORMING ARTS   The Rader family and a cast of 20 perform year-round in the **Ocean Opry Show,** 8400 Front Beach Rd., Panama City Beach (© **850/234-5464;** www.oceanopryshow.com), the area's answer to the Grand Ole Opry. There's a show every night at 8pm during the summer, less frequently during the off season. Popcorn, hot dogs, and soft drinks are available. Admission is about $20 for adults, half price for children ages 5 through 11. Prices jump to $30 or more when stars like Kitty Welles, B. J. Thomas, and the Wilkensons are in town, usually during winter. The box office opens at 9am Monday through Saturday, and reservations are recommended but not required.

THE CLUB & BAR SCENE   The **Breakers,** 12627 Front Beach Rd. (© **850/234-6060**), is the area's premier supper club, with unsurpassed Gulf views and music for dining and dancing. You'll swear The King has risen from the grave as "Elvis Presley" and other impersonators of **Clutch Rock 'n' Roll Cafe** perform here. The show is worth the $10 to $15 per-person cover charge. The beachfront **Harpoon Harry's Waterfront Cafe** is part of the same complex.

Romantic lounges with live entertainment are at the **Treasure Ship,** 3605 S. Thomas Dr. (© **850/234-8881**), where comedian-hypnotist Mike Harvey performs during summer in the top-floor Captain's Quarters; and at the **Boar's Head,** 17290 Front Beach Rd. (© **850/234-6628**). See "Where to Dine" and "Special Dining Experiences," above for more information.

The 20-something crowd likes to boogie all night at beach clubs such as **Schooners,** 5121 Gulf Dr. (© **850/235-3555**), where every table has a Gulf view; **Club La Vella,** a bikini-contest kind of place and one of Florida's largest nightclubs, also on the beach at 8813 Thomas Dr. (© **850/234-3866**); and **Sharkey's on the Gulf,** 15201 Front Beach Rd. (© **850/235-2420**). The clubs often stay open until 4am in summer while their bands play on. **Pineapple**

Willie's Lounge, beachside at 9900 S. Thomas Dr. (© **850/235-0928**), is open from 11am until 2am, serving ribs basted with Jack Daniel's and spotlighting live entertainment during summer and a host of sports-TVs year-round.

4 Apalachicola ★★

65 miles E of Panama City, 80 miles W of Tallahassee

Sometimes called Florida's Last Frontier (a claim that overlooks the Everglades), **Apalachicola** makes a fascinating day trip from Panama City Beach or Tallahassee, as well as a destination in its own right. The long, gorgeous beaches on **St. George Island,** 7 miles from town, are among America's best. Justifiably famous for Apalachicola oysters, the bays and estuaries are great for fishing and boating. And if you love nature, the area is also rich in wildlife preserves.

The charming little town of Apalachicola (pop. 2,600) was a major seaport each autumn from 1827 to 1861, when plantations in Alabama and Georgia shipped tons of cotton down the Apalachicola River to the Gulf. The town had a racetrack, an opera house, and a civic center that hosted balls, socials, and gambling. The population shrank during the mosquito-infested summer months, however, when yellow fever and malaria epidemics struck. It was during one of these outbreaks that Dr. John Gorrie of Apalachicola tried to develop a method of cooling his patients' rooms. In doing so, he invented the forerunner of the air conditioner, a device that made Florida tourism possible and life a whole lot more bearable for locals during summer months.

Apalachicola has traditionally made its living primarily from the Gulf and the lagoonlike bay protected by a chain of offshore barrier islands. Today, this area produces the bulk of Florida's oyster crop, and shrimping and fishing are major industries, too. The town has also been discovered by a number of urban expatriates, who have moved here, restored old homes, and opened interesting antiques and gift shops (there aren't many towns this size where you can buy Crabtree & Evelyn products).

ESSENTIALS

GETTING THERE   The nearest airport is 65 miles to the west at Panama City Beach (p. 614). From there you'll have to rent a car or take an expensive taxi ride. The Tallahassee airport is about 85 miles to the northeast (p. 629). **Croom's Transportation** (© **888/653-8132** or 850/653-2400) has airport shuttle service between Tallahassee and Apalachicola ($105 for one passenger, $10 for each additional person).

The scenic way to drive here is via the Gulf-hugging U.S. 98 from Panama City Beach, or via U.S. 319 and U.S. 98 from Tallahassee. From I-10, take exit 142 at Marianna, then follow Fla. 71 south to Port St. Joe, and then take U.S. 98 east to Apalachicola.

VISITOR INFORMATION   The **Apalachicola Bay Chamber of Commerce,** 99 Market St., Apalachicola, FL 32320 (© **850/653-9419;** fax 850/653-8219; www.apalachicolabay.org), supplies information about the area from its office on Market Street (U.S. 98) between Avenue D and Avenue E. The chamber is open Monday through Friday from 9:30am to 5pm.

TIME   The town is in the Eastern Time zone, like Orlando, Miami, and Tallahassee (it's 1 hr. ahead of Panama City Beach and the rest of the Panhandle). *Note:* Many shops are closed on Wednesday afternoon, when Apalachicolans go fishing.

BEACHES, PARKS & WILDLIFE REFUGES

Some experts consider the 9 miles of beaches in **St. George Island State Park** ★★★ to be among America's best. This pristine nature 9-mile long preserve occupies the eastern end of St. George Island, about 15 miles east of Apalachicola. A 4-mile-long paved road leads through the dunes to picnic areas, restrooms, showers, and a boat launch. An unpaved trail leads another 5 miles to the island's eastern end, but be careful: It's easy to get stuck in the soft sand, even in a four-wheel-drive sport-utility vehicle. From a hiking trail leading from the campground out a narrow peninsula on the bay side, you can see countless terns, snowy plovers, black skimmers, and other birds. Entry costs $3 for a vehicle with one occupant, $5 for vehicles with two to eight occupants, and $1 for pedestrians and bicyclists. Campsites cost $19. The park is open daily from 8am to sunset. Pets are allowed. For more information, contact the park at 1900 E. Gulf Beach Dr., St. George Island, FL 32328 (© **850/927-2111;** www.florida stateparks.org/stgeorgeisland).

There are no facilities whatsoever at the **St. Vincent National Wildlife Refuge,** southwest of Apalachicola and it's accessible only by boat. The U.S. Fish & Wildlife Service has left this 12,358-acre barrier island in its natural state, but visitors are welcome to walk through its pine forests, marshlands, ponds, dunes, and beaches. In addition to native species such as bald eagles and alligators, the island is home to a small herd of sambar deer from Southeast Asia. Red wolves are bred here for re-establishment in other wildlife areas. Access is by boat only. **St. Vincents Island Shuttle Service** (© 850/229-1065; www.stvincentisland. com), at Indian Pass, 21 miles west of Apalachicola via U.S. 98 and County Roads 30A and 30B, will take you to the island in a pontoon boat. If you bring your bike, they'll drop you on one end of the island and pick you up later at the other. Call for prices and reservations, which are required.

The refuge headquarters, at the north end of Market Street in town, has exhibits of wetland flora and fauna. It's open Monday through Friday from 8am to 4:30pm. Admission is free. For more information, contact the refuge at P.O. Box 447, Apalachicola, FL 32329 (© **850/653-8808**).

The huge **Apalachicola National Forest** (p. 642) begins a few miles northeast of town. It has a host of facilities, including canoeing and mountain-bike trails.

OUTDOOR ACTIVITIES

CRUISES Jeanni McMillan of **Journeys of St. George Island** ★ (© 850/927-3259; www.sgislandjourneys.com) takes guests on narrated nature cruises to the barrier islands and on canoe and kayak trips in the creeks and streams of the Apalachicola River basin. She also has night hikes with blue-crab netting, shelling excursions, and fishing and scalloping trips, plus excursions tailored exclusively for children. Prices range from $25 to $75 per person. Reservations are required, so call her to find out what she's offering when you'll be in town. Jeanni also rents canoes, kayaks, sailboats, and sailboards. She's closed January and February.

A less adventurous way to see the marshes, swamps, and shallow-water rivers is via a nature cruise with **EcoVentures, Inc.** (© 850/653-2593; www. apalachicolatours.com). It uses the *Osprey,* a 40-foot, all-weather boat that can carry up to 32 passengers. Fares are $20 for adults, $10 for children under 16. Call for schedule and reservations.

You can go afternoon or sunset sailing on the bay for hours on Captain Jerry Weber's 40-foot sloop *Wind Catcher* (© 850/653-3881). The 2½-hour voyages cost $35 for adults, $20 for children under 16, including snacks and soft drinks. Reservations are essential.

FISHING   You can't go oystering, but fishing is excellent in these waters, where trout, redfish, flounder, tarpon, shark, drum, and other fish abound. The chamber of commerce (see above) can help arrange charters on the local boats, many of which dock at the Rainbow Inn on Water Street. For guides, contact **Robinson Brothers Guide Service** (© **850/653-8896;** fax 850/653-3118; www.flaredfish.com). Rates run about $300 for a half day and $400 to $600 for a full day for up to four anglers.

EXPLORING THE TOWN

Start your visit by picking up a map and a self-guided tour brochure from the chamber of commerce (see above), and then stroll around Apalachicola's waterfront, business district, and Victorian-era homes.

Along Water Street, several tin warehouses date to the town's seafaring days of the late 1800s, as does the 1840s-era **Sponge Exchange** at Commerce Street and Avenue E. A highlight of the residential area, centered around Gorrie Square at Avenue D and 6th Street, is the Greek Revival–style **Trinity Episcopal Church,** built in New York and shipped here in 1837. At the water end of 6th Street, Battery Park has a children's playground. A number of excellent art galleries and gift shops are grouped on Market Street, Avenue D, and Commerce Street.

The showpiece at the **John Gorrie Museum State Park** ⚡, Avenue D at 6th Street (© **850/653-9347;** www.floridastateparks.org/johngorriemuseum), is a replica of Doctor Gorrie's cooling machine, a prototype of today's air conditioner: It really works! The park is open Thursday through Monday from 9am to 5pm; closed New Year's Day, Thanksgiving, and Christmas. Admission is $1, free for children 6 and under.

The newly renovated **Dixie Theater,** 21 Ave. E. (© **850/653-3200**), a 1912 movie house, hosts live theater and maintains the original ticket booth and facades restored to their original glory.

The **Estuarine Walk,** at the north end of Market Street on the grounds of the Apalachicola National Estuarine Research Reserve (© **850/653-8063**), contains aquariums full of fish and turtles, and displays of various other estuarine life. It's open Monday through Friday from 8am to 5pm. Admission is free.

WHERE TO STAY

Built in 1997, the 42-room **Best Western Apalach Inn,** 249 Hwy. 98 W. (© **800/528-1234** or 850/653-9131; fax 850/653-9136; www.apalachicola. com/bestwestern), a mile west of downtown, is the only national chain hotel here.

Apalachicola River Inn ⚡   The town's only waterfront accommodation, this two-story motel's rough-hewn exterior timbers make it look like one of the neighboring warehouses. Units in the main building all have views across a marina to Apalachicola Bay. Those on the second floor are larger and have balconies, making them preferable to the smaller downstairs units, whose doors open directly onto the marina's boardwalk. All rooms have been renovated, adding new carpeting, new windows, doors, and French Doors. Most of the upstairs rooms have shower-only bathrooms. Two rooms and a two-bedroom apartment in a building next door have whirlpool tubs. The lobby has been redone, adding the Frog Level Oyster Bar, a casual bar serving, what else, oysters. Boss Oyster is the inn's popular riverfront restaurant serving gulf water oysters cooked many ways such as Oysters Greektown, with feta cheese, garlic, olives, and parsley or the spicy Oysters Jalapeno. Facing the river, Caroline's Restaurant serves breakfast, lunch, and seafood dinners (it's a bit pricey at dinner but is a fine spot for an alfresco, dockside lunch). The Roseate Spoonbill Lounge, over the restaurant, is *the* local watering hole, with a grand view and music on an outdoor deck on weekends.

123 Water St., Apalachicola, FL 32320. ☎ **850/653-8139.** Fax 850/653-2018. www.apalachicolariverinn. com. 26 units. $95–$115 double; $125–$160 Jacuzzi suite; $200–$250 2-bedroom suite. AE, DC, DISC, MC, V. Pets accepted in smoking rooms ($10 nightly fee). **Amenities:** Restaurant; bar. *In room:* A/C, TV.

Coombs House Inn ★★★

The most luxurious accommodation here, this large bed-and-breakfast occupies two Victorian homes. The main house was built in 1905 by a lumber baron, and it shows: Polished black cypress paneling lines the entire central hallway and grand parlor. Each of the 10 guest rooms in the main house is tastefully decorated, with lots of Victorian reproductions. The Coombs Suite, with bay windows, a sofa, a four-poster bed, and its own whirlpool, is outstanding. The "Love Bungalow" has its own private entrance. Less grand but still impressive are eight rooms in another restored Victorian, known as the "Coombs House East," half a block away. One of these rooms has a whirlpool tub and bidet, and there's an apartment in the carriage house over there. One room in each house is equipped for guests with disabilities. A major truck route, U.S. 98, runs along the north side of both houses; request a south room to escape the periodic road noise. Guests are treated to complimentary wine receptions on weekends. The complimentary breakfast is hardly just Danish and coffee, but a home cooked extravaganza. All rooms are smoke-free.

80 6th St., Apalachicola, FL 32320. ☎ **850/653-9199.** Fax 850/653-2785. www.coombshouseinn.com. 18 units (all with bathroom). $79–$225 double. Rates include full breakfast. DISC, MC, V. **Amenities:** Access to nearby health club; free use of mountain bikes. *In room:* A/C, TV, dataport, fridge (3 units), hair dryer.

Gibson Inn ★★

Built in 1907 as a seaman's hotel and gorgeously restored, this cupola-topped inn is such a brilliant example of Victorian architecture that it's listed on the National Register of Historic Inns. No two guest rooms are alike (some still have the original sinks in the sleeping areas), but all are richly furnished with period reproductions. Nonguests are welcome to wander upstairs and peek into unoccupied rooms (whose doors are left open). Reservations are advised during summer and spring and fall weekends, and as much as 5 years ahead for the seafood festival in November. Grab a drink from the bar and relax in one of the high-back rockers on the old-fashioned veranda. The dining room serves excellent seafood and is open to all comers, so don't expect this to be private like a bed-and-breakfast; instead, you'll find yourself in a reborn, absolutely charming turn-of-the-20th-century hotel.

51 Ave. C, Apalachicola, FL 32320. ☎ **850/653-2191.** Fax 850/653-3521. www.gibsoninn.com. 31 units (all with bathroom). $90–$100 double; $105–$145 suite. AE, MC, V. **Amenities:** Restaurant; bar. *In room:* A/C, TV.

Rancho Inn

On the western edge of the historic district, this older, Spanish-look motel has been spiffed up by owners Mark and Mary Lynn Rodgers, who keep it clean and well maintained. Although simple when compared to the more expensive properties here, the motel rooms are spacious and comfortable, and all have microwave ovens and fridges. Restaurants are also within walking distance.

240 Hwy. 98 W., Apalachicola, FL 32320. ☎ **850/653-9435.** Fax 850/653-9180. www.ranchoinn.com. 32 units. $55–$150 double. AE, DISC, MC, V. Pets accepted ($6 fee). **Amenities:** Outdoor pool; bicycle rental. *In room:* A/C, TV, dataport, fridge, coffeemaker.

WHERE TO DINE

Townsfolk still plop down on the round stools at the marble-topped counter to order Coca-Colas and milkshakes at the **Old Time Soda Fountain & Lunch-eonette,** 93 Market St. (© 850/653-2606). This 1950s relic was once the town drugstore. It's open Monday through Saturday from 10am to 5pm.

The Boss Oyster ☆ SEAFOOD You've heard about the aphrodisiac proper-ties of Apalachicola oysters. Well, you can see if those properties are real at this rustic, dockside eatery, whose motto is "Shut Up and Shuck." In fact, this is one of the best places in Florida to try the bivalves raw, steamed, or under a dozen toppings ranging from capers to crab meat. They'll even steam three dozen of them and let you do the shucking. Steamed shrimp also are offered, as are deli-cious po'boy sandwiches. Most main courses come from the fryer, so consider this joint a great local experience, not fine dining. Sit at picnic tables inside, on a screened porch, or out on the dock.

125 Water St. (between aves. C and D). © 850/653-9364. Main courses $17–$22; oysters $4.50–$14; sand-wiches and baskets $7–$10. AE, DC, DISC, MC, V. Apr–Sept Sun–Thurs 11:30am–10pm, Fri–Sat 11:30am–11pm; Oct–Mar Sun–Thurs 11:30am–9pm, Fri–Sat 11:30am–10pm.

Chef Eddie's Magnolia Grill ☆☆☆ CONTINENTAL/CAJUN One of the top places to dine in Northwest Florida, Boston-bred chef-owner Eddie Cass's pleasant, homey restaurant offers nightly specials ranging from classic French rack of lamb and beef Wellington to fresh local seafood with New Orleans–style sauces. You will long remember Eddie's mahimahi Pontchartrain with cream and artichoke hearts. The snapper butter pecan and black-bean grouper are two other memorable dishes. Start with a bowl of spicy seafood gumbo, a consistent hit during the Florida Seafood Festival. No smoking inside.

99 11th St. (between aves. E and F). © 850/653-8000. www.chefeddiesmagnoliagrill.com. Reservations recommended. Main courses $12–$28. MC, V. Mon–Sat 6–9:30pm.

The Owl Cafe ☆☆ SEAFOOD Ensconced on the first floor of a two-story clapboard commercial building in the heart of downtown, this sophisticated restaurant ranks only behind Chef Eddie's Magnolia Grill as having the best cui-sine in town. Go for the nightly fresh seafood specials or opt for the terrific grouper with garlic, capers, and artichokes. Now paneled in rich wood, the walls are adorned with the works of noted local photographer Richard Bickel.

15 Ave. D (at Commerce St.). © 850/653-9888. Reservations recommended. Main courses $12–$25. MC, V. Mon–Sat 11:30am–3pm and 5:30–10pm.

Tamara's Cafe Floridita FLORIBBEAN/LATIN AMERICAN Tamara Saurez's store-front cafe offers a change of pace. Before settling in Apalachicola, Tamara was a TV producer in Venezuela, and her black-bean soup comes directly from the old country. Otherwise, you'll find Latino spices accentuating Floribbean fare, such as a creamy jalapeño sauce putting a little fire into pecan-encrusted grouper, and homemade mango chutney sweetening grouper stuffed with crab. Her paella is a winner, too.

17 Ave. E (at Commerce St.). © 850/653-4111. Reservations recommended. Main courses $12–$24. MC, V. Open daily 11am–10pm

APALACHICOLA AFTER DARK

Nocturnal diversions are scarce in this small town, but you can catch summer-stock performances of plays like *Same Time Next Year* in the lovingly restored, 1912-vintage **Dixie Theatre,** 21 Ave. D (© 850/653-3200). Tickets range from $10 to $25, depending on the show.

Locals like to have their after-work drinks in the fine old bar at the **Gibson Inn** and then hit the **Roseate Spoonbill Lounge,** in the Apalachicola River Inn (see "Where to Stay," above), where bands play on weekend evenings.

5 Tallahassee

163 miles W of Jacksonville, 191 miles E of Pensacola, 250 miles NW of Orlando

As a University of Miami alum, I was practically taught to hate Tallahassee, just because it's the home of the Miami Hurricanes' biggest rivals—Florida State University's Seminoles (or 'Noles as locals refer to them). Because I couldn't care less about football, I just chalked Tallahassee up to being the state capitol, and, later in life, command central for that pesky 2000 election bug known as the chad. Boy, was I wrong. It's not just about football and hanging chads at all. There's tons of charm and non-voting history here, too.

Tallahassee was selected as Florida's capital in 1823 because it was halfway between St. Augustine and Pensacola, then the state's major cities. That location puts it almost in Georgia, and, in fact, Tallahassee has more in common with Macon than with Miami. There's as much Old South ambience here as anywhere else you're likely to visit in Florida. You'll find lovingly restored 19th-century homes and buildings, including the 1845 Old Capitol. They all sit among so many towering pines and sprawling live oaks that you'll think you're in an enormous forest. The trees form virtual tunnels along Tallahassee's five official Canopy Roads, which are lined with historic plantations, ancient Native-American settlement sites and mounds, gorgeous gardens, quiet parks with picnic areas, and beautiful lakes and streams. And the nearby Apalachicola National Forest is a virtual gold mine of outdoor pursuits.

While tradition and history are important here, you'll also find the modern era, beginning with the New Capitol Building towering 22 stories over downtown. Usually sleepy Tallahassee takes on a very lively persona when the legislature is in session and when the football teams of Florida State University and Florida A&M University take to the gridiron.

If you're inclined to give your credit cards a workout, the nearby town of Havana is Florida's antiquing capital.

ESSENTIALS

GETTING THERE   AirTran (© 800/AIR-TRAN), **Delta** (© 800/221-1212), **Northwest** (© 800/225-2525), and **US Airways** (© 800/428-4322) serve **Tallahassee Regional Airport** (© **850/891-7802;** http://talgov.com/citytlh/aviation), 10 miles southwest of downtown on Southeast Capital Circle.

Alamo (© 800/327-9633), **Avis** (© 800/331-1212), **Budget** (© 800/527-0700), **Hertz** (© 800/654-3131), and **National** (© 800/CAR-RENT) have airport sites; **Dollar** (© 800/800-4000), **Enterprise** (© 800/325-8007), and **Thrifty** (© 800/367-2277) are nearby.

You can take a taxi to downtown for about $15.

Amtrak's transcontinental train the Sunset Limited stops in Tallahassee at 918½ Railroad Ave. (© **800/872-7245;** www.amtrak.com).

VISITOR INFORMATION   For information in advance of your arrival, contact the **Tallahassee Area Convention and Visitors Bureau,** 200 W. College Ave. (P.O. Box 1369), Tallahassee, FL 32302 (© **800/628-2866** or 850/413-9200; fax 850/487-4621; www.seetallahassee.com). The bureau's excellent quarterly visitor's guide has descriptions (including hours and admission fees) of just about everything going on here.

Go to the **Tallahassee Area Visitor Information Center,** 106 E. Jefferson St. across from the capitol (℃ **850/413-9200**), for free street and public-transportation maps, brochures, and pamphlets outlining tours of the historic districts and the Canopy Roads. The center is open Monday through Friday from 8am to 5pm, Saturday from 9am to noon.

For statewide information, a **Florida Welcome Center** is in the west foyer of the New Capitol Building (see below).

GETTING AROUND　Operated by TALTRAN, the city's public-transportation agency (℃ **850/891-5200;** www.state.fl.us/citytlh/taltran), the free **Old Town Trolley** is the best way to see the sights of historic downtown Tallahassee. You can get on or off at any point between Adams Street Commons, at the corner of Jefferson and Adams streets, and the Governor's Mansion (see the exact route on the "Downtown Tallahassee" map). The trolley runs Monday through Friday every 20 minutes between 7am and 6:30pm.

TALTRAN also provides city bus service from its downtown terminal at Tennessee and Adams streets ($1 adults, 50¢ kids 12 and under and seniors). Both the ticket booths there and at the Tallahassee Area Visitor Information Center have route maps and schedules.

For taxi service, call **Yellow Cab** (℃ **850/580-8080**) or **City Taxi** (℃ **850/ 562-4222**). Fares are $1.75 at flag fall, plus $1.50 per mile.

TIME　Tallahassee is in the Eastern Time zone, like Orlando, Miami, and Apalachicola. It's 1 hour ahead of the rest of the Panhandle.

EXPLORING THE CITY
THE CAPITOL COMPLEX

Florida's capitol complex, on South Monroe Street at Apalachee Parkway, dominates the downtown area and should be your first stop after the Tallahassee Area Visitor Information Center, just across Jefferson Street.

The **New Capitol Building** (℃ **850/488-6167**), a $43 million skyscraper, was built in 1977 to replace the 1845-vintage Old Capitol. State legislators meet here for at least 60 days, usually beginning in March. The chambers of the house and the senate have public viewing galleries. For a spectacular view, take the elevators to the 22nd-floor **observatory,** where, on a clear day, you can see all the way to the Gulf of Mexico. You can also view works by Florida artists while up there. The New Capitol is open Monday through Friday from 8am to 5pm.

Directly in front of the skyscraper is the strikingly white **Old Capitol** ✦ (℃ **850/487-1902;** http://dhr.dos.state.fl.us/museum/m_sites.html). With its majestic dome, this "Pearl of Capitol Hill" has been restored to its original beauty. An eight-room exhibit portrays Florida's political history. Turn-of-the-20th-century furnishings, cotton gins, and other artifacts are also of interest. The Old Capitol is open Monday through Friday from 9am to 4:30pm, Saturday from 10am to 4:30pm, and Sunday and holidays from noon to 4:30pm. Admission is free to the old and the new capitols.

The twin granite towers of the **Vietnam Veterans Memorial,** honoring Florida's Vietnam vets, are across Monroe Street from the Old Capitol. Next to it, facing Apalachee Parkway, the **Union Bank Museum** (℃ **850/561-2603**) is housed in Florida's oldest-surviving bank building. For a while, it was the Freedman's Savings and Trust Company, which served emancipated slaves. Now part of FAMU's Black Archives Research Center, it now houses a small but interesting collection of artifacts and documents reflecting black history and culture that are definitely worth a brief visit. Admission is free. Open Monday through Friday from 9am to 4pm.

Downtown Tallahassee

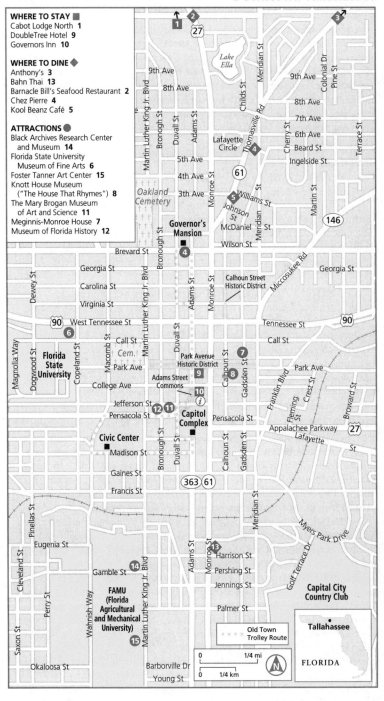

WHERE TO STAY ■
Cabot Lodge North **1**
DoubleTree Hotel **9**
Governors Inn **10**

WHERE TO DINE ◆
Anthony's **3**
Bahn Thai **13**
Barnacle Bill's Seafood Restaurant **2**
Chez Pierre **4**
Kool Beanz Café **5**

ATTRACTIONS ●
Black Archives Research Center
  and Museum **14**
Florida State University
  Museum of Fine Arts **6**
Foster Tanner Art Center **15**
Knott House Museum
  ("The House That Rhymes") **8**
The Mary Brogan Museum
  of Art and Science **11**
Meginnis-Monroe House **7**
Museum of Florida History **12**

The Old Town Trolley will take you to the lovely Georgian-style **Governor's Mansion,** north of the capitol at Adams and Brevard streets (© **850/488-4661**). Enhanced by a portico patterned after Andrew Jackson's columned antebellum home in Tennessee, the Hermitage, and surrounded by giant magnolia trees and landscaped lawns, the mansion is furnished with 18th- and 19th-century antiques and collectibles. Tours are given when the legislature is in session, usually beginning in March. Call for schedules and reservations.

Located adjacent to the Governor's Mansion, **The Grove** was home to Ellen Call Long, known as "The Tallahassee Girl," the first child born after Tallahassee was settled.

HISTORIC DISTRICTS

Although modern buildings have made inroads into the downtown area, Tallahassee makes an ongoing effort to preserve its historic homes and buildings.

Many of them are concentrated in three historic districts within an easy walk north of the capitol complex. The information center in the New Capitol (see "Essentials," above) distributes free brochures of walking tours that cover the three areas. Taken together, the tours are about 4 miles long and should take half a day. Most interesting is the Park Avenue District, 3 blocks north of the capitol complex, which you can see in about 1 hour.

ADAMS STREET COMMONS   This 1-block-long winding brick and landscaped area along Adams Street begins on the north side of the capitol complex (it's between Jefferson St. and College Ave.) and retains an old-fashioned town-square atmosphere. Restored buildings include the Governor's Club, a 1900s Masonic lodge, and Gallie's Hall, where Florida's first five African-American college students received their Florida A&M University diplomas in 1892. Restaurants, shops, and Gallie Alley are also here. Adams Street crosses Park Avenue 3 blocks north of the capitol complex. This is a good place for lunch at one of several cafes that cater to downtown office workers.

PARK AVENUE HISTORIC DISTRICT   The 7 blocks of Park Avenue between Martin Luther King Jr. Boulevard and North Meridian Street are a lovely promenade of beautiful trees, gardens, and outstanding old mansions. This broad avenue, with a shady median strip lined with moss-bearded live oaks, was originally named 200 Foot Street and then McCarty Street, but was later renamed Park Avenue to satisfy a snobbish Anglophile society matron who didn't want an Irish name imprinted on her son's wedding invitations.

Several Park Avenue historic homes are open to the public, including the **Knott House Museum,** at Calhoun Street (see "Museums, Galleries & Archaeological Sites," below). **The Columns,** at Duval Street, was built in the 1830s and is the city's oldest surviving building (it's now the home of the Tallahassee Chamber of Commerce). **The First Presbyterian Church,** at Adams Street, built in 1838, is the city's oldest church and has been an important African-American historic site since slaves were welcome to worship here without their masters' consent. **The Walker Library,** between Monroe and Calhoun streets, was one of Florida's first libraries, dating from 1903 (it's home to Springtime Tallahassee, which is the city's top special event). Just north of Park Avenue on Gadsden Street, the **Meginnis-Monroe House** contains the Lemoyne Art Gallery (see "Museums, Galleries & Archaeological Sites," below).

At Martin Luther King Jr. Boulevard, the adjacent **Old City Cemetery** and **Episcopal Cemetery** contain the graves of Prince Achille Murat, Napoleon's nephew, and Princess Catherine Murat, his wife and George Washington's grand-niece. Also buried here are two governors and numerous Confederate and Union soldiers who died at the Battle of Natural Bridge during the Civil War. The cemeteries are important to African-American history since a number of slaves and the first black Florida A&M graduates are interred here. The visitor information center in the New Capitol has a cemetery walking-tour brochure.

CALHOUN STREET HISTORIC DISTRICT The 3 blocks of Calhoun Street between Tennessee and Georgia streets, and running east on Virginia Street to Leon High School, sport elaborate homes built by prominent citizens between 1830 and 1880. A highlight here is the **Brokaw-McDougall House,** in front of Leon High School at the eastern end of Virginia Street, which was built in 1856.

MUSEUMS, GALLERIES & ARCHAEOLOGICAL SITES

Black Archives Research Center and Museum ⟨⚑⟩ Housed in the columned library built by Andrew Carnegie in 1908, and located on the grounds of the Florida Agricultural and Mechanical University (FAMU), this fascinating research center and museum displays one of the nation's most extensive collections of African-American artifacts, as well as such treasures as a 500-piece Ethiopian cross collection. The archives contain one of the world's largest collections on African-American history. Visitors can listen to tapes of gospel music and of elderly people reminiscing about the past. FAMU was founded in 1887, primarily as a black institution. Today it's acclaimed for its business, engineering, and pharmacy schools.

Martin Luther King Jr. Blvd. and Gamble St., on the Florida A&M University campus. 🕐 850/599-3020. www.famu.edu. Free admission. Mon–Fri 9am–4pm. Closed major holidays. Parking lot next to building.

Florida State University Museum of Fine Arts ⟨⚑⟩ This permanent, 4,000-piece collection features 16th-century Dutch paintings, 20th-century American paintings, Japanese prints, pre-Colombian artifacts, and much more. Touring exhibits are displayed every few weeks.

250 Fine Arts Building, Copeland and Call sts. (on the FSU campus). 🕐 850/644-6836. www.mofa.fsu.edu. Free admission. Sept–Apr Mon–Fri 9am–4pm, Sat–Sun 1–4pm (Sept–Apr only). Closed Aug.

Foster Tanner Art Center The focus in this gallery is on works by local, national, and international African-American artists, with a wide variety of paintings, sculptures, and more.

Florida A&M University (between Osceola and Gamble sts., off Martin Luther King Jr. Blvd.). 🕐 850/599-3161. www.famu.edu. Free admission. Mon–Fri 9am–5pm.

Knott House Museum ("The House That Rhymes") ⟨⚑⚑⟩ Adorned by a columned portico, this stately mansion was constructed in 1843, probably by a free black builder named George Proctor. Florida's first reading of the Emancipation Proclamation took place here in 1865. In 1928 it was purchased by politician William Knott, whose wife, Louella, wrote eccentric (read: kooky) rhymes about the house and its elegant Victorian furnishings, including the nation's largest collection of 19th-century gilt-framed mirrors, and about social, economic, and political events of the era. Attached by satin ribbons to tables, chairs, and lamps, her poems are the museum's most unusual feature. The house is in the Park Avenue Historic District and is listed in the National Register of Historic Places. It's preserved as it looked in 1928, when the Knott family left it and all of its contents to the city (it's now administered by the Museum of Florida History). The museum gift shop carries Victorian greeting cards, paper dolls, tin toy replicas, reprints of historic newspapers, and other nostalgic items.

301 E. Park Ave. (at Calhoun St.). ℂ 850/922-2459. http://dhr.dos.state.fl.us/museum/m_sites.html. Free admission. Wed–Fri 1–4pm; Sat 10am–4pm. 1-hr. tours depart on the hour.

The Mary Brogan Museum of Art and Science *(Kids)* This museum's mission statement: ". . . to stimulate interest in and understanding of the visual arts, sciences, mathematics, and technology through experiences that educate and inspire" pretty much says it all. Associated with the Smithsonian Institution, the museum has changing exhibitions, educational programs, and lectures as well as permanent science-museum-y exhibits.

350 S. Duval St. (at Pensacola St.). ℂ 850/513-0700. www.thebrogan.org. Admission $6 adults, $3.50 students 3–17, Senior Citizens 60 and over, college students, and military with ID; free for children under 2.

Meginnis-Monroe House ★★ This restored 1852 antebellum home is listed on the National Register of Historic Places and is a lovely setting for fine art. The home's **Lemoyne Art Gallery** is named in honor of Jacques LeMoyne, a member of a French expedition to Florida in 1564. Commissioned to depict the natives' dwellings and map the seacoast, LeMoyne was the first European artist known to have visited North America. Exhibits here include permanent displays by local artists, traveling exhibits, sculpture, pottery, and photography—everything from the traditional to the avant-garde. The gardens, with an old-fashioned gazebo, are spectacular during the Christmas holiday season. Programs of classical music are combined with visual arts during the year; check in advance for the current schedule.

125 N. Gadsden St. (between Park Ave. and Call St.). ℂ 850/222-8800. www.lemoyne.org. Admission $1, free Sun and every day for children 12 and under. Tues–Sat 10am–5pm; Sun 1–5pm. Closed holidays.

Mission San Luís de Apalachee ★ A Spanish Franciscan mission named San Luís was set up in 1656 on this hilltop, already a principal village of the Apalachee Indians. From then until 1704, it served as the capital of a chain of Spanish missions in Northwest Florida. The mission complex included a tribal council house, a Franciscan church, a Spanish fort, and residential areas. Based on extensive archaeological and historical research, the council house and the 10-by-50-foot thatch-roofed church have been reconstructed. They are both open to the public. So is a reconstruction of the 50-by-110-foot thatch-roof mission church. Interpretive markers are located across the 60-acre site, and self-guided tour brochures are available at the visitor center. Call for a schedule of ranger-led guided tours on weekends.

2021 Mission Rd. (between W. Tennessee and Tharpe sts.). ℂ 850/487-3711. http://dhr.dos.state.fl.us/bar/san_luis. Free admission. Tues–Sun 10am–4pm. Closed Thanksgiving, Christmas. From downtown, take Tennessee St. (U.S. 90) west to entrance on right past Ocala St.

Museum of Florida History ★ An 11-foot-tall mastodon greets you at this state history museum, where you look back 12,000 years to the first Native Americans to live in Florida (mastodons were very much alive back then). Ancient artifacts from Native American tribes are exhibited, plus such relics from Florida's past as a reconstructed steamboat and treasures from 16th- and 17th-century sunken Spanish galleons. Inquire about guided tours and special exhibits. Visitor parking is available in the garage around the corner on St. Augustine Street between Bronough and Duvall streets.

Lower level of R. A. Gray Building, 500 S. Bronough St. (at Pensacola St.). ℂ 850/245-6400. http://dhr.dos.state.fl.us/museum. Free admission (suggested donation $3 adults, $1 children). Mon–Fri 9am–4:30pm; Sat 10am–4:30pm; Sun and holidays noon–4:30pm. Closed Thanksgiving, Christmas.

PARKS & NATURE PRESERVES

Maclay State Gardens ★★   In 1923, New York financier Alfred B. Maclay and his wife, Louise, began planting the floral wonderland that surrounded their winter home on Lake Hall, on Tallahassee's northeastern outskirts. After her husband's death in 1944, Louise continued his dream of an ornamental garden to delight the public. In 1953, the land was bequeathed to the state of Florida. The more than 300 acres of flowers feature at least 200 varieties; 28 acres are devoted exclusively to azaleas and camellias. The surrounding park offers nature trails, canoe rentals, boating, picnicking, swimming, and fishing. The high blooming season is January through April, with the peak about mid-March. Beyond the house and gardens, the state park also includes Lake Overstreet, around which wind 5½ miles of hiking, biking, and horseback-riding trails, making this a major venue for those outdoor activities.

3540 Thomasville Rd. (U.S. 319, north of I-10). © 850/487-4556. www.ssnow.com/maclay. Admission to park $4 per vehicle with up to 8 passengers, $1 for pedestrians and cyclists. May–Dec free admission to gardens; Jan–Apr $4 adults, $2 children under 12. Park open daily 8am–sunset. Gardens daily 9am–5pm. Maclay House daily 9am–5pm Jan–Apr; closed May–Dec.

TRAVELING THE CANOPY ROADS

Graced by canopies of live oaks draped with Spanish moss, the St. Augustine, Miccousukee, Meridian, Old Bainbridge, and Centerville roads are the five official Canopy Roads leading out of Tallahassee. Driving is slow on these winding, two-lane country roads (the locals only reluctantly are turning some limited sections of them into four-lane highways); some of them are canopied for as much as 20 miles. Take along a picnic lunch, since there are few places to buy a meal along these tranquil byways.

The visitor information center in the New Capitol (p. 630) provides a useful driving guide map of the Canopy Roads and Leon County's country lanes.

If you have time for only one, take **Old Bainbridge Road,** which leads to the Lake Jackson Mounds State Archaeological Site in the northwest suburbs and then on to Havana, Florida's antiquing capital (see "Shopping," below).

SHOPPING

Antiques hounds flock to the little village of **Havana** ★★, 12 miles northwest of I-10 on U.S. 27. Havana used to make its living growing shade tobacco (the outer wrapper on cigars). When that industry fizzled in the 1960s, the town went with it. Things turned around 20 years later, however, when Havana began opening art galleries and antiques, handcrafts, and collectibles shops. Today, these are housed in lovingly restored, turn-of-the-20th-century brick buildings along Havana's commercial streets. Just drive into town on Main Street (U.S. 27), turn left on 7th Avenue, find a parking place, and start browsing. You'll have plenty of company on weekends.

⸢ Fun Fact High Flying

Florida State University's **Flying High Circus** (© 800/757-2146 or 850/644-6500; www.fsu.edu/~circus) calls itself the "Greatest Collegiate Show on Earth" and that's no small boast. It's arguably the grandest college circus in the country. Look for the big top and watch rehearsals during March, then enjoy performances (juggling, hand balancing, bicycle, and trapeze) the first 2 weekends in April ($5–$12).

Bradley's Country Store, about 8 miles north of I-10 on Centerville Road (© **850/893-1647;** www.bradleyscountrystore.com), sells more than 80,000 pounds of homemade sausage a year, both over the counter and from mail orders. You can also buy coarse-ground grits, country-milled corn meal, hogshead cheese, liver pudding, cracklings, and specially cured hams here. This friendly store, which is on the National Register of Historic Places, is also a sightseeing attraction with self-guided tours. It's open Monday through Friday from 8am to 6pm, Saturday from 8am to 5pm.

OUTDOOR ACTIVITIES & SPECTATOR SPORTS

BIKING & IN-LINE SKATING The 16-mile **Tallahassee–St. Marks Historic Railroad Trail State Park** (© **850/922-6007;** www.floridastateparks.org/stmarkstrail) is the city's most popular bike route. Constructed with the financial assistance of wealthy Panhandle cotton-plantation owners and merchants, this was Florida's oldest railroad, functioning from 1837 to 1984. Cotton and other products were transported from Tallahassee to St. Marks for shipment to other cities. In recent years, the tracks were removed and 16 miles of the historic trail were improved for joggers, hikers, bicyclists, and horseback riders. A paved parking lot is at the north entrance, on Woodville Highway (Fla. 363), just south of Southeast Capital Circle. See "Side Trips from Tallahassee," beginning on p. 640, for more about what you can see in the St. Marks area.

The **Apalachicola National Forest** also has extensive mountain-biking trails (p. 642), and there are 5½ miles of trails at **Maclay State Gardens** (see "Parks & Nature Preserves," above).

GOLF Play golf at outstanding Hilaman Park, 2737 Blair Stone Rd., where the **Hilaman Park Municipal Golf Course** features 18 holes (par 72), a driving range, racquetball and squash courts, and a swimming pool. Rental equipment is available at the club, and there's a restaurant, too (© **850/891-3935** for information and fees). Compared with most courses in Florida, greens fees are a steal: about $27 on weekdays, $32 on weekends, including cart (they're about $15 and $21, respectively, if you walk). The park also includes the recently renovated **Jake Gaither Municipal Golf Course,** at Bragg and Pasco streets (© **850/891-3942**), with a nine-hole, par-35 fairway and a pro shop. Call for fees.

The leading golf course is at the **Killearn Country Club and Inn** (© **800/476-4101** or 850/893-2186; www.killearncc.com), which once hosted the Sprint Classic. Moss-draped oaks enhance the beautiful 27-hole championship course, which is for members with reciprocal privileges only. Call for fees.

For course information online, go to www.golf.com and www.floridagolfing.com, or call the **Florida Sports Foundation** (© **850/488-8347**) or **Teebone Golfing** (© **866/833-2663**).

SPECTATOR SPORTS Tallahassee succumbs to football frenzy whenever the perennially powerful Seminoles of **Florida State University (FSU)** take to the gridiron. Call © **888/378-6653** or 850/644-1830 (www.seminoles.com) well in advance for tickets. Even when the Seminoles play on the road, everything except Tallahassee's many sports bars comes to a stop while fans watch the games on TV.

Semi-Tough: **The Prequel**

Burt Reynolds played defensive back for Florida State University's football team in 1957 and is still an avid 'Noles booster.

The **Florida A&M University (FAMU)** Rattlers are cheered on by the school's high-stepping, world-famous Marching 100 Band. Call ✆ **850/ 599-3230** or check the website at www.famu.edu/athletics for FAMU schedules and tickets.

Both FSU and FAMU have seasonal basketball, baseball, tennis, and track schedules. Call the numbers above for information.

WHERE TO STAY

There is no high or low season here, but every hotel and motel for miles around is completely booked during FSU and FAMU football weekends from September to November, at graduation in May, and, to a far lesser degree, weekdays during the 60-day legislative session that begins in March. Reserve well in advance or you may have to stay 60 miles or more from the city. For the schedules, call FSU or FAMU (see "Spectator Sports," above).

Most hotels are concentrated in three areas: downtown Tallahassee, north of downtown along North Monroe Street at exit 199 off I-10 (where you'll find most chains), and along Apalachee Parkway east of downtown.

Tax on all hotel and campground bills is 10% in Leon County.

Cabot Lodge North *Value* It looks like a random motel, really, but look closer. There's charm to be found here. A clapboard plantation-style house with a tin roof and a partially screened wraparound porch provides Southern country charm to distinguish this friendly motel from its nearby competitors. Guests can relax in straight-back rockers on the porch or on comfy sofas and easy chairs by a fireplace in the living room. Although the guest rooms in the two-story motel buildings out back don't hold up their end of the atmosphere factor, they're still quite satisfactory at these rates, and they give quick access to the outdoor swimming pool. Guests can also enjoy a complimentary continental breakfast buffet and evening cocktails.

2735 N. Monroe St., Tallahassee, FL 32303. ✆ **800/223-1964** or 850/386-8880. Fax 850/386-4254. www.cabotlodge.com. 160 units. $66–$88 double. Rates include continental breakfast, evening reception, and local phone calls. AE, DC, DISC, MC, V. **Amenities:** Outdoor pool; access to nearby health club; laundry service. *In room:* A/C, TV, dataport, hair dryer (king-size bedrooms only).

DoubleTree Hotel Most of the media covering the Bush-Gore 2000 election case before the Florida Supreme Court stayed at this 16-story hotel, one of the tallest buildings in town. The best thing about it is the location, just 2 blocks north of the Capitol Building at Park Avenue, and the views from the spacious rooms, especially those on the upper floors. It's usually booked solid by politicians and lobbyists during legislative sessions from March to May.

101 S. Adams St., Tallahassee, FL 32301. ✆ **800/222-8733** or 850/224-5000. Fax 850/513-9516. 243 units. $89–$169 double. AE, DC, DISC, MC, V. **Amenities:** Restaurant; bar; outdoor pool; exercise room; limited room service; laundry service; concierge-level rooms. *In room:* A/C, TV, dataport, coffeemaker, hair dryer, iron.

Governors Inn *★★* This is the place for legislators, lobbyists, groupies, and Southern gentry to stay, an elegantly furnished inn just half a block north of the Old Capitol in the Adams Street Commons historic district. It's very old school Washington, D.C. The building was once a livery stable, and part of its original architecture has been preserved, including the impressive beams. The guest rooms are distinctive, with four-poster beds, black-oak writing desks, rock-maple armoires, and antique accouterments. Of the suites, each one named for a Florida governor, one has a whirlpool bathtub; another has a loft bedroom with wood-burning fireplace. Complimentary continental breakfast and afternoon cocktails are presented in the pine-paneled Florida Room, and a restaurant across the street

---

Fun Fact   Count Them Out

Demand for hotel rooms during the weekends of Florida State University
football games is so great that the high-powered lawyers representing
then–Vice President Gore and then–Texas Governor George W. Bush had
to vacate their rooms when the University of Florida Gators came to play
the 'Noles during the 2000 presidential election dispute.

---

provides limited room service. Hang out in the bar area and eavesdrop on amusing political banter. The staff here is super friendly and helpful.

209 S. Adams St., Tallahassee, FL 32301. ℂ 800/342-7717 in Florida, or 850/681-6855. Fax 850/222-3105.
www.thegovinn.com. 40 units. $149–$159 double; $169–$229 suite. Rates include continental breakfast and
evening cocktails. AE, DC, DISC, MC, V. **Amenities:** Access to nearby health club; limited room service; laundry service. *In room:* A/C, TV, dataport.

Quality Inn & Suites *Value*   In contrast to most Quality Inns, this property
loses some of the motel, chain-gang feel in favor of a classy, marble-lined lobby
and guest rooms furnished with sofas and reclining wing chairs. A complimentary continental breakfast is served in a lounge with views of the inn's swimming
pool, and guests can partake of a free wine bar Monday through Thursday
evenings. A nearby restaurant will deliver food, and several fast-food and family-
style restaurants are within a short walk.

2020 Apalachee Pkwy., Tallahassee, FL 32301. ℂ 800/228-5151 or 850/877-4437. Fax 850/878-9964. www.
qualityinn.com. 100 units. $79 double; $129 suite. Rates include full breakfast, evening drinks, and local phone
calls. AE, DC, DISC, MC, V. **Amenities:** Outdoor pool; access to nearby health club; Jacuzzi; business center;
limited room service; laundry service. *In room:* A/C, TV, dataport, fridge, coffeemaker, hair dryer, iron, safe.

WHERE TO DINE

Numerous budget-priced fast-food and family chain restaurants lie along
Apalachee Parkway and North Monroe Street.

Anthony's ☆ SOUTHERN ITALIAN   Locals flock to Dick Anthony's elegantly relaxed trattoria, which supplies them with the city's best Italian cuisine.
Among his specialties is *pesce Venezia,* spinach fettuccine tossed in a cream sauce
with scallops, crab, and fish. Chicken piccata and chicken San Marino are also
favorites, and Dick's thick, juicy steaks are always popular with beef eaters. A
wall-size wine cupboard features choices from Italy and the United States by the
bottle or glass. Espresso pie leads the dessert menu.

1950 Thomasville Rd., at Bradford Rd. in the Betton Place Shops. ℂ 850/224-1447. Reservations recommended. Main courses $12–$23. AE, DC, DISC, MC, V. Daily 5–9pm.

Bahn Thai THAI/CANTONESE   Lamoi (Sue) Snyder and progeny have
been serving the spicy cuisine of her native Thailand at this store front since
1979. In deference to local Southerners, who may never have sampled anything
spicier than cheese grits, much of her menu is devoted to mild Cantonese-style
Chinese dishes. More adventurous diners, however, flock here to order such
authentic tongue-burners as *yon voon-sen,* a combination of shrimp, chicken,
bean threads, onions, lemon grass, ground peanuts, and the obligatory chile
peppers. Sue's specialty is her deliciously sweet, slightly gingered version of
Penang curry. You can ask her to turn down the heat in her other Thai dishes.
Come at lunch and sample it all from the all-you-can-eat buffet—a real bargain.

1319 S. Monroe St. (between Oakland Ave. and Harrison St.). ℂ **850/224-4765**. Main courses $6–$15. Lunch buffet $7. Dinner buffet $11. DISC, MC, V. Mon–Thurs 11am–2:30pm and 5–10pm; Fri 11am–2:30pm and 5–10:30pm; Sat 5–10:30pm.

Barnacle Bill's Seafood Restaurant SEAFOOD   There's always plenty of action at this noisy, very casual spot, a favorite of the downtown crowd, including journalists, bureaucrats, and politicians. Freshly shucked Apalachicola oysters are the stars at the enormous tile-topped raw bar in the middle of the room, but the menu offers a mélange of seafood to please the palates of the singles, couples, and families who flock here. The cooking is simple and usually done by Florida State University students working part-time jobs. Best bets are charcoal-grilled mahimahi, tuna, amberjack, and grouper. For a smoked sensation, try the mahimahi and amberjack cured on the premises. During nice weather, guests can sit at outdoor tables under a lean-to tent. A downstairs bar serves the regular seafood items plus sushi, deli sandwiches, and salads.

1830 N. Monroe St. (north of Tharpe St.). ℂ **850/385-8734**. www.barnaclebills.com. Main courses $8–$17 (most $10–$12); sandwiches and salads $5–$9. AE, DC, DISC, MC, V. Sun–Thurs 11am–11pm; Fri–Sat 11am–midnight.

Chez Pierre ⋆⋆ TRADITIONAL FRENCH   You become an instant Francophile in Florida at this chic restaurant in a beautifully restored 1920s brick home. French-born chef Eric Favier and his American wife and partner, Karen Cooley, offer traditional French cuisine either inside the house—where the walls are adorned with changing, for-sale works by local artists—or outside on a large deck nearly shaded by live oaks draped with Spanish moss. Opening to the deck, a bistro-style bar provides a light-fare menu between lunch and dinner. Chez Pierre offers daily specials to take advantage of fresh produce. Among the winners are rack of lamb, a version of Provençal-style ratatouille, and crab cakes with a luscious mustard and thyme demi-glacé. French table wines are moderately priced, and California house wines are also served. Live music regularly accompanies dining. No smoking except on the front porch, where stogies and brandy can be enjoyed while lounging in wicker chairs. Book as early as possible for Bastille Day (July 14), which sees a grand fete here.

1215 Thomasville Rd. (at 6th Ave.). ℂ **850/222-0936**. www.chezpierre.com. Reservations recommended. Main courses $15–$29. AE, DC, DISC, MC, V. Mon–Sat 11am–10pm; Sun 11am–2:30pm and 6–9pm.

Kool Beanz Cafe ⋆⋆ ECLECTIC   The coolest cafe in town, this noisy emporium of trendy cooking draws lots of patrons in their late 20s and early 30s who appreciate exciting blends of flavors. The joint is dimly lit but painted in bright pastels from the Caribbean. You'll find many island-style items on the constantly changing menu, including Jamaican jerk grouper served with black beans, rice, and a sweet tropical-fruit relish. You may want to get here early because more-inventive items like the seared but rare tuna crusted with spice and served with a terrific roasted-peanut sauce will sell out early, as will the curried lamb shank and the pork tenderloin marinated with orange molasses.

921 Thomasville Rd. (at Williams St.). ℂ **850/224-2466**. Main courses $13–$18. AE, DISC, MC, V. Mon–Fri 11am–2:30pm and 5:30–10pm; Sat 5:30–10pm.

TALLAHASSEE AFTER DARK

Check the "Limelight" section of Friday's *Tallahassee Democrat* (www.tallahassee democrat.com) for weekend entertainment listings.

As a college town, Tallahassee has numerous pubs and nightclubs with live dance music, not to mention a multitude of sports bars. Pick up a copy of ***Break*** and other entertainment tabloids at **Barnacle Bill's Seafood Restaurant** or other entertainment venues.

One of the best bars in town is **Bullwinkle's Saloon,** 620 W. Tennessee St. (© **850/224-0651**), a capital institution with a laid back vibe and even a Thirsty Moose Club in which members never pay a cover and drink free every Wednesday and Friday. For live music, **Floyd's Music Store,** 666 W. Tennessee St. (© **850/222-3506**), features local and national bands and, for the daring, a mosh pit that fills up quickly, so get there early. West Tennessee Street is where you'll find most of the happening bars in town.

The major performing-arts venue is the **Tallahassee–Leon County Civic Center,** 505 W. Pensacola St. (© **800/322-3602** or 850/222-0400; www.tlccc. org), which features a Broadway series, concerts, and sporting events including Florida State University (FSU) collegiate basketball games. Special concerts are presented by the **Tallahassee Symphony Orchestra** (www.tsolive.org) at FSU Ruby Diamond Auditorium, at College Avenue and Copeland Street (© **850/ 224-0461**). **The FSU Mainstage/School of Theatre,** at the Fine Arts Building on Call and Copeland streets (© **850/644-6500**), presents excellent productions from classic dramas to comedies.

SIDE TRIPS FROM TALLAHASSEE

The following excursions are generally on the way to Apalachicola, so if you're headed that way, plan to make a detour or two.

WAKULLA SPRINGS 🦀🦀

The world's largest and deepest freshwater spring is 15 miles south of Tallahassee in the 2,860-acre **Edward W. Ball Wakulla Springs State Park** 🦀🦀, on Fla. 267 just east of its junction with Fla. 61. Ball, a financier who administered the du Pont estate, turned the springs and the moss-draped surrounding forest into a preservation area. Divers have mapped an underwater cave system extending more than 6,000 feet back from the spring's mouth. Wakulla has been known to dispense an amazing 14,325 gallons of water per second at certain times. Mastodon bones, including those of Herman, now in Tallahassee's Museum of Florida History, were found in the caves. Also, the 1930s *Tarzan* movies starring Johnny Weissmuller were filmed here.

A free 10-minute orientation movie is offered at the park's theater at the waterfront. You can hike or bike along the nature trails, and swimming is allowed, but only in designated areas. *Note:* It's important to observe swimming rules here since alligators are present.

If the spring water is clear enough, 30-minute glass-bottom–boat sightseeing trips depart every 45 minutes daily, from 9:45am to 5pm during daylight savings time, 9:15am to 4:30pm the rest of the year. Even if the water is murky, you're likely to see alligators, birds, and other wildlife on 30-minute riverboat cruises, which operate during these same hours. Either boat ride costs $6 for adults, $4 for children under 13.

Entrance fees to the park are $4 per vehicle with up to eight passengers, $1 for pedestrians and bicyclists. The park is open daily from 8am to dusk.

For more information, contact the park at 550 Wakulla Springs Dr., Wakulla Springs, FL 32305 (© **850/224-5950;** fax 850/561-7251; www.floridastateparks. org/wakullasprings).

Where to Stay & Dine

Wakulla Springs Lodge 🦀 On the shore of Wakulla Springs, this dated but charming lodge is distinctive for its magnificent Spanish architecture and ornate old-world furnishings, such as rare Spanish tiles, black-granite tables, marble floors, and ceiling beams painted with Florida scenes by a German artist (supposedly Kaiser Wilhelm's court painter). The guest rooms are simple by today's standards (you'll get a marble bathroom and phone but no TV). By all means, ask for a room in the front, so you'll have a lake view. You don't have to be a lodge guest to enjoy the warm, smoky ambience of the great lobby with its huge stone fireplace and arched windows looking onto the springs, or to enjoy reasonably priced meals featuring Southern cuisine in the lovely Ball Room (reservations recommended). The fountain (a 60-ft.-long marble drugstore-style counter for old-fashioned ice-cream sodas) provides snacks and sandwiches. The only thing missing here are signs of taxidermy—no boar, deer, or bear heads perched high on the wall anywhere.

550 Wakulla Park Dr., Wakulla Springs, FL 32305. (C) 850/224-5950. Fax 850/561-7251. 27 units. $79–$99 double. AE, DISC, MC, V. **Amenities:** Restaurant. *In room:* A/C.

THE ST. MARKS AREA

Rich history lives in the area around the little village of **St. Marks,** 18 miles south of the capital at the end of both Fla. 363 and the Tallahassee–St. Marks Historic Railroad Trail State Park (p. 636).

After marching overland from Tampa Bay in 1528, the Spanish conquistador Panfilo de Narvaez and 300 men arrived at this strategic point at the confluence of the St. Marks and Wakulla Rivers near the Gulf of Mexico. Since their only avenue back to Spain was by sea, they built and launched the first ships made by Europeans in the New World. Some 11 years later, Hernando de Soto and his 600 men arrived here after following Narvaez's route from Tampa. They marked the harbor entrance by hanging banners in the trees, then moved inland. Two wooden forts were built here, one in 1679 and one in 1718, and a stone version was begun in 1739. The fort shifted among Spanish, British, and Native American hands until General Andrew Jackson took it away from the Spanish in 1819.

Parts of the old Spanish bastion wall and Confederate earthworks built during the Civil War are in the **San Marcos de Apalache Historic State Park,** reached by turning right at the end of Fla. 363 in St. Marks and following the paved road. A museum built on the foundation of the old marine hospital holds exhibits and artifacts covering the area's history. The site is open Thursday through Monday from 9am to 5pm, closed New Year's Day, Thanksgiving, and Christmas. Admission to the site is free; admission to the museum costs $1, free for children 6 and under. For more information, contact the site at 1022 DeSoto Park Dr., Tallahassee, FL 32301 ((C) **850/922-6007;** www.floridastateparks.org/sanmarcos).

De Soto's men marked the harbor entrance in what is now the **St. Marks Lighthouse and National Wildlife Refuge** (★), P.O. Box 68, St. Marks, FL 32355 ((C) **850/925-6121**). Operated by the U.S. Fish and Wildlife Service, this 65,000-acre preserve occupies much of the coast from the Aucilla River east of St. Marks to the Ochlockonee River west of Panacea and is home to more species of birds than anyplace else in Florida except the Everglades. The visitor center is 3½ miles south of U.S. 98 on Lighthouse Road (Fla. 59); turn south off U.S. 98 at Newport, about 2 miles east of St. Marks. Stop at the center for self-guided tour maps of the roads and extensive hiking trails, some of them built atop levees running through the marshland.

The 80-foot-tall **St. Marks Lighthouse,** 8 miles south of the visitor center, was built in 1842 of limestone blocks 4 feet thick at the base. The nearby beach is also a popular crabbing spot.

Tips A Ramshackle Riverside Lunch

Tallahasseeans love to drive or bike down to St. Marks and have a water-side lunch at **Posey's Oyster Bar,** at the end of Fla. 363 (© **850/925-6172**). Some nighttime patrons at this ramshackle wooden restaurant and bar can get rowdy, especially when country-and-western bands are playing on weekends, but it's a fine place for freshly shucked oysters or smoked mullet during the day. Be sure to walk all the way through the dining rooms to the bar beside the St. Marks River. Posey's opens daily at 10am (entrees are about $6–$11).

Admission to the refuge is $4 per vehicle, $1 for pedestrians and bicyclists (federal Duck Stamps and National Park Service passports accepted). The refuge is open daily from sunrise to sunset, the visitor center, Monday through Friday from 8am to 4pm and Saturday and Sunday from 10am to 5pm (closed all federal holidays). Contact the refuge for information about seasonal tours and hunting.

In 1865, during the final weeks of the Civil War, federal troops landed at the lighthouse and launched a surprise attack on Tallahassee. The Confederates quickly assembled an impromptu army of wounded soldiers, old men, and boys as young as 14. This ragtag bunch fought the Federal regulars for 5 days at what is now the **Natural Bridge Battlefield State Historic Site.** Surprisingly, the old men and boys won. As a result, Tallahassee remained the only Confederate state capital east of the Mississippi never to fall into Yankee hands. The historic site is on County Road 2192, 6 miles east of Woodville on the St. Marks River, halfway between Tallahassee and St. Marks. Follow the signs from Fla. 363 and go to the end of the pavement. It's open daily from 8am to sunset and admission is free. For more information, contact the San Marcos de Apalache Historic State Park (see above) or check www.floridastateparks.org/naturalbridge.

APALACHICOLA NATIONAL FOREST

The largest of Florida's three national forests, this huge preserve encompasses 600,000 acres stretching from Tallahassee's outskirts southward to the Gulf Coast and westward some 70 miles to the Apalachicola River. Included are a variety of woodlands, rivers, streams, lakes, and caves populated by a host of wildlife. There are picnic facilities with sheltered tables and grills, canoe and mountain-bike trails, campgrounds with tent and RV sites, and a number of other facilities, some of them especially designed for visitors with disabilities.

The **Leon Sinks Area** is closest to Tallahassee, 5½ miles south of Southeast Capital Circle on U.S. 319 near the Leon–Wakulla County line. Nature trails and boardwalks lead from one sinkhole (a lake formed when water erodes the underlying limestone) to another. The trails are open daily from 8am to 8pm.

A necessary stop before heading into this wilderness is the **Wakulla Area Ranger District,** 57 Taft Dr., Crawfordville, FL 32327 (© **850/926-3561;** fax 850/926-1904), a visitor center, which provides information about the forest and its facilities and sells topographical and canoe trail maps. The station is off U.S. 319, about 20 miles south of Tallahassee and 2 miles north of Crawfordville. It's open Monday through Thursday from 8am to 4:30pm, Friday from 8am to 4pm.

Index

Great Trips Like Great Days Begin with a Plan

FranklinCovey and Frommer's Bring You *Frommer's Favorite Places* Planner

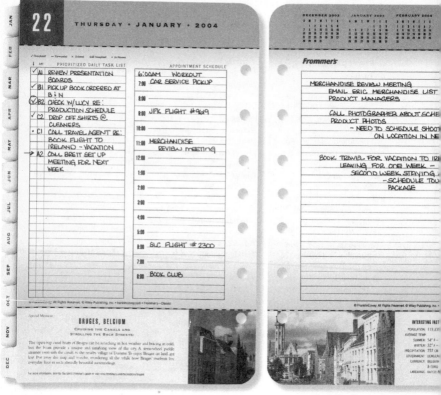

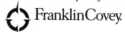

Classic Size Planning Pages $39.95

The planning experts at FranklinCovey have teamed up with the travel experts at Frommer's. The result is a full-year travel-themed planner filled with rich images and travel tips covering fifty-two of Frommer's Favorite Places.

- Each week will make you an expert about an intriguing corner of the world
- New facts and tips every day
- Beautiful, full-color photos of some of the most beautiful places on earth
- Proven planning tools from FranklinCovey for keeping track of tasks, appointments, notes, address/phone numbers, and more

Save 15%

when you purchase Frommer's Favorite Places travel-themed planner and a binder.

Order today before your next big trip.

www.franklincovey.com/frommers
Enter promo code 12252 at checkout for discount. Offer expires June 1, 2005.

◆ FranklinCovey.

Frommer's is a trademark of Arthur Frommer.

Travel Tip: He who finds the best hotel deal has more to spend on facials involving knobbly vegetables.

Hello, the Roaming Gnome here. I've been nabbed from the garden and taken round the world. The people who took me are so terribly clever. They find the best offerings on Travelocity. For very little cha-ching. And that means I get to be pampered and exfoliated till I'm pink as a bunny's doodah.

travelocity®

1-888-TRAVELOCITY / travelocity.com / America Online Keyword: Travel

Travel Tip: Make sure there's customer service for any change of plans — involving friendly natives, for example.

One can plan and plan, but if you don't book with the right people you can't seize le moment and canoodle with the poodle named Pansy. I, for one, am all for fraternizing with the locals. Better yet, if I need to extend my stay and my gnome nappers are willing, it can all be arranged through the 800 number at, oh look, how convenient, the lovely company coat of arms.

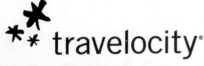

travelocity®

1-888-TRAVELOCITY / travelocity.com / America Online Keyword: Travel

Travel Tip: He who finds the best hotel deal has more to spend on facials involving knobbly vegetables.

Hello, the Roaming Gnome here. I've been nabbed from the garden and taken round the world. The people who took me are so terribly clever. They find the best offerings on Travelocity. For very little cha-ching. And that means I get to be pampered and exfoliated till I'm pink as a bunny's doodah.

travelocity®

1-888-TRAVELOCITY / travelocity.com / America Online Keyword: Travel